SHEPPARD'S BOOK DEALERS
IN THE BRITISH ISLES

Companion Volumes
SHEPPARD'S DIRECTORIES

Directories of Antiquarian & Secondhand Book Dealers

SHEPPARD'S BOOK DEALERS
IN EUROPE

SHEPPARD'S BOOK DEALERS
IN JAPAN

SHEPPARD'S BOOK DEALERS
IN AUSTRALIA & NEW ZEALAND

SHEPPARD'S BOOK DEALERS
IN NORTH AMERICA

SHEPPARD'S BOOK DEALERS
IN INDIA AND THE ORIENT

SHEPPARD'S BOOK DEALERS
IN LATIN AMERICA & SOUTHERN AFRICA

Other Directories
SHEPPARD'S INTERNATIONAL
DIRECTORY OF PRINT AND
MAP SELLERS
A DIRECTORY OF BUSINESSES IN THIRTY-EIGHT COUNTRIES

SHEPPARD'S INTERNATIONAL
DIRECTORY OF EPHEMERA DEALERS
A DIRECTORY OF BUSINESSES IN TWENTY-ONE COUNTRIES

Dealers in all regions can be found on our searchable web site:
www.sheppardsworld.co.uk

SHEPPARD'S
BRITISH ISLES

TWENTY-NINTH EDITION

WARWICKSHIRE
COUNTY LIBRARY

CONTROL No.

**A DIRECTORY OF
ANTIQUARIAN AND SECONDHAND
BOOK DEALERS IN THE
UNITED KINGDOM, THE CHANNEL ISLANDS,
THE ISLE OF MAN AND THE
REPUBLIC OF IRELAND**

RJ
RICHARD
JOSEPH
PUBLISHERS

First Edition published 1951
Twenty-ninth published 2006

RICHARD JOSEPH PUBLISHERS LIMITED
P.O. BOX 15, TORRINGTON
DEVON EX38 8ZJ
ENGLAND
TEL: 01805 625750 FAX: 01805 625376

E-MAIL:
For book sales:
office@sheppardsworld.co.uk
For enquiries and subscription to
Sheppard's World
info@sheppardsworld.co.uk

I.S.S.N. 0950-0715
10 Digit ISBN: 1 872699 84 7
13 Digit ISBN 978 1 872699 84 4

© RICHARD JOSEPH PUBLISHERS LIMITED 2006

MADE IN ENGLAND

Database and web site manager - Kevin Grimshire.
Printed and bound by
T J International, Padstow, Cornwall PL28 8RW

Editor's Note. Whilst every care is taken to ensure that the information given in this Directory is as accurate and complete as possible, the Publishers cannot accept any responsibility for any inaccuracies that occur or for any relevant information that was not available to the Publishers or its professional advisors at the time of going to press.

CONTENTS

SPECIALITY INDEX SUMMARY	8
INTRODUCTION	12
MISCELLANEOUS INFORMATION	
Abbreviations	14
Sizes of Books	15
Metric Conversions	16
The British Book Trade	17
ANTIQUARIAN BOOKSELLERS' ASSOCIATIONS	20
PERIODICALS – Literary Magazines and Book Trade Papers	24
CURRENT REFERENCE BOOKS	26
SUPPLIES AND SERVICES	
Book Auctioneers	32
Book Display and Storage Equipment	33
Book Fair Organisers	33
Catalogue Printers	34
Craft Bookbinders	36
Packaging Materials Suppliers	37
Remainder Merchants	39
Suppliers of Materials & Tools for Binding and Restoring	40
Useful Web Sites	42
INDEX OF CITIES AND TOWNS	45
USE OF THE DIRECTORY	51
GEOGRAPHICAL DIRECTORY OF DEALERS	
ENGLAND (see following pages)	53
THE CHANNEL ISLANDS	253
ISLE OF MAN	254
NORTHERN IRELAND	255
REPUBLIC OF IRELAND	257
SCOTLAND	262
WALES	276
ALPHABETICAL INDEXES	
List of dealers by name of Business	289
List of dealers with Web Sites	305
List of dealers by name of Proprietor	320
Speciality Index (see following pages)	329
Booksearch Service	475
Large Print Books	479
DISPLAYED ADVERTISEMENT INDEX	480

CONTENTS

ENGLAND (by Counties)

BEDFORDSHIRE	53
BERKSHIRE	55
BRISTOL (incl. Unitary Authority of Bristol)	58
BUCKINGHAMSHIRE	61
CAMBRIDGESHIRE	63
CHESHIRE	68
CORNWALL	72
CUMBRIA	76
DERBYSHIRE	81
DEVON	83
DORSET	90
DURHAM (incl. Unitary Authorities of Darlington, Hartlepool & Stockton-on-Tees)	96
EAST SUSSEX	98
EAST YORKSHIRE (incl. Unitary Authorities of East Riding & Kingston-upon-Hull)	105
ESSEX	108
GLOUCESTERSHIRE (incl. Unitary Authority of South Gloucestershire)	113
GREATER MANCHESTER (incl. the Unitary Authorities of Bolton, Bury, Manchester, Oldham, Rochdale, Salford, Stockport, Tameside, Trafford & Wigan)	118
HAMPSHIRE	122
HEREFORDSHIRE	128
HERTFORDSHIRE	130
ISLE OF WIGHT	134
KENT	136
LANCASHIRE	142
LEICESTERSHIRE	145
LINCOLNSHIRE (incl. the Unitary Authorities of North East Lincolnshire) & North Lincolnshire)	148
LONDON (EAST POSTAL DISTRICTS)	153
LONDON (EAST CENTRAL POSTAL DISTRICTS)	154
LONDON (NORTH POSTAL DISTRICTS)	155
LONDON (NORTH WEST POSTAL DISTRICTS)	158
LONDON (SOUTH EAST POSTAL DISTRICTS)	161
LONDON (SOUTH WEST POSTAL DISTRICTS)	164
LONDON (WEST POSTAL DISTRICTS)	169
LONDON (WEST CENTRAL POSTAL DISTRICTS)	174
LONDON (GREATER LONDON, OUTER)	178
MERSEYSIDE (incl. the Unitary Authorities of Knowsley, Liverpool, St. Helens, Sefton & Wirral)	182
NORFOLK	184
NORTH YORKSHIRE (incl. the Unitary Authorities of Cleveland, Middlesbrough, Redcar & York)	190
NORTHAMPTONSHIRE	196
NORTHUMBERLAND	198
NOTTINGHAMSHIRE	200
OXFORDSHIRE	202
RUTLAND	208
SHROPSHIRE	209
SOMERSET (incl. the Unitary Authorities of Bath & North East Somerset & North Somerset)	212
SOUTH YORKSHIRE (incl. the Unitary Authorities of Barnsley, Doncaster, Rotherham & Sheffield)	217
STAFFORDSHIRE	219
SUFFOLK	221
SURREY	226

TYNE AND WEAR (incl. the Unitary Authorities of Gateshead,
   Newcastle upon Tyne, North Tyneside, South Tyneside & Sunderland) 231
WARWICKSHIRE 232
WEST MIDLANDS (incl. the Unitary Authorities of Birmingham, Coventry,
   Dudley, Sandwell, Solihull, Walsall & Wolverhampton) 234
WEST SUSSEX 237
WEST YORKSHIRE (incl. the Unitary Authorities of Bradford, Calderdale,
   Kirklees, Leeds & Wakefield) 241
WILTSHIRE 246
WORCESTERSHIRE 250

ENGLAND (by Unitary Authorities)

To locate a dealer within a Unitary Authority, use the page references shown below in conjuction with the County Index shown above.

Barnsley 217	North Lincolnshire 148
Bath 212	North Tyneside 231
Birmingham 234	North Somerset 212
Bolton 118	Oldham 118
Bradford 241	Redcar 190
Bristol 58	Rochdale 118
Bury 118	Rotherham 217
Calderdale 241	St. Helens 182
Cleveland 190	Salford 118
Coventry 234	Sandwell 234
Darlington 96	Sefton 182
Doncaster 217	Sheffield 221
Dudley 234	Solihull 234
East Riding 105	South Gloucestershire 113
Gateshead 231	South Tyneside 231
Hartlepool 96	Stockport 118
Kingston-upon-Hull 105	Stockton-on-Tees 96
Kirklees 241	Sunderland 231
Knowsley 182	Tameside 118
Leeds 241	Trafford 118
Liverpool 182	Wakefield 241
Manchester 118	Walsall 234
Middlesbrough 190	Wigan 118
Newcastle upon Tyne 231	Wirral 182
North East Lincolnshire 148	Wolverhampton 234
North East Somerset 212	York 190

SPECIALITY INDEX

The following list has been created from the subjects provided by dealers' entry forms

Aboriginal 329	Atlases 345	Celtica 365
Academic/Scholarly 329	Author	Ceramics 365
Accountancy 330	– General 345	Charity 365
Acupuncture 330	– Specific (A–Z) 345	Chemistry 365
Adirondack Mountains, The 330	Authors	Chess 365
Adult 330	– British 357	Children's – General 365
Adventure 330	– Local 357	– Early Titles 365
Advertising 330	– National 357	– Illustrated 365
Aeronautics 331	– Women 357	Christmas 368
Aesthetic Movement 331	Autobiography 357	Churchilliana 368
Aesthetics 331	Autographs 357	Cinema/Film 368
African American Studies ... 331	Autolithography 358	Circus 369
Africana 331	Automobilia/Automotive 358	Cities 369
Agriculture 332	Avant-Garde 358	City of London 369
Aids Crisis, The 332	Aviation 358	Civil Engineering 369
Aircraft 332		Classical Studies 370
Alchemy 332	Banking and Insurance 359	Cockfighting 370
Almanacs 332	Beat Writers 359	Collectables 370
Alpinism/Mountaineering ... 332	Bell-Ringing (Campanology) 359	Collecting 370
Alternative Medicine 333	Belle-Lettres 359	Colonial 370
American Indians 333	Bibles 359	Colour-Plate 370
Americana 333	Biblical Studies 359	Comedy 370
Amish 333	Bibliography 359	Comic Books and
Animals and Birds 333	Bindings 360	Annuals 370
Annuals 334	Biography 360	Comics 371
Anthologies 334	Biology 362	Commerce - General 371
Anthropology 334	Black Studies 362	Communication 371
Anthroposophy 334	Book of Hours 357	Communism 371
Anti-Semitism 334	Book Arts 360	Company History 371
Antiquarian 334	Book of Hours 362	Computing 371
Antiques 336	Bookbinding 362	Conservation 371
Antiquities 337	Books about Books 362	Conspiracy 372
Apiculture 337	Books in Greek 362	Cookery - Professional 372
Applied Art 337	Botany 362	Cookery/Gastronomy 372
Arabica 337	Brewing 363	Cosmology 372
Archaeology 338	Bridge 363	Counselling 372
Architecture 338	British Books 363	Counterculture 372
Arms and Armour 339	Broadcasting 363	Countries and Regions
Army, The 340	Building and Construction ... 363	– General 372
Art - General 340	Bull Fighting 363	– Specific (A–Z) 373
–Afro-American 342	Buses/Trams 363	Country Houses 379
–Technique 342	Business Studies 363	County - Local 379
–Theory 342	Byzantium 363	Courtesy 379
Art Deco 342		Cowboys 379
Art History 342	Calligraphy 363	Crafts 379
Art Nouveau 343	Canadiana 364	Crime (True) 379
Art Reference 343	Canals/Inland Waterways ... 364	Criminology 380
Arthurian 343	Caricature 364	Critical Theory 380
Artists 343	Carpets 364	Crochet 380
Arts, The 344	Carriages and Driving 364	Cryptography 380
Asian Studies 344	Cartography 364	Cryptozoology 380
Assassinations 344	Cartoons 364	Cults 380
Astrology 344	Catalogues Raisonnés 365	Culture
Astronautics 344	Cats 365	– Foreign 380
Astronomy 344	Cattlemen 365	– National 380

SPECIALITY INDEX

- Popular........................ 380
Curiosa 380
Curiosities...................... 380
Cybernetics 380

D.I.Y (Do It Yourself)........ 380
Dance............................ 381
Decorative Art 381
Deep Sea Diving.............. 381
Design 381
Diaries........................... 381
Dictionaries..................... 381
Dinosaurs 381
Directories - General.......... 381
– British 382
Disneyana...................... 382
Divining......................... 382
Documents - General 382
Dogs............................. 382
Dolls and Dolls' Houses...... 382
Domesticity..................... 382
Drama........................... 382
Drawing......................... 382
Drugs............................ 382
Dyes 382

Early Imprints.................. 382
Earth Mysteries 383
Earth Sciences................. 383
Easter........................... 383
Eastern Philosophy............ 383
Ecclesiastical History and
  Architecture.................. 383
Ecology.......................... 383
Economics 383
Education and School........ 384
Egyptology...................... 384
Electronics 384
Emblemata..................... 384
Embroidery 384
Encyclopaedias................ 384
Engineering 384
English........................... 385
Engraving 385
Entertainment 385
Entomology..................... 385
Environment, The 385
Erotica........................... 385
Esoteric.......................... 385
Espionage 385
Ethics 386
Ethnography.................... 386
Ethnology 386
Etiquette........................ 386
European Books 386
Eurpean Studies................ 386
Evolution........................ 386
Ex-Libris 386
Examinations 386
Exhibitions 386
Expeditions 386
Exploration - General......... 386
–Polar............................ 386

Fables............................ 386
Fairgrounds..................... 387
Fairy/Folk Tales 387
Family 387
Famous People (A-Z) 387
Farming & Livestock.......... 387
Farriers.......................... 387
Fashion and Costume......... 387
Feminism....................... 387
Fiction
– General....................... 387
– 18th Century 389
– Adventure..................... 389
– Crime, Detective, Spy,
  Thrillers...................... 389
– Fantasy, Horror 390
– Historical 390
– Romantic 390
– Science Fiction 390
– Supernatural................. 391
– Westerns 391
– Women........................ 391
– Young Adult Mystery &
  Adventure 391
Fictional Chracters 391
Finance.......................... 391
Fine and Rare.................. 391
Fine Art 392
Fine Printing.................... 392
Fire and Firefighters........... 392
Firearms/Guns 392
First Editions................... 392
Fishes 393
Fisheries 393
Flora & Fauna 394
Flower Arranging............... 394
Folio Society, The 394
Folklore 394
Food and Drink 394
Fore-Edge Paintings........... 395
Foreign Texts................... 395
Forestry 395
Fossils........................... 395
Fourth Way..................... 385
Free Thought 385
Freemasonry and
  Anti-Masonry................. 395
French Foreign Legion 395
Freudiana 395
Fungi 395
Fur Trade 395
Furniture 396

Gambling........................ 396
Games 396
Gardening...................... 396
Gemmology 396
Gender Studies 397
Genealogy...................... 397
Genetics 397
Geography 397
Geology 397
Geophysics..................... 397

Ghosts 397
Glamour......................... 397
Glass............................. 398
Gnostics 398
Gold Rush 398
Goldsmiths..................... 398
Gothic Revival 398
Grand Canyon &
  Colorado River, The 398
Graphic Novels................. 398
Graphics......................... 398
Graphology 398
Guide Books.................... 398
Gynaecology 398
Gypsies 398

Hairdressing 398
Hand Bookbinding 398
Handwritten Books............ 398
Health 398
Heraldry......................... 399
Herbalism 399
Heritage 399
Hermeticism 399
Herpetology.................... 399
Himalayan Kingdoms......... 399
History
– General....................... 399
– Specific (A–Z)................ 401
History of Civilisation 404
History of Ideas................ 404
Hobbies 405
Holocaust 405
Homeopathy.................... 405
Homosexuality and
  Lesbianism 405
Horizon Writers................ 405
Horology 405
Horses 405
Horticulture..................... 405
Housekeeping.................. 405
Humanism 406
Humanities..................... 406
Humour 406
Hydrography 406
Hymnology 406
Hypnotism 406

Iconography 406
Illuminated Manuscripts...... 406
Illustrated 406
Incunabula 408
Industrial Design............... 408
Industry......................... 406
Institutions 408
Interior Design 408
International Affairs........... 408
Inventors & Inventions 408
Irish Interest 408

Jewellery 409
Journalism 409
Journals 396

SPECIALITY INDEX

Judaica 409
Jungiana 409
Juvenile 409

Kabbala/Cabbala/Cabala 410
Knitting 410
Ku Klux Klan 410

Lace 410
Landscape 410
Languages
– African 410
– Foreign 410
– National 410
Law - General 410
– Constitutional 411
Legal Paperwork 411
Leninism 411
Lepidopterology 411
Lettering 411
Letters 411
Library Science 411
Limited Editions 411
Linguistics 411
Literacy 411
Literary Criticism 411
Literary Travel 412
Literature
– General 412
– 19th C 415
– French 415
– Scottish 415
– Victorian 415
– Western American 415
Literature in Translation 415
Local Studies - Sussex 415
Locks and Locksmiths 415
Logging/Lumbering 415
Lost civilizations 415

Mafia 415
Magazines & Periodicals
– General 415
– Women's 416
Magic and
  Conjuring 416
Magnetism 416
Mammals 416
Management 416
Manuals
– General 416
– Seamanship 416
Manuscripts 416
Maps & Mapmaking 417
Marine Sciences 417
Maritime/Nautical
– General 417
– Log Books 418
Marque Histories
  (see also motoring) 418
Marxism 418
Mathematics 418
Mechanical Engneering 418

Media 418
Medicine 418
Medicine - History of 419
Medieval 419
Memoirs 419
Memorabilia 419
Metaphysics 419
Meteorology 419
Microscopy 419
Military 419
Military History 421
Military Uniforms 422
Mind, Body and Spirit 422
Mineralogy 422
Miniature Books 422
Mining 422
Minority Issues 422
Missionaries & Missions 422
Model Railways 422
Modern First Editions 408
Modern Art 422
Monographs 424
Motorbikes 424
Motoring 424
Mountain Men 424
Mountains 424
Movie & Television Scripts ... 424
Music
– General 424
– Specific (A–Z) 425
Musical Instruments
– General 426
– Guitars 426
Musicians 426
Mycology 426
Mysteries 426
Mysticism 426
Mythology 426

National Geographic 428
Native American 428
Natural Health 428
Natural History 428
Natural Sciences 429
Nature 430
Naturism 430
Naval 430
Navigation 430
Navy, The 430
Needlework 430
Neurology 431
New Age 431
New Naturalist 431
Newspapers
– General 431
Non-Fiction 431
Nostalgia 431
Numerology 431
Numismatics 431
Nursery Rhymes 431
Nurses / Doctors 431

Occult 431

Ocean Liners 432
Oceanography 432
Odd & Unusual 432
Oil Lamps 432
Oriental 432
Ornithology 432
Osteopathy 432
Ottoman Empire 433
Out of Print 433
Outdoors 433
Outlaws 433
Oxford Movement 433

Pacifism 433
Paddleboats 433
Paganism 433
Painting 433
Palaeography 433
Palaeontology 433
Palmistry and Fortune
  Telling 433
Paper Collectables 433
Papermaking 433
Parapsychology 434
Parish Registers 434
Performing Arts 434
Periodicals and Magazines
– see under Magazines and
  Periodicals
Petroleum Geology 434
Petroluem Technology 434
Pharmacy/Pharmacology 434
Philately 434
Philology 434
Philosophy 434
Photography 435
Phrenology 436
Physical Culture 436
Physics 436
Pirates 436
Plant Hunting 436
Plays 436
Poetry 436
Police Force Histories 437
Political History 437
Politics 437
Pomolgy 438
Pop-Up, 3D, Cut Out and
  Movable 438
Pornography 438
Pottery & Glass 438
Poultry 438
Prayer Books 438
Pre-Raphaelite 438
Precious Metals - Silver 438
Printed Textiles 438
Printing
– General 438
– North of England Privincial 438
– Printing and Mind of Man . 439
– Private Press 439
Proof Copies 439
Psychic 439

SPECIALITY INDEX

Psychoanalysis.................. 439
Psychology/Psychiatry 439
Psychotherapy.................. 440
Public Administration........ 440
Public Health................... 440
Public Houses 440
Public Schools.................. 440
Publishers
– General....................... 440
– Specific (A–Z)............... 440
Publishing....................... 441
Pulps............................. 441
Punk Fazines 442
Puppets and Marionettes.... 442
Puzzles........................... 442

Quakers, The 442

Radical Issues 442
Radio/Wireless 442
Railways & Railroads......... 442
Reference........................ 443
Registers......................... 443
Religion
– General....................... 443
– Specific (A–Z)............... 443
Religious Texts................. 445
River Thames................... 445
Ock Art 445
Romance......................... 445
Rosicrucianism 445
Royalty
– General....................... 445
– European 445
Rubaiyat of Omar Khayyam 445
Rugs 445
Rural Life........................ 445

Salvation Army 446
Satire............................. 446
School Registers/Rolls
  of Honour.................... 446
Science
– General....................... 446
– Forensic...................... 447
– History of.................... 447
– Pure and Applied........... 447
Scientific Instruments 447
Scientists 447
Scottish Enlightenment 447
Scottish Interest................ 447
Scouts and Guides............. 448
Scrimshaw....................... 448
Sculpture 448
Sea-Faring & Shipping....... 448
Seamanship 448
Secret Societies 448
Self-Help 448
Self-Improvement 448
Self-Sufficiency 448
Sets of Books................... 448
Sette of Odd Volumes........ 449

Sexology 449
Sheep/Shepherding............ 449
Sherlockiana 449
Ship Modelling 449
Shipbuilding & Shipping..... 449
Shipwrecks 449
Shorthand 449
Sigillography.................... 449
Signed Editions................. 449
Silversmiths 450
Sixties, The..................... 450
Slavery........................... 450
Small Press Published Books 450
Social Economics............... 450
Social History................... 450
Social Sciences.................. 450
Socialism 450
Sociology 451
South Seas....................... 451
Space............................. 451
Special Collections............. 451
Spiritual 451
Spiritualism 451
Sport
– General....................... 451
– Specific (A–Z) 452
Stained Glass 456
Steam Engines.................. 436
States of America
– Louisiana.................... 456
Statistics......................... 456
Steam Engines.................. 456
Stone Masonry 456
Suffragettes..................... 456
Sufism 456
Supernatural 456
Surgery........................... 456
Surrealism 456
Symbolism....................... 457

Tapestry 457
Taxidermy....................... 457
Teaching......................... 457
Technical 457
Technology...................... 457
Teddy Bears..................... 457
Television........................ 457
Texana 457
Textbooks 457
Textiles........................... 457
Theatre........................... 458
Theology......................... 458
Theosophy....................... 458
Therapy – Marital & Family . 459
Timber Technology 459
Topography
– General....................... 459
– Local......................... 460
Topology 463
Town Planning 463
Town Plans 463
Toys 463

Traction Engines 463
Trade Catalogues.............. 463
Trade Unions 463
Trades & Professions 463
Traditional Chinese Medicine 463
Traditions....................... 463
Transport 463
Travel
– General 464
– Specific (A–Z)............... 466
Trials 468
Tribal............................ 468
Trotskyism..................... 468
Typography 468

U.F.O.s 468
U.S. Presidents................. 469
Umbrellas/Parasols........... 469
Unexplained, The............. 469
University Histories.......... 469
University Press............... 469
University Texts 469
Urban History 469

Vatican and Papal
  History, The................. 469
Veterinary 469
Victorian Multi-Deckers..... 469
Victoriana 469
Vintage Cars 469
Vintage Paperbacks 469
Viticulture 469
Voyages and Discovery...... 469

War
– General 469
– Specific (A–Z)............... 471
Wargames 472
Watercolours 472
Weird and Wonderful 472
Welsh Interest................. 472
Western Americana 472
Whaling 472
Whisky.......................... 472
Windmills and Watermills .. 472
Wine............................. 472
Witchcraft 473
Women.......................... 473
Woodland Crafts 473
Woodwork..................... 473
Wolrd Fairs & Exhibitions.. 473
Writing.......................... 473

Year Books..................... 473
Yoga............................. 473
Youth Movements 473

Zoology 473
Zoos 473

INTRODUCTION

In the past twelve months we have experinced more changes than originally planned. In brief, these include a re-vamp of the cover design for our directories. This new style will be adopted for all future regional editions. After sixteen years, we felt it was time to give the printed reference sources a fresh look - though the contents follow the same tried and tested format of previous editions. Also, the series titles have been shortened, as in this editon, to Sheppard's British Isles as this is the way users refer to the book. During this time, we have also closed the web site that Nielsen Book Data hosted on which all dealers in the British Isles could edit and change their details. Our new site, Sheppard's World is growing rapidly as having completed this directory, we are now inviting dealers in other countries to register. Every business registered receives a free newsletter sent out weekly by e-mail. The new site offers dealers and collectors an alternative method of searching for books, one that complements the standard Internet web sites holding databases of titles. More features are planned, especially with the new telephone services available.

Perhaps the most significant and time consuming change has been the transfer of data from the web site hosted by Nielsen Book Data. After some four years of work, it became apparent that the main reason for creating the site was never likely to be realised by NBD, and we decided by mutual agreement to close the site. We could have found another host but it became obvious that merging the data onto our new site at www.sheppardsworld.co.uk would provide many more benfits to the trade.

The consequence of this decision was that we then had a major and time consuming task of merging the data: the problems were, as always, in the detail. Thankfully, all these are now in the past and dealers have already found the site more beneficial. Our new site is also the home for dealers overseas, and as we go to press, we have dealers listed in 35 countries. It is, we think, a site that is enhanced because we list dealers who are not linked to the Internet and when searching for a title within a subject, this will increase the search results. The site is also searchable, by geographical location and by book stock subject, but it differs from our previous site in that the user can select which dealers will receive their e-mailed booksearches, or offers. There are more details to be found on the web site and it's worth reading about the benefits as we add and improve the features from time to time.

The web site also lists businesses dealing in ephemera, and prints and maps. Book dealers can have more than one entry, as many also sell ephemera, or prints and maps.

All search results show the same information that appear in our directories, and the site allows users to e-mail dealers **but at no time** does the user see the actual e-mail address of the dealer. This is to protect dealers against the misuse of e-mail addresses lifted from the site by robotic and spidering programmes. Search results now also show the free text area that allows dealers to emphasise their main trading strengths and benefits. This field will appear in future printed directories as well. However, where dealer's list of speciality book stock classifications is extensive, only the first eight appear in the Geographical Section but dealers appear under all the appropriate headings in the index.

This year has seen the launch of a newsletter sent to all dealers registered on the web site. *Sheppard's Confidential* carries trade news, letters, list of auctions, and book fairs. It will shortly include book reviews and events. For the moment, the main theme is largely based on the British Isles but as each week passes, more and more news is appearing from overseas. The weekly newsletter is sent out free of charge, and dealers and trade related businesses, can advertise very effectively.

There is another benefit to publishing a newsletter. For years, we have commented that dealers are slow to update their business details, even when we know our e-mails get through. Treated as an annual task, the total number of e-mails that fail add to the delay to the publishing schedule. If we are not advised of the change, our newsletter and reminders to update their details do not get through. Now, we can spot the failed e-mails on a weekly basis. Thus we hope to minimise the annual problem of updating and have one of the better sites for collectors and dealers to use. Because changes are occurring rapidly, we believe users will make increasing use of the web site as the downside of printed directories is that once they have been published, some information is bound to become outdated.

It appears that changes are taking place in the trade too; the new and secondhand book trades appear to be getting closer. An increasing number of book dealers are now stocking new books in the subjects in which they specialise. And last October saw a large group of antiquarian dealers exhibiting at the Frankfurt Book Fair, an event not seen before.

For users of broadband, there is the use of the new Internet service Voice Over The Internet (VOIP for short). This telephone service offered by a number of providers certainly reduces the cost of calls substantially. On Skype for example, all calls to other Skype linked users are free, anywhere in the world and for any length of time. Calls to normal landlines are around the cheapest costs available. Add to this the capability of adding web cams, conference calls, and parallel ability to type messages, then it surely will not be long before dealers may be tempted by economy to adopt this service in a major way. The ability to show a book in close up to the potential buyer via VOIP could be a real boon for sales.

Statistics are not as comprehensive as we would like and in future years, these will cover more aspects of the trade. There are 1880 entries in this edition, a few more than last time and this edition contain a much smaller number who are known to be trading but have not updated their details. As always, our database has many more dealers. In detail, there are 705 trading from shops, and 895 from private premises. The balance of dealers trade solely via the Internet, or from a combination of storerooms, warehouses, offices or showrooms. Most dealers are, of course, linked to the Internet and total 1521.

By far the most notable change has been the large increase in book stock subjects held by dealers. This year the list of new subjects recorded has jumped by over 200. One reason may be that because there are no restrictions on the web site database, dealers are selecting more. Users might note though, that although all subjects selected by dealers are shown in the Speciality Index, there are only eight shown in the main geographical listings, otherwise the book would become too large (and too expensive).

For dealers who wish to register for the first time, there are two methods open. Those who are not linked to the Internet can write to us for a free dealer entry form, and those who can access our web site, can register on line. The site address is www.sheppardsworld.co.uk and the postal address is: The Editor, Richard Joseph Publishers Ltd, PO Box 15, Torrington, Devon, EX38 8ZJ.

Richard Joseph
June 2006

ABBREVIATIONS USED IN DESCRIBING BOOKS

Some booksellers and buyers use highly individualistic systems of abbreviations and others have adapted traditional terms for the Internet. The following are sufficiently well known to be generally used, but all other words should be written in full, and the whole typed if possible. Condition is described by the following scale:– Mint – Fine – Very good – Good – Fair – Poor

A.D.	Autograph document	Lea.	Leather
A.D.s.	Autograph document, signed	Ll.	Levant Morocco
A.D.*	Autograph document with seal	Ll.	Leaves
A.e.g.	All edges gilt	L.P.	Large paper
A.L.s.	Autograph letter, signed	M.	Mint
a.v.	Authorized version	Mco., mor	Morocco
B.A.R.	Book Auction Records	M.e.	Marbled edges
Bd.	Bound	M.S.(S.)	Manuscripts
Bdg.	Binding	N.d.	No date
Bds.	Boards	n.ed.	new edition
B.L.	Black letter	n.p.	no place (of publication)
C., ca.	Circa (approximately)	Ob., obl.	Oblong
C. & p.	Collated and perfect	Oct.	Octavo
Cat.	Catalogue	O.p.	Out of print
Cent.	Century	P.	Page
Cf.	Calf	P.f.	Post free
C.I.F.	Cost, insurance and freight	Pict.	Pictorial
Cl.	Cloth	Pl(s).	Plate(s)
Col(d).	Colour(ed)	Port.	Portrait
C.O.D.	Cash on delivery	P.P.	Printed privately
Cont.	Contemporary	Pp.	Pages
C.O.R.	Cash on receipt	Prelims.	Preliminary pages
Cr. 8vo.	Crown octavo	Pseud.	Pseudonym(ous)
d.e.	Deckle edges	Ptd.	Printed
Dec.	Decorated	q.v.	Quod Vide (which see)
D-j., d-w.	Dust jacket, dust wrapper	Qto.	Quarto
E.D.L.	Edition de luxe	Rev.	Revised
Edn.	Edition	Rom.	Roman letter
Endp., e.p.	Endpaper(s)	S.L.	Sine loco (without place of publication)
Eng., engr.	Engraved, engraving		
Ex-lib.	Ex-library	Sgd.	Signed
Facs.	Facsimile	Sig.	Signature
Fcp.	Foolscap	S.N.	Sine nomine (without name of printer)
F.	Fine		
F.,ff.	Folio, folios	Spr.	Sprinkled
Fo., fol.	Folio (book size)	T.e.g.	Top edge gilt
F.O.B.	Free on board	Thk.	Thick
Fp., front.	Frontispiece	T.L.s.	Typed letter, signed
Free	Post Free	T.p.	Title page
G.	Good	T.S.	Typescript
G., gt.	Gilt edges	Unbd.	Unbound
G.L.	Gothic letter	Uncut	Uncut (pages not trimmed)
Hf. bd.	Half bound	Und.	Undated
Illum.	Illuminated	V.d.	Various dates
Ill(s).	Illustrated, illustrations	V.g..	Very good
Imp.	Imperial	Vol,	Volume
Impft.	Imperfect	W.a.f.	With all faults
Inscr.	Inscribed, inscription	Wraps.	Wrappers
Ital.	Italic letter		

SIZES OF BOOKS

These are only approximate, as trimming varies and all sizes ignore the overlap of a book case.

	Octavo (8vo)		Quarto (4to)	
	Inches	Centimetres	Inches	Centimetres
FOOLSCAP	$6^{3}/_{4}$ x $4^{1}/_{4}$	17.1 x 10.8	$8^{1}/_{2}$ x $6^{3}/_{4}$	21.5 x 17.1
CROWN	$7^{1}/_{2}$ x 5	19.0 x 12.7	10 x $7^{1}/_{2}$	25.4 x 19.0
LARGE POST	$8^{1}/_{4}$ x $5^{1}/_{4}$	20.9 x 13.3	$10^{1}/_{2}$ x $8^{1}/_{4}$	26.6 x 20.9
DEMY	$8^{3}/_{8}$ x $5^{5}/_{8}$	22.3 x 14.2	$11^{1}/_{4}$ x $8^{3}/_{4}$	28.5 x 22.2
MEDIUM	9 x $5^{3}/_{4}$	22.8 x 14.6	$11^{1}/_{2}$ x 9	29.2 x 22.8
ROYAL	10 x $6^{1}/_{4}$	25.4 x 15.8	$12^{1}/_{2}$ x 10	31.7 x 25.4
SUPER ROYAL	$10^{1}/_{4}$ x $6^{3}/_{4}$	26.0 x 17.5	$13^{3}/_{4}$ x $10^{1}/_{4}$	34.9 x 26.0
IMPERIAL	11 x $7^{1}/_{2}$	27.9 x 19.0	15 x 11	38.0 x 27.9
FOOLSCAP FOLIO			$13^{1}/_{2}$ x $8^{1}/_{2}$	34.2 x 21.5
METRIC A5	$8^{1}/_{4}$ x $5^{7}/_{8}$	21.0 x 14.8		
A4	$11^{3}/_{4}$ x $8^{1}/_{4}$	29.7 x 21.0		
'A' FORMAT PAPERBACK		17.8 X 11.1		
'B' FORMAT PAPERBACK		19.8 X 12.9		

BRITISH PAPER SIZES (untrimmed)

Sizes of Printing Papers

	Inches	Centimetres
Foolscap	17 x $13^{1}/_{2}$	43.2 x 34.3
Double Foolscap	27 x 17	68.6 x 43.2
Crown	20 x 15	50.8 x 38.1
Double Crown	30 x 20	76.2 x 50.8
Quad Crown	40 x 30	101.6 x 76.2
Double Quad Crown	60 x 40	152.4 x 101.6
Post	$19^{1}/_{4}$ x $15^{1}/_{2}$	48.9 x 39.4
Double Post	$31^{1}/_{2}$ x $19^{1}/_{2}$	80.0 x 49.5
Double Large Post	33 x 21	83.8 x 53.3
Sheet and $^{1}/_{2}$ Post	$23^{1}/_{2}$ x $19^{1}/_{2}$	59.7 x 49.5
Demy	$22^{1}/_{2}$ x $17^{1}/_{2}$	57.2 x 44.5
Double Demy	35 x $22^{1}/_{2}$	88.9 x 57.2
Quad Demy	45 x 35	114.3 x 88.9
Music Demy	20 x $15^{1}/_{2}$	50.8 x 39.4
Medium	23 x 18	58.4 x 45.7
Royal	25 x 20	63.5 x 50.8
Super Royal	$27^{1}/_{2}$ x $20^{1}/_{2}$	69.9 x 52.1
Elephant	28 x 23	71.1 x 58.4
Imperial	30 x 22	76.2 x 55.9

Available from Richard Joseph Publishers Ltd
Sheppard's Book Dealers in
NORTH AMERICA

15th Edition   (Royal H/b plus CD-ROM)   £30.00 560pp

METRIC CONVERSIONS

SIZES

inches	m.m.	inches	m.m.
1/4	6	7 3/4	197
1/2	13	8	203
3/4	19	8 1/4	210
1	25	8 1/2	216
1 1/4	32	8 3/4	222
1 1/2	38	9	229
1 3/4	44	9 1/4	235
2	51	9 1/2	241
2 1/4	57	9 3/4	248
2 1/2	64	10	254
2 3/4	70	10 1/4	260
3	76	10 1/2	267
3 1/4	83	10 3/4	273
3 1/2	89	11	279
3 3/4	95	11 1/4	286
4	102	11 1/2	292
4 1/4	108	11 3/4	298
4 1/2	114	12	305
4 3/4	121	12 1/4	311
5	127	12 1/2	318
5 1/4	133	12 3/4	324
5 1/2	140	13	330
5 3/4	146	13 1/4	337
6	152	13 1/2	343
6 1/4	159	13 3/4	349
6 1/2	165	14	356
6 3/4	171	14 1/4	362
7	178	14 1/2	368
7 1/4	184	14 3/4	375
7 1/2	191	15	381

To convert inches to millimetres multiply by 25.4. Millimetres to inches may be found by multiplying by .0394.

WEIGHTS

lbs.	kgs.
1	0.45
2	0.91
3	1.36
4	1.81
5	2.27
6	2.72
7	3.18
8	3.63
9	4.08
10	4.54
11	4.99
12	5.44
13	5.90
14	6.35
15	6.80
16	7.26
17	7.71
18	8.16
19	8.62
20	9.07
21	9.53
22	9.98
23	10.43
24	10.89
25	11.34
26	11.79
27	12.25
28	12.70
56	25.40
112	50.80

To convert pounds to kilogrammes multiply by .4536. Kilogrammes to pounds may be found by multiplying by 2.205.

Looking for a dealer in the BRITISH ISLES?

Search on www.sheppardsworld.co.uk

or

reserve a copy of the next printed edition

THE BRITISH BOOK TRADE

NEW BOOKS

In the United Kingdom, marketing of new books is well organised and controlled by individual publishers. However, the British Book Trade has two highly organised trade associations, The Publishers Association and The Booksellers Association which represent a vast majority of their respective parts of the trade.

The Booksellers Association publishes an annual directory of members, listing 'over 3,900 bookselling outlets' in the current edition. This is an essential reference source used by all publishers. In addition, the Booksellers Association publishes an annual directory of book publishers, distributors and wholesalers.

The directory of B.A. Members includes not only general booksellers, but businesses that concentrate on specific subjects. Although, in fact, it confers no right to buy books at trade terms, entry in this directory confirms to publishers that they are eligible for trade terms.

Bibliographic information is supplied to the book trade through Nielsen BookData Ltd. Publishers supply information on the titles they have published and this is disseminated by this company to booksellers. Users of this directory will note the growing importance of this information in relation to the secondhand book trade.

THE BOOKSELLERS ASSOCIATION OF THE UNITED KINGDOM AND IRELAND LIMITED, 272 Vauxhall Bridge Road, London SW1V 1BA. Tel: (020) 7802-0802. Fax: (020) 7802-0803. E-Mail: mail@booksellers.org.uk. Web Site: www.booksellers.org.uk. Est: 1895 as the Associated Booksellers of Great Britain and Ireland and changed to its present name in 1999. Chief Executive: Tim Godfray. The Association's aims are: to provide services to help members increase book sales and develop the market for new books; to assist members to reduce costs; to improve distribution between publishers, booksellers and consumers; to represent booksellers' interests; and to provide a forum for members to discuss matters of common interest. It is not concerned with the secondhand or antiquarian trade: membership is open to all those engaged in the sale of new books, some of whom also sell secondhand and antiquarian books. The Association is governed by an Annual General MeetingConference and a Council which meets four times a year, delegating much work to specialist committees and encouraging members to join groups concerned with academic bookselling, Christian bookselling, children's bookselling etc. Book Tokens, and batch.co.uk - an electronic clearing house for the payment of accounts – are some of the services provided for members. The Association is linked with similar bodies overseas.

THE PUBLISHERS ASSOCIATION, 29B Montague Street, London WC1B 5BW. Tel: (020) 7691-9191. Fax: 7691-9199. E-Mail: mail@publishers.org.uk. Web: www.publishers.org.uk. Est: 1896. President: Stephen Page. Chief Executive: Ronnie Williams. Including the Trade Publishers Council, International Division, the Educational Publishers Council (School Books division), the Academic and Professional Publishers Division the Electronic Publishers Forum. The Association represents the interests of UK publishers of books, electronic publications and journals to governments, other bodies in the trade and the public at large. It seeks to promote the sales of British books by all suitable means, and provides members with a wide range of services and help on publishing problems and opportunities.

SECONDHAND AND ANTIQUARIAN BOOKS

Anyone who is so minded can enter this branch of the trade without any formality at all and, indeed, book lovers and collectors, buying items for their own libraries and selling duplicate or unwanted copies, have sometimes, almost unwittingly, drifted into a habit of rather casual regular dealing. This sounds easy and pleasant but, to enter seriously into business and make a profit in any way commensurate with the work involved, a great deal of expert knowledge is required.

Some dealers have large and handsome premises, but retail shops are now relatively few as most dealers now work from warehouses, storerooms, and private premises. In addition to these sales outlets, there are numerous book fairs of varying size around the country from which dealers trade. Many more though are trading via the Internet. While most dealers in secondhand and antiquarian books will try to obtain for a customer any required item which they do not have in stock, many specialists will now refer requests outside their speciality to other dealers.

Dealers offer titles for sale and advertise for titles wanted in the weekly magazine *Bookdealer*. Perhaps a word of advice may be given here: if a book is required, ask for it from as many dealers as possible, but make it clear whether you wish the bookdealer to advertise for it, and ask only one to do this. If a book-buyer goes from dealer to dealer asking to see if they can get a copy of some book for him, the probability is that six advertisements for it will appear in the next week's *Bookdealer*; the law of supply and demand will begin to operate, and the man who has a copy will feel that he has put too low a price on a book that is so eagerly sought, and will increase it accordingly.

The Internet has become a very useful tool to search for titles. In some respects, web sites devoted to the secondhand and antiquarian book trade are better organised than those for the new book trade. Those seeking information about this aspect will find *Sheppard's World* (www.sheppardsworld.co.uk) **very useful and there are others, some of which are listed on page forty-three.**

There is also a weekly newsletter for the trade, *Sheppard's Confidential*. This is supplied free to all dealers listed in Sheppard's directories. and carries auction and book fair calendars, trade news, letters, events and book reviews.

A distinctive feature of the secondhand book trade, however, is its high degree of specialisation. Almost every dealer has a particular interest, and some will be found who deal only in books on one subject, or indeed in the works of one author or group of authors. If one requires a secondhand or antiquarian book he should go or write directly to the specialist. This directory is intended to provide a handy guide that will enable the booklover to do this with the minimum of trouble, to fill its place as an essential reference book for the trade.

There are two national trade associations for antiquarian book dealers:

THE ANTIQUARIAN BOOKSELLERS' ASSOCIATION, Sackville House, 40 Piccadilly, London W1J 0DR. Tel: (020) 7439-3118. Fax: 7439-3119. E-Mail: admin@aba.org.uk. Web Site: www.aba.org.uk Est: 1906. President: Robert Frew. Vice President: Alan Shelley. Treasurer: Paul Minet. Administrators: John Critchley, Philippa Gibson, and Marianne Harwood. The Antiquarian Booksellers' Association includes the leading dealers in antiquarian, fine and scarce secondhand books throughout Great Britain as well as in some other countries. It is the founding member of the twenty similar associations, scattered throughout Europe, the Americas, and the Far East which together form the International League of Antiquarian Booksellers.

The Association seeks to provide a comprehensive service to its members. It organises the prestigious and renowned Antiquarian Book Fair each June at Olympia, London and a more broadly-based Book Fair at Chelsea Town Hall every autumn. Branch fairs are also held in Edinburgh. All members receive an informative newsletter each month and there is a fine reference library ready to answer their bibliographical queries. Their interests are further looked after by representatives sitting on various government bodies and dealing with such subjects as the export of manuscripts, the future of the British Library, the National Book Committee, the monitoring of V.A.T. and customs regulations both here and in the Common Market. The Association organises, through the year, a series of events – sporting, social, and educational – aimed at promoting friendship and understanding among colleagues at both national and international levels. There is a Benevolent Fund upon which members may call in times of financial difficulty. Members may also benefit from advantageous rates on credit card processing, and insurance negotiated on their behalf by the Association.

There are various ways in which the Association looks after the interest of the general public. By requiring of all its members a good experience of the trade, and high professional standards and ethics, it ensures that the public may approach with confidence any dealer displaying the A.B.A. badge. In rare cases of difficulty or dispute, the Association stands ready to arbitrate between dealer and client.

The public, especially institutions and public libraries, are further served by a sophisticated security system founded and developed by the Association and now copied throughout the world. It has already accounted for the apprehension of an impressive list of book-thieves and for the recovery and restoration to their rightful owners of many hundreds of stolen books.

THE BRITISH BOOK TRADE

From within its ranks, the Antiquarian Booksellers' Association can produce experts on most aspects of bibliography and book-collecting, and their collective expertise is available to the general public through the Association's office. A list of Members is published every two years and is available on request from the Administrators, or through the website.

PROVINCIAL BOOKSELLERS' FAIRS ASSOCIATION, The Old Coach House, 16 Melbourn Street, Royston, Hertfordshire SG8 7BZ. Tel: (01763) 248400. Fax: 248921. Fairs Information line: 249212. E-Mail: info@pbfa.org. Web: www.pbfa.org. Est: 1974. Chairman: George Newlands. Vice-Chairman: Adrian Pegg. Honorary Secretary: Roz Burmester. Honorary Treasurer: David Sedgwick. Administrator: Becky Wears.

The PBFA is the largest association of antiquarian and secondhand booksellers in Great Britain. With over 630 members it is also the largest in the world. It is non-profit making and co-operatively managed by its members through national and regional committees. The full-time administrative headquarters are in Royston.

The Association organises book fairs throughout the country – over 100 each year. Central to this programme are the monthly fairs held at the Hotel Russell in London and the international fairs held each June, at the Hotel Russell and Novotel London West. From January 2007, the monthly fairs will be held at the Holiday Inn Bloomsbury, Coram Street WC1 1HT.

Support for members and their dependents is available at times of distress through the Association's own charity, the Richard Condon Memorial Fund. The size of the membership allows the PBFA to negotiate advantageous rates for credit card processing, postal services, insurance and bulk purchasing.

The PBFA caters for a wide range of book collecting interests and aims to promote a broader interest in antiquarian and secondhand books. The PBFA provides safeguards for the public buying from its members and is committed to maintaining the highest trading standards. In addition a newsletter is published for members and an annual Directory of Members *(£5.50 inc. p&p)* and a nationwide calendar of book fairs *(free)* are available from the Royston office.

There is also an antiquarian and secondhand book-trade association for Wales:

WELSH BOOKSELLERS ASSOCIATION, c/o 44 Lion Street, Hay-on-Wye, Herefordshire HR3 5AA. Tel: (01497) 820322. Fax: 821150. Est: 1987. Chairman: Richard Booth. Secretary & Treasurer: Anna Cooper. The Association aims to encourage the development of secondhand and antiquarian bookselling in Wales. Books, maps, prints, manuscripts and ephemera all come within the scope of the Association. An annual leaflet giving details of each member is available by subscription from the Secretary, or any member.

PRIVATE LIBRARIES ASSOCIATION, Ravelston, South View Road, Pinner, Middlesex HA5 3YD. Est: 1956. Web: www.plabooks.org. The Private Libraries Association is an international society of book collectors with about 600 private members (about one quarter of them in America) and about 150 institutional members. The Association publishes a quarterly journal (*The Private Library*, which contains articles, notes and other items), an annual checklist of Private Press Books, a quarterly *Newsletter and Exchange List*, a *Members' List*, and other books about various aspects of book collecting. Annual subscription £25.

SOCIETY OF BOOKBINDERS, 2 Lower Faircox, Henfield, West Sussex BBN5 9UT. For all contacts, please use the web site: www.societyofbookbinders.com. Membership is open to anyone intersted in books, whether a binder or not, although most members are either binders already, or aspiring to learn the craft. Current Chairman: Gordon J. Hartley. Honorary Secretary: Mrs. J. Refern.

The web site includes a gallery of pictures showing the work of a number of members.

ANTIQUARIAN BOOKSELLERS' ASSOCIATIONS

Australia and New Zealand
AUSTRALIAN AND NEW ZEALAND ASSOCIATION OF ANTIQUARIAN BOOKSELLERS, (ANZAAB) 32 Maberley Crescent, Frankston, VIC 3199. Tel: (613) 5971-3230. Fax: (613) 9529-1298. E-mail: admin@anzaab.com. Web: www.anzaab.com. Est 1977. President: Louella Kerr. Vice-Presidents: Peter Tinsley. Secretary: Sam Haymes. Treasurer: Michael Sprod. 70 members.

Austria
VERBAND DER ANTIQUARE ÖSTERREICHS, Grünangergasse 4, A-1010 Wien, Austria. Tel: (01) 512 15 35. Fax: (01) 512 84 82. E-mail: sekretariat@hvb.at. Web: www.antiquare.at. President: Norbert Donhofer. 37 members

Belgium
LA CHAMBRE PROFESSIONNELLE BELGE DE LA LIBRAIRIE ANCIENNE ET MODERNE (C.L.A.M.). DE BELGISCHE BEROEPSKAMER VAN ANTIQUAREN (B.B.A.). Secretary: Mme Dominique Basteyns, CLAM-BBA, Galerie Bortier, 12-14, B-1000 Brussels. Fax: (+32) (02) 503 24 21. E-Mail: dominique.basteyns@skynet.be. Est: 1946. President: Henri Godts. Vice President: Jan Ceuleers. Treasurer: Alain Ferraton. Secretary: CLAM-BBA, the Belgium Antiquarian Booksellers' Association is affiliated to the International League of Antiquarian Booksellers (I.L.A.B)

Brazil
ASSOCIAÇÃO BRASILEIRA DE LIVERIROS ANTIQUÁRIOS, Rua Santos Dumont 677 25625-090 Centro Petrópolis, Brazil. Tel: (242) 42 03 76. Fax: (242) 31 16 95. Est: 1945 President: Mrs Ana Maria Bocayuva de Miranda Jordão. E-mail: sebofino@uol.com.br. 9 members.

Canada
ANTIQUARIAN BOOKSELLERS' ASSOCIATION OF CANADA, (A.B.A.C). c/o 783 Bank Street, Ottawa, Ontario K1S 3V5 Canada. President: Wilfrid M. de Freitas. Secretary: Charles Purpora (Tel: 604 320-0375). E-mail: charles@purporabooks.com. 70 members.

Czech Republic
SVAZ ANTIKVÁRU CR, Karlova 2, 110 00 Praha 1, Czech Republic. Tel: & Fax: (02) 22 22 02 86, 22 22 02 88. Est: 1922. President: Petr Meissner. E-mail: info@meissner.cz. 5 members

Denmark
DEN DANSKE ANTIKVARBOGHANDLERFORENING, P.O. Box 2028, DK-1012 Copenhagen K, Denmark. E-mail: info@antikvat.dk. Internet: www.antikvar.dk. Est: 1920. President: Poul Jan Poulsen. 35 members.

PROVINCIAL BY NAME

The PBFA has been running quality book fairs for more than quarter of a century. From our first event, held in London in 1972, and intended as a shop window for provincial book dealers (hence the name), to our current programme of fairs all round the country we offer the book collecting public and the secondhand book trade an unparalleled range of events to suit every taste and every pocket - large fairs, small fairs, in the North and in the South; specialist fairs, and general fairs with books on all subjects at prices ranging from £5 to £5,000. A PBFA book fair, large or small, stands out by its quality - quality of presentation, quality of organisation and quality of items offered.

Our fairs in the Hotel Russell have a well-deserved reputation as **the** place to buy books in London, and we will ensure that we continue to deserve this reputation when we move to a new venue in 2007. Each area of the United Kingdom now boasts its own regular major event; from Aberdeeen through Edinburgh, York, Harrogate, Cambridge, Oxford and Bath.

Visit out web site www.pbfa.org to see our full programme of quality fairslists of exhibitors, detailed information and maps for all fairs Our published calendar is also available post free from our HQ address below.

All PBFA members are established bookdealers who abide by a code of practice. Their trading details are readily accessible in the Directory of Members available at £4.00 (p + p extra) and through our online directory.

The PBFA relies on volunteers to run its affairs, be it on committees, managing a fair, or helping out with putting up posters or clearing up afterwards. We could not function without these hardworking members and however large we grow, we will retain our founding principles of working co-operatively to sell quality books at quality events.

WORLDWIDE BY REPUTATION

For further information on our renowned book fairs or how to join the PBFA contact:
Becky Wears, PBFA, The Old Coach House, 16 Melbourn St, Royston, Herts, SG8 7BZ.
Tel: 01763 248400, Fax: 01762 248921,
email: info@pbfa.org or visit our web site at www.pbfa.org

ANTIQUARIAN BOOKSELLERS' ASSOCIATIONS

Finland
SUOMEN ANTIKVARIAATTIYHDISTYS. (Finnish Antiquarian Booksellers Association), c/o Kampintorin Antikvaarinen Kirjakauppa, Fredrikinkatu 63, Helsinki, Finland. Tel: (09) 694 3306. Est: 1941. E-mail: timo.surojegin@pp.inet.fi. 23 members.

France
SYNDICAT NATIONAL DE LA LIBRAIRIE ANCIENNE ET MODERNE, 4 rue Gît-le-Cœur, F-75006 Paris, France. Tel: (01) 43 29 46 38. Fax: (01) 43 25 41 63. E-mail: slam-livre@wanadoo.fr. Web: www.slam-livre.fr. Est: 1914. President: Mr Frederic Castaing. 245 members.

Germany
VERBAND DEUTSCHER ANTIQUARE e.V., Herr Norbert Munsch, Seeblick 1, 56459 Elbingen. Tel: (0 64 35) 90 91 47. Fax: (0 64 35) 90 91 48. E-mail: buch@antiquare.de. Web: www.antiquare.de. Est: 1949. President: Eberhard Köstler. Aprroximately 300 members.

Italy
ASSOCIAZIONE LIBRAI ANTIQUARI D'ITALIA, via Parione 16, 50123 Florence, Italy. Tel: (039) 055 265 8317. Fax: (039) 055 214 831. E-mail: alai@alai.it. Web: www.alai.it. Est: 1947. President: Umberto Pregliasco. Vice President: Umberto Pregliasco. Treasurer: Piero Crini. 120 members.

Japan
THE ANTIQUARIAN BOOKSELLERS' ASSOCIATION OF JAPAN (ABAJ), 29 San-ei-cho, Shinjuku-ku, Tokyo 160-0008, Japan. Tel: (03) 3357-1411. Fax: (03) 3351-5855. Est: 1963. President: Mr Mitsuo Nitta. E-mail: antiq@yushodo.co.jp. 30 members.

Korea
ANTIQUARIAN BOOKSELLERS' ASSOCIATION OF KOREA (A.B.A.K.), Bi-Ja-Beol Bookshop, 2-123 Samhee-Sangga, Dapsipri 5-Dong, Dongdaemun-Gu, Souel, 130-035 Tel: (02) 242-97 75. President: Mr Ko Chang Suk. 31 members.

Netherlands
NEDERLANDSCHE VEREENIGING VAN ANTIQUAREN, Prinsegracht 15, 2512 EW Den Haag. Tel: 070-3649840. Fax: 070 3643340. Web: www.nvva.nl. President: Mr. Ton Kok. (E-mail: kok@xs4all.nl). 79 Members.

Norway
NORSK ANTIKVARBOKHANDLERFORENING, Postboks 1420, Vika N-0115 Oslo, Norway. Tel: (47) 23 31 02 80. Internet: www.antikvariat.no. President: Vidar Wangsmo. (E-mail: wangsmo@wangsmo.com. 20 members.

Spain
ADSCRIPTO IBERICA LIBRARIAE ANTIQUARIORUM (A.I.L.A.), San Miguel 12, E-07002 Palma de Mallorca, Spain. Tel: (971) 72 13 55. Fax: (971) 71 74 36. Internet: www.libreriaripoll.com. President: Mr Manuel Ripoll Billon.

ANTIQUARIAN BOOKSELLERS' ASSOCIATIONS

Sweden
SVENSKA ANTIKVARIATFÖRENINGEN, Box 22 549, SE-104 22 Stockholm, Sweden. Tel: (08) 654 80 86. Fax: (08) 654 80 06. E-Mail: main@svaf.se. Internet: www.svaf.se. President: Sten Rigselle. E-mail: antiquaria@telia.com

Switzerland
VEREINIGUNG DER BUCHANTIQUARE UND KUPFER-STICHHÄNDLER IN DER SCHWEIZ (V.E.B.U.K.U.) / SYNDICAT DE LA LIBRARIE ANCIENNE ET DU COMMERCE DE L'ESTAMPE EN SUISSE (S.L.A.C.E.S.), Route de Rolle, PO Box 17, CH-1162 St. prex. Tel: +41-21-806-1662. Fax: +41-21-806-3059. E-mail: f.bloch@bluewin.ch. President: Marcus Benz.

United Kingdom
THE ANTIQUARIAN BOOKSELLERS' ASSOCIATION, Sackville House, 40 Piccadilly, London W1J 0DR. Tel: (020) 7439-3118. Fax: 7439-3119. E-Mail: admin@aba.org.uk. Web Site: www.aba.org. Est: 1906. President: Robert Frew. Director: John Critchley.

PRIVATE LIBRARIES ASSOCIATION, Ravelston, South View Road, Pinner, Middlesex HA5 3YD. Est: 1956. The Private Libraries Association is an international society of book collectors with about 600 private members (about one third of them in America) and about 150 library members.

PROVINCIAL BOOKSELLERS FAIRS ASSOCIATION, The Old Coach House, 16 Melbourn Street, Royston, Hertfordshire SG8 7BZ. Tel: (01763) 248400. Fax: (01763) 248921. Fairs information line: (01763) 249212. E-Mail: info@pbfa.org. Web Site: www.pbfa.org. Est: 1974. Chairman: George Newlands. Vice-Chairman: Adrian Pegge. Honorary Secretary: Phil Salin. Becky Wears. Over 630 members.

WELSH BOOKSELLERS ASSOCIATION, c/o 44 Lion Street, Hay-on-Wye, Herefordshire HR3 5AA. Tel: (01497) 820322. Fax: 821150. E-Mail: WBA@richardbooth.demon.co.uk. Est. 1987. Chairman: Richard Booth. 29 members.

United States of America
ANTIQUARIAN BOOKSELLERS' ASSOCIATION OF AMERICA (A.B.A.A.), 20 West 44th Street, Fourth Floor, New York, N.Y. 10036-6604, U.S.A. Tel: (212) 944-8291. Fax: 944-8293. E-Mail: hq@abaa.org. Web Site: www.abaa.org. Est: 1949. President: David Lilburne. Over 456 members.

INTERNATIONAL LEAGUE OF ANTIQUARIAN BOOKSELLERS (I.L.A.B.) to which most national associations belong. President: Robert D. Fleck, 310 Delaware Street, Newcastle, DE 19720 USA. E-mail: oakknoll@oakknoll.com. General Secretary: Steven Temple, Steven Temple Books, 489 Queen Street West, Toronto, ON M5V 2B4 Canada. E-mail: books@steventemplebooks.com.

PERIODICALS
Literary Magazines and Book Trade Papers

Please note that magazine prices and subscriptions are given as a guide only, and are liable to change.

THE AFRICAN BOOK PUBLISHING RECORD (ABPR). Covers new and forthcoming African publications, as well as publishing articles & news. Est: 1975. Quarterly. Subscription: EURO 372.00 (price for 2004). Editor: Cécile Lomer. Published by: K.G. Saur Verlag GmbH, Ortlerstrasse 8, 81373 Muenchen, Germany; Postfach 70 16 20, 81316 Muenchen, Germany. Tel: +49-89-76902-0; Fax: +49-89-76902-150; E-mail: saur.info@thomson.com. Subscription enquiries to K.G. Saur Verlag.

ALMANACCO DEL BIBLIOFILO. Yearly. Publisher: Edizioni Rovello di Mario Scognamiglio, P.za Castello, 11, 20121 Milano, Italy. Tel: (02) 86464661 or (02) 866532. Fax: (02) 72022884. E-mail: edirovello@libero.it

ANTIQUES MAGAZINE. Weekly or fortnightly. Subscription. £52.00 – about 40 issues, plus 2 Antiques Fairs & Centres Guide (U.K.). Fortnightly £28.00 (U.K.); please call for overseas rates. Published by: H.P. Publishing, 2, Hampton Court Road, Harborne, Birmingham B17 9AE. Tel: (0121) 681-8000 (General enquiries); -8001 (Accounts); -8006 (Editorial). Subscriptions: Tel: (0121) 681 8003; Fax: (0121) 681-8005. E-Mail: subscriptions@antiquesmagazine.com. Web Site: www.antiquesmagazine.com.

ANTIQUES TRADE GAZETTE. Contains comprehensive weekly reports on antiquarian book sales worldwide plus auction calendar. Est: 1971. Weekly. Subscription: £74.00 (£133.00 North America £158.00 and rest of world, £135.00 Europe) a year. Published by: Metropress Ltd., 115 Shaftesbury Avenue, London WC2H 8AD. Tel: (020) 7420-6600. Editor: Ivan Macquisten. Antiquarian Books Editor: Ian McKay. Tel: (01795) 890475. Fax: 890014. E-mail: ianmckay1@btinternet.com

AUS DEM ANTIQUARIAT. German journal on Antiquarian booktrade by subscription. Published six times a year by MVB Marketing- und Verlagservice des Buchhandels GmbH, Grosser Hirschgraben 17-21, 60311 Frankfurt am Main (Postfach 100442, 60004 Frankfurt am Main), Germany. Tel: +49 (69) 1306 469. Fax: 1306 394. E-mail: antiquariat@mvb-online.de. Internet www.buch-antiquariat.de

BOOK AND MAGAZINE COLLECTOR. Biographies and bibliographies of collectable 19th and 20th century authors and illustrators, plus lists of books for sale and wanted. Est: 1984. Monthly. Subscription: £42.00 a year (13 issues, U.K.), £46.00 (Europe, Airmail), £53.00 (Rest of the World). Editor: Jonathan Scott. Publisher: John Dean. Published by: Diamond Publishing, Metropolis Int., Unit 101, Wales Farm Road, London W3 6UG Tel: (0870) 732-8080. Fax: (0870) 732-6060. E-mail: bmceditor@metropolis.co.uk

THE BOOK COLLECTOR. Est: 1952. Quarterly. Subscription: £47.00 (Europe & USA £50 [surface], Europe £51 and USA £58 [airmail], S E Asia & Australasia £50 [surface] and £60 [airmail]. Editor: Nicolas Barker. Published by: The Collector Ltd., 20 Maple Grove, London NW9 8QY. Tel: & Fax: (020) 8200-5004. E-mail: info@thebookcollector.co.uk.

THE BOOKDEALER. Trade weekly for secondhand and antiquarian books for sale and wanted. £52.00 a year or £26.00 for six months (incl. p. & p. within U.K.). Editor: Barry Shaw. Publisher: Alacrity, Eastern Wing, Banwell Castle, Weston-super-Mare BS29 6NX. Tel: (01934) 822971. Fax: 820682. E-mail: alacrity@dial.pipex .com.

BOOKS FROM FINLAND English-language journal presenting Finnish literature and writers. Est. 1967. Editor-in-chief: Kristina Carlson. Editors: Soila Lehtonen & Hildi Hawkins. Quarterly. Subscription: 20 euros a year (Finland and Scandinavia), 27 euros (all other countries). Published by: Finnish Literature Society, P.O. Box 259, FI-00171 Helsinki, Finland. Tel: +358 (0) 201 131345. E-mail: booksfromfinland@finlit.fi. Website: www.finlit.fi/booksfromfinland

THE BOOKSELLER. Journal of the book trade in Great Britain. Weekly. Subscription: £179.00 a year (U.K.), £185.00 (overseas, airmail extra). Editor-in-chief: Neill Denny. Published by: VNU Entertainment Media UK Ltd., 189 Shaftesbury Avenue, London WC2H 8TJ. Tel: (020) 7420-6006. Fax: 7420-6103.BOOK SOURCE MAGAZINE. Published since 1985, contains articles, news, reviews and information for the secondhand/antiquarian book trade in the USA. Subscription bi-monthly: $20.00 (1st class USA); $24.00 (library rate, Canada and Mexico); $48/£28.00 (overseas airmail). Editor: John C. Huckans. Published at: 2007 Syosett Drive, Cazenovia, NY 13035-9753. Tel: & Fax: (315) 655-8499. E-Mail: bsm@alltel.net. Web Site: www.booksourcemagazine.com.

BOOK WORLD MAGAZINE. Articles, reviews, advertisements and news of the book world in general. Monthly. Subscription: £50.00 (U.K.), $100.00 (surface mail U.S.), $140.00 (air mail U.S.). Published by: Christchurch Publishers Ltd., 2 Caversham Street, Chelsea, London SW3 4AH. Tel: & Fax: (020) 7351-4995.

PERIODICALS

CONTEMPORARY REVIEW. On politics, current affairs, theology, social questions, literature and the arts. Web: www.contemporaryreview.co.uk. Monthly. Subscription: £49.00 a year (U.K. surface mail), $195.00 (U.S.A. and Canada, airfreight), others on application. Editor: Dr. Richard Mullen. Published by: The Contemporary Review Co. Ltd., P.O. Box 1242, Oxford, OX1 4FJ, England. Tel: & Fax: (01865) 201529. E-mail: subscriptions@comtemporaryreview.co.uk. Editorial office: editorial@ comtemporaryreview.co.uk.

L'ESOPO. Bibliophile magazine. Quarterly. Published at: Edizioni Rovello di Mario Scognamiglio, P.za Castello, 11, 20121 Milano, Italy. Tel: (02) 86464661 or (02) 866532. Fax: (02) 72022884. E-mail: edirovello@libero.it

FINE BOOKS & COLLECTIONS (formerly OP Magazine). Dedicated to the out-of-print, collectible, and antiquarian book world. Six full colour issues a year. US Subscription $25. Published by OP Media LLC 4905 Pine Cone Drive, Suite 2, Durham NC 27707. E-mail: subscriptions@finebooksmagazine.com.

FOLIO. Produced 3-4 times a year, to members only. Editor: Kit Shepherd. Published by: The Folio Society Ltd., 44 Eagle Street, London WC1R 4FS. Web: www.foliosoc.co.uk. Tel: (020) 7400-4222.

THE LITERARY REVIEW. Covers books, arts and poetry. Est: 1978. Monthly. Subscription: £32.00 a year (U.K.), £39.00 (Europe), $75.00 (U.S.A. & Canada Airspeed), $104.00 (rest of the world Air Mail). Web: www.literaryreview.co.uk. Editor: Nancy Sladek. Published by: The Literary Review, 44 Lexington Street, London W1F 0LW. Tel: (020) 7437-9392. Fax: (020) 7734-1844.

MINIATURE BOOK NEWS. Est: 1965. Quarterly. (Now incorporated in the Miniature Book Society Newsletter – Subscription to both: $30.00 oer year, US, $35.00 Canada and $45.00 Overseas). Editor: Julian I. Edison. Published at: 8 St. Andrews Drive, St. Louis, Missouri 63124, U.S.A.

THE PRIVATE LIBRARY. Established 1957. Quarterly. Distributed free to members of the Private Libraries Association, annual subscription £25.00 ($40.00). Editors: David Chambers & Paul W. Nash. Sample copy free on request. Published by: The Private Libraries Association, Ravelston, South View Road, Pinner, Middlesex HA5 3YD.

PRIVATE PRESS BOOKS. An annual bibliography of books printed by private presses in the English speaking world. 1999 edition: 96 pp,;2000 edition 95pp; 2001 edition 64pp. £10.00 or $20.00 (£5.00 or $10.00 to PLA members) Editor: Paul W. Nash. Published by: The Private Libraries Association, Ravelston, South View Road, Pinner, Middlesex HA5 3YD.

QUILL AND QUIRE. Keeps its readers up-to-date on Canada's exciting book publishing scene and provides the earliest and most complete look at new Canadian books, with more than 500 titles reviewed each year. In addition, the Canadian Publishers Directory, which puts the book industry at your fingertips, is delivered free bi-annually. 12 issues a year for CAN$ 59.95; USA and Overseas CAN $95 (includes postage). Est: 1935. Editor: Derek Weiler. Published at: 111 Queen Street East, 3rd Floor, Toronto, Ontario M5C 1S2 Canada. Subscriptions tel: (905) 946-0406. Fax: 905 946-0410. Email: subscriptions@ quillandquire.com. Web: www.quillandquire.com.

RBR (RARE BOOK REVIEW). Magazine containing articles, book reviews, auction reports and catalogue news. Est: 1974. Subscription: £27 a year (U.K.), £35.00 (Europe), £45.00 (Rest of the World). Rare Book Review, 24 Maddox Street, London W1S 1PP Tel: +44 (0) 20 7529 4220. Fax: +44 (0) 20 7495 9499. E-mail: jeff@rarebookreview.com

TRIBUNE. Books Editor: Chris McLaughlin. Published by: Tribune Publications Ltd., 9 Arkright Road, London NW3 6AN. Subscriotion 1 year £64.00. Tel: (020) 7433-6410. E-mail: george@tribpub .demon.co.uk.

FREE TRADE MAGAZINES

BOOKSELLER.COM. A free e-mail newsletter where the latest trade news about the new book trade can be read. Register on www.bookseller.com

PN NEWS. An on-line international news service for the new book trade. To register: www.publishing news.co.uk

SHEPPARD'S CONFIDENTIAL. A free e-mail newsletter published weekly for the antiquarian and second-hand book trade: the latest news, calendars for book fairs and auctions. Events and book reviews as well as extensive coverage of views and opinions from members of the trade. Register on www.sheppardsworld.co.uk

CURRENT REFERENCE BOOKS

ABC OF BOOKBINDING. By Jane Greenfield. $39.95. Published by: Oak Knoll Press, 310 Delaware Street, New Castle, DE 19720, U.S.A. Tel: (302) 328-7232. Fax: 328-7274. E-Mail: oakknoll@ oakknoll.com. Sales rights: Worldwide outside of UK. Available in the UK from The Plough Press.

ABPC on CD-ROM. The auction season September 1975 to August 2005. $1680.76. Published by: Bancroft Parkman Inc., P.O. Box 1236, Washington, CT 06793, U.S.A. Tel: (860) 868-7408. Fax: (860) 868-0080. E-Mail: abpc@snet.net. Web Site: http://www.bookpricescurrent.com.

AMERICAN BOOKS ON FOOD & DRINK. By William R. Cagle & Lisa Killion Stafford. $95.00. Published by: Oak Knoll Press, 310 Delaware Street, New Castle, DE 19720, U.S.A. Tel: (302) 328-7232. Fax: 328-7274. E-Mail: oakknoll@oakknoll.com.

AMERICAN BOOK TRADE DIRECTORY. Profiles retail and antiquarian book dealers plus book and magazine wholesalers, distributors and jobbers in the United States. 2004/2005: £245 plus £15 post and handling. Available from: Information Today Ltd., Woodside, Hinksey Hill, Oxford OX1 5BE. Tel: (01865) 327813. Fax: (01865) 730232. E-mail: info.uk@infotoday.com. Web Site: www.infotoday.com.

THE ART OF BOOK–BINDING. By Edward Walker. $30.00. Published by: Oak Knoll Press, 310 Delaware Street, New Castle, DE 19720, U.S.A. Tel: (302) 328-7232. Fax: 328-7274. E-Mail: oakknoll@ oakknoll.com.

AT HOME WITH BOOKS. How book lovers live with and care for their libraries. By: Estelle Ellis, Caroline Seebohm, Christopher Simon Sykes. £19.95. Published by: Thames & Hudson, 181A High Holborn, London WC1V 7QX. Tel: (020) 7845-5000. Fax: 7845-5050. E-mail: sales@thameshudson.co.uk

BIBLIOGRAPHY OF HENRY JAMES. By Leon Edel & Dan Laurence. $80.00. Published by: Oak Knoll Press, 310 Delaware Street, New Castle, DE 19720, U.S.A. Tel: (302) 328-7232. Fax: 328-7274. E-Mail: oakknoll@oakknoll.com.

A & C BLACK COLOUR BOOKS. A collector's guide and bibliography 1900–1930. Author: Colin Inman. £30.00. Published in 1990 by Werner Shaw Ltd and distributed by Alacrity, Eastern Wing, Banwell Castle, Banwell, Weston-super-Mare, Somerset BS29 6NX. Tel: (01934) 820644, or 820478. Fax: (01934) 820682. E-mail: alacrity@dial.pipex.com. A bibliogrpahy covering 800 books in 50 series, with full historical account of this great publishing venture.

BOOKBINDING & CONSERVATION BY HAND: A working guide. By Laura S. Young. Hardback $35.00. Paperback $24.95. Published by: Oak Knoll Press, 310 Delaware Street, New Castle, DE 19720, U.S.A. Tel: (302) 328-7232. Fax: 328-7274. E-Mail: oakknoll@oakknoll.com.

BOOKDEALING FOR PROFIT. By Paul Minet. The philosophy behind the business as well as a look into the future and how the Internet is having a major effect on the trade. Hardback £10.00. Published by Richard Joseph Publishers Ltd, P.O. Box 15, Torrington, Devon EX38 8ZJ. UK. Tel: (01805) 625750. Fax: (01805) 625376. E-mail: admin@sheppardsworld.eclipse.co.uk. Web Site: www.sheppardsdirectories.com; and www.sheppardsworld.co.uk

BRITISH NATIONAL BIBLIOGRAPHY. Records new and forthcoming publications in the UK and Ireland. Options include: print (weekly list with cumulations), CD-ROM (monthly disc, fully cumulated) and MARC (weekly data file). Published by: The British Library, The Bibliographic Standards and Systems, Boston Spa, Wetherby, West Yorkshire LS23 7BQ. ENGLAND. Tel: (01937) 546548. Fax: 546586. E-mail: bss-info@bl.uk. Web Site: www.bl.uk. Orders and subscriptions: Turpin Distribution, Stratton Business Park, Pegasus Drive, Biggleswade, Bedfordshire SG18 8QB. Tel: (01767) 604955. Fax: 601640. E-mail: subscriptions@turpin-distribution.com.

LEWIS CARROLL AND THE PRESS. By Charles Lovett. $35.00. Published by: Oak Knoll Press & The British Library. Information from: Oak Knoll Press, 310 Delaware Street, New Castle, DE 19720, U.S.A. Tel: (302) 328-7232. Fax: 328-7274. E-Mail: oakknoll@oakknoll.com.

CHILDREN'S BOOKS IN ENGLAND. By F.J. Harvey Darton. $49.95. Published by: The British Library & Oak Knoll Press. Information from: Oak Knoll Press, 310 Delaware Street, New Castle, DE 19720, U.S.A. Tel: (302) 328-7232. Fax: 328-7274. E-Mail: oakknoll@oakknoll.com.

CILIP: the Chartered Institute of. 2004–2005. £44.95. Compilers: Kathryn Beecroft (ed.). Published by: Facet Publishing, 7 Ridgmount Street, London WC1E 7AE. Tel: (020) 7255-0590. Fax: 7255-0591. E-Mail: info@facetpublishing.co.uk. Web Site: www.facetpublishing.co.uk..

The Book Collector

In its fifty years of publication THE BOOK COLLECTOR has firmly established itself as the most interesting and lively current journal for collectors, bibliographers, antiquarian booksellers and custodians of rare books. Leading authorities contribute regularly on all aspects of bibliophily, from medieval manuscripts to modern first editions and each issue offers new and original insight into the world of books

Some back numbers of issues from 1956 to 1979 are available We hold complete volumes from 1980 to date.

Subscription rates and detailed list and prices from:
The Book Collector
20 MAPLE GROVE, LONDON NW9 8QY
Tel/fax 020-8200 5004
E-mail: info@thebookcollector.co.uk
Website: www.thebookcollector.co.uk

CURRENT REFERENCE BOOKS

W.H. DAVIES, A BIBLIOGRAPHY. By Sylvia Harlow. $78.00. Published by: Oak Knoll Press, 310 Delaware Street, New Castle, DE 19720, U.S.A. Tel: (302) 328-7232. Fax: 328-7274. E-Mail: oakknoll@ oakknoll.com.

DIRECTORY OF PUBLISHING: United Kingdom & Republic of Ireland. 2006 31st Ed. 216pp £75.00. ISBN: 0 826487 53 X . Published by Continuum, The Tower Building, 11 York Road, London SE1 7NX. ENGLAND. Tel: (020) 7922-0880. Fax: 7922-0881. Web: www.continuumbooks.com

THE ENCYCLOPEDIA OF PAPERMAKING AND BOOKBINDING: the definitive guide to making, embellishing and repairing paper and books by Heidi Reimer-Epp and Mary Reimer. 160 pages with 200m colour illustrations. Hardback £16.95. Published by The British Library; available from Turpin Distribution Ltd., Blackhorse Road, Letchworth, Hertfordshire SG6 1HN. E-mail turpin@tuirpinltd.com

THOMAS FROGNALL DIBDIN, 1776 - 1847: A BIBLIOGRAPHY. By John Windle & Karma Pippin. $85.00. Published by: Oak Knoll Press, 310 Delaware Street, New Castle, DE 19720, U.S.A. Tel: (302) 328-7232. Fax: 328-7274. E-Mail: oakknoll@oakknoll.com.

THE DICTIONARY OF 20TH CENTURY BOOK ILLUSTRATORS. By SAlan Home. £45.00. Published by: Antique Collectors Club, Sandy Lane, Old Martlesham, Woodbridge, Suffolk IP12 4SD. Tel: (01394) 389950. Fax: 389999. E-mail: sales@antique-acc.com

THE DICTIONARY OF 20TH CENTURY BRITISH BOOK ILLUSTRATORS. By Alan Horne. £45.00. Published by: Antique Collectors Club, Sandy Lane, Old Martlesham, Woodbridge, Suffolk IP12 4SD. Tel: (01394) 389950. Fax: 389999. E–mail: sales@antique-acc.com

DIRECTORY OF RARE BOOK AND SPECIAL COLLECTIONS IN THE UNITED KINGDOM AND REPUBLIC OF IRELAND. Editor: B.C. Bloomfield. 1997. £99.95. Published by: Facet Publishing, 7 Ridgmount Street, London WC1E 7AE. Tel: (020) 7255-0590. Fax: 7255-0591. E-Mail: info@facetpublishing.co.uk. Web Site: www.facetpublishing.co.uk.

ENCYCLOPEDIA OF THE BOOK. By: Geoffrey Ashall Glaister. Hardcover $75.00, Paperback $49.95. Published by Oak Knoll Press, 310 Delaware Street, New Castle, DE 19720, U.S.A. Tel: (302) 328-7232. Fax: 328-7274. E-Mail: oakknoll@oakknoll.com.

THE ENGLISH AS COLLECTORS. By Frank Herrmann. $49.95. Published by: Oak Knoll Press & John Murray Ltd. Information from: Oak Knoll Press, 310 Delaware Street, New Castle, DE 19720, U.S.A. Tel: (302) 328-7232. Fax: 328-7274. E-Mail: oakknoll@oakknoll.com. Sales Rights: Worldwide outside of the UK. Available in the UK from The Plough Press.

FIRST EDITIONS: A GUIDE TO IDENTIFICATION. 4th edition for 2001. $60.00. Editor: Edward N. Zempel. Published by: Spoon River Press, P.O. Box 3635, Peoria, IL 61612-3635, U.S.A. Tel: (309) 672-2665.

T.N. FOULIS: The History and Bibliography of an Edinburgh Publishing House. By Ian Elfick & Paul Harris. £30.00. Published by Werner Shaw Ltd and distributed by Alacrity, Eastern Wing, Banwell Castle, Banwell, Weston-super-Mare, Somerset BS29 6NX. Tel: (01934) 820644, or 820478. Fax: (01934) 820682. E-mail: alacrity@dial.pipex.com

GREATER LONDON HISTORY AND HERITAGE HANDBOOK: the millennium guide to historical, heritage and environmental networks and publications. 1999 edition, 189pp, £20 +£2p&p. New edition planned for 2006. Editor: Peter Marcan. Published by: Peter Marcan Publications, P.O. Box 3158, London SE1 4RA. Tel: (020) 7357-0368.

A GUIDE TO WORLD LANGUAGE DICTIONAIRIES. Andrew Dalby. 1998. £69.95. Published by Facet Publishing, 7 Ridgmount Street, London WC1E 7AE. Tel: (020) 7255 0590. Fax: (0)20 7255 0591. E-mail: info@facetpublishing.co.uk. Web Site: www.facetpublishing.co.uk.

HISTORY OF ENGLISH CRAFT BOOKBINDING TECHNIQUE. By Bernard C. Middleton. $55.00. Published by: Oak Knoll Press, 310 Delaware Street, New Castle, DE 19720, U.S.A. Tel: (302) 328-7232. Fax: 328-7274. E-Mail: oakknoll@oakknoll.com. Sales rights: Worldwide outside of UK. Available in the UK from The British Library

ELSPETH HUXLEY, A BIBLIOGRAPHY. By Robert Cross & Michael Perkin. $78.00. Published by: Oak Knoll Press, 310 Delaware Street, New Castle, DE 19720, U.S.A. Tel: (302) 328-7232. Fax: 328-7274. E-Mail: oakknoll@oakknoll.com

THE ILLUSTRATIONS OF W. HEATH ROBINSON: A COMMENTARY AND BIBLIOGRAPHY. By Geoffrey Beare. The bibliography which follows the long introduction to Heath Robinson's work as an illustrator, was compiled from primary sources. £18.95. Published by Werner Shaw Ltd and distributed by Alacrity, Eastern Wing, Banwell Castle, Banwell, Weston-super-Mare, Somerset BS29 6NX. Tel: (01934) 820644, or 820478. Fax: (01934) 820682. E-mail: alacrity@dial.pipex.com

CURRENT REFERENCE BOOKS

INTERNATIONAL DIRECTORY OF ANTIQUARIAN BOOKSELLERS. A world list of members of organisations belonging to the International League of Antiquarian Booksellers (I.L.A.B.). Published every 2 years: 2004-5 edition available October 2004. £15.00 + £2.00 p&p. Published by: I.L.A.B. Distributed in the UK by: The Antiquarian Booksellers' Association, Sackville House, 40 Piccadilly, London W1J 0DR. Tel: (020 7439-3118. Fax: (020) 7439-3119. E-mail: admin@aba.org.uk.

LIBRARIES AND INFORMATION SERVICES IN THE UNITED KINGDOM AND REPUBLIC OF IRELAND, 2005-226. £44.00. Published by: Facet Publishing, 7 Ridgmount Street, London WC1E 7AE. Tel: (020) 7255-0590. Fax: 7255-0591. E-mail: info@facetpublishing.co.uk. Web Site: www.facetpublishing.co.uk.

LITERARY MARKET PLACE. The directory of the book publishing industry for America and Canada. Published annually. 2006 edition. Priced US$299.95 plus $21.00 post and handling. Also, available online at www.infotoday.com. Fax: (01865) 730232. E-mail: info@infotoday.com.

LOCAL STUDIES LIBRARIANSHIP: A WORLD BIBLIOGRAPHY. Editor: Diana Dixon. 2001. £34.00. Published by Facet Publishing, 7 Ridgmount Street, London WC1E 7AE. Tel: (020) 7255 0590. Fax: (020) 7255 0591. E-mail: info@facetpublishing.co.uk. Web Site: www.facetpublishing.co.uk.

THE MARCAN VISUAL ARTS HANDBOOK: where to go for British contacts, expertise and speciality in the fine and applied arts. £25 + £2.50 p&p. To be published early 2006. This is an expansion of the visual arts section / history in the earlier version. Published by: Peter Marcan Publications, P.O. Box 3158, London SE1 4RA. Tel: (020) 7357-0368.

A MATTER OF TASTE. By William R. Cagle & Lisa Killion Stafford. $95.00. Published by: Oak Knoll Press, 310 Delaware Street, New Castle, DE 19720, U.S.A. Tel: (302) 328-7232. Fax: 328-7274. E-Mail: oakknoll@oakknoll.com.

THOMAS BIRD MOSHER: PIRATE PRINCE OF PUBLISHERS. By Philip R. Bishop. $125.00. Published by: Oak Knoll Press & The British Library. Information from: Oak Knoll Press, 310 Delaware Street, New Castle, DE 19720, U.S.A. Tel: (302) 328-7232. Fax: 328-7274. Sales rights: Worldwide outside of UK. Available in the UK from The British Library.

NEW SCIENCE OUT OF OLD BOOKS. Studies in manuscripts and early printed books in honour of A.I. Doyle. £80.00. Edited by: Richard Beadle and A.J. Piper. Published by: Ashgate Publishing Ltd., Gower House, Croft Road, Aldershot, Hampshire GU11 3HR. Distributed by Bookpoint. Tel: (01235) 827730. Fax: 400454.

NEW WORLDS IN OLD BOOKS. By Leona Rostenberg & Madeleine Stern. $25.00. Published by: Oak Knoll Press, 310 Delaware Street, New Castle, DE 19720, U.S.A. Tel: (302) 328-7232. Fax: 328-7274. E-Mail: oakknoll@oakknoll.com.

A POCKET GUIDE TO THE IDENTIFICATION OF FIRST EDITIONS. An essential guide to identifying first editions for collectors, dealers, librarians, cataloguers and auctioneers. 6th Edition $19.95 per copy plus $1 shipping 40% discount on 5 or more copies; shipping for 5 copies is $5 by Priority Mail. International orders: single copies shipping $2.50; five copies $8 by Air/Printed Matter. Published by: The Jumping Frog, McBride/Publisher, 56 Arbor Street, Hartford, CT 06106, U.S.A. Tel: (860) 523–1622. Web Site: www.mcbridepublisher.com.

PRINCE OF FORGERS. By Joseph Rosenblum. $39.95. Published by: Oak Knoll Press, 310 Delaware Street, New Castle, DE 19720, U.S.A. Tel: (302) 328-7232. Fax: 328-7274.

PROVENANCE RESEARCH IN BOOK HISTORY. By David Pearson. Hardback $45.00, paperback $29.95. Published by: Oak Knoll Press & The British Library. Information from: Oak Knoll Press, 310 Delaware Street, New Castle, DE 19720, U.S.A. Tel: (302) 328-7232. Fax: 328-7274. Sales Rights: North and South America; elsewhere, The British Library.

RESTORATION OF LEATHER BINDINGS. By Bernard C. Middleton. $39.95. Published by: Oak Knoll Press & The British Library. Information from: Oak Knoll Press, 310 Delaware Street, New Castle, DE 19720, U.S.A. Tel: (302) 328-7232. Fax: 328-7274. Sales Rights: Worldwide except the U.K. Available in the U.K. from The British Library.

VITA SACKVILLE–WEST, A BIBLIOGRAPHY. By Robert Cross & Ann Ravenscroft Hulme. $80.00. Published by: Oak Knoll Press, 310 Delaware Street, New Castle, DE 19720, U.S.A. Tel: (302) 328-7232. Fax: 328-7274. E-Mail: oakknoll@oakknoll.com.

SIR 'WALTER SCOTT: A BIBLIOGRAPHY HISTORY 1796 - 1832. By William B. Todd & Ann Bowden. $95.00. Published by: Oak Knoll Press, 310 Delaware Street, New Castle, DE 19720, U.S.A. Tel: (302) 328-7232. Fax: 328-7274. E-Mail: oakknoll@oakknoll.com.

STUDIES IN THE HISTORY OF BOOKBINDING. This book consists of articles on the history of bookbinding and related subjects. Grouped under seven headings ranging from general topics such as bookbinding as a subject for study and the need to preserve the book, to more detailed descriptions of individual bindings from the fifteenth to the twentieth century. £80.00. Published by: Ashgate Publishing Ltd., Gower House, Croft Road, Aldershot, Hampshire GU11 3HR. Distributed by Bookpoint. Tel: (01235) 827730. Fax: 400454.

JULIAN SYMONS, A BIBLIOGRAPHY. By John J. Walsdor and Julian Symons. $85.00. Published by: Oak Knoll Press, 310 Delaware Street, New Castle, DE 19720, U.S.A. Tel: (302) 328-7232. Fax: 328-7274.

THE TARTARUS PRESS GUIDE TO FIRST EDITION PRICES 2006/7. Edited by: R.B. Russell. £19.99 inc. p&p. Published by: Tartarus Press, Coverley House, Carlton-in-Coverdale, Leyburn, North Yorks DL8 4AY. Tel: & Fax: (01969) 640399. E-Mail: tartarus@pavilion.co.uk.

J.R.R. TOLKIEN, A DESCRIPTIVE BIBLIOGRAPHY. By Wayne G. Hammond. $94.00. Published by: Oak Knoll Press, 310 Delaware Street, New Castle, DE 19720, U.S.A. Tel: (302) 328-7232. Fax: 328-7274. E-Mail: oakknoll@oakknoll.com.

TASHA TUDOR: THE DIRECTION OF HER DREAMS. By William John & Priscilla T. Hare. $85.00. A definitive bibliography; collector's guide. Published by: Oak Knoll Press, 310 Delaware Street, New Castle, DE 19720, U.S.A. Tel: (302) 328-7232. Fax: 328-7274.

TRUE TO TYPE. By Ruari McLean. A Typographical Autobiography. £25.00. Published by Werner Shaw Ltd and distributed by Alacrity, Eastern Wing, Banwell Castle, Banwell, Weston-super-Mare, Somerset BS29 6NX. Tel: (01934) 820644, or 820478. Fax: (01934) 820682. E-mail: alacrity@dial.pipex.com

LEONARD WOOLF, A BIBLIOGRAPHY. By Leila Luedeking & Michael Edmonds. $78.00. Published by: Oak Knoll Press, 310 Delaware Street, New Castle, DE 19720, U.S.A. Tel: (302) 328-7232. Fax: 328-7274. E-Mail: oakknoll@oakknoll.com

TYPESETTING AND DESIGN

- CATALOGUES
- BOOKS
- BROCHURES
- ADVERTISEMENTS
- JACKETS
- LEAFLETS, etc...

Reasonable rates, plus discounts for bookdealers listed in Sheppard's 2005.

Contact: Claire Hudson on 01252 713423
or email: thurbansps@btinternet.com

12 Thurbans Road
Farnham
Surrey GU9 8TD

TPS
Thurbans Publishing Services

Bookdealer
the trade magazine for books wanted and for sale

For over 30 years a valued companion to the second-hand & antiquarian book trade,
Bookdealer *is the journal you can't afford to overlook*

Subscribe

… and access thousands of Books Wanted or For Sale. Keep up to date through the magazine's features, reviews and editorials. All this for around £1 an issue.

Advertise

… and know your ad will be seen by dealers throughout the UK and abroad. We can incorporate your existing artwork, or create an eye-catching display from scratch — free of charge!

Contact us for a free specimen copy and rate card

Visit the *Bookdealer* website at
www.alacrity.dial.pipex.com

Published by ALACRITY
Eastern Wing • Banwell Castle • Banwell • Weston-super-Mare BS29 6NX
Tel: 01934-822971/820478 • Fax 01934-820682 • e-mail: bookdealer@dsl.pipex.com

SUPPLIES AND SERVICES
BOOK AUCTIONEERS

BLOOMSBURY AUCTIONS, Bloomsbury House, 24 Maddox Street, London W1S 1PP. Tel: (020) 7495-9494. Fax: 7495-9499. E-Mail: info@bloomsburyauctions.com. Web site: www.bloomsburyauctions.com.

BONHAMS, 101 New Bond Street, London W1S 1SR Tel: (020) 7468-8351. Fax: 7465-0224. E-Mail: books@bonhams.com. View our catalogues on-line at www.bonhams.com. *At least 10 sales each season on books, maps, photographs, autographs and historical manuscripts.*

CAPES DUNN & CO., 38 Charles Street, Manchester M1 7DB. Tel: (0161) 273-1911. Fax: 273-3474. *Three to four sales per year. Catalogues can be accessed on* – www.ukauctioneers.com.

DOMINIC WINTER BOOK AUCTIONS, Mallard House, Broadway Lane, South Cerney, Nr Cirencester, Gloucestershire GL7 5UQ. Tel: (01285) 860006. Fax: 862461. E-Mail: info@dominicwinter.co.uk. Web: www.dominic winter.co.uk.

FINAN & CO., The Square, Mere, Wiltshire BA12 6DJ. Tel: (01747) 861411. Fax: 861944. E-Mail: post@finanandco.co.uk. Web Site: www.finanandco.co.uk. 3 auctions annually, including specialist books, manuscripts, photographs and ephemera. Enquireis to Julia Finan

GEORGE KIDNER, The Saleroom, Emsworth Road, Lymington, Hampshire SO41 8GN. Tel: (01590) 670070. Fax: 675167. E-Mail: info@georgekidner.co.uk. Web Site: www.georgekidner.co.uk. *4 sales a year, 200-300 lots per sale. Catalogues on subscription - £20 a year.* Enquiries to: Andrew Reeves.

GOLDING YOUNG & CO, Old Wharf Road, Grantham, Lincolnshire NG31 7AA. Tel: (01476) 565118. Fax: (01476) 561475. E-mail: enquiries@goldingyoung.com. Web Site: www.goldingyoung.com. Contact: Colin Young. *Established in 1900, Goldings currently hold 4 Fine Art sales per annum. Each sale has a dedicated book section. For vendors a Trade Rate Card is available upon request including some 0% commissions.*

HAMPTON & LITTLEWOOD AUCTIONEERS, The Auction Rooms, Alphin Brook Road, Alphington, Exeter, Devon EX2 8TH. Tel: (01392) 413100. Fax: (01392) 413110. E-Mail: enquiries@hamptonandlittlewood.co.uk. Web Site: www.hamptonandlittlewood.co.uk.

KEYS AUCTIONEERS, 8 Market Place, Aylsham, Norwich, Norfolk NR11 6EH. Tel: (01263) 733195. Fax: (01263) 732140. E-mail: mail@aylshamsalerooms.co.uk. Web Site: www.aylshamsalerooms.co.uk.

DAVID LAY, F.R.I.C.S., The Penzance Auction House, Alverton, Penzance, Cornwall TR18 4RE. Tel: (01736) 361414. Fax: 360035. E-Mail: david.lays@btopenworld.com. Web Site: www.invaluable.com. *2 book auctions a year in August & December.* Enquiries to: Mr. John Floyd.

MEALY'S LTD, Chatsworth Street, Castlecomer, County Kilkenny, Ireland. Tel: (056) 444-1229. Fax: (056) 444-1627. E-mail: info@mealys.com. Web site: www.mealys.com. Irelands leading auctioneers of rare, interesting and valuable books. Contact: Fonsie Mealy.

OUTHWAITE & LITHERLAND, Kingsway Galleries, Fontenoy Street, Liverpool L3 2BE. Tel: (0151) 236-6561. Fax: 236-1070. E-mail: auction@lots.uk.com. Web Site: www.lots.uk.com.

SCARBOROUGH PERRY FINE ARTS, Unit 2, Grange Industrial Estate, Southwick, West Sussex BN42 4EN. Tel: (01273) 870371. Fax: 595706. E-Mail: info@scarboroughfinearts.co.uk.

STRIDE & SON AUCTIONEERS, Southdown House, St. John's Street, Chichester, West Sussex PO19 1XQ. Tel: (01243) 780207. Fax: 786713. E-Mail: enquiries@stridesauctions.co.uk. Web Site: www.stridesauctions.co.uk or www.catmaker.co.uk. Appointment necessary for consultations. Book dept open Wednesdays 9am – 12.30pm for appointments. Buyers premium 15% + VAT. *3 auctions a year covering books, documents, ephemera, stamps & postcards.* Enquiries to: Derek White (ephemera) or Adriaan Van Noorden (books).

LAWRENCES AUCTIONEERS, The Linen Yard, South Street, Crewkerne, Somerset TA18 8AB. E-Mail: enquiries@lawrences.co.uk. Specialist book sales in January and July. *Also, fine art, silver and jewellery, furniture, pictures, collectables, militeria, and ceramics.*

THOMSON, RODDICK & MEDCALF, Coleridge House, Shaddongate, Carlisle CA2 5TU. Tel: (01228) 528939.

TRAFFORD BOOKS, P.O. Box 152, Salford, Manchester M17 1BP. Tel: (0161) 877 8818. Fax: (0161) 877 8819. Web Site: www.invaluable.co.uk/acorn. *Regular Public Auctions of books, autographs, ephemera, postcards and cigarette cards at our premises in Trafford Park, Manchester.* Specimen catalogues and vendors' terms available. Contact: George Wewiora.

P.F. WINDIBANK, The Dorking Halls, Reigate Road, Dorking, Surrey RH4 1SG. Tel: (01306) 884556/ 876280. Fax: 884669. E-Mail: sjw@windibank.co.uk. Web Site: www.windibank.co.uk.
WOOLLEY & WALLIS, Book Dept. at 51-61 Castle Street, Salisbury, Wiltshire SP1 3SU. Head of Dept: Paul Viney. Direct Line (01722) 424500. Direct Fax: (01722) 424508.

BOOK DISPLAY AND STORAGE EQUIPMENT, ETC

D AND M PACKAGING, 5a Knowl Road, Mirfield, West Yorkshire WF14 8DG. Tel: (01924) 495768. Fax: (01924) 491267. E-mail: packaging@dandmbooks.com. Web Site: www.bookcovers.co.uk. Contact: Daniel Hanson. *Suppliers of all types of covers for hardbacks, paperbacks and dust jackets. Also comprehensive range of packaging and book-care materials, adhesives, book cleaners, tapes, etc. Free catalogue on request. We supply both trade and private customers and have no minimum order.*
P.B.F.A., The Old Coach House, 16 Melbourn Street, Royston, Hertfordshire SG8 7BZ. Tel: (01763) 248400. Fax: 248921. *Folding bookshelves in natural beech and new books on book collecting.*
POINT EIGHT LTD., Unit 14, Narrowboat Way, Blackbrook Valley Industrial Estate, Dudley, West Midlands DY2 0EZ. Tel: (01384) 238282. Free Phone 0800 731 4887. Fax: 455746. E-mail: info@ point8.co.uk. Web Site: www.pointeight.co.uk. *Bookshop and P.O.S. display equipment designer and manufacturer in wood, metal, plastic etc..*
SEALINE BUSINESS PRODUCTS LIMITED, Media House, 27 Postwood Green, Hertford Heath, Herts., SG13 7QJ. Tel: (01992) 558001. Fax: (01992) 304569. E-mail: sales@sealinemediastorage.com. Web Site: www.sealinemediastorage.com. Contact: Sarah White. Crown Media – *An attractive ramge of multi purpose cabinets designed to house a variety, or mix, of media types including CD, DVD, Video, Microfilm, DAT Tapes, Cassettes, Index Cards and much more. Complete with lock and anti-tilt in a choice of colour finishes. Shelving, mobile solutions and fire resistant storage compliment the range. Please visit our web site for full details.*

BOOK-FAIR ORGANISERS

ANTIQUARIAN BOOKSELLERS ASSOCIATION. Est: 1906. International Book Fair held annually in London, in June, also in Chelsea (UK dealers only) in Autumn and, occasional book fairs elsewhere. *For complimentary tickts or handbook of members, please contact:* Antiquarian Booksellers' Association, Sackville House, 40 Piccadilly, London W1J 0DR. Tel: (020) 7439-3118. Fax: 7439-3119. E-Mail: admin@aba.org.uk. Web Site: www.aba.org.uk.
BOOK COLLECTORS PARADISE. Est: 1986. *Enquiries to:* Trudy Ashford. Tel: (01442) 824440. Book fairs organiser for Wing Book Fair, 1st Sunday each month – 10–4pm.
BUXTON BOOK FAIRS, 75 Chestergate, Macclesfield, Cheshire SK11 6DG. Tel: (01625) 425352. *Enquiries to*: Sally Laithwaite. 10 fairs a year, held at Pavilion Gardens.
CIANA LTD., 24 Langroyd Road, London SW17 7PL. Tel: (020) 8682 1969. Fax: 8682 1997. E-mail: enquiries@ciana.co.uk. Organisers of remainder and promotional book fairs, held in London in September and in Brighton in January.
CLENT BOOKS OF BEWDLEY, Rose Cottage, Habberley Road, Wribbenhall, Bewdley, Worcs. DY12 1JA. Tel: (01299) 401090. E-mail: clent.books@btinternet.com. Web Site: www.clentbooks.co.uk. Co-organiser of Waverley Book Fair (Est. 1981). Third Sunday of each month at Kinver, Nr. Kidderminster. Contact: Ivor Simpson. (Member of P.B.F.A. and Francis Brett Young Soc.).
HD FAIRS LTD. Independent organisers for over 20 years, running the largest UK monthly Book Fairs in London – 140 plus exhibitors. Fairs in Farnham, Surrey and Kempton Park Racecourse – widest choice of books both Antiquarian and modern, as well as printed collectables. Free diary of events available on request; new exhibitors always welcome. Phone, fax or write to HD Fairs Ltd: Wendy Collyer or Peter Sheridan, 38 Fleetside, West Molesey, Surrey KT8 2NF. Tel: (020) 8224-3609 Fax: (020) 8224 3576.
FOREST BOOKS, 7 High Street West, Uppingham, Rutland LE15 9QB. Tel: (01572) 821173. Fax: (0870) 1326314. E-Mail: forestbooks@rutlanduk.fsnet.co.uk. Web Site: http://homepages.primex.co.uk/~Forest. *3 Book Fairs organised annually: 2 at Farndon Memorial Hall, near Newark, Nottinghamshire and 1 at Uppingham School, Rutland.* Please phone or e-mail for booking details. Maps & photos on our web site.

GERRARDS CROSS BOOK FAIR. Est: 1974. Fairs held at the Memorial Centre, East Common, Gerrards Cross, Bucks. Dates for 2005: July 8; 16 September; 14 October; 18 November and 9 December. *Enquiries to:* Patty Lafferty on (01297) 21761. E-mail: patty@gxbooks.freeserve.co.uk

MISSING BOOK FAIRS. Est: 1994. Book fairs Cambridge (12 a year), Peterborough (6 a year), Orford (3 a year), Hatfield House (3 a year) and Dedham (1 a year). *Enquiries to:* Chris Missing, 'Coppers', Main Road, Great Leighs, Essex CM3 1NR. Tel: (01245) 361609. E-mail: missingbooks@ madasafish.com

NORTHWEST BOOK FAIRS. Many different venues throughout the year. *Enquiries to:* Greg Finn, 6 Knowsley View, Rainford, St Helens WA11 8SN. Tel: & Fax: (01744) 883780. E-mail: nwbookfairs@aol.com. Also: V & C Finn; Specialists in Folio Society books, 1200 volumes, 3 catalogues a year. View by appointment; private premises.

PROVINCIAL BOOKSELLERS' FAIRS ASSOCIATION. Est: 1974. Fairs held in Central London (monthly) and in more than 100 other towns in Great Britain. *Enquiries to:* Becky Wears, Provincial Booksellers' Fairs Association, The Old Coach House, 16 Melbourn Street, Royston, Herts, SG8 7BZ. Tel: (01763) 248400. Fax: 248921. Fairs Information Service: (24 hrs) (01763) 249212. E-Mail: info@pbfa.org. Web Site: www.pbfa.org. (See display advertisement).

SOUTHAMPTON BOOK FAIRS. Organiser: Bill Jackson. Tel: 023 8081 2624. E-mail: bill@ bilberry.ndo.co.uk. Venue: St Anne's School, Carlton Road, on Saturdays 10:00–16:00 1st July and 7th October. Entrance 50p (accompanied children free). Free parking on site. Refreshments available.

SUFFOLK BOOK MARKETS at Long Melford. *10 Book Markets are held each year at the Village Memorial Hall with around 20+ book and ephemera dealers in attendance.* Exhibitor enquiries, dates etc. from the organiser: K. McLeod, Boxford Books and Fairs, 3 Firs Farm Cottage, Boxford, Sudbury, Suffolk CO10 5NU. Tel: (01787) 210810. Fax: (01473) 823187.

TITLE PAGE BOOK FAIRS, 176 Elmbridge Avenue, Surbiton, Surrey KT5 9HF. Tel: & Fax: (020) 8399 8168. Mobile (07966) 162758. *Fairs in Surrey: Dorking 6 a year, Cobham 4 a year, Banstead 4 a year. Fairs in Kent: Bromley 4 a year. Dorking and Bromley open 10.00–15.30, Banstead and Cobbam open 09.15–15.30.* Contact Keith Alexander.

WAVERLEY FAIRS, 9 Hayley Park Road, Halesowen B63 1EJ. Tel: (0121) 550-4123. Kinver Book Fair established 1981. 3rd Sunday of every month. Also at Powick, Malvern, Worcestershire. (2nd Sunday)

WINCHETSRE BOOK FAIR. Organiser: Bill Jackson. Tel: 023 8081 2624. E-mail: bill@ bilberry.ndo.co.uk. Venue: Saxon Suite of Winchester Guildhall. Saturdays 10:00–16:00 15th July and 18th November. Entrance 50p (accompanied children free).

WORLD WAR BOOKFAIRS, Oaklands, Camden Park, Tunbridge Wells, Kent TN2 5AE. Tel: & Fax: (01892) 538465. E-Mail: wwarbooks@btinternet.com. Contact: Tim Harper. *Specialist military, aviation and naval bookfairs organised in London, Tunbridge Wells, Museum of Army Flying, Middle Wallop, Chatham and other locations from time to time.* Established in 1990, these are high quality fairs attracting some of the best specialist dealers in the UK.

CATALOGUE PRINTERS

ADVANCE BOOK PRINTING, Unit 9 Northmoor Park, Church Road, Northmoor, Oxfordshire OX29 5UH. Tel: (01865) 301737. E-mail: Advancebp@aol.com. Contact: L Simister. *Catalogues, booklets and short run books.*

THE DOLPHIN PRESS, 96 Whitehill Road, Whitehill Industrial Estate, Glenrothes, Fife. Tel: (01592) 771652. Fax: 630913. E-Mail: liz@dolphinpress.co.uk. Web : www.dolphinpress.co.uk *Catalogues and booklets printed.*

HOOVEY'S BOOKS, P.O. Box 27, St. Leonards-on-Sea, East Sussex TN37 6TZ. Tel & Fax: (01424) 753407. E-mail: hooveys@lineone.net. Web Site: www.hooveys.co.uk. We offer a budget-priced, 24 hour turnaround Catalogue Printing Service for book dealers – ask us to quote for your next catalogue – we aim to save you money. We are also suppliers of CoverClean the Trade cleaner for cloth covers, paperbacks and dust jackets (£12.95 plus £2.00 p&p), and LeatherBrite for cleaning/restoring leather bindings (£7.50 plus £1.00 p&p). Contact: Romney Hoovey.

JOSHUA HORGAN PRINT PARTNERSHIP, 246 Marston Road, Oxford OX3 0EL. Tel: (01865) 246762. Fax: (01865) 250555. E-mail: print@joshuahorgan.co.uk. Web Site: www.joshuahorgan.co.uk

Please let me take a little of your time...

Insurance is one of those matters we would all rather not think about - until something goes wrong!

Insurance is a complicated matter. It all seems so simple to begin with, pay your premium and sleep easily; that's all there is to it.

When things go wrong however - for example a burglary, missing parcel or even accidental damage by fire or flood - then anxious scrutiny of the policy can reveal that (a) you are under insured or (b) that the small print excludes your circumstances.

T.L. Dallas *(City)* **Ltd** are insurance brokers who have worked for the book trade for over 20 years, and arrange insurance cover for the PBFA and its members.

We are experienced in the needs of the antiquarian and secondhand bookseller and the particular requirements of the private collector - general house contents policies are rarely sufficient for substantial collections.

We can provide a bespoke package to suit *your* requirements. Allow us to guide you through the jargon and supply you with a policy that is right for your circumstances.

Please allow **T. L. Dallas** *(City)* **Ltd** to give you a no obligation quotation.

You may be pleasantly surprised at the cost of true peace of mind.

T.L. DALLAS *(City)*Ltd
Ibex House, 42-47 Minories
London, EC3N 1DY
Tel: 020 7816 0210
Fax: 020 7488 2421
Email: dowle@tldallas.com

Authorised and Regulated by the Financial Services Authority

We can arrange household and book collectors insurance at favourable terms

PARCHMENT PRINTERS, Printworks, Crescent Road, Cowley, Oxford OX4 2PB. Tel: (01865) 747547. Fax: 747551. E-mail: print@ParchmentUK.com. Web Site: www.PrintUK.com Specialist in short run production. Contact Ian Kinch.

CRAFT BOOKBINDERS

ATKINSON BOOK BINDERS, 19 Glenmore Business Park, Telford Road, Salisbury, Wiltshire SP2 7GL. Tel (01722) 329846. E-mail: atkinsonbinders@ukonline.co.uk

JOSEPHINE BACON, 179 Kings Cross Road, London WC1X 9BZ. Tel: (020) 7278 9490. Fax: 7278 2447. E-mail: bacon@langservice.com. *Specialist in foreign language material, judaica and cookery.*

GEORGE BAYNTUN, incorporating Robert Riviere, Manvers Street, Bath BA1 1JW. Tel: (01225) 466000. Fax: 482122. E-mail: ebc@georgebayntun.com. Web Site: www.georgebayntun.com. *Fine binding in leather, restoration and case-making since 1894 (and Robert Riviere since 1829).*

CLIVE BOVILL, "Greenburn" River Lane, East Bilney, Dereham NR20 4HS. Tel: (01362) 860174. *Letterpress fine bindings, gold tooling and design. Special interest in conservation of 17th to 19th century books.*

BRADY BOOKBINDERS, Library Building, Library Avenue, Lancaster University LA1 4YH. Tel: (01524) 592512. E-mail: gerard.brady@yahoo.co.uk. Contact: Gerard Brady. *Craft binding, thesis and book restoration.*

BRISTOL BOUND BOOKBINDING, 300 North Street, Ashton Gate, Bristol BS3 1JU. Tel & Fax: (0117) 9663300. E-mail: information@bristolbound.couk. Web Site: www.bristolbound.co.uk. Rachel and Richard James. *We are a husband and wife team first established in 1986 when Rachel gained distinctions in bookbinding from Brunel Technical College, Bristol. We aim to offer a professional, yet friendly service to our customers, whilst maintaining a high standard of workmanship. We undertake new and restoration binding, thesis and dissertation binding, limited editions, corporate presentation binding, binding of newspapers, journals, magazines, personal memoirs, visitors books, photograph albums, wedding albums and much more.*

PHILIP N. BROOK (BOOKBINDER AND BOOK RESTORER), Bell Hill Farm, Lindale in Cartmel, Grange over Sands, Cumbria LA11 6LD. Tel: (01539) 534241. *Bookbinding, book restoration and conservation. To include single volume restorations, fine binding, short run (up to 1,000) publishers. Case work. All aspects of bookbinding work considered. Serving collectors, libraries and dealers for over twenty-one years.*

FRANCIS BROWN CRAFT BOOKBINDER, 24 Camden Way, Dorchester, Dorset DT1 2RA. Tel: (01305) 266039. *Francis Brown is a journeyman bookbinder who undertakes all kinds of binding work, ranging from simple repairs to the restoration of antiquarian volumes, fine limited editions or designed bindings. He has restored books for Balliol College, Wimborne Minster chained library and the Thomas Hardy Memorial Collection in the County Museum in Dorchester.*

FIONA CAMPBELL, 158 Lambeth Road, London SE1 7DF. Tel: & Fax: (020) 7928-1633. E-mail: fcampbell@britishlibrary.net. *Fine bookbinding.*

CHALFONT BOOKBINDERS, Chesham Lane, Chalfont St Peter, Buckinghamshire SL9 0RJ. Tel: (01494) 601423. Fax: (01494) 874061. E-mail: bookbinding@epilepsynse.org.uk. *Quality binding and restoration by a team of very experienced craftsmen. Chalfont Bookbinding & Printing is a registered charity.*

CHIVERS-PERIOD, Aintree Avenue, White Horse Business Park, Trowbridge, Wiltshire BA14 0XB. Tel: (01225) 752888. Fax: (01225) 752666. E-mail: info@chivers-period.co.uk. Web Site: www.chivers-period.co.uk. Contact: Russell Pocock. *Binding, rebinding and repairing books since 1878. Conserving paper for a quarter of a century.*

CYRIL FORMBY BOOK CONSERVATOR, 19-21 Market Place, Ramsbottom, Lancashire BL0 0AJ. Tel: and Fax: (01706) 825771. E-mail: formbys@tiscali.co.uk. Web Site: www.artisanbooks.co.uk. *Craft Bookbinding and book restoration.*

CHRIS HICKS BOOKBINDER, 64 Merewood Avenue, Sandhills, Oxford OX3 8EF. Tel: (01865) 769346. E-Mail: chrishicksbookbinder@btinternet.com. Web Site: www.book-binder.co.uk. *Binding, rebinding, repairs, theses, slipcases, solander cases, fine bindings, short-run edition binding, blank books etc.*

FELICITY HUTTON, Langore House, Langore, Launceston, Cornwall PL15 8LD. Tel: (01566) 773831. E-Mail: pandfhutton@hotmail.com. *Bookbinding and restoration.*

SUPPLIES AND SERVICES

KINGSWOOD BOOKS, 17 Wick Road, Milborne Port, Sherborne, Dorset DT9 5BT. Tel: & Fax: (01963) 250280. E-mail: kingswoodbooks@btinternet.com. Web Site: www.kingswoodbooks.btinternet.co.uk. *Bookbinding & conservation.* Enquiries to A.J. Dollery.

D SANDERSON, Primrose Mill, London Road, Preston, Lancashire. Tel: (01772) 253594. Fax: (01772) 253592. E-mail: sanderson2003@aol.com. Contact: Mr J. Donerth. *Book restoration and print finishers.*

SALISBURY BOOKBINDERS, Woolstone Park, Backe, St Clears, Carmarthenshire, South Wales SA33 4EU. Tel: (01994) 230503. E-mail: salisburybinders@onetel.com. Web Site: www.salisburybookbinders.co.uk. Contact: Nancy Winfield. Established in 1840. *Specialists in fine bindings, book repair and conservation, edge gilding using genuine gold leaf. Also bind small runs up to 1,000 copies.*

CHARLES SYMINGTON, 145 Bishopthorpe Road, York YO23 1NZ. Tel: (01904) 633995. *Bookbinding and restoration.*

JAYNE TANDY (CRAFT BOOKBINDING AND RESTORATION), Bowhayes Cross, Williton, Somerset TA4 4NL. Tel: (01984) 632293. *Bookbinding, book restoration, conservation and repair.*

COLIN TATMAN, Corner House, 121A Lairgate, Beverley, E. Yorskire HU17 8JG. Tel: (01482) 880611 (day) & 882153 (evening). *Traditional craft bookbinding; paper repair; slipcases & book boxes; restoration & conservation.*

TEASDALE BOOKBINDERS, Caxton House, Corwen, Dengighshire LL21 0AA. Tel: (01490) 412 713. 7316. E-Mail: info@teasdalebookbinders.co.uk. *Hand bookbinding and restoration. Prop: Catherine Hore.*

TEMPLE BOOKBINDERS, 10 Quarry Road, Headington, Oxford OX3 8NU. Tel: (01865) 451940. E-Mail: enquiries@templebookbinders.co.uk. Web Site: www.templebookbinders.co.uk. Mr. Ian Barnes. *Hand bookbinder in fine leathers, vellum, linens, cloth & buckrams. Quality restorer of antiquarian books.*

TRADITIONAL BOOKCRAFTS, 28 Drayton Mill Court, Cheshire Street, Market Drayton, Shropshire TF9 1EF. Tel: (01630) 654410. *Craft bookbinder, antique and modern book repair and restoration, boxes, slipcases, gold tooling, handmade and scribed books. Established: 1983. Limited edition bindings. Prices on request. Prop: Monica Thornton.*

TUDOR BOOKBINDING LTD., 3 Lyon Close, Wigston, Leicestershire LE18 2BJ Tel: (0116) 2883988. Fax: (0116) 2884878. E-mail: sales@tudor-bookbinding.co.uk. *Antique and modern book restoration, repair and rebinding; gold tooling; single copy restorations work undertaken.*

PERIOD FINE BINDINGS, Yew Tree Farm, Stratford Road, Wootton Wawen, Warwickshire B95 6BY. Telephone: (01564) 793800. E-mail: periodfinebindings@tiscali.co.uk. Web Site: http://periodfinebindings.typepad.com/royal_bindings. *Restorer of antiquarian books using ancient formulae and hand-made materials. Fox marks, inkstains etc removed. Rare books bought, sold and valued.*

LIZ YOUNG – BOOKBINDER, The Old Rectory, Buckland, Nr. Aylesbury, Buckinghamshire HP22 5HU. Tel: (01296) 630461. E-mail: young.buckland@virgin.net. *Traditional craft bookbinding, restoration and photograph albums.*

PACKING MATERIALS SUPPLIERS

MACFARLANE GROUP PLC., **Group Head Office:** 21 Newton Place, Glasgow, Scotland G3 7PY. Tel: (0141) 333 9666. Fax: (0141) 333 1988. Web Site: www.macfarlanegroup.net

PACKING CASE MANUFACTURERS: **Grantham Branch:** PO Box 16, Alma Park Industrial Estate, Grantham, Lincolnshire NG31 9SF. Tel: (01476) 574747. Fax: (01476) 577444. **Westbury Branch:** Quartermaster Road, West Wilts Trading Estate, Westbury, Wiltshire BA13 4JT. Tel: (01373) 858555. Fax: (01373) 858999.

PACKAGING DISTRIBUTION: **Bristol Branch:** Western Approach Distribution Park, Severn Beach, Bristol BS35 4GG. Tel: (0870) 850 0542. Fax: (0870) 850 0543. **Exeter Branch**: Windsor Court,

SUPPLIES AND SERVICES

Visiting London?
Think PBFA!

The monthly Russell Book Fairs are a major source
of fresh material for dealers, collectors and librarians
Keep ALL our London dates in mind when
planning your next visit to London

MONTHLY LONDON BOOK FAIRS

HOTEL RUSSELL
Russell Square, WC1

Monthly one - day fairs 2006

July	Sun 9	August	Sun 13
September	Sun 10	October	Sun 8
November	Sun 12	December	Sun 10

Summer International Fairs 2007
2 Fairs in 2 locations

Fair One: Hotel Russell — Sun/Mon 3 - 4 June
Fair Two: Novotel London West
Shortlands, Hammersmith Fri/Sat 8 - 9 June

And for the specialists

Travel & Exploration Book Fair
Sunday 1 April 2007, 11-5
Royal Geographical Society, 1 Kensington Gore, SW7

And from January 2007 the PBFA London Book Fairs
will move to the
Holiday Inn Bloomsbury, Coram Street WC1N 1HT

January	Sun 14	February	Sun 11
March	Sun 11	April	Sun 8
May	Sun 13	July	Sun 8

Please note: all dates subject to change so please check our website
www.pbfa.org for latest information

Organised by the PBFA
The Old Coach House, 16 Melbourn St.,
Royston, Herts, Great Britain, SG8 7BZ
Tel: 01763 248400, Fax: 01763 248921

Manaton Close, Matford Business Park, Exeter, Devon EX2 8PF, Tel: (0870) 608 6110. Fax: (0870) 608 6111. **Coventry Branch:** Siskin Parkway East, Middlemarch Business Park, Coventry, West Midlands CV3 4PE. Tel: (0870) 608 6205. Fax: (0870) 608 6206. **Enfield Branch:** Unit 5, Delta Park, Millmarsh Lane, Enfield, EN3 7QJ. Tel: (0870) 850 0116. Fax: (0870) 850 0117. **Fareham Branch:** Unit 1, Stephenson Road, Midpoint 27, Segensworth, Fareham, Hampshire PO15 5RZ. Tel: (0870) 608 6160. Fax: (0870) 608 6161. **Glasgow Branch:** Unit 1 Linwood Industrial Estate, Burnbrae Road, Linwood, Paisley PA3 3BD. Tel: (0870) 150 4508. Fax: (0870) 150 4509. **Horsham Branch:** Oakhurst Business Park, Wilberforce Way, Southwater, West Sussex RH13 7NW. Tel: (0870) 608 6150. Fax: (0870) 608 6151. **Manchester Branch:** Empire Court, Trafford Park, Manchester M17 1TN. Tel: (0870) 150 4500. Fax: (0870) 150 4501. **Milton Keynes Branch:** Kingston Gateway, Whitehall Avenue, Milton Keynes, Buckinghamshire MK10 0BU. Tel: (0870) 150 4502. Fax: (0870) 150 4503. **Tyne & Wear Branch:** The Waterfront, Kingfisher Boulevard, Newburn Riverside, Tyne & Wear NE15 8NZ. Tel: (0870) 608 6100. Fax: (0870) 608 6101. **Sudbury Branch:** Windham Road, Chilton Industrial Estate, Sudbury, Suffolk CO10 2XD. Tel: (0870) 608 6140. Fax: (0870) 608 6141. **Telford Branch:** Unit D2, Horton Park Industrial Estate, Hortonwood 7, Telford, Shropshire TF7 4AP. Tel: (0870) 608 6120. Fax: (0870) 608 6121. **Wakefield Branch:** Unit H, Brunel Road, Wakefield 41 Industrial Estate, Wakefield WF2 0XG. Tel: (0870) 850 0118. Fax: (0870) 850 0119. **Wigan Branch:** Northgate Distribution Centre, Caxton Close, Wheatlea Park Industrial Estate, Wigan WN3 6XU. Tel: (0870) 150 4512. Fax: (0870) 150 4513.

Macfarlane Packaging provides a complete range of packaging materials, including New Book Pack and Super Book Pack, Postal bags and Easywrap.

D AND M PACKAGING, 5a Knowl Road, Mirfield, West Yorkshire WF14 8DG. Tel: (01924) 495768. Fax: (01924) 491267. E-mail: packaging@dandmbooks.com. Web Site: www.bookcovers.co.uk. Contact: Daniel Hanson. *Suppliers of all types of covers for hardbacks, paperbacks and dust jackets. Also comprehensive range of packaging and book-care materials, adhesives, book cleaners, tapes, etc. Free catalogue on request. We supply both trade and private customers and have no minimum order.*

PLASPAK, Piperell Way, Haverhill, Suffolk CB9 8QW (A Division of Marchant Manufacturing). Tel: (01440) 765300. Fax: 765302. E-mail: sales@marchant.co.uk. Web Site: www.plaspak.co.uk *Polythene manufacturer and specialist packaging.*

REMAINDER MERCHANTS

AWARD PUBLICATIONS LTD., The Old Riding School, Welbeck Estate, Worksop, Nottinghamshire S80 3LR. Tel: (01909) 478170. Fax: (01909) 484632. *E-mail: info@awardpublications.co.uk Genuine remainders for adults and children.*

BOOKMARK REMAINDERS LTD., Rivendell, Illand, Launceston, Cornwall PL15 7LS. Tel: (01566) 782 728. Fax: (01566) 782 059. E-mail: info@book-bargains.co.uk. WebSite: www.book-bargains.co.uk. Range of genuine remainders and bargain books. Trade sales only.

BLAKETON HALL LTD., Unit 1, 26 Marsh Green Road, Marsh Barton, Exeter EX2 8PN. Tel: (01392) 210602. Fax: 421165. E-Mail: sales@blaketonhall.co.uk. *Remainders and overstocks, including scientific, technical, academic, gardening, crafts & children's.* Enquiries to: Martin Shillingford.

FANSHAW BOOKS, Fanshaw House, 3/9 Fanshaw Street, London N1 6HX. Tel: (08453) 302511. Fax: (0207) 3502. E-Mail: info@roybloom.com. www.roybloom.com. *General remainders. Exhibits at all major book fairs.*

GRANGE BOOKS PLC., The Grange, Units 1–6 Kingsnorth Industrial Estate, Hoo, Nr. Rochester, Kent ME3 9ND. Tel: (01634) 256000. Fax: 255500. E-Mail: sales@grangebooks.co.uk. Web Site: www.grangebooks.co.uk. *Distributors of remainders, and publisher of promotional books and reprints to the adult illustrated non-fiction and children's market.*

JIM OLDROYD BOOKS, 14/18 London Road, Sevenoaks, Kent TN13 1AJ. Tel: (01732) 463356. Fax: 464486. E-Mail: paula@oldroyd.co.uk. Web site: www.oldroyd.co.uk. *Adult and children's remainders.*

SANDPIPER BOOKS LTD., Offices and Showroom, 24 Langroyd Road, London SW17 7PL. Tel: (020) 8767-7421. Fax: 8682-0280. E-Mail: enquiries@sandpiper.co.uk. *Scholarly and literary remainders, academic reprints and mail order.*

SUPPLIERS OF MATERIALS AND TOOLS FOR BINDING AND RESTORING BOOKS, ETC.

FALKINER FINE PAPERS, 76 Southampton Row, London WC1B 4AR. Tel: (020) 7831-1151. Fax: 7430-1248. E-mail: falkiner@ic24.net. Web: www.falkiner.com. *PAPERS. Wide selection of papers for repairs, marbled papers and coloured end papers. LEATHERS AND BOOKCLOTHS for repairs and bindings. BOOKS in print on bookbinding, calligraphy, typography, papermaking and printing history. All items can be supplied by post. Price lists available.*

FINE CUT GRAPHIC IMAGING LTD., Marlborough Road, Lancing Business Park, Lancing, West Sussex BN15 8UF. Tel: (01903) 751666. Fax: 750462. E-Mail: info@finecut.co.uk. Web Site: www.finecut.co.uk. *Manufacturers of bookbinders' finishing tools and accessories. 80 page catalogue available (also available on-line) showing brass type, handle letters, hand tools and brass rolls. Special designs to order.*

HARMATAN LEATHER LTD, Westfield Avenue, Higham Ferrers, Northamptonshire NN10 8AX. Tel: (01933) 412151. Fax: (01933) 412242. E-mail: marc@harmatan.co.uk. Web Site: www.harmatan.co.uk. Contact: Marc Lamb.

J. HEWIT AND SONS LIMITED, Kinauld Leather Works, Currie, Edinburgh, Scotland EH14 5RS. Tel: (0131) 449-2206. Fax: (0131) 451-5081. E-Mail: sales@hewit.com. Web Site: www.hewit.com. *BOOKBINDERS' TOOLS AND SUPPLIES, adhesive (paste, glue, P.V.A.), bone folders, brass type and type holders, brushes, knives, papers (marbled, etc.), presses, tapes, threads. BINDING LEATHERS, in a wide range of colours. BOOKCLOTHS, buckram, linen, cloth, mull, etc. BOOKBINDERS STARTER PACKS, basic tools to get you started.*

HOOVEY'S BOOKS, P.O. Box 27, St. Leonards-on-Sea, East Sussex TN37 6TZ. Tel & Fax: (01424) 753407. E-mail: hooveys@lineone.net. Web Site: www.hooveys.co.uk. *We offer a budget-priced, 24 hour turnaround Catalogue Printing Service for book dealers – ask us to quote for your next catalogue – we aim to save you money. We are also suppliers of CoverClean the Trade cleaner for cloth covers, paperbacks and dust jackets (£12.95 plus £2.00 p&p), and LeatherBrite for cleaning/restoring leather bindings (£7.50 plus £1.00 p&p).* Contact: Romney Hoovey.

ANN MUIR MARBLING, 1 St. Algar's Yard, West Woodlands, Frome, Somerset BA11 5ER. Tel: & Fax: (01985) 844786. E-mail: annmuir@marbling.freeserve.co.uk. Web Site: www.annmuirmarbling.co.uk. *Marbled paper in both modern and traditional patterns and colourways. Matching service for old papers in restoration work. New papers designed for individual projects. Send for catalogue of samples and price list.*

PAPERSAFE, 2 Green Bank, Adderley, Market Drayton TF9 3TH. Tel: (01630) 652217. E-Mail: philip@papersafe.demon.co.uk. Web Site: www.papersafe.demon.co.uk. *Suppliers of archival quality repair materials for book and paper collectors.*

PICREATOR ENTERPRISES LIMITED, 44 Park View Gardens, Hendon, London NW4 2PN. Tel: (020) 8202-8972. Fax: (020) 8202-3435. E-mail: info@picreator.co.uk. Web Site: www.picreator.co.uk. *Fine–art conservation and restoration materials. Manufacturers of Renaissance wax polish, Vulpex liquid soap and Groom/stick non–abrasive document dry cleaner. Bookdealers are increasingly undertaking basic cleaning and restorative treatment of books and paper. Picreator Enterprises supply professional products which are simple to use and advice is given on their application. The Company has held a Royal warrant of appointment to H.M. The Queen since 1984 as suppliers of products for (fine-art) restoration and conservation.*

RUSSELL BOOKCRAFTS, Unit 1, Bluntswood Hall, Throcking, Buntingford, Hertfordshire SG9 9RN. Tel: (01763) 281430. Fax: (01763) 281431. E-Mail: office@russels.com. Web Site: www.russels.com. *Major supplier of very fine leathers. Range includes the world renowned, and only genuine "OASIS" goatskin, calf and sheepskin skivers – handmade bookbinders' equipment includes, specially designed work benches, nipping presses, lying presses, ploughs, sewing frames and Digby Stuart presses. We offer a fine colour range of Buckrams and bookcloths, mulls, Jaconette, tapes, threads and headbands; a large selection of specialised papers, marbled end papers, & millboards. Tools include: paring knives, bridled glue brushes, decorative hand tools and brass letters. Backing hammers, bone folders, burnishing agates and all types of bookbinders adhesives.*

CONJURING WITH IDEAS

The first issue of

Textualities Magazine

MAGIC AFOOT
Out now £12 inc P&P

MAJOR FEATURES ON THE HISTORY OF CONJURING AND ROSSLYN CHAPEL

Orders to

Textualities, Main Point Books,

8 Lauriston Street, Edinburgh EH3 9DJ.

TEL: 0131 228 4837

Email: the.editor@textualities.net

Also, please visit www.textualities.net

– now over 300 book-related features

with new articles every week.

The Textualities office is at the back of Main Point Books, a secondhand book store in the heart of the historic West Port, Edinburgh's secondhand books quarter. Open Tuesday–Saturday. Visitors welcome.

USEFUL WEB SITES

Please note that in this selection the details are correct when going to press but changes and new ones may appear during the year. ***Those in bold are multi-search sites.*** *Some trade associations also offer book searching facilities, see pages 20–23.*

FOR SEARCHING TITLES

ABooksearch	www.abooksearch.com
Addall	**www.addall.com**
Advanced Book Exchange	www.abebooks.com
Abebooks Europe GmbH	www.abebooks.co.uk
ABookCoOp, Inc	www.tomfolio.com
Alibris	www.alibris.com
Amazon	www.amazon.com
Antiqbook (The Netherlands)	www.antiqbook.com
Antiquarian Booksellers Association of America (ABAA)	www.abaa.org
Barnes & Noble	www.bn.com
ANZAAB (Australia & New Zealand)	www.anzaab.com.au/anzaab
Bibliology	www.bibliology.com
Biblion	www.biblion.uk
Bibliophile	www.bibliophile.net
Bibliopoly (England)	www.bibliopoly.com
BiblioQuest International (Australia)	www.biblioz.com
Books and Collectibles	www.booksandcollectibles.co.au
Bookavenue (New York)	www.bookavenue.com
Bookfinder.com	**www.bookfinder.com**
Elephant Books	www.elephantbooks.com
Independent Booksellers Network (England)	www.ibooknet.co.uk
Independent OnLine Booksellers Association	www.iobabooks.com
International League of Booksellers (ILAB)	www.ilab-lila.com
The Internet Bookshop UK Ltd	www.ibuk.com
Maremagnum (Italy)	www.maremagnum
Powell's Books	www.powells.com
Provincial Book Fairs Association (PBFA)	www.booksatpbfa.com
Sheppard's World	www.sheppardsworld.co.uk
Strand Books (USA)	www.strandbooks.com
UKBookWorld	www.ukbookworld.com
Used Books Central (USA)	www.usedbookcentral.com
Zentrales Verzeichnis Antiquarischer Bücher (ZVAB, Germany)	www.zvab.com

FOR SEARCHING DEALERS

Advanced Book Exchange	www.abebooks.com
Sheppard's World	www.sheppardsworld.co.uk

GENERAL SEARCH SITES

Ask Jeeves	www.askjeeves.com
EBay	www.ebay.co.uk
Google	www.google.co.uk
Dog Pile	**www.dogpile.com**
Mamma	**www.mamma.com**

GAZELLE
Sales & Distribution Since 1988

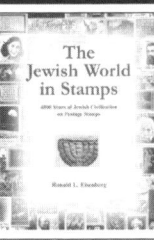

New Books at Competitive Discounts

ABOUT GAZELLE

Located in historic Lancaster, Gazelle is one of the most experienced book distribution companies in Europe and offers a flexible, fast and effective distribution service stretching across Great Britain, Ireland, Western and Eastern Europe. The company comprises an in-house team with many years experience in sales, distribution, warehousing and marketing. Additionally, Gazelle's Academic division provides specialist books to the academic and scholarly market.

OUR PRODUCTS

Gazelle has amassed a range of products from international publishers thus bringing variety to the UK market. Gazelle also handles posters, DVDs, anatomical models plus other learning materials. We handle over 30,000 titles spanning over 150 subject areas including:

ANTIQUES & COLLECTABLES
THE ARTS
ARCHAEOLOGY
ARCHITECTURE
AVIATION
BIOGRAPHY & AUTOBIOGRAPHY
CHILDRENS AND EDUCATIONAL
CINEMA
EDUCATION
FICTION
FIELD SPORTS
GARDENING
GENERAL & LITERARY FICTION
HISTORY
LITERATURE
MARITIME
MEDICINE
MILITARY HISTORY
MUSIC
NATURAL HISTORY
PHILOSOPHY
POETRY
POLITICS
RAILWAYS
RELIGION
SCIENCE
SPORT & LEISURE
TOPOGRAPHY
TRANSPORT
TRAVEL

HOW WE CAN HELP YOU

Orders received are processed by our friendly Customer Services staff, who maintain close personal contact with our customers. Using a variety of tried-and-tested courier services, we deliver your books, promptly and reliably. We are happy to provide point of sale materials: catalogues, posters, flyers etc to stimulate interest and encourage sales.

Contact us today for a catalogue in your specialist subject area

GAZELLE
White Cross Mills, Hightown, Lancaster LA1 4XS, United Kingdom
tel +44 (0) 1524 68765 / fax +44 (0) 1524 63232 / e-mail sales@gazellebooks.co.uk / web gazellebooks.co.uk

Rare Book Review

Each month the world's leading magazine for book dealers and book collectors brings you:

- Lively and informed news and views from the rare book world
- Every major international book fair previewed and reviewed
- Comprehensive auction reports with prices
- Dealer profiles
- Full listings of forthcoming auctions and fairs
- Reviews of the latest dealer websites
- Articles written by and about dealers of all countries
- Expertbibliographies on major and obscure authors
- Analysis of collections and single volumes
- Latest catalogues reviewed and recommended
- Entertaining and informative dealer features

Call
020 7529 4222
and mention 'Sheppard's' to get a year's subscription for just **£25**

FIND OUR NEW ISSUE IN BORDERS. NOW

WWW.RAREBOOKREVIEW.COM – OPENING UP THE WORLD OF BOOKS

INDEX OF CITIES AND TOWNS

Dealer locations listed alphabetically by country, city, town and village, as shown in the Geographical section.

ABERDEEN.................... 266	BARNARD CASTLE 96	BLEWBURY 202
ABERFELDY 275	BARNSTAPLE................ 83	BLUNTISHAM 63
ABERGAVENNY............ 280	BARROW–IN–FURNESS.. 76	BOGNOR REGIS 237
ABERYSTWYTH 277	BARTON–ON–HUMBER.. 148	BOLTON 118
ABINGDON................... 202	BASINGSTOKE 122	BOREHAM WOOD 130
ABOYNE....................... 267	BATH 212	BOSTON 148
ADARE 260	BATHEASTON 213	BOURNEMOUTH........... 90
ADDINGHAM, ILKLEY .. 241	BATLEY 241	BOXFORD 221
AIRDRIE 273	BEACONSFIELD 61	BRACKLEY 196
ALFRETON................... 81	BEADNELL 198	BRACKNELL.................. 55
ALFRISTON 98	BEAMINSTER................ 90	BRADFORD 241
ALNWICK..................... 198	BECCLES 221	BRADFORD ON AVON... 246
ALPRISTON 98	BECKENHAM 136	BRAINTREE................... 108
ALRESFORD 122	BEDDINGTON................ 226	BRECON........................ 281
ALSTON 76	BEDFORD...................... 53	BRENCHLEY.................. 136
ALTON 122	BEDWORTH.................. 232	BRENTWOOD 108
ALTRINCHAM 118	BELFAST 255	BRIDGE OF ALLAN 263
ALVERSTOKE 122	BERE ALSTON 83	BRIDGEND.................... 266
AMERSHAM 61	BERKELEY 113	BRIDGEWATER 213
AMMANFORD............... 276	BERKHAMSTED............. 130	BRIDGNORTH 209
ANDOVER 122	BETHESDA 279	BRIDLINGTON 105
ANSTRUTHER 265	BEULAH 281	BRIDPORT 91
APPLEBY-IN-	BEVERLEY 105	BRIGHOUSE 241
WESTMORLAND 76	BEWDLEY 250	BRIGHTON 98
ARBROATH 275	BEXHILL 98	BRINSCALL 142
ARMAGH 255	BEXLEY 136	BRISTOL....................... 58
ARUNDEL 237	BIDDENDEN 136	BRIXHAM 83
ASCOT 55	BIDEFORD 83	BROADSTAIRS 136
ASHBURTON 83	BIGGAR 273	BROCKLEY 161
ASHFORD..................... 136	BILLERICAY 108	BROUGH 76
ASHPERTON 128	BILLINGBOROUGH 148	BUCKINGHAM 61
ASHTEAD 226	BILLINGHAM 96	BUDE........................... 72
ASHTON-UNDER-LYNE . 118	BILLINGHAY 148	BUILTH WELLS............. 282
ATHERSTONE 232	BILLINGSHURST 237	BUNCLODY 261
AUSTWICK 190	BILSTON 234	BUNGAY 221
AXMINSTER 83	BIRCH 108	BURBAGE...................... 145
AYLESBURY 61	BIRCHWOOD 68	BURES 221
AYLSHAM 184	BIRKENHEAD................ 182	BURFORD 202
AYR............................. 273	BIRMINGHAM 234	BURTON UPON TRENT . 219
	BISHOP AUCKLAND...... 96	BURY............................ 142
BAKEWELL 81	BISHOP'S CASTLE.......... 209	BURY ST EDMUNDS 221
BALDERTON 200	BISHOP'S STORTFORD... 130	BUSHEY 130
BALLATER 266	BISHOPS CLEEVE 113	BUXTON 81
BALLINLOUGH, ... 257	BISHOPSTON................. 58	BY DUNBLANE............. 263
BALLYDEHOB................ 257	BLACKBURN 142	BYFLEET 226
BALLYGOWAN 255	BLACKPOOL 142	
BALLYNAHINCH 256	BLACKROCK 258	CALLANDER 263
BANBURY 202	BLAENAU FFESTINIOG . 279	CALLINGTON 72
BANGOR 256	BLAENAVON 287	CALNE......................... 246
BANGOR, GWYNEDD 279	BLAIR ATHOLL............. 275	CAMBORNE.................. 72
BANTRY....................... 257	BLANDFORD FORUM ... 90	CAMBRIDGE 63

INDEX OF CITIES AND TOWNS

CAMBRIDGE, GLOS	113
CAMPBELTOWN	273
CANTERBURY	136
CARDIFF	276
CARDIGAN	277
CARLISLE	76
CARMARTHEN	277
CARNDONAGH	258
CARNFORTH	142
CARRICK–ON–SHANNON	260
CARSHALTON, SURREY	178
CASTLE CAMPS	65
CASTLE CAREY	213
CASTLE DOUGLAS	263
CASTLE	68
CASTLETON	81
CATTERICK VILLAGE	190
CHALFORD STROUD	113
CHARD	213
CHARMOUTH	91
CHATHAM	137
CHATTERIS	65
CHEADLE	68
CHELMSFORD	108
CHELTENHAM	113
CHEPSTOW	279
CHESHAM	61
CHESHUNT	130
CHESTER	68
CHESTERFIELD	81
CHICHESTER	237
CHICKSANDS	53
CHIPPENHAM	246
CHIPPING CAMPDEN	114
CHIPPING NORTON	202
CHORLEY	142
CIRENCESTER	114
CLACTON-ON-SEA	108
CLAPTON–IN–GORDANO	213
CLARE	222
CLECKHEATON	241
CLEETHORPES	149
CLEVEDON	214
CLIFTON	59
CLITHEROE	143
CLONTARF	258
COCKERMOUTH	77
COLCHESTER	108
COLEFORD	114
COLERNE	246
COLYTON	84
COLLIERS WOOD	167
COLWYN BAY	277
COLYTON	84
COMBE MARTIN	84
CONWY	278
COOKHAM	55
COOTEHILL	257
CORBY GLEN	149
COVENTRY	234
COWES	134
COWFOLD	237
COWLEY	203
CREWE	68
CREWKERNE	214
CRICCIETH	280
CROMFORD	81
CROSBY	182
CROWBOROUGH	99
CROWTHORNE	55
CROYDON, SURREY	178
CULBOKIE	268
DACRE	190
DAGENHAM	109
DARLINGTON	96
DARTMOUTH	84
DAWLISH	84
DEAL	137
DEBENHAM	222
DEDDINGTON	203
DEREHAM	184
DEVIZES	246
DIDCOT	203
DIDSBURY	118
DINGWALL	268
DISS	184
DITCHLING	100
DOLGELLAU	280
DONAGHADEE	256
DONCASTER	217
DORCHESTER	91
DORCHESTER ON THAMES	203
DORKING	226
DOUGLAS	254
DOVER	137
DOWNHAM MARKET	184
DOWNPATRICK	256
DRIFFIELD	105
DROITWICH	250
DUBLIN	259
DUCKLINGTON	203
DUKINFIELD	118
DULVERTON	214
DUMFRIES	264
DUN LAOGHAIRE	259
DUNFERMLINE	265
DUNMANWAY	258
DUNSTABLE	53
DUNSTER	214
DURNESS	268
EAGLE	149
EAST GRINSTEAD	238
EAST HAGBOURNE	203
EAST HOATLY	100
EAST HORSLEY	226
EAST LOOE	72
EAST MOLESEY	226
EAST RUDHAM	184
EASTBOURNE	100
EASTCOTE	178
ECKINGTON	217
EDGWARE	178
EDINBURGH	269
EGGINGTON	53
EGHAM	227
EGREMONT	77
ELLESMERE	209
ELSTREE	131
ELY	65
EMSWORTH	123
ENFIELD	178
ENNIS	257
EPPING	109
EPSOM	227
EWELL	227
EXETER	84
EYE	222
FAIRFORD	115
FAKENHAM	184
FALMOUTH	72
FAREHAM	123
FARINGDON	203
FARNBOROUGH	123
FARNBOROUGH, KENT	137
FARNHAM	227
FARNINGHAM	137
FAVERSHAM	138
FELIXSTOWE	222
FENCE, NR. BURNLEY	143
FERNDALE	279
FILEY	190
FINCHINGFIELD	109
FINNINGHAM	222
FLAMBOROUGH	105
FLEET	123
FOCHABERS	267
FOLKESTONE	138
FORDINGBRIDGE	123
FORFAR	275
FORRES	267
FORT WILLIAM	268
FOWEY	73
FRAMLINGHAM	223
FRESHWATER	134
FRODSHAM	69
FROGGATT	82
FROME	214
GAINSBOROUGH	149
GALWAY	260

SUPPLIES AND SERVICES

GILLINGHAM 92	HEREFORD 128	KIDDERMINSTER 250
GILVERSOME 241	HERTFORD 131	KILLIECRANKIE 275
GLASGOW 273	HERTFORD HEATH 131	KILMARNOCK 274
GLASGOW 274	HEXHAM 198	KINETON 232
GLOSSOP 82	HIGH WYCOMBE 61	KING'S LYNN 186
GODALMING 227	HINCKLEY 145	KINGSBRIDGE 85
GODMANCHESTER 65	HINDLEY, WIGAN 143	KINGSCLERE 55
GORING–BY–SEA 238	HINDRINGHAM 185	KINGSTON 180
GORING–ON–THAMES... 204	HITCHIN 131	KINGSWINFORD 235
GORLESTON-ON-SEA 185	HOLBEACH 149	KINGTON 128
GOSPORT 123	HOLLAND-ON-SEA 110	KIRKBY STEPHEN 78
GRANGE–OVER–SANDS. 77	HOLMFIRTH 242	KIRKBY–IN–ASHFIELD .. 200
GRAVESEND 138	HOLT 185	KIRKCALDY 265
GRAYS 109	HONITON 85	KIRKCUDBRIGHT 264
GREAT DRIFFIELD 105	HOOK NORTON 204	KIRKELLA 106
GREAT DUNMOW 109	HORLEY 228	KIRKLINGTON 200
GREAT ELLINGHAM 185	HORNCASTLE 149	KIRKSTALL, LEEDS 243
GREAT LEIGHS 109	HORNDEAN 124	KIRKWALL 269
GREAT MALVERN 250	HORSHAM 238	KIRTON, BOSTON 150
GREAT MISSENDEN 61	HORWICH 118	KNARESBOROUGH 191
GREAT WALFORD 232	HOVE 101	KNUTSFORD 69
GREAT YARMOUTH 185	HOWDEN 106	
GREENFORD 178	HOYLAKE, WIRRAL 69	LAMPETER 277
GREENOCK 274	HUDDERSFIELD 242	LANCASTER 143
GREENWICH 161	HULL 106	LANCING 238
GUILDFORD 228	HUNSTANTON 186	LANGPORT 215
GUISBOROUGH 190	HUNTINGDON 66	LARBERT 263
GUNTHORPE 200	HUNTLY 268	LAUNCESTON 73
	HUNTON, MAIDSTONE .. 138	LEALHOLM 191
HADDENHAM, ELY 66	HURST 55	LEAMINGTON SPA 232
HADDINGTON 272	HYDE 69	LEATHERHEAD 228
HALESOWEN 235		LECHLADE 115
HALESWORTH 223		LEDBURY 128
HALIFAX 241	ILFORD 110, 179	LEEDS 243
HALTON 143	ILKLEY 243	LEICESTER 145
HALTWHISTLE 198	ILMINSTER 214	LEIGH ON SEA 110
HAMPTON 179	INGLETON 191	LEOMINSTER 128
HARLESTON 185	INNERLEITHEN 262	LETCHWORTH 131
HARPENDEN 131	INVERNESS 268	LEWES 102
HARROGATE 190	IPSWICH 223	LEYLAND, PRESTON 143
HARROW 179	IRCHESTER 196	LICHFIELD 219
HARWICH 110	IRVINE 274	LIMERICK 261
HASLEMERE 228	ISLE OF ARRAN 269	LINCOLN 150
HASSOCKS 238	ISLE OF COLONSAY 269	LIPHOOK 124
HASTINGS 100	ISLE OF IONA, ARGYLL 269	LISBURN 255
HAVANT 124	ISLEWORTH 179	LISS 124
HAWARTH 242	IVER 62	LITTLE HALLINGBURY . 110
HAY–ON–WYE 282		LITTLEBOROUGH 119
HAYES 179	JEDBURGH 262	LITTLEHAMPTON 238
HAYLING ISLAND 124		LITTLEOVER, DERBY 82
HEATHFIELD 101	KELSO 262	LIVERPOOL 182
HEBDEN BRIDGE 242	KEMPSFORD 115	LIVERSEDGE 244
HELENSBURGH 274	KENDAL 78	LLANDRINDOD WELLS . 284
HELMSLEY 191	KENILWORTH 232	LLANGAMMARCH
HELSTON 73	KENLEY, SURREY 179	WELLS 285
HENLEY ON THAMES ... 204	KENT 138	LLANGOLLEN 278
HENLEY–IN–ARDEN 232	KESWICK 78	LLANGURIG 285
HENLEY-ON–THAMES... 204	KEW, RICHMOND 180	LLANIDLOES 285
	KIBWORTH HARCOURT 145	

INDEX OF CITIES AND TOWNS

LLANRWST	278
LLANVAPLEY	280
LOCHCARRON	269
LONDERRY	255
LONDON (E)	153
LONDON (EC)	154
LONDON (N)	155
LONDON (NW)	158
LONDON (SE)	161
LONDON (SW)	164
LONDON (W)	169
LONDON (WC)	174
LONDON (O)	178
LONDONDERRY	255
LONG BURTON	92
LONG MELFORD	224
LONG PRESTON	191
LOOE	73
LOUGHBOROUGH	146
LOUTH	150
LOWER DARWEN	144
LOWESTOFT	224
LUDLOW	209
LYDD	138
LYME REGIS	92
LYMINGE	139
LYMINGTON	124
LYMM	69
LYMPSTONE	85
LYNG, NORWICH	186
LYTHAM ST. ANNES	144
MACCLESFIELD	69
MACHYNLLETH	285
MADELAY	210
MAIDENHEAD	55
MAIDSTONE	139
MALDON	110
MALMESBURY	247
MALVERN	251
MANCHESTER	119
MANNINGTREE	111
MANSFIELD	200
MARAZION	74
MARGATE	139
MARKET DEEPING	151
MARKET HARBOROUGH	147
MARLBOROUGH	247
MARPLE BRIDGE	70
MARSH GIBBON	204
MATLOCK	82
MELROSE	262
MELTON CONSTABLE	186
MELTON MOWBRAY	147
MERRIOTT	215
MIDHURST	239
MIDSOMER NORTON	215
MILBORNE PORT	93
MILLINGTON, YORK	106
MILTON KEYNES	62
MILVERTON	215
MINEHEAD	215
MIRFIELD	244
MITCHAM	228
MODBURY, IVYBRIDGE	85
MOFFAT	264
MOLD	279
MONKLEIGH	85
MONTGOMERY	285
MONTPELIER	115
MONTROSE	275
HAMBROOK	60
MORDEN, SURREY	180
MORETON–IN–MARSH	115
MORETONHAMPSTEAD	86
MORPETH	198
MOTTRAM IN LONGDENDALE	120
MOYARD	260
MUCH HADHAM	131
MUCH WENLOCK	210
NAILSEA	60
NAILSWORTH	115
NANTWICH	70
NEATH	281
NEW BARNET	132, 180
NEW BUCKENHAM	186
NEW MALDEN	228
NEW MILTON	124
NEW ROSS	261
NEW TREDEGAR	276
NEWARK	200
NEWBURY	55
NEWCASTLE UPON TYNE	231
NEWCASTLE–UNDER–LYME	219
NEWENT	115
NEWHAVEN	102
NEWMARKET	224
NEWNHAM ON SEVERN	115
NEWPORT (I.O.W.)	134
NEWPORT	281
NEWPORT ON TAY	265
NEWPORT PAGNELL	62
NEWQUAY	74
NEWTON ABBOT	86
NEWTOWN	285
NORMANTON	245
NORTH CHERITON	215
NORTH SHIELDS	231
NORTH WALSHAM	187
NORTHAMPTON	196
NORTHWICH	70
NORWICH	187
NOTTINGHAM	201
OAKHAMPTON	86
OBAN	274
OLD COLWYN	278
OLD COSTESSEY	188
OLDBURY	235
OLDHAM	120
ORPINGTON	139
OSTERLEY	180
OSWESTRY	210
OTLEY	245
OTTERTON	86
OUNDLE	196
OVER LANE	113
OVERTON	124
OXFORD	204
OXTED	228
PAIGNTON	86
PEASEDOWN ST. JOHN	215
PENN	62
PENRITH	78
PENZANCE	74
PERSHORE	251
PETERBOROUGH	66
PETERSFIELD	125
PETWORTH	239
PICKERING	191
PITLOCHRY	275
PLAISTOW	239
PLYMOUTH	86
PONTARDAWE	287
POOLE	93
PORT ERIN	254
PORTSLADE	103
PORTSMOUTH	125
PRENTON	182
PRESCOT	182
PRESTEIGNE	286
PRESTON	144
PUDDLETOWN	93
PURBROOK	125
QUEEN CAME	215
RADCLIFFE	120
RADLETT	132
RAINTON, THIRSK	192
RAMSBURY	247
RAMSGATE	139
RAYLEIGH	111
READING	56
REDCAR	96
REDLAND	60
REDMILE	201
RHYL	279

INDEX OF CITIES AND TOWNS

RICHMOND (N YORKS). 192	SOMERSET 213	TALGARTH 286
RICHMOND 228	SOMERTON 216	TAMWORTH................. 220
RICKMANSWORTH 132	SOUTH BRENT.............. 87	TARPORLEY 71
RINGWOOD................... 125	SOUTH KELSEY 151	TAUNTON 216
RIPON 192	SOUTH QUEENSFERRY . 272	TAVISTOCK 87
ROBERTSBRIDGE........... 103	SOUTHAMPTON............ 126	TEDDINGTON................ 181
ROCHDALE 120	SOUTHEND–ON–SEA 111	TEIGNMOUTH 88
ROCHE, ST. AUSTELL 74	SOUTHPORT 182	TELFORD 211
ROCHESTER 139	SOUTHSEA 126	TENBY 281
ROMSEY 125	SOUTHWOLD................. 225	TETBURY 117
ROSCREA 261	SPALDING 151	TEWKESBURY 117
ROSS–ON–WYE 128	ST. AGNES..................... 74	THIRSK 194
ROSSCARBERY 258	ST. ALBANS 132	THORNTON CLEVELEYS 144
ROTHERFIELD 103	ST. ANDREWS................ 266	THURCASTON 147
ROTHERHAM 217	ST. AUSTELL 74	TICEHURST 104
ROTHLEY...................... 147	ST. HELENS (I.O.W)........ 134	TINTERN....................... 281
RUGBY 232	ST. HELENS 144	TISBURY 248
RUNCORN..................... 70	ST. HELIER, JERSEY 253	TITCHFIELD, FAREHAM 126
RUSHDEN 196	ST. IVES 75	TIVERTON..................... 88
RYDE............................ 134	ST. JUST 74	TODMORDEN 245
RYE 103	ST. LEONARD'S–ON–SEA 103	TONBRIDGE 140
	ST. TEATH 75	TOOTING, LONDON 165
SAFFRON WALDEN 111	STAFFORD 219	TORQUAY 88
SALISBURY 247	STAITHES, CLEVELAND. 193	TORRINGTON................ 88
SALTBURN–BY–THE–SEA 192	STALBRIDGE 94	TOTNES......................... 89
SALTDEAN.................... 103	STAMFORD 151	TOWCESTER 196
SALTHOUSE 188	STANSTED..................... 111	TREGARON 277
SANDIACRE 201	STEYNING 239	TRING 132
SANDY 54	STILLORGAN.................. 259	TRURO 75
SAXMUNDHAM 224	STOBOROUGH 94	TUNBRIDGE WELLS....... 141
SCARBOROUGH............. 192	STOCKPORT 120	TURRIFF 268
SCONE 275	STOCKSFIELD................. 199	TWICKENHAM 181
SEA MILLS 60	STOCKTON–ON–TEES 194	
SEATON 87	STOKE GOLDINGTON ... 62	ULVERSTON.................. 80
SEDBERGH 79	STOKE SUB HAMDON ... 213	UPPINGHAM 208
SELBY 193	STOKE–ON–TRENT........ 220	UTTOXETER 220
SELKIRK 262	STONESFIELD................ 206	
SETTLE 193	STOURPORT-ON-	VALE, GUERNSEY......... 253
SEVENOAKS 140	SEVERN 251	VENTNOR 135
SHAFTESBURY 94	STOW–ON–THE–	VICARSTOWN............... 260
SHAMLEY GREEN......... 229	WOLD 116	
SHARNBROOK 54	STRATFORD–UPON	WADEBRIDGE 75
SHEFFIELD................... 217	–AVON 233	WALDERTON 239
SHENFIELD................... 111	STROUD........................ 116	WALLINGFORD 206
SHERBORNE 94	STUDLEY 233	WALLINGTON 229
SHERINGHAM 188	SUDBURY 225	WALMER DEAL 141
SHINFIELD 57	SUNBURY-ON-THAMES . 180	WALSALL 220
SHIPSTON-ON-STOUR ... 233	SURBITON 229	WALTON–ON–THAMES.. 229
SHOREHAM–BY–SEA 239	SUTTON 229	WANTAGE 207
SHREWSBURY 210	SUTTON COLDFIELD 235	WARBOROUGH 207
SIDCUP 140	SUTTON IN ASHFIELD .. 201	WAREHAM 94
SILVERSTONE............... 196	SUTTON, SURREY 180	WARFIELD 57
SIMONSBATH 215	SWANAGE 94	WARMINSTER 248
SITTINGBOURNE 140	SWANLAND................... 107	WARRINGTON............... 71
SKIPTON 193	SWANSEA 286	WARSASH 126
SLEAFORD 151	SWANTON ABBOT......... 188	WARWICK 233
SMARDEN 140	SWINDON 248	WATFORD..................... 132
SOLIHULL 235	SYDENHAM................... 162	WATTON 188

INDEX OF CITIES AND TOWNS

WELLING 181	WIGAN 120	WORCESTER 251
WELLINGBOROUGH 197	WIGTON 80	WORTHING 239
WELLINGTON 216	WIGTOWN 264	WYMONDHAM 189
WELLS–NEXT–THE–SEA . 189	WILLINGTON 97	
WELSHPOOL 286	WIMBORNE 95	YARKHILL 129
WELTON 80	WIMBORNE MINSTER ... 95	YARM 194
WEM 211	WINCHESTER 127	YARMOUTH 135
WEOBLEY 129	WINDERMERE 80	YORK 194
WEST BROMWICH 236	WINDLESHAM 229	YOUGHAL 258
WEST KINGTON 248	WINDSOR 57	YOXALL 220
WEST PENNARD 216	WINESTEAD, HULL 107	YOXFORD 225
WESTBURY 249	WINSFORD 71	YSTRAD MEURIG 282
WESTBURY-ON-SEVERN 117	WINTERTON 152	
WESTCLIFF–ON–SEA 111	WIRKSWORTH 82	ZEALS 249
WESTERHAM 141	WISBECH 67	
WESTON–SUPER–MARE . 216	WITHERSLACK 80	
WETHERBY 245	WITNEY 207	
WEYBRIDGE 229	WOKING 230	
WEYMOUTH 94	WOKINGHAM 57	
WHITBY 194	WOLVERHAMPTON 236	
WHITCHURCH 211	WOMBOURN 220	
WHITEHAVEN 80	WOMBWELL 218	
WHITLEY BAY 231	WOODBRIDGE 225	
WHITSTABLE 141	WOODFORD GREEN 112	
WICKFORD 112	WOOLER 199	
WICKHAM BISHOPS 112	WOOLWICH 161	
WIDEOPEN 183	WOOTTON BASSETT 249	

Atlanticweb.co.uk

Websites from £200

Wide ranging experience in the computer industry:

- 💻 Bookdealer websites
  - ▶ sell books online
  - ▶ secure sites

- 💻 Database design
  - ▶ online booksearches
  - ▶ stock control

- 💻 Makeovers for existing sites

All enquiries to: sales@atlanticweb.co.uk
Telephone: (01598) 760404

USE OF THE DIRECTORY

This directory is divided into four sections. The first is the *Geographical Directory of Dealers*, in which full details, where supplied, are given for each business or private dealer. These are listed alphabetically by town in which the shop or business premises are located. The details, as supplied by dealers, are presented in the following manner:

Name of business.	As provided. ■ Indicates that the type of premises is a Shop.
Postal address.	(∗) Indicates the dealer's preference for indexing or where we have imposed current county boundaries.
Prop:	Name of proprietor(s).
Web Site:	Web Site address. Users should ignore the full point at the end of the entry.
Tel:	Telephone number(s), together with the new codes followed by fax and/or mobile number. NOTE: If the code for the fax number is the same as for the telephone, it has sometimes been omitted.
E-Mail:	Electronic mail address. Users should ignore the full point at the end of the entry.
Est:	Date at which business was established.
Type of premises occupied:	Shop, private, mail order/internet, market stall or storeroom.
Opening times:	Of shop, or if premises are private, whether appointments to view stock may be made, or if postal business only.
Normal level of total stock:	Very small (less than 2,000), small (2,000–5,000), medium (5,000–10,000), large (10,000–20,000) or very large (more than 20,000).
Spec:	Subjects of books in which the dealer specialises. NB: only the first eight are shown in the Geographical Section. All dealers' subjects are shown in the Speciality Index
PR:	Price range of stock. This is intended as a guideline only.
CC:	Selection of Credit & Debit Cards eg. AE – American Express, DC – Diners Club, DI – Discovery, EC – Eurocard, JCB – Japanese Credit Bureau, MC – Mastercard, SO – Solo, SW – Switch, V – VISA.
Important lines of business:	Other than secondhand antiquarian books.
Cata:	Frequency and subject of catalogues, if issued.
Corresp:	Languages, other than English, in which correspondence may be conducted.
Mem:	Membership of book trade organisations, eg. A.B.A. – Antiquarian Booksellers' Association B.A. – Booksellers Association of Great Britain & Ireland P.A. – Publishers Association P.B.F.A. – Provincial Booksellers' Fairs Association

Entries that have been reviewed by the dealers since the last edition have [updated] after their entry. Those who have not responded to our mailings, either as e-mails or printed forms in the post have the date on which they last notified us of their information.

The next section is an alphabetical *Index of Businesses*, giving full name and county with the page on which their full entry is to be found.

There is then a new section, the *Index of Web Sites*, which lists dealers alphabetically with their page reference and web site.

This is followed by an alphabetical *Index of Proprietors*, giving their name and trading name followed by their page reference.

The fourth section is the *Speciality Index*. This is presented in alphabetical order by subject heading, giving the dealer's name, county and page on which their details may be found.

OLYMPIC GAMES

Jeux Olympiques – 𝔒𝔩𝔶𝔪𝔭𝔦𝔰𝔠𝔥𝔢 𝔖𝔭𝔦𝔢𝔩𝔢 – *Giochi Olimpichi*

1896 – 2004

Always Buying & Selling:

Official Reports - Programs - Books - Posters - Maps -
Tickets - Medals - Badges - Medallions - Collectables - etc.

Specializing in:
Olympic Games
History of Sport
Physical Education
Wrestling, Fencing
Rowing, Gymnastics
Sports & Athletics
Sport in Art
Sports Medicine
Graphic Illustrations of
  Sports & Athletics
Expositions & World's Fairs
1900 Paris, 1904 St. Louis

Historical research, writing & consulting services available.
Catalogs by subscription – Brokerage & Private Treaty sales.
Auctions – Consignments accepted – collection development.

HARVEY ABRAMS – BOOKS
P.O. Box 732 State College, P.A., U.S.A. 16804
Tel: (814) 237-8331 – Fax: (814) 237-8332
Email: Olympicbks@aol.com

BEDFORDSHIRE

BEDFORD

Books With Care, 7 Barford Road, Willington, Bedford, MK44 3QP. Prop: Gerald Ford. **Tel:** (01234) 831288. Fax: (01234) 831288. Web: www.bookswithcare.com. E-mail: shep@bookswithcare.com. Est: 1996. Private premises. postal only. Appointment necessary. Stock: Small. PR: £1–200. CC: MC; V; PayPal. [Updated]

Bunyan Books, 57 Purbeck Close, Goldington, Bedford, MK41 9LX. Prop: R.G. Sancto. Tel: (01234) 345518. E-mail: roderick@sanctofamily.fsnet.co.uk. Est: 2002. Private premises. Internet and postal. Appointment necessary. Stock: Large. PR: £10–500. Corresp: French, German. Notes: Advertises occasionally in Bookdealer. Also, restoration, repair and binding. [Updated]

The Eagle Bookshop, ■ 101 - 103 Castle Road, Bedford, MK40 3QP. Prop: Peter Budek. Tel: (01234) 269295. Fax: (01234) 290920. Web: www.eaglebookshop.co.uk. E-mail: info@eaglebookshop.co.uk. Est: 1991. Internet and postal. Shop open: **M:** 10:00–17:30; **T:** 10:00–17:30; **W:** 10:00–17:30; **Th:** 10:00–17:30; **F:** 10:00–17:30; **S:** 09:30–17:00; **Su:** 11:00–15:30. Stock: very large. Spec: Academic/Scholarly; Antiquarian; History - General; History of Ideas; Mathematics; Physics; Science - General; Technology. PR: £1–2,000. CC: MC; V; SW. Mem: PBFA. [Updated]

Kingsmere Books, 41 Haylands Way, Bedford, MK41 9BY. Prop: Brian Webb. Tel: 01234.302132. E-mail: a.webb3@ntlworld.com. Est: 1985. Private premises. Internet and postal. Spec: Biography; Natural History; Poetry; Topography - General. Corresp: French, Spanish. [Updated]

CHICKSANDS

Leslie H. Bolland Books, 1 Warren Court, Chicksands, SG17 5QB. Prop: Les & Anne Bolland. Tel: (01462) 815174. Fax: (01462) 814738. Web: www.bollandbooks.com. E-mail: lesbolland@aol.com. Est: 1997. Office and/or bookroom. Internet and postal. Appointment necessary. Stock: large. Spec: Academic/Scholarly; Advertising; Assassinations; Author - Buckeridge, A.; Crime (True); Criminology; Police Force Histories; Sport - Angling/Fishing. PR: £2–500. CC: MC; V; SW. Mem: PBFA. Also, a booksearch service. VAT No: GB 806 1492 42. [23/12/2004]

DUNSTABLE

Adrian Walker, 107 Great Northern Road, Dunstable, LU5 4BW. Tel: (01582) 605824. E-mail: adrian-walker@supanet.com. Est: 1965. Private premises. Postal only. Telephone first. Stock: very small Spec: Sport - Falconry. PR: £1–250. [Updated]

The Book Castle, ■ 12 Church St., Dunstable, Bedfordshire, LU5 4RU. Tel: (01582) 605670. Web: www.book-castle.co.uk. E-mail: bc@book-castle.co.uk. Shop open: **M:** 09:00–17:00; **T:** 09:00–17:00; **W:** 09:00–17:00; **Th:** 08:00–17:00; **F:** 09:00–17:00; **S:** 09:00–17:00. CC: AE; MC; V; Solo. Mem: PBFA. [Updated]

EGGINGTON

Robert Kirkman Ltd., Kings Cottage, Eggington, LU7 9PG. Tel: (01525) 210647. Fax: (01525) 211184. Web: www.robertkirkman.co.uk. E-mail: robertkirkmanltd@btinternet.com. Est: 1987. Private premises. Internet and postal. Appointment necessary. Stock: Small. Spec: Antiquarian; Authors - Bunyan, John, Churchill, Sir Winston; Autographs; Bibles; Bindings; First Editions; Fore-Edge Paintings. PR: £20–100. CC: MC; V. Mem: ABA; PBFA; BA; ILAB. Notes: Literary relics. [Updated]

Dealers – visit your entry at least once a year.
Check your details are correct. Go to:

www.sheppardsworld.co.uk

SANDY

H.J. Morgan, 47 Bedford Road, Sandy, SG19 1ES. Tel: (01767) 691383. E-mail: hedleymorgan@ntlworld.com. Est: 1980. Private premises. Postal only. Stock: Small. Spec: Academic/Scholarly; History - General; Literature; Travel - General. Mem: PBFA. VAT No: GB 467 3823 19. [Updated]

SHARNBROOK

Ouse Valley Books, 16 Home Close, Sharnbrook, Bedford, MK44 1PQ. Prop: Barrie Farnsworth. Tel: (01234) 782411. E-mail: ousevalleybooks@btconnect.com. Est: 1990. Private premises. Book Fairs Only. Appointment necessary. Stock: very small. Spec: Academic/Scholarly; Arts, The; History - British; Sport - Cycling; Topography - General; Topography - Local. PR: £5–500. Mem: PBFA . [Updated]

BERKSHIRE

ASCOT
Ian Cross, 83 Gainsborough Drive, Ascot, SL5 8TA. Tel: (01344) 872100. Fax: (01344) 872544. E-mail: ccross@btconnect.com. Est: 1972. Stock: small. Spec: Art. PR: £25–1,500. Corresp: Italian. [Updated]

BRACKNELL
Bookzone, 5 Flintgrove, Bracknell, RG12 2JN. Prop: John Bacon. Tel: (01344) 421770. E-mail: johnbacon@screaming.net. Est: 1990. Private premises. Internet and postal. Appointment necessary. Stock: small. Spec: Sport:- Athletics; Boxing; Cricket; Football (Soccer); Golf; Horse Racing (inc. Riding/Breeding/Equestrian); Rugby; Tennis. PR: £5–50. CC: MC; V; PayPal. Exhibits at bookfairs. Alternative Tel. No. (01344) 488825. [Updated]

COOKHAM
Jean Hedger, Poultons, Cookham, SL6 9LH. Prop: Jean Hedger. Tel: 01628 523911. Fax: 01628 528217. Web: www.booksatpbfa.com. E-mail: jeanhedger@btconnect.com. Est: 1977. Private premises. Internet and postal. Contactable at PBFA and ABA Book Fairs in UK and Biblion, Davies Mews, London. Spec: Artists; Authors:- Ahlberg, Janet & Allan; Aldin, Cecil; Ardizzone, Edward; Barker, Cecily M.; Barrie, J.M.; Caldicott, R.; Cook, Beryl. CC: D; JCB; MC; V. Cata: occasionally on Illustrated; Artwork; Children's; Stanley Spencer. Corresp: French; Spanish; German; Chinese (Mandarin). Mem: ABA; PBFA; BA; ILAB. Notes: I specialise in Illustrated Books and Original Artwork; Children's Books of the last three centuries; Reference Books related to these areas; Stanley Spencer. In addition I stock a small selection of books outside these subject areas. [Updated]

CROWTHORNE
Malcolm Applin, 21 Larkswood Drive, Crowthorne, RG45 6RH. Prop: Malcolm Applin. Tel: (01344) 776881. Est: 1993. Private premises. Postal only. Stock: small. Spec: Biography; Fiction - General; Fiction - Women; Literary Criticism; Poetry. PR: £5–250. [updated]

HURST
Christopher Edwards, Hatch Gate Farmhouse, Lines Road, Hurst, RG10 0SP. Prop: Christopher Edwards & Margaret Erskine. Tel: (0118) 934 0531. Fax: (0118) 934 0539. E-mail: chr.edwards@which.net. Est: 1992. Private premises. Internet Only. Appointment necessary. Stock: small. Spec: Early Imprints; History - General; Literature. CC: MC; V. Corresp: French. Mem: ABA; ILAB. [Updated]

KINGSCLERE
Wyseby House Books, ■ Kingsclere Old Bookshop, 2a George Street, Kingsclere, Nr. Newbury, RG20 5NQ. Dr. T. Oldham. Tel: (01635) 297995. Fax: (01635) 297677. Web: www.wyseby.co.uk. E-mail: info@wyseby.co.uk. Est: 1978. Internet and postal. Shop open: **M:** 09:00–17:00; **T:** 09:00–17:00; **W:** 09:00–17:00; **Th:** 09:00–17:00; **F:** 09:00–17:00; **S:** 09:00–17:00. Stock: Very large. Spec: Applied Art; Architecture; Art; Art History; Art Reference; Artists; Arts, The; Biology. PR: £1–1,000. CC: AE; JCB; MC. Mem: PBFA. VAT No: GB 295 3261 54. [Updated]

MAIDENHEAD
Valerie Peel, t/a Kiandra Associates Ltd., 40 Culley Way, Cox Green, Maidenhead, SL6 3PX. Tel: (01628) 822439. Fax: (01628) 826118. E-mail: valerie_peel@dogbooks.freeserve.co.uk. Est: 1985. Private premises. Internet and postal. Stock: small. Spec: Dogs. PR: £4–750. Notes: free booksearch. [Updated]

NEWBURY
Eastleach Books, Unit 53, Unity House, New Greenham Park, Newbury, RG19 6HU. Prop: Daniel Unwin. Tel: +44 (0)1635 817377. Fax: +44 (0)1635 817375. Web: www.eastleach-book.co.uk. E-mail: dan@bookville.freeserve.co.uk. Est: 1997. Internet and postal. Telephone first. Warehouse open: **M:** 09:00–18:00; **T:** 09:00–18:00; **W:** 09:00–18:00; **Th:** 09:00–18:00; **F:** 09:00–18:00; **S:** 09:00–18:00. Stock: very large. Spec: Academic/Scholarly; Alpinism/Mountaineering; Antiquarian; Applied Art; Art; Biography; History - General. PR: £2–4,500. CC: E; JCB; MC; V. Corresp: Little French. Mem: PBFA. [Updated]

Invicta Bookshop, ■ 8 Cromwell Place, Northbrook Street, Newbury, RG14 1AF. Prop: Simon & Tina Hall. Tel: (01635) 31176. Est: 1969. Shop open: **M:** 10:30–17:30; **T:** 10:30–17:30; **Th:** 10:30–17:30; **F:** 10:30–17:30; **S:** 10:30–17:30. Stock: large. Spec: Aviation; Cookery/Gastronomy; Military; Sport - Cricket; Topography - Local. PR: £1–200. CC: MC; V. Mem: PBFA. Also at: Hungerford Arcade Antiques Centre. [28/09/2004]

Railway Book and Magazine Search, The Warren, Curridge, Newbury, RG18 9DN. Prop: N.J. Bridger. Tel: (01635) 200507. Web: www.nevis-railway-bookshops.co.uk. Est: 1981. Private premises. Postal only. Stock: very small. Spec: Railways; Ephemera. PR: £1–200. Also at: Nevis Railway Bookshop, Goring-on-Thames, Oxon (q.v.) Nevis Railway Bookshop, Marlborough, Wiltshire (q.v.). [updated]

READING

Books for Amnesty, ■ 71 Wokingham Road, Reading, RG6 1LH. Prop: Amnesty International UK. Tel: 01189 661646. E-mail: readingbookshop@btconnect.com. Est: 2003. Shop open: **M:** 10.00–17:00; **T:** 10.00–17.00; **W:** 10.00–17.00; **Th:** 10.00–17:00; **F:** 10.00–17:00; **S:** 10.00–17:00. [Updated]

K.C. Brown, 11 Easington Drive, Lower Earley, Reading, RG6 3XN. Tel: (0118) 966-7013. Fax: (0118) 966-7013. Est: 1991. Private premises. Appointment necessary. [Updated]

Mary Butts Books, 219 Church Road, Earley, Reading, RG6 1HW. Prop: Mary Butts. Tel: (0118) 926-1793. E-mail: mary.butts@tiscali.co.uk. Est: 1985. Private premises. Internet and postal. Appointment necessary. M: 09:00–17:00; T: 09:00–17:00; W: 09:00–17:00; Th: 09:00–17:00; F: 09:00–17:00; S: 09:00–17:00. Stock: Medium. Spec: Applied Art; Architecture; Art; Art History; Art Reference; Artists; Children's; Decorative Art. PR: £2–50. Corresp: French. [Updated]

Footballana, 275 Overdown Road, Tilehurst, Reading, RG31 6NX. Prop: Bryan Horsnell. Tel: (0118) 942 4448. Fax: (0118) 942 4448. Private premises. Postal only. Stock: very small. Spec: Sport - Football (Soccer); Ephemera. PR: £5–100. Notes: also, pre-1950 football programmes, postcards and ephemera wanted. [Updated]

Forbury Fine Books, 46 Tredegar Road, Reading, RG4 8QF. Prop: Stephen Gardner. Tel: (0870) 063 8680. Fax: (0870) 286 6874. Web: www.forburyfinebooks.co.uk. E-mail: mail@forburyfinebooks.co.uk. Est: 2004. Private premises. Internet and postal. Appointment necessary: **M:** 09:00–18:00; **T:** 09:00–18:00; **W:** 09:00–18:00; **Th:** 09:00–18:00; **F:** 09:00–18:00. Stock: small. PR: £2–1,000. Also: Book Search. [Updated]

J.B. Books, 3 Wenlock Edge, Charvil, Reading, RG10 9QG. Prop: John A. Baker. Tel: (0118) 934-0679. Web: www.balloonbooks.co.uk. E-mail: jb.books@btopenworld.com. Est: 1978. Private premises. Postal only. Telephone first. Stock: small. Spec: Aviation; Sport - Ballooning. PR: £1–250. Corresp: French. [Updated]

Keegan's Bookshop, ■ Merchant's Place, (off Friar Street), Reading, RG1 1DT. Prop: John & Judith Keegan. Tel: (0118) 958-7253. Fax: (0118) 958-5220. Web: www.keegansbookshop.com. E-mail: enquiries@keegansbookshop.com. Est: 1979. Shop open: **M:** 09:00–17:30; **T:** 09:00–17:30; **W:** 09:00–17:30; **Th:** 09:00–17:30; **F:** 09:00–17:30; **S:** 09:00–17:30. Stock: medium. Spec: Aviation; Maritime/Nautical; Military; Military History; Naval; Railways; Topography - General; Topography - Local. PR: £1–100. CC: MC; V; SW. Corresp: Italian. [Updated]

Veronica Mayhew, Trewena, Behoes Lane, Woodcote, Reading, RG8 0PP. Tel: (01491) 680743. E-mail: veronica.mayhew@virgin.net. Est: 1972. Private premises. Appointment necessary. Stock: small. Spec: Animals and Birds; Apiculture; Cats; Farming & Livestock; Ornithology. PR: £1–500. VAT No: GB 537 6954 02. [Updated]

Searching for a title - and cannot find it on any Internet database?

Then try **www.sheppardsworld.co.uk**

By selecting the subject classification – then e-mail selected dealers who major in that subject.

SHINFIELD

Books & Bygones, 40 Hollow Lane, Shinfield, RG2 9BT. Prop: Pamela Pither and John Lilly. Tel: 0118 988 4346. Web: www.booksbygones.com. E-mail: booksbygones@btconnect.com. Est: 1990. Mail order only. Internet and postal. Spec: Cookery - Professional; Cookery/Gastronomy; Food & Drink. CC: MC; V. Maestro. Mem: Ibooknet. [Updated]

WARFIELD

Moss End Bookshop, ■ Moss End Garden Centre, Moss End, Warfield, Nr. Bracknell, RG42 6EJ. Prop: K. & M.A. Precious. Tel: (01344) 422110. Est: 1981. Shop open: **T:** 10:00–17:00; **W:** 10:00–17:00; **Th:** 10:00–17:00; **F:** 10:00–17:00; **S:** 10:00–17:00; **Su:** 10:00–17:00. Spec: Antiques; Rural Life; Sport - Field Sports PR: £2–250. CC: MC; V. Also, prints. [Updated]

WINDSOR

Brian Billing, 28 Athlone Square, Ward Royal, Windsor, SL4 1SS. Tel: (01753) 851343. Est: 1965. Private premises. Postal only. Stock: small. Spec: Economics; Natural History; Travel - General. PR: £2–250. [Updated]

Eton Antique Bookshop, ■ 88 High Street, Eton, Windsor, SL4 6AF. Prop: Maurice Bastians. Tel: (01753) 855534. Est: 1975. Shop open: **M:** 11:00–18:00; **T:** 11:00–18:00; **W:** 11:00–18:00; **Th:** 11:00–18:00; **F:** 11:00–18:00; **S:** 11:00–18:00; **Su:** 12:00–17:00. Stock: medium. Spec: Antiquarian; Antiques; Bindings; History - General; Literature; Military; Poetry; Sets of Books. PR: £3–2,000. CC: E; MC; V; Most others. Corresp: Spanish. Mem: Eton Traders Assoc. Notes: also old prints and maps, bookbinding and repairs. Notes: often open early and late - call first. VAT No: GB 787 1877 65. [Updated]

WOKINGHAM

John Townsend, 33, Bishop's Drive, Wokingham, RG40 1WA. Tel: (0118) 978-5463. Web: www.johntownsend.demon.co.uk. E-mail: john@johntownsend.demon.co.uk. Est: 1991. Private premises. Internet and postal. Contactable. Stock: medium. Spec: Genealogy; Heraldry; History - General; Manuscripts; Parish Registers; School Registers/Rolls of Honour; Topography - General; Topography - Local. PR: £10–200. Corresp: French, German. VAT No: GB 591 8061 25. [Updated]

BRISTOL

BISHOPSTON

Steve Liddle, 18 Morley Square, Bishopston, BS7 9DW. Tel: (0117) 924 4846. E-mail: steveandkath@liddles.fslife.co.uk. Est: 1983. Private premises. Internet and postal. Appointment necessary. Mem: ABA; PBFA; BA; ILAB. [Updated]

BRISTOL

Lesley Aitchison, 22 West Shrubbery, Redland, Bristol, BS6 6TA. Tel: (0117) 907-6899. Fax: (0117) 974-1962. Web: www.localhistory.co.uk/la. E-mail: lesley@localhistory.co.uk. Est: 1993. Private premises. Spec: Manuscripts; Topography - Local. PR: £10–1,000. Notes: also at these premises: Ambra Books. (q.v.) Also, sales particulars, maps & photographs [Updated]

Ambra Books, 22 West Shrubbery, Redland, Bristol, BS6 6TA. Prop: Ivor Cornish. Tel: (0117) 907-6899. Fax: (0117) 974-1962. Web: www.localhistory.co.uk/ambra. E-mail: ambra@localhistory.co.uk. Est: 1972. Private premises. Internet and postal. Appointment necessary. M: 09:00–17:00; **T:** 09:00–17:00; **W:** 09:00–17:00; **Th:** 09:00–17:17; **F:** 09:00–00:00; **S:** 09:00–12:00. Stock: small. Spec: Genealogy; History - Local; Topography - Local. PR: £10–3,000. CC: MC; V. SW. Corresp: French, Italian. Notes: Stock mainly covers West Country, Devon, Cornwall and Dorset. [Updated]

Avon Books, ■ 4 Waterloo Street, Clifton, Bristol, BS8 4 BT. Prop: John Ray. Tel: 0117 973 9848. E-mail: sales@avonbook.co.uk. Est: 1991. Shop open: M: 10:00–16:00; **T:** 10:00–16:00; **W:** 10:00–16:00; **Th:** 10:00–16:00; **F:** 10:00–16:00. [Updated]

Beware of the Leopard, Stalls 77 and 66 - 69, the Covered Market, Saint Nicholas Markets, Saint Nicholas Street, Bristol, BS1 1LJ. Prop: David Jackson. Tel: 01179 257277. E-mail: bewareoftheleopard@hotmail.com. Est: 1991. Market stand/stall: **M:** 10:00–17:00; **T:** 10:00–17:00; **W:** 10:00–17:00; **Th:** 10:00–17:00; **F:** 10:00–17:00; **S:** 10:00–17:00. Spec: Aircraft; Art Reference; Arts, The; Autobiography; Aviation; Cinema/Film; Classics, The; Computing. CC: MC; V. [Updated]

Bishopston Books, ■ 259, Gloucester Rd, Bristol, BS7 8NY. Prop: Bill Singleton. Tel: 0117 9445303. Web: www.ibooknet.co.uk. E-mail: bishopstonbooks@btinternet.com. Est: 1993. Shop open: **T:** 10.00–17.00; **W:** 10.00–17:30; **Th:** 10.00–17:30; **F:** 10.00–17:30; **S:** 09.30–16.30. CC: MC; V; Macstro. Mem: Ibooknet. [Updated]

Books for Amnesty, ■ 103 Gloucester Road, Bishopston, Bristol, BS7 8AT. Prop: Amnesty International U.K Tel: (0117) 942-2969. Est: 1998. Sho open: **M:** 10:00–16:30; **T:** 10:00–16:30; **W:** 10:00-16:30; **Th:** 10:00-16:30; **F:** 10:00–16:30; **S:** 11:00–17:00. Stock: medium. PR: £1–10. Mem: Bristol Book Fairs at BAWA. [Updated]

James Burmester, Pipley Old Farm, Upton Cheyney, Bristol, BS30 6NG. Prop: James & Rosamund Burmester. Tel: (0117) 932-7265. Fax: (0117) 932-7667. E-mail: james.burmester@btconnect.com. Est: 1985. Private premises. Appointment necessary. Stock: small. Spec: Agriculture. PR: £50–10,000. CC: MC; V. Mem: PBFA. VAT No: GB 404 6808 60. [Updateed]

Court Hay Books, Court Hay, 26 Church Road, Easton-in-Gordano, Bristol, BS20 0PQ. Prop: Howard and Gilian Walters. Tel: (01275) 372751. Web: www.courthaybooks.co.uk. E-mail: courthaybooks@btconnect.com. Est: 1990. Private premises. Internet and postal. Appointment necessary. Stock: small. Spec: Flower Arranging; Gardening - General; Horticulture. PR: £10–2,000. CC: AE; JCB; MC; V. [Updated]

Deverell Books, 86a Memorial Road, Hanham, Bristol, BS15 3LA. Prop: Paul Deverell Hughes. Tel: (0117) 961-6234. Fax: (0117) 373-8786. E-mail: pdhbooks@hotmail.com. Est: 2001. Private premises. Appointment necessary. Stock: very small. Spec: Books about Books; Children's; Illustrated. PR: £10–2,000. Mem: PBFA. [Updated]

Looking for a book dealer overseas? Then search Sheppard's on-line directories at:

www.sheppardsworld.co.uk

For overseas bookdealers

R.A. Gilbert, 4 Julius Road, Bishopston, Bristol, BS7 8EU. Tel: (0117) 924-6936. Fax: (0117) 924-4937. Est: 1963. Private premises. Appointment necessary. Stock: small. Spec: Alchemy; Folklore; Freemasonry & Anti-Masonry; Gnostics; Occult; Psychic; Religion - General; Theology. PR: £5–1,000. Corresp: French. Mem: PBFA. VAT No: GB 138 9728 22. [Updated]

Harlequin Books, ■ 122 High Street, Staple Hill, Bristol, BS16 5HH. Prop: Brian W. Ball. Tel: (0117) 970-1801. Fax: (0117) 970-1801. Web: www.harlequinbooks.co.uk. E-mail: harlequin.books@virgin.net. Est: 1994. Internet and postal. Shop open: **M:** 09:30–16:30; **T:** 09:30–16:30; **W:** 09:30–16:30; **Th:** 09:30–16:30; **F:** 09:30–16:30; **S:** 09:30–16:30. Stock: medium. Spec: Military; Military History; Railways; Topography - Local; Booksearch. PR: £1–250. CC: AE; JCB; MC; V. VAT No: GB 639 7296 86. [22/10/2004]

A.R. Heath, 62 Pembroke Road, Clifton, Bristol, BS8 3DX. Tel: (0117) 974-1183. Fax: (0117) 973-2901. Web: www.heathrarebooks.co.uk. E-mail: heath.rare-books@dsl.pipex.com. Est: 1964. Spec: Fine & Rare; Manuscripts. PR: £50–10,000. [Updated]

Higher Octave Books, ■ 58 Cotham Hill, Redland, Bristol, BS6 6JX. Prop: Kevin Fortey-Jones F.E.A.A. Tel: 0117 946 7772. Fax: 0117 973 0522. Web: www.higher-octave-books.co.uk. E-mail: royalfort@btconnect.com. Shop open: **M:** 10:00–18:00; **T:** 10:00–18:00; **W:** 10:00–18:00; **Th:** 10:00–18:00; **F:** 10:00–18:00; **S:** 10:00–18:00. CC: AE; E; MC; V. Notes: general stock; bookbinding, postcards and ephemera VAT No: GB 713 5195 47. [Updated]

Hinchliffe Books, Clematis Cottage, 15 Castle Street, Thornbury, Bristol, BS35 1HA. Prop: Geoffrey Hinchliffe. Tel: (01454) 415177. E-mail: geoff@sumbooks.co.uk. Est: 1972. Private premises. Appointment necessary. Stock: medium. Spec: Homeopathy; Industry; Mathematics; Physics; Science - General; Technology; Topography - General. PR: £2–200. VAT No: GB 520 4690 69. [Updated]

Arthur Hook, 54 Egerton Road, Bristol, BS7 8HL. Tel: (0117) 9144673. Web: www.hooksbooks.co.uk. E-mail: hooksbooks@blueyonder.co.uk. Est: 1997. Private premises. Internet and postal. Appointment necessary. Stock: very small. Spec: Atlases; City of London; Naval; Railways. [Updated]

A.J. Kitley, 31 Perrys Lea, Bradley Stoke, Bristol, BS32 0EE. Tel: (01454) 615261. Est: 1986. Private premises. Postal only. Stock: very small. Spec: Musical Instruments. PR: £1–150. [Updated]

Rachel Lee Rare Books, The Old Bakery, 30 Poplar Road, Warmley, Bristol, BS30 5JU. Prop: Rachel Lee. Tel: (0117) 960-6891. Fax: (0117) 960-6935. Web: www.rleerarebooks.co.uk. E-mail: rachellee.books@virgin.net. Est: 1979. Private premises. Internet and postal. Appointment necessary. Stock: small. Spec: Academic/Scholarly; Economics; History of Ideas; Humanities; Philosophy; Booksearch. PR: £30–20,000. CC: AE; MC; V. Mem: ABA; ILAB. Notes: also, a booksearch service for philosophy only. VAT No: GB 783 5078 02. [Updated]

M. G. Manwaring, 9 Glentworth Road, Bristol, BS6 7EG. Tel: 0117 942 2934. E-mail: malcolm@mgmanwaring.fsnet.co.uk. Est: 1975. Private premises. Open: **M:** 09:00–18:00; **T:** 09:00–18:00; **W:** 09:00–18:00; **Th:** 09:00–18:00; **F:** 09:00–18:00; **S:** 09:00–18:00. Spec: Applied Art; Architecture; Botany; Children's - Illustrated; Fine Art; Literature; Natural Sciences. CC: MC; V. Corresp: French. [Updated]

Paperbacks Plus, ■ Regent Street Shopping Arcade, 98 Regent Street, Kingswood, Bristol, BS15 8HP. Prop: Mr. T. Nicholls. Tel: (0117) 9566232. Web: www.pbplus.freeserve.co.uk. E-mail: books@pbplus.freeserve.co.uk. Est: 1994. Internet and postal. Shop open: **M:** 09:00–17:00; **T:** 09:00–17:00; **W:** 09:00–17:00; **Th:** 09:00–17:00; **F:** 09:00–17:00; **S:** 09:00–17:00. Spec: Biography; Children's; Fiction - General; Fiction - Crime, Detective, Spy, Thrillers; Fiction - Fantasy, Horror; Fiction - Science Fiction; Fiction - Women; Military History. PR: £1–20. [Updated]

S.P.C.K., ■ 79 Park Street, Bristol, BS1 5PF. Tel: (0117) 9273461. Fax: (0117) 9293525. Web: www.spck.org.uk. E-mail: bristol@spck.org.uk. Est: 1698. Shop open: **M:** 09:00–17:30; **T:** 09:00–17:30; **W:** 09:30–17:30; **Th:** 09:00–17:30; **F:** 09:00–17:30; **S:** 09:00–17:30. Stock: small. Spec: Prayer Books; Religion - Christian; Theology. PR: £1–250. CC: MC; V. Mem: PBFA. Notes: also, new technology. VAT No: GB 232 8071 82. [Updated]

Morris & Juliet Venables, 270 Henbury Road, Bristol, BS10 7QR. Prop: Morris & Juliet Venables. Tel: (0117) 950-7362. Fax: (0117) 959-2361. E-mail: morris.venables@ukgateway.net. Est: 1970. Private premises. Appointment necessary. Stock: medium. Spec: Academic/Scholarly; Advertising; Antiquarian; Art; Fine & Rare; Literary Criticism; Literature; Music - General. PR: £5–1,000. CC: MC; V. Mem: PBFA. VAT No: GB 397 3454 11. [Updated]

Gerald Baker, 28 Beaconsfield Road, Clifton, BS8 2TS. Tel: (0117) 974-4319. Web: www.gwrpublicity.co.uk. E-mail: gwrpublicity@btinternet.com. Postal only. Stock: very small. Spec: Railways. Notes: also, Ephemera. PR: £5–200. [Updated]

Bristol Books, Champion House, Moorend Farm Road, Hambrook, BS16 1SP. Prop: Garth O'Donnell. Tel: (0117) 910 9829. Web: www.abebooks.com/home/bs6books. E-mail: bs6books@aol.com. Est: 1985. Private premises. Internet and postal. Appointment necessary. Stock: medium. Spec: Art; Humanities; Literature; Pulps. PR: £1–50. CC: PayPal. [Updated]

Byass Rare Books, ■ 14 Clifton Arcade, Boyces Avenue, Clifton, BS8 4AA. Prop: Dean Byass. Tel: (0117) 974 2555. E-mail: byass@btopenworld.com. Est: 1994. Shop. Telephone first. Spec: Antiquarian; Fine & Rare; History of Ideas; Law - General; Literature; Medicine; Philosophy; Science - History of. PR: £50–10,000. CC: AE; MC; V. VAT No: GB 799 9334 44. [21/12/2004]

James Hawkes, 18 Caledonia Place, Clifton, BS8 4DJ. Tel: (0117) 317 9268. Web: www.abebooks.com/home/JAMESHAWKES/. E-mail: jameshawkes1977@yahoo.com. Private premises. Internet and postal. Telephone first. Stock: small. Spec: Academic/Scholarly; Antiquarian; Literary Criticism; Literature. PR: £20–1,500. CC: MC; V; Maestro SW. [Updated]

J. D. Patterson, 5 Cowper Road, Redland, BS6 6NY. Prop: John Patterson. Tel: 0117 973 6710. Fax: 0871 433 8209. Web: www.jdpatterson.co.uk. E-mail: john@jdpatterson.co.uk. Est: 1983. Private premises. Internet and postal. Appointment necessary. Spec: Aeronautics; Aircraft; Architecture; Aviation; Railroads; Railways. CC: MC; V. Cata: occasionally on UK Railways Aviation Architecture. Mem: PBFA. [Updated]

John Roberts Wine Books, 3 Weston Close, Sea Mills, BS9 2JG. Tel: 0117 373 7904. E-mail: wine.books@virgin.net. Est: 1977. Private premises. Internet and postal. Spec: Author - Simon, Andre L.; Viticulture; Whisky; Wine. Mem: ABA; ILAB. VAT No: GB 561 9002 57. [Updated]

NAILSEA

The Old Music Master, 16 Scotch Horn Way, Nailsea, BS48 1TE. Prop: Joseph Tooley. Tel: 01275 856320. E-mail: pokefun@btinternet.com. Est: 1962. Private premises. Appointment necessary. Spec: Music - Illustrated Sheet Music; Music - Printed, Sheet Music & Scores. Notes: main stock is illustrated music sheets. [Updated]

BUCKINGHAMSHIRE

AMERSHAM

Gill Bilski, 4 Sheepfold Lane, Amersham, HP7 9EL. Prop: Gill Bilski. Tel: (01494) 433895. Web: www.gillbilski.com. E-mail: gill@bilski.freeserve.co.uk. Est: 1983. Private premises. Internet and postal. Appointment necessary. Stock: very small. Spec: Authors: - Brent-Dyer, Elinor M.; Fairlie-Bruce, D.; Oxenham, Elsie; Children's; Booksearch. PR: £2–200. CC: via PayPal. Corresp: French. Also, a booksearch service. [Updated]

AYLESBURY

David Wilson, 95 Worlds End Lane, Weston Turville, Aylesbury, HP22 5RX. Tel: (01296) 612247. Est: 1969. Spec: Countries - Scotland; Natural History; Ornithology; Topography - Local. [Updated]

BEACONSFIELD

Barn Books, Old Hay Barn, Holtspur Top Lane, Beaconsfield, HP9 1BS. Prop: Elisabeth & Wolfgang Ansorge. Tel: (01494) 671122. Fax: (01494) 671122. E-mail: barnbooks@supanet.com. Est: 1991. Private premises. Internet and postal. Appointment necessary. Stock: small. Spec: Archaeology; Art; Cinema/Film; Collecting; Crafts; History - General; Military; Natural History. PR: £5–3,000. CC: PayPal. Corresp: German. VAT No: GB 578 4204 21. [Updated]

BUCKINGHAM

Corvus Books, 11 Parsons Close, Winslow, Buckingham, MK18 3BX. Prop: Chris Corbett. Tel: (01296) 713393. Fax: (01296) 713393. E-mail: corvusbooks@btinternet.com. Est: 1990. Private premises. Internet and postal. Appointment necessary. Stock: very small. Spec: Atlases; Colour-Plate; Natural History; Travel - General. PR: £50–5,000. CC: PayPal. Mem: PBFA. Notes: also attends 11 fairs a year at the Hotel Russell, London. [Updated]

E. & J. Shelley, Quakers Orchard, 12 Moreton Road, Buckingham, MK18 1LA. Prop: Jennifer Shelley. Tel: (01280) 812307. E-mail: shellbooks@btinternet.com. Est: 1996. Private premises. Postal only. Telephone first. Stock: large. Spec: Children's; First Editions; Illustrated; Literature; Poetry. PR: £10–2,000. [Updated]

CHESHAM

David Mundy at Nooks and Crannies, ■ 9 Market Square, Chesham, HP5 1HG. Prop: Dave Mundy. Tel: (020) 7482 7087. E-mail: dave.mundy@tiscali.co.uk. Est: 2000. Shop open: **M:** 09:30–17:30; **T:** 09:30–17:30; **W:** 09:30–17:30; **Th:** 09:30–17:30; **F:** 09:30–17:30; **S:** 09:30–17:30; **Su:** 11:00–16:30. Stock: very small. Spec: Antiques; Art; History - General; Topography - General; Travel - General. PR: £1–50. CC: MC; V. Notes: See also David Mundy at heritage Antiques, Berkhamstead, Hertfordshire. (q.v.) [Updated]

GREAT MISSENDEN

Martin Blackman, 6 Wychwood Rise, Great Missenden, HP16 0HB. Tel: (01494) 890839. Fax: (01494) 890839. E-mail: blackmanbooks@yahoo.co.uk. Est: 1993. PR: £5–200. [Updated]

HIGH WYCOMBE

Rivendale Press, P O Box 85, High Wycombe, HP14 4WZ. Prop: Steven Halliwell. Tel: 01494 562266. Fax: 01494 565533. Web: www.rivendalepress.com. E-mail: sales@rivendalepress.com. Est: 1998. Mail Order Only. Internet and postal. Telephone first. Open: **M:** 09:00–17:30; **T:** 09:00–17:30; **W:** 09:00–17:30; **Th:** 09:00–17:30; **F:** 09:00–17:30; **S:** 09:00–17:30; **Su:** 09:00–17:30; Closed for lunch: 13:00–14:00. Spec: Academic/Scholarly; Bibliography; Biography; Books about Books; Poetry; Private Press. CC: MC; V. Mem: PBFA. [Updated]

BUCKINGHAMSHIRE

IVER

Pemberley Books, ■ 18 Bathurst Walk, Richings Park, Iver, SL0 9AZ. Prop: Ian A. Johnson. Tel: (01753) 631114. Fax: (01753) 631115. Web: www.pemberleybooks.com. E-mail: info@ pemberleybooks.com. Est: 1985. Internet and postal. Shop open: **M:** 10:00–17:00; **T:** 10:00–17:00; **W:** 10:00–17:00; **Th:** 10:00–17:00; **F:** 10:00–17:00; **S:** 10:00–16:00. Stock: medium. Spec: Antiquarian; Botany; Entomology; Herpetology; Lepidopterology; Natural History; New Naturalist; Ornithology. PR: £5–8,000. CC: AE; E; JCB; MC; V. Corresp: German. Mem: PBFA; BA. Notes: also, new books on specialities. VAT No: GB 646 2266 34. [Updated]

MILTON KEYNES

Andromeda Books, 4 Glovers Lane, Milton Keynes, MK13 8LW. Prop: Annie and Mike Eynon. Tel: 01908 312046. Fax: 01908 312046. Web: www.m31books.co.uk. E-mail: andromedabooks@btopenworld.com. Est: 1998. Private premises. Postal only. Appointment necessary. Open: **M:** 09:00–17:30; **T:** 09:00–17:30; **W:** 09:00–17:30; **Th:** 09:00–17:30; **F:** 09:00–17:30; **S:** 09:00–17:30; **Su:** 09:00–17:30; Closed for lunch: 13:00–14:00. Spec: Art; Astronomy; Decorative Art. CC: AE; JCB; MC; V; Switch. Cata: quarterly. Mem: FSB. [Updated]

Daeron's Books, ■ 3 Timor Court, Stony Stratford, Milton Keynes, MK11 1EJ. Prop: Angela Gardner. Tel: (01908) 568989. Fax: (01908) 266199. Web: www.daerons.co.uk. E-mail: books@daerons.co.uk. Est: 1992. Internet and postal. Shop open: **M:** 09:30–17:15; **T:** 09:30–17:15; **W:** 09:30–17:15; **F:** 09:30–17:15; **S:** 09:30–17:15. Stock: medium. Spec: Antiquarian; Arthurian; Authors: - Chesterton, G.K.; Inklings, The; Kipling, Rudyard; Lewis, C.S.; MacDonald, George; Pratchett, Terry. PR: £1–500. CC: AE; D; E; JCB; MC; V. Mem: FSB SSBA. VAT No: GB 776 7066 85. [Updated]

Janian Comics / Computer Manuals, Chelworth House, 14 Chillery Leys, Willen, Milton Keynes, MK15 9LZ. Prop: Ian Kiddley. Tel: (07974) 155379. Web: www.janiancomics.com & janian.co.uk. E-mail: ian@janian.plus.com. Est: 1994. Private premises. Internet and postal. Appointment necessary. Stock: very large. Spec: Comics; Computing. PR: £0–1,500. CC: AE; MC; V; SW. Notes: Organiser of Milton Keynes Book Festival. VAT No: GB 639 9941 73. [Updated]

Periplus Books, 160 Waterside, Peartree Bridge, Milton Keynes, MK6 3DQ. Prop: John Phillips. Tel: (01908) 663579. Web: www.periplusbooks.co.uk. E-mail: john@periplusbooks.co.uk. Est: 1997. Private premises. Postal only. Appointment necessary. Stock: small. Spec: Geology; Marine Sciences; Meteorology. PR: £5–200. [Updated]

NEWPORT PAGNELL

Ken's Paper Collectables, ■ 29 High Street, Newport Pagnell, MK16 8AR. Prop: Ken Graham. Tel: (01908) 610003. Fax: (01908) 610003. Web: www.kens.co.uk. E-mail: ken@kens.co.uk. Est: 1983. Shop open: **M:** 09:30–17:00; **T:** 09:30–17:00; **W:** 09:30–17:00; **F:** 09:30–17:00; **S:** 09:30–16:00. Stock: large. Spec: Autographs; Comics; Magazines & Periodicals - General; Manuscripts; Newspapers; Paper Collectables; Ephemera. PR: £1–400. CC: MC; V. Mem: Ephemera Society. [Updated]

PENN

The Cottage Bookshop, ■ Elm Road, Penn, HP10 8LB. Prop: Mrs E. S. Tebbutt. Tel: 01494 812632. Est: 1951. Shop open: **T:** 10:00–17:00; **W:** 10:00–17:00; **Th:** 10:00–17:00; **F:** 10:00–17:00; **S:** 10:00–17:00. Mem: BA. [Updated]

STOKE GOLDINGTON

Fireside Books, Harebell Cottage, 14 Mount Pleasant, Stoke Goldington, MK16 8LL. Prop: John Coppock. Tel: (01908) 551199. Fax: (0870) 1617621. Web: www.firesidebooks.demon.co.uk. E-mail: john@firesidebooks.demon.co.uk. Est: 1998. Private premises. Postal only. Stock: very small. Spec: Author - Morton, H.V.; History - General; Rural Life; Topography - General; Topography - Local; Travel - General; Booksearch. PR: £5–300. CC: MC; V. [Updated]

CAMBRIDGESHIRE

BLUNTISHAM

Bluntisham Books, 4 East Street, Bluntisham, Huntingdon, PE28 3LS. Prop: D.W.H. & S. Walton. Tel: 01487 840449. Fax: 01487 840894. Web: www.bluntishambooks.co.uk. E-mail: contact@bluntishambooks.co.uk. Est: 1976. Private premises. Internet and postal. Spec: Countries - Antarctic, The; Countries - Arctic, The; Countries - Greenland; Countries - Polar; Travel - Polar; Whaling. CC: MC; V. Cata: occasionally. Notes: also, publishers of Antarctic book, including reprints of classics. VAT No: GB 344 2959 39. [Updated]

CAMBRIDGE

Book Barrow, 93 Cam Causeway, Chesterton, Cambridge, CB4 1TL. Tel: (01223) 424 429. E-mail: bookbarrow@ntlworld.com. Market stand/stall. Internet and postal. Open: **Th:** 09:30–16:00. Spec: Academic/Scholarly; Africana; American Indians; Esoteric; First Editions; Modern First Editions; Signed Editions. Mem: PBFA. [Updated]

Books & Collectables Ltd., ■ Unit 7/8, Railway Arches, Coldhams Road, Cambridge, CB1 3EW. Prop: A. Doyle, J. Cross, D.B. & M. Doyle & P. Brown Tel: (01223) 412845. Web: www.booksandcollectables.com. E-mail: ask@booksandcollectables.com. Est: 1993. Internet and postal. Shop open: **M:** 10:00–17:00; **T:** 10:00–17:00; **W:** 10:00–17:00; **Th:** 10:00–17:00; **F:** 10:00–17:00; **S:** 10:00–17:00; **Su:** 10:00–16:00. Stock: very large. Spec: Antiques; Art; Children's; Cinema/Film; Comic Books & Annuals; Comics; Cookery/Gastronomy; Fiction - General. PR: £1–300. [18/02/2004]

Bracton Books, 25 Lode Road, Lode, Cambridge, CB5 9ER. Prop: Mrs S.J. Harrison. Tel: (01223) 811976. Web: www.bractonbooks.co.uk. E-mail: bractonbooks@uk2.net. Est: 1981. Private premises. Postal only. Appointment necessary. Stock: large. Spec: Academic/Scholarly; American Indians; Anthropology; Archaeology; Biology; Books about Books; Countries - Africa; Countries - Americas, The. PR: £2–100. [Updated]

G. David, ■ 16 St. Edward's Passage, Cambridge, CB2 3PJ. Prop: D.C. Asplin, N.T. Adams & B.L. Collings. Tel: (01223) 354619. Fax: (01223) 324663. E-mail: gdavid.books@btinternet.com. Est: 1896. Shop open: **M:** 09:00–17:00; **T:** 09:00–17:00; **W:** 09:00–17:00; **Th:** 09:00–17:00; **F:** 09:00–17:00; **S:** 09:00–17:00. Stock: medium. Spec: Academic/Scholarly; Antiquarian; Bindings; Children's; Early Imprints; Fine & Rare; Illustrated; Literature. PR: £1–1,000. CC: JCB; MC; V. Corresp: Japanese, Swedish. Mem: ABA; PBFA. Exhibits at PBFA fair (June), York (September), ABA Chelsea (November). VAT No: GB 599 5999 44. [Updated]

de Visser Books, 309 Milton Road, Cambridge, CB4 1XQ. Prop: Erik de Visser. Tel: (01223) 500909. Fax: (01223) 500909. E-mail: devisserbooks@hotmail.com. Est: 1988. Private premises. Internet and postal. Appointment necessary. Stock: small. Spec: Academic/Scholarly; Countries:- Albania; Austria; Balkans, The; Baltic States; East Europe; Germany; Hungary. PR: £10–750. CC: JCB; MC; V; Delta, Solo. Cata: bi-monthly on Central & East Europe only. Corresp: French, Dutch, German. VAT No: GB 493 3891 05. [Updated]

Galloway & Porter Limited, ■ 30 Sidney Street, Cambridge, CB2 3HS. Prop: Mr Porter. Tel: (01223) 367876. Fax: (01223) 360705. E-mail: galpor1@aol.com. Est: 1900. Shop open: **M:** 08:45–17:00; **T:** 08:45–17:00; **W:** 08:45–17:00; **Th:** 08:45–17:00; **F:** 08:45–17:00; **S:** 09:00–17:15. Stock: large. Spec: Academic/Scholarly; Mythology. PR: £1–2,000. Mem: ABA; PBFA; BA; BT. Notes: also, remainders and bargain books. VAT No: GB 213 4374 92. [Updated]

The Haunted Bookshop, (Please see entry under 'Sarah Key', Cambridge) E-mail: sarah.key1@ntlworld.com. [Updated]

Available from Richard Joseph Publishers Ltd
MINIATURE BOOKS
by Louis W. Bondy

(A5 H/b)   221pp £24.00

CAMBRIDGESHIRE

J & J Burgess Booksellers, 2 St Thomas's Road, Cambridge, CB1 3TF. Prop: John Burgess, Janet Burgess. Tel: 01223 249037. E-mail: jandjburgess2@ntlworld.com. Est: 1997. Private premises. Postal only. Appointment necessary. Open: **M:** 09:00–17:30; **T:** 09:00–17:30; **W:** 09:00–17:30; **Th:** 09:00–17:30; **F:** 09:00–17:30; **S:** 09:00–17:30; **Su:** 09:00–17:30; Closed for lunch: 13:00–14:00. Spec: Africana; Aircraft; Archaeology; Author - General; Automobilia/Automotive; Aviation; Flora & Fauna; Fossils. [Updated]

Sarah Key, ■ The Haunted Bookshop, 9 St. Edward's Passage, Cambridge, CB2 3PJ. Prop: Sarah Key & Phil Salin. Tel: (01223) 312913. Fax: 0870 056 9392. E-mail: sarahkeybooks@tiscali.co.uk. Est: 1985. Shop open: **M:** 10:00–17:00; **T:** 10:00–17:00; **W:** 10:00–17:00; **Th:** 10:00–17:00; **F:** 10:00–17:00; **S:** 10:00–17:00. Stock: medium. Spec: Academic/Scholarly; Aeronautics; Annuals; Authors: - Ardizzone, Edward; Barker, Cecily M.; Blyton, Enid; Brent-Dyer, Elinor M.; Buckeridge, A. PR: £1–2,000. CC: AE; JCB; MC. Corresp: French. Mem: PBFA. Notes: also, local interest items & a booksearch service. VAT No: GB 572 9680 04. [Updated]

Paul Kunkler Books, 6 Hardwick Street, Cambridge, CB3 9JA. Tel: (01223) 321419. Fax: (01223) 321419. Private premises. Appointment necessary. Stock: very small. Spec: Art History; Manuscripts. [Updated]

Adam Mills Rare Books, 328 High Street, Cottenham, Cambridge, CB4 8TX. Tel: (01954) 250106. Fax: (01954) 250106. Web: www.abebooks.com. E-mail: adam@millsrb.freeserve.co.uk. Est: 1981. Private premises. Internet and postal. Appointment necessary. Stock: small. Spec: Bibliography; Books about Books; Fine Printing; Illustrated; Limited Editions; Literature; Private Press; Typography. CC: MC; V. Corresp: French, Italian. Mem: PBFA. [02/08/2004]

Peter Moore Bookseller, P.O. Box 66, Cambridge, CB1 3PD. Prop: Peter Moore. Tel: (01223) 411177. Web: www.aus-pacbooks.co.uk. E-mail: aus-pacbooks@lineone.net. Est: 1970. Office and/or bookroom. Internet and postal. Appointment necessary. Trading from: Unit 12, The Old Maltings, 135 Ditton Walk, Cambridge. Stock: small. Spec: Countries - Australia; Pacific, The; Papua New Guinea; Travel - Australasia/Australia. PR: £1–500. CC: JCB; MC; V. Mem: PBFA; BCSA. VAT No: GB 215 3610 02. [Updated]

Paul Neeve, Cambridge, CB4 3AQ. Prop: Paul Neeve. Tel: (07967) 227882. E-mail: p.neeve@ntlworld.com. Est: 1980. Market stand/stall. Stock: medium. PR: £1–25. VAT No: GB 215 8289 51. [Updated]

Mike Parker Books, 2 Mill Lane, Duxford, Cambridge, CB2 4PT. (*). Tel: (01223) 835935. Fax: (01223) 839737. E-mail: mjp@lineone.net. Est: 1995. Private premises. Internet and postal. Appointment necessary. Stock: small. Spec: Academic/Scholarly; Advertising; Modern First Editions. PR: £5–500. [Updated]

Plurabelle Books, The Grey Barn (Bldg 3), The Michael Young Centre, Purbeck Road, Cambridge, CB2 2HN. Dr. Michael Cahn. Tel: (01223) 415671. Fax: (01223) 413241. Web: www.plurabelle.co.uk. E-mail: books@plurabelle.co.uk. Est: 1993. Warehouse. Postal only. Telephone first. Stock: very large. Spec: Academic/Scholarly; Computing; Humanities; Linguistics; Literature; Philosophy; Science - General; Science - History of. PR: £8–500. CC: E; MC; V. Corresp: French, German, Italian. Mem: Tom Folio, IBookNnet. VAT No: GB 636 8493 00. [Updated]

Quest Booksearch, 24 Hawthorne Road, Stapleford, Cambridge, CB2 5DU. Prop: Dr. Rosemary Scott. Tel: (01223) 844080. Fax: (01223) 844080. E-mail: qbs2@lineone.net. Est: 1997. Private premises. Postal only. Stock: very small. Spec: Literature; Poetry; Booksearch. PR: £1–2,000. [Updated]

Rupert Books, 58/59 Stonefield, Bar Hill, Cambridge, CB3 8TE. Prop: Paulina M. & R. Dixon Smith. Tel: (01954) 781861. Web: www.rupert-books.co.uk. E-mail: sales@rupert-books.co.uk. Est: 1984. Private premises. Internet Only. Appointment necessary. Spec: Author - Conan Doyle, Sir Arthur; Crime (True); Sherlockiana. PR: £3–1,000. CC: JCB; V. [Updated]

New dealers in the British Isles can register their business on
www.sheppardsworld.co.uk

Frances Wetherell, 8 Highworth Avenue, Cambridge, CB4 2BG. Tel: (01223) 363537. E-mail: frances.wetherell@talk21.com. Est: 1988. Private premises. Postal only. Stock: very small. Spec: Art; Economics; Literature; Social History; Booksearch. PR: £10–100. Notes: also, a booksearch service. [Updated]

David White, The Old Guildhall, 4 Church Lane, Linton, Cambridge, CB1 6JX. Prop: David White. Tel: (01223) 894447. Web: www.davidwhitebooks.co.uk. E-mail: david@davidwhitebooks.co.uk. Est: 1987. Private premises. Internet and postal. Appointment necessary. Stock: very small. Spec: Medicine; Medicine - History of; Pharmacy/Pharmacology. PR: £10–2,000. CC: MC; V. [Updated]

Peter Wood, 51 Telegraph Street, Cottenham, Cambridge, CB4 8QU. Tel: (01954) 251056. Web: www.booksatpbfa.com. E-mail: peterwoodbooks@waitrose.com. Est: 1973. Private premises. Appointment necessary. Stock: small. Spec: Art; Broadcasting; Cinema/Film; Entertainment - General; Music - General; Performing Arts; Theatre; Ephemera. PR: £20–500. CC: MC; V. Mem: PBFA. Notes: contactable Monday to Friday 08:30 – 18:00. Attends Perfoming Arts fairs at National Theatre Apr-Oct. VAT No: GB 214 4339 88. [Updated]

CASTLE CAMPS

Harry Brett, Pepperpot Cottage, Bartlow Road, Castle Camps, Cambridge, CB1 6SX. Tel: (01799) 584515. Est: 1968. Private premises. Postal only. Stock: small. PR: £2–500. [Updated]

CHATTERIS

Joan Stevens, Books, ■ 3 High Street, Chatteris, PE16 6BE. Prop: Joan Stevens. Tel: (01354) 696874. Fax: (01354) 696874. E-mail: joan@stevens1989.fsnet.co.uk. Est: 2000. Shop. Appointment necessary. M: 10:00–17:00; **T:** 10:00–17:00; **W:** 10:00–17:00; **Th:** 10:00–17:00; **F:** 10:00–17:00. Stock: small. Spec: Art Reference; Black Studies; Feminism; Fiction - Women; First Editions; Free Thought; Illustrated; Limited Editions. PR: £1–200. Corresp: French. Notes: ring the door bell between 10:00 and 17:00, other times by appointment. [Updated]

ELY

P.G. Bright, 11 Ravens Court, Ely, CB6 3ED. Tel: (01353) 661727. E-mail: peter.bright2@btinternet.com. Est: 1982. Private premises. Appointment necessary. Stock: medium. Spec: Children's; Illustrated; Literature; Sport - Cricket. PR: £1–500. Mem: PBFA. Also at: The Bookshop, 24 Magdalene Street, Cambridge. [Updated]

Ely Books, 24 Downham Road, Ely, CB6 1AF. Prop: Michael G. Kousah. Tel: (01353) 661824. Web: www.elybooks.com. E-mail: elybooks@ntlworld.com. Est: 1986. Private premises. Internet Only. Appointment necessary. Stock: very small. Spec: Americana; Antiquarian; Author - General; Bindings; Biography; Illustrated; Lace; Literature - Victorian. PR: £5–2,000. Mem: PBFA. VAT No: GB 572 9042 32. [Updated]

Hereward Books, ■ 17 High Street, Haddenham, Ely, CB6 3XA. Prop: Roger J. Pratt. Tel: (01353) 740821. Fax: (01353) 741721. Web: www.herewardbooks.co.uk. E-mail: sales@herewardbooks.co.uk. Est: 1985. Internet and postal. Telephone first. Shop open: **S:** 10:00–13:00. Stock: medium. Spec: Bindings; Illustrated; Natural History; Sport - Angling/Fishing; Sport - Falconry; Sport - Field Sports; Travel - General. PR: £15–1,000. CC: JCB; MC; V; Debit. Mem: PBFA. VAT No: GB 382 3886 03. [Updated]

GODMANCHESTER

Godmanchester Books, Staughton House, 11 Post Street, Godmanchester, PE29 2BA. Prop: Doreen Lewis. Tel: (01480) 455020. Est: 1974. Private premises. Appointment necessary. Stock: small. Spec: History - Local; Topography - Local; Booksearch. PR: £1–100. [Updated]

Dealers who need to update their entry should visit their page on
www.sheppardsworld.co.uk

CAMBRIDGESHIRE

HADDENHAM

John Lewcock, 6 Chewells Lane, Haddenham, Ely, CB6 3SS. Prop: John Lewcock. Tel: (01353) 741960. Fax: (01353) 741710. Web: www.abebooks.com/home/maritime. E-mail: lewcock@maritime-bookseller.com. Est: 1984. Office and/or bookroom. Internet and postal. Telephone first. Stock: medium. Spec: Academic/Scholarly; Deep Sea Diving; Manuals - Seamanship (see also under Seamanship); Maritime/Nautical; Naval; Navigation; Shipbuilding and Shipping; Sport - Yachting. PR: £5–1,500. CC: AE; E; JCB; MC; V; Switch. Mem: ABA; PBFA; BA; ILAB; CEng/IEE. Notes: also, insurance & probate valuations. VAT No: GB 410 5334 04. [Updated]

HUNTINGDON

Roger Gaskell Rare Books, 17 Ramsey Road, Warboys, Huntingdon, PE28 2RW. Tel: (01487) 823059. Fax: (01487) 823070. Web: www.rogergaskell.com. E-mail: roger@rogergaskell.com. Est: 1989. Private premises. Postal only. Appointment necessary. Stock: very small. Spec: Engineering; Medicine; Science - General; Technology. PR: £100–10,000. CC: AE; MC; V. Cata: occasionally. Mem: ABA; ILAB. VAT No: GB 550 6050 74. [Updated]

MK Book Services, 7 East Street, Huntingdon, PE29 1WZ. Prop: Melvyn R King. Tel: (01480) 353710. Fax: (01480) 431703. E-mail: mkbooks@tiscali.co.uk. Est: 1983. Private premises. Postal only. Appointment necessary. Stock: very small. Spec: Authors - Local; Countries - Baltic States; Countries - South Atlantic Islands; Religion - Methodism; Sport - Horse Racing (inc. Riding/Breeding/Equestrian); Booksearch. PR: £1–50. CC: E; MC; V; UKMaestro. Mem: BA. VAT No: GB 958 0474 91. [Updated]

John Robertshaw, 5 Fellowes Drive, Ramsey, Huntingdon, PE26 1BE. Tel: (01487) 813330. Fax: (01487) 711901. E-mail: robertshaw.books@virgin.net. Est: 1983. Office and/or bookroom. Appointment necessary. Stock: small. Spec: Antiquarian; Foreign Texts; Languages - Foreign. Corresp: French, German. Mem: PBFA. VAT No: GB 360 1311 09. [Updated]

Ken Trotman, P.O.Box 505, Huntingdon, PE29 2XW. Prop: Richard & Roz Brown. Tel: (01480) 454292. Fax: (01480) 384651. Web: www.kentrotman.com. E-mail: rlbtrotman@aol.com. Est: 1949. Storeroom. Postal only. Appointment necessary. Spec: Military. PR: £5–1,500. CC: MC; V. Corresp: French. Mem: PBFA. VAT No: GB 386 4614 23. [Updated]

PETERBOROUGH

Francis Bowers Chess Suppliers, 1 Marriott Road, Oxney Road, Peterborough, PE1 5NQ. Tel: (01733) 897119. E-mail: chessbower@aol.com. Est: 1991. Private premises. Spec: Chess. PR: £1–1,000. [Updated]

Broadway Books, 144 Broadway, Peterborough, PE1 4DG. Prop: Alan & Marion Peasgood. Tel: (01733) 565055. Est: 1997. Private premises. Postal only. Stock: small. Spec: Architecture; Art; History - General; Literature; Topography - General; Travel - General. PR: £1–25. Corresp: Spanish. Notes: attends Cambridge Book Fair 2nd Tuesday each month. [Updated]

Brian Cocks Books, 18 Woodgate, Helpston, Peterborough, PE6 7ED. Prop: Brian Cocks. Tel: (01733) 252791. Fax: (01733) 252791. Web: www.aviationbookhouse.co.uk. E-mail: brianc@uku.co.uk. Est: 1982. Private premises. Postal only. Appointment necessary. Stock: small. Spec: Aviation; Booksearch. PR: £3–800. Corresp: French, German, Spanish. Mem: PBFA. VAT No: GB 513 933 431. [21/10/2004]

T.V. Coles, ■ 981 Lincoln Road, Peterborough, PE4 6AH. Tel: (01733) 577268. Est: 1982. Shop open: **M:** 09:30–15:30; **T:** 09:30–15:30; **W:** 09:30–15:30; **Th:** 09:30–15:30; **F:** 09:30–15:30; **S:** 09:30–15:30. Stock: small. Spec: Aviation; Military; Military History; Naval; Topography - General; Collectables; Ephemera. PR: £1–200. [Updated]

Paul Green, 83b London Road, Peterborough, PE2 9BS. Tel: Withheld. Est: 1998. Private premises. Postal only. Stock: very small. Spec: Naturism; Poetry. PR: £2–50. [Updated]

Available from Richard Joseph Publishers Ltd
BOOKWORMS, THE INSECT PESTS
by N. Hickin

Revised Edition (A5 H/b) 184pp £24.00

Peakirk Books, ■ Peakirk Book Shop, 15 St Pegas Road, Peakirk, Peterborough, PE6 7NF. Prop: Heather & Jeff Lawrence. Tel: 01733 253182. Web: www.peakirkbooks.com. E-mail: peakirkbooks@btinternet.com. Est: 1997. Shop open: **W:** 1:00–17:00; **Th:** 09:30–17:00; **F:** 09:30–17:00; **S:** 09:30–17:00; **Su:** 12.00–16.00. Spec: Author - Clare, John; Children's; General Stock; Juvenile; Topography - Local. CC: AE; MC; V. Notes: The shop is open at other times by appointment, and internet/postal days we are available everyday except for Tuesdays. Local topography includes the Fen. VAT No: GB 694 8457 71. [Updated]

Frank T. Popeley, 27 Westbrook Park Road, Woodston, Peterborough, PE2 9JG. Tel: (01733) 562386. Private premises. Postal only. Stock: small. Spec: Animals and Birds; Countries - Africa; Countries - Kenya; Countries - Tanzania; Countries - Uganda; Sport - Big Game Hunting; Tribal. PR: £1–1,000. Mem: Books on early administration in East Africa. [Updated]

Wizard Books, 106 Church Street, Deeping St. James, Peterborough, PE6 8HB. Prop: Stephen Blessett. Tel: (01778) 343175. Fax: (01778) 380538. E-mail: wizardbooks@aol.com. Private premises. Internet and postal. Stock: small. Spec: Arms & Armour; Arthurian; Cryptozoology; Divining; Ghosts; Magic & Conjuring; Military; Military History. PR: £5–100. CC: JCB; MC; V. [Updated]

WISBECH

Oasis Booksearch, ■ 88 Norfolk Street, Wisbech, PE13 2LF. Prop: R.G.M. & M.E. Welford. Tel: (01945) 420438. Fax: (01945) 465187. Web: www.ukbookworld.com/members/welford. E-mail: rwelford@onetel.com. Est: 1998. Internet and postal. Shop open: **T:** 09:00–17:00; **W:** 09:00–17:00; **Th:** 09:00–17:00; **F:** 09:00–17:00; **S:** 09:00–17:00. Stock: small. Spec: Authors: - Ballantyne, Robert M.; Lewis, C.S.; Morton, H.V.; Bibles; Mind, Body & Spirit; Prayer Books; Religion - Catholic; Religion - Christian. PR: £1–25. CC: AE; JCB; MC; V; PayPal. Mem: PBFA. [Updated]

CHESHIRE

BIRCHWOOD
Sensawunda Books, 59, Dunnock Grove, Birchwood, Warrington, WA3 6NW. Prop: Grant Flexman-Smith. Tel: 01925 838501. E-mail: grant@sensawunda.freeserve.co.uk. Est: 1994. Private premises. Postal only. Contactable. Spec: Fiction - Fantasy, Horror; Fiction - Science Fiction; First Editions; Signed Editions. Cata: occasionally on Science Fiction, Fantasy, Horror. [Updated]

CASTLE
KSC Books, 48 Chapel Street, Castle, Northwhich, CW8 1HD. Prop: Stuart Crook. Tel: 01606 79975. Fax: On request. E-mail: kscbooks@btinternet.com. Est: 1995. Private premises. Internet and postal. Spec: Academic/Scholarly; Author - Laithwaite, Eric; Canals/Inland Waterways; Engineering; Geology; History - British; Music - Folk & Irish Folk; Musical Instruments. CC: MC; V; Delta Electron Maestro Maestro-UK PayPal Solo. VAT No: GB 798 2130 04. [Updated]

CHEADLE
Geoff Booth Booksearch, 2 Hastings Close, Cheadle Hulme, Cheadle, SK8 7BE. Prop: Geoff Booth. Tel: (0161) 485-4246. Web: www.boothbookmark.com. E-mail: geoff.booth131@btopenworld.com. Est: 1980. Private premises. Internet and postal. Appointment necessary. Open: **M:** 09:00–16:00; **T:** 09:00–16:00; **W:** 09:00–16:00; **Th:** 09:00–16:00; **F:** 09:00–16:00; **S:** 09:00–12:00. Stock: small. Spec: Autobiography; Biography; Crime (True); Magic & Conjuring; Modern First Editions; Booksearch. PR: £5–400. CC: PayPal. Corresp: French, Spanish. [14/08/2004]

Tennis Collectables, 31 Syddall Avenue, Cheadle, SK8 3AA. Prop: Fiona & John Partington. Tel: (0161) 718-5378. Fax: (0161) 718-5378. E-mail: john@partbook.demon.co.uk. Private premises. Postal only. Stock: very small. Spec: Magazines & Periodicals - General; Sport - Tennis. PR: £2–200. CC: AE; JCB; MC; V. Also, a booksearch service. VAT No: GB 748 5252 10. [Updated]

Clifford Elmer Books Ltd., 8, Balmoral Avenue, Cheadle Hulme, Cheadle, SK8 5EQ. Prop: Clifford & Marie Elmer. Tel: 0161 485 7064. Web: www.cliffordelmerbooks.com. E-mail: sales@cliffordelmerbooks.com. Est: 1978. Private premises. Internet and postal. Appointment necessary. Open: **M:** 09:00–17:30; **T:** 09:00–17:30; **W:** 09:00–17:30; **Th:** 09:00–17:30; **F:** 09:00–17:30; **S:** 09:00–17:30. Closed for lunch: 13:00–14:00. Spec: American Indians; Americana; Antiquarian; Assassinations; Biography; Crime (True); Criminology; Famous People - Kennedy, John F. CC: MC; V. Cata: quarterly on Non-fiction crime and criminology. Mem: PBFA. [Updated]

CHESTER
Gildas Books, ■ 2, City Walls, Chester, CH1 2JG. Prop: Scott Lloyd, Sue Evans. Tel: 01244 311910. E-mail: scott.lloyd@btinternet.com. Est: 2005. Shop open: **M:** 10:00–16:00; **T:** 10:00–16:00; **W:** 10:00–16:00; **Th:** 10:00–16:00; **F:** 10:00–16:00; **S:** 10:00–16:00; **Su:** 10:00–16:00. Spec: Academic/Scholarly; Alpinism/Mountaineering; Arthurian; Authors:- Dick, Philip K; Barker, Clive; Cornwell, Bernard; Crowley, Aleister; King, Stephen. CC: MC; V. Notes: Specialists in Arthurian Studies, Welsh History, Sci-Fi, Popular Science [Updated]

Richard Nicholson of Chester, Stoneydale, Pepper Street, Christleton, Chester, CH3 7AG. Tel: (01244) 336004. Fax: (01244) 336138. Web: www.antiquemaps.com. E-mail: richard@antiquemaps.com. Est: 1961. Private premises. Postal only. Stock: very small. Spec: Atlases; Prints and Maps. PR: £10–3,000. CC: MC; V. Notes: see web site for stocks. VAT No: GB 159 3368 36. [Updated]

Stothert Old Books, ■ 4 Nicholas Street, Chester, CH1 2NX. Prop: Alan Checkley. Tel: (01244) 340756. E-mail: stothertbooks@yahoo.com. Est: 1970. Shop open: **M:** 10:00–17:00; **T:** 10:00–17:00; **W:** 10:00–17:00; **Th:** 10:00–17:00; **F:** 10:00–17:00; **S:** 10:00–17:00. Stock: medium. Spec: Antiquarian; Antiques; Art; Children's; History - General; Illustrated; Sport - General; Topography - General. PR: £1–1,000. CC: E; MC; V. Corresp: French. Mem: PBFA. Notes: Attends York and Haydock Park and other local fairs. VAT No: GB 691 9276 88. [17/01/2005]

CREWE
Copnal Books, ■ 18 Meredith Street, Crewe, CW1 2PW. Prop: Ruth Ollerhead. Tel: (01270) 580470. E-mail: copnalbooks@yahoo.co.uk. Est: 1980. Shop open: **M:** 09:30–16:30; **T:** 09:30–16:30; **W:** 09:30–16:30; **Th:** 09:30–16:30; **F:** 09:30–16:30; **S:** 09:30–16:30. Stock: large. Spec: Bibles; Children's; Theology; Topography - Local. PR: £1–50. Corresp: French. Notes: Open other times by appointment [Updated]

FRODSHAM

Cheshire Book Centre, ■ Lady Hayes, Kingsley Road, Frodsham, WA6 6SU. J. R. S. Hall. Tel: 01928 788743. Fax: 01928 788743. Web: www.cheshirebookcentre.com. E-mail: enquiries@ cheshirebookcentre.com. Est: 1950. Shop open: **M:** 10:00–17:00; **T:** 10:00–17:00; **W:** 10:00–17:00; **Th:** 10:00–17:00; **F:** 10:00–17:00; **S:** 10:00–17:00; **Su:** 11:00–17:00. Spec: Aeronautics; Agriculture; Alpinism/Mountaineering; Animals and Birds; Annuals; Antiquarian; Antiques; Applied Art. CC: E; MC; V. Corresp: French and German. [Updated]

GREAT BARROW

Henry Wilson Books, Unit 7, Barrowmore Estate, Great Barrow, CH3 7JS. Prop: Henry Wilson. Tel: 01829 740693. Web: www.henrywilsonbooks.co.uk. E-mail: hwrailwaybooks@aol.com. Est: 1983. Office and/or bookroom. Internet and postal. Appointment necessary. Spec: Author - Rolt, L.T.C.; Canals/Inland Waterways; Railways; Steam Engines; Traction Engines; Transport; Vintage Cars. CC: MC; V; Maestro. Cata: occasionally on railways, canals, LTC Rolt. Corresp: French, German. Mem: PBFA; FSB. Notes: also at Dales and Lakes Book Centre, 72 Main Street, Sedbergh, Cumbria, LA10 5AD, open daily 1000-1700. Tel. 01539 620125 (q.v.).VAT No: GB 439 7672 03. [Updated]

HOYLAKE

Marine and Cannon Books, Naval & Maritime Dept., 'Nilcoptra', 3 Marine Road, Hoylake, Wirral, CH47 2AS. Prop: Michael & Vivienne Nash and Diane Churchill-Evans. Tel: (0151) 632-5365. Fax: (0151) 632-6472. E-mail: michael@marinecannon.com. Est: 1983. Private premises. Internet and postal. Appointment necessary. Open: **M:** 09:00–18:00; **T:** 09:00–18:00; **W:** 09:00–18:00; **Th:** 09:00–18:00; **F:** 09:00–18:00; **S:** 09:00–17:00; Closed for lunch: 13:00–13:30. Stock: medium. Spec: Antiquarian; Aviation; History - General; Manuscripts; Maritime/Nautical; Military; Military History; Naval. PR: £10–20,000. CC: JCB; MC; V; Maestro. Mem: ABA; PBFA; ILAB. Notes: Outlets - RN Museum Portsmouth and Albert Dock Liverpool. VAT No: GB 539 4137 32. [Updated]

HYDE

J.A. Heacock, ■ 155, Market Street, Hyde, SK14 1HG. Prop: Joseph A. Heacock. Tel: 0161 3665098. E-mail: joseph@heacock.freeserve.co.uk. Est: 2000. Shop. Telephone first. Notes: Traditional secondhand and antiquarian bookshop, interesting and better than average stock, reasonable prices, trade and public welcome, usually open but prior phone call or e-mail is very strongly advised. [Updated]

KNUTSFORD

The Arts & Antiques Centre, ■ 113 King Street, Knutsford. Shop open: **T:** 10:00–17:00; **W:** 10:00–17:00; **Th:** 10:00–17:00; **F:** 10:00–17:00; **S:** 10:00–17:00. Spec: Topography - General. Notes: Cavern Books stock: general stock and topography. See also Cavern Books, Nantwich, Cheshire (q.v.). [Updated]

BC Books, 12 Mallard Close, Knutsford, WA16 8ES. Prop: Brian Corrigan. Tel: (01565) 654014. E-mail: brian@corrigan.demon.co.uk. Est: 1993. Private premises. Postal only. Stock: small. Spec: First Editions; History - Ancient; History - British; Humour; Literature. PR: £1–250. Corresp: French. [Updated]

Fiction First, The Old Chapel, Knolls Green Village, Knutsford, WA16 7BW. Tel: (01565) 872634. Web: www.abebooks.com. E-mail: richard.offer@virgin.net. Est: 1992. Private premises. Internet and postal. Appointment necessary. Stock: medium. Spec: Fiction - General; Fiction - Crime, Detective, Spy, Thrillers; Fiction - Fantasy, Horror; Fiction - Science Fiction; First Editions. PR: £10–2,000. CC: AE; MC; V. [Updated]

LYMM

K Books, 60 Mardale Crescent, Lymm, WA13 9PJ. Prop: Jef & Janet Kay. Tel: (01925) 755736. E-mail: jefkay@supanet.com. Est: 1994. Private premises. Appointment necessary. Stock: small. Spec: Astronautics; Authors:- Blyton, Enid; Charteris, Leslie; Children's; Comic Books & Annuals; Fiction - General; Fiction - Science Fiction; First Editions. PR: £1–100. Corresp: German. Mem: Followers of Rupert. [Updated]

MACCLESFIELD

George Longden, 71 Grimshaw Lane, Bollington, Macclesfield, SK10 5LY. Prop: George Longden. Tel: (01625) 572584. E-mail: longdengeorge@hotmail.com. Est: 1998. Private premises. Postal only. Stock: small. Spec: Cartoons; Comic Books & Annuals; Comics. PR: £2–200. Mem: PBFA. Notes: Exhibits at book fairs in the North and Midlands. [Updated]

CHESHIRE

Mereside Books, ■ 75 Chestergate, Macclesfield, SK11 6DG. Prop: Sally Laithwaite & Steve Kowalski. Tel: Shop (01625) 425352. Est: 1996. Shop open: **W:** 10:00–17:00; **Th:** 10:00–17:00; **F:** 10:00–17:00; **S:** 10:00–17:00. Stock: small. Spec: Illustrated. PR: £3–500. CC: E; JCB; MC; V. Mem: PBFA. Notes: Organisers of Buxton Book Fairs. [Updated]

Roger J. Treglown, Sunderland House, Sunderland Street, Macclesfield, SK11 6JF. Tel: (01625) 618978. Fax: (01625) 618978. E-mail: roger@rogerjtreglown.com. Est: 1980. Office and/or bookroom. Appointment necessary. Open: **M:** 09:00–17:30; **T:** 09:00–17:30; **W:** 09:00–17:30; **Th:** 09:00–17:30; **F:** 09:00–17:30. Spec: Antiquarian; Chess; Early Imprints; Esoteric; Odd & Unusual. PR: £2–2,000. CC: MC; V; Switch. Cata: bi-annually on chess and occasionally on antiquarian. Mem: ABA; PBFA. Notes: also valuations for probate etc. [Updated]

MARPLE BRIDGE

Talisman Books, ■ 42, Town Street, Marple Bridge, Stockport, SK65AA. Prop: Frank Leonard and Jean Cessford. Tel: 01614499271. E-mail: frank.talismanbooks@virgin.net. Est: 1989. Shop open: **M:** 12:00–17:00; **T:** 12:00–17:00; **Th:** 09:00–17:00; **F:** 09:00–17:00; **S:** 09:00–17:30. Spec: Authors:- Blyton, Enid; David, Elizabeth; King, Stephen; Pratchett, Terry; Children's - Early Titles; Cookery/Gastronomy; General Stock; Literature. CC: AE; MC; V. [Updated]

NANTWICH

Cavern Books, ■ Units 2-4 & 16, Dagfields Antique Centre, Audlem Rd, Walgherton, Nantwich, CW5 7LG. Prop: Harry Madden. Tel: (01270) 841594. Web: www.cavernbooks.co.uk. E-mail: cavernbks@aol.com. Est: 1997. Shop open: **M:** 10:00–17:00; **T:** 10:00–17:00; **W:** 10:00–17:00; **Th:** 10:00–17:00; **F:** 10:00–17:00; **S:** 10:00–17:00; **Su:** 10:00–17:00. Stock: very large. Spec: Americana; Annuals; Art; Buses/Trams; Canals/Inland Waterways; Crafts; Crime (True); Egyptology. PR: £1–1,500. CC: MC; V; SO, Maestro. Mem: Internet Bookshop, Gloucestershire (q.v.), Biblion, London W. (q.v.) & The Arts & Antiques Centre, Knutsford (qv). Also, CDs, Records (50s & 60s). VAT No: GB 823 5392 30. [Updated]

Guildmaster Books, 81 Welsh Row, Nantwich, CW5 5ET. Guildmaster. Tel: (01270) 629982. Fax: (01270) 629108. E-mail: guild.house@virgin.net. Est: 1986. Office and/or bookroom. Internet and postal. Appointment necessary. Open: Stock: very small. Spec: Agriculture; Antiquarian; Churchilliana; Culture - National; Firearms/Guns; Herbalism; History - British; Maritime/Nautical. PR: £10–500. Corresp: Most major cards. Mem: On request, US verified. [Updated]

J & D Jones, 2 Butler Way, Nantwich, CW5 7AS. Prop: J & D Jones. Tel: (01270) 583431. Fax: (01270) 623644. Web: www.jonesthebook.com. E-mail: jdjones@rmplc.co.uk. Est: 1990. Private premises. Internet and postal. Telephone first. Stock: small. Spec: Author - Brent-Dyer, Elinor M.; Children's; Children's - Illustrated; Illustrated. PR: £5–800. CC: PayPal. Corresp: French, German. [Updated]

Leona Thomas (Books), 84, London Road, Nantwich, CW5 6LT. Prop: Leona Thomas. Tel: (01270) 627779. Web: www.leonathomas.co.uk. E-mail: books@leonathomas.co.uk. Est: 1990. Private premises. Telephone first. Stock: small. Spec: Antiquarian; Antiques; Bindings; Books about Books; Folio Society, The; History - General; Poetry; Topography - Local. PR: £1–500. Corresp: French. Notes: Brewing books at Barleycorns, Welsh Row, Nantwich. [Updated]

NORTHWICH

Forest Books of Cheshire, Northwich, CW8 2AT. Prop: E.M. Mann. Tel: 01606 882388. E-mail: info@forest-books.co.uk. Est: 1988. Private premises. Appointment necessary. Spec: Architecture; Art History; Collecting; Drama; Fashion & Costume; History - Local; Humanities; Music - General. PR: £1–600. [Updated]

RUNCORN

Kirk Ruebotham, 16 Beaconsfield Road, Runcorn, WA7 4BX. Tel: (01928) 560540. Web: www.abebooks.com/home/kirk61. E-mail: kirk.ruebotham@ntlworld.com. Est: 1993. Private premises. Postal only. Stock: small. Spec: Crime (True); Fiction - Crime, Detective, Spy, Thrillers; Fiction - Fantasy, Horror; Fiction - Science Fiction; First Editions; Vintage Paperbacks. PR: £2–150. CC: PayPal. [Updated]

CHESHIRE

TARPORLEY

Marine & Cannon Books, Sandowne, Four Lanes End, Tiverton Heath, Tarporley, CW6 9HN. Prop: Mrs Diane Churchill-Evans (Military & Aviation Dept). Tel: (01829) 732524. Fax: (01829) 730710. E-mail: diane@marinecannon.com. Est: 1983. Private premises. Open: **M:** 09:00–18:00; **T:** 09:00–18:00; **W:** 09:00–18:00; **Th:** 09:00–18:00; **F:** 09:00–18:00; **S:** 09:00–17:00. Stock: medium. Spec: Academic/Scholarly; Antiquarian; Aviation; Military; Military History; Transport; War - General; Booksearch. PR: £10–20,000. CC: JCB; MC; V; Maestro. Mem: ABA; PBFA; ILAB. Notes: Occasional fairs and booksearch. VAT No: GB 539 4137 32. [Updated]

TIMPERLEY

Oopalba Books, 136 Moss Lane, Timperley, Altrincham, WA15 6JQ. Prop: Ann J. Ferguson. Tel: 0161 973 2065. E-mail: ann@oopalbalbooks.co.uk. Est: 1999. Mail order and Internet only. Appointment necessary. Stock size: Medium. Spec: Academic/Scholarly; Applied Art; Architecture; Art; Art Technique; Autobiography; Biography; Children's General, Early Titles, Illustrated; Cities - City of London; Cookery - Professional. PR: £1–100. CC: PayPal.Cheque/Postal order. Cata: online/internet. Notes: books listed on abebooks.com. [Updated]

WARRINGTON

Halson Books, The Oaks, Farnworth Road, Penketh, Warrington, WA5 2TT. Prop: Les Wilson. Tel: (01925) 726699. Web: www.users.zetnet.co.uk/halsongallery. E-mail: halson.gallery@zetnet.co.uk. Private premises. Internet and postal. Appointment necessary. Stock: large. Spec: Colour-Plate; Dogs; Natural History; Ephemera. CC: PayPal. Corresp: via Google language. [Updated]

Dr. B.L. Shakeshaft, Springfield, 15 Marlborough Crescent, Grappenhall, Warrington, WA4 2EE. Prop: Dr. B.L. Shakeshaft. Tel: (01925) 264790. E-mail: blsbooks@shakeshaft.wanadoo.co.uk. Est: 1999. Private premises. Postal only. Stock: very small. Spec: Americana; Animals and Birds; Annuals; Author - Watkins-Pitchford, Denys ('B.B.'); Authors - British; Biography; Children's; Children's - Illustrated. PR: £1–500. Cata: often on Ladybird books,Rupert annuals,New Naturalists. [Updated]

Naomi Symes Books, 2 Pineways, Appleton Park, Warrington, WA4 5EJ. Prop: Naomi Symes. Tel: 44 (0)1925 602898. Fax: 44 (0)1925 602898. Web: www.naomisymes.com. E-mail: books@naomisymes.com. Est: 1994. Private premises. Postal only. Contactable. **M:** 10:00–18:00; **T:** 10:00–18:00; **W:** 10:00–18:00; **Th:** 10:00–18:00; **F:** 10:00–18:00; **S:** 10:00–18:00; **Su:** 10:00–18:00. Stock: medium. Spec: Academic/Scholarly; Authors - Women; Feminism; Fiction - Women; History - General; History - 19th Century; History - British; History - European. PR: £5–1,000. CC: AE; D; E; JCB; MC; V; Maestro, Solo. Corresp: French. Mem: PBFA. Also: History A Level tuition; booksearch service; proof reading; copy editing and history resource centre on-line [Updated]

The Warrington Book Loft, ■ Osnath Works, Lythgoes Lane, Warrington, WA2 7XE. Prop: Mrs Pat Devlin. Tel: (01925) 633907. E-mail: WarringtonBkLoft@aol.com. Est: 1994. Shop. Open: **M:** 10:30–18:00; **T:** 10:30–18:00; **W:** 10:30–18:00; **Th:** 10:30–18:00; **F:** 10:30–18:00; **S:** 10:00–17:00. Stock: very large. Spec: Academic/Scholarly; Fiction - General; University Texts. PR: £1–50. CC: JCB; MC; V; Maestro, Solo. Notes: Over 40,000 books in stock. VAT No: GB 811 6681 37. [Updated]

WINSFORD

Blackman Books, 46 The Loont, Winsford, CW7 1EU. Prop: Margaret & Roger Blackman. Tel: (01606) 558527. Web: www.abebooks.com/home/rtmb. E-mail: books@blackmanbooks.freeserve.co.uk. Est: 1997. Private premises. Internet and postal. Appointment necessary. Stock: very small. PR: £10–1,000. CC: JCB; MC; V; Da, S. Corresp: French. [Updated]

CORNWALL

BUDE

David Eastwood Books, Ardoch Poundstock, Bude, EX23 0DF. Tel: (01288) 361847. E-mail: d_eastwood37@hotmail.com. Est: 1970. Private premises. Internet and postal. Appointment necessary. Stock: very small. Spec: Antiquarian; Children's - Illustrated; Fine & Rare; Illustrated; Limited Editions; Literature; Signed Editions. PR: £10–1,000. Also at: PBFA bookfairs. Mem: PBFA. Notes: Always interested in buying in any amount of books. [Updated]

CALLINGTON

Music By The Score, South Coombe, Downgate, Callington, PL17 8JZ. Prop: Eileen Hooper–Bargery. Tel: (01579) 370053. Fax: (01579) 370053. Web: www.musicbythescore.com. E-mail: musicbythescore@kernowserve.co.uk. Est: 1993. Private premises. Internet and postal. Appointment necessary. M: 10:00–20:00; **T:** 10:00–20:00; **W:** 10:00–20:00; **Th:** 10:00–20:00; **F:** 10:00–20:00; **S:** 10:00–20:00; Closed for lunch: 13:00–14:00. Stock: large. Spec: Music - General; Music - Composers; Music - Music Hall; Music - Musicians; Music - Opera; Music - Political Songs & Ballads; Music - Popular; Music - Printed, Sheet Music & Scores. PR: £4–40. CC: AE; MC; V; Switch. Notes: Stock also available through Biblio.com. All credit cards accepted. [Updated]

CAMBORNE

Humanist Book Services, 15 Basset Street, Camborne, TR14 8SW. Prop: Linnea Timson. Tel: (01209) 716470. Fax: (0870) 125 8049. Web: www.cornwallhumanists.org.uk. E-mail: humbooks@ukgateway.net. Est: 1964. Spec: Evolution; Free Thought; Humanism; Philosophy. PR: £1–15. [Updated]

EAST LOOE

Bosco Books, ■ The Old Hall Bookshop, Chapel Court, Shutta Road, East Looe, PL13 1BJ. Prop: Mr. & Mrs. S. Hawes. Tel: (01503) 263700. Fax: (01503) 263700. E-mail: boscobooks@aol.com. Est: 1971. Shop. Internet and postal. Open. Open: **T:** 10:30–17:00; **W:** 10:30–17:00; **Th:** 10:30–17:00; **F:** 10:30–17:00; **S:** 10:30–17:00. Stock: very large. Spec: Alpinism/Mountaineering; Archaeology; Architecture; Art; Art History; Art Reference; Biography; Crafts. PR: £1–750. CC: MC; V; SW. Corresp: French, Italian. [Updated]

FALMOUTH

Browsers Bookshop, ■13/15 St George's Arcade, Church Street, Falmouth, TR11 3DH. Prop: Crispin Crofts. Tel: 01326 313464. E-mail: cemeraldisle@aol.com. Est: 1980. Shop open: **M:** 09:00–17:30; **T:** 09:00–17:30; **W:** 09:00–17:30; **Th:** 09:00–17:30; **F:** 09:00–17:30; **S:** 09:00–17:30; **Su:** 09:00–17:30. CC: MC; V; Maestro. [Updated]

Isabelline Books, 2 Highbury House, 8 Woodlane Crescent, Falmouth, TR11 4QS. Prop: Michael Whetman. Tel: (01326) 210412. Fax: 0870 051 6387. Web: www.beakbook.demon.co.uk. E-mail: mikann@beakbook.demon.co.uk. Est: 1997. Private premises. Internet and postal. Appointment necessary. Stock: very small. Spec: Ornithology. PR: £10–2,000. CC: JCB; V. [Updated]

Dealers need to update their entry at least once a year. Visit your page on *www.sheppardsworld.co.uk*

FOWEY

Bookends of Fowey, ■4 South Street, Fowey, PL23 1AR. Tel: (01726) 833361. Web: www.bookendsoffowey.com. E-mail: info@bookendsoffowey.com. Est: 1985. Shop. Internet and postal. Open: **M:** 10:00–17:30; **T:** 10:00–17:30; **W:** 10:00–17:30; **Th:** 10:00–17:30; **F:** 10:00–17:30; **S:** 10:00–17:30; **Su:** 11:00–17:00. Stock: large. Spec: Authors:- du Maurier, Daphne; Quiller-Couch, Sir A.T.; Naval; Sport - Yachting; Topography - Local; Woodwork. CC: MC; V. VAT No: GB 813 0114 90. [Updated]

Ronald C. Hicks, Ardwyn, 22 Park Road, Fowey, PL23 1ED. Tel: (01726) 832739. Est: 1964. Private premises. Postal only. Stock: very small. Spec: Architecture; Art; History - Local; Maritime/Natical - Log Books; Booksearch. PR: £1–500. Notes: Books on Cornish history [Upadted]

Sue Moore, 37 Passage Street, Fowey, PL23 1DE. Prop: Susan M. Moore. Tel: (01726) 832397. Est: 1986. Private premises. Appointment necessary. Stock: small. Spec: Modern First Editions; Booksearch. PR: £2–50. [Updated]

HELSTON

The Helston Bookworm, ■ 9 Church Street, Helston, TR13 8TA. Prop: Ann & Malcolm Summers. Tel: (01326) 565079. Web: www.users.dialstart.net/~helstonb. E-mail: helstonb@btopenworld.com. Est: 1994. Internet and postal. Shop open: **M:** 10:00–17:30; **T:** 10:10–17:30; **W:** 10:00–17:30; **Th:** 10:00–17:30; **F:** 10:00–17:30; **S:** 10:00–14:00. Stock: large. Spec: Antiquarian; Topography - Local. PR: £1–300. CC: AE; MC; V. Mem: PBFA. [Updated]

J.T. & P. Lewis, 'Leaway', Tresowes Green, Ashton, Helston, TR13 9SY. Prop: John T. & Pearl Lewis. Tel: (01736) 762406. Web: www.http://ukbookworld.com/members/JTLANDPL. E-mail: JohnandPearl@aol.com. Est: 1990. Private premises. Internet and postal. Stock: small. Spec: Academic/Scholarly; Fiction - General; History - General; Modern First Editions; Odd & Unusual; Religion - General; Science - General; Theology. PR: £5–1,000. CC: PayPal. Notes: Payment via PayPal using JohnandPearl@aol.com. VAT No: GB 803 4711 59. [Updated]

Peter Clay, Heatherbank, North Corner, Coverack, Helston, TR12 6TH. Prop: Peter Clay. Tel: 01326280475. E-mail: pete.clay@virgin.net. Est: 1984. Private premises. Internet and postal. Appointment necessary. Spec: [Updated]

LAUNCESTON

Abbey Books, ■ White Hart Arcade, Launceston, PL15 8AA. Prop: Spencer Magill. Tel: 01566 779113. E-mail: SpencerMagill@aol.com. Est: 2003. Shop open: **M:** 09:00–17:00; **T:** 09:00–17:00; **W:** 09:00–17:00; **Th:** 09:00–17:00; **F:** 09:00–17:00; **S:** 09:00–16:00. Spec: Art Reference; Cinema/Film; Countries - Ireland; Fiction - General; Fiction - Crime, Detective, Spy, Thrillers; Fiction - Science Fiction; History - General; History - Irish. [Updated]

Charles Cox Rare Books, River House, Treglasta, Launceston, PL15 8PY. Tel: (01840) 261085. Fax: (01840) 261464. Web: www.abebooks.com. E-mail: charlescox@verso.fsnet.co.uk. Est: 1974. Private premises. Internet and postal. Appointment necessary. Stock: small. Spec: Antiquarian; Authors:- Browning, Robert; Byron, Lord; Hardy, Thomas; Housman, A.E.; Newman, Cardinal; Rossetti, C.; Ruskin, John. PR: £10–2,500. CC: JCB; MC; V; PayPal. Mem: ABA; ILAB. VAT No: GB 797 4887 40. [Updated]

R & B Graham Trading, The Bookshop, Church Street, Launceston, PL15 8AP. Prop: Richard & Beryl Graham. Tel: 01566 774107. Fax: 01566 777299. Web: www.cookery-books-online.com. E-mail: thebookshop@eclipse.co.uk. Est: 1999. Shop and/or gallery. Open: **M:** 09:00–17:30; **T:** 09:00–17:30; **W:** 09:00–17:30; **Th:** 09:00–17:30; **F:** 09:00–17:30; **S:** 09:00–17:30. Spec: Author - Quiller-Couch, Sir A.T.; Cookery - Professional; Cookery/Gastronomy. CC: E; JCB; MC; V. VAT No: GB 750 5071 55. [Updated]

LOOE

A. & R. Booksearch, High Close, Lanreath, Looe, PL13 2PF. Prop: Avis & Robert Ronald. Tel: (01503) 220246. Fax: (01503) 220965. Web: www.musicbooksrus.com. E-mail: robert.ronald@btopenworld.com. Est: 1984. Private premises. Postal only. Appointment necessary. Stock: medium. Spec: Music - Country & Western; Music - Jazz & Blues; Music - Popular; Music - Rock & Roll. PR: £1–500. Notes: also sell new books. [Updated]

CORNWALL

MARAZION

Andrew Stewart, Castledene, Turnpike Hill, Marazion, TR17 0BZ. Prop: Andrew Stewart. Tel: 01736 719333. E-mail: espaceblue@btopenworld.com. Est: 1978. Private premises. Appointment necessary. Spec: Classical Studies; Medieval; Printing; Theology. Corresp: French, German. VAT No: GB 328 0066 78. [Updated]

NEWQUAY

recollectionsbookshop.co.uk, Old Kiddlywink Cottage, Tresean, Newquay, TR8 5HN. Prop: Valerie Frith & Ray Frith. Tel: (01637) 830539. Web: www.recollectionsbookshop.co.uk. E-mail: railtonfrith@tiscali.co.uk. Est: 1996. Private premises. Internet and postal. Contactable. Stock: large. Spec: Railways; Topography - Local. PR: £4–100. CC: D; E; MC; V; PayPal. VAT No: GB 760 4240 56. [Updated]

PENZANCE

Green Meadow Books, 2 Bellair House, Bellair Road, Madron, Penzance, TR20 8SP. Prop: Sue Bell. Tel: (01736) 351708. Web: www.greenmeadowbooks.co.uk. E-mail: sue@bell83.fsnet.co.uk. Est: 1982. Private premises. Internet and postal. Appointment necessary. Stock: medium. Spec: Authors:- Blyton, Enid; Saville, M.; Children's; Children's - Illustrated; Illustrated; Ephemera. PR: £2–2,500. CC: MC; V; Switch. Notes: also, toys, games, ephemera & booksearch service. [Updated]

Mount's Bay Books, Sea Glimpses, 12 Garth Road, Newlyn, Penzance, TR18 5QJ. Prop: Tim Scott. Tel: (01736) 351335. Web: www.mountsbaybooks.co.uk. E-mail: sales@mountsbaybooks.co.uk. Est: 1994. Private premises. Internet and postal. Appointment necessary. Open: **M:** 10:00–17:00; **T:** 10:00–17:00; **W:** 10:00–17:00; **Th:** 10:00–17:00; **F:** 10:00–17:00; **S:** 10:00–16:00. Stock: very small. Spec: Authors:- Seymour, John; Tangye, D.; Natural History; Rural Life; Self-Sufficiency; Topography - Local. PR: £2–150. [Updated]

Newlyn & New Street Books, ■ New Street Bookshop, 4 New Street, Penzance, TR18 2LZ. Prop: Kelvin Hearn Tel: (1736) 362758. E-mail: eankelvin@yahoo.com. Est: 1992. Internet and postal. Shop open: **M:** 10:00–17:00; **T:** 10:00–17:00; **W:** 10:00–17:00; **Th:** 10:00–17:00; **F:** 10:00–17:00; **S:** 10:00–17:00. Stock: medium. Spec: Art; Topography - General; Topography - Local. PR: £1–350. CC: MC; V. [Updated]

ROCHE

Roger Collicott Books, Beacon Cottage, Belowda, Roche, St. Austell, PL26 8NQ. Prop: Roger Collicott. Tel: 01726 891885. Fax: 01726 891885. Web: www.www.rogercollicottbooks.com. E-mail: info@rogercollicottbooks.com. Est: 1978. Private premises. Appointment necessary. **M:** 10:00–17:30; **T:** 10:00–17:30; **W:** 10:00–17:30; **Th:** 10:00–17:30; **F:** 10:00–17:30; **S:** 10:00–17:30; **Su:** 10:00–17:30. Spec: Antiquarian; Bindings; County - Local; Directories - General; Dogs; Earth Sciences; Flora & Fauna; Fossils. CC: MC; V. Cata: quarterley on Antiquarian, Topography. History of Sciences. Mem: PBFA. [Updated]

ST. AGNES

Paul Hoare, Trevaunance Point House, Trevaunance Cove, St. Agnes, TR5 0RZ. Prop: Paul Hoare. Tel: 01872 553235. E-mail: paul.hoare@ntlworld.com. Est: 1990. Private premises. Internet and postal. Appointment necessary. Open: **M:** 09:00–17:30; **T:** 09:00–17:30; **W:** 09:00–17:30; **Th:** 09:00–17:30; **F:** 09:00–17:30; **S:** 09:00–17:30; **Su:** 09:00–17:30. Closed for lunch: 13:00–14:00. Spec: Publishers - Black, A. & C. Cata: occasionally on A&C Black, Illustrated & Topographic. Notes: specialist in A&C Black publications General Illustrated items. [Updated]

ST. JUST

Bosorne Books, ■ 4 Cape Cornwall Street, St. Just, TR19 7JZ. Prop: David James. Tel: 01736 787266. Est: 2003. Shop open: **T:** 10:00–17:00; **W:** 10:00–17:00; **Th:** 10:00–17:00; **F:** 10:00–17:00; **S:** 10:00–17:00; **Su:** 10:00–17:00. Notes: Café and bookshop. [Updated]

ST. AUSTELL

Neville Chapman, 24 Caudledown Lane, Stenalees, St. Austell, PL26 8TG. Tel: (01726) 850067. Web: www.abebooks.com/home/chapbooks. E-mail: chapbooks@aol.com. Est: 1992. Private premises. Internet and postal. Appointment necessary. Stock: small. Spec: Academic/Scholarly; Advertising; Author - Bellaires, George; Topography - Local. PR: £1–100. [21/12/2004]

ST. IVES

The Book Gallery, The Old Post Office Garage, Chapel Street, St. Ives, TR26 2LR. Prop: David Wilkinson. Tel: (01736) 793545. Web: www.abebooks.com/home/tinyworld. E-mail: books@bookgallery.co.uk. Est: 1991. Private premises. Internet and postal. Telephone first. Stock: small. Spec: Art; Art History; Art Reference; First Editions; Topography - Local; Ephemera. PR: £5–2,500. [Updated]

Tregenna Place Second Hand Books, ■ Tregenna Place, St. Ives, TR26 1AA. Prop: Linda Donaldson and Steven Macleod. Tel: 01736 799933. Est: 2004. Shop open: **M:** 10:00–17:00; **T:** 10:00–17:00; **W:** 10:00–17:00; **Th:** 10:00–17:00; **F:** 10:00–17:00; **S:** 10:00–17:00. CC: MC; V. Notes: General stock. [Updated]

ST. TEATH

Christopher Holtom, Aaron's, Treburgett, St. Teath, PL30 3LJ. Tel: (01208) 851062. Fax: (01208) 851062. Est: 1972. Private premises. Appointment necessary. Stock: medium. Spec: Antiquarian; Children's; Education & School; Fables; Folklore; Juvenile; Mathematics. PR: £3–150. Corresp: French. [Updated]

TRURO

Bonython Bookshop, ■16 Kenwyn Street, Truro, TR1 3BU. Prop: R.D. Carpenter. Tel: (01872) 262886. E-mail: bonythonbooks@btconnect.com. Est: 1996. Shop open: **M:** 10:30–16:30; **T:** 10:30–16:30; **W:** 10:30–16:30; **Th:** 10:30–16:30; **F:** 10:30–16:30; **S:** 10:30–16:30. Stock: medium. Spec: Archaeology; Authors:- du Maurier, Daphne; Tangye, D.; History - Local; Topography - Local; Booksearch; Ephemera. PR: £1–1,000. CC: D; E; JCB; MC; V. Corresp: French. Notes: also, booksearch and books on Cornwall. [Updated]

Just Books, ■ 9 Pydar Mews, Truro, TR1 2UX. Prop: Jennifer Wicks. Tel: (01872) 242532. E-mail: bookshopwren@yahoo.co.uk. Est: 1987. Shop open: **M:** 09:30–17:00; **T:** 09:30–17:00; **W:** 09:30–17:00; **Th:** 09:30–17:00; **F:** 09:30–17:00; **S:** 09:30–17:00. Stock: medium. Spec: Art; History - Local; Natural History; Topography - Local; Ephemera. PR: £1–1,000. CC: AE; E; JCB; MC; V. Notes: books on Cornwall and art books from America. VAT No: GB 789 3503 84. [Updated]

Westcountry Old Books, ■ 8 St.Mary's Street, Truro, TR12AF. Prop: David Neil. Tel: (01803) 322712. Web: www.abebooks.com. E-mail: westcountryoldbooks@btopenworld.com. Est: 1988. Shop open: **M:** 09:30–17:30; **T:** 09:30–17:30; **W:** 09:30–17:30; **Th:** 09:30–17:30; **F:** 09:30–17:30; **S:** 09:30–17:30. Stock: very small. Spec: Antiquarian; History - General; Literature. CC: E; JCB; MC; V. Mem: PBFA. Notes: also at Top Floor, S.P.C.K. Bookshop,1-2 Catherine Street, Exeter, Devon. [Updated]

WADEBRIDGE

Polmorla Books, Hostyn Mill, Burlawn, Wadebridge, PL27 7LD. Tel: (01208) 813345. Est: 2002. Private premises. Postal only. Stock: medium. Spec: History - General; History - Local; Literary Criticism; Literature; New Naturalist; Painting; Poetry; Women. [Updated]

CUMBRIA

ALSTON

Durham Book Centre, ■ Front Street, Alston, CA9 3HU. Prop: Mrs. A. Dumble. Tel: (01434) 381066. E-mail: ann@absolutely.fsnet.co.uk. Est: 1968. Shop open: **S:** 10:00–17:00; **Su:** 10:00–17:00. Stock: small. Spec: Ephemera. PR: £1–50. VAT No: GB 176 3861 34. [Updated]

APPLEBY-IN-WESTMORLAND

Barry McKay Rare Books, Kingstone House, Battlebarrow, Appleby-in-Westmorland, CA16 6XY. Prop: Barry McKay. Tel: 017683 52282. Fax: N/A. Web: www.barrymckayrarebooks.com. E-mail: barry.mckay@britishlibarry.net. Est: 1986. Shop and/or showroom; Appointment necessary. Open: **M:** 10.00–17.00; **T:** 10.00–17.00; **W:** 10.00–17.00; **Th:** 10.00–17.00; **F:** 10.00–17.00; **S:** 10.00–13.00. Spec: Advertising; Bibliography; Bindings; Book Arts; Bookbinding; Calligraphy; Early Imprints; Fine & Rare. CC: MC; V. Cata: bi-annually on Bibliography; rare and interesting books. Corresp: French. Mem: PBFA. VAT No: GB 448 5469 09. [Updated]

BARROW–IN–FURNESS

Americanabooksuk, 72 Park Drive, Barrow–in–Furness, LA13 9BB. Prop: Alan R. Beattie. Tel: (01229) 829722. E-mail: alan.rbeattie@virgin.net. Est: 1980. Private premises. Appointment necessary. Stock: very small. Spec: American Indians; Americana; Art; Cattlemen; Countries - Americas, The; Countries - U.S.A.; Cowboys; Exploration. PR: £3–150. CC: PayPal. Cata: annually on Western Americana. [Updated]

BROUGH

Summerfield Books Ltd, ■The Arches, Main Strreet, Brough, CA17 4AX. Prop: Jon & Sue Atkins. Tel: 01768341577. Fax: 01768341687. Web: www.summerfieldbooks.com. E-mail: info@summerfieldbooks.com. Est: 1986. Shop open: **M:** 09:30–16:30; **T:** 09:30–16:30; **Th:** 09:30–16:30; **F:** 09:30–16:30. Spec: Botany; Flora & Fauna; Forestry; Gardening - General; Horticulture; Natural Sciences; Nature; New Naturalist. CC: AE; E; JCB; MC; V. Cata: bi-annually on Botany, Forestry, Gardening, Horticulture. Corresp: French, German. Mcm: PBFA. Notes: We are specialist booksellers, selling from shop premises, by mail order and through the internet. Our stock is almost exclusively in the plant sciences, although we keep a small range of other natural history and local Cumbrian topography VAT No: GB 442816550. [Updated]

CARLISLE

Alauda Books, Unit 4, Carlisle Enterprise Centre, James Street, Carlisle, CA1 2PF. Prop: Michael Green. Tel: 01228 549694. E-mail: alaudabooks@hotmail.co.uk. Est: 1986. Storeroom. Book Fairs Only. Appointment necessary. Spec: Animals and Birds; Archaeology; Book Arts; Bookbinding; Botany; Cartography; Fishes; Flora & Fauna. Cata: annually on Natural History; Angling. Mem: PBFA. [Updated]

Bookcase, ■ 17 - 19 Castle Street, Carlisle, CA3 8SY. Prop: S. & G. Matthews. Tel: 01228 544560. E-mail: bookcasecarlisle@aol.com. Est: 1979. Shop open: **M:** 10:00–17:00; **T:** 10:00–17:00; **W:** 10:00–17:00; **Th:** 10:00–17:00; **F:** 10:00–17:00; **S:** 10:00–17:00. Spec: Antiquarian; Antiques; Art; Bibliography; Fiction - General; Languages - Foreign; Literary Criticism; Modern First Editions. CC: AE; MC; V. Corresp: French, German. Notes: Classical and jazz CDs (new) sold. Also booksearch. [Updated]

Dealers need to update their entry at least once a year. Visit your page on *www.sheppardsworld.co.uk*

Anne Fitzsimons, 3 Croft Park, Wetheral, Carlisle, CA4 8JH. Tel: (01228) 562184. Fax: (01228) 562184. Est: 1978. Private premises. Postal only. Stock: small. Spec: Cinema/Film; Circus; Dance; Magic & Conjuring; Music - General; Music - Music Hall; Music - Opera; Performing Arts. Mem: PBFA. [Updated]

COCKERMOUTH

Ian Dodsworth, 1 Banks Court, Market Place, Cockermouth, CA13 9NG. Prop: Ian Dodsworth. Tel: (01900) 823599. E-mail: ian@maurian.f9.co.uk. Est: 1986. Storeroom. Appointment necessary. Stock: small. PR: £1–150. Notes: attends day fairs in Northern England. [Updated]

The Printing House, ■ 102 Main Street, Cockermouth, CA13 9LX. Prop: David Winkworth. Tel: (01900) 824984. Web: www.printinghouse.co.uk. E-mail: info@printinghouse.co.uk. Est: 1968. Shop open: **M:** 09:00–17:00; **T:** 09:00–17:00; **W:** 09:00–17:00; **Th:** 09:00–17:00; **F:** 09:00–17:00; **S:** 09:00–17:00. Stock: large. PR: £1–500. CC: V. Mem: PBFA; BPS, PHT, PHS, AEPM. Notes: also art materials and picture framing. VAT No: GB 256 8544 27. [Updated]

EGREMONT

Esoteric Dreams Bookshop, ■ 1 St Bridgets Lane, Egremont, CA22 2BB. Prop: Mrs Sue Wright. Tel: 01946 821686. Web: www.amazon.co.uk/shops/esotericdreams. E-mail: suewright2000@btinternet.com. Est: 2004. Shop open: **T:** 10:00–16.00; **W:** 10.00–14.00; **Th:** 10.00–16.00; **F:** 10.00–16.00; **S:** 10.00–16.00. Spec: Alternative Medicine; Animals and Birds; Annuals; Art History; Authors:- Asimov, Isaac; Dinesen, Isak; Local; Women. Notes: We sell old and new books both in the shop and on the internet. We also sell postcards, local maps and unusual gifts. [Updated]

GRANGE–OVER–SANDS

Norman Kerr Booksellers, Priory Barn, Cartmel, Grange–over–Sands, LA11 6PX. Prop: Hilda & John Kerr. Tel: (015395) 36247 / 32508. Fax: Null. Web: www.kerrbooks.co.uk. E-mail: enquiries@kerrbooks.co.uk. Est: 1933. Shop and/or showroom. Telephone first. Open: **F:** 13:30–16:30; **S:** 13:30–16:30. Stock: medium. Spec: Antiquarian; Aviation; Canals/Inland Waterways; Engineering; Fine & Rare; Illustrated; Maritime/Nautical; Motoring. PR: £5–1,500. Mem: PBFA. Alternative tel: (015395) 32508. VAT No: GB 312 3475 89. [21/12/2004]

Over-Sands Books, ■ The Old Waiting Room, The Station, Grange-Over-Sands, LA11 6EH. Mr. S.R. Tyson. Tel: (01539) 534387. Web: www.oversandsbooks.co.uk. E-mail: over-sands.books@virgin.net. Est: 1995. Shop open: **M:** 11:00–17:00; **T:** 11:00–17:00; **W:** 11:00–17:00; **F:** 11:00–17:00; **S:** 11:00–17:00. Stock: small. Spec: Literature; Railways; Topography - General; Topography - Local; Booksearch; Ephemera. PR: £3–250. CC: PayPal. Notes: Opening times vary between November and March, call first. Also, a booksearch service. [Updated]

GRASMERE

Yewtree Books, ■ The Lakes Crafts & Antiques Gallery, 3 Oakbank Broadgate, Grasmere, LA22 9TA. Prop: Joe and Sandra Arthy. Tel: (015394) 35037. Fax: (015394) 44234. E-mail: lakescrafts@dsl.pipex.com. Est: 1990. Shop open: **M:** 10:00–17:00; **T:** 10:00–17:00; **W:** 10:00–17:00; **Th:** 10:00–17:00; **F:** 10:00–17:00; **S:** 10:00–17:00; **Su:** 10:00–17:00. Stock: small. Spec: Alpinism/Mountaineering; History - General; Railways; Sport - General; Topography - General; Topography - Local; Travel - General. PR: £1–300. CC: JCB; MC; V. [Updated]

Looking for ephemera? Then search Sheppard's on-line directories at:

www.sheppardsworld.co.uk

For all dealers selling ephemera

KENDAL

Kirkland Books, ■ 68, Kirkland, Kendal, LA9 5AP. Prop: Linden Burke. Tel: 0800 0112368. Fax: 0800 0112568. Web: www.kirklandbooks.co.uk. E-mail: enquiries@kirklandbooks.co.uk. Est: 1980. Shop open: **Th:** 10:00–17:00; **F:** 10:00–17:00; **S:** 10:00–17:00. Spec: Alpinism/Mountaineering; Authors:- Ransome, Arthur; Wainwright, Arthur; Exploration; Railways; Topography - Local; Transport. CC: AE; D; E; JCB; MC; V. Cata: occasionally on Alfred Wainwright, Arthur Ramsome. Notes: Kirkland Books is an established shop offering quality new, secondhand and antiquarian books specialising in: Mountaineering, The Lake District, Alfred Wainwright, Arthur Ransome and Railways. [Updated]

Left on The Shelf, Yard 91, Highgate, Kendal, LA9 4ED. Prop: Dave Cope. Tel: (01539) 729599. Web: www.abebooks.com/home/leftontheshelf. E-mail: leftontheshelf@phonecoop.coop. Est: 1992. Storeroom. Internet and postal. Telephone first. Stock: very large. Spec: History - Labour/ Radical Movements; Marxism; Pacifism; Radical Issues; Socialism; Trade Unions; War - Spanish Civil War; Booksearch. PR: £2–150. CC: MC; V. Corresp: French. Mem: PBFA. [Updated]

KESWICK

Jean Altshuler, 54 St. John Street, Keswick, CA12 5AB. Tel: (01768) 775745. E-mail: books@ jopplety.demon.co.uk. Est: 1996. Private premises. Internet and postal. Appointment necessary. Stock: small. Spec: Children's; Fiction - Science Fiction. PR: £5–200. [Updated]

Keswick Bookshop, ■ 4 Station Street, Keswick, CA12 5HT. Prop: Jane & John Kinnaird. Tel: (017687) 75535. Est: 1994. Shop. Telephone first. Open: **M:** 10:30–17:00; **T:** 10:30–17:00; **W:** 10:30–17:00; **Th:** 10:30–17:00; **F:** 10:30–17:00; **S:** 10:30–17:00. Stock: medium. Spcc: Antiques; Applied Art; Architecture; Art; Children's; Decorative Art; First Editions; Illustrated. PR: £1–300. CC: JCB; MC; V. Mem: PBFA. Notes: Winter opening - Saturday only (Nov-March) and Christmas holiday and New Year's day. And mail to: Winterbourne, 18 Houghton Road, Carlisle CA3 0LA. VAT No: GB 531 4987 33. [Updated]

KIRKBY STEPHEN

2 Ravens, ■ 2 Market Street, Kirkby Stephen, CA17 4QS. Prop: Val and Peter Harrison. Tel: 017683 71519. Est: 1997. Shop open: **W:** 10:00–16:00; **Th:** 10:00–16:00; **F:** 10:00–16:00; **S:** 10:00–16:00. Spec: New Age; Rural Life; Topography - Local. Notes: Telephone if making a special journey. [Updated]

The Book House, Ravenstonedale, Kirkby Stephen, CA17 4NG. Prop: Chris & Mary Irwin. Tel: (01539) 623634. Web: www.thebookhouse.co.uk. E-mail: mail@thebookhouse.co.uk. Est: 1963. Private premises. Open: **M:** 10:00–17:00; **W:** 10:00–17:00; **Th:** 10:00–17:00; **F:** 10:00–17:00; **S:** 10:00–17:00. Stock: large. Spec: Children's; Engineering; Fiction - General; Gardening - General; History - Industrial; Industry; Languages - Foreign; Languages - National. PR: £1–750. CC: AE; E; MC; V. Corresp: French, Italian. Mem: PBFA. VAT No: GB 113 8746 69. [Updated]

PENRITH

David A.H. Grayling, Verdun House, Main Street, Shap, Penrith, CA10 3NG. Prop: David A H Grayling. Tel: (01931) 716746. Fax: (01931) 716746. Web: www.davidgraylingbooks.co.uk. E-mail: graylingbook@ fsbdial.co.uk. Est: 1970. Private premises. Internet and postal. Appointment necessary. Stock: medium. Spec: Colour-Plate; Fine & Rare; Natural History; Scottish Interest; Sport - Angling/ Fishing; Sport - Big Game Hunting; Sport - Field Sports; Sport - Shooting. PR: £20–5,000. CC: AE; MC; V. Corresp: French, German. Mem: PBFA. Notes: Binding & restoration. Valuation for insurance & probate etc. Book search. VAT No: GB 154 6592 46. [Updated]

G.K. Hadfield, Old Post Office, Great Salkeld, Penrith, CA11 9LW. Prop: G.K. & J.V. Hadfield & N.R. Hadfield–Tilly. Tel: (01768) 870111. Web: www.gkhadfield-tilly.co.uk. E-mail: gkhadfield@ dial.pipex.com. Est: 1974. Shop and/or showroom; Internet and postal. Appointment necessary. Stock: large. Spec: Antiques; Astronomy; Bell-Ringing (Campanology); Furniture; Gemmology; Horology; Mathematics; Microscopy. CC: AE; JCB; MC; V; SO, ELEC. Corresp: French. Mem: B.H.I Notes: also, a booksearch service, antique clocks & materials for restoring antique clocks. Mobile: 07738 546488. VAT No: GB 114 809 578. [Updated]

Phenotype Books Ltd, 39 Arthur Street, Penrith, CA11 7TT. Prop: J.E. Mattley. Tel: (01768) 863049. Fax: (01768) 890493. Web: www.phenotypebooks.co.uk. E-mail: phenobooks@btconnect.com. Est: 1985. Private premises. Internet and postal. Telephone first. Stock: small. Spec: Agriculture; Animals and Birds; Carriages & Driving; Farming & Livestock; Farriers; Humanities; Magazines & Periodicals - General; Veterinary. PR: £5–1,800. Mem: PBFA. VAT No: GB 442 8614 47. [Updated]

SEDBERGH

The Bookseller, ■ 77 Main Street, Sedbergh, LA10 5AB. Prop: C. J. Chambers. Tel: 015396 20991. Fax: 015396 20589. E-mail: sedberghbooks@aol.com. Est: 1994. Shop open: **M:** 10:00–17:00; **T:** 10:00–17:00; **W:** 10:00–17:00; **Th:** 10:00–12:00; **F:** 10:00–17:00; **S:** 10:00–17:00. Spec: Children's; Children's - Illustrated. CC: AE; E; JCB; MC; V. Corresp: French. Notes: book repairs undertaken. [Updated]

Dales & Lakes Book Centre, ■ 72 Main Street, Sedbergh, LA10 5AD. Tel: 015396 20125. E-mail: booktown@sedbergh.org.uk. Est: 2005. Shop open: **M:** 10:00–17:00; **T:** 10:00–17:00; **W:** 10:00–17:00; **Th:** 10:00–17:00; **F:** 10:00–17:00; **S:** 10:00–17:00; **Su:** 10:00–17:00. Spec: Animals and Birds; Botany; Buses/Trams; Cookery/Gastronomy; Country Houses; Crafts; Drama; Fiction - General. CC: MC; V. Cata: annually. VAT No: GB 859 4936 61. [Updated]

R.F.G. Hollett and Son, 6 Finkle Street, Sedbergh, LA10 5BZ. Prop: C.G. & R.F.G. Hollett. Tel: (01539) 620298. Fax: (01539) 621396. Web: www.holletts-rarebooks.co.uk. E-mail: hollett@sedbergh.demon.co.uk. Est: 1959. Shop and/or showroom; Internet and postal. Appointment necessary. Stock: very large. Spec: Alpinism/Mountaineering; Antiquarian; Antiques; Biography; Children's; Collecting; Colour-Plate; Fine Art. PR: £30–50,000. CC: AE; E; JCB; MC; V; Maestro. Mem: ABA; ILAB; Valuations. VAT No: GB 343 4391 63. [Updated]

Orange Skies Books, ■ 46 Main Street, Sedbergh, LA10 5BL. Prop: David Johnston-Smith. Tel: 0161 408 1182. Web: www.orangeskies.co.uk. E-mail: orangeskiesmusic@gmail.com. Est: 2005. Shop open: **M:** 09:00–17:30; **T:** 09:00–17:30; **W:** 09:00–17:30; **Th:** 09:00–17:30; **F:** 09:00–17:30; **S:** 09:00–17:30; **Su:** 09:00–17:30. [Updated]

Sleepy Elephant Books & Artefacts, ■ 41 Main Street, Sedbergh, LA10 5BN. Prop: Avril Whittle and Partners. Tel: 015396 21770. Fax: 015396 21770. E-mail: avrilsbooks@aol.com. Est: 2003. Shop open: **M:** 09:00–17:30; **T:** 09:00–17:30; **W:** 09:00–17:30; **Th:** 09:00–17:30; **F:** 09:00–17:30; **S:** 09:00–17:30; **Su:** 12:00–17:00. Spec: Cookery/Gastronomy; Embroidery; Fiction - General; Furniture; Knitting; Rugs; Textiles; Theatre. Notes: art, craft and designs, especially textile arts. [Updated]

Westwood Books Ltd, ■ Leisure House, Sedbergh, LA10 5AH. Tel: 015396 21233. E-mail: evelyn@markwestwood.co.uk. Est: 1987. Shop open: **M:** 10:30–17:30; **T:** 10:30–17:30; **W:** 10:30–17:30; **Th:** 10:30–17:30; **F:** 10:30–17:30; **S:** 10:30–17:30; **Su:** 10:30–17:30. Spec: Academic/Scholarly; Alternative Medicine; Antiquarian; Archaeology; Architecture; Art; Art History; Art Reference. CC: JCB; MC; V. Corresp: French. Mem: ABA; PBFA; BA. Notes: New shop opens in 2006. [Updated]

Avril Whittle, Bookseller, Whittle's Warehouse, 7–9 (Rear) Bainbridge Road, Sedbergh, LA10 5AU. Prop: Avril Whittle. Tel: (015396) 21770. Fax: (015396) 21770. E-mail: avrilsbooks@aol.com. Est: 1980. Warehouse. Appointment necessary. Stock: medium. Spec: Crafts; Crochet; Decorative Art; Embroidery; Fashion & Costume; Illustrated; Interior Design; Needlework. PR: £1–600. CC: MC; V. Corresp: French. Notes: Sleepy Elephant Books & Artefacts, 16 Back Lane Dales & Lakes Booke Centre [coming soon]. VAT No: GB 379 7477 78. [Updated]

Henry Wilson Books, Dales and Lakes Book Centre, Main Street, Sedbergh, LA10 5AD. Prop: H.G.E. Wilson. Tel: (015396) 20125. E-mail: hwrailwaybooks@aol.com. Est: 2005. Shop and/or gallery. Open: **M:** 10:00–17:00; **T:** 10:00–17:00; **W:** 10:00–17:00; **Th:** 10:00–17:00; **F:** 10:00–17:00; **S:** 10:00–17:00; **Su:** 10:00–17:00. Stock: very small. Spec: Author - Rolt, L.T.C.; Buses/Trams; Canals/Inland Waterways; History - Industrial; Railways; Steam Engines; Traction Engines; Transport. PR: £2–500. CC: JCB; MC; V; Maestro. Cata: annually on railways, transport and industrial history. Corresp: French, German. Mem: PBFA; FSB. Also at Henry Wilson Books, Great Barrow, Cumbria (q.v.) Notes: New books & back issues of railway journals. VAT No: GB 439 7672 03. [Updated]

Dealers need to update their entry at least once a year. Visit your page on *www.sheppardsworld.co.uk*

ULVERSTON

Bookfare, Lowick Hall, Ulverston, LA12 8ED. Prop: Dr. A.C.I. Naylor. Tel: (01229) 885240. Fax: (01229) 885240. Web: www.bookfare.co.uk. E-mail: ambookfare@aol.com. Est: 1977. Private premises. Postal only. Contactable. Stock: small. PR: £6–300. CC: PayPal. Corresp: French. [Updated]

WELTON

The Little Bookshop, Sebergham Castle Houseon, Welton, Near Carlisle, CA5 7HG. Prop: Frank Grant. Tel: withheld. Fax: (016974) 76079. E-mail: fjg236@aol.com. Est: 1994. Private premises. Postal only. Appointment necessary. Stock: small. Spec: Alpinism/Mountaineering; Biography; Countries - Nepal; Geology; Palaeontology; Sport - Climbing & Trekking; Topography - Local. PR: £2–500. Notes: also, a booksearch service. [15/01/2005]

WHITEHAVEN

Michael Moon's Bookshop, ■ 19 Lowther Street, Whitehaven, CA28 7AL. Prop: Michael Moon. Tel: (01946) 599010. Fax: (09146) 599010. Est: 1970. Shop open: **M:** 09:30–17:00; **T:** 09:30–17:00; **W:** 09:30–17:00; **Th:** 09:30–17:00; **F:** 09:30–17:00; **S:** 09:30–17:00. Stock: very large. Spec: Cinema/Film; History - Local; Topography - Local; Booksearch. PR: £1–1,000. CC: JCB; MC; V. Mem: PBFA; SBA. Notes: Closed Wed - from January to Easter. Publisher on Cumbrian history. VAT No: GB 288 1073 42. [Updated]

WIGTON

Chelifer Books, Todd Close, Curthwaite, Wigton, CA7 8BE. Prop: Mike Smith & Deryn Walker. Tel: (01228) 711388. Web: www.military-books.biz. E-mail: militbks@aol.com. Est: 1985. Private premises. Internet and postal. Appointment necessary. Stock: small. Spec: American Indians; Antiquarian; Arms & Armour; Aviation; Military; Military History; Military Uniforms; War - General. PR: £5–1,500. CC: MC; V; Switch. Cata: bi-monthly– on general military. [Updated]

WINDERMERE

Bridge Books, 2 Sunnybrae Brook Road, Windermere. John Taylor. Tel: (01539) 445015. E-mail: jm.taylor@ic24.net. Est: 1993. Postal only. Spec: Poetry; Topography - Local. PR: £3–750. [Updated]

Fireside Bookshop, ■ 21 Victoria Street, Windermere, LA23 1AB. Prop: Mr R.D. Sheppard. Tel: (015394) 45855. Web: www.firesidebookshop.co.uk. E-mail: firesidebookshop@btconnect.com. Est: 1977. Shop open: **M:** 11:00–17:00; **T:** 11:00–17:00; **W:** 11:00–17:00; **Th:** 11:00–17:00; **F:** 11:00–17:00; **S:** 11:00–17:00; **Su:** 11:00–17:00. Stock: large. Spec: Academic/Scholarly; Aeronautics; Alpinism/Mountaineering; American Indians; Americana; Anthropology; Antiquarian; Art. PR: £1–1,000. CC: AE; JCB; MC; Switch. [Updated]

WITHERSLACK

Rosemary Dooley, Crag House, Witherslack, Grange–over–Sands, LA11 6RW. Prop: R.M.S. Dooley. Tel: (01539) 552286. Fax: (01539) 552013. Web: www.booksonmusic.co.uk. E-mail: rd@booksonmusic.co.uk. Est: 1992. Private premises. Postal only. Appointment necessary. Stock: medium. Spec: Academic/Scholarly; Music - General. PR: £3–500. CC: AE; E; MC; V. Mem: PBFA. VAT No: GB 393 1979 09. [Updated]

DERBYSHIRE

ALFRETON

John Titford, Yew Tree Farm, Hallfieldgate, Higham, Alfreton, DE55 6AG. Tel: (01773) 520389. Fax: (01773) 833373 E-mail: J.Titford@zen.co.uk. Est: 1987. Private premises. Postal only. Appointment necessary. Stock: small. Spec: Genealogy; History - General; Topography - General; Booksearch. PR: £2–1,000. Corresp: French Mem: PBFA. [Updated]

BAKEWELL

Country Books, Courtyard Cottage, Little Longstone, Bakewell, DE45 1NN. Prop: Richard J.T. Richardson. Tel: 01629 640670. Fax: 01629 640670. E-mail: DckRchrdsn7@aol.com. Est: 1992. Private premises. Book Fairs Only. Spec: Academic/Scholarly; Architecture; Farming & Livestock; Folklore; History - Local; Rural Life. CC: V. Cata: - quarterly. [Updated]

BUXTON

Birdnet Optics Ltd., ■ 5 London Road, Buxton, SK17 9PA. Prop: Paul and Sandi Flint. Tel: (01298) 71844. Fax: (01298) 27727. Web: www.birdnet.co.uk. E-mail: paulflint@birdnet.co.uk. Est: 1998. Shop open: **M:** 09:00–17:30; **T:** 09:00–17:30; **W:** 09:00–17:30; **Th:** 09:00–17:30; **F:** 09:00–17:30; **S:** 09:00–17:00. Stock: very small. Spec: Natural History; New Books; New Naturalist; Ornithology; Publishers - Poysers. PR: £1–2,000. CC: MC; V. [Updated]

Scrivener's Books & Bookbinding, ■ 42 High Street, Buxton, SK17 6HB. Prop: Alastar Scrivener. Tel: 01298 73100. Est: 1994. Shop open: **M:** 09:00–17:00; **T:** 09:00–17:00; **W:** 09:00–17:00; **Th:** 09:00–17:00; **F:** 09:00–17:00; **S:** 09:00–17:00; **Su:** 12:00–16:00; Closed for lunch: 13:00–14:00. Spec: Annuals; Antiquarian; Applied Art; Archaeology; Architecture; Art; Art - Technique; Art - Theory. CC: AE; D; E; JCB; MC; V. Notes: bookbinding, tuition, day courses, lectures. [Updated]

CASTLETON

Hawkridge Books, ■ The Cruck Barn, Cross Street, Castleton, Hope Valley, S33 8WH. Prop: Dr. J. & Mrs. I. Tierney. Tel: (01433) 621999. Web: www.hawkridge.co.uk. E-mail: books@hawkridge.co.uk. Est: 1995. Shop open: **M:** 10:00–17:30; **T:** 10:00–17:30; **W:** 10:00–17:30; **Th:** 10:00–17:30; **F:** 10:00–17:30; **S:** 10:00–17:30; **Su:** 12:00–17:30. Stock: large. Spec: Natural History; Ornithology. PR: £5–2,000. CC: AE; JCB; MC; V. Notes: also, barn bed & breakfast [Updated]

CHESTERFIELD

Ian Broddon, Meynell Close, Chesterfield, S40 3BL. Prop: Ian Briddon. Tel: 01246 208411. E-mail: i.b@briddonbuks.ablegratis.co.uk. Est: 2004. Private premises. Internet and postal. Contactable: **M:** 09:00–17:30; **T:** 09:00–17:30; **W:** 09:00–17:30; **Th:** 09:00–17:30; **F:** 09:00–17:30; **S:** 09:00–17:30; **Su:** 09:00–17:30; Closed for lunch: 13:00–14:00. Spec: Annuals; Antiquarian; Children's - Illustrated; Fine & Rare; First Editions; Food & Drink; Homosexuality & Lesbianism; Humour. [Updated]

Tilleys Vintage Magazine Shop, ■ 21 Derby Road, Chesterfield, S40 2EF. Prop: Antonius & Albertus Tilley. Tel: (01246) 563868. Web: www.tilleysmagazines.com. E-mail: Tilleysoldmags@aol.com. Est: 1978. Shop. Telephone first. Stock: very large. Spec: Comic Books & Annuals; Glamour; Magazines & Periodicals - General; Newspapers; Ephemera. PR: £1–100. CC: AE; MC; V. Corresp: Dutch. Notes: see also 281 Shoreham Street, Sheffield (q.v.) Mail order. 1 million + items in stock 1890s-present. [Updated]

CROMFORD

Scarthin Books, ■ The Promenade, Scarthin, Cromford, DE4 3QF. Prop: Dr. D.J. Mitchell. Tel: (01629) 823272. Fax: (01629) 825094. Web: www.scarthinbooks.com. E-mail: clare@scarthinbooks.com. Est: 1974. Shop open: **M:** 09:30–18:00; **T:** 09:30–18:00; **W:** 09:30–18:00; **Th:** 09:30–18:00; **F:** 09:30–18:00; **S:** 09:30–18:00; **Su:** 12:00–18:00. Stock: very large. Spec: Academic/Scholarly; Alpinism/Mountaineering; American Indians; Animals and Birds; Antiquarian; Architecture; Author - Uttley, Alison; History - Industrial. PR: £1–5,000. CC: MC; V. Corresp: French, German. Mem: BA; IPG. Notes: also, new books, publishers of local history and walking books. VAT No: GB 127 6427 64. [09/08/2004]

FROGGATT

Jarvis Books (incorporating 'Gastons' Books), Valleyside, Malthouse Lane, Froggatt, Hope Valley, S32 3ZA. Prop: Grant & Valerie Jarvis. Tel: (01433) 631 951. Web: www.mountainbooks.co.uk. E-mail: jarvis@mountainbooks.co.uk. Est: 1979. Private premises. Internet and postal. Telephone first. Stock: small. Spec: Alpinism/Mountaineering. CC: AE; MC; V. Mem: PBFA. VAT No: GB 439 5226 36. [Updated]

GLOSSOP

Andrews Books & Collectables, ■ Glossop Antique Centre, Brookfield, Glossop, SK14 6JE. Prop: Andrew R. Mays. Tel: 0161 351 1851. Fax: 0161 351 1851. Web: www.abebooks.com. E-mail: andrewsbooks@btinternet.com. Est: 1997. Shop open: **Th:** 10:00–16:00; **F:** 10:00–16:00; **S:** 10:00–16:00; **Su:** 10:00–16:00. Spec: Theology; Topography - General; Topography - Local. CC: PayPal. Notes: PayPal is for Internet transactions only. [Updated]

George St. Books, ■ 14 & 16 George Street, Glossop, SK13 8AY. Prop: Andrew Hancock. Tel: 01457 853413. Est: 1986. Shop open: **W:** 10:00–17:00; **Th:** 10:00–17:00; **F:** 10:00–17:00; **S:** 10:00–17:00. Spec: Alpinism/Mountaineering; Architecture; Art; Maritime/Nautical; Sport - Climbing & Trekking. CC: MC; V. [Updated]

LITTLEOVER

Bob Mallory (Books), 14 Dean Close, Littleover, Derby, DE23 4EF. Tel: 01332 511663. E-mail: rmalloryb@aol.com. Open: **M:** 09:00–17:30; **T:** 09:00–17:30; **W:** 09:00–17:30; **Th:** 09:00–17:30; **F:** 09:00–17:30; **S:** 09:00–17:30; **Su:** 09:00–17:30; Closed for lunch: 13:00–14:00. Spec: Autobiography; Automobilia/Automotive; Biography; Cinema/Film; Horses; Humour; Journalism; Management. Notes: also, Horse Racing, Gambling, Entertainment, Television, Cinema. [Updated]

MATLOCK

Hunter and Krageloh, Honeybee Cottage, In the Dale, Wensley, Matlock, DE4 2LL. Prop: J.A. Hunter. Tel: (01629) 732845. E-mail: hunterandkrageloh@btinternet.com. Est: 1993. Telephone first. Open: Spec: Alpinism/Mountaineering; Plant Hunting; Sport - Climbing & Trekking; Travel - Asia; Travel - Polar. PR: £1–12,000. Mem: PBFA. [Updated]

John O'Reilly - Mountain Books, Netherlea Barn, Bracken Lane, Holloway, Matlock, DE4 5AS. Tel: (01629) 534559. Fax: (01629) 534773. E-mail: johnoreill@aol.com. Est: 1972. Private premises. Postal only. Stock: very small. Spec: Alpinism/Mountaineering; Sport - Climbing & Trekking; Travel - Asia; Travel - Polar; Voyages & Discovery. PR: £5–500. CC: MC; V. [Updated]

WIRKSWORTH

Pastmasters, ■ 15 The Causeway, Wirksworth, DE4 4DL. Prop: Brian Jones. Tel: (01629) 823775. E-mail: brian@pastmasters.co.uk. Est: 1998. Shop open: **T:** 10:00–17:00; **F:** 10:00–17:00; **S:** 10:00–17:00. Stock: small. Spec: Journalism; Music - General; Plays; Theatre. PR: £1–40. Notes: also, classical cds. [Updated]

DEVON

ASHBURTON
The Dartmoor Bookshop, ■ 2 Kingsbridge Lane, Ashburton, TQ13 7DX. Prop: Mr. & Mrs. P.R. Heatley. Tel: (01364) 653356. Shop open: **W:** 09:30–17:30; **Th:** 09:30–17:30; **F:** 09:30–17:30; **S:** 09:30–17:30. Stock: very large. Spec: Alpinism/Mountaineering; Antiquarian; Architecture; Art; Art History; Art Reference; Artists; Fiction - General. PR: £1–250. CC: AE; JCB; MC; V. Mem: PBFA. VAT No: GB 365 7662 17. [Updated]

AXMINSTER
Bookquest, High Grange, Dalwood, Axminster, EX13 7ES. Prop: E.M. Chapman. Tel: (01404) 831317. Est: 1968. Private premises. Postal only. Spec: Booksearch. [Updated]

Books Plus, ■ 1 Bristol House, West Street, Axminster, EX13 5NS. Prop: Robert Starling. Tel: (01395) 578199. E-mail: books.plus@btconnect.com. Est: 1999. Shop open: **M:** 09:00–17:00; **T:** 09:00–17:00; **W:** 09:00–17:00; **Th:** 09:00–17:00; **F:** 09:00–17:00; **S:** 09:00–17:00. Stock: small. Spec: Cookery/Gastronomy; Military; Music - General; Railways; Sport - General. PR: £1–30. CC: D; E; MC; V; Solo Switch. Notes: also, videos & CDs, DVDs. [Updated]

W.C. Cousens, 'The Leat', Lyme Road, Axminster, EX13 5BL. Prop: William Clifford Cousens. Tel: (01297) 32921. Est: 1988. Private premises. Appointment necessary. Stock: small. Spec: Gardening - General; Topography - Local; Booksearch. PR: £1–200. Mem: PBFA. [Updated]

BARNSTAPLE
Tarka Books, ■ 5 Bear Street, Barnstaple, EX32 7BU. Prop: Fiona Broster. Tel: (01271) 374997. Web: www.tarkabooks.co.uk. E-mail: books@tarkabooks.co.uk. Est: 1988. Shop open: **M:** 09:45–17:00; **T:** 09:45–17:00; **W:** 09:45–17:00; **Th:** 09:45–17:00; **F:** 09:45–17:00; **S:** 09:45–17:00. Stock: very large. Spec: Author - Williamson, Henry; New Books. PR: £1–100. CC: MC; V; So. Mem: BA; FSB. Notes: also, a booksearch service. [Updated]

BERE ALSTON
The Victoria Bookshop, ■ 9 Fore Street, Bere Alston, PL20 7AA. Prop: Peter Churcher. Tel: (01822) 841638. E-mail: victoria_bookshop@btopenworld.com. Est: 2000. Shop and postal. Open: **T:** 10:30–16:30; **W:** 10:30–16:30; **Th:** 10:29–16:30; **F:** 10:30–16:30; **S:** 10:30–16:30. Stock: very large. Spec: Academic/Scholarly; Occult; Psychology/Psychiatry. PR: £3–600. CC: AE; MC; V; SW. Notes: over 80,000 books in stock. [Updated]

BIDEFORD
Allhalland Books, ■ 7 Allhalland St., Bideford, EX39 2JD. Prop: J.P. Simpson O'Gara and S. Sutherland. Tel: (01237) 479301. Est: 1997. Shop open: **M:** 09:00–17:00; **T:** 09:00–17:00; **W:** 09:00–17:00; **Th:** 09:00–17:00; **F:** 09:00–17:00; **S:** 09:00–17:00. Stock: small. Spec: Natural History; Topography - General. PR: £2–500. Notes: also, bookbinding. [Updated]

Peter Hames, ■ Devon Cottage, Churchill Way, Northam, Bideford, EX39 1NS. Prop: Peter Hames. Tel: (01237) 421065. Fax: (01237) 421065. E-mail: peterhames@hotmail.com. Est: 1980. Shop open: **M:** 09:30–17:30; **T:** 09:30–17:30; **W:** 09:30–17:30; **Th:** 09:30–17:30; **F:** 09:30–17:30; **S:** 09:30–17:30. Stock: small. Spec: Motoring; Music - Jazz & Blues; Topography - Local; Ephemera. PR: £1–100. Mem: PBFA. Notes: also at Barnstaple Market: Tues, Fri, Sat and South Molton Market: Thursday and book fairs in South West. Local topography includes Exmoor, and Lundy Island. [Updated]

BRIXHAM
Kate Armitage (Booksearch), 5 Park Court, Heath Road, Brixham, TQ5 9AX. Tel: (01803) 850277. E-mail: katesbooks2003@yahoo.co.uk. Private premises. Internet and postal. Spec: Children's; Maritime/Nautical; Military History; Modern First Editions. PR: £1–20. [Updated]

CHUDLEIGH
David Porteous Editions, PO Box 5, Chudleigh, Newton Abbot, TQ13 0YZ. Prop: David Porteous. Tel: 01626 853310. Fax: 01626 853663. E-mail: sales@davidporteous.com. Web: www.davidporteous.com. Private premises. Mail order only. Internet and postal. Stock: very small. Spec: art and crafts. [Updated]

COLYTON

Chandos Books, ■ London House, Market Place, Colyton, EX24 6JS. Prop: George Janssen. Tel: 01297 553344. E-mail: chandosbooks@hotmail.com. Est: 1997. Shop open: **M:** 10:00–16:00; **T:** 10:00–16:00; **W:** 10:00–16:00; **Th:** 10:00–16:00; **F:** 10:00–16:00; **S:** 10:00–13:00. Spec: Animals and Birds; Antiquarian; Architecture; Art; Bibles; Bindings; Bookbinding; Books about Books. Corresp: Dutch, German. Notes: bookbinding and book repairs on premises. [Updated]

COMBE MARTIN

Golden Books Group, Blurridge, Ridge Hill, Combe Martin, EX34 0NR. Tel: (01271) 883204. Web: www.abook4all.com. E-mail: ivan@abook4all.com. Est: 1991. Private premises. Internet Only. Appointment necessary. Open: **M:** 09:00–18:00; **T:** 09:00–18:00; **W:** 09:00–18:00; **Th:** 09:00–18:00; **F:** 09:00–18:00; **S:** 09:00–18:00; **Su:** 09:00–18:00. Stock: large. Spec: Antiquarian; Author - Dickens, Charles; Bindings. PR: £5–10,000. CC: MC; V; Switch. Mem: PBFA; LAPADA, CINOA. VAT No: GB 822 1619 54. [Updated]

DARTMOUTH

Compass Books, ■ 24 Lower Street, Dartmouth, TQ6 9AN. Prop: Emily and Lucie Wright. Tel: 01803 835915. Fax: 01803 835915. E-mail: books@compassmarine.co.uk. Est: 2000. Shop open: **M:** 10:00–16:00; **T:** 10:00–16:00; **W:** 10:00–16:00; **Th:** 10:00–16:00; **F:** 10:00–16:00; **S:** 10:00–16:00. Spec: History - Local; Maritime/Nautical; Topography - Local. CC: D; E; JCB; MC; V; Maestro, Solo. [Updated]

DAWLISH

Dawlish Books, ■ White Court, Beach Street, Dawlish, EX7 9PN. Prop: S. French. Tel: (01626) 866882 or 72. E-mail: frenchatavalon@aol.com. Est: 2000. Shop open: **M:** 11:00–16:30; **T:** 11:00–16:30; **W:** 11:00–16:30; **Th:** 11:00–16:30; **F:** 11:00–16:30; **S:** 11:00–16:30. Stock: medium. Spec: Comic Books & Annuals; Esoteric; New Age; Occult; Psychic; Spiritualism; U.F.O.s; Unexplained, The. PR: £1–100. Notes: Open 11:00–15:00 in winter. [Updated]

EXETER

Lisa Cox Music, The Coach House, Colleton Crescent, Exeter, EX 2 4DG. Prop: Ms. L. Cox. Tel: (01392) 490290. Fax: (01392) 277336. Web: www.lisacoxmusic.co.uk. E-mail: music@lisacoxmusic.co.uk. Est: 1984. Private premises. Internet and postal. Appointment necessary. Open: **M:** 10:00–17:00; **T:** 10:00–17:00; **W:** 10:00–17:00; **Th:** 10:00–17:00; **F:** 10:00–12:00. Stock: medium. Spec: Aids Crisis, The; Autographs; Manuscripts; Music - Printed, Sheet Music & Scores. PR: £100–50,000. CC: MC; V. Corresp: French. Mem: ABA; BA. VAT No: GB 631 4239 64. [Updated]

Exeter Rare Books, ■ 13a, Guildhall Shopping Centre, Exeter, EX8 5AX. Prop: R.C. Parry M.A Tel: (01392) 436021. Est: 1977. Shop open: **M:** 10:00–17:00; **T:** 10:00–17:00; **W:** 11:00–17:00; **Th:** 10:00–17:00; **F:** 10:00–17:00; **S:** 10:00–17:00; Closed for lunch: 13:00–14:00. Stock: medium. Spec: Topography - Local. PR: £2–500. CC: MC; V. Corresp: German Mem: ABA; PBFA. VAT No: GB 142 3267 91. [Updated]

John S. Hill, 78 Pinhoe Road, Exeter, EX4 7HL. Tel: (01392) 439753. Fax: (01392) 439753. E-mail: john@hill6383.fsnet.co.uk. Est: 1988. Private premises. Internet and postal. Appointment necessary. Stock: small. Spec: Fiction - Crime, Detective, Spy, Thrillers; Fiction - Science Fiction; First Editions; Military; Booksearch. PR: £5–1,500. [Updated]

Richard Connole, 12 Seabrook Avenue, Countess Wear, Exeter, EX2 7DW. Tel: 01392 201735. Web: www.yestervision.co.uk. E-mail: rconnole@hotmail.com. Internet and postal only. Telephone first. Medium stock. Cata: often.

Joel Segal Books, ■ 27 Fore Street, Topsham, Exeter, EX3 0HD. Prop: Joel Segal & Lily Neal. Tel: (01392) 877895. Web: www.joelsegalbooks.com. E-mail: lily@segalbooks.com. Est: 1993. Shop open: **M:** 10:30–17:00; **T:** 10:30–17:00; **W:** 10:30–17:00; **Th:** 10:30–17:00; **F:** 10:30–17:00; **S:** 10:30–17:00; Closed for lunch: 13:00–14:00. Stock: very large. Spec: Arts, The; Literature; Natural History; Social History; Topography - General; Topography - Local; Transport. PR: £1–300. CC: MC; V; debit. Corresp: French. Mem: Fed of Small Businesses. Notes: A valuation service, and ephemera. [Updated]

Westcountry Oldbooks, ■ S.P.C.K. Bookshop, 1-2 Catherine St., Exeter, EX11EX. Prop: David Neil. Tel: (01803) 322712. Web: www.abebooks.com. E-mail: westcountryoldbooks@btopenworld.com. Est: 1988. Shop open: **M:** 09:00–17:30; **T:** 09:00–17:30; **W:** 09:00–17:30; **Th:** 09:00–17:30; **F:** 09:00–17:30; **S:** 09:00–17:30. Stock: small. Spec: Antiquarian; Literature; Theology; Topography - General. CC: AE; D; JCB; MC; V. Mem: PBFA. [Updated]

HONITON

Ænigma Designs (Books), Whites Plot, Luppitt, Honiton, EX14 4RZ. Tel: (01404) 891560. Fax: (01404) 891560. Web: www.puzzlemuseum.com. E-mail: books@puzzlemuseum.com. Est: 1973. Private premises. Internet and postal. Appointment necessary. Stock: very small. Spec: Mathematics; Puzzles; Science - General; Collectables. PR: £5–500. CC: PayPal. [Updated]

High Street Books, ■ 150 High Street, Honiton, EX14 8JX. Prop: Geoff Tyson. Tel: (01404) 45570. Fax: (01404) 45570. Est: 1992. Shop open: **T:** 10:00–17:00; **W:** 10:00–17:00; **Th:** 10:00–17:00; **F:** 10:00–17:00; **S:** 10:00–17:00. Stock: large. Spec: Applied Art; Erotica; Maritime/Nautical; Military; Topography - General; Topography - Local; Travel - General; Ephemera. PR: £1–600. [Updated]

Graham York Rare Books, ■ 225 High Street, Honiton, EX14 1LB. Tel: (01404) 41727. Fax: (01404) 44993. Web: www.gyork.co.uk. E-mail: books@gyork.co.uk. Est: 1982. Shop. Internet and postal. Open: **M:** 09:30–17:00; **T:** 09:30–17:00; **W:** 09:30–17:00; **Th:** 09:30–17:00; **F:** 09:30–17:00; **S:** 09:30–17:00. Stock: large. Spec: Africana; Antiquarian; Art Reference; Author - Borrow, George; Countries - Spain; Gypsies; Lace; Travel - Europe. PR: £0–5,000. CC: AE; MC; V. Corresp: Spanish, French. Mem: ABA; PBFA; ILAB. VAT No: GB 429 2623 48. [Updated]

KINGSBRIDGE

Booktrace International, The Hald, Kernborough, Kingsbridge, TQ7 2LL. Prop: Richard Newbold. Tel: (01548) 511366. E-mail: booktrace@aol.com. Est: 1995. Private premises. Postal only. Spec: Booksearch. Notes: also, a booksearch service (main line of business) [22/12/2004]

LYMPSTONE

Reaveley Books, 1 Church Road, Lympstone, Nr Exmouth, EX8 5JU. Prop: Jane Johnson. Tel: (01395) 225462. Web: www.reaveleybooks.co.uk. E-mail: jane@johnsgrj.demon.co.uk. Est: 1998. Private premises. Internet and postal. Telephone first. Stock: small. Spec: Author - Murdoch, I.; Modern First Editions. PR: £5–500. CC: PayPal. Mem: FSB. Monthly newsletter sent on request - see www.reaveleybooks.co.uk. [Updated]

MARY TAVY

Margaret Faulkner, The Mallows, 24 Great Fellingfield, Mary Tavy, Tavistock, PL19 9QQ. Prop: Mary Faulkner. Tel: (01822) 810 650. E-mail: marg9@btinternet.com. Private premises. Postal Only. Telephone first. Stock: very small. Cata: occasionally. PR: £1 – 100. Corresp: a little French.

MODBURY

Lamb's Tales Books, 63 Brownston Street, Modbury, Ivybridge, PL21 0RQ. Prop: James & Elizabeth Lamb. Tel: (01548) 830317. Web: www.lambstales.co.uk. E-mail: books@lambstales.co.uk. Est: 1988. Private premises. Internet and postal. Contactable. Stock: small. Spec: Cookery/Gastronomy; Maritime/Nautical; Military. PR: £5–150. VAT No: GB 768 6509 77. [Updated]

MONKLEIGH

Catalyst Booksearch Services, Catsborough Cottage, Catsborough Cross, Monkleigh, Nr Bideford, EX39 5LE. Patrick Blosse. Tel: 01805 624056. Web: www.catalystbooksearch.co.uk. E-mail: books@catalystbooksearch.co.uk. Est: 1997. Private premises. Internet and postal. Appointment necessary. Open: **M:** 09:00–17:30; **T:** 09:00–17:30; **W:** 09:00–17:30; **Th:** 09:00–17:30; **F:** 09:00–17:30; **S:** 09:00–17:30; **Su:** 09:00–17:30; Closed for lunch: 13:00–14:00. Spec: Biography; Children's; History - General; Performing Arts; Politics. CC: PayPal. [Updated]

HAVE YOUR OWN WEB SITE

Features include an easy to use book stock database

For more details - see
www.sheppardsworld.co.uk

MORETONHAMPSTEAD

Moreton Books, ■ 3a The Square, Moretonhampstead, TQ13 8NF. Prop: Dave Jelfs. Tel: (01647) 441176. Web: www.moretonbooks.co.uk. E-mail: davejelfs@moretonbooks.co.uk. Est: 1994. Shop open: **M:** 10:00–17:00; **T:** 10:00–17:00; **W:** 10:00–17:00; **Th:** 10:00–17:00; **F:** 10:00–17:00; **S:** 10:00–17:00. Stock: medium. Spec: Antiquarian; Art History; Art Reference; Autobiography; Literature; Modern First Editions; Natural History; Poetry. PR: £1–500. CC: E; MC; V; SO, SW. Mem: PBFA; Notes: Viewing times may vary in winter. Stock include Dartmoor and West Country topography. [Updated]

NEWTON ABBOT

Gerard Brookes, 68a The Square, Chagford, Newton Abbot, TQ13 8AE. Prop: Gerard Brookes. Tel: (01647) 432670. Office and/or bookroom. Appointment necessary. Spec: Natural History. Mem: PBFA. [Updated]

DPE Books, PO Box 5, Chudleigh, Newton Abbot, TQ130YZ. Prop: David Porteous. Tel: 01626 853310. Web: www.davidporteous.com. E-mail: dp-ed@davidporteous.com. Mail Order Only. Postal only. Spec: Art - Technique; Art History; Crafts; Embroidery; Folklore; Hobbies; Housekeeping; Illustrated. VAT No: GB 441 2746 66. [Updated]

OAKHAMPTON

J C Books, ■ 9 The Arcade, Fore Street, Oakhampton, EX20 1EX. Tel: 01837 659339. Est: 1998. Shop open: **M:** 09:00–17:00; **T:** 09:00–17:00; **W:** 09:00–17:00; **Th:** 09:00–17:00; **F:** 09:00–17:00; **S:** 09:00–17:00.. Spec: History - Local; New Books; Railways; Science - General; Topography - Local; Transport. [Updated]

OTTERTON

The Book Shelf, Butterfly Cottage, Behind Hayes, Otterton, EX9 7JQ. Prop: Sandra George. Tel: (01395) 567565. Web: www.bookshelfuk.com. E-mail: sales@bookshelfuk.com. Est: 1994. Private premises. Internet and postal. Telephone first. Open: **M:** 08:00–18:00; **T:** 08:00–18:00; **W:** 08:00–18:00; **Th:** 08:00–18:00; **F:** 08:00–18:00; **S:** 08:00–14:00. Stock: medium. Spec: Autobiography; Biography; Illustrated; Modern First Editions; Poetry; Travel - General; Victoriana. PR: £5–1,200. CC: PayPal. Mem: PBFA. Notes: Antiques Centre, Quayside, Topsham, Devon. VAT No: GB 631 2242 85. [Updated]

PAIGNTON

David Way Angling Books, 10 Cedar Road, Preston, Paignton, TQ3 2DD. Prop: David Way. Tel: (01803) 390824. Est: 1990. Private premises. Appointment necessary. Stock: small. Spec: Sport - Angling/Fishing. PR: £1–120. Notes: stock majors in books on carp, barbel, pike, and bass. [Updated]

The Old Celtic Bookshop, ■ 43 Hyde Road, Paignton, TQ4 5BP. Prop: Michael Sutton. Tel: (01803) 558709. E-mail: michael.sutton2@virgin.net. Est: 1989. Shop open: **M:** 09:00–18:00; **T:** 09:00–18:00; **W:** 09:00–18:00; **Th:** 09:00–18:00; **F:** 09:00–18:00; **S:** 09:00–18:00; **Su:** 09:00–18:00. Stock: medium. Spec: Annuals; Children's; Children's - Early Titles; Children's - Illustrated; Comic Books & Annuals; Computing; Metaphysics; Railways. PR: £1–50. Notes: extended opening until 21:30 June to September. [Updated]

The Pocket Bookshop, ■ 159 Winner Street, Paignton, TQ3 3BP. Prop: Leon Corrall. Tel: (01803) 529804. Est: 1985. Shop open: **T:** 10:30–17:30; **W:** 10:30–17:30; **Th:** 10:30–17:30; **F:** 10:30–17:30; **S:** 10:30–17:30. PR: £1–50. Notes: open Mondays in from July to September. [Updated]

The Sheet Music Warehouse, Primley Mount, 17 Primley Park, Paignton, TQ3 3JP. Web: www.sheetmusicwarehouse.co.uk. E-mail: pianoman@globalnet.co.uk. Est: 1991. Warehouse; Internet and postal. Appointment necessary. Open: **M:** 09:00–17:30; **T:** 09:00–17:30; **W:** 09:00–17:30; **Th:** 09:00–17:30; **F:** 09:00–17:30; **S:** 09:00–17:30; **Su:** 09:00–17:30; Closed for lunch: 13:00–14:00. Spec: Music - General; Music - Chart Histories & Research; Music - Chart Histories and Research; Music - Classical; Music - Composers; Music - Country & Western; Music - Folk & Irish Folk; Music - Gregorian Chants. CC: PayPal. [Updated]

PLYMOUTH

Anne Harris Books & Bags Books, 38 Burleigh Park Road, Peverell, Plymouth, PL3 4QH. Tel: (01752) 775853. E-mail: anne.harris1@virgin.net. Est: 2000. Private premises. Postal only. Appointment necessary. Stock: very small. Spec: Architecture; Art; Plant Hunting; Travel - General. PR: £1–500. [Updated]

Bookcupboard, ■ Old Customs House, 18 The Parade, Barbican, Plymouth, PL1 2JW. Prop: A. Donoghue. Tel: (01752) 226311. Fax: (08701) 698629. E-mail: barbbook@globalnet.co.uk. Shop open: **M:** 10:30–16:30; **T:** 10:30–16:30; **W:** 10:30–16:30; **Th:** 10:30–16:30; **F:** 10:30–16:30; **S:** 10:30–16:30; **Su:** 10:30–16:30. Stock: very large. Spec: CC: AE; D; E; JCB; MC; V. Mem: FSB. [Updated]

The Bookcupboard, ■ 3 Mitre Court, Southside Street, Barbican, Plymouth, PL1 2LD. Prop: A Donnaghue. Tel: (01752) 226311. Fax: (0870) 169 8629. E-mail: barbbook@globalnet.co.uk. Est: 1999. Shop open: **M:** 10:30–16:00; **T:** 10:30–16:00; **W:** 10:30–16:00; **Th:** 10:30–16:00; **F:** 10:30–16:00; **S:** 10:30–16:00; **Su:** 10:30–16:00. Stock: very large. PR: £1–500. CC: AE; D; MC; V. [Updated]

books2books, 64, Glendower Road, Peverell, Plymouth, PL3 4LD. Prop: R.J.A. Paxton-Denny. Tel: 01752 510234. Web: www.abebooks/home/BOOKS2BOOKS E-mail: rpaxtonden@blueyonder.co.uk. Est: 1984. Private premises. Internet and postal. Contactable. Open: **M:** 08:00–23:30; **T:** 08:00–23:30; **W:** 08:00–23:30; **Th:** 08:00–23:30; **F:** 08:00–23:30; **S:** 08:00–23:30; **Su:** 08:00–23:30. Spec: Annuals; Author - 20th Century; Autobiography; Biography; Children's; Children's - Illustrated; Cinema/Film; Collectables. CC: MC; V; Debit cards. Cata: occasionally on Modern 1sts, Childrens, Illustrated, Biogs, Milit. Corresp: French, German Mem: Good quality general stock. View by arrangement,tel/email/mail.Ship worldwide.Insurance extra [Updated]

Cornerstone Books, ■ New Street Antiques Centre, 27 New Street, The Barbican, Plymouth, PL3 4LE. Prop: Mark Treece. Tel: (01752) 661165. Web: www.abe.books.com. E-mail: mark@streece.freeserve.co.uk. Est: 1985. Shop open: **M:** 10:00–17:00; **T:** 10:00–17:00; **W:** 10:00–17:00; **Th:** 10:00–17:00; **F:** 10:00–17:00; **S:** 10:00–17:00. Stock: large. PR: £1–100. Notes: General stock. [Updated]

Rods Books, ■ 20–21 Southside Street, Barbican, Plymouth, PL1 2LD. Prop: R.P. Murphy. Tel: (01752) 253546. E-mail: rmurphy980@aol.com. Est: 1996. Shop. Internet and postal. Spec: Deep Sea Diving; Fiction - Science Fiction; Fiction - Westerns; History - General; History - Ancient; History - British; History - Local; Maritime/Nautical. PR: £2–40. [Updated]

The Sea Chest Nautical Booksho, ■ Queen Anne's Battery Marina, Coxside, Plymouth, PL4 0LP. Prop: R.A. Dearn. Tel: (01752) 222012. Fax: (01752) 252679. Web: www.seachest.co.uk. E-mail: sales@seachest.co.uk. Est: 1987. Shop open: **M:** 09:00–17:00; **T:** 09:00–17:00; **W:** 09:00–17:00; **Th:** 09:00–16:00; **F:** 09:00–17:00; **S:** 09:00–17:00. Stock: small. Spec: Maritime/Nautical; Navigation; Sport - Yachting. PR: £2–750. CC: AE; MC; V. Mem: BA. Notes: also, new nautical books, pilots & charts, a booksearch service & British Admiralty chart agent. VAT No: GB 501 5928 65. [Updated]

SEATON

Hill House Books, Hill House, Highcliffe Crescent, Seaton, EX12 2PS. Prop: Phil Beard. Tel: (01297) 20377. E-mail: jphil.beard@lineone.net. Est: 1982. Private premises. Appointment necessary. Stock: very small. Spec: Advertising; Art; Art History; Photography. PR: £1–500. [Updated]

The End Bookshop, ■ 54 Queen Street, Seaton, EX12 2RB. Prop: Mark Elbro. Tel: 01297 20808. E-mail: maelbro@talk21.com. Est: 1993. Shop open: **M:** 09:30–16:00; **T:** 09:30–16:00; **W:** 09:30–16:00; **Th:** 09:30–13:00; **S:** 09:30–13:00. [Updated]

SOUTH BRENT

Patrick Pollak Rare Books, Moorview, Plymouth Road, South Brent, TQ10 9HT. Prop: Patrick & Jeanne Pollak. Tel: (01364) 73457. Fax: (01364) 649126. Web: www.rarevols.co.uk. E-mail: patrick@rarevols.co.uk. Est: 1973. Private premises. Internet and postal. Telephone first. Stock: small. Spec: Academic/Scholarly; Economics; Medicine; Natural Sciences; Photography; Science - General; Science - History of; Scientific Instruments. PR: £50–5,000. CC: AE; JCB; MC; V. Corresp: German, French. Mem: ABA; ILAB; Linnean Society. VAT No: GB 267 5364 31. [Updated]

Rosemary Stansbury, 25 Church Street, South Brent, TQ10 9AB. Tel: (01364) 72465. Est: 1985. Private premises. Appointment necessary. Stock: small. Spec: Children's. PR: £1–100. Notes: children's titles only. [Updated]

TAVISTOCK

Bookworm Alley, 36 Brook Street, Tavistock, PL19 0HE. Prop: Joan Williams. Tel: (01822) 617740. Web: www.bookwormalley.org.uk. E-mail: bookworm-alley@freenet.co.uk. Est: 2000. Private premises. Appointment necessary. Stock: small. Spec: Religion - Christian; Religion - Salvation Army. PR: £1–50. [Updated]

Lee Furneaux Books, 6 Lopes Road, Dousland, Yelverton, Tavistock, PL20 6NX. Prop: Lee Furneaux. Tel: (01822) 853243. Web: www.abebooks.com/home/madeleine. E-mail: lee@furneauxbooks. freeserve.co.uk. Est: 1987. Market stand/stall; Internet and postal. Telephone first. Shop At: Tavistock Market (Indoor Market and permanent shop). Open: **T:** 08:30–16:00; **W:** 08:30–16:00; **Th:** 08:30–16:00; **F:** 08:30–16:00; **S:** 08:30–16:00. Stock: small. Spec: Art; Children's; Crafts; Gardening - General; History - General; Literature; Mind, Body & Spirit; Music - Popular. PR: £1–100. CC: PayPal & via abebooks. Notes: open occasional Sundays - see local press. VAT No: GB 802 9873 14. [Updated]

TEIGNMOUTH

IKON, Magnolia House, New Road, Teignmouth, TQ14 8UD. Prop: Dr. Nicholas & Clare Goodrick–Clarke. Tel: (01626) 776528. Fax: (01626) 776528. E-mail: ikon@globalnet.co.uk. Est: 1982. Postal only. Spec: Alchemy; Esoteric; Herbalism; History - European; Literature in Translation; Natural Health; New Age. PR: £10–75. [Updated]

Milestone Books, ■ 43, Northumberland Place, Teignmouth, TQ14 8DE. Prop: V K & E C Marston. Tel: 01626 775436. Fax: 01626 777023. Web: www.milestonebooks.co.uk. E-mail: Info@milestonebooks.co.uk. Est: 1996. Shop. Internet and postal. Telephone first. Open: **M:** 09:30–17:30; **T:** 09:30–17:30; **W:** 09:30–17:30; **Th:** 09:30–17:30; **F:** 09:30–13:30; **S:** 09:30–17:30; Closed for lunch: 13:30–14:00. Spec: Aircraft; Aviation; Buses/Trams; Maritime/Nautical; Model Railways; Naval; Navigation; Navy, The. CC: AE; MC; V. Notes: We operate from within the Quayside Bookshop, which sells new books. VAT No: GB 585 7083 03. [Updated]

TIVERTON

Heartland Old Books, ■ 12–14 Newport Street, Tiverton, EX16 6NL. Prop: Jeremy Whitehorn. Tel: (01884) 254488. E-mail: jeremy@whitehorn.fsworld.co.uk. Est: 2001. Shop open: **M:** 10:00–17:00; **T:** 10:00–17:00; **W:** 10:00–17:00; **Th:** 10:00–17:00; **F:** 10:00–17:00; **S:** 10:00–17:00. Stock: medium. Spec: Military; Sport - Field Sports; Travel - General. PR: £1–500. Corresp: French. Mem: PBFA. Notes: easy parking in Pannier Market opposite [Updated]

Kelly Books Limited, 6, Redlands, Tiverton, EX16 4DH. Props: Len & Lynda Kelly. Tel: (01884) 256170. Fax: (0871) 242 0394. Web: www.kellybooks.co.uk. E-mail: len@kellybooks.co.uk. Est: 1972. Private premises. Internet and postal. Appointment necessary. Open: **M:** 09:00–18:00; **T:** 09:00–18:00; **W:** 09:00–18:00; **Th:** 09:00–18:00; **F:** 09:00–18:00; **S:** 09:00–18:00. Stock: medium. Spec: Advertising; Broadcasting; Cinema/Film; Journalism; Media; Radio/Wireless; Television; Ephemera. PR: £5–600. CC: AE; MC; V; SW. Mem: supply of back numbers of Radio Times, The Listener, and other radio magazines. VAT No: GB 799 7192 48. Updated]

TORQUAY

Colin Baker - Books for the Collector, 66 Marldon Road, Shiphay, Torquay, TQ2 7EH. Tel: (01803) 613356. E-mail: colinbakerbooks@ukonline.co.uk. Est: 1994. Private premises. Postal only. Appointment necessary. Stock: small. Spec: Authors: Betjeman, Sir John; Read, Miss; Tangye, D.; Children's; Children's - Illustrated; Illustrated; Topography - General; Topography - Local. PR: £5–500. [05/11/2004]

TORRINGTON

The Archivist, ■ Priory Cottage, Frithelstock, Torrington, EX38 8JH. Tel: (01805) 625750. Fax: (01805) 625376. E-mail: mjbooks@sheppardsworld.co.uk. Est: 1990. Internet and postal. Appointment necessary. Stock: very small. Spec: Cats; Journalism; Literature; Publishers - Joseph Ltd., Michael. PR: £1–1,000. [Updated]

Books Antiques & Collectables, ■ 3 Well Street, Torrington, EX38 8EP. Tel: (01805) 625624. E-mail: joannaford8@hotmail.com. Shop. open: **T:** 10:30–16:00; **W:** 10:30–16:00; **Th:** 10:00–16:00; **F:** 10:00–16:00; Closed for lunch: 13:00–14:00. Stock: very small. Spec: Art; Biography; Children's; Fiction - General; History - General; Philosophy; Plays; Poetry. PR: £1–25. [Updated]

Brown and Rivans Ltd, Heywood House, South Street, Torrington, EX38 8HE. Tel: 01805 623771. E-mail: david.brown78@btinternet.com. Office and/or bookroom. Internet and postal. Appointment necessary. CC: PayPal. [Updated]

River Reads Bookshop, ■ 21 South Street, Torrington, EX38 8AA. Tel: (01805) 625888. Fax: (01805) 625888. Web: www.riverreads.co.uk. E-mail: keitarmshw@aol.com. Est: 2002. Shop open: **M:** 10:00–16:00; **T:** 10:00–16:00; **W:** 10:00–13:00; **Th:** 10:00–16:00; **F:** 10:00–16:00; **S:** 10:00–16:00. Stock: large. Spec: Art; Children's; Cookery/Gastronomy; Fishes; Gardening - General; Health; Hobbies; Natural History. PR: £2–200. Notes: also, vintage fishing tackle, fishing prints and publishers of collector?s limited editions of 'BB' titles. [Updated]

TOTNES

Collards Bookshop, ■ 4 Castle Street, Totnes, TQ9 5NU. Prop: Belle Collard. Tel: (01548) 550246. Est: 1970. Shop open: **M:** 10:30–17:00; **T:** 10:30–17:00; **W:** 10:30–17:00; **Th:** 10:30–17:00; **F:** 10:30–17:00; **S:** 10:30–17:00. Stock: medium. PR: £1–300. Notes: Hours vary midweek January to March. [Updated]

Geoff Cox, Lower West Wing, Tristford House, Harberton, Totnes, TQ9 7RZ. Tel: (01803) 866181. E-mail: geoffcox46@hotmail.com. Est: 1978. Private premises. Appointment necessary. Stock: medium. Spec: Aviation; Canals/Inland Waterways; History - Industrial; Maritime/Nautical; Mining; Motoring; Railways; Social History. PR: £1–500. [Updated]

Harlequin, ■ 41 High Street, Totnes, TQ9 5NP. Prop: Paul Wesley. Tel: (01803) 865794. Est: 1983. Shop open: **M:** 10:00–17:30; **T:** 09:00–17:30; **W:** 10:00–17:30; **Th:** 10:00–17:30; **F:** 10:00–17:30; **S:** 10:00–17:30. Stock: medium. PR: £1–50. [Updated]

Pedlar's Pack Books, ■ 4 The Plains, Totnes, TQ9 5DR. Prop: Brenda Greysmith & Andy Collins. Tel: (01803) 866423. E-mail: books@thepedlarspack.co.uk. Est: 2003. Shop. Internet and postal. Open. Open: **M:** 10:00–17:00; **T:** 10:00–17:00; **W:** 10:00–17:00; **Th:** 10:00–17:00; **F:** 10:00–17:00; **S:** 10:00–17:00. Stock: large. Spec: Military. PR: £1–500. CC: JCB; MC; V; Switch. Notes: also, a booksearch service. [Updated]

Available from Richard Joseph Publishers Ltd
CLEANING, REPAIRING AND CARING FOR BOOKS
by Robert L. Shep

Revised Edition   148pp £12.00

DORSET

BEAMINSTER

John E. Spooner, 18 Glebe Court, Barnes Lane, Beaminster, DT8 3EZ. Tel: (01308) 862713. Est: 1975. Market stand/stall. Stock: small. Spec: Aviation; Military; Naval. PR: £5–100. [Updated]

BLANDFORD FORUM

The Dorset Bookshop, ■ 69 East Street, Blandford Forum, DT11 7DX. Prop: Ethan Golden. Tel: (01258) 452266. Est: 1950. Shop open: **M:** 10:00–17:00; **T:** 10:00–17:00; **W:** 10:00–17:00; **Th:** 10:00–17:00; **F:** 10:00–17:00; **S:** 10:00–17:00. Stock: small. PR: £1–100. Mem: BA. [Updated]

BOURNEMOUTH

African Studies, 67A Muscliffe Road, Winton, Bournemouth, BH9 1GA. Prop: Alan Painter. Tel: 01202 528678. Fax: 01202 528678. E-mail: alan.painter@africanstudies.com. Est: 1998. Private premises. Appointment necessary. **M:** 14:00–17:00; **T:** 08:00–17:00; **W:** 20:00–22:00; **Th:** 20:00–22:00; **F:** 20:00–22:00. Spec: Africana. Mem: Private Libraries Association. Notes: deals in Africana only, in indigenous peoples, anthropology, history, ethnology and ethnographic. [Updated]

Butler Books, 3 Denewood Road, Bournemouth, BH4 8EB. Prop: B.H. & M.E. Butler. Tel: (01202) 764185. Web: www.abebooks.com. E-mail: bandmbutler@telco4u.net. Est: 1980. Private premises. Postal only. Appointment necessary. Stock: medium. Spec: History of Ideas; Oriental; Religion - General; Religion - Christian; Religion - Jewish; Theology. PR: £10–5,000. CC: AE; JCB; MC; V; SW, Solo. Corresp: French, German. [Updated]

Dunstan Books, 13 Lascelles Road, Bournemouth, BH7 6NF. Tel: (01202) 246160. Fax: (01202) 246160. Web: www.abebooks.com.com. E-mail: dunstanbooks@aol.com. Est: 1992. Private premises. Internet and postal. Open: **M:** 09:00–18:00; **T:** 09:00–18:00; **W:** 09:00–18:00; **Th:** 09:00–18:00; **F:** 09:00–18:00; **S:** 09:00–17:00. Stock: small. Spec: Bridge; Crime (True); Fiction - Crime, Detective, Spy, Thrillers; Medicine; Politics; Psychotherapy; Sport - Golf. PR: £5–200. VAT No: GB 797 8711 57. [Updated]

Facet Books, 67 Bennett Road, Bournemouth, BH8 8RH. Prop: Mr James Allinson and Mrs Margit Allinson. Tel: (01202) 269269. Web: www.jallinson.freeserve.co.uk. E-mail: jim@jallinson.freeserve.co.uk. Est: 1982. Private premises. Internet and postal. Telephone first. Stock: large. Spec: Academic/Scholarly; Advertising; Aeronautics; Cartoons; Catalogues Raisonnes; Children's; Comedy; Comic Books & Annuals. PR: £1–2,500. CC: MC; V; Switch. Corresp: German. Mem: FSB. [Updated]

Holdenhurst Books, ■ 275, Holdenhurst Road, Bournemouth, BH8 8BZ. Prop: R.W. Reese. Tel: (01202) 397718. Est: 1985. Shop open: **M:** 10:00–17:00; **T:** 09:00–17:00; **Th:** 10:00–17:00; **F:** 10:00–17:00; **S:** 10:00–17:00. Stock: medium. Spec: Aeronautics; Freemasonry & Anti-Masonry; Furniture; Geology; Ghosts; Motorbikes / motorcycles; Motoring. PR: £5–150. [Updated]

P.F. & J.R. McInnes, 59, Richmond Park Road, Bournemouth, BH8 8TU. Tel: (01202) 394609. E-mail: jane.mcinnes@ntlworld.com. Est: 1981. Private premises. Appointment necessary. Stock: very small. Spec: Dogs; Sport - Boxing. PR: £1–3,000. Notes: Kennell Club Stud books 1903 & 1904, 1949-1990 [Updated]

H. & S.J. Rowan, ■ 459 Christchurch Road, Boscombe, Bournemouth, BH1 4AD. Tel: (01202) 398820. Est: 1969. Shop open: **M:** 09:00–18:00; **T:** 09:00–18:00; **W:** 09:00–18:00; **Th:** 09:00–18:00; **F:** 09:00–18:00; **S:** 09:00–18:00. Stock: large. Spec: Antiquarian; Antiques; Art; Aviation; Topography - Local. PR: £1–1,000. Notes: also, bookearch. VAT No: GB 185 3287 39. [Updated]

Sue Sims, 21 Warwick Road, Pokesdown, Bournemouth, BH7 6JW. Tel: (01202) 432562. E-mail: reggierhino@aol.com. Est: 1978. Private premises. Postal only. Contactable. Stock: very small. Spec: Authors:- Brent-Dyer, Elinor M.; Fairlie–Bruce, D.; Forest, A.; Oxenham, Elsie; Children's; Religion - Catholic; Booksearch. PR: £1–500. Corresp: French, German. Notes: Major stock of girl's books and school stories. [24/12/2004]

Yesterday Tackle & Books, Southbourne, Bournemouth. Prop: David Dobbyn. Tel: (01202) 476586. E-mail: d.dobin@ntlworld.com. Est: 1983. Private premises. Appointment necessary. Stock: very small. Spec: Author - Watkins-Pitchford, Denys ('B.B.'); Sport - Angling/Fishing; Ephemera. PR: £1–100. CC: AE; PayPal. Notes: fishing tackle and related items. [Updated]

Yesterday's Books, 6 Cecil Avenue, Bournemouth, BH8 9EH. Prop: David & Jessica L. Weir. Tel: (01202) 522442. E-mail: djl.weir@btinternet.com. Est: 1974. Office and/or bookroom. Internet and postal. Telephone first. Open: **M:** 09:00–17:00; **T:** 09:00–17:00; **W:** 09:00–17:00; **Th:** 09:00–17:00; **F:** 09:00–17:00; **S:** 09:00–13:00. Stock: medium. Spec: Anthropology; Countries - Africa; Egyptology; Ethnography; History - General; Literary Travel; Literature; Pacifism. PR: £5–500. CC: JCB; MC; V. Corresp: French, German. Mem: PBFA. [Updated]

BRIDPORT

Bridport Old Bookshop, ■ 11 South Street, Bridport, DT6 3NR. Prop: Caroline Mactaggart & Rosie Young. Tel: (01308) 425689. E-mail: caroline@TextBiz.com. Est: 1981. Shop open: **M:** 10:00–05:00; **T:** 10:00–05:00; **W:** 10:00–05:00; **Th:** 10:00–05:00; **F:** 10:00–05:00; **S:** 10:00–05:00. Stock: small. Spec: Children's. PR: £2–500. CC: MC; V. Mem: PBFA. [Updated]

Caroline Mactaggart, Manor Farmhouse, Swyre, Bridport, Dorchester, DT2 9DN. Tel: (01308) 898174. E-mail: caroline@textbiz.com. Est: 1984. Private premises. Contactable. M: 10:00–17:00; **T:** 10:00–17:00; **W:** 10:00–17:00; **Th:** 10:00–17:00; **F:** 10:00–17:00; **S:** 10:00–17:00. Stock: medium. Spec: Scottish Interest. PR: £5–500. CC: MC; V. Mem: PBFA. [Updated]

CHARMOUTH

The Lighthouse Books, ■ Langley House, The Street, Charmouth, DT6 6PE. Prop: Mr Jean Vaupres. Tel: (01297) 560634. Est: 2004. Shop open: **M:** 10:00–17:00; **T:** 10:00–17:00; **Th:** 10:00–17:00; **F:** 10:00–17:00; **S:** 10:00–17:00; **Su:** 10:00–17:00. Stock: medium. Spec: Architecture; Country Houses; Fashion & Costume; Folio Society, The; Irish Interest; Odd & Unusual; Sculpture; Travel - General. PR: £1–300. Corresp: French, Italian. Notes: outside school holidays, open 10:00 – 17:00 Friday to Monday: Easter to end October. Phone first at other times [14/12/2004]

DORCHESTER

The Dorchester Bookshop, ■ 3 Nappers Court, Charles Street, Dorchester, DT1 1EE. Prop: Michael J. Edmonds. Tel: (01305) 269919. Est: 1993. Shop open: **T:** 10:00–17:00; **W:** 10:00–17:00; **Th:** 10:00–17:00; **F:** 10:00–17:00; **S:** 10:00–17:00. Stock: medium. PR: £1–500. [Updated]

Marco Polo Travel & Adventure, Marco Polo House, West Bexington, Dorchester, DT2 9DE. Mark A. Culme-Seymour. Tel: (01308) 898420. Fax: (01308) 898416. Web: www.marcopolobooks.co.uk. E-mail: mark@marcopolobooks.co.uk. Est: 1977. Private premises. Internet and postal. Appointment necessary. Stock: very small. Spec: Travel - General. PR: £15–300. CC: MC; V. Notes: booksearch. VAT No: GB 717 8378 00. [Updated]

Judith Stinton, 21 Cattistock Road, Maiden Newton, Dorchester, DT2 OAG. Tel: (01300) 320778. Web: www.abebooks.com. E-mail: judithstinton@hardycountry.fsnet.co.uk. Est: 1989. Private premises. Internet and postal. Appointment necessary. Stock: very small. Spec: Children's; Literature; Topography - Local. PR: £1–100. [Updated]

Steve Walker Fine Books, 1 Sydenham Way, Dorchester, DT1 1DN. Tel: 01350 260690. E-mail: vectaphile@hotmail.com. Est: 1985. Private premises. Postal only. Appointment necessary. Stock: very small. Spec: Author - Hardy, Thomas; Author - Johnson, Samuel; Bookbinding; Books about Books; Languages - National; Literature; Occult; Religion - General. PR: £5–500. Mem: Society of Bookbinders. Bookbinding and Restoration. [Updated]

Woolcott Books, Kingston House, Higher Kingston, Dorchester, DT2 8QE. Prop: H.M. & J.R. St. Aubyn. Tel: (01305) 267773. Fax: (01305) 751899. Est: 1978. Private premises. Appointment necessary. Stock: small. Spec: Colonial; Countries - Africa; Countries - India; History - National; Military; Travel - Africa; Travel - Asia; Travel - Middle East. PR: £5–500. Notes: also, booksearch. [Updated]

Available from Richard Joseph Publishers Ltd
BOOK DEALING FOR PROFIT
by Paul Minet

(Quarto H/b) £10.00 144pp

DORSET

Words Etcetera Bookshop, ■ 2, Cornhill, Dorchester, DT1 1BA. Prop: Julian Nangle. Tel: 01305 267872. Fax: 01305 251919. Web: www.wordsetcetera.co.uk. E-mail: jnangle@wordsetcetera.co.uk. Est: 1974. Shop open: **M:** 10:00–17:00; **T:** 10:00–17:00; **W:** 10:00–17:00; **Th:** 10:00–17:00; **F:** 10:00–17:00; **S:** 10.00–17:30. Spec: Antiquarian; Art; Art History; Authors: Hardy, Thomas; Heaney, Seamus; Lawrence, T.E.; Powys Family, The; Woolf, Virginia. CC: MC; V. Cata: quarterly on Illustrated, Poetry, Mod firsts, T.Hardy. Corresp: French. Mem: PBFA; We have a few shelves rented out to other booksellers, specialising in antiquarian maps, collectible childrens,military history and Dorset topography. [Updated]

Stour Bookshop, ■ Bridge Street, Sturminster Newton, Dorset, DT10 1AP. Prop: Tony Butler. Tel: (01258) 473561. Est: 1982. Shop open: **M:** 10:00–18:00; **T:** 10:00–18:00; **W:** 10:00–18:00; **Th:** 10:00–18:00; **F:** 10:00–18:00; **S:** 10:00–13:00. Stock: very small. Spec: Aviation; Juvenile; Motoring; Vintage Cars. PR: £5–200. CC: MC; V. [Updated]

GILLINGHAM

DaSilva Puppet Books, 58 Shreen Way, Gillingham, SP8 4HT. Prop: Ray DaSilva. Tel: (01747) 835558. Fax: (01747) 835558. Web: www.puppetbooks.co.uk. E-mail: dasilva@puppetbooks.co.uk. Est: 1986. Private premises. Internet and postal. Appointment necessary. Open: **M:** 09:00–17:30; **T:** 09:00–17:30; **W:** 09:00–17:30; **Th:** 09:00–17:30; **F:** 09:00–17:30; Closed for lunch: 12:30–02:00. Stock: very small. Spec: Entertainment - General; Performing Arts; Puppets & Marionettes; Theatre; Ephemera. PR: £1–200. CC: MC; V; SW. Corresp: French. VAT No: GB 119 7586 34. [Updated]

Lilian Modlock, Southcote, Langham Lane, Wyke, Gillingham, SP8 5NT. Tel: (01747) 821875. Fax: (01747) 821875. E-mail: lilianmodlock@waitrose.com. Est: 1995. Private premises. Postal only. Appointment necessary. Stock: medium. Spec: Biography; Children's; Cinema/Film; Cookery/ Gastronomy; Illustrated; Landscape; Poetry; Topography - General. PR: £3–600. Notes: also, a booksearch service [Updated]

LONG BURTON

Grahame Thornton, Bookseller, Monghyr House, Spring Lane, Long Burton, Sherborne, DT9 5NZ. Prop: Grahame Thornton. Tel: 01963 210443. Fax: 01963 210443. Web: www.grahamethornton. f9.co.uk. E-mail: grahame@grahamethornton.f9.co.uk. Est: 1995. Private premises. Internet and postal. Contactable. M: 09:00–17:30; **T:** 09:00–17:30; **W:** 09:00–17:30; **Th:** 09:00–17:30; **F:** 09:00–17:30; **S:** 09:00–17:30; **Su:** 09:00–17:30; Closed for lunch: 13:00–14:00. Spec: Animals and Birds; Antiquarian; Autobiography; Belle-Lettres; Biography; Children's; Churchilliana; Classical Studies. CC: E; MC; V; Maestro. Cata: (lists) on Early Penguin, Antiquarian, Non Fiction, Medical. Corresp: French. Notes: Catalogues are not issued, but lists can be produced on demand. Visit my website to see the subjects covered. Regular stall at the monthly Sherborne Book Market VAT No: GB 608 6389 14. [Updated]

LYME REGIS

The Bookshop, ■ The Old Bonded Store, Marine Parade, The Cobb, Lyme Regis, DT7 3JF. Tel: 01297 444820. Est: 2003. Shop open: **M:** 11:00–16:00; **T:** 11:00–16:00; **W:** 11:00–16:00; **Th:** 11:00–16:00; **F:** 11:00–16:00; **S:** 11:00–16:00; **Su:** 11:00–16:00; Closed for lunch: –14:00. Spec: Children's; Fiction - General; History - General; Maritime/Nautical; Mind, Body & Spirit; Philosophy; Plays; Poetry. Notes: Opening hours stated apply to school holidays, otherwise Friday, Saturday and Sunday every week. Answerphone gives additonal days open. [Updated]

Lymelight Books & Prints, ■ 1 Drakes Way, Lyme Regis, DT7 3QP. Prop: Nigel Cozens. Tel: (01297) 443464. Fax: (01297) 443464. Web: www.lymelight-books.demon.co.uk. E-mail: nigel@lymelight-books.demon.co.uk. Est: 1994. Shop open: **M:** 10:00–18:00; **T:** 10:00–18:00; **W:** 10:00–18:00; **Th:** 10:00–18:00; **F:** 10:00–18:00; **S:** 10:00–18:00; **Su:** 10:00–18:00. Stock: medium. Spec: Antiquarian; Art; Atlases; Authors: Darwin, Charles; Fowles, John; Hardy, Thomas; Lawrence, T.E.; Children's - Illustrated. PR: £5–10,000. CC: AE; E; MC; V; Cirrus. Corresp: French. Mem: PBFA; Notes: bookbinding and booksearch. Print & mapsearch and restoration. VAT No: GB 684 4800 14. [Updated]

The Bookshop, ■ The Old Bonded Store, Marine Parade, The Cobb, Lyme Regis, BT7 3JF. Prop: Ms L. Forman. Tel: (01297) 444820. Est: 2003. Shop open: **F:** 11:00–16:30; **S:** 11:00–16:30. Stock: medium. Spec: Fiction - General; Maritime/Nautical; Poetry. PR: £1–100. Notes: open weekends in summer, phone first. Also, fossils. [Updated]

The Sanctuary Bookshop, 65 Broad Street, Lyme Regis, DT7 3QF. Prop: Bob & Mariko Speer. Tel: 00-44-(0)1297-445815. Web: www.lyme-regis.com. E-mail: books@lyme-regis.com. Est: 1982. Shop and/or showroom open: **M:** 10.30–17:30; **T:** 10.00–17:30; **W:** 10.00–17:30; **Th:** 10.00–17:30; **F:** 10.00–17:30; **S:** 10.00–17:30; **Su:** 10.00–17:30. Spec: Academic/Scholarly; Art History; Art Reference; Authors:- Fowles, John; Shute, Neville; Authors - Local; Bibliography; Biography. CC: AE; E; JCB; MC; V. Corresp: Japanese. Notes: general Bookshop on two floors + two floors above with B&B accomodation. Two doubles, each with private bath. Antiques and curiosa. John Fowles, Beryl Cook, and Hundertwasser stockists. Free booksearch. Japanese spoken. Internet Access [Updated]

MILBORNE PORT

Kingswood Books, 17 Wick Road, Milborne Port, Sherborne, DT9 5BT. Prop: Anne Rockall & Allan Dollery. Tel: (01963) 250280. Fax: (01963) 250280. Web: www. kingswoodbooks.btinternet.co.uk. E-mail: kingswoodbooks@btinternet.com. Est: 1985. Private premises. Internet and postal. Appointment necessary. Stock: medium. Spec: Academic/Scholarly; Advertising; Anthropology; Antiquarian; Archaeology; Art History; Egyptology; Genealogy. PR: £1–2,000. CC: JCB; MC; V; Switch. Mem: PBFA. Notes: Various book fairs listed on our web site. Also bookbinders & restorers. See our web site. [Updated]

POOLE

Bookstand, 53 Kings Ave., Poole, BH14 9QQ. Prop: Eleanor Smith & Wendy Marten. Tel: (01202) 716229. Fax: (01202) 734663. Web: www.abebooks.com/home/bookstand. E-mail: bookstand@lineone.net. Est: 1997. Private premises. Internet Only. Appointment necessary. Stock: small. Spec: Authors:- Thelwell, N; Wheatley, Dennis; Autographs; Humour; Illustrated; Manuscripts; Modern First Editions; Poetry. PR: £15–5,000. CC: MC; V. [Updated]

Branksome Books, 33a Kings Avenue, Poole, BH14 9QG. Prop: P.G. Bryer–Ash Tel: (01202) 730235. Est: 1988. Private premises. Appointment necessary. Open: Stock: very small. Spec: Author - Lawrence, T.E.; Sport - Angling/Fishing; Sport - Field Sports. PR: £5–200. Corresp: French, Spanish. [Updated]

R.H. & P. Haskell, 64 Winston Avenue, Branksome, Poole, BH12 1PG. Tel: (01202) 744310. Fax: (01202) 744310. E-mail: rhandp@btinternet.com. Est: 1973. Private premises. Postal only. Appointment necessary. Stock: very small. PR: £5–1,000. Notes: also, bookbinding service. [Updated]

Christopher Williams, 19 Morrison Avenue, Parkstone, Poole, BH12 4AD. Prop: Christopher & Pauline Williams. Tel: (01202) 743157. Fax: (01202) 743157. Web: www.abebooks.com/home/cw. E-mail: cw4finebooks@lineone.net. Est: 1967. Private premises. Internet and postal. Appointment necessary. Stock: very small. Spec: Arts, The; Bibliography; Cookery/Gastronomy; Crafts; Lace; Topography - Local. PR: £5–100. CC: MC; V. Mem: PBFA. [Updated]

PUDDLETOWN

The Antique Map and Bookshop, ■ 32 High Street, Puddletown, DT2 8RU. Prop: C.D. & H.M. Proctor. Tel: (01305) 848633. Fax: (01305) 848992. Web: www.puddletownbookshop.co.uk. E-mail: sales@puddletownbookshop.co.uk. Est: 1976. Internet and postal. Shop open: **M:** 09:00–17:00; **T:** 09:00–17:00; **W:** 09:00–17:00; **Th:** 09:00–17:00; **F:** 09:00–17:00; **S:** 09:00–17:00. Stock: medium. Spec: Authors:- Barnes, William; Conan Doyle, Sir Arthur; Hardy, Thomas; Henty, G.A.; Lawrence, T.E.; Wells, H.G.; Fine & Rare; Illustrated. PR: £5–3,000. CC: AE; JCB; MC, V; SW. Corresp: German. Mem: ABA; PBFA; ILAB. VAT No: GB 291 7495 21. [Updated]

Looking for a dealer in EPHEMERA?

Then search Sheppard's on-line directories at:

www.sheppardsworld.co.uk

SHAFTESBURY

Paul Goldman, Meadow View, East Orchard, Shaftesbury, SP7 0LG. Tel: (01747) 811380. Fax: (01747) 811380. Web: www.abebooks.com. E-mail: goldman@clara.net. Est: 1997. Private premises. Postal only. Appointment necessary. Stock: small. Spec: Academic/Scholarly; Art; Art History; Art Reference; Cartoons; Comedy; Humour; Illustrated. PR: £10–500. Corresp: French, Italian, Greek. Mem: ABA; PBFA; ILAB. [Updated]

Not Just Books, ■ 7a High Street, Shaftesbury, SP7 8QZ. Prop: F. W. Barrett-Selbie. Tel: 01747 850003. E-mail: ntrevor67@supanet.com. Est: 1996. Shop open: **W:** 10:00–16:30; **Th:** 10:00–17:30; **F:** 10:00–17:30; **S:** 10:00–17:30; Closed for lunch: 12:30–14:00. [Updated]

SHERBORNE

Chapter House Books, ■ Trendle Street, Sherborne, DT9 3NT. Prop: Claire Porter, Tudor Books Ltd. Tel: (01935) 816262. Web: www.chapterhouse-books.co.uk. E-mail: chapterhousebooks@tiscali.co.uk. Est: 1988. Shop open: **M:** 10:00–17:00; **T:** 10:00–17:00; **W:** 10:00–17:00; **Th:** 10:00–17:00; **F:** 10:00–17:00; **S:** 10:00–17:00. Stock: large. Spec: Booksearch. PR: £1–500. CC: MC; V. Also, 2nd hand CDs, videos and sheet music VAT No: GB 799 9885 07. [Updated]

Verandah Books, Stonegarth, The Avenue, Sherborne, DT9 3AH. Prop: Michael Hougham. Tel: (01935) 815900. Fax: (01935) 815900. Web: www.verandah.demon.co.uk. E-mail: mah@verandah.demon.co.uk. Est: 1992. Private premises. Postal only. Appointment necessary. Stock: medium. Spec: Author - Kipling, Rudyard; Countries - Afganistan; Countries - Burma; Countries - Himalayas, The; Countries - India; Countries - Nepal; Countries - Pakistan; Countries - South East Asia. PR: £10–500. [Updated]

STALBRIDGE

March House Books, March House, Thornhill Road, Stalbridge, DT10 2PS. Prop: Mrs. Barbara Fisher. Tel: (01963) 364403. Fax: (01963) 364405. Web: www.marchhousebooks.com. E-mail: books@marchhousebooks.com. Est: 1997. Private premises. Internet and postal. Stock: small. Spec: Children's; Illustrated. PR: £5–650. CC: PayPal. [Updated]

STOBOROUGH

Calluna Books, 54 Corfe Road, Stoborough, Wareham, BH20 5AF. Prop: Y. Gartshore. Tel: (01929) 552560 evenings. E-mail: neil&yuki@onaga54.freeserve.co.uk. Est: 1997. Private premises. Internet Only. Appointment necessary. Stock: small. Spec: Botany; Entomology; Natural History; New Naturalist; Ornithology. PR: £5–300. Notes: also, attends specialist bird fairs. [Updated]

SWANAGE

Reference Works Ltd., 9 Commercial Road, Swanage, BH19 1DF. Tel: (01929) 424423. Fax: (01929) 422597. Web: www.referenceworks.co.uk. E-mail: sales@referenceworks.co.uk. Est: 1984. Office and/or bookroom. Telephone first. Stock: small. Spec: Antiques; Ceramics; Decorative Art. PR: £5–800. CC: MC; V. [Updated]

WAREHAM

Reads, Beehive Cottage, East Stoke, Wareham, BH20 4JW. Prop: Reg Read & Anthony Hessey. Tel: (01929) 554971, or 5. E-mail: reginaldreads@aol.com. Est: 1998. Private premises. Postal only. Stock: small. Spec: Anthroposophy; Applied Art; Archaeology; Architecture; Art; Autobiography; Biography; Cinema/Film. PR: £5–3,000. CC: JCB; MC; V. Corresp: French. Mem: PBFA. Notes: Exhibits at major PBFA fairs. [Updated]

WEYMOUTH

Books Afloat, ■ 66 Park Street, Weymouth, DT4 7DE. Prop: John Ritchie. Tel: (01305) 779774. Est: 1983. Shop open: **M:** 09:30–17:30; **T:** 09:30–17:30; **W:** 09:30–17:30; **Th:** 09:30–17:30; **F:** 09:30–17:30; **S:** 09:30–17:30. Stock: large. Spec: Authors:- Hardy, Thomas; Powys Family, The; Aviation; Canals/Inland Waterways; Fiction - General; Maritime/Nautical; Military History; Navigation. PR: £1–140. Notes: also, maritime collectables, ephemera and postcards. [Updated]

The Nautical Antique Centre, ■ 3 Cove Passage, Hope Square, Weymouth, DT4 8TR. Prop: Mr D.C. Warwick. Tel: (01305) 777838. Web: www.nauticalantiques.org. E-mail: info@nauticalantiques.org. Est: 1989. Shop. Internet and postal. Telephone first. Open: **T:** 14:00–17:00; **W:** 10:00–17:00; **Th:** 10:00–17:00; **F:** 10:00–17:00; Closed for lunch: 13:00–14:00. Stock: very small. Spec: Judaica; Manuals - Seamanship (see also under Seamanship); Maritime/Natical - Log Books; Maritime/Nautical; Naval; Navigation; Shipbuilding and Shipping; Steam Engines. PR: £5–300. [Updated]

WIMBORNE MINSTER

John Graham, 52 Blandford Road, Corfe Mullen, Wimborne, BH21 3HQ. Prop: John Graham. Tel: (01202) 692397. Fax: (01202) 692397. Est: 1987. Private premises. Postal only. Stock: small. Spec: Biography; History - General; History - Industrial; History - Local; History - National; Social History; Booksearch; Ephemera. PR: £1–100. [Updated]

Minster Books, ■ 12 Corn Market, Wimborne Minster, BH21 1JL. Prop: John and Angela Child. Tel: 01202 883355. Web: www.minsterbooks.com. E-mail: minsterbooks@aol.com. Est: 1991. Shop open: **M:** 10:00–17:00; **T:** 10:00–17:00; **W:** 10:00–17:00; **Th:** 10:00–17:00; **F:** 10:00–17:00; **S:** 10:00–17:00; CC: MC; V. Notes: general stock. [Updated]

Looking for a dealer in PRINTS or MAPS?

Then search Sheppard's on-line directories at:

www.sheppardsworld.co.uk

DURHAM

BARNARD CASTLE

Book Aid, ■ 5 Galgate, Barnard Castle, DL12 8EQ. Prop: M J Abrahams. Tel: 01833 630209. Est: 1990. Shop open: **M:** 10:00–17:00; **T:** 10:00–17:00; **W:** 10:00–17:00; **Th:** 10:00–17:00; **F:** 10:00–17:00; **S:** 10:00–17:00. Spec: Theology. [Updated]

Books on the Bank, ■ 3 The Bank, Barnard Castle, DL12 8PH. Prop: Colin and Cathy Robinson. Tel: (01833) 695123. E-mail: bankbooks@btinternet.com. Est: 1999. Shop open: **T:** 10:00–16:00; **W:** 10:00–16:00; **Th:** 10:00–16:00; **F:** 10:00–16:00; **S:** 10:00–17:00. Stock: medium. Spec: Art Reference; History - General; Rural Life; Topography - Local; Ephemera. PR: £1–300. CC: AE; E; JCB; MC; V. Notes: Internet sales via abebooks.com. [Updated]

Curlews, ■ 11 Market Place, Barnard Castle, DL12 8NF. Prop: M. J. Abrahams. Tel: 01833 630455. Est: 1984. Shop. [Updated]

Greta Books, Lodge Farm, Scargill, Barnard Castle, DL12 9SY. Prop: Gordon Thomson. Tel: (01833) 621000. Fax: (01833) 621000. E-mail: Gretabooks@xemaps.com. Postal only. Spec: Authors:- Priestley, J.B.; Walsh, M.; Building & Construction; Countries - Scotland; Farming & Livestock; Fiction - General; First Editions; History - General. PR: £5–50. [Updated]

BILLINGHAM

Onepoundpaperbacks, 23 Roseberry Flats, The Causeway, Billingham, TS23 2LD. Prop: Stephen Phelps. Tel: 01642 643651. Web: www.onepoundpaperbacks.co.uk. E-mail: stephen.phelps@ntlworld.com. Est: 2003. Private premises. Internet Only. Spec: Adult; Fiction - Adventure; Fiction - Crime, Detective, Spy, Thrillers; Fiction - Fantasy, Horror; Fiction - Historical; Fiction - Romantic; Fiction - Science Fiction; Fiction - Westerns. CC: PayPal, Nochex, Moneybookers. Notes: Credit Card payments accepted through PayPal, Nochex, Moneybookers. [Updated]

BISHOP AUCKLAND

Vinovium Books, Wear Valley Business Centre, 27 Longfield Road, Bishop Auckland, DL14 6XB. Prop: Paul Hughes. Tel: (01388) 777770. Web: www.vinoviumbooks.co.uk. E-mail: enqrj@vinoviumbooks.co.uk. Est: 1996. Office and/or bookroom. Internet and postal. Appointment necessary. Stock: small. Spec: Academic/Scholarly; Antiquarian; History - Local; Military History; Sport - Angling/Fishing; Sport - Field Sports; Topography - Local. PR: £12–3,000. CC: JCB; MC; V; Switch. Mem: PBFA; DABA. VAT No: GB 746 9734 81. [Updated]

DARLINGTON

Combat Arts Archive, 12 Berkeley Road, Darlington, DL1 5ED. Prop: Mr. J. Sparkes. Tel: (01325) 465286. Web: www.combatbooks.co.uk. E-mail: johnsparkes@ntlworld.com. Est: 1995. Private premises. Postal only. Appointment necessary. Stock: small. Spec: Physical Culture; Sport - Boxing; Sport - Duelling; Sport - Fencing; Sport - Martial Arts; Sport - Weightlifting/Bodybuilding; Sport - Wrestling. PR: £1–150. CC: JCB; MC; V. [Updated]

Tony and Gill Tiffin, 144 Coniscliffe Road, Darlington, DL3 7RW. Prop: G.A. & M.G. Tiffin. Tel: (01325) 487274. E-mail: tony.tiffin@btinternet.com. Est: 1990. Private premises. Book Fairs Only. Appointment necessary. Stock: very large. Spec: Academic/Scholarly; Autobiography; Biography; Children's; Children's - Early Titles; Children's - Illustrated; Education & School; First Editions. PR: £1–1,000. Corresp: French. Mem: PBFA. Notes: attends PBFA and local book fairs. [Updated]

Jeremiah Vokes, ■ 61 Coniscliffe Road, Darlington, DL3 7EH. Prop: Jeremiah Vokes. Tel: (01325) 469449. Est: 1979. Shop open: **M:** 09:30–17:00; **T:** 09:30–17:00; **W:** 09:30–17:00; **Th:** 09:30–17:00; **F:** 09:30–17:00; **S:** 09:30–17:00; Closed for lunch: 12:00–13:00. Stock: medium. Spec: Fiction - Crime, Detective, Spy, Thrillers; Sherlockiana; Booksearch. PR: £1–1,000. Mem: PBFA. [Updated]

REDCAR

Xanadubooks, 16, Kirkleatham Lane, Redcar, TS10 5BZ. Prop: Sylvia & John Wallace. Tel: 01642 485516. Web: www.xanadubooks.co.uk. E-mail: sylvia@xanadubooks.co.uk. Est: 1987. Private premises. Internet and postal. Appointment necessary. Spec: Children's; Illustrated. CC: PayPal. [Updated]

STOCKTON-ON-TEES

P.R. Brown (Books), 39 Sussex Walk, Norton–on–Tees, Stockton-on-Tees, Cleveland, TS20 2RG. (*) Prop: P. Robinson–Brown. Tel: (01642) 871704. Est: 1975. Private premises. Appointment necessary. Stock: very small. Spec: Botany; History - Local; Ornithology; Prints and Maps. PR: £5–500. [Updated]

WILLINGTON

John Turton, ■ 83 High Street, Willington. Prop: John Turton. Tel: (01388) 747600. Fax: (01388) 746741. E-mail: johnturton@turtome.co.uk. Est: 1978. Shop open: **F:** 12:00–17:00; **S:** 10:00–17:00. Stock: large. Spec: Antiquarian; Bindings; Ecclesiastical History & Architecture; Free Thought; Genealogy; Heraldry; Journals; Military History. PR: £5–500. Notes: also at, 1-2 Cochrane Terrace, Willington (q.v.). [Updated]

John Turton, 1–2 Cochrane Terrace, Willington, Crook, DL15 0HN. Prop: John Turton. Tel: (01388) 745770. Fax: (01388) 746741. E-mail: johnturton@turtome.co.uk. Est: 1978. Private premises. Appointment necessary. Stock: large. Spec: Antiquarian; Bindings; Ecclesiastical History & Architecture; Free Thought; Genealogy; Heraldry; Journals; Military History. PR: £50–2,000. Notes: also at 83 High Street, Willington (q.v.) credit payments only by postal sales. [Updated]

Available from Richard Joseph Publishers Ltd
BOOKDEALING FOR PROFIT
by Paul Minet

Quarto H/b   £10.00 144pp

EAST SUSSEX

ALFRISTON

Much Ado Books, ■ 1 Steamer Cottage, High Street, Alfriston, BN26 5TY. Prop: Nash Robbins and Cate Olson. Tel: 01323 871222. Fax: 01323 871333. Web: www.muchadobooks.com. E-mail: shop@muchadobooks.com. Est: 2003. Shop open: **M:** 10:00–17:00; **T:** 10:00–17:00; **W:** 10:00–17:00; **Th:** 10:00–17:00; **F:** 10:00–17:00; **S:** 10:00–17:00; **Su:** 11:00–17:00. Spec: Art; Author - Bloomsbury Group, The; Children's; Cookery/Gastronomy; Fiction - General; Food & Drink. CC: MC; V. Mem: PBFA; Notes: literary lunches, and new books. [Updated]

David Summerfield Books, 4 Wingrove, The Tye, Alfriston, BN26 5TL. Tel: (01323) 870003. Est: 1987. Private premises. Appointment necessary. Stock: small. Spec: Sport - Cricket. PR: £5–500. [Updated]

BEXHIL

Raymond Elgar, 6 Blackfields Avenue, Bexhill, TN39 4JL. Prop: Raymond Elgar. Tel: (01424) 843539. Private premises. Postal only. Stock: very small. Spec: Bindings; Bookbinding; Magic & Conjuring; Music - General; Musical Instruments. [Updated]

BRIGHTON

Brighton Books, ■ 18 Kensington Gardens, Brighton, BN1 4AL. Prop: Paul Carmody & Catherine Clement. Tel: (01273) 693845. Fax: (01273) 693845. Est: 1996. Shop open: **M:** 10:00–18:00; **T:** 10:00–18:00; **W:** 10:00–18:00; **Th:** 10:00–18:00; **F:** 10:00–18:00; **S:** 10:00–18:00. Stock: large. Spec: Academic/Scholarly; Architecture; Art; Biography; Children's; Cinema/Film; Drama; Fiction - General. PR: £1–500. CC: AE; JCB; MC; V; SW. Corresp: French, German. [Updated]

Colin Page Books, ■ 36 Duke Street, Brighton, Prop: John Loska. Tel: 01273 325954. Est: 1969. Shop open: **M:** 09:30–17:30; **T:** 09:30–17:30; **W:** 09:30–17:30; **Th:** 09:30–17:30; **F:** 09:30–17:30; **S:** 09:30–17:30. CC: AE; D; MC; V. Mem: ABA; BA. Notes: attends ABA Olympia and Chelsea Fairs. VAT No: GB 550 5008 78. [Updated]

Cooks Books, 34 Marine Drive, Rottingdean, Brighton, BN2 7HQ. Prop: Tessa McKirdy. Tel: (01273) 302707. Fax: (01273) 301651. Est: 1975. Private premises. Appointment necessary. Stock: medium. Spec: Cookery/Gastronomy; Food & Drink; Ephemera. PR: £1–500. CC: MC; V. Corresp: French. VAT No: GB 509 0878 31. [Updated]

Dinnages Transport Publishing, P.O. Box 2210, Brighton, BN1 9WA. Prop: Mr. G. & Mrs. C. Dinnage. Tel: (01273) 601001. Fax: (0871) 433 8096. Web: www.Transport-Postcards.co.uk. E-mail: mail@dinnages.org.uk. Est: 1989. Storeroom. Internet and postal. Appointment necessary. Open: **S:** 12:00–16:00. Stock: very small. Spec: Buses/Trams; History - Local; Publishers - General; Railways; Transport; Collectables; Ephemera. PR: £1–25. CC: PayPal/Nox. Notes: Regular stall Maidstone Collectors Fair 5x pa plus others. Publisher of nostalgic transport & local photographs/postcards (& book distrubutor). [Updated]

Turner Donovan Military Books, 12 Southdown Avenue, Brighton, BN1 6EG. Tel: (01273) 566230. E-mail: tom@turnerdonovan.com. Est: 1985. Private premises. Postal only. Stock: medium. Spec: Countries - India; Military; Military History; War - Napoleonic; War - World War II; Ephemera. PR: £15–2,500. CC: MC; V. Notes: also, soldier's diaries, trench maps, memories and regimental histories. [Updated]

Elmo Books, The Lower Floor Workshop Floor, 7a Basin Road North, Brighton, BN41 1WA. Tel: 01273 439111. Web: www.stores.ebay.co.uk/elmo-books. E-mail: elmobooks@btconnect.com. Est: 2003. Warehouse; Internet Only. Contactable. Spec: Sport - General; Sport - Football (Soccer); Sport - Motor Racing. Notes: specialists in sports & motoring books. [Updated]

Fisher Nautical, Huntswood House, St. Helena Lane, Streat, Hassocks, Brighton, BN6 8SD. (*) Prop: S. & J. Fisher. Tel: (01273) 890273. Fax: (01273) 891439. Web: www.fishernauticalbooks.co.uk. E-mail: fishernautical@seabooks.fsnet.co.uk. Est: 1969. Private premises. Postal only. Telephone first. Stock: very large. Spec: Maritime/Nautical; Booksearch. PR: £10–3,000. CC: MC; V. Mem: PBFA. [Updated]

Invisible Books, Unit 8, 15-26 Lincoln Cottage Works, Lincoln Cottages, Brighton, BN2 9UJ. Prop: Paul Holman & Bridget Penney. Tel: (01273) 694574. Fax: (0870) 052 2755. Web: www.invisiblebooks.net. E-mail: invisible@invisiblebooks.demon.co.uk. Est: 1994. Storeroom. Internet and postal. Appointment necessary. Stock: medium. Spec: Academic/Scholarly; Counterculture; New Age. PR: £1–1,000. VAT No: GB 825 8052 27. [Updated]

Kenya Books, 31 Southdown Ave., Brighton, BN1 6EH. Prop: J. McGivney. Tel: (01273) 556029. Web: www.abebooks.com/home/kenyabooks. E-mail: info@kenyabooks.com. Private premises. Internet and postal. Open: **M:** 09:00–19:00; **W:** 09:00–19:00; **Th:** 09:00–19:00; **F:** 09:00–19:00; **S:** 09:00–19:00. Stock: medium. Spec: Africana; Countries - Africa; Countries - France; Countries - Indian Ocean, The; Countries - Ireland; Countries - Kenya; Countries - South Africa; Countries - Tanzania. PR: £1–500. Corresp: French; Swahili. [Updated]

Rainbow Books, ■ 28 Trafalgar Street, Brighton, BN1 4ED. Prop: Kevin Daly. Tel: (01273) 605101. Est: 1998. Shop open: **M:** 10:30–18:00; **T:** 10:30–18:00; **W:** 10:30–18:00; **Th:** 10:30–18:00; **F:** 10:30–18:00; **S:** 10:30–18:00. Stock: very large. PR: £1–20. [Updated]

Savery Books, ■ 257 Ditchling Road, Brighton, BN1 6JH. Prop: Marianne, James, Sarah & Anne Savery. Tel: 01273 503030. E-mail: saverybooks@aol.com. Est: 1992. Shop open: **M:** 10:00–16:00; **T:** 10:00–14:00; **W:** 10:00–14:00; **Th:** 10:00–16:00; **F:** 10:00–16:00; **S:** 10:00–16:00. Spec: Art History; Counselling; Gardening - General; History - Local; History - Military; History of Ideas; Military History; Mind, Body & Spirit. [Updated]

Liz Seeber, Old Vicarage, 3 College Road, Brighton, BN2 1JA. Tel: (01273) 684949. Web: www.lizseeberbooks.co.uk. E-mail: seeber.books@virgin.net. Est: 1994. Private premises. Postal only. Appointment necessary. Stock: small. Spec: Cookery/Gastronomy; Gardening - General; Booksearch. PR: £5–3,000. CC: MC; V. VAT No: GB 629 3954 04. [Updated]

Studio Bookshop, ■ 68 St. James's Street, Brighton, BN2 1PJ. Prop: Paul Brown. Tel: 01273-691253. Web: www.studiobookshop.co.uk. E-mail: studiobookshop@btconnect.com. Est: 1995. Shop open: **M:** 11.00–17:00; **T:** 11.00–17:00; **W:** 11.00–17:00; **F:** 11.00–17:00; **S:** 11.00–17:00. Spec: Academic/Scholarly; Antiques; Art; Art Reference; Artists; European Studies; Exhibitions; History - British. CC: JCB; MC; V; Maestro, Visa Electron. Cata: occasionally on Glass, Exhibition Catalogues. Corresp: French, Spanish. [Updated]

Trafalgar Bookshop, ■ 44 Trafalgar Street, Brighton, BN1 4ED. Prop: David Boland. Tel: (01273) 684300. Est: 1979. Shop open: **M:** 10:00–17:15; **T:** 10:00–17:15; **W:** 10:00–17:15; **Th:** 10:00–17:15; **F:** 11:00–17:15; **S:** 10:00–17:15. Stock: medium. Spec: Children's; Children's - Illustrated; Cinema/Film; Literature; Mind, Body & Spirit; Philosophy; Psychic; Sport - General. PR: £1–200. [Updated]

Waxfactor, ■ 24 Trafalgar Street, Brighton, BN1 4EQ. Prop: M. Driver. Tel: (01273) 673744. Est: 1985. Shop open: **M:** 10:00–17:30; **T:** 10:00–17:30; **W:** 10:00–17:30; **Th:** 10:00–17:30; **F:** 10:00–17:30; **S:** 10:00–17:30. Stock: medium. Spec: Art; Astrology; Cinema/Film; Esoteric; Fiction - Science Fiction; History - General; Literature; Occult. PR: £1–25. CC: JCB; MC; V; Mae, Solo. Notes: also, records & CDs, DVDs and tapes. [Updated]

CROWBOROUGH

Ray Hennessey Bookseller, Panfield House, Crowborough Hill, Crowborough, TN6 2HJ. Prop: Ray & Deanna Hennessey. Tel: (01892) 653704. Fax: (0870) 0548776. Web: www.rayhennesseybookseller.co.uk. E-mail: rayhen@books4.demon.co.uk. Est: 1954. Private premises. Internet and postal. Appointment necessary. Open: **M:** 10:00–17:00; **T:** 10:00–17:00; **W:** 10:00–17:00; **Th:** 10:00–17:00; **F:** 10:00–17:00; **S:** 10:00–17:00. Stock: medium. Spec: Africana; Antiquarian; Antiques; Applied Art; Art; Bibles; Canals/Inland Waterways; Children's - Illustrated. PR: £6–1,000. CC: AE; E; JCB; MC; V. Mem: PBFA. Notes: Olinda House, Rotherfield East, Sussex. Open to Public. [Updated]

Simply Read Books, Fielden Road, Crowborough, TN6 1TP. Prop: W.L. & W.P. Banks. Tel: 01892 664584. Web: www.abenooks.com. E-mail: Orders@simplyreadbooks.co.uk. Est: 1998. Private premises. Telephone first. Open: **M:** 09:00–17:30; **T:** 09:00–17:30; **W:** 09:00–17:30; **Th:** 09:00–17:30; **F:** 09:00–17:30; **S:** 09:00–17:30; **Su:** 09:00–17:30; Closed for lunch: 13:00–14:00. Spec: Crime (True); Modern First Editions; Travel - General; Booksearch. CC: MC; V. [Updated]

Dealers need to update their entry at least once a year.
Visit their page on
www.sheppardsworld.co.uk

DITCHLING

Kenneth Bal, 7 Mulberry Lane, Ditchling, BN6 8UH. Prop: Kenneth Ball. Tel: 01273 845000. Fax: 01273 844444. E-mail: kennethball@mistral.co.uk. Est: 1947. Storeroom. Appointment necessary. Spec: Journals; Marque Histories (see also motoring); Motorbikes / motorcycles; Motoring; Steam Engines; Traction Engines; Transport; Vintage Cars. PR: £5–1,000. Corresp: French. [Updated]

EAST HOATHLY

Claras Books, 20 High Street, East Hoathly, Nr Lewes, BN8 6EB. Prop: Jane Seabrook. Tel: 01825 840746. E-mail: claras@netway.co.uk. Est: 2000. Private premises. Internet and postal. Spec: CC: MC; V; Maestro. Notes: Large general stock. [Updated]

EASTBOURNE

Camilla's Bookshop, ■ 57 Grove Road, Eastbourne, BN21 4TX. Prop: Camilla Francombe & Stuart Broad. Tel: (01323) 736001. E-mail: camillasbooks@tiscali.co.uk. Est: 1976. Shop open: **M:** 10:00–17:30; **T:** 10:00–17:30; **W:** 10:00–17:30; **Th:** 10:00–17:30; **F:** 10:00–17:30; **S:** 10:00–17:30. Stock: very large. Spec: Aeronautics; Animals and Birds; Annuals; Arts, The; Aviation; Bindings; Botany; Children's. PR: £1–300. CC: E; MC; V; Mae, SO. Notes: Closed on Bank Holidays. VAT No: GB 583 7350 18. [Updated]

Roderick Dew, 10 Furness Road, Eastbourne, BN21 4EZ. Tel: (01323) 720239. Est: 1975. Private premises. Appointment necessary. Stock: small. Spec: Applied Art; Architecture; Bibliography; Fine Art. PR: £5–500. Corresp: French, German. [Updated]

Alan Gibbard Books, ■ 1 and 2 Calverley Walk, Eastbourne, BN21 4UP. Prop: Alan & Maria Tania Gibbard. Tel: (01323) 734128. Fax: (01323) 734128 Est: 1993. Shop open: **T:** 10:00–17:00; **W:** 10:00–17:00; **Th:** 10:00–17:00; **F:** 10:00–17:00; **S:** 10:00–17:00. Stock: medium. Spec: Natural History; Topography - Local; Travel - General. PR: £1–1,000. CC: AE; MC; V. Corresp: Italian, Spanish. Mem: PBFA. VAT No: GB 621 5744 53. [Updated]

Green Man Books, 14 Bath Road, Eastbourne, BN21 4UA. Prop: Jerry Bird. Tel: (01323) 735364. Web: www.greenman-books.co.uk. E-mail: greenmangallery@lineone.net. Est: 1999. Private premises. Appointment necessary. Spec: Antiquarian; Author - Powys Family, The; Esoteric; Fine & Rare; Folklore; Music - Folk & Irish Folk; Mythology; New Books. PR: £2–200. CC: D; E; JCB; MC; V; Maestro; Switch. Cata: occasionally. Mem: NMTA. Notes: also, new books, music, crafts and contemporary arts [Updated]

London & Sussex Antiquarian Books, Southwood, 15 Dittons Road, Eastbourne, BN21 1DR. Prop: Dr. G.B. Carruthers. Tel: (01323) 730857. Fax: (01323) 737550. E-mail: doctor.johnsons@virgin.net. Est: 1970. Postal only. Spec: Alternative Medicine; Dogs; Medicine - History of; Prints and Maps. PR: £10–100. [Updated]

Mellon's Books, ■ The Enterprise Centre, 1 Station Parade, Eastbourne, BN21 1BD. Tel: 01323749254. Web: www.mellonsbooks.co.uk. E-mail: mellonsbooks@yahoo.co.uk. Est: 2005. Shop open: **M:** 09:30–17:00; **T:** 10:00–16:00; **W:** 09:30–17:00; **Th:** 09:30–17:00; **F:** 09:30–17:00; **S:** 09:30–17:00; **Su:** Closed for lunch: 13:00–14:00. Spec: Academic/Scholarly; Author - 20th Century; Children's; Churchilliana; Cinema/Film; Cookery/Gastronomy; Drama; Famous People - Churchill, Sir Winston. CC: AE; MC; V; Maestro/Switch. Cata: occasionally. Corresp: Basic French. Updated]

R. & A. Books, 4 Milton Grange, 6 Arundel Road, Eastbourne, BN21 2EL. Prop: Robert Manning and Alan Millard. Tel: (01323) 647690. Web: www.raenterprises.co.uk/. E-mail: robert.manning@btinternet.com. Est: 2000. Private premises. Internet and postal. Stock: large. Spec: Academic/Scholarly; Advertising; Aeronautics; Africana; Agriculture; Almanacs; Alpinism/Mountaineering; Animals and Birds. PR: £1–500. Notes: worldwide orders accepted. Payment in sterling through PayPal. UK cheques accepted. [Updated]

HASTINGS

Boulevard Books, ■ Boulevard Book Shop, 32 George Street, Hastings, TN34 3EA. Prop: Graham Frost. Tel: 01424436521. Web: www.thehastingstrawler.co.uk. E-mail: hastingsbookshop@yahoo.co.uk. Est: 2004. Shop open: **M:** 10:30–17:30; **T:** 10:30–17:30; **W:** 10:30–17:30; **Th:** 10:30–17:30; **F:** 10:30–17:30; **S:** 10:30–17:30; **Su:** 10:30–17:30; Closed for lunch: 13:00–14:00. CC: Cash or Cheque only. Corresp: French German Swedish Dutch. Notes: open seven days a week and we only accept cash or cheques. [Updated]

Calendula Horticultural Books, 3 Amherst Garden, Hastings, TN34 1TU. Prop: Heiko Miles. Tel: (01424) 437591. Web: www.calendulabooks.com. E-mail: heiko@calendulabooks.com. Est: 1987. Private premises. Postal only. Stock: small. Spec: Flower Arranging; Gardening - General; Herbalism; Horticulture; Landscape; Ornithology; Plant Hunting. PR: £5–10,000. CC: JCB; V. [Updated]

Chthonios Books, 7 Tamarisk Steps, Off Rock-a-Nores Road, Hastings, TN34 3DN. Prop: Stephen Ronan. Tel: (01424) 433302. Web: www.esotericism.co.uk/index.htm. E-mail: service@esotericism.co.uk. Est: 1985. Private premises. Internet and postal. Telephone first. Stock: small. Spec: Alchemy; Classical Studies; Earth Mysteries; Egyptology; Hermeticism; Humanism; Literature in Translation; Occult. PR: £3–300. CC: MC; V; SW. SO. Corresp: French. [Updated]

High Street Book Shop, ■ High Street Book Shop, 78 High Street, Hastings, TN34 3EA. Prop: Graham Frost. Tel: 01424200833. E-mail: hastingsbookshop@yahoo.co.uk. Est: 1997. Shop open: **M:** 1030–17:30; **T:** 10:30–17:30; **W:** 10:30–17:30; **Th:** 10:30–17:30; **F:** 10:30–17:30; **S:** 10:30–17:30; **Su:** 10:30–17:30; Closed for lunch: 13:00–14:00. CC: cash or cheque only. Corresp: French, German, Italian, Spanish. Notes: we are open seven days a week and only accept cash or cheques [Updated]

Hoovey's Books, P.O. Box 27, St. Leonards–on–Sea, Hastings, TN37 6TZ. (*). Tel: (01424) 753407. Fax: (01424) 753407. Web: www.hooveys.co.uk. E-mail: books@hooveys.com. Est: 1968. Office and/or bookroom. Appointment necessary. Stock: small. Spec: Booksearch. Notes: catalogue printing, cleaning materials, jacket coverings. VAT No: GB 397 8504 94. [Updated]

Howes Bookshop, ■ Trinity Hall, Braybrooke Terrace, Hastings, TN34 1HQ. Prop: Miles Bartley. Tel: (01424) 423437. Fax: (01424) 460620. Web: www.howes.co.uk. E-mail: rarebooks@howes.co.uk. Est: 1921. Shop open: **M:** 09:30–17:00; **T:** 09:30–17:00; **W:** 09:30–17:00; **Th:** 09:29–17:00; **F:** 09:30–17:00; Closed for lunch: 13:00–14:00. Stock: large. Spec: Antiquarian; Bibliography; Bindings; Classical Studies; History - General; Literature; Theology; Topography - Local. PR: £1–5,000. CC: E; JCB; MC; V. Mem: ABA; PBFA. Notes: also, storeroom and attends bookfairs. [Updated]

Robert's Shop, ■ 68 High Street, Old Town, Hastings, TN34 3EW. Prop: Robert M. Mucci. Tel: (01424) 445340. Est: 1989. Shop open: **M:** 11:00–18:00; **T:** 11:00–18:00; **W:** 11:00–18:00; **Th:** 11:00–18:00; **F:** 11:00–18:00; **S:** 11:00–18:00; **Su:** 11:00–18:00. Stock: very small. Spec: Ephemera; Prints and Maps. PR: £1–10. [Updated]

Anthony Sillem, 9 Tackleway, Old Town, Hastings, TN34 3DE. Prop: Anthony Sillem. Tel: (01424) 446602. Fax: (01424) 446602. E-mail: tackletext@btopenworld.com. Est: 1994. Private premises. Appointment necessary. Stock: small. Spec: First Editions; Illustrated; Literature; Literature in Translation; Memoirs; Modern First Editions. PR: £10–2,000. CC: MC; V. Mem: PBFA. [Updated]

Underwater Books, 104d High Street, Hastings, TN24 3ES. Prop: J.A. Barak. Tel: (01424) 435905. Web: www.underwater-books.co.uk. E-mail: divingbooks@underwater-books.co.uk. Est: 1980. Office and/or bookroom. Internet and postal. Appointment necessary. Stock: very small. Spec: Sport - Diving/Sub-Aqua. PR: £10–150. CC: PayPal. Notes: books cover all aspects of diving. [Updated]

HEATHFIELD

Botting & Berry, ■ 41 High Street, Heathfield, TN21 8HU. Prop: John Botting and Dave Berry. Tel: (01435) 868555. Est: 2001. Shop open: **M:** 10:00–17:00; **T:** 10:00–17:00; **W:** 10:00–17:00; **Th:** 10:00–17:00; **F:** 10:00–17:00; **S:** 10:00–17:00. Stock: small. PR: £1–500. CC: MC; V. Notes: Fairs: Royal National, Bloomsbury, London. [Updated]

HOVE

J.F. Holleyman, 3 Portland Avenue, Hove, BN3 5NP. Tel: (01273) 410915. Private premises. Postal only. Appointment necessary. Stock: small. Spec: Photography. [Updated]

Are you making enough profit - if not then read

BOOKDEALING FOR PROFIT
by Paul Minet

Quarto H/b   Available from Richard Joseph Publishers Ltd   £10.00 144pp

Simon Hunter Antique Maps, 21 St Johns Road, Hove, BN3 2FB. Prop: Simon Hunter. Tel: (01273) 746983. Web: www.antiquemaps.org.uk. E-mail: simonhunter@fastnet.co.uk. Internet and postal. Stock: medium. PR: £5–1,000. CC: AE; E; JCB; MC; V. Corresp: French. Mem: IMCoS. Antique Maps only. VAT No: GB 587 4541 02. [Updated]

Whitehall Books, 3 Leighton Road, Hove, BN3 7AD. Prop: Peter Batten. Tel: (01273) 735252. Web: www.whitehallbooks.co.uk. E-mail: peterbatten@whitehallbooks.co.uk. Est: 1991. Private premises. Internet and postal. Appointment necessary. Stock: very small. Spec: Art; Crime (True); Criminology; Illustrated; Literary Criticism; Literature. PR: £1–100. Corresp: French, Russian. Notes: translation. Literary detective work and general literary information. [Updated]

LEWES

Richard Beaton, 24 Highdown Road, Lewes, BN7 1QD. Prop: Dr. Richard Beaton. Tel: (01273) 474147. Fax: (01273) 474147. Web: www.victorian-novels.co.uk. E-mail: richard@victorian-novels.co.uk. Est: 1996. Private premises. Internet and postal. Appointment necessary. Open: **M:** 09:00–18:00; **T:** 09:00–18:00; **W:** 09:00–18:00; **Th:** 09:00–18:00; **F:** 09:00–18:00; **S:** 09:00–18:00. Stock: small. Spec: Fiction - General; Literature - Victorian. PR: £5–1,000. CC: JCB; MC; V; SW. Corresp: French. Mem: PBFA. [Updated]

John Beck, 29 Mill Road, Lewes, BN7 2RU. Tel: (01273) 477555. Est: 1982. Office and/or bookroom. Postal only. Appointment necessary. Open: **M:** 10:00–16:00; **T:** 10:00–16:00; **W:** 10:00–16:00; **Th:** 10:00–16:00; **F:** 10:00–16:00; **S:** 10:00–16:00; **Su:** 10:00–16:00. Stock: small. Spec: Author - Blyton, Enid; Children's; Comic Books & Annuals; Comics; Juvenile; Ephemera. PR: £1–1,000. [Updated]

Bow Windows Book Shop, ■ 175 High Street, Lewes, BN7 1YE. Prop: Alan & Jennifer Shelley. Tel: (01273) 480780. Fax: (01273) 486686. Web: www.bowwindows.com. E-mail: rarebooks@bowwindows.com. Est: 1964. Shop open: **M:** 09:30–17:00; **T:** 09:30–17:00; **W:** 09:30–17:00; **Th:** 09:30–17:00; **F:** 09:30–17:00; **S:** 09:30–17:00. Stock: medium. Spec: Antiquarian; Artists; Author - Bloomsbury Group, The; Authors:- Rackham, Arthur; Sackville-West, Vita; Woolf, Virginia; Children's - Illustrated; Countries - China. PR: £1–5,000. CC: AE; MC; V. Corresp: German. Mem: ABA; PBFA; ILAB. VAT No: GB 370 1163 88. [28/07/2004]

Brimstones, Unit 6, Sewells Farm, Birdhole Lane, Barcombe, Lewes, BN8 5TJ. Prop: Geoff Kinderman. Tel: (01273) 401636. Fax: (01273) 400593. Web: www.brimstones.co.uk. E-mail: brimstonesZ@btconnect.com. Est: 1990. Storeroom. Contactable. Open: **M:** 09:00–16:00; **T:** 09:00–16:00; **W:** 09:00–16:00; **Th:** 09:00–16:00; **F:** 09:00–16:00. Stock: very large. Spec: Biography; History - General; International Affairs; Memoirs; Philosophy; Politics; Psychology/Psychiatry; Religion - General. PR: £1–500. CC: AE; MC; V; Maestro. VAT No: GB 550 1571 71. [Updated]

A. & Y. Cumming Limited, ■ 84 High Street, Lewes, BN7 1XN. Prop: A.J. Cumming. Tel: (01273) 472319. Fax: (01273) 486364. E-mail: a.y.cumming@ukgateway.net. Est: 1976. Shop open: **M:** 10:00–17:00; **T:** 10:00–17:00; **W:** 10:00–17:00; **Th:** 10:00–17:00; **F:** 10:00–17:00; **S:** 10:00–17:30. Stock: very large. Spec: Art; Bindings; Illustrated; Literature; Natural History; Topography - General; Travel - General. Mem: ABA. VAT No: GB 412 4098 80. [06/09/2004]

The Fifteenth Century Bookshop, ■ The Fifteenth Century House, 99/100 High Street, Lewes, BN7 1XH. Prop: Mrs S.J. Mirabaud. Tel: 01273 474160. Web: www.15thcenturybookshop.co.uk. E-mail: sj.mirabaud@tesco.net. Est: 1936. Shop open: **M:** 10:00–1730; **T:** 10:00–1730; **W:** 10:00–1730; **Th:** 10:00–1730; **F:** 10:00–1730; **S:** 10:00–1730. Spec: Authors:- Barker, Cecily M.; Bloomsbury Group, The; Blyton, Enid; Brent-Dyer, Elinor M.; Bruce, Mary Grant; Buckeridge, A.; Carroll, Lewis; Crompton, Richmal. CC: AE; MC; V. Corresp: French. Mem: PBFA. Notes: alternate web site: www.oldenyoungbooks.co.uk. [Updated]

Derek Wise, Berewood House, Barcombe, Lewes, BN8 5TW. Tel: (01273) 400559. Fax: (01273) 400559. E-mail: derekwise@pavilion.co.uk. Est: 1986. Private premises. Internet and postal. Appointment necessary. Stock: small. Spec: Author - Byron, Lord; Education & School; Literature; Maritime/Nautical; Military; Military History; Natural History; Naval. PR: £1–1,500. Corresp: French. Mem: PBFA. [13/10/2004]

NEWHAVEN

32 Seconds, ■ 32 High Street, Newhaven, BN9 9PD. Prop: G.G.J. Haynes. Tel: 01273 611350. Est: 2000. Shop open: **T:** 10:00–16:00; **W:** 10:00–16:00; **Th:** 10:00–16:00; **F:** 10:00–16:00; **S:** 10:00–16:00. Spec: Philately; Ephemera. [Updated]

PORTSLADE

Peter Scott, 14 Vale Road, Portslade, BN41 1GF. Prop: Peter Scott. Tel: (01273) 410576. Web: www.scottbooks.freeuk.com. E-mail: peter.scott45@btopenworld.com. Est: 1986. Private premises. Internet and postal. Appointment necessary. Stock: small. Spec: Academic/Scholarly; Art; History - General; Literature; Religion - General; Ephemera. PR: £1–200. [Updated]

ROBERTSBRIDGE

Spearman Books, ■ The Old Saddlery Bookshop, 56 High Street, Robertsbridge, TN32 5AP. Prop: John & Janet Brooman. Tel: (01580) 880631. Fax: (01580) 880631. E-mail: saddlerybooks@aol.com. Est: 1970. Shop open: **M:** 10:00–17:00; **T:** 10:00–17:00; **Th:** 10:00–17:00; **F:** 10:00–17:00; **S:** 09:00–17:00; Closed for lunch: 13:00–14:15. Stock: medium. Spec: Travel - General. PR: £1–1,000. Corresp: French. [Updated]

ROTHERFIELD

Kennedy & Farley, 2 Brook Cottages, New Road, Rotherfield, TN6 3JT. Prop: Helen Kennedy & Fran Farley. Tel: (01892) 853141. Web: www.kennedyandfarley.co.uk. E-mail: kennedyandfarley@care4free.net. Est: 1987. Private premises. Internet and postal. Telephone first. Stock: small. Spec: Modern First Editions; Sport - Horse Racing (inc. Riding/Breeding/Equestrian); Sport - Hunting. PR: £4–1,000. CC: PayPal. Corresp: French. Mem: PBFA. [Updated]

RYE

The Meads Book Service, ■ 4 & 5 Lion Street, Rye, TN31 7LB. Prop: Clive Ogden. Tel: (01797) 227057. Fax: (01797) 223769. E-mail: meadsbookservice@freenet.co.uk. Est: 1988. Shop open: **M:** 10:15–17:30; **T:** 10:15–17:30; **W:** 10:15–17:30; **Th:** 10:15–17:30; **F:** 10:15–17:30; **S:** 10:15–17:30; **Su:** 10:15–17:30. Stock: small. Spec: Antiquarian; Authors:- Benson, A.C.; Benson, E.F.; Benson, R.H.; Madox Ford, Ford; Thorndike, Russell; Wharton, Edith; Biography. PR: £1–200. Notes: also, a booksearch service. [Updated]

Rye Old Books, ■ 7 Lion Street, Rye, TN31 7LB. Prop: Ms Aoiffe Coleman. Tel: 01797 225410. Web: www.ukbookworld.com/members/ryeoldbooks. E-mail: rypeoldbooks@aol.com. Est: 1993. Shop open: **M:** 10:30–17:30; **T:** 10:30–17:30; **W:** 10:30–17:30; **Th:** 10:30–17:30; **F:** 10:30–17:30; **S:** 10:30–17:30; **Su:** 14:00–17:00. Spec: Antiquarian; Children's; Fiction - General; Fine & Rare; Illustrated; Irish Interest; Limited Editions; Literary Criticism. CC: E; MC; V. Notes: if calling in January - phone first. [Updated]

SALTDEAN

Ruth Kidson, 90 Lustrells Crescent, Saltdean, BN2 8FL. Prop: Mrs. G.R. Kidson. Tel: (01273) 307787. Web: www.ruthkidson.co.uk. E-mail: books@ruthkidson.co.uk. Est: 1992. Private premises. Internet and postal. Appointment necessary. Stock: small. PR: £5–800. CC: MC; V; Delta, Maestro. Mem: ABA; PBFA; ILAB; Rare Books Society. VAT No: GB 777 7852 58. [Updated]

N1 Books, 213 Marine Drive, Saltdean, BN2 8DA. Prop: Michael Sassen. Tel: 01273 301690. E-mail: michael@dogland.demon.co.uk. Est: 2001. Private premises. Internet and postal. Telephone first. Open: **M:** 11:00–23:30; **T:** 11:00–23:30; **W:** 11:00–23:30; **Th:** 11:00–23:30; **F:** 11:00–23:30; **S:** 11:00–23:30. Spec: Adult; Aeronautics; Antiquarian; Antiquities; Applied Art; Archaeology; Arms & Armour; Army, The. PR: £1 – 1,000. Cata: History, Illustrated, Bindings, Arts, Oddities. Corresp: none. [Updated]

ST. LEONARD'S–ON–SEA

John Gorton Booksearch, 22 Charles Road, St Leonard's-on-Sea, TN38 0QH. Prop: John Gorton. Tel: (0779) 1549 745. Est: 1983. Private premises. Appointment necessary. Stock: small. Spec: Art Reference; Fiction - Crime, Detective, Spy, Thrillers; Mathematics; Philosophy. PR: £1–200. Cata: occasionally on specialities. [Updated]

Bruce Holdsworth Books, Vale House, 9, Eversley Road, St Leonards-on-Sea, TN37 6QD. Prop: Bruce Holdsworth. Tel: (01424) 446400. Web: www.bruceholdsworthbooks.com. E-mail: Bruce@bruceholdsworthbooks.com. Est: 1993. Private premises. Internet and postal. Appointment necessary. Stock: medium. Spec: Art; Art History; Art Reference; Arts, The; Crafts; Decorative Art; Fine Art; Sculpture. PR: £15–5,000. CC: AE; JCB; MC; V; Maestro. Mem: PBFA; FRSA. Notes: Out of Print Art Book Search. New art books ordering service VAT No: GB 686 9604 74. [Updated]

The Book Jungle, ■ 24 North Street, St. Leonard's-on-Sea, TN38 0EX. Prop: Michael Gowen. Tel: (01424) 421187. Web: www.thebookjungle.co.uk. E-mail: mrgowen@yahoo.co.uk. Est: 1991. Shop. Internet and postal. Open: **T:** 10:00–16:00; **Th:** 10:00–16:00; **F:** 10:00–16:00; **S:** 10:00–16:00. Stock: large. PR: £1–20. [Updated]

Gerald Lee, Maritime Books, P.O. Box 7, St. Leonard's-on-Sea, TN38 8WX. Tel: (01424) 853006. Fax: (01424) 853006. E-mail: enquiries@leemaritimebooks.com. Est: 1990. Private premises. Internet and postal. Stock: small. Spec: Maritime/Nautical; Naval; Navigation; Ship Modelling; Shipbuilding and Shipping; Voyages & Discovery; Ephemera. PR: £2–400. CC: JCB; MC; V. VAT No: GB 690 7489 87. [Updated]

Raymond Kilgarriff, 15 Maze Hill, St. Leonard's-on-Sea, TN38 0HN. Tel: (01424) 426146. Web: www.ilab.org. E-mail: rmkilgarriff@btinternet.com. Est: 1947. Private premises. Internet and postal. Appointment necessary. Stock: very small. Spec: Academic/Scholarly; Antiquarian; Fine & Rare; History - General; Literature. PR: £100–2,000. CC: MC; V. Mem: ABA; ILAB. VAT No: GB 794 2047 15. [Updated]

TICEHURST

Piccadilly Rare Books, ■ Church Street, Ticehurst, TN5 7AA. Prop: Paul P.B. Minet. Tel: (01580) 201221. Web: www.picrare.com. E-mail: minet@btopenworld.com. Est: 1972. Shop. open: **M:** 10:00–17:00; **T:** 10:00–17:00; **W:** 10:00–17:00; **Th:** 10:00–17:00; **F:** 10:00–17:00; **S:** 10:00–18:00. Stock: large. Spec: Diaries; Royalty - General; Royalty - European. PR: £5–2,000. CC: AE; MC; V. Corresp: French, Greek, Spanish. Mem: ABA; PBFA. Notes: also, publishers of 'Royalty Digest' (monthly)1991-2005 and reprinters of scarce Royalty titles. Also owns Baggins Book Bazaar in Rochester (q.v.). VAT No: GB 583 9618 89. [Updated]

EAST YORKSHIRE

BEVERLEY

Beverley Old Bookshop, ■ 2 Dyer Lane, Beverley, HU17 8AE. Prop: Colin Tatman. Tel: (01482) 880611. Est: 1993. Shop open: **M:** 10:00–17:00; **T:** 10:00–17:00; **W:** 10:00–17:00; **Th:** 10:00–17:00; **F:** 10:00–17:00; **S:** 10:00–17:00. Stock: medium. Spec: Bookbinding; Children's; History - Local; Illustrated. PR: £1–200. Notes: also, book restoration. [Updated]

Countryman Books, 42, St Matthews Court, Beverley, HU17 8JH. Prop: Christine Swift. Tel: (01482) 869710. Fax: (01482) 869710. Web: www.countryman.co.uk. E-mail: books@countryman.co.uk. Private premises. Internet and postal. Telephone first. Open: Spec: Author - Aldin, Cecil; Dogs; Sport - Angling/Fishing; Sport - Big Game Hunting; Sport - Falconry; Sport - Hunting; Sport - Polo; Sport - Shooting. PR: £5–150. CC: MC; V; Switch. Mem: ABA. [Updated]

Eastgate Bookshop, ■ 11 Eastgate, Beverley, HU17 0DR. Prop: Barry Roper. Tel: (01482) 868579. E-mail: barry@eastgatebooks.karoo.co.uk. Est: 1983. Shop open: **W:** 10:00–17:00; **Th:** 10:00–17:00; **F:** 10:00–17:00; **S:** 10:00–16:30. Stock: large. Spec: Archaeology; Crime (True); History - Local; Military; Topography - Local; Travel - Asia; Booksearch. PR: £1–500. CC: JCB; MC; V; Switch. Notes: also at: Sarawak Books, Beverley (q.v.) n/a Open Monday and Tuesday by appointment only. VAT No: GB Null. [Updated]

Peter Riddell, Hall Cottage, Main St., Cherry Burton, Beverley, HU17 7RF. Tel: (01964) 551453. E-mail: bkscherryb@aol.com. Est: 1989. Private premises. Internet and postal. Appointment necessary. Stock: very small. Spec: Alpinism/Mountaineering; Countries - Central Asia; Countries - Polar. PR: £1–250. [Updated]

Sarawak Books, ■ 11 East Close, Molescroft, Beverley, HU17 7JN. Prop: Barry Roper. Tel: (01482) 868579. E-mail: eastgatebooks@eastgatebooks.caroo.co.uk. Est: 1965. Shop open: **W:** 10:00–17:00; **Th:** 10:00–17:00; **F:** 10:00–17:00; **S:** 10:00–17:00. Spec: Comedy; Countries - British North Borneo; Countries - Sarawak. CC: D; E; JCB; MC; V. Cata: annually on specialised subjects. [Updated]

BRIDLINGTON

Family-Favourites, 51 First Avenue, Bridlington, YO15 2JR. Prop: Shirley Jackson. Tel: 01262 6606061. E-mail: shirleyjackson@telco.4u.net. Est: 1989. Private premises. Postal only. Contactable. Medium stock. Spec: Autobiography; Biography; First editions, Large Print books. PR: £5–100.

J.L. Book Exchange, ■ 72 Hilderthorpe Road, Bridlington, YO15 3BQ. Prop: John Ledraw. Tel: (01262) 601285. Est: 1971. Shop open: **M:** 08:30–18:00; **T:** 08:30–18:00; **W:** 08:30–18:00; **Th:** 08:30–18:00; **F:** 08:30–18:00; **S:** 08:30–18:00; **Su:** 08:30–18:00. Stock: medium. PR: £1–80. Mem: PBFA. Notes: winter opening: Mon-Sat 09.30–17.30. [Updated]

DRIFFIELD

Solaris Books, Flat 4, 13 Lockwood St., Driffield, YO25 6RU. Prop: Jim Goddard. Tel: (01377) 272022. Web: www.solaris-books.co.uk. E-mail: jim@solaris-books.co.uk. Private premises. Internet and postal. Telephone first. Stock: medium. Spec: Fiction - Fantasy, Horror; Fiction - Science Fiction; Military History; Modern First Editions; Photography; Booksearch. PR: £2–1,200. CC: PayPal. [Updated]

FLAMBOROUGH

Resurgam Books, ■ The Manor House, Flamborough, Bridlington, York, YO15 1PD. Prop: Geoffrey Miller. Tel: (01262) 850943. Fax: (01262) 850943. Web: www.resurgambooks.co.uk. E-mail: gm@resurgambooks.co.uk. Est: 1998. Shop. Internet and postal. Open: **M:** 09:00–17:00; **T:** 09:00–17:00; **W:** 09:00–17:00; **Th:** 09:00–17:00; **F:** 09:00–17:00; **S:** 09:00–17:00; **Su:** 10:00–16:00. Stock: very small. PR: £1–400. CC: E; JCB; MC; V. [Updated]

GREAT DRIFFIELD

The Driffield Bookshop, ■ 21 Middle Street North, Great Driffield, YO25 6SW. Prop: G.R. Stevens. Tel: (01377) 254210. Est: 1981. Shop open: **M:** 10:00–17:30; **T:** 10:00–17:30; **W:** 10:00–17:30; **Th:** 10:00–17:30; **F:** 10:00–17:30; **S:** 10:00–17:30. Stock: medium. Spec: Fiction - Science Fiction; History - General; Literature; Military History; Modern First Editions; Travel - General. PR: £1–150. Cata: bi-annually on infrequent on collections. [Updated]

EAST YORKSHIRE

HOWDEN

Kemp Booksellers, ■ 5–7 Vicar Lane, Howden, DN14 7BP. Prop: Mike Kemp. Tel: 01430 432071. Fax: 01430 431666. Web: www.kempbooksellers.co.uk. E-mail: mike@kempbooksellers.co.uk. Est: 1979. Shop open: **T:** 10:00–17:00; **W:** 10:00–17:00; **Th:** 10:00–17:00; **F:** 10:00–17:00; **S:** 10:00–16:00; Closed for lunch: 13:00–13:30. Spec: Author - Peake, Mervyn; History - General; Topography - General; Topography - Local. CC: MC; V; Maestro. Cata: bi-annually – on British topography. Corresp: French. Mem: ABA; PBFA; ILAB. [Updated]

HULL

Bowie Books & Collectables, 19 Northolt Close, Hull, HU8 0PP. Prop: James Bowie. Tel: (01482) 374609. Web: www.freewebs.com/bowiebooksandcollectables/. E-mail: bowiebooks@hotmail.co.uk. Est: 2003. Private premises. Internet and postal. Appointment necessary. Open: **M:** 09:00–18:00; **T:** 09:00–18:00; **W:** 09:00–18:00; **Th:** 09:00–18:00; **F:** 09:00–18:00; **S:** 09:00–15:00. Stock: small. Spec: Antiquarian; Fiction - General; First Editions; Literature; Modern First Editions; Religion - General; Collectables. PR: £2–150. [Updated]

Harry Holmes Books, 85 Park Avenue, Hull, HU5 3EP. Prop: H.H. & P.A. Purkis. Tel: (01482) 443220. Est: 1989. Private premises. Appointment necessary. Stock: small. Spec: Alpinism/Mountaineering; Biography; Countries - Scotland; Literature; Religion - Christian; Spiritualism; Topography - Local; Travel - Polar. PR: £1–100. Corresp: French and German. Notes: Books on literary biography are also stocked. [Updated]

Hull hullbooks.com, ■ 165 Newland Avenue, Hull, HU5 2EP. Prop: Ian & Karren Barfield. Tel: 01482 444677. Web: www.hullbooks.com. E-mail: hullbooks@yahoo.co.uk. Est: 1991. Shop open: **M:** 10:00–17:00; **T:** 10:00–17:00; **W:** 10:00–17:00; **Th:** 10:00–17:00; **F:** 10:00–17:00; **S:** 10:00–17:00. Stock: large. Spec: Academic/Scholarly; History - Local; Humanities; Military; Social Sciences. PR: £2–200. CC: E; JCB; MC; V. Mem: PBFA. [Updated]

Hull Colin Martin - Bookseller, 3 Village Road, Garden Village, Hull, HU8 8QP. Prop: Colin and Jane Martin, L.L.B., B.A Tel: (01482) 585836. Web: www.colinmartinbooks.com. E-mail: enquiries@colinmartinbooks.com. Est: 1991. Storeroom. Internet and postal. Appointment necessary. Open: **M:** 10:00–16:00; **T:** 10:00 16:00; **W:** 10:00–16:00; **Th:** 10:00–16:00; **F:** 10:00–16:00. Stock: very large. Spec: Applied Art; Architecture; Art; Art History; Art Reference; Artists; Arts, The; Design. PR: £3–4,000. CC: AE; D; JCB; MC; V; SW, SO. Corresp: French, German, Italian. VAT No: GB 780 4607 24. [Updated]

KIRKELLA

East Riding Books, 13 Westland Road, Kirkella, HU10 7PH. Prop: Gill Carlile. Tel: (01482) 650674. Web: www.eastridingbooks.co.uk. E-mail: info@eastridingbooks.co.uk. Est: 1996. Private premises. Internet and postal. Stock: small. Spec: Music - General; Music - Classical; Music - Composers; Music - Jazz & Blues; Music - Musicians; Music - Opera; Musical Instruments. PR: £1–500. CC: JCB; MC; V. Mem: PBFA. VAT No: GB 747 0534 31. [Updated]

MILLINGTON

Quest Books, Harmer Hill, Millington, York, YO42 1TX. Prop: Dr. Peter Burridge. Tel: (01759) 304735. Fax: (01759) 306820. E-mail: QuestByz@aol.com. Est: 1984. Private premises. Postal only. Appointment necessary. Open: Stock: very small. Spec: Academic/Scholarly; Archaeology; Architecture; Classical Studies; Countries - Arabia; Countries - Asia Minor; Countries - Balkans, The; Countries - Cyprus. PR: £5–1,000. CC: JCB; MC; V. Mem: PBFA. [Updated]

Available from Richard Joseph Publishers Ltd
Sheppard's Book Dealers in JAPAN
Order the next edition - or search www.sheppardsworld.co.uk

SWANLAND

Cygnet Books, 86 Main Street, Swanland, HU14 3QR. Prop: Jackie Kitchen. Tel: 01482 635610. Web: www.cygnetbooks.co.uk. E-mail: jackie@cygnetbooks.co.uk. Est: 1995. Private premises. Internet and postal. Appointment necessary. Open: **M:** 09:00–17:30; **T:** 09:00–17:30; **W:** 09:00–17:30; **Th:** 09:00–17:30; **F:** 09:00–17:30; **S:** 09:00–13:00; Closed for lunch: 13:00–14:00. Spec: Children's; Children's - Early Titles; Children's - Illustrated; Christmas; Comic Books & Annuals; Disneyana. CC: MC; V. Cata: occasionally on Children's out of Print Books. Notes: booksearch for hard to find titles. [Updated]

WINESTEAD,

Alex Alec–Smith Books, The Old Rectory, Winestead, Hull, HU12 0NN. Tel: (01964) 630548. Fax: (01964) 631160. E-mail: alex@aasbooks.demon.co.uk. Est: 1985. Private premises. Appointment necessary. Stock: small. Spec: Author - Byron, Lord; Bibliography; Books about Books; Dictionaries; Literary Criticism; Literature; Topography - Local. PR: £5–3,000. CC: MC; V. Mem: ABA; PBFA; ILAB. VAT No: GB 433 6879 22. [Updated]

ESSEX

BILLERICAY

Engaging Gear Ltd., Lark Rise, 14 Linkdale, Billericay, CM12 9QW. Prop: D.E. Twitchett. Tel: (01277) 624913. Est: 1965. Private premises. Postal only. Stock: very small. Spec: Author - Moore, John; Horology; Sport - Cycling. PR: £5–500. Notes: stock includes titles on cycling history and travel. [Updated]

BIRCH

John Cowley, Auto–in–Print, Mill Lodge, Mill Lane, Birch, Colchester, CO2 0NG. Tel: (01206) 331052. Web: www.autoinprint.com. E-mail: cowley@autoinprint.freeserve.co.uk. Est: 1975. Private premises. Internet and postal. Appointment necessary. Stock: very large. Spec: Motoring; Booksearch; Ephemera. [Updated]

BRAINTREE

Lawful Occasions, 68 High Garrett, Braintree, CM7 5NT. Prop: M.R. Stallion. Tel: (01376) 551819. Fax: (01376) 326073. Web: www.lawfuloccasions.co.uk. E-mail: stallion@supanet.com. Est: 1997. Private premises. Internet and postal. Appointment necessary. Stock: very small. Spec: Crime (True); Criminology; Police Force Histories; Salvation Army; Science - Forensic; Booksearch. PR: £1–100. Corresp: French. Notes: stock and booksearch on police history only. Credit/debit cards accepted via PayPal. Publisher of bibliographies on police history. [Updated]

BRENTWOOD

Book End, ■ 36–38 Kings Road, Brentwood, CM14 4DW. Prop: G.E. & M.K. Smith. Tel: withheld. Est: 1980. Shop open: **M:** 10:00–17:30; **T:** 10:00–17:30; **W:** 10:00–17:30; **Th:** 10:00–13:00; **F:** 10:00–17:30; **S:** 10:00–17:00. Stock: medium. PR: £1–100. [Updated]

CHELMSFORD

Christopher Heppa, 48 Pentland Avenue, Chelmsford, CM1 4AZ. Prop: Christopher Heppa. Tel: (01245) 267679. E-mail: christopher@heppa4288.fsnet.co.uk. Est: 1982. Private premises. Internet and postal. Appointment necessary. Stock: medium. Spec: Authors:- Bates, H.E.; Buchan, John; Wodehouse, P.G.; Children's; Fiction - Crime, Detective, Spy, Thrillers; Fiction - Historical; First Editions; Illustrated. PR: £1–3,000. Corresp: Spanish. Mem: PBFA. [Updated]

CLACTON-ON-SEA

VOL:II, ■ VOL:II Out of print books, 14B St.John Road, Clacton-on-Sea, CO15 4BP. Prop: Andy Durrant. Tel: 01255 470448. Web: www.bookwormshop.com. E-mail: question@bookwormshop.com. Est: 2005. Shop. Open: **M:** 09:00–17:30; **T:** 09:00–17:30; **W:** 09:00–17:30; **Th:** 09:00–17:30; **F:** 09:00–17:30; **S:** 09:00–17:30. Spec: Fiction - General. CC: AE; E; JCB; MC; V; Solo, Electron, Switch, Maestro. Notes: part of the 'Bookworm' Group. [Updated]

COLCHESTER

Barcombe Services, 43 Church Lane, Colchester, CO3 4AE. Prop: Dr. Stephen M Williams. Tel: (01206) 510461. Web: www.homepage.ntlworld.com/steve.williams7/ner.htm. E-mail: steve.williams7@ntlworld.com. Est: 2004. Private premises. Internet and postal. Appointment necessary. Stock: very small. Spec: Academic/Scholarly; Education & School; History - General; Psychology/Psychiatry; Science - General. PR: £1–20. Corresp: French, German. [Updated]

Available from Richard Joseph Publishers Ltd
Sheppard's International Directory of EPHEMERA DEALERS
Order the next edition now – or search www.sheppardsworld.co.uk

Castle Bookshop, ■ 40 Osborne St., Colchester, CO2 7DB. Prop: J.R. Green. Tel: (01206) 577520. Fax: (01206) 577520. Est: 1947. Shop open: **M:** 09:00–17:00; **T:** 09:00–17:00; **W:** 09:00–17:00; **Th:** 09:00–17:00; **F:** 09:00–17:00; **S:** 09:00–17:00. Stock: very large. Spec: Archaeology; Aviation; First Editions; History - Local; Military History; Modern First Editions; Topography - General; Topography - Local. PR: £1–1,500. CC: MC; V. Mem: PBFA. Notes: none of our stock is on the Internet. VAT No: GB 360 3502 89. [Updated]

Farringdon Books, Shrubland House, 43 Mile End Road, Colchester, CO4 5BU. Prop: Alan Austin. Tel: (01206) 855 771. E-mail: alan@farringdon-books.demon.co.uk. Est: 1972. Private premises. Postal only. Stock: medium. Spec: Fiction - Crime, Detective, Spy, Thrillers; Fiction - Fantasy, Horror; Fiction - Science Fiction. PR: £1–200. [Updated]

GfB: the Colchester Bookshop, ■ 92 East Hill, Colchester, CO1 2QN. Prop: Pauline & Simon Taylor. Tel: (01206) 563138. Web: www.gfb.uk.net. E-mail: simon@gfb.uk.net. Est: 1983. Shop open: **M:** 10:00–17:30; **T:** 10:00–17:30; **W:** 10:00–17:30; **Th:** 10:00–17:30; **F:** 10:00–17:30; **S:** 10:00–17:30. Stock: very large. Spec: Academic/Scholarly; Archaeology; Architecture; Art; Art Reference; Gardening - General; History - Ancient; History - British. PR: £2–200. Corresp: French. VAT No: GB 759 8699 37. [Updated]

Quentin Books Ltd, 38 High Street, Wivenhoe, Colchester, CO7 9BE. Prop: Mr Paterson. Tel: (01206) 825433. Fax: (01206) 822990. E-mail: quentin_books@lineone.net. Est: 1990. Storeroom. Appointment necessary. Stock: medium. Spec: Bibliography; Bindings; Biography; Books about Books; History - General; History - American; Maritime/Nautical; Natural History. PR: £1–1,000. Corresp: French, German. Mem: Local topography majors on Essex. [Updated]

DAGENHAM

John Thorne, 19 Downing Road, Dagenham, RM9 6NR. Tel: (020) 8592-0259. Fax: (020) 8220-0082. Web: www.liquidliterature.co.uk. E-mail: liquidliterature@aol.com. Est: 1985. Private premises. Internet and postal. Stock: very small. Spec: Brewing; Public Houses; Viticulture; Whisky; Wine. PR: £1–300. CC: PayPal. [Updated]

EPPING

Browsers Bookshop, ■ 9 Station Road, Epping, CM16 4HA. Prop: Brian & Moira Carter. Tel: (01992) 572260. Est: 1990. Shop open: **Th:** 10:00–16:00; **F:** 10:00–16:00; **S:** 10:00–16:00. Stock: medium. PR: £1–800. [Updated]

FINCHINGFIELD

Brad Books, Finchingfield Antique Centre, Finchingfield, CM7 4JX. Prop: Arnold Bradbury. Tel: (01787) 460405. E-mail: arnold.bradbury@ukgateway.net. PR: £1–250. [Updated]

GRAYS

Phototitles.com, 50 Falcon Avenue, Grays, RM17 6SD. Prop: Steve Taylor. Tel: 07802 887319. Web: www.phototitles.com. E-mail: books@phototitles.com. Est: 2005. Mail Order Only. Internet Only. Contactable: **M:** 08:00–20:00; **T:** 08:00–20:00; **W:** 08:00–20:00; **Th:** 08:00–20:00; **F:** 08:00–20:00; **S:** 08:00–20:00; **Su:** 08:00–20:00; Closed for lunch: 13:30–14:00. Spec: Photography. CC: AE; E; JCB; MC; V. Cata: on Photography. Notes: Specialising in Rare, Signed and Out of Print Photographic Books. VAT No: GB 863 4039 23. [Updated]

GREAT DUNMOW

Clive Smith, Brick House, North Street, Great Dunmow, CM6 1BA. Tel: (01371) 873171. Fax: (01371) 873171. E-mail: clivesmith@route56.co.uk. Est: 1975. Private premises. Appointment necessary. Stock: small. Spec: Antiquarian; Cookery/Gastronomy; Medicine; Military; Natural History; Topography - General; Topography - Local; Travel - General. PR: £10–1,000. Corresp: French, Indonesian. VAT No: GB 571 600 167. [03/10/2004]

GREAT LEIGHS

Missing Books, 'Coppers', Main Road, Great Leighs, CM3 1NR. Prop: Chris Missing. Tel: (01245) 361609. E-mail: missingbooks@madasafish.com. Est: 1994. Private premises. Book Fairs Only. Stock: small. Spec: Architecture; Biography; City of London; Countries - England; History - Local; Publishers - Black, A. & C.; Rural Life; Topography - General. PR: £2–500. CC: MC; V. Mem: PBFA. [Updated]

HARWICH

The Book Annex, 18 Church Street, Harwich, CO12 3DS. Prop: Martin Ellingham / Peter J. Hadley. Tel: 01255 551667. Web: www.thebookannex.co.uk. E-mail: victoria@thebookannex.co.uk. Est: 2004. Shop and/or showroom; Telephone first. Spec: Art; Art - Technique; Art - Theory; Art History; Arts, The; Science - General; Science - Pure & Applied; University Press. CC: MC; V. Notes: Wide ranging stock of Academic Titles including many remainders / overstocks as well as strong sections in History, Science, Arts subjects, Literature and Media. Visitors welcome by chance or ideally by appointment [Updated]

Peter J. Hadley Bookseller, ■ 21 Market Street, Harwich, CI12 3DX. Tel: 01255 551667. Fax: 01255 551667. Web: www.hadley.co.uk. Est: 1982. Shop. Appointment necessary. Shop At: books@hadley.co.uk. Stock: small. Spec: Architecture; Country Houses; Decorative Art; Ecclesiastical History & Architecture; First Editions; Humanities; Literary Criticism; Literature. PR: £10–1,000. CC: MC; V. Mem: ABA. Notes: advise telephoning if travelling far. [Updated]

HOLLAND-ON-SEA

Bookworm, ■ Bookworm, 100 Kings Avenue, Holland-on-Sea, CO15 5EP. Tel: 01255 815984. Web: www.bookwormshop.com. E-mail: question@bookwormshop.com. Est: 1995. Shop open: **M:** 09:00–16:00; **T:** 09:00–16:00; **W:** 09:00–16:00; **Th:** 09:00–16:00; **F:** 09:00–16:00; **S:** 09:00–16:00. Spec: Children's; Military. CC: AE; E; JCB; MC; V; Maestro, Solo, Switch, Electron.[Updated]

ILFORD (SEE ALSO UNDER LONDON OUTER)

June Rhoda, 43 Redbridge Lane East, Ilford, IG4 5EU. Prop: J.R. Arnold. Tel: (020) 8550-5256. Est: 1983. Private premises. Postal only. Stock: very small. Spec: History - Local. PR: £1–100. [Updated]

LEIGH ON SEA

Caliver Books, ■ 816-818 London Road, Leigh on Sea, SS9 3NH. Prop: Dave Ryan. Tel: 01702 473986. Fax: 01702 473986. Web: www.caliverbooks.com. E-mail: dave@caliverbooks.com. Est: 1983. Shop open: **M:** 09:00–18:00; **T:** 09:00–18:00; **W:** 09:00–18:00; **Th:** 09:00–18:00; **F:** 09:00–18:00; **S:** 09:00–18:00; **Su:** 09:00–18:00. Spec: Arms & Armour; Byzantium; Colonial; Fashion & Costume; Firearms/Guns; History - General; Military; Military History. CC: E; MC; V; PayPal. Cata: occasionally on specialities. [Updated]

Leigh Gallery Books, ■ 135–137 Leigh Road, Leigh–on–Sea, SS9 1JQ. Prop: Barrie Gretton. Tel: (01702) 715477. Fax: (01702) 715477. Web: www.abebooks.com/home/BOO/. E-mail: leighgallerybooks@bigfoot.com. Est: 1983. Shop open: **Th:** 10:00–17:00; **F:** 10:00–17:00; **S:** 10:00–17:00. Stock: large. Spec: Art; Illustrated; Literature; Topography - Local; Ephemera; Prints and Maps. PR: £1–200. CC: AE; MC; V. [Updated]

Othello's Bookshop, ■ 1376 London Road, Leigh–On–Sea, SS9 2UH. Prop: F.G. Bush & M.A. Layzell. Tel: (01702) 473334. E-mail: othellos@hotmail.com. Est: 1999. Shop open. Stock: medium. PR: £6–200. [Updated]

LITTLE HALLINGBURY

Assinder Books, Windy Walls, Dell Lane, Little Hallingbury, CM22 7SH. Prop: N.M. & I. Assinder. Tel: 01279654479. Web: www.abebooks.com. E-mail: assinbooks@aol.com. Est: 1992. Private premises. Internet and postal. Telephone first. Stock: medium. Spec: Art Reference; Children's; Illustrated. PR: £2–300. Corresp: Norwegian. [Updated]

MALDON

All Books, ■ 2 Mill Road, Maldon, CM9 5HZ. Prop: Mr. Kevin Peggs. Tel: (01621) 856214. Web: www.allbooks.demon.co.uk. E-mail: kevin@allbooks.demon.co.uk. Est: 1970. Shop. Internet and postal. Open: **M:** 10:00–17:00; **T:** 10:00–17:00; **W:** 10:00–16:00; **Th:** 10:00–17:00; **F:** 10:00–16:00; **S:** 10:00–17:30; **Su:** 13:30–17:00. Stock: very large. Spec: Academic/Scholarly; Advertising; Aeronautics; Africana; Arts, The; Aviation; History - General; History - Renaissance, The. PR: £1–500. CC: MC; V. [Updated]

Philip Hopper, 29 Keeble Park, Maldon, CM9 6YG. Tel: 01621 850709. Est: 1985. Private premises. Internet and postal. Spec: Curiosities; Earth Mysteries; Folklore; Gypsies; Mind, Body & Spirit; Mysteries; Mysticism; Occult. Cata: quarterly on Occult, country life and angling. [Updated]

MANNINGTREE

John Drury Rare Books, Strandlands, Wrabness, Manningtree, CO11 2TX. Prop: David Edmunds. Tel: (01255) 886260. Fax: (01255) 880303. Web: www.johndruryrarebooks.com. E-mail: mail@johndruryrarebooks.com. Est: 1971. Private premises. Appointment necessary. Stock: small. Spec: Antiquarian; Economics; Education & School; Fine & Rare; History of Ideas; Humanities; Irish Interest; Law - General. PR: £30–3,000. CC: MC; V. Corresp: French. Mem: ABA. VAT No: GB 325 6594 41. [Updated]

RAYLEIGH

Fantastic Literature Limited, 35 The Ramparts, Rayleigh, SS6 8PY. Prop: Simon & Laraine Gosden. Tel: (01268) 747564. Fax: (01268) 747564. Web: www.fantasticliterature.com. E-mail: sgosden@netcomuk.co.uk. Est: 1984. Private premises. Internet and postal. Stock: large. Spec: Authors:- Blackwood, A.; King, Stephen; Pratchett, Terry; Wells, H.G.; Fiction - Crime, Detective, Spy, Thrillers; Fiction - Fantasy, Horror; Fiction - Historical; Fiction - Science Fiction. PR: £1–900. CC: E; MC; V; Switch. Corresp: French. Notes: also, booksearch and scans available of any title. [01/09/2005]

SAFFRON WALDEN

Lankester Antiques and Books, ■ The Old Sun Inn, Church Street and Market Hill, Saffron Walden, CB10 1HQ. Prop: Paul Lankester. Tel: (01799) 522685. E-mail: . Est: 1964. Shop open: **M:** 10:00–17:00; **T:** 10:00–17:00; **W:** 10:00–17:00; **Th:** 10:00–17:00; **F:** 10:00–17:00. Stock: very large. Spec: Ephemera; Prints and Maps. PR: £1–50. [Updated]

SHENFIELD

Booknotes, 6 York Road, Shenfield, CM15 8JT. Prop: Tony Connolly. Tel: (01277) 226130. Web: www.ascon.demon.co.uk. E-mail: booknotes@ascon.demon.co.uk. Est: 1985. Private premises. Internet and postal. Stock: medium. Spec: [Updated]

SOUTHEND–ON–SEA

Gage Postal Books, P.O. Box 105, Westcliff–on–Sea, Southend–on–Sea, SS0 8EQ. (*) Simon A. Routh. Tel: (01702) 715133. Fax: (01702) 715133. Web: www.gagebooks.com. E-mail: gagebooks@clara.net. Est: 1971. Storeroom. Internet and postal. Appointment necessary. Stock: very large. Spec: Ecclesiastical History & Architecture; Religion - General; Theology. PR: £3–1,000. CC: MC; V. Corresp: German. Mem: PBFA. [Updated]

Tony Peterson, 11 Westbury Road, Southend–on–Sea, SS2 4DW. Prop: Tony Peterson. Tel: (01702) 462757. Web: www.chessbooks.co.uk. E-mail: tony@chessbooks.co.uk. Est: 1993. Private premises. Internet and postal. Appointment necessary. Stock: very small. Spec: Chess. PR: £4–200. CC: PayPal. [Updated]

STANSTED

Paul Embleton, 12 Greenfields, Stansted, CM24 8AH. Tel: (01279) 812627. Fax: (01279) 817576. Web: www.abebooks.com/home/embleton. E-mail: paulembleton@btconnect.com. Est: 1994. Private premises. Internet and postal. Appointment necessary. Stock: small. Spec: Children's - Early Titles; Children's - Illustrated; Collecting; Illustrated; Military; Paper Collectables. PR: £5–1,000. CC: PayPal. Notes: also, a booksearch service. Books for picture postcard collectors [30/07/2005]

WESTCLIFF–ON–SEA

Clifton Books, 34 Hamlet Court Road, Westcliff–on–Sea, SS0 7LX. Prop: John R. Hodgkins. Tel: (01702) 331004. E-mail: jhodgk9942@aol.com. Est: 1970. Private premises. Internet and postal. Appointment necessary. Stock: large. Spec: Academic/Scholarly; Agriculture; Economics; History - British; Social History; Trade Unions; Transport. CC: AE; D; E; JCB; MC; V. Mem: PBFA. Notes: all related to West Ham. [Updated]

Available from Richard Joseph Publishers Ltd
BOOK DEALING FOR PROFIT
by Paul Minet
Quarto H/b £10.00 144pp

WESTCLIFF–ON–SEA

Marjon Books, 16 Mannering Gardens, Westcliff–on–Sea, SS0 0BQ. Prop: R.J. Cooper. Tel: (01702) 347119. Est: 1975. Private premises. Appointment necessary. Stock: very small. PR: £2–120. [Updated]

WICKFORD

Mr. H. Macfarlane, 40 Chaucer Walk, Wickford, SS12 9DZ. Tel: (01268) 570892. Web: www.tudorblackpress.co.uk. E-mail: jmba21803@blueyonder.co.uk. Est: 1997. Private premises. Internet and postal. Stock: very small. Spec: Astronomy; Medicine; Printing; Private Press; Science - General. PR: £2–150. Notes: also, a booksearch service (relating to scientific books only). [Updated]

WICKHAM BISHOPS

Baldwin's Scientific Books, Fossilis, 18 School Road, Wickham Bishops, Witham, CM8 3NU. Prop: Stuart A. Baldwin. Tel: 01621 891526. Fax: 01621 891522. Web: www.secondhandsciencebooks.com. E-mail: sbaldwin@fossilbooks.co.uk. Est: 1962. Private premises. Internet and postal. Appointment necessary. Open: **M:** 10:00–17:30; **T:** 10:00–17:30; **W:** 10:00–17:30; **Th:** 10:00–17:30; **F:** 10:00–17:30; **S:** 10:00–17:30; **Su:** 10:00–17:30. Spec: Antiquarian; Archaeology; Astronomy; Biography; Botany; Dinosaurs; Earth Sciences; Evolution. CC: MC; V. Cata: occasionally on Geology, palaeontology, science, natural history. Mem: PBFA. VAT No: GB 219 1793 51. [Updated]

WOODFORD GREEN

Handsworth Books, 8 Warners Close, Woodford Green, IG8 0TF. Prop: Stephen Glover. Tel: (07976) 329042. Fax: (0870) 0520258. Web: www.handsworthbooks.co.uk. E-mail: steve@handsworthbooks.demon.co.uk. Est: 1987. Private premises. Postal only. Stock: medium. Spec: Academic/Scholarly; Applied Art; Company History; Fine Art; History - General; Literary Criticism; Military History; Music - General. PR: £2–650. CC: AE; E; JCB; MC; V. Mem: PBFA. [Updated]

Salway Books, 47 Forest Approach, Woodford Green, IG8 9BP. Prop: Barry Higgs. Tel: (020) 8491 7766. Web: www.salwaybooks.co.uk. E-mail: salway.books@ntlworld.com. Est: 1993. Private premises. Stock: small. Spec: Aviation; Canals/Inland Waterways; Company History; Industry; Mining; Railways; Topography - Local; Traction Engines. PR: £1–500. CC: MC; V. Mem: PBFA. [Updated]

GLOUCESTERSHIRE

ALMONDSBURY

Michael Garbett Antiquarian Boooks, 1 Over Court Mews, Over Lane, Almondsbury, BS32 4DG. Prop: Michael & Jeanne Garbett. Tel: (01454) 617376. Fax: (01454) 617376. Web: www.michaelgarbett. theanswer.co.uk. E-mail: migarb@overcourtmews.freeserve.co.uk. Est: 1965. Private premises. Appointment necessary. Stock: small. Spec: Bindings; Miniature Books. Mem: ABA. VAT No: GB 358 1080 58. [Updated]

BERKELEY

Volumes of Motoring, Hertsgrove, Wanswell, Berkeley, GL13 9RR. Prop: Terry Wills. Tel: (01453) 811819. Fax: (01453) 811819. E-mail: twills@breathemail.net. Est: 1979. Private premises. Internet and postal. Appointment necessary. Open: **M:** 08:00–22:00; **T:** 08:00–22:00; **W:** 08:00–22:00; **Th:** 08:00–22:00; **F:** 08:00–22:00; **S:** 08:00–21:00; **Su:** 09:00–22:00. Stock: small. Spec: Motoring; Sport - Motor Racing. PR: £2–60. CC: MC; V. Notes: Wide range of motoring remainders available to the trade. [Updated]

BISHOPS CLEEVE

Courtyard Books, ■ Tarlings Yard, Church Road, Bishops Cleeve, Cheltenham, GL52 8RN. Tel: 01242 674335. Fax: 01242 674335. Web: www.courtyardbooks.co.uk. E-mail: post@courtyardbooks.co.uk. Est: 2000. Shop open: **M:** 09:00–17:00; **T:** 09:00–17:00; **W:** 09:00–17:00; **Th:** 09:00–17:00; **F:** 09:00–17:00; **S:** 09:00–17:00. Spec: Music - Jazz & Blues. CC: AE; MC; V. Cata: occasionally on JAZZ BOOKS. Notes: Comprehensive range of books on jazz. [Updated]

CAMBRIDGE

Internet Bookshop UK Ltd., ■ Unit 2, Wisloe Road, Cambridge, GL2 7AF. Prop: Mr. G. Cook. Tel: (01453) 890278. Fax: (0870) 442 5292. Web: www.ibuk.com. E-mail: orders@ibuk.com. Est: 1996. Shop. Internet and postal. Telephone first. Open: **M:** 09:00–17:00; **T:** 09:00–17:00; **W:** 09:00–17:00; **Th:** 09:00–17:00; **F:** 09:00–17:00. Stock: very large. Spec: Academic/Scholarly; Alpinism/ Mountaineering; Art; Aviation; Children's; Cookery/Gastronomy; Gardening - General; Military. PR: £8–1,000. CC: AE; MC; V; Switch. [Updated]

CHALFORD STROUD

Surprise Books, 14 Padin Close, Chalford Stroud, GL6 8FB. Prop: John Norman. Tel: 01453 887403. E-mail: surprisebooks@btopenworld.com. Est: 1995. Private premises. Internet and postal. Appointment necessary. Open: **M:** 09:00–17:30; **T:** 09:00–17:30; **W:** 09:00–17:30; **Th:** 09:00–17:30; **F:** 09:00–17:30; **S:** 09:00–17:30; **Su:** 09:00–17:30; Closed for lunch: 13:00–14:00. Spec: Annuals; Authors:- Dick, Philip K; Bainbridge, Beryl; Blyton, Enid; Charteris, Leslie; Cook, Beryl; Cornwell, Bernard; Crompton, Richmal. CC: MC; V. Mem: PBFA. VAT No: GB 811 2130 94. [Updated]

CHELTENHAM

David Bannister, 26 Kings Road, Cheltenham, GL52 6BG. Tel: (01242) 514287. Web: www.antiquemaps. co.uk. E-mail: db@antiquemaps.co.uk. Est: 1963. Private premises. Internet and postal. Appointment necessary. Stock: very small. Spec: Atlases; Cartography; Reference; Prints and Maps. PR: £10–5,000. CC: JCB; MC; V. VAT No: GB 391 9317 27. [Updated]

Cotswold Internet Books, Maida Vale Business Centre, Maida Vale Road, Cheltenham, GL53 7ER. Prop: John & Caro Newland. Tel: 261170 or (01242) 26. Web: www.cotsworldinternetbook.com. E-mail: john.newland@btconnect.com. Est: 1989. Warehouse; Internet and postal. Open: **M:** 08:30–18:00; **T:** 08:30–18:00; **W:** 08:30–18:00; **Th:** 08:30–18:00; **F:** 08:30–18:00; **S:** 09:00–18:00. Stock: very large. Spec: Aviation; Children's; Fiction - Crime, Detective, Spy, Thrillers. PR: £5–300. CC: AE; E; JCB; MC; V; Mae. Notes: Stock over 60,000. VAT No: GB 535 5039 51. [25/09/2004]

Bruce Marshall Rare Books, Foyers, 20 Gretton Road, Gotherington, Cheltenham, GL52 9QU. Tel: (01242) 672997. Fax: (01242) 675238. E-mail: marshallrarebook@aol.com. Private premises. Appointment necessary. Stock: very small. Spec: Atlases; Colour-Plate; Natural History; Travel - General. Mem: ABA; ILAB. [Updated]

Moss Books, ■ 8–9 Henrietta Street, Cheltenham, GL50 4AA. Prop: Christopher Moss. Tel: (01242) 222947. E-mail: chris.moss@virgin.net. Est: 1992. Shop open: **M:** 10:00–18:00; **T:** 10:00–18:00; **W:** 10:00–18:00; **Th:** 10:00–18:00; **F:** 10:00–18:00; **S:** 09:00–18:00. Stock: large. PR: £1–100. CC: JCB; MC; V. Corresp: Japanese. VAT No: GB 618 3105 62. [Updated]

Peter Lyons Books, ■ 11 Imperial Square, Cheltenham, GL50 1QB. Prop: Peter Lyons. Tel: (01242) 260345. Est: 2000. Shop open: **W:** 10:00–17:00; **Th:** 10:00–17:00; **F:** 10:00–17:00; **S:** 10:00–17:00. Stock: medium. Spec: Art; Art - Technique; Art - Theory; Art History; Art Reference; Artists; Arts, The; Children's. PR: £2–500. [Updated]

John Wilson Manuscripts Ltd, Painswick Lawn, 7 Painswick Road, Cheltenham, GL50 2EZ. Prop: John & Gina Wilson. Tel: (01242) 580344. Fax: (01242) 580355. Web: www.manuscripts.co.uk. E-mail: mail@manuscripts.co.uk. Est: 1967. Private premises. Internet and postal. Appointment necessary. Stock: very large. Spec: Autographs; Documents - General; Manuscripts; Ephemera. PR: £20–50,000. CC: AE; MC; V. Mem: ABA; ILAB; PADA. VAT No: GB 194 9050 39. [Updated]

CHIPPING CAMPDEN

Draycott Books, ■ 2 Sheep Street, Chipping Campden, GL55 6DX. Prop: Robert & Jane McClement. Tel: Business (01386) 841. E-mail: draycottbooks@hotmail.com. Est: 1981. Shop open: **M:** 10:00–17:00; **T:** 10:00–17:00; **W:** 10:00–17:00; **Th:** 10:00–17:00; **F:** 10:00–17:00; **S:** 10:00–17:00. Stock: medium. PR: £1–1,000. [Updated]

CIRENCESTER

Aviabooks, ■ 8 Swan Yard, West Market Place, Cirencester, GL7 2NH. Prop: Paul Gentil. Tel: (01285) 641700. Web: www.abebooks.com. E-mail: paul@gentil.demon.co.uk. Est: 1997. Shop open: **M:** 09:30–17:00; **T:** 09:30–17:00; **W:** 09:00–12:30; **Th:** 09:30–17:00; **F:** 09:30–17:00; **S:** 09:30–18:00. Stock: small. Spec: Aeronautics; Antiques; Applied Art; Architecture; Art; Art - Technique; Art History; Art Reference. PR: £1–1,000. CC: AE; MC; V; Maestro. Mem: PBFA. Notes: also, some book fairs & specialist events, bookbinding & repair service available. [Updated]

The Bookroom, ■ Cirencester Arcade, Market Place, Cirencester, GL7 2NX. Prop: Tetbury Old Books Ltd. Tel: (01285) 644214. Fax: (01285) 504458. E-mail: bookroom@tetbury.co.uk. Est: 1998. Shop open: **M:** 10:00–17:00; **T:** 10:00–17:00; **W:** 10:00–17:00; **Th:** 10:00–17:00; **F:** 10:00–17:00; **S:** 10:00–17:00; **Su:** 12:00–17:00. Stock: very small. PR: £3–100. CC: MC; V. Notes: also, prints and maps. [Updated]

COLEFORD

Past & Present Books, ■ 19a Gloucester Road, Coleford, GL16 8BH. Prop: Mr and Mrs J Saunders. Tel: 01594 833347. Shop open: **Th:** 16:00–17:30; **F:** 14:00–17:30; **S:** 10:00–17:30. Spec: Brewing; Industry; Mining; Topography - General; Topography - Local. Notes: major stockist of books on Gloucestershire - over 2,500. [Updated]

Are you making enough profit - if not then read

BOOKDEALING FOR PROFIT
by Paul Minet

Quarto H/b   Available from Richard Joseph Publishers Ltd   £10.00 144pp

Simon Lewis Transport Books, PO Box 9, Coleford, GL16 8YF. Prop: Simon Lewis. Tel: 01594 839369. Web: www.simonlewis.com. E-mail: simon@simonlewis.com. Est: 1985. Mail Order Only. Internet and postal. Appointment necessary. Open: **M:** 09:00–16:30; **T:** 09:00–16:30; **W:** 09:00–16:30; **Th:** 09:00–16:30; **F:** 09:00–16:30; Closed for lunch: 13:00–14:00. Spec: Buses/Trams; Motorbikes / motorcycles; Motoring; Railroads; Railways; Sport - Motor Racing; Traction Engines; Transport. CC: MC; V; Solo, Electron, Maestro. Cata: occasionaly on Car, Motorcycle, Truck & Bus, Rail. Notes: regular bookstall at Shelsley Walsh and Prescott speed hillclimb events & many other motor sport events during the season. VAT No: GB 575 9030 21. [Updated]

FAIRFORD

Jacques Gander, 14 Keble Lawns, Fairford, GL7 4BQ. Tel: (01285) 712988. E-mail: jacques@jgander.fsnet.co.uk. Private premises. Internet and postal. Spec: Children's; Modern First Editions. [Updated]

KEMPSFORD

Ximenes Rare Books Inc., Kempsford House, Kempsford, GL7 4ET. Prop: Stephen Weissman. Tel: (01285) 810640. Fax: (01285) 810650. E-mail: steve@ximenes.com. Est: 1965. Stock: small. Spec: Antiquarian. PR: £50–10,000. CC: MC; V. Corresp: French. Mem: ABA; PBFA; ILAB; ABAA. VAT No: GB 672 4533 30. [Updated]

LECHLADE

Evergreen Livres, The Old School, Kelmscot, Lechlade, GL7 3HG. Prop: N.S. O'Keeffe. Tel: (01367) 252558. Fax: (01367) 250081. E-mail: ocker@oxfree.com. Est: 1984. Private premises. Postal only. Stock: very small. Spec: Dogs; Farming & Livestock; Gardening - General; Horticulture; Natural History. PR: £2–500. [Updated]

MONTPELIER

Cooking = The Books, ■ 2 The Courtyard, Montpelier, Cheltenham, GL50 1SR. Prop: Dr Keith R. Harris. Tel: 01242 577908. E-mail: cooking@thebooks.fslife.co.uk. Est: 1995. Shop open: **M:** 09:00–17:00; **T:** 09:00–17:00; **W:** 09:00–17:00; **Th:** 09:00–17:00; **F:** 09:00–17:00; **S:** 09:00–17:00. Spec: Food & Drink; New Books. CC: JCB; MC; V; Mae, De. Notes: greetings cards - many handmade. New, out of print and used cookery books only. VAT No: GB 666 5230 26. [Updated]

MORETON–IN–MARSH

Jeffrey Formby Antiques, Orchard Cottage, East Street, Moreton–in–Marsh, GL56 0LQ. Tel: (01608) 650558. Fax: (01608) 650558. Web: www.formby-clocks.co.uk. E-mail: jeff@formby-clocks.co.uk. Est: 1993. Shop and/or gallery. Telephone first. Open: **F:** 10:00–17:00; **S:** 10:00–17:00. Stock: very small. Spec: Horology; Scientific Instruments. PR: £5–500. CC: E; JCB; MC; V. [Updated]

NAILSWORTH

Keogh's Books, ■ Market St, Nailsworth, GL6 0BX. Prop: J. Keogh. Tel: (01453) 833922. Web: www.keoghsbooks.co.uk. E-mail: joekeogh@keoghbooks.fsnet.co.uk. Est: 1985. Shop. Internet and postal. Open: **M:** 10:00–17:00; **T:** 10:00–17:00; **W:** 10:00–17:00; **Th:** 10:00–17:00; **F:** 10:00–17:00; **S:** 10:00–17:30. Stock: small. Spec: Art; Art History; Art Reference; Artists; Prints and Maps. PR: £2–200. CC: AE; MC; V; SW. [Updated]

NEWENT

Oakwood Books, 37 Church Street, Newent, GL18 1AA. Prop: Jim Haslem, A.L.A Tel: (01531) 821040. Web: www.abebooks.com/home/oakwoodbooks. E-mail: jim@haslem.fsnet.co.uk. Est: 1987. Private premises. Internet and postal. Appointment necessary. Stock: small. Spec: Topography - Local. PR: £2–450. [Updated]

NEWNHAM ON SEVERN

Christopher Saunders (Orchard Books), Kingston House, High Street, Newnham on Severn, GL14 1BB. Prop: Chris Saunders. Tel: (01594) 516030. Fax: (01594) 517273. Web: www.cricket-books.com. E-mail: chrisbooks@aol.com. Est: 1981. Office and/or bookroom. Appointment necessary. Open: **M:** 09:00–17:30; **T:** 09:00–17:30; **W:** 09:00–17:30; **Th:** 09:00–17:30; **F:** 09:00–17:30; **S:** 09:00–17:30; **Su:** 09:00–17:30; Closed for lunch: 13:00–14:00. Spec: Sport - Cricket. CC: MC; V; Maestro. Cata: quarterly on cricket. Mem: ABA; PBFA; ILAB. [Updated]

GLOUCESTERSHIRE

Marcus Niner, Newnham Old Books, 48 High Street, Newnham on Severn, GL14 1AA. Tel: (01594) 516088. E-mail: mail@ninerbooks.co.uk. Private premises. Telephone first. Stock: very small. Spec: Art; Literature; Topography - Local; Travel - General. PR: £10–2,000. CC: MC; V. Mem: PBFA. [Updated]

STOW-ON-THE-WOLD

Bookbox, ■ Chantry House, Sheep Street, Stow–on–the–Wold, GL54 1AA. Prop: Pat Brown & Connie Fisher. Tel: (01451) 831214. Web: www.Null. Est: 1987. Shop open: **M:** 11:00–17:00; **T:** 11:00–17:00; **Th:** 11:00–17:00; **F:** 11:00–17:00; **S:** 11:00–17:00; Closed for lunch: 13:00–14:15. Stock: medium. Spec: Arts, The; Author - Woolf, Virginia; Drama; Topography - General; Topography - Local. PR: £2–1,000. CC: MC; V. Mem: PBFA. Notes: NB In winter, telephone first. [Updated]

Wychwood Books, ■ Sheep Street, Stow–on–the–Wold, GL54 1AA. Prop: Miss. Lucy Baggott & Mr. Henry Baggott. Tel: 01451 831880. Fax: 01451 870631. Web: www.wychwoodbooks.com. E-mail: info@wychwoodbooks.com. Est: 2001. Shop open: **M:** 09:30–17:30; **T:** 09:30–17:30; **W:** 09:30–17:30; **Th:** 09:30–17:30; **F:** 09:30–17:30; **S:** 09:30–17:30. Stock: medium. Spec: Antiques; Architecture; Art; Children's; Cookery/Gastronomy; Literature; Modern First Editions; Natural History. PR: £3–4,000. CC: MC; V. Mem: PBFA. [Updated]

STROUD

Anthroposophical Books, Fromehall Mill - Blk 2, Rm 9, 2nd Flr, Lodgemore Lane, Stroud, GL5 3EH. Prop: H. & A. Tandree. Tel: (01453) 764 932. Fax: (01453) 764 932. E-mail: herb@philosophy-books.co.uk. Est: 1988. Office and/or bookroom. Appointment necessary. Open: **M:** 09:00–05:00. Stock: small. Spec: Anthroposophy; Author - Steiner, Rudolf; Occult. PR: £8–50. CC: MC; V. Corresp: French, German. [Updated]

The Blue Penguin, ■ Griffin Lodge, Griffin Mill, London Road, Stroud, GL52AZ. Prop: Steve Pritchard. Tel: (01453) 731027. E-mail: books@bluepenguin.fsnet.co.uk. Est: 1991. Shop open: **T:** 10:00–16:30; **W:** 10:00–16:30; **Th:** 10:00–16:30; **F:** 10:00–16:30; **S:** 10:00–16:30. Stock: medium. Spec: Booksearch; PR: £1–300. Corresp: 'Pidgeon' French. Notes: house clearances, antiques. Telephine if travelling far. [Updated]

Herb Tandree Philosophy Books, Fromehall Mill - Blk 2/Rm 9, Lodgemore Lane, Stroud, GL5 3EH. Herb Tandree. Tel: (01453) 764 932. Fax: (01453) 764 932. Web: www.philosophy-books.co.uk. E-mail: herb@philosophy-books.co.uk. Est: 2000. Private premises. Internet and postal. Appointment necessary. Open: Stock: medium. Spec: Academic/Scholarly; Economics; History of Ideas; Philosophy; Religion - General. CC: AE; JCB; MC. Corresp: French, German. VAT No: GB 783 4154 17. [Updated]

Ian Hodgkins and Company Limited, Upper Vatch Mill, The Vatch, Slad, Stroud, GL6 7JY. Prop: G.A. Yablon, I. Hoy, Simon Weager. Tel: (01453) 764270. Fax: (01453) 755233. Web: www.ianhodgkins.com. E-mail: i.hodgkins@dial.pipex.com. Est: 1974. Private premises. Internet and postal. Appointment necessary. Stock: medium. Spec: Applied Art; Art; Art Reference; Artists; Authors:- Austen, Jane; Brontes, The; Crane, Walter; Gaskell, E. PR: £5–5,000. CC: MC; V. Mem: ABA; PBFA; BA. [Updated]

Inprint, ■ 31 High Street, Stroud, GL5 1AJ. Prop: Joy & Mike Goodenough. Tel: (01453) 759731. Fax: (01453) 759731. Web: www.inprint.co.uk. E-mail: enquiries@inprint.co.uk. Est: 1978. Shop. Internet and postal. Open: **M:** 10:00–17:00; **T:** 10:00–17:00; **W:** 10:00–17:00; **Th:** 10:00–17:00; **F:** 10:00–17:00; **S:** 10:00–17:00. Stock: medium. Spec: Applied Art; Cinema/Film; Fine Art; Gardening - General; Performing Arts. PR: £5–500. CC: AE; D; E; JCB; MC; V. [Updated]

R & R Books, ■ Nelson Street, Stroud, GL5 2HL. Prop: Ruth Pyecroft. Tel: (01453) 755788. Web: www.inprint.co.uk/r&rbooks. E-mail: ruth@ruthpyecroftbooks.fsbusiness.co.uk. Est: 1994. Shop open: **M:** 10:00–17:30; **T:** 10:00–17:30; **W:** 10:00–17:30; **Th:** 10:00–17:30; **F:** 10:00–17:30; **S:** 10:00–17:30. Stock: medium. Spec: Advertising; Children's; Comic Books & Annuals; Comics; Culture - Popular; Earth Mysteries; Entertainment - General; Esoteric. PR: £1–20. CC: D; E; JCB; MC; V. [Updated]

Alan & Joan Tucker, The Bookshop, Old Stationmaster's House, Station Road, Stroud, GL5 3AR. Tel: (01453) 764738. Fax: (01453) 766899. Web: www.abebooks.com/home/SANDITON. E-mail: at80jt@globalnet.co.uk. Est: 1963. Storeroom. Internet and postal. Appointment necessary. Open: **M:** 09:30–17:00; **T:** 09:30–17:00; **W:** 09:30–17:00; **Th:** 09:30–17:00; **F:** 09:30–17:00; Closed for lunch: 12:00–14:15. Stock: very small. Spec: Arts, The; Authors - Women; Children's; Fine Printing; Limited Editions; Literary Criticism; Literary Travel; Literature. PR: £1–100. CC: MC; V. Mem: BA. Notes: please phone before visiting storeroom. Also, new maps. Stock also on www.bookline. VAT No: GB 275 0258 60. [Updated]

GLOUCESTERSHIRE

TETBURY

Tetbury Old Books Limited, ■ 4 The Chipping, Tetbury, GL8 8ET. Prop: Tetbury Old Books Ltd. Tel: (01666) 504330. E-mail: oldbooks@tetbury.co.uk. Est: 1994. Shop open: **M:** 10:00–18:00; **T:** 10:00–18:00; **W:** 10:00–18:00; **Th:** 10:00–18:00; **F:** 10:00–18:00; **S:** 10:00–18:00; **Su:** 11:00–18:00. Stock: small. Spec: Prints and Maps. PR: £1–5,000. CC: AE; E; JCB; MC; V; PayPal.com. Mem: TADA. [Updated]

TEWKESBURY

Cornell Books, ■ The Wheatsheaf, 132 High Street, Tewkesbury, GL20 5JR. Prop: Graham Cornell. Tel: (01684) 293337. E-mail: gtcornell@aol.com. Est: 1996. Shop open: **M:** 10:30–17:00; **T:** 10:30–17:00; **W:** 10:30–17:00; **Th:** 10:30–17:00; **F:** 10:30–17:00; **S:** 10:30–17:00. Stock: large. Spec: Author - Moore, John; Children's; Countries - England; Countries - Scotland; Countries - Wales; Prints and Maps. PR: £1–500. CC: AE; MC; V. Mem: PBFA. VAT No: GB 754 2601 43. [Updated]

WESTBURY-ON-SEVERN

Dive In Books, ■ Dive In, Lecture Hall, The Village, Westbury-on-Severn, GL14 1PA. Prop: Patricia Larkham. Tel: (01452) 760124. Fax: (01452) 760590. Web: www.diveinbooks.co.uk. E-mail: mydive@globalnet.co.uk. Est: 1975. Internet and postal. Shop open: **M:** 09:00–14:00; **T:** 09:00–14:00; **W:** 09:00–14:00; **Th:** 09:00–14:00; **F:** 09:00–14:00. Stock: small. Spec: Archaeology; Calligraphy; D.I.Y.; Deep Sea Diving; Maritime/Nautical; Natural History; Pacifism; Sport - Cycling. PR: £1–150. [Updated]

Available from Richard Joseph Publishers Ltd

Sheppard's Book Dealers in Latin America and Southern Africa

Order the next edition £24.00

GREATER MANCHESTER

ALTRINCHAM

Abacus Books, ■ 24 Regent Road, Altrincham. Prop: C D Lawton. Tel: 0161 928 5108. E-mail: abacusbookstore@yahoo.com. Est: 1979. Shop open: **T:** 10:00–17:00; **W:** 10:00–17:00; **Th:** 10:00–17:00; **F:** 10:00–17:00; **S:** 10:00–17:00. Spec: Art; Crafts; Gardening - General; Topography - Local. CC: MC; V. [Updated]

Christopher Baron, 15 Crossfield Road, Hale, Altrincham, WA15 8DU. Tel: (0161) 980-1014. Fax: (0161) 980-1415. Web: www.abebooks.com. E-mail: BaronBook@aol.com. Est: 1979. Private premises. Internet and postal. Stock: medium. Spec: Games; Horology; Locks & Locksmiths; Microscopy; Natural History; Science - General; Science - History of; Scientific Instruments. CC: JCB; MC; V; Maestro. Mem: PBFA. [Updated]

Edward Yarwood Rare Books, 61 Fairywell Road, Timperley, Altrincham, WA15 6XB. Tel: (withheld). Est: 1994. Private premises. Postal only. Stock: medium. Spec: Authors: Gurdjieff, W.I.; Wilson, Colin; Biography; Philosophy. PR: £5–250. Notes: book plates, manuscripts, booksearch and attends fairs. [Updated]

ASHTON-UNDER-LYNE

Marathon Books, 12 Lytham Close, Ashton-under-Lyne, Lancashire, OL6 9ER. Prop: Richard Bond. Tel: (0161) 343-2085. E-mail: richard.bond@jlservices.co.uk. Est: 1980. Private premises. Postal only. Appointment necessary. Stock: small. Spec: Psychology/Psychiatry; Sport - Athletics. Notes: also, a booksearch service. [Updated]

BOLTON

Siri Ellis Books, ■ The Last Drop Village, Bromley Cross, Bolton, BL7 9PZ. Prop: Siri E. Ellis. Tel: (01204) 597511. Web: www.siriellisbooks.co.uk. E-mail: mail@siriellisbooks.co.uk. Est: 1998. Shop. open: **M:** 12:00–17:00; **T:** 12:00–17:00; **Th:** 12:00–17:00; **F:** 12:00–17:00; **S:** 11:00–17:00; **Su:** 11:00–17:00. Stock: small. Spec: Children's; Children's - Illustrated; Illustrated. PR: £1–1,000. CC: AE; V; Switch. Mem: PBFA. Notes: booksearch for childhood favourites. [Updated]

CHEADLE

Mainly Fiction, 21 Tennyson Road, Cheadle, SK8 2AR. Prop: Christopher J. Peers. Tel: (0161) 428-6836. E-mail: mainly.fiction@ntlworld.com. Est: 1986. Private premises. Postal only. Spec: Children's; Fiction - Crime, Detective, Spy, Thrillers; First Editions; Modern First Editions. PR: £5–200. CC: V. Mem: PBFA. [Updated]

DIDSBURY

Barlow Moor Books, 29 Churchwood Road, Didsbury, M20 6TZ. Prop: Dr. Roger & Dr. L.A. Finlay. Tel: (0161) 434 5073. Fax: (0161) 448 2491. E-mail: books@barlowmoorbooks.com. Est: 1990. Private premises. Postal only. Contactable. Stock: very small. Spec: Corresp: French. VAT No: GB 560 9236 38. [Updated]

DUKINFIELD

Starlord Books, 72 Chester Avenue, Dukinfield, SK16 5BW. Prop: Starlord. Tel: 0161-338-8465. E-mail: Starlord@Starlord-Enterprises.freeserve.co.uk. Est: 1995. Private premises. Internet and postal. Appointment necessary. Open: **M:** 10:00–18:00; **T:** 09:00–12:00; **W:** 10:00–18:00; **Th:** 10:00–16:00; **F:** 12:00–16:00; **S:** 10:00–16:00; **Su:** 12:00–16:00. Stock: medium. Spec: Academic/Scholarly; Alternative Medicine; Astrology; Biography; Crime (True); Earth Mysteries; Esoteric; Metaphysics. PR: £1–100. [Updated]

HORWICH

Martin Bott (Bookdealers) Ltd., ■ 28-30 Lee Lane, Horwich, BL6 7BY. Prop: M.L.R. & M.H. Bott. Tel: (01204) 691489. Fax: (01204) 698729. Web: www.bottbooks.com. E-mail: martin.bott@btinternet.com. Est: 1997. Shop. Internet and postal. Telephone first. Open: **M:** 10:15–15:30; **T:** 10:15–15:00; **Th:** 10:15–15:00; **F:** 10:15–15:00; **S:** 10:30–16:00. Stock: large. Spec: Aviation; Buses/Trams; Canals/Inland Waterways; Company History; Engineering; Geology; Industry; Maritime/Nautical. PR: £1–1,000. CC: AE; JCB; MC; V; SW. Notes: booksearch for Railway & Industrial History titles only. [Updated]

LITTLEBOROUGH

George Kelsall Booksellers, ■ The Bookshop, 22 Church Street, Littleborough, OL15 9AA. Tel: (01706) 370244. E-mail: kelsall@bookshop22.fsnet.co.uk. Est: 1979. Shop open: **M:** 11:00–17:00; **T:** 13:00–17:00; **W:** 10:00–17:00; **Th:** 10:00–17:00; **F:** 10:00–17:00; **S:** 10:00–17:00. Stock: large. Spec: Architecture; Art History; Art Reference; History - General; History - Industrial; Politics; Social History; Topography - Local. PR: £1–500. CC: AE; MC; V. Mem: PBFA. VAT No: GB 306 0657 8. [26/07/2004]

MANCHESTER

The Bookshop, ■ 441 Wilmslow Road, Withington, Manchester, M20 4AN. Prop: Paul Johnson. Tel: (0161) 445 4345. Fax: (0161) 445 4345. Web: www.bookacademy.co.uk. E-mail: sales@bookacademy.co.uk. Est: 1996. Shop. Internet and postal. Open: **M:** 10:00–18:00; **T:** 10:00–18:00; **W:** 10:00–18:00; **Th:** 10:00–18:00; **F:** 10:00–18:00; **S:** 10:00–18:00; **Su:** 12:00–17:00. Stock: large. Spec: Academic/Scholarly; Black Studies; Culture - Popular; History - General; Holocaust; Homosexuality & Lesbianism; Irish Interest; Philosophy. PR: £1–50. CC: MC; V; Maestro. Notes: also at: The Bookshop, 11 Grove Street, Wilmslow, SK9 1DU & The Bookshop, 488 Wilbraham Rd, Chorlton, M21 9AS. [Updated]

Browzers, 2, Buckingham Road, Prestwich, Manchester, M25 9NE. Prop: Alan Seddon. Tel: 0161 771 32327. Fax: 161 773 2327. Web: www.browzers.co.uk. E-mail: alanseddon@tiscali.co.uk. Est: 1980. Mail Order Only. Internet and postal. Open: **M:** 09:00–17:30; **T:** 09:00–17:30; **W:** 09:00–17:30; **Th:** 09:00–17:30; **F:** 09:00–17:30; **S:** 09:00–17:30; **Su:** 09:00–17:30; Closed for lunch: 13:00–14:00. Spec: Antiques; Sport - Horse Racing (inc. Riding/Breeding/Equestrian). CC: MC; V. Cata: occasionally. Mem: ABA. [Updated]

Classic Crime Collections, 95a Boarshaw Road, Middleton, Manchester, M24 6AP. Prop: Rob Wilson. Tel: (0161) 653-4145. E-mail: Rob@mtwilson.freeserve.co.uk. Est: 1989. Private premises. Postal only. Stock: small. Spec: Authors:- Christie, Agatha; Creasey, John; Fleming, Ian; Buses/Trams; Canals/Inland Waterways; Crime (True); Fiction - Crime, Detective, Spy, Thrillers; Railways. PR: £2–400. Notes: also, a booksearch service. [Updated]

Franks Booksellers, Suite 33, 4th Floor, St Margaret's Chambers, 5 Newton Street, Piccadilly, Manchester, M1 1HL. Tel: (0161) 237-3747. Fax: (0161) 237-3747. Est: 1960. Office and/or bookroom open: **M:** 10:00–14:00; **T:** 10:00–14:00; **W:** 10:00–14:00; **Th:** 10:00–14:00; **F:** 10:00–14:00. Stock: small. Spec: Advertising; Autographs; Children's; Cinema/Film; Comic Books & Annuals; Magazines & Periodicals - General; Magic & Conjuring; Performing Arts. PR: £1–1,000. Notes: also, postcards. [Updated]

Gibbs Bookshop Ltd., ■ 13 Howard Road, Northenden, Manchester, M22 4EG. Tel: (0161) 998-2794. Fax: (0161) 998-2794. Web: www.gibbsbookshop.co.uk. E-mail: gibbsbookshop@beeb.net. Est: 1922. Internet and postal. Shop open: **M:** 10:00–17:00; **T:** 10:00–17:00; **W:** 10:00–17:00; **Th:** 10:00–17:00; **F:** 10:00–17:00; **S:** 10:00–17:00. Stock: very large. PR: £5–50. CC: JCB; MC; V. Mem: ABA. VAT No: GB 145 4624 68. [Updated]

Tim Kendall-Carpenter, 633 Wilmslow Road, Manchester, M20 6DF. Tel: (0161) 445-6172. Web: www.timkcbooks.com. E-mail: info@timkcbooks.com. Est: 1996. Private premises. Internet and postal. Appointment necessary. Stock: medium. Spec: First Editions; Modern First Editions; Poetry; Proof Copies. PR: £5–1,000. CC: AE; MC; V; Maestro. VAT No: GB 781 2657 13. [Updated]

The Little Bookshop, PO Box 134, Manchester, M8 4DJ. Prop: Valerie Clark. Tel: (0161) 740 1335. Web: www.littlebookshop.net. E-mail: info@littlebookshop.net. Est: 1989. Private premises. Internet and postal. Stock: medium. Spec: Arts; The; Autobiography; Biography; Fiction - General; History - General; Poetry; Religion - General; Travel - General. PR: £1–100. CC: PayPal. Notes: also sells new books under Thanatos Books. [Updated]

E.J. Morten (Booksellers), ■ 6–9 Warburton Street, Didsbury, Manchester, M20 6WA. Prop: John A. Morten. Tel: (0161) 445-7629. Fax: (0161) 448-1323. E-mail: morten.booksellers@lineone.net. Est: 1959. Shop open: **M:** 09:30–17:30; **T:** 09:30–17:30; **W:** 09:30–17:00; **Th:** 09:30–17:30; **F:** 09:30–17:30; **S:** 09:30–17:30. Stock: large. Spec: Military History; Sport - General; Travel - General. CC: MC; V; So, De. Corresp: French, German. Mem: PBFA; BA; ILAB; BT, NBL. [Updated]

Philip Nevitsky, P.O. Box 364, Manchester, M60 1AL. Tel: (0161) 228-2947. Fax: (0161) 236-0390. Est: 1974. Storeroom. Postal only. Stock: small. Spec: Cinema/Film; Entertainment - General; Music - Popular. [Updated]

V.M. Riley Books, 3 Leyburn Avenue, Stretford, Manchester, M32 8DZ. Prop: Mrs. Valerie M. Riley. Tel: (0161) 865-6543. Web: www.ukbookworld.com/members/vmriley. E-mail: val@rileyv.fsnet.co.uk. Est: 1989. Private premises. Postal only. Stock: small. PR: £1–50. [24/12/2004]

GREATER MANCHESTER

Star Lord Books, 72 Chester Avenue, Dukinfield, Cheshire, Manchester, SK16 5BW. Prop: Steve Starlord. Tel: (0161) 338-8465. E-mail: starlord@starlord-enterprises.freeserve.co.uk. Est: 1990. Private premises. Internet and postal. Appointment necessary. Stock: small. Spec: Astrology; Esoteric. PR: £1–100. [Updated]

Thanatos Books, PO Box 134, Manchester, M8 4DJ. Prop: Valerie Clark. Tel: 0161 740 1335. E-mail: info@littlebookshop.net. Est: 2000. Private premises. Internet and postal. CC: PayPal. Notes: for other details see under entry for The Little Bookshop, Manchester. [Updated]

The Treasure Island, 4 Evesham Road, Blackley, Manchester, M9 7EH. Prop: Ray Cauwood. Tel: (0161) 795 7750. Web: www.abebooks.com/home/RAYJC2000. E-mail: ray@the-treasure-island.com. Est: 2003. Private premises. Postal only. Appointment necessary. Stock: small. Spec: Animals and Birds; Art; Aviation; Languages - National; Maritime/Nautical; Medicine; Philately; Photography. PR: £1–50. CC: V. [Updated]

MOTTRAM IN LONGDENDALE

Rose Books, 26 Roe Cross Green, Mottram in Longdendale, Hyde, SK14 6LP. (*) Prop: E. Alan Rose. Tel: (01457) 763485. Fax: (01457) 763485. Est: 1990. Private premises. Appointment necessary. Stock: very small. Spec: History - Local; Religion - Christian; Theology. PR: £2–150. [Updated]

OLDHAM

Moorland Books, ■ 1 Smithy Lane, Uppermill, Oldham, OL3 6AH. Prop: Mrs. C.M. Bennett. Tel: (01457) 871306. E-mail: moorlandbooks@ntlworld.com. Est: 1982. Shop open: **T:** 10:30–16:00; **W:** 10:30–16:30; **Th:** 09:30–16:30; **F:** 10:30–16:30; **S:** 10:30–16:30; **Su:** 11:00–16:30. Stock: medium. Spec: Booksearch. PR: £1–100. CC: MC; V. [Updated]

Towpath Bookshop, ■ 27 High Street, Uppermill, Oldham, OL3 6HS. (*) Prop: Janet and Martin Byrom. Tel: (01457) 877078. Est: 1992. Shop open: **T:** 11:00–17:00; **W:** 10:30–17:00; **Th:** 10:30–17:00; **F:** 10:30–17:00; **S:** 10:30–17:00; **Su:** 11:00–17:00. Stock: very small. [Updated]

RADCLIFFE

Delph Books, 437, Bury and Bolton Road, Radcliffe, M26 4LJ. Prop: Frank Lamb. Tel: 0161 764 4488. E-mail: franklamb@delphbooks.freeserve.co.uk. Est: 1979. Private premises. Internet and postal. Telephone first. Open: **M:** 09:00–19:30; **T:** 09:00–19:30; **W:** 09:00–19:30; **Th:** 09:00–19:30; **F:** 09:00–19:30; **S:** 09:00–19:30; **Su:** 09:00–19:30. Spec: Company History; County - Local; Genealogy; History - Family; History - Military; Horology; Military History; Police Force Histories. CC: MC; V. Corresp: English French. Mem: PBFA. Notes: I also stand at book fairs in the North of England. I have a good stock of Lancs & Yorks Parish Registers, Co-op histories, Golf club histories, Clocks & Watches, Rolls of Honour, Lancs & Yorks Topography, Local History and Dialect. [Updated]

ROCHDALE

Rochdale Book Company, 59 Bagslate Moor Roadd, Rochdale, OL11 5YH. Prop: J.S. & S.M. Worthy. Tel: (01706) 658300. Fax: (01706) 713294. E-mail: worthybooks@aol.com. Est: 1971. Warehouse. Appointment necessary. Open: **S:** 10:30–17:30. Stock: large. Spec: Antiquarian; Architecture; Canals/Inland Waterways; Children's; Company History; Fine & Rare; History - Industrial; Illustrated. CC: MC; V. Mem: PBFA. [Updated]

STOCKPORT

Richard Coulthurst, 97 Green Pastures, Stockport, SK4 3RB. Tel: (0161) 431-3864. E-mail: richard.coulthurst@btinternet.com. Est: 1995. Private premises. Postal only. Stock: very small. Spec: Aviation; Canals/Inland Waterways; History - Industrial; Publishers - Oakwood Press; Railways; Steam Engines; Transport; Booksearch. PR: £5–100. [Updated]

Robin S. Hunt, 6 Alford Road, Heaton Chapel, Stockport, SK4 5AW. Prop: Robin Hunt. Tel: (0161) 285-9670. E-mail: robin@rashalf.freeserve.co.uk. Est: 1975. Postal only. Stock: very small. Spec: Crime (True); History - General; Nostalgia; Royalty - General; Social History. PR: £1–50. Notes: Very few books, mainly ephemera. [Updated]

WIGAN

R.D.M. & I.M. Price (Books), 25 Coniston Avenue, Whitley, Wigan, WN1 2EY. Prop: Robert and Irene Price. Tel: (01942) 242607. Est: 1997. Private premises. Postal only. Stock: very small. Spec: Autobiography; Biography; Colonial; Fiction - General; Booksearch. PR: £1–65. [Updated]

Rolling Stock Books, ■ 16, Upper Dicconson Street, Wigan, WN1 2AD. Prop: Nick Howell. Tel: (01942) 493949. E-mail: rollingstockbooks@fsmail.net. Est: 1996. Shop open: **T:** 09:30–17:00; **W:** 09:30–17:00; **Th:** 09:30–17:00; **F:** 09:30–17:00; **S:** 09:30–17:00. Stock: medium. Spec: Buses/Trams; Canals/Inland Waterways; Railways; Transport. PR: £5–500. Cata: occasionally on transport. Mem: PBFA. Notes: valuations booksearch some new books on transport. VAT No: GB 692 8123 15. [Updated]

Available from Richard Joseph Publishers Ltd
Sheppard's Book Dealers in
NORTH AMERICA
15th Edition   (Royal H/b, plus CD-ROM)   £30.00 560pp

HAMPSHIRE

ALRESFORD

Bolton Books, 60, The Dean, Alresford, SO24 9BD. Prop: David Bolton. Tel: (01962) 734435. Fax: (01962) 734435. Web: www.boltonbooks.com. E-mail: david@boltonbooks.com. Est: 1997. Private premises. Internet and postal. Appointment necessary. Stock: very small. Spec: Colour-Plate; Illustrated; Publishers - Black, A. & C.; Publishers - Foulis, T.N.; Topography - General. PR: £5–1,250. Mem: PBFA. Notes: also exhibits at bookfairs. [Updated]

Laurence Oxley Ltd, ■ The Studio Bookshop, 17 Broad Street, Alresford, Nr. Winchester, SO24 9AW. Prop: Anthony Oxley. Tel: (01962) 732188. E-mail: aoxley@freenet.co.uk. Est: 1950. Shop open: **M:** 09:00–17:00; **T:** 09:00–17:00; **W:** 09:00–17:00; **Th:** 09:00–17:00; **F:** 09:00–17:00; **S:** 09:00–17:00. Stock: large. Spec: Countries - Far East, The; Countries - India; Topography - General; Topography - Local. PR: £1–25,000. CC: AE; D; MC; V. Mem: ABA; BA; ABA, FATG. Notes: also, picture dealers, picture frame makers and restoration work. VAT No: GB 188 5081 31. [13/11/2004]

ALTON

Alton Secondhand Books, ■ 43 Normandy Street, Alton, GU34 1DQ. Prop: Mrs. J. Andrews. Tel: (01420) 89352. E-mail: joan.andrews@virgin.net. Est: 1989. Sho open: **M:** 09:30–17:30; **T:** 09:30–17:30; **W:** 09:30–17:00; **Th:** 09:30–17:30; **F:** 09:30–17:30; **S:** 09:30–17:00. Stock: medium. Spec: Booksearch. PR: £1–100. VAT No: GB 631 9874 13. [Updated]

Dance Books Ltd, The Old Bakery, 4 Lenten St., Alton, GU34 1HG. Prop: David Leonard. Tel: (01420) 86138. Fax: (01420) 86142. Web: www.dancebooks.co.uk. E-mail: dwl@dancebooks.co.uk. Est: 1960. Storeroom. Appointment necessary. Open: **M:** 10:00–17:00; **T:** 10:00–17:00; **W:** 10:00–17:00; **Th:** 10:00–17:00; **F:** 10:00–17:00. Stock: small. Spec: Dance. PR: £1–1,000. CC: AE; E; MC; V. Mem: BA. VAT No: GB 238 6405 53. [Updated]

Peter White Books, Westbrooke House, 76 High Street, Alton, GU34 1EN. Prop: Peter White. Tel: (01420) 86745. Fax: (01420) 86745. E-mail: pwbooks@btconnect.com. Est: 1995. Office and/or bookroom. Internet and postal. Telephone first. Stock: small. Spec: History - Local; Modern First Editions; Railways; Sport - Football (Soccer); Topography - General; Transport. PR: £4–60. CC: MC; V. Corresp: French. Mem: Also, stocks titles on local history in most counties [Updated]

Soldridge Books Ltd, Soldridge House, Soldridge Road, Medstead, Alton, GU34 5JF. Prop: Jan & John Lewis. Tel: (01420) 562811. Fax: (01420) 562811. Web: www.soldridgebooks.co.uk. E-mail: lewis@soldridgebooks.co.uk. Est: 1991. Private premises. Internet and postal. Appointment necessary. Open: **M:** 09:00–18:00; **T:** 09:00–18:00; **W:** 09:00–18:00; **Th:** 09:00–18:00; **F:** 09:00–18:00; **S:** 09:00–13:00. Stock: medium. Spec: Aeronautics; Aviation; Photography; Poetry. PR: £3–400. CC: MC; V; Maestro. Corresp: French. Mem: PBFA. VAT No: GB 799 6939 25. [Updated]

ALVERSTOKE

R.W. Forder, 12 St Mark's Road, Alverstoke, Gosport, PO12 2DA. Prop: R.W. Forder. Tel: (023) 9252-7965. E-mail: r.w.forder@btinternet.com. Est: 1985. Private premises. Internet and postal. Telephone first. Spec: Free Thought; Humanism; Radical Issues. PR: £1–200. Corresp: German. Notes: also, a booksearch service. [16/11/2004]

ANDOVER

Armchair Auctions, 98 Junction Road, Andover, SP10 3JA. Prop: George Murdoch. Tel: (01264) 362048. Fax: (01264) 362048. Est: 1989. Private premises. Stock: small. Spec: Aviation; Military; Naval; War - World War I; Booksearch; Prints and Maps. PR: £5–500. CC: AE; MC; V. Mem: Main activity: postal auctions. [Updated]

BASINGSTOKE

Byblos Antiquarian & Rare Book, Broadmead, 5 Worting Road, Basingstoke, RG21 8TL. Tel: (0207) 1930139. Web: www.byblos.uk.com. E-mail: Henry.Stanton@byblos.uk.com. Est: 2005. Private premises. Internet and postal. Stock: very small. Spec: Antiquarian; Fine & Rare; Booksearch. PR: £5–1,500. CC: MC; V. Corresp: French, Italian. Mem: IOAB. [Updated]

David Flint, 30 Barn Lane, Oakley, Basingstoke, RG23 7HT. Prop: David Flint. Tel: (01256) 781413. E-mail: davidaflint@aol.com. Est: 1985. Private premises. Postal only. Stock: small. Spec: Children's; Children's - Illustrated; Illustrated. PR: £1–200. [Updated]

Squirrel Antiques, 9a New Street, Joices Yard, Basingstoke, RG21 DQ. Prop: Alan Stone. Tel: (01256) 464885. Est: 1981. Office and/or bookroom. Open: **M:** 10:00–17:30; **T:** 10:00–17:30; **W:** 10:00–17:30; **Th:** 10:00–17:30; **F:** 10:00–17:30; **S:** 10:00–17:30. Stock: small. PR: £1–75. Mem: Small general stock. Also antiques, curios and jewelery. [Updated]

EMSWORTH

Bookends, ■ 7 High St., Emsworth, PO10 7AQ. Prop: Carol Waldron. Tel: (01243) 372154. Web: www.bookends.me.uk. E-mail: cawaldron@tinyworld.co.uk. Est: 1982. Shop open: **M:** 09:00–17:00; **T:** 09:00–17:00; **W:** 09:00–17:00; **Th:** 09:00–17:00; **F:** 09:00–17:00; **S:** 09:00–17:00; **Su:** 10:00–15:00. Stock: large. Spec: Booksearch. PR: £1–300. Corresp: French. [Updated]

Peter Hill, 3 Westbourne Avenue, Emsworth, PO10 7QT. Tel: (01243) 379956. Fax: (01243) 379956. E-mail: peterhill.books@btinternet.com. Est: 1986. Private premises. Appointment necessary. Open: **M:** 09:00–17:00; **T:** 09:00–17:00; **W:** 09:00–17:00; **Th:** 09:00–17:00; **F:** 09:00–17:00. Stock: small. Spec: Alpinism/Mountaineering; Classical Studies; Travel - General. PR: £10–2,000. Corresp: French. Mem: ABA; PBFA. [Updated]

FAREHAM

Portus Books, 9 Union Street, Fareham, PO16 9EB. Prop: Philip Elston. Tel: 01329 220419. Web: www.portusbooks.co.uk. E-mail: enquiry@portusbooks.co.uk. Private premises. Postal only. Telephone first. Spec: Author - Baker, Denys V.; Maritime/Nautical; Modern First Editions; Sport - Sailing; Travel - General. Corresp: German. Notes: All books are accurately described, professionally packaged and promptly dispatched. [Updated]

FARNBOROUGH

Farnborough Gallery, 26 Guildford Road West, Farnborough, GU14 6PU. Prop: P.H. Taylor. Tel: (01252) 518033. Fax: (01252) 511503. Web: www.farnboroughgallery.co.uk. E-mail: petert@btconnect.com. Est: 1978. Storeroom. Internet and postal. Appointment necessary. Open: **M:** 08:00–18:00; **T:** 08:00–18:00; **W:** 08:00–18:00; **Th:** 08:00–18:00; **F:** 08:00–18:00; **S:** 08:00–17:00. Spec: Academic/Scholarly; Art; Art - Technique; First Editions; History - General; Military; Military History; Prints and Maps. PR: £5–1,000. CC: AE; MC; V. Mem: Fine Art Trade Guild. Notes: Picture framing , mount cutting, framed artwork for sale. VAT No: GB 296 4807 13. [10/10/2004]

FLEET

War & Peace Books, 32 Wellington Ave., Fleet, GU51 3BF. Prop: Dr G.M. Bayliss. Tel: (01252) 677902. Fax: (01252) 677902. Web: www.abebooks.com. E-mail: gwyn.bayliss@ntlworld.com. Est: 1998. Private premises. Postal only. Contactable. Stock: very small. Spec: Aviation; Biography; Literary Travel; Literature; Maritime/Nautical; Military; Military History; Naval. PR: £5–100. [Updated]

FORDINGBRIDGE

Bristow & Garland, ■ 45–47 Salisbury Street, Fordingbridge, SP6 1AB. Prop: David Bristow & Victoria Garland. Tel: (01425) 657337. Fax: (01425) 657337. Web: www.bristowandgarland.co.uk. E-mail: mail@bristowandgarland.fsnet.co.uk. Est: 1970. Shop open: **M:** 10:00–17:00; **F:** 10:00–17:00; **S:** 10:00–17:00. Stock: small. Spec: Autographs; Fine & Rare; Manuscripts. PR: £5–5,000. CC: JCB; MC. [Updated]

GOSPORT

Richard Martin Bookshop & Gallery, ■ 19-23 Stoke Road, Gosport, PO12 1LS. Tel: (023) 9252-0642. Fax: (023) 9252-0642. Web: www.richardmartingallery.co.uk. E-mail: enquiries@richardmartingallery.co.uk. Est: 1976. Shop open: **T:** 10:30–16:30; **Th:** 10:30–16:30; **F:** 10:30–16:30; **S:** 10:30–13:00; Closed for lunch: 13:00–14:15. Stock: medium. Spec: Illustrated; Maritime/Nautical; Topography - General; Travel - General; Prints and Maps. PR: £10–3,000. CC: MC; V. Mem: PBFA. Notes: also, restoration work, frames and mounts. VAT No: GB 430 6603 81. [Updated]

Available from Richard Joseph Publishers Ltd
Sheppard's Book Dealers in
AUSTRALIA & NEW ZEALAND
Order the next edition now £30.00

Sub Aqua Prints and Books, 3 Crescent Road, Alverstoke, Gosport, PO12 2DH. Prop: Kevin F. Casey. Tel: (023) 9252 0426. Fax: (023) 9250 2428. Web: www.buyhistoryprints.com. E-mail: kevin@ buyhistoryprints.com. Est: 1991. Private premises. Internet and postal. Appointment necessary. Open: Stock: small. Spec: Deep Sea Diving; Marine Sciences; Maritime/Nautical; Naval; Collectables; Ephemera; Prints and Maps. PR: £5–1,000. CC: JCB; MC; V. [Updated]

HAVANT

Tobo Books, 6 The Oakwood Centre, Downley Road, Havant, PO9 2NP. Prop: Matthew Wingett. Tel: 02392472000. Web: www.tobo-books.com. E-mail: sheppards@tobo-books.com. Est: 2000. Office and/or bookroom. Internet Only. Appointment necessary. Open: **M:** 09:00–17:00; **T:** 09:00–17:00; **W:** 09:00–17:00; **Th:** 09:00–17:00; **F:** 09:00–17:00. Stock: small. Spec: Antiquarian; Architecture; Authors:- Byron, Lord; Cruickshank, G.; Dickens, Charles; Fleming, Ian; Greene, Graham; Milne, A.A. PR: £1–20,000. CC: JCB; MC; V. Corresp: Schoolboy French; Schoolboy Spanish. Mem: PBFA. VAT No: GB 812 1985 36. [Updated]

HAYLING ISLAND

DBS Childrens Collectable Books, 43 Sea Front, Hayling Island, PO11 0AN. Prop: Dennis Cowan. Tel: 02392 637456. Fax: 02392 637456. Web: www.dbschildrenscollectablebooks.com. E-mail: dbsbooks@ hotmail.com. Est: 1998. Private premises. Open: **M:** 10:30–17:30; **T:** 10:30–17:30; **W:** 10:30–17:30; **Th:** 10:30–17:30; **F:** 10:30–17:30. [Updated]

HORNDEAN

Milestone Publications Goss & Crested China Club, 62 Murray Road, Horndean, PO8 9JL. Prop: Mrs. Lynda Pine. Tel: (023) 9259-7440. Fax: (023) 9259-1975. Web: www.gosschinaclub.demon.co.uk. E-mail: info@gosschinaclub.co.uk. Est: 1975. Shop and/or showroom. Open: **M:** 09:00–16:00; **T:** 09:00–16:00; **W:** 09:00–16:00; **Th:** 09:00–16:00; **F:** 09:00–16:00. Stock: small. Spec: Authors:- Goss, W.H.; Hall S.C.; Jewett, S.O.; Ceramics; Ephemera. PR: £1–40. CC: E; JCB; MC; V; all others. Mem: F.R.S.A. Notes: Open at other times by appointment Also, dealers in souvenir ware china, Goss & Crested china c.1850-1940, heraldic porcelain & new books of the same topics. [Updated]

LIPHOOK

Pauline Harries Books, 4 Willow Close, Liphook, GU30 7HX. Tel: (01428) 723764. Fax: (01428) 722367. Web: www.abebooks.com/home/paulineharriesbooks. E-mail: pauline.harriesbooks@tiscali.co.uk. Est: 1982. Private premises. Appointment necessary. Stock: medium. Spec: Booksearch. PR: £2–1,000. CC: JCB; MC; V; Delta. Mem: PBFA. [Updated]

LISS

William Duck, Highfield Farm, Hatch Lane, Liss, GU33 7NH. Prop: William Duck. Tel: (01730) 895594. Fax: (01730) 894548. Est: 1963. Private premises. Appointment necessary. Stock: very small. Spec: Architecture; Arms & Armour; Astronautics; Aviation; Canals/Inland Waterways; Cities; Civil Engineering; Decorative Art. PR: £10–5,000. Mem: ABA; PBFA. [Updated]

LYMINGTON

M. & B. Clapham, ■ 4 Priestmands Place, Lymington, SO41 9GA. Prop: Peter Clapham. Tel: (01590) 677019. Est: 1978. Shop open: **M:** 10:00–17:00; **T:** 10:00–17:00; **W:** 10:00–17:00; **Th:** 10:00–17:00; **F:** 10:00–17:00; **S:** 09:00–17:00. Stock: medium. Spec: Music - General; Sport - Yachting. CC: MC; V. [Updated]

NEW MILTON

J.H. Day, 33 Ashley Common Road, Ashley, New Milton, BH25 5AL. Prop: J.H. Day. Tel: (01425) 619406. Web: www.abebooks.com. E-mail: jamesjday@aol.com. Est: 1983. Private premises. Internet and postal. Appointment necessary. Open: Stock: medium. Spec: Sport - Horse Racing (inc. Riding/ Breeding/Equestrian). PR: £5–200. CC: PayPal. Notes: Lymington Antique Centre Hampshire UK. [Updated]

OVERTON

David Esplin, 30 High Street, Overton, RG25 3HA. Tel: (01256) 771108. E-mail: books@ esplin.fsworld.co.uk. Est: 1978. Private premises. Postal only. Stock: small. Spec: Medicine - History of; Science - History of; Technology. PR: £5–1,000. CC: MC; V; SW, So. Corresp: French. [Updated]

PETERSFIELD

The Petersfield Bookshop, ■ 16a Chapel Street, Petersfield, GU32 3DS. Prop: Frank, Ann, John & David Westwood. Tel: (01730) 263388. Fax: (01730) 269426. Web: www.petersfieldbookshop.com. E-mail: sales@petersfieldbookshop.com. Est: 1918. Shop open: **M:** 09:00–17:30; **T:** 09:00–17:30; **W:** 09:00–17:30; **Th:** 09:00–17:30; **F:** 09:00–17:30; **S:** 09:00–17:30. Spec: Sport - Angling/Fishing; Travel - General. PR: £1–2,000. CC: AE; D; MC; V. Mem: ABA; PBFA; BA; ILAB. Notes: also, maps, prints, new books, art materials, picture framing & a booksearch service. VAT No: GB 192 6013 72. [Updated]

David Schutte, 'Waterside', 119 Sussex Road, Petersfield, GU31 4LB. Tel: (01730) 269115. Fax: (01730) 231177. Web: www.http://davidschutte.co.uk. E-mail: david.schutte@virgin.net. Est: 1980. Private premises. Internet and postal. Appointment necessary. Spec: Authors:- Blyton, Enid; Buckeridge, A.; Crompton, Richmal; Johns, W.E.; Ransome, Arthur; Richards, Frank; Saville, M.; Wodehouse, P.G PR: £3–1,500. CC: MC; V. Mem: PBFA. [Updated]

PORTSMOUTH

Alexander Books, ■ 62 Castle Road, Southsea, Portsmouth, PO5 3AZ. Prop: Michael Wilson. Tel: 023 927 53207. Web: www.alexanderbooks.com. E-mail: michael@alexanderbooks.com. Est: 2003. Shop open: **S:** 10:00–17:00. [Updated]

Art Reference Books, 3 Portswood Road, Portsmouth, PO2 9QX. Prop: Andy Ralph. Tel: (02392) 790861. Fax: (02392) 650756. Web: www.artreferencebooks.com. E-mail: artreferencebooks@hotmail.com. Est: 1999. Private premises. Internet and postal. Appointment necessary. Stock: medium. Spec: Antiquarian; Antiques; Applied Art; Architecture; Art; Art History; Art Reference; Artists. PR: £2–1,000. [Updated]

Jade Mountain, ■ 17–19 Highland Road, Southsea, Portsmouth, PO4 9DA. Prop: Ian Stemp. Tel: (023) 92 732951. E-mail: ianstemp@btinternet.com. Est: 1992. Internet and postal. Shop open: **M:** 09:30–17:30; **W:** 09:30–17:30; **F:** 09:30–17:30; **S:** 09:30–17:30. Stock: large. Spec: Animals and Birds; Cinema/Film; Dictionaries; Fiction - General; Food & Drink; Gardening - General; History - General; Languages - Foreign. PR: £1–80. [Updated]

PURBROOK

Hobgoblin Books, 66 Privett Road, Purbrook, PO7 5JW. Prop: Jacqueline & Philip Barrett. Tel: (023) 9271-3129. E-mail: goblinbook@aol.com. Est: 1988. Private premises. Appointment necessary. Stock: medium. Spec: Authors - Women; Countries - China; Countries - Japan; Folklore; Medieval; Women. PR: £5–500. CC: PayPal. [Updated]

RINGWOOD

E. Chalmers Hallam, Trees, 9 Post Office Lane, St. Ives, Ringwood, BH24 2PG. Prop: Laura Hiscock. Tel: (01425) 470060. Fax: (01425) 470060. Web: www.hallam-books.co.uk. E-mail: laura@hallam-books.co.uk. Est: 1946. Private premises. Appointment necessary. Stock: large. Spec: Anthropology; Author - Watkins-Pitchford, Denys ('B.B.'); Cockfighting; Countries - Africa; Countries - India; Dogs; Firearms/Guns; Fishes. PR: £5–5,000. CC: MC; V; Debit card. Mem: PBFA. [Upadted]

ROMSEY

Bufo Books, 32 Tadficld Road, Romscy, SO51 5AJ. Prop: Ruth Allen & Peter Hubbard. Tel: (01794) 517149. Fax: (08700) 516786. Web: www.bufobooks.demon.co.uk. E-mail: bufo@bufobooks.demon.co.uk. Est: 1979. Private premises. Internet and postal. Appointment necessary. Stock: medium. Spec: Children's; Military; War - General. PR: £1–200. CC: MC; V; Bartercard. Corresp: French. Mem: PBFA. Notes: attends bookfairs. VAT No: GB 522 4988 32. [Updated]

Available from Richard Joseph Publishers Ltd
BOOKDEALING FOR PROFIT
by Paul Minet

Quarto H/b   £10.00 144pp

SOUTHAMPTON

Vincent G. Barlow, 24 Howerts Close, Warsash, Southampton, SO31 9JR. Tel: (01489) 582431. E-mail: vg.books@ntlworld.com. Est: 1981. Storeroom. Appointment necessary. Stock: small. Spec: Art Reference; Catalogues Raisonnes; Children's; Decorative Art; Fine Printing; Illustrated; Interior Design; Limited Editions. PR: £3–2,000. Mem: PLA; IBIS. Notes: attends monthly fairs at Royal National. Also prints. [Updated]

Broadwater Books, 62 Britannia Gardens, Hedge End, Southampton, SO30 2RP. Prop: J.E. Dancy. Tel: (01489) 786035. E-mail: john@jdancy.fsnet.co.uk. Est: 1988. Private premises. Postal only. Stock: large. Spec: Countries - England; Countries - Melanesia; Countries - Scotland; History - General; Religion - General; Theology; Travel - General. PR: £1–400. Notes: also, wants lists welcomed. [Updated]

W.E. Jackson, 6 Shepherds Close, Bartley, Southampton, SO40 2LJ. Prop: Bill Jackson. Tel: (02380) 812640. E-mail: bill@bilberry.ndo.co.uk. Est: 1988. Private premises. Postal only. Telephone first. Stock: small. PR: £1–100. Notes: also organisor of Southampton and Winchester Book Fairs - and attends other fairs. [Updated]

Morley Case, 24 Wildburn Close, Calmore, Southampton, SO40 2SG. Prop: David Case. Tel: (023) 8086-4264. Web: www.abebooks.com/home/case. E-mail: morleycase@aol.com. Est: 1973. Private premises. Internet and postal. Appointment necessary. Stock: small. Spec: Art; Aviation; Military; Sport - Golf. PR: £5–200. [Updated]

Peter Rhodes, Bookseller, ■ 21 Portswood Road, Southampton, SO17 2ES. Tel: (02380) 399003. E-mail: peterrhodes.books@virgin.net. Est: 1996. Shop open: **T:** 10:00–17:00; **W:** 10:00–17:00; **Th:** 10:00–17:00; **F:** 10:00–17:00; **S:** 10:00–17:00. Stock: large. Spec: Anthropology; Author - 20th Century; Children's - Illustrated; Countries - India; Photography; Theatre. Notes: insurance and probate valuation. also coffee shop. [Updated]

Signature Books, 22 Taranto Road, Southampton, SO16 5PN. Prop: Mrs Rowena Adams. Tel: (023) 8078 7756. Web: www.signaturebookco.com. E-mail: signaturebookco@aol.com. Est: 2002. Private premises. Internet and postal. Stock: very small. Spec: Children's; Countries - Polar; Fiction - General; Maritime/Nautical; Military; Natural History; Performing Arts; Poetry. PR: £5–160. [Updated]

SOUTHSEA

Palladour Books, 23, Eldon Street, Southsea, PO5 4BS. Prop: Jeremy & Anne Powell. Tel: (02392) 826935. Fax: (02392) 826935. E-mail: jeremy.powell@ntlworld.com. Est: 1985. Private premises. Internet and postal. Appointment necessary. Stock: very small. Spec: First Editions; Literature; Magazines & Periodicals - General; Military; Poetry; School Registers/Rolls of Honour; War - General; War - World War I. PR: £1–500. [Updated]

TITCHFIELD

Ardis Books, 3 Mill Street, Titchfield, Fareham, PO14 4AB. Prop: Robert Newbury. Tel: 01329 517724. Web: www.ardis.co.uk. E-mail: RNewbury@ardis.co.uk. Est: 1989. Mail Order Only. Internet Only. Telephone first. Open: **M:** 09:00–17:30; **T:** 09:00–17:30; **W:** 09:00–17:30; **Th:** 09:00–17:30; **F:** 09:00–17:30; **S:** 09:00–17:30; **Su:** 09:00–17:30; Closed for lunch: 13:00–14:00. Spec: Antiquarian; Authors:- Johns, W.E.; Saville, M.; Bibles; Business Studies; Comics; Commerce - General; Computing. VAT No: GB 522 2143 96. [Updated]

WARSASH

Warsash Nautical Bookshop, ■ 6 Dibles Road, Warsash, Southampton, SO31 9HZ. Prop: Mr. Andrew Marshall. Tel: (01489) 572384. Fax: (01489) 885756. Web: www.nauticalbooks.co.uk. E-mail: orders@nauticalbooks.co.uk. Est: 1973. Shop. Internet and postal. Open: **M:** 09:00–17:30; **T:** 09:00–17:30; **W:** 09:00–17:30; **Th:** 09:00–17:30; **F:** 09:00–17:30; **S:** 09:30–17:00. Stock: small. Spec: Academic/Scholarly; Maritime/Natical - Log Books; Maritime/Nautical; Navigation; Booksearch; Prints and Maps. PR: £5–500. CC: AE; D; E; JCB; MC; V. Mem: BA. VAT No: GB 108 3293 82. [Updated]

WINCHESTER

Boris Books, Winnall Manor Farm, Wales Street, Winchester, SO23 0HA. Prop: Pam Stevenson. Tel: (01962) 890355. Web: www.borisbooks.co.uk. E-mail: pam@borisbooks.fsnet.co.uk. Est: 1995. Office and/or bookroom. Internet and postal. Appointment necessary. Open: **M:** 09:30–16:30; **T:** 09:30–16:30; **W:** 09:30–16:30; **Th:** 09:30–16:30; **F:** 09:30–16:30; Closed for lunch: 13:15–14:15. Stock: small. Spec: Author - Heyer, Georgette; Children's; Fiction - General; Fiction - Historical; First Editions; Illustrated; Literature; Music - General. PR: £1–200. CC: MC; V. Mem: PBFA. VAT No: GB 717 6806 15. [Updated.]

Peter M. Daly, 6 Ronald Bowker Court, Greenhill Road, Winchester, SO22 5EA. Prop: Peter M. Daly. Tel: (01962) 867732. Fax: (01962) 867732. E-mail: petermdaly@rarebooks.fsnet.co.uk. Est: 1978. Private premises. Internet and postal. Appointment necessary. Stock: small. Spec: Africana; Agriculture; Alpinism/Mountaineering; Animals and Birds; Antiquarian; Countries - Afganistan; Countries - Africa; Countries - Arabia. PR: £1–1,000. CC: JCB; MC; V; SW. Mem: PBFA. VAT No: GB 411 8630 76. [Updated]

H.M. Gilbert & Son, 5 Rooks Down, Winchester, SO22 4QN. Prop: Richard Gilbert. Tel: (023) 8022-6420. Est: 1859. Private premises. Appointment necessary. Open: Stock: small. Spec: Antiquarian; Literature; Topography - General; Topography - Local. PR: £1–500. CC: MC; V. Mem: PBFA. [Updated]

John Barton, 84, Old Kennels Lane, Winchester, SO22 4JT. Tel: 01962 866543. E-mail: jg.barton@virgin.net. Est: 1966. Private premises. Postal only. Appointment necessary. Spec: Archaeology; History - Local; Topography - Local. Cata: occasionally. [Updated]

Kingsgate Books & Prints, ■ Kingsgate Arch, Winchester, SO23 9PD. Prop: Michael Fowkes. Tel: (01962) 864710. Fax: (01962) 864710. Est: 1992. Shop open: **M:** 12.30–17:00; **T:** 12:30–17:00; **W:** 12:30–17:00; **Th:** 12:30–17:00; **F:** 12:30–17:00; **S:** 10:00–17:00. Stock: very small. Spec: Art History; Art Reference; History - Local; Literary Criticism; Literature; Natural History; Poetry; Prints and Maps. PR: £1–150. CC: MC; V; Any. [Updated]

Oxfam Books and Music, ■ 74 Parchment St., Winchester, SO23 8AT. Prop: Oxfam. Tel: (01962) 841627. Web: www.oxfam.org.uk/shops. E-mail: shopf4034@btinternet.com. Est: 1989. Shop open: **M:** 09:00–17:00; **T:** 09:00–17:00; **W:** 09:30–17:00; **Th:** 09:30–17:00; **F:** 09:00–17:00; **S:** 09:00–17:00. Stock: small. Spec: Academic/Scholarly; Art; Children's; Fiction - General; Health; History - General; Natural History; Religion - General. PR: £1–150. CC: MC; V. [Updated]

S.P.C.K., ■ 24 The Square, Winchester, SO23 9EX. Tel: (01962) 866617. Fax: (01962) 890312. E-mail: winchester@spck.org.uk. Est: 1698. Shop open: **M:** 09:00–16:30; **T:** 08:00–17:30; **W:** 09:00–17:30; **Th:** 09:00–17:30; **F:** 09:00–17:30; **S:** 08:00–17:30. Stock: large. Spec: Religion - Christian; Theology; Booksearch. PR: £1–300. CC: MC; V. Mem: BA. Notes: also, wide Christian booksearch service. VAT No: GB 232 8071 82. [Updated]

Sen Books, 3 Long Barrow Close, South Wonston, Winchester, SO21 3ED. Prop: Andrew Duckworth. Tel: (01962) 884405. Fax: (01962) 884405. E-mail: andrew.duckworth_senbooks@btopenworld.com. Est: 1975. Private premises. Appointment necessary. Stock: small. Spec: Authors:- Trollope, Anthony; White, Gilbert; Booksearch; Ephemera; Prints and Maps. PR: £1–200. [Updated]

The Winchester Bookshop, ■ 10a St George's Street, Winchester, SO23 8BG. Prop: Messrs Barnes, Brown and Green. Tel: 01962863483. E-mail: winchester.books@btinternet.com. Est: 1991. Open: **M:** 10.00–1700; **T:** 10:00–17:00; **W:** 10:00–17:00; **Th:** 10:00–17:00; **F:** 10:00–17:00; **S:** 10:00–17:30. Spec: CC: MC; V; Most debit cards. Corresp: German. Notes: a general bookshop, with particular strengths in Winchester local history, fishing and literature. Some good antiquarian and modern firsts are stocked [Updated]

HEREFORDSHIRE

ASHPERTON

Books for Content, Spring Grove Farm, Wood End, Ashperton, Ledbury, HR8 2RS. Prop: H.M. Jones. Tel: (01432) 890279. Est: 1989. Private premises. Postal only. Stock: small. Spec: Agriculture; Author - Street, A.G.; Cookery/Gastronomy; Crafts; Farming & Livestock; Gardening - General; Horticulture; Rural Life. PR: £3–100. [Updated]

HAY–ON–WYE (SEE ALSO UNDER POWYS, WALES)

HEREFORD

Acer Books, Penworlodd Farm, Rowlestone, Hereford, HR2 0DS. Prop: Kevin Desforges BSc (Hons). Tel: (01981) 241176. Fax: (01981) 241176. E-mail: acerbooks@bigfoot.com. Est: 1998. Private premises. Postal only. Contactable. Open: **M:** 09:00–18:00; **T:** 09:00–18:00; **W:** 09:00–18:00; **Th:** 09:00–18:00; **F:** 09:00–18:00; **S:** 09:00–18:00. Stock: medium. Spec: Animals and Birds; Botany; Conservation; Forestry; Geography; Landscape; Natural History; New Naturalist. PR: £1–3,000. Notes: exhibits at natural history fairs, inc. British Birdwatching Fair. [Updated]

The New Strand Bookshop, ■ Eardisley, Hereford, HR3 6PW. Prop: R. & A. Cardwell. Tel: (01544) 327285. Shop open: **W:** 09:30–18:00; **Th:** 09:30–18:00; **F:** 09:30–18:00; **S:** 09:30–18:00; **Su:** 09:30–18:00. Stock: very large. Spec: Children's; Fiction - General; Fiction - Crime, Detective, Spy, Thrillers; Fiction - Science Fiction; Natural History. PR: £1–250. [Updated]

B.A. & C.W.M. Pratt, Huntington House, Huntington Lane, Hereford, HR4 7RA. Tel: (01432) 350927. Fax: (01432) 350927. Est: 1967. Private premises. Postal only. Spec: Medicine. [Updated]

KINGTON

Castle Hill Books, ■ 12 Church Street, Kington, HR5 3AZ. Prop: Peter Newman. Tel: (01544) 231195/ 23116. Fax: (01544) 231161. Web: www.castlehillbooks.co.uk. E-mail: sales@castlehillbooks.co.uk. Est: 1987. Shop open: **M:** 10:30–13:00; **T:** 10:30–13:00; **W:** 10:30–13:00; **Th:** 10:30–13:00; **F:** 10:30–13:00; **S:** 10:30–16:00. Stock: very large. Spec: Agriculture; Antiquarian; Archaeology; History - General; History - Local; Natural History; Topography - General; Topography - Local. PR: £3–15,000. CC: MC; V. Mem: PBFA. Notes: also, new books. and maps in stock. VAT No: GB 489 2054 19. [Updated]

LEDBURY

Keith Smith Books, ■ 78b The Homend, Ledbury, HR8 1BX. Prop: Keith Smith. Tel: Day (01531) 635336. E-mail: keith@ksbooks.demon.co.uk. Est: 1986. Shop open: **T:** 10:00–17:00; **W:** 10:00–17:00; **Th:** 10:00–17:00; **F:** 10:00–17:00; **S:** 10:00–17:00. Stock: medium. Spec: Authors:- Dymock Poets, The; Masefield, John; Embroidery; History - Local; Needlework; Poetry; Rugs; Topography - Local. PR: £1–250. CC: E; JCB; MC; V; De, SW. [Updated]

LEOMINSTER

Hummingbird Books, ■ 16 South Street, Leominster, HR6 8JB. Prop: Jill Gibbs. Tel: (01568) 616471. Web: www.hummingbirdbooks@btinternet.com. E-mail: hummingbirdbooks@btinternet.com. Est: 2001. Shop open: **M:** 10:00–17:30; **T:** 10:00–17:30; **Th:** 10:00–17:30; **F:** 10:00–17:30; **S:** 09:00–16:00. Stock: medium. Spec: Illustrated; Military History; Sport - General; Topography - General. CC: MC; V. Notes: Concession at 6 Broad Street, Hay-on-Wye. [Updated]

ROSS–ON–WYE

Ross Old Books, ■ 51 & 52 High Street, Ross–on–Wye, HR9 5HH. Prop: Phil Thredder. Tel: +44 (0)1989 567458. Web: www.rossoldbooks.co.uk. E-mail: enquiries@rossoldbooks.co.uk. Est: 1986. Shop. Internet and postal. Open: **W:** 10:00–17:00; **Th:** 10:00–17:00; **F:** 10:00–17:00; **S:** 10:00–17:00. Stock: medium. Spec: Folio Society, The; History - Local; Topography - General; Prints and Maps. PR: £1–1,000. CC: AE; MC; V; SW, SO. Mem: PBFA; BA. Notes: also, British county maps. VAT No: GB 435 3892 33. [Updated]

WEOBLEY

Hereford Booksearch (John Trevitt, Church Road, Weobley, HR4 8SD. Tel: 01544 318388. E-mail: john@trevitt.freeserve.co.uk. Est: 2004. Private premises. Postal only. Appointment necessary. Stock: very small. [13/10/2004

Weobley Bookshop, ■ Broad Street, Weobley, HR4 8SA. Prop: Karen Stout. Tel: 01544 319292. Web: www.weobleybookshop.co.uk. E-mail: sales@weobleybookshop.co.uk. Est: 1999. Shop open: **M:** 10.00–17.00; **T:** 10.00–17.00; **W:** 10.00–17.00; **Th:** 10.00–17.00; **F:** 10.00–17.00; **S:** 10.00–17.00; Closed for lunch: 13.15–14:00. Spec: New Books; Ephemera. CC: MC; V. Notes: new and secondhand books, CDs and greetings cards [Updated]

YARKHILL

David Warnes Books, One Pound Cottage, Yarkhill, HR1 3TA. Tel: 01432 890275. E-mail: davidwarnesbooks@aol.com. Private premises. Book Fairs Only. Telephone first. Open: **M:** 09:00–17:30; **T:** 09:00–17:30; **W:** 09:00–17:30; **Th:** 09:00–17:30; **F:** 09:00–17:30; **S:** 09:00–17:30; **Su:** 09:00–17:30; Closed for lunch: 13:00–14:00. Spec: Alpinism/Mountaineering; Anthropology; Countries - Afganistan; Countries - Alaska; Countries - Arabia; Countries - Armenia; Countries - Asia; Countries - Balkans, The. Mem: PBFA. [Updated]

Sheppard's Book Dealers in
JAPAN
Order the next printed edition – or search on www.sheppardsworld.co.uk

HERTFORDSHIRE

BERKHAMSTED

David Mundy at Heritage Antiques, ■ 24 Castle Street, Berkhamsted, HP4 2DD. Prop: David Mundy. Tel: (020) 7482 7087. E-mail: dave.mundy@tiscali.co.uk. Est: 1994. Shop open: **M:** 10:00–17:30; **T:** 10:00–17:30; **W:** 10:00–17:30; **Th:** 10:00–17:30; **F:** 10:00–17:30; **S:** 10:00–17:30; **Su:** 10:00–17:30. Stock: small. Spec: Art; Fiction - General; History - General; Military; Sport - General; Topography - General; Topography - Local. PR: £1–50. CC: MC; V. Notes: See also Nooks & Crannies, Chesham, Buckingahmshire HP5 1HG (q.v.). [Updated]

Richard Frost, 'Sunhaven', Northchurch Common, Berkhamsted, HP4 1LR. Tel: (01442) 862011. E-mail: richardfrost4@btinternet.com. Est: 1989. Private premises. Book Fairs Only. Telephone first. Stock: medium. Spec: Biography; First Editions; History - General; Literary Criticism; Philately; Topography - General; Travel - General. PR: £1–200. [Updated]

Red Star Books, 4 Hamilton Road, Berkhamsted, HP4 3EF. Prop: Conor Pattenden. Tel: (01442) 870775. Web: www.abebooks.com/home/conorpattenden. E-mail: redstarbooks@btopenworld.com. Est: 2001. Private premises. Internet and postal. Appointment necessary. Stock: medium. Spec: Academic/Scholarly; History - Anarchism; History - Labour/ Radical Movements; Marxism; Politics; Radical Issues; Social History; Socialism. PR: £2–1,000. [Updated]

BISHOP'S STORTFORD

Sheila Rainford, White Pine Cottage, High St., Henham, Bishop's Stortford, CM22 6AS. Tel: (01279) 851129. Fax: (01279) 851129. E-mail: sheilarainford@talk21.com. Est: 1983. Private premises. Internet and postal. Stock: small. Spec: Banking & Insurance; Cookery/Gastronomy; Economics; History - Industrial; Industry; Literature. PR: £5–1,000. CC: V. Corresp: French and German. Mem: PBFA. VAT No: GB 632 2122 89. [Updated]

Ray Smith, 'Lynwood', 111 Parsonage Lane, Bishop's Stortford, CM23 5BA. Tel: (01279) 324780. Fax: (01279) 324780. E-mail: raymond.smith63@ntlworld.com. Est: 1994. Private premises. Appointment necessary. Stock: very small. Spec: Countries - South Africa; Travel - Africa. PR: £5–250. Notes: also, Especially books on Cecil Rhodes, Rhodesiana and Southern Africa. [Updated]

Edwin Trevorrow, 5 Pryors Close, Bishop's Stortford, CM23 5JX. Tel: (01279) 652902. Est: 1994. Private premises. Appointment necessary. Stock: small. Spec: Biography; Fiction - General; Fiction - Historical; Fiction - Science Fiction; First Editions; Literature; Modern First Editions; Vintage Paperbacks. PR: £1–200. [Updated]

www.AntiqueWatchStore.com, Grooms Cottage, Elsenham Hall, Bishops Stortford, CM22 6DP. Tel: 01279-814 946. Fax: 01279-814 962. Web: www.antiquewatchstore.com. E-mail: info@davidpenney.co.uk. Est: 1994. Private premises. Internet and postal. Appointment necessary. Stock: very small. Spec: Antiques. PR: £1–20,000. CC: AE; MC; V. Mem: FBHI. VAT No: GB 354 3041 82. [Updated]

BOREHAM WOOD

Baggins Books, ■ 120 Shenley Road, Boreham Wood, WD6 1EF. Prop: Matt Fowler. Tel: 020 8236 0966. E-mail: bagginsbooks@yahoo.co.uk. Est: 2003. Shop. Open: **M:** 09:00–17:30; **T:** 09:00–17:30; **W:** 09:00–17:30; **Th:** 09:00–17:30; **F:** 09:00–17:30; **S:** 09:00–17:30; **Su:** 09:00–17:30; Closed for lunch: 13:00–14:00. [Updated]

BUSHEY

Aviation Book Supply, ■ 10 Pasture Close, Bushey, WD23 4HP. Prop: R.K. Tomlinson. Tel: (020) 8386 1880. Web: www.aero-shop.co.uk. Est: 1996. Shop. Appointment necessary. Stock: medium. Spec: Aviation. PR: £5–250. [Updated]

CHESHUNT

Denis W. Amos, 10 Mill Lane, Cheshunt, Waltham Cross, EN8 0JH. Tel: (01992) 630486. Est: 1948. Private premises. Postal only. Stock: large. Spec: Gambling; Sport - General; Sport - Football (Soccer); Sport - Horse Racing (inc. Riding/Breeding/Equestrian); Sport - Olympic Games, The; Sport - Tennis. [Updated]

ELSTREE

Elstree Books, 12 West View Gardens, Elstree, WD6 3DD. Prop: Mrs. S. Herbert. Tel: (020) 8953-2999. Web: www.abebooks.com. E-mail: elstreebooks@hotmail.com. Est: 1991. Postal only. Spec: Fine & Rare; First Editions; Illustrated; Limited Editions; Private Press; Signed Editions; Topography - General; Travel - General. PR: £2–250. Notes: mainly booksearch via abebook.com. [Updated]

HARPENDEN

Mavis Eggle, 34 Cowper Road, Harpenden, AL5 5NG. Tel: (01582) 762603. Fax: (01582) 762603 Est: 1979. Private premises. Appointment necessary. Stock: small. Spec: Antiquarian; Social History; Sport - Angling/Fishing; Technology; Ephemera. PR: £1–500. Mem: PBFA. [Updated]

HERTFORD

Gillmark Gallery, 25 Parliament Square, Hertford, SG14 1EX. Prop: Mark Pretlove & Gill Woodhouse Tel: (01992) 534444. Fax: (01992) 554734. Web: www.gillmark.com. E-mail: gillmark@btinternet.com. Est: 1997. Market stand/stall. Open: **T:** 10:00–17:00; **W:** 10:00–17:00; **Th:** 10:00–14:00; **F:** 10:00–17:00; **S:** 10:00–05:00. Stock: medium. Spec: Antiquarian; Atlases; Natural History; Topography - General; Topography - Local; Booksearch; Prints and Maps. PR: £1–3,000. CC: AE; JCB; MC; V. VAT No: GB 740 8541 36. [Updated]

HERTFORD HEATH

G Collins Bookdealers, 18 Postwood Green, Hertford Heath, SG13 7QJ. Tel: 01992 509928. Fax: 01992 584190. E-mail: badnbrowne@aol.com. Mail Order Only. Postal only. Spec: Sport - Yachting; Topography - Local. Cata: on Hertfordshire topography sailing history. Notes: specialist in Hertfordshire books. [Updated]

HITCHIN

Adrem Books, 7 Bury End, Hitchin, SG5 3QB. Prop: David Braybrooke. Tel: 01462712668. Fax: 01462712668. E-mail: braybrooke35@AOL.com. Est: 1992. Private premises. Internet and postal. Appointment necessary. Open: **M:** 06:00–24:00; **T:** 06:00–24:00; **W:** 06:00–24:00; **Th:** 06:00–24:00; **F:** 06:00–24:00; **S:** 06:00–24:00; **Su:** 06:00–24:00; Closed for lunch: 06:00–24:00. Spec: Academic/Scholarly; Adult; Aeronautics; Publishers - General; Puzzles; Railroads; Reference; Religion - General. CC: AE; E; MC; V. [Updated]

Eric T. Moore Books, ■ 24 Bridge Street, Hitchin, SG5 2DF. Prop: John Leeson. Tel: (01462) 450497. Web: www.erictmoore.co.uk. E-mail: booksales@erictmoore.co.uk. Est: 1965. Shop. Internet and postal. Open: **M:** 08:30–18:00; **T:** 08:30–18:00; **W:** 08:30–18:00; **Th:** 08:30–18:00; **F:** 08:30–18:00; **S:** 08:30–18:00; **Su:** 11:00–17:00. Stock: very large. Spec: CC: MC; V. VAT No: GB 759 7801 77. [Updated]

Phillips of Hitchin (Antiques), ■ The Manor House, Hitchin, SG5 1JW. Prop: Jerome Phillips. Tel: (01462) 432067. Fax: (01462) 441368. Est: 1884. Shop open: **M:** 09:00–17:30; **T:** 09:00–17:30; **W:** 09:00–17:30; **Th:** 09:00–17:30; **F:** 09:00–17:30. Stock: medium. Spec: Antiques; Applied Art; Architecture; Interior Design; Woodwork; Booksearch. PR: £5–3,000. CC: AE; E; MC; V. Corresp: French, German, Italian, Spanish, Russian, Portuguese. Mem: PBFA Notes: open Saturdays by appointment. Also, antique furniture. VAT No: GB 197 1842 28. [Updated]

LETCHWORTH

Gaullifmaufry Books, ■ 50 Leys Avenue, Letchworth Garden City, SG6 3EQ. Prop: Barry Meaden. Tel: (01462) 678912. Web: www.ukbookworld.com/members/spitfire. E-mail: barrymeaden@waitrose.com. Est: 1998. Shop. Open: **M:** 10:00–17:00; **T:** 10:00–17:00; **W:** 10:00–17:00; **Th:** 10:00–17:00; **F:** 10:00–17:00; **S:** 10:00–17:00. Stock: small. Spec: Aboriginal; Academic/Scholarly; Aeronautics; Army, The; Aviation; Military; Military History; Natural History. Cata: quarterly. PR: £5–200. [Updated]

MUCH HADHAM

H.M. Fletcher, Wynches Barn, Much Hadham, SG10 6BA. Prop: Marina & Keith R. Fletcher Tel: (01279) 843883. Fax: (01279) 842830. E-mail: keith@hmfletcher.co.uk. Est: 1902. Private premises. Telephone first. Spec: Antiquarian; Bindings; Fine & Rare; Illustrated; Incunabula. PR: £50–20,000. CC: MC; V. Corresp: French. Mem: ABA; PBFA; ILAB. VAT No: GB 626 2128 60. [Updated]

HERTFORDSHIRE

NEW BARNET

ForensicSearch, 17 Greenacres, Glyn Avenue, New Barnet, EN4 9PJ. Prop: Nick Danks and Samantha Sproates Tel: (020) 8440-8896. Est: 1999. Private premises. Postal only. Stock: very small. Spec: Crime (True); Science - Forensic; Booksearch. PR: £2–200. [Updated]

RADLETT

G.L. Green Ltd., 18 Aldenham Avenue, Radlett, WD7 8HX. Prop: G. L. Grenn. Tel: (01923) 857077. Fax: (01923) 857077. Web: www.glgreen.co.uk. E-mail: orders@glgreen.co.uk. Est: 1972. Storeroom. Internet and postal. Appointment necessary. Stock: small. Spec: Deep Sea Diving; Maritime/Nautical; Naval; Shipbuilding and Shipping; War - World War I; War - World War II; Ephemera. PR: £1–1,000. CC: AE; JCB; V; PayPal. Notes: Booksearch service. [Updated]

RICKMANSWORTH

Clive A. Burden Ltd., Elmcote House, The Green, Croxley Green, Rickmansworth, WD3 3HN. Tel: (01923) 778097. Fax: (01923) 896520. Web: www.caburden.com. E-mail: pburden@caburden.com. Est: 1966. Private premises. Appointment necessary. Stock: very large. Spec: Academic/Scholarly; Atlases; Botany; Cartography; Illustrated; Natural History; Topography - General; Topography - Local. PR: £5–10,000. Mem: ABA; ILAB; IMCoS. Also, decorative books. [Updated]

ST. ALBANS

Reg & Philip Remington, 23 Homewood Road, St. Albans, AL1 4BG. Tel: (020) 7836-9771. Fax: 01727 893532. Web: www.remingtonbooks.com. E-mail: philip@remingtonbooks.com. Est: 1979. Private premises. Appointment necessary. Spec: American Indians; Colour-Plate; Travel - Africa; Travel - Americas; Travel - Asia; Travel - Australasia/Australia; Travel - Middle East; Travel - Polar. PR: £5–5,000. CC: MC; V. Cata: bi-annually on specialised subjects. Mem: ABA; BA; ILAB. [Updated]

Paton Books, ■ 34 Holywell Hill, St. Albans, AL1 1DE. Prop: Richard & Josie Child. Tel: (01727) 853984. Fax: (01727) 865764. Web: www.patonbooks.co.uk. E-mail: patonbooks@aol.com. Est: 1962. Shop open: **M:** 09:00–18:00; **T:** 09:00–18:00; **W:** 09:00–18:00; **Th:** 09:00–18:00; **F:** 09:00–18:00; **S:** 09:00–18:00. Stock: very large. Spec: Art; Fiction - General; First Editions; History - General; Religion - General; Transport; Travel - General. PR: £1–400. CC: D; JCB; MC; V; Switch, SO. Corresp: French. [Updated]

RM Books, 18 Cornwall Road, St. Albans, AL1 1SH. Prop: Robert Moore. Tel: (01727) 830058. Web: www.rmbooks.co.uk. E-mail: rmbooks@verulamium94.freeserve.co.uk. Est: 1988. Private premises. Postal only. Stock: very small. Spec: Medicine; Medicine - History of; Science - General; Science - History of. PR: £10–100. Mem: PBFA. [Updated]

TRING

Book Collectors Paradise, 38 Windmill Way, Tring, HP23 4HH. Prop: Trudy Ashford. Tel: (01442) 824440. Est: 1985. Book Fairs Only. Open: **Su:** 10:00–16:00. PR: £1–100. Notes: At Wing - 1st Sunday every month. [Updated]

David Ford Books, Midwood, Shire Lane, Cholesbury, Tring, HP23 6NA. Tel: (01494) 758663. E-mail: dford.books@ukgateway.net. Est: 1985. Private premises. Internet and postal. Telephone first. Stock: large. Spec: Animals and Birds; Art History; Cinema/Film; Egyptology; Fiction - General; First Editions; Gardening - General; History - General. PR: £1–500. CC: JCB; MC; V. Mem: PBFA. Notes: also at, The Gillmark Gallery, Parliament Square, Hertford. [Updated]

WATFORD

G. & R. Leapman Ltd., 37 Hogarth Court, High Street, Bushey, Watford, WD23 1BT. Prop: Gillian Leapman. Tel: (020) 8950-2995. Fax: (020) 8950-4131. E-mail: gleapman1@compuserve.com. Est: 1970. Private premises. Appointment necessary. Stock: very small. Spec: Countries - Caribbean, The; Travel - Americas; Booksearch; Prints and Maps. PR: £10–1,000. Corresp: French. VAT No: GB 197 6103 41. [Updated]

Peter Taylor & Son, 1 Ganders Ash, Leavesden, Watford, WD25 7HE. Prop: Peter Taylor. Tel: (01923) 663325. E-mail: taylorbooks@clara.co.uk. Est: 1973. Storeroom. Postal only. Contactable. Stock: medium. Spec: Academic/Scholarly; Antiquarian; Archaeology; Art History; Bibliography; Biography; Ecclesiastical History & Architecture; Fine & Rare. PR: £15–1,000. CC: MC; V. Corresp: French. [Updated]

Westons Booksellers Ltd., 44 Stratford Road, Watford, WD17 4NZ. Prop: Jeremy Weston. Tel: (01923) 229081. Fax: (01923) 243343. Web: www.westons.co.uk. E-mail: books@westons.co.uk. Est: 1977. Private premises. Appointment necessary. Stock: medium. Spec: Engineering; Medicine; Science - General; Technology. PR: £3–300. CC: E; MC; V. VAT No: GB 225 0259 93. [Updated]

Norman Wright, 60 Eastbury Road, Watford, WD19 4JL. Tel: (01923) 232383. Est: 1989. Private premises. Postal only. Stock: small. Spec: Children's; Comic Books & Annuals; Comics. PR: £5–500. [Updated]

ISLE OF WIGHT

COWES

The Bookroom, ■ 37 Goss Street, Cowes, PO31 7TA. Prop: M.C. & V.F. Edmondson. Tel: 01983 873897. E-mail: mothergoose4books@btinternet.com. Shop open: **M:** 10:30–17:00; **T:** 10:30–17:00; **W:** 10:30–17:00; **Th:** 10:30–17:00; **F:** 10:30–17:00; **S:** 10:30–17:00. Notes: also at Mothergoose Bookshop, St Helens, and The Bookroom, Yarmouth. [Updated]

Curtle Mead Books, 105 Curtle Mead, Baring Road, Cowes, PO31 8DS. Prop: John Lucas. Tel: (01983) 294312. E-mail: lucas@curtlemead.demon.co.uk. Est: 1999. Private premises. Telephone first. Stock: medium. Spec: Maritime/Nautical; Natural History; Naval; Navigation; Ornithology; Ship Modelling; Shipbuilding and Shipping; Sport - Yachting. PR: £1–500. CC: PayPal. Corresp: German. Mem: PBFA. [Updated]

FRESHWATER

David G. Bancroft, Little Orchard, Court Road, Freshwater, PO40 9NU. Tel: (01983) 759069. Est: 1995. Private premises. Postal only. Stock: small. Spec: Aviation; Ephemera. PR: £3–150. Notes: Catalogues also include gliding and technical aspects of aviation. [Updated]

Cameron House Books, ■ Dimbola Lodge, Terrace Lane, Freshwater Bay, PO40 9QE. Prop: L.J. Sklaroff. Tel: (01983) 754960. Web: www.cameronhousebooks.com. E-mail: ljs@cambooks-dimbola.freeserve.co.uk. Est: 1994. Shop. Internet and postal. Open: **T:** 10:00–16:00; **W:** 10:00–16:00; **Th:** 10:00–16:00; **F:** 10:00–16:00; **S:** 10:00–16:00; **Su:** 10:00–16:00. Stock: medium. Spec: Authors:- Cameron, Julia Margaret; Keeping, Charles; Peake, Mervyn; Tennyson, Lord Alfred; Fine & Rare; First Editions; Illustrated; Limited Editions. PR: £1–3,000. Corresp: French, German, Spanish. Mem: PLA. Notes: also, a booksearch service [Updated]

NEWPORT

Firsts in Print, 95 St. John's Road, Newport, PO30 1LS. Prop: Peter Elliston. Tel: (01983) 521748. Web: www.firsts-in-print.co.uk. E-mail: peter@firsts-in-print.co.uk. Est: 1984. Private premises. Internet and postal. Appointment necessary. Open: **M:** 09:00–17:00; **T:** 09:00–17:00; **W:** 09:00–17:00; **Th:** 09:00–17:00; **F:** 09:00–17:00. Stock: medium. Spec: Children's; Fiction - Crime, Detective, Spy, Thrillers; Fiction - Fantasy, Horror; Literature; Modern First Editions; Proof Copies; Signed Editions. PR: £3–1,000. CC: MC; V; Switch/Mae. Notes: also at, Corner House, 68-70 Lugley St, Newport, Isle of Wight. VAT No: GB 768 9507 66. [Updated]

RYDE

Heritage Books, ■ 7 Cross Street, Ryde, PO33 2AD. Prop: Rev. D.H. Nearn. Tel: (01983) 562933. Fax: (01983) 812634. E-mail: heritagebooksryde@btconnect.com. Est: 1978. Shop open: **M:** 10:00–17:00; **T:** 10:00–17:00; **W:** 10:00–17:00; **F:** 10:00–17:00; **S:** 10:00–17:00. Stock: large. Spec: Countries - Africa; Countries - Isle of Wight; Theology. PR: £1–500. CC: MC; V. Corresp: French, Portuguese. VAT No: GB 339 0615 58. [Updated]

Kalligraphia (formerly Charmouth Bounty Books), 66 Bettesworth Road, Ryde, PO33 3EJ. Prop: Louisa Mamakou. Tel: 00 44 (0) 1983 562702. Web: www.kalligraphia.com. E-mail: books@kalligraphia.com. Est: 2003. Private premises. Internet and postal. Appointment necessary. Spec: Archaeology; Astronomy; Biography; Cartography; Children's; Countries - Greece; Dinosaurs; Earth Sciences. CC: MC; V; PayPal. Cata: quarterly, on Earth Sciences; Nat. History; Greece & Cyprus etc. Corresp: Greek; French. [Updated]

The Ryde Bookshop, ■ 135 High Street, Ryde, PO33 2RJ. Prop: M.D. Sames. Tel: (01983) 565227. E-mail: rydebookshop@yahoo.co.uk. Est: 1988. Shop open: **M:** 09:00–17:00; **T:** 09:00–17:00; **W:** 09:00–17:00; **Th:** 09:00–17:00; **F:** 09:00–17:00; **S:** 09:00–17:00. Stock: very large. PR: £1–200. CC: E; JCB; MC; V. Mem: BA. Notes: also, new books. [Updated]

ST. HELENS

Mothergoose Bookshop, ■ West Green House, Upper Green Road, St. Helens, PO33 1XB. Prop: M.C. and V.F. Edmondson. Tel: 01983 874063. E-mail: mothergoose4books@btinternet.com. Est: 1980. Shop open: **M:** 10:30–17:00; **T:** 10:30–17:00; **W:** 10:30–17:00; **Th:** 10:30–17:00; **F:** 10:30–17:00; **S:** 10:30–17:00. Spec: Alpinism/Mountaineering; Maritime/Nautical; Military; Prints and Maps. Notes: also at The Bookroom, Cowes and The Bookroom, Yarmouth. [Updated]

VENTNOR

Shirley Lane Books, St. Lawrence Dene, Undercliff Drive, Ventnor, PO38 1XJ. Prop: Shirley Lane. Tel: (01983) 852309. Web: www.abebook.co.uk. E-mail: shirleylane@talk21.com. Est: 1976. Private premises. Internet and postal. Appointment necessary. Stock: small. Spec: Authors - Women; Feminism; Women. PR: £1–500. Corresp: French. [Updated]

Ventnor Rare Books, ■ 32 Pier Street, Ventnor, PO38 1SX. Prop: Nigel & Teresa Traylen. Tel: (01983) 853706 Fax: (01983) 854706. E-mail: vrb@andytron.demon.co.uk. Est: 1989. Shop open: **M:** 10:00–17:00; **T:** 10:00–17:00; **Th:** 10:00–17:00; **F:** 10:00–17:00; **S:** 10:00–17:00. Stock: medium. Spec: Academic/Scholarly; Antiquarian; Art Reference; Bibliography; Bindings; Fiction - General; Literature; Military History. PR: £1–500. CC: MC; V; UK Switch. Corresp: French. Mem: ABA; PBFA; ILAB. VAT No: GB 566 5246 19. [Updated]

YARMOUTH

Alan Argent, Two Ways, Sconce Road, Norton, Yarmouth, PO41 0RT. Alan Argent. Tel: (01983) 760851. E-mail: alanthebook@aol.com. Storeroom. Appointment necessary. Open: Stock: very small. Spec: Maritime/Nautical; Seamanship; Sport - Sailing. PR: £3–100. Notes: also, attends the occasional bookfair. [Updated]

Available from Richard Joseph Publishers Ltd
Sheppard's International Directory of
EPHEMERA DEALERS
Order the next printed edition – or search on www.sheppardsworld.co.uk

KENT

ASHFORD
Woodside Books, 1 Woodside Cottages, Westwell Lane, Ashford, TN26 1JB. Prop: Ann Gipps. Tel: (01233) 624495. E-mail: ann.gipps@btinternet.com. Est: 1991. Private premises. Internet and postal. Appointment necessary. Stock: very small. Spec: Botany; Entomology; Natural History; Ornithology. PR: £1–500. CC: MC; V. [Updated]

BECKENHAM
Julia Sesemann, 10 Kemerton Road, Beckenham, BR3 6NJ. Prop: Julia Sesemann. Tel: (020) 8658-6123. Est: 1977. Private premises. Appointment necessary. Stock: very small. Spec: Author - Blyton, Enid; Children's; Comic Books & Annuals; Illustrated; Juvenile. PR: £2–250. [Updated]

BEXLEY
Ruskin Books, 42 Red Lodge Road, Joydens Wood, Bexley, DA5 2JP. Prop: Frederick W. Lidyard. Tel: 01322 558291. E-mail: fwlidyard@aol.com. Private premises. Contactable. Spec: Booksearch. Notes: mainly a booksearch service [Updated]

BIDDENDEN
P.R. & V. Sabin (Printed Works, Saxton House, The Nightingales, Biddenden, TN27 8HN. Tel: (01580) 715603. Fax: (01580) 714603. E-mail: paulsabin@btopenworld.com. Private premises. Appointment necessary. Stock: medium. Spec: Illustrated; Limited Editions; Private Press. Mem: PBFA. [Updated]

BRENCHLEY
Anthony Whittaker, Four Seasons, Chill Mill Green, Brenchley, Tonbridge, TN12 7AL. Prop: Anthony Whittaker. Tel: 01892 723494. E-mail: bookant@hotmail.com. Est: 1980. Private premises. Telephone first. Open: **M:** 09:00–17:30; **T:** 09:00–17:30; **W:** 09:00–17:30; **Th:** 09:00–17:30; **F:** 09:00–17:30; **S:** 09:00–17:30; **Su:** 09:00–17:30; Closed for lunch: 13:00–14:00. Spec: Applied Art; Children's; Illustrated; Natural History; Topography - Local. CC: MC; V. Mem: PBFA. [Updated]

BROADSTAIRS
Island Books, Woodland Cottages, Dane Court Gardens, St Peters, Broadstairs, CT10 2SD. Tel: (01843) 869203. Fax: (01843) 869203. E-mail: island@swauk.freeserve.co.uk. Est: 1974. Private premises. Internet and postal. Appointment necessary. Stock: medium. Spec: Academic/Scholarly; Aeronautics; Agriculture; Animals and Birds; Antiquarian; Applied Art; Archaeology; Architecture. PR: £10–10,000. CC: AE; JCB; MC; V. [10/10/2004]

CANTERBURY
The Canterbury Bookshop, ■ 37 Northgate, Canterbury, CT1 1BL. Prop: David Miles. Tel: (01227) 464773. Fax: (01227) 780073. E-mail: canterburybookshop@btconnect.com. Est: 1980. Shop open: **M:** 10:00–17:00; **T:** 10:00–17:00; **W:** 10:00–17:00; **Th:** 10:00–17:00; **F:** 10:00–17:00; **S:** 10:00–17:00. Stock: small. Spec: Children's; Illustrated; Juvenile; Typography; Prints and Maps. PR: £1–2,000. CC: MC; V. Mem: ABA; PBFA; BA; ILAB. Notes: fairs attended: all London, ABA, Olympia, Chelsea and in USA. [Updated]

Chaucer Bookshop, ■ 6-7, Beer Cart Lane, Canterbury, CT1 2NY. Prop: Sir Robert Sherston-Baker, Bt Tel: 01227 453912. Fax: 01227 451893. Web: www.chaucer-bookshop.co.uk. E-mail: chaucerbooks@btconnect.com. Est: 1956. Shop open: **M:** 10am–5pm; **T:** 10:00–17:00; **W:** 110:00–17:00; **Th:** 10:00–17:00; **F:** 10:00–17:00; **S:** 10:00–17:00. Spec: Antiques; Art; Art History; Arts, The; Autobiography; Biography; Fiction - General; Gardening - General. CC: AE; D; E; JCB; MC; V; Switch / Solo. Mem: ABA; PBFA; BA; ILAB. Notes: within the city walls, less than 5 minutes walk from the Cathedral [Updated]

Little Stour Books, North Court House, West Stourmouth, Nr Preston, Canterbury, CT3 1HT. Prop: Colin Button. Tel: (01227) 722371. Fax: (01227) 722021. Web: www.littlestourbooks.com. E-mail: sales@littlestourbooks.com. Est: 1996. Private premises. Internet and postal. Appointment necessary. Stock: very large. Spec: Authors: Blyton, Enid; Buckeridge, A.; Crompton, Richmal; Henty, G.A.; Johns, W.E.; Maclean, Alistair; Oxenham, Elsie; Rackham, Arthur. PR: £6–500. CC: E; JCB; MC; V; SW, SO. Mem: PBFA. [Updated]

Oast Books, 1 Denstead Oast, Chartham Hatch, Canterbury, CT4 7SH. Prop: Bill & Jennie Reading. Tel: (01227) 730808. Web: www.http://members.aol.com/oastbooks/home.htm. E-mail: oastbooks@aol.com. Est: 1997. Market stand/stall; Postal only. Stock: small. Spec: Counselling; Psychoanalysis; Psychology/Psychiatry; Psychotherapy. PR: £2–40. CC: PayPal. [18/01/2005]

Tiger Books, Yew Tree Cottage, Westbere, Canterbury, CT2 0HH. Prop: Dr. Bryan & Mrs. Sylvia Harlow. Tel: (01227) 710030. Fax: (01227) 712066. E-mail: tiger@sharlow.fsbusiness.co.uk. Est: 1988. Private premises. Internet and postal. Appointment necessary. Stock: large. Spec: Antiquarian; Author - Dickens, Charles; Fiction - Women; Literary Travel; Literature; Literature in Translation; Magazines & Periodicals - General; Booksearch. PR: £10–5,500. CC: E; JCB; MC; V. Mem: ABA; PBFA; ILAB. Notes: also, a booksearch service. [Updated]

CHATHAM

Roadmaster Books, P.O. Box 176, Chatham, ME5 9AQ. Prop: Malcolm & Sue Wright. Tel: (01634) 862843. Fax: (01634) 201555. E-mail: info@roadmasterbooks.co.uk. Est: 1976. Private premises. Postal only. Spec: Canals/Inland Waterways; Company History; Conservation; Dolls & Dolls' Houses; Flower Arranging; Geography; Geology; Motoring. PR: £1–350. Corresp: French. Notes: To contact publishing business use info@roadmasterpublishing.co.uk. VAT No: GB 619 3009 52. [Updated]

Sandstone Books, 14 Seymour Road, Chatham, ME5 7AE. Prop: Verne Sanderson. Tel: 01634 306437. Web: www.sandstonebooks.co.uk. E-mail: verne@sandstonebooks.co.uk. Est: 1989. Private premises. Internet and postal. Appointment necessary. Open: **M:** 09:00–17:30; **T:** 09:00–17:30; **W:** 09:00–17:30; **Th:** 09:00–17:30; **F:** 09:00–17:30; **S:** 09:00–17:30; **Su:** 09:00–17:30; Closed for lunch: 13:00–14:00. Spec: Cata: bi-annually on modern first editions. [Updated]

DEAL

Books, ■ 168 High Street, Deal, CT14 6BQ. Prop: Peter Ritchie. Tel: (01304) 368662. Shop open: **Th:** 10:00–17:00; **F:** 10:00–17:00; **S:** 10:00–17:00. Stock: medium. Spec: Antiques; Architecture; Art; Collecting. PR: £2–300. [Updated]

J. Clarke–Hall Limited, 75 Middle Street, Deal, CT14 6HN. Prop: S.M. Edgecombe. Tel: (01304) 375467. Est: 1934. Private premises. Appointment necessary. Stock: very small. Spec: Authors:- Carroll, Lewis; Johnson, Samuel. PR: £5–750. Cata: occasionally on Samuel Johnson and his world. Notes: Attends Bonnington Fair in June. [Updated]

McConnell Fine Books, ■ The Golden Hind, 85 Beach Street, Deal, CT14 6JB. Prop: Nick McConnell. Tel: (01304) 375086. Web: www.abebooks.com/home/sandwichfinebooks. E-mail: mcconnellbooks@aol.com. Est: 1972. Shop. Telephone first. Open: **W:** 10:30–17:00; **Th:** 10:30–17:00; **F:** 10:30–17:00; **S:** 10:30–17:00. Stock: medium. Spec: Antiquarian; Bindings; Maritime/Nautical. PR: £2–1,000. CC: MC; V. Corresp: French, Russian. Mem: ABA; PBFA; ILAB. [Updated]

DOVER

Pat Castleton, 26, Kearsney Avenue, Dover, CT16 3BU. Prop: Pat Castleton. Tel: 01304 330371. E-mail: patriciacastleton@hotmail.com. Est: 2002. Private premises. Internet and postal. Telephone first. Open: **M:** 09:00–17:30; **T:** 09:00–17:30; **W:** 09:00–17:30; **Th:** 09:00–17:30; **F:** 09:00–17:30; **S:** 09:00–17:30; **Su:** 09:00–17:30; Closed for lunch: 13:00–14:00. Spec: Agriculture; Aircraft; Art Reference; Autobiography; Aviation; Biography; Botany; Cats. CC: PayPal, Cheque. Corresp: French. Notes: Homepage on Abebooks.com - www.abebooks.com/home/PATCASTLETON. [Updated]

FARNBOROUGH

Lewis First Editions, 9 Ferndale Way, Farnborough, BR6 7EL. Prop: David Fordyce. Tel: (01689) 854261. Web: www.abebooks.com/home/davidfordyce/. Est: 2000. Internet and postal. Stock: small. Spec: Author - Lewis, C.S.; Author - Saville, M.; Author - Shute, Neville; Modern First Editions. PR: £5–2,000. [Updated]

FARNINGHAM

Wadard Books, ■ 6 High Street, Farningham, DA4 0DG. Tel: (01322) 863151. E-mail: wadardbooks@btinternet.com. Est: 2001. Shop open: **T:** 10:00–18:00; **Th:** 10:00–18:00; **F:** 10:00–18:00; **S:** 10:00–18:00. Stock: medium. Spec: Alchemy; Antiquarian; Art; Aviation; Children's; Children's - Early Titles; Children's - Illustrated; Churchilliana. PR: £1–5,000. CC: AE; JCB; MC; V. VAT No: GB 586 5906 86. [Updated]

FAVERSHAM

Faversham Books, 49 South Road, Faversham, ME13 7LS. Prop: Mr. & Mrs. C.M. Ardley. Tel: (01795) 532873. Est: 1979. Private premises. Postal only. Spec: Author - Kipling, Rudyard. PR: £5–1,000. Corresp: French. [Updated]

John O'Kill, 'Coulthorn Lodge', 9 Ospringe Road, Faversham, ME13 7LJ. Tel: (01795) 534510. E-mail: john.o'kill@virgin.net. Est: 1990. Private premises. Postal only. Stock: small. Spec: Antiquarian; Illustrated. PR: £1–500. [18/10/2004]

FOLKESTONE

Jenny Hurst, The Old Coach House, Rectory Lane, Lyminge, Folkestone, CT18 8EG. Prop: Jenny Hurst. Tel: (01303) 862693. Web: www.abebooks.com. E-mail: intabooks@btopenworld.com. Est: 1996. Private premises. Internet and postal. Stock: medium. Spec: Academic/Scholarly; Alternative Medicine; Autobiography; Biography; Children's; Fiction - General; Food & Drink; Health. PR: £5–100. [Updated]

MilitaryHistoryBooks.com, PO Box 590, Folkestone, CT20 2WX. Prop: Ian H. & Gillian M. Knight. Tel: (01303) 246500. Fax: (01303) 245133. Web: www.militaryhistorybooks.com. E-mail: info@militaryhistorybooks.com. Est: 1970. Private premises. Internet and postal. Appointment necessary. Open: **M:** 10:00–17:00; **T:** 10:00–17:00; **W:** 10:00–17:00; **Th:** 10:00–17:00; **F:** 10:00–17:00; **S:** 09:00–14:00. Stock: large. Spec: Arms & Armour; Aviation; Espionage; Firearms/Guns; Military; Military History; War - General; Wargames. PR: £10–500. CC: AE; D; E; JCB; MC; V; SW. VAT No: GB 770 7124 36. [Updated]

Nick Spurrier, 27 Plain Road, Folkestone, CT20 2QF. Tel: (01303) 246100. Fax: (01303) 245800. Web: www.nick-spurrier.co.uk. E-mail: spurrier@btconnect.com. Est: 1977. Private premises. Internet and postal. Appointment necessary. Stock: medium. Spec: Black Studies; Company History; Economics; Feminism; History - General; Marxism; Pacifism; Philosophy. PR: £1–50. CC: JCB; MC. VAT No: GB 362 1931 64. [Updated]

Marrin's Bookshop, ■ 149 Sandgate Road, Folkestone, CT20 2DA. Prop: Patrick Marrin. Tel: 01303 253016. Fax: 01303 850956. Web: www.marrinbook.co.uk. E-mail: patrick@marrinbook.co.uk. Est: 1945. Shop open: **T:** 09:30–17:30; **W:** 09:30–17:30; **Th:** 09:30–17:30; **F:** 09:30–17:30; **S:** 09:30–17:30. Spec: Antiquarian; Topography - Local. CC: MC; V; Debit. Cata: bi-annually on Kent Topography. Corresp: French, Italian. Mem: ABA; PBFA; BA; ILAB. Notes: We specialize in Kent Books, Prints, Maps and Ephemera and have in addition, a good selection of Antiquarian and secondhand books. VAT No: GB 316 6132 80. [Updated]

GRAVESEND

L.J. Berry Books and Pictures, 4, Manor Road, Gravesend, DA12 1AA. Tel: (020) 8854-6753. E-mail: lesberry@berrybooks.freeserve.co.uk. Est: 1987. Shop and/or gallery. Open: **F:** 10:30–17:30; **S:** 09:00–17:00. Spec: Archaeology; Architecture; Art; Art History; Art Reference; Design; Fine Art; History - General. PR: £5–200. [Updated]

HUNTON

Jill Howell, Hopview Cottage, 1, Hilltop, Hunton, Maidstone, ME15 0QP. Prop: Jill Howell. Tel: 01622 820 899. Fax: 01622 820 899. E-mail: jillphotobooks@aol.com. Est: 1993. Private premises. Postal only. Appointment necessary. Spec: Photography. Cata: quarterly on Photography. Corresp: French. [Updated]

Stanley Fish & Co., 215a Upper Grosvenor Road, Tunbridge Wells, Kent, TN1 2EG. Robin Peterson. Tel: (01892) 546431. Web: www.stanleyfish.com. E-mail: stanleyfishbooks@aol.com. Est: 1992. Storeroom. Appointment necessary. Stock: medium. PR: £1–300. CC: MC; V; Maestro. VAT No: GB 621 7154 64. [Updated]

LYDD

Anthony Neville, New hall, High Street, Lydd, TN29 9AJ. Tel: 01797 320180. Fax: 01797 320140. E-mail: neville.anthony@talk21.com. Est: 1985. Private premises. Appointment necessary. Spec: Art; Author - James, Henry; Foreign Texts; Illustrated; Private Press. CC: MC; V. Cata: 10 a year on specialities. Corresp: French, German and Russian. Mem: ABA; PBFA; BA. VAT No: GB 515 9087 34. [Updated]

LYMINGE

Scott Brinded, 17 Greenbanks, Lyminge, CT18 8HG. Tel: (01303) 862258. Fax: (01303) 862660. Est: 1991. Private premises. Internet and postal. Stock: small. Spec: Antiquarian; Bibliography; Books about Books; Literature; Palaeography; Papermaking; Printing; Topography - General. PR: £1–5,000. CC: MC; V. Mem: ABA; PBFA. Notes: also, UK distributors for Martin Publishing, Oak Knoll Press. VAT No: GB 624 9315 38. [Updated]

Periwinkle Press, ■ 2 Rose Cottages, Woodland Road, Lyminge, Folkstone, CT18 8DR. Prop: Antony & Clare Swain. Tel: (01303) 863595. Fax: Mobile (07709) 918361. E-mail: cswain1805@aol.com. Est: 1968. Shop. Internet and postal. Open: **M:** 10:00–17:00; **T:** 10:00–17:00; **W:** 10:00–14:00; **Th:** 10:00–17:00; **F:** 10:00–17:00; **S:** 10:00–17:00. Stock: medium. Spec: Author - Ardizzone, Edward; Rural Life; Topography - Local; Transport; Prints and Maps. PR: £1–100. CC: AE; JCB; V; PayPal. Mem: PBFA. Notes: also, trade & retail print and picture framers, colourists, restoration. [Updated]

MAIDSTONE

Peter Blest, Little Canon Cottage, Wateringbury, Maidstone, ME18 5PJ. Prop: Peter & Jan Blest. Tel: (01622) 812940. E-mail: pmblest@aol.com. Est: 1974. Private premises. Postal only. Stock: very large. Spec: Agriculture; Animals and Birds; Botany; Cockfighting; Entomology; Flower Arranging; Gardening - General; Herbalism. PR: £5–5,000. CC: AE; JCB; MC; V. Cata: bi-annually on Natural History, Gardening & Botanical, Sporting. Corresp: French. Mem: PBFA. [Updated]

Cobnar Books, 567 Red Hill, Wateringbury, Maidstone, ME18 5BE. Prop: Larry Ilott. Tel: (01622) 813230. Fax: (0870) 056 7232. Web: www.cobnarbooks.com. E-mail: books@cobnar.demon.co.uk. Private premises. Postal only. Appointment necessary. Stock: small. Spec: Antiquarian; Bibliography; Printing; Topography - Local. PR: £10–2,000. CC: MC; V. Mem: PBFA. VAT No: GB 702 4681 56. [Updated]

Wealden Books, 39 Adisham Drive, Maidstone, ME16 0NP. Prop: Alfred & C.A. King. Tel: (01622) 762581. E-mail: wealdenbooks@talk21.com. Est: 1980. Private premises. Appointment necessary. Stock: large. Spec: Fiction - General; History - Local; Topography - General; Topography - Local. PR: £2–1,000. Notes: Main stream subjects are on and about Kent, Surrey and Sussex. VAT No: GB 304 1457 96. [Updated]

MARGATE

Sun House Books, 72 Northumberland Avenue, Margate, CT9 3LY. Tel: (0709) 2841342. Fax: (0709) 2024636. Web: www.sunhousebooks.co.uk. E-mail: sales@sunhousebooks.co.uk. Est: 1999. Private premises. Internet Only. Appointment necessary. Stock: small. Spec: Academic/Scholarly; Architecture; Civil Engineering; Ecclesiastical History & Architecture; Engineering; History - Design; Interior Design; Teaching. PR: £3–200. CC: PayPal. [Updated]

ORPINGTON

Roland Books, 60 Birchwood Road, Petts Wood, Orpington, BR5 1NZ. Prop: A.R. Hughes. Tel: (01689) 838872. Fax: (01689) 838872. E-mail: py32@dial.pipex.com. Private premises. Internet and postal. Open: **M:** 09:00–17:00; **T:** 09:00–17:00; **W:** 09:00–17:00; **Th:** 09:00–17:00; **F:** 09:00–17:00. Stock: medium. Spec: Advertising; Animals and Birds; Annuals; Antiques; Architecture; Art; Autobiography; Biography. PR: £1–75. CC: MC; V; Switch. [Updated]

RAMSGATE

Yesteryear Railwayana, Stablings Cottage, Goodwin Road, Ramsgate, CT11 0JJ. Prop: Patrick & Mary Mullen. Tel: 01843 587283. Fax: 01843 587283. Web: www.yesrail.com. E-mail: mullen@yesrail.com. Est: 1978. Private premises. Internet and postal. Stock: large. Spec: Railways; Ephemera; Prints and Maps. PR: £1–500. CC: AE; JCB; MC. [Updated]

ROCHESTER

Baggins Book Bazaar Ltd., ■ 19 High Street, Rochester, ME1 1PY. Manager: Godfrey George. Tel: (01634) 811651. Fax: (01634) 840591. Web: www.bagginsbooks.co.uk. E-mail: godfreygeorge@btconnect.com. Est: 1986. Shop open: **M:** 10:00–18:00; **T:** 10:00–18:00; **W:** 10:00–18:00; **Th:** 10:00–18:00; **F:** 10:00–18:00; **S:** 10:00–18:00; **Su:** 10:00–18:00. Stock: very large. Spec: Booksearch. PR: £1–200. CC: AE; D; E; JCB; MC; V; Maestro. VAT No: GB 472 9061 36. [23/10/2004]

Stained Glass Books, 13, Parkfields, Rochester, ME2 2TW. Prop: K.R. & S.J. Hill. Tel: (01634)719050. Web: www.glassconservation.com. E-mail: bookmail@glassconservation.com. Est: 1987. Private premises. Postal only. Contactable. Stock: very small. Spec: Glass; Stained Glass. PR: £5–500. [Updated]

SEVENOAKS

Roderick M. Barron, P.O. Box 67, Sevenoaks, TN13 3WW. Tel: (01732) 742558. Fax: (01732) 742558. Web: www.barron.co.uk. E-mail: rod@barron.co.uk. Est: 1989. Private premises. Internet and postal. Spec: Atlases; Prints and Maps. PR: £100–10,000. CC: AE; MC; V. Cata: Occasionally Corresp: French, German. Mem: ABA; IMCoS. VAT No: GB 602 6465 60. [Updated]

Garwood & Voigt, 55 Bayham Road, Sevenoaks, TN13 3XE. Prop: Nigel Garwood & Rainer G. Voigt Tel: (01732) 460025. Fax: (01732) 460026. Web: www.garwood-voigt.com. E-mail: gv@garwood-voigt.com. Est: 1977. Office and/or bookroom. Appointment necessary. Stock: small. Spec: Atlases; Cookery/Gastronomy; Prints and Maps. CC: E; MC; V. Corresp: German, French. Mem: ABA; PBFA; ILAB; IMCoS. [Updated]

Geophysical Books, 82 Granville Rd., Sevenoaks, TN13 1HA. Prop: Miss Bobbie Smith. Tel: 01732 456018. Web: www.geophysicalbooks.com. E-mail: geo.books@which.net. Est: 1986. Private premises. Telephone first. Open: **M:** 09:00–17:30; **T:** 09:00–17:30; **W:** 09:00–17:30; **Th:** 09:00–17:30; **F:** 09:00–17:30; **S:** 09:00–17:30; Closed for lunch: 13:00–14:00. Spec: Geology; Geophysics; Petroleum Geology; Petroleum Technology. CC: MC; V. Corresp: French. [Updated]

Martin Wood Cricket Books, 1c Wickenden Road, Sevenoaks, TN13 3PJ. Tel: (01732) 457205. Fax: (01732) 457205. Web: www.martinwoodcricketbooks.co.uk. Est: 1970. Private premises. Appointment necessary. Stock: small. Spec: Sport - Cricket; Ephemera. PR: £1–500. [Updated]

SIDCUP

Mark W. Corder, 9 Townshend Close, Sidcup, DA14 5HY. Prop: Mark Corder. Tel: (020) 8309-5665. Web: www.mark.corder.btinternet.co.uk. E-mail: mark.corder@btinternet.com. Est: 1988. Private premises. Internet and postal. Appointment necessary. Open: **M:** 08:00–00:00. Stock: small. Spec: Academic/Scholarly; History - British; Reference; Theology; Topography - Local. PR: £10–500. [Updated]

SITTINGBOURNE

J. & J. Fox Books, 48 Woodstock Road, Sittingbourne, ME10 4HN. Prop: M.V. Fox. Tel: (01795) 470310. Fax: (01795) 470310. Est: 1981. Storeroom. Appointment necessary. Stock: small. Spec: Antiquarian; Cookery/Gastronomy; Maritime/Nautical; Military; Typography; Ephemera. PR: £10–1,500. Corresp: French, Portugese, Spanish. Mem: PBFA. [Updated]

Underwater Antiques, 12 West Lane, Sittingbourne, ME10 3AA. Tel: (01795) 472664. E-mail: philsidey@aol.com. Est: 1980. Private premises. Postal only. Stock: very small. Spec: Military; Sport - Diving/Sub-Aqua. PR: £3–500. CC: AE; D; E; MC; V; PayPal, Sw. Notes: attends book fairs. [Updated]

SMARDEN

Mrs Janet Cameron, The Meeting House, Smarden, TN27 8NR. Tel: (01233) 770552. Est: 1992. Private premises. Postal only. Stock: small. Spec: [Updated]

TONBRIDGE

C. & A.J. Barmby, 140 Lavender Hill, Tonbridge, TN9 2AY. Prop: Chris & Angela Barmby. Tel: (01732) 771590. Fax: (01732) 771590. Web: www.bookpilot@aol.com. E-mail: bookpilot@aol.com. Est: 1981. Storeroom. Internet and postal. Appointment necessary. Stock: large. Spec: Antiquarian; Antiques; Applied Art; Archaeology; Architecture; Art; Art Reference; Author - 20th Century. PR: £5–4,000. CC: MC; V; SW, DE. VAT No: GB 367 4200 58. [14/01/2005]

Chas J. Sawyer, P.O. Box 333, Tonbridge, TN9 1WJ. Prop: Richard Sawyer. Tel: 01732 369388. Fax: 01732 369388. E-mail: cjsbks@btinternet.com. Est: 1894. Private premises. Internet and postal. Appointment necessary. Open: **M:** 09:00–17:30; **T:** 09:00–17:30; **W:** 09:00–17:30; **Th:** 09:00–17:30; **F:** 09:00–17:30; **S;** Closed for lunch: 13:00–14:00. Spec: Africana; Authors:- Burton, R.F.; Carroll, Lewis; Chapman, Abel; Churchill, Sir Winston; Autographs; Bibliography; Bindings. CC: MC; V; PayPal. Cata: online/Internet on Churchilliana, Africana, inc Ephemera. Notes: Insurance and Consultancy work undertaken based on 40 years experience of antiquarian booktrade [Updated]

Grant Demar Books, 15 White Cottage Road, Tonbridge, TN10 4PX. Prop: Grant Demar. Tel: (01732) 360208. Web: www.garntdemarbooks.co.uk. E-mail: grantdemar@tiscali.co.uk. Est: 1977. Private premises. Appointment necessary. Stock: small. Spec: Animals and Birds; Conservation; Entomology; Natural History; Ornithology; Zoology. PR: £1–1,000. Cata: annually. [Updated]

KENT 141

Tony Skelton, The Old School House, Shipbourne, Tonbridge, TN11 9PB. Prop: D.A.L. Skelton. Tel: (01732) 810481. E-mail: tskelt@waitrose.com. Est: 1992. Private premises. Internet and postal. Contactable. Open: **M:** 08:08–20:20; **T:** 08:08–20:20; **W:** 08:00–20:00; **Th:** 08:00–20:00; **F:** 08:00–20:00; **S:** 09:00–20:00; **Su:** 09:00–20:00. Stock: small. Spec: Countries - Ireland; First Editions; Literature; Modern First Editions; Publishers - Penguin; Booksearch. PR: £5–500. Corresp: French, German. Mem: PBFA. VAT No: GB 796 5067 79. [Updated]

P. & F. Whelan, 68 The Drive, Tonbridge, TN9 2LR. Prop: Tony & Mary Whelan. Tel: (01732) 354882. Fax: (01732) 354882. E-mail: whelanirishbooks@lineone.net. Est: 1986. Private premises. Postal only. Stock: small. Spec: Countries - Ireland; History - National; Irish Interest. PR: £5–250. [Updated]

TUNBRIDGE WELLS

The Secondhand Bookshop, ■ 13 Nevill Street, Tunbridge Wells, TN2 5RU. Prop: David Neal. Tel: (01892) 547005. Est: 1988. Shop open: **M:** 10:00–16:30; **T:** 10:00–16:30; **Th:** 10:00–16:30; **F:** 10:00–16:30; **S:** 10:00–16:30. Stock: medium. PR: £1–500. VAT No: GB 725 4573 27. [Updated]

Hall's Bookshop, ■ 20–22 Chapel Place, Tunbridge Wells, TN1 1YQ. Prop: Sabrina Izzard. Tel: (01892) 527842. Fax: (01892) 527842. E-mail: sabizzard@waitrose.com. Est: 1898. Shop open: **M:** 09:30–17:00; **T:** 09:30–17:00; **W:** 09:30–17:00; **Th:** 09:30–17:00; **F:** 09:30–17:00; **S:** 09:30–17:00. Stock: large. Spec: Art; Bindings; Biography; History - General; Literature; Natural History; Topography - General; Travel - General. Mem: PBFA. [Updated]

Pantiles Bookshop, ■ The Corn Exchange, The Pantiles, Tunbridge Wells, TN2 5TE. Prop: Steve and Val Marshall. Tel: 01892 618191. Web: www.pantilesbooksop.co.uk. E-mail: pantiles@corn3.wanadoo.co.uk. Est: 2004. Shop open: **M:** 09:00–17:30; **T:** 09:00–17:30; **W:** 09:00–17:30; **Th:** 09:00–17:30; **F:** 09:00–17:30; **S:** 09:00–17:30; **Su:** 10:00–17:00. CC: AE; MC; V. Notes: a well stocked mainly non-fiction bookshop specialising in Sport, Railway, Military, Cinema, Mind, Body, Spirit and books on Kent. [Updated]

Politicos.co.uk, PO Box 279, Tunbridge Wells, TN2 4WJ. Prop: Iain Dale. Tel: (0870) 850 1110. Fax: (0870) 850 0176. Web: www.politicos.co.uk. E-mail: iain.dale@politicos.co.uk. Est: 1996. Warehouse; Internet and postal. Stock: very large. Spec: Autobiography; Autographs; Biography; History - National; Memoirs; Politics. PR: £1–1,000. CC: AE; MC; V; SW. Mem: PBFA. Notes: also, new books [Updated]

World War Books, Oaklands, Camden Park, Tunbridge Wells, TN2 5AE. Prop: Tim Harper. Tel: (01892) 538465. Fax: (01892) 538465. Web: www.worldwarbooks.com. E-mail: wwarbooks@btinternet.com. Est: 1993. Private premises. Internet and postal. Contactable. Stock: medium. Spec: Aviation; Holocaust; Maritime/Nautical; Military; School Registers/Rolls of Honour; War - General. PR: £10–5,000. CC: MC; V. Mem: PBFA; OMRS. [Updated]

WALMER

Twiggers Booksearch, 44 The Strand, Walmer Deal, CT14 7DX. Prop: M. Thiry. Tel: (013) 0436 5511. Fax: (013) 0437 5209. Web: www.twiggers.com. E-mail: booksearch@twiggers.com. Est: 1980. Private premises. Postal only. Contactable. Open: **M:** 09:00–17:30; **T:** 09:00–17:30; **W:** 09:00–17:30; **Th:** 09:00–17:30; **F:** 09:00–17:30; **S:** 10:00–16:00. Stock: very small. Spec: Booksearch. CC: SW. VAT No: GB 726 1475 36. [Updated]

WESTERHAM

Derek Stirling Bookseller, 1 Quebec Avenue, Westerham, TN16 1BJ. Tel: (01959) 561 822. Fax: (01959) 561 822. E-mail: derekfs@dialstart.net. Est: 1999. Private premises. Internet and postal. Appointment necessary. Stock: very small. Spec: Academic/Scholarly; Advertising; Antiquarian; Author - Dickens, Charles; Author - Hardy, Thomas; Bibles; Ex-Libris; Fables. PR: £10–2,000. [Updated]

The Design Gallery 1850-1950, 5 The Green, Westerham, RH7 6NR. Prop: Chrissie Painell. Tel: (01959) 561234. Web: www.designgallery.co.uk. E-mail: sales@designgallery.co.uk. Spec: Bindings; Crafts. Notes: also, Victorian fine bindings, and original illustrations. [Updated]

WHITSTABLE

Alan & Margaret Edwards, 10 Meteor Avenue, Whitstable, CT5 4DH. Tel: (01227) 262276. Fax: (01227) 261158. E-mail: a.m.books@lineone.net. Est: 1988. Private premises. Postal only. Appointment necessary. Stock: small. Spec: Ecclesiastical History & Architecture; Theology; Topography - General. PR: £1–500. Corresp: French, German. Notes: Exhibits at book fairs. [Updated]

LANCASHIRE

BLACKBURN

Neil Summersgill, Pigeon Hall, Abbott Brow, Mellor, Blackburn, BB2 7HT. Tel: (01254) 813559. E-mail: summersgillbooks@btinternet.com. Est: 1984. Private premises. Internet and postal. Appointment necessary. Stock: very small. Spec: Antiquarian; Atlases; Autographs; Bindings; Letters; Manuscripts; Natural History; Sport - Field Sports. PR: £10–5,000. CC: MC; V. Mem: PBFA. [Updated]

BLACKPOOL

Book Mad, ■ 151 Church Street, Blackpool, FY1 3NX. Prop: Nick Street. Tel: 01253 291969. E-mail: bookmad151@hotmail.com. Est: 1991. Shop open: **M:** 10:00–17:30; **T:** 10:00–17:30; **W:** 10:00–17:30; **Th:** 10:00–17:30; **F:** 10:00–17:30; **S:** 10:00–17:30; **Su:** 10:00–16:00; Closed for lunch: 10:00–16:00. Spec: out-of-print; Prints and Maps. [Updated]

Bob Dobson, 3 Staining Rise, Staining, Blackpool, FY3 0BU. Tel: (01253) 895678. Fax: (01253) 895678. E-mail: peggie@peggiedobson.wanadoo.co.uk. Est: 1969. Private premises. Appointment necessary. Stock: large. Spec: History - Local; Topography - Local. PR: £1–100. Mem: Incl: books on Lancashire, Yorkshire and Cheshire. Notes: also publishes as Landy Publishing VAT No: GB 534 3982 30. [Updated]

John McGlynn, 173 Newton Drive, Blackpool, FY3 8ND. Tel: (01253) 300100. Fax: (01253) 300020. Web: www.vintagetechnology.org. E-mail: johnmcglynn@blueyonder.co.uk. Est: 1996. Private premises. Postal only. Stock: medium. Spec: Motoring; Transport. PR: £10–200. Notes: also, collectables and ephemera. vintage@blackpool.net. [Updated]

BRINSCALL

Modern Firsts Etc., Hilltops, Windsor Drive, Brinscall, PR6 8PX. Prop: R.J. Leek. Tel: (01254) 830861. Est: 1985. Private premises. Postal only. Stock: very small. Spec: Autographs; First Editions; Painting. PR: £1–500. [Updated]

BURY

Richard Byrom Textile Bookroom, 3 Hawkshaw Lane, Bury, BL8 4JZ. Prop: Richard Byrom. Tel: (01204) 883110. Fax: (01204) 880155. Est: 1984. Private premises. Appointment necessary. Stock: large. Spec: Carpets; Company History; Crochet; Embroidery; Fashion & Costume; Industry; Knitting; Lace. PR: £1–500. [Updated]

CARNFORTH

The Carnforth Bookshop, ■ 38–42 Market Street, Carnforth, LA5 9JX. Prop: P. & G. Seward. Tel: (01524) 734588. Fax: (01524) 735893. Web: www.carnforthbooks.co.uk. E-mail: carnforthbkshop@aol.com. Est: 1977. Internet and postal. Shop open: **M:** 09:00–17:30; **T:** 09:00–17:30; **W:** 09:00–17:30; **Th:** 09:00–17:30; **F:** 09:00–17:30; **S:** 09:00–17:30. Stock: very large. Spec: Alpinism/Mountaineering; Art; Art History; Biography; Classical Studies; Fiction - General; Fine & Rare; History - General. PR: £1–500. CC: AE; E; JCB; MC; V. Mem: BA; Booksearch. VAT No: GB 306 8293 93. [Updated]

CHORLEY

Bowland Bookfinders, 88 Bury Lane, Withnell, Chorley, PR6 8SD. Prop: D.S. Suttie. Tel: (01254) 830619. E-mail: david@bookfind.freeserve.co.uk. Est: 1987. Private premises. Postal only. Appointment necessary. Spec: Academic/Scholarly; Advertising; War - General; Booksearch. [Updated]

Available from Richard Joseph Publishers Ltd
Sheppard's Book Dealers in EPHEMERA
Order the next edition now – or search on www.sheppardsworld.co.uk

Browse Books, 10 Silverdale Close, Worden Park, Leyland, Chorley, PR25 3BY. Prop: T.B. Bowe. Tel: (01772) 431608. E-mail: b_bowe@hotmail.com. Est: 1989. Display/stand; Internet and postal. Telephone first. Open: **M:** 10:00–17:00; **T:** 10:00–17:00; **W:** 10:00–20:00; **Th:** 10:00–15:00; **F:** 10:00–17:00; **S:** 10:00–16:00; **Su:** 10:00–17:00. Spec: Antiques; Buses/Trams; Crafts; Embroidery; Gardening - General; Humour; Motoring; Poetry. PR: £2–50. Notes: Extensive Sheet Music Stock. [13/12/2004]

CLITHEROE

Bowdon Books, ■ 33 Lowergate, Clitheroe, BB7 1AD. Prop: Gordon & Gillian Hill. Tel: (01200) 425333. Est: 1987. Shop open: **Th:** 10:00–16:00; **F:** 10:00–16:30; **S:** 10:00–16:30. Stock: medium. Spec: Topography - Local. PR: £5–500. CC: JCB; MC; V; Switch. [Updated]

Moorside Books Ltd, ■ Moorside Cottage, Whalley Old Road, Billington, Clitheroe, BB7 9JF. Prop: David Sedgwick. Tel: (01254) 824104. Web: www.abebooks.com/home/DFSBOOKS/. E-mail: dsbooks@easynet.co.uk. Est: 1985. Shop. Internet and postal. Open: **T:** 10:00–17:00; **Th:** 10:00–17:00; **F:** 10:00–17:00; **S:** 10:00–17:00. Stock: small. Spec: Astronomy; Author - Lawrence, T.E.; Bindings; Physics; Science - General; Science - History of; Travel - Asia; Travel - Middle East. PR: £5–10,000. CC: MC; V; Maestro. Mem: PBFA. Notes: also at, 29 Moor Lane, Clitheroe, Lancs. VAT No: GB 787 8011 92. [Updated]

Roundstone Books, ■ 29 Moor Lane, Clitheroe, BB7 1BE. Prop: Jo Harding. Tel: (01200) 444242. Web: www.roundstonebooks.co.uk. E-mail: joharbooks@aol.com. Est: 1995. Shop open: **T:** 09:00–17:00; **Th:** 09:00–17:00; **F:** 09:00–17:00; **S:** 09:00–17:00. Spec: Alternative Medicine; Biography; Children's; County - Local; Drama; History - General; Languages - Foreign; Literary Criticism. PR: £1–100. CC: JCB; MC; V; Debit cards. Notes: free booksearch service. [Updated]

FENCE

Pendleside Books, 359 Wheatley Lane Road, Fence, Nr. Burnley, BB12 9QA. Prop: E. & B. Sutcliffe. Tel: (01282) 615617. Est: 1974. Private premises. Appointment necessary. Stock: very small. Spec: Entomology; Mycology; Topography - Local. PR: £5–500. Corresp: French, Italian. [Updated]

HALTON

Mark Towers, 45 Beech Road, Halton, LA2 6QQ. Tel: (01524) 811556. Web: www.royoftherovers.com. E-mail: mark@royoftherovers.com. Est: 1999. Private premises. Postal only. Contactable. Spec: Comic Books & Annuals; Comics. PR: £2–50. [Updated]

HINDLEY

Wiend Books, Unit 1 Hindley Business Centre, Platt Lane, Hindley , Wigan, WN2 3PA. Prop: Paul Morris. Tel: (07976) 604203. Web: www.wiendbooks.co.uk. E-mail: wiendbooks@lycos.co.uk. Est: 1997. Office and/or bookroom. Appointment necessary. Open: **M:** 09:00–17:30; **W:** 09:00–17:30; **Th:** 09:00–17:30; **F:** 09:00–17:30; **S:** 09:00–13.00. Spec: Africana; Annuals; Architecture; Art; Astronomy; Autobiography; Automobilia/Automotive; Aviation. Mem: PBFA. [Updated]

LANCASTER

Hardback Hotel, 68, Windermere Road, Lancaster, LA1 3EZ. Prop: Jonathan Bean. Tel: 07763 814587. Web: www.hardbackhotel.co.uk. E-mail: mail@hardbackhotel.co.uk. Est: 2001. Private premises. Internet Only. Open: **M:** 09:00–17:30; **T:** 09:00–17:30; **W:** 09:00–17:30; **Th:** 09:00–17:30; **F:** 09:00–17:30; **S:** 09:00–17:30; **Su:** 09:00–17:30; Closed for lunch: 13:00–14:00. Spec: Fiction - General; Fiction - Crime, Detective, Spy, Thrillers; Fiction - Science Fiction; First Editions. CC: PayPal. Notes: modern fiction first editions and proof copies [Updated]

Interstellar Master Traders, ■ 33 North Road, Lancaster, LA1-1NS. Prop: P. Pinto. Tel: +44-1524-382181. Web: www.i-m-t.demon.co.uk/. E-mail: ppshepp@i-m-t.demon.co.uk. Est: 1985. Shop. Internet and postal. Open: **M:** 10:00–19:00; **T:** 10:00–19:00; **W:** 10:00–19:00; **Th:** 10:00–19:00; **F:** 10:00–19:00; **S:** 10:00–19:00. Stock: large. Spec: Fiction - Fantasy, Horror; Fiction - Science Fiction. PR: £0–750. Notes: Titles want-listed 'til found / deleted by customer. [Updated]

LEYLAND

Great Grandfather's, ■ 82 Towngate, Leyland, Preston, PR25 2LR. Prop: Greg D. Smith. Tel: (01772) 422268. E-mail: books@greatgrandfathers.fsnet.co.uk. Est: 1985. Shop open: **T:** 10:00–17:30; **Th:** 10:00–17:30; **F:** 10:00–17:30; **S:** 10:00–17:30. Stock: large. PR: £1–200. Corresp: French, German. Mem: PBFA. Notes: open other times by appointment. Large general stock [Updated]

LOWER DARWEN

Red Rose Books, Brook Mill Complex, Branch Road, Lower Darwen, BB3 0PR. Prop: K.M. Tebay. Tel: (01254) 290029. Web: www.redrosebooks.co.uk. E-mail: info@redrosebooks.co.uk. Est: 1993. Office and/or bookroom. Internet and postal. Appointment necessary. Stock: small. PR: £1–1,000. CC: AE; MC; V. Mem: PBFA. VAT No: GB 693 2135 32. [Updated]

LYTHAM ST. ANNES

Robert F. Butterworth, 33 Eldon Court, Glen Eldon Road, Lytham St. Annes, FY8 2BH. Prop: Robert F Butterworth. Tel: (01253) 729031. Fax: (01253) 729031. E-mail: rfbutters@compuserve.com. Est: 1982. Private premises. Internet and postal. Appointment necessary. Stock: small. Spec: Maritime/Nautical; Ephemera. PR: £1–750. Notes: Antique Centre, St.George's Road, St.Annes. [Updated]

PRESTON

B D McManmon, 6 SeaView, Walmer Bridge, Preston, PR4 5GH. Prop: Barry McManmon. Tel: 01772 612727. E-mail: barry@mcmanmon.fsbusiness.co.uk. Est: 1982. Private premises. Appointment necessary. Spec: Academic/Scholarly; Military; Travel - General. CC: AE; D; E; JCB; MC; V; Debit cards. Mem: ABA; ILAB. Notes: stock includes books on academiin history. [Updated]

Halewood & Sons, ■ 37 Friargate, Preston, PR1 2AT. Tel: (01772) 252603. E-mail: halewoodandsons@aol.com. Est: 1867. Shop open: **M:** 09:30–17:30; **T:** 09:30–17:30; **W:** 09:30–17:30; **Th:** 09:30–17:30; **F:** 09:30–17:30; **S:** 09:30–17:30. Stock: very large. Spec: Countries - Africa; Countries - Americas, The; Countries - Australia; Booksearch; Prints and Maps. CC: AE; MC; V; Solo, Maestro. Corresp: French, German, Spanish. Mem: ABA; PBFA; BA. Cata: occasionally. Notes: open Sunday by appointment. [Updated]

O'Connor Fine Books, 9 Garrison Road, Fulwood, Preston, PR2 8AL. Prop: John and Evelyn O'Connor. Tel: 01297 32431. E-mail: oconnorfinebooks@hotmail.com. Est: 2002. Private premises. Appointment necessary. Stock: very small. Spec: Bibliography; Folio Society, The; Printing. Corresp: French. [Updated]

Pamona Books, Canberra Road, Preston, PR25 3JH. Prop: Mr. D. W. Heald. Tel: 01772 452198. E-mail: pamonabooks@aol.com. Private premises. Postal only. Contactable. Spec: Fiction - General. [Updated]

Preston Book Company, ■ 68 Friargate, Preston, PR1 2ED. Prop: M. Halewood. Tel: (01772) 252613. E-mail: prestonrarebooks@halewood221b.freeserve.co.uk. Est: 1960. Shop. Internet and postal. Open: **M:** 10:00–17:00; **T:** 10:00–17:00; **W:** 10:00–17:00; **Th:** 10:00–17:00; **F:** 10:00–17:00; **S:** 10:00–17:00. Stock: large. Spec: Americana; Atlases; Author - Conan Doyle, Sir Arthur; Colour-Plate; Sherlockiana; Travel - General. PR: £10–1,000. CC: JCB; MC; V. [Updated]

ST. HELENS

Harvest Books, 25 Thickwood Moss Lane, Rainford, St. Helens, WA11 8QL. Prop: Mrs. Janet Christie. Tel: (01744) 885747. E-mail: harvestbooks@btinternet.com. Est: 1998. Private premises. Internet and postal. Appointment necessary. Stock: very small. Spec: Cookery/Gastronomy; Food & Drink; Rural Life; Social History; Booksearch. PR: £5–100. Mem: PBFA. Notes: attends some fairs. Stock also at Dales and Lakes, Sedberg. [Updated]

THORNTON CLEVELEYS

Seabreeze Books, 39 Woodfield Road, Thornton Cleveleys, FY5 4EQ. Prop: Martin L. Johnson. Tel: (01253) 850075. Est: 1994. Private premises. Appointment necessary. Stock: medium. Spec: Antiquarian; Art; Books about Books; Children's; Churchilliana; Fiction - General; Limited Editions; Literature - Victorian. PR: £1–5,000. Notes: Skipton Antiques Centre, Skipton (q.v.). [Updated]

LEICESTERSHIRE

BURBAGE

Michael D. Raftery (Books), 12 Salem Road, Burbage, LE10 2DT. Prop: Mike Raftery. Tel: Home (01455) 611017. Est: 1976. Shop and/or gallery. Open: **M:** 11:00–16:00; **T:** 11:00–16:00; **W:** 11:00–16:00; **Th:** 11:00–16:00; **F:** 11:00–16:00; **S:** 11:00–16:00; **Su:** 11:00–16:00. Stock: small. Spec: Booksearch. PR: £1–30. CC: AE; D; E; JCB; MC; V. Notes: also, a booksearch service and tea rooms. [Updated]

HINCKLEY

Caduceus Books, 28 Darley Road, Burbage, Hinckley, LE10 2RL. Prop: Ben Fernee. Tel: (01455) 250542. Fax: (0870) 055-2982. Web: www.caduceusbooks.com. E-mail: ben@caduceusbooks.com. Est: 1989. Private premises. Appointment necessary. Stock: very small. Spec: Alchemy; Astrology; Esoteric; Occult; Supernatural; Witchcraft. PR: £1–1,000. CC: MC; V; Switch. Notes: also, manuscripts, associated items. [Updated]

KIBWORTH HARCOURT

The Countryman Gallery, The Croft, 14 Leicester Road, Kibworth Harcourt, LE8 0NN. Prop: Pamela M. Turnbull. Tel: (0116) 279-3211. E-mail: pamturnbull@countrymansgallery.fsnet.co.uk. Est: 1980. Private premises. Appointment necessary. Stock: small. Spec: Children's; Dogs; Ornithology; Poultry; Sport - Angling/Fishing; Sport - Field Sports; Sport - Hunting; Sport - Shooting. PR: £1–500. CC: MC; V. Notes: Shop also at above premises but appointment necessary. [Updated]

LEICESTER

Aucott & Thomas, 45 Mount Ave., Barwell, Leicester, LE9 8AJ. Tel: (01455) 450195. Fax: (01455) 450195. Web: www.aucott.com. E-mail: books@aucott.co.uk. Est: 1996. Private premises. Appointment necessary. Open: **M:** 09:00–18:00; **T:** 09:00–18:00; **W:** 09:00–18:00; **Th:** 09:00–18:00; **F:** 09:00–18:00; **S:** 09:00–18:00. Stock: small. Spec: Authors:- Bell, Adrian; Moore, John; Children's; Fiction - Crime, Detective, Spy, Thrillers; Music - Folk & Irish Folk; Sport - Angling/Fishing; Sport - Horse Racing (inc. Riding/Breeding/Equestrian). PR: £5–25. CC: AE; JCB; MC; V. Mem: I.B.N. VAT No: GB 800 2360 90. [Updated]

Black Cat Bookshop, ■ 90 Charles St., Leicester, LE1 1GE. Prop: Philip & Karen Woolley. Tel: (0116) 251-2756. Fax: (0116) 281-3545. Web: www.blackcatbookshop.com. E-mail: blackcatuk@aol.com. Est: 1987. Shop. Internet and postal. Open: **M:** 09:30–17:00; **T:** 09:30–17:00; **W:** 09:30–17:00; **Th:** 09:30–17:00; **F:** 09:30–17:00; **S:** 09:30–17:00. Stock: large. Spec: Authors:- Conan Doyle, Sir Arthur; Fleming, Ian; Children's; Comic Books & Annuals; Comics; Counterculture; Countries - Melanesia; Countries - Mexico. PR: £1–500. CC: E; JCB; MC; V; SW, De. Mem: PBFA. Notes: attends book fairs - Midlands and North. [22/11/2004]

Clarendon Books, ■ 144 Clarendon Park Road, Leicester, LE2 3AE. Prop: Julian Smith. Tel: (0116) 270-1856. E-mail: clarendonbooks@aol.com. Est: 1985. Shop open: **M:** 10:00–17:00; **T:** 10:00–17:00; **W:** 10:00–17:00; **Th:** 10:00–17:00; **F:** 10:00–17:00; **S:** 10:00–17:00. Stock: medium. Spec: History - General; History - Local; Literary Criticism; Literature. PR: £1–1,000. CC: E; JCB; MC; V; Mae, SO. Mem: PBFA. [Updated]

Cottage Books, Gelsmoor, Coleorton, Leicester, LE67 8HR. Prop: Jennifer M. Boyd–Cropley. Tel: None. Est: 1970. Private premises. Postal only. Stock: medium. Spec: Agriculture; Architecture; Canals/Inland Waterways; Crafts; Fairgrounds; Folklore; Gypsies; History - Local. PR: £1–2,000. Mem: PBFA. [Updated]

Rebecca Dearman Rare Books, ■ 2 Francis Street, Stonygate, Leicester, LE2 BD. Prop: Rebecca Dearman. Tel: (0116) 270-9666. Est: 1967. Shop. Internet and postal. Open: **T:** 09:00–17:00; **W:** 09:00–17:00; **Th:** 09:00–17:00; **F:** 09:00–17:00; **S:** 09:00–17:00. Stock: medium. PR: £1–1,000. [Updated]

Alfred Lenton, ■ 27 Saint Nicholas Place, Leicester, LE1 4LD. Prop: Philip Lenton. Tel: (0116) 262-7827. Est: 1942. Shop. Telephone first. Stock: small. Spec: Art; Arts, The; Illustrated; Literature; Natural History; Science - General; Prints and Maps. PR: £1–100. [Updated]

Bruce Main–Smith & Co. Ltd., 132, Saffron Road, Wigston, Leicester, LE18 4UP. (*) D.R. & M.E. Mitchell (Directors). Tel: (0116) 277-7669. Fax: (0116) 277-7669. Web: www.brucemainsmith.com. E-mail: sales@brucemainsmith.com. Est: 1972. Spec: Motorbikes / motorcycles. PR: £4–100. CC: MC; V; SW. Notes: also, virtually a complete stock of all new motor cycle books, plus 4,000 photocopied manuals, spares lists & brochures [Updated]

Maynard & Bradley, ■ 1 Royal Arcade, Silver Street, Leicester, LE1 5YW. Prop: David Maynard & Stephen Bradley Tel: (0116) 253-2712. Web: www.maynardandbradley.com. E-mail: orderds@maynardandbradley.com. Est: 1971. Shop open: **M:** 09:15–17:15; **T:** 09:15–17:15; **W:** 09:15–17:15; **Th:** 09:15–17:15; **F:** 09:15–17:15; **S:** 09:00–17:00. Stock: medium. Spec: Bindings; Colour-Plate; Cookery/Gastronomy; Illustrated; Private Press; Sport - Cricket; Sport - Field Sports; Topography - General. PR: £1–3,000. CC: E; MC; V; So, Mae. Mem: PBFA. Notes: also, booksearch, pictures, picture-framing, conservation services, print colouring & decorative mount cutting service (trade). VAT No: GB 416 3807 58. [Updated]

Pooks Motor Books, ■ Unit 4 Victoria Road, Fowke Street, Rothley, Leicester, LE7 7PJ. (*) Barrie Pook & John Pook. Tel: (0116) 237-6222. Fax: (0116) 237-6491. Web: www.abebooks.com. E-mail: pooks.motorbooks@virgin.net. Shop open: **M:** 09:00–17:00; **T:** 09:00–17:00; **W:** 09:00–17:00; **Th:** 09:00–17:00; **F:** 09:00–17:00. Stock: very large. Spec: Biography; Marque Histories (see also motoring); Motorbikes / motorcycles; Motoring; Transport; Vintage Cars; Collectables; Ephemera. PR: £3–1,000. CC: MC; V. Mem: FSB. Notes: also, sales catalogues for cars & motorcycles. Open at other times by appointment [Updated]

Rosanda Books, 11 Whiteoaks Road, Oadby, Leicester, LE2 5YL. Prop: David Baldwin BA, M. Phil, & Joyce Baldwin. Tel: (0116) 2713880. E-mail: dbaldwin@themutual.net. Est: 1994. Private premises. Appointment necessary. Spec: History - Ancient; History - British; History - European; History - Middle Ages. PR: £2–50. [15/10/2004]

Tin Drum Books, ■ 68 Narborough Road, Leicester, LE3 0BR. Prop: Valerie & Ian Smalley Tel: (0116) 224-8409. E-mail: tindrum@ntlworld.com. Est: 1986. Shop open: **M:** 10:00–18:00; **T:** 10:00–18:00; **W:** 10:00–18:00; **Th:** 10:00–18:00; **F:** 10:00–18:00; **S:** 10:00–18:00. Stock: medium. PR: £1–10. Notes: Notes: also, bookbinding. [Updated]

Treasure Trove Books, ■ 21 Mayfield Road, Leicester, LE2 1LR. Prop: Linda Sharman. Tel: (0116) 2755933. E-mail: sales@treasuretrovebks.plus.com. Est: 1993. Shop. Internet Only. Open: **M:** 09:30–17:30; **T:** 09:30–17:30; **W:** 09:30–17:30; **Th:** 09:30–17:30; **F:** 09:30–17:30; **S:** 09:30–17:30. Stock: very large. Spec: Annuals; Authors:- Bellaires, George; Blyton, Enid; Brent-Dyer, Elinor M.; Buckeridge, A.; Christie, Agatha; Johns, W.E.; Potter, Beatrix. PR: £1–500. [03/02/2004]

Tony Yates Antiquarian Books, 3 Melton Avenue, Leicester, LE4 7SE. Tel: (0116) 266-1891. Web: www.TonyYatesBooks@Btopenworld.com. E-mail: tonyyatesbooks@btopenworld.com. Est: 1989. Private premises. Appointment necessary. Stock: small. Spec: Antiquarian; Children's - Early Titles; Dictionaries; Education & School; History - Local; Illustrated; Literature; Topography - Local. PR: £5–1,000. Mem: PBFA. [Updated]

LOUGHBOROUGH

Booklore, 6 The Green, East Leake, Loughborough, LE12 6ld. (*) Prop: Ralph & Simon Corbett. Tel: (01509) 820614. E-mail: Ralphcorbett@aol.com. Private premises. Internet and postal. Appointment necessary. Open: **M:** 09:30–17:30; **T:** 09:30–17:30; **W:** 09:30–17:30; **Th:** 09:30–17:30; **F:** 09:30–17:30; **S:** 09:00–16:00. Stock: large. Spec: Antiquarian; Bindings. PR: £10–1,000. CC: MC; V. Mem: ABA; PBFA. VAT No: GB 815 6907 13. [22/12/2004]

Eric Goodyer, Natural History, Hathern, Loughborough, LE12 5LE. Prop: Sue Duerdoth & Eric Goodyer. Tel: (01509) 844473. Fax: (01509) 844473. Web: www.abebooks.com/home/ERICGOODYER/. E-mail: eric.goodyer@ntlworld.com. Est: 1992. Stock: very small. Spec: Antiquarian; Natural History. PR: £5–300. CC: PayPal. [Updated]

Malcolm Hornsby, Antiquarian and Secondhand Books, ■ 41 Churchgate, Loughborough, LE11 1UE. Prop: Malcolm Hornsby. Tel: (01509) 269860. Web: www.hornsbybooks.co.uk. E-mail: info@hornsbybooks.co.uk. Est: 1993. Shop open: **M:** 10:00–17:30; **T:** 10:00–17:30; **W:** 10:00–17:30; **Th:** 10:00–17:30; **F:** 10:00–17:30; **S:** 10:00–17:30. Stock: medium. Spec: Academic/Scholarly; Antiquarian; Art; Aviation; History - General. CC: AE; E; JCB; MC; V. Corresp: French, German, Greek. Mem: PBFA. [Updated]

Magis Books, 64 Leopold Street, Loughborough, LE11 5DN. Prop: Tom Clarke. Tel: 01509210626. Fax: 01509238034. Web: www.www.magis.co.uk. E-mail: enquiries@magis.co.uk. Est: 1975. Private premises. Internet and postal. Telephone first. Open: **M:** 09:00–17:30; **T:** 09:00–17:30; **W:** 09:00–17:30; **Th:** 09:00–17:30; **F:** 09:00–17:30; **S:** 09:00–17:30; **Su:** 09:00–17:30; Closed for lunch: 13:00–14:00. Spec: Alchemy; Divining; Esoteric; Folklore; Ghosts; Graphology; Hermeticism; Homeopathy. CC: MC; V. Cata: bi-monthly on Esoteric, occult, Eastern & Western philosophies,. Mem: PBFA. [Updated]

MARKET HARBOROUGH

Bowden Books, 14 Station Road, Great Bowden, Market Harborough, LE16 7HN. Prop: Terry Bull. Tel: (01858) 466832. Est: 1986. Private premises. Postal only. Stock: very small. Spec: Architecture; Art; Colour-Plate; Publishers - Black, A. & C.; Topography - General; Travel - General. PR: £5–750. Corresp: French, Italian. Mem: PBFA. Notes: book fairs. [Updated]

Christine's Book Cabin, ■ 7 Coventry Road, Market Harborough, LE16 9BX. Prop: Malcolm & Christine Noble. Tel: (01858) 433233. Web: www.bookcabin.co.uk. E-mail: malcolm@bookcabin.co.uk. Est: 1992. Shop open: **M:** 10:00–16:30; **T:** 10:00–16:30; **Th:** 10:00–16:30; **F:** 10:00–16:30; **S:** 10:00–16:30. Stock: small. Spec: Booksearch; Ephemera. PR: £1–400. CC: AE; JCB; MC; V. Notes: General stock. [Updated]

MELTON MOWBRAY

Witmeha Productions, The Orchard, Wymondham, Melton Mowbray, LE14 2AZ. [Updated]

ROTHLEY

Whig Books Ltd., 11 Grangefields Drive, Rothley. Prop: Dr. J. Pollock & Mrs. A. Hinchliffe. Tel: (0116) 237-4420. Est: 1985. Private premises. Appointment necessary. Stock: very small. Spec: Art; History - General; Literature. PR: £1–500. Mem: PBFA. [Updated]

THURCASTON

Ian Kilgour (Sporting Books), 3 Hall Farm Road, Thurcaston, LE7 7JF. Prop: Ian Kilgour. Tel: (0116) 235-0025. E-mail: sportingbooks@ntlworld.com. Est: 1972. Private premises. Internet and postal. Appointment necessary. Stock: small. Spec: Cockfighting; Dogs; Farming & Livestock; Firearms/Guns; Rural Life; Sport - Angling/Fishing; Sport - Field Sports; Sport - Hunting. PR: £2–500. [Updated]

LINCOLNSHIRE

BARTON–ON–HUMBER

Humber Books, Rozel House, 4 St. Mary's Lane, Barton–on–Humber, DN18 5EX. Prop: Peter M. Cresswell. Tel: (01652) 634958. Fax: (01652) 634965. Web: www.netguides.co.uk/uk/humber.html. E-mail: pmc@humberbooks.co.uk. Est: 1972. Spec: Antiquarian; Bibles; Hymnology; Manuscripts; Religion - Christian; Religion - Methodism; Religion - Non conformity; Religion - Protestantism. PR: £20–2,000. [Updated]

BILLINGBOROUGH

Brockwells Booksellers, Unit 1C, White Leather Square, Billingborough, NG34 0QP. Prop: Matthew & Richard Peace. Tel: (01529)241222. Fax: (01529)455890. Web: www.brockwells.co.uk. E-mail: books @brockwells.co.uk. Est: 1997. Warehouse; Internet and postal. Telephone first. Open: **M:** 09:00–16:00; **T:** 09:00–16:00; **W:** 09:00–16:00; **Th:** 09:00–16:00; **F:** 09:00–16:00. Stock: large. Spec: Academic/Scholarly; Antiquarian; Business Studies; Engineering; History - General; Military History; Politics; Travel - General. PR: £7–2,250. CC: AE; MC; V; Maestro. Mem: Bibliographical Society. Notes: prints and maps selling. New boook sales, secure credit card facility on website. [29/10/2004]

Alan Redmouth Books, 25 High Street, Billingborough, Sleaford, NG34 0QB. Prop: Mrs E. Redmond. Tel: 01529 240215. Est: 1981. Storeroom. Open: **S:** 10:00–17:00; **Su:** 10:00–17:00. Notes: also open on Bank Holidays but closed between 1 November and 1 March. [Updated]

BILLINGHAY

Not JUST Books, 27-29 High Street, Billinghay, Lincoln, LN4 4AU. Prop: Maggy Browne. Tel: (01526) 860294. Fax: (0870) 7059623. Web: www.njbonline.com. E-mail: books@notjustbooks.f9.co.uk. Est: 1981. Private premises. Internet and postal. Appointment necessary. Stock: medium. Spec: Biography; Crime (True); Fiction - General; Fire & Fire Fighters; History   General; Police Force Histories; Politics; Publishers - Chambers. PR: £5–50. CC: AE; JCB; MC; V; Switch. Mem: FSB. Notes: props for Theatre, Film and TV. Mailroom supplies, Dustjacket sleeving , PB covers etc etc.[Updated]

BOSTON

Libra Books, Church House, Wigtoft, Boston, PE20 2NJ. Prop: Paul & Linda Daunter. Tel: (01205) 460829. Fax: (01205) 460829. Web: www.: ukbookworld.com/members/LibraBooks. E-mail: libra.books@btinternet.com. Est: 1994. Private premises. Internet and postal. Telephone first. Stock: large. Spec: Biography; Ex-Libris; Fiction - General; Fiction - Crime, Detective, Spy, Thrillers; Fiction - Historical; Fiction - Science Fiction; Fiction - Women; Gardening - General. PR: £1–100. [Updated]

HUMBER BOOKS

THEOLOGY & BIBLES
PRINTED BEFORE 1700

Regular Catalogues issued free (including later works)

Specialising in the Protestant Reformation,
Puritanism & Nonconformity

Books also purchased

4 ST MARY'S LANE, BARTON-ON-HUMBER, DN18 5EX.
Tel: (01652) 634958 Fax: (01652) 634965.
Email: pmc@humberbooks.co.uk   Website: www.humberbooks.co.uk

CLEETHORPES

Soccer Books Limited, 72 St Peter's Avenue, Cleethorpes, DN35 8HU. Prop: John, Michael & Glenys Robinson. Tel: 01472-696226. Fax: 01472-698546. Web: www.soccer-books.co.uk. E-mail: info@soccer-books.co.uk. Est: 1982. Office and/or bookroom. Postal only. Contactable. Open: **M:** 09:00–17:00; **T:** 09:00–17:00; **W:** 09:00–17:00; **Th:** 09:00–17:00; **F:** 09:00–12.00; Closed for lunch: 13:00–14:00. Spec: New Books; Railways; Sport - Football (Soccer). CC: AE; E; JCB; MC; V; Maestro. Cata: bi-monthy on soccer. Mem: PBFA. Notes: Publishers of 15 to 20 titles each year and mailorder suppliers of other publishers new and used football books throughout the world VAT No: GB 546 5008 49. [Updated]

CORBY GLEN

Anchor Books, 20 Walsingham Drive, Corby Glen, NG33 4TA. Prop: Mr. C.R. Dunn. Tel: 01476 550103. E-mail: c.r.dunn@btinternet.com. Est: 1990. Private premises. Postal only. Stock: medium. Spec: Aeronautics; Aviation; Canals/Inland Waterways; History - General; Maritime/Nautical; Military; Naval. CC: MC; V. Corresp: German. Mem: PBFA. [Updated]

EAGLE

J. & J. Books, Holly Cottage, 14 Scarle Lane, Eagle, LN6 9EJ. Prop: Jim & Jan Rayner. Tel: (01522) 869597. Fax: (01522) 869597. Web: www.jandjbooks.com. E-mail: jim.rayner@virgin.net. Est: 1994. Private premises. Stock: small. Spec: Fiction - Crime, Detective, Spy, Thrillers; Natural History; Publishers - Penguin; Topography - Local; Vintage Paperbacks. PR: £4–500. CC: MC; V. Mem: PBFA. Notes: also, a booksearch service. [Updated]

GAINSBOROUGH

Hemswell Antique Centre, Caenby Corner Estate, Hemswell Cliff, Gainsborough, DN21 5TJ. Prop: Mr. R. Miller Tel: (01427) 668389. Fax: 668935. E-mail: info@Hemswell-Antiques.com. Est: 1986. Shop and/or gallery. Open: **M:** 10:00–17:00; **T:** 10:00–17:00; **W:** 10:00–17:00; **Th:** 10:00–17:00; **F:** 10:00–17:00; **S:** 10:00–17:00; **Su:** 10:00–17:00. CC: AE; D; E; JCB; MC; V. [Updated]

HOLBEACH

P. Cassidy (Bookseller), ■ 1 Boston Road, Holbeach, PE12 7LR. Prop: Patrick Cassidy. Tel: (01406) 426322. Web: www.ukbookworld.com/members/7676. E-mail: bookscass@aol.com. Est: 1975. Shop open: **M:** 10:00–17:30; **T:** 10:00–17:30; **W:** 10:00–17:30; **Th:** 10:00–17:30; **F:** 10:00–17:30; **S:** 10:00–17:30. Stock: medium. Spec: Topography - Local; Prints and Maps. PR: £1–250. CC: AE; MC; V; PayPal. [Updated]

HORNCASTLE

Good for Books, ■ Good for Books, 23 North Street, Horncastle, LN9 5DX. Prop: Richard & Sarah Ingram-Hill. Tel: 01507 525021. Fax: 01507 524415. Web: www.goodforbooks.co.uk. E-mail: books@goodforbooks.co.uk. Est: 2004. Shop open: **M:** 10.00–16:30; **T:** 10.00–16:30; **W:** 10:00–16:30; **Th:** 10:00–16:30; **F:** 10:00–16:30; **S:** 10:00–16:30. Spec: Animals and Birds; Antiquarian; Architecture; Art; Author - 20th Century; Aviation; Biography; Children's. Notes: shop divided into 3 rooms - Good for Books - eclectic mix! Books Two - all books £2.00 or under. Book 3 - all books 3 for £1.00. A coke burning stove adds to an ambient browsing atmosphere during the winter months!. [Updated]

Are you making enough profit - if not then read

BOOKDEALING FOR PROFIT
by Paul Minet

Quarto H/b   Available from Richard Joseph Publishers Ltd   £10.00 144pp

Jabberwock Books, ■ 14 - 16 St Lawrence Street, Horncastle, LN9 5BJ. Prop: Robert Flanagan and Pauline Flanagan. Tel: 01507 522112. Web: www.jabberwockbooks.co.uk. E-mail: info@jabberwockbooks.co.uk. Est: 1986. Shop open: **M:** 10:00–17:00; **T:** 10:00–17:00; **W:** 10.00–17:00; **Th:** 10:00–17:00; **F:** 10:00–17:00; **S:** 10:00–17:00; **Su:** 10:00–17:00. [Updated]

Roger Lucas Booksellers, 44 Queen Street, Horncastle, LN9 6BG. Prop: Roger Lucas. Tel: 01507 522261. E-mail: Rogerbks@aol.com. Est: 1984. Private premises. Internet and postal. Appointment necessary. Open: **M:** 09:00–13:00; **T:** 09:00–13:00; **W:** 09:00–13:00; **Th:** 09:00–13:00; **F:** 09:00–13:00. Spec: Art; Crafts; Fiction - General; Literary Criticism; New Age. CC: MC; V; PayPal. Notes: We are a small, family-run firm of booksellers who have been trading for over 20 years. Our aim has always been to supply decent condition books on a wide variety of subjects at sane prices. [Updated]

KIRTON

D.C. Books, 11 Hemington Way, Kirton, Boston, PE20 1EA. Prop: D.J. & C. Lidgett. Tel: (01205) 724507. Fax: (01205) 724507. E-mail: dave.lidgett@fsmail.net. Est: 1984. Private premises. Internet and postal. Stock: very small. Spec: Travel - General; Booksearch. PR: £3–5. [Updated]

LINCOLN

Aardvark Books, 19 Vanwell Drive, Waddington, Lincoln, LN6 9LT. Prop: Peter & Elizabeth Taylor. Tel: 01522 722671. E-mail: pete@aardvarkcricketbooks.co.uk. Est: 1998. Private premises. Appointment necessary. Open: **M:** 09:00–17:00; **T:** 09:00–17:00; **W:** 09:00–17:00; **Th:** 09:00–17:00; **F:** 09:00–17:00; **S:** 09:00–17:00. Spec: Sport - Cricket. Cata: quarterly on Wisden Cricketers Almanacks. Mem: FSB. Notes: a major dealer in Wisden Cricketers Almanacks. Also, book restoration. [Updated]

Autumn Leaves, ■ 19 The Green, Nettleham, Lincoln, LN2 2NR. Prop: Ian & Sue Young. Tel: (01522) 750779. E-mail: leaves@onetel.com. Est: 1997. Shop open: **T:** 09:15–16:30; **W:** 09:30–16:30; **Th:** 09:30–16:30; **F:** 09:15–17:00; **S:** 09:15–12:30. Stock: medium. Spec: Antiques; Art; Cookery/Gastronomy; Drama; Entertainment - General; Fiction - General; Health; History - General. PR: £2–100. CC: AE; JCB; MC; V; Maestro. Corresp: French, German, Swedish. VAT No: GB 737 8648 80. [Updated]

Chapter & Verse, 17 Queensway, Lincoln, LN2 4AJ. Prop: Roy Fines. Tel: (01522) 523202. E-mail: roy@fines18.freeserve.co.uk. Est: 1977. Private premises. Internet and postal. Appointment necessary. Open: **M:** 09:00–18:00; **T:** 09.00–18:00; **W:** 09:00–18:00; **Th:** 09:00–18:00; **F:** 09:00–18:00; **S:** 09:00–18:00; **Su:** 09:00–18:00. Stock: very small. Spec: Topography - Local; Ephemera; Prints and Maps. PR: £1–5,000. CC: AE; MC; V; SW. Corresp: German. [Updated]

Eden Books, PO Box 38, Alford, Lincoln, LN13 3AB. Tel: 01507 466150. Web: www.edenbooks.com. E-mail: edenbooks@aol.com. Est: 1999. Private premises. Internet and postal. Spec: Sport - Football (Soccer); Sport - Rugby. CC: AE; MC; V. Cata: on-line/Internet on Football, Rugby. Mem: PBFA. VAT No: GB 762 3914 22. [Updated]

Golden Goose Books, ■ 20–21 Steep Hill, Lincoln, LN2 1LT. Prop: Mrs Anna Cockram & Richard West–Skinn. Tel: (01522) 522589. E-mail: harlequin@acockram.fsbusiness.co.uk. Est: 1984. Shop. Internet Only. Open: **M:** 11:00–17:00; **T:** 11:00–17:00; **Th:** 11:00–17:00; **F:** 11:00–17:00; **S:** 11:00–17:15. Spec: Antiques; Art; Illustrated. Mem: PBFA; Harlequin Gallery, 20-22, Steep Hill, Lincoln (q.v.). [Updated]

Harlequin Gallery, ■ 22 Steep Hill, Lincoln, LN2 1LT. Prop: Richard West–Skinn. Tel: (01522) 522589. E-mail: harlequin@acockram.fsbusiness.co.uk. Est: 1964. Shop. Internet Only. Open: **M:** 11:00–17:00; **T:** 11:00–17:00; **W:** 12:00–16:00; **Th:** 11:00–17:00; **F:** 11:00–17:00; **S:** 11:00–17:00. Stock: very large. Spec: Prints and Maps. PR: £1–20,000. Notes: Golden Goose Books, 20-21, Steep Hill, Lincoln LN2 1LT. General stock. Also, Golden Goose Globe restorers, R.W. & S.J. West-Skinn. Sometimes open at 10:00. [Updated]

Readers Rest, ■ 13–14 Steep Hill, Lincoln, LN2 1LT. Prop: Nick Warwick. Tel: (01522) 543217. Est: 1982. Shop open: **M:** 09:30–16:00; **T:** 09:30–16:00; **W:** 09:30–16:00; **Th:** 09:30–16:00; **F:** 09:30–16:00; **S:** 09:30–16:00; **Su:** 11:00–16:00. Stock: very large. PR: £1–50. Notes: Readers Rest Hall of Books, Steep Hill, Lincoln. [Updated]

LOUTH

Mostly Mysteries Bookstore, 64 Legbourne Road, Louth, LN11 8ER. Prop: Victor H. Brown & Mary Brown. Tel: 01507 354990. E-mail: victro3@operamail.com. Est: 1985. Storeroom. Appointment necessary. Spec: Mysteries. [Updated]

MARKET DEEPING

Cornucopia Books, 2 Godsey Crescent, Market Deeping, PE6 8HX. Prop: Roy Dennis. Web: www.cornucopiabooks.co.uk. E-mail: mycornucopia@btinternet.com. Est: 1986. Mail Order Only. Internet and postal. Contactable. Spec: Academic/Scholarly; Advertising; Aeronautics; Aircraft; American Indians; Animals and Birds; Antiques; Applied Art. CC: PayPal. Notes: I am disabled and deal by Internet Only. Most major credit cards can be accepted from my website using PayPal. [Updated]

SLEAFORD

Phillip Austen, 50 Main Street, Ewerby, Sleaford, NG34 9PJ. Tel: (01529) 461074. E-mail: phillip.austen@militarybooks.f9.co.uk. Est: 1989. Private premises. Postal only. Stock: medium. Spec: Military. CC: D; E; JCB; MC; V. Mem: PBFA. [Updated]

Mark Evans, 34 Northgate, Sleaford, NG34 7DA. Prop: Mark Evans. Tel: (0798) 1938165. Est: 1985. Private premises. Postal only. Stock: very small. Spec: Cinema/Film; Music - General; Sport - General; Television; Theatre; Booksearch. PR: £3–100. [29/09/2004]

Julian Roberts Fine Books, Hill House, Braceby, Sleaford, NG34 0TA. Tel: (01529) 497271. Fax: (01529) 497271. Web: www.jrfinebooks.com. E-mail: jrfinebooks@aol.com. Private premises. Appointment necessary. Stock: small. PR: £10–5,000. CC: MC; V. Mem: PBFA. Notes: General stock. [Updated]

Westgate Bookshop, ■ 45 Westgate, Sleaford, NG34 7PU. Prop: Geoffrey Almond. Tel: (01529) 304276. Web: www.abebooks.com/home/WESTGATEBOOKSHOP/. E-mail: geoff.almond@btinternet.com. Est: 1986. Shop open: **M:** 10:00–17:00; **T:** 10:00–17:00; **W:** 10:00–17:00; **F:** 10:00–17:00; **S:** 10:00–17:00. Stock: small. PR: £1–15. CC: MC; V. [Updated]

SOUTH KELSEY

Winghale Books Ltd., Grassmere Cottage, Brigg Road, South Kelsey, LN7 6PH. Directors: Irwin & Hilary Johnston. Tel: (01652) 678752. E-mail: winghale@enterprise.net. Est: 1984. Private premises. Internet and postal. Appointment necessary. Stock: medium. Spec: Academic/Scholarly; Classical Studies; Colonial; Ecclesiastical History & Architecture; History - National; Philosophy; Politics. PR: £10–200. CC: AE; MC; V. Mem: PBFA. VAT No: GB 365 1833 46. [Updated]

SPALDING

Bookshop at the Plain, Holbeach, Spalding, PE12 7AU. Prop: M.D. Watts. Tel: (01406) 422 942. E-mail: wattsmc@aol.com. Est: 1987. Private premises. Appointment necessary. Stock: medium. Spec: History - General; Literature; Religion - General; Travel - General. PR: £3–250. CC: MC; V. [Updated]

Robin Peake, 26 Balmoral Avenue, Spalding, PE11 2RN. Tel: (01775) 724050. E-mail: robin.peake@btinternet.com. Est: 1989. Postal only. Spec: Motorbikes / motorcycles; Motoring; Vintage Cars. PR: £2–250. [Updated]

Michael Prior, 34 Fen End Lane, Spalding, PE12 6AD. Prop: Michael Prior. Tel: (01775) 761851. E-mail: mikevprior1@msn.com. Est: 1970. Private premises. Internet and postal. Appointment necessary. Stock: medium. Spec: Advertising; Aeronautics; Authors: - Churchill, Sir Winston; Forester, C.S.; Masefield, John; Aviation; Maritime/Nautical; Military. PR: £10–250. Cata: annually – infrequent on maritime. Corresp: French. [Updated]

STAMFORD

Andrew Burroughs Books, 3 Empingham Road, Stamford, PE9 2RH. Tel: (01780) 751363. Fax: (01780) 765140. E-mail: militarybooks@andrewburroughs.co.uk. Private premises. Postal only. Spec: Maritime/Nautical; Military; Military History; Naval; War - World War I; War - World War II. PR: £5–500. [Updated]

Robert Humm & Co., ■ Station House, Gresley Drive, Stamford, PE9 2JN. Prop: Robert Humm and Clare Humm. Tel: (01780) 766266. Fax: (01780) 757929. Web: www.roberthumm.co.uk. E-mail: books@roberthumm.co.uk. Est: 1974. Internet and postal. Shop open: **M:** 09:30–17:30; **T:** 09:30–16:30; **W:** 09:30–17:30; **Th:** 09:30–17:30; **F:** 09:30–17:30; **S:** 09:30–17:30. Stock: very large. Spec: Aviation; Canals/Inland Waterways; History - Industrial; Maritime/Nautical; Railways; Transport. PR: £5–10,000. CC: E; JCB; MC; V; SW. Corresp: French. [Updated]

St. Mary's Books & Prints, ■ 9 St. Mary's Hill, Stamford, PE9 2DP. Prop: N.A.M., M.G.D. P.A. Tyers. Tel: (01780) 763033. Fax: (01780) 763033. Web: www.stmarysbooks.com. E-mail: orders@stmarysbooks.com. Est: 1971. Internet Only. Shop open: **M:** 08:00–18:00; **T:** 08:00–18:00; **W:** 08:00–18:00; **Th:** 08:00–18:00; **F:** 08:00–18:00; **S:** 08:00–18:00; **Su:** 09:00–18:00. Stock: large. Spec: Academic/Scholarly; Archaeology; Architecture; Authors:- Aldin, Cecil; Fleming, Ian; Rackham, Arthur; Rowling, J.K.; Watkins-Pitchford, Denys ('B.B.'). PR: £10–50,000. CC: AE; D; E; JCB; MC; V. Corresp: German, Latin, French, Spanish, Italian. Notes: Open Sundays. Bookbinding, Valuations, Book Search & major stock of Wisdens. [Updated]

St. Paul's Street Bookshop, ■ 7 St. Paul's Street, Stamford, PE9 2BE. Prop: James Blessett. Tel: (01780) 482748. Fax: (01778) 380538. E-mail: stpaulsbookshop@aol.com. Est: 1986. Shop open: **M:** 10:00–17:00; **T:** 10:00–17:00; **Th:** 10:00–17:00; **F:** 10:00–17:00; **S:** 10:00–17:00. Stock: medium. Spec: Motoring; Sport - Motor Racing; Topography - Local. PR: £1–500. CC: E; MC; V. Corresp: French, German. Mem: PBFA. Notes: also, catalogues on motorsport. VAT No: GB 551 0471 74. [Updated]

Staniland (Booksellers), ■ 4/5 St. George's Street, Stamford, PE9 2BJ. Prop: V.A. & B.J. Valentine Ketchum. Tel: (01780) 755800. Fax: (01780) 755800. E-mail: stanilandbooksellers@btinternet.com. Est: 1972. Internet Only. Shop open: **M:** 10:00–17:00; **T:** 10:00–17:00; **W:** 10:00–17:00; **F:** 10:00–17:00; **S:** 10:00–17:00; Closed for lunch: 13:00–14:00. Stock: large. Spec: Academic/Scholarly; Applied Art; Archaeology; Architecture; Art; Art History; Art Reference; Bindings. PR: £1–3,800. CC: MC; V. Mem: PBFA. VAT No: GB 200 8434 08. [22/12/2004]

Undercover Books, ■ 30 Scotgate, Stamford, PE9 2YQ. Tel: 01780 438098. Fax: 01780 763963. Web: www.usedbooknews.com. E-mail: undercoverbooks@btinternet.com. Est: 1990. Shop. Internet and postal. Open: **M:** 10:00–16:00; **T:** 10:00–16:00; **W:** 10:00–16:00; **Th:** 10:00–16:00; **F:** 10:00–16:00; **S:** 10:00–16:00. Stock: very large. Spec: Crime (True); Criminology; Espionage; Law - General; Police Force Histories; Travel - Europe; Booksearch. CC: AE; D; E; JCB; MC; V; SW, De. Corresp: Any. Notes: Police History Ass. listed on 8 Internet web sites. VAT No: GB 797 0827 78. [07/08/2004]

WINTERTON

Richard Williams (Bookdealer), 4-A Enterprise Way, Roxby Road, Winterton, DN15 9SU. Prop: Richard Williams. Tel: (01724) 733011. Web: www.http://rwilliamsbookdealer.mysite.wanadoo-members/. E-mail: rich@rahwilliams.freeserve.co.uk. Est: 1975. Private premises. Appointment necessary. Stock: very large. Spec: Authors: Wallace, Edgar; Bibliography; Cinema/Film; Crime (True); Fiction - General; Fiction - Crime, Detective, Spy, Thrillers; Fiction - Fantasy, Horror; Fiction - Romantic. PR: £2–200. CC: MC; V. Corresp: French, German. [Updated]

LONDON
(EAST LONDON POSTAL DISTRICTS)

Antique City Bookshop, ■ 2 - 3 Antique City Market, 98 Wood Street, Walthamstow, London, E17 3HX. Prop: Alan Stone. Tel: 020 8520 8300. Est: 1994. Shop open: **M:** 10:30–16:30; **T:** 10:30–17:30; **F:** 10:30–17:30; **S:** 10:30–16:30. [Updated]

Bibliophile Books, Unit 5 Industrial Estate, Thomas Road, London, E14 7BN. Prop: A. Quigley. Tel: (0207) 515-9222. Fax: (0207) 538-4115. Web: www.bibliophilebooks.com. E-mail: customercare@bibliophilebooks.co.uk. Est: 1978. Storeroom. Open: **M:** 08:30–17:00; **T:** 08:30–17:00; **W:** 08:30–17:00; **Th:** 08:30–17:00; **F:** 08:30–17:00. Stock: medium. Spec: First Editions; Signed Editions; Social History. PR: £1–30. CC: AE; MC; V. Corresp: French, German, Spanish. Notes: also, re-prints & remainders. VAT No: GB 242 6934 55. [Updated]

Birchden Books, 3 Edith Road, East Ham, London, E1 1DE. Prop: Michael Vetterlein. Tel: (020) 8472-3654. E-mail: mike@mvetterlein.freeserve.co.uk. Est: 2001. Private premises. Postal only. Appointment necessary. Stock: very small. Spec: Ecclesiastical History & Architecture; Illuminated Manuscripts; Sculpture; Stained Glass; Topography - Local. PR: £2–500. [Updated]

Brian Troath Books, 106 Graham Road, London, E8 1BX. Prop: Brian Troath. Tel: 020 7254 2912. Web: www.ukbookworld.com/members/ariel. E-mail: briantroathbooks@onetel.com. Private premises. Appointment necessary. Open: **M:** 09:00–17:30; **T:** 09:00–17:30; **W:** 09:00–17:30; **Th:** 09:00–17:30; **F:** 09:00–17:30; **S:** 09:00–17:30; **Su:** 09:00–17:30; Closed for lunch: 13:00–14:00. Spec: Books about Books; Cinema/Film; Classical Studies; Drama; Fine & Rare; First Editions; History - General; Limited Editions. Cata: occasionally (very). [Updated]

Crimes Ink, 35 Moreton Close, Upper Clapton, London, E5 9EP. Prop: Nigel S. Piercy. Tel: (020) 8806-1895. E-mail: crimesink@q-serve.com. Est: 1987. Private premises. Appointment necessary. Stock: medium. Spec: Assassinations; Crime (True); Criminology; Espionage; Fiction - General; Fiction - Crime, Detective, Spy, Thrillers; Fiction - Science Fiction; Law - General. PR: £1–150. CC: Via abecom. Corresp: French. [Updated]

David Houston - Bookseller, 26 North Birkbeck Road, London, E11 4JG. Prop: David Houston. Tel: 020 8556 9048. Fax: 020 8556 9048. Web: www.abebooks.com/home/dghbooks. E-mail: scotsbooks@aol.com. Est: 1997. Private premises. Internet and postal. Open: **M:** 09:00–17:30; **T:** 09:00–17:30; **W:** 09:00–17:30; **Th:** 09:00–17:30; **F:** 09:00–17:30; **S:** 09:00–17:30; **Su:** 09:00–17:30; Closed for lunch: 13:00–14:00. Spec: Countries - Scotland; Literature - Scottish. CC: MC; V. Cata: occasionally – Scottish Books, Scottish Literature. Notes: Postal business only. [Updated]

I.D. Edrich, 17 Selsdon Road, Wanstead, London, E11 2QF. Prop: I. D. & S. Edrich. Tel: (020) 8989-9541. Web: www.idedrich.co.uk. E-mail: idedrich@idedrich.co.uk. Est: 1966. Private premises. Postal only. Contactable. Open: **M:** 09:00–17:00; **T:** 09:00–17:00; **W:** 09:00–17:00; **Th:** 09:00–17:00; **F:** 09:00–17:00. Stock: large. PR: £3–1,000. Corresp: French. VAT No: GB 410 1439 10. [Updated]

Dr Jeremy Parrott, 31A Beacontree Avenue, Elm Road, Mannamead, Walthamstow, London, E17 4BU. Tel: (0208) 5274315. Web: www.abebooks.com. E-mail: jeremy@invitel.hu. Est: 1985. Private premises. Internet and postal. Appointment necessary. Stock: large. Spec: Authors:- Beckett, S.; Benson, E.F.; Stevenson, Robert Louis; Twain, Mark; Verne, Jules; Bibliography; Books about Books; Countries - Hungary. PR: £5–1,000. Corresp: French, German, Spanish, Hungarian. Notes:: Book search for any book in Hungarian. [Updated]

M.A. Stroh, Riverside House, Leaside Road, Upper Clapton, London, E5 9LU. Tel: (0208) 806 3690. Fax: (0208) 806 3690. Web: www.webspawner.com/users/Buttonbook/. E-mail: patent@stroh.demon.co.uk. Est: 1956. Storeroom. Appointment necessary. Open: **M:** 10:00–22:00; **T:** 10:00–22:00; **W:** 10:00–22:00; **Th:** 10:00–22:00; **F:** 10:00–22:00. Stock: very large. Spec: Mathematics; Medicine; Science - General; Technology. PR: £10–1,000. Corresp: French. [Updated]

LONDON
(EAST CENTRAL POSTAL DISTRICTS)

Amwell Book Company, ■ 53 Amwell Street, London, EC1R 1UR. Prop: Charlotte Robinson. Tel: 020 7837 4891. E-mail: sixrobins@aol.com. Est: 1981. Shop open: **M:** 11.00–18.00; **T:** 11:00–18:00; **W:** 11:00–18.00; **Th:** 11:00–18.00; **F:** 11.00–18.00; **S:** 12.00–17.00. Spec: Applied Art; Architecture; Art; Art - Theory; Art History; Art Reference; Artists; Arts, The. CC: MC; V. Cata: occasionally on Architecture, Modern Firsts, childrens & Illustra. Corresp: French, Italian. Mem: PBFA; FSB. [Updated]

Elizabeth Crawford, 5 Owen's Row, London, EC1V 4NP. Prop: Elizabeth Crawford. Tel: (020) 7278-9479. Fax: (020) 7278-9479. E-mail: E.Crawford@sphere20.freeserve.co.uk. Est: 1984. Private premises. Postal only. Appointment necessary. Stock: very small. Spec: Authors - Women; Women; Ephemera. PR: £5–5,000. Mem: PBFA. [08/12/2004]

Andrew Sclanders (Beatbooks), Apt. 32 St Paul's View, 15 Amwell Street, London, EC1R 1UP. Prop: Andrew Sclanders. Tel: (020) 7278-5034. Fax: (020) 7278-5034. Web: www.beatbooks.com. E-mail: sclanders@beatbooks.com. Est: 1990. Private premises. Internet and postal. Appointment necessary. Stock: small. Spec: Art; Authors:- Burroughs, William; Kerouac, Jack; Avant-Garde; Beat Writers; Counterculture; Music - Rock & Roll. PR: £5–2,500. CC: AE; E; JCB; MC; V. [08/12/2004]

LONDON
(NORTH POSTAL DISTRICTS)

Alpha Books, 60 Langdon Park Road, London, N6 5QG. Prop: Tony Maddock. Tel: (020) 8348-2831. Fax: (020) 8348-2831. Web: www.abebooks.com/home/alphabks. E-mail: alpha@dircon.co.uk. Est: 1983. Private premises. Appointment necessary. Stock: medium. Spec: Academic/Scholarly; Alchemy; Astrology; Egyptology; Esoteric; Folklore; Freemasonry & Anti-Masonry; Hermeticism. PR: £1–500. CC: MC; V. [Updated]

G.W. Andron, 162a Brunswick Park Road, London, N11 1HA. Tel: (020) 8361-2409. Est: 1972. Private premises. Postal only. Stock: medium. Spec: Aeronautics; Aviation; Bibliography; Bookbinding; Books about Books; Maritime/Nautical; Military; Military History. PR: £1–100. [Updated]

Antique Prints of the World, 6 Livingstone Road, Palmers Green, London, N13 4SD. Prop: Mr Mel Menelaou. Tel: (020) 8292-0622. Fax: (020) 8292-0622. Web: www.antique19thcenturyprints.com. E-mail: mel@worldprints.freeserve.co.uk. Est: 1994. Private premises. Appointment necessary. Spec: Countries - Cyprus; Countries - Greece; Collectables; Ephemera; Prints and Maps. CC: PayPal. Corresp: Greek. [Updated]

Atlas, 17 Pitfield Street, London, N1 6HB. Prop: Alastair Brotchie. Tel: (0370) 784185. Fax: (020) 7490-8742. E-mail: atlaspress@compuserve.com. Est: 1996. Spec: Art Reference; Counterculture; Foreign Texts; Literature in Translation; Surrealism. PR: £40–500. Notes: also, a publisher. [Updated]

Bannatyne Books, 6 Bedford Road, London, N8 8HL. Prop: Mr. & Mrs. Court. Tel: (020) 8340-1953. Est: 1980. Private premises. Postal only. Spec: Author - Buchan, John. PR: £2–300. [Updated]

Cavendish Rare Books Ltd, 19 Chesthunte Road, London, N17 7PU. Prop: Barbara Grigor-Taylor. Tel: 0208 808 4595. Fax: 0208 808 4595. E-mail: grigorbooks@aol.com. Est: 1976. Private premises. Appointment necessary. Spec: Alpinism/Mountaineering; Exploration - Polar Regions; Maritime/Nautical - History; Voyages & Discovery. CC: MC; V; Debit cards. Cata: bi-annually. Corresp: French, Spanish. Mem: ABA; ILAB. VAT No: GB on application. [Updated]

Church Street Bookshop, ■ 142 Stoke Newington Church Street, London, N16 0JU. Prop: Tim Watson Tel: 0207 241 5411. Web: www.abebooks.com. E-mail: churchstreetbookshopn16@btopenworld.com. Est: 1984. Shop open: **M:** 11:30–18:00; **T:** 11:30–18:00; **W:** 11:30–18:00; **Th:** 11:30–18:00; **F:** 11:30–18:00; **S:** 11:00–18:00; **Su:** 11:30–18:00. Spec: Academic/Scholarly. CC: MC; V. [Updated]

Decorum Books, 24 Cloudesley Square, London, N1 0HN. Prop: David Soames. Tel: 020 7278 1838. Web: www.decorunbooks.co.uk. E-mail: decorumbooks@lineone.net. Est: 1971. Office and/or bookroom. Appointment necessary. Open: **M:** 09:30–17:30; **T:** 09:30–17:30; **W:** 09:30–17:30; **Th:** 09:30–17:30; **F:** 09:30–17:30; Closed for lunch: 13:00–14:00. Spec: Art; Art Reference; Cinema/Film; Design; Music - General; Music - Printed, Sheet Music & Scores; Theatre. CC: MC; V; Mae, So. Cata: monthly 12 per annum. Corresp: French, German. Notes: Art & Design is a major subject stocked VAT No: GB 230 3437 06. [Updated]

Erian Books, 24 Woodside Avenue, Highgate, London, N6 4SS. Prop: Dr. Eric Nieman Tel: (020) 8444-9851. E-mail: eric@enieman.fsnet.co.uk. Est: 1992. Postal only. Spec: Medicine; Medicine - History of; Neurology; Poetry; Psychology/Psychiatry; Science - History of; Booksearch. PR: £15–750. [Updated]

Fantasy Centre, ■ 157 Holloway Road, London, N7 8LX. Prop: Ted Ball & Erik Arthur. Tel: (020) 7607-9433. Fax: (020) 7607-9433. Web: www.fantasycentre.biz E-mail: books@fantasycentre.biz. Est: 1972. Shop open: **M:** 10:00–18:00; **T:** 10:00–18:00; **W:** 10:00–18:00; **Th:** 10:00–18:00; **F:** 10:00–18:00; **S:** 10:00–18:00. Stock: medium. Spec: Fiction - Fantasy, Horror; Fiction - Science Fiction. CC: E; MC; V. VAT No: GB 227 3306 83. [Updated]

Fisher & Sperr, ■ 46 Highgate High Street, London, N6 5JB. Tel: (020) 8340-7244. Fax: (020) 8348-4293. Est: 1939. Shop open: **M:** 10:30–17:00; **T:** 10:30–17:00; **W:** 10:30–17:00; **Th:** 10:30–17:00; **F:** 10:30–17:00; **S:** 10:00–17:30. Stock: very large. Spec: Art; Art History; Folio Society, The; Literary Criticism; Philosophy; Sets of Books; Topography - General; Collectables. PR: £1–100. CC: AE; D; E; JCB; MC; V. Corresp: French. Mem: ABA; ILAB. Notes: bookbinding. VAT No: GB 229 2603 70. [Updated]

Nicholas Goodyer, 8 Framfield Road, Highbury Fields, London, N5 1UU. Tel: (020) 7226-5682. Fax: (020) 7354-4716. Web: www.nicholasgoodyer.com. E-mail: email@nicholasgoodyer.com. Private premises. Internet and postal. Telephone first. Open: **M:** 10:00–17:00; **T:** 10:00–17:00; **W:** 10:00–17:00; **Th:** 10:00–17:00; **F:** 10:00–17:00. Stock: very small. Spec: Animals and Birds; Architecture; Art; Botany; Colour-Plate; Decorative Art; Fashion & Costume; Gardening - General. CC: MC; V. Corresp: French, German, Italian, Spanish, Portuguese. Mem: ABA; PBFA. Notes: business operates by appointment or by chance, weekdays. VAT No: GB 629 6750 05. [Updated]

F. & J. Hogan, 31 Tranmere Road, Edmonton, London, N9 9EJ. Prop: Frederick & Joan Hogan. Tel: (020) 8360-6146. Est: 1969. Private premises. Postal only. Stock: small. Spec: Atlases; Caricature; Cartography; Prints and Maps. PR: £5–1,000. [Updated]

Idle Genius Books, 115 Cluse Court, St. Peter Street, London, N1 8PE. Prop: Philip Obeney. Tel: (020) 7704-3193. E-mail: p.obeney@btopenworld.com. Est: 2000. Storeroom. Appointment necessary. Stock: small. Spec: Archaeology; Authors:- Christie, Agatha; Wolfe, Thomas; Fiction - Science Fiction; Literature; Modern First Editions; Topography - Local. PR: £5–400. Notes: attends HD Book Fairs. Also, ephemera on London in wartime. [Updated]

InterCol London, 43 Templars Crescent, London, N3 3QR. Prop: Yasha Beresiner. Tel: (020) 8349-2207. Fax: (020) 8346-9539. Web: www.intercol.co.uk. E-mail: yasha@itercol.co.uk. Est: 1981. Private premises. Internet and postal. Stock: small. Spec: Cartography; Erotica; Freemasonry & Anti-Masonry; Gambling; Games; Numismatics; Topography - General. PR: £5–500. CC: AE; E; JCB; MC; V; PayPal. Corresp: French, Italian, Spanish, Turkish, Hebrew. Mem: ANA; IBNS; IMCoS; IPCS. VAT No: GB 350 6069 69. [Updated]

M. Eric Korn, 32 North Grove, London, N15 5QP. Prop: Eric Korn. Tel: 0208 800 1302. Fax: 0208 800 1302. E-mail: eric@mekornbooks.freeserve.co.uk. Office and/or bookroom. Appointment necessary. Spec: Antiquarian; Author - Darwin, Charles; Juvenile; Languages - Foreign; Natural History. Corresp: French, Russian, Spanish. Mem: ABA; PBFA. [Updated]

Barrie Marks Limited, 24 Church Vale, Fortis Green, London, N2 9PA. Tel: (020) 8883-1919. Spec: Fine & Rare; Illustrated; Limited Editions; Literature; Private Press. [Updated]

Ian McKelvie, 45 Hertford Road, London, N2 9BX. Tel: (020) 8444-0567. Fax: (020) 8444-0567. Web: www.http://ukbookworld.com/members/Dudley1. E-mail: ianmckelvie@supanet.com. Est: 1969. Private premises. Internet and postal. Appointment necessary. Stock: large. Spec: Author - Bloomsbury Group, The; Fiction - General; Fiction - Crime, Detective, Spy, Thrillers; First Editions; Limited Editions; Literature; Modern First Editions; Plays. CC: AE; JCB; MC; V; Maestro. [Updated]

Mountaineering Books, 6 Bedford Road, London, N8 8HL. Prop: Mr. R. & Mrs. A. Court. Tel: (020) 8340-1953. Est: 1990. Private premises. Appointment necessary. Stock: very small. Spec: Alpinism/Mountaineering. PR: £10–500. [Updated]

Nicolas - Antiquarian Bookseller, 59 Fallowcourt Avenue, London, N12 0BE. Tel: (020) 8445-9835. Fax: (020) 8446-9615. Web: www.nicolasrarebooks.com. E-mail: nicolas@nicolasbooks.demon.co.uk. Est: 1971. Private premises. Internet and postal. Spec: Canals/Inland Waterways; Countries - Cyprus; Countries - Greece; Countries - Malta; Countries - Turkey; History - General; Topography - General; Travel - General. Mem: ABA; PBFA; BA; ILAB. Notes: also, pictures. [Updated]

Pendleburys Bookshop, Church House, Portland Avenue, Stamford Hill, London, N16 6HJ. Prop: Jonathan Pendlebury Tel: (020) 8809-4922. Web: www.pendleburys.com. E-mail: books@pendleburys.com. Est: 1984. Open: **M:** 10:00–17:00; **T:** 10:00–17:00; **Th:** 10:00–17:00; **F:** 10:00–17:00; **S:** 10:00–17:00. Stock: very large. Spec: Bibles; Ecclesiastical History & Architecture; History of Ideas; Philosophy; Prayer Books; Religion - General; Religion - Christian; Religion - Islam. PR: £1–300. Mem: PBFA. [Updated]

Ripping Yarns (Celia Mitchell)

355 Archway Road
London N6 4EJ
Tel: 020 8341 6111
Fax: 020 7482 5056

Antiquarian & secondhand stock bought and sold
All subjects but especially **CHILDREN'S**
Highgate Tube. Free car parking (1 hour) just north of shop in Archway Road
Email: yarns@rippingyarns.co.uk. Web site: www.rippingyarns.co.uk

Weekdays 11.00-5.00
Saturdays 11.00-5.00
Sundays 11.00-4.00

LONDON NORTH POSTAL DISTRICTS

John Price, 8 Cloudesley Square, London, N1 0HT. Tel: (020) 7837-8008. Fax: (020) 7278-4733. Web: www.johnpriceantiquarianbooks.com. E-mail: books@jvprice.com. Est: 1988. Private premises. Internet and postal. Appointment necessary. Stock: very small. Spec: Antiquarian; Cookery/ Gastronomy; History of Ideas; Literature; Music - Musicians; Performing Arts; Philosophy; Scottish Interest. PR: £45–4,500. CC: AE; E; MC; V. Corresp: French, German. Mem: ABA; PBFA; BA; ILAB. [Updated]

Richard Thornton Books, 25 Beechdale, Winchmore Hill, London, N21 3QE. Prop: Richard Thornton. Tel: 020 8886 8202. E-mail: richard.thorntonbooks@btinternet.com. Est: 1997. Office and/or bookroom. Telephone first. Open: **M:** 09:30–21:30; **T:** 09:30–21:30; **W:** 09:30–21:30; **Th:** 09:30–21:30; **F:** 09:30–21:30; **S:** 09:30–21:30; **Su:** 09:30–21:30. Spec: Arts, The; Autobiography; Bindings; Children's; History - General; History - Local; Literature; Military. CC: AE; D; E; JCB; MC; V. Cata: occasionally. Mem: PBFA. [Updated]

Ripping Yarns, ■ 355 Archway Road, London, N6 4EJ. Prop: Celia Mitchell. Tel: (020) 8341-6111. Fax: (020) 7482-5056. Web: www.rippingyarns.co.uk. E-mail: yarns@rippingyarns.co.uk. Est: 1984. Shop. Internet and postal. Open: **T:** 11:00–17:00; **W:** 11:00–17:00; **Th:** 11:00–17:00; **F:** 11:00–17:00; **S:** 10:00–17:00; **Su:** 11:00–16:00. Stock: very large. Spec: Children's; Illustrated; Literature. PR: £1–500. Corresp: French Spanish. Mem: PBFA. [Updated]

Susanne Schulz–Falster, 22 Compton Terrace, London, N1 2UN. Prop: Susanne Schulz-Falster. Tel: (020) 7704-9845. Fax: (020) 7354-4202. E-mail: sfalster@btinternet.com. Est: 1997. Private premises. Appointment necessary. Stock: very small. Spec: Antiquarian; Early Imprints; Economics; History of Ideas; Linguistics; Philosophy; Printing; Women. PR: £100–10,000. CC: MC; V. Corresp: German, Italian, French. Mem: ABA; ILAB; VDA. Notes: Booksearch, building collections, valuations. VAT No: GB 714 4200 79. [Updated]

Robert Temple, 65 Mildmay Road, London, N1 4PU. Prop: P.J. Allen. Tel: (020) 7254-3674. Fax: (020) 7254-3674. Web: www.telinco.co.uk/RobertTemple/. E-mail: roberttemple@telinco.co.uk. Est: 1977. Warehouse; Internet and postal. Appointment necessary. Stock: medium. Spec: Academic/Scholarly; Anthologies; Antiquarian; Fiction - General; Fiction - Crime, Detective, Spy, Thrillers; Fiction - Fantasy, Horror; Fiction - Historical; Fiction - Science Fiction. PR: £5–15,000. CC: PayPal. Corresp: French. Notes: Credit and Debit cards taken via the PayPal secure server only (VISA, non-corporate AmEx, MasterCard, Discover, Switch, Solo). VAT No: GB 292 2648 41. [Updated]

John Trotter Books, 80 East End Road, London, N3 2SY. Prop: John Trotter. Tel: (020) 8349-9484. Web: www.bibliophile.net/John-Trotter-Books.htm. E-mail: jtrotter@freenetname.co.uk. Est: 1973. Office and/or bookroom. Internet and postal. Open: **M:** 09:00–17:00; **T:** 09:09–17:00; **W:** 09:00–17:00; **Th:** 09:00–17:00; **Su:** 10:00–13:00. Stock: large. Spec: Countries - Middle East, The; History - Ancient; Religion - Jewish; Travel - Middle East; Booksearch; Prints and Maps. PR: £5–1,500. CC: MC; V. Corresp: French, German, Italian. Mem: PBFA. [Updated]

Tyger Press, 41 Cheverton Road, London, N19 3BA. Prop: Alaric Bamping. Tel: (020) 7272-3234. Fax: (020) 7272-8898. Web: www.abebooks.com. E-mail: tygerpress@clara.net. Est: 1984. Postal only. Spec: Genealogy; History - General; History - Local; Manuscripts; Topography - General. PR: £1–750. [Updated]

Graham Weiner, 78 Rosebery Road, London, N10 2LA. Tel: (020) 8883-8424. Fax: (020) 8444-6505. E-mail: graham.weiner@btopenworld.com. Est: 1973. Private premises. Internet and postal. Appointment necessary. Stock: medium. Spec: Academic/Scholarly; Chemistry; Geology; History - General; Medicine; Physics; Science - General; Science - History of. PR: £20–2,500. CC: MC; V. Corresp: French. Mem: ABA; ILAB; IEE. VAT No: GB 230 6110 23. [Updated]

Woburn Books, 5 Caledonian Road, London, N1 9DX. Prop: Andrew Burgin. Tel: (020) 7263 5196. Fax: (020) 7263-5196. Web: www.abebooks/home/woburnbooks. E-mail: woburn@burgin.freeserve.co.uk. Est: 1991. Office and/or bookroom. Internet and postal. Stock: medium. Spec: Academic/Scholarly; Africana; Anthropology; Antiquarian; Architecture; Art; Arts, The; Avant-Garde. PR: £1–5,000. CC: JCB; MC; V; SW. Mem: PBFA. [28/05/2003]

LONDON
(LONDON NORTH WEST POSTAL DISTRICTS)

Aurelian Books, 31 Llanvanor Road, London, NW2 2AR. Prop: David Dunbar. Tel: (020) 8455 9612. E-mail: dgldunbar@aol.com. Est: 1970. Private premises. Appointment necessary. Stock: small. Spec: Colour-Plate; Conservation; Entomology; Lepidopterology; Natural History. PR: £5–5,000. CC: MC; V; SW. Mem: PBFA. [Upadted]

H. Baron, 121 Chatsworth Road, London, NW2 4BH. Prop: Christel Wallbaum. Tel: (020) 8459-2035. Fax: (020) 8459-2035. Est: 1949. Private premises. Postal only. Spec: Autographs; Iconography; Letters; Music - General. CC: E; MC; V. Corresp: French, German. Mem: ABA. VAT No: GB 227 1452 82. [Updated]

The Book Depot, 111 Woodcote Avenue, Mill Hill, London, NW7 2PD. Prop: Conrad Wiberg. Tel: (020) 8906-3708. E-mail: conrad@adword.fsnet.co.uk. Est: 1980. Postal only. Spec: Booksearch. PR: £5–10. [Updated]

Cranhurst Books, 20 Cranhurst Road, Willesden Green, London, NW2 4LN. Prop: Heidi Stransky. Tel: (020) 8452-7845. Fax: (020) 8452-0689. E-mail: HStransky@aol.com. Est: 1997. Private premises. Appointment necessary. Stock: small. Spec: Children's; Comic Books & Annuals; Modern First Editions; Ephemera. PR: £5–2,500. [Updated]

Keith Fawkes, ■ 1–3 Flask Walk, Hampstead, London, NW3 1HJ. Prop: Keith Fawkes. Tel: (020) 7435-0614. Est: 1970. Shop open: **M:** 10:00–18:00; **T:** 09:00–18:00; **W:** 10:00–18:00; **Th:** 09:00–18:00; **F:** 10:00–18:00; **S:** 10:00–18:00; **Su:** 13:00–18:00. Stock: large. PR: £1–100. Notes: also, bric a brac. VAT No: GB 232 0644 04. [Updated]

Fishburn Books, 43 Ridge Hill, London, NW11 8PR. Prop: Jonathan Fishburn. Tel: (0208) 455-9139. Fax: (0208) 922-5008. Web: www.fishburnbooks.com. E-mail: fishburnbooks@yahoo.co.uk. Est: 2000. Private premises. Appointment necessary. Spec: Countries - Middle East, The; Holocaust; Judaica; Religion - Hebraica; Religion - Jewish. PR: £15–5,000. CC: AE; MC; V. Mem: PBFA. VAT No: GB 805 4965 16. [Updated]

Fortune Green Books, 74 Fortune Green Road, London, NW6 1DS. Prop: Eric Stevens & Jane Bell. Tel: (020) 7435-7545. E-mail: belleric@dircon.co.uk. Est: 1992. Office and/or bookroom. Internet and postal. Appointment necessary. Stock: medium. Spec: Academic/Scholarly; Art; Feminism; Fiction - General; Fiction - Women; Literary Criticism; Literature; Women. PR: £1–50. CC: MC; V. Mem: PBFA. [Updated]

Stephen Foster, ■ 95 Bell Street, London, NW1 6TL. Prop: Stephen Foster. Tel: (020) 7724-0876. Fax: (020) 7724-0927. Web: www.95bellstreet.com. E-mail: stephen.foster@sfbooks.co.uk. Est: 1987. Shop open: **M:** 10:30–18:00; **T:** 10:30–18:00; **W:** 10:30–18:00; **Th:** 10:30–18:00; **F:** 10:30–18:00; **S:** 10:30–18:00. Stock: medium. Spec: Antiquarian; Antiques; Architecture; Art History; Art Reference; Artists; Arts, The; Decorative Art. PR: £1–1,000. CC: AE; JCB; MC; V; Switch, Maestro. Mem: ABA; PBFA; ILAB. Notes: ibooknet. stock at Biblion, Davies Mews Also, a booksearch service; new books at a discount. VAT No: GB 521 5504 81. [Updated]

Hellenic Bookservices, ■ 91 Fortess Road, Kentish Town, London, NW5 1AG. Prop: M. Williams & Andrew Stoddart. Tel: (020) 7267-9499. Fax: (020) 7267-9498. Web: www.hellenicbooks.com. E-mail: info@hellenicbookservice.com. Est: 1966. Shop open: **M:** 09:30–18:00; **T:** 09:30–18:00; **W:** 09:30–18:00; **Th:** 09:30–18:00; **F:** 09:30–18:00; **S:** 10:00–17:00. Stock: large. Spec: Academic/Scholarly; Books in Greek; Byzantium; Classical Studies; Countries - Cyprus; Countries - Greece; Foreign Texts; Guide Books. PR: £1–500. CC: AE; JCB; MC; V. Corresp: Modern Greek. Mem: PBFA. Notes: also, a booksearch service, school supplies – all subjects. [Updated]

HAVE YOUR OWN WEB SITE
Features include an easy to use book stock database

For more details - see
www.sheppardsworld.co.uk

Hosains Books, 12 Honeybourne Road, West Hampstead, London, NW6 1JJ. Prop: Mrs. Y. Hosain and Mr. K.S. Hosain. Tel: (020) 7794-7127. Web: www.indoislamica.com. Est: 1979. Private premises. Appointment necessary. Spec: Oriental; Ottoman Empire; Travel - Africa; Voyages & Discovery; Prints and Maps. Cata: bi-annually. PR: £100–5,000. CC: MC; V. [Updated]

C.R. Johnson Rare Book Collect, 4, Keats Grove, Hampstead, London, NW3 2RT. Prop: C.R. Johnson & C.A. Forster. Tel: (020) 7794-7940. Fax: (020) 7433-3303. Web: www.crjohnson.com. E-mail: mail@crjohnson.com. Est: 1970. Private premises. Internet and postal. Appointment necessary. Stock: very large. Spec: Authors - Women; Fiction - General; Literature. PR: £50–5,000. CC: MC; V. Mem: PBFA; CERL. [Updated]

Terence Kaye - Bookseller, 52 Neeld Crescent, London, NW4 3RR. Prop: H Terence Kaye. Tel: (020) 8202-8188. Fax: (020) 8202-8188. E-mail: kforbook@onetel.com. Est: 1996. Office and/or bookroom. Appointment necessary. Open: **M:** 09:00–20:00; **T:** 09:00–20:00; **W:** 09:00–20:00; **Th:** 09:00–20:00; **F:** 09:00–18:00; **S:** 10:00–20:00; **Su:** 10:00–20:00. Stock: small. Spec: Cinema/Film; Circus; Drama; Entertainment - General; Fairgrounds; Music - Music Hall; Performing Arts; Television. PR: £10–200. Corresp: Hebrew. Notes: Ephemera Society. Also, a booksearch service (specialist subjects only), and library/collection development. [Updated]

Lee Jackson, Suite 53, 176 Finchley Road, London, NW3 6BT. Prop: Lee Jackson. Tel: 020 7625 2157. Web: www.leejacksonmaps.com. E-mail: leejackson@btinternet.com. Est: 1973. Private premises. Internet and postal. Spec: Americana; Atlases; Countries - Germany; Prints and Maps. CC: MC; V. Corresp: Spanish. Mem: PBFA; IMCOS, IAMA. VAT No: GB 673 2310 54. [Updated]

Loretta Lay Books, 24 Grampian Gardens, London, NW2 1JG. Prop: Loretta Lay. Tel: 020 8455 3069. Web: www.laybooks.com. E-mail: lorettalay@hotmail.com. Est: 2001. Mail Order Only. Internet and postal. Telephone first. Open: **M:** 09:00–17:30; **T:** 09:00–17:30; **W:** 09:00–17:30; **Th:** 09:00–17:30; **F:** 09:00–17:30; **S:** 09:00–17:30; **Su:** 09:00–17:30. Spec: Authors:- Tully, Jim; Upfield, Arthur; Wilson, Colin; Crime (True); Criminology; Espionage; Fiction - Crime, Detective, Spy, Thrillers; Ghosts. CC: JCB; MC; V; Delta, Switch, Solo. Cata: annually – all true crime. Notes: A comprehensive stock of true crime and specialising in Jack the Ripper. [Updated]

Richard Lucas, 114 Fellows Road, London, NW3 3JH. Prop: Richard Lucas. Tel: (020) 7449-9431. Est: 1975. Private premises. Appointment necessary. Stock: medium. Spec: Brewing; Cookery/Gastronomy; Etiquette; Food & Drink; Herbalism; Public Houses; Travel - General; Viticulture. PR: £10–1,000. [Updated]

Moss Books, 14 Manor Park Gardens, Edgware, London, HA8 7NA. Tel: (020) 8386-2707. Fax: (020) 8386-2707. E-mail: moss.books@ntlworld.com. Est: 2002. Market stand/stall; Internet and postal. Appointment necessary. Stock: medium. Spec: Archaeology; Architecture; Ceramics; Ecclesiastical History & Architecture; Lepidopterology; Odd & Unusual; Ornithology; Pacifism. PR: £5–800. CC: PayPal. VAT No: GB 805 4666 26. [Updated]

Neil's Books, 151 Fordwych Road, London, NW2 3NG. Prop: Neil Aptaker. Tel: (020) 8452–0933. Fax: (02082) 2082434. E-mail: neilsbooks@lineone.net. Est: 1990. Internet and postal. Open: **M:** 10:00–18:45; **Th:** 10:00–18:45. Stock: medium. Spec: Fiction - General; Modern First Editions. PR: £2–200. [Updated]

Primrose Hill Books, 134 Regents Park Road, London, NW1 8XL. Tel: (0207) 586 2027. Fax: (0207) 722 9653. E-mail: phbooks@btconnect.com. Est: 1987. Storeroom. Internet and postal. Appointment necessary. Stock: medium. Spec: Biography; First Editions; Poetry; Theatre. PR: £4–1,000. CC: AE; E; JCB; MC; V. Mem: PBFA. VAT No: GB 523 4672 53. [Updated]

Paul Rassam, Flat 5, 18 East Heath Road, London, NW3 1AJ. Tel: (020) 7794-9316. E-mail: paul@rassam.demon.co.uk. Est: 1972. Private premises. Appointment necessary. Stock: very small. Spec: Autographs; First Editions; Literature; Manuscripts. CC: MC; V. Mem: ABA. [Updated]

Robert G Sawers Ltd, No.5, Inglewood Road, London, NW6 1OT. Tel: (0207) 794 9618. Fax: (0207) 794 9571. Web: www.bobsawers@clara.net. E-mail: bobsawers@clara.net. Est: 1970. Private premises. Internet and postal. Appointment necessary. Stock: very small. Spec: Countries - Far East, The; Countries - Japan. Corresp: French, Spanish, Japanese. Mem: ABA. VAT No: GB 233 701 02. [Updated]

Sevin Seydi Rare Books, 13 Shirlock Road, London, NW3 2HR. Prop: Sevin Seydi & Maurice Whitby. Tel: (020) 7485 9801. Fax: (020) 7428 9313. E-mail: sevin@seydi.fsnet.co.uk. Est: 1970. Private premises. Internet and postal. Appointment necessary. Stock: large. Spec: Architecture; Art History; Bindings; Classical Studies; Countries - Greece; Countries - Italy; Countries - Turkey; Early Imprints. CC: MC; V. Corresp: French, Turkish. Mem: PBFA. [Updated]

Unsworths Booksellers, ■ 101 Euston Road, London, NW1 2RA. Prop: Charlie Unsworth. Tel: (020) 7436 9836. Fax: (020) 7383 7557. Web: www.unsworths.com. E-mail: books@unsworths.com. Est: 1986. Shop open: **M:** 10:00–18:30; **T:** 10:00–18:30; **W:** 10:00–18:30; **Th:** 10:00–18:30; **F:** 10:00–18:30; **S:** 10:00–18:30; **Su:** 12:00–17:00. Stock: very large. Spec: Academic/Scholarly; Antiquarian; Archaeology; Art History; Bibliography; Bindings; Books about Books; Byzantium. PR: £3–5,000. CC: AE; D; E; JCB; MC; V. Corresp: Latin, French, Portuguese. Mem: ABA; ILAB. VAT No: GB 480 1145 75. [Updated]

Walden Books, ■ 38 Harmood Street, London, NW1 8DP. Prop: David Tobin. Tel: 020 7267-8146. Fax: 020 7267-8147. Web: www.ukbookworld/members/waldenbooks. E-mail: waldenbooks@lineone.net. Est: 1979. Shop open: **Th:** 10:30–18:30; **F:** 10:30–18:30; **S:** 10:30–18:30; **Su:** 10:30–18:30. Stock: medium. Spec: Academic/Scholarly; Advertising; Applied Art; Architecture; Art; Art History; Literature; Philosophy. PR: £1–1,000. CC: AE; MC; V. Mem: PBFA. VAT No: GB 564 4805 26. [Updated]

Eva M. Weininger, Antiquarian Bookseller, 79 Greenhill, London, NW3 5TZ. Tel: (020) 7435-2334. Est: 1979. Private premises. Appointment necessary. Stock: very small. Spec: Courtesy; Culture - Foreign; Culture - National; Etiquette; History of Ideas; Social History. PR: £10–150. [Updated]

J. & S. Wilbraham, 1 Wise Lane, Mill Hill, London, NW7 2RL. Prop: John and Shahin Wilbraham. Tel: (0208) 9593709. Web: www.wilbraham.demon.co.uk. E-mail: john@wilbraham.demon.co.uk. Est: 1981. Private premises. Postal only. Contactable. Stock: very small. Spec: Antiquarian; Children's; Literature. PR: £10–1,000. CC: AE; MC; V. Corresp: French. [Updated]

LONDON
(SOUTH EAST POSTAL DISTRICTS)

Hava Books, 110 Aspinall Road, Brockley, SE4 2EG. Prop: J. Havercroft. Tel: (0207) 6398339. E-mail: salesmailbox-hava@yahoo.co.uk. Est: 1998. Private premises. Internet Only. Appointment necessary. Stock: medium. Spec: Antiquarian; Dictionaries; Illustrated; Languages - Foreign; Sets of Books. PR: £5–5,000. CC: PayPal. Corresp: French, Spanish. Mem: PBFA; PayPal. VAT No: GB 782 4918 92. [Updated]

Marcet Books, ■ 4a, Nelson Road, Greenwich, SE10 9JB. Prop: Martin Kemp. Tel: 020 8853 5408. Web: www.marcetbooks.co.uk. E-mail: info@marcetbooks.co.uk. Est: 1980. Shop open: **M:** 10:00–17:30; **T:** 10:00–17:30; **W:** 10:00–17:30; **Th:** 10:00–17:30; **F:** 10:00–17:30; **S:** 09:00–17:30; **Su:** 10:00–17:30. Spec: Africana; Aircraft; Arabica; Art History; Canals/Inland Waterways; Cartography; City of London; Cookery - Professional. CC: MC; V; PayPal. Cata: occasionally on Foreign Travel. [Updated]

Stephen E. Tilston, 7 Dartmouth House, Dartmouth Row, Greenwich, SE10 8BF. Prop: Steve & Frances Tilston. Tel: (020) 8691 3108. Web: www.ukbookworld.com/members/tilston. E-mail: tilston@attglobal.net. Est: 1985. Private premises. Internet and postal. Appointment necessary. Stock: medium. Spec: Architecture; Art; Biography; Cookery/Gastronomy; Fiction - General; History - General; Maritime/Nautical; Military. PR: £5–1,000. CC: MC; V; Maestro. [Updated]

The Book Palace, Jubilee House, Bedwardine Road, Crystal Palace, London, SE19 3AP. Prop: G West. Tel: 020 8768 0022. Fax: 020 8768 0563. Web: www.bookpalace.com. E-mail: books@bookpalace.com. Est: 1997. Warehouse; Internet and postal. Appointment necessary. Open: **M:** 10:00–18:00; **T:** 10:00–18:00; **W:** 10:00–18:00; **Th:** 10:00–18:00; **F:** 10:00–18:00. Spec: Annuals; Art; Art - Theory; Art History; Art Reference; Artists; Arts, The; Author - Burroughs, Edgar R CC: AE; MC; V; Maestro. Cata: occasionally on Popular culture. Corresp: Dutch, French. Notes: Wholesale on many titles. VAT No: GB 756458884. [Updated]

The Bookshop on the Heath Ltd, ■ 74 Tranquil Vale, Blackheath, London, SE3 0BW. Prop: Richard Platt. Tel: (020) 88524786. Fax: (020) 88564211. Web: www.bookshopontheheath.co.uk. E-mail: richard@bookshopontheheath.co.uk. Est: 2003. Shop open: **M:** 12:00–18:00; **T:** 10:00–18:00; **W:** 10:00–18:00; **F:** 10:00–18:00; **S:** 10:00–18:00; **Su:** 12:00–18:00. Stock: medium. Spec: Art Deco; Author - Fleming, Ian; Children's; Fiction - Crime, Detective, Spy, Thrillers; Modern First Editions; Topography - Local. PR: £1–5,000. CC: MC; V; Switch. Corresp: German, Mandarin. Mem: Biblion, 1-7 Davies Mews, Mayfair, London W1. VAT No: GB 831 1125 78. [Updated]

Fiona Campbell, 158 Lambeth Road, London, SE1 7DF. Tel: (020) 7928-1633. Fax: (020) 7928-1633. E-mail: fcampbell@britishlibrary.net. Est: 1970. Private premises. Appointment necessary. Stock: small. Spec: Countries - Italy; Travel - General; Travel - Europe. CC: JCB; MC; V. Corresp: French, German and Italian. Mem: ABA; PBFA; ILAB. Notes: also, a booksearch service, and bookbinding. [03/01/2005]

Marcus Campbell Art Books, ■ 43 Holland Street, Bankside, London, SE1 9JR. Prop: Marcus Campbell. Tel: (020) 7261-0111. Fax: (020) 7261-0129. Web: www.marcuscampbell.co.uk. E-mail: info|@marcuscampbell.co.uk. Est: 1998. Shop. Internet and postal. Open: **M:** 10:30–18:00; **T:** 10:30–18:00; **W:** 10:30–18:00; **Th:** 10:30–18:00; **F:** 10:30–18:00; **S:** 10:30–18:00; **Su:** 12:00–18:00. Stock: very large. Spec: Art; Art Reference; Artists; Monographs; Ephemera. PR: £2–2,000. CC: AE; E; MC; V; Switch. Corresp: French. Mem: PBFA. VAT No: GB 605 8695 15. [Updated]

Chapter Two, Fountain House, Conduit Mews, Woolwich, SE18 7AP. Manager: Miss P. Brachotte. Tel: (020) 8316-5389. Fax: (020) 8854-5963. Web: www.chaptertwobooks.org.uk. E-mail: chapter2uk@aol.com. Est: 1976. Office and/or bookroom. Internet and postal. Telephone first. Open: **M:** 09:00–17:00; **T:** 09:00–17:00; **W:** 09:00–17:00; **Th:** 09:00–17:00; **F:** 06:00–17:00; Closed for lunch: 13:00–14:30. Stock: medium. Spec: Authors:- Baring-Gould, S.; Blyton, Enid; Bunyan, John; Johns, W.E.; Bibles; Children's; Countries - Africa; Countries - Asia. PR: £2–3,500. CC: AE; MC; V. Corresp: Afrikaans, French, German, Dutch, Spanish, Norwegian. Notes: Chapter Two Christian Bookshop, 199 Plumstead Common Rd Plumstead Common, London SE18 2UJ. Also, publisher/retailer of new books & foreign language Christian literature, Bible distributor, archive & booksearch service. [Updated]

Nigel A. Clark, 28 Ulundi Road, Blackheath, London, SE3 7UG. Tel: (020) 8858-4020. Est: 1975. Private premises. Postal only. Appointment necessary. Stock: very small. Spec: Antiques; Art History; Art Reference; Artists; Ceramics; Collecting; Horology; Numismatics. PR: £1–100. Notes: also, British coins. VAT No: GB 311 6080 06. [Updated]

Collectable Books, 15 West Park, London, SE9 4RZ. Partners: Tom & Sue Biro. Tel: (020) 8851-8487. Web: www.collectablebooks.co.uk. E-mail: biro@collectablebooks.co.uk. Est: 1992. Private premises. Appointment necessary. Stock: very small. Spec: Antiquarian; Architecture; Arts, The; Food & Drink; Health; Medicine; Natural History; Religion - General. PR: £10–20,000. CC: E; JCB; MC; V; SO, SW. Corresp: French, German, Italian, Hungarian, Portuguese. Mem: ABA; PBFA; ILAB. VAT No: GB 299 3282 10. [Updated]

Eclectica, 48 Rosendale Road, London, SE21 8DP. Prop: Michael Coupe. Tel: (0208) 761-4138. Storeroom. Appointment necessary. Stock: very small. PR: £1–2,000. [Updated]

Peter Ellis, Bookseller, ■ 18 Cecil Court, London, WC2N 4HE. Tel: (020) 7836 8880. Fax: (020) 8318-4748. Web: www.peter-ellis.co.uk. E-mail: ellisbooks@lineone.net. Est: 1999. Shop open: **M:** 10:30–19:00; **T:** 10:30–19:00; **W:** 10:30–19:00; **Th:** 10:30–19:00; **F:** 10:30–19:00; **S:** 10:30–17:30. Stock: medium. Spec: Academic/Scholarly; Advertising; Art; Artists; Arts, The; Beat Writers; Biography; Children's. PR: £10–1,000. CC: AE; MC; V. Corresp: French, German. Mem: ABA; ILAB. VAT No: GB 751 8751 12. [Updated]

Enscot Books, 17 Crantock Road, Catford, London, SE6 2QS. Prop: Michael Enscot and Philip Enscot. Tel: (020) 8698 1976. Fax: (020) 8698 1976. E-mail: smith.pipe@virgin.net. Est: 1998. Private premises. Stock: small. Spec: Fiction - Historical; Modern First Editions. PR: £2–50. Corresp: French, German. [Updated]

Jane Gibberd, ■ 20 Lower Marsh, London, SE1 7RJ. Tel: (020) 7633-9562. Est: 1968. Shop open: **W:** 11:00–19:00; **Th:** 11:00–19:00; **F:** 11:00–19:00. Stock: small. PR: £1–25. [Updated]

Junk & Spread Eagle, ■ 9 Greenwich South Street, Greenwich, London, SE10 8NW. Prop: Tobias Moy. Tel: (020) 8305-1666. Est: 1960. Shop open: **M:** 10:00–18:00; **T:** 10:00–18:00; **W:** 10:00–18:00; **Th:** 10:00–18:00; **F:** 10:00–18:00; **S:** 10:00–18:00; **Su:** 10:00–18:00; Closed for lunch: 13:00–14:00. Stock: medium. Spec: Advertising; Animals and Birds; Antiquarian; Arts, The; Author - Churchill, Sir Winston; Bindings; Children's; Children's - Illustrated. PR: £3–100. CC: D; E; JCB; MC; V; SW. Mem: Also, ephemera, collectables and antiques. [Updated]

Kirkdale Bookshop, ■ 272 Kirkdale, Sydenham, SE26 4RS. Prop: Ms. Geraldine A. Cox. Tel: (020) 8778-4701. Fax: (020) 8776-6293. E-mail: kirkdalebookshop@hotmail.com. Est: 1966. Shop open: **M:** 09:00–17:30; **T:** 09:00–17:30; **W:** 09:00–17:30; **Th:** 09:00–17:30; **F:** 09:00–17:30; **S:** 09:00–17:30. Stock: medium. Spec: CC: MC; V. Mem: BA. Notes: also, new books, greetings cards plus small art gallery. [[Updated]

Peter Marcan, Bookseller, P.O. Box 3158, London, SE1 4RA. Prop: Peter Marcan. Tel: (020) 7357 0368. Est: 2000. Private premises. Appointment necessary. Open: **M:** 10:00–19:00; **T:** 10:00–19:00; **W:** 10:00–19:00; **Th:** 10:00–19:00; **F:** 10:00–19:00; **S:** 10:00–19:00. Stock: very small. Spec: Music - Classical; Social History; Topography - General; Topography - Local. PR: £3–50. Notes: Books on 18th - 20th C British art, Greater London and S. East England topography. Publishing - reprints, directories, catalogues. [Updated]

Herbert Murch Booksend, 258/260 Creek Road, Greenwich, London, SE10 9SW. Prop: D. Murch. Tel: (020) 8858 2414. E-mail: herbertmurch@btinternet.com. Est: 1974. Private premises. Postal only. Spec: Arts, The; Biography; Literature; Media; Collectables. PR: £8–25. Cata: occasionally. Notes: Business being re-organised spring 2006. Has large stock of biographies in first half 20th Century. [Updated]

Hilary Rittner Booksearch, 30 Crooms Hill, Greenwich, London, SE10 8ER. Prop: Hilary Rittner. Tel: (020) 8858-7759. Private premises. Postal only. Spec: Artists; Author - Ardizzone, Edward; Illustrated; Booksearch. [Updated]

Rogers Turner Books, 87 Breakspears Road, London, SE4 1TX. Prop: P.J.Turner. Tel: (0208) 692-2472. Fax: (0208) 692- 2472. E-mail: rogersturner@compuserve.com. Est: 1976. Private premises. Appointment necessary. Open: **Th:** 10:00–18:00; **F:** 10:00–18:00. Stock: small. Spec: Horology; Science - General; Science - History of; Scientific Instruments; Technology. CC: AE; D; JCB; MC; V. Corresp: French, German, Spanish. Mem: ABA; PBFA. [Updated]

John Rolfe, 39 Combe, Blackheath, London, SE3 7PZ. Prop: John Rolfe. Tel: (020) 8858-3349. Web: www.abebooks.com/home/johnrolfe. E-mail: johnrolfebooks@tinyworld.co.uk. Private premises. Internet and postal. Appointment necessary. Stock: very small. Spec: Dogs. PR: £5–500. [Updated]

Michael Silverman, P.O. Box 350, London, SE3 0LZ. Tel: (020) 8319-4452. Fax: (020) 8856-6006. Web: www.michael-silverman.com. E-mail: ms@michael-silverman.com. Est: 1989. Private premises. Postal only. Appointment necessary. Stock: medium. Spec: Art; Autographs; Documents - General; History - General; Letters; Literature; Manuscripts. CC: AE; MC; V. Mem: ABA; ILAB. VAT No: GB 532 9017 59. [23/12/2004]

Anthony J. Simmonds, ■ 66 Royal Hill, Greenwich, London, SE10 8RT. Prop: Anthony & Setitia Simmonds. Tel: (020) 8692 1794. E-mail: anthony@anthonysimmonds.demon.co.uk. Shop open: **T:** 10:00–18:00; **W:** 10:00–18:00; **Th:** 10:00–18:00; **F:** 10:00–18:00; **S:** 10:00–18:00; **Su:** 10:00–18:00. Spec: Maritime/Nautical; Naval; Booksearch. PR: £1–5,000. CC: MC; V. Cata: occasionally on specialities, naval and maritime history. Mem: PBFA. [02/02/2006]

Warwick Leadlay Gallery, 5 Nelson Road, Greenwich, London, SE10 9JB. Tel: (020) 8858-0317. Web: www.warwickleadlay.com. E-mail: info@warwickleadlay.com. Est: 1974. Shop and/or gallery. Open: **M:** 09:30–17:30; **T:** 09:30–17:30; **W:** 09:30–17:30; **Th:** 09:30–17:30; **F:** 09:30–17:30; **S:** 09:30–17:30; **Su:** 11:00–17:30. Stock: very small. Spec: Naval. PR: £5–500. CC: AE; D; JCB; MC; V. [Updated]

Searching for a title - and cannot find it on any Internet database?

Then try searching for a dealer specialising in the subject on www.sheppardsworld.co.uk

Select the subject classification – then chose the dealer to send your request to.

LONDON
(SOUTH WEST POSTAL DISTRICTS)

Allsworth Rare Books, P.O.Box 134, 235 Earls Court Road, London, SW5 9FE. Tel: (020) 7377-0552. Fax: (020) 7377-0552. Web: www.allsworthbooks.com. E-mail: jenny@allsworthbooks.com. Est: 2002. Office and/or bookroom. Appointment necessary. Spec: Africana; Photography; Sport - Big Game Hunting; Travel - General; Travel - Asia; Travel - Middle East; Voyages & Discovery. PR: £50–50,000. CC: MC; V; Maestro. Mem: ABA; PBFA; ILAB. Notes: stock may be viewed (by appt.) at central London office Valuations. VAT No: GB 798 7327 57. [Updated]

Ancient Art Books (and at Bibion), 34 East Sheen Ave., East Sheen, London, SW14 8AS. Prop: D.G. Giles. Tel: (020) 8878-8951. Fax: (020) 8878-9201. Web: www.gilesancientart.com. E-mail: Ancientartbooks@aol.com. Est: 1999. Private premises. Internet and postal. Appointment necessary. Stock: small. Spec: Antiques; Applied Art; Archaeology; Glass. PR: £10–15,000. Notes: also at Biblion, London. [Updated]

Ash Rare Books, 43 Huron Road, London, SW17 8RE. Prop: Laurence Worms. Tel: (020) 8672-2263. Web: www.ashrare.com. E-mail: books@ashrare.com. Est: 1946. Private premises. Internet and postal. Appointment necessary. Open: **M:** 10:00–17:00; **T:** 10:00–17:00; **W:** 10:00–17:00; **Th:** 10:00–17:00; **F:** 10:00–17:00. Stock: medium. Spec: Bibliography; City of London; First Editions; Poetry; Prints and Maps. PR: £20–5,000. CC: AE; D; E; JCB; MC; V. Mem: ABA; ILAB. VAT No: GB 244 2896 45. [Updated]

Book Mongers, ■ 439 Coldharbour Lane, London, SW9 8LN. Prop: Patrick Kelly. Tel: (020) 7738-4225. Fax: (020) 7738-4225. Web: www.freespace.virgin.net/book.mongers. E-mail: book.mongers@virgin.net. Est: 1992. Shop open: **M:** 10:30–18:30; **T:** 10:30–18:30; **W:** 10:30–18:30; **Th:** 10:30–18:30; **F:** 10:30–18:30; **S:** 10:30–18:30. Stock: very large. PR: £1–10. CC: D; E; JCB; MC; V; Mae. So. [Updated]

Classic Bindings Ltd, ■ 61 Cambridge Street, Pimlico, London, SW1V 4PS. Prop: Mr. Sasha Poklewski–Koziell. Tel: (020) 7834-5554. Fax: (020) 7630-6632. Web: www.classicbindings.net. E-mail: info@classicbindings.net. Est: 1988. Shop open: **M:** 09:30–17:30; **T:** 09:30–17:30; **W:** 09:30–17:30; **Th:** 09:30–17:30; **F:** 09:30–17:30. Stock: large. Spec: Architecture; Art; Bindings; Biography; Foreign Texts; History - General; Poetry; Religion - Christian. PR: £10–5,000. CC: E; MC; V. VAT No: GB 562 2080 66. [02/11/2004]

Robin de Beaumont, 25 Park Walk, Chelsea, London, SW10 0AJ. Tel: (0207) 352-3440. Fax: (0207) 352-1260. Web: www.abebooks.com/home/RDEBOOKS. E-mail: rdebooks@aol.com. Est: 1980. Private premises. Internet and postal. Telephone first. Stock: small. Spec: Art; Bindings; Illustrated; Victoriana. PR: £20–3,000. CC: MC; V. Corresp: French. Mem: ABA; BA; ILAB. [Updated]

J.C.Deyong Books, 17 Cadogan Court, Draycott Avenue, London, SW3 3BX. Prop: J.C. Deyong. Tel: (0207) 5818665. Fax: (0207) 5810031. Web: www.jcdeyong.co.uk. E-mail: snowsmithbooks@hotmail.com. Est: 1973. Private premises. Internet and postal. Appointment necessary. Stock: very small. Spec: Ethnology; Travel - Africa; Travel - Asia; Travel - Asia, South East; Travel - Australasia/Australia; Travel - Islamic World; Travel - Middle East; Tribal. CC: MC; V. Corresp: French. Mem: PBFA. VAT No: GB No. [Updated]

Earlsfield Bookshop, ■ 513 Garratt Lane, Wandsworth, London, SW18 4SW. Prop: Charles Dixon. Tel: (020) 8946-3744. Est: 1995. Shop open: **M:** 16:00–18:00; **T:** 16:00–18:00; **W:** 16:00–18:00; **Th:** 16:00–18:00; **F:** 11:00–18:00; **S:** 10:00–17:00. Stock: small. PR: £1–50. [Updated]

Searching for a title – and cannot find it on any Internet database?

Then try www.sheppardsworld.co.uk

Select the subject classification – requests and offers can be made to selected specialist dealers

LONDON SOUTH WEST POSTAL DISTRICTS 165

Fine Art, 75, Tooting, London, SW11 1DP. Prop: Robert Walker. Tel: 0208 6961921. Fax: 0208 6961921. Web: www.fineart.tm. E-mail: sheppards@fineart.tm. Est: 1991. Private premises. Internet and postal. Appointment necessary. Open: **M:** 10:00–17:00; **T:** 10:00–17:00; **W:** 10:00–17:00; **Th:** 10:00–17:00; **F:** 10:00–17:00. Stock: small. Spec: Antiquarian; Arts, The; Bindings; Colour-Plate; Early Imprints; First Editions; Fore-Edge Paintings; Illuminated Manuscripts. PR: £100–1,000. CC: AE; MC; V. Mem: PBFA. Notes: please contact by e-mail, or telephone. Internet expert for the trade. [Updated]

Harfield Books of London, 81 Replingham Road, Southfields, London, SW18 5LU. Prop: P.V. Eastman. Tel: (020) 8871-0880. Fax: (020) 8871-0880. Web: www.harfieldbooks.com. E-mail: internet@harfieldbooks.com. Est: 1989. Warehouse; Internet and postal. Appointment necessary. Stock: very large. Spec: Academic/Scholarly; Booksearch. Notes: also, a booksearch service & academic publishing. [Updated]

Edmund Pollinger Rare Books, 27, Bramham Gardens, London, SW5 0JE. Prop: Edmund Pollinger. Tel: 0207 244 8498. Fax: 0207 244 8498. Web: www.etpollinger.com. E-mail: etpollinger@hotmail.com. Est: 2004. Office and/or bookroom. Contactable. Open: **M:** 10:00–17:30; **T:** 10:00–17:30; **W:** 10:00–17:30; **Th:** 10:00–17:30; **F:** 10:00–17:30; Closed for lunch: 12:00–14:00. Spec: Adventure; Africana; Animals and Birds; Apiculture; Author - Selous, Frederick; Curiosa; Entomology; Erotica. CC: MC; V. Cata: bi-annually on natural history, game hunting, fishing, food, drink. Corresp: French. Mem: PBFA. Notes: usually somebody here all the time, but call first to be sure. [Updated]

Europa Books, 15 Luttrell Avenue, Putney, London, SW15 6PD. Prop: Paul Hetherington PhD., F.S.A Tel: (020) 8788-0312. Fax: (020) 8788-0312. E-mail: phetherington@ukonline.co.uk. Est: 1985. Private premises. Appointment necessary. Stock: small. Spec: Antiquarian; Architecture; Art; Art - Technique; Art - Theory; Art History; Art Reference. PR: £10–2,000. CC: MC; V. Corresp: French, German, Italian. Mem: PBFA. Notes: appointments can be made at most times. [Updated]

Exedra Booksearch Ltd., 40 Peterborough Road, London, SW6 3BN. Prop: Jonathan Tootell. Tel: (020) 7731-8500. Fax: (020) 7731-8400. Web: www.exedra.co.uk. E-mail: info@exedra.co.uk. Est: 1999. Postal only. Contactable. Open: **M:** 09:00–18:00; **T:** 09:00–18:00; **W:** 09:00–18:00; **Th:** 09:00–18:00; **F:** 09:00–18:00; **S:** 09:00–14:00. Stock: very small. Spec: Booksearch. CC: MC; V. Corresp: French. [Updated]

Folios Limited, Flat 5, 193/195 Brompton Road, London, SW3 1LZ. Prop: Mr. Badr El–Hage. Tel: (020) 7581-2706. Fax: (020) 7581-2563. E-mail: folios@folios.demon.co.uk. Est: 1990. Private premises. Appointment necessary. Spec: Countries - Africa; Countries - Arabia; Religion - Islam; Prints and Maps. PR: £5–1,000. CC: MC; V. Cata: occasionally. Corresp: Arabic, French. [Updated]

Paul Foster Bookshop, ■ 119 Sheen Lane, London, SW14 8AE. Tel: (020) 8876-7424. Fax: (020) 8876 7424. E-mail: paulfosterbooks@btinternet.com. Est: 1990. Shop. Internet and postal. Open: **W:** 10:30–18:00; **Th:** 10:30–18:00; **F:** 10:30–18:00; **S:** 10:30–18:00. Stock: medium. Spec: Antiquarian; Art; Authors:- 20th Century; Churchill, Sir Winston; Bindings; Children's; Children's - Illustrated; First Editions. PR: £5–10,000. CC: JCB; MC; V. Mem: ABA; PBFA; ILAB. [Updated]

Gardener & Cook, 40, Peterborough Road, London, SW6 3BN. Prop: Jonathan Tootell & Simon Cobley. Tel: 020 7751 3377. Fax: 020 7731 8500. Web: www.gardenerandcook.com. E-mail: info@gardenerandcook.com. Est: 2005. Office and/or bookroom. Appointment necessary. Open: **M:** 09:00–17:30; **T:** 09:00–17:30; **W:** 09:00–17:30; **Th:** 09:00–17:30; **F:** 09:00–17:30; **S:** 09:00–17:30. Spec: Antiquarian; Food & Drink; Gardening - General. CC: AE; MC; V. Cata: occasionally on Gardening & Cookery. [Updated]

Geneva Books, 58 Elms Road, London, SW4 9EW. Tel: (020) 7627-4070. Est: 1985. Private premises. Appointment necessary. Spec: Religion - General. PR: £1–350. Annually. [Updated]

Gloucester Road Bookshop, ■ 123 Gloucester Road, London, SW7 4TE. Prop: Nick Dennys. Tel: (020) 7370-3503. Fax: (020) 7373-0610. E-mail: manager@gloucesterbooks.co.uk. Est: 1983. Shop open: **M:** 09:30–22:30; **T:** 09:30–22:30; **W:** 09:30–22:30; **Th:** 09:30–22:30; **F:** 09:30–22:30; **S:** 10:30–18:30; **Su:** 10:30–18:30. Stock: large. Spec: Antiques; Architecture; Art; Author - Greene, Graham; Children's; Fiction - General; History - General; Literature. PR: £1–5,000. CC: E; MC; V. [Updated]

Grays of Westminster, ■ 40 Churton Street, Pimlico, London, SW1V 2LP. Prop: Gray Levett & Nick Wynne. Tel: (020) 7828-4925. Fax: (020) 7976-5783. Web: www.graysofwestminster.co.uk. E-mail: info@graysofwestminster.co.uk. Est: 1985. Shop. Internet and postal. Open: **M:** 10:00–17:29; **T:** 10:00–17:30; **W:** 10:00–17:30; **Th:** 10:00–17:30; **F:** 10:00–17:30; **S:** 10:00–13:00. Spec: Photography. PR: £10–200. CC: AE; D; E; MC; V; Maestro. Corresp: Japanese, Italian, Polish, German. Notes: also, new, secondhand and vintage Nikon cameras. VAT No: GB 503 1317 05. [Updated]

SOUTH WEST POSTAL DISTRICTS

Robin Greer, 434 Fulham Palace Road, London, SW6 6HX. Prop: Robin Greer. Tel: (020) 7381-9113. Web: www.rarerobin.com. E-mail: rarities@rarerobin.com. Est: 1966. Private premises. Appointment necessary. Stock: small. Spec: Arthurian; Author - Lang, Andrew; Children's; Children's - Illustrated; Illustrated. PR: £1–5,000. CC: MC; V. Corresp: Spanish. Mem: ABA; PBFA; ILAB. [Updated]

Hanshan Tang Books, Unit 3 Ashburton Centre, 276 Cortis Road, London, SW15 3AY. Prop: John Cayley, John Constable, Myrna Chua. Tel: 0208 788 4464. Fax: 02087801565. Web: www.hanshan.com. E-mail: hst@hanshan.com. Est: 1973. Office and/or bookroom. Internet and postal. Appointment necessary. Open: **M:** 10:00–17:00; **T:** 10:00–17:00; **W:** 10:00–17:00; **Th:** 10:00–17:00; **F:** 10:00–17:00. Spec: Antiquarian; Antiques; Antiquities; Archaeology; Architecture; Art; Art History; Art Reference. CC: AE; MC; V. Cata: quarterly on East Asian Art and Archaeology. Mem: ABA; BA. VAT No: GB 749 5193 91. [Updated]

Peter Harrington Antiquarian B, ■ 100 Fulham Road, Chelsea, London, SW3 6HS. Tel: (020) 7591-0220. Fax: (020) 7225-7054. Web: www.peter-harrington-books.com. E-mail: mail@peter-harrington-books.com. Est: 1969. Shop open: **M:** 10:00–18:00; **T:** 10:00–18:00; **W:** 10:00–18:00; **Th:** 10:00–18:00; **F:** 10:00–18:00; **S:** 10:00–18:00. Stock: very large. Spec: Aeronautics; Antiquarian; Architecture; Atlases; Autographs; Bibles; Bindings; Botany. PR: £10–100,000. CC: AE; E; JCB; MC; V; SO, SW. Corresp: Polish, Spanish. Mem: ABA; PBFA; ILAB. VAT No: GB 701 5578 50. [Updated]

Thomas Heneage Art Books, ■ 42 Duke Street, St. James's, London, SW1Y 6DJ. Tel: (020) 7930-9223. Fax: (020) 7839-9223. Web: www.heneage.com. E-mail: artbooks@heneage.com. Est: 1977. Shop open: **M:** 09:30–18:00; **T:** 09:30–18:00; **W:** 09:30–18:00; **Th:** 09:30–18:00; **F:** 09:30–18:00. Stock: medium. Spec: Antiques; Applied Art; Arms & Armour; Art; Art History; Carpets; Catalogues Raisonnes; Ceramics. PR: £2–30,000. CC: MC; V. Notes: also, a booksearch service and publishers of Art Book Survey. Open at other times by appointment. [Updated]

Hesketh & Ward Ltd., 31 Britannia Road, London, SW6 2HJ. Prop: Viscount Bangor. Tel: (020) 7736-5705. Fax: (020) 7736-1089. E-mail: heskward@btopenworld.com. Est: 1985. Private premises. Appointment necessary. Stock: very small. Spec: Foreign Texts. PR: £80–5,000. Corresp: French, Italian. Mem: ABA. Notes: stock is mainly 16th century Continental, especially Italian. VAT No: GB 394 8008 27. [Updated]

Hünersdorff Rare Books, P.O. Box 582, London, SW10 9RP. Prop: Richard von Hünersdorff. Tel: (020) 7373-3899. Fax: (020) 7370-1244. Web: www.abebooks.com/hunersdorff/home. E-mail: huner.rarebooks@dial.pipex.com. Est: 1969. Private premises. Appointment necessary. Spec: Architecture; Countries - South America; Gardening - General; Landscape; Languages - Foreign; Literature; Medicine; Science - General. PR: £25–500,000. CC: MC; V. Corresp: German, Spanish, French. Mem: ABA; ILAB. [Updated]

Andrew Hunter–Rare Books, Box 9, 34 Buckingham Palace Road, London, SW1W 0RH. Tel: (020) 7834-4924. Fax: (020) 7834-4924. Web: www.rarebookhunter.com. E-mail: andrew@rarebookhunter.com. Est: 2001. Private premises. Appointment necessary. Stock: very small. Spec: Literature; Medicine; Science - General; Scottish Interest. PR: £200–25,000. Corresp: French, Spanish. Mem: ABA. VAT No: GB 782 2863 04. [Updated]]

Romilly Leeper, 12 Bolton Garden Mews, London, SW10 9LW. Prop: Romilly Leeper. Tel: (020) 7373-8370. Fax: (020) 7370-3226. Est: 1986. Private premises. Appointment necessary. Stock: small. Spec: Sport - Horse Racing (inc. Riding/Breeding/Equestrian); Travel - Asia, South East. PR: £6–100. Corresp: French, German, Portuguese. [Updated]

Mandalay Bookshop, 36c Sisters Avenue, London, SW11 5SQ. Prop: Nicholas Greenwood. Tel: (0207) 223-8987. Fax: (0207) 223-8987. Web: www.mandalaybookshop.com. E-mail: info@mandalaybookshop.biz. Est: 1994. Private premises. Internet and postal. Stock: small. Spec: Animals and Birds; Anthropology; Botany; Colonial; Countries - Burma; Countries - China; Countries - India; Countries - South East Asia. PR: £5–1,500. CC: PayPal. Corresp: French, German, Burmese, Thai. Notes: WWII includes the Burma Campaign. [Updated]

Michael Graves-Johnston, 54 Stockwell Park Road, London, SW9 0DA. Prop: Michael Graves-Johnston. Tel: +4420-7274-2069. Fax: +4420-7738-3747. E-mail: Books@gravesjohnston.demon.co.uk. Est: 1978. Private premises. Postal only. Appointment necessary. Stock: large. Spec: Africana; American Indians; Anthropology; Archaeology; Byzantium; Countries - Africa; Countries - Sudan, The; Egyptology. PR: £5–25,000. CC: AE; E; MC; V. Cata: quarterly. Mem: ABA; BA; ILAB. VAT No: GB 238 2333 72. [Updated]

My Back Pages, 8-10 Balham Station Road, London, SW16 6RT. Prop: Douglas Jeffers. Tel: 0208 675 9346. Fax: 0208 769 9741. E-mail: douglasjeffers@aol.com. Open: **M:** 10:10–20:00; **T:** 10:00–20:00; **W:** 10:00–20:00; **Th:** 10:00–20:00; **F:** 10:00–20:00; **S:** 10:00–19:00; **Su:** 11:00–18:00. Stock: very large. Spec: Academic/Scholarly; Architecture; Art; Cinema/Film; Countries - India; Egyptology; Fashion & Costume; Folio Society, The. CC: AE; JCB; MC. VAT No: GB 5620 221 84. [Updated]

Nibris Books, 14 Ryfold Road, Wimbledon Park, London, SW19 8BZ. Prop: Nigel Israel. Tel: (020) 8946-7207. Fax: (020) 8946-7207. E-mail: nibris_books@yahoo.com. Est: 1980. Private premises. Postal only. Appointment necessary. Stock: small. Spec: Gemmology; Horology; Jewellery; Mineralogy; Collectables; Ephemera; Prints and Maps. PR: £10–500. Notes: included in clasifications: gem stones, engraved gems, crown jewels regalia & ceremony VAT No: GB 446 2021 80. [Updated]

Paul Orssich, 2 St. Stephen's Terrace, South Lambeth, London, SW8 1DH. Tel: (020) 7787-0030. Fax: (020) 7735-9612. Web: www.orssich.com. E-mail: paulo@orssich.com. Est: 1980. Private premises. Internet and postal. Telephone first. Stock: very large. Spec: Academic/Scholarly; Advertising; Author - Cervantes Saavedra, Miguel de; Bull Fighting; Countries - Andorra; Countries - Central America; Countries - Gibraltar; Countries - Mexico. PR: £25–5,000. CC: MC; V. Corresp: Spanish, Catalan, French, German, Italian. Mem: PBFA. Notes: open any time by appointment. VAT No: GB 442 4102 94. [Updated]

Hugh Pagan Limited, P.O. Box 4325, London, SW7 1DD. Tel: (020) 7589-6292. Fax: (020) 7589-6303. Web: www.hughpagan.com. E-mail: enquiries@hughpagan.com. Est: 1987. Appointment necessary. Spec: Architecture; Fine Art. CC: MC; V. Cata: occasionally, Mem: ABA. [Updated]

Nigel Phillips, 5 Burleigh Place, Cambalt Road, Putney Hill, London, SW15 6ES. Tel: (020) 8788 2664. Fax: (020) 8780 1989. Web: www.nigelphillips.com. E-mail: nigel@nigelphillips.com. Est: 1981. Private premises. Appointment necessary. Stock: medium. Spec: Antiquarian; History of Ideas; Medicine; Science - General; Science - History of; Technology. PR: £15–50,000. CC: MC; V. Mem: ABA; ILAB. [26/07/2004]

Russell Rare Books, ■ 239A Fulham Road, Chelsea, London, SW3 6HY. Tel: (020) 7351-5119. Fax: (020) 7376-7227. Web: www.russellrarebooks.com. E-mail: c.russell@russellrarebooks.com. Est: 1977. Shop open: **M:** 14:00–18:00; **T:** 14:00–18:00; **W:** 14:00–18:00; **Th:** 14:00–18:00; **F:** 14:00–18:00. Stock: very small. Spec: Atlases; Bindings; Natural History; Social History; Travel - General; Prints and Maps. PR: £200–10,000. CC: V. Mem: ABA; PBFA; ILAB. Notes: when closed: telephone 07768 004152 usually open but appointment advisable [Updated]

SaBeRo Books, 27 Cavendish Road, Colliers Wood, SW19 2ET. Prop: Ron, Bethani and Sarah Travis. Tel: 44 (0) 20 85 40 60 2. E-mail: saberobooks@blueyonder.co.uk. Est: 2002. Private premises. Internet and postal. Contactable. Open: **M:** 09:00–17:00; **T:** 09:00–17:00; **W:** 09:00–17:00; **Th:** 09:00–17:00; **F:** 09:00–17:00; **S:** 09:00–17:00. Stock: medium. PR: £2–500. [Updated]

Sandpiper Books Ltd., 24 Langroyd Road, London, SW17 7PL. Prop: Robert Collie. Tel: (020) 8767-7421. Fax: (020) 8682-0280. Web: www.sandpiper.co.uk. E-mail: enquiries@sandpiper.co.uk. Est: 1983. Office and/or bookroom. Internet and postal. Appointment necessary. Open: **M:** 09:00–17:00; **T:** 09:00–17:00; **W:** 09:00–17:00; **Th:** 09:00–17:00; **F:** 09:00–17:00. Stock: medium. Spec: Academic/Scholarly; Classical Studies; Medieval. PR: £1–100. CC: MC; V. [Updated]

Sims Reed Limited, ■ 43a Duke Street, London, SW1Y 6DD. Prop: John Sims. Tel: 020 7493 5660. Fax: 020 7493 8468. Web: www.simsreed.com. E-mail: info@simsreed.com. Est: 1978. Shop open: **M:** 10:00–18:00; **T:** 10:00–18:00; **W:** 10:00–18:00; **Th:** 10:00–18:00; **F:** 10:00–18:00. Spec: Antiquarian; Art; Artists; Illustrated; Prints and Maps. CC: AE; E; MC; V; Maestro. Mem: PBFA; ILAB. Notes: Open at other times by appointment. VAT No: GB 242 9715 52. [Updated]

Tsbbooks, 214 Ferndale Road, London, SW9 8AG. Tel: (0207) 7330965. E-mail: tsbbooks@hotmail.com. Est: 1989. Internet and postal. Stock: small. Spec: Homosexuality & Lesbianism; Booksearch. PR: £4–450. [Updated]

Mary Wells, 24 Minehead Road, London, SW16 2AW. Prop: Mary Wells. Tel: (020) 8769-0778. Fax: (020) 8769-0778. Est: 1980. Market stand/stall; Book Fairs Only. Stock: small. Spec: Booksearch. PR: £1–500. Notes: attends Bloomsbury Fair, Royal National. [Updated]

Whistler's Books, 11 Ashbourne Terrace, Wimbledon, London, SW19 1QX. Prop: Ronald H. Ashworth. Tel: (020) 8540-7370. Est: 1993. Private premises. Appointment necessary. Stock: very small. Spec: Building & Construction; Chess; Company History; Electronics; Engineering; Industry; Mathematics; Music - Composers. PR: £5–50. [Updated]

Worlds End Bookshop, ■ 357 Kings Road, London, SW3 5ES. Prop: Stephen Dickson. Tel: 020 7352 9376. E-mail: stevdcksn@btinternet.com. Est: 1990. Shop open: **M:** 10:00–18:30; **T:** 10:00–18:30; **W:** 10:00–18:30; **Th:** 10:00–18:30; **F:** 10:00–18:30; **S:** 10:00–18:30; **Su:** 10:00–18:30. Spec: Antiquarian; Antiques; Architecture; Art; Avant-Garde; Beat Writers; Biography; Children's - Illustrated. CC: AE; JCB; MC; V; Switch. Notes: 20% discounts every Saturday, Sunday & Monday. 40% discounts every Bank Holiday. [Updated]

Wykeham Books, 64 Ridgway, Wimbledon, London, SW19 4RA. Prop: H.S.G. Mather. Tel: (020) 8879-3721. Web: www.bibliographies.co.uk. E-mail: wykbooks@msn.com. Est: 1976. Private premises. Internet and postal. Stock: medium. Spec: Author - Kipling, Rudyard; Bibliography; Books about Books. PR: £5–15,000. Mem: PBFA. [Updated]

LONDON

(LONDON WEST POSTAL DISTRICTS)

Al Saqi Books, ■ 26 Westbourne Grove, London, W2 5RH. Prop: Arab Books Ltd Tel: (020) 7229-8543. Fax: (020) 7229-7492. E-mail: alsaqibooks@aol.com. Est: 1978. Shop open: **M:** 10:00–18:00; **T:** 10:00–18:00; **W:** 10:00–18:00; **Th:** 10:00–18:00; **F:** 10:00–18:00; **S:** 10:00–18:00. Stock: medium. Spec: Academic/Scholarly; Antiquarian; Architecture; Art; Authors - Women; Canals/Inland Waterways; Cookery/Gastronomy; Countries - Central Asia. PR: £5–800. CC: AE; D; E; JCB; MC; V. Corresp: French, Arabic. Notes: also, important stock of Arabic books, also new books. VAT No: GB 242 6953 51. [Updated]

Altea Gallery, 35 Saint George St., London, W1S 2FN. Prop: Mr. Massimo De Martini. Tel: (020) 7491 0010. Fax: (020) 7491 0015. Web: www.alteagallery.com. E-mail: info@alteagallery.com. Est: 1993. Shop and/or gallery. Internet and postal. Open: **M:** 10:00–18:00; **T:** 10:00–18:00; **W:** 10:00–18:00; **Th:** 10:00–18:00; **F:** 10:00–18:00; **S:** 11:00–16:00. Stock: medium. Spec: Astronomy; Atlases; Geography; Maritime/Nautical; Topography - General; Topography - Local; Travel - General; Voyages & Discovery. PR: £50–10,000. CC: AE; E; JCB; MC; V. Corresp: Italian. Mem: ABA; PBFA; ILAB; IMCoS. Notes: also, map search, colouring & restoration VAT No: GB 649 5809 86. [Updated]]

David Batterham, 36 Alexander Street, London, W2 5NU. Tel: (020) 7229-3845. E-mail: david.batterham @virgin.net. Est: 1966. Private premises. Appointment necessary. Stock: small. Spec: Applied Art; Architecture; Caricature; Fashion & Costume; Illustrated; Journals; Technology; Typography. PR: £5–5,000. CC: MC; V. Corresp: French. [Updated]

Nicholas Bernstein, 2 Vaughan Avenue, London, W6 0XS. Prop: Nicholas Bernstein. Tel: (020) 874 17140. Est: 1986. Private premises. Appointment necessary. Stock: medium. Spec: Antiquarian; Bibles; Bindings; Curiosities; Dictionaries; Economics; Fiction - General; History of Ideas. PR: £25–5,000. Corresp: French. Mem: PBFA. Notes: appointments: 7 days a week. Exhibits at monthly PBFA fairs at Hotel Russell. [Updated]

Biblion Ltd, ■ 1–7 Davies Mews, London, W1K 5AB. Director: Leo Harrison. Manager: Stephen Poole. Tel: (020) 7629-1374. Fax: (020) 7629-1374. Web: www.biblion.com. E-mail: info@biblion.co.uk. Est: 1999. Internet and postal. Shop open: **M:** 10:00–18:00; **T:** 10:00–18:00; **W:** 10:00–18:00; **Th:** 10:00–18:00; **F:** 10:00–18:00; **S:** 10:00–18:00. Stock: large. Spec: Alpinism/Mountaineering; Antiquarian; Applied Art; Architecture; Art; Bibles; Bibliography; Bindings. PR: £10–50,000. CC: E; JCB; MC; V. [Updated]

J. & S.L. Bonham, Flat 14, 84 Westbourne Terrace, London, W2 6QE. Prop: John & Suzanne Bonham. Tel: (020) 7402-7064. Fax: (020) 7402-0955. Web: www.bonbooks.dial.pipex.com. E-mail: bonbooks@dial.pipex.com. Est: 1976. Private premises. Internet and postal. Appointment necessary. Stock: medium. Spec: Alpinism/Mountaineering; Countries - Africa; Countries - Australia; Countries - Polar; Topography - General; Travel - General; Travel - Africa; Travel - Americas. PR: £10–2,000. CC: MC; V; SW, SO. Corresp: German. Mem: ABA; PBFA; ILAB; Valuations. VAT No: GB 362 1962 53. [Updated]

The Book Business, 90 Greenford Avenue, London, W7 3QS. Prop: Giles Levete. Tel: (020) 8840-1185. E-mail: bookbusiness@homechoice.co.uk. Est: 1990. Private premises. Internet and postal. Appointment necessary. Stock: very small. Spec: Academic/Scholarly; Children's; Literature; Modern First Editions; Odd & Unusual; Travel - General. PR: £10–2,000. CC: AE; JCB; MC; V. Mem: PBFA.[Updated]]

Books & Things, P.O. Box 17768, London, W8 6ZD. Prop: M.M. Steenson. Tel: (020) 7370-5593. Fax: (020) 7370-5593. Web: www.booksandthings.co.uk. E-mail: martin@booksandthings.co.uk. Est: 1972. Warehouse; Internet and postal. Stock: small. Spec: Advertising; Applied Art; Art Reference; Children's - Illustrated; Decorative Art; Illustrated; Magazines & Periodicals - General; Modern First Editions. PR: £20–1,000. CC: E; JCB; MC. Mem: ABA; PBFA; ILAB. Notes: also, a booksearch service [23/07/2004]

Don Kelly Books, Admiral Vernon L16-20, 141-149 Portobello Rd, London, W11. Prop: Don Kelly. Tel: 020 7731 0482. Fax: 020 7731 0482. E-mail: donkellybooks@btinternet.com. Est: 1978. Market stand/ stall. Shop at: P.O.Box 44132, London SW6 2RP. Open: **S:** 07.30–15.30. Spec: Antiques; Antiquities; Art Deco; Art History; Art Nouveau; Art Reference; Arts, The; Carpets. CC: MC; V. Cata: on reference books for the Art & Antique trade. Notes: also at: P.O.Box 44132, London SW6 2RP. I also exhibit at The Olympia Fine Art and Antique Fair three times a year. Although I am only open on Saturdays, a selection of my stock can be viewed by appointment throughout the week. VAT No: GB 563 2239 49. [Updated]

Marc–Antoine du Ry Medieval M, medievalmodern, 13 New Burlington Street, London, W1S 3BG. Tel: 0044 (0) 207 287 905. Fax: (cell) 0044 (0) 777 0888 166. Web: www.medievalart.uk.com. E-mail: info@marcdury.co.uk. Est: 1995. Shop and/or gallery. Internet and postal. Appointment necessary. Open: **W:** 11:00–18:00; **Th:** 11:00–18:00; **F:** 11:00–18:00; **S:** 11:00–18:00. Spec: Book of Hours; Illuminated Manuscripts; Manuscripts; Medieval. PR: £100–100,000. Corresp: French; Italian. Notes: also contactable in Belgium on 0032 (0) 475 866073. VAT No: GB 735 7640 1. [21/12/2004]

Elton Engineering Books, 27 Mayfield Avenue, London, W4 1PN. Tel: (0208) 747 0967. E-mail: elton_engineering_books@compuserve.com. Est: 1985. Private premises. Internet and postal. Appointment necessary. Stock: very small. Spec: Architecture; Building & Construction; Engineering; Naval; Railways; Transport. PR: £30–8,000. CC: MC; V. Corresp: French, German. Mem: ABA; ILAB. VAT No: GB 429 7966 90. [Updated]

James Fergusson Books & Manuscripts, 39 Melrose Gardens, London, W6 7RN. Tel: 020 7602 3536. Fax: 020 7602 0502. E-mail: jamesfergusson@btinternet.com. Est: 1986. Private premises. Postal only. Appointment necessary. Closed for lunch: 13:00–14:00. Spec: Letters; Manuscripts. Cata: occasionally. Notes: also, 19th & 20th century literary association copies, autographs and photographs. [Updated]

Simon Finch Rare Books Ltd., ■ 53 Maddox Street, London, W1S 2PN. Tel: (020) 7499-0974. Fax: (020) 7499-0799. Web: www.simonfinch.com. E-mail: rarebooks@simonfinch.com. Est: 1981. Shop open: **M:** 10:00–18:00; **T:** 10:00–18:00; **W:** 10:00–18:00; **Th:** 10:00–18:00; **F:** 10:00–18:00. Spec: Art; Autographs; Bindings; Design; Early Imprints; Literature; Manuscripts; Medicine. PR: £1–500,000. CC: AE; MC; V; SW. Cata: annually. [Updated]

First State Books, 35 Talbot Road, London, W2 5JG. Prop: Euan Stuart. Tel: (020) 7792-2672. Fax: (020) 7792-2672. Web: www.firststatebooks.com. E-mail: info@firststatebooks.com. Est: 2001. Private premises. Internet and postal. Spec: Children's; Fiction - General; First Editions; Modern First Editions. PR: £15–100. CC: AE; D; E; JCB; MC; V; Maestro, Solo. [Updated]

Sam Fogg Ltd, ■ 15d Clifford Street, London, W1S 4JZ. Tel: (020) 7534-2100. Fax: (020) 7534-2122. Web: www.samfogg.com. E-mail: info@samfogg.com. Est: 1978. Appointment necessary. Open: **M:** 09:30–17:30; **T:** 09:30–17:30; **W:** 09:30–17:30; **Th:** 09:30–17:30; **F:** 09:30–17:30. Stock: small. Spec: Manuscripts. CC: MC; V. Corresp: French, German. Mem: ABA. VAT No: GB 467 6893 80. [Updated]

Richard Ford, 70 Chaucer Road, London, W3 6DP. Tel: (020) 8993-1235. Fax: (020) 8752-1431. E-mail: richard.rmford@btopenworld.com. Est: 1982. Private premises. Appointment necessary. Stock: very small. Spec: Autographs; Bibliography; Documents - General; Manuscripts; Publishing; Ephemera. PR: £10–1,000. Corresp: French, Italian. Notes: also, historical documents. [21/12/2004]

Fosters Bookshop, ■ 183 Chiswick High Road, London, W4 2DR. Prop: W.A. & M.A. Foster. Tel: (020) 8995-2768. E-mail: willmaf@btinternet.com. Est: 1968. Open: **Th:** 10:30–17:00; **F:** 10:30–17:00; **S:** 10:30–17:00. Stock: medium. Spec: Applied Art; Architecture; Art; Bindings; Children's; First Editions; Illustrated; Sets of Books. PR: £2–1,000. Mem: PBFA. [Updated]

Robert Frew Ltd, ■ 31 Maddox Street, London, W1S 2PB. Tel: (020) 7290 3800. Fax: (020) 72903801. Web: www.robertfrew.com. E-mail: shop@robertfrew.com. Est: 1993. Shop open: **M:** 10:00–18:00; **T:** 10:00–18:00; **W:** 10:00–18:00; **Th:** 10:00–18:00; **F:** 10:00–18:00; **S:** 10:00–14:00. Spec: Antiquarian; Atlases; Author - Churchill, Sir Winston; Bindings; Cartography; Encyclopaedias; History - General; Illustrated. PR: £10–30,000. CC: AE; D; E; JCB; MC; V. Mem: ABA; PBFA; ILAB0. Notes: book packing and shipping VAT No: GB 625 8877 92. [Updated]

Fuller D'Arch Smith, 37b New Cavendish Street, London, W1G 8JR. Prop: Jean Overton Fuller & Timothy D'Arch Smith. Tel: (020) 7722-0063. Fax: (020) 7722-0063. Est: 1969. Private premises. Appointment necessary. Stock: very small. PR: £5–500. Corresp: French, German, Italian, Russian [Updated]

Hab Books, 35 Wellington Road, Ealing, London, W5 4UJ. Prop: T. Habraszewski. Tel: (020) 8932-5058. Fax: (020) 8932-5058. E-mail: tom@habbks.freeserve.co.uk. Est: 1981. Private premises. Postal only. Spec: Biography; Countries - East Europe; Countries - Russia; Foreign Texts; Politics; Theology. [Updated]

Adrian Harrington, 64a Kensington Church Street, Kensington, London, W8 4DB. Tel: (020) 7937-1465. Fax: (020) 7368-0912. Web: www.harringtonbooks.co.uk. E-mail: rare@harringtonbooks.co.uk. Est: 1971. Spec: Antiquarian; Art; Authors:- General; Churchill, Sir Winston; Conan Doyle, Sir Arthur; Cornwell, Bernard; Dickens, Charles; Fleming, Ian. PR: £10–50,000. CC: AE; MC; V. Mem: ABA; PBFA. Notes: also, bookbinding. [Updated]

G. Heywood Hill Limited, ■ 10 Curzon Street, London, W1J 5HH. Tel: (020) 7629-0647. Fax: (020) 7408-0286. Web: www.gheywoodhill.com. E-mail: old@gheywoodhill.com. Est: 1936. Shop open: **M:** 09:00–17:30; **T:** 09:00–17:30; **W:** 09:00–17:30; **Th:** 09:00–17:30; **F:** 09:00–17:30; **S:** 09:00–12:30. Stock: medium. Spec: Architecture; Children's; History - General; Illustrated; Literature; Natural History; Booksearch. PR: £5–10,000. CC: MC; V; Switch. Corresp: French, German, Spanish, Italian. Mem: ABA; BA. Notes: also, new books & a booksearch service. VAT No: GB 239 4090 56. [Updated]

Judith Hodgson, 11 Stanwick Road, London, W14 8TL. Tel: (020) 7603-7414. Fax: (020) 7602-1431. E-mail: judith.hodgson@btinternet.com. Est: 1986. Private premises. Postal only. Appointment necessary. Stock: small. Spec: Antiquarian; Countries - Latin America; Countries - Portugal; Countries - Spain. Corresp: French, Spanish, Portuguese. Mem: ABA; ILAB. VAT No: GB 446 0649 44. [Updated]

Kay Books, Roger's Arcade, 65 Portobello Road, London, W11 2QB. Prop: Peter Degnan. Tel: (020) 8640-7779. Fax: (Mobile) 07940 833870. E-mail: peter@pdegnan.fsnet.co.uk. Est: 1968. Private premises. Telephone first. Spec: Bindings; Topography - General; Travel - General. [Updated]

Robert J. Kirkpatrick, 6 Osterley Park View Road, London, W7 2HH. Tel: (020) 8567-4521. E-mail: rkirkpatrick.molesworth@virgin.net. Est: 1986. Private premises. Postal only. Appointment necessary. Stock: very small. Spec: Juvenile; Memoirs; Public Schools. PR: £1–100. [Updated]

Maggs Brothers Limited, ■ 50 Berkeley Square, London, W1J 5BA. Tel: (020) 7493-7160. Fax: (020) 7499-2007. Web: www.maggs.com. E-mail: postmaster@maggs.com. Est: 1853. Shop open: **M:** 09:30–05:00; **T:** 09:30–05:00; **W:** 09:30–05:00; **Th:** 09:30–05:00; **F:** 09:30–05:00. Stock: very large. Spec: Author - Blake, N.; Autographs; Bibliography; Bindings; Early Imprints; Fine Printing; Geology; Illuminated Manuscripts. PR: £5–5,000,000. CC: V. Corresp: Japanese, Mandarin, German, French, Italian, Spanish. Mem: ABA; PBFA; BA; ILAB; BADA. [Updated]

Marlborough Rare Books Ltd, ■ 144/146 New Bond Street, London, W1S 2TR. Prop: Jonathan Gestetner. Tel: (020) 7493-6993. Fax: (020) 7499-2479. E-mail: sales@mrb-books.co.uk. Est: 1948. Shop open: **M:** 09:30–17:30; **T:** 09:30–17:30; **W:** 09:30–17:30; **Th:** 09:30–17:30; **F:** 09:30–17:30. Stock: medium. Spec: Architecture; Bibliography; Bindings; Colour-Plate; Country Houses; Fine Art; Illustrated; Landscape. PR: £50–50,000. CC: E; MC; V. Corresp: French, German. Mem: ABA; ILAB. [12/10/2004]

Melvin Tenner, 51 Gayford Road, London, W12 9BY. Prop: Melvin Tenner. Tel: 020 8740 6677. Fax: 010 8740 6960. Est: 1980. Private premises. Appointment necessary. Spec: International Affairs; Booksearch. Notea: Also, a booksearch service. [Updated]

Orbis Books (London) Ltd., 206 Blythe Road, London, W14 0HH. Dir: Mr. Jerzy Kulczycki & Dr. Aleksandra Kulczycka. Fax: (020) 8742-7686. E-mail: bookshop@orbis-books.co.uk. Est: 1944. Spec: Countries - East Europe; Countries - Poland; Countries - Russia; Foreign Texts. PR: £2–20,000. Notes: also, new books, booksearch, large print books, CDs & cassettes of Polish music. [Updated]

Diana Parikian, Rare Books, 3 Caithness Road, London, W14 0JB. Tel: (020) 7603-8375. Fax: (020) 7602-1178. E-mail: dparikian@mac.com. Est: 1960. Private premises. Appointment necessary. Spec: Emblemata; Fine & Rare; Foreign Texts; Iconography. PR: £200–10,000. Corresp: French, Italian. Cata: annually. ABA. VAT No: GB 194 5853 21. [Updated]

New dealers in the British Isles can register their business on

www.sheppardsworld.co.uk

Pickering & Chatto, ■ 36 St. George Street, London, W!S 2FA. Tel: (020) 7491-2656. Fax: (020) 7491-9161. Web: www.pickering-chatto.com. E-mail: j.hudson@pickering-chatto.com. Est: 1820. Shop open: **M:** 09:30–17:30; **T:** 09:30–17:30; **W:** 09:30–17:30; **Th:** 09:30–17:30; **F:** 09:30–17:30. Stock: small. Spec: Chemistry; Early Imprints; Economics; Education & School; Health; Humanities; Incunabula; Literature. PR: £100–10,000. CC: MC; V. Corresp: French. Mem: ABA; PBFA; ILAB. VAT No: GB 691 3252 35. [Updated]

William Poole, 97 New Bond Street, London, W1S 1SL. Tel: (020) 7629-8738. Est: 1979. Private premises. Appointment necessary. Stock: small. Spec: Academic/Scholarly; Classical Studies; Fine & Rare; Foreign Texts; Humanism; Publishers - General. Notes: also books by Foulis Press. [Updated]

Portobello Books, ■ 328 Portobello Road, London, W10 5RU. Prop: Lawrence Thompson. Tel: 020 8964 3166. Fax: 020 8964 3166. Web: www.portobello-books.com. E-mail: sales@portobello-books.com. Est: 1985. Shop open: **T:** 11:00–17:00; **W:** 11:00–17:00; **Th:** 11:00–17:00; **F:** 11:00–17:00; **S:** 09:00–17:00. Spec: Anthropology; Architecture; Art - Technique; Art History; Astronomy; Biography; Children's - Illustrated; Cinema/Film. CC: AE; D; E; JCB; MC; V. Cata: occasionally on various subjects. Notes: we are a second hand book shop, specialising in out of print books. Not open on Mondays or Sundays. [Updated]

Jonathan Potter Ltd., 125 New Bond Street, London, W1S 1DY. Tel: (020) 7491-3520. Fax: (020) 7491-9754. Web: www.jpmaps.co.uk. E-mail: jpmaps@attglobal.net. Est: 1975. Shop and/or gallery. Open: **M:** 10:00–18:00; **T:** 10:00–18:00; **W:** 10:00–18:00; **Th:** 10:00–18:00; **F:** 10:00–18:00. Spec: Atlases; Cartography; Reference; Prints and Maps. PR: £30–30,000. CC: AE; D; MC; V. Mem: ABA; PBFA; ILAB. Notes: also, reference books on the history of cartography & framing & paper restoration services. [Updated]

Bernard Quaritch Ltd., ■ 8 Lower John Street, Golden Square, London, W1F 9AU. Prop: John Koh. Tel: (020) 7734-2983. Fax: (020) 7437-0967. Web: www.quaritch.com. E-mail: rarebooks@quaritch.com. Est: 1847. Shop open: **M:** 09:30–17:30; **T:** 09:30–17:30; **W:** 09:30–17:30; **Th:** 09:30–17:30; **F:** 09:30–17:30. Stock: large. Spec: Alchemy; Antiquarian; Architecture; Art; Bibliography; Cookery/Gastronomy; Early Imprints; Economics. PR: £100–500,000. CC: AE; MC; V; SW. Corresp: French, German, Italian, Spanish, Russian. Mem: ABA; PBFA; ILAB; SLAM, VDA, BADA. VAT No: GB 840 1358 54. [05/10/2004]

Leslie Robert, t/a Hyde Park Books, 74 Devonport, Southwick Street, London, W2 2QH. Tel: (020) 7402 9567. E-mail: hydeparkbooks@dsl.pipex.com. Est: 1978. Private premises. Internet and postal. Appointment necessary. Spec: First Editions; Modern First Editions. PR: £20–500. [02/02/2006]

A.F. Sephton, 16 Bloemfontein Avenue, Shepherds Bush, London, W12 7BL. Prop: A.F. Sephton. Tel: (020) 8749-1454. Est: 1966. Private premises. Appointment necessary. Stock: very small. Spec: Artists; Colour-Plate; Illustrated; Social History; Prints and Maps. PR: £10–100. [Updated]

Bernard J. Shapero Rare Books, ■ 32 St. George Street, London, W1S 2EA. Tel: (020) 7493-0876. Fax: (020) 7229-7860. Web: www.shapero.com. E-mail: rarebooks@shapero.com. Est: 1979. Shop. Internet and postal. Open: **M:** 09:30–18:30; **T:** 09:30–18:30; **W:** 09:30–18:30; **Th:** 09:30–18:30; **F:** 09:30–18:30; **S:** 11:00–17:00. Stock: large. Spec: Academic/Scholarly; Africana; Alchemy; Alpinism/Mountaineering; American Indians; Americana; Animals and Birds; Anthropology. PR: £50–100,000. CC: AE; D; E; JCB; MC; V; SW. Corresp: French, German, Italian, Spanish, Dutch. Mem: ABA; PBFA; BA; ILAB. VAT No: GB 466 5294 16. [Updated]

Sokol Books Ltd, P.O. Box 2409, London, W1A 2SH. Prop: C.J. Sokol. Tel: (020) 7499-5571. Fax: (020) 7629-6536. E-mail: books@sokol.co.uk. Est: 1977. Appointment necessary. Spec: Antiquarian; Classical Studies; Early Imprints; Fine & Rare; History of Ideas; Incunabula; Literature; Science - History of. PR: £100–100,000. Mem: ABA; ILAB. [Updated]

Henry Sotheran Limited, ■ 2–5 Sackville Street, Piccadilly, London, W1S 3DP. Tel: (020) 7439-6151. Fax: (020) 7434-2019. Web: www.sotherans.co.uk. E-mail: sotherans@sotherans.co.uk. Est: 1761. Shop open: **M:** 09:30–18:00; **T:** 09:30–18:00; **W:** 09:30–18:00; **Th:** 09:30–18:00; **F:** 09:30–18:00; **S:** 10:00–16:00. Stock: very large. Spec: Architecture; Art; Bindings; Children's; Churchilliana; Illustrated; Literature; Natural History. PR: £20–100,000. CC: AE; D; MC; V. Mem: ABA; PBFA; ILAB. VAT No: GB 689 7172. [Updated]

Saint Swithin's Illustrated & Children's Books, 87 Portobello Road, London, London W, W11 2QB. Mrs. Margaret Davies. Tel: (020) 8573-8556. Shop and/or showroom; Appointment necessary. Spec: Advertising; Artists; Cats; Children's; Children's - Illustrated; Christmas; Circus; Decorative Art. Notes: None of the stock is shown on the Internet. [Updated]

Sue Lowell Natural History Books, 101 Cambridge Gardens, London, W10 6JE. Prop: Sue Lowell. Tel: (020) 8960-4382. Web: www.abebooks.com. E-mail: sue4382@aol.com. Est: 1972. Private premises. Internet and postal. Appointment necessary, callers are asked to telephone first. Open: **M:** 10:00–19:00; **T:** 10:00–19:00; **W:** 10:00–19:00; **Th:** 19:00–00:00; **F:** 19:00–00:00; **S:** 09:00–13:00; **Su:** 10:00–16:00. Stock: medium. Spec: Academic/Scholarly; Advertising; Aeronautics; Animals and Birds; Art Reference; Botany; Gardening - General; Medicine - History of. PR: £10–4,000. CC: MC; V. Corresp: French. Notes: also, booksearch. [Updated]

The Travel Bookshop, 13-15 Blenheim Crescent, Notting Hill, London, W11 2EE. Prop: Sarah Anderson. Tel: (020) 7229-5260. Fax: (020) 7243-1552. Web: www.thetravelbookshop.co.uk. E-mail: post@thetravelbookshop.co.uk. Est: 1979. Spec: New Books; Travel - General. PR: £1–200. Notes: also, new books on travel [Updated]

Patrick Tuft, The Vicarage, Chiswick Mall, London, W4 2PJ. Prop: Patrick Tuft. Tel: (withheld). Private premises. Postal only. Stock: very small. Spec: Bibles; Bibliography; History - General; Religion - Christian; Vatican and Papal History, The. [Updated]

Valentine Rare Books, 20 Fitzroy Square, London, W1T 6EJ. Prop: Gaston Chappell Tel: 020 7387 5454. E-mail: vrb@easynet.co.uk. Est: 1983. Office and/or bookroom. Appointment necessary. Spec: Authors:- Austen, Jane; Dickens, Charles; Hardy, Thomas; James, Henry; British; Fiction - 18th Century; Fine & Rare; Literature. PR: £20–10,000. Cata: occasionally on Fiction (mostly 19th century). Mem: ABA; PBFA; ILAB. VAT No: GB 504 6399 43. [Updated]

Mrs. Teresa White, Flat 4, 79 St. Helen's Gardens, London, W10 6LJ. Prop: Mrs. Teresa White. Tel: not disclosed. Private premises. Postal only. Stock: small. Spec: Ephemera. PR: £1–100. [Updated]

LONDON
(WEST CENTRAL POSTAL DISTRICTS)

Any Amount of Books, ■ 56 Charing Cross Road, London, WC2H 0QA. Tel: (020) 7836-3697. Fax: (020) 7240-1769. Web: www.anyamountofbooks.com. E-mail: charingx@anyamountofbooks.com. Est: 1975. Shop. Internet and postal. Open: **M:** 10:30–21:30; **T:** 10:30–21:30; **W:** 10:29–21:30; **Th:** 10:30–21:30; **F:** 10:30–21:30; **S:** 10:30–21:30; **Su:** 11:30–20:30. Spec: Academic/Scholarly; Antiquarian; Art Reference; Collectables; Ephemera. PR: £1–25,000. CC: AE; JCB; MC; PAYPAL. Mem: ABA; BA. Notes: also, books by the yard, i.e. for furnishing, film sets etc. & valuations. [Updated]

Atlantis Bookshop, ■ 49a Museum Street, London, WC1A 1LY. Prop: Bali Beskin & Geraldine Beskin. Tel: (020) 7405-2120. Web: www.atlantisbookshop.demon.co.uk. E-mail: atlantis@theatlantisbookshop.com. Est: 1922. Shop. Internet and postal. Open: **M:** 10:30–18:00; **T:** 10:30–18:00; **W:** 10:30–18:00; **Th:** 10:30–18:00; **F:** 10:30–18:00; **S:** 10:30–18:00. Stock: small. Spec: Alchemy; Archaeology; Authors:- Crowley, Aleister; Spare, Austin Osman; Countries - Egypt; Mythology; Occult; Paganism. PR: £4–40. CC: AE; MC; V; SW. [Updated]

Josephine Bacon, 179 Kings Cross Road, London, WC1X 9BX. Tel: (020) 7278 9490. Fax: (020) 7278 2447. E-mail: bacon@americanization.com. Private premises. Spec: Cookery/Gastronomy; Judaica; Languages - Foreign. [Updated]

Bertram Rota Ltd., ■ 31 Long Acre (First Floor), Covent Garden, London, WC2E 9LT. Tel: (020) 7836-0723. Fax: (020) 7497 9058. Web: www.bertramrota.co.uk. E-mail: bertramrota@compuserve.com. Est: 1923. Shop open: **M:** 09:30–17:30; **T:** 09:30–17:30; **W:** 09:30–17:30; **Th:** 09:30–17:30; **F:** 09:30–17:30. Stock: medium. Spec: Antiquarian; Autographs; First Editions; Literature; Modern First Editions; Private Press; Booksearch. CC: E; JCB; MC; V. Mem: ABA; ILAB. Notes: also, a booksearch service. [Updated]

Steve Burak, ■ 18, Leigh Street, off Judd Street, London, WC1H 9EW. Prop: Steve Burak. Tel: (020) 7388-1153. E-mail: SteveBurakLondon@yahoo.com. Est: 2002. Shop. Telephone first. Open: **M:** 11:00–19:00; **T:** 11:00–19:00; **W:** 11:00–19:00; **Th:** 11:00–19:00; **F:** 11:00–19:00; **S:** 11:00–19:00. Stock: large. Spec: Academic/Scholarly; Antiquarian; Ephemera; Prints and Maps. PR: £5–1,000. Corresp: French. Notes: also, ephemera artwork and various eclectica. [Updated]

Collinge & Clark, ■ The Bookshop, 13 Leigh Street, London, WC1H 9EW. Prop: Michael Collinge & Oliver Clark. Tel: 0207 387 7105. Fax: 0207 388 1315. E-mail: collingeandclark@aol.com. Est: 1987. Shop open: **M:** 11:00–18:30; **T:** 11:00–18:30; **W:** 11:00–18:30; **Th:** 11:00–18:30; **F:** 11:00–18:30. Spec: Book Arts; Books about Books; Engraving; Fine Printing; Limited Editions; Printing; Private Press; Typography. CC: AE; MC; V. Cata: bi-annually on Private Press & Typography. Corresp: Francais, Deutsch. Mem: PBFA. VAT No: GB 523 1738 64. [Updated]

Delectus Books, 27 Old Gloucester Street, London, WC1N 3XX. Prop: Michael R. Goss. Tel: (020) 8963-0979. Fax: (020) 8963-0502. Web: www.delectusbooks.co.uk. E-mail: mgdelectus@aol.com. Est: 1987. Private premises. Internet and postal. Stock: very large. Spec: Academic/Scholarly; Aesthetic Movement; Anthropology; Astrology; Authors:- Blackwood, A.; Huysmans, J.K.; Machen, Arthur; Countries - Ireland. PR: £20–5,000. CC: E; JCB; MC; V; SW, So. Corresp: French, German, Spanish, Dutch. VAT No: GB 532 3080 82. [Updated]

David Drummond at Pleasures of, 11 Cecil Court, Charing Cross Road, London, WC2N 4EZ. Prop: David Drummond. Tel: (020) 7836-1142. Fax: (020) 7836-1142. E-mail: drummond@popt.fsnet.co.uk. Est: 1967. Open: **M:** 11:00–05:45; **S:** 11:00–02:30; Closed for lunch: 02:30–03:30. Spec: Children's; Circus; Illustrated; Magic & Conjuring; Performing Arts. PR: £10–500. Notes: also, juvenile illustrated. [Updated]

Need a web site?
Basic web sites from £220
for details visit
www.sheppardsworld.co.uk

Francis Edwards (London) Limit, ■ 13 Great Newport Street, Charing Cross Road, London, WC2H 7JA. Tel: (020) 7240 7279. Fax: (020) 7836-5977. Web: www.francisedwards.co.uk. E-mail: sales@femilitary.demon.co.uk. Shop open: **M:** 10:00–19:00; **T:** 10:00–19:00; **W:** 10:00–19:00; **Th:** 10:00–19:00; **F:** 10:00–19:00; **S:** 10:00–19:00. Stock: small. Spec: Architecture; Art; Aviation; Bindings; Economics; Folklore; History - General; Law - General. PR: £15–5,000. CC: AE; D; E; JCB; MC; V. Corresp: Spanish. Mem: ABA; PBFA; ILAB. VAT No: GB 594 2720 23. [Updated]

Fine Books Oriental Ltd., ■ 38 Museum Street, London, WC1A 1LP. Prop: Jeffrey Somers. Tel: (020) 7242-5288. Fax: (020) 7242-5344. Web: www.finebooks.demon.co.uk. E-mail: oriental@finebooks.demon.co.uk. Est: 1977. Shop open: **M:** 09:30–18:00; **T:** 09:30–18:00; **W:** 09:30–18:00; **Th:** 09:30–18:00; **F:** 09:30–18:00; **S:** 11:00–19:00. Stock: medium. Spec: Aviation; Canals/Inland Waterways; Cartoons; Countries - Asia; Countries - India; Countries - Japan; Psychic; Religion - Oriental. PR: £3–15,000. CC: AE; D; JCB; MC; V; SW, SOLO. Corresp: Japanese. Mem: PBFA. [Updated]

Gay's The Word, ■ 66 Marchmont Street, London, WC1N 1AB. Prop: Noncyp Ltd Tel: (020) 7278-7654. Web: www.gaystheword.co.uk. E-mail: sales@gaystheword.co.uk. Est: 1979. Shop open: **M:** 10:00–18:30; **T:** 10:00–18:30; **W:** 10:00–18:30; **Th:** 10:00–18:30; **F:** 10:00–18:30; **S:** 10:00–18:30; **Su:** 14:00–18:30. Spec: Homosexuality & Lesbianism; New Books. PR: £1–60. CC: AE; D; E; JCB; MC; V; Switch. Cata: quarterly. Notes: Also, new books. [Updated]

Gekoski Booksellers, ■ Pied Bull Yard, 15a Bloomsbury Square, London, WC1A 2LP. Prop: R.A. Gekoski, P.A. Grogan & J.A.M. Irvine Tel: (020) 7404-6676. Fax: (020) 7404-6595. Web: www.gekoski.com. E-mail: rick@gekoski.com. Est: 1982. Shop open: **M:** 10:00–17:30; **T:** 10:00–17:30; **W:** 10:00–17:30; **Th:** 10:00–17:30; **F:** 10:00–17:30. Stock: small. Spec: First Editions; Letters; Manuscripts. PR: £100–1,000. CC: MC; V. Mem: ABA. VAT No: GB 418 5464 40. [Updated]

Grosvenor Prints, 19 Shelton Street, London, WC2H 9JN. Nigel Talbot. Tel: 020 7836 1979. Fax: 020 7379 6695. Web: www.grosvenorprints.com. E-mail: grosvenorprints@btinternet.com. Est: 1979. Shop and/or gallery. Open: **M:** 10:00–18:00; **T:** 10:00–18:00; **W:** 10:00–18:00; **Th:** 10:00–18:00; **F:** 10:00–18:00; **S:** 11:00–16:00. Spec: Animals and Birds; Art Reference; Fine Art; Painting; Printing. CC: AE; MC; V; Maestro/Switch. Mem: ABA; BA; ILAB. Cata: occasionally. VAT No: GB 217 6907 49. [Updated]

Jarndyce Antiquarian Bookselle, 46 Great Russell Street, (opp. British Museum), London, WC1B 3PA. Brian Lake & Janet Nassau. Tel: (020) 7631-4220. Fax: (020) 7631-1882. Web: www.jarndyce.co.uk. E-mail: books@jarndyce.co.uk. Est: 1969. Shop and/or showroom; Internet and postal. Open: **M:** 10:30–17:30; **T:** 10:30–17:30; **W:** 10:30–17:30; **Th:** 10:30–17:30; **F:** 10:30–17:30. Stock: large. Spec: Antiquarian; Authors:- Austen, Jane; Byron, Lord; Dickens, Charles; Economics; Education & School; First Editions; Literature. PR: £5–5,000. CC: AE; MC; V. Corresp: French. Mem: ABA; PBFA; ILAB; BBA. Notes: valuations and book search within our specialist areas. VAT No: GB 524 0890 57. [Updated]

Judd Books, ■ 82 Marchmont Street, London, WC1N 1AG. Prop: Nigel Kemp & A. Donaldson. Tel: (020) 7387-5333. E-mail: hb@juddbooks.demon.co.uk. Est: 1995. Shop open: **M:** 11:00–19:00; **T:** 11:00–19:00; **W:** 11:00–19:00; **Th:** 11:00–19:00; **F:** 11:00–19:00; **S:** 11:00–19:00; **Su:** 11:00–18:00. Stock: large. Spec: Architecture; Art; Cinema/Film; Drama; Feminism; History - General; Homosexuality & Lesbianism; Interior Design. PR: £1–100. CC: AE; E; MC; V. Corresp: French, Spanish. [Updated]

The Maghreb Bookshop, ■ 45 Burton Street, London, WC1H 9AL. Prop: Mohamed Ben Madani. Tel: (020) 7388-1840. Fax: (020) 7388-1840. Web: www.maghreview.com. E-mail: maghreb@maghrebreview.com. Est: 1981. Shop open: **M:** 09:00–18:00; **T:** 09:00–18:00; **W:** 08:00–18:00; **Th:** 09:00–18:00; **F:** 09:00–18:00; **S:** 09:00–18:00. Spec: Academic/Scholarly; Anthropology; Archaeology; Architecture; Authors - Women; Colonial; Countries - Middle East, The; Countries - North Africa. Corresp: Arabic, French. VAT No: GB 735 8794 81. [Updated]

Marchpane, ■ 16 Cecil Court, Charing Cross Road, London, WC2N 4HE. Prop: Kenneth R. Fuller. Tel: (020) 7836-8661. Fax: (020) 7497-0567. Web: www.marchpane.com. E-mail: K_Fuller@btclick.com. Est: 1989. Shop open: **M:** 11:00–18:00; **T:** 11:00–18:00; **W:** 11:00–18:00; **Th:** 11:00–18:00; **F:** 11:00–18:00; **S:** 11:00–18:00. Spec: Author - Carroll, Lewis; Children's; Illustrated; Punk Fanzines; War - WWII Home Front UK (1939-45). PR: £1–2,000. CC: AE; E; JCB; MC; V. Cata: occasionally. Debit. Cata: occasionnally. Mem: ABA; PBFA; ILAB. [Updated]

Tim Bryars Ltd, ■ 8 Cecil Court, London, WC2N 4HE. Prop: Tim Bryars. Tel: (020) 7836-1901. Fax: (020) 7836-1910. Web: www.timbryars.co.uk. E-mail: tim@timbryars.co.uk. Est: 2004. Shop open: **M:** 11:00–18:00; **T:** 11:00–18:00; **W:** 11:00–18:00; **Th:** 11:00–18:00; **F:** 11:00–18:00; **S:** 12:00–17:00. Stock: very large. Spec: Atlases; Cartography; Classical Studies; Early Imprints; Fine & Rare; Natural History; Topography - General. PR: £10–30,000. CC: MC; V. Mem: ABA; ILAB; IAMA. VAT No: GB 839 6884 58. [Updated]

Pholiota Books, 179 Kings Cross Road, London, WC1X 9BZ. Prop: Josephine Bacon. Tel: (020) 7278-9490. Fax: (020) 7278-2447. Web: www.pholiota.cc. E-mail: bacon@pholiota.cc. Est: 1996. Storeroom. Internet and postal. Telephone first. Open: **M:** 09:09–18:18. Stock: medium. Spec: Academic/Scholarly; Botany; Cookery/Gastronomy; Languages - Foreign; Literature in Translation; Travel - Middle East; Wine; Ephemera. PR: £1–60. Corresp: French, Hebrew, Russian, German, Italian, Spanish. Mem: ATA, ITI. Notes: translations to and from any language. VAT No: GB 778 0611 12. [Updated]

Photo Books International, ■ 99 Judd Street, London, WC1H 9NE. Prop: Bill Herbert & Jasper Howard. Tel: (020) 7813-7363. Fax: (020) 7813-7363. Web: www.pbi-books.com. E-mail: pbi@britishlibrary.net. Est: 1998. Internet and postal. Shop open:**W:** 11:00–18:00; **Th:** 11:00–18:00; **F:** 11:00–18:00; **S:** 11:00–18:00. Stock: medium. Spec: Photography. PR: £5–200. CC: AE; MC; V. Mem: PBFA; BA. VAT No: GB 730 6914 40. [Updated]

Henry Pordes Books Ltd., ■ 58-60 Charing Cross Road, London, WC2H 0BB. Prop: Gino Della–Ragione. Tel: (020) 7836 9031. Fax: (020) 7240 4232. Web: www.henrypordesbooks.com. E-mail: info@henrypordesbooks.com. Est: 1980. Shop open: **M:** 10:00–19:00; **T:** 10:00–19:00; **W:** 10:00–19:00; **Th:** 10:00–19:00; **F:** 10:00–19:00; **S:** 10:00–23:00; **Su:** 13:00–18:00. Spec: Academic/Scholarly; Advertising; Aeronautics; Africana; Antiques; Archaeology; Architecture; Art. PR: £1–2,000. CC: AE; MC; V. Mem: PBFA. [23/12/2004]

Arthur Probsthain, ■ 41 Great Russell Street, London, WC1B 3PE. Prop: Arthur Probsthain. Tel: (020) 7636-1096. Fax: (020) 7636-1096. E-mail: ap@oriental-african-books.com. Est: 1902. Shop open: **M:** 09:30–17:30; **T:** 09:30–17:30; **W:** 09:30–17:30; **Th:** 09:30–17:30; **F:** 09:30–17:30; **S:** 11:00–16:00. Spec: Countries - Africa; Oriental. CC: AE; D; E; JCB; MC; V. Cata: quarterly on specialised subjects. [Updated]

Quinto of Charing Cross Road, ■ 48a Charing Cross Road, London, WC2H 0BB. Prop: Hay Cinema Bookshop Ltd Tel: (0207) 379 7669. Fax: (0207) 836-5977. Web: www.haycinemabookshop.co.uk. E-mail: sales@femilitary.demon.co.uk. Est: 1905. Shop open: **M:** 09:00–21:00; **T:** 09:00–21:00; **W:** 09:00–21:00; **Th:** 09:00–21:00; **F:** 09:00–21:00; **S:** 09:00–21:00; **Su:** 12:00–08:00. Stock: very large. Spec: Art; Fiction - General; History - General; Literature; Medicine; Military History; Music - General; Philosophy. PR: £1–100. CC: AE; D; E; JCB; MC; V. Corresp: Spanish. VAT No: GB 594 2720 23. [Updated]

Quinto of Great Russell Street, ■ 63 Great Russell Street, London, WC1B 3BF. Tel: (0207) 430 2535. Fax: (0207) 430 2566. Web: www.haycinemabookshop.co.uk. E-mail: sales@quintogrs.co.uk. Est: 2002. Shop open: **M:** 10:00–19:00; **T:** 10:00–19:00; **W:** 10:00–19:00; **Th:** 10:00–19:00; **F:** 10:00–19:00; **S:** 10:00–19:00; **Su:** 10:00–19:00. Stock: very large. Spec: Art; Fiction - General; History - General; Literature; Medicine; Military; Music - General; Natural History. PR: £5–1,000. CC: AE; D; E; JCB; MC; V. Corresp: Spanish. VAT No: GB 594 2720 23. [Updated]

Omega Bookshop, ■ 27 Cecil Court, London, WC2N 4EZ. Prop: Angus O'Neill. Tel: (020) 7836-3336. Web: www.omegabookshop.com. E-mail: angus@omegabookshop.com. Est: 2005. Shop. Internet and postal. Open: **M:** 10:00–18:00; **T:** 10:00–18:00; **W:** 10:00–18:00; **Th:** 10:00–18:00; **F:** 10:00–18:00; **S:** 10:00–17:00. Spec: Antiques; Applied Art; Architecture; Art; Illustrated; Literature; Modern First Editions. CC: E; MC; V. Mem: ABA; ILAB. Notes: valuations. [Updated]

Roe and Moore, ■ 29 Museum Street, London, WC1A 1LH. Prop: Anthony and Deana Roe. Tel: (020) 7636 4787. E-mail: roeandmoore@fsbdial.co.uk. Est: 1992. Shop open: **M:** 10:30–18:00; **T:** 10:30–18:00; **W:** 10:30–18:00; **Th:** 10:30–18:00; **F:** 10:30–18:00; **S:** 10:30–18:00. Stock: medium. Spec: Art; Art Reference; Artists; Children's; Design; Fine Art; Illustrated; Juvenile. PR: £1–3,000. CC: MC; V. [Updated]

Spink & Son Limited, 69 Southampton Row, Bloomsbury, London, WC1B 4ET. Tel: (020) 7563-4000. Fax: (020) 7563-4068. Web: www.spink-online.com. E-mail: info@spink.com. Est: 1666. Shop and/or gallery. Open: **M:** 09:30–17:30; **T:** 09:30–17:30; **W:** 09:30–17:30; **Th:** 09:30–17:30; **F:** 09:30–17:30. Stock: medium. Spec: Military; Numismatics; Philately. PR: £1–5,000. CC: AE; D; E; JCB; MC; V. [Updated]

Tindley & Chapman, ■ 4 Cecil Court, London, WC2N 4HE. Prop: James Tindley, Ron Chapman. Tel: (0207) 240-2161. Fax: (0207) 379-1062. Est: 1975. Shop open: **M:** 10:00–17:30; **T:** 10:00–17:30; **W:** 10:00–17:30; **Th:** 10:00–17:30; **F:** 10:00–17:30; **S:** 11:00–17:00. Stock: medium. Spec: Fiction - General; Fiction - Crime, Detective, Spy, Thrillers; Fiction - Women; First Editions; Literature; Poetry. PR: £10–5,000. CC: MC; V. Mem: PBFA. Notes: see Ron Chapman, London SW10 9LW (q.v.). [Updated]

Travis & Emery Music Bookshop, ■ 17 Cecil Court, off Charing Cross Road, London, WC2N 4EZ. Tel: (020) 7240-2129. Fax: (020) 7497-0790. Web: www.travis-and-emery.com. E-mail: shepenq@travis-and-emery.com. Est: 1960. Shop open: **M:** 10:15–18:45; **T:** 10:15–18:45; **W:** 10:15–18:45; **Th:** 10:15–18:45; **F:** 10:15–18:45; **S:** 10:15–18:45; **Su:** 11:30–17:30; Closed for lunch: 14:00–14:45. Stock: very large. Spec: Bell-Ringing (Campanology); Bibliography; Music - General; Music - Classical; Music - Composers; Music - Folk & Irish Folk; Music - Jazz & Blues; Music - Music Hall. PR: £0–5,000. CC: MC; V. Mem: ABA; PBFA; ILAB. Notes: also, secondhand sheet music & new music books, plus prints VAT No: GB 239 5258 39. [Updated]

Ulysses, ■ 40 Museum Street, London, WC1 1LU. Prop: Peter Jolliffe. Tel: (020) 7831-1600. E-mail: ulyssesbooks@fsbdial.co.uk. Est: 1990. Shop open: **M:** 10:30–18:00; **T:** 10:30–18:00; **W:** 10:30–18:00; **Th:** 10:30–18:00; **F:** 10:30–18:00; **S:** 10:30–18:00. Stock: large. Spec: Illustrated; Modern First Editions. PR: £5–1,000. CC: AE; MC; V. Mem: ABA; PBFA. [Updated]

Waterstone's, ■ 82 Gower Street, London, WC1E 6EQ. Prop: HMV Media Group. Tel: (020) 7636-1577. Fax: (020) 7580-7680. Web: www.waterstones.co.uk/gowerst. E-mail: secondhand@gowerst.waterstones.co.uk. Est: 1936. Shop open: **M:** 09:30–20:00; **T:** 10:00–20:00; **W:** 09:30–20:00; **Th:** 09:30–20:00; **F:** 09:30–20:00; **S:** 09:30–19:00; **Su:** 12:00–18:00. Stock: medium. Spec: Academic/Scholarly. CC: AE; D; MC; V. Notes: Dept. also sells academic remainders and is situated within large, well-known bookshop. [Updated]

Watkins Books Ltd., ■ 19–21 Cecil Court, off Charing Cross Road, London, WC2N 4EZ. Tel: (020) 7836-2182. Fax: (020) 7836-6700. Web: www.watkinsbooks.com. E-mail: service@watkinsbooks.com. Est: 1894. Shop open: **M:** 11:00–19:00; **T:** 11:00–19:00; **W:** 11:00–19:00; **Th:** 11:00–19:00; **F:** 11:00–19:00; **S:** 11:00–19:00. Stock: large. Spec: Esoteric; Mind, Body & Spirit; Mythology; Occult. PR: £50–500. CC: MC; V; Sw. [Updated]

Wildy & Sons Ltd, ■ Lincoln's Inn Archway, Carey Street, London, WC2A 2JD. Prop: John Sinkins. Tel: 02072425778. Fax: 02074300897. Web: www.wildy.co.uk. E-mail: info@wildy.co.uk. Est: 1830. Shop open: **M:** 09:00–18:00; **T:** 09:00–18:00; **W:** 09:00–18:00; **Th:** 09:00–18:00; **F:** 09:00–18:00. Spec: Law - General; Law - Constitutional. CC: AE; D; MC; V. Cata: monthly on Law. Notes: Exclusively sell law books and sets, new and secondhand (including antiquarian) VAT No: GB 233 5262 84. [Updated]

Nigel Williams Rare Books, ■ 25 Cecil Court, Charing Cross Road, London, WC2N 4EZ. Tel: (020) 7836-7757. Fax: (020) 7379-5918. Web: www.nigelwilliams.com. E-mail: sales@nigelwilliams.com. Est: 1989. Internet and postal. Shop open: **M:** 10:00–18:00; **T:** 10:00–18:00; **W:** 10:00–18:00; **Th:** 10:00–18:00; **F:** 10:00–18:00; **S:** 10:00–18:00. Stock: large. Spec: Authors: - Christie, Agatha; Fleming, Ian; Greene, Graham; Joyce, James; Wodehouse, P.G.; Fables; Fiction - General; Fiction - Historical. PR: £5–10,000. CC: AE; D; E; JCB; MC; V. Mem: ABA; PBFA; ILAB. VAT No: GB 574 3776 05. [Updated]

LONDON
GREATER LONDON OUTER

CARSHALTON

Crosby Nethercott Books, 16 Kings Avenue, Carshalton, Surrey, SM5 4NX. (*) Prop: D.W. Beer. Tel: (020) 8643 4124. E-mail: crosbybooks@cwcom.net. Est: 1991. Private premises. Internet and postal. Appointment necessary. Stock: small. Spec: Author - Rolt, L.T.C.; Canals/Inland Waterways; Company History; History - Industrial; Railways. PR: £5–100. Corresp: French, German. Notes: Also, a booksearch service. [Updated]

Croydon Bookshop, ■ 304 Carshalton Road, Carshalton, London, SM5 3QB. Prop: Mrs. P.F. Reding & P.J. Rogers. Tel: (020) 8643-6857. Est: 1954. Shop open: **T:** 10:30–17:30; **W:** 10:30–17:30; **Th:** 10:30–17:30; **F:** 10:30–17:30; **S:** 10:30–17:30. Stock: medium. PR: £2–100. Corresp: French, German, Spanish. [Updated]

CROYDON

Steve Archer, 11 Bedford Place, Croydon, Surrey, CR0 2BS. (*). Tel: (020) 8686 3736. Web: www.ukbookworld.com/members/stevearcher. E-mail: stevearcher2000@yahoo.co.uk. Est: 2000. Private premises. Internet and postal. Stock: small. Spec: Autobiography; Biography; Canals/Inland Waterways; Literary Travel; Literature; Modern First Editions; Booksearch. PR: £2–200. CC: PayPal. [Updated]

EASTCOTE

The Eastcote Bookshop, ■ 156/160 Field End Road, Eastcote, Middlesex, HA5 1RH. Prop: Eileen & David May. Tel: (020) 8866-9888. Fax: (020) 8905-9387. Est: 1993. Shop open: **T:** 12:00–16:00; **Th:** 12:00–16:00; **F:** 12:00–16:00; **S:** 10:00–17:00. Stock: very large. Spec: Alpinism/Mountaineering; American Indians; Annuals; Antiques; Art; Canals/Inland Waterways; Children's; Cinema/Film. PR: £2–500. CC: MC; V. Mem: PBFA. Notes: occasional fairs. [Updated]

EDGWARE

Two Jays Bookshop, ■ 119 High Street, Edgware, HA8 7DB. Prop: Joyce and Mark Matthews. Tel: (020) 8952-1349. Est: 1977. Shop open: **T:** 09:00–17:00; **W:** 09:00–17:00; **Th:** 09:00–17:00; **F:** 09:00–17:00; **S:** 09:00–17:00. Stock: large. PR: £2–100. [Updated]

ENFIELD

Terence J. McGee, 20 Slades Close, Enfield, Middlesex, EN2 7EB. Prop: T.J. & J.I. McGee. Tel: (020) 8366-5727. E-mail: tmcgee@globalnet.co.uk. Est: 1972. Private premises. Appointment necessary. Open: **S:** 09:00–19:00; **Su:** 09:00–19:00. Stock: small. Spec: Author - Betjeman, Sir John; Cinema/Film; Comics; Counterculture; Countries - Italy; Education & School; Music - General; Music - Music Hall. PR: £1–500. Corresp: French, German, Italian, Spanish. Mem: Brit. Ephemera Society. Notes: also, sound recordings & record tapes (inc. 16s, 33s, 45s,78s and CDs) [Updated]

Felicity J. Warnes, ■ 82 Merryhills Drive, Enfield, Middlesex, EN2 7PD. Prop: F. J. Warnes. Tel: (020) 8367-1661. Fax: (020) 8372-1035. E-mail: felicity@fjwarnes.u-net.com. Est: 1978. Shop. Appointment necessary. Stock: large. Spec: Embroidery; Fashion & Costume; Jewellery; Knitting; Lace; Military; Social History; Textiles. PR: £5–200. CC: MC; V. Mem: PBFA; ES. [Updated]

GREENFORD

Jack Ben–Nathan, 22 Teignmouth Gardens, Perivale, Greenford, UB6 8BX. (*). Tel: (020) 8997-6574. E-mail: jack.ben-nathan@the-sun.co.uk. Est: 1980. Private premises. Appointment necessary. Open: Stock: very small. Spec: Sport - Billiards/Snooker/Pool; Booksearch. PR: £3–300. [Updated]

Books B.C., 58 Elton Avenue, Greenford, Middlesex, UB6 0PP. Prop: Martin McCrory. Tel: (020) 8864-0580. Est: 1987. Private premises. Postal only. Appointment necessary. Stock: very small. Spec: Archaeology; Egyptology; Fiction - Fantasy, Horror; Fiction - Science Fiction; History - Ancient. PR: £1–500. [Updated]

HAMPTON HILL

Bates Books, 95 High Street, Hampton Hill, Middlesex, TW12 1NH. Prop: Garry and Jackie Bates. Tel: (020) 8941-6782. E-mail: gbates@dsl.pipex.com. Est: 2002. Private premises. Postal only. Telephone first. Stock: small. Spec: Children's; First Editions; Illustrated. PR: £2–30. [Updated]

HAMPTON

R. W. Clements, 114 High Street, Hampton, Middlesex, TW12 2ST. Prop: R. W. Clements. Tel: (020) 8979-3069. Est: 1992. Private premises. Appointment necessary. Stock: large. Spec: Archaeology; Art; Autobiography; Biography; Children's; Drama; Fiction - General; History - General. PR: £5–1,000. Notes: all speciality subjects shown relate to Ireland. Also, ephemera and prints related to Ireland [Updated]

R. S. & P. A. Scowen, 9 Birchwood Grove, Hampton, TW12 3DU. Prop: Roger Scowen. Tel: +44 (0) 20 8979 7429. E-mail: patscowen@waitrose.com. Est: 1987. Private premises. Internet and postal. Appointment necessary. Open: **M:** 09:00–17:30; **T:** 09:00–17:30; **W:** 09:00–17:30; **Th:** 09:00–17:30; **F:** 09:00–17:30; **S:** 09:00–17:30; **Su:** 09:00–17:30; Closed for lunch: 13:00–14:00. Spec: Bridge; Chess; Games; Sport - Billiards/Snooker/Pool. Notes: we specialise in indoor games of skill, for example: chess, bridge, draughts, checkers, snooker, billiards. [Updated]

HARROW

medievalbookshop, 118 Vaughan Road, West Harrow, Harrow, Middlesex, HA1 4ED. Prop: Nick Gorman. Tel: (07950) 147504. Web: www.medievalbookshop.co.uk. E-mail: admin@medievalbookshop.co.uk. Est: 2001. Private premises. Internet and postal. Stock: small. Spec: Academic/Scholarly; Archaeology; History - Middle Ages; History - Renaissance, The; Medieval; Religion - General. PR: £1–200. CC: PayPal. [Updated]

HAYES

The Churchill Book Specialist, 25a Station Road, Hayes, UB3 4BD. Prop: Mark Weber. Tel: (020) 8573-6370. Web: www.wscbooks.com. E-mail: mark@wscbooks.com. Est: 1987. Private premises. Internet and postal. Appointment necessary. Stock: medium. Spec: Author - Churchill, Sir Winston; Military; War - World War I; War - World War II; Ephemera. PR: £5–10,000. CC: MC; V. Mem: ABA. Notes: send mail to PO Box 90689, Tucson, AZ 85752 USA. [21/12/2004]

ILFORD (SEE ALSO UNDER ESSEX)

Porcupine Books, 37 Coventry Road, Ilford, Essex, IG1 4QR. (*) Prop: Brian Ameringen. Tel: (0208) 554-3799. Web: www.porcupine.demon.co.uk. E-mail: brian@porcupine.demon.co.uk. Est: 1998. Private premises. Internet and postal. Appointment necessary. Open: **M:** 08:00–21:00; **T:** 08:00–21:00; **W:** 18:00–21:00; **Th:** 18:00–21:00; **F:** 20:00–21:00; **S:** 18:00–21:00; **Su:** 08:00–21:00. Stock: medium. Spec: Fiction - Crime, Detective, Spy, Thrillers; Fiction - Fantasy, Horror; Fiction - Science Fiction. PR: £1–2,500. [Updated]

ISLEWORTH

Chaters Motoring Booksellers, ■ 8 South Street, Isleworth, Middlesex, TW7 7DH. Prop: C. Stroud. Tel: (020) 8568-9750. Fax: (020) 8569-8273. Web: www.chaters.co.uk. E-mail: books@chaters.co.uk. Est: 1957. Shop open: **M:** 09:00–17:30; **T:** 09:00–17:30; **W:** 09:00–17:30; **Th:** 09:00–17:30; **F:** 09:00–17:30; **S:** 10:00–17:00. Spec: Motorbikes / motorcycles; Motoring; New Books. PR: £1–500. CC: JCB; MC; V; plus Debit Cata: b-annually. Mem: BA. Notes: also, new books in specialities & a booksearch service. [Updated]

KENLEY

David & Lynn Smith, The Hermitage, 21 Uplands Road, Kenley, Surrey, CR8 5EE. Tel: (020) 8660-9908. Fax: (020) 8660-9908. E-mail: smithbookskenley@tiscali.co.uk. Est: 1980. Storeroom. Appointment necessary. Stock: small. Spec: Biology; Medicine; Medicine - History of; Pharmacy/Pharmacology; Science - General; Science - History of; Scientific Instruments. PR: £10–500. CC: JCB; MC; V. Mem: PBFA. [Updated]

KEW

Criterion Books, 6 Nylands Avenue, Kew, Richmond, TW9 4HH. Prop: Terence Crimmings. Tel: (020) 8876-1773. Fax: (020) 8876-1773. E-mail: terry.crimmings@tinyworld.co.uk. Est: 1992. Private premises. Postal only. Appointment necessary. Stock: very small. Spec: Author - Durrell, Lawrence; Biography; Horizon Writers; Illustrated; Literary Travel; Literature; Modern First Editions; Poetry. PR: £10–350. [Updated]

KINGSTON

Modern First Editions, 32 Woodlands Avenue, New Malden, Surrey, Kingston, KT3 3UQ. (*) Prop: Nicholas & Helen Burrows. Tel: (020) 8942-2677. Fax: (020) 8942-2679. E-mail: nick@burrbook.demon.co.uk. Est: 1993. Private premises. Internet and postal. Appointment necessary. Stock: small. Spec: Countries - Melanesia; Countries - Mexico; Fiction - General; Fiction - Science Fiction; First Editions; Limited Editions; Modern First Editions. PR: £5–500. CC: AE; MC; V. [Updated]

MORDEN

A. Burton–Garbett, 35 The Green, Morden, Surrey, SM4 4HJ. Tel: (020) 8540-2367. Fax: (020) 8540-4594. Est: 1959. Private premises. Appointment necessary. Stock: small. Spec: Countries - Caribbean, The; Countries - Central America; Countries - Mexico; Countries - South America. PR: £5–1,000. [Updated]

NEW BARNET

Chandos Books, 111 Park Road, New Barnet, Hertfordshire, EN4 9QR. Prop: Stan Brett. Tel: (020) 8449-9457. E-mail: stanbrett@f2s.com. Est: 1970. Private premises. Internet and postal. Appointment necessary. Stock: small. Spec: Bibliography; Humanities. PR: £10–300. Mem: PBFA. [Updated]

OSTERLEY

Osterley Bookshop, ■ 168a Thornbury Road, Osterley, Middlesex, TW7 4QE. Prop: Pennie Smith & Tony Vesely. Tel: (020) 8560-6206. E-mail: avesely@linconc.net. Est: 1973. Internet and postal. Open. Shop open: **M:** 09:30–17:30; **T:** 09:30–17:30; **W:** 09:30–17:30; **Th:** 09:30–17:30; **F:** 09:30–17:30; **S:** 09:30–17:30; **Su:** 09:30–17:30. Stock: medium. PR: £3–150. CC: AE; JCB; MC; V; Maestro. Notes: Large general stock. [Updated]

SUNBURY-ON-THAMES

Cecilia Marsden, 98 Manor Lane, Sunbury-on-Thames, TW16 6JB. Prop: Cecilia Marsden. Tel: 01932 785705. E-mail: mairob@tiscali.co.uk. Est: 1993. Private premises. Postal only. Appointment necessary. Spec: Fiction - Crime, Detective, Spy, Thrillers. [Updated]

SUTTON

Mike Park, 351 Sutton Common Road, Sutton, Surrey, SM3 9HZ. Prop: Mike Park & William To. Tel: (020) 8641-7796. Fax: (020) 8641-3330. E-mail: mikeparkbooks@aol.com. Est: 1974. Private premises. Appointment necessary. Open: **M:** 09:00–17:00; **T:** 09:00–17:00; **W:** 09:00–17:00; **Th:** 09:00–17:00; **F:** 09:00–17:00. Stock: small. Spec: Botany; Flower Arranging; Forestry; Gardening - General; Herbalism; Horticulture; Landscape; Natural History. PR: £1–1,000. CC: E; MC; V. Mem: PBFA. [Updated]

Searching for a title - and cannot find it on any Internet database?

Then try **www.sheppardsworld.co.uk**

Select dealers by book subject classification – then mail requests to selected dealers who may not have uploaded the title to any Internet Search database.

TEDDINGTON

Chris Hollingshead Horticulture, 10 Linden Grove, Teddington, TW11 8LT. (*). Tel: (0208) 977 6051. E-mail: c.hollingshead@btinternet.com. Est: 1995. Private premises. Open: **M:** 09:30–08:00; **T:** 09:30–18:00; **W:** 09:30–18:00; **Th:** 09:30–18:00; **F:** 09:30–18:00. Stock: small. Spec: Agriculture; Botany; Gardening - General; Herbalism; Horticulture; Landscape; Mycology; Natural History. PR: £5–3,000. CC: MC; V. Mem: PBFA. Notes: & garden history, design landscape and architecture; farming, botanical academic & antiquarian. [Updated]

TWICKENHAM

Books on Spain, P.O. Box 207, Twickenham, TW2 5BQ. (*) Prop: Keith Harris. Tel: (020) 8898-7789. Fax: (020) 8898-7789 (24 hours). E-mail: booksonspainplus@aol.com. Est: 1993. Private premises. Internet and postal. Stock: large. Spec: Antiquarian; Bull Fighting; Countries - Andorra; Countries - Central America; Countries - Cuba; Countries - Gibraltar; Countries - Latin America; Countries - Mexico. PR: £5–1,000. CC: AE; JCB; MC; V; Switch. Corresp: Spanish, Portuguese, French. Mem: PBFA. VAT No: GB 720 5623 63. [Updated]

Anthony C. Hall, Antiquarian Bookseller, ■ 30 Staines Road, Twickenham, TW2 5AH. Prop: Anthony C. Hall. Tel: (020) 8898-2638. Fax: (020) 8893-8855. Web: www.hallbooks.co.uk. E-mail: achallbooks@intonet.co.uk. Est: 1966. Shop open: **M:** 10:00–17:00; **Th:** 10:00–17:00; **F:** 10:00–17:00; Closed for lunch: 12:30–01:30. Stock: small. Spec: Countries - Africa; Countries - Asia; Countries - East Europe; Countries - Middle East, The; Countries - Russia; History - Industrial; Travel - Africa; Travel - Asia. PR: £10–1,000. CC: MC; V. Corresp: French, German, Russian, Spanish. Mem: ABA; PBFA. Notes: large specialist stock seen by appointment only. VAT No: GB 224 2699 61. [Updated]

John Ives Bookseller, 5 Normanhurst Drive, St. Margarets, Twickenham, TW1 1NA. (*). Tel: (020) 8892-6265. Fax: (020) 8744-3944. Web: www.ukbookworld.com/members/johnives. E-mail: jives@btconnect.com. Est: 1978. Private premises. Internet and postal. Appointment necessary. Stock: small. Spec: Antiques; Architecture; Art Reference; Ceramics; Collecting; Fashion & Costume; Jewellery; Needlework. PR: £5–500. CC: JCB; MC; V. Mem: PBFA. VAT No: GB 409 8526 30. [Updated]

Marble Hill Books, 35, Napoleon Road, St Margarets Twickenham, TW1 3EW. Prop: Philip Dawson. Tel: 020 8892 0511. Web: www.marblehillbooks.com. E-mail: info@marblehillbooks.com. Est: 1999. Mail Order Only. Internet and postal. Telephone first. Spec: American Indians; Antiquarian; Architecture; Author - 20th Century; Countries - Africa; Countries - Antarctic, The; Countries - Far East, The; Countries - Latin America. CC: AE; JCB; MC; V; Maestro/Switch. Cata: online/Internet0 – Modern First Editions; Antiquarian; General. Corresp: French; German. Notes: also at Title Page Book Fairs. [Updated]

John Prescott - The Bookseller, ■ Paul Hoffmann House, 57 York Street, Twickenham, TW1 3LP. Prop: John Prescott. Tel: (020) 8940-3066. E-mail: johnprescott@avdv.demon.co.uk. Est: 1998. Shop open: **F:** 10:30–18:00; **S:** 10:30–18:00. Stock: medium. Spec: Antiques; Archaeology; Architecture; Art; Art History; Cinema/Film; Countries - South America; Fables. PR: £1–100. Corresp: German, French, Spanish, Dutch. Notes: SHOP SALES ONLY. [Updated]

Stephen Miller, 19 Clifden Road, Twickenham, Middlesex, TW1 4LU. Tel: (020) 8892-0331. Est: 1981. Private premises. Stock: very small. Spec: Antiquarian. PR: £1–500. Corresp: French. [Updated]

WELLING

Falconwood Transport & Militar, ■ 5 Falconwood Parade, The Green, Welling, DA16 2PL. (*) Prop: A.M. Doran. Tel: (020) 8303-8291. Fax: (020) 8303-8291. E-mail: falconw@globalnet.co.uk. Est: 1985. Shop open: **Th:** 09:30–17:30; **F:** 09:30–17:30; **S:** 09:30–17:30. Stock: medium. Spec: Aviation; Engineering; Maritime/Nautical; Military; Motorbikes / motorcycles; Motoring; Railways; Traction Engines. PR: £5–50. CC: E; JCB; MC; V. VAT No: GB 427 0309 76. [Updated]

MERSEYSIDE

BIRKENHEAD

Grange Old Bookshop, ■ 32 Oxton Road, Birkenhead, Wirral, CH41 2QT. Prop: Paul A. Dearden. Tel: 0151 653 3090. Est: 1992. Shop open: **T:** 11:30–17:30; **W:** 11:30–17:30; **Th:** 11:30–17:30; **F:** 11:30–17:30; **S:** 11:30–17:30. Notes: also sells postcards. [Updated]

CROSBY

Ahbooks, 12 College Green Road, Crosby, Crosby, L23 3DR. Prop: Andrew Harty. Tel: 0151 284 4446 (M. 0785 1128145). Web: www.ahbooks.co.uk. E-mail: ah_books@yahoo.co.uk. Est: 2000. Storeroom. Internet and postal. Appointment necessary. Shop At: Unit 5 Parrs Corner Marsh Lane/Stanley Rd, Bootle, L20. Spec: Fiction - General; Modern First Editions. CC: PayPal. Notes: also at: Unit 5 Parrs Corner, Marsh Lane/Stanley Rd, Bootle, L20. VAT No: GB 867 1615 04. [Updated]

LIVERPOOL

Black Voices, 2, Saville Road, Liverpool, L13 4DP. T. Aitman. Tel: (0151) 475 2936. E-mail: tonyaitman@blackvoices.freeserve.co.uk. Est: 1992. Private premises. Internet and postal. Appointment necessary. Open: Stock: very small. Spec: Africana; Black Studies; Booksearch. PR: £3–2,000. Notes: also booksearches in specialist subjects. [Updated]

Hylton Booksearch, 23 Chelsea Court, West Derby, Liverpool, L12 6RS. Prop: Mr. R.A. Hylton. Tel: (0151) 259-5163. Web: www.rahylton@btinternet.com. E-mail: hylton.booksearch@btinternet.com. Est: 1992. Private premises. Postal only. Appointment necessary. Stock: very small. Spec: Author - General; Modern First Editions; Booksearch. PR: £5–500. CC: V; PayPal. Notes: also trade as "liverpoolbooqshop" on Amazon Internet Site. [Updated]

Modern Welsh Publications Ltd., 32 Garth Drive, Liverpool, L18 6HW. Prop: Professor D. Ben Rees. Tel: (0151) 724 1989. Fax: (0151) 724-5691. E-mail: ben@garthdrive.fsnet.co.uk. Est: 1962. Private premises. Postal only. Stock: medium. Spec: Countries - Wales; History - General; Literature in Translation; Politics; Theology; Ephemera. Corresp: Welsh. [Updated]

Reid of Liverpool, ■ 105 Mount Pleasant, Liverpool, L3 5TB. Prop: Gerard Fitzpatrick. Tel: (0151) 709-2312. E-mail: liverpoolbooks@btconnet.com. Est: 1980. Shop open: **M:** 10:30–17:30; **T:** 10:30–17:30; **W:** 10:30–17:30; **Th:** 10:30–17:30; **F:** 10:30–17:30; **S:** 10:30–17:30. Stock: very large. Spec: Academic/Scholarly; Culture - Popular; Esoteric; Fiction - General; Mind, Body & Spirit; Mysticism; Odd & Unusual; Psychology/Psychiatry. PR: £1–1,000. [Updated]

PRENTON

Thin Read Line, 11 St. Andrews Road, Prenton, CH43 1TB. Tel: 0151 652 4483. Fax: 0151 652 4483. E-mail: richmond_dutton@hotmail.com. Est: 1995. Private premises. Postal only. Contactable. Open: **M:** 09:00–17:30; **T:** 09:00–17:30; **W:** 09:00–17:30; **Th:** 09:00–17:30; **F:** 09:00–17:30; **S:** 09:00–17:30; **Su:** 09:00–17:30; Closed for lunch: 13:00–14:00. Spec: Aeronautics; Africana; Agriculture; Aircraft; Animals and Birds; Antiques; Arms & Armour; Army, The. [Updated]

PRESCOT

Nostalgia Unlimited, 19 Dunbeath Avenue, Rainhill, Prescot, L35 0QH. Tel: (0151) 426-2046. Est: 1988. Private premises. Postal only. Stock: small. Spec: Christmas; Collecting; Comic Books & Annuals; Comics; Magazines & Periodicals - General; Newspapers; Nostalgia. PR: £1–35. [Updated]

SOUTHPORT

Broadhurst of Southport Ltd., ■ 5 & 7 Market Street, Southport, PR8 1HD. Prop: Laurens R. Hardman. Tel: (01704) 532064 & 534. Fax: (01704) 542009. Web: www.ckbroadhurst.com. E-mail: litereria@aol.com. Est: 1926. Shop open: **M:** 09:00–17:30; **T:** 09:00–17:30; **W:** 09:00–17:30; **Th:** 09:00–17:30; **F:** 09:00–17:30; **S:** 09:00–17:30. Stock: very large. Spec: Architecture; Art; Bibliography; Biography; Children's; Fiction - General; Fine & Rare; History - General. PR: £5–10. CC: MC; V. Corresp: French. Mem: ABA; PBFA; BA; ILAB. Notes: also, bookbinding & restoration service, new books on all subjects & a booksearch service. [Updated]

Cover to Cover, 252 Balmoral Drive, Southport, PR9 8QA. Prop: Arthur Reeve. Tel: (01704) 231443. Web: www.covers.freeuk.com. E-mail: covers@freeuk.com. Est: 1996. Private premises. Internet and postal. Telephone first. Spec: Applied Art; Architecture; Art; Ceramics; Cinema/Film; Circus; Crafts; Crochet. PR: £1–300. [Updated]

Kernaghans, ■ 57–65 Wayfarers Arcade, Lord Street, Southport, PR8 1NT. Prop: Alwyn & Bryan Kernaghan. Tel: (01704) 546329. Fax: (01704) 546329. E-mail: kernaghanbooks@hotmail.com. Est: 1972. Shop open: **M:** 10:00–17:00; **T:** 10:00–17:00; **W:** 10:00–17:00; **Th:** 10:00–17:00; **F:** 10:00–17:00; **S:** 10:00–17:00. Stock: very large. Spec: Countries - Ireland; Fine & Rare; Irish Interest; Natural History; Pop-Up, Movable & Cut Out; Religion - Christian; Theology; Topography - Local. PR: £5–5,000. CC: AE; MC; V. Mem: PBFA. [Updated]

Don Mulyan, 48 Clairville, Lulworth Road, Southport, PR8 2FA. Prop: Don Mulyan. Tel: (01704) 568429. Fax: (01704) 568429. E-mail: donmulyan@onetel.com. Est: 1970. Private premises. Appointment necessary. Open: **M:** 10:00–20:00; **T:** 10:00–20:00; **W:** 10:00–20:00; **Th:** 10:00–20:00; **F:** 10:00–20:00; **S:** 10:00–20:00. Stock: very small. Spec: Countries - Isle of Man; Countries - Norway; Topography - Local. Notes: specialist in Norway pre 1940. [Updated]

Parkinsons Books, ■ In Parkinson's Ginnel, 359-363 Lord Street, Southport, PR8 1NH. Tel: 01704-547016. Web: www.parki.com. E-mail: sheppards@parki.com. Shop open: **M:** 10:00–17:00; **T:** 10:00–17:00; **W:** 10:00–17:00; **Th:** 10:00–17:00; **F:** 10:00–17:00; **S:** 10:00–17:00; **Su:** 13:00–17:00. Spec: Biology; Botany; Chemistry; History - General; History of Ideas; Languages - Foreign; Linguistics; Literary Criticism. CC: AE; JCB; MC; V; Most major cards. Notes: we occupy three floors on the main shopping street, between Monsoon & Lakeland. The stock is is well classified, with a leaning towards the academic. We also sell coins, antiquities, tropical shells, fossils, mineral specimens & crystals. [Updated]

Rosemary Books, 27 Cedar Street, Southport, PR8 6NQ. Prop: Eileen M. Golborn. Tel: (01704) 542134. Est: 1985. Private premises. Appointment necessary. Stock: very small. Spec: Books about Books; Children's; Fiction - General; First Editions; Juvenile; Poetry; Religion - Christian; Collectables. [Updated]

ST. HELENS

V. & C. Finn, 6 Knowsley View, Rainford, St. Helens, WA11 8SN. Tel: (01744) 883780. Est: 1992. Private premises. Appointment necessary. Stock: small. Spec: Folio Society, The. PR: £1–200. Notes: also, organiser of North West Book Fairs (see prelims). [Updated]

WIDEOPEN

Christopher Handley, 38 Beacon Drive, Wideopen, NE13 7HB. Tel: (0191) 2367759. E-mail: christopherhandley@cdsh2.fsnet.co.uk. Est: 1990. Private premises. Postal only. Stock: very small. Spec: Diaries. PR: £3–200. [Updated]

NORFOLK

AYLSHAM

Burebank Books, ■ 44, Red Lion Street, Aylsham, NR11 6ER. Prop: Roger M Crouch. Tel: 01263 735710. Fax: 01263 735703. E-mail: roger.crouch@freenet.co.uk. Est: 1993. Shop. Open: **M:** 10:00–17:00; **T:** 10:00–17:00; **W:** 10:00–17:00; **Th:** 10:00–17:00; **F:** 10:00–17:00; **S:** 09:00–17:00; Closed for lunch: 13:00–14:00. Spec: Archaeology; Countries - Japan; History - Local; Landscape; Maritime/Nautical. CC: MC; V; Solo, Switch. Corresp: Italian, Japanese. [Updated]

Mayhew Books, 8 Sears Close, Aylsham, NR11 6JB. Prop: John & Linda Mayhew. Tel: (01263) 731305. Est: 1989. Private premises. Postal only. Stock: very small. Spec: Booksearch. PR: £1–100. [Updated]

DEREHAM

Village Books, ■ 20a High Street, Dereham, NR19 1DR. Prop: Mr Jack James. Tel: (01362) 853066. Fax: (01362) 853066. E-mail: villagebkdereham@aol.com. Est: 1996. Shop open: **M:** 09:30–16:30; **T:** 09:30–16:30; **Th:** 09:30–16:30; **F:** 09:30–16:30; **S:** 09:00–16:00. Stock: very large. Spec: Art; History - General; Medicine; Military History. PR: £1–100. CC: PayPal. [23/12/2004]

DISS

Church Street Books, ■ 6 Church Street, Diss, IP22 4AD. Prop: Andy Vidion. Tel: 01379 652020. E-mail: atvidion@yahoo.co.uk. Est: 2005. Shop open: **M:** 10:00–17:30; **T:** 10:00–17:30; **Th:** 10:00–17:30; **F:** 10:00–17:30; **S:** 10:00–17:30; **Su:** 09:00–17:30. Spec: Alpinism/Mountaineering; Autobiography; Aviation; Counterculture; Dictionaries; Fiction - General; Free Thought; Guide Books. [Updated]

Riderless Horse Books, Oakfields, Redgrave Road, Blo Norton, Diss, IP22 2JA. (*) Prop: Richard B. Hamburger. Tel: (01379) 898481. Fax: +44 (0)870 912 1193. E-mail: riderlesshorse@clara.co.uk. Est: 1991. Private premises. Internet and postal. Appointment necessary. Stock: small. Spec: Author - Paul Bowles; First Editions; Literary Criticism; Literature; Literature in Translation; Magazines & Periodicals - General; Poetry. PR: £2–1,000. CC: MC; V. Cata: occasionally on Literature, Modern Poetry, First Editions. Corresp: French. Mem: PBFA. [Updated]

Michael Taylor Rare Books, Hoblins, One Eyed Lane, Weybread, Diss, IP21 5TT. Tel: (01379) 853889. Fax: (01379) 853889. E-mail: michael@hoblins.demon.co.uk. Est: 1984. Private premises. Appointment necessary. Stock: small. Spec: Bibliography; Calligraphy; Illustrated; Private Press; Typography. PR: £5–1,000. CC: MC; V. Mem: PBFA. [Updated]

DOWNHAM MARKET

Richard Everett, Sandfield House, 58 Lynn Road, Downham Market, PE38 9NN. Prop: Richard & Jenny Everett. Tel: (01366) 382074. Est: 1983. Office and/or bookroom. Appointment necessary. Stock: large. Spec: Children's; Illustrated; Publishers - Warnes; Topography - Local; Collectables. PR: £2–400. Mem: PBFA. Notes: also at: Southwold Antiques Centre, Suffolk (q.v.). [Updated]

EAST RUDHAM

Victor Sutcliffe, Mulberry Coach House, East Rudham, PE31 8RD. Prop: Victor Sutcliffe. Tel: (01485) 528463. Web: www.victorsutcliffe.demon.co.uk. E-mail: vhs@victorsutcliffe.demon.co.uk. Est: 1970. Private premises. Internet and postal. Appointment necessary. Stock: very small. Spec: Military History. PR: £15–5,000. CC: MC; V. [Updated]

FAKENHAM

The Dancing Goat Bookshop, ■ 5 Oak Street, Fakenham, NR21 9DX. Prop: Michael Goss. Tel: (01328) 855757. E-mail: dancinggoatbooks@talk21.com. Est: 1998. Shop open: **M:** 10:00–16:00; **T:** 10:00–16:00; **W:** 10:00–16:00; **Th:** 10:00–16:00; **F:** 10:00–16:00; **S:** 10:00–16:00. Stock: medium. Spec: American Indians; Americana; Folklore; Music - Folk & Irish Folk; Music - Popular; Music - Rock & Roll; Ornithology; Poetry. PR: £1–100. Notes: also a coffee shop (coffee, tea, home made cakes & light lunches). [Updated]

GORLESTON-ON-SEA

C. & J. Read - Gorleston Books, Unit 10, Longs Industrial Estate, Englands Lane, Gorleston-on-Sea, NR31 6NE. Prop: Cynthia & John Read. Tel: (01493) 656511. E-mail: jc@bookshop1.fsbusiness.co.uk. Est: 1993. Storeroom. Internet and postal. Telephone first. Stock: medium. Spec: Aeronautics; Collecting; Fashion & Costume; History - General; Maritime/Nautical; Military; Natural History; Rural Life. PR: £1–1,000. CC: AE; MC; V; Maestro. Mem: PBFA. [Updated]

GREAT ELLINGHAM

John Knowles, Brick Kiln Farm, Hingham Road, Great Ellingham, Nr. Attleborough, NR17 1JE. Prop: John Knowles. Tel: (01953) 452257. Fax: (01953) 452733. E-mail: enquire@johnknowlesbooks.com. Est: 1985. Private premises. Internet and postal. Appointment necessary. Stock: small. Spec: Marque Histories (see also motoring); Motorbikes / motorcycles; Motoring; Sport - Motor Racing; Transport. PR: £5–1,000. CC: E; JCB; MC; V; SW. Corresp: French, German. [Updated]

GREAT YARMOUTH

R.F. & C. Ward, 27 Kent Square, Great Yarmouth, NR30 2EX. Frank & Carol Ward. Tel: (01493) 856280. Fax: (01493) 853909. Web: www.ashbook.co.uk. E-mail: wardf@dsl.pipex.com. Est: 1985. Private premises. Postal only. Stock: very large. Spec: Fiction - General; Fiction - Crime, Detective, Spy, Thrillers; Fiction - Science Fiction; Fiction - Westerns; First Editions; War - General. PR: £1–500. CC: AE; JCB; MC; V. [Updated]

HARLESTON

Black Cat Books, Meadow Cottage, High Road, Wortwell, Harleston, IP20 0EN. Prop: Ann Morgan–Hughes. Tel: (01986) 788826. Fax: (01986) 788826. Web: www.blackcatbooks.co.uk. E-mail: ann@blackcatbooks.co.uk. Est: 1984. Office and/or bookroom. Telephone first. Stock: small. Spec: Colour-Plate; Cookery/Gastronomy; Courtesy; Embroidery; Etiquette; Fashion & Costume; Food & Drink; Hairdressing. PR: £10–2,000. CC: MC; V. Cata: occasionally. Corresp: French, German, Greek. Mem: ABA; PBFA; ILAB. Notes: Visitors are most welcome, but please telephone first to make sure I am at home and to ask for directions. VAT No: GB 446 3847 25. [Updated]

Riviera Books, ■ 9 Market Place, Harleston, IP20 9AD. Prop: David Chatten. Tel: (01379) 855123. E-mail: rivierabooks@fsmail.net. Est: 1999. Shop open: **T:** 10:00–16:30; **W:** 10:00–16:30; **Th:** 10:00–13:00; **F:** 10:00–16:30; **S:** 10:00–16:30. Stock: large. PR: £2–200. CC: MC; V. Corresp: French. [Updated]

HINDRINGHAM

Fullerton's Booksearch, The Dukes House, 1 Moorgate Road, Hindringham, Fakenham, NR21 0PT. Humphrey Boon. Tel: 01328 87 87 81. Fax: 01328 87 87 82. E-mail: fullertons.books@virgin.net. Est: 1991. Private premises. Postal only. Appointment necessary. Open: **M:** 09:00–17:00; **T:** 09:00–17:00; **W:** 09:00–17:00; **Th:** 09:00–17:00; **F:** 09:00–17:00. Spec: Booksearch. PR: £18–2,000. CC: JCB; MC; V; Debit. VAT No: GB 631 8838 22. [Updated]

HOLT

Jackdaw Books, ■ 10 New Street, Holt, NR25 6JJ. Prop: Mick & Eleanor Finn. Tel: (01263) 711658. Fax: (01263) 710056. Web: www.jackdawbooks.co.uk. E-mail: eleanor.finn@btopenworld.com. Est: 1997. Internet and postal. Shop open: **M:** 09:00–16:00; **T:** 09:00–16:00; **W:** 09:00–16:00; **F:** 09:00–16:00; **S:** 09:00–16:00. Stock: large. Spec: Academic/Scholarly; Antiquarian; Archaeology; History - British; History - Local; Topography - Local. PR: £5–3,500. CC: JCB; MC; V; Switch. Mem: PBFA. VAT No: GB 784 6478 72. [Updated]

Searching for a title - and cannot find it on any Internet database?

Then try www.sheppardsworld.co.uk

Select dealers by book subject classification – then mail requests to selected dealers who may not have uploaded the title to any Internet Search database.

Simon Finch Nofolk, ■ 5 Fish Hill, Holt, NR25 6BD. Tel: 01263 712650. Fax: 01263 711153. Web: www.simonfinchnorfolk.com. E-mail: simonfinch.norfolk@virgin.net. Est: 2003. Shop open: **M:** 10:00–17:00; **T:** 10:00–17:00; **W:** 10:00–17:00; **Th:** 10:00–17:00; **F:** 10:00–17:00; **S:** 10:00–17:00. Spec: Art; Illustrated; Literature; Natural History; Sport - Field Sports. CC: AE; JCB; MC; V; Debit. [Updated]

HUNSTANTON

Musicalania, 8B Melton Drive, Hunstanton, PE36 5DD. Prop: David Burkett. Tel: (01485) 534282. E-mail: musicalania@btinternet.com. Est: 1973. Private premises. Internet and postal. Telephone first. Stock: small. Spec: Music - General; Music - Composers; Music - Popular. PR: £1–50. Corresp: French and German. [Updated]

KING'S LYNN

Bookends, ■ 4 King Street, King's Lynn, PE30 1ES. Prop: Iain Dempster. Tel: 01553 766086. Est: 2002. Shop open: **M:** 10:00–17:00; **T:** 10:00–17:00; **Th:** 10:00–17:00; **F:** 10:00–17:00; **S:** 10:00–17:00. CC: AE; MC; V; Maestro. Notes: also, prints and fine art cards. Open on Sundays during summer. [Updated]

Brazenhead Ltd., Greenside, Market Place, Burnham Market, King's Lynn, PE31 8HD. Prop: H.S. Kenyon. Tel: (01328) 730700. Fax: (01328) 730929. Web: www.brazenhead.co.uk. E-mail: brazenheadbook@aol.com. Est: 1996. Shop and/or gallery. Internet and postal. Open: **M:** 09:30–17:00; **T:** 09:30–17:00; **W:** 09:30–17:00; **Th:** 09:30–17:00; **F:** 09:30–17:00; **S:** 09:30–17:00. Stock: very large. Spec: Architecture; Art; Children's; History - Local; Military; Collectables; Ephemera. PR: £1–10,000. CC: MC; V; Switch. [Updated]

John Lowe, 7 Orchard Grove, West Lynn, King's Lynn, PE34 3LE. Tel: (01553) 661271. E-mail: john@lowebooks.fsnet.co.uk. Est: 1982. Spec: Academic/Scholarly; Advertising; Aeronautics; Alternative Medicine; Archaeology; Folklore; History - British; Topography - General. PR: £2–200. Mem: PBFA. [Updated]

Torc Books, ■ 9 Hall Road, Snettisham, King's Lynn, PE31 7LU. Prop: Heather Shepperd. Tel: (01485) 541188 and 5. Est: 1977. Shop open: **F:** 10:00–16:00; **S:** 10:00–16:00. Stock: medium. PR: £1–100. Notes: open other times by appointment. [Updated]

LYNG

Lyngheath Books, 51 Pightle Way, Lyng, Norwich, NR9 5RL. Prop: Tim Holt. Tel: 01603 879037. Web: www.lyngheathbooks.co.uk. E-mail: lyngheathbooks@hotmail.com. Est: 1999. Private premises. Internet and postal. Appointment necessary. Open: **M:** 09:00–17:30; **T:** 09:00–17:30; **W:** 09:00–17:30; **Th:** 09:00–17:30; **F:** 09:00–17:30; **S:** 09:00–17:30; **Su:** 09:00–17:30; Closed for lunch: 13:00–14:00. Spec: Autobiography; Biography; Sport - General. CC: UK Bank sterling cheque. Corresp: French. Notes: The main focus of Lyngheath Books is book searching. Only a small stock of books is held - mainly biography and autobiography. Web site being updated. [Updated]

MELTON CONSTABLE

Enigma Books, Stow House, 3 Thornton Close, Briston, Melton Constable, NR24 2LZ. A.E.R.M. Stevens. Tel: (01263) 861609. E-mail: stevens@stowhouse3060.fsnet.co.uk. Est: 1976. Private premises. Postal only. Appointment necessary. Stock: very small. Spec: First Editions; Ghosts; Occult; Supernatural. PR: £5–1,000. [Updated]

NEW BUCKENHAM

John Underwood Antiquarian Books, Hill House, Chapel Street, New Buckenham, NR16 2BB. Prop: John Underwood. Tel: 01953 860746. Web: www.abebooks.com. E-mail: mrjunder@aol.com. Est: 1991. Office and/or bookroom. Telephone first. Open: **Th:** 1400–17:30; **F:** 09:00–17:30; **S:** 09:00–17:30; **Su:** 09:00–17:30. Spec: Antiquarian; Author - Norton, Mary; Author - White, T.H.; Book of Hours; Calligraphy; Children's; Children's - Illustrated; Crime (True). CC: Cheques /Cash. Mem: PBFA. Notes: Book Fairs with PBFA. London Fair most months. Bookroom open by appointment, telephone, leave message, or e-mail. Small quality stock of Antiquarian, Children's, Newspapers, Manuscripts, Medieval leaves,True Crime, some Modern Firsts. [Updated]

NORTH WALSHAM

C.J. Murphy, 5 Burton Avenue, North Walsham, NR28 0EW. Tel: (01692) 402831. Web: www.abebooks.com/home/Chrismurphy/home. E-mail: chris@cmurphy6.fsnet.co.uk. Est: 1999. Private premises. Postal only. Telephone first. Stock: medium. Spec: Academic/Scholarly; Annuals; Antiquarian; Art Reference; Atlases; Author - General; Autobiography; Children's. PR: £1–1,000. Corresp: english only. Notes:: Also, a booksearch service. [Updated]

NORWICH

Bookshelf – Aviation Books, St. Catherines, The Green, Hickling, Norwich, NR12 0XR. Prop: Roger Billings. Tel: (01692) 598183. Fax: (01692) 598751. Web: www.aviation-bookshelf.co.uk. E-mail: airbooks2@aol.com. Est: 1996. Private premises. Postal only. Telephone first. Spec: Aviation; Booksearch. PR: £1–300. CC: AE; MC; V. Cata: quarterly on Aviation. Mem: PBFA. VAT No: GB 728 5963 88. [Updated]

Carlton Books, 44 Langley Road, Chedgrave, Norwich, NR14 6HD. Prop: A.P. Goodfellow. Tel: (01508) 520124. Est: 1974. Private premises. Appointment necessary. Stock: small. Spec: History - Local; Natural History; Ornithology; Topography - Local. PR: £1–500. Mem: PBFA. [Updated]

J. & D. Clarke, The Elms, 19 Heigham Grove, Norwich, NR2 3DQ. Tel: (01603) 619226. E-mail: jonddclarke@norwichnorfolk.freeserve.co.uk. Est: 2004. Private premises. Postal only. Stock: very small. Spec: Topography - General; Topography - Local. PR: £1–500. Mem: PBFA; Attends local PBFA fairs. [Updated]

John Debbage, 28 Carterford Drive, Norwich, NR3 4DW. Tel: (01603) 488015. Fax: (01603) 788933. E-mail: norvicsales@btopenworld.com. Private premises. Internet and postal. Spec: Topography - Local; Ephemera; Prints and Maps. Cata: occasionally. [Updated]

J.R. & R.K. Ellis, ■ 53 St. Giles Street, Norwich, NR2 1JR. Tel: (01603) 623679. Est: 1960. Shop open: **M:** 08:30–18:00; **T:** 08:30–18:00; **W:** 08:30–18:00; **Th:** 08:30–18:00; **F:** 08:30–18:00; **S:** 08:30–18:00; **Su:** 10:00–16:00. Stock: large. PR: £1–100. Notes: also at market stalls. [Updated]

Firstpagebooks, Oakdale House, Church Road Bergh Apton, Norwich, NR15 1BP. Prop: Mr Kim Sergeant. Tel: 01508 558484. Fax: 01508 558484. Web: www.firstpagebooks.com. E-mail: kim@firstpagebooks.com. Est: 2002. Mail Order Only. Internet and postal. Contactable: **M:** 09.30–17:00; **T:** 09:30–17:00; **W:** 09.30–17:00; **Th:** 09:30–17:00; **F:** 09:30–17:00; **S:** 09:30–17:00; **Su:** 09:30–17:00. Spec: Authors:- Francis, Dick; Greene, Graham; Autobiography; Autographs; Children's; Cinema/Film; Comedy; Comic Books & Annuals. Cata: occasionally on Modern First Editions, Giles, Rupert, Cricket,. Corresp: Japanese. Notes: General booksellers, specialising in Modern First Editions, Rock/Pop music, Cricket, Rupert, Football, Giles, Military as well as stockists in Sport & Pop memorabilia. [Updated]

Freeman's Corner Shop, ■ 52 King Street, Norwich, NR2 1AB. Prop: J.G. & A.H. Freeman. Tel: 01603 493210. E-mail: sales@tomblandbookshop.co.uk. Est: 1987. Shop open: **M:** 09:30–17:00; **T:** 09:30–17:00; **W:** 09:30–17:00; **Th:** 09:30–17:00; **F:** 09:30–17:00; **S:** 09:30–16:30. Notes: also at, Tombland Bookshop, Norwich (q.v.) [Updated]

Freya Books & Antiques, St. Mary's Farm, Cheney's Lane, Tacolneston, Norwich, NR16 1DB. Prop: Colin Lewsey. Tel: (01508) 489252. Web: www.freyaantiques.co.uk. E-mail: freyaantiques@yahoo.co.uk. Est: 1971. Storeroom. Appointment necessary. Stock: medium. Spec: Fiction - General; Juvenile; Booksearch; Ephemera. PR: £1–50. CC: MC; V. Corresp: French, Danish. Notes: also, 3,000sq ft antique furniture. Organisor of book fairs. [Updated]

Hawes Books, 8 Keswick Road, Cringleford, Norwich, NR4 6UG. Prop: T.L.M. & H.J. Hawes. Tel: (01603) 452043. Est: 1980. Private premises. Appointment necessary. Stock: large. Spec: Genealogy; History - Local; History - National; Topography - General. PR: £2–200. VAT No: GB 342 4870 57. [Updated]

Katnap Arts, 1 Whitefields, Norwich Road, Saxlingham Nethergate, Norwich, NR15 1TP. Prop: Margaret Blake. Tel: 01508 498323. Fax: 01508 498323. Web: www.katnap.co.uk. E-mail: mail@katnaparts.plus.co.uk. Est: 1999. Private premises. Internet and postal. Contactable. Open: **M:** 09:00–17:30; **T:** 09:00–17:30; **W:** 09:00–17:30; **Th:** 09:00–17:30; **F:** 09:00–17:30; **S:** 09:00–17:30; **Su:** 09:00–17:30; Closed for lunch: 13:00–14:00. Spec: Annuals; Architecture; Art; Art History; Art Reference; Children's; Entertainment - General; First Editions. CC: MC; V. [Updated]

David Lake, 36 Colney Lane, Cringleford, Norwich, NR4 7RE. Tel: 07909 896 809. E-mail: djl@netcom.co.uk. Est: 1990. Private premises. Postal only. Stock: small. Spec: Antiquarian; Children's - Illustrated; Colour-Plate; Topography - Local. PR: £5–500. [Updated]

Steven Simpson Books, 5 Hardingham Road, Hingham, Norwich, NR9 4LX. Prop: S.J. Simpson. Tel: 01953-850-471. Fax: 01953-850-471. Web: www.stevensimpsonbooks.com. E-mail: info@stevensimpsonbooks.com. Est: 1986. Mail Order Only. Internet and postal. Open: **M:** 09:00–17:30; **T:** 09:00–17:30; **W:** 09:00–17:30; **Th:** 09:00–17:30; **F:** 09:00–17:30; **S:** 09:00–17:30; **Su:** 09:00–17:30; Closed for lunch: 13:00–14:00. Spec: Botany; Fishes; Herpetology; Zoology. CC: E; MC; V. Corresp: German, French, Spanish, Portuguese. Notes: Exclusive UK book trade distributors for Aqualog Verlag A.C.S. GmbH., Birgit Schmettkamp Verlag and Verlag Eugen Ulmer (Stuttgart). All titles from these publishers can be ordered directly from us or through any good UK bookshop VAT No: GB 711 6055 70. [Updated]

The Dormouse Bookshop, ■ 29 Elm Hill, Norwich, NR3 1HG. Prop: Philip Goodbody. Tel: 01603 621021. E-mail: dormouse1@btopenworld.com. Est: 1985. Shop open: **M:** 10:00–16:00; **T:** 10:00–16:00; **W:** 10:00–16:00; **Th:** 10:00–16:00; **F:** 10:00–16:00; **S:** 10:00–17:00. Spec: Authors:- Blyton, Enid; Johns, W.E.; Children's; Fiction - General; History - General; History - Local; History - Military; Military History. CC: MC; V. Notes: Book lovers welcomed. [Updated]

Tombland Bookshop, ■ 8 Tombland, Norwich, NR3 1HF. Prop: J.G. & A.H. Freeman. Tel: 01603 490000. Fax: 01603 760610. E-mail: sales@tomblandbookshop.co.uk. Est: 1973. Shop open: **M:** 09.30–17.00; **T:** 09.30–17.00; **W:** 09.30–17.00; **Th:** 09.30–17.00; **F:** 09.30–17.00; **S:** 09.30–16.30. Spec: Academic/Scholarly; Archaeology; Architecture; Art; Biography; Literary Criticism; Military; Military History. CC: E; MC; V; PayPal. Notes: also at, Freeman's Corner Bookshop, Norwich (q.v.). Booksearch and bookbinding. VAT No: GB 366 6678 01. [Updated]

OLD COSTESSEY

Wensumbooks, ■ 53 The Street, Old Costessey, NR8 5DD. Prop: Elke Katherina McKinlay. Tel: 01603 746315. Web: www.abebooks.com. E-mail: mckinlay@wensumbooks.wanadoo.co.uk. Est: 2005. Shop open: **T:** 10:00–17:00; **W:** 10:00–17:00; **Th:** 10:00–17:00; **F:** 10:00–17:00; **S:** 10:00–17:00; Closed for lunch: 13:00–14:00. Spec: Ornithology; Ephemera; Prints and Maps. CC: PayPal. Corresp: German. [Updated]

SALTHOUSE

John Hart, Salt Barn, Bard Hill, Salthouse, NR25 7XB. Tel: (01263) 741380. Fax: (01263) 741700. E-mail: johnhartbks@btopenworld.com. Est: 1987. Private premises. Appointment necessary. Stock: small. Spec: Literature. PR: £20–2,000. CC: MC; V. Corresp: French. Mem: ABA; PBFA. VAT No: GB 529 2455 28. [Updated]

SHERINGHAM

Peter Pan Bookshop, ■ 5 The Courtyard, Station Road, Sheringham, NR26 8RF. Prop: Peter Cox. Tel: (01263) 824411. Est: 1994. Shop open: **M:** 10:30–17:00; **T:** 10:30–17:00; **W:** 10:30–17:00; **Th:** 10:30–17:00; **F:** 10:30–17:00; **S:** 10:30–17:00; **Su:** 12:00–16:00. Stock: small. PR: £1–20. Notes: Peter's Bookshop, 19 St Peter's Road (q.v.) Secondhand books published after 1990. [Updated]

Peter's Bookshop, ■ 19 St. Peter's Road, Sheringham, NR26 8QY. Prop: Peter Cox. Tel: (01263) 823008. Est: 1984. Shop open: **M:** 10:00–17:30; **T:** 10:00–17:30; **W:** 10:00–17:30; **Th:** 10:00–17:30; **F:** 10:00–17:30; **S:** 10:00–17:30; **Su:** 13:00–17:00. Stock: very large. Spec: Children's; Fiction - General; Literature; Ephemera; Large Print Books. PR: £1–100. Notes: The Peter Pan Bookshop, Sheringham, Norfolk (q.v.) Winter hours: (Nov. to Mar.) Mon./Tue. & Thurs. to Sat. 10:30–16:30. [Updated]

SWANTON ABBOT

Hamish Riley-Smith, Swanton Abbot Hall, Swanton Abbot, NR10 5DJ. Prop: Hamish Riley-Smith. Tel: 01692538244. Web: www.riley-smith.com. E-mail: hamish@riley-smith.com. Est: 1974. Private premises. Internet and postal. Appointment necessary. Open: **M:** 09:00–17:30; **T:** 09:00–17:30; **W:** 09:00–17:30; **Th:** 09:00–17:30; **F:** 09:00–17:30; **S:** 09:00–17:30; **Su:** 09:00–17:30; Closed for lunch: 13:00–14:00. Spec: Antiquarian; Arabica; Economics; History - Economic Thought; Philosophy; Printing and Mind of Man; Science - History of; Scottish Enlightenment. Cata: occasionally on Economics, Philosophy, PMM, Sciences, Arithimetic. [Updated]

WATTON

J.C. Books, 55 High Street, Watton, IP25 6AB. Prop: C.F. & J.A. Ball & T.F. Robinson. Tel: (01953) 883488. E-mail: j_c_books@lineone.net. Est: 1992. Shop open: **M:** 10:00–16:30; **T:** 10:00–16:30; **W:** 10:00–16:30; **F:** 10:00–16:30; **S:** 10:00–16:30. Stock: medium. Spec: Theatre. PR: £1–1,000. CC: MC; V. Mem: PBFA. Notes: exhibits at PBFA fairs. [Updated]

WELLS-NEXT-THE-SEA
The Old Station Pottery & Book, ■ 2/4 Maryland, Wells–Next–The–Sea, NR23 1LX. Prop: Thom Borthwick. Tel: (01328) 710847. E-mail: oldstation.books@btinternet.com. Est: 1996. Shop open: **M:** 09:00–17:00; **W:** 09:00–17:00; **F:** 09:00–17:00; **S:** 09:00–17:00; **Su:** 09:00–17:00; Closed for lunch: 12:30–13:30. Stock: large. Spec: Children's; Topography - General. PR: £1–50. CC: PayPal. [Updated]

WYMONDHAM
The Bookshop, ■ 1 Town Green, Wymondham, NR18 OPN. Prop: M. & A.C. Thompson. Tel: (01953) 602244. Web: www.abebooks.com/home/MANDACTHOMPSON. E-mail: mac.thompson@btopenworld.com. Est: 1975. Shop open: **M:** 10:45–16:45; **T:** 10:30–16:45; **Th:** 10:30–16:45; **F:** 10:30–16:45; **S:** 10:00–17:00. Stock: medium. Spec: Comics; Entertainment - General; Music - General; Topography - General. PR: £1–300. [Updated]

Turret House, ■ 27 Middleton Street, Wymondham, NR18 0AB. Prop: Dr. D.H. & R.A. Morgan. Tel: (01953) 603462. E-mail: hughmorgan@turrethouse.demon.co.uk. Est: 1972. Shop. Telephone first. Stock: very small. Spec: Astronomy; Mathematics; Medicine; Microscopy; Natural Sciences; Science - General; Science - History of; Scientific Instruments. PR: £1–1,000. CC: MC; V. Mem: PBFA. Notes: usually open Monday – Saturday 09:00–18:00 but telephone first to save a wasted journey. VAT No: GB 282 1349 63. [Updated]

NORTH YORKSHIRE

AUSTWICK

Austwick Hall Books, Austwick Hall, Town Head, Austwick, LA2 8BS. Prop: Michael Pearson. Tel: 015242 51794. E-mail: Austwickhall@btinternet.com. Est: 2000. Private premises. Internet Only. Appointment necessary. Open: **M:** 09:00–17:30; **T:** 09:00–17:30; **W:** 09:00–17:30; **Th:** 09:00–17:30; **F:** 09:00–17:30; **S:** 09:00–17:30; **Su:** 09:00–17:30; Closed for lunch: 13:00–14:00. Spec: Academic/Scholarly; Antiquarian; Biology; Botany; Evolution; Exploration; Farriers; Geology. [Updated]

CATTERICK VILLAGE

Brock Books, 43 High Street, Catterick Village, DL10 7LL. Prop: Jude Haslam. Tel: (01748) 818729. Web: www.brockbooks.com. E-mail: judehaslam@btopenworld.com. Est: 2002. Private premises. Internet and postal. Appointment necessary. Open: **M:** 09:00–17:30; **T:** 09:00–17:30; **W:** 09:00–17:30; **Th:** 09:00–17:30; **F:** 11:00–17:30; **S:** 10:00–17:00; **Su:** 10:00–17:00. Stock: very small. Spec: Animals and Birds; Annuals; Art; Authors: Johns, W.E.; Kipling, Rudyard; Morris, William; Morton, H.V.; Ratcliffe, Dorothy Una. PR: £5–500. CC: PayPal. Corresp: Spanish. Notes: illustrations, book restoration. [Updated]

DACRE

Theatreshire Books, Dacre Hall, Dacre, HG3 4ET. Prop: Catherine Shire. Tel: (01423) 780497. Fax: (01423) 781957. E-mail: theatreshire@theatresearch.co.uk. Est: 2000. Private premises. Internet and postal. Appointment necessary. Stock: small. Spec: Architecture; Cinema/Film; Engineering; Fire & Fire Fighters; Performing Arts; Theatre. PR: £1–5,000. [Updated]

FILEY

Professional Book Services, 10 Hope Street, Filey, YO14 9DL. Prop: Peter Jacques. Tel: (01723) 515170. Web: www.bookspluspictures.com. E-mail: books@bookspluspictures.com. Est: 1996. Private premises. Internet and postal. Stock: very small. Spec: Booksearch. PR: £2–50. CC: PayPal. VAT No: GB 758 7448 73. [31/07/2005]

GUISBOROUGH

K.A. McCaughtrie, 7 Grosvenor Square, Guisborough, TS14 6PB. Tel: (01287) 633663. Est: 1986. Private premises. Postal only. Appointment necessary. Stock: very small. Spec: Biography; Crime (True); Fiction - Crime, Detective, Spy, Thrillers. PR: £1–50. [Updated]

The Guisborough Bookshop, 4 Chaloner Street, Guisborough, North Yorkshire, TS14 6QD. Tel: (01287) 639018. E-mail: books@guisboroughbookshop.com. [Updated]

HARROGATE

Richard Axe Rare & Out of Print Books, ■ 12 Cheltenham Crescent, Harrogate, HG1 1DH. Prop: Richard Axe. Tel: (01423) 561867. Fax: (01423) 561837. E-mail: rja@tiscali.co.uk. Est: 1981. Shop open: **T:** 10:00–17:30; **W:** 10:00–17:30; **Th:** 10:00–17:30; **F:** 10:00–17:30; **S:** 10:00–17:30. Stock: very large. Spec: Antiquarian; Antiques; Art History; Ceramics; Cookery/Gastronomy; History - General; Literary Criticism; Literature. PR: £2–1,000. CC: AE; D; E; JCB; MC; V. Mem: PBFA. Notes: Libraries purchased throughout UK. Open at other times by appointment. [Updated]

Books (For All), ■ 23a Commercial Street, Harrogate, HG1 1UB. Prop: Jenny Todd. Tel: (01423) 561982. E-mail: booksforall@amserve.net. Est: 1998. Shop open: **M:** 10:30–17:00; **T:** 10:30–17:00; **W:** 10:30–17:00; **Th:** 10:30–17:00; **F:** 10:30–17:00; **S:** 10:30–17:00. Stock: large. Spec: Art History; Biography; Children's; Cookery/Gastronomy; Esoteric; Fiction - Science Fiction; History - General; Horticulture. PR: £1–100. CC: MC; V; SW. [Updated]

Macbuiks, 7 Leadhall Crescent, Harrogate, HG2 9NG. Prop: Sally Mackenzie. Tel: 01423870978. E-mail: macbuiks@ntlworld.com. Est: 1997. Private premises. Internet and postal. Appointment necessary. Open: **M:** 09:00–17:30; **T:** 09:00–17:30; **W:** 09:00–17:30; **Th:** 09:00–17:30; **F:** 09:00–17:30; **S:** 09:00–17:30; **Su:** 09:00–17:30. Spec: Author - Kipling, Rudyard; Children's; Children's - Illustrated; Crafts; Gardening - General; Wine. CC: PayPal. Mem: Ibooknet. [Updated]

HELMSLEY

Helmsley Antiquarian & Secondhand Books, ■ The Old Fire Station, Borogate, Helmsley, YO62 5BN. Prop: Myles Moorby. Tel: (01439) 770014. Est: 1985. Shop open: **M:** 10:00–17:00; **T:** 10:00–17:00; **W:** 09:00–17:00; **Th:** 10:00–17:00; **F:** 10:00–17:00; **S:** 10:00–17:00; **Su:** 12:00–17:00. Stock: medium. Spec: Architecture; Art; Topography - Local. PR: £1–100. CC: MC; V. VAT No: GB 390 4976 18. [Updated]

INGLETON

John Killeen, 16 Main Street, Ingleton, LA6 3HF. Tel: (015242) 41021. Est: 1974. Private premises. Open: **M:** 09:00–17:00; **T:** 09:00–17:00; **W:** 09:00–17:00; **Th:** 09:00–17:00; **F:** 09:00–17:00. Stock: medium. Spec: Literature; Marxism; Philosophy; Religion - Catholic; Topography - Local; Travel - General. PR: £4–1,000. Corresp: French. Mem: PBFA. Notes: attends fairs in Northern England. Irregular opening hours. [Updated]

KNARESBOROUGH

Pennymead Books, 1 Brewerton Street, Knaresborough, HG5 8AZ. Prop: David Druett. Tel: (01423) 865962. Fax: (01423) 547057. Web: www.pennymead.com. E-mail: pennymead@aol.com. Est: 1984. Private premises. Internet and postal. Telephone first. Stock: small. Spec: Carriages & Driving; Colonial; Countries - Bermuda; Countries - Caribbean, The; Countries - Cuba; Countries - Dominican Republic; Countries - Puerto Rico; Countries - Siam. PR: £5–5,000. CC: JCB; MC; V. Mem: PBFA. Notes: also, postage stamp auctioneer. VAT No: GB 387 9262 94. [07/10/2004]

LEALHOLM

Stepping Stones Bookshop, ■ Stepping Stones, Lealholm, near Whitby, YO21 2AJ. Prop: Judith & Lawrence Davies. Tel: (01947) 897382. E-mail: info@steppingstonesantiques.co.uk. Est: 1970. Shop open: **M:** 10:00–17:00; **T:** 10:00–17:00; **W:** 10:00–17:00; **Th:** 09:00–17:00; **F:** 10:00–17:00; **S:** 10:00–17:00; **Su:** 10:00–17:00. Stock: medium. Spec: Children's; Children's - Illustrated. PR: £1–100. [Updated]

LONG PRESTON

Books at the Warehouse, Barn Cottage, Church Street, Long Preston, BD23 4NJ. Prop: Jo Lunt. Tel: (01729) 840152. E-mail: jo.lunt3@tiscali.co.uk. Est: 1993. Private premises. Postal only. Appointment necessary. Stock: medium. Spec: Publishers - Penguin; Ephemera. PR: £1–100. Corresp: French, German. [Updated]

PICKERING

Alan Avery, 15 Middleton Road, Pickering, YO18 8AL. Prop: Alan Avery. Tel: (01751) 476863. Web: www.abebooks.com/home/avery. E-mail: avery_uk@yahoo.com. Est: 1988. Private premises. Postal only. Appointment necessary. Open: **M:** 09:00–17:00; **T:** 09:09–17:17; **W:** 09:00–17:00; **Th:** 09:00–17:00; **F:** 09:00–17:00; **S:** 09:00–13:00. Stock: small. Spec: Folio Society, The. PR: £5–60. CC: AE; MC; V. [Updated]

Sybil Buckley, ■ Pickering Antique Centre, Southgate, Pickering, YO18 8BN. Tel: (01751) 477210. E-mail: buckleysbooks@lineone.net. Est: 1998. Shop open: **M:** 10:00–17:00; **T:** 10:00–17:00; **W:** 10:00–17:00; **Th:** 10:00–17:00; **F:** 10:00–17:00; **S:** 10:00–17:00; **Su:** 10:00–17:00. Stock: small. PR: £1–200. CC: MC; V; DELTA [Updated]

Are you making enough profit? If in doubt then read

BOOKDEALING FOR PROFIT
by Paul Minet

Quarto H/b　　　　　　　　　　　　　　　　　　　　　　　　　　　　£10.00 144pp

Cobweb Books, ■ Ye Olde Corner Shoppe, 1 Pickering Road, Thornton–Le–Dale, Pickering, YO18 7LG. Prop: Robin & Sue Buckler. Tel: (01751) 476638. Web: www.cobwebbooks.co.uk. E-mail: robin@cobweb-books-yorks.fsnet.co.uk. Shop open: **M:** 10:00–17:00; **T:** 10:00–17:00; **W:** 10:00–17:00; **Th:** 10:00–17:00; **F:** 10:00–17:00; **S:** 10:00–17:00; **Su:** 10:00–17:00. Stock: very large. Spec: Antiquarian; Aviation; First Editions; Illustrated; Military; Motoring; Railways; Topography - General. PR: £1–1,000. CC: AE; E; JCB; MC; V; SW. [Updated]

Inch's Books, 6 Westgate, Pickering, YO18 8BA. Prop: Peter & Eleanor Inch. Tel: (01751) 474928. Fax: (01751) 475939. Web: www.inchsbooks.co.uk. E-mail: inchs.books@dial.pipex.com. Est: 1986. Office and/or bookroom. Telephone first. Open: **M:** 09:00–17:00; **T:** 09:00–17:00; **W:** 09:00–17:00; **Th:** 09:00–17:00; **F:** 09:00–17:00. Stock: medium. Spec: Architecture; Building & Construction; Cities; Design; History - Design; Landscape; Town Planning; Urban History. PR: £10–2,000. CC: MC; V; SW. Corresp: French. Mem: ABA; PBFA; ILAB. Notes: also, books on international exhibitions. VAT No: GB 412 1286 94. [Updated]

RAINTON

Pandion Books, 10 Carr Close, Rainton, Thirsk, YO7 3QE. Prop: Les Wray. Tel: 01845 578224. E-mail: pandionbks@aol.com. Est: 1980. Private premises. Internet and postal. Appointment necessary. Spec: Natural History; Ornithology. CC: MC; V. Cata: annually. Mem: PBFA. [Updated]

RICHMOND

Richmond Books, ■ 20 Trinity Church Square, Richmond, DL10 4QN. Prop: Bob & Gail Ions. Tel: (01325) 377332. E-mail: richmondbooks@ions.ndo.co.uk. Est: 1995. Shop. Internet and postal. Open: **M:** 09:30–16:30; **T:** 09:30–16:30; **W:** 09:30–16:30; **Th:** 09:30–16:30; **F:** 09:30–16:30; **S:** 09:30–16:30; **Su:** 10:00–16:30. Stock: medium. Spec: Art; Aviation; Biography; Fiction - General; Fiction - Crime, Detective, Spy, Thrillers; History - General; Literature; Maritime/Nautical. PR: £1–200. [Updated]

J.P. Vokes, Linton House, 43 Bargate, Richmond. Prop: Jonathan Peter Vokes. Tel: (01748) 824946. Fax: (01748) 824946. Est: 1972. Private premises. Postal only. Stock: small. Spec: Fiction - General; Gardening - General; Horticulture; Military History; Natural History; Topography - General; Travel - General. PR: £1–500. Notes: also, a booksearch service. [Updated]

RIPON

Hornseys' of Ripon, ■ 3 Kirkgate, Ripon, HG4 1PA. Prop: Bruce, Susan & Daniel Hornsey. Tel: (01765) 602878. E-mail: dan@hornseys.com'. Est: 1976. Shop open: **M:** 09:00–17:30; **T:** 09:00–17:30; **W:** 09:00–17:30; **Th:** 09:00–17:30; **F:** 09:00–17:30; **S:** 09:00–17:30. Stock: very large. Spec: Alpinism/Mountaineering; Architecture; Aviation; Children's; Fashion & Costume; History - General; Military History; Motoring. PR: £1–8,000. CC: MC; V; Switch. [Updated]

SALTBURN–BY–THE–SEA

Saltburn Bookshop, ■ 3 Amber Street, Saltburn–by–the–Sea, TS12 1DT. Prop: Jösef Thompson. Tel: (01287) 623335. E-mail: aflaj@tiscali.co.uk. Est: 1978. Shop open: **M:** 11:00–17:00; **T:** 11:00–17:00; **W:** 11:00–17:00; **Th:** 11:00–17:00; **F:** 11:00–17:00; **S:** 11:00–17:00; Closed for lunch: 13:00–14:00. Stock: medium. Spec: Booksearch. PR: £1–100. Notes: winter opening hours: Wed to Sat 11:00-16:00. (Closed for lunch 13:00–14:00). [Updated]

SCARBOROUGH

Antiquary Ltd., (Bar Bookstore), ■ 4 Swanhill Road, Scarborough, YO11 1BW. Prop: Michael Chaddock. Tel: (01723) 500141. Web: www.ukbookworld.com/members/Barbooks. E-mail: antiquary@btinternet.com. Est: 1976. Shop open: **T:** 10:30–17:00; **W:** 10:30–17:00; **Th:** 10:30–17:00; **F:** 10:30–17:00; **S:** 10:30–18:00. Stock: medium. Spec: Academic/Scholarly; Art; Author - Housman, A.E.; History - General; Literature; Topography - General; Topography - Local; Booksearch. PR: £1–450. Mem: PBFA. [Updated]

The Bookshelf, ■ 6 Victoria Road, Scarborough, YO11 1SD. Prop: Mrs. Leslie Anne Stones. Tel: (01723) 381677. Web: www.bookshelf.scarborough.co.uk. E-mail: bookshelf@scarborough.co.uk. Est: 2000. Shop open: **M:** 10:00–17:00; **T:** 10:00–17:00; **W:** 10:00–17:00; **Th:** 10:00–17:00; **F:** 10:00–17:00; **S:** 10:00–17:00. Stock: small. PR: £1–100. Corresp: Some French. [Updated]

Richard Dalby, 4 Westbourne Park, Scarborough, YO12 4AT. Tel: (01723) 377049. Est: 1976. Private premises. Postal only. Stock: very small. Spec: Fiction - Fantasy, Horror; Fiction - Supernatural; Ghosts; Literature. Mem: PBFA. [Updated]

Doodles Bookshop, ■ 45 Newborough, Scarborough, YO11 1NF. Prop: Nicholas Paul Ironside. Tel: 016723 379079. E-mail: doodleboos@fsmail.net. Est: 2004. Shop open: **M:** 10:00–17:00; **T:** 10:00–17:00; **W:** 10:00–17:00; **Th:** 10:00–17:00; **F:** 10:00–17:00; **S:** 10:00–17:00; **Su:** 10:00–17:00. Notes: open in winter: 11:00 – 16:00. [Updated]

Reeves Technical Books, San Marino, Limestone Road, Burniston, Scarborough, YO13 0DG. Prop: W.H. & L.I. Reeves. Tel: 01723 870267. Fax: 01723 870267 (Ring First). Web: www.reevestechnicalbooks.co.uk. E-mail: busterjut@yahoo.co.uk. Est: 1975. Private premises. Telephone first. Open: **M:** 09:00–17:30; **T:** 09:00–17:30; **W:** 09:00–17:30; **Th:** 09:00–17:30; **F:** 09:00–17:30; **S:** 09:00–17:30; **Su:** 09:00–17:30; Closed for lunch: 13:00–14:00. Spec: Academic/Scholarly; Annuals; Architecture; Botany; Bridge; Building & Construction; Catalogues Raisonnes; Civil Engineering. CC: PayPal. Cata: occasionally on Carpentry, Wood Machining, Furniture, Building Co. Notes: I specialise in books mainly for the building industry (woodworking in all its forms). With a few exceptions all my Books are of a technical nature with no fiction. [Updated]

Book Emporium, ■ 2, Queen Street, Scarborough, YP11 1HA. Prop: Shaun Lofthouse. Tel: 01723506057. Fax: 01723506057. E-mail: shaunlofthouse@netscape.net. Est: 1989. Shop open: **M:** 10:00–17:00; **T:** 10:00–17:00; **W:** 10:00–17:00; **Th:** 10:00–17:00; **F:** 10:00–17:00; **S:** 10:00–17:00; **Su:** 10:00–17:00. Spec: CC: MC; V. Notes: we believe that each customer is important. [Updated]

SELBY

Anthony Vickers, 23 Baffam Gardens, Selby, YO8 9AY. Tel: (01757) 705949. E-mail: anthonyvickers@bun.com. Est: 1993. Private premises. Internet and postal. Telephone first. Stock: small. Spec: Academic/Scholarly; Advertising; Aeronautics; Aesthetic Movement; Alpinism/Mountaineering; Alternative Medicine; Archaeology; Architecture. PR: £5–500. Mem: PBFA. [Updated]

SETTLE

Peter M. Thornber, 3 School Hill, Settle, BD24 9HB. Tel: (01729) 824067. E-mail: hastathaas@hotmail.com. Est: 1997. Private premises. Appointment necessary. Stock: small. Spec: Agriculture; Antiquarian; Ecclesiastical History & Architecture; Farming & Livestock; Modern First Editions; Religion - Christian; Theology. PR: £5–500. Corresp: French. Notes: also, valuations, consultancy and researcher, commissions at auctions. [Updated]

SKIPTON

Grove Rare Books, ■ The Old Post Office, Bolton Abbey, Skipton, BD23 6EX. Prop: Andrew & Janet Sharpe. Tel: (01756) 710717. Fax: (01756) 711098. Web: www.grovebookshop.co.uk. E-mail: antiquarian@groverarebooks.co.uk. Est: 1984. Shop open: **T:** 10:00–17:00; **W:** 10:00–17:00; **Th:** 10:00–17:00; **F:** 10:00–17:00; **S:** 10:00–17:00; Closed for lunch: 13:00–14:00. Stock: medium. Spec: Bindings; Fiction - General; Illustrated; Literature; Rural Life; Sets of Books; Sport - Angling/Fishing; Sport - Field Sports. PR: £10–3,000. CC: JCB; MC; V; SW, SO. Mem: ABA; PBFA; BA. VAT No: GB 756 1269 18. [Updated]

C. L. Hawley, 26 Belgrave Street, Skipton, BD23 1QB. Prop: Catherine Hawley. Tel: (01756) 792380. Web: www.clhawley.co.uk. E-mail: clh@clhawley.co.uk. Est: 2000. Private premises. Postal only. Stock: small. Spec: Academic/Scholarly; Arts, The; Biography; Children's; History - General; History - Local; Humanities; Literary Criticism. PR: £2–250. CC: JCB; MC; V; debit cds. Mem: Ibooknet. Also, a booksearch service. [Updated]

Skipton Antiques Centre, ■ Cavendish Square, Skipton, BD23 2AB. Tel: (01756) 797667. Shop open: **M:** 11:00–16:30; **T:** 11:00–16:30; **W:** 11:00–16:30; **Th:** 11:00–16:30; **F:** 11:00–16:30; **S:** 11:00–16:30; **Su:** 11:00–16:30. PR: £1–5,000. Notes: Display stock from Seabreeze, for details see under Thornton Cleveleys, Lancs. (q.v.). [Updated]

STAITHES

John L. Capes (Books, Maps & Prints), Church Street, Staithes, Cleveland, TS13 5DB. Tel: (01947) 840 790. Web: www.johncapes.co.uk. E-mail: capes@staithes.fsbusiness.co.uk. Est: 1969. Private premises. Appointment necessary. Stock: very small. Spec: Academic/Scholarly; Antiquarian; Fine Art; Topography - Local; Prints and Maps. PR: £10–2,000. Mem: PBFA. [Updated]

STOCKTON–ON–TEES

Norton Books, 18 Wolviston Road, Billingham, Stockton–on–Tees, Cleveland, TS22 5AA. Prop: C. Casson. Tel: (01642) 553965. Fax: (01642) 553965. E-mail: sales@ricardmarketing.com. Est: 1981. Private premises. Internet and postal. Appointment necessary. Spec: Antiquarian; Authors:- Beckett, S.; Crane, Hall; Crosby, Harry & Caresse; Cunard, Nancy; Durrell, Lawrence; Eliot, T.S.; Hemingway, Ernest. PR: £10–2,000. Mem: PBFA. [Updated]

THIRSK

Potterton Books, The Old Rectory, Sessay, Thirsk, YO7 3LZ. Prop: Clare Jameson. Tel: (01845) 501218. Fax: (01845) 501439. Web: www.pottertonbooks.co.uk. E-mail: enquiries@pottertonbooks.co.uk. Est: 1982. Spec: Antiquarian; Antiques; Applied Art; Architecture; Art Reference; Carpets; Ceramics; Decorative Art. PR: £5–5,000. CC: AE; D; MC; V. Notes: also, booksearch [Updated]

WHITBY

Endeavour Books, ■ 1 Grape Lane, Whitby, YO22 4BA. Tel: (01947) 821331. Web: www.enbooks.co.uk. E-mail: linda@enbooks.co.uk. Est: 1989. Internet and postal. Shop open: **M:** 10:30–17:00; **T:** 10:30–17:00; **W:** 10:30–17:00; **Th:** 10:30–17:00; **F:** 10:30–17:00; **S:** 10:30–17:00; **Su:** 10:30–17:00. Stock: large. PR: £3–50. CC: MC; V. [Updated]

John R. Hoggarth, Thorneywaite House, Glaisdale, Whitby, YO21 2QU. Prop: John R. Hoggarth. Tel: 01947 897338. Web: www.johnrhoggarth.co.uk. E-mail: john@johnrhoggarth.co.uk. Est: 1979. Private premises. Internet and postal. Telephone first. Open: **M:** 09:00–17:30; **T:** 09:00–17:30; **W:** 09:00–17:30; **Th:** 09:00–17:30; **F:** 09:00–17:30; **S:** 09:00–17:30; **Su:** 09:00–17:30; Closed for lunch: 13:00–14:00. Spec: Annuals; Antiques; Authors:- Baden-Powell, Lord Robert; Milligan, Spike; Collecting; Famous People - Baden Powell, Lord & Lady R.S.S.; Juvenile; Music - Classical. CC: PayPal. [Updated]

YARM

Richard J. Hodgson (Books), Manor Farm, Kirklevington, Yarm, TS15 9PY. Prop: Richard Hodgson. Tel: (01642) 780445. E-mail: rjhodgsonbooks@clara.co.uk. Est: 1989. Private premises. Appointment necessary. Stock: medium. Spec: Agriculture; Colour-Plate; Ex-Libris; Farming & Livestock; Guide Books; Illustrated; Magic & Conjuring; Natural History. PR: £1–1,000. Mem: PBFA. [02/11/2004]

YORK

Barbican Bookshop, ■ 24 Fossgate, York, YO1 9TA. Prop: Christian Literature Stalls Ltd. Tel: (01904) 653643. Fax: (01904) 653643. Web: www.barbicanbookshop.co.uk. E-mail: mail@barbicanbookshop.co.uk. Est: 1960. Shop open: **M:** 09:00–17:30; **T:** 09:15–17:30; **W:** 09:00–17:30; **Th:** 09:00–17:30; **F:** 09:15–17:30; **S:** 09:00–17:30. Stock: large. Spec: Aeronautics; Aviation; Bibles; Buses/Trams; Canals/Inland Waterways; Ecclesiastical History & Architecture; Folio Society, The; History - General. PR: £1–500. CC: E; JCB; MC; V. Mem: PBFA; BA; York Tourism Bureau. Notes: also, new books, remainders, cards & videos/dvds. VAT No: GB 169 3696 12. [Updated]

Boer War Books, 8 Mill Lane, Heworth, York, YO31 7TE. Prop: E. A. Hackett. Tel: 01904 415829. Fax: 01904 415829. E-mail: ahackett9@aol.com. Est: 1969. Private premises. Postal only. Spec: Countries - South Africa; Military; Military History. [Updated]

Courtney & Hoff, Hutton Hall Farm, Hutton Wendasley, York, YO26 7LZ. Prop: Gerrit van Hoff. Tel: (01904) 738885. Fax: Mob: 07762 378540. E-mail: evh@hotmail.com. Est: 1986. Storeroom. Appointment necessary. Stock: small. Spec: Antiquarian; Architecture; Bindings; Ecclesiastical History & Architecture; Stone Masonry. PR: £1–900. Corresp: Dutch. Mem: PBFA. Notes: abstract & figurative sculpture; also vellum and leather. [Updated]

Empire Books, 12 Queens Staith Mews, York, YO1 6HH. Prop: Colin Hinchcliffe. Tel: (01904) 610679. Fax: (01904) 641664. E-mail: colin@empirebooks.org.uk. Est: 1990. Private premises. Internet and postal. Appointment necessary. Stock: large. Spec: Academic/Scholarly; Advertising; Aeronautics; Aesthetic Movement; Africana; Agriculture; Alchemy; Almanacs. PR: £3–1,000. CC: MC; V; PayPal. VAT No: GB 647 2977 92. [Updated]

Fossgate Books, ■ 36 Fossgate, York, YO1 9TF. Prop: Alex Helstrip. Tel: (01904) 641389. E-mail: alexhelstrip@hotmail.com. Est: 1992. Shop open: **M:** 10:00–17:30; **T:** 10:00–17:30; **W:** 10:00–17:30; **Th:** 10:00–17:30; **F:** 10:00–17:30; **S:** 10:00–17:30. Stock: very large. Spec: Academic/Scholarly; Antiquarian; Folio Society, The; History - General. PR: £2–300. CC: MC; V. [Updated]

Knapton Bookbarn, Back Lane, Knapton, York, YO26 6QJ. Tel: (01904) 339493. E-mail: . Est: 1996. Postal only. Spec: Natural History; Topography - General; Travel - General. PR: £5–100. [Updated]

Lucius Bookshop & Gallery, ■ 50 Fossgate, York, YO1 9TF. Prop: James Hallgate & Georgina Harris. Tel: 01904 640111. Fax: 01904 640444. Web: www.luciusbooks.com. E-mail: info@luciusbooks.com. Est: 1993. Shop open: **T:** 10:00–18:00; **W:** 10:00–18:00; **Th:** 10:00–18:00; **F:** 10:00–18:00; **S:** 10:00–18:00. Stock: very small. Spec: Authors: Aldin, Cecil; Barker, Cecily M.; Blyton, Enid; Bramah, Ernest; Brent-Dyer, Elinor M.; Burroughs, William; Carr, John Dickson; Carroll, Lewis. PR: £30–20,000. CC: D; E; JCB; MC; V; Debit. Cata: occasionally. Corresp: French. Mem: ABA; PBFA; ILAB. VAT No: GB 766 9110 08. [Updated]

Philip Martin Music Books, 22 Huntington Road, York, YO31 8RL. Prop: Martin & Eleanor Dreyer. Tel: (01904) 636111. Fax: (01904) 658889. E-mail: musicbooks@philipmartin.demon.co.uk. Est: 1975. Open: **T:** 10:00–17:30; **W:** 10:00–17:30; **Th:** 10:00–17:30; **F:** 10:00–17:30; **S:** 10:00–17:30; Closed for lunch: 13:00–14:00. Spec: Music - General; Music - Composers; Music - Opera; Music - Printed, Sheet Music & Scores; Musical Instruments. PR: £1–75. Notes: also, a comprehensive display of new books about music. [Updated]

Minster Gate Bookshop, ■ 8 Minster Gates, York, YO1 7HL. Prop: Nigel Wallace. Tel: (01904) 621812. Fax: (01904) 622960. Web: www.minstergatebooks.co.uk. E-mail: rarebooks@minstergatebooks.co.uk. Est: 1970. Shop. Internet and postal. Open: **M:** 10:00–17:30; **T:** 10:00–17:30; **W:** 10:00–17:30; **Th:** 10:00–17:30; **F:** 10:00–17:30; **S:** 10:00–17:30; **Su:** 11:00–19:00. Stock: large. Spec: Arthurian; Children's; Folklore; Illustrated; Literature; Booksearch. PR: £1–500. CC: MC; V. Corresp: French. Mem: PBFA. Notes: also, a free booksearch service. VAT No: GB 450 7122 78. [Updated]

Janette Ray Rare and Out of Print Books, ■ 8 Bootham, York, YO30 7BL. Prop: Janette Ray. Tel: (01904) 623088. Fax: (01904) 620814. Web: www.janetteray.co.uk. E-mail: books@janetteray.co.uk. Est: 1995. Shop. Internet and postal. Open: **F:** 09:30–17:30; **S:** 09:30–17:30. Stock: medium. Spec: Applied Art; Architecture; Design; Fine Art; Interior Design; Landscape; Photography. PR: £20–8,000. CC: E; MC; V. Corresp: French, Spanish. Mem: ABA; PBFA; ILAB. Notes: We also sell original drawings & photographic material. Valuations undertaken. VAT No: GB 698 7195 56. [Updated]

Ken Spelman, ■ 70 Micklegate, York, YO1 6LF. Prop: Peter Miller & Tony Fothergill. Tel: (01904) 624414. Fax: (01904) 626276. Web: www.kenspelman.com. E-mail: rarebooks@kenspelman.com. Est: 1948. Shop open: **M:** 09:00–17:30; **T:** 09:00–17:30; **W:** 09:00–17:30; **Th:** 09:00–17:30; **F:** 09:00–17:30; **S:** 09:00–17:30. Stock: very large. Spec: Academic/Scholarly; Antiquarian; Fine Art; History - General; Horticulture; Literature; Booksearch; Ephemera. PR: £1–10,000. CC: E; MC; V; SW. Mem: ABA; PBFA; BA; ILAB. Cata: quarterly. Notes: also, valuations & a booksearch service & on-line search and ordering. [Updated]

Jeffrey Stern Antiquarian Book, Little Hall, Heslington, York, YO10 5EB. Tel: (01904) 413711. Fax: (01904) 412761. Web: www.abebooks.com/home/STARLIN. E-mail: jeffrey@sternj.demon.co.uk. Est: 1971. Internet and postal. Spec: Academic/Scholarly; Anthropology; Antiquarian; Architecture; Art; Biography; Business Studies; Computing. PR: £25–2,000. CC: MC; V. Cata: online/Internet. [Updated]

Stone Trough Books, ■ 38 Fossgate, York, YO1 9TF. Prop: George Ramsden. Tel: (01904) 670323. Fax: (01944) 768465. E-mail: george@stonetrough.demon.co.uk. Est: 1981. Shop open: **T:** 10:00–17:30; **W:** 10:00–17:30; **Th:** 10:00–17:30; **F:** 10:00–17:30; **S:** 10:00–17:30. Stock: small. Spec: Art; Literature. PR: £2–200. CC: MC; V. Cata: occasionally. Corresp: French, German. Mem: PBFA. VAT No: GB 237 5500 70. [Updated]

Westfield Books, 28, Easthorpe Drive, York, YO26 6NR. Prop: A E Cunningham. Tel: 01904 794711. E-mail: westfieldbooks@btopenworld.com. Est: 1992. Mail Order Only. Internet and postal. Contactable. Spec: Antiquarian; Law - General. CC: PayPal. Mem: PBFA. VAT No: GB 827 4126 32. [Updated]

NORTHAMPTONSHIRE

BRACKLEY

The Old Hall Bookshop, ■ 32 Market Place, Brackley, NN13 7DP. Prop: John & Lady Juliet Townsend. Tel: 01280 704146. Web: www.oldhallbooks.com. E-mail: books@oldhallbooks.com. Est: 1977. Shop open: **M:** 09:30–17:30; **T:** 09:30–17:30; **W:** 09:30–17:30; **Th:** 09:30–17:30; **F:** 09:30–17:30; **S:** 09:30–17:30. Stock: medium. Spec: Children's; Topography - Local; Travel - General; Booksearch; Prints and Maps; Prints and Maps. PR: £1–10,000. CC: AE; JCB; MC; V; Maestro. Mem: ABA; PBFA; BA; ILAB. Notes: new books, fast order service, Book Tokens, book search etc. [Updated]

IRCHESTER

Jane Badger Books, Manor House Farm, High St, Irchester, Wellingborough, NN29 7AA. Prop: Jane Badger. Tel: (01922) 410943. Web: www.janebadgerbooks.co.uk. E-mail: janebadger.books@btinternet.com. Est: 2002. Mail Order Only. Internet and postal. Appointment necessary. Spec: Children's; Horses; Sport - Horse Racing (inc. Riding/Breeding/Equestrian); Sport - Hunting. CC: PayPal. Cata: quarterly on Pony Books and Equine Non-Fiction. [Updated]

NORTHAMPTON

Occultique, 30 St. Michael's Avenue, Northampton, NN1 4JQ. Prop: Michael John Lovett. Tel: (01604) 627727. Fax: (01604) 603860. Web: www.occultique.co.uk. E-mail: enquiries@occultique.co.uk. Est: 1973. Private premises. Internet and postal. Appointment necessary. Stock: medium. Spec: Alchemy; Alternative Medicine; American Indians; Astrology; Authors:- Crowley, Aleister; Spare, Austin Osman; Earth Mysteries; Egyptology. PR: £1–1,000. CC: PayPal. Notes: also, new books, essential oils, herbs & occult paraphernalia. [Updated]

Roosterbooks, 7 Elysium Terrace, Northampton, NN2 6EN. Tel: 01604 720983. Fax: 01604 720983. E-mail: roosterbooks@aol.com. Est: 1997. Private premises. Internet and postal. Appointment necessary. Stock: large. PR: £3–3,000. CC: MC; V. VAT No: GB 655 1461 40. [Updated]

Ryeland Books, 18 St. George's Place, Northampton, NN2 6EP. Prop: Alan & Joy Riley. Tel: (01604) 716901. E-mail: amriley@ryeland.demon.co.uk. Est: 1998. Private premises. Appointment necessary. Stock: small. Spec: Architecture; Art History; Children's; History - General; Literary Criticism; Literature; Natural History. PR: £3–1,000. Mem: PBFA. [Updated]

OUNDLE

Geraldine Waddington Books & P, ■ 3 West Street, Oundle, PE8 4EJ. Tel: (01832) 275028. Fax: (01832) 275028. Web: www.geraldinewaddington.com. E-mail: g.waddington@dial.pipex.com. Est: 1984. Internet and postal. Shop open: **M:** 10:00–17:00; **T:** 10:00–17:00; **Th:** 10:00–17:00; **F:** 10:00–17:00; **S:** 10:00–17:00. Stock: medium. Spec: Art Reference; Engraving; Ex-Libris; Folio Society, The; Illustrated; Private Press; Prints and Maps. PR: £2–500. CC: MC; V. Mem: PBFA. VAT No: GB 745 9396 81. [Updated]

RUSHDEN

Booksmart, 4 Manning Rise, Rushden, NN10 0LY. Prop: Andy Wagstaff. Tel: (01933) 357416. Web: www.booksmart.co.uk. E-mail: wagstaa@hotmail.com. Est: 1990. Postal only. Spec: Ephemera. PR: £1–10. [Updated]

SILVERSTONE

Collectors Carbooks, ■ 2210 Silverstone Technolgy Park, Silverstone Circuit, Silverstone, NN12 8TN. Prop: Chris Knapman. Tel: (01327) 855888. Fax: (01327) 855999. Web: www.collectorscarbooks.com. E-mail: info@collectorscarbooks.com. Est: 1993. Internet and postal. Shop open: **M:** 10:00–17:00; **T:** 10:00–17:00; **W:** 10:00–17:00; **Th:** 10:00–17:00; **F:** 10:00–17:00; **S:** 10:00–16::00. Stock: large. Spec: Marque Histories (see also motoring); Motorbikes / motorcycles; Motoring; Sport - Motor Racing; Transport; Vintage Cars; Booksearch. PR: £1–1,200. CC: MC; V. Notes: open certain race Saturdays 08:30–14:30. Also, a free booksearch service VAT No: GB 649 2588 91. [Updated]

Mr. Pickwick of Towcester, Lavender Cottage, Shutlanger, Towcester, NN12 7RR. Prop: William Mayes. Tel: (01604) 862006. Fax: (01604) 862006. Web: www.yell.co.uk.sites/pickwickbookfinders. Est: 1963. Private premises. Internet and postal. Stock: very large. Spec: Author - Dickens, Charles; Biography; Books about Books; Fiction - General; Literature; Magazines & Periodicals - General; Memoirs; Newspapers. PR: £3–300. [Updated]

WELLINGBOROUGH

Lost Books, 103 Leyland Trading Estate, Wellingborough, NN8 1RT. Prop: Meisterco Limited. Tel: (01933) 228828. Fax: (01933) 228828. Web: www.lostbooks.net. E-mail: gareth@lostbooks.net. Est: 2000. Warehouse; Internet and postal. Appointment necessary. Open: **M:** 09:00–17:30; **T:** 09:00–17:30; **W:** 09:00–17:30; **Th:** 09:00–17:30; **F:** 09:00–17:30; **S:** 09:00–17:00. Stock: very large. Spec: Arms & Armour; History - General; Military; Military History; Naval; War - General; War - Napoleonic; War - World War I. PR: £5–5,000. CC: AE; MC; V. Corresp: German, French. Notes: also, book Search. VAT No: GB 818 7468 87. [Updated]

The Park Gallery & Bookshop, ■ 16 Cannon Street, Wellingborough, NN8 4DJ. Prop: J.A. Foster. Tel: (01933) 222592. Web: www.ukbookworld.com/members/parkbookshop. E-mail: judy@parkbookshop.freeserve.co.uk. Est: 1979. Internet and postal. Shop open: **M:** 10:00–17:30; **T:** 10:00–17:30; **W:** 10:00–17:30; **Th:** 10:00–14:30; **F:** 10:00–17:30; **S:** 10:00–18:00. Stock: medium. Spec: Antiquarian; Antiques; Author - Bates, H.E.; Biography; Children's; Fiction - General; Military; Railways. PR: £1–500. Notes: also, a booksearch service, collectables, ephemera, prints & maps, plus picture framing. [Updated]

NORTHUMBERLAND

ALNWICK

Barter Books, ■ Alnwick Station, Alnwick, NE66 2NP. Prop: Stuart & Mary Manley. Tel: (01665) 604888. Fax: (01665) 604444. Web: www.barterbooks.co.uk. E-mail: bb@barterbooks.co.uk. Est: 1991. Shop open: **M:** 09:00–19:00; **T:** 09:00–19:00; **W:** 09:00–19:00; **Th:** 09:00–19:00; **F:** 09:00–19:00; **S:** 09:00–19:00; **Su:** 09:00–19:00. Stock: very large. PR: £1–13,000. CC: AE; JCB; MC; V. Corresp: French. Mem: IOBA. Notes: Barter Books, Seahouses, Northumberland open rest of the year, Mon-Sun 09:00–17.00. VAT No: GB 414 3504 88. [Updated]

BEADNELL

Shearwater Bed & Books, Shearwater, 78 Harbour Road, Beadnell, Northumberland, NE67 5BE. Prop: John Lumby. Tel: (01665) 720654. E-mail: shearwaterbooks@yahoo.co.uk. Est: 1965. Private premises. Internet and postal. Appointment necessary. Stock: very small. Spec: Natural History; New Naturalist; Ornithology. PR: £10–500. Notes: Booksearch & bookbinding + B&B . Attends British Bird Watching Fair. [Updated]

HALTWHISTLE

Newcastle Bookshop@Haltwhistle, ■ Market Square, Haltwhistle, NE49 OBG. Prop: Valerie Levitt. Tel: (01434) 320 103. Web: www.newcastlebookshop.com. E-mail: newcstlbk@aol.com. Est: 1975. Shop. Internet and postal. Open:**Th:** 11:00–16:00; **F:** 11:00–16:00; **S:** 11:00–16:00. Stock: medium. Spec: Art; Art History; Art Reference; Illustrated; Photography. CC: AE; JCB; MC; V; SW. Notes: bookbinding and repair service. Also, old prints. [Updated]

HEXHAM

Alex Fotheringham, East Chesterhope, West Woodburn, Hexham, NE48 2RQ. Tel: (01434) 270046 Fax: (01434) 632931. Private premises. Appointment necessary. Stock: very small. Spec: Antiquarian; Architecture; Art; Bibliography; Literature; Theology. PR: £20–2,500. Mem: ABA; PBFA. VAT No: GB 646 1882 17. [Updated]

Hencotes Books & Prints, ■ 8 Hencotes, Hexham, NE46 2EJ. Prop: Penny Pearce. Tel: (01434) 605971. E-mail: enquiries@hencotesbooks.onyxnet.co.uk. Est: 1981. Shop open: **M:** 10:30–17:00; **T:** 10:30–17:00; **W:** 10:30–17:00; **F:** 10:30–17:00; **S:** 10:30–17:00. Stock: medium. Spec: Booksearch. PR: £1–1,000. CC: JCB; MC; V; SW. Mem: PBFA. Notes: Attends P.B.F.A. and local fairs. VAT No: GB 796 9893 26. [Updated]

Newgate Books and Translations, 3 Quatre Bras, Hexham, NE46 3JY. Prop: Davina and John Dwyer. Tel: (01434) 607650. Fax: (01434) 607650. E-mail: newgate.books@virgin.net. Est: 1987. Private premises. Postal only. Contactable. Open: **M:** 09:00–18:00; **T:** 09:00–18:00; **W:** 09:00–18:00; **Th:** 09:00–18:00; **F:** 09:00–18:00; **S:** 09:00–12:00; Closed for lunch: 12:45–14:15. Stock: small. Spec: Conservation; Environment, The; Fiction - Crime, Detective, Spy, Thrillers; Music - Classical. PR: £5–300. Corresp: French, German. Notes: booksearch. French - English Translation. [Updated]

Priestpopple Books, ■ 9b Priestpopple, Hexham, NE46 1PF. Prop: John B. Patterson. Tel: (01434) 607773. E-mail: priestpopple.books@tinyworld.co.uk. Est: 1997. Shop open: **M:** 09:00–17:00; **T:** 09:00–17:00; **W:** 09:00–17:00; **Th:** 09:00–17:00; **F:** 09:00–17:00; **S:** 09:00–17:00. Stock: very large. Spec: Academic/Scholarly; Art Reference; Author - General; Author - Carlyle, Thomas; Children's; Cinema/Film; Crafts; Dogs. PR: £1–500. Notes: also, sheet music and used LPs. [Updated]

MORPETH

Intech Books, 14 Bracken Ridge, Morpeth, NE61 3SY. Prop: Mr. D. J. Wilkinson. Tel: (01670) 519102. Fax: (01670) 515815. E-mail: djw.intech@virgin.net. Est: 1981. Private premises. Internet and postal. Appointment necessary. Stock: small. Spec: Children's; Comic Books & Annuals; Fiction - General; First Editions; Topography - Local; Prints and Maps. PR: £1–100. Notes: also, a booksearch service. [Updated]

STOCKSFIELD

Leaf Ends, Leaf End, Ridley Mill, Stocksfield, NE43 7QU. Prop: Moira Tait. Tel: 01661 844261. Fax: 01661 844261. Web: www.abebooks.com. E-mail: alexander.tait@virgin.net. Est: 1995. Mail Order Only. Internet and postal. Appointment necessary. Spec: Children's. CC: MC; V. Notes: No set opening hours but contactable at any time, mixed general stock, over 5,000 childrens' books, stock listed on abebooks.com and viewable by appointment. VAT No: GB 747 2468 08. [Updated]

WOOLER

Hamish Dunn Antiques & Books, ■ 17 High Street, Wooler, NE71 6BU. Tel: (01668) 281341. Est: 1986. Shop open: **M:** 09:00–16:00; **T:** 09:00–16:00; **W:** 09:00–16:00; **Th:** 09:00–12:00; **F:** 09:00–16:00; **S:** 09:00–16:00. Stock: small. Spec: Ephemera; Prints and Maps. PR: £1–100. CC: AE; D; V. [Updated]

NOTTINGHAMSHIRE

BALDERTON

Anthony W. Laywood, Kercheval House, 70 Main Street, Balderton, Newark, NG24 3NN. Prop: Antony Laywood. Tel: (01636) 659031. Fax: (01636) 659219. E-mail: books@anthonylaywood.co.uk. Est: 1965. Private premises. Internet and postal. Appointment necessary. Open: **M:** 09:00–17:30; **T:** 09:00–17:30; **W:** 09:00–17:30; **Th:** 09:00–17:30; **F:** 09:00–17:30. Stock: medium. Spec: Antiquarian. PR: £25–3,000. [Updated]

GUNTHORPE

Letterbox Books, The Coach House, Gunthorpe, NG14 7ES. Prop: Bob Dakin. Tel: (0115) 966-4349. E-mail: enquiries@letterboxbooks.plus.com. Est: 1993. Private premises. Internet and postal. Stock: very small. Spec: Alpinism/Mountaineering; History - Local; Sport - Caving (Spelaeology); Sport - Potholing; Topography - General; Topography - Local; Booksearch; Ephemera. PR: £1–200. [Updated]

KIRKBY–IN–ASHFIELD

Kyrios Books, ■ 11 Kingsway, Kirkby–in–Ashfield, NG17 7BB. Prop: Keith Parr. Tel: (01623) 452556 answerphone. Web: www.kyriosbooks.co.uk. E-mail: keith@kyriosbooks.co.uk. Est: 1989. Shop. Internet and postal. Telephone first. Open: **M:** 09:00–16:30; **T:** 09:00–16:30; **W:** 09:00–16:00; **Th:** 09:00–16:30; **F:** 09:00–16:30; **S:** 09:00–16:30; Closed for lunch: 12:00–13:00. Stock: large. Spec: Autobiography; Ecclesiastical History & Architecture; Philosophy; Prayer Books; Religion - General; Religion - Christian; Theology. PR: £1–100. Mem: FSB. [Updated]

KIRKLINGTON

Karen Miller, Church Farm Cottage, Church Lane, Kirklington, NG22 8NA. Prop: Karen Miller. E-mail: karen@miller1964.freeserve.co.uk. Est: 1994. Mail Order Only. Internet and postal. Spec: Archaeology; Fiction - Historical; History - Ancient; History - British; History - European; History - Middle Ages. Cata: quarterly on ancient and medieval history (fact and fiction). Notes: I only deal in ancient and medieval history books. I operate a booksearch service (for ancient and medieval history books only). [Updated]

MANSFIELD

Fiona Edwards, 33 Crompton Road, Mansfield, NG19 7RG. Tel: 07710 410325. Prop: Fiona Edwards. E-mail: fionaedwardsbks@aol.com. Est: 1994. Private premises. Appointment necessary. Spec: Art; Cookery/Gastronomy; Music - General; Sport - General; Booksearch; Ephemera. CC: AE; JCB; MC; V. Mem: PBFA. Notes: also, ephemera and exhibits at PBFA fairs. [Updated]

R. W. Price, 19 Park Avenue, Mansfield, NG18 2AU. Prop: Mr G.D. Price. Tel: (01623) 629858. Web: www.gdprice.com. E-mail: gdp@gdprice.freeserve.co.uk. Est: 1986. Private premises. Internet and postal. Stock: very large. Spec: Beat Writers; Children's; Comedy; Erotica; Espionage; Fiction - General; Fiction - Crime, Detective, Spy, Thrillers; Fiction - Fantasy, Horror. PR: £0–100. [Updated]

NEWARK

Gladstone Books, ■ Curio Cafe Antique Centre, 57–59 Castle gate, Newark, NG24 1BG. Prop: Prof. Ben Mepham. Tel: 01636 813601. E-mail: ben.mepham@btopenworld.com. Est: 2005. Shop open: **M:** 09:30–16:30; **T:** 09:30–16:30; **W:** 09:30–16:30; **Th:** 09:30–16:30; **F:** 09:30–16:30; **S:** 09:30–16:30; **Su:** 11:00–16:30. Notes: Exhibits at fairs. [Updated]

Lawrence Books, Newark Antiques Centre, Lombard Street, Newark–on–Trent, NG24 1XP. Prop: Arthur Lawrence. Tel: (01636) 605865. Est: 1987. Market stand/stall. Open: **M:** 09:30–17:00; **T:** 09:30–17:00; **W:** 09:30–17:00; **Th:** 09:30–17:00; **F:** 09:30–17:00; **S:** 09:30–17:00; **Su:** 11:00–16:00. Stock: small. Spec: Aviation; Diaries; History - General; Letters; Maritime/Nautical; Military; Poetry; Topography - Local. PR: £1–200. Notes: exhibits at book fairs, bookbinding. Alternative tel: (01636) 701619. [Updated]

NOTTINGHAM

Artco, 6 Grantham Road, Radcliffe on Trent, Nottingham, NG12 2HD. Prop: Mr. H. Boehm. Tel: (0115) 933-3530. Fax: (0115) 911-9746. Est: 1970. Private premises. Appointment necessary. Stock: small. Spec: Applied Art; Art; Art Reference; Artists; Arts, The; Colour-Plate; Foreign Texts; Illustrated. PR: £10–1,000. CC: MC; V. Corresp: German. [Updated]

Geoffrey Blore's Bookshop, ■ 484 Mansfield Road, Sherwood, Nottingham, NG5 2BF. Tel: (0115) 969-1441. Est: 1987. Shop open: **M:** 10:30–17:00; **T:** 10:30–17:00; **W:** 10:30–17:00; **Th:** 10:30–17:00; **F:** 10:30–17:00; **S:** 10:30–17:00. Stock: very large. [Updated]

Guy Davis, Antiquarian Books, 61 Bakerdale Road, Bakersfield, Nottingham, NG3 7GJ. Tel: (0115) 940-3835. Fax: (0115) 940-0093. Est: 1970. Spec: Bindings; Fore-Edge Paintings; Prints and Maps. PR: £50–5,000. [Updated]

A. Holmes, 82 Highbury Avenue, Nottingham, NG6 9DB. Prop: A. Holmes. Tel: (0115) 979-5603. E-mail: aholmesbooks@ntlworld.com. Est: 1997. Private premises. Postal only. Telephone first. Open: Stock: very large. Spec: Biography; Gypsies; History - General; Military; Travel - General. PR: £5–1,000. [Updated]

Jermy & Westerman, ■ 203 Mansfield Road, Sherwood, Nottingham, NG1 3FS. G.T. Prop: G. Blore. Tel: (0115) 947-4522. Est: 1977. Shop open: **M:** 11:00–17:00; **T:** 11:00–17:00; **W:** 11:00–17:00; **Th:** 11:00–17:00; **F:** 11:00–17:00; **S:** 11:00–17:00. Stock: medium. Spec: Illustrated; Literature; Topography - Local. Notes: see also Geoffrey Blore's Bookshop, Nottingham. [Updated]

Frances Wakeman Books, PO Box 8039, Nottingham, NG5 2WN. Prop: Frances & Paul Wakeman. Tel: (0115) 875 3944. Fax: none. Web: www.fwbooks.com. E-mail: info@fwbooks.com. Est: 1970. Private premises. Internet and postal. Appointment necessary. Stock: very small. Spec: Bibliography; Books about Books; Papermaking; Printing; Private Press; Publishing; Typography. PR: £100–6,000. CC: AE; E; JCB; MC; V. Mem: PBFA: Notes: also, publishing books about books VAT No: GB 685 4226 14. [Updated]

REDMILE

Forest Books, Overfields, 1, Belvoir Road, Redmile, NG13 0GL. Tel: (01949) 842360. Fax: (01949) 844196. Web: www.forestbooks.co.uk. E-mail: bib@forestbooks.co.uk. Est: 1979. Private premises. Internet and postal. Appointment necessary. Stock: medium. Spec: Bibliography; Bindings; Bookbinding; Books about Books; Papermaking; Printing; Typography. PR: £5–5,000. CC: MC; V. Mem: PBFA. [Updated]

SANDIACRE

A.E. Beardsley, 14 York Avenue, Sandiacre, NG10 5HB. Tony and Irene Beardsley. Tel: (0115) 917-0082. Web: www.ukbookworld.com/members/aebbooks. E-mail: aebbooks@ntlworld.com. Est: 1991. Private premises. Appointment necessary. Stock: small. Spec: Countries - Malaysia; Topography - General; Travel - General; Booksearch. PR: £4–400. Notes: exhibits at Buxton Book Fair - 1,000 books on www.abebooks.com. [Updated]

SUTTON IN ASHFIELD

Kingfisher Book Service, 6 Ash Grove, Skegby, Sutton in Ashfield, NG17 3FH. Prop: Malcolm Walters. Tel: (01623) 552530. Fax: (01623) 552530. Web: www.kingfisher-books.co.uk. E-mail: quotes@kingfisher-books.co.uk. Est: 1991. Private premises. Postal only. Stock: very small. Spec: Fiction - General; Military; War - General; Booksearch. PR: £3–100. CC: AE; E; JCB; MC; V. [Updated]

OXFORDSHIRE

ABINGDON

Bennett & Kerr Books, Millhill Warehouse, Church Lane, Steventon, Abingdon, OX13 6SW. (*) Prop: Edmund Bennett & Andrew Kerr Tel: (01235) 820604. Fax: (01235) 821047. Web: www.abebooks.com/home/bennettkerr. E-mail: bennettkerr@aol.com. Est: 1982. Storeroom. Internet and postal. Telephone first. Open: **M:** 09:30–17:30; **T:** 09:30–17:30; **W:** 09:30–17:30; **Th:** 09:30–17:30; **F:** 09:30–17:30; **S:** 10:00–13:00; Closed for lunch: 13:15–14:15. Stock: medium. Spec: Academic/Scholarly; Art History; Ecclesiastical History & Architecture; History - General; Iconography; Literary Criticism; Medieval; Palaeography. PR: £5–1,000. CC: MC; V; Switch. Corresp: French, Italian. Mem: ABA; PBFA; ILAB. Notes: selection at Oxbow Books, Park End Place, Oxford. VAT No: GB 348 7058 28. [Updated]

B. & N. Kentish, Old Farmhouse, Longworth, Abingdon, OX13 5ET. Tel: (01865) 820711. E-mail: briankentish@yahoo.co.uk. Private premises. Postal only. Spec: Atlases. Cata: annually. Notes: also see entry in Sheppard's Prints & Map Sellers. [Updated]

Mary Mason, 55 Winterborne Road, Abingdon, OX14 1AL. Prop: Mary Mason. Tel: (01235) 559929. Web: www.masonpeett.co.uk. E-mail: marymason@mmbooks.freeserve.co.uk. Est: 1988. Private premises. Internet and postal. Appointment necessary. Stock: medium. Spec: Art; Author - Ardizzone, Edward; Children's; Illustrated; Juvenile. PR: £1–1,000. CC: PayPal. Corresp: French. Notes: booksearch. [Updated]

PsychoBabel Books & Journals, 56b Milton Park, Abingdon, OX14 4RX. Prop: Chris Edwards. Tel: 01235 861411. Fax: 01235 861422. Web: www.psychobabel.co.uk. E-mail: psychobabel@btconnect.com. Est: 2003. Warehouse; Internet and postal. Contactable. Open: **M:** 08:30–18:00; **T:** 08:30–18:00; **W:** 08:30–18:00; **Th:** 08:30–18:00; **F:** 08:30–18:00; **S:** 10:00–14:00; **Su:** 10:00–14:00. Spec: Biblical Studies; Celtica; Communism; Eastern Philosophy; Ecclesiastical History & Architecture; Economics; Encyclopaedias; European Books. CC: AE; MC; V; PayPal. Corresp: German, French, Spanish. VAT No: GB 824 8827 00. [Updated]

BANBURY

Books, The Old Forge, Upper Brailes, Banbury, OX15 5AT. Prop: Mrs E.M. Pogmore. Tel: (01608) 685260. Web: www.pogmore@marg3.freeserve.co.uk. E-mail: pogmore@marg3.freeserve.co.uk. Est: 1985. Private premises. Postal only. Contactable. Stock: small. Spec: Author - Fleming, Ian; Autobiography; Cookery/Gastronomy; Modern First Editions; Poetry; Tapestry. PR: £1–200. [Updated]

BLEWBURY

Blewbury Antiques, ■ London Road, Blewbury, OX11 9NX. Prop: Eric Richardson. Tel: (01235) 850366. Est: 1971. Shop open: **M:** 10:00–18:00; **Th:** 10:00–18:00; **F:** 10:00–18:00; **S:** 10:00–18:00; **Su:** 10:00–18:00. Stock: very small. Notes: also, collectables, garden ornaments. [Updated]

BURFORD

The Classics Bookshop, Greyhounds, 23 Sheep Street, Burford, OX18 4LS. Prop: Anne and Philip Powell-Jones. Tel: 01993 822969. Fax: 01993 822969. Web: www.classicsbookshop.co.uk. E-mail: sales@classicsbookshop.com. Est: 1975. Office and/or bookroom. Open: **W:** 10:00–17:00; **S:** 10:00–17:00; Closed for lunch: 13:00–14:00. Spec: Archaeology; Art; Classical Studies; English; History - Ancient; Sport - Angling/Fishing. CC: AE; MC; V. Cata: quarterly on Latin and Greek Classics. Mem: PBFA. VAT No: GB 298 2963 94. [Updated]

CHIPPING NORTON

Four Shire Bookshops, PO Box 231, Chipping Norton, OX7 9AP. Prop: Linda Osgood. Tel: (01608) 651451. Fax: (01608) 650827. E-mail: fourshirebooks@aol.com. Est: 1981. Private premises. Internet Only. Appointment necessary. Open: **M:** 09:30–16:00; **T:** 09:30–16:00; **W:** 09:30–16:00; **Th:** 09:30–17:00; **F:** 09:30–17:00; **S:** 08:30–17:00; Closed for lunch: 13:00–14:00. Stock: medium. Spec: Crafts; Embroidery; Needlework; Booksearch. PR: £1–100. CC: E; JCB; MC; V. Mem: FSB. [Updated]

Greensleeves, P.O. Box 156, Chipping Norton, OX7 3XT. Prop: P.R. & C. Seers. Tel: (01608) 676140. Fax: (01608) 676140. Web: www.greensleevesbooks.co.uk. E-mail: greensleeves@v21mail.co.uk. Est: 1982. Private premises. Postal only. Stock: medium. Spec: Alternative Medicine; Anthroposophy; Astrology; Esoteric; Health; Herbalism; Homeopathy; Metaphysics. PR: £1–500. CC: MC; V; Switch. Mem: BA. Notes: also, new books and booksearch service. VAT No: GB 596 3357 96. [Updated]

Kellow Books, ■ 6 Market Place, Chipping Norton, OX7 5NA. Prop: Peter & Jan Combellack. Tel: (01608) 644293. Est: 1998. Shop open: **M:** 10:00–16:30; **T:** 10:00–16:30; **W:** 10:00–16:30; **Th:** 10:00–16:30; **F:** 10:00–16:30. Stock: medium. Spec: Children's; Company History; Fiction - General; Maritime/Nautical; Military History; Natural History; Ornithology; Topography - General. PR: £2–800. CC: AE; D; E; JCB; MC; V; All cards. [Updated]

COWLEY

Thornton's Bookshop, 65 St Luke's Road, Cowley, Oxford, OX4 3JE. Prop: W.A. Meeuws. Tel: (01865) 779832. Fax: (01865) 321126. Web: www.thorntonsbooks.co.uk. E-mail: thorntons@booknews.demon.co.uk. Est: 1835. Private premises. Internet and postal. Contactable. Stock: medium. Spec: Classical Studies; Fine & Rare; History - General; History - Ancient; Languages - Foreign; Philosophy; Theology; Topography - General. PR: £15–1,000. CC: JCB; MC; V; Maestro. Corresp: French, Dutch, German, Spanish, Italian. Mem: ABA; BA; ILAB; BASEES. VAT No: GB 194 4663 31. [21/11/2004]

DEDDINGTON

Brian Carter, 13 High Street, Deddington, OX15 0SJ. Brian Carter. Tel: (01869) 337341. E-mail: carterbe@lineone.net. Est: 1974. Private premises. Postal only. Contactable. Stock: small. Spec: Ecclesiastical History & Architecture; Oxford Movement; Philosophy; Theology. PR: £5–500. CC: MC; V. Notes: we take telephone calls from 09:00 to 21:00 all week. [Updated]

DIDCOT

The Parlour Bookshop, ■ 30 Wantage Road, Didcot, OX11 0BT. Prop: Roy Burton. Tel: (01235) 818989. Fax: (01235) 814494. Est: 1995. Shop open: **W:** 10:00–16:00; **Th:** 10:00–16:00; **F:** 10:00–16:00; Closed for lunch: 12:45–13:45. Stock: small. Spec: Military; Railways; Topography - General. PR: £1–50. Notes: Closed Bank Holidays, Good Friday, Easter Monday, Christmas Eve to 4 January. [Updated]

Wayside Books & Cards, Wayside Wellshead, Harwell, Didcot, OX11 0HD. Prop: J.A.B. & J.L. Gibson. Tel: (01235) 835256. E-mail: gibsonjab@aol.com. Est: 1985. Private premises. Postal only. Open in Summer. Stock: medium. Spec: Arms & Armour; Astronomy; Biography; Countries - Melanesia; Fiction - Science Fiction; Journals; Law - General; Physics. PR: £1–100. [Updated]

DORCHESTER ON THAMES

Pablo Butcher, Overy Mill, Dorchester on Thames, OX10 7JU. Tel: (01865) 341445. Fax: (01865) 340180. Est: 1974. Private premises. Appointment necessary. Stock: small. Spec: Art; Ethnography; Photography; Travel - Africa; Travel - Americas; Travel - Asia, South East; Travel - India; Travel - Islamic World. Mem: ABA; PBFA; ILAB. [Updated]

DUCKLINGTON

Demetzy Books, Manor House, 29 Standlake Road, Ducklington, OX29 7UX. Prop: Paul & Marie Hutchinson. Tel: 01993 702209. Fax: 01993 702209. E-mail: demetzybooks@tiscali.co.uk. Est: 1971. Market stand/stall. Shop At: 113 Portobello Road London W.11. Open: **S:** 07:00–15.00. Spec: Antiquarian; Juvenile; Miniature Books; Natural Sciences; Surgery; Travel - General. CC: JCB; MC; V. Mem: ABA; PBFA; BA; ILAB. [Updated]

EAST HAGBOURNE

E.M. Lawson & Company, Kingsholm, East Hagbourne, OX11 9LN. Prop: W.J. & K.M. Lawson. Tel: (01235) 812033. Est: 1919. Private premises. Appointment necessary. Stock: very small. Spec: Antiquarian; Countries - Africa; Americas, The; Australasia; Economics; Literature; Medicine; Science - General. Cata: occasionally on general subjects. Mem: ABA; ILAB. [Updated]

FARINGDON

E.W. Classey Limited, 9 Regal Way, Faringdon, SN7 7BX. Prop: Peter & E.W. Classey. Tel: (01367) 244700. Fax: (01367) 244800. Web: www.classeybooks.com. E-mail: bugbooks@classey.demon.co.uk. Est: 1949. Office and/or bookroom. Internet and postal. Open: **M:** 09:00–04:00; **T:** 09:00–04:00; **W:** 09:00–04:00; **Th:** 09:00–04:00; **F:** 09:00–03:00. Stock: large. Spec: Entomology; Natural History; Booksearch. PR: £1–15,000. CC: E; MC; V. Notes: also, natural history publisher, new books [Updated]

N.W. Jobson, 8 Weston Cottages, Buscot Wick, Faringdon, SN7 8DN. Prop: Nigel Jobson. Tel: (01367) 252240. E-mail: jobbobookfinder@tiscali.co.uk. Est: 1981. Private premises. Postal only. Stock: small. Spec: Booksearch. PR: £1–100. [Updated]

GORING–ON–THAMES

Nevis Railway Books, ■ 3 Barbara's, The Orchard, Goring–on–Thames, RG8 9HB. Prop: N.J. Bridger. Tel: (01491) 873032. Web: www.nevis-railway-bookshops.co.uk. Est: 1992. Shop open: **M:** 10:00–17:00; **T:** 10:00–17:00; **W:** 10:00–17:00; **Th:** 10:00–17:00; **F:** 10:00–17:00; **S:** 10:00–17:00; Closed for lunch: 13:00–14:15. Stock: very small. Spec: Railways. PR: £1–50. Notes: Railway Book & Magazine Search, Newbury, Berks. (qv.) Nevis railway Bookshops, Marlborough, Wilts (q.v). [Updated]

HENLEY ON THAMES

Jonkers Rare Books, 24 Hart Street, Henley on Thames, RG9 2AU. Tel: (01491) 576427. Web: www.jonkers.co.uk. E-mail: info@jonkers.co.uk. Est: 1990. Shop and/or showroom; Open: **M:** 10:00–17:30; **T:** 10:00–17:30; **W:** 10:00–17:30; **Th:** 10:00–17:30; **F:** 10:00–17:30; **S:** 10:00–17:30. Stock: small. Spec: Children's; Children's - Illustrated; Literature; Modern First Editions. PR: £25–1,000,000. CC: AE; E; MC; V. Cata: quarterly on specialist subjects. Corresp: Italian, French, Spanish. Mem: ABA; PBFA; BA; ILAB. [Updated]

Richard Way Booksellers, ■ 54 Friday Street, Henley–on–Thames, RG9 1AH. Prop: Richard Way & Diana Cook. Tel: (01491) 576663. Fax: (01491) 576663. Est: 1978. Shop open: **M:** 10:00–17:30; **T:** 10:00–17:30; **W:** 10:00–17:30; **Th:** 10:00–17:30; **F:** 10:00–17:30; **S:** 10:00–17:30. Stock: small. Spec: River Thames; Sport - Rowing. PR: £1–200. CC: E; JCB; V; Switch. Mem: ABA. [Updated]

HOOK NORTON

Orangeberry Books, Rowan House, Queens Street, Hook Norton, Banbury, OX15 5PH. Prop: Paul Tranter. Tel: (01608) 737928. Fax: (01608) 730810. Web: www.orangeberry.co.uk. E-mail: books@orangeberry.co.uk. Est: 1995. Private premises. Internet and postal. Telephone first. Stock: medium. Spec: Literature; Poetry; Science - General; Technology; Travel - General. PR: £5–1,000. CC: E; MC; V; Maestro. Corresp: French. Mem: IBN. VAT No: GB 800 0734 85. [Updated]

MARSH GIBBON

Dusty Old Books Ltd, 7 Pear Tree Farm, Marsh Gibbon, OX27 0GB. Prop: Paul Poornan. Tel: (01869) 278 160. Fax: (01869) 278 163. Web: www.dustyoldbooks.com. E-mail: paul@dustyoldbooks.com. Spec: Agriculture; Antiquarian; History - General; Medicine; Travel - General; Veterinary. PR: £20–200. [Updated]

OXFORD

Antiques on High, ■ 85 High Street, Oxford, OX1 4BG. Prop: Paul Lipson amd Sally Young. Tel: (01865) 251075. Est: 1997. Shop open: **M:** 10:00–17:00; **T:** 10:00–17:00; **W:** 10:00–17:00; **Th:** 10:00–17:00; **F:** 10:00–17:00; **S:** 10:00–17:00; **Su:** 11:00–17:00. Stock: medium. Spec: Antiques; Architecture; Art; Art History; Autobiography; Biography; Children's; Collecting. PR: £1–200. CC: AE; E; JCB; MC; V. Notes: has stock for 'Books on High' and 'Music Bookshop'. [Updated]

PROJECT PORTMANTEAUX - EVERY MAN A DEBTOR

Give thought - Virtue can be fun

Project Portmanteaux the outcome of the creative thinking of Gordon Rattray-Taylor is a project which brings hope to the excluded young. In the first instance the gifted who by misfortune have missed their footing on the upper rungs of the educational ladder. While mammon demands that we fund raise, our immediate plangent need is for fine minds willing to help keep the good ship charity on course. Mind Tune the young. Let your educational success endow theirs.

Be a mentor on the net:

mind-a-mind.com   guru-4u.com   entente-serieurse.com

This advertisement is sponsored by Game Advice, 71 Rose Hill, OX4 4JR GB

Arcadia, ■ 4 St. Michael's Street, Oxford, OX1 2DU. Tel: (01865) 241757. Est: 1975. Shop open: **M:** 10:00–17:30; **T:** 10:00–17:30; **W:** 10:00–17:30; **Th:** 10:00–17:30; **F:** 10:00–17:30; **S:** 10:00–18:00. Stock: very small. Spec: Publishers - Penguin; Ephemera; Prints and Maps. PR: £1–50. CC: AE; D; E; JCB; MC; V. Mem: PBFA Notes: mainly prints and postcards. [Updated]

Ars Artis, 31 Abberbury Road, Oxford, OX4 4ET. Prop: G.B. & H.J. Lowe. Tel: 01865 770714. Est: 1976. Private premises. Appointment necessary. Spec: Applied Art; Architecture; Art History; Art Reference; Artists; Catalogues Raisonnes; Fine Art; Photography. VAT No: GB 119 1785 58. [Updated]

Blackwell's Music Shop, ■ 23-25 Broad Street, Oxford, OX1 3AX. Tel: (01865) 333580. Fax: (01865) 728020. Web: www.blackwell.co.uk/printedmusic. E-mail: books.music@blackwell.co.uk. Est: 1955. Shop. Internet and postal. Open: **M:** 09:00–18:00; **T:** 09:30–18:00; **W:** 09:00–18:00; **Th:** 09:00–18:00; **F:** 09:00–18:00; **S:** 09:00–18:00; **Su:** 11:00–17:00. Stock: very large. Spec: Music - General; Music - Classical; Music - Composers; Music - Musicians; Music - Opera. PR: £2–175. CC: MC; V. [Updated]

Blackwell's Rare Books, ■ 48 - 51 Broad Street, Oxford, OX1 3BQ. Tel: (01865) 333555. Fax: (01865) 794143. Web: www.rarebooks.blackwell.co.uk. E-mail: rarebooks@blackwell.co.uk. Est: 1879. Shop. Internet and postal. Open: **M:** 09:00–18:00; **T:** 09:30–18:00; **W:** 09:00–18:00; **Th:** 09:00–18:00; **F:** 09:00–18:00; **S:** 09:00–20:00. Stock: small. Spec: Classical Studies; Juvenile; Literature; Modern First Editions; Private Press; Travel - General. PR: £20–20,000. CC: MC; V. Corresp: French, German, Russian. Mem: ABA; PBFA; BA; ILAB. Notes: vast range of new books, particularly in academic subjects [Updated]

Game Advice, 71 Rose Hill, Oxford, OX4 4JR. Prop: Alick Elithorn. Tel: (01865) 777317. Fax: (01865) 433050. Web: www.game-advice.com. E-mail: a.elithorn@ntlworld.com. Est: 1975. Private premises. Internet and postal. Telephone first. Stock: large. Spec: Academic/Scholarly; Anthropology; Children's; Computing; Education & School; Fore-Edge Paintings; Games; History of Ideas. PR: £3–9,000. Corresp: French. Notes: also, chess sets, antique games & puzzles, chess prints, educational software, computer & personal consultancy, booksearch & loan. [Updated]

Hanborough Books, The Foundry, Church Hanborough, Nr. Witney, Oxford, OX29 8AB. Prop: Dennis Hall. Tel: (01993) 881260. Fax: (01993) 883080. Web: www.parrotpress.co.uk. E-mail: dennis@parrotpress.co.uk. Est: 1970. Private premises. Appointment necessary. Stock: small. Spec: Antiquarian; Illustrated; Limited Editions; Private Press; Typography. PR: £5–650. CC: MC; V. VAT No: GB 490 6827 17. [Updated]

The Inner Bookshop, ■ 111 Magdalen Road, Oxford, OX4 1RQ. Prop: R.E. Ashcroft & A.S. Cheke. Tel: (01865) 245301. Fax: (01865) 245521. Web: www.innerbookshop.com. E-mail: mail@innerbookshop .com. Est: 1982. Shop. Internet and postal. Open: **M:** 10:00–17:45; **T:** 10:00–17:45; **W:** 10:00–17:45; **Th:** 10:00–17:45; **F:** 10:00–17:45; **S:** 10:00–17:45. Stock: large. Spec: Academic/Scholarly; Alchemy; Alternative Medicine; American Indians; Anthroposophy; Arthurian; Astrology; Cryptozoology. PR: £1–1,000. CC: E; MC; V; SW, SO. Corresp: French. Mem: BA; FSB. Notes: also, new books on specialities & tarot cards, New Age music, bargain books and a passive booksearch service. [Updated]

Leabeck Books, Meadowbrook Farm, Sheepwash Lane, Steventon, Oxford, OX13 6SD. Prop: Tony Sloggett. Tel: (01235) 820914. E-mail: tony.sloggett@britishlibrary.net. Est: 1993. Private premises. Internet and postal. Appointment necessary. Stock: small. Spec: Antiques; Art; Children's; First Editions; History - General; Illustrated; Literature; Travel - General. PR: £5–200. Corresp: French, German. Notes: also at Antiques on High, 85 High Street, Oxford, OX1 4BG. [Updated]

Chris Morris Secondhand & Antiquarian Books, 67 Home Close, Wolvercote, Oxford, OX2 8PT. Tel: (01865) 557806. E-mail: chrisandbarbara@yahoo.com. Est: 1992. Private premises. Internet and postal. Stock: small. Spec: Cinema/Film; Motoring; Music - General; Sport - Motor Racing; Television. PR: £1–75. Notes: also, a booksearch service. [Updated]

Oxfam Bookshop St Giles, ■ 56 St Giles, Oxford, OX1 3LU. Manager: Jen Elford. Tel: 01865 310145. Web: www.oxfamstgiles.co.uk. E-mail: stgiles56@yahoo.co.uk. Est: 1987. Shop open: **M:** 10:00–17:30; **T:** 10:00–17:30; **W:** 10:00–17:30; **Th:** 10:00–17:30; **F:** 10:00–17:30; **S:** 10:00–17:30. Spec: CC: E; JCB; MC; V; Switch, Maestro. Cata: monthly but on-line only. Corresp: French, German, Italian. [Updated]

St Philip's Books, ■ 82 St. Aldates, Oxford, OX1 1RA. Prop: Christopher James Zealley. Tel: (01865) 202182. Fax: (01865) 202184. Web: www.stphilipsbooks.co.uk. E-mail: sales@stphilipsbooks.co.uk. Est: 1995. Internet and postal. Shop open: **M:** 10:00–17:00; **T:** 10:00–17:00; **W:** 10:00–17:00; **Th:** 10:00–17:00; **F:** 10:00–17:00; **S:** 10:00–17:00. Stock: large. Spec: Academic/Scholarly; Antiquarian; Art History; Art Nouveau; Authors:- Inklings, The; Lewis, C.S.; Newman, Cardinal; Bibles. PR: £1–2,000. CC: MC; V; SO, SW. Mem: PBFA. Notes: religious books bought nationwide. VAT No: GB 717 925 021. [Updated]

Waterfield's, ■ 52 High Street, Oxford, OX1 4AS. Prop: Robin Waterfield Ltd. Tel: (01865) 721809. Est: 1973. Shop open: **M:** 09:45–17:45; **T:** 09:45–17:45; **W:** 09:45–17:44; **Th:** 08:45–17:45; **F:** 09:45–17:45; **S:** 09:45–17:45. Stock: large. Spec: Academic/Scholarly; Antiquarian; Arts, The; First Editions; History - General; Humanities; Literary Criticism; Literature. PR: £1–5,000. CC: MC; V. Corresp: French Mem: ABA; PBFA. Notes: Catalogues also on 17th and 18thC books VAT No: GB 195 8007 39. [Updated]

STONESFIELD

Austin Sherlaw-Johnson, Woodland View, Churchfields, Stonesfield, OX29 8PP. Tel: (01993) 898223. E-mail: austin.sherlaw-johnson@virgin.net. Est: 2001. Private premises. Appointment necessary. Open: **M:** 09:00–17:00; **T:** 09:00–17:00; **W:** 09:00–17:00; **Th:** 09:00–17:00; **F:** 09:00–17:00. Stock: medium. Spec: Music - General; Music - Composers; Music - Opera; Musical Instruments. PR: £1–500. Notes: also at: Malvern Bookshop, Malvern, Worcestershire (q.v.) Antiques on High, 85 High Street, Oxford. [Updated]

WALLINGFORD

Toby English, ■ 10 St. Mary's Street, Wallingford, OX10 0EL. Tel: (01491) 836389. Fax: (01491) 836389. Web: www.tobyenglish.com. E-mail: toby@tobyenglish.com. Est: 1981. Shop open: **M:** 09:30–17:00; **T:** 09:30–17:00; **W:** 09:30–17:00; **Th:** 09:30–16:45; **F:** 09:30–16:45; **S:** 09:30–17:00. Stock: large. Spec: Academic/Scholarly; Architecture; Art; Author - Inklings, The; First Editions; Private Press; Topography - Local; Typography. PR: £1–500. CC: AE; JCB; MC; V; SW. Cata: annually. Mem: PBFA. Notes: also, a booksearch service. [Updated]

Tooley, Adams & Co, PO Box 174, Wallingford D.O., OX10 0RB. Prop: Steve Luck. Tel: 01491 838298. Fax: 01491834616. Web: www.tooleys.co.uk. E-mail: steve@tooleys.co.uk. Est: 1979. Private premises. Internet and postal. Telephone first. Open: **M:** 09:00–17:00; **T:** 09:00–17:00; **W:** 09:00–17:00; **Th:** 09:00–17:00; **F:** 09:00–17:00. Spec: Antiquarian; Caricature; Cartography; Geography; River Thames. CC: AE; D; E; JCB; MC; V. Cata: occasionally on Maps, Atlases, Views, Cartobibliographies. Corresp: French, Spanish. Mem: ABA; BA; ILAB; International Antiquarian Mapdealers Assoc. VAT No: GB 371 2110 01. [Updated]

```
        Bed and Books              Birds and Beauty

        The High Road to the islands
           lined with literature
                  Voyages-Heureux.com
```

```
    If you like to see and feel before you buy the books you will
    love: You will buy from and stay with one of the partners who
    support the "entente-serieuse.com" These you will find listed
    near a scenic route at "not-the-M40.com." which brings you to
                         Game-Advice
         A Mecca for "medics-beyond-medicine.com"

      On the ground @ 71 Rose Hill OX4 4JR +44 1865 777 317
```

WANTAGE
Parrott Books, ■ Regent Mall, Town Centre, Wantage, OX12 8BU. Tel: (01367) 820251. Fax: (01367) 820210. E-mail: parrottbooks@aol.com. Est: 1997. Shop open: **M:** 08:30–17:30; **T:** 08:30–17:30; **W:** 08:30–17:30; **Th:** 08:30–17:30; **F:** 08:30–17:30; **S:** 08:30–17:00. Stock: very large. Spec: Alpinism/Mountaineering; Animals and Birds; Archaeology; Architecture; Art Reference; Biography; Children's; Cookery/Gastronomy. PR: £2–50. [Updated]

WARBOROUGH
Nineteenth Century Books, St. Mary's Cottage, 61 Thame Road, Warborough, Wallingford, OX10 7EA. Prop: Dr. Ann M. Ridler. Tel: (01865) 858379. Fax: (01865) 858575. Web: www.ukbookworld.com/members/papageno. E-mail: annridlersoutter@warboro.fsnet.co.uk. Est: 1984. Private premises. Internet and postal. Stock: small. Spec: Biography; Books about Books; History - General; Literature; Natural History; Philology; Poetry; Topography - General. PR: £5–500. CC: MC; V. Corresp: French, Spanish. Mem: PBFA. [Updated]

WITNEY
Church Green Books, ■ 46 Market Square, Witney, OX28 6AL. Prop: Roger & Margaret Barnes. Tel: (01993) 700822. Web: www.churchgreen.co.uk. E-mail: books@churchgreen.co.uk. Est: 1992. Shop open: **M:** 10:00–16:00; **T:** 10:00–16:00; **W:** 10:00–16:00; **Th:** 10:00–16:00; **F:** 10:00–16:00. Stock: medium. Spec: Bell-Ringing (Campanology); Music - Folk & Irish Folk; Rural Life; Topography - Local; Booksearch. PR: £1–300. CC: MC; V. Mem: PBFA. Notes: valuations of Bell-ringing books. [Updated]

RUTLAND

UPPINGHAM

The Rutland Bookshop, ■ 13 High Street West, Uppingham, LE15 9QB. Prop: Mr & Mrs Edward Baines. Tel: (01572) 823450. Est: 1979. Shop open: **T:** 11:00–17:00; **W:** 11:00–17:00; **Th:** 11:00–17:00; **F:** 11:00–17:00; **S:** 11:00–17:00. Stock: medium. Spec: Education & School; Farming & Livestock; Farriers; Fiction - General; Gardening - General; Literary Criticism; Natural History; Odd & Unusual. PR: £1–500. Corresp: French, German. Mem: PBFA. Notes: attends Burghley Horse Trials, Rutland Water Bird Fair and Rutland & Leicester Agricultural Show. [Updated]

Forest Books, ■ 7 High Street West, Uppingham, Rutland, LE15 9QB. Prop: David Siddons. Tel: (01572) 821173. Fax: (0870) 1326314. Web: www.homepages.primex.co.uk/~forest. E-mail: forestbooks@rutlanduk.fsnet.co.uk. Est: 1986. Shop open: **M:** 10:30–17:00; **T:** 10:30–17:00; **W:** 10:30–17:00; **Th:** 10:30–17:00; **F:** 10:30–17:00; **S:** 10:30–17:00; **Su:** 13:30–16:30. Stock: very large. Spec: Booksearch; Ephemera. PR: £1–500. CC: JCB; MC; V. Corresp: French. Notes: also, fairs organiser, copying and design. VAT No: GB 424 4691 51. [Updated]

SHROPSHIRE

BISHOP'S CASTLE

Autolycus, ■ 10 Market Square, Bishop's Castle, SY9 5DN. Prop: David & Jay Wilkinson. Tel: (01588) 630078. Fax: (01588) 630078. Web: www.booksonline.uk.com. E-mail: Autolycusbc@aol.com. Est: 1996. Internet and postal. Shop open: **M:** 11:00–16:30; **T:** 11:00–16:30; **W:** 11:00–16:30; **Th:** 11:00–16:30; **F:** 11:00–17:00; **S:** 10:30–17:00. Stock: medium. Spec: Antiquarian; Children's; Children's - Early Titles; Children's - Illustrated; First Editions; Illustrated; Literature; Modern First Editions. PR: £1–1,500. CC: MC; V; PayPal, Maestro. Corresp: French, German. Notes: Please telephone if travelling from afar as opening hours may vary. VAT No: GB 771 9717 90. [07/10/2004]

Yarborough House Bookshop, ■ Yarborough House, The Square, Bishop's Castle, SY9 5BN. Prop: Carol Wright. Tel: (01588) 638318. E-mail: mail@yarboroughhouse.com. Est: 1980. Shop open: **T:** 10:00–17:30; **Th:** 10:00–17:30; **F:** 10:00–17:30; **S:** 09:00–17:30; **Su:** 10:00–17:30. Stock: medium. Spec: Fiction - General; Collectables. PR: £1–20. CC: AE; D; E; JCB; MC; V. Notes: also 4,000 secondhand classic records 4,000 classic CDs and coffee house. [Updated]

BRIDGNORTH

The Bookpassage, ■ 57a High Street, Bridgnorth, WV16 4DX. Prop: David Lamont Tel: (01746) 768767. E-mail: bookman@btconnect.com. Est: 1990. Shop open: **M:** 09:00–17:15; **T:** 09:00–17:15; **W:** 08:00–17:15; **Th:** 09:00–17:15; **F:** 09:00–17:15; **S:** 09:00–17:15. Stock: large. Spec: Ephemera. PR: £1–500. Notes: open occasionally on Sundays. [Updated]

Bookstack & D.J. Creece (Bookbinder), The Bindery Book Store, 3 Castle Terrace, Bridgnorth, WV16 4AH. Prop: Elizabeth Anderton (Books), Dermott Creece (Binder). Tel: (01746) 768008. Fax: (01756) 768008. E-mail: djcbookbinder@onetel.com. Est: 1975. Storeroom. Appointment necessary. Open: **M:** 09:00–17:00; **T:** 09:00–17:00; **W:** 09:00–17:00; **Th:** 13:00–17:00; **F:** 09:00–15:00; **S:** 10:00–12:00. Stock: very small. Spec: Pre-Raphaelites. PR: £1–200. [Updated]

ELLESMERE

Glyn's Books, 6 The Avenue, Lyneal, Ellesmere, SY12 OQJ. Prop: Glyn Watson. Tel: (01948) 710591. Fax: (01948) 710442. Web: www.glynsbooks.com. E-mail: glyn@glynsbooks.com. Est: 1986. Private premises. Internet and postal. Spec: Astrology; First Editions; History - General; Literature; Booksearch. CC: AE; D; E; JCB; MC; V. Notes: also, a major international booksearch service. [Updated]

LUDLOW

Ampersand Books, Ludford Mill, Ludlow, SY8 1PR. Prop: Michael Dawson. Tel: (01584) 877813. Fax: (01584) 877519. Web: www.ampersandbooks.co.uk. E-mail: popups@ampersandbooks.co.uk. Est: 1982. Private premises. Appointment necessary. Stock: small. Spec: Children's; Children's - Illustrated; Pop-Up, Movable & Cut Out; Collectables; Ephemera. PR: £5–1,000. Notes: also, repairing of pop-ups & moveables [Updated]

Lyndon Barnes - Books, 3 Mortimer Drive, Ludlow, SY8 4JW. Prop: Lyndon Barnes. Tel: (01568) 780641. Fax: (01568) 780641. Web: www.abebooks.co.uk. E-mail: lyndonbarnes@clara.co.uk. Est: 1988. Private premises. Internet and postal. Contactable. Open: **M:** 09:00–17:00; **T:** 09:00–17:00; **W:** 09:00–17:00; **Th:** 09:00–17:00; **F:** 09:00–17:00; **S:** 09:00–17:00; **Su:** 09:00–17:00. Stock: very small. Spec: Music - Classical; Music - Country & Western; Music - Jazz & Blues; Music - Popular; Music - Rock & Roll. PR: £2–100. CC: PayPal. Notes: all stock on abebooks. [Updated]

Innes Books, 22 Julian Road, Ludlow, SY8 1HA. Prop: Pat Innes. Tel: (01584) 878146. Web: www.innesbooks.co.uk. E-mail: patricia@innesbooks.fsnet.co.uk. Est: 1997. Private premises. Internet and postal. Appointment necessary. Open: **M:** 09:00–10:00; **T:** 09:00–10:00; **W:** 09:00–10:00; **Th:** 09:00–10:00; **F:** 09:00–10:00; **S:** 10:00–06:00; **Su:** 10:00–05:00. Stock: small. Spec: Academic/Scholarly; Children's; Fiction - General; Illustrated; Literature; Modern First Editions. PR: £3–600. CC: PayPal. VAT No: GB 812 5174 53. [Updated]

Offa's Dyke Books, Old School House, Downton-on-the Rock, Ludlow, SY8 2HX. Prop: S.R. Bainbridge. Tel: (01584) 856212. Fax: (01584) 856757. E-mail: books@offas-dyke.fsnet.co.uk. Est: 1974. Private premises. Appointment necessary. Spec: Academic/Scholarly; Advertising; Antiquarian; Antiques; Art; Bindings; Fine & Rare; Literature. CC: PayPal. VAT No: GB 393 9270 15. [Updated]

Olynthiacs, 19 Castle View Terrace, Ludlow, SY8 2NG. Prop: Neil MacGregor. Tel: (01584) 872671. Web: www.ukbookworld.com/members/olynthiacs. E-mail: juvenal@martial.fsnet.co.uk. Est: 1735. Storeroom. Postal only. Contactable. **M:** 09:00–18:00; **T:** 09:00–18:00; **W:** 09:00–18:00; **Th:** 09:00–18:00; **F:** 09:00–18:00; **S:** 09:00–18:00; Closed for lunch: 13:00–14:00. Stock: medium. Spec: Author - Wodehouse, P.G.; Biography; Classical Studies; Ecclesiastical History & Architecture; Fiction - General; History - General; Linguistics; Philology. PR: £5–500. [Updated]

MADELAY

C. R. Moore, Park House, Park Lane, Madelay, TF7 5HF. Prop: C. R. Moore. Tel: 01952 585231. Est: 1995. Private premises. Appointment necessary. Spec: Antiquarian; Bindings; Genealogy; Heraldry; Printing; Sport - General; Sport - Football (Soccer); Topography - Local. Notes: exhibits at bookfairs. [Updated]

MUCH WENLOCK

Good Books, Hill Top Farm, Hill Top, Much Wenlock, TF13 6DJ. Prop: Judith Goodman. Tel: (01746) 785250. Web: www.abebooks.com. E-mail: jude_good@btinternet.com. Est: 1996. Private premises. Appointment necessary. Spec: Children's; Private Press; Railways; Sport - Angling/Fishing; Sport - Field Sports. PR: £1–200. [Updated]

P.J. Mead, 6 Blakeway Hollow, Much Wenlock, TF13 6AR. Tel: (01952) 727591. E-mail: meadbooks@yahoo.com. Est: 1976. Private premises. Postal only. Spec: Antiquarian; Bibliography; Bindings; Books about Books; Juvenile; Miniature Books; Sport - General. PR: £10–1,000. Mem: PBFA. VAT No: GB 349 3412 50. [Updated]

Wenlock Books, ■ 12 High Street, Much Wenlock, TF13 6AA. Prop: Anna Dreda. Tel: (01952) 727877. Fax: (01952) 727877. Web: www.wenlockbooks.co.uk. E-mail: info@wenlockbooks.co.uk. Est: 1985. Shop open: **M:** 10:00–17:00; **T:** 10:00–17:00; **W:** 10:00–17:00; **Th:** 10:00–17:00; **F:** 10:00–17:00; **S:** 10:00–17:00. Stock: medium. PR: £10–25. CC: MC; V. Mem: BA. VAT No: GB 823 8745 08. [Updated]

OSWESTRY

Bookworld, ■ 32 Beatrice Street, Oswestry, SY11 1QG. Prop: John Cranwell. Tel: (01691) 657112. Fax: (01691) 657112. Web: www.tgal.co.uk/bookworld. E-mail: jc.bookworld@arrowweb.co.uk. Est: 1993. Shop open: **M:** 09:00–17:00; **T:** 09:00–17:00; **W:** 09:00–17:00; **Th:** 08:00–17:00; **F:** 09:00–17:00; **S:** 09:00–17:00. Stock: medium. Spec: Alpinism/Mountaineering; Antiques; Autobiography; Children's; Cookery/Gastronomy; Crafts; Dictionaries; Gardening - General. PR: £1–1,500. CC: E; JCB; MC; V. [Updated]

SHREWSBURY

Candle Lane Books, ■ 28 & 29, Princess Street, Shrewsbury, SY1 1LW. Prop: John & Margaret Thornhill. Tel: (01743) 365301. Est: 1974. Shop open: **M:** 09:30–17:00; **T:** 09:00–17:00; **W:** 09:00–17:00; **Th:** 09:00–17:00; **F:** 09:00–17:00; **S:** 09:00–17:00. Stock: very large. Spec: Booksearch. PR: £1–3,000. CC: MC; V. [Updated]

Gemini–Books, 66 Oakfield Road, Copthorne, Shrewsbury, SY3 8AE. Prop: Geoff and Rosalie Davies. Tel: (01743) 343750. E-mail: enquiries@gemini-books.co.uk. Est: 2000. Storeroom. Appointment necessary. Open: **M:** 10:00–16:00; **T:** 10:00–16:00; **W:** 10:00–16:00; **Th:** 10:00–16:00; **F:** 10:00–16:00; **S:** 10:00–16:00; **Su:** 10:00–16:00. Stock: medium. Spec: Children's; Fiction - General. PR: £4–300. CC: AE; JCB; MC; V. Notes: Exhibits at Kinver Book Fair in Staffordshire (3rd Sunday every month). [Updated]

Oriental and African Books, 33 Whitehall Street, Shrewsbury, SY2 5AD. Prop: Paul D. Wilson. Tel: (01743) 352575. Fax: (01743) 363432. Web: www.africana.co.uk E-mail: paul@africana.co.uk. Est: 1982. Office and/or bookroom. Internet and postal. Telephone first. Stock: large. Spec: Academic/Scholarly; Africana; Black Studies; Countries - Africa; Countries - Middle East, The; Travel - Africa; Travel - Middle East. PR: £25–2,000. CC: E; JCB; MC; V. Corresp: French, Arabic. VAT No: GB 434 0550 82. [Updated]

The Victorian Gallery, ■ 40 St. John's Hill, Shrewsbury, SY1 1JQ. Prop: R.D. Vernon. Tel: (01743) 356351. Fax: (01743) 356351. E-mail: victoriangallery@xln.co.uk. Est: 1987. Shop open: **M:** 09:00–17:00; **T:** 09:00–17:00; **W:** 09:00–17:00; **Th:** 09:00–17:00; **F:** 09:00–17:00. Stock: very large. PR: £6–600. CC: accepted. [Updated]

SHROPSHIRE

TELFORD

Andrew Cox, 16, Garbett Road Aquaduct, Telford, TF4 3RX. Prop: Andrew Cox. Tel: (01952) 590630. E-mail: andyaituk@aol.com. Est: 2000. Private premises. Postal only. Telephone first. Stock: small. Spec: Antiquarian; Authors:- Austen, Jane; Verne, Jules; Wells, H.G.; Children's - Illustrated; Fiction - Historical; Fiction - Science Fiction. PR: £10. [Updated]

WEM

Black Five Books, ■ 54 High Street, Wem, SY4 5DW. Prop: Ken Simpson. Tel: 0845 166 4084. Web: www.black5books.co.uk. E-mail: black5books@wemshropshire.freeserve.co.uk. Est: 1984. Shop. Internet and postal. Telephone first. Open: **M:** 10:30–17:00; **T:** 10:30–17:00; **Th:** 10:30–17:00; **F:** 10:30–17:00; **S:** 10:30–17:00; Closed for lunch: 13:30–15:00. Stock: very large. Spec: Aviation; Biography; Children's; Education & School; Fiction - General; Fiction - Historical; History - General; History - Ancient. PR: £1–200. CC: MC; V; Maestro. Mem: BA. VAT No: GB 701 2786 58. [Updated]

Booksets.com Ltd, Unit 5 & 6, Wem Business Park, New Street, Wem, SY4 5JX. Tel: (01948) 710345. Fax: 0870 0521838. Web: www.booksets.com. E-mail: sales@booksets.com. Est: 1974. Warehouse; Internet Only. Contactable. Stock: very large. Spec: Academic/Scholarly; Computing; Magazines & Periodicals - General; Reference; Special Collections; University Texts; Ephemera. PR: £5–5,000. CC: AE; MC; V; Maestro. VAT No: GB 696 1311 25. [Updated]

Kabristan Archives, 19 Foxleigh Grove, Wem, SY4 5BS. Prop: Eileen Hewson FRGS. Tel: (01939) 234061. E-mail: kabristan@talk21.com. Est: 2004. Private premises. Internet and postal. Stock: very small. Spec: Countries - India; Countries - Ireland; Geography; Publishing. PR: £5–100. [02/11/2004]

WHITCHURCH

Barn Books, ■ Pear Tree Farm, Norbury, Whitchurch, SY13 4HZ. Prop: Mary Perry. Tel: (01948) 663742. Fax: (01948) 663742. Web: www.barnbooks.co.uk. E-mail: barnbooks@barnbooks.co.uk. Est: 1985. Shop open: **F:** 10:00–17:30; **S:** 10:00–17:30; **Su:** 10:00–17:30. Spec: Agriculture; Farming & Livestock; Gardening - General; History - Local; Horticulture; Rural Life; Topography - Local; Ephemera. PR: £1–500. Notes: also, open on Bank Holidays. [Updated]

SOMERSET

BATH

Bath Book Exchange, ■ 35 Broad Street, Bath, BA1 5LP. Tel: (01225) 466214. Est: 1959. Shop open: **M:** 09:30–17:00; **T:** 09:30–17:00; **W:** 09:30–17:00; **Th:** 09:30–17:00; **F:** 09:30–17:00; **S:** 09:30–17:00; Closed for lunch: 13:00–14:00. Stock: medium. Spec: Booksearch. PR: £1–10. [Updated]

Bath Old Books, ■ 9c Margarets Buildings, Bath, BA1 2LP. Prop: Chris Phillips. Tel: (01225) 422244. E-mail: batholdbooks@yahoo.co.uk. Est: 1990. Shop open: **M:** 10:00–17:00; **T:** 10:00–17:00; **W:** 10:00–17:00; **Th:** 10:00–17:00; **F:** 10:00–17:00; **S:** 10:00–17:00. Stock: large. Spec: Antiquarian; Art; Children's - Illustrated; Literature; Topography - Local. CC: JCB; MC; V. Corresp: French. Mem: PBFA. Notes: Booksearch, Valuations. [Updated]

George Bayntun, ■ Manvers Street, Bath, BA1 1JW. E.W.G. Prop: Bayntun–Coward. Tel: (01225) 466000. Fax: (01225) 482122. Web: www.georgebayntun.com. E-mail: ebc@georgebayntun.com. Est: 1894. Shop open: **M:** 09:00–17:30; **T:** 09:00–17:30; **W:** 09:00–17:30; **Th:** 09:00–17:30; **F:** 09:00–17:30; **S:** 09:30–13:00; Closed for lunch: 13:00–14:00. Stock: small. Spec: Bindings; Children's; Children's - Illustrated; Fine & Rare; First Editions; Illustrated; Literature; Poetry. PR: £10–5,000. CC: MC; V; SW, SO. Corresp: French. Mem: ABA; PBFA. Notes: also, bindery incorporating the famous binding firm of Robert Riviere & Son, est. 1829. VAT No: GB 137 5073 71. [Updated]

Camden Books, Bath, BA15JD. Prop: Victor Suchar. Tel: (01225) 337026. Web: www.camdenbooks.com. E-mail: suchcam@msn.com. Est: 1984. Private premises. Internet and postal. Stock: small. Spec: Academic/Scholarly; Architecture; Art History; Biography; Civil Engineering; Classical Studies; Company History; Diaries. PR: £10–2,000. CC: Cheque. Mem: PBFA. Notes: online business only. [Updated]

Janet Clarke, 3 Woodside Cottages, Freshford, Bath, BA2 7WJ. Prop: Janet Clarke. Tel: (01225) 723186. Fax: (01225) 722063. Web: www.janetclarke.com. E-mail: janetclarke@ukgateway.net. Est: 1973. Private premises. Postal only. Stock: small. Spec: Cookery/Gastronomy; Food & Drink; Wine; Ephemera. PR: £5–3,000. CC: PayPal. Cata: occasionally on specialities. Mem: ABA; BA; ILAB. [Updated]

Peter Goodden Books Ltd, 7 Clarendon Villas, Widcombe Hill, Bath, BA2 6AG. Tel: (01225) 310986. E-mail: peter.goodden@ukonline.co.uk. Est: 1976. Internet and postal. Stock: small. Spec: Music - General; Musical Instruments. PR: £5–1,500. CC: JCB; MC; V. Corresp: Simple French. Mem: PBFA. VAT No: GB 195 9854 90. [Updated]

George Gregory, Manvers Street, Bath, BA1 1JW. Prop: Charlotte Bayntun-Coward. Tel: (01225) 466000. Fax: (01225) 482122. E-mail: julie@georgebayntun.com. Est: 1846. Shop and/or gallery. Open: **M:** 09:00–17:30; **T:** 09:00–17:30; **W:** 09:00–17:30; **Th:** 09:00–17:30; **F:** 09:00–17:30; **S:** 09:30–13:00; Closed for lunch: 13:00–14:00. Stock: large. Spec: Literature; Prints and Maps. PR: £1–200. CC: MC; V. Notes: Engraved portraits and views. [Updated]

Hugh Ashley Rayner, 4 Malvern Buildings, Fairfield Park, Bath, BA1 6JX. Prop: Hugh A. Rayner. Tel: (01225) 463552. Fax: (01225) 463552. Web: www.indiabooks.co.uk. E-mail: hughrayner@indiabooks.co.uk. Private premises. Internet and postal. Appointment necessary. Open: **M:** 10:00–19:00; **T:** 10:00–19:00; **W:** 10:00–19:00; **Th:** 10:00–19:00; **F:** 10:00–19:00; **S:** 10:00–19:00; **Su:** 12:00–18:00. Stock: small. Spec: Countries - Asia; Countries - Burma; Countries - Central Asia; Countries - Himalayas, The; Countries - India; Countries - Sri Lanka; Photography; Travel - Asia. PR: £35–500. CC: AE; D; JCB; MC; V. Corresp: German. Mem: PBFA. Notes: valuations, library cataloguing. [Updated]

Solitaire Books, Holly Lawn, Prospect Place, Beechen Cliff, Bath, BA2 4QP. Prop: Martyn Thomas. Tel: (01225) 469441. Fax: 0870 135 8843. E-mail: solitaire@hollylawn.org. Est: 1994. Private premises. Postal only. Stock: very small. Spec: Books about Books; Printing; Private Press; Typography. PR: £30–5,000. CC: PayPal. Corresp: Dutch, French, Spanish. [Updated]

The Traveller's Bookshelf, Canal House, 64 Murhill, Limpley Stoke, Bath, BA2 7FQ. Prop: Jenny Steadman. Tel: (01225) 722589. E-mail: jenny@travellersbookshelf.co.uk. Est: 1991. Private premises. Internet and postal. Spec: Countries - Afganistan; Countries - Albania; Countries - Arabia; Countries - Armenia; Countries - Asia Minor; Countries - Balkans, The; Countries - Central Asia; Countries - China. PR: £20–5,000. CC: MC; V; Switch. Mem: ABA; PBFA; ILAB. VAT No: GB 779 2193 85. [Updated]

BATHEASTON

Libris (Weston) Books, 68 London Road West, Batheaston, BA1 7DA. Tel: (01225) 858809. E-mail: libriswestonbooks@hotmail.com. Private premises. Book Fairs Only. Spec: Aviation; Countries - Antarctic, The; History - General; Performing Arts; Poetry; Topography - General. Mem: PBFA. [Updated]

BARRINGTON

R.G. Watkins, Book and Print Room, 7 Water Street, Barrington, Ilminster, TA19 0JR. Tel: (01460) 54188. Web: www.rgwatkins.co.uk/. E-mail: inquiries@rgwatkins.co.uk. Est: 1985. Office and/or bookroom. Appointment necessary. Open: **F:** 10:00–05:00. Stock: small. Spec: Arts, The; Author - Lawrence, T.E.; Collecting; History - General; Booksearch; Prints and Maps. PR: £1–500. CC: AE; MC; V. Corresp: French. Mem: PBFA. Notes: also, a booksearch service [Updated]

BRIDGEWATER

R.W. Millard, 112 Wembdon Hill, Bridgater, Somerset, TA6 7QA. [Updated]

Wembdon Books, 112 Wembdon Hill, Bridgewater, TA6 7QA. Ray Millard. Tel: (01278) 424060. Est: 1987. Private premises. Internet and postal. Stock: very small. Spec: Antiquarian; Diaries; Military; Topography - Local; Travel - General; War - World War II; Booksearch. PR: £3–150. [Updated]

CASTLE CAREY

Avedikian Rare Books, Bank House, Castle Carey, BA7 7AW. Prop: Stephen James Avedikian. Tel: 01963 359680. Web: www.militarybookshop.com. Open: **M:** 09:00–17:30; **T:** 09:00–17:30; **W:** 09:00–17:30; **Th:** 09:00–17:30; **F:** 09:00–17:30; **S:** 09:00–17:30; **Su:** 09:00–17:30; Closed for lunch: 13:00–14:00. Spec: Author - Lawrence, T.E.; Aviation; History - Military; Voyages & Discovery; War - World War I. Mem: ABA. [Updated]

CHARD

P.J. Baron - Scientific Book Sales, Lakewood, Chard, TA20 4AJ. Prop: Dr. P. Baron. Tel: (01460) 66319. Fax: (01460) 66319. Web: www.books.free-online.co.uk. E-mail: pb@sciencebaron.demon.co.uk. Est: 1975. Private premises. Internet and postal. Stock: small. Spec: Biology; Botany; Chemistry; Ecology; Engineering; Mathematics; Medicine; Natural History. PR: £5–150. CC: MC; V; SW, Delta, PayPal. Cata: online/Internet. Corresp: French. VAT No: GB 549 4779 82. [Updated]

CLAPTON–IN–GORDANO

Avonworld Books, 1 Swancombe, Clapton–in–Gordano, BS20 7RR. Prop: Michael C. Ross. Tel: (01275) 842531. Fax: (01275) 849221. Web: www.avonworld-booksource.co.uk. E-mail: books@avonworld.demon.co.uk. Est: 1984. Office and/or bookroom. Internet and postal. Appointment necessary. Open: **M:** 09:00–18:00; **T:** 09:00–18:00; **W:** 09:00–18:00; **Th:** 09:00–18:00; **F:** 09:00–18:00; Closed for lunch: 13:00 14:00. Stock: small. Spec: Art; Authors:- Buchan, John; Coward, Noel; Graves, Robert; Kipling, Rudyard; Sayers, Dorothy; Literature; Modern First Editions. PR: £1–500. CC: MC; V. Corresp: German (post only, not e-mail). Mem: PBFA. Notes: valuations for insurance or probate of private collections in our author specialities. VAT No: GB 496 6867 66. [Updated]

Searching for a title - and cannot find it on any Internet database?

Try www.sheppardsworld.co.uk

Select dealers by book subject classification – then mail requests to selected dealers who may not have uploaded the title to any Internet Search database

CLEVEDON

Clevedon Books, Canbourne Cottage, 6 Seavale Road, Clevedon, BS21 7QB. Prop: George & Wendy Douthwaite. Tel: (01275) 872304. Fax: (01275) 342817. E-mail: clevedonbooks@globalnet.co.uk. Est: 1970. Private premises. Internet and postal. Appointment necessary. Open: **Th:** 11:00–16:30; **F:** 11:00–16:30; **S:** 11:05–16:30; Closed for lunch: 13:00–14:15. Stock: very large. Spec: Architecture; Art History; Geology; History - Industrial; History of Ideas; Science - History of; Transport; Travel - General. PR: £10–3,000. CC: JCB; MC; V; Debit. Mem: PBFA. Notes: also at 27 Copse Road, Clevedon. (q.v.) Also, colouring & mounting service. [Updated]

K.W. Cowley, Bookdealer, Trinity Cottage, 153 Old Church Road, Clevedon, BS21 7TU. Tel: (01275) 872247. E-mail: kencowley@blueyonder.co.uk. Est: 1987. Private premises. Postal only. Telephone first. Stock: small. Spec: Anthologies; Books about Books; Cinema/Film; Fiction - Crime, Detective, Spy, Thrillers; Fiction - Fantasy, Horror; Fiction - Science Fiction; Ghosts; Pulps. PR: £1–100. [Updated]

CREWKERNE

Gresham Books, ■ 31 Market Street, Crewkerne, TA18 7JU. Prop: James Hine. Tel: (01460) 77726. Fax: (01460) 52479. Web: www.greshambooks.co.uk. E-mail: jameshine@btconnect.com. Est: 1972. Shop open: **M:** 10:00–17:00; **T:** 10:00–17:00; **W:** 10:00–17:00; **Th:** 10:00–17:00; **F:** 10:00–17:00; **S:** 10:00–17:00. Stock: medium. Spec: Antiquarian; Antiques; Architecture; Cookery/Gastronomy; Fashion & Costume; Food & Drink; Needlework; Sport - Golf. PR: £1–1,000. CC: AE; MC; V; Switch. Mem: ABA; PBFA. [29/09/2004]

Anne Hine / Gresham Books, ■ 31 Market Street, Crewkerne, TA18 7JU. Tel: (01460) 77726. Fax: (01460) 52479. E-mail: annehine@gresham-books.demon.co.uk. Est: 1994. Shop open: **M:** 10:00–17:00; **T:** 10:00–17:00; **W:** 10:00–17:00; **Th:** 10:00–17:00; **F:** 10:00–17:00; **S:** 10:00–17:00. Stock: very small. Spec: Publishers - Warnes. CC: AE; MC; V. Notes: also, provides a booksearach service for all plant related books, and Japanese gardening. [Updated]

DULVERTON

Rothwell & Dunworth, ■ 2 Bridge Street, Dulverton, TA22 9HJ. Tel: 01398 323169. E-mail: rothwellm@aol.com. Est: 1975. Shop open: **M:** 10:30–17:15; **T:** 10:30–17:15; **W:** 10:30–17:15; **Th:** 10:30–17:15; **F:** 10:30–17:15; **S:** 10:30–17:15; **Su:** 11:00–16:00. Spec: Aircraft; Antiquarian; Architecture; Army, The; Art History; Author - Aldin, Cecil; Autobiography; History - General. CC: MC; V; Debit. Mem: ABA. [Updated]

DUNSTER

Cobbles Books, ■ 14 - 16 Church Street, Dunster, TA24 6SH. Prop Adrian Corley. Tel: 01643 821305. Fax: 01643 821305. E-mail: books@cobbles1416.fsnet.co.uk. Est: 2003. Shop open: **M:** 10:30–17:00; **T:** 10:30–17:00; **W:** 10:30–17:00; **F:** 10:30–17:00; **S:** 10:30–17:00; **Su:** 10:30–17:00. Spec: Antiques; Art; Aviation; Biography; Fiction - General; Folio Society, The; History - General; History - British. CC: MC; V. Notes: opening times may vary between November and March. Please telephone for details [Updated]

FROME

Upper–Room Books, ■ Above Antiques & Country Living, Vallis Way, Babcox, Frome, BA11 3BA. Prop: Victor Adams. Tel: (01373) 467125. Fax: (01373) 467125. Web: www.vabooks.com. E-mail: victoradams@vabooks.co.uk. Est: 1990. Shop. Internet and postal. Open: **M:** 09:30–17:30; **T:** 09:30–17:30; **W:** 09:30–17:30; **Th:** 09:30–17:30; **F:** 09:30–17:30; **S:** 09:30–17:30. Stock: medium. Spec: Art; Artists; Author - Morris, William; Crafts; Furniture; Woodwork. PR: £5–1,000. CC: JCB; MC; V. Mem: PBFA. [Updated]

ILMINSTER

David Clarke Books, P.O. Box 24, Ilminster, TA19 0YU. Prop: David Clarke. Tel: (01460) 242330. E-mail: dclarke@lineone.net. Est: 1999. Private premises. Internet and postal. Appointment necessary. Stock: medium. Spec: Aeronautics; Farming & Livestock; Fiction - General; Gardening - General; History - British; Horticulture; Natural History; Railways. PR: £4–300. Corresp: French. [Updated]

Ile Valley Bookshop, ■ 10 Silver Street, Ilminster, TA19 0DJ. Prop: Chris Chapman. Tel: (01460) 57663. Fax: (01460) 57188. E-mail: ilevalley@aol.com. Est: 1985. Shop. Stock: very small. [Updated]

LANGPORT

Keeble Antiques, ■ Cheapside, Langport, TA10 9PW. Prop: Clive Keeble. Tel: (01458) 259627. Fax: (01458) 259627. Web: www.keebleantbks.co.uk. E-mail: clive@keebleantiques.com. Est: 1998. Shop. Internet and postal. Open: **M:** 09:00–18:00; **T:** 09:00–18:00; **W:** 09:00–18:00; **Th:** 09:00–18:00; **F:** 09:00–18:00; **S:** 09:00–18:00; **Su:** 10:00–16:30. Stock: medium. Spec: Antiques; Art; Carriages & Driving; Natural History; Private Press; Rural Life; Topography - Local; Travel - General. PR: £1–1,000. [Updated]

MERRIOTT

Richard Budd, The Coach House, Glebelands, Merriott, TA16 5RE. Prop: Richard Budd. Tel: (01460) 78297. E-mail: richardbudd@btconnect.com. Est: 1972. Private premises. Postal only. Appointment necessary. Stock: small. Spec: Author - Beckett, S.; First Editions; Limited Editions; Literary Criticism; Literature; Poetry. PR: £10–5,400. CC: E; MC; V. Corresp: French. Mem: ABA; PBFA; ILAB. Notes: also, attends 50 bookfairs a year. [Updated]

MIDSOMER NORTON

Tom Randall, Welton Hill Cottage, Welton Grove, Midsomer Norton, Radstock, BA3 2TS. (*). Tel: (01761) 418926. E-mail: Null. Est: 1987. Spec: Ethnology; Folklore; Mythology; Topography - Local; Traction Engines; Transport. PR: £2–500. Notes: also, a booksearch service [Updated]

MILVERTON

Cat Lit, Loundshay Manor Cottage, Preston Bowyer, Milverton, TA4 1QF. Tel: (01823) 401527. Fax: (01823) 401527. E-mail: amolibros@aol.com. Est: 2002. Private premises. Postal only. Appointment necessary. Spec: Cats; Dogs; Sport - Field Sports. [Updated]

MINEHEAD

Rare Books & Berry, ■ High Street, Porlock, Minehead, TA24 8PT. Prop: Helen & Michael Berry. Tel: (01643) 863255. Fax: (01643) 863092. Web: www.rarebooksandberry.co.uk. E-mail: search@rarebooksandberry.co.uk. Est: 1992. Shop open: **M:** 09:30–17:00; **T:** 09:30–17:00; **W:** 09:30–17:00; **Th:** 09:30–17:00; **F:** 09:30–17:00; **S:** 09:30–17:00; Closed for lunch: 13:00–14:00. Stock: medium. Spec: Author - Edwards, Lionel; Sport - Angling/Fishing; Sport - Hunting; Topography - Local. PR: £1–1,000. CC: MC; V; S, SW. VAT No: GB 801 1222 04. [Updated]

NORTH CHERITON

Paper Pleasures, Holt Farm, North Cheriton, BA8 0AQ. Prop: Lesley Tyson. Tel: (01963) 33718. Web: www.paperpleasures.com. E-mail: books@paperpleasures.com. Est: 1998. Private premises. Postal only. Appointment necessary. Stock: small. Spec: Art; Erotica; Ex-Libris; Glamour; Homosexuality & Lesbianism; Literature; Magazines & Periodicals - General; Photography. PR: £5–2,000. CC: MC; V; Switch. Mem: PBFA. [Updated]

PEASEDOWN ST. JOHN

BookLovers.co.uk, ■ The Post Office, 12 Bath Road, Peasedown St. John, BA2 8DH. Prop: David Gower-Spence. Tel: 0845 009 4455. Fax: 0845 009 1786. Web: www.booklovers.co.uk. E-mail: dgs@booklovers.co.uk. Est: 1997. Shop. Internet and postal. Open: **M:** 09:00–17:30; **T:** 09:00–17:30; **W:** 09:00–13:00; **Th:** 09:00–17:30; **F:** 09:00–17:30; **S:** 09:00–12:30; Closed for lunch: 13:00–14:00. Spec: Booksearch. CC: AE; MC; V. [Updated]

QUEEN CAMEL

Steven Ferdinando, The Old Vicarage, Queen Camel, Nr. Yeovil, BA22 7NG. Tel: (01935) 850210. E-mail: stevenferdinando@onetel.com. Est: 1977. Office and/or bookroom. Telephone first. Stock: medium. Spec: Agriculture; Authors:- Hardy, Thomas; Powys Family, The; Illustrated; Irish Interest; Literature; Topography - Local; Travel - General. PR: £10–800. CC: MC; V. Mem: PBFA. Notes: See Bath Old Books, Bath. (q.v.). [Updated]

SIMONSBATH

Spooner & Co, Mead Cottage, Honeymead, Simonsbath, TA24 7JX. Prop: Brian John Spooner. Tel: (01643) 831562. Fax: (01643) 831562. E-mail: spoonerb@supanet.com. Est: 1985. Private premises. Appointment necessary. Stock: small. Spec: Antiquarian; Archaeology; Architecture; Bibliography; Ecclesiastical History & Architecture; Genealogy; Heraldry; History - Local. PR: £3–230. Notes: also, booksearch, bookbinding and repairs. [Updated]

SOMERTON

Simon's Books, ■ Broad Street, Somerton. Prop: Bryan Ives. Tel: (01458) 272313. Est: 1978. Shop open: **M:** 10:00–16:30; **T:** 10:00–16:30; **W:** 09:00–16:30; **Th:** 09:00–16:30; **F:** 10:00–16:30; **S:** 10:00–16:30. Stock: large. PR: £1–100. [Updated]

TAUNTON

Badger Books, 2 The Orchard, Dowell Close, Taunton, TA2 6BN. Prop: Janet & Nic Tall. Tel: (01823) 323180. Web: www.badgerbooks.co.uk. E-mail: janetnic@badgerbooks.co.uk. Est: 2002. Private premises. Internet and postal. Appointment necessary. Stock: small. Spec: Authors:- Blyton, Enid; Brent-Dyer, Elinor M.; Forest, A.; Children's. PR: £1–200. Corresp: German. [Updated]

Boxwood Books & Prints, Ashbrook House, Winsford, Minehead, Taunton, TA24 7HN. (*) Prop: Peter & Catherine Nicholls. Tel: (01643) 851588. Fax: (01643) 851588. E-mail: boxwood.books@virgin.net. Est: 1995. Private premises. Appointment necessary. Stock: very small. Spec: Art Reference; Illustrated; Printing; Private Press; Prints and Maps. PR: £50–1,500. CC: MC; V. Mem: PBFA. Notes: attends Private Press Fair only. [Updated]

Dene Barn Books & Prints, Brackenbury, Ash Priors, Taunton, TA4 3NF. Prop: Derek Cundy. Tel: (01823) 433103. Est: 1990. Private premises. Appointment necessary. Stock: very small. Spec: Botany; Natural History; Topography - Local; Prints and Maps. PR: £10–500. Notes: picture framing and mounting. [Updated]

The Eastern Traveller, 52 Mountway Road, Bishops Hull, Taunton, TA1 5LS. Prop: Geoffrey Mullett. Tel: (01823) 327012. E-mail: books@gamullett'fsnet.co.uk. Est: 1979. Postal only. Spec: History - General; Military; Military History; Travel - General; Travel - Africa; Travel - Asia; Travel - Middle East; Voyages & Discovery. PR: £5–50. [Updated]

Russell Needham Books, 5 Silver St., Milverton, Taunton, TA4 1LA. (*). Tel: (01823) 400470. Fax: (0870) 0561167. Web: www.needhambooks.demon.co.uk. E-mail: russell@needhambooks.demon.co.uk. Private premises. Internet and postal. Stock: very small. Spec: Academic/Scholarly; Alchemy; Author - Bennett, J.G.; Foreign Texts; Fourth Way; Literature; Modern First Editions; Mysticism. PR: £5–300. Corresp: French Francais. [Updated]

WELLINGTON

Peter J. Ayre, Greenham Hall, Greenham, Wellington, TA21 0JJ. Tel: (01823) 672603. Fax: (01823) 672307. E-mail: peterjayre@aol.com. Est: 1980. Private premises. Internet and postal. Appointment necessary. Stock: small. Spec: Africana; Countries - Africa; Countries - Kenya; Countries - Tanzania; Natural History; Sport - Big Game Hunting; Travel - Africa. PR: £10–5,000. CC: JCB; MC; V. Mem: PBFA. Notes: also, a booksearch service. [Updated]

Mary Sharpe, 55 Twitchen, Holcombe Rogus, Wellington, TA21 0PS. Tel: (01823) 672304. Est: 1995. Private premises. Postal only. Stock: small. Spec: Authors:- Austen, Jane; Brontes, The; Burney, Fanny; Eliot, G.; Gaskell, E.; Hardy, Thomas; Children's; Illustrated. PR: £5–200. Mem: PBFA. Notes: exhibits at bookfairs. [Updated]

WEST PENNARD

Eddie Baxter - Books, The Old Mill House, West Pennard, BA6 8ND. Prop: Josie Matthews. Tel: (01749) 890369. Fax: (01749) 890369. Est: 1956. Private premises. Postal only. Stock: very small. Spec: Dance; Music - General; Music - Jazz & Blues; Booksearch. [Updated]

WESTON–SUPER–MARE

Manna Bookshop, ■ 30 Orchard Street, Weston–Super–Mare, BS23 1RQ. Prop: Peter Fairington. Tel: (01934) 636228. Est: 1981. Shop open: **M:** 10:00–17:00; **T:** 10:00–17:00; **W:** 10:00–17:00; **Th:** 10:00–17:00; **F:** 10:00–17:00; **S:** 10:00–17:00. Stock: large. PR: £1–100. Notes: (Sometimes closed on Thursday). [Updated]

Sterling Books, ■ 43a Locking Road, Weston-Super-Mare, BS23 3DG. Prop: David Nisbet. Tel: (01934) 625056. Web: www.abe.com. E-mail: sterling.books@talk21.com. Est: 1966. Shop open: **T:** 10:00–17:30; **W:** 10:00–17:30; **Th:** 10:00–13:00; **F:** 10:00–17:30; **S:** 10:00–17:30. Stock: very large. Spec: Academic/Scholarly; Advertising; Aeronautics; Antiquarian; Art; Bindings; Crafts; History - General. PR: £1–1,500. CC: AE; D; E; JCB; MC; V. Mem: ABA; ILAB; ABA. Notes: also, bookbinding & restoration, picture-framing & a booksearch service. [Updated]

SOUTH YORKSHIRE

DONCASTER

Hedgerow Books, 10 Whitbeck Close, Wadworth, Doncaster, DN11 9DZ. Prop: Peter & Elizabeth Hedge. Tel: (01302) 856311. Web: www.hedgerowbooks.com. E-mail: info@hedgerowbooks.com. Est: 1988. Private premises. Internet and postal. Appointment necessary. Open: **M:** 09:00–21:00; **T:** 09:00–21:00; **W:** 09:00–21:00; **Th:** 09:00–21:00; **F:** 09:00–21:00; **S:** 09:00–12:30; Closed for lunch: 12:30–14:00. Stock: small. Spec: Ecclesiastical History & Architecture; History - Industrial; Sport - Boxing; Sport - Football (Soccer). PR: £1–500. CC: MC; V; Switch. Mem: PBFA. VAT No: GB 657 8581 80. [Updated]

Saxton Books Ltd, 18 Saxton Avenue, Doncaster, DN4 7AX. Tel: 01302 371600. Fax: 01302 371071. Web: www.saxtonbooks.com. E-mail: becky@capitalbooks.co.uk. Est: 1997. Private premises. Internet and postal. Stock: very small. Spec: Authors:- Austen, Jane; Bates, H.E.; Bramah, Ernest; Flint, William Russell; Rand, Ayn; Shute, Neville; Economics; Engraving. PR: £10–1,000. [Updated]

ECKINGTON

The Bibliophile, 42, Fern Close, Eckington, S21 4 HE. (*) Michael P. Russell. Tel: (01246) 434025. Fax: (01246) 434025. E-mail: mpr@supanet.com. Est: 1997. Spec: Freemasonry & Anti-Masonry; Medicine; Printing; Collectables; Ephemera. PR: £1–50. [Updated]

ROTHERHAM

Anthony Singleton, 6 Birkwood Terrace, Braithwell, Rotherham, S66 7AE. Tel: (01709) 813396. E-mail: ajsingleton.books@virgin.net. Est: 1996. Private premises. Postal only. Stock: very small. Spec: History - General; Rural Life; Theology; Topography - General; Travel - General. [Updated]

SHEFFIELD

Annie's Books, 28 Blackbrook Drive, Sheffield, S10 4LS. Prop: Chris. Tel: (0114) 2306494. Fax: (0114) 2306494. Web: www.anniesbooks.co.uk. E-mail: wrentrading@talk21.com. Est: 1999. Private premises. Internet and postal. Appointment necessary. Open: M: 09:00–17:00; **T:** 09:00–17:00; **W:** 09:00–17:00; **Th:** 09:00–17:00; **F:** 09:00–17:00. Stock: small. Spec: Adventure; Animals and Birds; Author - Blyton, Enid; Cats; Children's; Modern First Editions; Booksearch. PR: £1–200. CC: AE; MC; V; SW. [Updated]

Baedekers & Murray Guides, 11 St. Quentin Drive, Sheffield, S17 4PN. Prop: Dr. R.H. Hickley. Tel: (0114) 236-6306. Web: www.roger_hickley@dial.Pipex.com. E-mail: roger_hickley@dial.pipex.com. Est: 1991. Private premises. Appointment necessary. Stock: very small. Spec: Guide Books; Travel - General. PR: £10–500. Corresp: French, German, Swedish, Finnish. [Updated]

Chantrey Books, 24 Cobnar Road, Sheffield, S8 8QB. Prop: Clare Brightman. Tel: (0114) 274-8958. E-mail: chantrey.24@btinternet.com. Est: 1981. Spec: Botany; Cookery/Gastronomy; Food & Drink; Gardening - General; Herbalism; Illustrated; Plant Hunting; Rural Life. PR: £5–500. Mem: PBFA. [Updated]

Alan Hill Books, Unit 4, Meersbrook Works, Sheffield, S8 9FT. Prop: Alan Hill. Tel: (01142) 556242. E-mail: alanhillbooks@supanet.com. Est: 1980. Shop and/or showroom; Internet and postal. Telephone first. Open: **M:** 10:30–14:30; **T:** 10:30–14:30; **W:** 10:30–14:30; **Th:** 10:30–14:30; **F:** 10:30–14:30. Stock: large. Spec: Academic/Scholarly; Genealogy; Topography - Local. PR: £5–500. CC: MC; V. VAT No: GB 533 9950 19. [Updated]

The Porter Bookshop, ■ 227 Sharrowvale Road, Sheffield, S11 8ZE. Prop: Margot Armitage. Tel: (0114) 266-7762. Est: 1988. Shop. Telephone first. Stock: medium. Spec: Academic/Scholarly; Crime (True); Humanities; Literature. [Updated]

Rare & Racy, ■ 164–166 Devonshire Street, Sheffield, S3 7SG. Prop: Allen Capes & Joseph Mhlongo. Tel: (0114) 270-1916. Web: www.rareandracy.co.uk. E-mail: shop@rareandracy.fsnet.co.uk. Est: 1969. Shop open: **M:** 10:00–18:00; **T:** 10:00–18:00; **W:** 10:00–18:00; **Th:** 10:00–18:00; **F:** 10:00–18:00; **S:** 10:00–18:00. Spec: Gardening - General; History - Local; Topography - Local. PR: £1–250. CC: MC; V; Solo, Maestro. Mem: PBFA. [Updated]

Tilleys Vintage Magazine Shop, ■ 281 Shoreham Street, Sheffield, S1 4SS. Antonius & Albertus Tilley Tel: (0114) 275-2442. Web: www.tilleysmagazines.com. E-mail: antonjusttilley@yahoo.co.uk. Est: 1978. Shop open: **T:** 10:00–16:30; **W:** 10:00–16:30; **Th:** 10:00–16:30; **F:** 10:00–16:30; **S:** 10:00–16:30. Stock: very large. Spec: Comic Books & Annuals; Comics; Magazines & Periodicals - General; Spiritualism; Ephemera; Prints and Maps. PR: £1–200. CC: AE; MC; V. Notes: also at 21 Derby Road, Chesterfield (q.v.). [Updated]

WOMBWELL

Bijou Books, Nimrod, 55 Aldham House Lane, Wombwell, S73 8RG. Prop: Maureen Firth, Dr. Gregory Firth (Assistant). Tel: (01226) 755012. Fax: (01226) 755012. E-mail: maureenfirth@blueyonder.co.uk. Est: 1982. Private premises. Internet and postal. Stock: small. Spec: Art Reference; Arts, The; Biography; Ceramics; Cookery/Gastronomy; Illustrated; Limited Editions; Literature. PR: £1–500. CC: PayPal. [Updated]

STAFFORDSHIRE

BURTON UPON TRENT

Ian J. Sherratt, Rhoslyn, Victoria St. Yoxall, Burton upon Trent, DE13 8NG. Tel: Not supplied. Est: 1989. Private premises. Postal only. Stock: small. PR: £1–20. [Updated]

LICHFIELD

Mike Abrahams, 14 Meadowbrook Road, Lichfield, WS13 7RN. Tel: (01543) 256200. Est: 1979. Private premises. Appointment necessary. Spec: Antiques; Banking & Insurance; Canals/Inland Waterways; Children's; Collecting; Comic Books & Annuals; Cookery/Gastronomy; Crime (True). PR: £1–500. [Updated]

Steve Brown (Books), 2 Curborough Cottages, Watery Lane, Lichfield, WS13 8ER. Prop: Steve Brown. Tel: (01543) 264498. Web: www.abebooks.com/home/sbbooks. E-mail: steve.brown26@virgin.net. Est: 1992. Private premises. Internet and postal. Appointment necessary. Stock: small. Spec: Sport - Horse Racing (inc. Riding/Breeding/Equestrian). PR: £5–500. Corresp: French. Mem: PBFA. Notes: also at: Curborough Hall Antiques Centre, Watery Lane, Lichfield. [Updated]

David Clegg, 6 Longbridge Road, Lichfield, WS14 9EL. Prop: David Clegg. Tel: (01543) 252117. Est: 1984. Private premises. Postal only. Stock: very small. Spec: Occult; Religion - General; Travel - General. PR: £5–20. [Updated]

Terry W. Coupland, 15 Harwood Road, Lichfield, WS13 7PP. Tel: (01543) 256599. E-mail: tcfortypo@btinternet.com. Est: 1980. Private premises. Appointment necessary. Stock: small. Spec: Bookbinding; Children's; Illustrated; Juvenile; Papermaking; Printing; Private Press; Publishing. PR: £5–1,500. Mem: PBFA. Notes: Attends PBFA fairs. [Updated]

Colin Shakespeare Books, 3 Chestnut Drive, Shenstone, Lichfield, WS14 0JH. Prop: Colin & Lilian Shakespeare. Tel: (01543) 480978. Est: 1991. Private premises. Postal only. Contactable. Open: **M:** 09:00–21:00; **T:** 09:00–21:00; **W:** 09:00–21:00; **Th:** 09:00–21:00; **F:** 09:00–21:00. Stock: small. Spec: Literature; Topography - General. PR: £3–1,500. [Updated]

The Staffs Bookshop, 4 and 6 Dam Street, Lichfield, WS13 6AA. Prop: Miss Hawkins. Tel: (01543) 264093. Fax: (01543) 264093. Web: www.staffsbookshop.co.uk. E-mail: contact@staffsbookshop.co.uk. Est: 1938. Shop and/or gallery. Internet and postal. Open: **M:** 09:30–17:30; **T:** 09:30–17:30; **W:** 09:30–17:30; **Th:** 09:30–17:30; **F:** 09:30–17:30; **S:** 09:30–17:30. Stock: very large. Spec: Author - Johnson, Samuel; Children's; Dolls & Dolls' Houses; History - General; Literature; Theology; Topography - Local. PR: £1–1,000. CC: MC; V; Maestro. Notes: Prints, Sheet Music, Ephemera. VAT No: GB 784 5011 28. [Updated]

NEWCASTLE–UNDER–LYME

Pomes Penyeach, 25 Curzon Street, Basford, Newcastle–under–Lyme, ST5 0PD. Prop: Paul Robinson. Tel: (01782) 630729. Web: www.abebooks.com. E-mail: books@pomes-penyeach.co.uk. Est: 1985. Private premises. Appointment necessary. Stock: small. Spec: Academic/Scholarly; Children's; First Editions; History - General; Literary Criticism; Literature; Modern First Editions; Philosophy. PR: £1–500. CC: AE; MC; V; Delta. Mem: PBFA. Notes: also, a booksearch service. [Updated]

Keith Twigg Toy Books, 27 Lansdell Avenue, Porthill, Newcastle-under-Lyme, ST5 8ET. Tel: (01782) 642932. Est: 1970. Postal only. Spec: Dolls & Dolls' Houses; Toys. PR: £20–200. [Updated]

STAFFORD

Ray Roberts (Booksellers), Whiston Hall Mews, Whiston Hall, Whiston, Nr. Penkridge, Stafford, ST19 5QH. Tel: (01785) 712232. Fax: (01785) 712232 Est: 1980. Private premises. Appointment necessary. Stock: small. Spec: Motoring; Traction Engines; Travel - General; Vintage Cars; Collectables. PR: £1–500. CC: AE; MC; V. Notes: also: author and publisher – Bentley Specials & Special Bentleys. [Updated]

STAFFORDSHIRE

STOKE–ON–TRENT

Abacas Books & Cards, ■ 56–60 Millrise Road, Milton, Stoke–on–Trent, ST2 7BW. Prop: Dave & Margaret Mycock. Tel: (01782) 543005. Est: 1980. Shop open: **M:** 09:00–17:00; **T:** 09:00–17:00; **W:** 09:00–17:00; **Th:** 09:00–17:00; **F:** 09:00–17:00; **S:** 09:00–13:00. Stock: medium. Spec: Art; Autobiography; Bindings; Biography; Ceramics; Cookery/Gastronomy; Fiction - General; Gardening - General. PR: £1–200. Notes: attends Buxton Book Fairs. VAT No: GB 478 7684 71. [Updated]

Acumen Books, Rushton House, 167 Nantwich Road, Audley, Stoke-on-Trent, ST7 8DL. Managing Director: C.B. Pearson. Tel: (01782) 720753. Fax: (01782) 720798. Web: www.acumenbooks.co.uk. E-mail: shep@acumenbooks.co.uk. Est: 1978. Open: **M:** 10:00–15:00; **Th:** 10:00–15:00. Spec: Sport - Cricket. PR: £1–20. CC: MC; V. Mem: ACU&S MCIArb. [Updated]

Cartographics, 49 Grange Road, Biddulph, Stoke–on–Trent, ST8 7RY. R.J. & S.W. Prop: Dean. Tel: (01782) 513449. Web: www.cartographics.co.uk. E-mail: carto@tesco.net. Est: 1969. Private premises. Internet and postal. Appointment necessary. Stock: very large. Spec: Canals/Inland Waterways; Cartography; Ephemera; Prints and Maps. PR: £1–500. Corresp: French (limited!). Notes: Map drawing-repair-mounting-conservation. Historical research from cartographic sources. VAT No: GB 318 9820 32. [Updated]

TAMWORTH

G. & J. Chesters, ■ 14 Market Street, Polesworth, Tamworth, B78 1HW. Prop: Geoff & Jean Chester. Tel: (01827) 894743. Web: www.abebooks.com/home/geoffchesters. E-mail: gandjchesters@tiscali.co.uk. Est: 1970. Shop open: **M:** 10:00–17:00; **T:** 10:00–17:00; **W:** 10:00–21:00; **Th:** 10:00–17:00; **F:** 10:00–17:00; **S:** 10:00–17:00. Stock: very large. Spec: Academic/Scholarly; Anthropology; Criminology; Economics; Geography; Geology; History - General; Linguistics. PR: £1–1,000. CC: AE; MC; V; Maestro. Mem: PBFA. VAT No: GB 112 6448 93. [Updated]

UTTOXETER

J.O. Goodwin, Woodcrofts Farm, Highwood, Uttoxeter, ST14 8PS. Prop: J.O. Goodwin. Tel: (01889) 562792. Est: 1965. Private premises. Appointment necessary. Stock: small. Spec: Prints and Maps. PR: £1–200. VAT No: GB 125 9041 83. [Updated]

WALSALL

SETI Books, 3C, Kingswood Drive, Walsall, WS6 6NX. Prop: David J Ward. Tel: 01922 413277. Fax: 01922 413277. E-mail: davidjward@setibooks.freeserve.co.uk. Est: 2002. Private premises. Internet and postal. Telephone first. Stock: very small. Spec: Cryptozoology; Earth Mysteries; Esoteric; Ghosts; Metaphysics; Mind, Body & Spirit; New Age; Occult. PR: £1–175. [Updated]

WOMBOURN

Rookery Bookery, 39 Rookery Road, Wombourn, WV5 0JH. Prop: Colin Hardwick. Tel: (01902) 895983. Est: 1987. Private premises. Appointment necessary. Stock: very small. PR: £1–250. Corresp: French. [Updated]

YOXALL

Ray Sparkes (Books), The Hollies, Bond End, Yoxall, DE13 8NH. Tel: (01543) 472274. Est: 1987. Private premises. Appointment necessary. Stock: small. Spec: Directories - General; Directories - British. PR: £2–3,000. Cata: quarterly. Mem: PBFA. VAT No: GB 478 2190 24. [Updated]

SUFFOLK

BECCLES

Besleys Books, ■ 4 Blyburgate, Beccles, NR34 9TA. Prop: Piers & Gabby Besley. Tel: (01502) 715762. Fax: (01502) 675649. Web: www.besleysbooks.demon.co.uk. E-mail: piers@besleysbooks. demon.co.uk. Shop open: **M:** 09:30–17:00; **T:** 09:30–17:00; **Th:** 09:30–17:00; **F:** 09:30–17:00; **S:** 09:30–17:00. Stock: large. Spec: Gardening - General; Illustrated; Natural History. PR: £1–1,000. CC: JCB; MC; V. Mem: ABA; PBFA. [Updated]

BOXFORD

Dolphin Books, Old Coach House, Broad Street, Boxford, CO10 5DX. Prop: Mrs. Rita Watts. Tel: (01787) 211630. Web: www.wwwukbookworld.com/members/DOLPHINBOOKS. E-mail: rwdolphinbooks@aol.com. Est: 1988. Private premises. Internet and postal. Appointment necessary. Stock: small. Spec: Arts, The; Authors - Women; Autobiography; Biography; History - General; History - Women; Literature; Memoirs. PR: £5–50. Notes: selected Stock also listed on Biblion.com and Alibris.com. Booksearch service. [Updated]

BUNGAY

Bardsley's Books, ■ 22 Upper Olland Street, Bungay, NR35 1BH. Prop: W.N.A. & D.H. Bardsley. Tel: (01986) 892077. Web: www.bardsleysbooks.co.uk. E-mail: antonybardsley@easynet.co.uk. Est: 1998. Shop open: **M:** 10:00–17:30; **T:** 10:00–17:30; **Th:** 10:00–17:30; **F:** 10:00–17:30; **S:** 10:00–17:30. Stock: very large. Spec: Antiquarian; Art; Bibles; Books about Books; Cinema/Film; Countries - Mexico; Countries - Poland; Ecclesiastical History & Architecture. PR: £1–250. Notes: also, cards, O.S. Maps, CDs & new books to order. [Updated]

Beaver Booksearch, 33 Hillside Road East, Bungay, NR35 1JU. Prop: Sarah Coulthurst & Nicholas Watts. Tel: (01986) 896698. Fax: (01986) 896698. Web: www.beaverbooksearch.co.uk. E-mail: nick@beaverbooksearch.co.uk. Est: 1995. Private premises. Postal only. Stock: small. Spec: Bridge; Booksearch. PR: £1–50. CC: AE; MC; V; SW. Notes: also, a booksearch service. VAT No: GB 638 1296 25. [Updated]

Scorpio Books, Autumn Cottage, Low Street, Ilketshall St Margaret, Bungay, NR35 1QZ. Prop: Lorna & Patrick Quorn. Tel: 01986 781721. Web: www.abe.com/home/scorpiobooks. E-mail: scorpiobooks.suffolk@virgin.net. Est: 1987. Private premises. Postal only. Appointment necessary. Spec: Aircraft; History - Military; History - Women; Music - Jazz & Blues; Performing Arts; Women. CC: JCB; MC; V. Cata: occasionally on Jazz, Military History, Aviation, Womens' Studies. Mem: PBFA. [Updated]

BURES

Major Iain Grahame, Daws Hill, Lamarsh, Bures, CO8 5EX. Prop: Major Iaian Grahame. Tel: (01787) 269213. Fax: (01787) 269634. Web: www.iaingrahamerarebooks.com. E-mail: majorbooks@ compuserve.com. Est: 1979. Private premises. Internet and postal. Telephone first. Open: **M:** 09:00–21:00; **T:** 09:00–21:00; **W:** 09:00–21:00; **Th:** 09:00-21:00; **F:** 09:00–21:00; **S:** 09:00–17:00; **Su:** 09:00–17:00. Medium stock. Spec: Fine and Rare; Natural History; Sport - Field Sports. PR: £5 – 50,000. CC: AE; MC; V. Cata: 2 a year on Sporting, Natural History and Africana. Corresp: French, Italian. Mem: ABA. Notes: also, booksearch. VAT: No: GB 341 7566 51. [Updated]

BURY ST EDMUNDS

Bury Bookshop, ■ 28A Hatter Street, Bury St Edmunds, IP33 1NE. Prop: Joe and Sheila Wakerley. Tel: (01284) 703107. Fax: 01284 755936. E-mail: burybooks@btconnect.com. Est: 1980. Shop open:**M:** 09:00–17:00; **T:** 09:00–17:00; **W:** 09:00–17:00; **Th:** 09:00–1700; **F:** 09:00–17:00; **S:** 09:00–17:30. Spec: County - Local; History - Local; Topography - Local. CC: AE; E; MC; V. Notes: major stock of books on and about Suffolk. [Updated]

Churchgate Books, ■ 47 Churchgate Street, Bury St Edmunds, IP33 1RG. Prop: Stephen Cook. Tel: (01284) 604604. E-mail: thebookman@btinternet.com. Shop open: **M:** 09:30–17:00; **T:** 09:30–17:00; **W:** 09:30-15:30; **Th:** 09:30-17:00; **F:** 09:30–17:00; **S:** 09:30–17:00. Small stock. Spec: East Anglia; Military History; Children's. Notes: also collectables, bookbinding and booksearch.

Sally Smith Books, 13 Manor Garth, Pakenham, Bury St Edmunds, IP31 2LB. Tel: (01359) 230431. Web: www.sallysmithbooks.co.uk. E-mail: sally@sallysmithbooks.co.uk. Est: 1989. Private premises. Internet Only. Appointment necessary. Stock: medium. Spec: Antiques; Art Reference; Bibliography; Biography; Children's; Crafts; Fiction - General; Literature - Victorian. PR: £1–1,000. Corresp: French. [Updated]

Janet Carters, 40 Church Lane, Barton Mills, Bury St. Edmunds, IP28 6AY. Tel: (01638) 717619. Fax: (01638) 717619. E-mail: cartersbooks@aol.com. Est: 1978. Private premises. Appointment necessary. Stock: small. Spec: Sport - Horse Racing (inc. Riding/Breeding/Equestrian). PR: £2–500. [Updated]

CLARE

Trinders' Fine Tools, ■ Malting Lane, Clare, Sudbury, CO10 8NW. Prop: Peter and Rosemary Trinder. Tel: (01787) 277130. Fax: (01787) 277677. Web: www.trindersfinetools.co.uk/. E-mail: peter@trindersfinetools.co.uk. Est: 1975. Shop. Internet and postal. Open: **M:** 10:00–17:00; **T:** 10:00–17:00; **Th:** 10:00–17:00; **F:** 10:00–17:00; **S:** 10:00–17:00; Closed for lunch: 13:00–14:00. Stock: small. Spec: Antiques; Applied Art; Architecture; Art; Art Reference; Artists; Arts, The; Building & Construction. PR: £2–500. CC: AE; JCB; MC; V. Mem: PBFA. Notes:. please phone before travelling lest we be closed!. VAT No: GB 299 6575 77. [Updated]

DEBENHAM

David Shacklock (Books), ■ 27 High St., Debenham, IP14 6QN. Prop: David Shacklock. Tel: (01728) 861286. E-mail: riley01@globalnet.co.uk. Est: 1986. Shop open: **T:** 10:00–17:00; **F:** 14:00–20:00; **S:** 10:00–16:00. Stock: medium. Spec: Annuals; Anthologies; Authors:- Baring-Gould, S.; Henty, G.A.; Biography; Fiction - General; Guide Books; History - General. PR: £1–150. CC: D; JCB; MC; V; Maestro. Notes: Townsend Mill, Halstead. Closed Tuesday 13:00–14:00. [Updated]

EYE

Elizabeth Nelson, Owl Cottage, 153 The Street, Stoke Ash, Eye, IP23 7EW. Tel: (01379) 678481. Fax: (01379) 678481. E-mail: eliznelson@owlcot.demon.co.uk. Est: 1982. Private premises. Appointment necessary. Stock: small. Spec: Antiques; Art; Aviation; Maritime/Nautical; Military. PR: £5–1,500. CC: MC; V. Mem: PBFA. VAT No: GB 428 0755 47. [Updated]

Thomas Rare Books, Valley Farm House, Yaxley, Eye, IP23 8BX. Prop: G.L. Thomas. Tel: (01379) 783288. Fax: (01379) 783288. Web: www.abebooks.com. E-mail: thomasrarebooks@btinternet.com. Est: 1978. Private premises. Postal only. Spec: Antiquarian; Prints and Maps. PR: £10–10,000. CC: JCB; V. Mem: PBFA. [Updated]

FELIXSTOWE

Books Only, ■ 84 Garrison Lane, Felixstowe, IP11 7RQ. Prop: Colin E. Sharman. Tel: (01394) 285546. Web: www.booksonly.co.uk. E-mail: colin.sharman@btopenworld.com. Est: 1980. Shop. Internet and postal. Open: **M:** 10:00–17:0; **T:** 10:00–17:00; **W:** 10:00–17:00; **Th:** 10:00–17:00; **F:** 10:00–17:00; **S:** 10:00–17:00. Stock: small. Spec: Comedy; Cookery/Gastronomy; Photography; Politics; Topography - Local. PR: £1–200. Notes: also at, Needham Market Antiques Centre. [Updated]

Poor Richard's Books, ■ 17 Orwell Road, Felixstowe, IP11 7EP. Prop: Dick Moffat. Tel: 01394 283138. E-mail: moffatsfx@aol.com. Est: 1997. Shop open: **M:** 09:30–17:00; **T:** 09:30–17:00; **W:** 09:30–17:00; **Th:** 09:30–17:00; **F:** 09:30–17:00; **S:** 09:00–17:00. Spec: Fiction - General; Fiction - Women; Literature; New Naturalist; Ornithology; Performing Arts; Poetry; Sport - Cricket. CC: MC; V; SO, SW. Corresp: French. Mem: PBFA. Notes: booksearch and book repairs. [Updated]

Treasure Chest Books, ■ Null, 61 Cobbold Road, Felixstowe, IP11 7BH. Prop: R. & R. Green. Tel: (01394) 270717. Est: 1982. Shop open: **M:** 09:30–17:30; **T:** 09:30–17:30; **W:** 09:30–17:30; **Th:** 09:30–17:30; **F:** 09:30–17:30; **S:** 09:30–17:30. Stock: very large. Spec: Art; Aviation; Cinema/Film; Occult; Topography - Local; Transport; Collectables; Ephemera. CC: E; JCB; MC. Mem: PBFA. Notes: none of our stock is on the Internet. [Updated]

FINNINGHAM

Abington Bookshop, Primrose Cottage, Westhorpe Road, Finningham, IP14 4TW. Prop: J. Haldane. Tel: (01449) 780303. Fax: (01449) 780202. E-mail: absand@.tiscali.co.uk. Est: 1971. Private premises. Appointment necessary. Stock: small. Spec: Carpets; Tapestry; Textiles; Travel - Asia. PR: £1–5,000. Corresp: French, German. Notes: also new books. VAT No: GB 213 3817 89. [Updated]

FRAMLINGHAM

Mrs. V.S. Bell (Books), ■ 19 Market Hill, Framlingham, Nr. Woodbridge, IP13 9BB. Tel: (01728) 723046. E-mail: rvbell@breathe.com. Est: 1974. Shop open: **M:** 10:00–16:00; **T:** 10:00–16:00; **W:** 10:00–13:00; **Th:** 10:00–16:00; **F:** 10:00–16:00; **S:** 09:00–16:00. Stock: medium. Spec: Fiction - Crime, Detective, Spy, Thrillers; Booksearch. PR: £2–200. [Updated]

Mrs. A. Kent (Books), ■ 19 Market Hill, Framlingham, Nr. Woodbridge, IP13 9BB. Tel: (01728) 723046. Est: 1974. Shop open: **M:** 10:00–16:00; **T:** 10:00–16:00; **W:** 10:00–12:00; **Th:** 10:00–14:00; **F:** 10:00–14:00; **S:** 09:00–16:00; Closed for lunch: 13:00–14:00. Stock: medium. Spec: Fiction - Crime, Detective, Spy, Thrillers; Booksearch. PR: £1–100. [Updated]

HALESWORTH

Andrew Jones, 25 Rectory Street, Halesworth, IP19 8AE. Tel: (01986) 835944. E-mail: andrewjones. history@dsl.pipex.com. Est: 1977. Private premises. Postal only. Stock: very small. Spec: Academic/Scholarly; Fine & Rare; History - General. PR: £5–1,000. [Updated]

IPSWICH

Roy Arnold, ■ 77 High Street, Needham Market, Ipswich, IP6 8AN. Tel: (01449) 720110. Fax: (01449) 722498. Web: www.royarnold.com. E-mail: books@royarnold.com. Est: 1976. Shop. Internet and postal. Open: **M:** 10:10–17:17; **T:** 10:10–17:17; **W:** 10:10–17:17; **Th:** 10:10–17:17; **F:** 10:10–17:17; **S:** 10:00–17:00. Stock: medium. Spec: Antiquarian; Antiques; Applied Art; Rural Life; Scientific Instruments; Windmills & Watermills; Woodwork. PR: £4–3,000. CC: MC; V. Mem: PBFA; TATHS, SOT, EAIA, MWTCA. Notes: also, new books on specialities & a booksearch service. VAT No: GB 334 0169 85. [Updated]

The Art Book Company, 35 Belstead Road, Ipswich, IP2 8AU. Prop: Priscilla Pilkington. Tel: (01473) 602133. Fax: (01473) 602133. E-mail: artbookco@totalise.co.uk. Est: 1974. Postal only. Open: **M:** 09:30–18:30; **T:** 09:30–18:30; **W:** 09:30–18:30; **Th:** 09:30–18:30; **F:** 09:30–12:30; Closed for lunch: 13:30–16:30. Stock: small. Spec: Architecture; Art History; Artists; Catalogues Raisonnes; Fine Art; Publishers - General; Publishers - Arabis Books; Publishers - Hacker Art Books. PR: £15–1,000. VAT No: GB 728 7258 02. [Updated]

Claude Cox Old & Rare Books, ■ College Gateway Bookshop, 3 & 5 Silent Street, Ipswich, IP1 1TF. Prop: Anthony Brian Cox. Tel: (01473) 254776. Fax: (01473) 254776. Web: www.claudecox.co.uk. E-mail: books@claudecox.co.uk. Est: 1944. Shop open: **W:** 10:00–17:00; **Th:** 10:00–17:00; **F:** 10:00–17:00; **S:** 10:00–17:00. Stock: medium. Spec: Antiquarian; Art Reference; Bibliography; Bindings; Books about Books; Ex-Libris; Fine Printing; Fore-Edge Paintings. CC: E; JCB; MC; V; SW. Mem: ABA; PBFA; ILAB; PLA, PHS. Notes: binding repairs, Suffolk Prints & Maps. VAT No: GB 304 7952 56. [Updated]

Footrope Knots, 501 Wherstead Road, Ipswich, IP2 8LL. Prop: Des & Liz Pawson. Tel: (01473) 690090. E-mail: knots@footrope.fsnet.co.uk. Est: 1981. Private premises. Postal only. Appointment necessary. Stock: very small. Spec: Crafts; Maritime/Nautical; Sport - Yachting. PR: £1–100. [Updated]

The Idler, ■ 37 High Street, Hadleigh, Ipswich, IP7 5AF. Prop: Bryan & Jane Haylock. Tel: (01473) 827752. Est: 1980. Shop open: **M:** 09:30–17:00; **T:** 09:30–17:00; **W:** 09:30–12:00; **Th:** 09:30–17:00; **F:** 09:30–17:00; **S:** 09:30–17:00. Stock: medium. Spec: Art; New Books; Booksearch. PR: £1–100. Notes: also, new books, publisher's remainders, art materials, greetings cards. VAT No: GB 410 6933 74. [Updated]

Bookmark www.sheppardsworld.co.uk

to order Sheppard's directories and related titles – and to search for overseas

book dealers – ephemera dealers – print & map sellers

LONG MELFORD

Lime Tree Books, ■ Hall Street, Long Melford, CO10 9JF. Bryan Marsh. Tel: (01787) 311532. E-mail: limetreebooks@tiscali.co.uk. Est: 1992. Shop open: **M:** 10:00–17:00; **T:** 10:00–17:00; **W:** 10:00–17:00; **Th:** 10:00–17:00; **F:** 10:00–17:00; **S:** 10:00–17:00; **Su:** 10:00–17:00. Stock: medium. PR: £1–200. CC: MC; V. VAT No: GB 623 0516 79. [Updated]

LOWESTOFT

A Book For All Reasons, Rockville House, 6 Pakefield Road, Lowestoft, NR33 0HS. Prop: G. A. Michael Sims. Tel: 01502 581011. Fax: 01502 574891. Web: www.abfar.co.uk. E-mail: books@abfar.co.uk. Est: 1994. Private premises. Internet and postal. Appointment necessary. Open: **M:** 09:00–18:00; **T:** 09:00–18:00; **W:** 09:00–18:00; **Th:** 09:00–18:00; **F:** 09:00–18:00; **S:** 09:00–18:00; Closed for lunch: 13:00–16:00. Spec: Authors:- Heyer, Georgette; Yates, Dornford; Fiction - General; Fiction - Historical; Fiction - Romantic; History - Local; Naval; Topography - Local. CC: MC; V; Switch, Maestro. Mem: PBFA; ibooknet. Notes: also on www.ibooknet.com. VAT No: GB 770 1056 57. [Updated]

R. W. Lamb, Talbot House, 158 Denmark Road, Lowestoft, NR32 2EL. Tel: (01502) 564306. Fax: (01502) 564306. E-mail: talbot@rwlamb.co.uk. Est: 1972. Private premises. Internet and postal. Appointment necessary. Spec: Classical Studies. [Updated]

John Rolph, ■ Manor House, Pakefield Street, Lowestoft, NR33 0JT. Tel: (01502) 572039. Est: 1952. Shop open: **T:** 11:00–17:00; **W:** 11:00–17:00; **F:** 11:00–17:00; **S:** 11:00–17:00; Closed for lunch: 13:00–14:30. Stock: medium. PR: £1–100. [Updated]

NEWMARKET

Miles Apart, 5 Harraton House, Exning, Newmarket, CB8 7HF. Prop: Ian Mathieson. Tel: 01638 577627. Fax: 01638 577874. Web: www.sthelena.se. E-mail: imathieson2000@yahoo.co.uk. Est: 1994. Private premises. Appointment necessary. Open: **M:** 09:00–09:00; **T:** 09:00–09:00; **W:** 09:00–09:00; **Th:** 09:00–09:00; **F:** 09:00–09:00; **S:** 09:00–09:00; **Su:** 09:00–09:00; Closed for lunch: 13:00–09:00. Spec: Countries - Falklands, The; Countries - South Atlantic Islands; Travel - General; Travel - Polar; War - Napoleonic. CC: MC; V. Cata: bi-annually on South Atlantic Islands, Antarctic and Travel. Mem: PBFA. Notes: specialising in islands of South Atlantic - St Helena, Ascension, Tristan, Falklands also the Antarctic and general travel. [Updated]

C.D. Paramor, 25 St. Mary's Square, Newmarket, CB8 0HZ. Tel: (01638) 664416. E-mail: cdparamor@btopenworld.com. Est: 1974. Private premises. Appointment necessary. Stock: medium. Spec: Cinema/Film; Dance; Entertainment - General; Music - General; Performing Arts; Television; Theatre; Windmills & Watermills. PR: £1–350. [Updated]

R.E. & G.B. Way, Brettons, Burrough Green, Newmarket, CB8 9NA. Prop: Greg Way. Tel: 01638 507217. Fax: 01638 508058. Web: www.geocities.com/regbway. E-mail: waybks@msn.com. Est: 1958. Private premises. Telephone first. Open: **M:** 08:30–17:30; **T:** 08:30–17:30; **W:** 08:30–17:30; **Th:** 08:30–17:30; **F:** 08:30–17:30; **S:** 08:30–17:30. Spec: Animals and Birds; Natural History; Private Press; Sport - Big Game Hunting; Sport - Field Sports. VAT No: GB 103 4378 02. [Updated]

SAXMUNDHAM

Chapel Books, The Chapel, Westleton, Saxmundham, IP17 3AA. Prop: Robert Jackson. Tel: 01728 648616. Web: www.chapelbooks.com. E-mail: bob.thechapel@virgin.net. Est: 1982. Shop and/or gallery. Open: **M:** 12.00–17:0; **T:** 12.00–17:0; **W:** 12.00–17:0; **Th:** 12.00–17:0; **F:** 12.00–17:0; **S:** 12.00–17:0; **Su:** 12.00–17:0; Closed for lunch: 12.00–17:00. Spec: CC: AE; MC; V; Maestro. [Updated]

Keith A. Savage, ■ 35 High Street, Saxmundham, IP17 1AJ. Prop: Keith Savage. Tel: 01728 604538. Fax: 01986 872231(answerphone). Est: 1992. Shop open: **M:** 10:30–13:00; **T:** 10:30–17:00; **W:** 10:30–17:00; **F:** 10:30–17:00; **S:** 10:30–13:00. Stock: small. Spec: Children's; Comic Books & Annuals; Comics; Ephemera; Prints and Maps. PR: £1–150. [Updated]

Sax Books, ■ 4a High Street, Saxmundham, IP17 1DF. Prop: Richard W.L. Smith, MVO. Tel: (01728) 605775. E-mail: richard@saxbooks.co.uk. Est: 2000. Shop open: **W:** 10:00–16:00; **Th:** 10:00–16:00; **F:** 10:00–16:00; **S:** 10:00–16:00. Stock: medium. PR: £1–250. Notes: also open on Tuesdays 10-4 in Summer and near to Christmas. [Updated]

SOUTHWOLD

Richard Everett, ■ Southwold Antiques Centre, Buckenham Mews, 83 High Street, Southwold, IP18 6DS. Tel: (01502) 723060. Shop open: **M:** 10:00–17:00; **T:** 10:00–17:00; **W:** 10:00–17:00; **Th:** 10:00–17:00; **F:** 10:00–17:00; **S:** 10:00–17:00; **Su:** 11:00–17:00. Stock: small. Spec: Children's; Publishers - Warnes; Topography - Local. PR: £2–50. Mem: PBFA; Richard Everett at Downham Market, Norfolk (q.v.) Local topography includes Adrian Bell. [Updated]

SUDBURY

Beckham Books Ltd., Chilton Mount, Newton Road, Sudbury, CO102RS. Prop: Mrs. J. E. Beckham. Tel: (01787) 373683. Fax: (01787) 375441. Web: www.beckhambooks.com. E-mail: beckhambooks1@btconnect.com. Est: 1998. Office and/or bookroom. Internet and postal. Telephone first. Stock: very large. Spec: Theology. PR: £1–2,000. CC: AE; D; E; JCB; MC; V. Mem: PBFA. VAT No: GB 750 9305 36. [Updated]

Parade Bookshop, ■ 10 North Street Parade, Sudbury, CO10 1GL. Prop: Mrs. G. Cawthorn. Tel: 01787 881626. Est: 1975. Shop open: **M:** 10:00–16:30; **T:** 10:00–16:30; **Th:** 10:00–16:30; **F:** 10:00–16:30; **S:** 10:00–16:30. [Updated]

Suffolk Rare Books, 7 New Street, Sudbury, CO10 1JB. Prop: T.M. Cawthorn. Tel: (01787) 372075. Web: www.abebooks.com. E-mail: morrisbooks@hotmail.com. Est: 1975. Private premises. Telephone first. Open: **T:** 10:30–16:30; **Th:** 10:30–16:30; **F:** 10:30–16:30; **S:** 10:30–16:30. Stock: medium. Spec: Aviation; History - Local; Maritime/Nautical; Military; Railways; Topography - General; Topography - Local; Transport. PR: £1–40. [Updated]

Derek Vanstone - Aviation Book, Tymperley Farm, Great Henny, Sudbury, CO10 7LX. Tel: (01787) 269291. Fax: (01787) 269291. Web: www.aircraftbooks.com. E-mail: derek.vanstone@lineone.net. Est: 1996. Private premises. Internet and postal. Contactable. Open: **M:** 09:00–18:00; **T:** 09:00–18:00; **W:** 09:00–18:00; **Th:** 09:00–18:00; **F:** 09:00–18:00; **S:** 09:00–13:00. Stock: small. Spec: Aviation; Maritime/Nautical; Military. PR: £1–200. CC: AE; MC; V. Cata: occasionally. Mem: PBFA. VAT No: GB 711 3364 72. [Updated]]

WOODBRIDGE

W.H. Collectables, 24 Ipswich Road, Woodbridge, IP12 4BU. Prop: Michael Wheeler. Tel: (01394) 385021. Fax: (01394) 385021. Est: 1981. Storeroom. Appointment necessary. Open: **M:** 09:00–20:00; **T:** 09:00–20:00; **W:** 09:00–20:00; **Th:** 09:00–20:00; **F:** 09:00–20:00. Stock: large. Spec: Aeronautics; Alpinism/Mountaineering; Americana; Banking & Insurance; Children's; Colonial; Comics; Documents - General. PR: £10–500. CC: D; MC; V. Corresp: German. Mem: ES. Notes: stock also covers Australia, Canada and New Zealand. [Updated]

YOXFORD

Skoob Russell Square, Woodhill Farm, Willow Marsh Lane, Yoxford, IP17 3JR. Prop: Chris Edwards. Tel: 07816 027 642. Web: www.skoob.com. E-mail: skoobrussellsquare@hotmail.com. Est: 1979. Private premises. Internet and postal. Appointment necessary. Stock: very large. Spec: Academic/Scholarly; Anthropology; Architecture; Art; Art Reference; Biography; Cinema/Film; Classical Studies. PR: £1–500. CC: AE; E; MC; V. VAT No: GB 824 8827 00. [Updated]

SURREY

ASHTEAD

Nigel Smith Books, 2 Bagot Close, Ashtead, KT21 1NS. Tel: (01372) 272517. Web: www.bagotbooks. com. E-mail: info@bagotbooks.com. Est: 1999. Private premises. Internet and postal. Stock: medium. PR: £2–300. CC: PayPal. Notes: especially British topography. [Updated]

BEDDINGTON

Mrs. Patricia Clear, 33 Cedars Road, Beddington, CR0 4PU. Prop: Mrs Patricia Clear. Tel: (020) 8681-0251. E-mail: patandray@blueyonder.co.uk. Est: 1990. Private premises. Postal only. Telephone first. Stock: small. Spec: Children's. PR: £1–120. [Updated]

BYFLEET

Joppa Books Ltd., ■ 68 High Road, Byfleet, KT14 7QL. Prop: Nadeem M. Elissa. Tel: (01932) 336777. Fax: (01932) 348881. Web: www.joppabooks.com. E-mail: joppa@joppabooks.com. Est: 1989. Shop. Internet and postal. Open: **M:** 10:00–14:00; **T:** 10:00–16:00; **W:** 10:00–16:00; **Th:** 10:00–16:00; **F:** 10:00–16:00; Closed for lunch: 12:00–14:00. Stock: large. Spec: Academic/Scholarly; Antiquarian; Archaeology; Canals/Inland Waterways; Carriages & Driving; Countries - Middle East, The; Egyptology; History - National. PR: £5–5,000. CC: AE; MC; V; SW. Corresp: Arabic, French. Mem: PBFA. VAT No: GB 493 7403 24. [Updated]

DORKING

A.J. Coombes, 24 Horsham Road, Dorking, RH4 2JA. Prop: John Coombes. Tel: (01306) 880736. Fax: (01306) 743641. E-mail: john.coombes@ukgateway.net. Est: 1967. Private premises. Appointment necessary. Stock: small. Spec: Architecture; History - General; History - British; History - Local; Topography - General; Topography - Local. Corresp: German. Mem: ABA. VAT No: GB 210 5273 14. [Updated]

C.C. Kohler, 12 Horsham Road, Dorking, RH4 2JL. Tel: (01306) 881532. Fax: (01306) 742438. E-mail: cornflwr@cornflwr.demon.co.uk. Est: 1963. Storeroom. Appointment necessary. Stock: medium. Spec: Special Collections. Corresp: German. Mem: ABA; ILAB. VAT No: GB 293 7862 08. [Updated]

EAST HORSLEY

Emjay Books, Ashdene, High Park Avenue, East Horsley, KT24 5DF. Prop: M. Gardner. Tel: (01483) 283373. E-mail: emjaybooks@lineone.net. Est: 1990. Private premises. Internet and postal. Appointment necessary. Stock: large. Spec: American Indians; Authors:- Bates, H.E.; Byron, Lord; Christie, Agatha; Francis, Dick; Tangye, D.; Motoring; Private Press. PR: £5–3,000. Notes: also, a booksearch service. [Updated]

Rowan House Books, Rowans, Norrels Ride, East Horsley, KT24 5EH. Prop: George Spranklins. Tel: (01483) 282482. Fax: (01483) 285924. Web: www.abebooks.com. E-mail: gsprankling@aol.com. Est: 1995. Private premises. Internet and postal. Appointment necessary. Stock: medium. Spec: Children's; First Editions; Illustrated. PR: £10–500. CC: MC; V. [Updated]

EAST MOLESEY

Books Bought & Sold, ■ 68 Walton Road, East Molesey, KT8 0DL. Prop: P.J. Sheridan & W.J. Collyer. Tel: (020) 8224-3609. Fax: (020) 8224-3576. Web: www.booksinstore.co.uk. E-mail: sheridan@ books.keyuk.com. Est: 1985. Shop open: **T:** 10:00–17:00; **W:** 10:00–17:00; **Th:** 10:00–17:00; **F:** 10:00–17:00; **S:** 10:00–17:00. Stock: medium. Spec: Aeronautics; Aviation; Children's; History - General; Illustrated; Military; Motoring; Railways. PR: £1–900. CC: D; E; JCB; MC; V. Notes: organisers of HD Book Fairs. VAT No: GB 644 1831 46. [Updated]

Londinium Books, 10 Summer Avenue, East Molesey, KT8 9LU. Prop: Eric & Jean Mahoney Tel: (020) 8398-7165. Web: www.abebooks.com. E-mail: j.jm.mahoney@talk21.com. Market stand/stall. **M:** 11:00–18:30; **S:** 11:00–18:30; **Su:** 11:00–18:30. [Updated]

EGHAM

Blacklock's, ■ 8 Victoria Street, Englefield Green, Egham, TW20 0QY. Prop: Graham Dennis. Tel: (01784) 438025. Est: 1988. Shop open: **M:** 09:00–17:00; **T:** 09:00–17:00; **W:** 09:00–17:00; **Th:** 09:00–17:00; **F:** 09:00–17:00; **S:** 09:00–13:00; Closed for lunch: 13:00–14:00. Stock: small. Spec: Sport - Polo; Prints and Maps. PR: £2–250. CC: MC; V. Notes: prints on Venice. [Updated]

Corfe Books, ■ 'Corfe', Mount Lee, Egham, TW20 9PD. Prop: Mark Hayhoe. Tel: (01932) 850674. Est: 2001. Shop open: **T:** 10:00–16:00; **W:** 10:00–16:00; **Th:** 10:00–16:00; **F:** 10:00–17:45; **S:** 10:00–17:45. Stock: large. Spec: Aeronautics; Animals and Birds; Antiques; Archaeology; Architecture; Espionage; Fiction - General; History - General. PR: £1–300. [Updated]

EPSOM

Vandeleur Antiquarian Books, 6 Seaforth Gardens, Stoneleigh, Epsom, KT19 0NR. Prop: E.H. Bryant. Tel: (020) 8393-7752 (24h. Fax: (020) 8393-7752 (24hrs). Est: 1971. Private premises. Appointment necessary. Stock: small. Spec: Alpinism/Mountaineering; Antiquarian; Bindings; Sport - Big Game Hunting; Sport - Rowing; Travel - Africa; Travel - Americas; Travel - Asia. PR: £5–2,000. Mem: PBFA. Notes: exhibits at bookfairs. Also, rowing prints and Indian Mogul-style paintings. Maps. [Updated]

EWELL

Ewell Bookshop Ltd, ■ 9A High Street, Ewell Village, Epsom, KT17 1SG. Prop: Steven Fordham. Tel: 0208 3931283. E-mail: ewellbookshop@aol.com. Est: 2002. Shop open: **T:** 10:00–17:00; **W:** 10:00–17:00; **Th:** 10:00–17:00; **F:** 13:00–18:00; **S:** 10:00–17:00. Stock: medium. Spec: Aviation; Military History; Naval; Railways; Topography - General; Topography - Local; Transport; Booksearch. PR: £1–200. [Updated]

J.W. McKenzie Ltd, ■ 12 Stoneleigh Park Road, Ewell, Epsom, KT19 0QT. Tel: (0208) 393 7700. Fax: (0208) 393 1694. Web: www.mckenzie-cricket.co.uk. E-mail: jwmck@netcomuk.co.uk. Est: 1971. Shop. Internet and postal. Open: **M:** 09:00–17:00; **T:** 09:00–17:00; **W:** 09:00–17:00; **Th:** 09:00–17:00; **F:** 09:00–17:00; **S:** 10:00–13:00; Closed for lunch: 13:00–14:00. Stock: medium. Spec: Sport - Cricket. CC: E; JCB; MC; V. [Updated]

FARNHAM

Bodyline Books, The Oast House, Park Row, Farnham, GU9 7JH. Prop: Giles Lyon & Mike Scott. Tel: 01252 727222. Web: www.bodylinebooks.com. E-mail: info@bodylinebooks.com. Est: 1996. Private premises. Postal only. Contactable. Open: **M:** 09:00–17:30; **T:** 09:00–17:30; **W:** 09:00–17:30; **Th:** 09:00–17:30; **F:** 09:00–17:30; **S:** 09:00–17:30; **Su:** 09:00–17:30; Closed for lunch: 13:00–14:00. Spec: Sport - General; Sport - Angling/Fishing; Sport - Archery; Sport - Athletics; Sport - Badminton; Sport - Basketball; Sport - Billiards/Snooker/Pool; Sport - Bowls. CC: MC; V; Switch, Delta. Cata: quarterly on all sports. [Updated]

Derek Burden, 1 Boundstone Road, Wrecclesham, Farnham, GU10 4TH. Prop: Derek Burden. Tel: (01252) 793615. Fax: (01252) 794789. E-mail: dweburden@aol.com. Est: 1967. Private premises. Internet and postal. Appointment necessary. Stock: large. Spec: Graphics; Illustrated; Prints and Maps. PR: £0–1,000. [Updated]

Valentine Rare Books, Potters Hatch House, Crondall, Nr. Farnham, GU10 5PW. Prop: Anthony Surtees. Tel: (01252) 851495. Est: 1983. Private premises. Appointment necessary. Stock: small. Spec: Fiction - General; Fiction - Historical; Fiction - Romantic; Fiction - Women; Literature; Literature in Translation; Travel - General; Travel - Middle East. PR: £20–10,000. [Updated]

GODALMING

Crouch Rare Books, Syringa, Tuesley Lane, Godalming, GU7 1SB. Prop: A.S. Crouch. Tel: (01483) 420390. Fax: (01483) 421371. Web: www.crbooks.co.uk. E-mail: tcrouch@crbooks.co.uk. Est: 1970. Storeroom. Internet and postal. Telephone first. Open: **M:** 09:00–17:30; **T:** 09:00–17:30; **W:** 09:00–17:30; **F:** 09:00–17:30; **S:** 09:00–17:30; Closed for lunch: 13:00–14:00. Stock: medium. Spec: Academic/Scholarly; Antiquarian; Archaeology; Classical Studies; Countries - Cyprus; Countries - Greece; Crafts; Ecclesiastical History & Architecture. PR: £2–1,000. CC: AE; JCB; MC; V; Switch. Corresp: French, Greek, Latin. Notes: also, publishers. VAT No: GB 417 6129 55. [Updated]

GUILDFORD

Apocalypse, 51 Woking Road, Guildford, GU1 1QD. Prop: Richard Grenville Clark. Tel: 01483 841550. Fax: 01483 841550. E-mail: richardg.clark1000@ntlworld.com. Est: 1996. Mail Order Only. Internet and postal. Appointment necessary. Spec: Academic/Scholarly; Adult; Aesthetic Movement; Aesthetics; Aircraft; Alchemy; Amish; Animals and Birds. CC: PayPal. Cata: on Non-Fiction and Fiction of all kinds. Corresp: Some French. Notes: We also publish books on art, education,poetry and fiction [see: www.apocalypsepress.co.uk]. [Updated]

Anglo-American Rare Books, Galleons Lap, P.O. Box 71, Haslemere, GU27 1YT. Prop: Jack Laurence. Tel: 01428 606462. E-mail: anglobooks@aol.com. Private premises. Postal only. Spec: Americana; Authors:- Eliot, T.S.; Greene, Graham; Hemingway, Ernest; James, Henry; Mailer, Norman; Sassoon, Siegfried; Fiction - General. Mem: PBFA. [Updated]

G. Bickford-Smith (formerly Snowden Smith Books), Linden, Holdfast Lane, Haslemere, GU27 2EY. Prop: Gilian Bickford-Smith. Tel: 01428 641363. Fax: 01428 641363. E-mail: g.bickfordsmith@virgin.net. Est: 1975. Private premises. Internet and postal. Spec: Colonial; Ethnography; International Affairs; Travel - Africa; Travel - Asia; Travel - Balkans; Travel - Islamic World; Travel - Middle East. Cata: occasionally on specialities listed. [Updated]

HORLEY

Reigate Galleries, Cedar Cottage, Haroldslea Drive, Horley, RH6 9PH. Prop: K. & J. Morrish. Tel: (01293) 773426. Est: 1960. Private premises. Postal only. Appointment necessary. Stock: small. PR: £5–300. CC: MC; V. Mem: PBFA. [Updated]

LEATHERHEAD

Dandy Lion Editions, ■ 63, High Street, Leatherhead, KT22 8AQ. Prop: Angela McCarthy. Tel: (01372) 377785. Web: www.dandylioneditions.co.uk. E-mail: angela@dandylioneditions.co.uk. Est: 1995. Shop. Internet and postal. Open:**T:** 10:00–16:30; **W:** 10:00–16:30; **Th:** 10:00–16:30; **F:** 10:00–16:30; **S:** 09:00–17:00. Stock: medium. Spec: Academic/Scholarly; Art; Biography; Children's; Children's - Illustrated; Early Imprints; Entertainment - General; Folio Society, The. PR: £1–100. CC: JCB; MC. Notes: Internet & Postal sales. [Updated]

MITCHAM

J.G. Natural History Books, 149 Sherwood Park Road, Mitcham, CR4 1NJ. Prop: J. Greatwood. Tel: (020) 8764-4669. Fax: (020) 8764-4669. Web: www.reptilebooks.com. E-mail: jgbooks@btinternet.com. Est: 1969. Private premises. Internet and postal. Appointment necessary. Spec: Gemmology; Herpetology; New Books. PR: £10–500. CC: PayPal. Notes: also, new books. [Updated]

NEW MALDEN

Steve Baxter, 13 Westbury Road, New Malden, KT3 5BE. Tel: (020) 8942-4431. Fax: (020) 8942-2249. E-mail: baxterfinebooks@aol.com. Private premises. Postal only. Stock: small. Spec: Antiquarian; Bindings; Churchilliana; Fine & Rare; First Editions; History - General; Literature; Sets of Books. CC: AE; JCB; MC; V. Mem: ABA; PBFA; ILAB. VAT No: GB 711 1425 88. [Updated]

OXTED

Postings, P.O. Box 1, Oxted, RH8 0FD. Prop: R.N. Haffner. Tel: (01883) 722646. Fax: (01883) 722646. E-mail: postingsauctions@yahoo.co.uk. Est: 1992. Private premises. Postal only. Stock: very small. Spec: Aviation; History - Postal; Philately; Railways; Sport - Ballooning; Topography - Local; Transport; Ephemera. PR: £5–300. CC: E; JCB; MC; V. Mem: PTS. Notes: also, postcards. [Updated]

Secondhand Bookshop, ■ 56 Station Road West, Oxted, RH8 9EU. Prop: David Neal. Tel: (01883) 715755. Est: 1993. Shop open: **M:** 10:00–17:00; **T:** 10:00–17:00; **W:** 10:00–17:00; **Th:** 10:00–17:00; **F:** 10:00–17:00; **S:** 10:00–17:00. Stock: medium. PR: £1–400. Notes: Books in the Basement, Oxted (q.v.) Browsers's Coffee Shop, Lingfield, Surrey Also, at home, by appointment. VAT No: GB 725 4573 27. [Updated]

RICHMOND

W & A Houben, ■ 2, Church Court, Richmond, TW9 1JL. Prop: CJW & AKD Dunlop. Tel: 020 8940 1055. E-mail: houbens@tiscali.co.uk. Est: 1963. Shop open: **M:** 10:00–18:00; **T:** 10:00–18:00; **W:** 10:00–18:00; **Th:** 10:00–18:00; **F:** 10:00–18:00; **S:** 10:00–18:00. CC: MC; V. VAT No: GB 215 9473 53. [Updated]

SHAMLEY GREEN

Eric Thompson, Hullhatch, Shamley Green, Guildford, GU5 0TG. Tel: (01483) 893694. Fax: (01483) 892219. Est: 1978. Private premises. Appointment necessary. Stock: large. Spec: Motoring; Booksearch. PR: £5–750. [Updated]

SURBITON

The Bookroom, ■ 146 Chiltern Drive, Surbiton, KT5 8LS. Prop: Keith Alexander. Tel: 020 8404 6644. Web: www.abebooks.com/home/keithalexander. E-mail: kmabooks@aol.com. Est: 2002. Shop open: **W:** 11:00–18.00; **Th:** 11:00–18.00; **F:** 11:00–18.00; **S:** 10:00–18.00. Spec: Architecture; Art; Art History; Art Reference; Artists; Autobiography; Biography; Ceramics. CC: JCB; MC; V; Solo Maestro. [Updated]

Caissa Books, 5 Pembroke Avenue, Berrylands, Surbiton, KT5 8HN. Prop: Mike Sheehan. Tel: (020) 8399 6591. Fax: (020) 8399 6591. E-mail: caissa.books@tinyworld.co.uk. Est: 1980. Postal only. Contactable. Open: **M:** 14:00–20:00; **T:** 14:00–20:00; **W:** 14:00–20:00; **Th:** 14:00–20:00; **F:** 14:00–20:00. Stock: small. Spec: Chess; Collectables; Ephemera; Prints and Maps. PR: £3–3,000. CC: MC; V. Corresp: French and German. [Updated]

SUTTON

Nonsuch Books, 176 Mulgrave Road, Cheam, Sutton, SM2 6JS. Prop: Robert and Lynette Gleeson. Tel: (020) 8770 7875. E-mail: nonsuch.books@virgin.net. Est: 1990. Private premises. Postal only. Appointment necessary. Open: **M:** 09:00–17:00; **T:** 09:00–17:00; **W:** 09:00–17:00; **Th:** 09:00–17:00; **F:** 09:00–17:00; **S:** 09:00–17:00. Stock: small. Spec: Archaeology; Architecture; Art; Art History; Art Reference; History - General; Illustrated; Literature. PR: £5–200. [Updated]

WALLINGTON

RGS Books, 3 Dower Street, Wallington, SM6 0RG. Tel: (0208) 647 2003. Fax: (0208) 647 2003. E-mail: rgsbooks@btinternet.com. Est: 1960. Private premises. Internet and postal. Stock: large. Spec: Academic/Scholarly; Antiquarian; Antiques; Architecture; Art; Artists; Arts, The; Author - Wells, H.G PR: £2–500. Mem: PLA; SB. Notes: stocks titles on history of London. [Updated]

WALTON–ON–THAMES

Fred Lake, 104 Kings Road, Walton–on–Thames, KT12 2RE. Tel: (01932) 227824. Private premises. Postal only. Stock: very small. Spec: Magazines & Periodicals - General; Sport - Archery; Sport - Field Sports. PR: £1–150. [Updated]

WEYBRIDGE

Fun in Books, P.O. Box 608, Weybridge, KT13 3BL. Prop: Michael J. White. Tel: (01932) 852625. E-mail: mail@melitzer.freeserve.co.uk. Est: 1994. Storeroom. Postal only. Spec: Freemasonry & Anti-Masonry; Glamour; Humour; Collectables; Ephemera. PR: £5–1,000. CC: MC; V. [Updated]

Mrs. D.M. Green, 7 Tower Grove, Weybridge, KT13 9LX. Tel: (01932) 241105. Est: 1974. Private premises. Appointment necessary. Stock: very small. Spec: Atlases; Topography - General; Prints and Maps. PR: £1–3,500. Mem: IMCos. [Updated]

WINDLESHAM

Cold Tonnage Books, 22 Kings Lane, Windlesham, GU20 6JQ. Prop: Andy Richards. Tel: (01276) 475388. Web: www.andy@coldtonnage.com. E-mail: andy@coldtonnage.com. Est: 1989. Private premises. Internet and postal. Appointment necessary. Stock: medium. Spec: Fiction - Science Fiction. PR: £5–500. CC: MC; V. VAT No: GB 530 1816 81. [Updated]

New dealers in the British Isles can register their business on
www.sheppardsworld.co.uk

WOKING

Glenwood Books, Highlands, Cedar Road, Hook Heath, Woking, GU22 0JJ. Prop: Lesleyanne Woolvett. Tel: (01483) 725628. Fax: (01420) 541173. E-mail: lawoolvett@hotmail.com. Est: 1994. Private premises. Book Fairs Only. Contactable. Stock: very small. Spec: Antiques; Cookery/Gastronomy; Literature - Victorian; Topography - Local; Booksearch. PR: £5–100. [Updated]

Goldsworth Books, ■ 47 Goldsworth Road, Woking, GU21 6JY. Prop: Brian & Joyce Hartles. Tel: (01483) 767670. Fax: (01483) 767670. Web: www.goldsworthbooks.com. E-mail: brian@goldsworthbooks.com. Est: 1986. Shop. Internet and postal. Open: **T:** 10:00–16:00; **W:** 10:00–16:00; **Th:** 10:00–16:00; **F:** 10:00–16:00; **S:** 09:30–16:30. Stock: very large. Spec: Booksearch; Prints and Maps. PR: £1–5,000. CC: JCB; V. Mem: PBFA. VAT No: GB 641 2513 73. [Updated]

Peter Kennedy, ■ 2 Shirley Place, Knaphill, Woking, GU21 2PL. Tel: (01483) 797293. E-mail: peter@peterkennedy.com. Est: 1972. Shop open: **S:** 08:00–16:00. Spec: Atlases; Botany; Illustrated; Natural History; Prints and Maps. CC: V. Mem: ABA. Notes: also, antique prints. Appointment necessary Mon-Friday. [Updated]

World War II Books, P.O. Box 55, Woking, GU22 8HP. Prop: C.G. Palmer. Tel: (01483) 722880. Fax: (01483) 721548. Web: www.worldwarbooks.co.uk. E-mail: ww2books@churchill.net.uk. Est: 1982. Postal only. Spec: War - World War II. PR: £4–500. [Updated]

TYNE AND WEAR

NEWCASTLE UPON TYNE

Frank Smith Maritime Aviation, ■ 92 Heaton Road, Newcastle upon Tyne, NE6 5HL. Prop: Alan Parker. Tel: (0191) 265-6333. Fax: (0191) 224-2620. E-mail: books@franksmith.freeserve.co.uk. Est: 1981. Shop. Internet and postal. Open: **M:** 10:00–16:00; **T:** 10:00–16:00; **W:** 10:00–16:00; **Th:** 10:00–16:00; **F:** 09:00–16:00. Stock: large. Spec: Aviation; Maritime/Nautical; Motoring; Shipbuilding and Shipping; Sport - Yachting. PR: £4–1,000. CC: AE; E; JCB; MC; V. Corresp: German, French, Dutch. Mem: PBFA. VAT No: GB 297 9302 12. [Updated]

Stalagluft Books, 73 Titan House, Berry Close, Newcastle Upon Tyne, NE63DQ. Prop: Richard Cartwright. Tel: 0191 209 1720. Web: www.stores.ebay.co.uk/STALAGLUFT. E-mail: ric59@blueyonder.co.uk. Est: 2002. Private premises. Internet and postal. Telephone first. Open: **M:** 09:00–20:00; **T:** 09:00–20:00; **W:** 09:00–20:00; **Th:** 09:00–20:00; **F:** 09:00–20:00; **S:** 09:00–22:00; **Su:** 09:00–22.00. Spec: Academic/Scholarly; Archaeology; Autobiography; Ex-Libris; Fine & Rare; Geology; History - British; Hymnology. CC: MC; V. Notes: Specialise in obscure, out of print titles & wide selection of Ex-Reference library material. Local interest including Northumberland, Durham. [Updated]

Robert D. Steedman, ■ 9 Grey Street, Newcastle upon Tyne, NE1 6EE. Prop: D.J. Steedman. Tel: (0191) 232-6561. Est: 1907. Shop open: **M:** 09:00–17:00; **T:** 09:00–17:00; **W:** 09:00–17:00; **Th:** 09:00–17:00; **F:** 09:00–17:00; **S:** 09:00–12:30. Stock: large. PR: £1–5,000. CC: JCB; MC; V; S, SW. Mem: ABA; BA. VAT No: GB 177 1638 41. [Updated]

NORTH SHIELDS

Keel Row Books, ■ 11 Fenwick Terrace, Preston Road, North Shields, NE29 0LU. Tel: Withheld. Est: 1980. Shop open: **M:** 10:30–17:00; **T:** 10:30–17:00; **Th:** 10:30–17:00; **F:** 10:30–17:00; **S:** 10:30–17:00; **Su:** 11:00–16:00. Stock: very large. Spec: Alpinism/Mountaineering; Art; Children's; Cinema/Film; Comic Books & Annuals; Crime (True); Military; Military History. PR: £1–700. [Updated]

WHITLEY BAY

The Rider Haggard Society, 27 Deneholm, Monkseaton, Whitley Bay, NE25 9AU. Prop: Roger Allen. Tel: (0191) 252-4516. Fax: (0191) 252-4516. E-mail: rb27allen@aol.com. Stock: very small. Spec: Author - Haggard, Sir Henry Rider; Author - Heyer, Georgette; Author - Stoker, B.; Booksearch. PR: £2–300. Corresp: French, Spanish. Mem: Also, a booksearch service and editor for the Rider Haggard Society. [Updated]

WARWICKSHIRE

ATHERSTONE

Throckmorton's Bookshop, ■ 16 Market Place, Atherstone, CV9 1EX. Prop: Peter Playdon and Molly Rogers. Tel: 01827 717570. E-mail: throckmortons@hotmail.com. Est: 2005. Shop open: **M:** 10:00–17:00; **T:** 10:00–17:00; **W:** 10:00–17:00; **F:** 10:00–17:00; **S:** 10:00–17:00; **Su:** 12:00–16:00. CC: MC; V. Corresp: French, Spanish. [Updated]

BEDWORTH

Astley Book Farm, ■ Astley Lane, Bedworth, CV12 0NE. Prop: Vivienne Mills and Sarah Exley. Tel: 02476 490235. Web: www.astleybookfarm.com. E-mail: astleybookfarm@yahoo.co.uk. Est: 2004. Shop open: **M:** 10:00–17:00; **T:** 10:00–17:00; **W:** 10:00–17:00; **Th:** 10:00–17:00; **F:** 10:00–17:00; **S:** 10:00–17:00; **Su:** 10:00–17:00. Spec: CC: AE; MC; V. Notes: Approximately 50,000 titles in stock. VAT No: GB 831 8247 29. [Updated]

GREAT WALFORD

NV Books, 4 Carters Leaze, Great Walford, CV36 5NS. Prop: Tom Verrall. Tel: 0800 0830281. Web: www.abebooks.com/home/nvrarebooks. E-mail: nvbooks@nvmanagement.co.uk. Est: 2005. Private premises. Appointment necessary. Open: **M:** 09:00–18:00; **T:** 09:00–18:00; **W:** 09:00–18:00; **Th:** 09:00–18:00; **F:** 09:00–18:00; **S:** 09:00–18:00; **Su:** 09:00–18:00. Spec: Antiquarian; First Editions; Limited Editions; Modern First Editions; Signed Editions. CC: MC; V; Solo, Maestro, Visa Electron. Cata: monthly on latest acquisitions by e-mail. VAT No: GB 783 9189 70. [Updated]]

HENLEY–IN–ARDEN

Arden Books & Cosmographia, 11 Pound Field, Wootton Wawen, Henley–in–Arden, B95 6AQ. Prop: David Daymond. Tel: (01564) 793476. Est: 1998. Private premises. Postal only. Stock: small. Spec: Antiques; Art; Biography; Canals/Inland Waterways; Children's; Crafts; Food & Drink; Gardening - General. PR: £1–50. Corresp: French, German. [Updated]

KENILWORTH

Frank & Stella Allinson, 25 Brooke Road, Kenilworth, CV8 2BD. Tel: (01926) 854662. Web: www.ukbookworld.com. E-mail: fandsallinson@onetel.com. Est: 1989. Private premises. Postal only. Appointment necessary. Spec: Alpinism/Mountaineering; Children's - Illustrated; Military; Modern First Editions; Natural History; Sport - General; Transport. PR: £3–40. CC: D; E; JCB; MC; V; Solo, Switch, PayPal. Mem: PBFA. [Updated]

KINETON

Kineton Books, ■ Bookshop, Southam Street, Kineton, CV35 0LP. Prop: J Neal. Tel: (01926) 640700. Web: www.kinetonbooks.co.uk. E-mail: josie@kinetonbooks.co.uk. Est: 1998. Shop open: **W:** 10:00–17:00; **Th:** 10:00–17:00; **F:** 10:00–17:00; **S:** 10:00–16:00. Stock: medium. Spec: Annuals; Author - Milligan, Spike; Children's; Illustrated; Publishers - Ladybird Books. PR: £1–200. [Updated]

LEAMINGTON SPA

Alexander's Books, 58 Greatheed Road, Leamington Spa, CV32 6ET. Prop: Andrew Parkes. Tel: (01926) 314508. E-mail: agmparkes@btinternet.com. Est: 1987. Private premises. Appointment necessary. Spec: Biography; Children's; History - General; Illustrated; Literature; Medieval; Topography - General; Booksearch. PR: £2–500. Corresp: French, Italian. [Updated]

RUGBY

Central Bookshop, ■ 4 Central Buildings, Railway Terrace, Rugby, CV21 3EL. Prop: J. & A. Sewell. Tel: 01788 577853. Web: www.central-bookshop.com. E-mail: centralbookshop@aol.com. Est: 1996. Shop open: **M:** 09:30–17:00; **T:** 09:30–13:00; **W:** 00.00–00.00; **Th:** 09:30–17:00; **F:** 09:30–17.00; **S:** 09.30–17.00; **Su:** 00.00–00.00. Spec: Art; Esoteric; Fine Art; Folio Society, The; History - General; Military; Military History; Modern First Editions. CC: AE; E; JCB; MC; V; Switch, Solo. [Updated]

SHIPSTON-ON-STOUR

Paper Moon Books, 61 Telegraph Street, 61 Telegraph Street, Shipston-on-Stour, CV36 4DA. Prop: Elaine Fletcher. Tel: 01608 661308. Fax: Shop (01451) 870404. Est: 1977. Shop and/or showroom. Open: **M:** 10:00–17:00; **T:** 10:00–17:00; **W:** 10:00–17:00; **Th:** 10:00–17:00; **F:** 10:00–17:00; **S:** 10:00–17:00; **Su:** 11:00–17:00. Spec: Bibles; Bindings; Literature; Poetry; Prayer Books. PR: £5–300. CC: D; E; JCB; MC; V; Solo, Switch. [Updated]

STRATFORD–UPON–AVON

Paul Meekins Books, Valentines, Long Marston, Stratford–upon–Avon, CV37 8RG. Prop: Paul Meekins. Tel: (01789) 722434. Fax: (01789) 722434. Web: www.paulmeekins.co.uk. E-mail: paul@paulmeekins.co.uk. Est: 1989. Private premises. Internet and postal. Appointment necessary. Stock: large. Spec: Arms & Armour; Fashion & Costume; Firearms/Guns; History - General; History - Ancient; History - British; History - Middle Ages; Medicine - History of. PR: £2–200. CC: MC; V; Meastro. [Updated]

Chaucer Head Bookshop, ■ 21, Chapel Street, Stratford-Upon-Avon, CV37 6EP. Prop: Richard and Vanessa James. Tel: 01789 415691. Web: www.stratford-upon-avonbooks.co.uk. E-mail: richard@chaucerhead.co.uk. Shop open: **M:** 10.00–17:30; **T:** 10.00–17:30; **W:** 10.00–17:30; **Th:** 10.00–17:30; **F:** 10.00–17:30; **S:** 10.00–17:30. Spec: Author - Shakespeare, William; Drama; Topography - Local. CC: MC; V; Switch, Visa Debit. Corresp: French, German. [Updated]

The Stratford Bookshop, ■ 45a, Rother Street, Stratford-upon-Avon, CV37 6LT. Prop: Sue and John Hill. Tel: 01789 298362. Web: www.thestratfordbookshop.co.uk. E-mail: thestratfordbookshop@btinternet.com. Shop open: **M:** 10:00–18:00; **T:** 10:00–18:00; **W:** 10:00–18:00; **Th:** 10:00–18:00; **F:** 10:00–18:00; **S:** 10:00–18:00. Spec: General. CC: MC; V; Switch ; Maestro. VAT No: GB 785 7543 76. [Updated]

STUDLEY

Brewin Books Ltd., Doric House, 56 Alcester Road, Studley, B80 7NP. Director: K.A.F. Brewin. Tel: (01527) 854228. Fax: (01527) 852746. Web: www.brewinbooks.com. E-mail: admin@brewinbooks.com. Est: 1973. Office and/or bookroom. Internet and postal. Telephone first. Open: **M:** 09:00–17:00; **T:** 09:00–17:00; **W:** 09:00–17:00; **Th:** 09:00–17:00; **F:** 09:00–17:00; Closed for lunch: 13:00–13:30. Stock: medium. Spec: Aviation; Genealogy; Motoring; New Books; Railways; Steam Engines; Topography - Local; Transport. Mem: BA. Notes: also, publishers of local history books. VAT No: GB 705 0077 73. [Updated]

WARWICK

Duncan M. Allsop, ■ 68 Smith Street, Warwick, CV34 4HU. Tel: (01926) 493266. Fax: (01926) 493266. Web: www.abe.com. E-mail: duncan.allsop@btopenworld.com. Est: 1966. Shop. Book Fairs Only. Open: **M:** 11:00–16:30; **T:** 10:00–17:00; **W:** 10:00–17:00; **Th:** 10:00–17:00; **F:** 10:00–17:00; **S:** 10:00–17:00. Stock: large. Spec: Antiquarian; Bindings; Fine & Rare. PR: £5–3,000. CC: MC; V; SW, SO. Cata: occasionally. Mem: ABA; BA. [Updated]

WOOTTON WAWEN

Period Fine Bindings, Yew Tree Farm, Wootton Wawen, Nr. Stratford Upon Avon, B95 6BY. Prop: Paul Tronson. Tel: 01564 793800. Fax: 0121 706 1623. Web: www.periodfinebindings.typepad.com/royal_bindings/. E-mail: periodfinebindings@tiscali.co.uk. Est: 20. Shop and/or showroom; Contactable. Open: **M:** 09:00–17:30; **T:** 09:00–17:30; **W:** 09:00–17:30; **Th:** 09:00–17:30; **F:** 09:00–17:30; **S:** 09:00–13:30; Closed for lunch: 13:00–14:00. Spec: Antiquarian; Antiquities; History - General; Illuminated Manuscripts. CC: AE; MC; V. Mem: Master Bookbinder of London Alliance. Notes: Exceedingly rare books for sale and restoration – 15-19th century including some exceptional variant tudor pieces. Book valuations given and advice on books as pension investments. [Updated]

WEST MIDLANDS

BILSTON
Christine M. Chalk 17 Regent Street, Bilston, WV14 6AP. Tel: (01902) 403978. Fax: (01902) 403978. E-mail: ChristineMChalk@aol.com. Est: 1996. Private premises. Postal only. Stock: very small. Spec: Art; Artists; Children's - Illustrated; Fiction - General; Illustrated. PR: £1–200. [Updated]

BIRMINGHAM
Afar Books International, 11 Church Place, 135 Edward Road, Balsall Heath, Birmingham, B12 9JQ. Prop: Alf Richardson. Tel: (0121) 440-3918. Est: 1990. Private premises. Postal only. Stock: medium. Spec: Anthropology; Black Studies; Colonial; Countries - Africa; Countries - Caribbean, The; Countries - Egypt; Egyptology; Voyages & Discovery. PR: £1–300. Notes: only telephone evenings or Sunday. [Updated]

Albion Books, Beechcroft, 15 Woodlands Road, Saltley, Birmingham, B8 3AG. Prop: John Bentley. Tel: (0121) 328 2878. Est: 1984. Private premises. Postal only. Stock: small. Spec: Military; Military History; War - General; War - World War I. PR: £1–150. Notes: open at irregular times. Also, booksearch [Updated]

Birmingham Books, 202 Witton Lodge Road, Birmingham, B23 5BW. Prop: Mike Attree. Tel: (0121) 3845318. E-mail: mike.attree@blueyonder.co.uk. Est: 2004. Private premises. Internet and postal. Appointment necessary. Spec: Alpinism/Mountaineering; Authors:- Fleming, Ian; Greene, Graham; Children's - Illustrated; Fiction - Crime, Detective, Spy, Thrillers; Fiction - Fantasy, Horror; Fiction - Science Fiction; Folio Society, The. [Updated]

Elmfield Books, 24 Elmfield Crescent, Moseley, Birmingham, B13 9TN. Prop: Liz Palmer. Tel: (0121) 689-6246. Web: www.elmfieldbooks.co.uk. E-mail: elmfieldbooks@blueyonder.co.uk. Est: 1999. Private premises. Internet and postal. Appointment necessary. Stock: small. Spec: Cookery/Gastronomy; Food & Drink; Illustrated; Natural History; Topography - General; Topography - Local. PR: £5–500. Mem: PBFA. Notes: attend bookfairs and other events. [Updated]

Heritage, P.O. Box 3075, Edgbaston, Birmingham, B15 2EW. Prop: Gill & Jem Wilyman. Tel: 0121 440 2734. Fax: 0121 440 1382. E-mail: Heritagebook@aol.com. Est: 1985. Private premises. Postal only. Telephone first. Spec: Antiquarian; Atlases; Bindings; Cartography; Directories - General; Engraving; Ex-Libris; Fine & Rare. Cata: occasionally on Ex-Libris, Heraldry, Maps, Private Press,. Mem: PBFA. Notes: we also exhibit at PBFA Book Fairs. [Updated]

Moseley Books, 7 Cornerstone, Birmingham, B13 8EN. Tel: (0121) 442 6062. Web: www.moseleybooks.co.uk. E-mail: john@moseleybooks.co.uk. Est: 2002. Storeroom. Internet and postal. Stock: small. Spec: Classical Studies; Humanities; Philosophy; Politics. PR: £2–50. [Updated]

Robin Doughty - Fine Books, 100a Frederick Road, Stechford, Birmingham, B33 8AE. Prop: Robin Doughty. Tel: 01210 783 7289. E-mail: robin.doughty@btinternet.com. Est: 1994. Private premises. Postal only. Stock: small. Spec: Antiquarian; Art; Illustrated; Literature; Private Press; Religion - General; Religion - Quakers; Topography - General. PR: £10–2,500. Mem: PBFA. [Updated]

David Temperley, 19 Rotton Park Road, Edgbaston, Birmingham, B16 9JH. Prop: David Temperley. Tel: (0121) 454 0135. Fax: (0121) 454 1124. Est: 1969. Private premises. Appointment necessary. Stock: medium. Spec: Atlases; Autolithography; Bindings; Colour-Plate; Decorative Art; Fine & Rare; Illustrated; Miniature Books. [Updated]

Stephen Wycherley, ■ 508 Bristol Road, Selly Oak, Birmingham, B29 6BD. Prop: Stephen & Elizabeth Wycherley. Tel: (0121) 471-1006. Est: 1971. Shop open: **M:** 10:00–17:00; **T:** 10:00–17:00; **Th:** 10:00–17:00; **F:** 10:00–17:00; **S:** 10:00–17:00. Stock: large. PR: £1–500. Corresp: French, Dutch. Mem: PBFA. Notes: summer (July-August) open on Thursdays, Fridays and Saturdays only. [Updated]

COVENTRY
Malcolm Harris (Books), 154 Avon Street, Coventry, CV2 3GP. Tel: (withheld). Private premises. Postal only. Stock: very small. Spec: Autobiography; Fiction - Crime, Detective, Spy, Thrillers; Modern First Editions; Signed Editions; Theatre; Booksearch; Ephemera. [Updated]

Silver Trees Books, Silver Trees Farm, Balsall St., Balsall Common, Coventry, CV7 7AR. Prop: Brian and Elaine Hitchens. Tel: (01676) 533143. Fax: (01676) 533143. Web: www.abebooks.com. E-mail: brian.hitchens@tesco.net. Private premises. Postal only. Telephone first. Stock: medium. Spec: Author - Crompton, Richmal; Ceramics; Gardening - General; Military; Modern First Editions. PR: £3–1,500. CC: AE; JCB; MC; V; Switch. Corresp: French. [Updated]

Uncle Phil's, Wit's End, 10 Mary Slessor Street, Coventry, CV3 3BY. Tel: 02476 639989. Web: www.uncluephilsbooks.co.uk. E-mail: pjames@unclephilsbooks.co.uk. Mail Order Only. Apointment necessary. Stock: large. PR: £5 – 500. CC: MC, V, Switch, Maestro, PayPal. Cata: online/Internet on general stock. Mem: Ibooknet. Notes: we are an on-line and mail order business only. [Updated]

HALESOWEN

Anvil Books, ■ 52 Summer Hill, Halesowen, B63 3BU. Prop: J.K. Maddison and C.J.Murtagh. Tel: (0121) 550-0600. E-mail: jkm@anvilbookshalesowen.co.uk. Est: 1997. Shop. Internet and postal. Open:T: 10:00–17:00; **Th:** 10:00–17:00; **S:** 10:00–17:00. Stock: medium. Spec: Canals/Inland Waterways; History - Industrial; Industry; Maritime/Nautical; Navigation; Railways; Shipbuilding and Shipping; Topography - General. PR: £1–200. [Updated]

Janus Books / Waverley Fairs, Newlands, 9 Hayley Park, Hayley Green, Halesowen, B63 1EJ. Prop: Royston Thomas Slim. Tel: (0121) 550-4123. Est: 1968. Private premises. Postal only. Stock: small. Spec: Motoring; Topography - General; Topography - Local; War - General; Ephemera; Prints and Maps. PR: £1–500. Notes: (Incl: books on Black Country & Midland Local History) Also, book fair organiser – see prelims: Kinver, Powick (Malvern) and Bromsgrove Antique Fairs. [Updated]

KINGSWINFORD

Wright Trace Books, 70 Ash Crescent, Kingswinford, DY6 8DH. Prop: Colin Mickleright and Pam Wright. Tel: (01384) 341211. E-mail: bandogge-books@blueyonder.co.uk. Est: 2001. Private premises. Postal only. Stock: very small. Spec: Animals and Birds; Annuals; Dogs; Modern First Editions; Booksearch. PR: £5–1,000. CC: PayPal. [Updated]

OLDBURY

Anthony Dyson, 57 St John's Road, Oldbury, B68 9SA. Tel: (0121) 544-5386. Est: 1973. Private premises. Appointment necessary. Stock: small. Spec: Fashion & Costume; Fiction - Crime, Detective, Spy, Thrillers; Literary Criticism; Literature. [Updated]

SOLIHULL

Fifth Element, 15 St. Lawrence Close, Knowle, Solihull, B93 0EU. Prop: Michael Rogers. Tel: (01564) 773106. E-mail: fifthelement@postmaster.co.uk. Est: 1996. Private premises. Postal only. Spec: Author - Wilson, Colin; Beat Writers; Counterculture. Corresp: German. [Updated]

Helion & Company Ltd, 26 Willow Road, Solihull, B91 1UE. D. Rogers. Tel: (0121) 705-3393. Fax: (0121) 711-4075. Web: www.helion.co.uk. E-mail: books@helion.co.uk. Est: 1992. Private premises. Postal only. Stock: very large. Spec: Academic/Scholarly; Archaeology; Arms & Armour; Aviation; Countries - Germany; Firearms/Guns; History - General; History - 19th Century. PR: £1–3,500. CC: AE; E; JCB; MC; V; Switch. Cata: quarterly – on military history. Corresp: German, French, Spanish. Mem: IPG. Notes: also, a free booksearch service. VAT No: GB 797 4185 72. [Updated]

SUTTON COLDFIELD

Patrick Walcot, 60 Sunnybank Road, Sutton Coldfield, B73 5RJ. Prop: Patrick Walcot. Tel: (0121) 382-6381. Fax: 0870 0511 418. Web: www.walcot.demon.co.uk. E-mail: patrick@walcot.demon.co.uk. Est: 1980. Private premises. Internet and postal. Appointment necessary. Stock: very small. Spec: Travel - Polar. PR: £10–5,000. [Updated]

WALSALL

A.J. Mobbs, 65 Broadstone Avenue, Walsall, WS3 1JA. Tel: (01922) 477281. Fax: (01922) 477281. Web: www.mobbs.birdbooks.btinternet.co.uk. E-mail: mobbs.birdbooks@btinternet.com. Est: 1982. Private premises. Internet and postal. Appointment necessary. Stock: small. Spec: Academic/Scholarly; Entomology; Herpetology; Natural Health; Natural History; Ornithology. PR: £1–200. [Updated]

J. & M.A. Worrallo, 29 Trees Road, The Delves, Walsall, WS1 3JU. Prop: John & Mark Anthony Worrallo. Tel: (01922) 721224. Web: www.ukbookworld.com/members/worras. E-mail: jworrallo@aol.com. Est: 1980. Private premises. Postal only. Appointment necessary. Stock: small. Spec: Booksearch. PR: £1–100. Notes: also, a booksearch service [Updated]

WEST BROMWICH

Books at Star Dot Star, Flat 23 Salisbury House, Lily Street, West Bromwich, B71 1QD. Prop: Bruce Tober. Tel: (0121) 553-4284. Web: www.star-dot-star.net. E-mail: books@star-dot-star.net. Est: 2003. Private premises. Internet and postal. Appointment necessary. Stock: small. PR: £5–1,000. CC: JCB; MC; V; PayPal. [Updated]

WOLVERHAMPTON

Books & Bygones (Pam Taylor), ■ 19 Hollybush Lane, Penn, Wolverhampton, WV4 4JJ. Prop: Pam Taylor. Tel: (01902) 334020. Fax: (01902) 334747. Est: 1987. Shop open: **S:** 08:30–17:00; **Su:** 08:30–17:00. Stock: medium. Spec: Authors - Women; Autographs; Dictionaries; Fiction - Science Fiction; History - General; History - Industrial; Magic & Conjuring; Performing Arts. PR: £1–10. Notes: open other times by appointment only. [Updated]

R. & S. Crombie, 73 Griffiths Drive, Wednesfield, Wolverhampton, WV11 2JN. Tel: (01902) 733462. E-mail: royandsheila@rcrombie.freeserve.co.uk. Est: 1995. Private premises. Book Fairs Only. Telephone first. PR: £1–100. [Updated]

GS Cricket Books / The Old Book Shop, ■ 53 Bath Road, Chapel Ash, Wolverhampton, WV1 4EL. Gerry Stack. Tel: 01902 421055. Fax: 01902 569597. E-mail: gscricketbooks@hotmail.co.uk. Est: 2005. Shop open: **T:** 10.00–16.30; **W:** 10.00–16.30; **Th:** 10.00–16.30; **F:** 09.00–16.30; **S:** 11.00–16.30. Spec: Sport - Cricket. Cata: bi-annually. [Updated]

Mogul Diamonds, 17 High Street, Albrighton, Wolverhampton, WV7 3JT. Prop: Gerald Leach. Tel: (01902) 372288. Web: www.ukbookworld.com/members/mogul. E-mail: moguldiamonds @btopenworld.com. Est: 1999. Spec: Biography; Biology; History - Local; Music - General; Topography - Local; Ephemera. PR: £1–200. Notes: specialises in books about Shropshire. [Updated]

The Old Bookshop, ■ 53 Bath Road, Wolverhampton, WV1 4EL. Prop: Jerry Stack. Tel: 01902 421055. E-mail: gscricketbooks@hotmail.co.uk. Est: 1967. Shop open: **T:** 10:00–16:30; **W:** 10:00–16:30; **Th:** 10:00–16:30; **F:** 09:00–16:30; **S:** 11:00–16:30. Spec: Art; Embroidery; History - General; Literature; Needlework; Theology; Topography - Local. [Updated]

WEST SUSSEX

ARUNDEL

Baynton–Williams Gallery, ■ 37a High Street, Arundel, BN18 9AG. Prop: Sarah & Roger Baynton–Williams Tel: (01903) 883588. Fax: (01903) 883588. Web: www.baynton-williams.com. E-mail: gallery@baynton-williams.freeserve.co.uk. Est: 1946. Shop open: **M:** 10:00–18:00; **T:** 10:00–18:00; **W:** 10:00–18:00; **Th:** 10:00–18:00; **F:** 10:00–18:00; **S:** 10:00–18:00. Stock: very small. Spec: Atlases; Travel - General; Prints and Maps. PR: £100–15,000. Notes: also, prints & maps. [Updated]

Kim's Bookshop, ■ 10 High Street, Arundel, BN18 9AB. Prop: Mrs L Flowers. Tel: (01903) 882680. E-mail: kimbookshoparundel@yahoo.co.uk. Est: 2003. Shop open: **M:** 10:00–17:00; **T:** 10:00–17:00; **W:** 10:00–17:00; **Th:** 10:00–17:00; **F:** 10:00–17:00; **S:** 10:00–17:00; **Su:** 10:30–17:00. Stock: large. Spec: Antiquarian; Arts, The; Fiction - General; History - General; Music - General; Natural History; Topography - General; Topography - Local. CC: MC; V. Corresp: Spanish. Notes: also at 19 Crescent Road, Worthing, West Sussex, BN11 1RL, and at 28 South Street, Chichester, West Sussex, PO19 1EL. Open on Bank Holidays 10:30–17:00. [Updated]

BILLINGSHURST

Bianco Library, Oaklands, West Chiltington Lane, Broadford Bridge, Billingshurst, RH13 9EA. Prop: Anthony Bianco. Tel: 01403 741038. Fax: 01403 741038. Web: www.biancolibrary.com. E-mail: sales@biancolibrary.com. Est: 1999. Private premises. Internet Only. Spec: Architecture; Art; Bibliography; Biography; Botany; Canals/Inland Waterways; Collecting; Colour-Plate. CC: PayPal. Notes: web site has advanced search facility & multiple picture gallery. We have 70 book categories - see website. [Updated]

BOGNOR REGIS

mcbooks, 21 Upper Bognor Road, Bognor Regis, PO21 1JA. Prop: Emma Laing. Tel: 01243 868614. Web: www.meadowcroftbooks.demon.co.uk. E-mail: emma@meadowcroftbooks.demon.co.uk. Est: 1996. Private premises. Internet and postal. Telephone first. Open: **M:** 09:00–17:30; **T:** 09:00–17:30; **W:** 09:00–17:30; **Th:** 09:00–17:30; **F:** 09:00–17:30; **S:** 09:00–17:30; **Su:** 09:00–17:30; Closed for lunch: 13:00–14:00. Spec: CC: MC; V; Maestro. Notes: primarily booksearch. VAT No: GB 699 0227 01. [Updated]

CHICHESTER

The Chichester Bookshop, ■ 39 Southgate, Chichester, PO19 1DP. Prop: Chris Lowndes. Tel: (01243) 785473. E-mail: redbooks@fsmail.net. Est: 1994. Shop open: **M:** 09:30–17:00; **T:** 09:30–17:00; **W:** 09:30–17:00; **Th:** 09:30–17:00; **F:** 09:30–17:00; **S:** 09:30–17:00. Stock: very large. Spec: Politics; Topography - Local. PR: £1–1,000. [01/10/2004]

Peter Hancock Antiques, ■ 40–41 West Street, Chichester, PO19 1RP. Tel: (01243) 786173. Fax: (01243) 778865. Est: 1965. Shop open: **T:** 10:00–17:30; **W:** 10:00–17:30; **Th:** 10:00–17:30; **F:** 10:00–17:30; **S:** 10:30–17:30. Stock: small. Spec: Aeronautics; Alpinism/Mountaineering; Americana; Antiquarian; Military; Ephemera; Prints and Maps. PR: £5–500. CC: AE; E; JCB; MC; V. Notes: also, antiques. VAT No: GB 192 8554 28. [Updated]

Kim's Bookshop, ■ 28 South Street, Chichester, PO19 1EL. Prop: Mrs L Flowers. Tel: (01243) 778477. E-mail: kimbookshopchichester@yahoo.co.uk. Est: 2004. Shop open: **M:** 10:00–17:00; **T:** 10:00–17:00; **W:** 10:00–17:00; **Th:** 10:00–17:00; **F:** 10:00–17:00; **S:** 10:00–17:00. Stock: large. Spec: Academic/Scholarly; Antiquarian; Arts, The; Fiction - General; History - General; Music - General; Natural History; Topography - General. PR: £1–1,000. CC: MC; V. Corresp: Spanish. Notes: also, 19 Crescent Road, Worthing, West Sussex, BN11 1RL and at 10 High Street, Arundel, West Sussex, BN18 9AB. VAT No: GB 825 9120 31. [Updated]

COWFOLD

Michael Phelps, Allfreys House, Bolney Road, Cowfold, RH13 8AZ. Tel: (01403) 754222. Fax: (01403) 864730. E-mail: phelobooks@tiscali.co.uk. Est: 1974. Spec: Aeronautics; Alchemy; Astronomy; Aviation; Botany; Brewing; Chemistry; Engineering. PR: £10–100. [Updated]

WEST SUSSEX

EAST GRINSTEAD

The Bookshop, ■ Tudor House, 22 High Street, East Grinstead, RH19 3AW. Prop: J. & H. Pye. Tel: (01342) 322669. Shop open: **M:** 09:00–17:30; **T:** 09:00–17:30; **W:** 09:00–17:30; **Th:** 09:00–17:30; **F:** 09:00–17:30; **S:** 09:00–17:30. Stock: medium. Spec: History - General; Booksearch. CC: AE; MC; V. Mem: BA. VAT No: GB 472 9663 08. [Updated]

GORING–BY–SEA

Barry Jones, Daymer Cottage, 28 Marine Crescent, Goring–by–Sea, BN12 4JF. Prop: Barry Jones. Tel: (01903) 244655. Fax: (01903) 244655. Est: 1990. Private premises. Appointment necessary. Stock: medium. Spec: Railways; Traction Engines; Transport; Ephemera. PR: £1–500. Notes: appointments only between 09:00 and 21:00. Railway Collectors Fairs Organiser. [Updated]

HASSOCKS

Post Mortem Books Ltd, 58 Stanford Ave, Hassocks, BN6 8JH. Prop: Ralph Spurrier. Tel: (01273) 843066. Fax: (0870) 161-7332. Web: www.postmortembooks.com. E-mail: ralph@pmbooks.demon.co.uk. Est: 1979. Private premises. Internet and postal. Appointment necessary. Open: **M:** 08:00–18:00; **T:** 08:00–18:00; **Th:** 08:00–18:00; **F:** 10:00–16:00; **S:** 10:00–13:00. Stock: medium. Spec: Fiction - Crime, Detective, Spy, Thrillers. PR: £5–1,000. CC: AE; MC; V; Maestro. [Updated]

HORSHAM

Horsham Rare Books, P.O. Box 770, Horsham, RH12 9BA. Tel: 01403 252187. Web: www.horshamrarebooks.com. Private premises. Internet and postal. Contactable. Open: **M:** 09:00–17:30; **T:** 09:00–17:30; **W:** 09:00–17:30; **Th:** 09:00–17:30; **F:** 09:00–17:30; **S:** 09:00–17:30; **Su:** 09:00–17:30; Closed for lunch: 13:00–14:00. Spec: Antiquarian; Art; Aviation; Bindings; Biography; History - General; History - Local; Motoring. CC: AE; MC; V; Maestro. Mem: PBFA. [Updated]

Merlin Books, P.O. Box 153, Horsham, RH12 2YG. Prop: Mike Husband. Tel: (01403) 257626. Fax: (01403) 257626. Web: www.merlinbooks.com. E-mail: info@merlinbooks.com. Est: 1990. Private premises. Internet and postal. Telephone first. Stock: very small. Spec: Motorbikes / motorcycles; Booksearch. PR: £2–60. CC: E; JCB; MC; V. [21/12/2004]

LANCING

Paul Evans Books, 13 Berriedale Drive, Sompting, Lancing, BN15 OLE. Tel: (01903) 764655. Fax: (01903) 764655. Web: www.paulevansbooks.com. E-mail: paulevans@paulevansbooks.com. Est: 1991. Private premises. Postal only. Appointment necessary. Stock: small. Spec: Art; Author - Bloomsbury Group, The; Authors:- Sackville-West, Vita; Woolf, Virginia; Publishers - Hogarth Press. PR: £5–30,000. Notes: also, art by members of the Bloomsbury Group. [Updated]

LITTLEHAMPTON

Chris Adam Smith Modern First Editions, 9, Western Road, Littlehampton, BN17 5NP. Prop: Chris Adam Smith. Tel: 01903 722392. Web: www.adamsmithbooks.com. E-mail: chrisadamsmith@btinternet.com. Est: 1993. Mail Order Only. Internet Only. Appointment necessary. Open: **T:** 09:00–17:30; **W:** 09:00–17:30; **Th:** 09:00–17:30; **F:** 09:00–17:30. Spec: Modern First Editions. CC: AE; D; MC; V; Switch Maestro. Cata: occasionally on Crime, Maritime, Children's, Science Fiction. Notes: we cover most modern fiction in fine first edition and signed copies are a specialty. [Updated]

JB Books & Collectables, 14 Kingsmead, Thornlea Park, Littlehampton, BN17 7QS. Prop: Mrs J. Brittain. Tel: (01903) 725819. Fax: (01903) 725819. Web: www.jbbooks.co.uk. E-mail: jan@jbbooks.co.uk. Est: 1997. Private premises. Internet and postal. Telephone first. Open: **M:** 09:00–17:30; **T:** 09:00–17:30; **W:** 09:00–17:30; **Th:** 09:00–17:30; **F:** 09:00–17:30; **S:** 09:00–17:00; Closed for lunch: 13:00–14:00. Stock: small. Spec: Children's; Illustrated; Literature. PR: £1–500. CC: JCB; MC; V; Maestro. Mem: PBFA. [Updated]

South Downs Book Service, Garden Cottage, 39c Arundel Road, Littlehampton, BN17 7BY. Prop: Ms. J.A. Bristow. Tel: (01903) 723401. Fax: (01903) 726318. Est: 1994. Private premises. Appointment necessary. Open: **M:** 08:00–20:00; **T:** 08:00–20:00; **W:** 08:00–20:00; **Th:** 08:00–20:00; **F:** 08:00–20:00; **S:** 08:00–20:00; **Su:** 08:00–20:00. Stock: very small. Spec: Academic/Scholarly; Antiquarian; Ecclesiastical History & Architecture; Literature - Victorian; Social History; Ephemera; Prints and Maps. PR: £4–600. Notes: accredited valuers and cataloguers to libraries to leading private libraries [Updated]

MIDHURST

Canon Gate Books, 2 The Common off Carron Lane, Midhurst, GU29 9LF. Prop: Philip & Wendy Pegler. Web: www.canongate-thoughtful-books.com. E-mail: member@canongate.fsbusiness.co.uk. Est: 1986. Private premises. Internet and postal. Stock: very small. Spec: Oriental; Religion - General; Religion - Christian; Booksearch. PR: £5–1,000. VAT No: GB 543 8777 05. [Updated]

Wheeler's Bookshop, ■ Red Lion Street, Midhurst, GU29 9PB. Tel: 01730 817666. Web: www.wheelersbookshop.co.uk. E-mail: simon@wheelersbookshop.co.uk. Shop open: **M:** 10:00–17:00; **T:** 10:00–17:00; **W:** 10:00–17:00; **Th:** 10:00–17:00; **F:** 10:00–17:00; **S:** 10:00–17:00. Spec: General Stock; New Books. CC: MC; V. Notes: thousands of secondhand books on many and varied subjects, plus a wide range of in-print titles. The shop has recently expanded upstairs, to accommodate even more books. Please call in if you are in the area. [Updated]

PETWORTH

Tim Boss, North Street, Petworth, GU28 0DD. Prop: Tim Boss. Tel: (01798) 343170. Est: 1993. Private premises. Postal only. Stock: small. Spec: Ephemera; Prints and Maps. PR: £1–350. Notes: also, 10,000 inexpensive prints; some maps. Exhibits at bookfairs. [Updated]

Muttonchop Manuscripts, ■The Playhouse Gallery, Lombard Street, Petworth, GU28 0AG. Prop: Roger S. Clarke. Tel: 01798 344471. Fax: 01798 344471. E-mail: rogmutton@aol.com. Est: 1992. Shop. open **W:** 10:00–16:00; **S:** 10:00–16:00. Spec: Agriculture; Antiquarian; Bibliogrpahy; Bindings; Books about Books; Fables; Farming & Livestock; Manuscripts. PR: £5–5,000 CC: D; Switch; Solo. VAT No: GB 704 6864 26. [Updated]

Petworth Antique Market (Bookroom), East Street, Petworth, GU28 0AB. Prop: Doris Rayment. Tel: (01798) 342073. Web: www.petworthantiquecentre.co.uk. E-mail: info@petworthantiquecentre.co.uk. Est: 1965. Shop and/or gallery. Open: **M:** 10:00–17:00; **T:** 10:00–17:00; **W:** 10:00–17:00; **Th:** 10:00–17:00; **F:** 10:00–17:00; **S:** 10:00–17:30. Spec: Antiques; Art; Bindings; Rural Life; Sport - Angling/Fishing; Sport - Field Sports. PR: £1–400. CC: MC; V; Maestro, Solo. [Updated]

PLAISTOW

Explorer Books, Fallow Chase, Durfold Wood, Plaistow, RH14 0PL. Prop: JI. & S.J. Simper. Tel: (01483) 200286. Fax: (01483) 200286. E-mail: explbooks@aol.com. Est: 1985. Private premises. Appointment necessary. Stock: very small. Spec: Countries - Antarctic, The; Countries - Arctic, The; Countries - Greenland; Countries - Polar; Travel - Polar; Voyages & Discovery; Ephemera. PR: £10–1,000. [Updated]

SHOREHAM–BY–SEA

Sansovino Books, 9 Mill Lane, Shoreham–By–Sea, BN43 5AG. Prop: Q. & R. Barry. Tel: (01273) 455753. Est: 1991. Storeroom. Appointment necessary. Stock: medium. Spec: First Editions; Literature; Maritime/Nautical; Military; Private Press; Booksearch. PR: £5–200. Notes: also at: Sansovino, Stokelsy, Cleveland [Updated]

STEYNING

dgbbooks, 15 Ingram Road, Steyning, BN44 3PF. Prop: Denise Bennett. Tel: (01903) 814895. E-mail: dgbbooks@talk21.com. Internet Only. Spec: Authors - Women; Biography; Fiction - General. PR: £5–50. [Updated]

WALDERTON

John Henly, 1 Brooklands, Walderton, Chichester, PO18 9EE. Tel: (023) 9263-1426. Fax: (023) 9263-1544. E-mail: johnhenly@aol.com. Est: 1986. Private premises. Postal only. Appointment necessary. Stock: small. Spec: Geology; Mineralogy; Natural History; Palaeontology. CC: MC; V. Mem: PBFA. VAT No: GB 582 5689 92. [Updated]

WORTHING

Badgers Books, ■ 8–10 Gratwicke Road, Worthing, BN11 4BH. Prop: Ray Potter & Meriel Cocks. Tel: (01903) 211816. E-mail: ray@badgersbooks.freeserve.co.uk. Est: 1982. Shop open: **M:** 09:00–17:30; **T:** 09:00–17:30; **W:** 09:00–17:30; **Th:** 09:00–17:30; **F:** 09:00–17:30; **S:** 09:00–18:00. Stock: large. Spec: CC: E; JCB; MC; V; SW, EL, SO. VAT No: GB 587 5552 89. [Updated]

Kim's Bookshop, ■ 19 Crescen Road, Worthing, BN11 1RL. Prop: Mrs L Flowers. Tel: (01903) 206282. E-mail: kimbookshop@hotmail.com. Est: 1971. Shop open: **M:** 09:30–17:30; **T:** 09:30–17:30; **W:** 09:30–17:30; **Th:** 09:30–17:30; **F:** 09:30–17:30; **S:** 09:30–17:30. Stock: very large. Spec: Antiquarian; Arts, The; Fiction - General; History - General; Music - General; Natural History; Topography - General; Topography - Local. PR: £1–1,000. CC: E; MC; V. Corresp: Spanish. Notes: also at 10 High Street, Arundel, West Sussex, BN18 9AB 28 South Street, Chichester, West Sussex, PO19 1EL. VAT No: GB 717 5863 08. [Updated]

Optimus Books Ltd, ■ 8 Ann Street, Worthing, BN11 1NX. Tel: (01903) 205895. Fax: (01903) 213438. E-mail: optimusbooks@easynet.co.uk. Est: 1975. Shop. Internet and postal. Telephone first. Open: **M:** 09:00–17:30; **T:** 09:00–17:30; **W:** 09:00–17:30; **Th:** 09:00–17:30; **F:** 09:00–17:30; **S:** 09:00–17:30. Stock: medium. Spec: Gardening - General; Native American. CC: MC; V. Mem: PBFA; BA. Notes: Shop likely to close shortly but intend to remain a book dealer. VAT No: GB 193 7839 11. [Updated]

WEST YORKSHIRE

ADDINGHAM

TP Children's Bookshop, ■ 71 Main Street, Addingham, Ilkley, LS29 0PS. Prop: Louise Harrison. Tel: 01943 830095. E-mail: tpbooks@btinternet.com. Est: 2005. Shop open: **F:** 10:00–16:00; **S:** 10:00–16:00. Spec: Annuals; Authors:- Brent-Dyer, Elinor M.; Fairlie–Bruce, D.; Hill, Lorna; Johns, W.E.; Oxenham, Elsie; Saville, M.; Children's. CC: MC; V. Mem: PBFA. Notes: have traded for 5 years from private premises. Also, attends book fairs at least once a month. Open at other times by appointment. [Updated]

BATLEY

Vintage Motorshop, ■ 749 Bradford Road, Batley, WF17 8HZ. Prop: R. & C. Hunt. Tel: (01924) 470773. Fax: (01924) 470773. Web: www.vintagemotorshop.co.uk. E-mail: books@vintagemotorshop.co.uk. Est: 1976. Shop. Appointment necessary. Stock: medium. Spec: Motorbikes / motorcycles; Motoring; Traction Engines; Transport; Vintage Cars. PR: £1–30. CC: MC; V. [Updated]

BRADFORD

The Idle Booksellers, 7 Town Lane, Idle, Bradford, BD10 8PR. Prop: Ros Stinton & Michael Compton. Tel: (01274) 613737. E-mail: idlebooks@bd108pr.freeserve.co.uk. Est: 1990. Private premises. Telephone first. Stock: small. Spec: Authors: Brontes, The; Gissing, George; Genealogy; Topography - Local. PR: £1–600. Mem: PBFA. [Updated]

Woodbine Books, 15 Stone Street, Bradford, BD15 9JR. Prop: Colin Neville. Tel: (01274) 824759. Web: www.abebooks.com/home/woodbine. E-mail: woodbine@blueyonder.co.uk. Private premises. Internet and postal. Appointment necessary. Stock: very small. Spec: Artists; Author - Webb, Mary; Bindings; Engraving; Fine & Rare; First Editions; Illustrated; Natural History. PR: £5–1,300. Mem: PBFA; FPBA, PLA. [Updated]

BRIGHOUSE

Northern Herald Books, 5 Close Lea, Rastrick, Brighouse, HD6 3AR. Prop: R.W. Jones. Tel: (01484) 721845. E-mail: bobjones_nhb@talk21.com. Est: 1985. Private premises. Postal only. Stock: large. Spec: Academic/Scholarly; Economics; Free Thought; Politics; Social History; Social Sciences; Socialism; Trade Unions. PR: £1–100. Corresp: French. Mem: PBFA. [Updated]

Sparrow Books, 10 Peaseland Close, Cleckheaton, BD19 3HA. Tel: (01274) 876995. Fax: (01274) 876995. E-mail: apinnock@cix.co.uk. Est: 1992. Private premises. Internet and postal. Stock: medium. Spec: Academic/Scholarly; Architecture; Geography; Geology; Politics; Topography - General; Topography - Local; Booksearch. PR: £1–80. Notes: exhibits at Leeds Book Fairs. [Updated]

GILVERSOME

Moorhead Books, Suffield Cottage, Gildersome Lane, Gilversome, Gilversome, LS27 7BA. Frank Spicer. Tel: 0113 285 2264. E-mail: frank@moorheadbooks.co.uk. Est: 1964. Private premises. Appointment necessary. Open: **M:** 09:00–17:30; **T:** 09:00–17:30; **W:** 09:00–17:30; **Th:** 09:00–17:30; **F:** 09:00–17:30; **S:** 09:00–17:30; **Su:** 09:00–17:30; Closed for lunch: 13:00–14:00. Spec: Annuals; Art; Bibliography; Bindings; Children's; Colour-Plate; Cookery/Gastronomy; Miniature Books. Notes: also, attends Pudsey Book Fair. [Updated]

HALIFAX

M.R. Clark, 18 Balmoral Place, Halifax, HX1 2BG. Tel: (01422) 357475. Web: www.abebooks.com. Est: 1980. Private premises. Appointment necessary. Stock: medium. Spec: Gardening - General; Natural History. Notes: also, booksearch and stock also on www.books@pbfa.co.uk. [Updated]

HAWARTH

Yorkshire Relics, ■ 11 Main Street, Hawarth, BD21 8DA. Prop: Colin and Jacqueline Ruff. Tel: 01535 642218. Est: 1999. Shop open: **M:** 12:00–17:00; **T:** 12:00–17:00; **W:** 12:00–17:00; **Th:** 12:00–17:00; **F:** 12:00–17:00; **S:** 12:00–17:00; **Su:** 12:00–17:00. Spec: Annuals; Children's; Comic Books & Annuals; Comics; Magazines & Periodicals - General; Music - Popular; Music - Rock & Roll; Vintage Paperbacks. [Updated]

Hatchard & Daughters, ■ 91 Main Street, Haworth. Prop: Mary Hatchard. Tel: (01535) 648720. Web: www.brontebooks.co.uk. Est: 2001. Shop open: **F:** 12:30–17:00; **S:** 10:30–17:00; **Su:** 12:30–17:00. Spec: Author - Brontes, The. PR: £5–200. Notes: also at 56 Market Street, Hebden Bridge, West Yorkshire. (q.v.). [Updated]

HEBDEN BRIDGE

Christopher I. Browne, Hawdon Hall, Hebden Bridge, HX7 7AL. Prop: CI. .Browne. Tel: (01422) 844744. Fax: (01422) 844744. Web: www.gilbertandsullivanonline.com. E-mail: sales@gilbertandsullivanonline.com. Est: 1998. Private premises. Internet and postal. Telephone first. Stock: medium. Spec: Music - Classical; Music - Music Hall; Music - Opera; Music - Printed, Sheet Music & Scores; Performing Arts. CC: AE; MC; V. Mem: SASS/G&S Society. [Updated]

Hatchard & Daughters, ■ 56 Market Street, Hebden Bridge, HX7 6HJ. Prop: Mary Hatchard Tel: (01422) 845717. E-mail: books@maryhatchard.fsnet.co.uk. Est: 1989. Shop open: **F:** 12:30–17:00; **S:** 10:30–17:00; **Su:** 12:30–17:00. Spec: Art; Natural History. PR: £1–50. Notes: see also, in Haworth, N. Yorks. (q.v.). [Updated]

The Glass Key, Old Town Mill, Wadsworth, Hebden Bridge, HX7 8SW. Prop: James Fraser. Tel: 01422 846265. Web: www.ibooknet.co.uk. E-mail: glasskey@3-c.coop. Est: 1990. Mail Order Only. Postal only. Contactable. Open: **Th:** 09:00–17:30; **F:** 09:00–17:30; **S:** 09:00–17:30; **Su:** 09:00–17:30; Closed for lunch: 13:00–14:00. Spec: Antiques; Author - 20th Century; Fiction - Crime, Detective, Spy, Thrillers; Fiction - Fantasy, Horror; Fiction - Science Fiction; Fiction - Supernatural; First Editions; Food & Drink. CC: AE; JCB; MC; V. Corresp: French. Mem: Ibooknet. Notes: Retail premises recently closed. Currently trading via the internet only. [Updated]

HOLMFIRTH

Beardsell Books, ■ Toll House Bookshop, 32–34 Huddersfield Road, Holmfirth, HD9 2JS. Prop: Elaine V. Beardsell. Tel: (01484) 686541. Fax: (01484) 688406. Web: www.toll-house.co.uk. E-mail: tollhouse.bookshop@virgin.net. Est: 1977. Shop. Internet and postal. Open: **M:** 09:00–17:00; **T:** 09:00–17:00; **W:** 09:00–17:00; **Th:** 09:00–17:00; **F:** 09:00–17:00; **S:** 09:00–17:30; **Su:** 13:00–16:30. Stock: very large. Spec: Antiquarian; History - General; History - Local. PR: £1–1,000. CC: MC; V. Mem: PBFA. [Updated]

Daisy Lane Books, ■ 15 Towngate, Holmfirth, HD9 1HA. Prop: J. & B. Townsend–Cardew Tel: (01484) 688409. Est: 1990. Shop open: **M:** 09:30–17:00; **T:** 09:30–17:00; **W:** 09:30–17:00; **Th:** 09:30–17:00; **F:** 09:30–17:00; **S:** 09:30–17:00; **Su:** 09:30–17:00. Stock: large. [Updated]

Madalyn S. Jones, Horsegate Hill House, 3 Town End Road, Wooldale, Holmfirth, HD9 1AH. Prop: Madalyn S. Jones. Tel: (01484) 681580. Fax: (01484) 681580. Web: www.madalynjonesbooks.co.uk. E-mail: madalynjonesbooks@yahoo.co.uk. Est: 1978. Private premises. Appointment necessary. Stock: very small. Spec: Sculpture; Ephemera; Prints and Maps. PR: £1–250. Mem: PBFA. Notes: general stock and a booksearch service. [Updated]

HUDDERSFIELD

Aphra Books, See under 'Susan Taylor Books', Huddersfield, HD4 6XZ. Prop: Susan Taylor. Tel: 01484 662120. Open: **M:** 09:00–17:30; **T:** 09:00–17:30; **W:** 09:00–17:30; **Th:** 09:00–17:30; **F:** 09:00–17:30; **S:** 09:00–17:30; **Su:** 09:00–17:30; Closed for lunch: 13:00–14:00. [Updated]

Childrens Bookshop, ■ 37/39 Lidget Street, Lindley, Huddersfield, HD3 3JF. Prop: Sonia & Barry Benster. Tel: (01484) 658013. Fax: (01484) 460020. E-mail: barry@hudbooks.demon.co.uk. Est: 1975. Shop open: **M:** 09:00–17:30; **T:** 09:00–17:30; **W:** 09:00–17:30; **Th:** 09:00–17:30; **F:** 09:00–17:30; **S:** 09:00–17:00. Stock: small. Spec: Author - Dickens, Charles; Children's; Medicine; Medicine - History of. CC: JCB; MC. Mem: BA. [Updated]

Elaine Lonsdale Books, 4 Scar Top, Golcar, Huddersfield, HD7 4DT. Prop: Elaine Lonsdale. Tel: 01484 644193. E-mail: Lainelonsdale@yahoo.co.uk. Est: 1990. Spec: Author - Alcotts, The; Authors - Women; Literary Criticism; Literature; Poetry; Social History; Topography - General; Women. PR: £1–100. Notes: also, bookbinder [Updated]

William H. Roberts, The Crease, 113 Hill Grove, Salendine Nook, Huddersfield, HD3 3TL. Tel: (01484) 654463. Fax: (01484) 654463. Web: www.williamroberts-cricket.com. E-mail: william.roberts2@virgin.net. Est: 1997. Private premises. Internet and postal. Telephone first. Spec: Sport - Cricket; Collectables; Ephemera. CC: V. Mem: PBFA. [Updated]

Susan Taylor Books, 2 Top of the Hill, Thurstonland, Huddersfield, HD4 6XZ. Prop: Susan Taylor. Tel: 01484 662120. E-mail: susan@mosleyr.freeserve.co.uk. Est: 1987. Mail Order Only. Internet and postal. Telephone first. Spec: Domesticity; Feminism; Fiction - Women; Housekeeping; Spiritual; Textiles; Women. Cata: occasionally on Women. [Updated]

Nick Tozer Railway Books, 62 Parkgate, Huddersfield, HD4 7NG. Nick Tozer. Tel: (01484) 663811. Fax: (01484) 663811. Web: www.railwaybook.com. E-mail: nick@railwaybook.com. Est: 1997. Office and/or bookroom. Internet and postal. Appointment necessary. Stock: medium. Spec: Railways; Booksearch. PR: £0–50. CC: PayPal. [Updated]

ILKLEY

Fine Books at Ilkley, 41 Manley Road, Ilkley, LS29 8QP. Prop: Dr. F.P. Williams. Tel: (01943) 600168. Fax: (01943) 603828. E-mail: finebooksilkley@dialstart.net. Est: 1979. Private premises. Appointment necessary. Spec: Antiquarian; Bindings; Children's - Illustrated; Technical; Travel - Africa; Travel - Americas; Travel - Asia, South East; Travel - China. PR: £10–1,000. Mem: ABA; PBFA. VAT No: GB 427 7108 51. [Updated]

Greenroom Books, 9 St. James Road, Ilkley, LS29 9PY. Prop: Geoff Oldham. Tel: (01943) 607662. E-mail: greenroombooks@blueyonder.co.uk. Est: 1991. Private premises. Contactable. Open: **M:** 09:00–18:00; **T:** 09:00–18:00; **W:** 09:00–18:00; **Th:** 09:00–18:00; **F:** 09:00–18:00; **S:** 09:00–18:00. Stock: small. Spec: Academic/Scholarly; Cinema/Film; Comedy; Dance; Drama; Entertainment - General; Fashion & Costume; Performing Arts. PR: £8–50. CC: PayPal. Corresp: French. Notes: No shop, work from home, booksearch. [Updated]

Skyrack Books, ■ 20 Skipton Road, Ilkley, LS29 9EJ. Prop: Steven Dyke. Tel: (01943) 601598. Fax: (01943) 601598. Est: 2000. Shop open: **T:** 10:00–17:00; **W:** 10:00–17:00; **Th:** 10:00–17:00; **F:** 10:00–17:00; **S:** 10:00–17:00; Closed for lunch: 13:00–14:00. Stock: medium. Spec: Canals/Inland Waterways; History - Industrial; History - Local; New Books; Railways; Topography - Local; Booksearch. PR: £1–100. Mem: BA. Notes: and stocks on Yorkshire, new books, book tokens. [Updated]

Mark Sutcliffe, 14 St. John's Avenue, Addingham, Ilkley, LS29 0QB. Tel: (01943) 830117. Fax: (01943) 830117. Web: www.marksutcliffebooks.com. E-mail: msfe@btinternet.com. Est: 1996. Private premises. Internet and postal. Appointment necessary. Stock: very small. Spec: Authors:- Blake, N.; Chandler, Raymond; Crofts, Freeman Wills; Hammett, Dashiell; Fiction - Crime, Detective, Spy, Thrillers; First Editions; Publishers - Collins (Crime Clb, The). PR: £5–3,000. CC: E; JCB; MC; V. Mem: PBFA. [Updated]

KIRKSTALL

The Bookshop, Kirkstall, ■ 10 Commercial Road, Kirkstall, Leeds, LS5 3AQ. Prop: R.A. & P.P. Brook. Tel: (0113) 278-0937. Fax: (0113) 278-0937. E-mail: book.shop@btinternet.com. Est: 1982. Shop open: **M:** 10:15–17:30; **T:** 10:15–17:30; **W:** 10:15–16:30; **Th:** 10:15–16:30; **F:** 10:15–17:30; **S:** 10:15–17:30. Stock: large. Spec: Antiquarian. PR: £1–2,000. CC: MC; V. [Updated]

LEEDS

Bates & Hindmarch, 2 Cumberland Road, Headingley, Leeds, LS6 2EF. Prop: Jeffery Bates. Tel: (0113) 278-3306. Web: www.abebooks.com. E-mail: jefferybates@aol.com. Est: 1987. Private premises. Appointment necessary. Stock: small. Spec: Antiquarian; Bindings; Cartoons; Countries - Afganistan; Countries - Asia; Countries - Central Asia; Countries - India; Countries - Tibet. PR: £20–1,000. CC: AE; JCB; MC. Mem: PBFA. VAT No: GB 417 9947 06. [Updated]

John Blanchfield, 5 Stanmore Place, Leeds, LS4 2RR. Prop: John Blanchfield. Tel: (0113) 274-2406. E-mail: john@blanchfield.demon.co.uk. Est: 1984. Private premises. Internet and postal. Appointment necessary. Stock: medium. Spec: Academic/Scholarly; History - Industrial; Industry. PR: £5–500. CC: JCB; V. Cata: annually. Mem: PBFA; and PBFA book fairs. VAT No: GB 405 5743 61. [Updated]

John Bonner, 82a Allerton Grange Rise, Moortown, Leeds, LS17 6LH. Tel: (0113) 2695012. E-mail: johnbonner@btinternet.com. Est: 1990. Private premises. Postal only. Stock: small. Spec: Aviation; Biography; Military. PR: £1–250. [Updated]

Bryony Books, 11 Woodhall Avenue, Leeds, LS5 3LH. Prop: Joan & Bill Martin. Tel: (0113) 258-7283. Est: 1976. Private premises. Appointment necessary. Stock: very small. Spec: Children's. PR: £2–100. Notes: please note: limited trading only. [Updated]

Elephant Books, ■ off Midland Road, Nr. Hyde Park Corner, Leeds, LS6 1BQ. Prop: Neil Whitworth. Tel: (0113) 274-4021. Est: 1987. Shop open: **M:** 10:00–18:00; **T:** 10:00–18:00; **W:** 10:00–18:00; **Th:** 10:00–18:00; **F:** 10:00–18:00; **S:** 10:00–18:00. Stock: large. Spec: Arts, The; Beat Writers; Literature; Philosophy; Psychology/Psychiatry. PR: £1–100. CC: AE; D; E; JCB; MC; V; Solo. Corresp: German, French, Spanish. [Updated]

Find That Book, 74 Oxford Avenue, Guiseley, Leeds, LS20 9BX. Prop: David Herries. Tel: (01943) 872699. Web: www.findthatbook.demon.co.uk. E-mail: david@findthatbook.demon.co.uk. Est: 1991. Private premises. Postal only. Spec: Booksearch. [Updated]

Leeds Bookseller, 3 Wedgewood Drive, Roundhay, Leeds, LS8 1EF. Prop: J.B. Wilkinson. Tel: (0113) 266-7183. Est: 1980. Private premises. Postal only. Stock: very small. Spec: Academic/Scholarly; Palaeography. PR: £1–8. [Updated]

Old Cathay Fine Books, 80 Lovell Park Grange, Sheepscar, Leeds, LS7 1DT. Prop: Ian Edwards. Tel: (0113) 248-1421. E-mail: ianedwards@ntlworld.com. Est: 1986. Private premises. Internet and postal. Stock: small. Spec: Banking & Insurance; Children's - Illustrated; Colour-Plate; Economics; Politics; Social Sciences; Socialism; Topography - General. PR: £5–1,000. Cata: annually on children's, colour, illustrated, academic. Notes: Business incorporates 'Academic and Scholarly Fine Books'. Catalogue includes titles on children's, colour, illustrated, academic and economics [Updated]

Peregrine Books (Leeds), 27 Hunger Hills Avenue, Horsforth, Leeds, LS18 5JS. Prop: J. & M.A. Whitaker. Tel: (0113) 258-5495. Est: 1986. Private premises. Appointment necessary. Stock: small. Spec: Natural History; Travel - General. PR: £5–3,000. Notes: also publishers of books on natural history. [Updated]

David Spenceley Books, 75 Harley Drive, Leeds, LS13 4QY. Prop: David Spenceley. Tel: (0113) 257-0715. Web: www.abebooks.com/home/davidspenceleybooks. E-mail: davidspenceley@email.com. Est: 1990. Private premises. Internet and postal. Contactable. Open: **M:** 09:00–17:00; **T:** 09:00–17:00; **W:** 09:00–17:00; **Th:** 09:00–17:00; **F:** 09:00–17:00; **S:** 09:00–17:00; **Su:** 09:00–17:00; Closed for lunch: 12:00–14:00. Stock: medium. Spec: Academic/Scholarly; Arms & Armour; Country Houses; Ecclesiastical History & Architecture; History - British; History - Middle Ages; History - Renaissance, The; History - Women. PR: £1–200. Notes: outside quoted opening hours - contactable at all reasonable times. [Updated]

Graham Sykes, 81 Gledhow Park Grove, Leeds, LS7 4JW. Tel: (0113) 262-1547. Est: 1985. Private premises. Postal only. Stock: small. Spec: Fine Art; First Editions; History - General; Natural History; Palaeontology; Photography; Topography - General; Travel - General. Mem: PBFA. [Updated]

Woodlands Books, 65 Gledhow Wood Road, Leeds, LS8 4DG. Prop: Bill & Valerie Astbury. Tel: (0113) 266-7834. Est: 1986. Private premises. Postal only. Stock: small. Spec: Music - General; Music - Musicians. PR: £2–150. [Updated]

LIVERSEDGE

Heckmondwike Book Shop, ■ 66 Union Road, Liversedge, WF15 7JF. Prop: David Sheard. Tel: (01924) 505666. E-mail: david.sheard@ntlworld.com. Est: 1984. Shop. Internet and postal. Telephone first. Open: **S:** 10:00–14:00. Stock: large. Spec: Author - Wheatley, Dennis; Fiction - General; Fiction - Crime, Detective, Spy, Thrillers; Fiction - Science Fiction; Publishers - Pan; Publishers - Penguin; Publishers - Puffin; Vintage Paperbacks. PR: £1–500. Notes: will open shop at other times by arrangement. VAT No: GB 427 5900 45. [Updated]

MIRFIELD

D. & M. Books, 5a Knowl Road, Mirfield, WF14 8DQ. Prop: Daniel J. Hanson. Tel: (01924) 495768. Fax: (01924) 491267. Web: www.dandmbooks.com. E-mail: daniel@dandmbooks.com. Est: 1989. Warehouse; Internet and postal. Telephone first. Stock: small. Spec: Cartoons; Children's; Comic Books & Annuals; Comics; Booksearch. PR: £10–1,000. CC: JCB; MC; V. Mem: PBFA. Notes: suppliers and manufacturers of book jacket covers and mailing supplies. VAT No: GB 686 8348 71. [Updated]

NORMANTON

Andrew Warrender, 4 West Street, Normanton, WF6 2AP. Tel: (01924) 892117. Fax: (01924) 215327. Web: www.warrender.demon.co.uk. E-mail: andrew@4yourprinting.co.uk. Est: 1995. Private premises. Postal only. Stock: small. Spec: Author - Fleming, Ian; Modern First Editions. PR: £1–150. [Updated]

OTLEY

Books Upstairs, ■ 9 Newmarket, Otley, LS21 3AE. Prop: John Hepworth. E-mail: buxupstairs@onetel.com. Est: 2002. Shop open: **T:** 11:00–16:00; **F:** 11:00–16:00; **S:** 11:00–16:00. [Updated]

Chevin Books, ■ 19 Manor Square, Otley, LS21 3AP. Simon Michael. Tel: (01943) 466599. E-mail: chevinbooks@yahoo.co.uk. Est: 1996. Shop open: **Th:** 10:00–17:00; **F:** 10:00–17:00; **S:** 10:00–17:00. Stock: medium. Spec: Architecture; Art History; Aviation; Folio Society, The; Literature; Military; Motoring; Natural History. PR: £1–1,000. CC: MC; V. [Updated]

TODMORDEN

Border Bookshop, ■ 61a & 63 Halifax Road, Todmorden, OL14 5BB. Prop: Victor H. Collinge. Tel: (01706) 814721. Web: www.borderbookshop.co.uk. E-mail: collinge@borderbookshop.fsnet.co.uk. Est: 1980. Shop open: **M:** 10:00–17:00; **W:** 10:00–17:00; **Th:** 10:00–17:00; **F:** 10:00–17:00; **S:** 10:00–17:00; Closed for lunch: 13:00–14:00. Stock: large. Spec: Children's; Comic Books & Annuals; Comics; Magazines & Periodicals - General; Nostalgia; Sport - Cricket; Sport - Football (Soccer); Ephemera. CC: E; JCB; MC; V. Corresp: French. Notes: also, new books, book tokens & book ordering service. [27/09/2004]

John Eggeling Books, Claremont South, 56 Burnley Road, Todmorden, OL14 5LH. Prop: John Eggeling. Tel: (01706) 816487. Fax: (01706) 816487. E-mail: todmordenbooks@ndirect.co.uk. Est: 1972. Private premises. Internet and postal. Appointment necessary. Stock: medium. Spec: Anthologies; Calligraphy; Colonial; Countries - Australasia; Fables; Fiction - General; Fiction - Crime, Detective, Spy, Thrillers; Fiction - Fantasy, Horror. PR: £2–1,000. CC: MC; V; Switch. Notes: also, a booksearch service. [Updated]

Magpie Books, Mellor Barn Farm, Peel Cottage Road, Walsden, Todmorden, OL14 7QJ. Prop: Graeme Roberts. Tel: (01706) 815005. Web: www.magpie-books.co.uk. E-mail: magpie@mellorbarn.co.uk. Private premises. Internet and postal. Appointment necessary. Stock: medium. PR: £5–2,000. CC: AE; JCB; MC; V. Mem: Ibooknet. Notes: large general stock. [Updated]

Judith Mansfield, Claremont South, 56 Burnley Road, Todmorden, OL14 5LH. Prop: Judith Mansfield. Tel: (01706) 816487. Fax: (01706) 816487. Web: www.abebooks.com/home/TODBOOKS/. E-mail: todmordenbooks@ndirect.co.uk. Est: 1983. Private premises. Internet and postal. Appointment necessary. Stock: medium. Spec: Crochet; Embroidery; Fashion & Costume; Knitting; Lace; Needlework; Textiles. PR: £2–500. CC: MC; V; PayPal. Mem: PBFA; Textile Society. [Updated]

WETHERBY

Steve Schofield Golf Books, 29 Nichols Way, Wetherby, LS22 6AD. Tel: (01937) 581276. Fax: (01937) 581276. E-mail: golfbooks@steveschofield.com. Est: 1993. Private premises. Postal only. Contactable. Open: **M:** 09:00–17:00; **T:** 09:00–17:00; **W:** 09:00–17:00; **Th:** 09:00–17:00; **F:** 09:00–17:00. Stock: very small. Spec: Sport - Golf. PR: £10–1,500. CC: MC; V. [Updated]

WILTSHIRE

BRADFORD ON AVON

Ex Libris, ■ 1 The Shambles, Bradford on Avon, BA15 1JS. Prop: Roger Jones. Tel: (01225) 863595. Fax: (01225) 863595. Web: www.ex-librisbooks.co.uk. E-mail: roger.jones@ex-librisbooks.co.uk. Est: 1980. Shop. Internet and postal. Open: **M:** 09:00–17:30; **T:** 09:00–17:30; **W:** 09:00–17:30; **Th:** 09:00–17:30; **F:** 09:00–17:30; **S:** 09:00–17:30. PR: £1–10. CC: AE; JCB; MC. Mem: PBFA. Notes: also, new books publishing as Ex Libris Press. [Updated]

CALNE

Clive Farahar & Sophie Dupre, Horsebrook House, XV The Green, Calne, SN11 8DQ. Tel: (01249) 821121. Fax: (01249) 821202. Web: www.farahardupre.co.uk. E-mail: sophie@farahardupre.co.uk. Est: 1978. Private premises. Internet and postal. Appointment necessary. Open: **M:** 09:00–17:00; **T:** 09:00–17:00; **W:** 09:00–17:00; **Th:** 09:00–17:00; **F:** 09:00–17:00; **S:** 10:00–13:00; Closed for lunch: 13:00–14:00. Stock: large. Spec: Antiquarian; Autographs; Documents - General; Letters; Literature; Manuscripts; Photography; Royalty - General. PR: £10–10,000. CC: AE; JCB; MC; V. Corresp: French. Mem: ABA; ILAB; PADA Manuscript Society. VAT No: GB 341 0770 87. [Updated]

CHIPPENHAM

Vernon Askew Books, Preston East Farm, Nr. Lyneham, Chippenham, SN15 4DX. Prop: Vernon Askew. Tel: (01249) 892177 and 8. Fax: (01249) 892177. E-mail: vernonaskewbooks@tiscali.co.uk. Est: 1997. Storeroom. Appointment necessary. Stock: very large. Spec: Alpinism/Mountaineering; Aviation; Bibliography; Biography; Bull Fighting; Byzantium; Churchilliana; Countries - Cyprus. PR: £3–75. Corresp: Swedish. Notes: Contactable all week [Updated]

Ben Bass, Greyne House, Marshfield, Chippenham, SN14 8LU. Tel: (01225) 891279. E-mail: benbassbooks@hotmail.com. Est: 1689. Storeroom. Open: **M:** 08:00–20:00; **T:** 08:00–20:00; **W:** 08:00–20:00; **Th:** 08:00–20:00; **F:** 08:00–20:00. Stock: large. Spec: Author - Machen, Arthur; Biography; Countries - Spain; Fiction - General; First Editions; Literature; Booksearch. PR: £2–20. Corresp: French, German, Italian, Spanish. [Updated]

Granny's Attic, ■ The Old Citadel, Attic Rooms, Bath Road, Chippenham, SN15 2AA. Tel: 01249 715327. Est: 2005. Shop open: **M:** 09:45–16:00; **T:** 09:45–16:00; **W:** 09:45–16:00; **Th:** 09:45–16:00; **F:** 09:45–16:00; **S:** 09:45–16:00. Notes: General stock. [Updated]

Tony Pollastrone Railway Books, 4, Wells Close, Chippenham, SN14 0QD. Prop: Tony Pollastrone. Tel: 01249 444298. Web: www.tp-railbooks.co.uk. E-mail: sales@tp-railbooks.co.uk. Est: 2004. Private premises. Open: **M:** 09:00–17:30; **T:** 09:00–17:30; **W:** 09:00–17:30; **Th:** 09:00–17:30; **F:** 09:00–17:30; **S:** 09:00–17:30. Spec: Buses/Trams; Canals/Inland Waterways; General Stock; History - Industrial; Motoring; Railways; Transport. CC: JCB; MC; V; Switch/Maestro. Cata: bi-annually on Railways, Canals, Industrial History. Mem: Specialising in railways, and related subjects. Also carry a small stock of general interest subjects. Please visit my website for full details VAT No: GB 840 9362 23. [Updated]

COLERNE

Chris Phillips, 28 Roundbarrow Close, Colerne, Chippenham, SN14 8EF. Prop: Chris Phillips. Tel: (01225) 742755. E-mail: batholdbooks@yahoo.co.uk. Est: 1997. Private premises. Book Fairs Only. Stock: small. Spec: Antiquarian; Art; Children's - Illustrated; Literature; Technology. PR: £1–500. CC: JCB; MC; V. Corresp: French. Mem: PBFA. Notes: booksearch, valuations for insurance or Probate. [Updated]

DEVIZES

D'Arcy Books, ■ The Chequers, High Street, Devizes, SN10 1AT. Prop: Colin & Jenifer MacGregor. Tel: Shop (01380) 726922. E-mail: darcybooks@btclick.com. Est: 1974. Shop open: **M:** 10:00–17:30; **T:** 10:00–17:30; **W:** 10:00–17:30; **Th:** 10:00–17:30; **F:** 10:00–17:30; **S:** 10:00–17:30. Stock: large. Spec: Archaeology; Architecture; Arts, The; Aviation; Children's; Cookery/Gastronomy; Fiction - General; Gardening - General. Notes: also, a booksearch, bookbinding & repair service. VAT No: GB 196 1414 55. [Updated]

MALMESBURY

Earth Science Books, Old Swan House, Swan Barton, Sherston, Malmesbury, SN16 0LJ. Prop: Geoff Carss. Tel: (01666) 840995. Web: www.earthsciencebooks.com. E-mail: geoff@earthsciencebooks.com. Est: 2002. Private premises. Internet and postal. Contactable. Stock: very small. Spec: Academic/Scholarly; Advertising; Animals and Birds; Geology; Hydrography; Natural History; Natural Sciences; Palaeography. PR: £3–10,000. [Updated]

MARLBOROUGH

Anthony Spranger, 67 London Road, Marlborough, SN8 2AJ. Prop: Anthony Spranger. Tel: 01672 516338. E-mail: sprangerbooks@hotmail.com. Private premises. Appointment necessary. Spec: Alpinism/Mountaineering; Autobiography; Biography; Performing Arts. CC: AE; D; E; JCB; MC; V; SW. Corresp: French. Mem: PBFA. [Updated]

John Bevan Catholic Bookseller, Romans Halt, Mildenhall, Marlborough, SN8 2LX. Tel: (01672) 519817. Web: www.catholic-books.co.uk. E-mail: johnbevan@catholicbooks.co.uk. Est: 1978. Storeroom. Internet and postal. Appointment necessary. Stock: medium. Spec: Religion - Christian. PR: £1–500. CC: MC; V. Corresp: French, German. Mem: PBFA. [23/07/2004]

Katharine House Gallery, ■ Katharine House, The Parade, Marlborough, SN8 1NE. Prop: Christopher Gange. Tel: (01672) 514040. E-mail: chrisgange@fsmail.net. Est: 1983. Shop open: **T:** 10:00–17:30; **W:** 10:00–17:30; **Th:** 10:00–17:30; **F:** 10:00–17:30; **S:** 10:00–17:30. Stock: medium. Spec: Antiques; Art; Illustrated; Modern First Editions. PR: £3–300. CC: MC; V. Notes: also, 20thC British art and antiques. [Updated]

Military Parade Bookshop, The Parade, Marlborough, SN8 1NE. Prop: Graham & Peter Kent. Tel: (01672) 515470 Fax: (01980) 630150. Web: www.militaryparadebooks.com. E-mail: enquiry@militaryparadebooks.com. Est: 1988. Spec: Aviation; Maritime/Nautical; Military History. PR: £2–150. [Updated]

Nevis Railway Bookshops, ■ Katharine House Gallery, The Parade, Marlborough, SN8 1NE. Prop: N.J. Bridger. Tel: Shop (01672) 514040. Web: www.nevis-railway-bookshops.co.uk. Est: 1988. Shop open: **T:** 10:00–17:30; **W:** 10:00–17:30; **Th:** 10:00–17:30; **F:** 10:00–17:30; **S:** 10:00–17:30. Stock: medium. Spec: Archaeology; Canals/Inland Waterways; Railways; Ephemera. PR: £1–75. Notes: Railway Book and Magazine Search, Newbury, Berks (q.v.) Nevis Railway Bookshop, Goring-on-Thames, Oxon (q.v.) Mainly industrial archeology. [Updated]

RAMSBURY

Heraldry Today, ■ Parliament Piece, Ramsbury, Nr. Marlborough, SN8 2QH. Prop: Rosemary Pinches. Tel: (01672) 520617. Fax: (01672) 520183. Web: www.heraldrytoday.co.uk. E-mail: heraldry@heraldrytoday.co.uk. Est: 1954. Shop open: **M:** 09:30–16:30; **T:** 09:30–16:30; **W:** 09:30–16:30; **Th:** 09:30–16:30; **F:** 09:30–16:30. Stock: large. Spec: Biography; Ex-Libris; Genealogy; Heraldry; History - General; Royalty - General; School Registers/Rolls of Honour; Booksearch. PR: £1–5,000. CC: E; MC; V; Maestro. Corresp: French. Mem: ABA; ILAB. Notes: also, back-numbers of journals, new books, periodicals & a booksearch service VAT No: GB 238 8244 41. [Updated]

SALISBURY

Badger, Boxwood, Broadchalke, Salisbury, SP5 5EP. Prop: Peter Bletsoe. Tel: (01722) 326033. Est: 1987. Market stand/stall. Open: **M:** 10:00–17:00; **T:** 10:00–17:00; **W:** 10:00–17:00; **Th:** 10:00–17:00; **F:** 10:00–17:00. Stock: small. Spec: Prints and Maps. PR: £5–200. CC: AE; D; E; JCB; MC; V. [Updated]

Ellwood Books, ■ 38 Winchester Street, Salisbury, SP1 1HG. Prop: Mark Harrison and Helen Ford. Tel: (01722) 322975. Web: www.ellwoodbooks.com. E-mail: info@ellwoodbooks.com. Est: 2001. Shop open: **M:** 10:30–17:00; **T:** 10:30–17:00; **Th:** 10:30–17:00; **F:** 10:30–17:00; **S:** 10:30–17:00. Stock: medium. Spec: Fiction - General; Fine & Rare; Literary Criticism; Modern First Editions; Poetry; Signed Editions; Topography - General; Topography - Local. PR: £1–50. CC: E; JCB; MC; V; Switch/Sol. Mem: PBFA. Notes: also attends London & Farnham HD bookfairs, some PBFA fairs & Internet trading. VAT No: GB 832 0693 40. [Updated]

John & Judith Head, The Barn Book Supply, 88 Crane Street, Salisbury, SP1 2QD. Tel: (01722) 327767. Fax: (01722) 339888. Web: www.johnandjudithhead.co.uk. E-mail: info@johnandjudithhead.co.uk. Est: 1958. Office and/or bookroom. Open: **M:** 09:30–00:00; **T:** 09:30–00:00; **W:** 09:30–00:00; **Th:** 09:30–00:00; **F:** 09:30–00:00. Stock: medium. Spec: Sport - Angling/Fishing; Sport - Field Sports. PR: £1–18,000. CC: AE; D; E; JCB; MC; V; Mae, So. Mem: ABA. Notes: open on Saturday by appointment. [Updated]

WILTSHIRE

Rosemary Pugh Books, 59b Old Sarum Airfield, Salisbury, SP4 6DZ. Prop: Mrs. R M Pugh, Mr J M Pugh, Mr A.E. Pugh. Tel: 01722 330132. Fax: 01722 330132. Web: www.rosemarypughbooks.co.uk. E-mail: rosemarypugh@btopenworld.com. Est: 1990. Storeroom. Internet and postal. Telephone first. Open: **M:** 08:00–16:00; **T:** 08:00–16:00; **W:** 08:00–16:00; **Th:** 08:00–16:00. Spec: Bibles; Ecclesiastical History & Architecture; Ecology; Feminism; Gnostics; Holocaust; Hymnology; Iconography. CC: JCB; MC; V; Delta, Maestro, Solo, Fortoak,. Cata: occasionally on areas within Theology. Mem: FSB. VAT No: GB 699 1250 01. [Updated]

Water Lane Bookshop, ■ 24, Water Lane, Salisbury, SP2 7TE. Prop: Peter Shouler. Tel: 01722 337929. Web: www.www.waterlanebooks.co.uk. E-mail: inquiries@dorsetrarebooks.co.uk. Est: 2000. Shop open: **M:** 10:00–17:00; **T:** 10:00–17:00; **W:** 10:00–17:00; **Th:** 10:00–17:00; **F:** 10:00–17:00; **S:** 10:00–17:00. Spec: Antiquarian; Antiques; Art; Art - Technique; Art - Theory; Art History; Art Reference; Artists. CC: MC; V. Mem: PBFA. VAT No: GB 723 3951 38. [Updated]

SWINDON

Peter Barnes, 138 Ermin Street, Stratton St Margaret, Swindon, SN3 4NQ. Prop: Peter Barnes. Tel: (01793) 821327. Est: 2001. Private premises. Postal only. Stock: small. Spec: Aviation; History - General; Magazines & Periodicals - General; Military; Military History; Naval; Topography - General; Topography - Local. PR: £1–50. Notes: exhibits at book fairs. [Updated]

Bookmark (Children's Books), Fortnight, Wick Down, Broad Hinton, Swindon, SN4 9NR. Prop: Anne & Leonora Excell. Tel: (01793) 731693. Fax: (01793) 731782. E-mail: leonora-excell@btconnect.com. Est: 1973. Private premises. Book Fairs Only. Appointment necessary. Open: **M:** 09:00–18:00; **T:** 09:00–18:00; **W:** 09:00–18:00; **Th:** 09:00–18:00; **F:** 09:00–18:00; **S:** 10:00–18:00. Stock: medium. Spec: Authors:- Aldin, Cecil; Ardizzone, Edward; Brent-Dyer, Elinor M.; Crane, Walter; Dahl, Roald; - Henty, G.A.; Keeping, Charles; Author - Potter, Beatrix. PR: £5–2,000. CC: E; JCB; MC; V; Switch. Mem: PBFA. Notes: also, a specialist booksearch service leonora-excell@btconnect.com. [Updated]

Collectors Corner, ■ 227 Kingshill, Swindon, SN1 4NG. Prop: Fred Stevens. Tel: (01793) 521545. Est: 1986. Shop open: **M:** 10:30–16:45; **T:** 10:30–16:45; **Th:** 10:30–16:45; **F:** 10:30–16:45; **S:** 10:30–16:45. Stock: very small. Spec: Collecting; Military; Railways; Topography - Local; Transport; Collectables; Ephemera; Prints and Maps. PR: £1–100. Notes: Stock includes: postcards, cigarette cards, coins, medals, badges, toys, and ephemera. [Updated]

Ice House Books, Hard Crag, Foxhill, Swindon, SN4 0DR. Prop: Mr Simon Miles. Tel: 01793 791975. Web: www.icehousebooks.co.uk. E-mail: shop@icehousebooks.co.uk. Est: 2000. Warehouse; Internet and postal. Appointment necessary. Shop At: Unit A Pigeon House Lane, Stratton St. Margaret, Swindon, SN3 4QH. Open: **M:** 09:00–18:00; **T:** 09:00–18:00; **W:** 09:00–18:00; **Th:** 09:00–18:00; **F:** 09:00–18:00; **S:** 09:00–18:00; **Su:** 09:00–18:00; Closed for lunch: 13:00–14:00. Spec: Academic/ Scholarly; Arts, The; Evolution; History - General; Natural History; Philology; Politics; Science - General. CC: MC; V; SW. Cata: weekly website updates. Notes: also at: Unit A Pigeon House Lane, Stratton St. Margaret, Swindon, SN3 4QH. Spec: Acadameic and professional non-fiction; sciences; arts; social sciences; equestrian; classics; politics; humanities. Relocated under new ownership from Leicester. [Updated]

TISBURY

Heatons, ■ 2–3 High Street, Tisbury, SP3 6PS. Prop: Ros King. Tel: (01747) 873025 and 8. Fax: (01747) 870059. Web: www.heatons-of-tisbury.co.uk. E-mail: rosking@freenetname.co.uk. Shop. Internet and postal. Open: **M:** 09:00–16:30; **F:** 09:00–16:30; **S:** 09:00–16:30. Stock: very large. Spec: Ephemera; Prints and Maps. PR: £1–2,000. Notes: also, engravings, maps, Arts & Crafts, Art Nouveau & Deco furniture and decorative items especially glass. [Updated]

WARMINSTER

Sturford Books, Landfall, 35 Corton, Warminster, BA12 0SY. Prop: Maria & Robert Mayall. Tel: (01985) 850478/85058. E-mail: maria@booksfortravel.org.uk. Est: 1993. Private premises. Appointment necessary. Stock: small. Spec: Architecture; Art; Fiction - General; Foreign Texts; Literature; Poetry; Travel - General; Booksearch. PR: £5–800. CC: MC; V. [Updated]

WEST KINGTON

Peter Barnitt, Latimer's Yard, West Kington, Chippenham, SN14 7JJ. Tel: (01249) 782099. E-mail: barnitt.latlo@virgin.net. Private premises. Appointment necessary. Stock: very small. Spec: Fine Printing; Private Press. PR: £20–3,000. [Updated]

WESTBURY

Aardvark Books, 50 Bratton Road, Westbury, BA13 3EP. Prop: Clive & Caroline Williams. Tel: (01225) 867723. Fax: (01225) 867723. Web: www.aardvarkmilitarybooks.com. E-mail: aardvarkbooks@blueyonder.co.uk. Est: 1998. Private premises. Internet and postal. Telephone first. Open: **M:** 09:00–19:00; **T:** 09:00–19:00; **W:** 09:00–19:00; **Th:** 09:00–19:00; **F:** 09:00–19:00; **S:** 09:00–19:00; **Su:** 09:00–07:00. Stock: large. Spec: Military History; War - World War I; War - World War II. PR: £5–250. CC: MC; V; Switch. [Updated]

Zardoz Books, 20 Whitecroft, Dilton Marsh, Westbury, BA13 4DJ. Prop: M. & L. Flanagan. Tel: (01373) 865371. Web: www.zardozbooks.co.uk. E-mail: zardoz@blueyonder.co.uk. Est: 1990. Warehouse; Internet and postal. Appointment necessary. Stock: very large. Spec: Books about Books; Cinema/Film; Crime (True); Early Imprints; Fiction - General; Fiction - Fantasy, Horror; Fiction - Science Fiction; Fiction - Westerns. PR: £2–100. CC: MC; V. [Updated]

WOOTTON BASSETT

G. Jackson, 10 Dryden Place, Wootton Bassett, SN4 8JP. Prop: Geoffrey Jackson. Tel: (01793) 849660. Fax: (01793) 849660. E-mail: geoffsj.jackson@tiscali.co.uk. Est: 2001. Private premises. Appointment necessary. Open: **M:** 09:30–17:30; **T:** 09:30–17:30; **W:** 09:30–17:30; **Th:** 09:30–17:30; **F:** 09:30–17:30. Stock: small. Spec: Antiquarian; Antiques; Art Reference; Irish Interest; Military History; Modern First Editions; Natural History; Sport - General. PR: £25–9,000. CC: MC; V; PayPal. [Updated]

ZEALS

Hurly Burly Books, 47 Zeals Rise, Zeals, BA12 6PL. Prop: Moira Lord. Tel: (01747) 840691. E-mail: hurlyburly@fsmail.net. Est: 1995. Storeroom. Appointment necessary. Shop At: Words Etc, Dorchester, Dorset. Stock: small. Spec: Children's; Children's - Illustrated; Illustrated. CC: E; JCB; MC; V; Solo, Switch. Notes: also at: Words Etc, Dorchester, Dorset. [Updated]

WORCESTERSHIRE

BESFORD

Louise Ross Books, 28 Besford Court, Besford, Nr. Worcester, WR8 9LZ. Tel: (01368) 550461. E-mail: louise.ross@btclick.com. Est: 1977. Private premises. Postal only. Contactable. Stock: very small. Spec: Children's; Illustrated; Literature. PR: £25–5,000. [Updated]

BEWDLEY

Clent Books of Bewdley, Rose Cottage, Habberley Road, Bewdley, DY12 1JA. Prop: Ivor Simpson. Tel: (01299) 401090. Web: www.clentbooks.co.uk. E-mail: clent.books@btinternet.com. Est: 1977. Private premises. Book Fairs Only. Stock: medium. Spec: Antiquarian; Fine & Rare; History - Local; Military; Topography - Local. PR: £20–200. Prop: Book Fair Organiser. [31/07/2004]

DROITWICH

Grant Books, The Coach House, New Road, Cutnall Green, Droitwich, WR9 0PQ. Prop: Bob & Shirley Grant. Tel: (01299) 851588. Fax: (01299) 851446. Web: www.grantbooks-memorabilia.com. E-mail: golf@grantbooks.co.uk. Est: 1972. Office and/or bookroom. Open: **M:** 09:00–17:00; **T:** 09:00–17:00; **W:** 09:00–17:00; **Th:** 09:00–17:00; **F:** 09:00–17:00. Stock: small. Spec: Antiquarian; Sport - Golf. PR: £10–2,500. CC: AE; D; MC; V. Mem: PBFA; BGCS; GCS(USA). Notes: open at other times by appointment. VAT No: GB 275 8638 10. [Updated]

M. & D. Books, ■ 16 High Street, Droitwich Spa, WR9 8EW. Prop: Mike Hebden. Tel: (01905) 775814. Est: 1996. Shop open: **T:** 10:00–17:00; **W:** 10:00–17:00; **Th:** 10:00–17:00; **F:** 10:00–17:00; **S:** 09:30–17:00. Stock: medium. Spec: Topography - Local. PR: £1–250. CC: AE; JCB; MC; V; SW. [Updated]

GREAT MALVERN

The Malvern Bookshop, ■ 7 Abbey Road, Great Malvern, WR14 3ES. Prop: Howard and Julie Hudson. Tel: (01684) 575915. Fax: (01684) 575915. E-mail: browse@malvernbookshop.co.uk. Est: 1955. Shop open: **M:** 10:00–17:00; **T:** 10:00–17:00; **W:** 10:00–17:00; **Th:** 10:00–17:00; **F:** 10:00–17:00; **S:** 10:00–17:00; Closed for lunch: 10:00–17:00. Stock: large. Spec: Academic/Scholarly; Advertising; Antiques; Archaeology; Architecture; Art; Aviation; Bindings. PR: £1–1,000. Notes: also, a booksearch service. In winter, call before visiting as closed some weeks. [22/11/2004]

Wildside Books, Rectory House, 26 Priory Road, Great Malvern, WR14 3DR. Prop: Chris & Christine Johnson. Tel: (01684) 562 818. Fax: (01684) 566 491. Web: www.wildsidebooks.co.uk. E-mail: enquire@wildsidebooks.co.uk. Est: 1982. Private premises. Internet and postal. Appointment necessary. Stock: small. Spec: Animals and Birds; Ecology; Fine & Rare; Natural History; Natural Sciences; New Naturalist; Ornithology; Rural Life. PR: £15–10,000. CC: E; MC; V; SW. Notes: Gallery: specialising in wildlife art from 18th-21st Century. VAT No: GB 162 5737 56. [Updated]

KIDDERMINSTER

Lion Books, 52 Blackwell St, Kidderminster, DY10 2EE. Prop: Colin Raxter. Tel: (0156) 745060. Web: www.lionbooks.co.uk. E-mail: info@lionbooks.co.uk. Est: 1987. Private premises. Internet and postal. Open: **T:** 10:30–17:00; **Th:** 10:30–17:00; **F:** 10:30–17:00; **S:** 10:30–14:00; Closed for lunch: 13:00–14:00. Stock: medium. Spec: Sport - Angling/Fishing; Sport - Cricket; Sport - Football (Soccer); Sport - Motor Racing; Sport - Rugby. PR: £1–1,000. CC: E; JCB; MC; V; PayPal. Mem: PBFA. [Updated]

M. & M. Baldwin, ■ 24 High St, Cleobury Mortimer, Kidderminster, DY14 8BY. Tel: (01299) 270110. Fax: (01299) 270110. E-mail: mb@mbaldwin.free-online.co.uk. Est: 1978. Shop open: **W:** 14:00–18:00; **S:** 10:14–13:18; Closed for lunch: 13:00–14:00. Stock: medium. Spec: Author - Rolt, L.T.C.; Aviation; Canals/Inland Waterways; Crafts; Cryptography; Espionage; Maritime/Nautical; Military. PR: £1–500. CC: AE; MC; V. Corresp: French. Mem: Fed. of Small Businesses. Notes: also, publisher of books. VAT No: GB 547 6638 05. [Updated]

Salsus Books, Elderfield Gardens, 42 Coventry Street, Kidderminster, DY10 2BT. Prop: Dr. D.T. Salt. Tel: (01562) 742081. Fax: (01562) 824583. E-mail: salsus@books93.freeserve.co.uk. Est: 1991. Private premises. Internet and postal. Appointment necessary. Stock: medium. Spec: Academic/Scholarly; Advertising; Aeronautics; Ecclesiastical History & Architecture; Religion - General; Religion - Christian; Religion - Muslim; Theology. PR: £1–250. CC: JCB; MC; V; SW. Mem: PBFA. [Updated]

MALVERN

Jonathan Gibbs Books, The Lakes Cottages, Drake Street, Welland, Malvern, WR13 6LN. Prop: Jonathan and Angela Gibbs. Tel: (01684) 593169. Web: www.jgibbsbooks.co.uk. E-mail: info@jgibbsbooks.co.uk. Est: 2001. Private premises. Internet and postal. Appointment necessary. Stock: small. Spec: Academic/Scholarly; Antiquarian; Literature; Music - General; Music - Classical; Music - Printed, Sheet Music & Scores; Performing Arts; Sport - Horse Racing (inc. Riding/Breeding/Equestrian). PR: £10–1,000. CC: AE; MC; V. Mem: PBFA. [Updated]

Golden Age Books, PO Box 45, Malvern, WR14 1XT. Prop: Tony Byatt, Adrian and Gillian Ainge. Tel: (05511) 436803. Web: www.ukbookworld.com/members/goldenage. E-mail: enquiries@goldenagebooks.co.uk. Est: 1981. Private premises. Internet and postal. Appointment necessary. Stock: small. Spec: Academic/Scholarly; Bibles; Religion - General; Religion - Christian; Religion - Jewish; Theology. PR: £1–500. CC: E; JCB; MC; V; SW. Notes: also, new Biblical books. [Updated]

St. Ann's Books, Rectory House, 26 Priory Road, Malvern, WR14 3DR. Prop: Chris & Christine Johnson. Tel: (01684) 562818. Fax: (01684) 566491. Web: www.wildsidebooks.co.uk. E-mail: enquire@wildsidebooks.co.uk. Est: 1982. Private premises. Internet and postal. Appointment necessary. Stock: small. Spec: Art; Botany; Gardening - General; Natural History; Ornithology; Zoology. PR: £20–20,000. CC: MC; V; SW, Mae. [Updated]

PERSHORE

Coach House Books, ■ 17a Bridge Street, Pershore, WR10 1AJ. Prop: Michael & Sue Ellingworth. Tel: (01386) 554633. Fax: (01386) 554633. E-mail: sue.chb@virgin.net. Est: 1982. Shop. Telephone first. Open: **W:** 09:00–05:00. Stock: medium. Spec: Architecture; Art Reference; Author - Lawrence, T.E.; Folio Society, The; Horticulture; Limited Editions; Military; Ornithology. PR: £5–2,000. CC: AE; D; MC; V. Corresp: French. Mem: BA. VAT No: GB 396 2460 27. [14/10/2004]

Ian K. Pugh Books, ■ 40 Bridge Street, Pershore, WR10 1AT. Tel: (01386) 552681. Mob: 07968 429112. E-mail: iankpugh.books@virgin.net. Est: 1974. Shop open: **M:** 10:30–15:30; **T:** 10:30–15:30; **W:** 10:30–15:30; **Th:** 10:30–15:30; **F:** 10:30–15:30; **S:** 09:30–17:00. Stock: medium. Spec: Fine Art; Horticulture; Illustrated; Collectables. PR: £1–7,000. [Updated]

Sedgeberrow Books, ■ Retail Market, Cherry Orchard, Pershore, WR10 1EY. Prop: Mrs. Jayne Winter. Tel: (01386) 751830. Web: www.abebooks.com/home/SEDGEBERROW. E-mail: sales@sedgeberrowbooks.co.uk. Est: 1985. Shop open: **W:** 09:00–17:00; **Th:** 09:00–17:00; **F:** 09:00–17:00; **S:** 09:00–17:00. Stock: large. Spec: Authors:- Moore, John; Young, Francis Brett; Aviation; History - Local; Military; Mind, Body & Spirit; Railways; Topography - General. PR: £1–300. CC: MC; V; Switch. [Updated]

STOURPORT-ON-SEVERN

P. and P. Books, Dairy Cottage, Yarhampton, Stourport, Stourport-on-Severn, DY13 0UY. Prop: J.S. Pizey. Tel: (01299) 896996. Fax: (01299) 896996. E-mail: pandpbooks_jim@compuserve.com. Est: 1982. Private premises. Appointment necessary. Stock: very small. Spec: Archaeology; Egyptology; Travel - Middle East. PR: £5–2,000. CC: JCB. Corresp: French, German. Mem: ABA; PBFA. VAT No: GB 441 7426 59. [16/11/2004]

WORCESTER

Ann & Mike Conry, 14, St George's Square, Worcester, WR1 1HX. Tel: 01905 25330. Web: www.abe.com. E-mail: irishallsorts@aol.com. Est: 1998. Private premises. Internet and postal. Spec: Irish Interest; Modern First Editions; Sport - General; Sport - Football (Soccer); Travel - General. Notes: For sale through Abe but direct contact available. [Updated]

Available from Richard Joseph Publishers Ltd
BOOKDEALING FOR PROFIT
by Paul Minet

Quarto H/b £10.00 144pp

WORCESTERSHIRE

Bookworms of Evesham, ■ 81 Port Street, Evesham, Worcester, WR11 3LF. Prop: T.J. Sims. Tel: (01386) 45509. Fax: (01386) 45509. Est: 1971. Shop open: **T:** 10:00–17:00; **W:** 10:00–17:00; **Th:** 10:00–17:00; **F:** 10:00–17:00; **S:** 10:00–17:00. Stock: medium. Spec: Art; History - General; Literature; Military; Topography - Local; Transport; Travel - General. Mem: PBFA. Notes: fairs attended - Cheltenham, Bath, Cirencester; and Churchdown Book Fair. [Updated]

Davies Fine Books, 21 Droitwich Road, Worcester, WR3 7LG. Prop: Richard Davies. Tel: (01905) 23919. Web: www.daviesfinebooks.biblion.com. E-mail: daviesfinebooks@yahoo.co.uk. Est: 2002. Private premises. Internet and postal. Contactable. Stock: small. Spec: Antiquarian; Gardening - General; Illustrated; Natural History; Travel - General. CC: AE; JCB; MC; V. Corresp: French. Mem: PBFA. VAT No: GB 823 3339 44. [Updated]

Graduate Books, 5 Rectory Lane, Shrawley, Worcester, WR6 6TW. Tel: (01905) 620786. E-mail: davidrobertvirr@aol.com. Est: 1985. Private premises. Internet and postal. Appointment necessary. Stock: very small. Spec: Mind, Body & Spirit; Music - Popular; Philosophy; Psychology/Psychiatry. PR: £3–300. Corresp: French. [Updated]

Priory Books, ■ 10 Church Walk, Malvern, Worcester, WR14 2XH. Prop: Paul Sheath. Tel: (01684) 560258. E-mail: priorybooks@tiscali.co.uk. Est: 1985. Shop open: **M:** 09:30–17:15; **T:** 09:30–17:15; **W:** 09:30–17:15; **Th:** 09:30–17:15; **F:** 09:30–17:15; **S:** 09:30–17:15. Stock: medium. Spec: History - Local; Poetry; Railways; Topography - General. PR: £1–500. CC: AE; MC; V; Maestro. Notes: free booksearch and new book ordering. VAT No: GB 819 3353 21. [Updated]

Restormel Books, 1 East Comer, St. John's, Worcester, WR2 6BE. Prop: Roy Slade. Tel: (01905) 422290. Est: 1978. Display/stand. Open: **M:** 10:00–17:00; **T:** 10:00–17:00; **W:** 10:00–17:00; **Th:** 10:00–17:00; **F:** 10:00–17:00; **S:** 10:00–17:00. Stock: small. Spec: Collecting; Topography - Local; Collectables. PR: £1–50. Corresp: French, Spanish. Mem: PBFA. Notes: attends PBFA fairs in Midlands. [Updated]

Worcester Rare Books, c/o 22 Oakland Close, Upton Upon Severn, Worcester, WR8 0ES. D.I. Lloyd. Tel: (01905) 28780. E-mail: rarebooks@worcester74. freeserve.co.uk. Est: 1972. Private premises. Internet and postal. Appointment necessary. Stock: very small. Spec: Academic/Scholarly; Antiquarian; Architecture; Medicine; Philosophy; Science - General; Science - History of. PR: £10–200. CC: MC; V. Corresp: French, German. Mem: PBFA. [Updated]

CHANNEL ISLANDS

GUERNSEY

VALE

Channel Islands Galleries Limited, ■ Les Clospains, Rue de L'Ecole, Vale, Guernsey, GY3 5LL. Prop: Geoffrey P. & Christine M. Gavey Tel: Shop (01481) 247337. Fax: (01481) 243538. E-mail: geoff.gavey@cigalleries.f9.co.uk. Est: 1967. Shop. Postal only. Open: **M:** 10:00–17:00; **T:** 10:00–17:00; **W:** 10:00–17:00; **Th:** 10:00–13:00; **F:** 10:00–17:00; **S:** 10:00–13:00. Stock: small. Spec: Antiquarian; Atlases; History - General; Natural History; Topography - General; Topography - Local; Prints and Maps. PR: £5–4,000. CC: E; MC; V. Corresp: French, German. Notes: also, antique maps, prints, watercolours and paintings - featuring The Channel Islands, coins & CI bank notes. [Updated]

JERSEY

ST. HELIER

Books and Things, ■ First Tower, St. Helier, Jersey, JE2 3LN. Prop: Bob Burrow. Tel: 01534 759949. Fax: n/a. Web: www.newnats.com. E-mail: bob@newnats.com. Est: 1998. Shop open: **M:** 12:00–17:00; **T:** 12:00–17:00; **W:** 12:00–17:00; **Th:** 12:00–17:00; **F:** 12:00–17:00; **S:** 10:00–17:00; **Su:** 10:00–17:00. Stock: medium. Spec: New Naturalist. PR: £1–5,000. Corresp: English. [Updated]

ISLE OF MAN

DOUGLAS

Garretts Antiquarian Books, 4 Summerhill, Douglas, IM2 4PJ. Prop: Mr. Jonathon Hall. Tel: (01624) 675065. Web: www.isleofmanbooks.com. E-mail: garrettsbooks_iom@yahoo.co.uk. Est: 1987. Private premises. Internet and postal. Telephone first. Stock: small. Spec: Countries - Isle of Man; History - Local; Topography - Local. PR: £1–1,000. CC: AE; JCB; MC; V. Mem: PBFA. [Updated]

PORT ERIN

Bridge Bookshop Ltd, Shore Road, Port Erin, IM9 6HL. Tel: 01624 833376. Fax: 01624 835381. E-mail: bbs@manx.net. [Updated]

NORTHERN IRELAND

CO. ANTRIM

BELFAST

P. & B. Rowan, Carleton House, 92 Malone Road, Belfast, BT9 5HP. Prop: Peter & Briad Rowan. Tel: (028) 9066-6448. Fax: (028) 9066-3725. E-mail: peter@pbrowan.thegap.com. Est: 1973. Private premises. Appointment necessary. Stock: large. Spec: Economics; Fine & Rare; History - General; Irish Interest; Law - General; Literature; Manuscripts; Medicine - History of. PR: Euro 25 upwards. Corresp: French. Mem: PBFA; IADA. [Updated]

The Bell Gallery, 13 Adelaide Park, Belfast, BT9 6FX. Prop: James Nelson Bell. Tel: 02890 662998. Fax: 02890 381524. Web: www.bellgallery.com. E-mail: bellgallery@btinternet.com. Est: 1965. Shop and/or gallery. Spec: Countries - Ireland; Irish Interest. PR: £10–100. Notes: also, Irish paintings & sculpture. [Updated]

LISBURN

JIRI Books, 11 Mill Road, Lisburn, BT27 5TT. Prop: Jim & Rita Swindall. Tel: (028) 9082-6443. Fax: (028) 9082-6443. Web: www.abebooks.com/home/WJS/. E-mail: jiri.books@dnet.co.uk. Est: 1978. Private premises. Postal only. Appointment necessary. Stock: medium. Spec: Antiquarian; Irish Interest; Literature; Poetry; Travel - General. CC: MC; V. Mem: Organises Annual Belfast Book Fair. Next fair 11th November 2006. [Updated]

CO. ARMAGH

ARMAGH

Craobh Rua Books, 12 Woodford Gardens, Armagh, BT60 2AZ. Prop: James Vallely. Tel: (028) 3752-6938. E-mail: craobh@btinternet.com. Est: 1990. Private premises. Internet and postal. Appointment necessary. Stock: medium. Spec: Antiquarian; First Editions; History - National; Irish Interest; Literature; Scottish Interest; Topography - General; Travel - General. PR: £1–400. CC: MC; V. Cata: monthly. Corresp: French. Mem: PBFA. Notes: also, a booksearch service. [Updated]

CO. DERRY

LONDERRY

George Harris, 163 Legavallon Road, Dungiven, Londerry, BT47 4QN. Prop: George Harris. Tel: (02877) 740012. Est: 1976. Private premises. Appointment necessary. Stock: medium. Spec: Aeronautics; Arms & Armour; Aviation; Irish Interest; Military; Military History; Naval; War - General. PR: £5–500. Corresp: French. Mem: PBFA. Notes: Attends PBFA fairs. [Updated]

Foyle Books, ■ 12 Magazine Street, Londonderry, BT48 6HH. Prop: Ken Thatcher & Art Byrne. Tel: (028) 7137-2530. E-mail: foylebookshopni@btconnect.com. Est: 1984. Shop open: **M:** 11:00–17:00; **T:** 11:00–17:00; **W:** 11:00–17:00; **Th:** 11:00–17:00; **F:** 11:00–17:00; **S:** 10:00–17:00. Stock: very large. Spec: Academic/Scholarly; Countries - Ireland; Foreign Texts; History - National; Irish Interest; Theology. PR: £1–200. Corresp: French. Gaelic. Notes: also, a booksearch service. [Updated]

CO. DOWN

BALLYGOWAN

Saintfield Antiques & Fine Boo, Vestry Hall, 49 Vestry Road, Ballygowan, BT23 6HQ. (*) Prop: Joseph Leckey. Tel: (028) 97528428. Fax: (028) 97528428. Web: www.antiquesireland.com. E-mail: home@antiquesireland.com. Est: 1988. Private premises. Internet and postal. Appointment necessary. Stock: medium. Spec: Fine & Rare; Irish Interest; Literature; Travel - General. PR: £1–500. [Updated]

BALLYNAHINCH

Davidson Books, 34 Broomhill Road, Ballynahinch, BT24 8QD. Prop: Arthur Davidson. Tel: (028) 9756-2502. Fax: (028) 9756-2502. Est: 1958. Private premises. Appointment necessary. Stock: medium. Spec: History - National; Irish Interest; Literature; Topography - Local; Ephemera; Prints and Maps. [Updated]

BANGOR

Books Ulster, 12 Bayview Road, Bangor, BT19 6AL. Prop: D.A. Rowlinson. Tel: (028) 914-70310. Web: www.booksulster.com. E-mail: orders@booksulster.com. Est: 1995. Private premises. Postal only. Stock: large. Spec: Irish Interest. PR: £1–500. CC: JCB; MC; V. [Updated]

DONAGHADEE

Prospect House Books, Prospect House, 4 MIllisle Road, Donaghadee, BT21 0HY. Web: www.antiquarianbooksellers.co.uk. E-mail: rarebooks.phb@btopenworld.com. Private premises. Internet and postal. Appointment necessary. Spec: Africana; Agriculture; Animals and Birds; Archaeology; Architecture; Art; Asian Studies; Banking & Insurance. CC: MC; V. Cata: occasionally on Irish, travel, natural history, medicine, philoso. [Updated]

DOWNPATRICK

Bookline, 35 Farranfad Road, Downpatrick, BT30 8NH. Prop: Lady Faulkner. Tel: (028) 4481-1712. Web: www.abebooks.com/home/bookline. E-mail: BooklineUK@aol.com. Est: 1988. Spec: Animals and Birds; Cats; Children's; Dogs; History - Irish; Illustrated; Private Press; Sport - Field Sports. PR: £5–500. Notes: also, a booksearch service. [Updated]

REPUBLIC OF IRELAND

CO. CAVAN

COOTEHILL

Sillan Books, Richelieu, Drumgreen, Cootehill. Prop: Patricia H. Smyth. Tel: 0044 49 5552343. Fax: 00444 49 5552343. Web: www.abebooks.com. E-mail: greenaway@eircom.net. Est: 1990. Mail Order Only. Postal only. Telephone first. PR: Euro 5–350. CC: MC; V. Cata: on Irish/Childrens/Religion/ History/Biography/General. [Updated]

CO. CLARE

ENNIS

Orchid Book Distributors, Unit 2, Fitzpatrick Centre, Tulla Road, Ennis. Tel: 00 353 65 6842 862. Fax: 00 353 65 6842 862. Web: www.orchidbooks.org. E-mail: info@orchidbooks.org. Est: 2002. Shop and/or showroom; Internet and postal. Open: **T:** 10.00–18.00; **W:** 10.00–18.00; **Th:** 10.00–18.00; **F:** 10.00–18.00; **S:** 10.00–18.00; Closed for lunch: 13:00–14:00. Spec: Acupuncture; American Indians; Art - Theory; Eastern Philosophy; Esoteric; Health; Herbalism; Homeopathy. PR: Euro 5–350. CC: PayPal. Corresp: Dutch, French, German. VAT No: IE 5333275R. [Updated]

CO. CORK

BALLINLOUGH

Royal Carbery Books Ltd., Lissadell, 36 Beechwood Park, Ballinlough. Prop: G. & M. Feehan. Tel: (021) 4294191. Fax: (021) 4294191. Est: 1976. Private premises. Appointment necessary. Stock: medium. Spec: Folklore; Guide Books; History - General; History - Local; Irish Interest; Literary Travel; Military; Music - Folk & Irish Folk. PR: Euro 3 upwards. [Updated]

BALLYDEHOB

Barbara and Jack O'Connell (t/a Schull Books), The Bookshop, Ballydehob, Ballydehob. Prop: Barbara & Jack O'Connell. Tel: (+ 353) [0]28 37317. Fax: (+ 353) [0]28 37317. Web: www.schullbooks.com. E-mail: schullbooks@eircom.net. Est: 1981. Office and/or bookroom. Telephone first. Open: **M:** 10:00–19:00; **T:** 10:00–19:00; **W:** 10:00–19:00; **Th:** 10:00–19:00; **F:** 10:00–19:00; **S:** 10:00–19:00. Stock: medium. Spec: Irish Interest; Military History; Booksearch. PR: Euro 10–500. CC: MC; V. Corresp: French, German, Irish. Notes: Summer shop, Ballydehob village, June - Sept. [Updated]

BANTRY

Karen Millward, Coorycommane, Coomhola, Bantry. Prop: Karen Millward. Tel: 00353-27-53898. Web: www.ukbookworld.com/members/irishmaid. E-mail: karenmillward@eircom.net. Est: 2001. Private premises. Internet and postal. Telephone first. Open: **M:** 09:00–17:30; **T:** 09:00–17:30; **W:** 09:00–17:30; **Th:** 09:00–17:30; **F:** 09:00–17:30; **S:** 09:00–17:30; **Su:** 09:00–17:30; Closed for lunch: 13:00–14:00. Spec: Authors:- Frost, Robert; Joyce, James; Russell, W; Thomas, Edward; Wilde, Oscar; Biography; Countries - Ireland; General Stock. PR: Euro 5–500. CC: MC; V; Sterling or Euro Cheques. Notes: Irish Books A Speciality. [Updated]

Michael J Carroll, Sunville House, Wolfe Tone Square, Bantry. Prop: Michael J Carroll. Tel: +353 (0) 27 50064. Fax: + 353 (0) 27 52042. Web: www.www.abe.com. E-mail: bantrydesigns@iol.ie. Private premises. Internet and postal. Appointment necessary. Spec: Celtica; Countries - Ireland; Ecclesiastical History & Architecture; Folklore; History - Local; Maritime/Nautical; Medieval. PR: Euro 10–300. Notes: specialising in Irish History [Updated]

DUNMANWAY

Darkwood Books, Darkwood, Dunmanway. Prop: Annette Sheehan. Tel: (023) 55470. Fax: (023) 55224. Web: www.darkwoodbooks.com. E-mail: darkwood@indigo.ie. Est: 2000. Private premises. Postal only. Stock: medium. Spec: Architecture; Art; Art History; Art Reference; Artists; Biography; Countries - Ireland; History - General. PR: £1–500. CC: MC; V. [Updated]

ROSSCARBERY

C.P. Hyland, 4 Closheen Lane, Rosscarbery. Prop: Cal & Joan Hyland. Tel: (023) 48063. Fax: (023) 48658. Web: www.cphyland.com. E-mail: calbux@iol.ie. Est: 1966. Private premises. Internet and postal. Telephone first. Open: **M:** 10:00–17:30; **T:** 10:00–17:30; **W:** 10:00–17:30; **Th:** 10:00–17:30; **F:** 10:00–17:30; **S:** 10:00–17:30; **Su:** 12:00–17:30. Stock: large. Spec: Countries - Ireland; Irish Interest; Languages - National. PR: £1–10,000. CC: MC; V. Corresp: Gaelic. [Updated]

YOUGHAL

Alan Prim, ■ 6 South Main St., Youghal. Prop: Alan Prim. Tel: (0035) 324 92781. E-mail: waprim@hotmail.com. Est: 1998. Shop open: **M:** 10:00–18:00; **T:** 10:00–18:00; **W:** 10:00–18:00; **Th:** 10:00–18:00; **F:** 10:00–18:00; **S:** 10:00–18:00; **Su:** 14:00–17:30; Closed for lunch: 13:30–14:00. Stock: medium. PR: £3–100. CC: AE; MC; V. Corresp: French, Spanish. [Updated]]

CO. DONEGAL

CARNDONAGH

The Bookshop, ■ Court Place, Carndonagh. Prop: Michael Herron. Tel: (07493) 74389. Est: 1989. Shop open: **M:** 14:00–18:00; **T:** 14:00–18:00; **Th:** 14:00–18:00; **F:** 14:00–18:00; **S:** 14:00–18:00; **Su:** 14:00–18:00. Stock: very large. Spec: Antiquarian; First Editions; History - Local; Irish Interest; Medicine; Philosophy; Religion - Christian; Science - General. PR: £1–100. Notes: also, half price sales in August, December and Easter. [Updated]

CO. DUBLIN

BLACKROCK

Carraig Books Ltd., ■ 73 Main Street, Blackrock. Prop: Sean L. Day. Tel: (01) 2882575. Fax: (01) 2834209. E-mail: carraigb@indigo.ie. Est: 1968. Shop open: **M:** 09:30–17:00; **T:** 09:30–17:00; **W:** 09:30–17:00; **Th:** 09:30–17:00; **F:** 09:30–17:00; **S:** 09:30–17:00; Closed for lunch: 13:00–14:00. Spec: Irish Interest; Religion - Catholic. PR: £2–100. CC: AE; MC; V. Cata: monthly or about 10 a year on specialities. Notes: also, back-numbers of Irish journals. [Updated]

Samovar Books, 63 Ardagh Park, Blackrock. Prop: Louis Hemmings. Tel: 00-353-1-2104990. Fax: 0000. Web: www.samovarbooks.com. E-mail: louis@samovarbooks.com. Est: 1993. Private premises. Internet Only. Open: **M:** 09:00–17:30; **T:** 09:00–17:30; **W:** 09:00–17:30; **Th:** 09:00–17:30; **F:** 09:00–17:30; **S:** 09:00–17:30; **Su:** 09:00–17:30; Closed for lunch: 13:00–14:00. Spec: Africana; Agriculture; Archaeology; Architecture; Autobiography; Biblical Studies; Biography; British Books. PR: £10–50. CC: MC; V. Cata: online/Internet – theology. topography, politics, history, Irish. Corresp: none. Mem: Librarians Christian Fellowship. Notes: Ireland's only online used theology book dealer. [Updated]

CLONTARF

Read Ireland, 392 Clontarf Road, Clontarf. Prop: Gregory Carr. Tel: 353 18532063. Fax: 353 18532063. Web: www.readireland.ie. E-mail: gregcarr@readireland.ie. Est: 1995. Private premises. Internet Only. Appointment necessary. Open: **M:** 09:00–17:30; **T:** 09:00–17:30; **W:** 09:00–17:30; **Th:** 09:00–17:30; **F:** 09:00–17:30; **S:** 09:00–17:30; **Su:** 09:00–17:30; Closed for lunch: 13:00–14:00. Spec: Authors:- Beckett, S.; Heaney, Seamus; Yeats, W.B.; Countries - Ireland; History - Irish; Irish Interest. PR: Euro 5–100. CC: MC; V. Cata: weekly on Irish Interest only. Notes: Ireland's Irish Interest Specialist Internet Booksellers. VAT No: IE 5093937G. [Updated]

DUBLIN

Cathach Books Ltd, ■ Cathach Books Ltd, 10 Duke Street, Dublin, 2. Prop: David Cunningham. Tel: +353 16718676. Fax: +353 1675120. Web: www.rarebooks.ie. E-mail: info@rarebooks.ie. Est: 1988. Shop open: **M:** 09:30–17:45; **T:** 09:30–17:45; **W:** 09:30–17:45; **Th:** 09:30–17:45; **F:** 09:30–17:45; **S:** 09:30–17:45. PR: Euro 10–20,000. CC: AE; JCB; V; Laser. Cata: occasionally on Literature, History (mostly Irish interest). Mem: ABA; BA; ILAB. Notes: together with our general stock, we offer an excellent selection of rare and first edition books by Oscar Wilde, James Joyce and William Butler Yeats. In addition, we stock a wide variety of Books on Irish History. [Updated]

De Burca Rare Books, 'Cloonagashel', 27 Priory Drive, Blackrock, Dublin. Prop: Eamonn & Vivien de Burca. Tel: (01) 288-2159. Fax: (01) 283-4080. Web: www.deburcararebooks.com. E-mail: deburca@indigo.ie. Est: 1979. Private premises. Internet and postal. Telephone first. Stock: large. Spec: Bindings; Countries - Ireland; Culture - National; Genealogy; History - National; Incunabula; Irish Interest; Literature. PR: £5–30,000. CC: JCB; MC. Corresp: French, German, Italian. Mem: ABA; PBFA; ILAB. Notes: also, manuscripts of Irish interest, a worldwide mail order service & publishers of fine historical books. VAT No: IE 16193333M. [Updated]

James Fenning, Antiquarian Books, 12 Glenview, Rochestown Avenue, Dun Laoghaire, Dublin. Prop: Jim & Chris Fenning. Tel: (01) 2857855. Fax: (01) 2857919. E-mail: fenning@indigo.ie. Est: 1969. Private premises. Internet and postal. Appointment necessary. Open: **M:** 08:00–16:00; **T:** 08:00–16:00; **W:** 08:00–16:00; **F:** 08:00–17:00. Stock: small. Spec: Antiquarian. PR: £20–15,000. CC: MC; V. Mem: ABA. VAT No: IE 9T568850. [Updated]

Glenbower Books, 46 Howth Road, Clontarf, Dublin, Dublin 3. Prop: Martin Walsh. Tel: (01) 833-5305. Web: www.abebooks.com/home/GLENBOWERBOOKS. E-mail: oldbook@eircom.net. Private premises. Postal only. Stock: medium. Spec: Academic/Scholarly; Antiquarian. PR: £3–340. CC: MC; V. [Updated]

Obscurebooks, 17 St. Peters Crescent, Walkinstown, Dublin. Prop: Tom Murray. Tel: +353-1-4567830. Web: www.obscurebooks.co.uk. E-mail: obscurebooks@yahoo.co.uk. Est: 2005. Mail Order Only. Internet Only. Appointment necessary. Open: **M:** 09:00–17:30; **T:** 09:00–17:30; **W:** 09:00–17:30; **Th:** 09:00–17:30; **F:** 09:00–17:30; **S:** 09:00–17:30; **Su:** 09:00–17:30; Closed for lunch: 13:00–14:00. PR: Euro 5–100. CC: V. [Updated]

Stokes Books, ■ 19 Market Arcade, South Great George's Street, Dublin 2. Prop: Stephen Stokes. Tel: (01) 671-3584. Fax: (01) 671-3181. Web: www.usedbooksirleand.ie. E-mail: stokesbooks@eircom.net. Est: 1982. Shop open: **M:** 11:00–18:00; **T:** 11:00–18:00; **W:** 11:00–18:00; **Th:** 11:00–18:00; **F:** 11:00–18:00; **S:** 11:00–18:00. Spec: Culture - National; Irish Interest; Languages - Foreign; Literature; Philosophy; Theology. PR: Euro 20–1,000. CC: AE; MC; V. Cata: bi-annually. Corresp: German. [Updated]

Taney Books, ■ Rear No. 7, Main St. Dundrum, Dublin. Prop: Morrough Lacy. Tel: 2157880. E-mail: maplacy@eircom.net. Est: 1982. Shop. Telephone first. Open: **M:** 11:00–17:30; **T:** 11:00–17:30; **W:** 11:00–17:30; **Th:** 11:00–17:30; **F:** 11:00–17:30; **S:** 11:00–17:30. Spec: Antiquarian; Cartography; Countries - Ireland; Prints and Maps. PR: US$ 1–150. Notes: Attends Temple Bar Book Market, Temple Bar Square Dublin 2. Phone 186 1902892 11:00-18:00 Saturday and Sunday. [Updated]

Greene's Bookshop Ltd, ■ 16 Clare St., Dublin 2, Tel: 00-353-1-6762554. Fax: 00-353-1-6789091. Web: www.greenesbookshop.com. E-mail: info@greenesbookshop.com. Est: 1843. Shop. Internet and postal. Open: **M:** 09:00–17:30; **T:** 09:00–17:30; **W:** 09:00–17:30; **Th:** 09:09–17:30; **F:** 09:00–17:30; **S:** 09:00–17:00. Stock: medium. Spec: Countries - Ireland; Irish Interest. CC: AE; D; MC; V. Mem: PBFA. VAT No: IE 48100860. [Updated]

DUN LAOGHAIRE

Naughton Booksellers, ■ 8 Marine Terrace, Dun Laoghaire. Prop: Susan Naughton. Tel: +353 1 280 4392. Web: www.naughtonsbooks.com. E-mail: sales@naughtonsbooks.com. Est: 1976. Shop open: **M:** 10:00–17:00; **T:** 10:00–17:00; **W:** 10:00–17:00; **Th:** 10:00–17:00; **F:** 10:00–17:00; **S:** 10:00–17:00. Spec: Academic/Scholarly; Anthologies; Antiquarian; Art History; Arts, The; Author - General; Book Arts; Books about Books. PR: Euro 5–500. CC: AE; MC; V. VAT No: IE 8495489V. [Updated]

STILLORGAN

Dublin Bookbrowsers, 12 Weirview Drive, Stillorgan. Prop: Dave Downes. Tel: (00353) 872636347. Fax: (00353) 1210300. Web: www.abebooks.com. E-mail: dave@dubbookbrowsers.com. Est: 1996. Private premises. Appointment necessary. Stock: large. Spec: Irish Interest. PR: £1–20,000. CC: MC; V. Mem: PBFA. [Updated]

CO. GALWAY

GALWAY

Charlie Byrne's Bookshop, ■ Middle Street, Galway. Prop: Charlie Byrne. Tel: (0035) 391 561766. Fax: (0035) 391 561766. Web: www.charliebyrne.com. E-mail: info@charliebyrne.com. Shop. Internet and postal. Open: **M:** 09:00–18:00; **T:** 09:00–18:00; **W:** 09:00–18:00; **Th:** 09:00–18:00; **F:** 09:00–20:00; **S:** 09:00–18:00; **Su:** 12:00–18:00. PR: Euro 1–300. CC: AE; MC; V. [Updated]

Kenny's Book Export Co., Kilkerrin Park, Liosban, Tuam Road, Galway. Tel: (091) 709350. Fax: (091) 709351. E-mail: conor@kennys.ie. Est: 1999. Office and/or bookroom. Open: **M:** 09:00–17:00; **T:** 09:00–17:00; **W:** 09:00–17:00; **Th:** 09:00–17:00; **F:** 09:00–17:00. Stock: very large. PR: Euro 2–16,000. CC: AE; D; JCB; MC; V. Mem: ABA; BA. Notes: Kenny's Bookshop & Art Gallery, Galway (q.v). VAT No: IE 6328356V. [Updated]

Kennys Bookshops and Art Galleries Limited, ■ Art Galleries Ltd, High Street, Galway. Managing Director: Mr. Conor Kenny. Tel: (091) 562739 and 534760. Fax: (091) 568544. Web: www.kennys.ie. E-mail: conor@kennys.ie. Est: 1940. Shop open: **M:** 09:00–18:00; **T:** 09:00–18:00; **W:** 09:00–18:00; **Th:** 09:00–18:00; **F:** 09:00–18:00; **S:** 09:00–18:00. Stock: very large. Spec: Americana; Anthropology; Archaeology; Architecture; Art Reference; Author - 20th Century; Authors - Women; Bindings. PR: Euro 1–5,000. CC: AE; D; E; JCB; MC; V; Laser. Cata: weekly. Corresp: French, Italian. Mem: ABA; BA; ILAB. Notes: additional web site: www.kennyscollections.com. Kennys Export Book Co., Galway (q.v) Also, a booksearch service, in-house fine bindings & large comtemporary Irish Art Gallery VAT No: IE 2238521A. [Updated]

MOYARD

The House of Figgis Ltd, Ross House, Moyard. Prop: Neville Figgis. Tel: (095) 41092. Fax: (095) 41261. E-mail: figgisbooks@eircom.net. Private premises. Appointment necessary. Stock: small. Spec: Early Imprints; Irish Interest; Literature; Modern First Editions. CC: MC; V. VAT No: 9 N 543 415. [Updated]

CO. LAOIS

VICARSTOWN

Courtwood Books, Vicarstown, Stradbally, Vicarstown. Prop: PJ Tynan. Tel: (0502) 26384. E-mail: lbloom@eircom.net. Est: 1984. Private premises. Internet and postal. Appointment necessary. Stock: medium. Spec: Academic/Scholarly; Advertising; Authors:- Beckett, S.; Joyce, James; Wilde, Oscar; Engineering; History - Local; Irish Interest. PR: £1–500. CC: MC; V. Notes: also, organiser of annual Kilkenny book fair (August). [Updated]

CO. LEITRIM

CARRICK–ON–SHANNON

Trinity Rare Books, ■ Bridge Street, Carrick–on–Shannon. Prop: Nick Kaszuk. Tel: 00353 71 9622144. Web: www.trinityrarebooks.com. E-mail: nickk@iol.ie. Est: 1999. Shop open: **M:** 09:30–18:00; **T:** 09:30–18:00; **W:** 09:30–18:00; **Th:** 09:30–18:00; **F:** 09:30–18:00; **S:** 09:30–18:00. Stock: large. Spec: Antiquarian; Art; Arts, The; Autobiography; Avant-Garde; Beat Writers; Bindings; Biography. PR: £3–150. Corresp: French, German. [Updated]

CO. LIMERICK

ADARE

George Stacpoole, ■ Main Street, Adare. Prop: George Stacpoole. Tel: (061) 396409. Fax: (061) 396733. Web: www.georgestacpooleantiques.com. E-mail: stacpoole@iol.ie. Shop open: **M:** 10:00–17:30; **T:** 10:00–17:30; **W:** 10:00–17:30; **Th:** 10:00–17:30; **F:** 10:00–17:30; **S:** 10:00–17:30. Spec: History - Local; Sport - Field Sports; Booksearch; Prints and Maps. PR: £5–2,000. CC: AE; E; JCB; MC; V. Mem: IADA. [Updated]

LIMERICK

The Celtic Bookshop, ■ 2 Rutland Street, Limerick. Prop: Caroline O'Brien. Tel: (061) 401155. E-mail: celticbk@iol.ie. Est: 1982. Shop. Internet and postal. Telephone first. Open: **M:** 10:00–17:00; **T:** 10:00–17:00; **W:** 10:00–17:00; **Th:** 10:00–17:00; **F:** 10:00–17:00; **S:** 10:00–17:00. Stock: medium. Spec: Academic/Scholarly; Antiquarian; Countries - Ireland; Fiction - General; History - General. PR: £3–1,000. CC: MC; V. Corresp: Irish. VAT No: GB 322566i. [Updated]

O'Brien Books & Photo Gallery, ■ 26 High Street, Limerick. Prop: John O'Brien. Tel: (061) 412833. E-mail: ob.books@oceanfree.net. Est: 1988. Shop open: **T:** 10:30–17:30; **W:** 10:30–00:17; **Th:** 10:30–17:30; **F:** 10:30–17:30; **S:** 10:00–17:30; Closed for lunch: 13:00–13:30. Stock: medium. Spec: Art; Art History; Biography; Cinema/Film; Fiction - General; Folio Society, The; History - General; Irish Interest. PR: £1–400. CC: D; E; JCB; MC; V. VAT No: GB 192 620 9a. [Updated]

CO. TIPPERARY

ROSCREA

Roscrea Bookshop, ■ Rosemary Square, Roscrea, N/A. Tel: 00-353-505-22894. Fax: 00-353-505-22895. Web: www.roscreabookshop.com. E-mail: info@roscreabookshop.com. Est: 1997. Shop open: **M:** 07:30–19:00; **T:** 07:30–19:00; **W:** 07:30–00:20; **Th:** 07:30–19:00; **F:** 07:30–19:00; **S:** 07:30–20:00; **Su:** 07:30–14:00. Stock: large. Spec: Academic/Scholarly; Africana; Agriculture; American Indians; Bibles; Children's; Children's - Illustrated; Christmas. PR: £3–50. CC: AE; D; MC; V. Corresp: French. Mem: BA. VAT No: GB 327613 4P. [Updated]

CO. WEXFORD

BUNCLODY

Fuchsia Books, Ballypreacus, Bunclody. Prop:. Mary Mackey. Tel: 054 75577. E-mail: maryjmackey@ercom.net. Private premises. Internet and postal. Contactable. Stock: small. Spec: History - National; Irish Interest; Booksearch; Prints and Maps. PR: £10–500. [Updated]

NEW ROSS

Britons Catholic Library, Riverview, Arthurstown, New Ross. Prop: Mr. N.M. Gwynne. Tel: (51) 389111. E-mail: riverview@esatclear.ie. Est: 1976. Private premises. Appointment necessary. Stock: small. Spec: Religion - Catholic. PR: £2–100. Notes: Stock majors on traditional Catholic titles. [Updated]

SCOTLAND

Including the Unitary Authorities of Aberdeenshire, Angus, Argyll & Bute, Borders, Clackmannan, Dumfries & Galloway, Dumbarton & Clydebank, Dundee, East Ayrshire, East Dunbartonshire, East Lothian, East Renfrewshire, Edinburgh, Falkirk, Fife, Glasgow, Highland, Inverclyde, Mid Lothian, Moray, North Ayrshire, North Lanarkshire, Orkney Islands, Perthshire & Kinross, Renfrewshire, Shetland Islands, South Ayrshire, South Lanarkshire, Stirling, Western Isles and West Lothian

BORDERS

INNERLEITHEN

Spike Hughes Rare Books, Willow Bank, Damside, Innerleithen, EH44 6HR. Tel: (01896) 830019. Fax: (01896) 831499. E-mail: spike@buik.demon.co.uk. Est: 1981. Private premises. Internet and postal. Appointment necessary. Stock: small. Spec: Countries - Scotland; Fine & Rare; History - General; History - Local; History - National; Literature; Philosophy; Social History. PR: £10–5,000. CC: MC; V. Mem: ABA. VAT No: GB 345 4470 55. [Updated]

JEDBURGH

G. & R. Stone, Hap House, 5 Allerton Court, Jedburgh, TD8 6RT. Prop: Gillian & Ralph Stone. Tel: (01835) 864147. Fax: (01835) 864147. Est: 1972. Private premises. Appointment necessary. Open: Spec: Agriculture; Antiquarian; Natural History; Poetry; Women. PR: £5–100. CC: MC; V. Cata: occasionally. Mem: PBFA. [Updated]

KELSO

Border Books, ■ The Bookshop, 47–51 Horsemarket, Kelso, TD5 7AA. Prop: Ronald C. Hodges. Tel: (01573) 225861. E-mail: ron.borderbooks@virgin.net. Est: 1981. Shop open: **M:** 10:30–16:00; **T:** 10:30–16:00; **W:** 10:30–16:00; **Th:** 10:30–16:00; **F:** 10:30–16:00; **S:** 10:30–16:00. Spec: Countries - Scotland; History - Local; Journals; Military; Sport - Field Sports; Topography - Local; Transport; Travel - General. PR: £1–500. Notes: closed Wednesdays in winter. [Updated]

MELROSE

Stroma Books, Charlesfield, St. Boswells, Melrose, TD6 0HH. Tel: (01835) 824169. Web: www.stromabooks.co.uk. E-mail: kenny@stromabooks.fsnet.co.uk. Est: 2000. Private premises. Internet and postal. Stock: medium. Spec: Academic/Scholarly; Art; Biography; Children's; Children's - Illustrated; Cinema/Film; Countries - Scotland; Entertainment - General. PR: £1–500. CC: JCB; MC; V; M, SW, SO. [Updated]

SELKIRK

Wheen O'Books, Glyndwr, Mill St., Selkirk, TD7 5AE. Prop: Margaret Tierney. Tel: (01750) 21009. Web: www.wheenobooks.com. E-mail: megtie@aol.com. Est: 1997. Private premises. Internet Only. Telephone first. Stock: large. PR: £2–1,500. CC: PayPal. Notes: general stock. [Updated]

Looking for a dealer in PRINTS or MAPS?

– go to Sheppard's on-line directories at:

www.sheppardsworld.co.uk

CENTRAL

BRIDGE OF ALLAN

Bridge of Allan Books, ■ 2 Henderson Street, Bridge of Allan, FK9 4HT. Prop: Dr Andrew Jennings. Tel: (01786) 834483. Web: www.bridgeofallanbooks.com. E-mail: books@bridgeofallanbooks.com. Est: 1985. Shop. Internet and postal. Open: **M:** 10:00–17:00; **T:** 10:00–17:00; **W:** 10:00–17:00; **Th:** 10:00–17:00; **F:** 10:00–17:00; **S:** 10:00–17:00. Stock: large. Spec: Academic/Scholarly; Alpinism/ Mountaineering; Anthroposophy; Antiquarian; Countries - Scotland; History - Local; Literature; Topography - Local. PR: £1–700. CC: AE; D; E; MC; V; Solo, Maestro. Notes: Scottish history and Gaelic culture research, free booksearch service. [Updated]

DUNBLANE

Sheriffmuir Books, Glentye, Sheriffmuir, by Dunblane, FK15 OLN. Tel: 01786 822269. E-mail: sheriffmuirbooks@hotmail.com. Private premises. Postal only. Open in Summer: **M:** 00.00–17:30; **T:** 00.00–17:30; **W:** 00.00–17:30; **Th:** 00.00–17:30; **F:** 09:00–17:30; **S:** 09:00–17:30; **Su:** 09:00–17:30. [Updated]

CALLANDER

HP Bookfinders, Mosslaird, Brig O'Turk, Callander, FK17 8HT. Tel: (01877) 376377. Fax: (01877) 376377. Web: www.hp-bookfinders.co.uk. E-mail: martin@hp-bookfinders.co.uk. Est: 1986. Private premises. Internet and postal. Contactable. Stock: very small. Spec: Booksearch. CC: E; JCB; MC; V; SW. [Updated]

Kings Bookshop Callander, ■ 91–93 Main Street, Callander, Trossachs, FK17 8BQ. Prop: Ian William King & Sally Evans. Tel: (01877) 339 449. E-mail: sally.king@btinternet.com. Est: 1987. Shop open: Spec: Bindings; Classical Studies; Scottish Interest. PR: £1–1,000. Notes: shop open Monday through to Sunday. Closed Wednesday. NB When sending e-mails - add 'bookshop' to subject field. [Updated]

LARBERT

Dave Simpson, Lorne Villa, 161 Main Street, Larbert, FK5 4AL. Tel: (01324) 558628. Fax: (01324) 558628. Web: www.dave.simpson3@virgin.net. E-mail: dave.simpson3@virgin.net. Est: 2000. Private premises. Internet and postal. Contactable. Stock: small. Spec: Antiquarian; Children's; Literature; Modern First Editions; Signed Editions. PR: £10–300. CC: E; JCB; MC; V; SW. [Updated]

DUMFRIES & GALLOWAY

CASTLE DOUGLAS

Benny Gillies Books Ltd, ■ 33 Victoria Street, Kirkpatrick Durham, Castle Douglas, DG7 3HQ. Prop: Benny Gillies. Tel: 01556 650412. Web: www.www.bennygillies.co.uk. E-mail: benny@ bennygillies.co.uk. Est: 1979. Shop. Telephone first. Open: **M:** 10:00–17:00; **T:** 10:00–17:00; **W:** 10:00–17:00; **Th:** 10:00–17:00; **F:** 10:00–17:00; **S:** 10:00–17:00. Spec: Countries - Scotland; County - Local; Scottish Interest; Topography - Local; Prints and Maps. CC: AE; MC; V. Cata: occasionally on Scotland. Corresp: French. Mem: PBFA. Notes: Specialist dealer in Scottish material only (Books maps and prints). Kirkpatrick Durham is situated 6 miles from Castle Douglas. Please telephone before making a special journey especially in winter. VAT No: GB 499 0638 93. [Updated]

Available from Richard Joseph Publishers Ltd

MINIATURE BOOKS
by Louis W. Bondy

(A5 H/b)   221pp £24.00

DUMFRIES

Anwoth Books, ■ Mill on the Fleet, Gatehouse of Fleet, Dumfries, DG7 2HS. Prop: Anwoth Books Ltd. Tel: (01557) 814774. Est: 1991. Shop open: **M:** 10:30–17:00; **T:** 10:30–17:00; **W:** 10:30–17:00; **Th:** 10:30–17:00; **F:** 10:30–17:00; **S:** 10:30–17:00; **Su:** 10:30–17:00. Stock: large. Spec: Art; Children's; Ornithology; Poetry; Scottish Interest. PR: £1–50. CC: JCB; MC; V. Notes: winter opening: November to March open Friday to Sunday only. [Updated]

KIRKCUDBRIGHT

Solway Books, ■ 14 St. Cuthbert's Street, Kirkcudbright, DG6 4DU. Prop: Mrs Beverley Chadband. Tel: 01557 330635. E-mail: beverley.chadband@btinternet.com. Est: 2003. Shop open: **M:** 09:00–17:00; **T:** 09:00–17:00; **W:** 09:00–17:00; **Th:** 09:00–17:00; **F:** 09:00–17:00; **S:** 10:00–17:00. Spec: Ephemera; Prints and Maps. PR: £1–300. CC: JCB; MC; V; Switch Mem: BA. [Updated]

Vailima Books, ■ 61 High Street, Kirkcudbright, DG6 4JZ. Prop: Elizabeth Kirby. Tel: (01557) 330583. E-mail: vailimabooks@supanet.com. Est: 1988. Shop open: **M:** 10:00–17:00; **T:** 10:00–17:00; **Th:** 10:00–17:00; **F:** 10:00–17:00; **S:** 10:00–17:00. Stock: small. Spec: Railways; Transport. PR: £1–20. [Updated]

MOFFAT

Moffat Book Exchange, ■ 5 Well Street, Moffat, DF10 9DP. Prop: Andy Armstrong. Tel: (01683) 220059. E-mail: dandrewarmstrong@aol.com. Est: 1998. Shop open: **M:** 10:00–16:30; **W:** 10:00–16:30; **Th:** 10:00–16:30; **F:** 10:00–16:30; **S:** 10:00–17:00; **Su:** 13:00–16:00; Closed for lunch: 13:00–14:00. Spec: Fiction - General. PR: £1–25. Notes: stock: stock includes large slection of paperback fiction. [Updated]

WIGTOWN

AA1 Books at Windy Hill, ■ Unit 3, Duncan Park, Wigtown, DG8 9JD. Prop: Marion Richmond. Tel: (01988) 402653. Web: www.bookavenue/hosted/AA1. E-mail: AA1books@supanet.com. Est: 2001. Shop open: **M:** 10:00–17:00; **T:** 10:00–17:00; **W:** 10:00–17:00; **Th:** 10:00–17:00; **F:** 10:00–17:00; **S:** 08:00–17:00; **Su:** 11:00–15:00. Stock: very large. Spec: Children's; Espionage; Fiction - Crime, Detective, Spy, Thrillers; Fiction - Fantasy, Horror; Fiction - Science Fiction; Fiction - Westerns; Ghosts; History - General. PR: £1–150. CC: AE; MC; V. Corresp: French, German. Notes: also, new books. In association with Ming Books. [Updated]

A.P. & R. Baker Limited, The Laigh House, Church Lane, Wigtown, DG8 9HT. Prop: Anthony P. & Rosemary Baker. Tel: (01988) 403348. Fax: (01988) 403443. Web: www.apandrbaker.co.uk. E-mail: rosemaryapandrb@yahoo.co.uk. Est: 1974. Private premises. Postal only. Telephone first. Open: Spec: Archaeology; History - General. PR: £2–500. CC: MC; V. [Updated]

Byre Books, ■ 24 South Main St., Wigtown, DG8 9EH. Prop: Laura Mustian, Shani Mustian and Chris Ballance. Tel: (01988) 402133. Web: www.byrebooks.co.uk. E-mail: info@byrebooks.co.uk. Est: 2000. Shop. Internet and postal. Open: **M:** 10:00–17:30; **T:** 10:00–17:30; **W:** 10:00–17.30; **Th:** 10:00–17:30; **F:** 10:00–17:30; **S:** 10:00–17:30; **Su:** 10:00–17:30. Stock: small. Spec: American Indians; Arthurian; Author - Shakespeare, William; Celtica; Children's; Cinema/Film; Countries - Scotland; Dance. PR: £3–100. CC: E; JCB; MC; V; Switch, Delta. Corresp: French, Spanish. Cata: occasionally. Mem: Wigtown Book Trades Ass. Notes: during the winter we are usually closed on a Wednesday, and our opening hours are 10:00-16:00. Please call before visiting for exact times during your stay VAT No: GB 789 1742 76. [Updated]

G. C. Books Ltd., Unit 10 Book Warehouse, Bladnoch Bridge Estate, Wigtown, DG8 9AB. Prop: Beverley and Keith Chadband. Tel: 01988 402 688. Fax: 01988 402 688. E-mail: sales@gcbooks.demon.co.uk. Est: 2005. Warehouse; Internet and postal. Open: **M:** 10.00–17.00; **T:** 10.00–17.00; **W:** 10.00–17.00; **Th:** 10.00–17.00; **F:** 10.00–17.00; **S:** 10.00–17.00. Spec: Academic/Scholarly; Africana; Aircraft; Antiquarian; Archaeology; Architecture; Atlases; Autobiography. CC: MC; V. Cata: occasionally as required. Mem: FSB. Notes: visitors, Trade Overseas Enquiries Welcome - Free Booksearch Service - International Shipping. [Updated]

M.E. McCarty, Bookseller, ■ 13 North Main St., Wigtown, DG8 9HL. Tel: (01988) 402062. E-mail: moi@orkneybooks.co.uk. Est: 2000. Shop open: **M:** 10:00–17:00; **T:** 10:00–17:00; **W:** 10:00–17:00; **Th:** 10:00–17:00; **F:** 10:00–17:00; **S:** 10:00–17:00; **Su:** 10:00–17:00. Spec: Literature; Maritime/Nautical; Travel - General. PR: £1–100. CC: AE; JCB; MC; V; Maestro, Solo. Corresp: French, German, Norwegian. Mem: PBFA. Notes: also at 54 Junction Road, Kirkwall (q.v.). [Updated]

Ming Books, Beechwood House, Acre Place, Wigtown, DG8 9DU. Prop: Mrs Marion Richmond. Tel: (01988) 402653. Fax: (0709) 221-8017. Web: www.mingbooks.supanet.commcom. E-mail: mingbooks@supanet.com. Est: 1982. Office and/or bookroom. Internet and postal. Appointment necessary. Open: **M:** 10:00–18:00; **T:** 10:00–18:00; **W:** 10:00–18:00; **Th:** 10:00–18:00; **F:** 10:00–18:00; **S:** 10:00–18:00; **Su:** 11:00–15:00; Closed for lunch: 12:00–13:00. Stock: very large. Spec: Crime (True); Espionage; Fiction - Crime, Detective, Spy, Thrillers; Fiction - Science Fiction; First Editions; History - General; Modern First Editions; Scottish Interest. PR: £4–1,000. CC: AE; MC; V; SW. Corresp: German and French. Mem: Wigtown Book Town. Also at: AA1 BOOKS AT WINDY HILL, Unit 3 Duncan Park, Wigtown. VAT No: GB 432 9993 15. [Updated]

Reading Lasses, ■ 17 South Main Street, Wigtown, DG8 9EH. Prop: Angela Everitt. Tel: 00 (44) 1988 403266. Web: www.reading-lasses.com. E-mail: books@reading-lasses.com. Est: 1997. Shop open: **M:** 10:00–17:00; **T:** 10:00–17:00; **W:** 10:00–17:00; **Th:** 10:00–17:00; **F:** 10:00–17:00; **S:** 10:00–17:00; **Su:** 12:00–17:00. Spec: Academic/Scholarly; Adult; African-American Studies; Africana; Alternative Medicine; Anthropology; Art; Asian Studies. CC: MC; V. Mem: PBFA. [Updated]

Transformer, ■ 26 Bladnoch, Wigtown, DG8 9AB. Prop: C.A. Weaver. Tel: 0044 (0) 1988-403455. Web: www.abebooks.com/home/TRANSFORMER/home.htm. E-mail: transformer@tesco.net. Est: 1998. Shop. Internet and postal. Open in Summer. Stock: very large. Spec: Academic/Scholarly; Children's; Culture - Foreign; Education & School; Espionage; Fiction - Crime, Detective, Spy, Thrillers; Fiction - Fantasy, Horror; Fiction - Science Fiction. PR: £1–400. Corresp: French. [Updated]

FIFE

ANSTRUTHER

Rising Tide Books, 51 John Street, Cellardyke, Anstruther, KY10 3BA. Prop: Stephen Checkland. Tel: (01333) 310948. Fax: (01333) 310948. E-mail: stevecheckland@risingtidebooks.com. Est: 1997. Private premises. Book Fairs Only. Appointment necessary. Stock: very small. Spec: Illustrated; Modern First Editions; Scottish Interest. PR: £5–500. Mem: PBFA. [Updated]

DUNFERMLINE

Larry Hutchison (Books), 27 Albany Street, Dunfermline, KY12 OQZ. Tel: (01383) 725566. Fax: (01383) 620394. Web: www.larryhutchisobooks.com. E-mail: larry@larryhutchisonbooks.com. Est: 1987. Private premises. Appointment necessary. Stock: medium. Spec: Antiquarian; Countries - Scotland; Fine & Rare; Folklore; Genealogy; History - General; Literature; Military. PR: £5–5,000. CC: AE; MC; V. Corresp: most major European. Mem: PBFA. Notes: also, a booksearch service. VAT No: GB 716 9500 30. [31/10/2004]

Gary Walker, Swallowdrum Cottage, Milesmark, Dunfermline, KY12 9BB. Prop: Gary Walker. Tel: (01383) 737977. Private premises. Stock: small. PR: £2–500. Mem: Open daily. [Updated]

KIRKCALDY

R. Campbell Hewson Books, 6 West Albert Road, Kirkcaldy, KY1 1DL. Tel: (01592) 262051. Est: 1996. Private premises. Appointment necessary. Open: Stock: small. Spec: Author - Burton, R.F.; Ethnography; Rural Life; Sport - Big Game Hunting; Travel - Africa; Voyages & Discovery. PR: £10–3,500. [Updated]

NEWPORT ON TAY

Gordon Bettridge, 4 Myrtle Terrace, Newport on Tay, DD6 8DN. Tel: (01382) 542377. Est: 1984. Private premises. Postal only. Spec: Advertising; Bibliography; Books about Books; Calligraphy; Illustrated; Journals; Papermaking; Printing. PR: £1–75. [Updated]

Mair Wilkes Books, 3 St. Mary's Lane, Newport on Tay, DD6 8AH. Tel: (01382) 542260. E-mail: mairwilkes.books@zoom.co.uk. Est: 1969. Storeroom. Open: **T:** 10:00–16:30; **W:** 10:00–16:30; **Th:** 10:10–16:30; **F:** 10:00–16:30; **S:** 10:00–17:00; Closed for lunch: 12:30–14:00. Spec: Academic/Scholarly; Bindings; Fine & Rare; History of Ideas; Medicine - History of; Modern First Editions; Neurology; Psychology/Psychiatry. PR: £2–1,000. CC: AE; MC; V; PaypPal. Cata: bi-annually on Scottish Interests. Mem: PBFA. Notes: Scottish Antiques Ctre, Abernyte, Inchture, Perthshire. VAT No: GB 397 9923 69. [Updated]

ST. ANDREWS

The Quarto Bookshop, ■ 8 Golf Place, St. Andrews, KY16 9JA. Prop: M. Squires. Tel: (01334) 474616. E-mail: quartobooks@btconnect.com. Est: 1969. Shop open: **M:** 10:00–17:30; **T:** 10:00–17:30; **W:** 10:00–17:30; **Th:** 10:00–17:30; **F:** 10:00–17:30; **S:** 10:00–17:30; **Su:** 12:00–17:00. Stock: medium. Spec: Countries - Scotland; History - Local; Sport - Golf; Topography - Local; Booksearch. PR: £1–500. CC: MC; V. Corresp: French, Spanish. Mem: BA. Notes: also, a booksearch service. [Updated]

GRAMPIAN

ABERDEEN

Clifford Milne Books, 6 Hill Crest Place, Aberdeen, AB2 7BP. Tel: (01224) 697654. Est: 1994. Private premises. Postal only. Spec: Art; Countries - Scotland; Modern First Editions; Sport - Golf. CC: PayPal. Mem: PBFA. Notes: selected titles from Elizabeth Ferguson, Aberdeen (q.v.). [Updated]

Elizabeth Ferguson, 34 Woodburn Avenue, Aberdeen, AB15 8JQ. Tel: (01224) 315949. Fax: (01224) 315949. E-mail: efergusonbooks@aol.com. Est: 2000. Postal only. Stock: small. Spec: Booksearch. PR: £5–500. Corresp: French, German. Notes: very small stock at Aberdeen Antique and Art Centre, Aberdeen (q.v.). [Updated]

Old Aberdeen Bookshop, ■ 140 Spital, Aberdeen, AB24 3TU. Tel: 01224 658355. E-mail: cscottpaul@btinternet.com. Est: 1996. Shop open: **M:** 10:00–17:30; **T:** 10:00–17:30; **W:** 10:00–17:30; **Th:** 10:00–17:30; **F:** 10:00–17:30; **S:** 11:00–17:00. Stock: medium. Spec: Esoteric; Literary Criticism; Literature; Military. PR: £1–20. CC: D; MC; V. [Updated]

Winram's Bookshop, ■ 32/36 Rosemount Place, Aberdeen, AB25 2XB. Prop: Mrs. Margaret Davidson. Tel: (01224) 630673. Fax: (01224) 631532. Est: 1977. Shop open: **M:** 10:00–17:30; **T:** 10:00–17:30; **W:** 10:00–13:00; **Th:** 10:00–17:30; **F:** 10:00–17:30; **S:** 10:00–17:30. Stock: medium. Spec: Scottish Interest. PR: £1–1,000. [Updated]

BALLATER

Deeside Books, ■ 22 Bridge Street, Ballater, AB35 5QP. Prop: Bryn Wayte. Tel: 01339 754080. Fax: 01339 754080. E-mail: deesidebk@aol.com. Est: 1998. Shop open: **M:** 10:00–17:00; **T:** 10:00–17:00; **W:** 10:00–17:00; **Th:** 10:00–17:00; **F:** 10:00–17:00; **S:** 10:00–17:00; **Su:** 12:00–17:00. Spec: CC: AE; JCB; MC; V. Mem: PBFA. VAT No: GB 716 9705 12. [Updated]

McEwan Fine Books, Glengarden, Ballater, AB35 5UB. Prop: Dr. Peter McEwan. Tel: (01339) 755429. Fax: (01339) 755995. E-mail: pjmm@easynet.co.uk. Est: 1968. Private premises. Postal only. Stock: medium. Spec: Countries - Antarctic, The; Countries - Polar; Heraldry; History - Family; Natural History; Ornithology; Plant Hunting; Sport - Angling/Fishing. PR: £5–5,000. CC: E; MC; V; LAPADA. Cata: quarterly. Notes: also at Rhod McEwan Golf Books (q.v.) and works of art. [Updated]

Rhod McEwan Golf, Glengarden, Ballater, AB35 5UB. Tel: (013397) 55429. Fax: (013397) 55995. Web: www.rhodmcewan.com. E-mail: teeoff@rhodmcewan.com. Est: 1985. Private premises. Appointment necessary. Stock: medium. Spec: Sport - Golf. PR: £3–5,000. CC: E; MC; V; PayPal, Debit. Cata: bi-annually. Corresp: German, Hungarian, Russian. Mem: ABA; ILAB. Notes: at same premises: McEwan Fine Books. (q.v.) Also, golf posters and paintings VAT No: GB 605 2115 89. [Updated]

BRIDGEND

Kevin S. Ogilvie Modern First, Tolquhon, Bridgend, Ellon, AB41 8LX. Tel: 07841 289308. E-mail: kevinsogilvie@boltblue.com. Est: 1991. Private premises. Postal only. Spec: Children's; Fiction - Crime, Detective, Spy, Thrillers; First Editions; Modern First Editions; Signed Editions. PR: £7–100. Cata: occasionally. [Updated]

DINNET

Jane Jones Books, ■ The Old Shop, Dinnet, Aboyne, AB34 5JY. Prop: Jane Jones. Tel: 013398 85662. Fax: 013398 85662. E-mail: jjbooks@tiscali.co.uk. Est: 2003. Shop open: **M:** 11.00–18.00; **T:** 11.00–18.00; **Th:** 11.00–18.00; **F:** 11.00–18.00; **S:** 10.30–18.00; **Su:** 11.30–17.30. Spec: Adventure; Agriculture; Animals and Birds; Antiquarian; Authors - National; Children's; Children's - Illustrated; Dogs. Cata: on General stock Corresp: French. Mem: PBFA. Notes: my stock is general with an emphasis on Natural History, Scottish, Illustrated and childrens. I do have a booksearch facility. Not all of my stock is on show at the shop. [Updated]

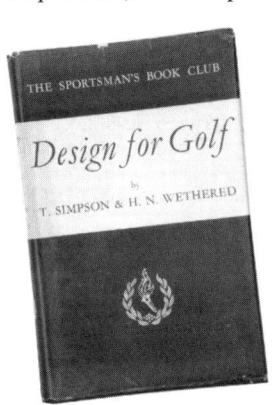

FOCHABERS

Alba Books, Maxwell Street, Fochabers, IV32 7DE. Prop: Mike Seton. Tel: (01343) 820575. Fax: (01343) 820780. Web: www.albabooks.com. E-mail: Albabooks@dial.pipex.com. Est: 1997. Warehouse; Internet and postal. Appointment necessary. Stock: very large. Spec: Alternative Medicine; Art; Biology; Countries - Scotland; Education & School; Gynaecology; Literature; Maritime/Nautical. PR: £2–200. CC: AE; E; MC; V; Switch. Corresp: French, German. Mem: IBooknet. VAT No: GB 751 3324 56. [Updated]

Marianne Simpson, ■ 61/63 High Street, Fochabers, IV32 7DU. Tel: (01343) 821192. Est: 1990. Shop open: **M:** 10:00–16:00; **T:** 10:00–16:00; **W:** 10:00–16:00; **Th:** 10:00–16:00; **F:** 10:00–16:00; **S:** 10:00–16:00; Closed for lunch: 13:00–14:00. Stock: small. PR: £1–100. Corresp: French. Notes: Winter opening: Oct to Easter - Tues, Thurs & Sat 10:00-16:00. Closed lunch. [Updated]

FORRES

The Moray Bookshop, ■ Logie Steading Visitor Centre, Dunphail, Forres, IV36 2QN. Prop: Helen Trussell. Tel: (01309) 611373. E-mail: helen.trussell@hotmail.com. Est: 1999. Shop open: **M:** 11:00–17:00; **T:** 11:00–17:00; **W:** 11:00–17:00; **Th:** 11:00–17:00; **F:** 11:00–17:00; **S:** 11:00–17:00; **Su:** 11:00–17:01. Stock: large. PR: £1–500. CC: JCB; MC; V; Maestro Switch. [Updated]

HUNTLY

Orb's Bookshop, ■ 33a Deveron Street, Huntly, AB54 8BY. Prop: Anne Lamb. Tel: (01466) 793765. E-mail: info@orb.demon.co.uk. Est: 2001. Shop open: **M:** 09:15–17:00; **T:** 09:15–17:00; **W:** 09:15–17:00; **Th:** 09:15–17:00; **F:** 09:15–17:00; **S:** 09:15–17:00; Closed for lunch: 13:00–14:00. Spec: Animals and Birds; Authors:- Barrie, J.M.; Borrow, George; Buchan, John; Burns, Robert; Francis, Dick; Heyer, Georgette; Kipling, Rudyard. CC: MC; V; Maestro. Corresp: French. Mem: BA; FSB. Notes: also, new books. Open Saturdays 9:15 to 16:00 (no lunch break). [Updated]

RHOD McEWAN GOLF

Specialist dealer in antiquarian, out-of-print and elusive books on golf

Annuals	Histories
Architecture	Humour
Biographies	Instructionals
Cigarette Cards	Magazines
Club Histories	Rules
Ephemera	Tournament Histories
Essays	Turf Management
Fiction	Upkeep
Handbooks	Women's Golf

I am always looking to purchase golf books in any quantity

Ballater, Royal Deeside, Aberdeenshire AB35 5UB
Telephone: (013397) 55429 Fax: (013397) 55995
E-mail: teeoff@rhodmcewan.com www.rhodmcewan.com

TURRIFF

Grampian Books, Glendale house, Fyvie, Turriff, AB53 8SJ. Prop: David Fleming. Tel: 01888 544577. E-mail: grampianbooks@btinternet.com. Est: 1990. Private premises. Internet and postal. Appointment necessary. Spec: Almanacs; Antiquarian; Architecture; Bibliography; Countries - Scotland; Ecclesiastical History & Architecture; Folklore; Genealogy. CC: MC; V. Cata: quarterly on Scottish books ; Books by Scottish authors. Corresp: French Spanish. Mem: PBFA. VAT No: GB 553 1059 63. [Updated]

HIGHLAND

CULBOKIE

Tom Coleman, 2 Schoolcroft, Culbokie, IV7 8LB. Tel: (01349) 877502. Fax: (01349) 877502. E-mail: tomcoleman@tesco.net. Private premises. Postal only. Appointment necessary. Stock: medium. Spec: Scottish Interest. PR: £10–1,000. CC: PayPal. [Updated]

DINGWALL

Mercat Books, ■ 6 Church Street, Dingwall, IV15 9HP. Tel: 01349 865593. Fax: 01349 865593. Web: www.mercatbooks.com. E-mail: mercat.books@zetnet.co.uk. Est: 1994. Shop. Open in Summer. Open: **M:** 10.00–17.00; **T:** 10.00–17.00; **W:** 10.00–16.00; **Th:** 10.00–17.00; **F:** 09:00–17:30; **S:** 09:00–17:30; **Su:** 09:00–17:30; Closed for lunch: 13:00–14:00. [Updated]

DURNESS

Loch Croispol Bookshop & Restaurant, ■ 17C, Balnakeil, Durness, IV27 4PT. Prop: Kevin Crowe. Tel: 01971-511777. Web: www.scottish-books.net. E-mail: lochcroispol@btopenworld.com. Est: 1999. Shop open: **M:** 10.00–17.00; **T:** 10.00–17:00; **W:** 10:00–17:00; **Th:** 10:00–17:00; **F:** 10:00–17:00; **S:** 10:00–17:00; **Su:** 10:00–16.00. Spec: Countries - Scotland; History - Scottish; Literature - Scottish; Poetry; Scottish Enlightenment; Scottish Interest; Seafaring & Shipping. CC: MC; V; Maestro, PayPal. Notes: We specialise in Scottish titles. We also have a large stock of poetry. We also stock general adult and children's titles. Members of the international cooperative of independent booksellers: www.worldbookmarket.com. VAT No: GB 734 9262 18. [Updated]

FORT WILLIAM

Don McGavin, 14 Lanark Place, Fort William, PH33 6UD. Prop: Don McGavin. Tel: (01397) 703157. Private premises. Appointment necessary. Stock: very small. Spec: Ephemera. PR: £1–100. Corresp: French. [Updated]

Creaking Shelves, Arkaig Cottage, Fort William, Inverness-shire, PH33 6RN. Prop: Chris Robinson. Tel: (01397) 702886. Web: www.abebooks.com. E-mail: cr@lochaber.almac.co.uk. Est: 1998. Private premises. Postal only. Open in Summer. Stock: very small. Spec: Alpinism/Mountaineering; Countries - Scotland; Natural History; New Naturalist. PR: £5–500. [Updated]

INVERNESS

Leakey's Bookshop Ltd, ■ Church Street, Inverness, IV1 1EY. Prop: Charles Leakey. Tel: (01463) 239947. Est: 1979. Shop open: **M:** 10:00–17:30; **T:** 10:00–17:30; **W:** 10:00–17:30; **Th:** 10:00–17:30; **F:** 10:00–17:30; **S:** 10:00–17:30. Stock: very large. Spec: Countries - Scotland; Culture - National; Scottish Enlightenment; Scottish Interest; Topography - Local; Prints and Maps. CC: E; JCB; MC; V. [Updated]

LOCHCARRON

Blythswood Bookshop, ■ Main Street, Lochcarron, IV54 8YD. Blythswood Trade. Tel: (01520) 722337. Fax: (01520) 722264. Web: www.blythswood.org. E-mail: blythswoodbookshop@lineone.net. Est: 1984. Shop. Internet and postal. Open: **M:** 10:00–16:00; **T:** 10:00–16:00; **W:** 10:00–16:00; **Th:** 10:00–16:00; **F:** 10:00–16:00. Stock: medium. Spec: Biography; First Editions; Religion - General; Religion - Christian; Theology; Booksearch; Collectables. PR: £2–200. CC: MC; V. Mem: BA; Also at: Portree, Isle of Skye. Dingwell, Ross-shire. Stornoway, Isle of Lewis, and Cromer, Norfolk. Also, new books VAT No: GB 742 9279 06. [Updated]

ISLES OF SCOTLAND

ISLE OF ARRAN
Barnhill Books, Old Schoolhouse, Kilmory, Isle of Arran, KA27 8PQ. Prop: John Rhead. Tel: (01770) 870368. E-mail: rheadz@btinternet.com. Est: 1985. Private premises. Postal only. Spec: Alpinism/ Mountaineering; Gardening - General; Natural History; Ornithology; Plant Hunting; Sport - Big Game Hunting; Sport - Falconry; Sport - Field Sports. PR: £5–2,000. [Updated]

Audrey McCrone, Windyridge, Whiting Bay, Isle of Arran, KA27 8QT. Tel: (01770) 700564. Fax: (01770) 700564. Web: www.ukbookworld.com/members/finora. E-mail: a.mccrone@btinternet.com. Est: 1980. Private premises. Internet and postal. Telephone first. Stock: small. Spec: Animals and Birds; Anthologies; Antiquarian; Archaeology; Art History; Astronomy; Biography; Children's. PR: £5–200. [Updated]

ISLE OF COLONSAY
Colonsay Bookshop, ■ Isle of Colonsay, Argyll, Isle of Colonsay, PA61 7YR. Prop: Kevin & Christa Byrne. Tel: (01951) 200232. Fax: (01951) 200232. Web: www.colonsay.org.uk. E-mail: bookshop@colonsay.org.uk. Est: 1988. Shop. Open in Summer. Stock: very small. Spec: Countries - Scotland; Scottish Interest. PR: £1–300. CC: MC; V; Switch. Notes: also, new books & publisher. [Updated]

ISLE OF IONA
The Iona Bookshop, ■ The Old Printing Press Building, Isle of Iona, Argyll, PA76 6SL. Prop: Angus L. & Alison Johnston. Tel: (01681) 700699. Est: 1978. Shop open: **M:** 10:30–16:30; **T:** 10:30–16:30; **W:** 10:30–16:30; **Th:** 10:30–16:30; **F:** 10:30–16:30; **S:** 10:30–16:30; **Su:** 10:30–16:30. Stock: small. Spec: Countries - Scotland; History - Local; Topography - Local. PR: £1–500. Notes: winter: open by appointment only. Also, Celtic tapestry kits. [Updated]

WESTERN ISLES
M.E.McCarty, Bookseller, ■ 54 Junction Road, Kirkwall, KW15 1AG. Prop: Moi McCarty. Tel: 01856 870860. E-mail: moi@orkneybooks.co.uk. Est: 1986. Shop. Postal only. Appointment necessary. Open: **M:** 10:30–17:00; **T:** 10:30–17:00; **W:** 10:30–17:00; **Th:** 10:30–17:00; **F:** 10:30–17:00; **S:** 10:30–17:00; **Su:** 12:00–17:00; Closed for lunch: 13:00–1:00. Stock: medium. Spec: Literature; Maritime/ Nautical; Travel - General. PR: £1–100. CC: AE; JCB; MC; V; Maestro, Solo. Mem: PBFA; 13 North Main Street, Wigtown, Scotland (q.v.). [Updated]

LOTHIAN

EDINBURGH
Archways Sports Books, P.O. Box 13018, Edinburgh, EH14 2YA. Prop: Iain C. Murray. Web: www.archwaysbooks.com. E-mail: archways@blueyonder.co.uk. Est: 1992. Mail Order Only. Internet and postal. Appointment necessary. Spec: Sport - General; Sport - American Football; Sport - Athletics; Sport - Basketball; Sport - Boxing; Sport - Cricket; Sport - Cycling; Sport - Football (Soccer). CC: AE; JCB; MC; V. Cata: occasionally on Sports. [Updated]

Armchair Books, ■ 72-74 West Port, Edinburgh, EH1 2LE. Prop: David Govan. Tel: (0131) 229-5927. Web: www.armchairbooks.co.uk. E-mail: wlytle@ireland.com. Est: 1989. Shop open: **M:** 10:00–19:00; **T:** 10:00–19:00; **W:** 10:00–19:00; **Th:** 10:00–19:00; **F:** 10:00–18:00; **S:** 10:00–18:00; **Su:** 10:00–18:00. Stock: large. Spec: Africana; Annuals; Art; Authors:- Belloc, Hilaire; Buchan, John; Chesterton, G.K.; Conan Doyle, Sir Arthur; Kipling, Rudyard. PR: £1–1,000. CC: MC; V. [Updated]

Aurora Books Ltd, ■ 6 Tanfield, Edinburgh, EH3 5DA. Prop: Tom and Annabel Chambers. Tel: 00 44 (0)131 557 8466. Fax: 00 44 (0)131 557 8466. Web: www.aurorabooks.co.uk. E-mail: aurorabooks@btconnect.com. Est: 2003. Shop open: **M:** 10:00–18:00; **T:** 10:00–18:00; **W:** 10:00–18:00; **Th:** 10:00–18:00; **F:** 10:00–18:00; **S:** 10:00–18:00. Spec: Art; Artists; Arts, The; Author - General; Author - 20th Century; Biography; Children's; Countries - General. CC: AE; JCB; MC; V; Maestro, Solo, Visa Electron. VAT No: GB 808 8104 30. [Updated]

Peter Bell, ■ 68 West Port, Edinburgh, EH1 2LD. Tel: (0131) 556-2198. Fax: (0131) 229-0562. Web: www.peterbell.net. E-mail: books@peterbell.net. Est: 1980. Shop open: **M:** 10:00–17:00; **T:** 10:00–17:00; **W:** 10:00–17:00; **Th:** 10:00–17:00; **F:** 10:00–17:00; **S:** 10:00–17:00. Stock: medium. Spec: Academic/Scholarly; Antiquarian; Biography; Ecclesiastical History & Architecture; History - General; History - British; History - European; History - Scottish. PR: £1–500. CC: MC; V. Mem: ABA; PBFA. VAT No: GB 416 0959 50. [Updated]

Blacket Books, 1 Leadervale Terrace, Edinburgh, EH16 6NX. Prop: Elizabeth and Ian Laing. Tel: (0131) 666-1542. Web: www.blacketbooks.co.uk. E-mail: liz@blacketbooks.co.uk. Est: 1985. Private premises. Internet and postal. Telephone first. Stock: small. Spec: Children's; Military; Scottish Interest. PR: £10–1,500. CC: JCB; MC; V. Mem: PBFA. [Updated]

Bookworm, ■ 210 Dalkeith Road, Edinburgh, EH16 5DT. Prop: Peter Ritchie. Tel: (0131) 662-4357. Est: 1986. Shop. Open: **M:** 09:30–17:30; **T:** 09:30–17:30; **W:** 09:30–17:30; **Th:** 09:30–17:30; **F:** 09:30–17:30; **S:** 09:30–17:15. Stock: medium. Spec: Arms & Armour; Art History; Egyptology; Fiction - General; Firearms/Guns; Freemasonry & Anti-Masonry; History - General; Literature. CC: AE; JCB; MC; V; SW. [Updated]

Antiquarian Books Maps & Prints

Old & rare books on Fine Art, Architecture, Scotland, Edinburgh & Literature

Maps and Prints from the 17th–19th century

Open 10.30am–5.45pm Mon–Sat

The Old Town Bookshop

8 Victoria Street, Edinburgh
Tel: 0131 225 9237
www.oldtownbookshop.co.uk

The Bookworm, ■ 210 Dalkeith Road, Edinburgh, EH16 5DT. Prop: Peter Ritchie. Tel: 0131 662 4357. Web: www.scottishbookworm.com. E-mail: petertyhebook@btinternet.com. Est: 1989. Shop. Open: **M:** 09:30–17:30; **T:** 09:30–17:30; **W:** 09:30–17:30; **Th:** 09:30–17:30; **F:** 09:30–17:30; **S:** 09:30–17:30. Spec: Art Reference; Fiction - General; Firearms/Guns; History - General; Military; Military History; Naval; Scottish Interest. [Updated]

Broughton Books, ■ 2a Broughton Place, Edinburgh, EH1 3RX. Prop: Peter Galinsky. Tel: (0131) 557-8010. Est: 1963. Shop open: **T:** 12:00–18:00; **W:** 12:00–18:00; **Th:** 12:00–18:00; **F:** 12:00–18:00; **S:** 09:30–17:30. Stock: large. Spec: History - General; Humanities; Literature. PR: £2–250. Corresp: Flemish, French, Frisian, German, Dutch, Spanish. Notes: Essential oils, chess sets. [Updated]

Duncan & Reid, ■ 5 Tanfield, Edinburgh, EH3 5DA. Prop: Maraget Duncan. Tel: 0131 556 4591. Est: 1978. Shop open: **T:** 11:00–17:00; **W:** 11:00–17:00; **Th:** 11:00–17:00; **F:** 11:00–17:00; **S:** 11:00–17:00. Spec: Antiquarian; Antiques; Art; Fashion & Costume; Literature; Scottish Interest. CC: MC; V. Corresp: French and German. [Updated]

Grant & Shaw Ltd., 10 Leslie Place, Edinburgh, EH4 1NH. Prop: A.S. Grant. Tel: (0131) 332 8088. Fax: (0131) 332 9080. E-mail: agrant4227@aol.com. Est: 1989. Spec: Antiquarian. PR: £20–10,000. [Updated]

Jay Books, Rowll House, Roull Grove, Edinburgh, EH12 7JP. Prop: D.J. Brayford. Tel: (0131) 316-4034. Fax: (0131) 467-0309. Web: www.jaybooks.demon.co.uk. E-mail: djb@jaybooks.demon.co.uk. Est: 1977. Private premises. Internet and postal. Appointment necessary. Open: **M:** 09:00–21:00; **T:** 09:00–21:00; **W:** 09:00–21:00; **Th:** 09:00–21:00; **F:** 09:00–21:00; **S:** 09:00–21:00; **Su:** 09:00–21:00. Stock: small. Spec: Botany; Gardening - General; Natural History; Science - General; Science - History of; Technology. PR: £20–1,000. CC: MC; V. Corresp: Spanish, German, French. Mem: ABA; PBFA; ILAB. Notes: also, valuations. [Updated]

Main Point Books, ■ 8 Lauriston Street, Edinburgh, EH3 9DJ. Prop: Richard Browne. Tel: (0131) 228 4837. Fax: (0131) 228 4837. Est: 2001. Shop open: **T:** 11:00–17:00; **W:** 11:00–17:00; **Th:** 11:00–17:00; **F:** 11:00–17:00; **S:** 11:00–00:00. Stock: medium. Spec: Alpinism/Mountaineering; Esoteric; Fiction - General; Literature; Poetry; Scottish Interest; Sport - Climbing & Trekking; Theology. [Updated]

McNaughtan's Bookshop, ■ 3a and 4a Haddington Place, Leith Walk, Edinburgh, EH7 4AE. Prop: Elizabeth A. Strong Tel: (0131) 556-5897. Fax: (0131) 556 8220. Web: www.mcnaughtansbookshop.com. E-mail: mcnbooks@btconnect.com. Est: 1957. Shop open: **T:** 09:30–17:30; **W:** 09:30–17:30; **Th:** 09:30–17:30; **F:** 09:30–17:30; **S:** 09:30–17:30. Stock: very large. Spec: Antiquarian; Architecture; Art; Children's; Literature; Scottish Interest. PR: £1–3,500. CC: JCB; MC; V; Maestro. Mem: ABA; ILAB. VAT No: GB 327 3505 69. [Updated]

The Old Town Bookshop, ■ 8 Victoria Street, Edinburgh, EH1 2HG. Prop: Ronald Wilson. Tel: (0131) 225-9237. Fax: (0131) 229-1503. Web: www.oldtownbookshop.co.uk. Est: 1992. Shop open: **M:** 10:30–17:45; **T:** 10:30–17:45; **W:** 10:30–17:45; **Th:** 10:30–17:45; **F:** 10:30–17:45; **S:** 10:00–17:45. Stock: medium. Spec: Architecture; Art; Art Reference; Bindings; Botany; Catalogues Raisonnes; Children's; Country Houses. PR: £1–3,000. CC: JCB; MC; V; SW. Mem: PBFA. Notes: exhibits at 18 book fairs around the country [Updated]

David Page, 47 Spottiswoode Road, Edinburgh, EH9 1DA. Tel: (0131) 447-4553. Fax: (0131) 447-4553. E-mail: dcampbellpage@blueyonder.co.uk. Private premises. Telephone first. Stock: small. Spec: Alpinism/Mountaineering; Natural History; Plant Hunting; Travel - General; Travel - Africa; Travel - Asia; Travel - Middle East; Travel - Polar. Corresp: French, German. [21/12/2004]

Pinnacle Books, 13 Westgarth Avenue, Edinburgh, EH13 0BB. Tel: 0131 441 3870. Web: www.pinnaclebooks.net. E-mail: pinnaclebooks@blueyonder.co.uk. Private premises. Internet and postal. Appointment necessary. Spec: Alpinism/Mountaineering; Exploration; Mountain Men; Mountains; Scottish Interest; Sport - Skiing; Travel - Americas; Travel - Asia. Cata: occasionally on Mountaineering. Mem: PBFA. [Updated]

Andrew Pringle Booksellers, ■ 62 West Port, Edinburgh, EH1 2LD. Tel: (0131) 228-8880. Web: www.pringlebooks.co.uk. E-mail: andrew@pringlebooks.co.uk. Est: 1988. Shop. Stock: medium. Spec: Antiquarian; Art; Biography; History - National; Literature; Modern First Editions; Scottish Interest; Prints and Maps. PR: £3–500. CC: JCB; V; Switch. Corresp: French. Mem: PBFA. [Updated]

Robertson Books, 60 Craigcrook Road, Edinburgh, EH4 3PJ. Prop: Vanessa Robertson. Tel: 0131 343 3118. Web: www.robertsonbooks.co.uk. E-mail: vanessa@robertsonbooks.co.uk. Est: 2003. Private premises. Internet and postal. Spec: Children's. CC: cheque. Cata: bi-annually on children's books. Mem: Ibooknet. [Updated]

Second Edition, ■ 9 Howard Street, Edinburgh, EH3 5JP. Prop: Mrs. Maureen E. and W.A. Smith. Tel: (0131) 556-9403. Web: www.secondeditionbookshop.co.uk. E-mail: secondedition@tiscali.co.uk. Est: 1978. Shop open: **M:** 10:30–17:30; **T:** 10:30–17:30; **W:** 10:30–17:30; **Th:** 10:30–17:30; **F:** 10:30–17:30; **S:** 09:30–17:30. Stock: large. Spec: Architecture; Art; Children's; Fine Art; Illustrated; Literature; Medicine; Military History. PR: £10–500. Corresp: Spanish. [Updated]

The Old Children's Bookshelf, ■ 175 Canongate, Edinburgh, EH8 8BN. Prop: Shirley Neilson. Tel: 0131 558 3411. E-mail: shirleyOCB@aol.com. Shop open: **M:** 10:30–17:00; **T:** 10:30–17:00; **W:** 10:30–17:00; **Th:** 10:30–17:00; **F:** 10:30–17:00; **S:** 10:00–17:00; **Su:** 11:00–16:30. Spec: Annuals; Children's; Children's - Illustrated; Comics; Education & School; Juvenile; Pop-Up, Movable & Cut Out; Scouts & Guides. CC: MC; V. Cata: quarterly on children's books only. Mem: PBFA. Notes: exhibits at PBFA fairs. [Updated]

Till's Bookshop, ■ 1 Hope Park Crescent, (Buccleugh Street), Edinburgh, EH8 9NA. Tel: (0131) 667-0895. Web: www.tillsbookshop.co.uk. E-mail: tillsbookshop@btconnect.com. Est: 1986. Shop. Internet and postal. Open: **M:** 12:00–19:30; **T:** 12:00–19:30; **W:** 12:00–19:30; **Th:** 12:00–19:30; **F:** 12:00–19:30; **S:** 11:00–18:00; **Su:** 12:00–17:30. Stock: large. Spec: Cinema/Film; Comic Books & Annuals; Drama; Entertainment - General; Feminism; Fiction - General; Fiction - Crime, Detective, Spy, Thrillers; Fiction - Fantasy, Horror. PR: £2–100. CC: E; MC; V; De, SW, SO. Notes: also, cinema posters. [Updated]

John Updike Rare Books, 7 St. Bernard's Row, Edinburgh, EH4 1HW. Prop: John S. Watson & Edward G. Nairn. Tel: (0131) 332-1650. Fax: (0131) 332-1347. Est: 1965. Private premises. Appointment necessary. Stock: medium. Spec: Books about Books; Children's; Churchilliana; Drama; Fine & Rare; Fine Printing; First Editions; Illustrated. Mem: ABA. [Updated]

HADDINGTON

Yeoman Books, 37 Hope Park Crescent, Haddington, East Lothian, EH41 3AN. Prop: D.A. Hyslop. Tel: (01620) 822307. E-mail: yeomanbooks@talk21.com. Est: 1924. Private premises. Appointment necessary. Stock: very small. Spec: Aviation; Military; Military History; Motorbikes / motorcycles; Motoring; War - General. PR: £5–150. Mem: PBFA. Notes: also attends PBFA book fairs. [Updated]

SOUTH QUEENSFERRY

Marion Shearer, 41 Moubray Grove, South Queensferry, West Lothian, EH30 9PB. Tel: (0131) 331-1978. Private premises. Postal only. Stock: very small. PR: £2–200. [Updated]

STRATHCLYDE

AIRDRIE

Brown-Studies, Woodside Cottage, Longriggend, Airdrie, ML6 7RU. (*) Prop: Mr. M.G. & Mrs. B.J. Brown. Tel: (01236) 843826. Fax: (01236) 842545. Web: www.brown-studies-books.co.uk. E-mail: brownstudies@clara.co.uk. Est: 1990. Private premises. Internet and postal. Appointment necessary. Open: **M:** 09:00–20:00; **T:** 09:00–20:00; **W:** 09:00–20:00; **Th:** 09:00–20:00; **F:** 09:00–20:00; **S:** 09:00–20:00; **Su:** 09:00–20:00. Stock: very large. Spec: Artists; Author - Read, Miss; Building & Construction; Cookery/Gastronomy; D.I.Y. (Do It Yourself); Ecology; Gardening - General; Herbalism. PR: £3–300. CC: E; MC; V; Switch. Mem: Ibooknet. VAT No: GB 556 6923 05. [Updated]

AYR

Ainslie Books, ■ 1 Glendoune St., Girvan, Ayr, KA26 0AA. Prop: Gordon Clark. Tel: (01465) 715453. Fax: (01465) 715453. Web: www.ainsliebooks.co.uk. E-mail: ainslie.books@btopenworld.com. Shop. Internet and postal. Open: **M:** 10:00–17:00; **T:** 10:00–17:00; **W:** 10:00–17:00; **Th:** 10:00–17:00; **F:** 10:00–17:00; **S:** 10:00–17:00. Stock: large. Spec: Academic/Scholarly; Advertising; Aeronautics; Africana; Shorthand; Booksearch. PR: £1–200. CC: MC; V. [Updated]

BIGGAR

Karen Thomson, South Lindsaylands, Biggar, ML12 6NR. Tel: (01899) 221991. Fax: (01899) 221955. Est: 1987. Private premises. Postal only. Stock: very small. Spec: Antiquarian; Dictionaries; Medieval; Philology. Corresp: French, German. VAT No: GB 527 7505 33. [Updated]

CAMPBELTOWN

The Old Bookshelf, ■ 8 Cross Street, Campbeltown, PA28 6HU. Prop: David and Davina Tomlinson. Tel: (01586) 551114. Web: www.theoldbookshelf.co.uk. E-mail: theoldbookshelf@aol.com. Est: 2001. Shop. Internet and postal. Open: **M:** 11:00–17:00; **T:** 11:00–17:00; **W:** 11:00–17:00; **Th:** 11:00–17:00; **F:** 11:00–17:00; **S:** 10:00–16:00. Stock: large. Spec: Scottish Interest. PR: £2–3,000. CC: AE; E; JCB; MC; V; Meastro. Mem: ibooknet. VAT No: GB 808 8668 81. [Updated]

GLASGOW

Alba Secondhand Music, ■ 55 Otago Street, Glasgow, G12 8PQ. Prop: Robert Lay. Tel: (0141) 357 1795. Web: www.albamusick.co.uk. E-mail: robert@albamusick.co.uk. Est: 1994. Shop open: **M:** 11:00–17:30; **T:** 11:00–17:30; **W:** 11:00–17:30; **Th:** 11:00–17:30; **F:** 11:00–17:30; **S:** 11:00–17:30. Stock: large. Spec: Music - Classical. PR: £1–100. CC: MC; V. Notes: shop located behind Otago cafe & open at other times by appointment. [Updated]

Jack Baldwin 34 Hamilton Park Avenue, Glasgow, G12 8DT. Prop: Jack Baldwin. Tel: (0141) 334-8684. Fax: (0141) 334-8684. Web: www.jackbaldwin.dial.pipex.com. E-mail: jackbaldwin@dial.pipex.com. Est: 1985. Private premises. Internet and postal. Appointment necessary. Stock: small. Spec: Antiquarian; Countries - Baltic States; Countries - Mexico; Countries - Portugal; Countries - Russia; Countries - South America; Countries - Spain; Foreign Texts. PR: £5–1,000. CC: JCB; MC; V. Cata: bi-annually. Corresp: French, German, Italian, Spanish, Portuguese. [Updated]

Caledonia Books, ■ 483 Great Western Road, Kelvinbridge, Glasgow, G12 8HL. Prop: Maureen Smillie & Charles McBride. Tel: (0141) 334-9663. Fax: (0141) 334-9663. Web: www.caledoniabooks.co.uk. E-mail: caledoniabooks@aol.com. Est: 1984. Shop open: **M:** 10:00–18:00; **T:** 10:00–18:00; **W:** 10:00–18:00; **Th:** 10:00–18:00; **F:** 10:00–18:00; **S:** 10:00–18:00. Spec: Art; Art History; Bibliography; Biography; Cinema/Film; Countries - Poland; Drama; Fiction - General. PR: £2–200. CC: MC; V. [Updated]

Cooper Hay Rare Books, ■ 182 Bath Street, Glasgow, G2 4HG. Prop: Cooper Hay and Marianne Hay. Tel: (0141) 333-1992. Fax: (0141) 333-1992. Web: www.abebooks.com/home/haybooks. E-mail: chayrbooks@aol.com. Est: 1985. Shop open: **M:** 10:00–17:30; **T:** 10:00–17:30; **W:** 10:00–17:30; **Th:** 10:00–17:30; **F:** 10:00–17:30; **S:** 10:00–13:00; Closed for lunch: 13:00–14:15. Stock: medium. Spec: Art; Bindings; Books about Books; Children's - Illustrated; Countries - Scotland; Fine & Rare; Fine Art; History - Scottish. PR: £5–5,000. CC: MC; V. Mem: ABA. Notes: attends ABA fairs in Edinburgh and Chelsea. VAT No: GB 402 9241 83. [Updated]

Eddie's Books and Cards, Argyle Market Centre, 28 Argyle Street, Glasgow, G2 8AD. Prop: Edward E. Cowan. Tel: (0141) 226-3050. E-mail: info@eddiebookcards.co.uk. Est: 1982. Market stand/stall; Open: **M:** 09:30–17:00; **T:** 09:30–17:00; **W:** 09:30–17:00; **Th:** 09:30–17:00; **F:** 09:30–17:00; **S:** 09:30–17:30. Stock: medium. Spec: Collectables; Ephemera. PR: £1–6. Notes: also, greetings cards, remainders, calandars and jigsaws and remainders. [Updated]

The Studio, ■ De Courcy's Arcade, 5-21 Cresswell Lane, Glasgow, G12 8AA. Prop: Liz McKelvie. Tel: (0141) 334 8211. Web: www.wglasgowwestend.co.uk/shopping/antiques/studio. E-mail: lizthestudio@aol.com. Est: 1997. Shop open: **T:** 10:00–17:30; **W:** 10:00–17:30; **Th:** 10:00–17:30; **F:** 10:00–17:30; **S:** 10:00–17:30; **Su:** 12:00–17:00. Stock: small. Spec: Bindings; Children's - Illustrated; Decorative Art; History - Local; Publishers - Blackie. PR: £5–1,000. CC: D; E; JCB; MC; V; SW, MAE. Notes: also, books about Glasgow and Glasgow style antques, furnishings, metalware, textiles, ceramics - circa 1900. [Updated]

Thistle Books, 61 Otago Street, Glasgow, G12 8PQ. Prop: Robert Dibble. Tel: (0141) 334 8777. Est: 1997. Open: **M:** 11:00–17:30; **T:** 11:00–17:30; **W:** 11:00–17:30; **Th:** 11:00–17:30; **F:** 11:00–17:30; **S:** 11:00–17:30. Stock: large. Spec: Fiction - General; History - General; History - National; History - Scottish; Literature - Scottish; Modern First Editions; Scottish Interest. PR: £1–100. [Updated]

GREENOCK

Westwords, ■ 14 Newton Street, Greenock, PA16 8UJ. Tel: (01475) 892467. Est: 1982. PR: £1–50. [Updated]

HELENSBURGH

McLaren Books, 22 John Street, Helensburgh, G84 8BA. Tel: (01436) 676453. Fax: (01436) 673747. Web: www.mclarenbooks.co.uk. E-mail: george@mclarenbooks.demon.co.uk. Est: 1976. Office and/or bookroom. Open: **F:** 10:00–17:00; **S:** 10:00–17:00. Stock: medium. Spec: Manuals - Seamanship (see also under Seamanship); Maritime/Natical - Log Books; Maritime/Nautical; Naval; Navigation; Ship Modelling; Shipbuilding and Shipping; Sport - Canoeing/Kayaks. PR: £5–2,000. CC: MC; V; Switch. Mem: ABA; PBFA; ILAB. Notes: open at other times by appointment. VAT No: GB 293 0008 81. [Updated]

IRVINE

D. Webster, 43 West Road, Irvine, KA12 8RE. Tel: (01294) 272257. Fax: (01294) 276322. Est: 1958. Private premises. Appointment necessary. Stock: small. Spec: Circus; Physical Culture; Sport - Highland Games; Sport - Weightlifting/Bodybuilding; Sport - Wrestling; Booksearch; Collectables; Ephemera. PR: £5–40. Notes: also, booksearch. [Updated]

KILMARNOCK

Roberts Books, 8, Main Road, Waterside, Kilmarnock, KA3 6JB. Prop: Richard Roberts. Tel: (01560) 600349. Fax: (01560) 600349. E-mail: robertsbooks@btinternet.com. Est: 1976. Private premises. Internet and postal. Appointment necessary. Stock: small. Spec: Academic/Scholarly; Mathematics; Science - General; Science - History of; Scottish Interest; Technical; Technology. PR: £5–450. Corresp: French, German. Mem: Book Market Organiser in Scotland. [Updated]

OBAN

Bygone Books, Terok Nor, Ardconnel Hill, Oban, PA34 5DY. Prop: Isaac Lipkowitz. Tel: (01631) 563928. E-mail: lipkowitz@hotmail.com. Est: 1987. Private premises. Postal only. Appointment necessary. Stock: very small. Spec: Illustrated; Mysticism; Occult; Paganism. PR: £1–200. [Updated]

Looking for a bookdealer in Australia or New Zealand?

Then search on:

www.sheppardsworld.co.uk

TAYSIDE

ABERFELDY
Freader's Books, ■ 8 Dunkeld Street, Aberfeldy, PH15 2DA. Prop: Christopher Rowley. Tel: (01887) 829519. Fax: (01887) 829519. E-mail: Rowley@freaders.freeserve.co.uk. Est: 1991. Shop open: **M:** 10:00–16:00; **T:** 10:00–16:00; **Th:** 10:00–16:00; **F:** 10:00–16:00; **S:** 10:00–16:00; Closed for lunch: 13:00–14:00. Stock: very small. Spec: Natural History; Physics; Scottish Interest; Topography - General; Topography - Local. PR: £4–200. Mem: BA. [Updated]

ARBROATH
A Jolly Good Read, 94 Brechin Road, Arbroath, DD11 1SX. Tel: (01241) 877552. Web: www.ajollygoodread.co.uk. E-mail: books@ajollygoodread.co.uk. Est: 2004. Private premises. Internet and postal. Contactable. Stock: small. Spec: Children's. PR: £5–500. CC: PayPal. [Updated]

BLAIR ATHOLL
Atholl Browse, ■ by the Station, Blair Atholl, PH18 5SG. Prop: John and Mary Herdman. Tel: 01796 481530. Web: www.athollbrowse.co.uk. E-mail: mary@athollbrowse.co.uk. Est: 1989. Shop open: **M:** 12:00–17:00; **T:** 12:00–17:00; **W:** 12:00–17:00; **Th:** 12:00–17:00; **F:** 12:00–17:00; **S:** 12:00–17:00; **Su:** 12:00–17:00. Spec: Scottish Interest. Notes: open March-November. Extended hours during summer [Updated]

FORFAR
Hilary Farquharson, Deuchar Farm, Fern, Forfar, DD8 3QZ. Prop: H. Farquharson. Tel: (01356) 650278. Fax: (01356) 650417. E-mail: deucharfarm@btopenworld.com. Est: 1992. Private premises. Book Fairs Only. Appointment necessary. Open: **M:** 08:00–21:00; **T:** 08:00–21:00; **W:** 08:00–21:00; **Th:** 08:00–20:00; **F:** 08:00–21:00; **S:** 08:00–21:00; **Su:** 21:00–22:00. Stock: medium. Spec: Agriculture; Antiquarian; Countries - Scotland; Genealogy; Motoring; Scottish Interest; Topography - General; Topography - Local. PR: £5–1,000. CC: JCB; V. Mem: PBFA. [Updated]

KILLIECRANKIE
Atholl Fine Books, Clunemore, Killiecrankie, Pitlochry, PH16 5LS. Prop: Nancy Foy Cameron. Tel: 01796 473470. E-mail: nancy.foy@btinternet.com. Est: 1988. Private premises. Appointment necessary. Open: **M:** 09:00–17:30; **T:** 09:00–17:30; **W:** 09:00–17:30; **Th:** 09:00–17:30; **F:** 09:00–17:30; **S:** 09:00–17:30; **Su:** 09:00–17:30; Closed for lunch: 13:00–14:00. Spec: Bindings; History - Family; History - Local; Literature - Scottish; Scottish Interest; Topography - General; Topography - Local. CC: MC; V. Corresp: French. [Updated]

MONTROSE
Devanha Military Books, 4 Castle Terrace, Inverbervie, Montrose, DD10 0RE. Prop: Nick Ducat. Tel: (01561) 361387. E-mail: nickducat@devbooks.fsnet.co.uk. Est: 2001. Private premises. Postal only. Stock: small. Spec: Military; Military History. PR: £5–350. [Updated]

PITLOCHRY
Glacier Books, Ard–Darach, Strathview Terrace, Pitlochry, PH16 5AT. Prop: Chris Bartle. Tel: (01796) 470056. Fax: (01796) 470056. Web: www.glacierbooks.com. E-mail: sales@glacierbooks.com. Est: 1999. Private premises. Internet and postal. Telephone first. Stock: medium. Spec: Alpinism/Mountaineering; Calligraphy; Countries - Antarctic, The; Countries - Canada; Countries - France; Countries - Greenland; Countries - Himalayas, The; Countries - Iceland. PR: £1–3,000. [Updated]

SCONE
Bookseeker, 5 Isabella Place, Scone, PH2 6TE. Prop: Paul Thompson. Tel: (01738) 553582. E-mail: bookseeker@scone18.fsnet.co.uk. Private premises. Postal only. Notes: Booksearch only. [Updated]

WALES

The Unitary Authorities of Caerphilly, Cardiff, Carmarthenshire, Ceredigion, Conwy, Denbighshire, Dyfed, Flintshire, Gwynedd, Monmouthshire, Neath Port Talbot, Newport, Powys, Rhondda Cynon Taff, Swansea and Wrexham.

CAERPHILLY

NEW TREDEGAR
Tom Saunders, 9 Woodland Terrace, New Tredegar, NP24 6LL. Tel: (01443) 836946. Fax: (02920) 371921. E-mail: saunderstgc@tiscali.co.uk. Est: 1989. Private premises. Postal only. Telephone first. Stock: small. Spec: Academic/Scholarly; Biography; Chess; Children's; Education & School; Politics; Religion - General; Sport - American Football. PR: £3–50. [Updated]

CARDIFF

CARDIFF
Bear Island Books, ■ Cardiff Central Market, St. Mary Street, Cardiff, CF10 1AU. Tel: (029) 2038 8631. E-mail: bearislandbooks@talk21.com. Shop open: **M:** 10:00–17:00; **T:** 10:00–17:00; **W:** 10:00–17:00; **Th:** 10:00–17:00; **F:** 10:00–17:00; **S:** 10:00–17:00. Spec: History - Local; Topography - Local; Welsh Interest. CC: PayPal. [Updated]
Capital Bookshop, ■ 27 Morgan Arcade, Cardiff, CF10 1AF. Prop: A.G. Mitchell. Tel: (029) 2038-8423. E-mail: capitalbooks@cardiffwales.fsnet.co.uk. Est: 1981. Shop open: **M:** 10:00–17:30; **T:** 10:00–17:30; **W:** 10:00–17:30; **Th:** 10:00–17:30; **F:** 10:00–17:30; **S:** 10:00–17:30. Stock: large. Spec: Antiquarian; Countries - Wales; Booksearch; Prints and Maps. PR: £1–500. CC: E; MC; V; Maestro, Solo. Mem: PBFA. [27/09/2004]
Len Foulkes, 28 St. Augustine Road, Heath, Cardiff, CF14 4BE. Tel: (029) 2062-7703. Est: 1971. Private premises. Postal only. Stock: very large. PR: £5–100. Notes: now semi-retired. [Updated]
Whitchurch Books Ltd., ■ 67 Merthyr Road, Whitchurch, Cardiff, CF14 1DD. Prop: Mr. G.L. Canvin. Tel: (029) 2052-1956. Fax: (029) 2062-3599. E-mail: whitchurchbooks@btopenworld.com. Est: 1994. Shop open: **T:** 10:00–17:30; **W:** 10:00–17:30; **Th:** 10:00–17:30; **F:** 10:00–17:30; **S:** 10:00–17:30. Stock: very large. Spec: Anthropology; Archaeology; Art History; Arthurian; Byzantium; Cookery/Gastronomy; Countries - Wales; Ecclesiastical History & Architecture. PR: £1–100. CC: AE; D; E; JCB; MC; V; SW; S; EL. Mem: WBA. Notes: also, a booksearch service. VAT No: GB 648 3263 23. [Updated]
Nicholas Willmott Bookseller, 97 Romilly Road, Canton, Cardiff, CF5 1FN. Prop: Nicholas Willmott & Judith Wayne. Tel: (029) 2037-7268. Fax: (029) 2037-7268. Web: www.members.lycos.co.uk/nicholaswillmott/id17.htm. E-mail: willmott_wayne@hotmail.com. Est: 1982. Private premises. Postal only. Contactable. Stock: large. Spec: Authors - Women; Autobiography; Biography; Drama; Feminism; Fiction - General; History - General; Humour. PR: £2–500. Corresp: French. Notes: Freelance tenor. VAT No: GB 368 3564 19. [Updated]

CARMARTHENSHIRE

AMMANFORD
Stobart Davies Limited, Stobart House, Pontyclerc, Penybanc Road, Ammanford, SA18 3HP. Tel: (01269) 593100. Fax: (01269) 596116. Web: www.stobartdavies.com. E-mail: sales@stobartdavies.com. Est: 1989. Office and/or bookroom. Internet and postal. Open: **M:** 09:00–17:00; **T:** 09:00–17:00; **W:** 09:00–17:00; **Th:** 09:00–17:00; **F:** 09:00–17:00. Stock: very large. Spec: Building & Construction; Crafts; D.I.Y. (Do It Yourself); Forestry; Woodwork. PR: £3–60. CC: AE; D; MC; V. Mem: BA. [Updated]

CARMARTHEN

Sue Lloyd-Davies, 94 St. Catherine Street, Carmarthen, SA31 1RF. Prop: Sue Lloyd-Davies. Tel: (01267) 235462. Fax: (01267) 235462. E-mail: sue@lloyd-davies.fsnet.co.uk. Est: 1979. Private premises. Internet and postal. Telephone first. Open: **M:** 10:00–16:00; **T:** 10:00–16:00; **W:** 10:00–16:00; **Th:** 10:00–16:00; **F:** 10:00–16:00; **S:** 10:00–16:00. Stock: medium. Spec: Children's; Children's - Illustrated; First Editions; Illustrated; Literature; Travel - General; Welsh Interest; Booksearch. PR: £5–2,000. CC: E; JCB; MC; V; Switch etc. Corresp: French Japanese Welsh. Mem: PBFA; WBA. Notes: also, a booksearch service. [Updated]

CEREDIGION

ABERYSTWYTH

Colin Hancock, Ty'N–Y–Llechw, Aberystwyth, SY24 5BX. Prop: Colin Hancock. Tel: 01970 828709. Fax: 01970 828709. E-mail: colin-hancock@wales-books.demon.co.uk. Est: 1998. Private premises. Appointment necessary. Spec: Antiquarian; Archaeology; Countries - Wales; Culture - National; History - Local; Languages - National; Music - General; Welsh Interest. Corresp: French, Welsh. [Updated]

Ystwyth Books, ■ 7 Princess Street, Aberystwyth, SY23 1DX. Prop: Mrs. H.M. Hinde. Tel: (01970) 639479. Est: 1976. Shop open: **M:** 09:30–17:15; **T:** 09:30–17:15; **W:** 09:30–17:15; **Th:** 09:30–17:15; **F:** 09:30–17:15; **S:** 09:30–17:15. Stock: medium. Spec: Countries - Wales; History - Industrial; Technology; Topography - Local. PR: £2–100. CC: MC; V. Mem: BA. VAT No: GB 124 7218 86. [Updated]

CARDIGAN

Books in Cardigan, ■ 2, Pwllhai, Cardigan, SA43 1BZ. Prop: Mary Sinclair. Tel: (0121) 39682517. Web: www.http://cardiganbooks.hypermart.net/. E-mail: csinclair@lineone.net. Est: 1986. Shop. Internet and postal. Open: **M:** 09:00–17:00; **T:** 09:00–17:00; **W:** 09:00–17:00; **Th:** 09:00–17:00; **F:** 09:00–17:00; **S:** 09:00–17:00. Stock: large. Spec: Corresp: French, Spanish, Portuguese. Notes: Cardigan Market Stall open 6 days a week [Updated]

LAMPETER

Barry Thomas Poultry Books, The Vicarage, Felinfach, Lampeter, SA48 8AE. Tel: (01570) 470944. Fax: (01570) 471557. E-mail: barry.thomas3@tiscali.co.uk. Est: 1976. Private premises. Internet and postal. Contactable. Open: **M:** 09:00–21:00; **T:** 09:00–21:00; **W:** 09:00–21:00; **Th:** 09:00–21:00; **F:** 09:00–21:00. Stock: very small. Spec: Cockfighting; Poultry; Ephemera; Prints and Maps. PR: £1–1,000. Corresp: French, German, Welsh. [08/12/2004]

TREGARON

Nigel Bird (Books), Bryn Hir, Llwynygroes, Tregaron, SY25 6PY. Prop: Nigel Bird. Tel: (01974) 821281. Fax: (01974) 821548. Web: www.nigelbirdbooks.co.uk. E-mail: nigelbird.books@virgin.net. Est: 1985. Private premises. Internet and postal. Appointment necessary. Stock: medium. Spec: Author - Rolt, L.T.C.; Canals/Inland Waterways; Railways; Transport. PR: £1–200. CC: E; JCB; MC; V. Notes: also, a booksearch service for specialist subjects only. [Updated]

CONWY

COLWYN BAY

Bay Bookshop, 14 Seaview Road, Colwyn Bay, LL29 8DG. Prop: A.P. Morley. Tel: (01492) 531642. E-mail: andy@baybookshop.fsnet.co.uk. Est: 1971. Spec: Collectables; Ephemera; Prints and Maps. PR: £1–500. Notes: shop at Bay Bookshop, Rhos-on-Sea. (q.v.). [Updated]

Colwyn Books, ■ 66 Abergele Road, Colwyn Bay, LL29 7PP. Prop: John & Linda Beagan. Tel: (01492) 530683. E-mail: colwynbooks@fsmail.net. Est: 1989. Shop open: **M:** 09:30–17:00; **T:** 09:30–17:00; **W:** 09:30–13:00; **Th:** 09:30–17:00; **F:** 09:30–17:00; **S:** 09:30–17:00; Closed for lunch: 13:00–13:30. Stock: medium. Spec: Countries - France; Foreign Texts; New Books; Publishers - Haynes Publishing; Theology; Booksearch. PR: £1–15. Corresp: Welsh. Mem: Welsh Booksellers Assoc. Notes: catalogues: French, Theology and Modern First Editions. [Updated]

WALES

D. Gathern, 42a Seaview Road, Colwyn Bay, LL29 8DG. Prop: David Gathern. Tel: 01492 532569. E-mail: deagathern@btinternet.com. Private premises. Appointment necessary. Open: **M:** 09:30–16:30; **T:** 09:30–16:30; **W:** 09:30–16:30; **Th:** 09:30–16:30; **F:** 09:30–16:30; **S:** 09:30–16:30. Stock: medium. Spec: Sport - General; Sport - Baseball; Sport - Football (Soccer). CC: PayPal. [Updated]

owenbooks65, 13 Wynn Drive, Old Colwyn, Colwyn Bay, LL29 9DE. Prop: Jack Owen. Tel: (01492) 516600. E-mail: owenbooks65@hotmail.com. Est: 1989. Private premises. Internet Only. Appointment necessary. Stock: small. Spec: Countries - Europe; Countries - France; Languages - African; Languages - Foreign; Languages - National. CC: PayPal. Corresp: French, Italian. Mem: WBA. Notes: on Amazon. [Updated]

Rhos Point Books, ■ 85 The Promenade, Rhos–on–Sea, Colwyn Bay, LL28 4PR. Prop: Gwyn & Beryl Morris. Tel: (01492) 545236. Fax: (01492) 540862. Web: www.ukbookworld.com/members/brynglas. E-mail: rhos.point@btinternet.com. Est: 1986. Shop. Open: **M:** 10:00–17:30; **T:** 10:00–17:30; **W:** 10:00–17:30; **Th:** 10:00–17:30; **F:** 10:00–17:30; **S:** 10:00–17:30; **Su:** 11:00–17:30. Stock: medium. Spec: Antiquarian; Welsh Interest. PR: £1–300. CC: AE; MC; V. Corresp: Welsh. [Updated]

Yesterday's News, 43 Dundonald Road, Colwyn Bay, LL29 7RE. Prop: Elfed Jones. Tel: (01492) 531195. Web: www.giftnewspapers.co.uk/. E-mail: elfedjones@btinternet.com. Est: 1967. Private premises. Open: **M:** 09:00–21:00; **T:** 09:00–21:00; **W:** 09:00–21:00; **Th:** 09:00–21:00; **F:** 09:00–21:00; **S:** 09:00–21:00; **Su:** 09:00–00:00. Stock: very large. Spec: Broadcasting; Canadiana; Churchilliana; Cinema/Film; Comic Books & Annuals; Comics; Crime (True); Entertainment - General. PR: £5–50. Corresp: German, Welsh. Notes: majors in newspapers, periodicals and paper ephemera. [Updated]

CONWY

Roz Hulse, Llanrwst Road, Conwy, LL27 0JR. Prop: Roz Hulse. Tel: (01492) 641676. Web: www.rozhulse.com. E-mail: roz@rozhulse.com. Est: 2004. Private premises. Internet and postal. Appointment necessary. Stock: small. Spec: Academic/Scholarly; Antiquarian; Atlases; Colour-Plate; Illustrated; Natural History; Private Press; Travel - General. PR: £40–5,000. CC: MC; V. [Updated]

LLANRWST

Prospect Books, 10 Trem Arfon, Llanrwst, LL26 0BP. Prop: M. R. Dingle. Tel: 01492 640111. Web: www.gunbooks.co.uk. E-mail: mike@gunbooks.co.uk. Est: 1982. Private premises. Appointment necessary. Open: **M:** 09:00–15:30; **T:** 09:00–15:30; **W:** 09:00–15:30; **Th:** 09:00–15:30; **F:** 09:00–15:30. Spec: Arms & Armour; Firearms/Guns. CC: JCB; MC; V; Maestro/Switch. Cata: quarterly on weapons. Notes: specialist books on weaponry. [Updated]

OLD COLWYN

J V Owen, 13 Wynn Drive, Old Colwyn, LL29 9DE. Tel: (01492) 516600. Fax: (01492) 516600. E-mail: owenbooks65@hotmail.com. Est: 2003. Private premises. Appointment necessary. Stock: small. Spec: Foreign Texts. PR: £1–100. Corresp: French, German, Italian. [Updated]

E. Wyn Thomas, Old Quarry, 9 Miners Lane, Old Colwyn, LL29 9HG. Prop: E. Wyn Thomas. Tel: (01492) 515336. Est: 1947. Private premises. Appointment necessary. Stock: small. Spec: Countries - Wales; Fiction - General; History - General; Natural History; Topography - Local; Prints and Maps. PR: £1–1,000. Corresp: Welsh. [Updated]

DENBIGHSHIRE

LLANGOLLEN

Books, ■ 17 Castle Street, Llangollen, LL20 8NY. Prop: Mr. Thor Sever. Tel: (01978) 860334. Web: www.llangollen.org.uk/pages/books.htm. E-mail: books@easynet.co.uk. Est: 1983. Shop open: **M:** 10:00–17:00; **T:** 10:00–17:00; **W:** 10:00–17:00; **Th:** 10:00–17:00; **F:** 10:00–17:00; **S:** 10:00–17:00; **Su:** 10:00–17:00. Spec: Alpinism/Mountaineering; American Indians; Art; Astrology; Cinema/Film; Countries - Melanesia; Folklore; Gardening - General. PR: £3–50. CC: JCB; MC; V. [12/09/2005]

RHYL
Siop y Morfa, ■ 109 Stryd Fawr, Rhyl, Sir Ddinbych, LL18 1TR. Prop: Dafydd Timothy. Tel: (01745) 339197. Web: www.siopymorfa.com. E-mail: dafydd@siopymorfa.com. Est: 1980. Shop. Internet and postal. Open: **M:** 09:30–17:30; **T:** 09:30–17:30; **W:** 09:30–17:30; **Th:** 09:30–17:30; **F:** 09:30–16:30; **S:** 09:30–17:30; Closed for lunch: 13:00–14:00. Stock: medium. Spec: History - National; Literature; Welsh Interest. PR: £5–200. CC: AE; JCB; MC; V; Solo. Corresp: French, Cymraeg/Welsh. Mem: PBFA. VAT No: GB 771 0696 20. [Updated]

FLINTSHIRE

MOLD
BOOKS4U, 7 The Firs, Mold, CH7 1JX. Prop: Norman MacDonald. Tel: (01352) 751121. Web: www.http://ukbookworld.com/members/bks4u. E-mail: norman_macdonald@btinternet.com. Est: 1997. Private premises. Appointment necessary. Spec: Academic/Scholarly; Annuals; Antiquarian; Children's - Illustrated; Fiction - General; Folio Society, The; Limited Editions; Modern First Editions. PR: £4–1,500. CC: PayPal. Corresp: Welsh. [Updated]

GLAMORGAN

FERNDALE
Norman F. Hight, 149 North Road, Ferndale, CF43 4RA. Tel: (01443) 756552. E-mail: norman.f.hight@care4free.net. Est: 1998. Private premises. Internet and postal. Appointment necessary. Open: **M:** 10:00–19:00; **T:** 10:00–18:00; **W:** 10:00–19:00; **Th:** 10:00–19:00; **F:** 10:00–18:00; **S:** 10:00–14:00. Stock: small. Spec: Fiction - Crime, Detective, Spy, Thrillers; Fiction - Fantasy, Horror; Fiction - Science Fiction; Modern First Editions. PR: £1–200. CC: PayPal. [Updated]

GWENT

CHEPSTOW
Glance Back Books, 17 Upper Church Street, Chepstow, NP6 5EX. Prop: Greg Lance-Watkins. Tel: (01291) 626562. Web: www.glanceback.co.uk. E-mail: greg@glanceback.demon.co.uk. Est: 1981. Private premises. Internet and postal. PR: £1–2,000. CC: PayPal. Notes: large general stock. [Updated]

GWYNEDD

BANGOR
The Muse Bookshop, ■ 43 Holyhead Road, Bangor, LL57 2EU. Prop: Huw Jones. Tel: (01248) 362072. Fax: (01248) 362072. E-mail: themusebookshop@yahoo.co.uk. Est: 1992. Shop open: **M:** 09:00–17:30; **T:** 09:00–17:30; **W:** 09:00–17:30; **Th:** 09:00–18:30; **F:** 09:00–17:30; **S:** 10:00–16:30. Stock: medium. Spec: Aboriginal; Academic/Scholarly; Accountancy; Adirondack Mountains, The; Adult; Alpinism/Mountaineering; Natural History; New Naturalist. PR: £0–500. CC: MC; V. Mem: BA. Notes: also, new books. [Updated]

BETHESDA
A.E. Morris, ■ 40 High Street, Bethesda, LL57 3AN. Tel: (01248) 602533. Est: 1987. Shop open: **M:** 10:00–17:00; **T:** 10:00–17:00; **W:** 10:00–17:00; **Th:** 10:00–17:00; **F:** 10:00–17:00; **S:** 10:00–17:00. Spec: Prints and Maps. PR: £1–100. [Updated]

BLAENAU FFESTINIOG
P. & D. Doorbar, Min-y-ffordd, Bethania, Blaenau Ffestiniog, LL41 3LZ. Prop: Mr. K.P. & Mr. D.L. Doorbar. Tel: (01766) 831995. Fax: (01766) 831995. Web: www.doorbar.co.uk/books/. E-mail: books@doorbar.co.uk. Est: 1991. Private premises. Internet Only. Contactable. Stock: small. Spec: Art; Children's; Children's - Illustrated; Dogs; Gypsies; Illustrated; Rural Life. PR: £5–500. Mem: PBFA. [Updated]

Siop Lyfrau'r Hen Bost, ■ 45 High Street, Blaenau Ffestiniog, LL41 3AA. Prop: Elin Angharad Jones. Tel: (01766) 831802. E-mail: elin.henbost@virgin.net. Est: 1988. Postal and shop. Open: **M:** 10:00–17:00; **T:** 10:00–17:00; **W:** 10:00–17:00; **Th:** 10:00–17:00; **F:** 10:00–17:00; **S:** 10:00–17:00. Stock: medium. Spec: Countries - Wales; History - Local; Journals; Literature; New Books; Welsh Interest; Ephemera. PR: £1–200. Mem: BA; WBA. Notes: also, back-numbers of Welsh journals [Updated]

CRICCIETH

Capel Mawr Collectors Centre, ■ 21 High Street, Criccieth, LL52 0BS. Prop: Alun & Dee Turner. Tel: (01766) 523600. E-mail: capelmawr@aol.com. Est: 1998. Shop. Open: **M:** 11:00–17:00; **T:** 11:00–17:00; **W:** 11:00–17:00; **Th:** 11:00–17:00; **F:** 11:00–17:00; **S:** 11:00–17:00; **Su:** 11:00–16:00. Stock: very large. Spec: Cinema/Film; Comics; Cookery/Gastronomy; Counterculture; Fiction - General; Food & Drink; Sport - General; Theology. PR: £1–100. CC: AE; E; JCB; MC; V. Mem: Winter opening Thursday, Friday, Saturday 10:00–17:00. Notes: also, collectables & ephemera. [Updated]

DOLGELLAU

Cader Idris Books, ■ 2 Maldwyn House, Finsbury Square, Cader Road, Dolgellau, LL40 1TR. Prop: Barbara Beeby & Son. Tel: (01654) 703849. Web: www.abebooks.com/home/dvbookshop. E-mail: beeb@dvbookshop.fsnet.co.uk. Est: 1988. Shop open: Stock: medium. Spec: Arms & Armour; Firearms/Guns; Military; Sport - Archery; Welsh Interest. PR: £1–500. CC: AE; JCB; MC; V. Mem: WBA. Notes: also at Dyfi Valley Bookshop, 6, Doll St., Machynlleth, Powys. Please telephone before calling. [Updated]

MONMOUTHSHIRE

ABERGAVENNY

Books for Writers, 'Avondale', 13 Lansdown Drive, Abergavenny, NP7 6AW. Prop: Ms. Sonia A. Hughes. Tel: (01873) 853967. Est: 1999. Private premises. Postal only. Stock: very small. Spec: Biography; Fiction - General; Reference; Booksearch. PR: £2–50. [Updated]

Skirrid Books, 58 Poplars Road, Mardy, Abergavenny, NP7 6LX. Prop: Mrs. G.M. Parry. Tel: (01873) 857004. E-mail: skirbook@skirbook.freeserve.co.uk. Est: 1995. Private premises. Appointment necessary. Stock: small. Spec: Fiction - Supernatural. PR: £5–200. CC: E; JCB; MC; V; PayPal. [Updated]

LLANVAPLEY

Monmouth House Books, Monmouth House, Llanvapley, Abergavenny, NP7 8SN. Prop: Richard Sidwell. Tel: (01600) 780236. Fax: (01600) 780532. Web: www.monmouthhousebooks.co.uk. E-mail: monmouthhousebooks@compuserve.com. Est: 1985. Private premises. Postal only. Appointment necessary. Stock: small. Spec: Architecture; Booksearch. PR: £5–1,000. Mem: Also, booksearch & stock lists on architecture only. Publishes facsimile reprints of early architectural books. VAT No: GB 615 8003 63. [Updated]

Open 7 Days
Catalogues by Post & E-mail
Books Bought
Wants Match Service
Visa/Amex

Stella BOOKS

Monmouth Road
Tintern
Monmouthshire
NP16 6SE
01291 689755

50,000 Rare and Out of Print Books

Specialists in UK Topography, Childrens and Illustrated Books
*** Winner UK Outstanding Customer Service Award ***
Email: enquiry@stellabooks.com   Web: www.stellabooks.com

TINTERN

Stella Books, ■ Monmouth Road, Tintern, NP16 6SE. Prop: Chris Tomaszewski. Tel: (01291) 689755. Fax: (01291) 689998. Web: www.stellabooks.com. E-mail: enquiry@stellabooks.com. Est: 1990. Internet, and Shop open: **M:** 09:30–17:30; **T:** 09:30–17:30; **W:** 09:30–17:30; **Th:** 09:30–17:30; **F:** 09:30–17:30; **S:** 09:30–17:30; **Su:** 09:30–17:30. Stock: very large. Spec: Authors:- Blyton, Enid; Johns, W.E.; Rackham, Arthur; Cats; Children's; Children's - Illustrated; Countries - Wales; Dogs. PR: £1–3,000. CC: AE; JCB; MC; V. Corresp: French. Mem: PBFA; Ibooknet.co.uk. Notes: also at: Rose's Books., 14 Broad Street, Hay-On-Wye, HR3 5DB (q.v.). Wants matching. Over 4,000 different catalogues issued quarterly. VAT No: GB 667 0422 36. [Updated]

NEATH PORT TALBOT

NEATH

www.rugbyrelics.com, 61 Leonard Street, Neath, SA11 3HW. Prop: Dave Richards. Tel: (01639) 646725. Fax: (01639) 638142. Web: www.rugbyrelics.com. E-mail: sales@rugbyrelics.com. Est: 1991. Private premises. Postal only. Appointment necessary. Stock: very small. Spec: Sport - Boxing; Sport - Cricket; Sport - Football (Soccer); Sport - Golf; Sport - Rugby; Prints and Maps. PR: £2–2,000. CC: MC; V. [Updated]

PEMBROKESHIRE

NEWPORT

Carningli Centre, ■ East St, Newport, SA42 0SY. Prop: Ann Gent. Tel: 01239 820724. Web: www.carningli.co.uk. E-mail: info@carningli.co.uk. Est: 1982. Shop open: **M:** 10:00–17:30; **T:** 10:00–17:30; **W:** 10:00–17:30; **Th:** 10:00–17:30; **F:** 10:00–17:30; **S:** 10:00–17:30. Spec: Agriculture; Animals and Birds; Anthologies; Antiques; Art; Countries - Wales; D.I.Y. (Do It Yourself); Farming & Livestock. CC: AE; MC; V; Maestro. VAT No: GB 491 0134 72. [Updated]

TENBY

Cofion Books, ■ Bridge Street, Tenby, SA70 7BU. Prop: Albie Smosarki. Tel: (01834) 845741. Fax: (01834) 843864. Web: www.cofion.com. E-mail: albie@cofion.com. Est: 1994. Shop open: **M:** 10:30–17:30; **T:** 10:30–17:30; **W:** 10:30–17:30; **Th:** 10:30–17:30; **F:** 10:30–17:30; **S:** 10:30–17:30; **Su:** 11:30–17:30. Stock: very large. Spec: Animals and Birds; Art; Art Reference; Arthurian; Astrology; Autobiography; Biography; Esoteric. PR: £1–500. [Updated]

POWYS

BEULAH

Myra Dean Illustrated Books, Crossways, Beulah, LD5 4UB. Prop: Myra Dean. Tel: (01591) 620647. Web: www.myradean-illustatedbooks.co.uk. E-mail: myra.dean@hotmail.co.uk. Est: 1984. Private premises. Internet and postal. Telephone first. Stock: very small. Spec: Children's; Illustrated; Private Press. PR: £5–2,000. CC: MC; V; Switch. Cata: quarterly. [Updated]

BRECON

Andrew Morton Books, ■ 11 Lion Yard, Brecon, LD3 7BA. Tel: (01874) 620086. E-mail: sales@mortonbooks.co.uk. Est: 1999. Shop open: **M:** 09:30–17:30; **T:** 09:30–17:30; **W:** 09:30–17:30; **Th:** 09:30–17:30; **F:** 09:30–17:30; **S:** 09:30–17:30. Stock: very large. Spec: Art; Children's; Crafts; History - General; Literature; Military. PR: £2–30. CC: MC; V; SW, SO. Notes: Also at: 7 Lion Street, Brecon. Also, open on Sundays in season. [Updated]

Garfi Books, ■ Bron y Graig, Pontrhydygroes, Ystrad Meurig, SY25 6DN. (*) Prop: Barbara & Salvatore Garfi. Tel: 01974 282684. E-mail: garfibooks@btinternet.com. Est: 2000. Shop At: The Book Unit, Brecon Antiques Centre, 22a High St., Brecon, Powys LD3 7LA. Open: **M:** 10:00–17:00; **T:** 10.00–17:00; **W:** 10.00–17:00; **Th:** 10.00–17.00; **F:** 10:00–17:00; **S:** 10:00–17:00. Spec: Alpinism/ Mountaineering; Archaeology; Art; Author - Armour, G. D.; Biography; Children's; Crime (True); Criminology. CC: MC; V; Maestro & Switch. Notes: open Sundays from Easter to Christmas. 11:00-16:00. [Updated]

BUILTH WELLS

Louise Boer, Arthurian Books, The Rectory, Rhosgoch, Builth Wells, LD2 3JU. Prop: Louise Boer. Tel: (01497) 851260. Fax: (01497) 851260. E-mail: louise.boer@btinternet.com. Est: 1996. Private premises. Internet and postal. Contactable. Open: Stock: medium. Spec: Academic/Scholarly; Arthurian; Business Studies; Literary Criticism. PR: £2–150. CC: MC; V. Corresp: Dutch. [Updated]

HAY–ON–WYE

The Addyman Annexe, ■ 27 Castle Street, Hay-on-Wye, HR3 5DF. Prop: Derek Addyman and Anne Brichto. Tel: 01497 821600. Web: www.hay-on-wyebooks.com. E-mail: madder@hay-on-wyebooks.com. Shop open: **M:** 10:30–17:30; **T:** 10:30–17:30; **W:** 10:30–17:30; **Th:** 10:30–17:30; **F:** 10:30–17:30; **S:** 10:30–17:30; **Su:** 10:30–17:30. Spec: Bindings; Literature; Military; Modern First Editions. CC: MC; V; Maestro. [Updated]

Addyman Books, ■ 39 Lion Street, Hay–on-Wye, HR3 5AA. Prop: Derek Addyman & Anne Brichto. Tel: (01497) 821136. Fax: (01497) 821732. Web: www.hay-on-wyebooks.com. E-mail: madness@hay-on-wyebooks.com. Est: 1987. Shop. Internet and postal. Open: **M:** 10:00–17:30; **T:** 10:00–17:30; **W:** 10:00–17:30; **Th:** 10:00–17:30; **F:** 10:00–17:30; **S:** 10:00–17:30; **Su:** 10:30–17:30. Stock: large. Spec: Anthologies; Antiquarian; Archaeology; Architecture; Art; Arthurian; Arts, The; Astronomy. PR: £1–20,000. CC: MC; V; De, SW. Notes: also at Murder & Mayhem, 5 Lion St., Hay-on-Wye (q.v) The Addyman Annexe, 27 Castle St., Hay-on-Wye, (q.v.).

C. Arden, Bookseller, ■ 'Radnor House', Church Street, Hay–on–Wye, HR3 5DQ. Prop: Chris & Catherine Arden. Tel: (01497) 820471. Fax: (01497) 820498. Web: www.WWW.ardenbooks.co.uk. E-mail: c.arden@virgin.net. Est: 1993. Internet and postal. Shop open: **M:** 10:00–17:00; **F:** 10:00–17:00; **S:** 10:00–17:00; **Su:** 10:00–17:00. Stock: medium. Spec: Antiquarian; Biology; Botany; Conservation; Ecology; Entomology; Evolution; Fine & Rare. PR: £3–10,000. CC: JCB; MC; V. Mem: PBFA. [Updated]

B. and K. Books of Hay-on-Wye, Riverside, Newport Street, Hay–on–Wye, HR3 5BG. Prop: Betty & Karl Showler. Tel: (01497) 820386. Web: www.hay-on-wye.co.uk/bkbooks Est: 1966. Private premises. Appointment necessary. Stock: very small. Spec: Apiculture. PR: £6–600. Notes: also at storeroom. [Updated]

Richard Booth's Bookshop Ltd, ■ 44 Lion Street, Hay–on–Wye, HR3 5AA. Director: Mr. Richard Booth. Tel: (01497) 820322. Fax: (01497) 821150. Web: www.richardbooth. demon.co.uk. E-mail: postmaster@richardbooth.demon.co.uk. Est: 1961. Shop open: **M:** 09:00–17:30; **T:** 09:00–17:30; **W:** 09:00–17:30; **Th:** 09:00–17:30; **F:** 09:00–19:00; **S:** 09:00–19:00; **Su:** 11:00–17:30. Stock: very large. Spec: Agriculture; Archaeology; Atlases; Children's; Cookery/Gastronomy; Countries - Mexico; Economics; Fiction - Science Fiction. PR: £1–1,000. CC: AE; D; JCB; MC; V. Mem: WBA. Notes: also at Hay Castle, Hay-on-Wye. (q.v.) Paperbacks & magazines. NB: add 'via Hereford' after Hay-on-Wye when sending by post. VAT No: GB 412 774 460. [Updated]

Boz Books, ■ 13a Castle Street, Hay–on–Wye, HR3 5DF. Prop: Peter Harries. Tel: (01497) 821277. Fax: (01497) 821277. Web: www.bozbooks.co.uk. E-mail: peter@bozbooks.co.uk. Est: 1987. Shop. Internet and postal. Open: **M:** 10:00–17:00; **T:** 10:00–17:00; **W:** 10:00–17:00; **Th:** 10:00–17:00; **F:** 10:00–17:00; **S:** 10:00–17:00; Closed for lunch: 13:00–14:00. Stock: medium. Spec: Author - Dickens, Charles; Fiction - General; Literature; Literature - 19th C. PR: £5–10,000. CC: JCB; MC; V. Mem: ABA. Notes: Opening times vary in winter. VAT No: GB 489 1240 27. [Updated]

The Children's Bookshop, ■ Toll Cottage, Pontvaen, Hay-on-Wye, HR3 5EW. Prop: Judith M Gardner. Tel: (01497) 821083. Web: www.childrensbookshop.com. E-mail: judith@childrensbookshop.com. Est: 1980. Internet and postal. Shop open: **M:** 09:30–17:30; **T:** 09:30–17:30; **W:** 09:30–17:30; **Th:** 09:30–00:30; **F:** 09:31–17:30; **S:** 09:30–17:30; **Su:** 09:35–17:30. Stock: medium. Spec: Children's; Booksearch. PR: £5–500. CC: JCB; MC; V. Corresp: French, German. Notes: booksearch service. [Updated]

davidleesbooks.com, ■ Marches Gallery, 2 Lion Street, Hay–on–Wye, HR3 5AA. Prop: David Lees. Tel: (01497) 822969. Web: www.davidleesbooks.com. E-mail: julie@davidleesbooks.com. Est: 1985. Shop. Internet and shop: **M:** 11:00–17:00; **T:** 11:00–17:00; **W:** 11:00–17:00; **Th:** 11:00–17:00; **F:** 11:00–17:00; **S:** 11:00–17:00; **Su:** 11:00–17:00. Stock: medium. PR: £0–1,000. CC: MC; V; Debit Card. VAT No: GB 488 7008 07. [Updated]

Marijana Dworski Books, Travel, ■ Backfold, Hay–on–Wye, HR3 5EQ. Prop: Marijana Dworski. Tel: (01497) 820200. Fax: (01497) 820200. Web: www.dworskibooks.com. E-mail: sales@dworskibooks.com. Est: 1991. Shop open: **M:** 10:30–17:00; **T:** 10:30–17:00; **W:** 10:30–17:00; **Th:** 10:30–17:00; **F:** 10:30–17:00; **S:** 10:30–17:30; Closed for lunch: 13:00–14:00. Stock: medium. Spec: Academic/Scholarly; American Indians; Anti-Semitism; Antiquarian; Arabica; Atlases; Biography; Byzantium. PR: £1–1,000. CC: D; JCB; V; debit. Corresp: French, German, Croatian. Notes: NB add ' via Hereford' after Hay-on-Wye when sending by post. VAT No: GB 794 1222 28. [Updated]

Francis Edwards in Hay–on–Wy, ■ The Old Cinema, Castle Street, Hay–on–Wye, HR3 5DF. Prop: Hay Cinema Bookshop Ltd. Tel: (01497) 820071. Fax: (01497) 821900. Web: www.francisedwards.co.uk. E-mail: sales@francisedwards.demon.co.uk. Est: 1855. Shop open: **M:** 09:00–19:00; **T:** 09:00–19:00; **W:** 09:00–19:00; **Th:** 09:00–19:00; **F:** 09:00–19:00; **S:** 09:00–19:00; **Su:** 11:30–17:30. Stock: medium. Spec: Architecture; Art; Economics; Folklore; History - General; Law - General; Literature; Medicine. PR: £20–10,000. CC: AE; D; E; JCB; MC; V; Switch. Mem: ABA; PBFA; ILAB. Notes: NB add 'via Hereford' after Hay-on-Wye when sending by post. VAT No: GB 594 2720 23. [Updated]

Hancock & Monks Music Emporium, ■ 6 Broad Street, Hay–on–Wye, HR3 5DB. Prop: Eric Hancock & Jerry Monks. Tel: (01591) 610555. Fax: (01591) 610555. Web: www.hancockandmonks.co.uk. E-mail: jerry@hancockandmonks.co.uk. Est: 1974. Internet and postal. Shop open: **M:** 10:00–17:00; **T:** 10:00–17:00; **W:** 10:00–17:00; **Th:** 10:00–17:00; **F:** 10:00–17:00; **S:** 10:00–17:00; **Su:** 10:00–17:00. Stock: medium. Spec: Music - General; Music - Classical; Music - Composers; Music - Jazz & Blues; Music - Music Hall; Music - Musicians; Music - Opera; Music - Printed, Sheet Music & Scores. PR: £1–250. CC: MC; V; Maestro. Notes: also, CDs, DVDs, sheet music & scores. VAT No: GB 139 8108 51. [Updated]

Hay Castle (Booth Books), ■ Hay Castle, Hay–on–Wye, HR3 5DL. Prop: Hope Booth (Richard Booth Bookshops Ltd.) Tel: (01497) 820503. Fax: (01497) 821314. Web: www.boothbooks.co.uk. E-mail: books@haycastle.freeserve.co.uk. Est: 1987. Shop open: **M:** 09:30–17:30; **T:** 09:30–17:30; **W:** 09:30–17:30; **Th:** 09:30–17:30; **F:** 09:30–17:30; **S:** 09:30–17:30; **Su:** 09:30–17:30. Stock: very large. Spec: American Indians; Architecture; Art; Cinema/Film; Crafts; Humour; Photography; Railways. PR: £1–2,500. CC: AE; MC; V. Corresp: French Mem: WBA. Notes: also at 44 Lion Street, Hay–on–Wye (q.v.). Also, photographic images from 1850s onwards. NB: add 'via Hereford' after Hay-on-Wye when sending by post. [Updated]

Hay Cinema Bookshop Ltd., ■ Castle Street, Hay–on–Wye, HR3 5DF. Tel: (01497) 820071. Fax: (01497) 821900. Web: www.haycinemabookshop.co.uk. E-mail: sales@haycinemabookshop.co.uk. Est: 1982. Shop open: **M:** 09:00–19:00; **T:** 09:00–19:00; **W:** 09:00–19:00; **Th:** 09:00–19:00; **F:** 09:00–19:00; **S:** 09:00–19:00; **Su:** 11:30–17:30. Stock: very large. Spec: Academic/Scholarly; Aeronautics; Applied Art; Art; Calligraphy; Cinema/Film; Cookery/Gastronomy; Economics. PR: £1–25. CC: AE; D; JCB; MC; V. Mem: ABA; PBFA. Notes: also at Quinto, 48a Charing Cross Road, London WC2H 0BB (q.v.) Quinto, 63 Great Russell Street, London WC1B 3BF. Fine and Antiquarian books in all subjects via our sister business Francis Edwards. VAT No: GB 594 2720 23. [Updated]

HCB Wholesale, Unit 2, Forest Road Enterprise Park, Hay–on–Wye, HR3 5DS. Tel: (01497) 820333. Fax: (01497) 821192. E-mail: sales@hcbwholesale.co.uk. Est: 2002. Storeroom. Open: **M:** 09:00–18:00; **T:** 09:00–18:00; **W:** 09:00–18:00; **Th:** 09:00–18:00; **F:** 09:00–18:00. Stock: very large. Spec: CC: AE; D; E; JCB; MC; V. Notes: Main stock: publishers' returns, academic overstocks, and remainders. NB: add 'via Hereford' after Hay-on-Wye when sending by post. [24/01/2005]

Kestrel Books, 6 De Breos Court, Hay-on-Wye, HR3 5DL. Prop: Stephen Cook. Tel: 01497 822890. Fax: 01497 822891. Web: www.hay-kestrel.com. E-mail: david@hay-kestrel.com. Est: 2005. Private premises. Appointment necessary. Stock: very small. Spec: Modern First Editions. PR: £25–2,000. CC: MC; V. Cata: quarterly. VAT No: GB 863 5090 18. [Updated]

Looking for a dealer in EPHEMERA?

Then search Sheppard's on-line directories at:

www.sheppardsworld.co.uk

Murder & Mayhem, ■ 5 Lion Street, Hay–on–Wye, HR3 5AA. Prop: Derek Addyman & Anne Brichto. Tel: (01497) 821613. Fax: (01497) 821732. Web: www.hay-on-wyebooks.com. E-mail: madness@hay-on-wyebooks.com. Est: 1997. Shop open: **M:** 10:30–17:30; **T:** 10:30–17:30; **W:** 10:30–17:30; **Th:** 10:30–17:30; **F:** 10:30–17:30; **S:** 10:30–17:30. Stock: medium. Spec: Crime (True); Criminology; Fiction - Crime, Detective, Spy, Thrillers; Fiction - Fantasy, Horror; Sherlockiana. PR: £1–1,000. Notes: also at Addyman Books, 39 Lion Street, Hay-on-Wye (q.v.). [Updated]

O'Donoghue Books, PO Box 162, Hay-on-Wye, HR3 5WZ. Prop: Sean O'Donoghue. Tel: 01497 822831. Web: www.intertextuality.com. E-mail: odonoghue.books@virgin.net. Est: 1994. Private premises. Internet Only. Stock: large. Spec: Academic/Scholarly; Biography; Philosophy; Politics; Psychology/Psychiatry; Social Sciences. PR: £10–50. CC: MC; V; Switch. Mem: Ibooknet. VAT No: GB 751 8509 19. [Updated]

Outcast Books, ■ 15a Broad St., Hay–on–Wye, HR3 5DB. Prop: David Howard. Tel: (01497) 821292. Web: www.ukbookworld.com/members/outcastbooks. E-mail: outcastbooks@supanet.com. Est: 1993. Shop open: **M:** 10:30–17:00; **T:** 10:30–17:00; **W:** 10:30–17:00; **Th:** 10:30–17:00; **F:** 10:30–17:00; **S:** 11:30–17:00; **Su:** 12:00–14:00. Stock: small. Spec: Academic/Scholarly; Alternative Medicine; Medicine; Psychoanalysis; Psychology/Psychiatry; Psychotherapy; Social Sciences. PR: £1–150. CC: AE; E; JCB; MC; V. Mem: Welsh Booksellers Assoc. NB: add 'via Hereford' after Hay-on-Wye when sending by post. [Updated]

Oxford House Books, ■ Montpelier, 21 Broad Street, Hay-on-Wye, HR3 5DB. Prop: Paul Harris. Tel: (01497) 820191. Web: www.oxfordhousebooks.com. E-mail: oxfordbook@aol.com. Est: 2003. Shop open: **T:** 10:30–17:30; **W:** 10:30–17:30; **Th:** 10:30–17:30; **F:** 10:30–17:30; **S:** 10:30–17:30; **Su:** 10:30–17:30. CC: MC; V; Electron, Maestro, Solo, Delta. [Updated]

The Poetry Bookshop, ■ Ice House, Brook Street, Hay–on–Wye, HR3 5BQ. Prop: Christopher Prince. Tel: (01497) 821812. Fax: (01497) 821812. Web: www.poetrybookshop.co.uk. E-mail: info@poetrybookshop.co.uk. Est: 1998. Internet and postal. Shop open: **M:** 10:00–18:00; **T:** 10:00–18:00; **W:** 10:00–18:00; **Th:** 10:00–18:00; **F:** 10:00–18:00; **S:** 10:00–18:00; **Su:** 11:00–17:00. Stock: large. Spec: Academic/Scholarly; Anthologies; Antiquarian; Autobiography; Beat Writers; Bindings; Biography; Counterculture. PR: £1–10,000. CC: MC; V; Maestro. Mem: All subjects that relate to poets and poetry inc criticism, biography, readers guides, work in translation and anthologies VAT No: GB 831 777 901. [29/09/2004]

Rose's Books, ■ 14 Broad Street, Hay–on–Wye, HR3 5DB. Tel: (01497) 820013. Fax: (01497) 820031. Web: www.rosesbooks.com. E-mail: enquiry@rosesbooks.com. Est: 1982. Shop. Internet and postal. Open: **M:** 09:30–17:30; **T:** 09:30–17:30; **W:** 09:30–17:30; **Th:** 09:30–17:30; **F:** 09:30–17:30; **S:** 09:30–17:30; **Su:** 09:30–17:30. Stock: large. Spec: Children's; Children's - Illustrated; Illustrated; Publishers - Ladybird Books. PR: £1–2,000. CC: AE; JCB; MC; V; SW. Mem: PBFA. Notes: also on www.ibooknet.co.uk. Bookmatch service - we can let you know when a book comes into stock. VAT No: GB 667 0422 36. [Updated]

Mark Westwood Books, ■ High Town, Hay–on–Wye, HR3 5AE. Tel: (01497) 820068. Fax: (01497) 821641. E-mail: books@markwestwood.co.uk. Est: 1987. Shop open: **M:** 10:30–17:30; **T:** 10:30–17:30; **W:** 10:30–17:30; **Th:** 10:30–17:30; **F:** 10:30–17:30; **S:** 10:30–17:30; **Su:** 10:30–17:30. Stock: very large. Spec: Folio Society, The; History - General; Mathematics; Medicine; Medicine - History of; New Naturalist; Philosophy; Psychology/Psychiatry. PR: £5–1,000. CC: E; JCB; MC; V. Corresp: French. Mem: ABA; PBFA. VAT No: GB 315 3343 88. [Updated]

Y Gelli Auctions, Broad Street, Hay-on-Wye, HR3 5DB. Prop: Michael Bowers. Tel: (01497) 821179. Fax: (01497) 820978. Web: www.invakuable.com/ygelli. E-mail: auction@ygelli.demon.co.uk. Est: 1988. Saleroom. Open: **T:** 10:00–18:00; **W:** 10:00–18:00; **Th:** 10:00–18:00; **F:** 10:00–18:00. Spec: CC: MC; V. [Updated]

LLANDRINDOD WELLS

Udo K.H. Polczynski, Rose & Crown, Llanbadarn Fynydd, Llandrindod Wells, LD1 6YH. Prop: Udo K.H. Polczynski. Tel: 01597 840569. Fax: 01597 840569. Est: 1984. Private premises. Appointment necessary. Stock: medium. Spec: Anthropology; Archaeology; History - Science; Philology; Philosophy. PR: £10–5,000. Cata: occasionally on special collections. Corresp: French, German, Malay, Polish, Russian, Spanish. [Updated]

LLANGAMMARCH WELLS

Dally Books & Collectables, Berthllwyd, Beulah, Llangammarch Wells, LD5 4UN. Prop: Andrew Dally. Tel: (01591) 610892. Web: www.dallybooks.com. E-mail: andrew@thedallys.com. Est: 2001. Market stand/stall. Internet and postal. Contactable. Stock: small. Spec: Memorabilia; Military; Military History; War - General; War - World War I; War - World War II; Welsh Interest; Collectables. PR: £1–200. [Updated]

LLANIDLOES

Dead Mens Minds.co.uk, Neuadd Ddu, LLangurig, Llanidloes, SY18 6RX. Prop: Tristan Winston-Smith. Tel: (01686) 440730. Web: www.TPOBooks.co.uk. E-mail: tpobooks@aol.com. Est: 2000. Private premises. Internet and postal. Stock: very small. Spec: Antiquarian. PR: £10–2,000. CC: MC; V; Switch. [Updated]

Dusty Books, The Old Woollen Mill, Shortbridge Street, Llanidloes, SY18 6AD. Prop: Bernard Conwell. Tel: (01686) 411247. Fax: (01686) 411247. Web: www.dustybooks.co.uk. E-mail: alex@dustybooks.co.uk. Postal only. Spec: Authors:- Farnol, Jeffery; Forester, C.S.; Heyer, Georgette; Sabatini, R.; Shute, Neville; Cookery/Gastronomy; Crafts; Food & Drink. PR: £5–250. [Updated]

The Great Oak Bookshop, ■ Great Oak Street, Llanidloes, SY18 6BW. Prop: B. Boswell. Tel: (01686) 412959. Web: www.midwales.com/gob. E-mail: goodbooks@btinternet.com. Est: 1988. Shop. Internet and postal. Open: **M:** 09:32–17:30; **T:** 09:31–17:30; **W:** 09:29–17:30; **Th:** 09:31–17:30; **F:** 09:30–17:30; **S:** 09:31–16:30. Stock: very large. Spec: Autobiography; Biography; Countries - Wales; Welsh Interest; Booksearch. PR: £1–50. CC: AE; E; JCB; MC; V. Corresp: German, French. Mem: BA; WBA. Notes: also, new books, booksearch service, greetings cards & a resident parrot. [Updated]

MACHYNLLETH

Coch-y-Bonddu Books Ltd., ■ Papyrus, Pentrerhedyn Street, Machynlleth, SY20 8DJ. Prop: Paul Morgan. Tel: (01654) 702837. Fax: (01654) 702857. Web: www.anglebooks.com. E-mail: paul@anglebooks.com. Est: 1982. Internet and postal. Shop open: **M:** 09:00–17:00; **T:** 09:00–17:00; **W:** 09:00–17:00; **Th:** 09:00–17:00; **F:** 09:00–17:00; **S:** 09:00–17:00. Stock: large. Spec: Animals and Birds; Conservation; Dogs; Fishes; Forestry; Natural History; Ornithology; Rural Life. PR: £1–2,000. CC: AE; D; E; JCB; MC; V. Corresp: French, German, Spanish, Portuguese, Welsh. Mem: PBFA; BA. Notes: we stock new books in our fields, as well as remainders, s/hand and antiquarian. [Updated]

Martin's Books, Zion Chapel, Llanwrin, Machynlleth, SY20 8QH. Prop: Martin Ashby. Tel: (01650) 511595. E-mail: martin.ashby@martin-ashby.demon.co.uk. Est: 2000. Storeroom. Internet and postal. Appointment necessary. Spec: Animals and Birds; Biography; Botany; Fiction - General; First Editions; Natural History; Ornithology; Poetry. PR: £6–500. [03/11/2005]

MONTGOMERY

Castle Bookshop, The Old Rectory, Llandyssil, Montgomery, SY15 6LQ. Prop: C.N., E.J. & S.J. Moore. Tel: (01686) 668484. Fax: (01686) 668842. Web: www.archaeologybooks.co.uk. E-mail: castlebooks@dial.pipex.com. Est: 1987. Office and/or bookroom. Telephone first. Open: Stock: large. Spec: Archaeology; Architecture; Countries - Wales; Welsh Interest. PR: £5–1,000. CC: JCB; MC; V; Switch. Mem: ABA; PBFA; ILAB. VAT No: GB 482 4054 51. [Updated]

NEWTOWN

David Archer, The Pentre, Kerry, Newtown, SY16 4PD. Prop: David Archer & Alison Brown. Tel: (01686) 670382. Web: www.david-archer-maps.co.uk. E-mail: david@david-archer-maps.co.uk. Est: 1985. Private premises. Internet and postal. Telephone first. Open: **M:** 08:30–20:00; **T:** 08:30–20:00; **W:** 08:30–20:00; **Th:** 08:30–20:00; **F:** 08:30–20:00; **S:** 09:00–13:00. Stock: very large. Spec: Cartography; Geography; Geology; Transport; Prints and Maps. PR: £1–150. Mem: Welsh Booksellers Assoc. [Updated]

Available from Richard Joseph Publishers Ltd
BOOKWORMS, THE INSECT PESTS
by N. Hickin

Revised Edition (A5 H/b) 184pp £24.00

WALES

Carta Regis Ltd, Agriculture House, Old Kerry Road, Newtown, SY16 4LE. Prop: David Pugh. Tel: (01686) 624274. Web: www.davidp@cartaregis.com. E-mail: davidp@cartaregis.com. Est: 1997. Office and/or bookroom. Internet and postal. Telephone first. Open: **M:** 10:00–17:00; **T:** 10:00–17:00; **W:** 10:00–17:00; **Th:** 10:00–17:00; **F:** 10:00–17:00; **S:** 10:00–17:00. Stock: large. Spec: Academic/ Scholarly; Agriculture; Alpinism/Mountaineering; Animals and Birds; Antiques; Arts, The; First Editions; Fore-Edge Paintings. PR: £5–300. CC: MC; V; PayPal. Notes: new Books. Altenative web site: www.cartaregisbooks.co.uk Book Search. VAT No: GB 850 5402 50. [Updated]

D.M. Newband, Drefor Cottage, Kerry, Newtown, SY16 4PQ. D.M. Newband. Tel: (01686) 670205. Fax: please ask. Web: www.davidnewbandbooks.co.uk. E-mail: enquiries@davidnewbandbooks. co.uk. Est: 1983. Office and/or bookroom. Internet and postal. Appointment necessary. Open: **M:** 09:00–19:00; **T:** 09:00–19:00; **W:** 09:00–19:00; **Th:** 09:00–19:00; **F:** 09:00–19:00; **S:** 09:00–19:00; **Su:** 10:00–18:00. Stock: small. Spec: Railways; Steam Engines; Transport. PR: £1–200. CC: PayPal. Notes: also, a booksearch service; valuation service railways only. [Updated]

Tant Yn Ellen Books, Draenllwynellen, Sarn, Newtown, SY16 4ET. Prop: Jim and June Crundwell. Tel: 01686 668475. Est: 2002. Private premises. Appointment necessary. Open: **M:** 09:00–17:30; **T:** 09:00–17:30; **W:** 09:00–17:30; **Th:** 09:00–17:30; **F:** 09:00–17:30; **S:** 09:00–17:30; **Su:** 09:00–17:30; Closed for lunch: 13:00–14:00. Spec: Botany; Children's; Children's - Illustrated; Cookery/Gastronomy; Entomology; Gardening - General; Natural History; Poetry. Notes: exhibits at book fairs. [Updated]

PRESTEIGNE

Antique & Book Shop, ■ 2 Hereford Street, Presteigne, LD8 2AW. Prop: A. L. Bird. Tel: (01544) 260316. Est: 1988. Shop open: **M:** 10:00–17:00; **T:** 10:00–17:00; **W:** 10:00–17:00; **Th:** 10:00–17:00; **F:** 10:00–17:00; **S:** 10:00–17:00. Stock: large. Spec: Topography - Local. PR: £1–200. Notes: open on Sundays by appointment. [Updated]

Tony Bird, 2 Hereford Street, Presteigne, LD8 2AW. Tel: (01544) 260316. Private premises. Spec: Topography - Local. [Updated]

Kingshead Books, ■ 45 High St., Presteigne, Powys. Prop: Ivan Monckton. Tel: (01547) 560100. (Hom. Est: 1983. Shop open: **M:** 10:00–17:00; **T:** 10:00–17:00; **W:** 09:00–17:00; **Th:** 10:00–17:00; **F:** 10:00–17:00; **S:** 10:00–17:00. Stock: medium. Spec: Natural History; Welsh Interest. PR: £1–250. Notes: open as above in summer. Winter: Saturdays & various others. Phone first. [Updated]

TALGARTH

The Strand Bookshop, ■ Regent Street, Talgarth, LD3 0DB. Prop: Ms Kate Cardwell. Tel: (01874) 711195. Shop open: **M:** 10:00–15:30; **Th:** 10:00–15:30; **F:** 10:00–15:30; **S:** 10:00–17:00; **Su:** 09:00–17:00. Stock: medium. PR: £1–50. [Updated]

WELSHPOOL

D. & J. Young, Fairview Cottage, Groes Llwyd, Welshpool, SY21 9BZ. Prop: David & Joy Young. Tel: (01938) 553149. Web: www.abebooks.com. E-mail: joy_young@lineone.net. Est: 1985. Private premises. Postal only. Appointment necessary. Stock: small. Spec: Calligraphy; Embroidery; Fashion & Costume; Knitting; Lace; Textiles. PR: £1–300. [Updated]

SWANSEA

SWANSEA

Dylans Bookstore, ■ Salubrious House, 23 King Edward Road, Swansea, SA1 4LL. Prop: Jeff and Elizabeth Towns. Tel: 01792 655255. Web: www.dylans.com. E-mail: jefftowns@dylans.com. Est: 1970. Postal and shop, open: **M:** 10:00–16:30; **T:** 10.00–16:30; **W:** 10.00–16:30; **Th:** 10.00–16:30; **F:** 10.00–16.30; **S:** 10.00–13.00. Spec: Academic/Scholarly; African-American Studies; Antiquarian; Arthurian; Authors:- Steadman, Ralph; Thomas, Dylan; Thomas, Edward; Watkins, Vernon. CC: JCB; MC; V. Cata: occasionally on Dylan Thomas, Wales, women. Corresp: French. Mem: ABA; PBFA; BA; ILAB. Mem: Welsh Booksellers Association. Notes: we have two open shops in Swansea - the other is in the Dylan Thomas Centre. We exhibit at bookfairs and sell on the Internet. [Updated]

PONTARDAWE

Mollie's Loft Books, 31 Cilmaengwyn, Pontardawe, SA8 4QL. Prop: M.J.P. Evans. Tel: (01792) 863556. Web: www.Molliesloft.com. E-mail: books@mollies.freeserve.co.uk. Est: 1998. Private premises. Internet and postal. Appointment necessary. Stock: small. Spec: Science - General; Technology; Welsh Interest. PR: £5–150. CC: MC; V; Switch. Corresp: French. [Updated]

J.M. Farringdon, Ariel Cottage, 8 Hadland Terrace, West Cross, Swansea, SA3 5TT. Prop: M.G. Farringdon. Tel: (01792) 405267. Fax: (01792) 405267. E-mail: bellbooks@aol.com. Est: 1970. Private premises. Internet and postal. Appointment necessary. Stock: very small. Spec: Antiquarian; Authors:- Masefield, John; Ransome, Arthur; Bell-Ringing (Campanology). PR: £20–1,000. Notes: also, a booksearch service & publishing as 'Ariel House Publications'. VAT No: GB 558 2330 40. [Updated]

TORFAEN

BLAENAVON

Blaenavon Books, ■ 71 Broad Street, Blaenavon, NP4 9NH. Prop: James Hanna. Tel: (01495) 793093. E-mail: blaenavonbooks@yahoo.co.uk. Est: 2003. Shop open: **M:** 10:00–17:00; **T:** 10:00–17:00; **W:** 10:00–17:00; **Th:** 10:00–17:00; **F:** 10:00–17:00; **S:** 09:00–17:00; **Su:** 10:00–17:00. Stock: medium. Spec: Art; Design; Photography. PR: £1–100. CC: MC; V; SW, SO. Notes: only open Sundays in summer. Large general stock. [Updated]

Broadleaf Books, ■ 12 Broad Street, Blaenavon, NP4 9ND. Prop: Joanna Chambers and Latagrifrith-Unny. Tel: (01495) 792852. E-mail: broadleaf12@aol.com. Est: 2003. Shop open: **M:** 10:00–17:00; **T:** 10:00–17:00; **W:** 10:00–17:00; **F:** 10:00–17:00; **S:** 10:00–17:00; **Su:** 11:00–16:00. Stock: medium. Spec: Children's; Design; Natural History; Photography. PR: £1–50. CC: V. [Updated]

Browning Books, ■ 33 Broad Street, Blaenavon, NP4 9NF. Prop: Stephanie and Andrew Nummelin. Tel: (01495) 790089. Web: www.browningbooks.co.uk. E-mail: info@browningbooks.co.uk. Est: 2001. Shop. Internet and postal. Open:**T:** 10:00–17:00; **W:** 10:00–17:00; **Th:** 10:00–17:00; **F:** 10:00–17:00; **S:** 10:00–17:00. Stock: medium. Spec: Children's; Children's - Illustrated; Languages - National; Mining; New Books; Railways; Steam Engines; Transport. PR: £1–150. CC: AE; E; JCB; MC; V; MAE, ELEC. Mem: MC. [Updated]

Queen Victoria PH, Prince Street, Blaenavon, NP4 9BD. Prop: Kim Winstone. Tel: 01495 791652. Web: www.webster.uk.net/queenvictoriainn. E-mail: queenvictoriainn@webster.uk.net. Est: 2003. Storeroom. Open: **M:** 11:00–23:00; **T:** 11:00–23:00; **W:** 11:00–23:00; **Th:** 11:00–23:00; **F:** 11:00–23:00; **S:** 11:00–23:00; **Su:** 12:00–20:30. Spec: Cookery/Gastronomy; Gardening - General; Military; Military History. Notes: Accommodation available. In Good Beer Guide. [Updated]

The Railway Shop, ■ 13a Broad Street, Blaenavon, NP4 9ND. Prop: Peter Hunt. Tel: (01495) 792263. E-mail: railway@pontypoolandblaenavon.freeserve.co.uk. Est: 1998. Shop open: **M:** 11:00–17:30; **T:** 11:00–17:30; **W:** 11:00–17:30; **Th:** 11:00–17:30; **F:** 11:00–17:30; **S:** 11:00–16:00. Stock: large. Spec: Railways; Shipbuilding and Shipping; Transport. PR: £1–20. CC: MC; V. [Updated]

BOOK SEARCH

TRIED ABEBOOKS, ALIBRIS, BIBLIOPHILE, ET AL?

IF YOUR SEARCHES SHOW NO RESULTS IT'S NOT THEIR FAULT
WHEN THIS HAPPENS – TRY A NEW METHOD FOR BOOKSEARCH

Most book dealers do not have the time, or resources, to create records of all their current stock to show on Internet search engines. So although dealers may specialise in specific subjects, a substantial number of titles in those subjects will not be available to your searches.

When your searches fail, Sheppard's World offers you a quick method of locating dealers who specialise in the subject of the book you seek, and provides a platform to enable you to rapidly send numerous and individiual e-mail requests.

It is as easy a writing the original, then copying and pasting it.

Best of all, you can chose which dealers to write to with your request.

For more information
Visit Sheppard's World on
www.sheppardsworld.co.uk

ALPHABETICAL INDEX BY NAME OF BUSINESS

(Business name followed by county, some of which have been abbreviated)

2 Ravens, Cumbria	78
32 Seconds, East Sussex	102
Ænigma Designs (Books), Devon	85
A. & R. Booksearch, Cornwall	73
AA1 Books, Dumfries & Galloway	264
Aardvark Books, Wiltshire	249
Aardvark Books, Lincolnshire	150
Abacus Books, Greater Manchester	118
Abacus Gallery, Staffordshire	220
Abbey Books, Cornwall	73
Abington Bookshop, Suffolk	222
Abrahams (Mike), Staffordshire	219
Acer Books, Herefordshire	128
Acumen Books, Staffordshire	220
Addyman Annexe (The), Powys	282
Addyman Books, Powys	282
Adrem Books, Hertfordshire	131
Afar Books International, W Midlands	234
African Studies, Dorset	90
ahbooks, Merseyside	182
Ainslie Books, Strathclyde	273
Aitchison (Lesley), Bristol	58
Al Saqi Books, London W	169
Alan Prim, Co. Cork	258
Alan Redmouth Books, Lincolnshire	148
Alauda Books, Cumbria	76
Alba Books, Grampian	267
Alba Secondhand Music, Strathclyde	273
Albion Books, W Midlands	234
Alec–Smith Books (Alex), East Yorkshire	107
Alexander Books, Hampshire	125
Alexander's Books, Warwickshire	232
All Books, Essex	110
Allhalland Books, Devon	83
Allinson (Frank & Stella), Warwickshire	232
Allsop (Duncan M.), Warwickshire	233
Allsworth Rare Books Ltd., London	164
Alpha Books, London N	155
Altea Antique Maps & Books, London W	169
Alton Secondhand Books, Hampshire	122
Altshuler (Jean), Cumbria	78
Ambra Books, Bristol	58
Americanabooksuk, Cumbria	76
Amnesty International UK, Berkshire	56
Amos (Denis W.), Hertfordshire	130
Ampersand Books, Shropshire	209
Amwell Book Company, London SE	154
Anchor Books, Lincolnshire	149
Ancient Art Books, London SW	164
Andrew Morton (Books), Powys	281
Andrew Stewart, Cornwall	74
Andrews Books & Collectables, Derbyshire	82
Andromeda Books, Buckinghamshire	62
Andron (G.W.), London N	155
Anglo-American Rare Books, Surrey	228
Ann & Mike Conry, Worcestershire	251
Anne Harris Books & Bags Booksearch, Devon	86
Annie's Books, South Yorkshire	217
Anthony Neville, Kent	138
Anthony Spranger, Wiltshire	247
Anthony Whittaker, Kent	136
Anthroposophical Books, Gloucestershire	116
Antiquary Ltd., (Bar Bookstore), North Yorkshire	192
Antique & Book Shop, Powys	286
Antique City Bookshop, London E	153
Antique Map and Bookshop (The), Dorset	93
Antique Prints of the World, London N	155
Antiques on High, Oxfordshire	204
Anvil Books, W Midlands	235
Anwoth Books, Dumfries & Galloway	264
Any Amount of Books, London WC	174
Aphra Books, West Yorkshire	242
Apocalypse, Surrey	228
Applin (Malcolm), Berkshire	55
Arcadia, Oxfordshire	205
Archer (David), Powys	285
Archer (Steve), London Outer	178
Archivist (The), Devon	88
Archways Sports Books, Lothian	269
Arden Books & Cosmographia, Warwickshire	232
Arden, Bookseller (C.), Powys	282
Ardis Books, Hampshire	126
Argent (Alan), Isle of Wight	135
Armchair Auctions, Hampshire	122
Armchair Books, Lothian	270
Armitage (Booksearch), (Kate), Devon	83
Arnold (Roy), Suffolk	223
Ars Artis, Oxfordshire	205
Art Book Company, (The), Suffolk	223
Art Reference Books, Hampshire	125
Artco, Nottinghamshire	201
Arts & Antiques Centre (The), Cheshire	69
Ash Rare Books, London SW	164
Askew Books (Vernon), Wiltshire	246
Assinder Books, Essex	110
Astley Book Farm, Warwickshire	232
Atholl Browse, Tayside	275
Atholl Fine Books, Tayside	275
Atlantis Bookshop, London WC	174
Atlas, London N	155
Aucott & Thomas, Leicestershire	145
Aurelian Books, London NW	158
Aurora Books Ltd, Lothian	270
Austen (Phillip), Lincolnshire	151
Austwick Hall Books, Lancaster	190
Autobooks Ltd., East Sussex	100
Autolycus, Shropshire	209
Autumn Leaves, Lincolnshire	150
Avedikian Rare Books, Somerset	213
Avery (Alan), North Yorkshire	191

289

ALPHABETICAL INDEX: Business (A – B)

Aviabooks, Gloucestershire 114
Aviation Book Supply, Hertfordshire 130
Avon Books, Bristol................................ 58
Avonworld Books, Somerset...................... 213
Axe Rare & Out of Print
 Books (Richard), North Yorkshire 190
Ayre (Peter J.), Somerset 216

B D McManmon, Lancashire 144
B. and K. Books, Powys............................ 282
Bacon (Josephine), London WC 174
Badger, Wiltshire..................................... 247
Badger Books, Somerset 216
Badgers Books, West Sussex...................... 239
Baedekers & Murray Guides, South Yorkshire 217
Baggins Book Bazaar Ltd., Kent 139
Baggins Books, Hertfordshire...................... 130
Baker (Gerald), Bristol............................. 59
Baker - Books for the Collector (Colin), Devon 88
Baker Limited (A.P. & R.), Dumfries &
 Galloway... 264
Baldwin (Jack), Strathclyde 273
Baldwin (M. & M.), Shropshire 250
Baldwin's Scientific Books, Essex 112
Bancroft (David G.), Isle of Wight 134
Bannatyne Books, London N 155
Bannister (David), Gloucestershire................ 113
Barbican Bookshop, North Yorkshire 194
Barcombe Services, Essex........................... 108
Bardsley's Books, Suffolk.......................... 221
Barlow (Vincent G.), Hampshire................... 126
Barlow Moor Books, Greater Manchester 118
Barmby (C. & A.J.), Kent......................... 140
Barn Books, Shropshire............................. 211
Barn Books, Buckinghamshire..................... 61
Barnes (Peter), Wiltshire 248
Barnes - Books (Lyndon), Shropshire 209
Barnhill Books, Isle of Arran 269
Barnitt (Peter), Wiltshire........................... 248
Baron (Christopher), Greater Manchester....... 118
Baron (H.), London NW........................... 158
Baron - Scientific Book Sales (P.J.), Somerset.. 213
Barron (Robert M.), Kent.......................... 140
Barry McKay Rare Books, Cumbria............. 76
Barter Books, Northumberland 198
Baskerville Books, Kent 141
Bass (Ben), Wiltshire 246
Bates & Hindmarch, West Yorkshire 243
Bates Books, London Outer 179
Bath Book Exchange, Somerset................... 212
Bath Old Books, Somerset 212
Batterham (David), London W 169
Baxter (Steve), Surrey 228
Baxter - Books (Eddie), Somerset................. 216
Bay Bookshop, Conwy.............................. 277
Baynton–Williams Gallery, West Sussex......... 237
Bayntun (George), Somerset 212
BC Books, Cheshire................................. 69
Bear Island Books, Cardiff........................ 276
Beardsell Books, West Yorkshire 242
Beardsley (A.E.), Nottinghamshire................ 201
Beaton (Richard), East Sussex 102

Beaver Booksearch, Suffolk 221
Beck (John), East Sussex 102
Beckham Books Ltd., Suffolk 225
Bell (Books) (Mrs. V.S.), Suffolk................. 223
Bell (Peter), Strathclyde 270
Bell Gallery (The), Co. Antrim................... 255
Ben–Nathan (Jack), London Outer............... 178
Bennett & Kerr Books, Oxfordshire.............. 202
Benny Gillies Books Ltd, Dumfries &
 Galloway.. 263
Bernstein (Nicholas), London W.................. 169
Berry (L.J.), Kent 138
Bertram Rota Ltd., London WC 174
Besleys Books, Suffolk 221
Bettridge (Gordon), Fife 265
Bevan (John), Wiltshire............................. 247
Beverley Old Bookshop, East Yorkshire 105
Beware of the Leopard, Bristol.................... 58
Bianco Library, West Sussex...................... 237
Biblion, London W.................................. 169
Bibliophile (The), South Yorkshire 217
Bibliophile Books, London E..................... 153
Billing (Brian), Berkshire 57
Bilski (Gill), Buckinghamshire..................... 61
Birchden Books, London E 153
Bird (Tony), Powys.................................. 286
Bird Books (Nigel), Ceredigion.................... 277
Birdnet Optics Ltd., Derbyshire................... 81
Birmingham Books, W Midlands................. 234
Bishopston Books, Bristol.......................... 58
Black Cat Books, Norfolk.......................... 185
Black Cat Bookshop, Leicestershire 145
Black Five Books, Shropshire 211
Black Voices, Merseyside 182
Blacket Books, Lothian 270
Blacklock's, Surrey.................................. 227
Blackman (Martin), Buckinghamshire 61
Blackman Books, Cheshire........................ 71
Blackwell's Music Shop, Oxfordshire 205
Blackwell's Rare Books, Oxfordshire............. 205
Blaenavon Books, Torfaen 287
Blanchfield (John), West Yorkshire............... 243
Blest (Peter), Kent 139
Blewbury Antiques, Oxfordshire 202
Blore's Bookshop (Geoffrey), Nottinghamshire 201
Blue Penguin (The), Gloucestershire.............. 116
Bluntisham Books, Cambridgeshire 63
Blythswood Bookshop, Highland 269
Bob Mallory (Books), Derbyshire................. 82
Bodyline Books, Surrey............................. 227
Boer (Louise), Arthurian Books, Powys......... 282
Boer War Books, North Yorkshire............... 194
Bolland Books (Leslie H.), Bedfordshire......... 53
Bolton Books, Hampshire.......................... 122
Bonham (J. & S.L.), London W 169
Bonner (John), West Yorkshire.................... 243
Bonython Bookshop, Cornwall.................... 75
Book Aid, Durham.................................. 96
Book Annex (The), Essex 110
Book Barrow, Cambridgeshire 63
Book Business (The), London W 169
Book Castle, (The), Bedfordshire 53

ALPHABETICAL INDEX: Business (B – B)

Book Collectors Paradise, Hertfordshire......... 132
Book Depot (The), London NW 158
Book End, Essex 108
Book For All Reasons (A.), Suffolk............... 224
Book Gallery (The), Cornwall..................... 75
Book House (The), Cumbria 78
Book Jungle (The), East Sussex 104
Book Mad, Lancashire 142
Book Mongers, London SW 164
Book Palace (The), London SE 161
Book Shelf (The), Devon 86
Bookbox, Gloucestershire 116
Bookcase, Cumbria 76
Bookcupboard, Devon 87
Bookcupboard (The), Devon 87
Bookends, Hampshire 123
Bookends, Norfolk 186
Bookends of Fowey, Cornwall 73
Bookfare, Cumbria 80
Bookline, Co. Down 256
Booklore, Leicestershire 146
BookLovers.co.uk, Somerset 215
Bookmark (Children's Books), Wiltshire 248
Booknotes, Essex 111
Bookpassage (The), Shropshire 209
Bookquest, Devon 83
Bookroom (The), Isle of Wight 134
Bookroom (The), Surrey 229
Bookroom (The), Gloucestershire 114
Books, Kent 137
Books, Oxfordshire 202
Books, Denbighshire 278
Books & Bygones, Berkshire 57
Books & Bygones (Pam Taylor), W Midlands . 236
Books & Collectables Ltd., Cambridgeshire 63
Books & Things, London W 169
Books (For All), North Yorkshire 190
Books Afloat, Dorset 94
Books and Things, Channel Islands 253
Books Antiques & Collectables, Devon 88
Books at Star Dot Star, W Midlands 236
Books at the Warehouse, North Yorkshire 191
Books B.C., London Outer 178
Books Bought & Sold, Surrey 226
Books for Amnesty, Bristol 58
Books for Content, Herefordshire 128
Books for Writers, Monmouthshire 280
Books in Cardigan, Ceredigion 277
Books on Spain, London Outer 181
Books on the Bank, Durham 96
Books Only, Suffolk 222
Books Plus, Devon 83
Books Ulster, Co. Down 256
Books Upstairs, West Yorkshire 245
Books With Care, Bedfordshire 53
books2books, Devon 87
BOOKS4U, Flintshire 279
Bookseeker, Tayside 275
Bookseller (The), Cumbria 79
Bookshelf (The),, North Yorkshire 192
Bookshelf – Aviation Books, Norfolk 187
Bookshop (The), Co. Donegal 258

Bookshop (The), Greater Manchester............ 119
Bookshop (The), Norfolk 189
Bookshop (The), West Sussex 238
Bookshop (The), Dorset 92
Bookshop at the Plain, Lincolnshire.............. 151
Bookshop on the Heath, The, London SE...... 161
Bookshop, Kirkstall (The), West Yorkshire..... 243
Booksmart, Northamptonshire 196
Bookstack & D.J. Creece (Bookbinder),
  Shropshire 209
Bookstand, Dorset 93
Booktrace International, Devon 85
Bookworld, Shropshire 210
Bookworm, Lothian 270
Bookworm, Essex 110
Bookworm (The), Lothian 271
Bookworm Alley, Devon 87
Bookworms of Evesham, Worcestershire 252
Bookzone, Berkshire 55
Booth (Booksearch Service), (Geoff), Cheshire . 68
Booth Books, Powys 282
Border Books, Borders 262
Border Bookshop, West Yorkshire 245
Boris Books, Hampshire 127
Bosco Books, Cornwall 72
Bosorne Books, Cornwall 74
Boss (Tim), West Sussex 239
Bott, (Bookdealers) Ltd., (Martin), Greater
  Manchester 118
Botting & Berry, East Sussex 101
Boulevard Books, East Sussex 100
Bow Windows Book Shop, East Sussex 102
Bowden Books, Leicestershire 147
Bowdon Books, Lancashire 143
Bowers Chess Suppliers (Francis),
  Cambridgeshire 66
Bowie Books & Collectables, East Yorkshire... 106
Bowland Bookfinders, Lancashire 142
Boxwood Books & Prints, Somerset 216
Boz Books, Powys 282
Bracton Books, Cambridgeshire 63
Brad Books, Essex 109
Bradley–Cox (Mary), Dorset 90
Branksome Books, Dorset 93
Brazenhead Ltd., Norfolk 186
Brett (Harry), Cambridgeshire 65
Brewin Books Ltd., Warwickshire 233
Brian Troath Books, London E 153
Bridge Books, Cumbria 80
Bridge Bookshop Ltd, Isle of Man 254
Bridge of Allan Books, Central 263
Bridport Old Books, Dorset 91
Bright (P.G.), Cambridgeshire 65
Brighton Books, East Sussex 98
Brimstones, East Sussex 102
Brinded (Scott), Kent 139
Bristol Books, Bristol 60
Bristow & Garland, Hampshire 123
Britons Catholic Library, Co. Wexford 261
Broadhurst of Southport Ltd., Merseyside...... 182
Broadleaf Books, Torfaen 287
Broadwater Books, Hampshire 126

ALPHABETICAL INDEX: Business (B – C)

Broadway Books, Cambridgeshire 66
Brock Books, North Yorkshire 190
Brockwells Booksellers, Lincolnshire 148
Brookes (Gerard), Devon......................... 86
Broughton Books, Lothian 271
Brown (Books) (P.R.), Durham 97
Brown (Books) (Steve), Staffordshire............. 219
Brown (K.C.), Berkshire 56
Brown and Rivans Ltd, Devon................... 88
Brown-Studies, Strathclyde 273
Browne (Christopher I.), West Yorkshire 242
Browning Books, Torfaen 287
Browse Books, Lancashire 143
Browsers Bookshop, Cornwall.................... 72
Browsers Bookshop, Essex 109
Browzers, Greater Manchester 119
Bryony Books, West Yorkshire 244
Buckley (Sybil), North Yorkshire 191
Budd (Richard), Somerset 215
Bufo Books, Hampshire 125
Bunyan Books, Bedfordshire...................... 53
Burak (Steve), London WC 174
Burden Ltd., (Clive A.), Hertfordshire 132
Burebank Books, Norfolk 184
Burmester (James), Bristol........................ 58
Burroughs (Andrew), Lincolnshire............... 151
Burton–Garbett (A.), London Outer 180
Bury Bookshop, Suffolk 221
Butcher (Pablo), Oxfordshire 203
Butler Books, Dorset 90
Butterworth (Robert F.), Lancashire 144
Butts Books (Mary), Berkshire 56
Byblos Antiquarian & Rare Book, Hampshire . 122
Bygone Books, Strathclyde 274
Byre Books, Dumfries & Galloway............... 264
Byrom Textile Bookroom (Richard),
 Lancashire 142

Cader Idris Books, Gwynedd 280
Caduceus Books, Leicestershire 145
Caissa Books, Surrey 229
Caledonia Books, Strathclyde..................... 273
Calendula Horticultural Books, East Sussex.... 101
Caliver Books, Essex 110
Calluna Books, Dorset 94
Camden Books, Somerset 212
Cameron (Mrs Janet), Kent...................... 140
Cameron House Books, Isle of Wight 134
Camilla's Bookshop, East Sussex 100
Campbell (Fiona), London SE 161
Campbell Art Books (Marcus), London SE 161
Campbell Hewson Books (R.), Fife 265
Candle Lane Books, Shropshire 210
Canon Gate Books, West Sussex 239
Canterbury Bookshop (The), Kent 136
Capel Mawr Collectors Centre, Gwynedd....... 280
Capes (Books, Maps & Prints) (John L.),
 North Yorkshire................................ 193
Capital Bookshop, Cardiff 276
Carlton Books, Norfolk 187
Carnforth Bookshop (The), Lancashire.......... 142
Carningli Centre, Pembrokeshire................. 281

Carraig Books Ltd., Co. Dublin 258
Carta Regis, Powys 286
Carter, (Brian), Oxfordshire...................... 203
Carters (Janet), Suffolk........................... 222
Cartographics, Staffordshire...................... 220
Cassidy (Bookseller) (P.), Lincolnshire........... 149
Castle Bookshop, Essex 109
Castle Bookshop, Powys......................... 285
Castle Hill Books, Herefordshire 128
Castleton (Pat), Kent 137
Cat Lit, Somerset 215
Catalyst Booksearch Services, Devon 85
Cathach Books Ltd, Co. Dublin 259
Cavendish Rare Books Ltd, London N 155
Cavern Books, Cheshire 70
Cecilia Marsden, London Outer.................. 180
Celtic Bookshop (The), Co. Limerick 261
Central Bookshop, Warwickshire 232
Chalk (Old & Out of Print Books)
 (Christine M.), W Midlands 234
Chalmers Hallam (E.), Hampshire............... 125
Chandos Books, London Outer 180
Chandos Books, Devon........................... 84
Channel Islands Galleries Limited,
 Channel Islands................................ 253
Chantrey Books, South Yorkshire 217
Chapel Books, Suffolk 224
Chapman (Neville), Cornwall..................... 74
Chapter & Verse, Lincolnshire 150
Chapter House Books, Dorset.................... 94
Chapter Two, London SE 161
Charlie Byrne's Bookshop, Co. Galway 260
Chas J. Sawyer, Kent 140
Chaters Motoring Booksellers, London Outer . 179
Chaucer Bookshop, Kent......................... 136
Chaucer Head Bookshop, Warwickshire 233
Chelifer Books, Cumbria 80
Cheshire Book Centre, Cheshire 69
Chesters (G. & J.), Staffordshire.................. 220
Chevin Books, West Yorkshire 245
Chichester Bookshop (The), West Sussex 237
Children's Bookshop (The), Herefordshire...... 282
Childrens Bookshop, West Yorkshire............ 242
Chris Adam Smith Modern First Editions,
 West Sussex 238
Chris Phillips, Wiltshire 246
Christine's Book Cabin, Leicestershire 147
Christopher Saunders (Orchard Books),
 Gloucestershire 115
Chthonios Books, East Sussex.................... 101
Church Green Books, Oxfordshire 207
Church Street Books, Norfolk 184
Church Street Bookshop, London N............. 155
Churchgate Books, Suffolk 221
Churchill Book Specialist (The), London Outer. 179
Clapham (M. & B.), Hampshire 124
Claras Books, East Sussex........................ 100
Clarendon Books, Leicestershire 145
Clark (M.R.), West Yorkshire.................... 241
Clark (Nigel A.), London SE..................... 162
Clarke (J.&D), Norfolk 187
Clarke (Janet), Somerset 212

ALPHABETICAL INDEX: Business (C – D)

Clarke Books (David), Somerset 214
Clarke–Hall (J.) Limited, Kent 137
Classey Limited (E.W.), Oxfordshire 203
Classic Bindings Ltd, London SW 164
Classic Crime Collections, Greater Manchester 119
Classics Bookshop (The), Oxfordshire 202
Clear (Mrs. Patricia), Surrey 226
Clegg (David), Staffordshire........................ 219
Clements (R.W.), London Outer 179
Clent Books, Worcestershire 250
Clevedon Books, Somerset 214
Clifford Elmer Books Ltd., Cheshire 68
Clifford Milne Books, Grampian 266
Clifton Books, Essex 111
Coach House Books, Worcestershire............. 251
Cobbles Books, Somerset........................... 214
Cobnar Books, Kent 139
Cobweb Books, North Yorkshire.................. 192
Coch-y-Bonddu Books, Powys 285
Cocks Books (Brian), Cambridgeshire 66
Cofion Books, Pembrokeshire 281
Cold Tonnage Books, Surrey 229
Coleman (Tom), Highland 268
Coles (T.V.), Cambridgeshire 66
Colin Hancock, Ceredigion 277
Colin Page Books, East Sussex 98
Collards Bookshop, Devon 89
Collectable Books, London SE 162
Collectables (W.H.), Suffolk 225
Collectors Carbooks, Northamptonshire 196
Collectors Corner, Wiltshire........................ 248
Collinge & Clark, London WC 174
Colonsay Bookshop, Isle of Colonsay 269
Colwyn Books, Conwy.............................. 277
Combat Arts Archive, Durham 96
Compass Books, Devon 84
Cooking = The Books, Gloucestershire......... 115
Cooks Books, East Sussex.......................... 98
Coombes (A.J.), Surrey 226
Cooper Hay Rare Books, Strathclyde............ 273
Copnal Books, Cheshire 68
Corder (Mark W.), Kent 140
Corfe Books, Surrey 227
Cornell Books, Gloucestershire.................... 117
Cornerstone Books, Devon 87
Cornucopia Books, Lincolnshire 151
Corvus Books, Buckinghamshire.................. 61
Cotswold Internet Books, Gloucestershire 113
Cottage Books, Leicestershire...................... 145
Cottage Bookshop (The), Buckinghamshire..... 62
Coulthurst (Richard), Greater Manchester 120
Country Books, Derbyshire 81
Countryman Books, East Yorkshire 105
Countrymans Gallery (The), Leicestershire...... 145
Coupland (Terry W.), Staffordshire 219
Court Hay Books, Bristol 58
Courtney & Hoff, North Yorkshire 194
Courtwood Books, Co. Laois...................... 260
Courtyard Books, Gloucestershire 113
Cousens (W.C.), Devon 83
Cover to Cover, Merseyside........................ 183
Cowley, Auto–in–Print (John), Essex 108

Cowley, Bookdealer (K.W.), Somerset........... 214
Cox (Geoff), Devon 89
Cox Music (Lisa), Devon........................... 84
Cox Old & Rare Books (Claude), Suffolk....... 223
Cox Rare Books (Charles), Cornwall 73
Cox, Andrew, Shropshire........................... 211
Cranhurst Books, London NW 158
Craobh Rua Books, Co. Armagh................. 255
Crawford (Elizabeth), London EC................ 154
Creaking Shelves, Highland 268
Crimes Ink, London E 153
Criterion Books, London Outer................... 180
Crombie (R. & S.), W Midlands................. 236
Crosby Nethercott Books, London Outer....... 178
Cross (Ian), Berkshire 55
Crouch Rare Books, Surrey........................ 227
Croydon Bookshop, London Outer 178
Cumming Limited (A. & Y.), East Sussex 102
Curlews, Durham 96
Curtle Mead Books, Isle of Wight................ 134
Cygnet Books, East Yorkshire 107

D'Arcy Books, Wiltshire............................ 246
D. & M. Books, West Yorkshire 244
D.C. Books, Lincolnshire........................... 150
Daisy Lane Books, West Yorkshire 242
Dalby (Richard), North Yorkshire 192
Dales and Lakes Book Centre, Cumbria 79
Dally Books & Collectables, Powys 285
Daly (Peter M.), Hampshire 127
Dance Books Ltd, Hampshire 122
Dancing Goat Bookshop (The), Norfolk 184
Dandy Lion Editions, Surrey 228
Darkwood Books, Co. Cork....................... 258
Dartmoor Bookshop (The), Devon............... 83
DaSilva Puppet Books, Dorset 92
David (G.), Cambridgeshire........................ 63
David Houston - Bookseller, London E......... 153
David Summerfield Books, East Sussex 98
David Warnes Books, Herefordshire............. 129
David Way Angling Books, Devon 86
davidleesbooks.com, Powys 283
Davidson Books, Co. Down....................... 256
Davies Fine Books, Worcestershire............... 252
Davis, Antiquarian Books (Guy),
   Nottinghamshire.................................. 201
Dawlish Books, Devon.............................. 84
Day (J.H.), Hampshire 124
DBS Childrens Collectable Books, Hampshire . 124
de Beaumont (Robin), London SW 164
De Burca Rare Books, Co. Dublin 259
de Visser Books, Cambridgeshire 63
Dead Mens Minds.co.uk, Powys 285
Dean Byass, Bristol 60
Dean Illustrated Books (Myra), Powys 281
Dearman Rare Books (Rebecca), Leicestershire 145
Debbage (John), Norfolk 187
Decorum Books, London N 155
Deeside Books, Grampian.......................... 266
Delectus Books, London WC..................... 174
Delph Books, Greater Manchester................ 120
Demar Books (Grant), Kent 140

ALPHABETICAL INDEX: Business (D – F)

Demetzy Books, Oxfordshire 203
Dene Barn Books & Prints, Somerset 216
Derek Stirling Bookseller, Kent 141
Design Gallery 1850-1950 (The), Kent 141
Devanha Military Books, Tayside 275
Deverell Books, Bristol 58
Dew (Roderick), East Sussex 100
Deyong Books (J.C.), London SW 164
dgbbooks, West Sussex 239
Dinnages Transport Publishing, East Sussex.... 98
Dobson (Bob), Lancashire 142
Dodsworth (Ian), Cumbria 77
Dolphin Books, Suffolk 221
Don Kelly Books, London W 170
Donovan Military Books (Tom), East Sussex .. 98
Doodles Bookshop, North Yorkshire 193
Dooley (Rosemary), Cumbria 80
Doorbar (P. & D.), Gwynned 279
Dorchester Bookshop (The), Dorset 91
Dorset Bookshop (The), Dorset 90
Downie Fine Books Ltd., (Robert),
   Shropshire 211
DPE Books, Devon 86
Draycott Books, Gloucestershire 114
Driffield Bookshop (The), East Yorkshire 105
Drummond Pleasures of Past Times (David),
   London WC 174
Drury Rare Books (John), Essex 111
Du Ry Medieval Manuscripts (Marc–Antoine),
   London W 170
Dublin Bookbrowsers, Co. Dublin 259
Duck (William), Hampshire 124
Duncan & Reid, Lothian 271
Dunn Antiques & Books (Hamish),
   Northumberland 199
Durham Book Centre, Cumbria 76
Dusty Books, Powys 285
Dusty Old Books Ltd., Oxfordshire 204
Dworski Books, Travel & Language
   Bookshop (Marijana), Herefordshire 283
Dylans Bookstore, Glamorgan 286
Dyson (Anthony), W Midlands 235

Eagle Bookshop (The), Bedfordshire 53
Earlsfield Bookshop, London SW 164
Earth Science Books, Wiltshire 247
East Riding Books, East Yorkshire 106
Eastcote Bookshop (The), London Outer 178
Eastern Books of London, London SW 165
Eastern Traveller (The), Somerset 216
Eastgate Bookshop, East Yorkshire 105
Eastleach Books, Berkshire 55
Eastwood Books (David), Cornwall 72
Eclectica, London SE 162
Eddie's Books and Cards, Strathclyde 274
Eden Books, Lincolnshire 150
Edmund Pollinger Rare Books, London SW ... 165
Edrich (I.D.), London E 153
Edwards (Alan & Margaret), Kent 141
Edwards (Christopher), Berkshire 55
Edwards (London) Limited (Francis),
   London WC 175

Edwards in Hay–on–Wye (Francis),
   Herefordshire 283
Eggeling Books (John), West Yorkshire 245
Eggle (Mavis), Hertfordshire 131
Elaine Lonsdale Books, West Yorkshire 242
Elephant Books, West Yorkshire 244
Elgar (Raymond), East Sussex 98
Ellis (J.R. & R.K.), Norfolk 187
Ellis, Bookseller (Peter), London SE 162
Ellwood Editions, Wiltshire 247
Elmfield Books, W Midlands 234
Elmo Books, East Sussex 98
Elstree Books, Hertfordshire 131
Elton Engineering Books, London W 170
Ely Books, Cambridgeshire 65
Embleton (Paul), Essex 111
Emjay Books, Surrey 226
Empire Books, North Yorkshire 194
Endeavour Books, North Yorkshire 194
Engaging Gear Ltd., Essex 108
English (Toby), Oxfordshire 206
Enigma Books, Norfolk 186
Enscot Books, London SE 162
Erian Books, London N 155
Esoteric Dreams Bookshop, Cumbria 77
Esplin (David), Hampshire 124
Eton Antique Bookshop, Berkshire 57
Europa Books, London SW 165
Evans (Mark), Lincolnshire 151
Evans Books (Paul), West Sussex 238
Everett (Richard), Norfolk 184
Everett (Richard, at the Southwold Antiques
   Centre, Suffolk 225
Evergreen Livres, Gloucestershire 115
Ewell Bookshop, Surrey 227
Ex Libris, Wiltshire 246
Exedra Booksearch Ltd., London SW 165
Exeter Rare Books, Devon 84
Explorer Books, West Sussex 239

Facet Books, Dorset 90
Falconwood Transport & Military
   Bookshop, London Outer 181
Family-Favourites, East Yorkshire 105
Fantastic Literature, Essex 111
Fantasy Centre, London N 155
Farahar & Dupre (Clive & Sophie), Wiltshire .. 246
Farnborough Gallery, Hampshire 123
Farquharson, (Hilary), Tayside 275
Farringdon (J.M.), Swansea 287
Farringdon Books, Essex 109
Faversham Books, Kent 138
Fawkes (Keith), London NW 158
Fenning (James), Co. Dublin 259
Ferdinando (Steven), Somerset 215
Ferguson (Elizabeth), Grampian 266
Fiction First, Cheshire 69
Fifteenth Century Bookshop (The), E Sussex .. 102
Fifth Element, W Midlands 235
Finch Rare Books Ltd. (Simon), London W ... 170
Find That Book, West Yorkshire 244
Fine Art, London SE 165

ALPHABETICAL INDEX: Business (F – G)

Fine Books at Ilkley, West Yorkshire............ 243
Fine Books Oriental Ltd., London WC 175
Finn (V. & C.), Merseyside 183
Fiona Edwards, Nottinghamshire................. 200
Fireside Books, Buckinghamshire................ 62
Fireside Bookshop, Cumbria 80
First State Books, London W 170
firstpagebooks, Norfolk............................. 187
Firsts in Print, Isle of Wight 134
Firth (Bijou Books & Photography)
  (Maureen), South Yorkshire 218
Fishburn Books, London NW 158
Fisher & Sperr, London N 155
Fisher Nautical, East Sussex 98
Fitzsimons (Anne), Cumbria....................... 77
Fletcher (H.M.), Hertfordshire 131
Flint (David), Hampshire........................... 122
Fogg Rare Books & Manuscripts (Sam),
  London W... 170
Folios Limited, London SW 165
Footballana, Berkshire 56
Footrope Knots, Suffolk............................ 223
Forbury Fine Books, Berkshire 56
Ford (Richard), London W 170
Ford Books (David), Hertfordshire............... 132
Forder (R.W.), Hampshire.......................... 122
ForensicSearch, Hertfordshire 132
Forest Books, Nottinghamshire 201
Forest Books, Rutland 208
Forest Books of Manchester, Cheshire 70
Formby Antiques (Jeffrey), Gloucestershire..... 115
Fortune Green Books, London NW 158
Fossgate Books, North Yorkshire 194
Foster (Stephen), London NW 158
Foster Bookshop (Paul), London SW 165
Fosters Bookshop, London W 170
Fotheringham (Alex), Northumberland.......... 198
Foulkes (Len), Cardiff............................... 276
Four Shire Bookshops, Oxfordshire.............. 202
Fox Books (J. & J.), Kent.......................... 140
Foyle Books, Co. Derry 255
Franks Booksellers, Greater Manchester 119
Freader's Books, Tayside........................... 275
Freeman's Corner Shop, Norfolk 187
Frew Limited (Robert), London W 170
Freya Books & Antiques, Norfolk................ 187
Frost (Richard), Hertfordshire..................... 130
Fuchsia Books, Co. Wexford 261
Fuller D'Arch Smith, London W 170
Fullerton's Booksearch, Norfolk 185
Fun in Books, Surrey 229
Furneaux Books (Lee), Devon 88

G Collins Bookdealers, Hertfordshire............ 131
G. Bickford-Smith (formerly Snowden Smith
  Books), Surrey...................................... 228
G. C. Books Ltd., Dumfries & Galloway 264
Gage Postal Books, Essex 111
Galloway & Porter Limited,
  Cambridgeshire 63
Game Advice, Oxfordshire 205
Gander, (Jacques), Gloucestershire 115

Garbett Antiquarian Books (Michael),
  Gloucestershire 113
Gardener & Cook, London SW 165
Garfi Books, Ceredigion 282
Garretts Antiquarian Books, Isle of Man 254
Garwood & Voigt, Kent............................. 140
Gaskell Rare Books (Roger), Cambridgeshire.. 66
Gathern (D.), Conwy................................ 278
Gaullifmaufry Books, Hertfordshire.............. 131
Gay's The Word, London WC 175
Gekoski (R.A.), London WC 175
Gemini–Books, Shropshire 210
Geneva Books, London SW 165
Geophysical Books, Kent........................... 140
George St. Books, Derbyshire 82
GfB: the Colchester Bookshop, Essex........... 109
Gibbard (A. & T.), East Sussex 100
Gibberd (Jane), London SE 162
Gibbs Books, (Jonathan), Worcestershire 251
Gibbs Bookshop Ltd., Greater Manchester..... 119
Gilbert (R.A.), Bristol............................... 59
Gilbert and Son (H.M.), Hampshire 127
Gildas Books, Cheshire 68
Gillmark Gallery, Hertfordshire................... 131
Glacier Books, Tayside.............................. 275
Gladstone Books, Nottinghamshire 200
Glance Back Books, Gwent........................ 279
Glenbower Books, Co. Dublin 259
Glenwood Books, Surrey 230
Gloucester Road Bookshop, London SW....... 165
Glyn's Books, Shropshire 209
Godmanchester Books, Cambridgeshire 65
Golden Age Books, Worcestershire.............. 251
Golden Books Group, Devon 84
Golden Goose Books, Lincolnshire............... 150
Goldman (Paul), Dorset 94
Goldsworth Books, Surrey 230
Good Books, Shropshire 210
Good for Books, Lincolnshire 149
Goodden (Peter), Somerset 212
Goodwin (J.O.), Staffordshire 220
Goodyer (Nicholas), London N................... 156
Goodyer, Natural History Books (Eric),
  Leicestershire.. 146
Graduate Books, Worcestershire 252
Graham (John), Dorset 95
Grahame (Major Iain), Suffolk.................... 221
Grahame Thornton, Bookseller, Dorset 92
Grampian Books, Grampian....................... 268
Grange Old Bookshop, Merseyside.............. 182
Granny's Attic, Wiltshire........................... 246
Grant & Shaw Ltd., Lothian 271
Grant Books, Worcestershire 250
Grayling (David A.H.), Cumbria.................. 78
Grays of Westminster, London SW 165
Great Grandfather's, Lancashire................... 143
Great Oak Bookshop (The), Powys 285
Green (Mrs. D.M.), Surrey......................... 229
Green (Paul), Cambridgeshire 66
Green Ltd. (G.L.), Hertfordshire.................. 132
Green Man Books, East Sussex 100
Green Meadow Books, Cornwall 74

ALPHABETICAL INDEX: Business (G – H)

Greene's Bookshop Ltd, Co. Dublin 259
Greenroom Books, West Yorkshire 243
Greensleeves, Oxfordshire 202
Greer (Robin), London SW 166
Gregory (George), Somerset 212
Gresham Books, Somerset 214
Greta Books, Durham 96
Grosvenor Prints, London WC 175
Grove Bookshop (The), North Yorkshire 193
GS Cricket Books / The Old Book Shop, W Midlands 236
Guildmaster Books, Cheshire 70
Guisborough Bookshop (The), N Yorkshire ... 190
Hab Books, London W 171

Hadfield (G.K.), Cumbria 78
Hadley Bookseller (Peter J.), Essex 110
Halewood & Sons, Lancashire 144
Hall's Bookshop, Kent 141
Hall, (Anthony C.) Antiquarian Bookseller, London Outer 181
Halson Books, Cheshire 71
Hames (Peter), Devon 83
Hamish Riley-Smith, Norfolk 188
Hanborough Books, Oxfordshire 205
Hancock & Monks, Powys 283
Hancock (Peter), West Sussex 237
Handley (Christopher), Newcastle Upon Tyne . 183
Handsworth Books, Essex 112
Hanshan Tang Books, London SW 166
Hardback Hotel, Lancashire 143
Harlequin, Devon 89
Harlequin Books, Bristol 59
Harlequin Gallery, Lincolnshire 150
Harries (Pauline), Hampshire 124
Harrington (Adrian), London W 171
Harrington Antiquarian Bookseller (Peter), London SW 166
Harris (Books), (Malcolm), W Midlands 234
Harris (George J.), Co. Derry 255
Hart (John), Norfolk 188
Harvest Books, Lancashire 144
Haskell (R.H. & P.), Dorset 93
Hatchard & Daughters, West Yorkshire 242
Hatchard & Daughters, West Yorkshire 242
Haunted Bookshop (The), Cambridgeshire ... 63
Hava Books, London SE 161
Hawes Books, Norfolk 187
Hawkes (James), Bristol 60
Hawkridge Books, Derbyshire 81
Hawley (C.L.), North Yorkshire 193
Hay Castle, Powys 283
Hay Cinema Bookshop Ltd., Herefordshire ... 283
HCB Wholesale, Powys 283
Head (John & Judith), Wiltshire 247
Heartland Old Books, Devon 88
Heath (A.R.), Bristol 59
Heatons, Wiltshire 248
Heckmondwike Book Shop, West Yorkshire ... 244
Hedgerow Books, South Yorkshire 217
Helion & Company, W Midlands 235
Hellenic Bookservices, London NW 158

Helmsley Antiquarian & Secondhand Books, North Yorkshire 191
Helston Bookworm (The), Cornwall 73
Hemswell Antique Centre, Lincolnshire 149
Hencotes Books & Prints, Northumberland ... 198
Heneage Art Books (Thomas), London SW ... 166
Henly (John), West Sussex 239
Hennessey Bookseller (Ray), East Sussex 99
Heppa (Christopher), Essex 108
Heraldry Today, Wiltshire 247
Herb Tandree Philosophy Books, Gloucestershire 116
Hereford Booksearch (John Trevitt), Herefordshire 129
Hereward Books, Cambridgeshire 65
Heritage, W Midlands 234
Heritage Books, Isle of Wight 134
Hesketh & Ward Ltd., London SW 166
Heywood Hill Limited (G.), London W 171
Hicks (Ronald C.), Cornwall 73
High Street Book Shop, East Sussex 101
High Street Books, Devon 85
Higher Octave Books, Bristol 59
Hight (Norman F.), Glamorgan 279
Hill (John S.), Devon 84
Hill (Peter), Hampshire 123
Hill Books (Alan), South Yorkshire 217
Hill House Books, Devon 87
Hinchliffe Books, Bristol 59
Hine (Anne), Somerset 214
Hobgoblin Books, Hampshire 125
Hodgkins and Company Limited (Ian), Gloucestershire 116
Hodgson (Books) (Richard J.), North Yorkshire 194
Hodgson (Judith), London W 171
Hogan (F. & J.), London N 156
Holdenhurst Books, Dorset 90
Holdsworth Books (Bruce), East Sussex 103
Hollett and Son (R.F.G.), Cumbria 79
Holleyman (J.F.), East Sussex 101
Hollingshead (Chris), London Outer 181
Holmes (A.), Nottinghamshire 201
Holmes Books (Harry), East Yorkshire 106
Holtom (Christopher), Cornwall 75
Hook (Arthur), Bristol 59
Hoovey's Books, East Sussex 101
Hornsby, Antiquarian and Secondhand Books (Malcolm), Leicestershire 146
Hornsey's, North Yorkshire 192
Horsham Rare Books, West Sussex 238
Hosains Books, London NW 159
House of Figgis Ltd (The), Co. Galway 260
Howes Bookshop, East Sussex 101
HP Bookfinders, Central 263
Hünersdorff Rare Books, London SW 166
Hughes Rare Books (Spike), Borders 262
hullbooks.com, East Yorkshire 106
Humanist Book Services, Cornwall 72
Humber Books, Lincolnshire 148
Humm & Co. (Robert), Lincolnshire 151
Hummingbird Books, Herefordshire 128

ALPHABETICAL INDEX: Business (H – K)

Hunt (Robin S.), Greater Manchester 120
Hunter and Krageloh, Derbyshire 82
Hunter–Rare Books (Andrew), London SW.... 166
Hurly Burly Books, Wiltshire 249
Hurst (Jenny), Kent 138
Hutchison (Books) (Larry), Fife.................... 265
Hyland (C.P.), Co. Cork............................. 258
Hylton Booksearch, Merseyside 182

Ian Briddon, Derbyshire............................. 81
Ice House Books, Wiltshire 248
Idle Booksellers (The), West Yorkshire 241
Idle Genius Books, London N 156
Idler (The), Suffolk 223
IKON, Devon 88
Inch's Books, North Yorkshire..................... 192
Inner Bookshop (The), Oxfordshire 205
Innes Books, Shropshire 209
Inprint, Gloucestershire.............................. 116
Intech Books, Northumberland 198
InterCol London, London N 156
Internet Bookshop UK Ltd., Gloucestershire .. 113
Interstellar Master Traders, Lancashire 143
Invicta Bookshop, Berkshire 56
Invisible Books, East Sussex 98
Iona Bookshop (The), Isle of Iona 269
Isabelline Books, Cornwall 72
Island Books, Kent 136
Ives Bookseller (John), London Outer 181

J & D Jones, Cheshire 70
J & J Burgess Booksellers, Cambridgeshire 64
J C Books, Devon 86
J. & J. Books, Lincolnshire 149
J.A. Heacock, Cheshire 69
J.B. Books, Berkshire................................. 56
J.C. Books, Norfolk 188
J.G. Natural History Books, Surrey 228
J.L. Book Exchange, East Yorkshire............. 105
Jabberwock Books, Lincolnshire.................. 150
Jackdaw Books, Norfolk 185
Jackson (M.W.), Wiltshire........................... 249
Jackson (W.E.), Hampshire 126
Jade Mountain, Hampshire 125
James Fergusson Books & Manuscripts,
  London W.. 170
Jane Badger Books, Northamptonshire 196
Jane Jones Books, Grampian....................... 267
Janian Comics / Computer Manuals,
  Buckinghamshire 62
Janus Books, W Midlands 235
Jarndyce Antiquarian Booksellers,
  London WC.. 175
Jarvis Books, Derbyshire 82
Jay Books, Lothian 271
JB Books & Collectables, West Sussex........... 238
Jean Hedger, Berkshire............................... 55
Jermy & Westerman, Nottinghamshire 201
Jill Howell, Kent 138
Jiri Books, Co. Antrim............................... 255
Jobson (N.W.), Oxfordshire......................... 204
John Barton, Hampshire............................. 127

John Gorton Booksearch, East Sussex........... 103
John R. Hoggarth, North Yorkshire............. 194
John Underwood Antiquarian Books, Norfolk 186
Johnson Rare Book Collections (C.R.),
  London NW 159
Jolly Good Read (A.), Tayside.................... 275
Jones (Andrew), Suffolk 223
Jones (Barry), West Sussex......................... 238
Jones (Madalyn S.), West Yorkshire 242
Jonkers Rare Books, Oxfordshire................. 204
Joppa Books Ltd., Surrey 226
Judd Books, London WC 175
Junk & Spread Eagle, London SE................ 162
Just Books, Cornwall................................ 75

K Books, Cheshire.................................... 69
K.S.C. Books, Cheshire.............................. 68
Kabristan Archives, Shropshire 211
Kalligraphia (formerly Charmouth
  Bounty Books), Isle of Wight.................... 134
Karen Millward, Co. Cork......................... 257
Katharine House Gallery, Wiltshire 247
Katnap Arts, Norfolk 187
Kay Books, London W.............................. 171
Kaye - Bookseller (Terence), London NW...... 159
Keeble Antiques, Somerset 215
Keegan's Bookshop, Berkshire 56
Keel Row Books, Tyne and Wear 231
Kellow Books, Oxfordshire 203
Kelly Books, Devon 88
Kelsall (George), Greater Manchester............ 119
Kemp Booksellers, East Yorkshire 106
Ken's Paper Collectables, Buckinghamshire 62
Kendall–Carpenter (Tim), Greater Manchester 119
Kennedy & Farley, East Sussex 103
Kennedy (Peter), Surrey 230
Kenny's Book Export Co., Co. Galway 260
Kenny's Bookshops and Art Galleries Ltd,
  Co. Galway 260
Kent (Books) (Mrs. A.), Suffolk 223
Kentish (B. & N.), Oxfordshire.................... 202
Kenya Books, East Sussex 99
Keogh's Books, Gloucestershire................... 115
Kernaghans, Merseyside 183
Kerr (Norman), Cumbria........................... 77
Kestrel Books, Powys 283
Keswick Bookshop, Cumbria...................... 78
Kevin S. Ogilvie Modern First Editions,
  Grampian 266
Key Books (Sarah), Cambridgeshire 64
Kidson (Ruth), East Sussex........................ 103
Kilgarriff (Raymond), East Sussex................ 104
Kilgour (Sporting Books) (Ian), Leicestershire . 147
Killeen (John), North Yorkshire................... 191
Kim's Bookshop, West Sussex 237, 240
Kineton Nooks, Warwickshire 232
King Street Bookshop (The), Norfolk 185
Kingfisher Book Service, Nottinghamshire...... 201
Kings Bookshop Callander, Central.............. 263
Kingsgate Books & Prints, Hampshire........... 127
Kingshead Books, Wales 286
Kingsmere Books, Bedfordshire................... 53

ALPHABETICAL INDEX: Business (K – M)

Kingswood Books, Dorset 93
Kirkcudbright Books, Dumfries & Galloway... 264
Kirkdale Bookshop, London SE 162
Kirkland Books, Cumbria 78
Kirkman Ltd., (Robert), Bedfordshire 53
Kirkpatrick (Robert J.), London W 171
Kitley (A.J.), Bristol 59
Knapton Bookbarn, North Yorkshire 194
Knowles (John), Norfolk 185
Kohler (C.C.), Surrey 226
Korn (M. Eric), London N 156
Kunkler Books (Paul), Cambridgeshire 64
Kyrios Books, Nottinghamshire 200

Lake (David), Norfolk 187
Lake (Fred), Surrey 229
Lamb (R.W.), Suffolk 224
Lamb's Tales Books, Devon 85
Lane Books (Shirley), Isle of Wight 135
Lankester Antiques and Books, Essex 111
Larkham Books (Patricia), Gloucestershire 117
Lawful Occasions, Essex 108
Lawrence Books, Nottinghamshire 200
Lawson & Company (E.M.), Oxfordshire 203
Lawton (J.), Surrey 227
Laywood (Anthony W.), Nottinghamshire 200
Leabeck Books, Oxfordshire 205
Leaf Ends, Northumberland 199
Leakey's Bookshop, Highland 268
Leapman Ltd. (G. & R.), Hertfordshire 132
Lee Jackson, London NW 159
Lee Rare Books (Rachel), Bristol 59
Lee, Maritime Books (Gerald), East Sussex 104
Leeds Bookseller, West Yorkshire 244
Leeper (Romilly), London SW 166
Left on The Shelf, Cumbria 78
Leigh Gallery Books, Essex 110
Lenton (Alfred), Leicestershire 145
Letterbox Books, Nottinghamshire 200
Lewcock (John), Cambridgeshire 66
Lewis (J.T. & P.), Cornwall 73
Lewis First Editions, Kent 137
Libra Books, Lincolnshire 148
Libris (Weston) Books, Somerset 213
Liddle (Steve), Bristol 58
Lighthouse Books (The), Dorset 91
Lime Tree Books, Suffolk 224
Lion Books, Worcestershire 250
Little Bookshop (The), Greater Manchester 119
Little Bookshop (The), Cumbria 80
Little Stour Books, Kent 136
Lloyd-Davies (Sue), Carmarthenshire 277
Loch Croispol Bookshop & Restaurant,
  Highland 268
Londinium Books, Surrey 226
London & Sussex Antiquarian Book & Print
  Services, East Sussex 100
Longden (George), Cheshire 69
Loretta Lay Books, London NW 159
Lost Books, Northamptonshire 197
Lowe (John), Norfolk 186
Lucas (Richard), London NW 159

Lucius Books, North Yorkshire 195
Lymelight Books & Prints, Dorset 92
Lyngheath Books, Norfolk 186

M. & D. Books, Worcestershire 250
Macbuiks, North Yorkshire 190
Macfarlane (Mr. H.), Essex 112
Mactaggart (Caroline), Dorset 91
Maggs Brothers Limited, London W 171
Maghreb Bookshop (The), London WC 175
Magis Books, Leicestershire 147
Magpie Books, West Yorkshire 245
Main Point Books, Lothian 271
Main–Smith & Co. Ltd. (Bruce), Leicestershire 146
Mainly Fiction, Greater Manchester 118
Mair Wilkes Books, Fife 265
Malvern Bookshop (The), Worcestershire 250
Mandalay Bookshop, London SW 166
Manna Bookshop, Somerset 216
Mannwaring (M.G.), Bristol 59
Mansfield (Judith), West Yorkshire 245
Marathon Books, Greater Manchester 118
Marble Hill Books, Middlesex 181
Marcan, Bookseller (Peter), London SE 162
Marcet Books, London SE 161
March House Books, Dorset 94
Marchpane, London WC 175
Marco Polo Travel & Adventure Books, Dorset 91
Marine & Cannon Books, Cheshire 71
Marine and Cannon Books, Cheshire 69
Marine Workshop Bookshop, Dorset 92
Marjon Books, Essex 112
Marks Limited (Barrie), London N 156
Marlborough Rare Books Ltd., London W 171
Marrin's Bookshop, Kent 138
Marshall Rare Books (Bruce), Gloucestershire. 113
Martin - Bookseller (Colin), East Yorkshire.... 106
Martin Bookshop & Gallery (Richard),
  Hampshire 123
Martin Music Books (Philip), North Yorkshire 195
Martin's Books, Powys 285
Mason (Mary), Oxfordshire 202
Mayhew (Veronica), Berkshire 56
Mayhew Books, Norfolk 184
Maynard & Bradley, Leicestershire 146
mcbooks, West Sussex 237
McCarty, Bookseller (M.E.), Western Isles 269
McCarty, Bookseller (M.E.),
  Dumfries & Galloway 264
McCaughtrie (K.A.), North Yorkshire 190
McConnell Fine Books, Kent 137
McCrone (Audrey), Isle of Arran 269
McEwan Fine Books, Grampian 266
McEwan Golf Books (Rhod), Grampian 268
McGavin (Don), Highland 268
McGee (Terence J.), London Outer 178
McGlynn (John), Lancashire 142
McInnes (P.F. & J.R.), Dorset 90
McKelvie (Ian), London N 156
McKenzie (J.W.), Surrey 227
McLaren Books, Strathclyde 274
McNaughtan's Bookshop, Lothian 271

ALPHABETICAL INDEX: Business (M – O)

Mead (P.J.), Shropshire 210
Meads Book Service (The), East Sussex 103
medievalbookshop, London Outer 179
Meekins Books (Paul), Warwickshire 233
Mellon's Books, East Sussex 100
Melvin Tenner, London W 171
Mercat Books, Highland 268
Mereside Books, Cheshire 70
Merlin Books, West Sussex 238
Michael Graves-Johnston, London SW 166
Michael J Carroll, Co. Cork 257
Miles Apart, Suffolk 224
Milestone Books, Devon 88
Milestone Publications Goss & Crested China, Hampshire 124
Military Parade Bookshop, Wiltshire 247
MilitaryHistoryBooks.com, Kent 138
Millard (R.W.), Somerset 213
Miller (Karen), Nottinghamshire 200
Miller (Stephen), London Outer 181
Mills Rare Books (Adam), Cambridgeshire 64
Ming Books, Dumfries & Galloway 265
Minster Books, Dorset 95
Minster Gate Bookshop, North Yorkshire 195
Missing Books, Essex 109
MK Book Services, Cambridgeshire 66
Mobbs (A.J.), W Midlands 235
Modern First Editions, London Outer 180
Modern Firsts Etc, Lancashire 142
Modern Welsh Publications Ltd., Merseyside .. 182
Modlock (Lilian), Dorset 92
Moffat Book Exchange, Dumfries & Galloway 264
Mogul Diamonds, W Midlands 236
Mollie's Loft, Swansea 287
Monmouth House Books, Monmouthshire 280
Moon's Bookshop (Michael), Cumbria 80
Moore (C.R.), Shropshire 210
Moore (Eric T.), Hertfordshire 131
Moore (Peter), Cambridgeshire 64
Moore (Sue), Cornwall 73
Moorhead Books, West Yorkshire 241
Moorland Books, Greater Manchester 120
Moorside Books, Lancashire 143
Moray Bookshop (The), Grampian 267
Moreton Books, Devon 86
Morgan (H.J.), Bedfordshire 54
Morley Case, Hampshire 126
Morris (A.E.), Gwynedd 279
Morris Secondhand & Antiquarian Books (Chris), Oxfordshire 205
Morten (Booksellers) (E.J.), Greater Manchester 119
Moseley Books, W Midlands 234
Moss Books, London NW 159
Moss Books, Gloucestershire 114
Moss End Bookshop, Berkshire 57
Mostly Mysteries Bookstore, Lincolnshire 150
Mothergoose Bookshop, Isle of Wight 134
Mount's Bay Books, Cornwall 74
Mountaineering Books, London N 156
Mr. Pickwick of Towcester, Northamptonshire 196
Much Ado Books, East Sussex 98

Mulyan (Don), Merseyside 183
Mundy (David), Hertfordshire 130
Mundy (David), Buckinghamshire 61
Murch Booksend, (Herbert), London SE 162
Murder & Mayhem, Powys 284
Murphy (C.J.), Norfolk 187
Muse Bookshop (The), Gwynedd 279
Music By The Score, Cornwall 72
Musicalania, Norfolk 186
Muttonchop Manuscripts, West Sussex 239
My Back Pages, London SW 167

N V Books, Warwickshire 232
N1 Books, East Sussex 103
Naughton Booksellers, Co. Dublin 259
Nautical Antique Centre (The), Dorset 94
Needham Books, (Russell), Somerset 216
Neeve (P.), Cambridgeshire 64
Neil Summersgill, Lancashire 142
Neil's Books, London NW 159
Nelson (Elizabeth), Suffolk 222
Nevis Railway Books, Oxfordshire 204
Nevis Railway Bookshops (The Antique & Book Collector), Wiltshire 247
Nevitsky (Philip), Greater Manchester 119
New Strand Bookshop (The), Herefordshire ... 128
Newband (D.M.), Powys 286
Newcastle Bookshop, Northumberland 198
Newgate Books and Translations, Northumberland 198
Newlyn & New Street Books, Cornwall 74
Nibris Books, London SW 167
Nicholson of Chester (Richard), Cheshire 68
Nicolas - Antiquarian Booksellers & Art Dealers, London N 156
Niner (Marcus), Gloucestershire 116
Nineteenth Century Books, Oxfordshire 207
Nonsuch Books, Surrey 229
Northern Herald Books, West Yorkshire 241
Norton Books, North Yorkshire 194
Nostalgia Unlimited, Merseyside 182
Not JUST Books, Lincolnshire 148
Not Just Books, Dorset 94

O'Brien Books & Photo Gallery, Co. Limerick 261
O'Connor Fine Books, Lancashire 144
O'Donoghue Books, Powys 284
O'Kill (John), Kent 138
O'Reilly - Mountain Books (John), Derbyshire 82
Oakwood Books, Gloucestershire 115
Oasis Booksearch, Cambridgeshire 67
Oast Books, Kent 137
Obscurebooks, Co. Dublin 259
Occultique, Northamptonshire 196
Offa's Dyke Books, Shropshire 209
Old Aberdeen Bookshop, Grampian 266
Old Bookshelf (The), Strathclyde 273
Old Bookshop (The), W Midlands 236
Old Cathay Fine Books, West Yorkshire 244
Old Celtic Bookshop (The), Devon 86
Old Hall Bookshop (The), Northamptonshire 196

ALPHABETICAL INDEX: Business (O – P)

Old Station Pottery & Bookshop (The), Norfolk ... 189
Old Town Bookshop (The), Lothian ... 271
Olynthiacs, Shropshire ... 210
Onepoundpaperbacks, Cleveland ... 96
Oopalba Books, Cheshire ... 71
Optimus Books Ltd, West Sussex ... 240
Orange Skies Books, Cumbria ... 79
Orangeberry Books, Oxfordshire ... 204
Orb's Bookshop, Grampian ... 268
Orbis Books (London) Ltd., London W ... 171
Orchid Book Distributors, Co. Clare ... 257
Oriental and African Books, Shropshire ... 210
Orssich (Paul), London SW ... 167
Osterley Bookshop, London Outer ... 180
Othello's Bookshop, Essex ... 110
Ouse Valley Books, Bedfordshire ... 54
Outcast Books, Herefordshire ... 284
Over-Sands Books, Cumbria ... 77
Owen (J.V.), Conwy ... 278
owenbooks65, Conwy ... 278
Oxfam Books and Music, Hampshire ... 127
Oxfam Bookshop St Giles, Oxfordshire ... 205
Oxford House Books, Powys ... 284
Oxley (Laurence), Hampshire ... 122

P. and P. Books, Worcestershire ... 251
Pagan Limited (Hugh), London SW ... 167
Page (David), Lothian ... 271
Palladour Books, Hampshire ... 126
Pamona Books, Lancashire ... 144
Pandion Books, North Yorkshire ... 192
Pantiles Bookshop, Kent ... 141
Paper Moon Books, Warwickshire ... 233
Paper Pleasures, Somerset ... 215
Paperbacks Plus, Bristol ... 59
Parade Bookshop, Suffolk ... 225
Paragon Books, Somerset ... 214
Paralos Ltd., London WC ... 175
Paramor (C.D.), Suffolk ... 224
Parikian, Rare Books (Diana), London W ... 171
Park (Mike), London Outer ... 180
Park Gallery & Bookshop (The), Northamptonshire ... 197
Parker Books (Mike), Cambridgeshire ... 64
Parkinsons Books, Merseyside ... 183
Parlour Bookshop (The), Oxfordshire ... 203
Parrott (Jeremy), London E ... 153
Parrott Books, Oxfordshire ... 207
Past & Present Books, Gloucestershire ... 114
Pastmasters, Derbyshire ... 82
Paton Books, Hertfordshire ... 132
Patterson (J.D.), Bristol ... 60
Paul Hoare, Cornwall ... 74
Peake (Robin), Lincolnshire ... 151
Peakirk Books, Cambridgeshire ... 67
Pedlar's Pack Books, Devon ... 89
Peel (Valerie), Berkshire ... 55
Pemberley Books, Buckinghamshire ... 62
Pendleburys Bookshop, London N ... 156
Pendleside Books, Lancashire ... 143
Pennymead Books, North Yorkshire ... 191

Peregrine Books (Leeds), West Yorkshire ... 244
Period Fine Bindings, Warwickshire ... 233
Periplus Books, Buckinghamshire ... 62
Periwinkle Press, Kent ... 139
Peter Clay, Cornwall ... 73
Peter Lyons Books, Gloucestershire ... 114
Peter Pan Bookshop, Norfolk ... 188
Peter White, Hampshire ... 122
Peter's Bookshop, Norfolk ... 188
Petersfield Bookshop (The), Hampshire ... 125
Peterson (Tony), Essex ... 111
Petworth Antique Market (Bookroom), West Sussex ... 239
Phelps (Michael), West Sussex ... 237
Phenotype Books, Cumbria ... 78
Philip Hopper, Essex ... 110
Phillips (Nigel), London SW ... 167
Phillips of Hitchin (Antiques) Ltd., Hertfordshire ... 131
Pholiota Books, London WC ... 176
Photo Books International, London WC ... 176
Phototitles.com, Essex ... 109
Piccadilly Rare Books, East Sussex ... 104
Pickering & Chatto, London W ... 172
Pinnacle Books, Lothian ... 271
Plurabelle Books, Cambridgeshire ... 64
Pocket Bookshop (The), Devon ... 86
Poetry Bookshop (The), Powys ... 284
Polczynski (Udo K.H.), Powys ... 284
Politico's.co.uk, Kent ... 141
Pollak (P.M.), Devon ... 87
Polmorla Books, Cornwall ... 75
Pomes Penyeach, Staffordshire ... 219
Pooks Motor Books, Leicestershire ... 146
Poole (William), London W ... 172
Poor Richard's Books, Suffolk ... 222
Popeley (Frank T.), Cambridgeshire ... 67
Porcupine Books, London Outer ... 179
Pordes Books Ltd., (Henry), London WC ... 176
Porter Bookshop (The), South Yorkshire ... 217
Portobello Books, London W ... 172
Portus Books, Hampshire ... 123
Post Mortem Books, West Sussex ... 238
Postings, Surrey ... 228
Potter Limited (Jonathan), London W ... 172
Potterton Books, North Yorkshire ... 194
Pratt (B.A. & C.W.M.), Herefordshire ... 128
Prescott - The Bookseller (John), London Outer ... 181
Preston Book Company, Lancashire ... 144
Price (John), London N ... 157
Price (R.D.M. & I.M.) (Books), Greater Manchester ... 120
Price (R.W.), Nottinghamshire ... 200
Priestpopple Books, Northumberland ... 198
Primrose Hill Books, London NW ... 159
Pringle Booksellers (Andrew), Lothian ... 271
Printing House (The), Cumbria ... 77
Prior (Michael), Lincolnshire ... 151
Priory Books, Worcestershire ... 252
Probsthain (Arthur), London WC ... 176
Professional Book Services, North Yorkshire ... 190

ALPHABETICAL INDEX: Business (P – S)

Prospect Books, Conwy............................. 278
Prospect House Books, Co. Down 256
PsychoBabel Books & Journals, Oxfordshire... 202
Pugh Books (Ian K.), Worcestershire 251
Pyecroft (Ruth), Gloucestershire 116

Quaritch Ltd., (Bernard), London W 172
Quarto Bookshop (The), Fife...................... 266
Queen Victoria PH, Torfaen....................... 287
Quentin Books Ltd, Essex 109
Quest Books, East Yorkshire 106
Quest Booksearch, Cambridgeshire................ 64
Quinto of Charing Cross Road, London WC.. 176
Quinto of Great Russell Street, London WC... 176

R M Books, Hertfordshire 132
R & B Graham Trading, Cornwall................ 73
R. & A. Books, East Sussex 100
R. S. & P. A. Scowen, Middlesex................ 179
R.E. & G.B. Way, Suffolk 224
Raftery Books (Michael D.), Leicestershire 145
Railway Book and Magazine Search, Berkshire 56
Railway Shop (The), Torfaen...................... 287
Rainbow Books, East Sussex 99
Rainford (Sheila), Hertfordshire................... 130
Randall (Tom), Somerset 215
Rare & Racy, South Yorkshire.................... 217
Rare Books & Berry, Somerset.................... 215
Rassam (Paul), London NW 159
Ray Rare and Out of Print Books (Janette), North Yorkshire..................................... 195
Rayner (Hugh Ashley), Somerset 212
Read Ireland, Co. Dublin 258
Readers Rest, Lincolnshire 150
Reading Lasses, Dumfries & Galloway 265
Reads, Dorset... 94
Reaveley Books, Devon.............................. 85
recollectionsbookshop.co.uk, Cornwall 74
Red Rose Books, Lancashire 144
Red Star Books, Hertfordshire 130
Rees & O'Neill Rare Books, London WC 176
Reeves Technical Books, North Yorkshire...... 193
Reference Works Ltd., Dorset...................... 94
Reid of Liverpool, Merseyside..................... 182
Reigate Galleries, Surrey............................ 228
Remington (Reg & Philip), Hertfordshire 132
Restormel Books, Worcestershire 252
Resurgam Books, East Yorkshire 105
RGS Books, Surrey................................... 229
Rhoda (June), Essex................................. 110
Rhodes, Bookseller (Peter), Hampshire 126
Rhos Point Books, Conwy 278
Richard Connole 84
Richard Thornton Books, London N............. 157
Richmond Books, North Yorkshire 192
Riddell (Peter), East Yorkshire 105
Rider Haggard Society (The), Tyne and Wear . 231
Riderless Horse Books, Norfolk 184
Riley Books (V.M.), Greater Manchester 119
Ripping Yarns, London N 157
Rising Tide Books, Fife............................. 265
Rittner Booksearch (Hilary), London SE 162

Rivendale Press, Buckinghamshire................. 61
River Reads Bookshop, Devon..................... 89
Riviera Books, Norfolk 185
Roadmaster Books, Kent............................ 137
Robert (Leslie), London W 172
Robert G Sawers Ltd, London NW 159
Robert's Shop, East Sussex 101
Roberts (Booksellers), (Ray), Staffordshire...... 219
Roberts (William H.), West Yorkshire........... 243
Roberts Books, Strathclyde 274
Roberts Fine Books (Julian), Lincolnshire 151
Roberts Wine Books (John), Bristol.............. 60
Robertshaw (John), Cambridgeshire............... 66
Robertson Books, Lothian 271
Robin Doughty - Fine Books, W Midlands 234
Rochdale Book Company, Greater Manchester................................. 120
Rods Books, Devon 87
Roe and Moore, London WC..................... 176
Roger Collicott Books, Cornwall 74
Roger Lucas Booksellers, Lincolnshire........... 150
Rogers Turner Books, London SE 162
Roland Books, Kent.................................. 139
Rolfe (John), London SE........................... 162
Rolling Stock Books, Greater Manchester 121
Rolph (John), Suffolk 224
Rookery Bookery, Staffordshire.................... 220
Roosterbooks, Northamptonshire.................. 196
Rosanda Books, Leicestershire 146
Roscrea Bookshop, Co. Tipperary................. 261
Rose Books, Greater Manchester 120
Rose's Books, Herefordshire....................... 284
Rosemary Books, Merseyside...................... 183
Rosemary Pugh Books, Wiltshire 248
Ross & Company Ltd., (Louise), Worcestershire 250
Ross Old Books & Prints, Herefordshire........ 128
Rothwell & Dunworth, Somerset 214
Roundstone Books, Lancashire 143
Rowan (H. & S.J.), Dorset........................ 90
Rowan (P. & B.), Co. Antrim 255
Rowan House Books, Surrey 226
Royal Carbery Books Ltd., Co. Cork 257
Roz Hulse, Conwy................................... 278
Ruebotham (Kirk), Cheshire....................... 70
Rugby Relics, West Glamorgan.................... 281
Rupert Books, Cambridgeshire..................... 64
Ruskin Books, Kent.................................. 136
Russell (Charles), London SW 167
Rutland Bookshop (The), Rutland 208
Ryde Bookshop (The), Isle of Wight............ 134
Rye Old Books, East Sussex 103
Ryeland Books, Northamptonshire................ 196

S.P.C.K., Bristol...................................... 59
S.P.C.K., Hampshire................................. 127
SaBeRo Books, London SW....................... 167
Sabin (Printed Works) (P.R. & V.), Kent 136
Saint Ann's Books, Worcestershire 251
Saint Mary's Books & Prints, Lincolnshire 152
Saint Paul's Street Bookshop, Lincolnshire 152
Saint Philip's Books, Oxfordshire................. 205

Saint Swithin's Illustrated & Children's
  Books, London W 172
Saintfield Antiques & Fine Books, Co. Down.. 255
Salsus Books, Worcestershire 250
Saltburn Bookshop, North Yorkshire............ 192
Salway Books, Essex 112
Samovar Books, Co. Dublin........................ 258
Sandpiper Books Ltd., London SW 167
Sandstone Books, Kent 137
Sansovino Books, West Sussex 239
Sarawak Books, East Yorkshire................... 105
Saunders (Tom), Caerphilly 276
Savage (Keith A.), Suffolk 224
Savery Books, East Sussex   99
Sax Books, Suffolk.................................... 224
Scarthin Books, Derbyshire   81
Schofield Golf Books (Steve), West Yorkshire . 245
Schull Books, Co. Cork.............................. 257
Schulz–Falster Rare Books (Susanne),
  London N 157
Schutte (David), Hampshire 125
Sclanders (Beatbooks), (Andrew), London EC . 154
Scorpio Books, Suffolk............................... 221
Scott (Peter), East Sussex 103
Scrivener's Books & Bookbinding, Derbyshire . 81
Sea Chest Nautical Bookshop (The), Devon ... 87
Seabreeze Books, Lancashire....................... 144
Second Edition, Lothian.............................. 272
Secondhand Bookshop, Surrey 228
Sedgeberrow Books & Framing, Worcestershire 251
Seeber (Liz), East Sussex 99
Segal Books (Joel), Devon 84
Sen Books, Hampshire................................ 127
Sensawunda Books, Cheshire 68
Sephton (A.F.), London W 172
Sesemann (Julia), Kent................................ 136
SETI Books, Staffordshire........................... 220
Seydi Rare Books (Sevin), London NW......... 159
Shacklock Books (David), Suffolk 222
Shakeshaft (Dr. B.), Cheshire....................... 71
Shakespeare Books (Colin), Staffordshire 219
Shapero Rare Books (Bernard J.), London W . 172
Sharpe (Mary), Somerset 216
Shaun Lofthouse, North Yorkshire............... 193
Shearer (Marion), Lothian 272
Shearwater Bed & Books (formerly John
  Lumby Nat. History Bks), Northumberland.. 198
Sheet Music Warehouse (The), Devon 86
Shelley (E. & J.), Buckinghamshire................ 61
Sheriffmuir Books, Central.......................... 263
Sherlaw-Johnson (Austin), Oxfordshire 206
Sherratt (Ian J.), Staffordshire 219
Sidey, Bookdealer (Philip), Kent 140
Signature Books, Hampshire........................ 126
Sillan Books, Co. Cavan............................. 257
Sillem (Anthony), East Sussex..................... 101
Silver Trees Books, W Midlands.................. 234
Silverman (Michael), London SE 163
Simmonds (Anthony J.), London SE 163
Simon Finch Nofolk, Norfolk...................... 186
Simon Hunter Antique Maps, East Sussex...... 102
Simon Lewis Transport Books, Gloucestershire 115

Simon's Books, Somerset 216
Simply Read Books, East Sussex 99
Simpson (Dave), Central............................. 263
Simpson (Marianne), Grampian.................... 267
Sims (Sue), Dorset 90
Sims Reed Limited, London SW.................. 167
Singleton (Anthony), South Yorkshire........... 217
Siop Lyfrau'r Hen Bost, Gwynedd 280
Siop y Morfa, Denbighshire 279
Siri Ellis Books, Greater Manchester............. 118
Skelton (Tony), Kent.................................. 141
Skipton Antiques Centre, North Yorkshire..... 193
Skirrid Books, Monmouthshire.................... 280
Skoob Russell Square, Suffolk..................... 225
Skyrack Books, West Yorkshire 243
Sleepy Elephant Books & Artefacts, Cumbria.. 79
Smith (Clive), Essex 109
Smith (David & Lynn), London Outer 179
Smith (Ray), Hertfordshire.......................... 130
Smith Books (Keith), Herefordshire.............. 128
Smith Books, (Nigel), Surrey 226
Smith Books, (Sally), Suffolk 222
Smith Maritime Aviation Books (Frank),
  Tyne and Wear...................................... 231
Soccer Books Limited, Lincolnshire.............. 149
Sokol Books Ltd., London W...................... 172
Solaris Books, East Yorkshire...................... 105
Soldridge Books Ltd, Hampshire 122
Solitaire Books, Somerset........................... 212
Sotheran Limited (Henry), London W........... 172
South Downs Book Service, West Sussex 238
Sparkes (Books) (Ray), Staffordshire............ 220
Sparrow Books, West Yorkshire 241
Spearman Books, East Sussex 103
Spelman (Ken), North Yorkshire 195
Spenceley Books (David), West Yorkshire 244
Spink & Son Limited, London WC 176
Spooner & Co, Somerset 215
Spooner (John E.), Dorset 90
Spurrier (Nick), Kent 138
Squirrel Antiques, Hampshire 123
Stacpoole (George), Co. Limerick 260
Staffs Bookshop (The), Staffordshire............. 219
Stained Glass Books, Kent 139
Stalagluft Books, Tyne and Wear................. 231
Staniland (Booksellers), Lincolnshire............. 152
Stanley Fish & Co., Kent............................ 138
Stansbury (Rosemary), Devon...................... 87
Star Lord Books, Greater Manchester............ 120
Starlord Books, Greater Manchester 118
Steedman (Robert D.), Tyne and Wear 231
Stella Books, Monmouthshire 281
Stepping Stones Bookshop, North Yorkshire .. 191
Sterling Books, Somerset 216
Stern Antiquarian Bookseller (Jeffrey), North
  Yorkshire 195
Steven Simpson Books, Norfolk 188
Stevens (Joan), Cambridgeshire 65
Stinton (Judith), Dorset 91
Stobart Davies Limited, Carmarthwnshire 276
Stokes Books, Co. Dublin........................... 259
Stone Trough Books, North Yorkshire.......... 195

ALPHABETICAL INDEX: Business (S – V)

Stone, (G.& R.), Borders 262
Stothert Old Books, Cheshire 68
Stour Bookshop, Dorset 92
Strand Bookshop (The), Powys 286
Stroh (M.A.), London E 153
Stroma Books, Borders 262
Studio (The), Strathclyde 274
Studio Bookshop, East Sussex 99
Sturford Books, Wiltshire 248
Sub Aqua Prints and Books, Hampshire 124
Sue Lowell Natural History Books, London W 173
Suffolk Rare Books, Suffolk 225
Summerfield Books Ltd, Cumbria 76
Sun House Books, Kent 139
Surprise Books, Gloucestershire 113
Susan Taylor Books, West Yorkshire 243
Sutcliffe (Mark), West Yorkshire 243
Sutcliffe (Victor), Norfolk 184
Sykes (Graham), West Yorkshire 244
Symes Books (Naomi), Cheshire 71

Talisman Books, Cheshire 70
Taney Books, Co. Dublin 259
Tant Yn Ellen Books, Powys 286
Tarka Books, Devon 83
Taylor & Son (Peter), Hertfordshire 132
Taylor Rare Books (Michael), Norfolk 184
Temperley (David), W Midlands 234
Temple (Robert), London N 157
Tennis Collectables, Cheshire 68
Tetbury Old Books, Gloucestershire 117
Thanatos Books, Greater Manchester 120
The Dormouse Bookshop, Norfolk 188
The End Bookshop, Devon 87
The Glass Key, West Yorkshire 242
The Old Children's Bookshelf, Lothian 272
The Old Music Master, Bristol 60
The Sanctuary Bookshop, Dorset 93
The Stratford Bookshop, Warwickshire 233
The Winchester Bookshop, Hampshire 127
Theatreshire Books, North Yorkshire 190
Thin Read Line, Merseyside 182
Thistle Books, Strathclyde 274
Thomas (Barry), Ceredigion 277
Thomas (E. Wyn), Conwy 278
Thomas Rare Books, Suffolk 222
Thompson (Eric), Surrey 229
Thomson (Karen), Strathclyde 273
Thornber (Peter M.), North Yorkshire 193
Thorne (John), Essex 109
Thorntons of Oxford Ltd., Oxfordshire 203
Throckmorten's Bookshop, Warwickshire 232
Tiffin (Tony and Gill), Durham 96
Tiger Books, Kent 137
Till's Bookshop, Lothian 272
Tilleys Vintage Magazine Shop, South Yorkshire 218
Tilleys Vintage Magazine Shop, Derbyshire ... 81
Tilston (Stephen E.), London SE 161
Tin Drum Books, Leicestershire 146
Tindley & Chapman, London WC 176
Titford (John), Derbyshire 81

Tobo Books, Hampshire 124
Tombland Bookshop, Norfolk 188
Tony Pollastrone Railway Books, Wiltshire 246
Tooley, Adams & Co, Oxfordshire 206
Torc Books, Norfolk 186
Towers (Mark), Lancashire 143
Townsend (John), Berkshire 57
Towpath Bookshop, Greater Manchester 120
Tozer Railway Books (Nick), West Yorkshire . 243
TP Children's Bookshop, West Yorkshire 241
Trafalgar Bookshop, East Sussex 99
Transformer, Dumfries & Galloway 265
Travel Bookshop (The), London W 173
Traveller's Bookshelf (The), Somerset 212
Travis & Emery Music Bookshop, London WC 177
Treasure Chest Books, Suffolk 222
Treasure Island (The), Greater Manchester 120
Treasure Trove Books, Leicestershire 146
Tregenna Place Second Hand Books, Cornwall 75
Treglown (Roger J.), Cheshire 70
Trevorrow (Edwin), Hertfordshire 130
Trinders' Fine Tools, Suffolk 222
Trinity Rare Books, Co. Leitrim 260
Trotman (Ken), Cambridgeshire 66
Trotter Books (John), London N 157
Tsbbooks, London SW 167
Tucker (Alan & Joan), Gloucestershire 116
Tuft (Patrick), London W 173
Turret House, Norfolk 189
Turton (John), Durham 97
Twigg (Keith), Staffordshire 219
Twiggers Booksearch, Kent 141
Two Jays Bookshop, London Outer 178
Tyger Press, London N 157

Ulysses, London WC 177
Undercover Books, Lincolnshire 152
Underwater Books, East Sussex 101
Unsworths Booksellers, London NW 160
Updike Rare Books (John), Lothian 272
Upper–Room Books, Somerset 214

Vailima Books, Dumfries & Galloway 264
Valentine Rare Books, Surrey 227
Valentine Rare Books, London W 173
Vandeleur Antiquarian Books, Surrey 227
Vanstone - Aviation Books, (Derek), Suffolk 225
Venables (Morris & Juliet), Bristol 59
Ventnor Rare Books, Isle of Wight 135
Verandah Books, Dorset 94
Vickers (Anthony), North Yorkshire 193
Victoria Bookshop (The), Devon 83
Victorian Gallery (The), Shropshire 210
Village Books, Norfolk 184
Vinovium Books, Durham 96
Vintage Motorshop, West Yorkshire 241
Vokes (Jeremiah), Durham 96
Vokes Books Ltd., North Yorkshire 192
VOL:II, Essex 108
Volumes of Motoring, Gloucestershire 113

ALPHABETICAL INDEX: Business (W – Z)

W & A Houben, Surrey 228
Wadard Books, Kent 137
Waddington Books & Prints (Geraldine),
  Northamptonshire 196
Wakeman Books (Frances), Nottinghamshire .. 201
Walcot (Patrick), W Midlands 235
Walden Books, London NW 160
Walker (Adrian), Bedfordshire 53
Walker (Gary), Fife 265
Walker Fine Books (Steve), Dorset 91
War & Peace Books, Hampshire 123
Ward (R.F. & C.), Norfolk 185
Warnes (Felicity J.), London Outer 178
Warrender (Andrew), West Yorkshire 245
Warrington Book Loft (The), Cheshire 71
Warsash Nautical Bookshop, Hampshire 126
Warwick Leadley Gallery, London SE 163
Water Lane Bookshop, Wiltshire 248
Waterfield's, Oxfordshire 206
Waterstone's, London WC 177
Watkins (R.G.), Somerset 213
Watkins Books Ltd., London WC 177
Waxfactor, East Sussex 99
Way Booksellers (Richard), Oxfordshire 204
Wayside Books and Cards, Oxfordshire 203
Wealden Books, Kent 139
Webb Books (John), South Yorkshire 217
Webster (D.), Strathclyde 274
Weiner (Graham), London N 157
Weininger Antiquarian Books (Eva M.),
  London NW 160
Wells (Mary), London SW 167
Wembdon Books, Somerset 213
Wenlock Books, Shropshire 210
Wensum Books, Norfolk 188
Weobley Bookshop, Herefordshire 129
Westcountry Old Books, Cornwall 75
Westcountry Oldbooks, Devon 84
Westfield Books, North Yorkshire 195
Westgate Bookshop, Lincolnshire 151
Westons, Hertfordshire 133
Westwood Books (Mark), Powys 284
Westwood Books Ltd, Cumbria 79
Westwords, Strathclyde 274
Wetherell (Frances), Cambridgeshire 65
Wheeler's Bookshop, West Sussex 239
Wheen O'Books, Borders 262
Whelan (P. & F.), Kent 141
Whig Books Ltd., Leicestershire 147
Whistler's Books, London SW 167
Whitchurch Books Ltd., Cardiff 276
White (David), Cambridgeshire 65
White (Mrs. Teresa), London W 173
Whitehall Books, East Sussex 102
Whittle, Bookseller (Avril), Cumbria 79
Wiend Books, Lancashire 143
Wilbraham (J. & S.), London NW 160
Wildside Books, Worcestershire 250
Wildy & Sons Ltd, London WC 177
Williams (Bookdealer), (Richard), Lincolnshire 152
Williams (Christopher), Dorset 93
Williams Rare Books (Nigel), London WC 177

Willmott Bookseller (Nicholas), Cardiff 276
Wilson (David), Buckinghamshire 61
Wilson (Manuscripts) Ltd., (John),
  Gloucestershire 114
Winghale Books, Lincolnshire 151
Winram's Bookshop, Grampian 266
Wise (Derek), East Sussex 102
Witmehá Productions, Leicestershire 147
Wizard Books, Cambridgeshire 67
Woburn Books, London N 157
Wood (Peter), Cambridgeshire 65
Wood Cricket Books (Martin), Kent 140
Woodbine Books, West Yorkshire 241
Woodlands Books, West Yorkshire 244
Woodside Books, Kent 136
Woolcott Books, Dorset 91
Worcester Rare Books, Worcestershire 252
Words Etcetera Bookshop, Dorset 92
World War Books, Kent 141
World War II Books, Surrey 230
Worlds End Bookshop, London SW 168
Worrallo (J. & M.A.), W Midlands 235
Wright (Norman), Hertfordshire 133
Wright Trace Books, W Midlands 235
www.AntiqueWatchStore.com, Hertfordshire... 130
Wycherley (Stephen), W Midlands 234
Wychwood Books, Gloucestershire 116
Wykeham Books, London SW 168
Wyseby House Books, Berkshire 55
Xanadubooks, Cleveland 96

Ximenes Rare Books Inc., Gloucestershire 115

Y Gelli Auctions, Powys 284
Yarborough House Bookshop, Shropshire 209
Yarwood Rare Books (Edward), Greater
  Manchester 118
Yates Antiquarian Books (Tony), Leicestershire 146
Yeoman Books, Lothian 272
Yesterday Tackle & Books, Dorset 90
Yesterday's Books, Dorset 91
Yesterday's News, Conwy 278
Yesteryear Railwayana, Kent 139
Yewtree Books, Cumbria 77
York (Graham), Devon 85
Yorkshire Relics, West Yorkshire 242
Young (D. & J.), Powys 286
Ystwyth Books, Ceredigion 277

Zardoz Books, Wiltshire 249

ALPHABETICAL INDEX OF DEALERS WITH WEB SITES

Ænigma Designs (Books), (See page 85) .... www.puzzlemuseum.com
A. & R. Booksearch, (See page 73)... www.musicbooksrus.com
AA1 Books, (See page 264) www.bookavenue/hosted/AA1
Aardvark Books, (See page 249) .... www.aardvarkmilitarybooks.com
Acumen Books, (See page 220).. www.acumenbooks.co.uk
Addyman Annexe (The), (See page 282) .... www.hay-on-wyebooks.com
Addyman Books, (See page 282).. www.hay-on-wyebooks.com
ahbooks, (See page 182) .... www.ahbooks.co.uk
Ainslie Books, (See page 273)... www.ainsliebooks.co.uk
Aitchison (Lesley), (See page 58) .... www.localhistory.co.uk/la
Alba Books, (See page 267)... www.albabooks.com
Alba Secondhand Music, (See page 273) .... www.albamusick.co.uk
Alexander Books, (See page 125) .... www.alexanderbooks.com
All Books, (See page 110) .... www.allbooks.demon.co.uk
Allinson (Frank & Stella), (See page 232).. www.ukbookworld.com
Allsop (Duncan M.), (See page 233) .... www.abe.com
Allsworth Rare Books Ltd., (See page 164)... www.allsworthbooks.com
Alpha Books, (See page 155) .... www.abebooks.com/home/alphabks
Altea Antique Maps & Books, (See page 169) .... www.alteagallery.com
Ambra Books, (See page 58).. www.localhistory.co.uk/ambra
Ampersand Books, (See page 209)... www.ampersandbooks.co.uk
Ancient Art Books, (See page 164) .... www.gilesancientart.com
Andrews Books & Collectables, (See page 82) .... www.abebooks.com
Andromeda Books, (See page 62) www.m31books.co.uk
Ann & Mike Conry, (See page 251) .... www.abe.com
Annie's Books, (See page 217).. www.anniesbooks.co.uk
Antiquary Ltd., (Bar Bookstore), (See page 192) .... www.ukbookworld.com/members/Barbooks
Antique Map and Bookshop (The), (See page 93).......................... www.puddletownbookshop.co.uk
Antique Prints of the World, (See page 155) www.antique19thcenturyprints.com
Any Amount of Books, (See page 174) .... www.anyamountofbooks.com
Archer (David), (See page 285)... www.david-archer-maps.com
Archer (Steve), (See page 178) .... www.ukbookworld.com/members/stevearcher
Archways Sports Books, (See page 269).. www.archwaysbooks.com
Arden, Bookseller (C.), (See page 282) .... www.WWW.ardenbooks.co.uk
Ardis Books, (See page 126) .... www.ardis.co.uk
Armchair Books, (See page 270) .... www.armchairbooks.co.uk
Arnold (Roy), (See page 223)... www.royarnold.com
Art Reference Books, (See page 125).. www.artreferencebooks.com
Ash Rare Books, (See page 164) .... www.ashrare.com
Assinder Books, (See page 110) .... www.abebooks.com
Astley Book Farm, (See page 232) .... www.astleybookfarm.com
Atholl Browse, (See page 275) .... www.athollbrowse.co.uk
Atlantis Bookshop, (See page 174) .... www.atlantisbookshop.demon.co.uk
Aucott & Thomas, (See page 145) .... www.aucott.com
Aurora Books Ltd, (See page 270) .... www.aurorabooks.co.uk
Autolycus, (See page 209) .... www.booksonline.uk.com
Avedikian Rare Books, (See page 213) .... www.militarybookshop.com
Avery (Alan), (See page 191) .... www.abebooks.com/home/avery
Aviabooks, (See page 114) .... www.abebooks.com
Aviation Book Supply, (See page 130)... www.aero-shop.co.uk
Avonworld Books, (See page 213).. www.avonworld-booksource.co.uk

B. and K. Books, (See page 282).. www.hay-on-wye.co.uk/bkbooks.
Badger Books, (See page 216) .... www.badgerbooks.co.uk
Baedekers & Murray Guides, (See page 217).. www.roger_hickley@dial.Pipex.com
Baggins Book Bazaar Ltd., (See page 139)... www.bagginsbooks.co.uk

ALPHABETICAL INDEX: Web Sites (B – B)

Baker (Gerald), (See page 59) .... www.gwrpublicity.co.uk
Baker Limited (A.P. & R.), (See page 264) .... www.apandrbaker.co.uk
Baldwin (Jack), (See page 273) .... www.jackbaldwin.dial.pipex.com
Baldwin's Scientific Books, (See page 112) .... www.secondhandsciencebooks.com
Bannister (David), (See page 113)... www.antiquemaps.co.uk
Barbican Bookshop, (See page 194) .... www.barbicanbookshop.co.uk
Barcombe Services, (See page 108) www.homepage.ntlworld.com/steve.williams7/ner.htm
Bardsley's Books, (See page 221).. www.bardsleysbooks.co.uk
Barn Books, (See page 211).. www.barnbooks.co.uk
Barnes - Books (Lyndon), (See page 209) .... www.abebooks.com
Baron (Christopher), (See page 118).. www.abebooks.com
Baron - Scientific Book Sales (P.J.), (See page 213) .... www.books.free-online.co.uk
Barron (Robert M.), (See page 140)... www.barron.co.uk
Barry McKay Rare Books, (See page 76)... www.barrymckayrarebooks.com
Barter Books, (See page 198) .... www.barterbooks.co.uk
Bates & Hindmarch, (See page 243).. www.abebooks.com
Baynton–Williams Gallery, (See page 237)... www.baynton-williams.com
Bayntun (George), (See page 212) .... www.georgebayntun.com
Beardsell Books, (See page 242)... www.toll-house.co.uk
Beardsley (A.E.), (See page 201) .... www.ukbookworld.com/members/aebbooks
Beaton (Richard), (See page 102) .... www.victorian-novels.co.uk
Beaver Booksearch, (See page 221).. www.beaverbooksearch.co.uk
Beckham Books Ltd., (See page 225) .... www.beckhambooks.com
Bell (Peter), (See page 270) .... www.peterbell.net
Bell Gallery (The), (See page 255) .... www.bellgallery.com
Bennett & Kerr Books, (See page 202) .... www.abebooks.com/home/bennettkerr
Benny Gillies Books Ltd, (See page 263).. www.www.bennygillies.com
Bertram Rota Ltd., (See page 174) .... www.bertramrota.co.uk
Besleys Books, (See page 221) .... www.besleysbooks.demon.co.uk
Bevan (John), (See page 247).. www.catholic-books.co.uk
Bianco Library, (See page 237) .... www.biancolibrary.com
Biblion, (See page 169)... www.biblion.com
Bibliophile Books, (See page 153).. www.bibliophilebooks.com
Bilski (Gill), (See page 61).. www.gillbilski.com
Bird Books (Nigel), (See page 277) .... www.nigelbirdbooks.co.uk
Birdnet Optics Ltd., (See page 81)... www.birdnet.co.uk
Bishopston Books, (See page 58) .... www.ibooknet.co.uk
Black Cat Books, (See page 185)... www.blackcatbooks.co.uk
Black Cat Bookshop, (See page 145).. www.blackcatbookshop.com
Black Five Books, (See page 211).. www.black5books.co.uk
Blacket Books, (See page 270).. www.blacketbooks.co.uk
Blackman Books, (See page 71)... www.abebooks.com/home/rtmb
Blackwell's Music Shop, (See page 205) .... www.blackwell.co.uk/printedmusic
Blackwell's Rare Books, (See page 205) .... www.rarebooks.blackwell.co.uk
Bluntisham Books, (See page 63) .... www.bluntishambooks.co.uk
Blythswood Bookshop, (See page 269)... www.blythswood.org
Bodyline Books, (See page 227) .... www.bodylinebooks.com
Bolland Books (Leslie H.), (See page 53).. www.bollandbooks.com
Bolton Books, (See page 122)... www.boltonbooks.com
Bonham (J. & S.L.), (See page 169) .... www.bonbooks.dial.pipex.com
Book Annex (The), (See page 110) .... www.thebookannex.co.uk
Book Castle, (The), (See page 53).. www.book-castle.co.uk
Book For All Reasons (A.), (See page 224)... www.abfar.co.uk
Book Gallery (The), (See page 75) .... www.abebooks.com/home/tinyworld
Book House (The), (See page 78) .... www.thebookhouse.co.uk
Book Jungle (The), (See page 104).. www.thebookjungle.co.uk
Book Mongers, (See page 164) .... www.freespace.virgin.net/book.mongers
Book Palace (The), (See page 161) .... www.bookpalace.com
Book Shelf (The), (See page 86) .... www.bookshelfuk.com
Bookends, (See page 123)... www.bookends.me.uk
Bookends of Fowey, (See page 73) .... www.bookendsoffowey.com
Bookfare, (See page 80).. www.bookfare.co.uk

Bookline, (See page 256)	www.abebooks.com/home/bookline
BookLovers.co.uk, (See page 215)	www.booklovers.co.uk
Booknotes, (See page 111)	www.ascon.demon.co.uk
Bookroom (The), (See page 229)	www.abebooks.com/home/keithalexander
Books, (See page 278)	www.llangollen.org.uk/pages/books.htm
Books, (See page 202)	www.pogmore@marg3.freeserve.co.uk
Books & Bygones, (See page 57)	www.booksbygones.com
Books & Collectables Ltd., (See page 63)	www.booksandcollectables.com
Books & Things, (See page 169)	www.booksandthings.co.uk
Books and Things, (See page 253)	www.newnats.com
Books at Star Dot Star, (See page 236)	www.star-dot-star.net
Books Bought & Sold, (See page 226)	www.booksinstore.com
Books in Cardigan, (See page 277)	www.http://cardiganbooks.hypermart.net/
Books Only, (See page 222)	www.booksonly.co.uk
Books Ulster, (See page 256)	www.booksulster.com
Books With Care, (See page 53)	www.bookswithcare.com
books2books, (See page 87)	www.abebooks.com/home/BOOKS2BOOKS.
BOOKS4U, (See page 279)	www.http://ukbookworld.com/members/bks4u
Bookshelf (The),, (See page 192)	www.bookshelf.scarborough.com
Bookshelf – Aviation Books, (See page 187)	www.aviation-bookshelf.co.uk
Bookshop (The), (See page 119)	www.bookacademy.co.uk
Bookshop (The), (See page 189)	www.abebooks.com/home/MANDACTHOMPSON
Bookshop on the Heath, The, (See page 161)	www.bookshopontheheath.co.uk
Booksmart, (See page 196)	www.booksmart.co.uk
Bookstand, (See page 93)	www.abebooks.com/home/bookstand
Bookworld, (See page 210)	www.tgal.co.uk/bookworld
Bookworm, (See page 110)	www.bookwormshop.com
Bookworm (The), (See page 271)	www.scottishbookworm.com
Bookworm Alley, (See page 87)	www.bookwormalley.org.uk
Booth (Booksearch Service), (Geoff), (See page 68)	www.boothbookmark.com
Booth Books, (See page 282)	www.richardbooth.demon.co.uk
Border Bookshop, (See page 245)	www.borderbookshop.co.uk
Boris Books, (See page 127)	www.borisbooks.co.uk
Bott, (Bookdealers) Ltd., (Martin), (See page 118)	www.bottbooks.com
Boulevard Books, (See page 100)	www.thehastingstrawler.co.uk
Bow Windows Book Shop, (See page 102)	www.bowwindows.com
Bowie Books & Collectables, (See page 106)	www.freewebs.com/bowiebooksandcollectables/
Boz Books, (See page 282)	www.bozbooks.co.uk
Bracton Books, (See page 63)	www.bractonbooks.co.uk
Bradley–Cox (Mary), (See page 90)	www.marybradleycox.com
Brazenhead Ltd., (See page 186)	www.brazenhead.co.uk
Brewin Books Ltd., (See page 233)	www.brewinbooks.com
Brian Troath Books, (See page 153)	www.ukbookworld.com/members/ariel
Bridge of Allan Books, (See page 263)	www.bridgeofallanbooks.com
Brimstones, (See page 102)	www.brimstones.co.uk
Bristol Books, (See page 60)	www.abebooks.com/home/bs6books
Bristow & Garland, (See page 123)	www.bristowandgarland.co.uk
Broadhurst of Southport Ltd., (See page 182)	www.ckbroadhurst.com
Brock Books, (See page 190)	www.brockbooks.com
Brockwells Booksellers, (See page 148)	www.brockwells.co.uk
Brown (Books) (Steve), (See page 219)	www.abebooks.com/home/sbbooks
Brown-Studies, (See page 273)	www.brown-studies-books.co.uk
Browne (Christopher I.), (See page 242)	www.gilbertandsullivanonline.com
Browning Books, (See page 287)	www.browningbooks.co.uk
Browzers, (See page 119)	www.browzers.co.uk
Bufo Books, (See page 125)	www.bufobooks.demon.co.uk
Burden Ltd., (Clive A.), (See page 132)	www.caburden.com
Butler Books, (See page 90)	www.abebooks.com
Byblos Antiquarian & Rare Book, (See page 122)	www.byblos.uk.com
Byre Books, (See page 264)	www.byrebooks.co.uk
Cader Idris Books, (See page 280)	www.abebooks.com/home/dvbookshop

Caduceus Books, (See page 145) .... www.caduceusbooks.com
Caledonia Books, (See page 273) .... www.caledoniabooks.co.uk
Calendula Horticultural Books, (See page 101) .... www.calendulabooks.com
Caliver Books, (See page 110) .... www.caliverbooks.com
Camden Books, (See page 212) .... www.camdenbooks.com
Cameron House Books, (See page 134) .... www.cameronhousebooks.com
Campbell Art Books (Marcus), (See page 161) .... www.marcuscampbell.co.uk
Canon Gate Books, (See page 239) .... www.canongate-thoughtful-books.com
Capes (Books, Maps & Prints) (John L.), (See page 193) .... www.johncapes.com
Carnforth Bookshop (The), (See page 142) .... www.carnforthbooks.co.uk
Carningli Centre, (See page 281) .... www.carningli.co.uk
Carta Regis, (See page 286) .... www.davidp@cartaregis.com
Cartographics, (See page 220) .... www.cartographics.co.uk
Cassidy (Bookseller) (P.), (See page 149) www.ukbookworld.com/members/7696
Castle Bookshop, (See page 285) .... www.archaeologybooks.co.uk
Castle Hill Books, (See page 128) .... www.castlehillbooks.co.uk
Catalyst Booksearch Services, (See page 85) .... www.catalystbooksearch.co.uk
Cathach Books Ltd, (See page 259) .... www.rarebooks.ie
Cavern Books, (See page 70) .... www.cavernbooks.co.uk
Central Bookshop, (See page 232) .... www.central-bookshop.com
Chalmers Hallam (E.), (See page 125) .... www.hallam-books.co.uk
Chapel Books, (See page 224) .... www.chapelbooks.com
Chapman (Neville), (See page 74) .... www.abebooks.com/home/chapbooks
Chapter House Books, (See page 94) .... www.chapterhouse-books.co.uk
Chapter Two, (See page 161) .... www.chaptertwobooks.org.uk
Charlie Byrne's Bookshop, (See page 260) .... www.charliebyrne.com
Chaters Motoring Booksellers, (See page 179) .... www.chaters.co.uk
Chaucer Bookshop, (See page 136) .... www.chaucer-bookshop.co.uk
Chaucer Head Bookshop, (See page 233) .... www.stratford-upon-avonbooks.co.uk
Chelifer Books, (See page 80) .... www.military-books.biz
Cheshire Book Centre, (See page 69) .... www.cheshirebookcentre.com
Chesters (G. & J.), (See page 220) .... www.abebooks.com/home/geoffchesters
Children's Bookshop (The), (See page 282) .... www.childrensbookshop.com
Chris Adam Smith Modern First Editions, (See page 238) .... www.adamsmithbooks.com
Christine's Book Cabin, (See page 147) .... www.bookcabin.co.uk
Christopher Saunders (Orchard Books), (See page 115) .... www.cricket-books.com
Chthonios Books, (See page 101) .... www.esotericism.co.uk/index.htm
Church Green Books, (See page 207) .... www.churchgreen.co.uk
Church Street Bookshop, (See page 155) .... www.abebooks.com
Churchill Book Specialist (The), (See page 179) .... www.wscbooks.com
Clark (M.R.), (See page 241) .... www.abebooks.com
Clarke (Janet), (See page 212) .... www.janetclarke.com
Classey Limited (E.W.), (See page 203) .... www.classeybooks.com
Classic Bindings Ltd, (See page 164) .... www.classicbindings.net
Classics Bookshop (The), (See page 202) .... www.classicsbookshop.co.uk
Clent Books, (See page 250) .... www.clentbooks.co.uk
Clifford Elmer Books Ltd., (See page 68) .... www.cliffordelmerbooks.com
Cobnar Books, (See page 139) .... www.cobnarbooks.com
Cobweb Books, (See page 192) .... www.cobwebbooks.co.uk
Coch-y-Bonddu Books, (See page 285) .... www.anglebooks.com
Cocks Books (Brian), (See page 66) .... www.aviationbookhouse.co.uk
Cofion Books, (See page 281) .... www.cofion.com
Collectable Books, (See page 162) .... www.collectablebooks.com
Collectors Carbooks, (See page 196) .... www.collectorscarbooks.com
Colonsay Bookshop, (See page 269) .... www.colonsay.org.uk
Combat Arts Archive, (See page 96) .... www.combatbooks.co.uk
Cooper Hay Rare Books, (See page 273) .... www.abebooks.com/home/haybooks
Corder (Mark W.), (See page 140) .... www.mark.corder.btinternet.co.uk
Cornerstone Books, (See page 87) .... www.abe.books.com
Cornucopia Books, (See page 151) .... www.cornucopiabooks.co.uk
Cotswold Internet Books, (See page 113) .... www.cotsworldinternetbook.com
Countryman Books, (See page 105) .... www.countryman.co.uk

ALPHABETICAL INDEX: Web Sites (C – E)

Court Hay Books, (See page 58) .... www.courthaybooks.co.uk
Courtyard Books, (See page 113) .... www.courtyardbooks.co.uk
Cover to Cover, (See page 183) .... www.covers.freeuk.com
Cowley, Auto–in–Print (John), (See page 108) .... www.autoinprint.com
Cox Music (Lisa), (See page 84) .... www.lisacoxmusic.com
Cox Old & Rare Books (Claude), (See page 223) .... www.claudecox.co.uk
Cox Rare Books (Charles), (See page 73) .... www.abebooks.com
Creaking Shelves, (See page 268) .... www.abebooks.com
Crouch Rare Books, (See page 227) .... www.crbooks.co.uk
Cygnet Books, (See page 107) .... www.cygnetbooks.co.uk

D. & M. Books, (See page 244) .... www.dandmbooks.com
Dally Books & Collectables, (See page 285) .... www.dallybooks.com
Dance Books Ltd, (See page 122) .... www.dancebooks.co.uk
Dandy Lion Editions, (See page 228) .... www.dandylioneditions.co.uk
Darkwood Books, (See page 258) .... www.darkwoodbooks.com
DaSilva Puppet Books, (See page 92) .... www.puppetbooks.co.uk
David Houston - Bookseller, (See page 153) .... www.abebooks.com/home/dghbooks
davidleesbooks.com, (See page 283) .... www.davidleesbooks.com
Davies Fine Books, (See page 252) .... www.daviesfinebooks.biblion.com
Day (J.H.), (See page 124) .... www.abebooks.com
DBS Childrens Collectable Books, (See page 124) .... www.dbschildrenscollectablebooks.com
de Beaumont (Robin), (See page 164) .... www.abebooks.com/home/RDEBOOKS
De Burca Rare Books, (See page 259) .... www.deburcararebooks.com
Dead Mens Minds.co.uk, (See page 285) .... www.TPOBooks.co.uk
Dean Illustrated Books (Myra), (See page 281) .... www.myradean-illustatedbooks.co.uk
Dearman Rare Books (Rebecca), (See page 145) .... www.rebeccadearmanrarebooks.co.uk
Decorum Books, (See page 155) .... www.decorunbooks.co.uk
Delectus Books, (See page 174) .... www.delectusbooks.co.uk
Demar Books (Grant), (See page 140) .... www.garntdemarbooks.co.uk
Design Gallery 1850-1950 (The), (See page 141) .... www.designgallery.co.uk
Deyong Books (J.C.), (See page 164) .... www.jcdeyong.co.uk
Dinnages Transport Publishing, (See page 98) .... www.Transport-Postcards.co.uk
Dolphin Books, (See page 221) .... www.wwwukbookworld.com/members/DOLPHINBOOKS
Dooley (Rosemary), (See page 80) .... www.booksonmusic.co.uk
Doorbar (P. & D.), (See page 279) .... www.doorbar.co.uk/books/
Downie Fine Books Ltd., (Robert), (See page 211) .... www.booksets.com
DPE Books, (See page 86) .... www.davidporteous.com
Drury Rare Books (John), (See page 111) .... www.johndruryrarebooks.com
Du Ry Medieval Manuscripts (Marc–Antoine), (See page 170) .... www.medievalart.uk.com
Dublin Bookbrowsers, (See page 259) .... www.abebooks.com
Dusty Books, (See page 285) .... www.dustybooks.co.uk
Dusty Old Books Ltd., (See page 204) .... www.dustyoldbooks.com
Dworski Books, Travel & Language Bookshop (Marijana), (See page 283) .... www.dworskibooks.com
Dylans Bookstore, (See page 286) .... www.dylans.com

Eagle Bookshop (The), (See page 53) .... www.eaglebookshop.co.uk
Earth Science Books, (See page 247) .... www.earthsciencebooks.com
East Riding Books, (See page 106) .... www.eastridingbooks.co.uk
Eastern Books of London, (See page 165) .... www.harfieldbooks.com
Eastleach Books, (See page 55) .... www.eastleach-book.co.uk
Eden Books, (See page 150) .... www.edenbooks.com
Edmund Pollinger Rare Books, (See page 165) .... www.etpollinger.com
Edrich (I.D.), (See page 153) .... www.idedrich.co.uk
Edwards (London) Limited (Francis), (See page 175) .... www.francisedwards.co.uk
Edwards in Hay–on–Wye (Francis), (See page 283) .... www.francisedwards.co.uk
Ellis, Bookseller (Peter), (See page 162) .... www.peter-ellis.co.uk
Ellwood Editions, (See page 247) .... www.ellwoodbooks.co.uk
Elmfield Books, (See page 234) .... www.elmfieldbooks.co.uk
Elmo Books, (See page 98) .... www.stores.ebay.co.uk/elmo-books
Elstree Books, (See page 131) .... www.abebooks.com
Ely Books, (See page 65) .... www.elybooks.com

ALPHABETICAL INDEX: Web Sites (E – G)

Embleton (Paul), (See page 111) .... www.abebooks.com/home/embleton
Endeavour Books, (See page 194) .... www.enbooks.co.uk
English (Toby), (See page 206) .... www.tobyenglish.com
Esoteric Dreams Bookshop, (See page 77) .... www.amazon.co.uk/shops/esotericdreams
Evans Books (Paul), (See page 238) .... www.paulevansbooks.com
Ex Libris, (See page 246) .... www.ex-librisbooks.co.uk
Exedra Booksearch Ltd., (See page 165) .... www.exedra.co.uk

Facet Books, (See page 90)... www.jallinson.freeserve.co.uk
Fantastic Literature, (See page 111) .... www.fantasticliterature.com
Fantasy Centre, (See page 155) .... www.fantasycentre.biz.
Farahar & Dupre (Clive & Sophie), (See page 246)................................... www.farahardupre.co.uk
Farnborough Gallery, (See page 123) .... www.farnboroughgallery.co.uk
Fiction First, (See page 69)... www.abebooks.com
Fifteenth Century Bookshop (The), (See page 102) www.15thcenturybookshop.co.uk
Finch Rare Books Ltd. (Simon), (See page 170)... www.simonfinch.com
Find That Book, (See page 244) .... www.findthatbook.demon.co.uk
Fine Art, (See page 165) .... www.fineart.tm
Fine Books Oriental Ltd., (See page 175) .... www.finebooks.demon.co.uk
Fireside Books, (See page 62) .... www.firesidebooks.demon.co.uk
Fireside Bookshop, (See page 80) .... www.firesidebookshop.co.uk
First State Books, (See page 170) .... www.firststatebooks.com
firstpagebooks, (See page 187) .... www.firstpagebooks.com
Firsts in Print, (See page 134) .... www.firsts-in-print.co.uk
Fishburn Books, (See page 158) .... www.fishburnbooks.com
Fisher Nautical, (See page 98) .... www.fishernauticalbooks.co.uk
Fogg Rare Books & Manuscripts (Sam), (See page 170).................................... www.samfogg.com
Forbury Fine Books, (See page 56)... www.forburyfinebooks.co.uk
Forest Books, (See page 201) .... www.forestbooks.co.uk
Forest Books, (See page 208) .... www.homepages.primex.co.uk/~forest
Formby Antiques (Jeffrey), (See page 115)... www.formby-clocks.com
Foster (Stephen), (See page 158) www.95bellstreet.com
Frew Limited (Robert), (See page 170) .... www.robertfrew.com
Freya Books & Antiques, (See page 187) .... www.freyaantiques.co.uk
Furneaux Books (Lee), (See page 88) .... www.abebooks.com/home/madeleine

Gage Postal Books, (See page 111)... www.gagebooks.com
Game Advice, (See page 205).. www.game-advice.com
Garbett Antiquarian Books (Michael), (See page 113)....................... www.michaelgarbett.theanswer.co.uk
Gardener & Cook, (See page 165) .... www.gardenerandcook.com
Garretts Antiquarian Books, (See page 254)... www.isleofmanbooks.com
Garwood & Voigt, (See page 140)... www.garwood-voigt.com
Gaskell Rare Books (Roger), (See page 66).. www.rogergaskell.com
Gaullifmaufry Books, (See page 131) .... www.ukbookworld.com/members/spitfire
Gay's The Word, (See page 175)... www.gaystheword.co.uk
Gekoski (R.A.), (See page 175)... www.gekoski.com
Geophysical Books, (See page 140) .... www.geophysicalbooks.com
GfB: the Colchester Bookshop, (See page 109)... www.gfb.uk.net
Gibbs Books, (Jonathan), (See page 251) .... www.jgibbsbooks.co.uk
Gibbs Bookshop Ltd., (See page 119)... www.gibbsbookshop.co.uk
Gillmark Gallery, (See page 131) .... www.gillmark.com
Glacier Books, (See page 275) .... www.glacierbooks.com
Glance Back Books, (See page 279) .... www.glanceback.co.uk
Glenbower Books, (See page 259) .... www.abebooks.com/home/GLENBOWERBOOKS
Glyn's Books, (See page 209) .... www.glynsbooks.com
Golden Age Books, (See page 251)................................ www.ukbookworld.com/members/goldenage
Golden Books Group, (See page 84) www.abook4all.com
Goldman (Paul), (See page 94) .... www.abebooks.com
Goldsworth Books, (See page 230) .... www.goldsworthbooks.com
Good Books, (See page 210)... www.abebooks.com
Good for Books, (See page 149) .... www.goodforbooks.co.uk
Goodyer (Nicholas), (See page 156) .... www.nicholasgoodyer.com

ALPHABETICAL INDEX: Web Sites (G – H)

Goodyer, Natural History Books (Eric), (See page 146) .... www.abebooks.com/home/ERICGOODYER/
Grahame (Major Iain), (See page 221)... www.IainGrahameRareBooks.com
Grahame Thornton, Bookseller, (See page 92) www.grahamethornton.f9.co.uk
Grant Books, (See page 250) .... www.grantbooks-memorabilia.com
Grayling (David A.H.), (See page 78) .... www.davidgraylingbooks.co.uk
Grays of Westminster, (See page 165) .... www.graysofwestminster.co.uk
Great Oak Bookshop (The), (See page 285) .... www.midwales.com/gob
Green Ltd. (G.L.), (See page 132) .... www.glgreen.co.uk
Green Man Books, (See page 100) .... www.greenman-books.co.uk
Green Meadow Books, (See page 74)... www.greenmeadowbooks.co.uk
Greene's Bookshop Ltd, (See page 259) .... www.greenesbookshop.com
Greensleeves, (See page 202).. www.greensleevesbooks.co.uk
Greer (Robin), (See page 166) .... www.rarerobin.com
Gresham Books, (See page 214)... www.greshambooks.co.uk
Grosvenor Prints, (See page 175) .... www.grosvenorprints.com
Grove Bookshop (The), (See page 193)... www.grovebookshop.co.uk

Hadfield (G.K.), (See page 78) .... www.gkhadfield-tilly.co.uk
Hadley Bookseller (Peter J.), (See page 110) .... www.hadley.co.uk
Hall, (Anthony C.) Antiquarian Bookseller, (See page 181) .... www.hallbooks.co.uk
Halson Books, (See page 71)... www.users.zetnet.co.uk/halsongallery
Hamish Riley-Smith, (See page 188) .... www.riley-smith.com
Hanborough Books, (See page 205) .... www.parrotpress.co.uk
Hancock & Monks, (See page 283)... www.hancockandmonks.co.uk
Handsworth Books, (See page 112)... www.handsworthbooks.co.uk
Hanshan Tang Books, (See page 166) .... www.hanshan.com
Hardback Hotel, (See page 143) .... www.hardbackhotel.co.uk
Harlequin Books, (See page 59)... www.harlequinbooks.co.uk
Harries (Pauline), (See page 124)............................... www.abebooks.com/home/paulineharriesbooks
Harrington (Adrian), (See page 171) .... www.harringtonbooks.co.uk
Harrington Antiquarian Bookseller (Peter), (See page 166)................. www.peter-harrington-books.com
Hatchard & Daughters, (See page 242) .... www.brontebooks.co.uk
Hawkes (James), (See page 60)................................... www.abebooks.com/home/JAMESHAWKES/
Hawkridge Books, (See page 81)... www.hawkridge.co.uk
Hawley (C.L.), (See page 193) .... www.clhawley.co.uk
Hay Castle, (See page 283).. www.boothbooks.co.uk
Hay Cinema Bookshop Ltd., (See page 283) .... www.haycinemabookshop.co.uk
Head (John & Judith), (See page 247) .... www.johnandjudithhead.co.uk
Heath (A.R.), (See page 59) .... www.heathrarebooks.co.uk
Heatons, (See page 248) .... www.heatons-of-tisbury.co.uk
Hedgerow Books, (See page 217) .... www.hedgerowbooks.com
Helion & Company, (See page 235) .... www.helion.co.uk
Hellenic Bookservices, (See page 158) .... www.hellenicbooks.com
Helston Bookworm (The), (See page 73) .... www.users.dialstart.net/~helstonb
Heneage Art Books (Thomas), (See page 166) .... www.heneage.com
Hennessey Bookseller (Ray), (See page 99) .... www.rayhennesseybookseller.co..uk
Heraldry Today, (See page 247) .... www.heraldrytoday.co.uk
Herb Tandree Philosophy Books, (See page 116)............................... www.philosophy-books.com
Hereward Books, (See page 65) .... www.herewardbooks.co.uk
Heywood Hill Limited (G.), (See page 171)... www.gheywoodhill.com
Higher Octave Books, (See page 59) .... www.higher-octave-books.co.uk
Hodgkins and Company Limited (Ian), (See page 116) .... www.ianhodgkins.com
Holdsworth Books (Bruce), (See page 103) .... www.bruceholdsworthbooks.com
Hollett and Son (R.F.G.), (See page 79) .... www.holletts-rarebooks.co.uk
Hook (Arthur), (See page 59).. www.hooksbooks.co.uk
Hoovey's Books, (See page 101) .... www.hooveys.co.uk
Hornsby, Antiquarian and Secondhand Books (Malcolm), (See page 146)....... www.hornsbybooks.co.uk
Horsham Rare Books, (See page 238) .... www.horshamrarebooks.co.uk
Hosains Books, (See page 159) .... www.indoislamica.com
Howes Bookshop, (See page 101) .... www.howes.co.uk
HP Bookfinders, (See page 263)... www.hp-bookfinders.co.uk
Hünersdorff Rare Books, (See page 166) .... www.abebooks.com/hunersdorff/home

hullbooks.com, (See page 106)... www.hullbooks.com
Humanist Book Services, (See page 72).. www.cornwallhumanists.org.uk
Humber Books, (See page 148).. www.netguides.co.uk/uk/humber.html
Humm & Co. (Robert), (See page 151).. www.roberthumm.co.uk
Hummingbird Books, (See page 128) .... www.hummingbirdbooks@btinternet.com
Hunter–Rare Books (Andrew), (See page 166)... www.rarebookhunter.com
Hurst (Jenny), (See page 138)... www.abebooks.com
Hutchison (Books) (Larry), (See page 265) .... www.larryhutchisobooks.com
Hyland (C.P.), (See page 258) .... www.cphyland.com
Hylton Booksearch, (See page 182)... www.rahylton@btinternet.com

Ice House Books, (See page 248) .... www.icehousebooks.co.uk
Inch's Books, (See page 192).. www.inchsbooks.co.uk
Inner Bookshop (The), (See page 205)... www.innerbookshop.com
Innes Books, (See page 209) .... www.innesbooks.co.uk
Inprint, (See page 116) .... www.inprint.co.uk
InterCol London, (See page 156) .... www.intercol.co.uk
Internet Bookshop UK Ltd., (See page 113) .... www.ibuk.com
Interstellar Master Traders, (See page 143) .... www.i-m-t.demon.co.uk/
Invisible Books, (See page 98) .... www.invisiblebooks.net
Isabelline Books, (See page 72).. www.beakbook.demon.co.uk
Ives Bookseller (John), (See page 181) .... www.ukbookworld.com/members/johnives

J & D Jones, (See page 70)... www.jonesthebook.com
J. & J. Books, (See page 149)... www.jandjbooks.com
J.B. Books, (See page 56).. www.balloonbooks.co.uk
J.G. Natural History Books, (See page 228)... www.reptilebooks.com
Jabberwock Books, (See page 150)... www.jabberwockbooks.co.uk
Jackdaw Books, (See page 185) .... www.jackdawbooks.co.uk
Jane Badger Books, (See page 196)... www.janebadgerbooks.co.uk
Janian Comics / Computer Manuals, (See page 62).................. www.janiancomics.com & janian.co.uk
Jarndyce Antiquarian Booksellers, (See page 175).. www.jarndyce.co.uk
Jarvis Books, (See page 82) .... www.mountainbooks.co.uk
Jay Books, (See page 271) .... www.jaybooks.demon.co.uk
JB Books & Collectables, (See page 238).. www.jbbooks.co.uk
Jean Hedger, (See page 55)... www.booksatpbfa.com
Jiri Books, (See page 255) .... www.abebooks.com/home/WJS/
John R. Hoggarth, (See page 194)... www.johnrhoggarth.co.uk
John Underwood Antiquarian Books, (See page 186) .... www.abebooks.com
Johnson Rare Book Collections (C.R.), (See page 159) .... www.crjohnson.com
Jolly Good Read (A.), (See page 275) .... www.ajollygoodread.co.uk
Jones (Madalyn S.), (See page 242)... www.madalynjonesbooks.com
Jonkers Rare Books, (See page 204) .... www.jonkers.co.uk
Joppa Books Ltd., (See page 226) .... www.joppabooks.com

Kalligraphia (formerly Charmouth Bounty Books), (See page 134).................... www.kalligraphia.com
Karen Millward, (See page 257)..................................... www.ukbookworld.com/members/irishmaid
Katnap Arts, (See page 187)... www.katnap.co.uk
Keeble Antiques, (See page 215) .... www.keebleantbks.co.uk
Keegan's Bookshop, (See page 56) .... www.keegansbookshop.com
Kelly Books, (See page 88).. www.kellybooks.co.uk
Kemp Booksellers, (See page 106) .... www.kempbooksellers.co.uk
Ken's Paper Collectables, (See page 62) .... www.kens.co.uk
Kendall–Carpenter (Tim), (See page 119) .... www.timkcbooks.com
Kennedy & Farley, (See page 103).. www.kennedyandfarley.co.uk
Kenny's Bookshops and Art Galleries Ltd, (See page 260)..................................... www.kennys.ie
Kenya Books, (See page 99) .... www.abebooks.com/home/kenyabooks
Keogh's Books, (See page 115) .... www.keoghsbooks.co.uk
Kerr (Norman), (See page 77) .... www.kerrbooks.co.uk
Kidson (Ruth), (See page 103) .... www.ruthkidson.co.uk
Kilgarriff (Raymond), (See page 104) .... www.ilab.org
Kineton Nooks, (See page 232) .... www.kinetonbooks.co.uk

ALPHABETICAL INDEX: Web Sites (K – M)

Kingfisher Book Service, (See page 201).. www.kingfisher-books.co.uk
Kingswood Books, (See page 93) .... www.kingswoodbooks.btinternet.co.uk
Kirkland Books, (See page 78) .... www.kirklandbooks.co.uk
Kirkman Ltd., (Robert), (See page 53) .... www.robertkirkman.co.uk
Kyrios Books, (See page 200)... www.kyriosbooks.co.uk

Lamb's Tales Books, (See page 85).. www.lambstales.co.uk
Lane Books (Shirley), (See page 135) .... www.abebook.co.uk
Larkham Books (Patricia), (See page 117) .... www.diveinbooks.co.uk
Lawful Occasions, (See page 108)... www.lawfuloccasions.co.uk
Leaf Ends, (See page 199)... www.abebooks.com
Lee Jackson, (See page 159)... www.leejacksonmaps.com
Lee Rare Books (Rachel), (See page 59)... www.rleerarebooks.co.uk
Left on The Shelf, (See page 78) .... www.abebooks.com/home/leftontheshelf
Leigh Gallery Books, (See page 110).. www.abebooks.com/home/BOO/
Lewcock (John), (See page 66) .... www.abebooks.com/home/maritime
Lewis (J.T. & P.), (See page 73)....................... www.http://ukbookworld.com/members/JTLANDPL
Lewis First Editions, (See page 137)................................. www.abebooks.com/home/davidfordyce/
Libra Books, (See page 148)................................... www.: ukbookworld.com/members/LibraBooks
Lion Books, (See page 250).. www.lionbooks.co.uk
Little Bookshop (The), (See page 119) .... www.littlebookshop.net
Little Stour Books, (See page 136).. www.littlestourbooks.com
Loch Croispol Bookshop & Restaurant, (See page 268) .... www.scottish-books.net
Londinium Books, (See page 226) .... www.abebooks.com
Loretta Lay Books, (See page 159) .... www.laybooks.com
Lost Books, (See page 197).. www.lostbooks.net
Lucius Books, (See page 195).. www.luciusbooks.com
Lymelight Books & Prints, (See page 92) .... www.lymelight-books.demon.co.uk
Lyngheath Books, (See page 186)... www.lyngheathbooks.co.uk

Macfarlane (Mr. H.), (See page 112) .... www.tudorblackpress.co.uk
Maggs Brothers Limited, (See page 171) .... www.maggs.co.uk
Maghreb Bookshop (The), (See page 175) .... www.maghreview.com
Magis Books, (See page 147) .... www.www.magis.co.uk
Magpie Books, (See page 245).. www.magpie-books.co.uk
Main–Smith & Co. Ltd. (Bruce), (See page 146)....................................... www.brucemainsmith.com
Mandalay Bookshop, (See page 166) .... www.mandalaybookshop.com
Mansfield (Judith), (See page 245).. www.abebooks.com/home/TODBOOKS/
Marble Hill Books, (See page 181)... www.marblehillbooks.com
Marcet Books, (See page 161) .... www.marcetbooks.co.uk
March House Books, (See page 94) .... www.marchhousebooks.com
Marchpane, (See page 175).. www.marchpane.com
Marco Polo Travel & Adventure Books, (See page 91) .... www.marcopolobooks.co.uk
Marrin's Bookshop, (See page 138) .... www.marrinbook.co.uk
Martin - Bookseller (Colin), (See page 106).. www.colinmartinbooks.com
Martin Bookshop & Gallery (Richard), (See page 123) .... www.richardmartingallery.co.uk
Mason (Mary), (See page 202)... www.masonpeett.co.uk
Maynard & Bradley, (See page 146) .... www.maynardandbradley.com
mcbooks, (See page 237).. www.meadowcroftbooks.demon.co.uk
McConnell Fine Books, (See page 137)........................... www.abebooks.com/home/sandwichfinebooks
McCrone (Audrey), (See page 269) .... www.ukbookworld.com/members/finora
McEwan Golf Books (Rhod), (See page 266) .... www.rhodmcewan.com
McGlynn (John), (See page 142) .... www.vintagetechnology.org
McKelvie (Ian), (See page 156) www.http:/ukbookworld.com/members/Dudley1
McKenzie (J.W.), (See page 227) .... www.mckenzie-cricket.com
McLaren Books, (See page 274) .... www.mclarenbooks.co.uk
McNaughtan's Bookshop, (See page 271) .... www.mcnaughtansbookshop.com
medievalbookshop, (See page 179) .... www.medievalbookshop.co.uk
Meekins Books (Paul), (See page 233) .... www.paulmeekins.co.uk
Mellon's Books, (See page 100) .... www.mellonsbooks.co.uk
Mercat Books, (See page 268) .... www.mercatbooks.com
Merlin Books, (See page 238) .... www.merlinbooks.com

Michael J Carroll, (See page 257) .... www.abe.com
Miles Apart, (See page 224) .... www.sthelena.se
Milestone Books, (See page 88) .... www.milestonebooks.co.uk
Milestone Publications Goss & Crested China, (See page 124) .... www.gosschinaclub.demon.co.uk
Military Parade Bookshop, (See page 247) .... www.militaryparadebooks.com
MilitaryHistoryBooks.com, (See page 138) .... www.militaryhistorybooks.com
Mills Rare Books (Adam), (See page 64) .... www.abebooks.com
Ming Books, (See page 265) .... www.mingbooks.supanet.commcom
Minster Books, (See page 95) .... www.minsterbooks.com
Minster Gate Bookshop, (See page 195) .... www.minstergatebooks.co.uk
Mobbs (A.J.), (See page 235) .... www.mobbs.birdbooks.btinternet.co.uk
Mogul Diamonds, (See page 236) .... www.ukbookworld.com/members/mogul
Mollie's Loft, (See page 287) .... www.Molliesloft.com
Monmouth House Books, (See page 280) .... www.monmouthhousebooks.co.uk
Moore (Eric T.), (See page 131) .... www.erictmoore.co.uk
Moore (Peter), (See page 64) .... www.aus-pacbooks.co.uk
Moorside Books, (See page 143) .... www.abebooks.com/home/DFSBOOKS/
Moreton Books, (See page 86) .... www.moretonbooks.co.uk
Morley Case, (See page 126) .... www.abebooks.com/home/case
Moseley Books, (See page 234) .... www.moseleybooks.co.uk
Mount's Bay Books, (See page 74) .... www.mountsbaybooks.co.uk
Mr. Pickwick of Towcester, (See page 196) .... www.yell.co.uk.sites/pickwickbookfinders
Much Ado Books, (See page 98) .... www.muchadobooks.com
Murder & Mayhem, (See page 284) .... www.hay-on-wyebooks.com
Murphy (C.J.), (See page 187) .... www.abebooks.com/home/Chrismurphy/home
Music By The Score, (See page 72) .... www.musicbythescore.com

N V Books, (See page 232) .... www.abebooks.com/home/nvrarebooks
Naughton Booksellers, (See page 259) .... www.naughtonsbooks.com
Nautical Antique Centre (The), (See page 94) .... www.nauticalantiques.org
Needham Books, (Russell), (See page 216) .... www.needhambooks.demon.co.uk
Nevis Railway Books, (See page 204) .... www.nevis-railway-bookshops.co.uk
Nevis Railway Bookshops (See page 247) .... www.nevis-railway-bookshops.co.uk
Newband (D.M.), (See page 286) .... www.davidnewbandbooks.co.uk
Newcastle Bookshop, (See page 198) .... www.newcastlebookshop.com
Nicholson of Chester (Richard), (See page 68) .... www.antiquemaps.com
Nicolas - Antiquarian Booksellers & Art Dealers, (See page 156) .... www.nicolasrarebooks.com
Nineteenth Century Books, (See page 207) .... www.ukbookworld.com/members/papageno
Not JUST Books, (See page 148) .... www.njbonline.com

O'Donoghue Books, (See page 284) .... www.intertextuality.com
Oakwood Books, (See page 115) .... www.abebooks.com/home/oakwoodbooks
Oasis Booksearch, (See page 67) .... www.ukbookworld.com/members/welford
Oast Books, (See page 137) .... www.http://members.aol.com/oastbooks/home.htm
Obscurebooks, (See page 259) .... www.obscurebooks.co.uk
Occultique, (See page 196) .... www.occultique.co.uk
Old Bookshelf (The), (See page 273) .... www.theoldbookshelf.co.uk
Old Hall Bookshop (The), (See page 196) .... www.oldhallbooks.com
Old Town Bookshop (The), (See page 271) .... www.oldtownbookshop.co.uk
Olynthiacs, (See page 210) .... www.ukbookworld.com/members/olynthiacs
Onepoundpaperbacks, (See page 96) .... www.onepoundpaperbacks.co.uk
Orange Skies Books, (See page 79) .... www.orangeskies.co.uk
Orangeberry Books, (See page 204) .... www.orangeberry.co.uk
Orchid Book Distributors, (See page 257) .... www.orchidbooks.org
Oriental and African Books, (See page 210) .... www.africana.co.uk
Orssich (Paul), (See page 167) .... www.orssich.com
Outcast Books, (See page 284) .... www.ukbookworld.com/members/outcastbooks
Over-Sands Books, (See page 77) .... www.oversandsbooks.co.uk
Oxfam Books and Music, (See page 127) .... www.oxfam.org.uk/shops
Oxfam Bookshop St Giles, (See page 205) .... www.oxfamstgiles.co.uk
Oxford House Books, (See page 284) .... www.oxfordhousebooks.com

ALPHABETICAL INDEX: Web Sites (P – R)

Pagan Limited (Hugh), (See page 167).. www.hughpagan.com
Pantiles Bookshop, (See page 141)... www.pantilesbooksop.co.uk
Paper Pleasures, (See page 215) .... www.paperpleasures.com
Paperbacks Plus, (See page 59).. www.pbplus.freeserve.co.uk
Paralos Ltd., (See page 175) .... www.timbryars.co.uk
Park Gallery & Bookshop (The), (See page 197) .... www.ukbookworld.com/members/parkbookshop
Parkinsons Books, (See page 183) .... www.parki.com
Parrott (Jeremy), (See page 153) .... www.abebooks.com
Paton Books, (See page 132)... www.patonbooks.co.uk
Patterson (J.D.), (See page 60) .... www.jdpatterson.co.uk
Peakirk Books, (See page 67) .... www.peakirkbooks.com
Pemberley Books, (See page 62)... www.pemberleybooks.com
Pendleburys Bookshop, (See page 156) .... www.pendleburys.com
Pennymead Books, (See page 191)... www.pennymead.com
Period Fine Bindings, (See page 233) .... www.periodfinebindings.typepad.com/royal_bindings/
Periplus Books, (See page 62)... www.periplusbooks.co.uk
Petersfield Bookshop (The), (See page 125) .... www.petersfieldbookshop.com
Peterson (Tony), (See page 111) .... www.chessbooks.co.uk
Petworth Antique Market (Bookroom), (See page 239) .... www.petworthantiquecentre.co.uk
Phenotype Books, (See page 78) .... www.phenotypebooks.co.uk
Phillips (Nigel), (See page 167) .... www.nigelphillips.com
Pholiota Books, (See page 176)... www.pholiota.cc
Photo Books International, (See page 176) .... www.pbi-books.com
Phototitles.com, (See page 109)... www.phototitles.com
Piccadilly Rare Books, (See page 104) .... www.picrare.com
Pickering & Chatto, (See page 172) .... www.pickering-chatto.com
Pinnacle Books, (See page 271).. www.pinnaclebooks.net
Plurabelle Books, (See page 64) .... www.plurabelle.co.uk
Poetry Bookshop (The), (See page 284) .... www.poetrybookshop.co.uk
Politico's.co.uk, (See page 141) .... www.politicos.co.uk
Pollak (P.M.), (See page 87) .... www.rarevols.co.uk
Pomes Penyeach, (See page 219) .... www.abebooks.com
Pooks Motor Books, (See page 146) .... www.abebooks.com
Porcupine Books, (See page 179).. www.porcupine.demon.co.uk
Pordes Books Ltd., (Henry), (See page 176) .... www.henrypordesbooks.com
Portobello Books, (See page 172) .... www.portobello-books.com
Portus Books, (See page 123).. www.portusbooks.co.uk
Post Mortem Books, (See page 238) .... www.postmortembooks.com
Potter Limited (Jonathan), (See page 172) .... www.jpmaps.com
Potterton Books, (See page 194) .... www.pottertonbooks.co.uk
Price (John), (See page 157)... www.johnpriceantiquarianbooks.com
Price (R.W.), (See page 200) .... www.gdprice.com
Pringle Booksellers (Andrew), (See page 271) .... www.pringlebooks.co.uk
Printing House (The), (See page 77)... www.printinghouse.co.uk
Professional Book Services, (See page 190) .... www.bookspluspictures.com
Prospect Books, (See page 278) .... www.gunbooks.com
Prospect House Books, (See page 256) .... www.antiquarianbooksellers.co.uk
PsychoBabel Books & Journals, (See page 202)..................................... www.psychobabel.co.uk
Pyecroft (Ruth), (See page 116) .... www.inprint.co.uk/r&rbooks

Quaritch Ltd., (Bernard), (See page 172) .... www.quaritch.com
Queen Victoria PH, (See page 287)... www.webster.uk.net/queenvictoriainn
Quinto of Charing Cross Road, (See page 176)................................ www.haycinemabookshop.co.uk
Quinto of Great Russell Street, (See page 176).............................. www.haycinemabookshop.co.uk

R M Books, (See page 132)... www.rmbooks.co.uk
R & B Graham Trading, (See page 73)....................................... www.cookery-books-online.com
R. & A. Books, (See page 100).. www.raenterprises.co.uk/
R.E. & G.B. Way, (See page 224) .... www.geocities.com/regbway
Railway Book and Magazine Search, (See page 56)...................... www.nevis-railway-bookshops.co.uk
Rare & Racy, (See page 217) .... www.rareandracy.co.uk
Rare Books & Berry, (See page 215).. www.rarebooksandberry.co.uk

Ray Rare and Out of Print Books (Janette), (See page 195) .... www.janetteray.co.uk
Rayner (Hugh Ashley), (See page 212) .... www.indiabooks.co.uk
Read Ireland, (See page 258) .... www.readireland.ie
Reading Lasses, (See page 265) .... www.reading-lasses.com
Reaveley Books, (See page 85) .... www.reaveleybooks.co.uk
recollectionsbookshop.co.uk, (See page 74) .... www.recollectionsbookshop.co.uk
Red Rose Books, (See page 144) .... www.redrosebooks.co.uk
Red Star Books, (See page 130) .... www.abebooks.com/home/conorpattenden
Rees & O'Neill Rare Books, (See page 176) .... www.omegabookshop.com
Reeves Technical Books, (See page 193) .... www.reevestechnicalbooks.co.uk
Reference Works Ltd., (See page 94) .... www.referenceworks.co.uk
Remington (Reg & Philip), (See page 132) .... www.remingtonbooks.com
Resurgam Books, (See page 105) .... www.resurgambooks.co.uk
Rhos Point Books, (See page 278) .... www.ukbookworld.com/members/brynglas
Richard Connole (See page 84) .... www.yestervision.co.uk
Riley Books (V.M.), (See page 119) .... www.ukbookworld.com/members/vmriley
Ripping Yarns, (See page 157) .... www.rippingyarns.co.uk
Rivendale Press, (See page 61) .... www.rivendalepress.com
River Reads Bookshop, (See page 89) .... www.riverreads.co.uk
Robert G Sawers Ltd, (See page 159) .... www.bobsawers@clara.net
Roberts (William H.), (See page 243) .... www.williamroberts-cricket.com
Roberts Fine Books (Julian), (See page 151) .... www.jrfinebooks.com
Robertson Books, (See page 271) .... www.robertsonbooks.co.uk
Roger Collicott Books, (See page 74) .... www.rogercollicottbooks.com
Rolfe (John), (See page 162) .... www.abebooks.com/home/johnrolfe
Roscrea Bookshop, (See page 261) .... www.roscreabookshop.com
Rose's Books, (See page 284) .... www.rosesbooks.com
Rosemary Pugh Books, (See page 248) .... www.rosemarypughbooks.co.uk
Ross Old Books & Prints, (See page 128) .... www.rossoldbooks.co.uk
Roundstone Books, (See page 143) .... www.roundstonebooks.co.uk
Rowan House Books, (See page 226) .... www.abebooks.com
Roz Hulse, (See page 278) .... www.rozhulse.com
Ruebotham (Kirk), (See page 70) www.abebooks.com/home/kirk61
Rugby Relics, (See page 281) .... www.rugbyrelics.com
Rupert Books, (See page 64) .... www.rupert-books.co.uk
Russell (Charles), (See page 167) .... www.russellrarebooks.com
Rye Old Books, (See page 103) .... www.ukbookworld.com/members/ryeoldbooks

S.P.C.K., (See page 59) .... www.spck.org.uk
Saint Ann's Books, (See page 251) .... www.wildsidebooks.co.uk
Saint Mary's Books & Prints, (See page 152) .... www.stmarysbooks.com
Saint Philip's Books, (See page 205) .... www.stphilipsbooks.co.uk
Saintfield Antiques & Fine Books, (See page 255) .... www.antiquesireland.com
Salway Books, (See page 112) .... www.salwaybooks.co.uk
Samovar Books, (See page 258) .... www.samovarbooks.com
Sandpiper Books Ltd., (See page 167) .... www.sandpiper.co.uk
Sandstone Books, (See page 137) .... www.sandstonebooks.co.uk
Scarthin Books, (See page 81) .... www.scarthinbooks.com
Schull Books, (See page 257) .... www.schullbooks.com
Schutte (David), (See page 125) .... www.http://davidschutte.co.uk
Sclanders (Beatbooks), (Andrew), (See page 154) .... www.beatbooks.com
Scorpio Books, (See page 221) .... www.abe.com/home/scorpiobooks
Scott (Peter), (See page 103) .... www.scottbooks.freeuk.com
Sea Chest Nautical Bookshop (The), (See page 87) .... www.seachest.co.uk
Second Edition, (See page 272) .... www.secondeditionbookshop.co.uk
Sedgeberrow Books & Framing, (See page 251) .... www.abebooks.com/home/SEDGEBERROW
Seeber (Liz), (See page 99) .... www.lizseeberbooks.co.uk
Segal Books (Joel), (See page 84) .... www.joelsegalbooks.com
Shapero Rare Books (Bernard J.), (See page 172) .... www.shapero.com
Sheet Music Warehouse (The), (See page 86) .... www.sheetmusicwarehouse.co.uk
Signature Books, (See page 126) .... www.signaturebookco.com
Sillan Books, (See page 257) .... www.abebooks.com

ALPHABETICAL INDEX: Web Sites (S – T) 317

Silver Trees Books, (See page 234) .... www.abebooks.com
Silverman (Michael), (See page 163) .... www.michael-silverman.com
Simon Finch Nofolk, (See page 186) .... www.simonfinchnorfolk.com
Simon Hunter Antique Maps, (See page 102) .... www.antiquemaps.org.uk
Simon Lewis Transport Books, (See page 115) .... www.simonlewis.com
Simply Read Books, (See page 99) .... www.abenooks.com
Simpson (Dave), (See page 263) .... www.dave.simpson3@virgin.net
Sims Reed Limited, (See page 167) .... www.simsreed.com
Siop y Morfa, (See page 279) .... www.siopymorfa.com
Siri Ellis Books, (See page 118) .... www.siriellisbooks.co.uk
Skoob Russell Square, (See page 225) .... www.skoob.com
Smith Books, (Nigel), (See page 226) .... www.bagotbooks.com
Smith Books, (Sally), (See page 222) .... www.sallysmithbooks.co.uk
Soccer Books Limited, (See page 149) .... www.soccer-books.co.uk
Solaris Books, (See page 105) .... www.solaris-books.co.uk
Soldridge Books Ltd, (See page 122) .... www.soldridgebooks.co.uk
Sotheran Limited (Henry), (See page 172) .... www.sotherans.co.uk
Spelman (Ken), (See page 195) .... www.kenspelman.com
Spenceley Books (David), (See page 244) .... www.abebooks.com/home/davidspenceleybooks
Spink & Son Limited, (See page 176) .... www.spink-online.com
Spurrier (Nick), (See page 138) .... www.nick-spurrier.co.uk
Stacpoole (George), (See page 260) .... www.georgestacpooleantiques.com
Staffs Bookshop (The), (See page 219) .... www.staffsbookshop.co.uk
Stained Glass Books, (See page 139) .... www.glassconservation.com
Stalagluft Books, (See page 231) .... www.stores.ebay.co.uk/STALAGLUFT
Stanley Fish & Co., (See page 138) .... www.stanleyfish.com
Stella Books, (See page 281) .... www.stellabooks.com
Sterling Books, (See page 216) .... www.abe.com
Stern Antiquarian Bookseller (Jeffrey), (See page 195) .... www.abebooks.com/home/STARLIN
Steven Simpson Books, (See page 188) .... www.stevensimpsonbooks.com
Stinton (Judith), (See page 91) .... www.abebooks.com
Stobart Davies Limited, (See page 276) .... www.stobartdavies.com
Stokes Books, (See page 259) .... www.usedbooksirleand.ie
Stroh (M.A.), (See page 153) .... www.webspawner.com/users/Buttonbook/
Stroma Books, (See page 262) .... www.stromabooks.co.uk
Studio (The), (See page 274) .... www.wglasgowwestend.co.uk/shopping/antiques/studio
Studio Bookshop, (See page 99) .... www.studiobookshop.co.uk
Sub Aqua Prints and Books, (See page 124) .... www.buyhistoryprints.com
Sue Lowell Natural History Books, (See page 173) .... www.abebooks.com
Suffolk Rare Books, (See page 225) .... www.abebooks.com
Summerfield Books Ltd, (See page 76) .... www.summerfieldbooks.com
Sun House Books, (See page 139) .... www.sunhousebooks.co.uk
Sutcliffe (Mark), (See page 243) .... www.marksutcliffebooks.com
Sutcliffe (Victor), (See page 184) .... www.victorsutcliffe.demon.co.uk
Symes Books (Naomi), (See page 71) .... www.naomisymes.com

Tarka Books, (See page 83) .... www.tarkabooks.co.uk
Temple (Robert), (See page 157) .... www.telinco.co.uk/RobertTemple/
The Glass Key, (See page 242) .... www.ibooknet.co.uk
The Sanctuary Bookshop, (See page 93) .... www.lyme-regis.com
The Stratford Bookshop, (See page 233) .... www.thestratfordbookshop.co.uk
Thomas Rare Books, (See page 222) .... www.abebooks.com
Thorne (John), (See page 109) .... www.liquidliterature.co.uk
Thorntons of Oxford Ltd., (See page 203) .... www.thorntonsbooks.com
Till's Bookshop, (See page 272) .... www.tillsbookshop.co.uk
Tilleys Vintage Magazine Shop, (See page 218) .... www.tilleysmagazines.com
Tilleys Vintage Magazine Shop, (See page 81) .... www.tilleysmagazines.com
Tilston (Stephen E.), (See page 161) .... www.ukbookworld.com/members/tilston
Tobo Books, (See page 124) .... www.tobo-books.com
Tony Pollastrone Railway Books, (See page 246) .... www.tp-railbooks.co.uk
Tooley, Adams & Co, (See page 206) .... www.tooleys.co.uk
Towers (Mark), (See page 143) .... www.royoftherovers.com

ALPHABETICAL INDEX: Web Sites (T – W)

Townsend (John), (See page 57).. www.johntownsend.demon.co.uk
Tozer Railway Books (Nick), (See page 243)... www.railwaybook.com
Transformer, (See page 265) .... www.abebooks.com/home/TRANSFORMER/home.htm
Travel Bookshop (The), (See page 173).. www.thetravelbookshop.co.uk
Travis & Emery Music Bookshop, (See page 177)................................... www.travis-and-emery.com
Treasure Island (The), (See page 120)................................ www.abebooks.com/home/RAYJC2000
Trinders' Fine Tools, (See page 222) .... www.trindersfinetools.co.uk/
Trinity Rare Books, (See page 260) .... www.trinityrarebooks.com
Trotman (Ken), (See page 66).. www.kentrotman.com
Trotter Books (John), (See page 157) .... www.bibliophile.net/John-Trotter-Books.htm
Tucker (Alan & Joan), (See page 116)................................ www.abebooks.com/home/SANDITON
Twiggers Booksearch, (See page 141) .... www.twiggers.com
Tyger Press, (See page 157) .... www.abebooks.com

Undercover Books, (See page 152) .... www.usedbooknews.com
Underwater Books, (See page 101) .... www.underwater-books.co.uk
Unsworths Booksellers, (See page 160) .... www.unsworths.com
Upper–Room Books, (See page 214)... www.vabooks.com

Vanstone - Aviation Books, (Derek), (See page 225).................................... www.aircraftbooks.com
Verandah Books, (See page 94) .... www.verandah.demon.co.uk
Vinovium Books, (See page 96) .... www.vinoviumbooks.com
Vintage Motorshop, (See page 241) .... www.vintagemotorshop.co.uk
VOL:II, (See page 108)... www.bookwormshop.com

Waddington Books & Prints (Geraldine), (See page 196) .... www.geraldinewaddington.com
Wakeman Books (Frances), (See page 201).. www.fwbooks.com
Walcot (Patrick), (See page 235) .... www.walcot.demon.co.uk
Walden Books, (See page 160) .... www.ukbookworld/members/waldenbooks
War & Peace Books, (See page 123) .... www.abebooks.com
Ward (R.F. & C.), (See page 185) .... www.ashbook.com
Warrender (Andrew), (See page 245) .... www.warrender.demon.co.uk
Warsash Nautical Bookshop, (See page 126)... www.nauticalbooks.co.uk
Warwick Leadley Gallery, (See page 163).. www.warwickleadlay.com
Water Lane Bookshop, (See page 248) .... www.www.waterlanebooks.co.uk
Waterstone's, (See page 177).. www.waterstones.co.uk/gowerst
Watkins (R.G.), (See page 213) .... www.rgw.eurobell.co.uk/
Watkins Books Ltd., (See page 177) .... www.watkinsbooks.com
Webb Books (John), (See page 217).. www.saxtonbooks.com
Wenlock Books, (See page 210) .... www.wenlockbooks.co.uk
Wensum Books, (See page 188) .... www.abebooks.com
Weobley Bookshop, (See page 129) .... www.weobleybookshop.co.uk
Westcountry Old Books, (See page 75) .... www.abebooks.com
Westcountry Oldbooks, (See page 84) .... www.abebooks.com
Westgate Bookshop, (See page 151).................. www.abebooks.com/home/WESTGATEBOOKSHOP/
Westons, (See page 133) .... www.westons.co.uk
Wheeler's Bookshop, (See page 239) .... www.wheelersbookshop.co.uk
Wheen O'Books, (See page 262) .... www.wheenobooks.com
White (David), (See page 65) .... www.davidwhitebooks.co.uk
Whitehall Books, (See page 102) .... www.whitehallbooks.co.uk
Wiend Books, (See page 143) .... www.wiendbooks.co.uk
Wilbraham (J. & S.), (See page 160) .... www.wilbraham.demon.co.uk
Wildside Books, (See page 250) .... www.wildsidebooks.co.uk
Wildy & Sons Ltd, (See page 177)... www.wildy.co.uk
Williams (Bookdealer), (Richard), (See page 152) www.http://rwilliamsbookdealer.mysite.wanadoo-members/
Williams (Christopher), (See page 93).. www.abebooks.com/home/cw
Williams Rare Books (Nigel), (See page 177)... www.nigelwilliams.com
Willmott Bookseller (Nicholas), (See page 276) www.members.lycos.co.uk/nicholaswillmott/id17.htm
Wilson (Manuscripts) Ltd., (John), (See page 114) .... www.manuscripts.co.uk
Woburn Books, (See page 157) .... www.abebooks/home/woburnbooks
Wood (Peter), (See page 65) .... www.booksatpbfa.com
Wood Cricket Books (Martin), (See page 140)............................. www.martinwoodcricketbooks.co.uk

ALPHABETICAL INDEX: Web Sites (W – Z)

Woodbine Books, (See page 241) .... www.abebooks.com/home/woodbine
Words Etcetera Bookshop, (See page 92) .... www.wordsetcetera.co.uk
World War Books, (See page 141) .... www.worldwarbooks.com
World War II Books, (See page 230) .... www.worldwarbooks.co.uk
Worrallo (J. & M.A.), (See page 235) .... www.ukbookworld.com/members/worras
www.AntiqueWatchStore.com, (See page 130) .... www.antiquewatchstore.com
Wychwood Books, (See page 116) .... www.wychwoodbooks.com
Wykeham Books, (See page 168) .... www.bibliographies.co.uk
Wyseby House Books, (See page 55) .... www.wyseby.co.uk

Xanadubooks, (See page 96) .... www.xanadubooks.co.uk

Y Gelli Auctions, (See page 284) .... www.invakuable.com/ygelli
Yates Antiquarian Books (Tony), (See page 146) .... www.TonyYatesBooks@Btopenworld.com
Yesterday's News, (See page 278) .... www.giftnewspapers.co.uk/
Yesteryear Railwayana, (See page 139) .... www.yesrail.com
York (Graham), (See page 85) .... www.gyork.co.uk
Young (D. & J.), (See page 286) .... www.abebooks.com

Zardoz Books, (See page 249) .... www.zardozbooks.co.uk

ALPHABETICAL INDEX BY NAME OF PROPRIETOR

Adams (N.T.) = G. David 63
Adams (V.) = Upper–Room Books 214
Addyman (D.) = Addyman Books 282
Addyman (D.) = Murder & Mayhem 284
Ainge (G.) = Golden Age Books 251
Aitman (T.) = Black Voices......................... 182
Allcoat (K.) = Tarka Books 83
Allen (P.J.) = Robert Temple....................... 157
Allen (R.) = Bufo Books 125
Allinson (J. & M.) = Facet Books................ 90
Allsop (D.) = Duncan M. Allsop 233
Almond (G.) = Westgate Bookshop............... 151
Altshuler (J.) = Jean Altshuler...................... 78
Ameringen (B.) = Porcupine Books 179
Anderson (S.) = The Travel Bookshop Ltd...... 173
Anderton (E.) = Bookstack & D.J. Creece....... 209
Andrews (Mrs. J.) = Alton Secondhand Books. 122
Ansorge (E. & W.) = Barn Books.................. 61
Applin (M.) = Malcolm Applin 55
Aptaker (N.) = Neil's Books........................ 159
Archer (D.) = David Archer 285
Ardley (C.M.) = Faversham Books 138
Armishaw (K.& S.) = River Reads Bookshop .. 89
Armitage (M.) = The Porter Bookshop 217
Armstrong (A.) = Moffat Book Exchange 264
Arnold (J.R.) = June Rhoda........................ 110
Arthur (E.J.L.) = Fantasy Centre.................. 155
Ashby (M.) = Martin's Books...................... 285
Ashcroft (R.E.) = The Inner Bookshop 205
Ashford (T.) = Book Collectors Paradise 132
Ashworth (R.H.) = Whistler's Books 167
Askew Books (V.) = Vernon Askew Books...... 246
Asplin (D.C.) = G. David 63
Astbury (B. & V.) = Woodlands Books 244
Attree (M.) = Birmgham Books 234
Austen (P.) = Phillip Austen....................... 151
Austin (A.) = Farringdon Books................... 109

Bacon (J.) = Pholiota Books....................... 176
Bacon (J) = Bookzone 55
Baggott (L. & H.) = Wychwood Books 116
Bainbridge (S.R.) = Offa's Dyke Books 209
Baine (Mr & Mrs) = The Rutland Bookshop ... 208
Baker (J.A.) = J.B. Books 56
Baldwin (D. & J.) = Rosanda Books 146
Ball (B.W.) = Harlequin Books 59
Ball (C.F. & J.A.) = J.C. Books 188
Ball (E.W.) = Fantasy Centre 155
Ballance (C.) = Byre Books 264
Bamping (A.) = Tyger Press 157
Bangor (Viscount) = Hesketh & Ward Ltd...... 166
Banwell (M.) = Baskerville Books 141
Barfield (I.&K.) = hullbooks.com.................. 106
Barnes, Brown and Green = Winchester
  Bookshop.. 127
Barnes (R. & M.) = Church Green Books....... 207

Baron (Dr. P.J.) = P.J. Baron - Scientific Book Sales 213
Barrett (J. & P.) = Hobgoblin Books 125
Barry (Q. & R.) = Sansovino Books.............. 239
Bartle (C.) = Glacier Books......................... 275
Bartley (M.) = Howes Bookshop 101
Bastians(M) = Eton Antique Bookshop.......... 57
Bates (G. & J.) = Bates Books 179
Bates (J.) = Bates & Hindmarch 243
Batten (P.) = Whitehall Books 102
Bayliss (Dr G.M) = War & Peace Books 123
Bayntun-Coward (C.) = George Gregory 212
Bayntun–Coward (G.) = George Bayntun 212
Beard (P.) = Hill House Books.................... 87
Beardsell (E.V.) = Beardsell Books 242
Beattie (A.) = Americanabooksuk 76
Beckham (J.E.) = Beckham Books Ltd. 225
Beeby (B. & Son) = Cader Idris Books........... 280
Beer (D.W.) = Crosby Nethercott Books 178
Bell (J.) = Fortune Green Books................... 158
Bell (S.) = Green Meadow Books 74
Bennett (Mrs. C.M.) = Moorland Books......... 120
Bennett (D.) = dgbbooks............................ 239
Benster (S. & B.) = Childrens Bookshop......... 242
Bentley (J.) = Albion Books 234
Beresiner (Y.) = InterCol London 156
Bertsein (N.) = Nicholas Bernstein 169
Berry (D.) = Botting & Berry 101
Berry (M.) = Rare Books & Berry 215
Besley (P.& G.) = Besleys Books 221
Biro (T. & S.) = Collectable Books................. 162
Blackman (M. & R.) = Blackman Books 71
Blessett (J.) = St. Paul's Street Bookshop 152
Blessett (S.) = Wizard Books 67
Bletsoe (P.) = Badger................................ 247
Blore (G.T.) = Jermy & Westerman.............. 201
Boehm (H.) = Artco................................. 201
Boland (D.) = Trafalgar Bookshop................ 99
Bond (R.) = Marathon Books...................... 118
Boon (H.) = Fullerton's Booksearch 185
Borthwick (T.) = The Old Station Pottery &
  Bookshop.. 189
Boss (T.) = Tim Boss 239
Boswell (B.) = The Great Oak Bookshop........ 285
Botting (J.) = Botting & Berry 101
Bowe (T.B.) = Browse Books...................... 143
Bowers (M.) = Y Gelli Auctions 284
Bowie (J.) = Bowie Books & Collectables........ 106
Boyd–Cropley (J.M.) = Cottage Books............ 145
Brachotte (P.) = Chapter Two...................... 161
Bradbury (A.) = Brad Books, ... 109
Bradley (S.) = Maynard & Bradley 146
Brayford (D.J.) = Jay Books 271
Brett (S.) = Chandos Books 180
Brewin (K.A.F.) = Brewin Books Ltd 233
Brichto (A.) = Addyman Books 282
Brichto (A.) = Murder & Mayhem................ 284

ALPHABETICAL INDEX: Proprietor (B – C)

Bridger (N.J.) = Nevis Railway Books............ 204
Bridger (N.J.) = Railway Book and Magazine Search 56
Bridger (N.J.) = Nevis Railway Bookshops...... 247
Brightman (C.) = Chantrey Books 217
Bristow (J.A.) = South Downs Book Service.... 238
Brittain (J.) = JB Books & Collectables 238
Broad (S.) = Camilla's Bookshop.................. 100
Brook (R.A. & P.P.) = The Bookshop, Kirkstall... 243
Brooman (J. & J.) = Spearman Books............ 103
Brotchie (A.) = Atlas................................. 155
Brown (A.) = David Archer 285
Brown (M.G. & B.J.) = Brown-Studies........... 273
Brown (P.) = Bookbox............................... 116
Brown (R. & R.) = Ken Trotman.................. 66
Browne (M.) = Premier Books & Prints.......... 148
Browne (R.) = Main Point Books 271
Bryant (E.H.) = Vandeleur Antiquarian Books . 227
Bryer–Ash (P.G.) = Branksome Books 93
Bryers (T.) = Tim Bryers Ltd....................... 175
Buck (J.) = Polmorla Books 75
Buckler (R. & S.) = Cobweb Books............... 192
Budek (P.M. & M.M.) = The Eagle Bookshop . 53
Bull (T.) = Bowden Books 147
Burca (E.) = De Burca Rare Books............... 259
Burca (V.) = De Burca Rare Books............... 259
Burden (C.) = Clive A. Burden Ltd. 132
Burden (D.) = J. Lawton............................ 227
Burgin (A.) = Woburn Books 157
Burkett (D.) = Musicalania 186
Burmester (J.R.)....................................... 58
Burridge (Dr. Peter) = Quest Books............... 106
Burrow (b.) = Books and Things 253
Burrows (N. & H.) = Modern First Editions.... 180
Burton (R.F.) = The Parlour Bookshop.......... 203
Bush (F.) = Othello's Bookshop 110
Butler (T.) = Stour Bookshop 92
Button (C.) = Little Stour Books 136
Byatt (T.) = Golden Age Books 251
Byrne (A.) = Foyle Books........................... 255
Byrne (C.) = Charlie Byrne's Bookshop.......... 260
Byrne (K. & C.) = Colonsay Bookshop 269
Byrom (J.) = Towpath Bookshop 120
Byrom (R.) = Richard Byrom Textile Bookroom 142

Cahn (M.) = Plurabelle Books 64
Canvin (G.L.) = Whitchurch Books Ltd. 276
Cardwell (R. & A.) = The New Strand Bookshop 128
Carlile (G.) = East Riding Books.................. 106
Carmody (P.) = Brighton Books................... 98
Carpenter (R.D.) = Bonython Bookshop 75
Carruthers (Dr. G.B.) = London & Sussex Ant. Book & Print 100
Carter (B. & M.) = Browsers Bookshop 109
Case (D.) = Morley Case 126
Casey (K.F.) = Sub Aqua Prints and Books 124
Casson (C.) = Norton Books 194
Cauwood (R.) = The Treasure Island............ 120

Cawthorn (T.M.) = Suffolk Rare Books 225
Chadband (Mrs. B.) = Solway Books............. 264
Chaddock (M.) = Antiquary Ltd. (Bar Bookstore).. 192
Chambers (J.) = Broadleaf Books 287
Chapman (C.) = Paragon Books................... 214
Chapman (E.M.) = Bookquest 83
Chapman (R.) = Tindley & Chapman............ 176
Chappell (G.) = Valentine Rare Books 227
Chatten (D.) = Riviera Books...................... 185
Checkland (S.) = Rising Tide Books.............. 265
Checkley (A.) = Stothert Old Books 68
Cheke (A.S.) = The Inner Bookshop.............. 205
Child (R. & J.) = Paton Books..................... 132
Christian Literature Stalls = Barbican Bookshop 194
Christie (J.) = Harvest Books...................... 144
Churcher (P.R.) = The Victoria Bookshop 83
Churchill–Evans (D.) = Marine and Cannon Books.. 69
Churchill-Evans (Mrs D.) = Marine & Cannon Books.. 71
Clark (A. & G.) = Ainslie Books 273
Clarke (J.) = Janet Clarke.......................... 212
Clarke (R.) = Muttonchop Manuscripts.......... 239
Clarke (V.) = The Little Bookshop................ 119
Clegg (D.) = David Clegg 219
Clement (C.) = Brighton Books.................... 98
Cockram (A.) = Golden Goose Books 150
Cocks (M.) = Badgers Books....................... 239
Collard (B.) = Collards Bookshop 89
Collie (R.) = Sandpiper Books Ltd................ 167
Collinge (V.H.) = The Border Bookshop......... 245
Collins (A.) = Pedlar's Pack Books 89
Collyer (W.J.) = Books Bought & Sold 226
Combellack (P. & J.) = Kellow Books............ 203
Compton (M.) = The Idle Booksellers 241
Connolly (T.) = Booknotes 111
Conway (Ms. S.A.) = Books for Writers......... 280
Conwell (B.) = Dusty Books........................ 285
Cook (D.) = Richard Way Booksellers........... 204
Cook (M.) = Internet Bookshop UK Ltd........ 113
Cook (S.) = Churchgate Books 221
Cooper (R.J.) = Marjon Books 112
Cope (D.) = Left on The Shelf 78
Coppock (C.) = Fireside Books 62
Coppock (J.) = Fireside Books 62
Corbett (C.) = Corvus Books....................... 61
Corbett (R.) = Booklore............................. 146
Corbett (S.) = Booklore............................. 146
Cornell (G.) = Cornell Books 117
Cornish (I.) = Ambra Books 58
Corrall (L.) = The Pocket Bookshop 86
Coulthurst (S.) = Beaver Booksearch 221
Coupe (M.) = Eclectica 162
Court (Mr. & Mrs.) = Bannatyne Books......... 155
Court (R. & A.) = Mountaineering Books....... 156
Cowan (E.E.) = Eddie's Books and Cards 274
Cox (G.A.) = Kirkdale Bookshop 162
Cox (A.B.) = Claude Cox Old & Rare Books .. 223
Cox (L.) = Lisa Cox Music 84
Cox (P.) = Peter Pan Bookshop 188

ALPHABETICAL INDEX: Proprietor (C –F)

Cox (P.) = Peter's Bookshop 188
Cozens (N.) = Lymelight Books & Prints 92
Cranwell (J.) = Bookworld 210
Cresswell (P.M.) = Humber Books 148
Crimmings (T.) = Criterion Books 180
Cross (J.) = Books & Collectables Ltd. 63
Crouch (A.S.) = Crouch Rare Books 227
Culme-Seymour (M.A.) = Marco Polo
  Travel & Adventure Books, ... 91
Cundy (D.) = Dene Barn Books & Prints 216

Dakin (B.) = Letterbox Books 200
Dale (I.) = Politicos.co.uk 141
Daly (K.) = Rainbow Books 99
Dancy (J.E. & A.B.) = Broadwater Books 126
Danks (N.) = ForensicSearch 132
D'Arch Smith (T.) = Fuller D'Arch Smith 170
Daunter (P. & L.) = Libra Books 148
Davidson (M.) = Winram's Bookshop 266
Davies (G.&R.) = Gemini–Books 210
Davies (J. & L.) = Stepping Stones Bookshop .. 191
Davies (R.) = Davies Fine Books 252
Dawson (M.) = Ampersand Books 209
Daymond (D.) = Arden Books &
  Cosmographia 232
de Visser (E.) = de Visser Books 63
Dean (R.J. & S.W.) = Cartographics 220
Dearn (R.A.) = The Sea Chest Nautical
  Bookshop 87
Degnan (P.) = Kay Books 171
Della–Ragione (G.) = Henry Pordes
  Books Ltd. 176
Demar (G.) = Grant Demar Books 140
De Martini (M.) = Altea Antique Maps
  & Books 169
Dennis (G.) = Blacklock's 227
Dennys (N.) = Gloucester Road Bookshop 165
Desforges (K.) = Acer Books 128
Devlin (Mrs P.) = The Warrington Book Loft .. 71
Deyong (J.C.) = Deyong Books (J.C.) 164
Dibble (R.) = Thistle Books 274
Dinnage (Mr G. & C.) = ... 98
Dixon (C.) = Earlsfield Bookshop 164
Dobbyn (D. & A.) = Yesterday Tackle
  and Books 90
Dollery (A.) = Kingswood Books 93
Donaldson (A.) = Judd Books 175
Doran (A.) = Falconwood Transport &
  Military Bookshop 181
Douthwaite (G. & W.) = Clevedon Books 214
Downes (D.) = Dublin Bookbrowsers 259
Doyle (A.) = Books & Collectables Ltd. 63
Dreda (A.) = Wenlock Books 210
Dreyer (M. & E.) = Philip Martin Music
  Books 195
Driver (M.) = Waxfactor 99
Druett (D.) = Pennymead Books 191
Ducat (N.) = Devanha Military Books 275
Duckworth (A.) = Sen Books 127
Duerdoth (S.) = Eric Goodyer, Natural History
  Books 146
Dumble (Mrs. A.) = Durham Book Centre 76

Dunbar (D.) = Aurelian Books 158
Dunn (C.R.) = Anchor Books 149
Dwyer (D.&J.) = Newgate Books and
  Translations 198
Dyke (S.) = Skyrack Books 243

Eastman (P.V.) = Eastern Books of London 165
Edgecombe (S.M.) = J. Clarke–Hall Limited 137
Edmonds (M.J.) = The Dorchester Bookshop .. 91
Edmunds (D.R.D.) = John Drury Rare Books . 111
Edwards (C.) = Christopher Edwards 55
Edwards (I.) = Old Cathay Fine Books 244
Elgar (R.) = Raymond Elgar 98
Elissa (N.M.) = Joppa Books Ltd. 226
Elithorn (A.) = Game Advice 205
Ellingworth (M. & S.) = Coach House Books .. 251
Elliston (P.) = Firsts in Print, ... 134
Erskine (M.) = Christopher Edwards 55
Evans (M.) = Mollie's Loft 287
Evans (M.) = Mark Evans 151
Evans (S.) = Kings Bookshop Callander, ... 263
Excell (A. & L.F.) = Bookmark (Children's
  Books) 248

Fairnington (P.) = Manna Bookshop 216
Farley (F.) = Kennedy & Farley 103
Farnsworth (B.) = Ouse Valley Books 54
Faulkner (Lady) = Bookline 256
Feehan (G. & M.) = Royal Carbery Books Ltd. 257
Fenning (J. & C.) = James Fenning,
  Antiquarian Books 259
Ferguson (A.J.) = Oopalba Books 71
Fernee (B.) = Caduceus Books 145
Figgis (N.) = The House of Figgis Ltd 260
Fines (R.) = Chapter & Verse 150
Finlay (Dr. R. & Dr L.A.) = Barlow Moor
  Books 118
Finn (M. & E.) = Jackdaw Books 185
Finn (T.) = Twiggers Booksearch 141
Firth (M.) = Bijou Books 218
Fishburn (J.) = Fishburn Books 158
Fisher (B.) = March House Books 94
Fisher (C.) = Bookbox 116
Fitzpatrick (G.) = Reid of Liverpool 182
Flanagan (M. & L.) = Zardoz Books 249
Flint (D.) = David Flint 122
Flint (P.) = Birdnet Optics Ltd. 81
Flowers (L.) = Kim's Bookshop 237, 240
Ford (G.) = G.F. Book Services 53
Ford (J.) = Books Antiques & Collectables 88
Fordham (S.) = Ewell Bookshop 227
Fordyce (D.) = Lewis First Editions 137
Forman (L.) = The Bookshop 92
Forster (C.A.) = C.R. Johnson Rare Book
  Collections 159
Foster (J.A.) = The Park Gallery & Bookshop . 197
Foster (P.) = Paul Foster Bookshop 165
Foster (W.A.&M.A.) = Fosters Bookshop 170
Fothergill (T.) = Ken Spelman 195
Fowkes (M.) = Kingsgate Books & Prints 127
Francombe (C.) = Camilla's Bookshop 100
French (S.) = Dawlish Books 84

ALPHABETICAL INDEX: Proprietor (F – H)

Frith (V. & R.) = recollectionsbookshop.co.uk . 74
Galinsky (P.) = Broughton Books 271
Gange (C.) = Katharine House Gallery 247
Gardner (J. & M.) = The Children's Bookshop 282
Gardner (M.) = Emjay Books 226
Gardner (S.) = Forbury Fine Books 56
Gartshore (Y.) = Calluna Books 94
Garwood (N.) = Garwood & Voigt 140
Gavey (G.P.& C.M.) = Channel Islands Galleries Ltd. 253
Gentil (P.) = Aviabooks 114
George (G.) = Baggins Book Bazaar Ltd. 139
George (S.) = The Book Shelf 86
Gestetner (J.) = Marlborough Rare Books Ltd. 171
Gibbs (J.) = Hummingbird Books 128
Gibson (J.A.B. & J.L.) = Wayside Books & Cards 203
Gilbert (R.A.) = R.A. Gilbert 59
Giles (D. G.) = Ancient Art Books 164
Gipps (A.) = Woodside Books 136
Gleeson (L.) = Nonsuch Books 229
Gleeson (R.) = Nonsuch Books 229
Glover (S.) = Handsworth Books 112
Goddard (J.) = Solaris Books 105
Goddard (M.) = Rose's Books 284
Golborn (E.M.) = Rosemary Books 183
Golden (E.) = Dorset Bookshop, The 90
Goodenough (M.) = Inprint 116
Goodfellow (A.P.) = Carlton Books 187
Goodrick–Clarke (Dr. N. & C.) = IKON 88
Goodwin (J.O.) = J.O. Goodwin 220
Goodyer (E.) = Eric Goodyer, Natural History Books 146
Gorman (N.) = medievalbookshop 179
Gorton (J.) = John Gorton Booksearch 103
Gosden (S.G.) = Fantastic Literature 111
Goss (M.) = The Dancing Goat Bookshop 184
Goss (M.R.) = Delectus Books 174
Goulding (J.) = Optimus Books Ltd 240
Govan (D.) = Armchair Books 270
Gowen (M.) = The Book Jungle 104
Graham (K. & J.) = Ken's Paper Collectables .. 62
Grant (B.& S.) = Grant Books 250
Grant (F.) = The Little Bookshop 80
Graves-Johnston (M.) = Michael Graves-Johnston 166
Greatwood (J.) = J.G. (Natural History Books) 228
Green (J.R.) = Castle Bookshop 109
Green (R.&R.) = Treasure Chest Books 222
Green (W.M. & O.D.) = Angel Books ....
Greenwood (N.) = Right Now Books (Burma) . 166
Gregory (Dr G.) = Bijou Books 218
Gretton (B.) = Leigh Gallery Books 110
Greysmith (B.) = Pedlar's Pack Books............ 89
Grogan (P.) = R.A. Gekoski 175
Gwynne (Mr. N.M.) = Britons Catholic Library 261

Habraszewski (T.) = Hab Books 171
Hadfield (G.K. & J.V.) = G.K. Hadfield 78
Hadfield–Tilly (N.R.) = G.K. Hadfield 78
Haffner (R.N.) = Postings 228

Haldane (J.) = Abington Bookshop 222
Halewood (M.) = Preston Book Company 144
Hall (D.) = Hanborough Books 205
Hall (J.) = Garretts Antiquarian Books 254
Hall (S.&T.) = Invicta Bookshop 56
Hallgate (J.) = Lucius Books 195
Hamburger (R.B.) = Riderless Horse Books 184
Hancock (E.) = Hancock & Monks 283
Hanna (J.) = Blaenavon Books 287
Hanson (D. & M.) = D. & M. Books 244
Harding (J.) = Roundstone Books................. 143
Hardman (L.R.) = Broadhurst of Southport Ltd.. 182
Hardwick (C.) = Rookery Bookery 220
Harlow (Dr. B.J. & S.) = Tiger Books........... 137
Harper (T.) = World War Books 141
Harries (P.) = Boz Books 282
Harries (P.) = Pauline Harries Books 124
Harris (K.) = Books on Spain 181
Harrison (L.) = Biblion 169
Harrison (S.J.) = Bracton Books 63
Hartles (D.B. & J.) = Goldsworth Books 230
Haslam (J.) = Brock Books 190
Haslem (J.) = Oakwood Books 115
Havercroft (J.) = Hava Books 161
Hawes (S. & J.) = Bosco Books 72
Hawkin (S.) = The Staffs Bookshop 219
Hay Cinema Bookshop Ltd = Francis Edwards in Hay–on–Wye 283
Hayhoe (M.) = Corfe Books 227
Haylock (B. & J.) = The Idler 223
Heald (D.W.) = Pamona Books 144
Hearn (K.) = Newlyn & New Street Books 74
Heatley (Mr. & Mrs. P.R.) = The Dartmoor Bookshop 83
Hebden (M.) = M. & D. Books.................... 250
Hedge (P. & E.) = Hedgerow Books.............. 217
Helstrip (A.) = Fossgate Books 194
Herbert (Mrs. S.) = Elstree Books 131
Herbert (W.) = Photo Books International 176
Herries (D.) = Find That Book 244
Herron (M.) = The Bookshop 258
Hessey (A.) = Reads................................. 94
Hetherington (P.) = Europa Books 165
Hewson (E.) = Kabristan Archives 211
Hickley (Dr. R.H.) = Baedekers & Murray Guides... 217
Hill (A.) = Alan Hill Books........................ 217
Hill (G. & G.) = Bowdon Books 143
Hill (K.R.) = Stained Glass Books 139
Hill (S.J.) = Stained Glass Books 139
Hinchcliffe (C.) = Empire Books 194
Hinchliffe (Mrs. A.) = Whig Books Ltd. 147
Hinde (H.M.) = Ystwyth Books 277
Hine (J.) = Gresham Books 214
Hiscock (L.) = E. Chalmers Hallam 125
Hitchens (B. & E.) = Silver Trees Books 234
HMV Media Group = Waterstone's 177
Hinchliffe (G.) = Hinchliffe Books................ 59
Hodgkins (J.R.) = Clifton Books 111
Holman (P.) = Invisible Books 98
Holtom (C.) = Christopher Holtom 75

ALPHABETICAL INDEX: Proprietor (H – L)

Hooper–Bargery (E.) = Music By The Score 72
Hornseys' (B.,S., &D.) = Hornseys' 192
Horsnell (B.) = Footballana 56
Hosain (K.S.) = Hosains Books.................... 159
Hosain (Mrs. Y.) = Hosains Books 159
Hougham (M.) = Verandah Books................ 94
Howard (D.) = Outcast Books 284
Howard (J.) = Photo Books International 176
Howell (N.) = Rolling Stock Books............... 121
Hoy (I.) = Ian Hodgkins and Company
  Limited... 116
Hubbard (P.) = Bufo Books 125
Hudson (H.G.) = The Malvern Bookshop....... 250
Hughes (A.R.) = Roland Books,................... 139
Hughes (P.) = Vinovium Books.................... 96
Hughes (P.D.) = Deverell Books................... 58
Hulse (R.) = Roz Hulse 278
Humm (C.) = Robert Humm & Co............... 151
Humm (R.) = Robert Humm & Co 151
Hunt (R. & C.) = Vintage Motorshop............ 241
Hunter (J.A.) = Hunter and Krageloh............ 82
Husband (M.) = Merlin Books..................... 238
Hutchison (C. & R.) = Chapter House Books .. 94
Hyslop (D.A.) = Yeoman Books 272

Ilott (L.) = Cobnar Books 139
Innes (P.) = Innes Books 209
Ions (B. & G.) = Richmond Books 192
Irvine (J.A.M.) = R.A. Gekoski................... 175
Irwin (C. & M.) = The Book House 78
Israel (N.) = Nibris Books 167
Ives (B.) = Simon's Books........................... 216
Izzard (S.) = Hall's Bookshop 141

Jacksin (S.) = Family Favourites................... 105
Jacques (P.) = Professional Book Services 190
James (J.A.R.) = Village Books 184
Jameson (C.) = Potterton Books................... 194
Jeffers (D.) = My Back Pages 167
Johnson (C.R.) = C.R. Johnson Rare Book
  Collections.. 159
Johnson (C. & C.) = On the Wild Side........... 250
Johnson (I.A.) = Pembury Books.................. 62
Johnson (J.) = Reaveley Books..................... 85
Johnson (M.L.) = Seabreeze Books 144
Johnson (P.) = The Bookshop...................... 119
Johnston (A.L. & A.) = The Iona Bookshop ... 269
Johnston (I. & H.) = Winghale Books........... 151
Jolliffe (P.) = Ulysses 177
Jones (B.) = Pastmasters............................. 82
Jones (B.) = Barry Jones 238
Jones (E.A.) = Siop Lyfrau'r Hen Bost........... 280
Jones (E.) = Yesterday's News 278
Jones (H.M.) = Books for Content................ 128
Jones (N.) = Musebookshop........................ 279
Jones (R.) = Ex Libris 246
Jones (R.W.) = Northern Herald Books 241

Karlou (P.G.) = Crouch Rare Books 227
Kaszuk (N.) = Trinity Rare Books 260
Kay (J. & J.) = K Books 69
Keegan (J.&J.) = Keegan's Bookshop 56

Kelly (L.&L.) = Kelly Books Limited 88
Kelly (P.) = Book Mongers.........................164
Kemp (N.) = Judd Books 175
Kennedy (H.) = Kennedy & Farley 103
Kenny (C.) = ...260
Kent (G. & P.) = Military Parade Bookshop ...247
Kenyon (H.S.) = Brazenhead Ltd 186
Kernaghan (A.&B.) = Kernaghans 183
Key (S.) = Sarah Key Books 64
Kaindra Associates Ltd = Valerie Peel 55
Kiddley (I.) = Janian Comics / Computer
  Manuals...62
Kinderman (G.) = Brimstones......................102
King (A. & C.A.) = Wealden Books..............139
King (I. W.) = Kings Bookshop Callander, ...263
King (R.) = Heatons 248
Kinnaird (J. & J.) = Keswick Bookshop 78
Kirby (E.) = Vailima Books 264
Kitley (A.J.) = A.J. Kitley..........................59
Knapman (C.) = Collectors Carbooks 196
Knight (I.H. & G.M.) =
  MilitaryHistoryBooks.com 138
Kousah (M.G.) = Ely Books 65
Kowalski (S.) = Mereside Books..................70
Kunkler (P.) = Paul Kunkler Books 64

Laing (E.) = Blacket Books.........................270
Laithwaite (S.) = Mereside Books 70
Lake (B.) = Jarndyce Antiquarian Booksellers ..175
Lamb (J. & E.) = Lamb's Tales....................85
Lamont (D.) = The Bookpassage 209
Larkham (P.) = Dive In Books 117
Lawrence (A.) = Lawrence Books 200
Lay (R.) = Alba Secondhand Music 273
Layzell (M.) = Othello's Bookshop...............110
Leach (G.) = Mogul Diamonds 236
Leckey (J.) = Saintfield Antiques and Fine
  Books...255
Ledraw (J.) = J.L. Book Exchange 105
Lee (R.) = Rachel Lee Rare Books 59
Leek (R.J.) = Modern Firsts Etc...................142
Leeper (R.) = Romilly Leeper 166
Leonard (D.) = Dance Books Ltd. 122
Levete (G.) = The Book Business..................169
Levett (G.) = Grays of Westminster...............165
Levitt (V.) = Newcastle Bookshop.................198
Lewis (D. & J.) = Bookshop (Godmanchester) . 65
Lewis (J. & J.) = Photography at Soldridge
  Books...122
Lewsey (C.) = Freya Books & Antiques.........187
Liddle (S.) = Steve Liddle 58
Lidgett (D.J. & C.) = D.C. Books 150
Lidyard (F.W.) = Ruskin Books 136
Lipson (P.) = Antiques on High 204
Lloyd (D.J.) = Worcester Rare Books 252
Loh (C.Y.) = Skoob Russell Square 225
Longton (Mrs. C.L.) = Moorland Books 120
Lovett (M. J.) = Occultique.........................196
Lowndes (C.) = The Chichester Bookshop 237
Lucas (R.) = Richard Lucas 159
Luck (S.) = Tooley, Adams & Co. 206
Lumby (J.) = Shearwater Bed & Books 198

ALPHABETICAL INDEX: Proprietor (L – P)

Lunt (J.) = Books at the Warehouse 191

McBride (C.) = Caledonia Books 273
McCarthy (A.) = Dandy Lion Ediitons 228
McClement (R.H. & J.M.) = Draycott Books .. 114
McConnell (N.) = McConnell Fine Books 137
McCrory (M.) = Books B.C. 178
MacDonald (N.) = BOOKS4U 279
McGavin (D.) = Don McGavin 268
MacGregor (C. & J.) = D'Arcy Books 246
MacGregor (N.) = Olynthiacs 210
Mackey (M.) = Fuchsia Books 261
McKirdy (T.) = Cooks Books 98
MacTaggart (C.) = Bridport Old Books 91
Madani (M.B.) = The Maghreb Bookshop 175
Madden (H.) = Cavern Books 70
Maddison (J.K.) = Anvil Books 235
Maddock (T.) = Alpha Books 155
Mair (J.) = Mair Wilkes Books 265
Manley (S. & M.) = Barter Books 198
Manning (R.) = R. & A. Books 100
Marcan (P.) = Peter Marcan 162
Marsh (B.) = Lime Tree Books 224
Marshall (A.) = Warsash Nautical Bookshop ... 126
Marten (W.) = Bookstand 93
Martin (J. & B.) = Bryony Books 244
Mather (H.S.G) = Wykeham Books 168
Matthews (J.) = Eddie Baxter - Books............ 216
Matthews (J. & M.) = Two Jays Bookshop 178
Mattley (J.E.) = Phenotype Books................. 78
May (E. & D.) = The Eastcote Bookshop 178
Mayall (M. & R.) = Sturford Books 248
Mayes (W.) = Mr. Pickwick of Towcester 196
Maynard (D.) = Maynard & Bradley 146
McGivney (J.) = Kenya Books 99
McKelvie (L.) = The Studio 274
Meaden (B.) = Gaullifmaufry Books.............. 131
Meeuws (W.A.) = Thorntons of Oxford Ltd. ... 203
Menelaou (M.) = Antique Prints of
   the World... 155
Michael (S.) = Otley Books 245
Micklewright (C.) = Wright Trace Books 235
Miles (D.) = The Canterbury Bookshop 136
Miles (H.) = Calendula Horticultural Books ... 101
Miles (S.) = Ice House Books 248
Millard (A.) = R. & A. Books,..................... 100
Millard (R.) = Wembdon Books 213
Miller (G.) = Resurgam Books..................... 105
Miller (P.) = Ken Spelman.......................... 195
Minet (P.P.B.) = Piccadilly Rare Books 104
Missing (C.) = Missing Books...................... 109
Mitchell (A.G.) = Capital Bookshop.............. 276
Mitchell (C.) = Ripping Yarns 157
Mitchell (D.R. & M.E.) = Bruce Main–Smith
   & Co. Ltd.. 146
Mitchell (Dr. D.J.) = Scarthin Books 81
Monckton (I.) = Kingshead Books 286
Monks (J.) = Hancock & Monks 283
Moore (C.N., E.J. & S.J.) = Castle Bookshop .. 285
Moore (R.) = R M Books 132
Morgan (Dr. D.H. & R.A.) = Turret House 189
Morgan (P.) = Coch-y-Bonddu Books............ 285

Morgan–Hughes (A.) = Black Cat Books 185
Morley (A.P.) = Bay Bookshop 277
Morris (G. & B.) = Rhos Point Books 278
Morrish (K. & J.) = Reigate Galleries 228
Morton (A.) = Andrew Morton Books............ 281
Moreton (D.) = Moreton Books......................86
Moy (R.F.) = Spread Eagle Bookshop 162
Mucci (R. M.) = Robert's Shop 101
Mullen (P. & M.) = Yesteryear Railwayana..... 139
Mullett (G.&A.) = The Eastern Traveller 216
Mundy (D.) = David Mundy at Nooks and
   Crannies... 61
Mundy (D.) = David Mundy at Heritage
   Antiques 130
Murdoch (G.) = Armchair Auctions 122
Murphy (R.P.) = Rods Books....................... 87
Murtagh (C.J.) = Anvil Books 235
Mustin (L.) = Byre Books........................... 264
Mycock (D. & M.) = Abacus Books and Cards 220

Nairn (E.G.) = John Updike Rare Books........ 272
Nash (M. & V.) = Marine and Cannon Books . 69
Nassau (J.) = Jarndyce Antiquarian Booksellers 175
Naylor (Dr. A.C.I.) = Bookfare..................... 80
Neal (D.) = Secondhand Bookshop 228
Neal (j.) = Kineton Books 232
Neal (L.) = Joel Segal Books 84
Nearn (Rev. D.H.) = Heritage Books.............. 134
Neil (D.) = Westcountry Oldbooks 84
Neil (D.) = Westcountry Old Books 75
Neville (C.) = Woodbine Books.................... 241
Newbold (R.) = Booktrace International......... 85
Newland (J.& C.) = Cotswold Internet Books .. 113
Newlands (G.M.D.) = McLaren Books 274
Newman (P.) = Castle Hill Books 128
Nicholls (P. & C.) = Boxwood Books & Prints . 216
Nicholls (T.) = Paperbacks Plus.................... 59
Nisbet (D.) = Sterling Books 216
Noble (C. & M.) = Christine's Book Cabin 147
Nummelin (S.&A.) = Browning Books 287

O'Brien (C.) = The Celtic Bookshop.............. 261
Obeney (P.) = Idle Genius Books.................. 156
O'Connell (B. & J.) = Schull Books.............. 257
O'Connor (J.&E.) = O'Connor Fine Books 144
O'Donnell (G.) = Bristol Books.................... 60
Ogden (C.) = The Meads Book Service 103
O'Keeffe (N.S.) = Evergreen Livres 115
Oldham (G.) = Greenroom Books 243
Oldham (Dr. T.) = Wyseby House Books 55
Ollerhead (P.E.) = Copnal Books.................. 68
Ondaatje (C.) = Rare Books & Berry............. 215
O'Neill (A.) = Rees & O'Neill Rare Books 176
Osgood (L.) = Four Shire Bookshops 202
Overton Fuller (J.) = Fuller D'Arch Smith 170
Owen (J.) = owenbooks65........................... 278
Owen (J.V.) = Colwyn Books 277

Painell (C.) = The Design Gallery 1850-1950.... 141
Palmer (E.) = Elmfield Books,..................... 234
Papworth (M.J.) = Hunter and Krageloh......... 82
Park (M.) = Mike Park............................... 180

ALPHABETICAL INDEX: Proprietor (P – S)

Parker (A.) = Frank Smith Maritime Aviation . 231
Parker (M.) = Mike Parker Books 64
Parmoor (Lord) = Bernard Quaritch Ltd 172
Parr (K.) = Kyrios Books 200
Parry (G.M.) = Skirrid Books 280
Parry (R.C.) = Exeter Rare Books 84
Partington (F. & J.) = Tennis Collectables 68
Pattenden (C.) = Red Star Books 130
Patterson (J.B.) = Priestpopple Books 198
Pawson (D. & L.) = Footrope Knots 223
Peace (R.) = Brockwells Booksellers 148
Pearce (P.) = Hencotes Books & Prints 198
Peasgood (A. & M.) = Broadway Books 66
Peers (C.J.) = Mainly Fiction 118
Peggs (K.) = All Books 110
Pegler (P. & W.) = Canon Gate Bookshop 239
Penney (B.) = Invisible Books 98
Perry (I.) = The Strand Bookshop 286
Perry (M.) = Barn Books........................... 211
Peterson (R.) = Stanley Fish & Co. 138
Phil (M.) = Rosanda Books 146
Phillips (C.) = Chris Phillips 246
Phillips (C.) = Bath Old Books.................... 212
Phillips (J.) = Phillips of Hitchin 131
Phillips (J.) = Periplus Books 62
Phillips (S.D.) = Bygone Books 274
Piercy (N.S.) = Crimes Ink........................ 153
Pilkington (P.) = The Art Book Company....... 223
Pinches (R.) = Heraldry Today 247
Pine (L.) = Milestone Publications Goss
  & Crested China 124
Pinto (P.) = Interstellar Master Traders 143
Pipe (M.) = Enscot Books 162
Pizey (J.S.) = P. and P. Books 251
Platt (R.) = Bookshop on the Heath, The 161
Pogmore (Mrs. E.M.) = Books..................... 202
Poklewski–Koziell (S.) = Classic Bindings....... 164
Pollock (Dr. J.) = Whig Books Ltd. 147
Pook (B.&J.) = ... 146
Poole (S.) = Biblion 169
Potter (R.) = Badgers Books 239
Powell (J. & A.) = Palladour Books 126
Pratt (R.J.) = Hereward Books..................... 65
Pretlove (M.) = Gillmark Gallery.................. 131
Prince (C.) = The Poetry Bookshop............... 284
Pritchard (S.) = The Blue Penguin................ 116
Proctor (C.D. & H.M.) = The Antique Map
  & Bookshop..................................... 93
Pugh (D.) = Carta Regis 286
Pugh (J.M.); (A.E.); (Mrs R.M.) = Rosemary
  Pugh Books 248
Purkis (H.H. & P.A.) = Harry Holmes Books .. 106
Pye (J. & H.) = The Bookshop.................... 238

Quigley (A.) = Bibliophile Books 153

Ralph (A.) = Art Reference Books 125
Ramsden (G.) = Stone Trough Books 195
Raxter (C.) = Lion Books.......................... 250
Rayner (J. & J.) = J. & J. Books 149
Read (C. & J.) = The King Street Bookshop.... 185
Reading (B. & J.) = Oast Books 137

Reding (Mrs. P.F.) = Croydon Bookshop 178
Reese (R.W.) = Holdenhurst Books............... 90
Reeve (A.) = Cover to Cover....................... 183
Rees (D.) = Kestrel Books, Powys 283
Rhead (J.) = Barnhill Books....................... 269
Richards (A.) = Cold Tonnage Books 229
Richards (D.) = Rugby Relics..................... 281
Richardson (A.) = Afar Books International.... 234
Richardson (E.) = Blewburst Antiques 202
Richmond (M.) = AA1 Books 264
Richmond (M.) = Ming Books.................... 265
Ridler (Dr. A.M.) = Nineteenth Century Books. 207
Riley (A. & J.) = Ryeland Books, ... 196
Riley (V.M.) = V.M. Riley Books 119
Ritchie (J.) = Books Afloat 94
Ritchie (P.) = Bookworm........................... 270
Ritchie (P.) = Books................................ 137
Robert (L.) = Hyde Park Books 172
Roberts (G.) = Magpie Books..................... 245
Robinson (C.) = Books on the Bank 96
Robinson (C.) = Creaking Shelves................ 268
Robinson (J. M. & G.) = Soccer Books.......... 149
Robinson (P. & S.) = Pomes Penyeach 219
Robinson (T.F.) = J.C. Books..................... 188
Robinson–Brown (P.) = P.R. Brown (Books)... 97
Rockall (A.) = Kingswood Books 93
Roe (A.&D.) = Roe and Moore 176
Rogers (D.) = Helion & Company 235
Rogers (M.) = Fifth Element 235
Rogers (P.J.) = Croydon Bookshop 178
Rogers (P.J.) = Rogers Turner Books 162
Ronald (A.) = A. & R. Booksearch 73
Ronald (R.) = A. & R. Booksearch 73
Ronan (S.) = Chthonios Books 101
Roper (B.) = Eastgate Bookshop 105
Ross (M.C.) = Avonworld Books 213
Routh (S.A.) = Gage Postal Books................ 111
Rowley (F.) = Freader's Books 275
Rowlinson (D.A.) = Books Ulster................. 256
Russell (M.P.) = The Bibliophile 217

St. Aubyn (H.M. & J.R.) = Woolcott Books.... 91
Salin (P.) = Sarah Key Books 64
Salt (D.T.) = Salsus Books......................... 250
Sames (M.D.) = The Ryde Bookshop 134
Sancto (R.G.) = Bunyan Books 53
Savage (K.) = Keith Savage 224
Savery (M. J. S. & A.) = Savery Books 99
Scott (Dr. R.) = Quest Booksearch 64
Scott (T.) = Mount's Bay Books................... 74
Scott Paul (C.) = Old Aberdeen Bookshop 266
Sedgwick (D.) = Moorside Books 143
Seers (P.R. & C.) = Greensleeves 202
Segal (J.) = Joel Segal Books 84
Sephton (A.F.) = A.F Sephton 172
Sesemann (J.) = Luia Sesemann.................... 136
Seton (M.) = Alba Books 267
Sever (T.P.) = Books................................ 278
Seward (P.& G) = The Carnforth Bookshop.... 142
Seydi (S.) = Sevin Seydi Rare Books 159
Shakeshaft (B.L.) = Dr. B. Shakeshaft 71
Shakespeare (C. & L.) = Colin Shakespeare 219

ALPHABETICAL INDEX: Proprietor (S – T)

Sharman (L.) = Treasure Trove Books 146
Sharman (C.E.) = Books Only 222
Sharpe (A.&J.) = Grove Rare Books 193
Sheard (D.) = Heckmondwike Book Shop 244
Sheath (.P.) = Priory Books......................... 252
Sheehan (A.) = Darkwood Books 258
Sheehan (M.) = Caissa Books 229
Sheffield (R.) = Roosterbooks 196
Shelley (A. & J.) = Bow Windows Book Shop.. 102
Shelly (E.& J.) = E.J. Shelly 61
Sheppard (R.D.) = Fireside Bookshop............ 80
Shepperd (H.) = Torc Books 186
Sheridan (P.J.) = Books Bought & Sold.......... 226
Shire (C.) = Theatreshire Books 190
Showler (B. & K.) = B. and K. Books 282
Siddons (D.) = Forest Books 208
Sidwell (R.) = Monmouth House Books 280
Simper (J.I. & S.J.) = Explorer Books 239
Simpson (I.) = Clent Books......................... 250
Simpson (K.M.L.) = Black Five Books 211
Simpson O'Gara (J.P.) = Allhalland Books...... 83
Sims (T.J.) = Bookworms of Evesham............ 252
Sinclair (M.) = Books in Cardigan 277
Sklaroff (L.J.) = Cameron House Books 134
Slade (R.) = Restormel Books 252
Slim (R.T.) = Janus Books & Antiques 235
Sloggett (T.) = Leabeck Books 205
Smillie (M.) = Caledonia Books.................... 273
Smith (E.) = Bookstand 93
Smith (G.D.) = Great Grandfather's.............. 143
Smith (G.E. & M.K.) = Book End................ 108
Smith (J.) = Clarendon Books...................... 145
Smith (K.) = Keith Smith Books 128
Smith (M.) = Chelifer Books 80
Smith (M.E & W.A.) = Second Edition.......... 272
Smith (M.) = Enscot Books......................... 162
Smith (N.) = Nigel Smith Books................... 226
Smith (P.M. & R.D.) = Rupert Books 64
Smith (R.W.L.) = Sax Books 224
Smosarki (A.) = Cofion Books...................... 281
Somers (J.) = Fine Books Oriental Ltd. 175
Sparkes (J.) = Combat Arts Archive 96
Spranklins (G.) = Rowan House Books.......... 226
Sproates (S.) = ForensicSearch 132
Spurrier (R.) = Post Mortem Books 238
Squires (M.) = The Quarto Bookshop............ 266
Stallion (M.R.) = Lawful Occasions............... 108
Starling (R.) = Books Plus 83
Steadman (J.) = The Traveller's Bookshelf....... 212
Steenson (M.M.) = Books & Things 169
Stemp (I.) = Jade Mountain 125
Stevens (A.E.R.M.) = Enigma Books 186
Stevens (E.) = Fortune Green Books 158
Stevens (F.) = Collectors Corner................... 248
Stevens (G.R.) = The Driffield Bookshop........ 105
Stevens (J.) = Joan Stevens......................... 65
Stevenson (P.A.) = Boris Books.................... 127
Stewart (I.) = Sun House Books 139
Stinton (R.) = The Idle Booksellers 241
Stoddart (A.) = Hellenic Bookservices 158
Stone (A.) = Squirrel 123
Stones (L. A.) = The Bookshelf.................... 192

Stransky (H.) = Cranhurst Books 158
Strong (E.A.) = McNaughtan's Bookshop....... 271
Stroud (F.P.A.) = Chaters Motoring
  Booksellers 179
Stuart (E.) = First State Books..................... 170
Suchar (V. & E.) = Camden Books 212
Summers (A. & M.) = The Helston Bookworm 73
Surtees (A.) = Valentine Rare Books 227
Sutcliffe (E.) = Pendleside Books 143
Highland (S.) = Allhalland Books.................. 83
Suttie (D.S.) = Bowland Bookfinders 142
Sutton (M.) = The Old Celtic Bookshop......... 86
Swain (A. & C.) = Periwinkle Press 139
Swift (H. & C.) = Countryman Books............ 105
Swindall (J. & R.) = Jiri Books 255

Tall (J. & N.) = Badger Books..................... 216
Tandree (H. & A.) = Anthroposophical Books. 116
Tandree (H.) = Rachel Lee Rare Books.......... 59
Tatam (J.) = Puss in Books......................... 215
Tatman (C.) = Beverley Old Bookshop.......... 105
Taylor (P.H.) = Farnborough Bookshop &
  Gallery 123
Taylor (P. & S.) = Greyfriars Books 109
Taylor (P.) = Books & Bygones.................... 236
Tebay (K.M.) = Red Rose Books 144
Thatcher (K.) = Foyle Books....................... 255
Thomas (M.) = Solitaire Books.................... 212
Thompson (J.) = Saltburn Bookshop 192
Thompson (M. & A.C.) = The Bookshop 189
Thompson (P.) = Bookseeker....................... 275
Thomson (G.) = Greta Books 96
Thornhill (J. & M.) = Candle Lane Books 210
Thredder (P.) = Ross Old Books & Prints....... 128
Tierney (Dr. J. & Mrs. I.) = Hawkridge
  Books.. 81
Tierney (M.) = Wheen O'Books,................... 262
Tilley (A. & A.) = Tilleys Vintage
  Magazine Shop 81
Timothy (D.) = Siop y Morfa 279
Timson (L.) = Humanist Book Services 72
Tindley (J.) = Tindley & Chapman 176
To (W.) = Mike Park 180
Tober (B.) = Bruce Tober 236
Tobin (D.) = Walden Books 160
Todd (J.) = Books (For All) 190
Tomaszewski (C.) = Stella Books 281
Tomlinson (D.&D.) = The Old Bookshelf 273
Tomlinson (R.K.) = Aviation Book Supply 130
Tootell (J.) = Exedra Booksearch Ltd............. 165
Townsend (J. & J.) = The Old Hall Bookshop . 196
Townsend–Cardew (J. & B.) = Daisy Lane
  Books.. 242
Tozer (N.) = Roscrea Bookshop.................... 243
Tranter (P.) = Orangeberry Books................. 204
Travis (R., B., and S.) = SaBeRo Books.......... 167
Traylen (N. & T.) = Ventnor Rare Books 135
Treece (M.) = Cornerstone Books................. 87
Trinder (R.) = Trinders' Fine Tools............... 222
Trussell (H.) = The Moray Bookshop 267
Tuft (P.) = Patrick Tuft............................. 173
Turnbull (P.M.) = The Countryman's Gallery .. 145

ALPHABETICAL INDEX: Proprietor (T – Z)

Turner (A. & D.) = Capel Mawr Collectors Centre 280
Turner (A.J.) = Rogers Turner Books 162
Turner (L.M.) = Bath Book Exchange 212
Twitchett (D.E.) = Engaging Gear Ltd. 108
Tyers (N.A.M., M.G.D. & P.A.) = St. Mary's Books & Prints 152
Tynan (P.) = Courtwood Books 260
Tyson (G.) = High Street Books 85
Tyson (L.) = Paper Pleasures 215
Tyson (S.R.) = Over-Sands Books 77

Unny (L.) = Broadleaf Books 287
Unwin (D.) = Eastleach Books 55

Vidion (A.) = Church Street Books 184
Valentine Ketchum (V.A. & B.J.) = Staniland (Booksellers)... 152
Vallely (J.) = Craobh Rua Books 255
Vaupres (J.) = The Lighthouse Books 91
Voigt (R.G.) = Garwood & Voigt 140

Wagstaff (A.) = Booksmart 196
Wakeman (P. & F.) = Frances Wakeman Books... 201
Waldron (C.) = Bookends............................ 123
Walker (D.) = Chelifer Books 80
Walker (G.) = Gary Walker 265
Walker (R.) = Fine Art 165
Wallace (N.) = Minster Gate Bookshop.......... 195
Wallbaum (C.) = H. Baron 158
Walsh (M.) = Glenbower Books 259
Walters (H. & G.) = Court Hay Books 58
Walters (M.) = Kingfisher Book Service 201
Ward (D.J.) = SETI Books 220
Warwick (D.C.) = The Nautical Antique Centre 94
Warwick (N.) = Readers Rest 150
Watson (J.S.) = John Updike Rare Books....... 272
Watts (M.D.) = Bookshop at the Plain........... 151
Watts (N.) = Beaver Booksearch 221
Watts (R.) = Dolphin Books 221
Way (D.) = David Way Angling Books.......... 86
Way (R.) = Richard Way Booksellers 204
Wayne (N.) = Nicholas Willmott Bookseller 276
Weaver (C.A.) = Transformer 265
Weber (M) = The Churchill Book Specialist 179
Weir (D. & J.L.) = Yesterday's Books............ 91
Weissman (S.) = Ximenes Rare Books Inc....... 115
Welford (R.G.M.& M.E.) = Oasis Booksearch . 67
Wells (M.) = Mary Wells............................ 167
Wesley (P.) = Harlequin 89
Weston (J.) = Westons Booksellers Ltd 133
West–Skinn (R.) = Harlequin Gallery 150
West–Skinn (R.) = Golden Goose Books 150
Westwood (F.) = The Petersfield Bookshop 125
Wheeler (M.A.) = W.H. Collectables 225
Whetman (M.) = Isabelline Books................. 72
Whitaker (J. & M.A.) = Peregrine Books (Leeds) 244
Whitby (M.) = Sevin Seydi Rare Books.......... 159
White (M.J.) = Fun in Books 229

Whitehorn (J.) = Heartland Old Books........... 88
Whitworth (N.) = Elephant Books 244
Wiberg (C.) = The Book Depot.................... 158
Wicks (J.) = Just Books 75
Wilkes (A.) = Mair Wilkes Books................. 265
Wilkinson (D. & T.) = The Book Gallery 75
Wilkinson (D.J.) = Intech Books 198
Wilkinson (D.&J.) = Autolycus 209
Wilkinson (J.B.) = Leeds Bookseller 244
Williams (C. & C.) = Aardvark Books 249
Williams (J.) = Bookworm Alley................... 87
Williams (M.) = Hellenic Bookservices 158
Williams (Dr. S.M.) = Barcombe Services 108
Willmott (N.) = Nicholas Willmott Bookseller.. 276
Wills (T.) = Volumes of Motoring................. 113
Wills (Mrs. V.) = Bridge of Allan Books......... 263
Wilson (H.G.E.) = Dales and Lakes Book Centre... 79
Wilson (J.) = John Wilson (Manuscripts) Ltd... 114
Wilson (L.) = Halson Books........................ 71
Wilson (P.D.) = Oriental and African Books.... 210
Wilson (R.) = Classic Crime Collections 119
Wilson (R.) = The Old Town Bookshop 271
Winkworth (D.) = The Printing House........... 77
Winston–Smith (M. & S.) = Dead Mens Minds.co.uk 285
Winter (Mrs.J.) = Sedgeberrow Books & Framing.. 251
Wise (C.) = Atlantis Bookshop..................... 174
Woodhouse (G.) = Gillmark Gallery 131
Woolley (P. & K.) = Black Cat Bookshop....... 145
Woolvett (L.) = Glenwood Books 230
Worms (L.) = Ash Rare Books 164
Worthy (J.S. & S.) = Rochdale Book Company 120
Wren (C.) = Annie's Books 217
Wright (C.) = Yarborough House Bookshop ... 209
Wright (M. & S.) = Roadmaster Books.......... 137
Wright (P.) = Wright Trace Books 235
Wynne (N.) = Grays of Westminster 165

Yablon (G.A.) = Ian Hodgkins and Company Limited... 116
Young (I. & S.) = Autumn Leaves 150
Young (R.) = Bridport Old Books 91
Young (S.) = Antiques on High 204

Zealley (C.J.) = St. Philip's Books 205

SPECIALITY INDEX
Index of dealers by stock speciality followed by county

ABORIGINAL
Gaullifmaufry Books, Hertfordshire.............. 131
Muse Bookshop (The), Gwynedd................. 279

ACADEMIC/SCHOLARLY
Adrem Books, Hertfordshire...................... 131
Ainslie Books, Strathclyde.......................... 273
Al Saqi Books, London W......................... 169
All Books, Essex 110
Alpha Books, London N 155
Antiquary Ltd., (Bar Bookstore), North Yorkshire.................................... 192
Any Amount of Books, London WC............ 174
Apocalypse, Surrey 228
Austwick Hall Books, Lancaster 190
B D McManmon, Lancashire 144
Barcombe Services, Essex........................... 108
Bell (Peter), Strathclyde 270
Bennett & Kerr Books, Oxfordshire.............. 202
Blanchfield (John), West Yorkshire.............. 243
Boer (Louise), Arthurian Books, Powys......... 282
Bolland Books (Leslie H.), Bedfordshire 53
Book Barrow, Cambridgeshire 63
Book Business (The), London W 169
BOOKS4U, Flintshire.............................. 279
Bookshop (The), Greater Manchester........... 119
Bowland Bookfinders, Lancashire 142
Bracton Books, Cambridgeshire.................. 63
Bridge of Allan Books, Central 263
Brighton Books, East Sussex....................... 98
Brockwells Booksellers, Lincolnshire 148
Burak (Steve), London WC........................ 174
Burden Ltd., (Clive A.), Hertfordshire 132
Camden Books, Somerset 212
Capes (Books, Maps & Prints) (John L.), North Yorkshire.................................... 193
Carta Regis, Powys 286
Celtic Bookshop (The), Co. Limerick 261
Chapman (Neville), Cornwall...................... 74
Chesters (G. & J.), Staffordshire.................. 220
Church Street Bookshop, London N............ 155
Clifton Books, Essex 111
Corder (Mark W.), Kent 140
Cornucopia Books, Lincolnshire 151
Country Books, Derbyshire 81
Courtwood Books, Co. Laois...................... 260
Crouch Rare Books, Surrey....................... 227
Dandy Lion Editions, Surrey 228
David (G.), Cambridgeshire....................... 63
de Visser Books, Cambridgeshire 63
Delectus Books, London WC..................... 174
Derek Stirling Bookseller, Kent 141
Dooley (Rosemary), Cumbria 80
Downie Fine Books Ltd., (Robert), Shropshire 211
Dworski Books, Travel & Language Bookshop (Marijana), Herefordshire.......... 283

Dylans Bookstore, Glamorgan 286
Eagle Bookshop (The), Bedfordshire............ 53
Earth Science Books, Wiltshire................... 247
Eastern Books of London, London SW......... 165
Eastleach Books, Berkshire........................ 55
Ellis, Bookseller (Peter), London SE 162
Empire Books, North Yorkshire.................. 194
English (Toby), Oxfordshire 206
Facet Books, Dorset................................. 90
Farnborough Gallery, Hampshire 123
Fireside Bookshop, Cumbria 80
Fortune Green Books, London NW 158
Fossgate Books, North Yorkshire 194
Foyle Books, Co. Derry 255
G. C. Books Ltd., Dumfries & Galloway 264
Galloway & Porter Limited, Cambridgeshire ... 63
Game Advice, Oxfordshire 205
Gaullifmaufry Books, Hertfordshire.............. 131
GfB: the Colchester Bookshop, Essex............ 109
Gibbs Books, (Jonathan), Worcestershire 251
Gildas Books, Cheshire 68
Glenbower Books, Co. Dublin 259
Golden Age Books, Worcestershire.............. 251
Goldman (Paul), Dorset 94
Greenroom Books, West Yorkshire 243
Handsworth Books, Essex.......................... 112
Hawkes (James), Bristol 60
Hawley (C.L.), North Yorkshire 193
Hay Cinema Bookshop Ltd., Herefordshire 283
Helion & Company, West Midlands 235
Hellenic Bookservices, London NW.............. 158
Herb Tandree Philosophy Books, Gloucestershire 116
Hill Books (Alan), South Yorkshire.............. 217
Hornsby, Antiquarian and Secondhand Books (Malcolm), Leicestershire 146
hullbooks.com, East Yorkshire.................... 106
Hurst (Jenny), Kent 138
Ice House Books, Wiltshire 248
Inner Bookshop (The), Oxfordshire 205
Innes Books, Shropshire 209
Internet Bookshop UK Ltd., Gloucestershire .. 113
Invisible Books, East Sussex 98
Island Books, Kent 136
Jackdaw Books, Norfolk 185
Jones (Andrew), Suffolk 223
Joppa Books Ltd., Surrey.......................... 226
K.S.C. Books, Cheshire............................ 68
Key Books (Sarah), Cambridgeshire 64
Kilgarriff (Raymond), East Sussex................ 104
Kim's Bookshop, West Sussex.................... 237
Kingswood Books, Dorset 93
Lee Rare Books (Rachel), Bristol 59
Leeds Bookseller, West Yorkshire 244
Lewcock (John), Cambridgeshire 66
Lewis (J.T. & P.), Cornwall....................... 73

329

SPECIALITY INDEX

Lowe (John), Norfolk 186
Maghreb Bookshop (The), London WC 175
Mair Wilkes Books, Fife............................. 265
Malvern Bookshop (The), Worcestershire....... 250
Marine & Cannon Books, Cheshire 71
medievalbookshop, London Outer................ 179
Mellon's Books, East Sussex....................... 100
Mobbs (A.J.), West Midlands 235
Morgan (H.J.), Bedfordshire....................... 54
Murphy (C.J.), Norfolk.............................. 187
Muse Bookshop (The), Gwynedd.................. 279
My Back Pages, London SW....................... 167
Naughton Booksellers, Co. Dublin 259
Needham Books, (Russell), Somerset 216
Northern Herald Books, West Yorkshire 241
O'Donoghue Books, Powys......................... 284
Offa's Dyke Books, Shropshire.................... 209
Oopalba Books, Cheshire........................... 71
Oriental and African Books, Shropshire......... 210
Orssich (Paul), London SW........................ 167
Ouse Valley Books, Bedfordshire 54
Outcast Books, Herefordshire 284
Oxfam Books and Music, Hampshire............ 127
Parker Books (Mike), Cambridgeshire 64
Pholiota Books, London WC....................... 176
Plurabelle Books, Cambridgeshire 64
Poetry Bookshop (The), Powys.................... 284
Pollak (P.M.), Devon................................ 87
Pomes Penyeach, Staffordshire 219
Poole (William), London W 172
Pordes Books Ltd., (Henry), London WC 176
Porter Bookshop (The), South Yorkshire 217
Priestpopple Books, Northumberland............ 198
Quest Books, East Yorkshire 106
R. & A. Books, East Sussex 100
Reading Lasses, Dumfries & Galloway 265
Red Star Books, Hertfordshire 130
Reeves Technical Books, North Yorkshire...... 193
Reid of Liverpool, Merseyside..................... 182
RGS Books, Surrey................................... 229
Rivendale Press, Buckinghamshire................ 61
Roberts Books, Strathclyde 274
Roscrea Bookshop, Co. Tipperary................ 261
Roz Hulse, Conwy.................................... 278
Saint Mary's Books & Prints, Lincolnshire 152
Saint Philip's Books, Oxfordshire................. 205
Salsus Books, Worcestershire 250
Sandpiper Books Ltd., London SW.............. 167
Saunders (Tom), Caerphilly 276
Scarthin Books, Derbyshire 81
Scott (Peter), East Sussex 103
Shapero Rare Books (Bernard J.),
 London W... 172
Skoob Russell Square, Suffolk..................... 225
South Downs Book Service, West Sussex 238
Sparrow Books, West Yorkshire 241
Spelman (Ken), North Yorkshire 195
Spenceley Books (David), West Yorkshire 244
Stalagluft Books, Tyne and Wear................. 231
Staniland (Booksellers), Lincolnshire............. 152
Starlord Books, Greater Manchester 118
Sterling Books, Somerset 216

Stern Antiquarian Bookseller (Jeffrey),
 North Yorkshire................................... 195
Stroma Books, Borders 262
Studio Bookshop, East Sussex..................... 99
Sue Lowell Natural History Books, London W 173
Sun House Books, Kent 139
Symes Books (Naomi), Cheshire 71
Taylor & Son (Peter), Hertfordshire.............. 132
Temple (Robert), London N....................... 157
The Sanctuary Bookshop, Dorset................. 93
Tiffin (Tony and Gill), Durham................... 96
Tombland Bookshop, Norfolk 188
Transformer, Dumfries & Galloway.............. 265
Unsworths Booksellers, London NW 160
Venables (Morris & Juliet), Bristol 59
Ventnor Rare Books, Isle of Wight 135
Vickers (Anthony), North Yorkshire............. 193
Victoria Bookshop (The), Devon 83
Vinovium Books, Durham 96
Walden Books, London NW 160
Warrington Book Loft (The), Cheshire.......... 71
Warsash Nautical Bookshop, Hampshire 126
Waterfield's, Oxfordshire 206
Waterstone's, London WC......................... 177
Weiner (Graham), London N 157
Westwood Books Ltd, Cumbria 79
Winghale Books, Lincolnshire 151
Woburn Books, London N 157
Worcester Rare Books, Worcestershire 252

ACCOUNTANCY
Muse Bookshop (The), Gwynedd.................. 279

ACUPUNCTURE
Orchid Book Distributors, Co. Clare............. 257

ADIRONDACK MOUNTAINS, THE
Muse Bookshop (The), Gwynedd.................. 279

ADULT
Adrem Books, Hertfordshire....................... 131
Apocalypse, Surrey 228
Muse Bookshop (The), Gwynedd.................. 279
N1 Books, East Sussex.............................. 103
Onepoundpaperbacks, Cleveland.................. 96
Reading Lasses, Dumfries & Galloway 265

ADVENTURE
Annie's Books, South Yorkshire 217
Edmund Pollinger Rare Books, London SW ... 165
Jane Jones Books, Grampian...................... 267

ADVERTISING
Ainslie Books, Strathclyde......................... 273
All Books, Essex 110
Barry McKay Rare Books, Cumbria............. 76
Bettridge (Gordon), Fife............................ 265
Bolland Books (Leslie H.), Bedfordshire 53
Books & Things, London W....................... 169

SPECIALITY INDEX

Bowland Bookfinders, Lancashire 142
Chapman (Neville), Cornwall 74
Cornucopia Books, Lincolnshire 151
Courtwood Books, Co. Laois 260
Derek Stirling Bookseller, Kent 141
Earth Science Books, Wiltshire 247
Ellis, Bookseller (Peter), London SE 162
Empire Books, North Yorkshire 194
Facet Books, Dorset 90
Franks Booksellers, Greater Manchester 119
Hill House Books, Devon 87
Junk & Spread Eagle, London SE 162
Kelly Books, Devon 88
Kingswood Books, Dorset 93
Lowe (John), Norfolk 186
Malvern Bookshop (The), Worcestershire 250
Offa's Dyke Books, Shropshire 209
Orssich (Paul), London SW 167
Parker Books (Mike), Cambridgeshire 64
Pordes Books Ltd., (Henry), London WC 176
Prior (Michael), Lincolnshire 151
Pyecroft (Ruth), Gloucestershire 116
R. & A. Books, East Sussex 100
Roland Books, Kent 139
Saint Swithin's Illustrated & Children's Books,
 London W 172
Salsus Books, Worcestershire 250
Sterling Books, Somerset 216
Sue Lowell Natural History Books, London W 173
Venables (Morris & Juliet), Bristol 59
Vickers (Anthony), North Yorkshire 193
Walden Books, London NW 160

AERONAUTICS
Adrem Books, Hertfordshire 131
Ainslie Books, Strathclyde 273
All Books, Essex 110
Anchor Books, Lincolnshire 149
Andron (G.W.), London N 155
Aviabooks, Gloucestershire 114
Barbican Bookshop, North Yorkshire 194
Books Bought & Sold, Surrey 226
Camilla's Bookshop, East Sussex 100
Cheshire Book Centre, Cheshire 69
Clarke Books (David), Somerset 214
Collectables (W.H.), Suffolk 225
Corfe Books, Surrey 227
Cornucopia Books, Lincolnshire 151
Empire Books, North Yorkshire 194
Facet Books, Dorset 90
Fireside Bookshop, Cumbria 80
Gaullifmaufry Books, Hertfordshire 131
Hancock (Peter), West Sussex 237
Harrington Antiquarian Bookseller (Peter),
 London SW 166
Harris (George J.), Co. Derry 255
Hay Cinema Bookshop Ltd., Herefordshire 283
Holdenhurst Books, Dorset 90
Island Books, Kent 136
Key Books (Sarah), Cambridgeshire 64
King Street Bookshop (The), Norfolk 185

Lowe (John), Norfolk 186
N1 Books, East Sussex 103
Patterson (J.D.), Bristol 60
Phelps (Michael), West Sussex 237
Pordes Books Ltd., (Henry), London WC 176
Prior (Michael), Lincolnshire 151
R. & A. Books, East Sussex 100
Salsus Books, Worcestershire 250
Soldridge Books Ltd, Hampshire 122
Sterling Books, Somerset 216
Sue Lowell Natural History Books, London W 173
Thin Read Line, Merseyside 182
Vickers (Anthony), North Yorkshire 193

AESTHETIC MOVEMENT
Apocalypse, Surrey 228
Delectus Books, London WC 174
Empire Books, North Yorkshire 194
Vickers (Anthony), North Yorkshire 193

AESTHETICS
Apocalypse, Surrey 228

AFRICAN-AMERICAN STUDIES
Dylans Bookstore, Glamorgan 286
Reading Lasses, Dumfries & Galloway 265

AFRICANA
African Studies, Dorset 90
Ainslie Books, Strathclyde 273
All Books, Essex 110
Allsworth Rare Books Ltd., London 164
Armchair Books, Lothian 270
Ayre (Peter J.), Somerset 216
Black Voices, Merseyside 182
Book Barrow, Cambridgeshire 63
Chas J. Sawyer, Kent 140
Daly (Peter M.), Hampshire 127
Edmund Pollinger Rare Books, London SW ... 165
Empire Books, North Yorkshire 194
G. C. Books Ltd., Dumfries & Galloway 264
Hennessey Bookseller (Ray), East Sussex 99
J & J Burgess Booksellers, Cambridgeshire 64
Kenya Books, East Sussex 99
Marcet Books, London SE 161
Michael Graves-Johnston, London SW 166
Oriental and African Books, Shropshire 210
Pordes Books Ltd., (Henry), London WC 176
Prospect House Books, Co. Down 256
R. & A. Books, East Sussex 100
Reading Lasses, Dumfries & Galloway 265
Roscrea Bookshop, Co. Tipperary 261
Samovar Books, Co. Dublin 258
Shapero Rare Books (Bernard J.), London W . 172
Thin Read Line, Merseyside 182
Wiend Books, Lancashire 143
Woburn Books, London N 157
York (Graham), Devon 85

SPECIALITY INDEX

AGRICULTURE
Barn Books, Shropshire 211
Blest (Peter), Kent 139
Books for Content, Herefordshire 128
Booth Books, Powys 282
Burmester (James), Bristol 58
Carningli Centre, Pembrokeshire 281
Carta Regis, Powys 286
Castle Hill Books, Herefordshire 128
Castleton (Pat), Kent 137
Cheshire Book Centre, Cheshire 69
Clifton Books, Essex 111
Cottage Books, Leicestershire 145
Daly (Peter M.), Hampshire 127
Dusty Old Books Ltd., Oxfordshire 204
Empire Books, North Yorkshire 194
Farquharson, (Hilary), Tayside 275
Ferdinando (Steven), Somerset 215
Guildmaster Books, Cheshire 70
Hodgson (Books) (Richard J.), North
   Yorkshire 194
Hollingshead (Chris), London Outer 181
Island Books, Kent 136
Jane Jones Books, Grampian 267
Muttonchop Manuscripts 239
Phenotype Books, Cumbria 78
Prospect House Books, Co. Down 256
R. & A. Books, East Sussex 100
Roscrea Bookshop, Co. Tipperary 261
Samovar Books, Co. Dublin 258
Stone, (G.& R.), Borders 262
Thin Read Line, Merseyside 182
Thornber (Peter M.), North Yorkshire 193

AIDS CRISIS, THE
Cox Music (Lisa), Devon 84

AIRCRAFT
Apocalypse, Surrey 228
Beware of the Leopard, Bristol 58
Castleton (Pat), Kent 137
Cornucopia Books, Lincolnshire 151
G. C. Books Ltd., Dumfries & Galloway 264
J & J Burgess Booksellers, Cambridgeshire 64
Marcet Books, London SE 161
Milestone Books, Devon 88
Patterson (J.D.), Bristol 60
Rothwell & Dunworth, Somerset 214
Scorpio Books, Suffolk 221
Thin Read Line, Merseyside 182

ALCHEMY
Alpha Books, London N 155
Apocalypse, Surrey 228
Atlantis Bookshop, London WC 174
Caduceus Books, Leicestershire 145
Chthonios Books, East Sussex 101
Empire Books, North Yorkshire 194
Gilbert (R.A.), Bristol 59
IKON, Devon 88

Inner Bookshop (The), Oxfordshire 205
Magis Books, Leicestershire 147
Needham Books, (Russell), Somerset 216
Occultique, Northamptonshire 196
Phelps (Michael), West Sussex 237
Quaritch Ltd., (Bernard), London W 172
Shapero Rare Books (Bernard J.), London W . 172
Wadard Books, Kent 137

ALMANACS
Empire Books, North Yorkshire 194
Grampian Books, Grampian 268
R. & A. Books, East Sussex 100

ALPINISM/MOUNTAINEERING
Allinson (Frank & Stella), Warwickshire 232
Anthony Spranger, Wiltshire 247
Askew Books (Vernon), Wiltshire 246
Barnhill Books, Isle of Arran 269
Biblion, London W 169
Birmingham Books, West Midlands 234
Bonham (J. & S.L.), London W 169
Books, Denbighshire 278
Bookworld, Shropshire 210
Bosco Books, Cornwall 72
Bridge of Allan Books, Central 263
Carnforth Bookshop (The), Lancashire 142
Carta Regis, Powys 286
Cavendish Rare Books Ltd, London N 155
Cheshire Book Centre, Cheshire 69
Church Street Books, Norfolk 184
Collectables (W.H.), Suffolk 225
Creaking Shelves, Highland 268
Daly (Peter M.), Hampshire 127
Dartmoor Bookshop (The), Devon 83
David Warnes Books, Herefordshire 129
Eastcote Bookshop (The), London Outer 178
Eastleach Books, Berkshire 55
Empire Books, North Yorkshire 194
Fireside Bookshop, Cumbria 80
Garfi Books, Ceredigion 282
George St. Books, Derbyshire 82
Gildas Books, Cheshire 68
Glacier Books, Tayside 275
Hancock (Peter), West Sussex 237
Hill (Peter), Hampshire 123
Hollett and Son (R.F.G.), Cumbria 79
Holmes Books (Harry), East Yorkshire 106
Hornsey's, North Yorkshire 192
Hunter and Krageloh, Derbyshire 82
Internet Bookshop UK Ltd., Gloucestershire .. 113
Jarvis Books, Derbyshire 82
Keel Row Books, Tyne and Wear 231
Kirkland Books, Cumbria 78
Letterbox Books, Nottinghamshire 200
Little Bookshop (The), Cumbria 80
Main Point Books, Lothian 271
Mothergoose Bookshop, Isle of Wight 134
Mountaineering Books, London N 156
Muse Bookshop (The), Gwynedd 279
O'Reilly - Mountain Books (John), Derbyshire 82

SPECIALITY INDEX

Page (David), Lothian................................. 271
Parrott Books, Oxfordshire 207
Pinnacle Books, Lothian............................. 271
R. & A. Books, East Sussex 100
Riddell (Peter), East Yorkshire 105
Scarthin Books, Derbyshire 81
Shapero Rare Books (Bernard J.), London W. 172
Vandeleur Antiquarian Books, Surrey 227
Vickers (Anthony), North Yorkshire.............. 193
Yewtree Books, Cumbria............................ 77

ALTERNATIVE MEDICINE
Alba Books, Grampian 267
Empire Books, North Yorkshire 194
Esoteric Dreams Bookshop, Cumbria............ 77
Greensleeves, Oxfordshire 202
Hurst (Jenny), Kent 138
Inner Bookshop (The), Oxfordshire 205
London & Sussex Antiquarian Book & Print
   Services, East Sussex................................ 100
Lowe (John), Norfolk 186
Occulture, Northamptonshire...................... 196
Outcast Books, Herefordshire 284
Reading Lasses, Dumfries & Galloway........... 265
Roundstone Books, Lancashire 143
Starlord Books, Greater Manchester 118
Vickers (Anthony), North Yorkshire.............. 193
Westwood Books Ltd, Cumbria 79

AMERICAN INDIANS
Americanabooksuk, Cumbria....................... 76
Book Barrow, Cambridgeshire 63
Books, Denbighshire................................. 278
Bracton Books, Cambridgeshire.................... 63
Byre Books, Dumfries & Galloway................ 264
Chelifer Books, Cumbria 80
Clifford Elmer Books Ltd., Cheshire.............. 68
Cornucopia Books, Lincolnshire 151
Dancing Goat Bookshop (The), Norfolk........ 184
Dworski Books, Travel & Language Bookshop
   (Marijana), Herefordshire......................... 283
Eastcote Bookshop (The), London Outer 178
Emjay Books, Surrey................................. 226
Fireside Bookshop, Cumbria 80
Hay Castle, Powys.................................... 283
Inner Bookshop (The), Oxfordshire 205
Marble Hill Books, Middlesex...................... 181
Michael Graves-Johnston, London SW........... 166
Occulture, Northamptonshire...................... 196
Orchid Book Distributors, Co. Clare............. 257
Remington (Reg & Philip), Hertfordshire 132
Roscrea Bookshop, Co. Tipperary................. 261
Scarthin Books, Derbyshire 81
Shapero Rare Books (Bernard J.), London W. 172

AMERICANA
Americanabooksuk, Cumbria....................... 76
Anglo-American Rare Books, Surrey 228
Cavern Books, Cheshire 70
Clifford Elmer Books Ltd., Cheshire.............. 68

Collectables (W.H.), Suffolk 225
Dancing Goat Bookshop (The), Norfolk........ 184
Ely Books, Cambridgeshire 65
Fireside Bookshop, Cumbria 80
Hancock (Peter), West Sussex 237
Kenny's Bookshops and Art Galleries Ltd,
   Co. Galway 260
Lee Jackson, London NW 159
Preston Book Company, Lancashire 144
Shakeshaft (Dr. B.), Cheshire....................... 71
Shapero Rare Books (Bernard J.), London W. 172

AMISH
Apocalypse, Surrey 228

ANIMALS AND BIRDS
Acer Books, Herefordshire 128
Alauda Books, Cumbria............................ 76
Annie's Books, South Yorkshire 217
Apocalypse, Surrey 228
Blest (Peter), Kent 139
Bookline, Co. Down................................. 256
Brock Books, North Yorkshire..................... 190
Camilla's Bookshop, East Sussex 100
Carningli Centre, Pembrokeshire.................. 281
Carta Regis, Powys................................... 286
Chandos Books, Devon............................. 84
Cheshire Book Centre, Cheshire 69
Coch-y-Bonddu Books, Powys 285
Cofion Books, Pembrokeshire 281
Corfe Books, Surrey 227
Cornucopia Books, Lincolnshire 151
Dales & Lakes Book Centre, Cumbria 79
Daly (Peter M.), Hampshire 127
Demar Books (Grant), Kent........................ 140
Earth Science Books, Wiltshire..................... 247
Edmund Pollinger Rare Books, London SW... 165
Esoteric Dreams Bookshop, Cumbria............ 77
Ford Books (David), Hertfordshire................ 132
Good for Books, Lincolnshire...................... 149
Goodyer (Nicholas), London N 156
Grahame Thornton, Bookseller, Dorset 92
Grosvenor Prints, London WC.................... 175
Island Books, Kent 136
Jade Mountain, Hampshire 125
Jane Jones Books, Grampian....................... 267
Junk & Spread Eagle, London SE................. 162
Mandalay Bookshop, London SW 166
Martin's Books, Powys 285
Mayhew (Veronica), Berkshire 56
McCrone (Audrey), Isle of Arran 269
Orb's Bookshop, Grampian........................ 268
Parrott Books, Oxfordshire 207
Phenotype Books, Cumbria........................ 78
Popeley (Frank T.), Cambridgeshire.............. 67
Prospect House Books, Co. Down 256
R. & A. Books, East Sussex 100
R.E. & G.B. Way, Suffolk 224
Roland Books, Kent.................................. 139
Scarthin Books, Derbyshire 81
Shakeshaft (Dr. B.), Cheshire....................... 71

SPECIALITY INDEX

Shapero Rare Books (Bernard J.), London W . 172
Sue Lowell Natural History Books, London W 173
Thin Read Line, Merseyside 182
Treasure Island (The), Greater Manchester 120
Wildside Books, Worcestershire 250
Wright Trace Books, West Midlands 235

ANNUALS

Armchair Books, Lothian 270
Book Palace (The), London SE 161
books2books, Devon 87
BOOKS4U, Flintshire 279
Brock Books, North Yorkshire 190
Camilla's Bookshop, East Sussex 100
Cavern Books, Cheshire 70
Cheshire Book Centre, Cheshire 69
Eastcote Bookshop (The), London Outer 178
Esoteric Dreams Bookshop, Cumbria............ 77
Ian Briddon, Derbyshire 81
John R. Hoggarth, North Yorkshire............. 194
Katnap Arts, Norfolk 187
Key Books (Sarah), Cambridgeshire 64
Kineton Nooks, Warwickshire 232
Moorhead Books, West Yorkshire 241
Murphy (C.J.), Norfolk 187
Old Celtic Bookshop (The), Devon............... 86
R. & A. Books, East Sussex 100
Reeves Technical Books, North Yorkshire...... 193
Roland Books, Kent 139
Scrivener's Books & Bookbinding, Derbyshire . 81
Shacklock Books (David), Suffolk 222
Shakeshaft (Dr. B.), Cheshire..................... 71
Surprise Books, Gloucestershire................... 113
The Old Children's Bookshelf, Lothian.......... 272
TP Children's Bookshop, West Yorkshire 241
Treasure Trove Books, Leicestershire 146
Wiend Books, Lancashire 143
Wright Trace Books, West Midlands 235
Yorkshire Relics, West Yorkshire................. 242

ANTHOLOGIES

Addyman Books, Powys............................ 282
Carningli Centre, Pembrokeshire................... 281
Cowley, Bookdealer (K.W.), Somerset........... 214
Eggeling Books (John), West Yorkshire 245
McCrone (Audrey), Isle of Arran................. 269
Naughton Booksellers, Co. Dublin 259
Poetry Bookshop (The), Powys.................... 284
Shacklock Books (David), Suffolk 222
Temple (Robert), London N 157

ANTHROPOLOGY

Afar Books International, West Midlands 234
Apocalypse, Surrey 228
Bracton Books, Cambridgeshire.................... 63
Chalmers Hallam (E.), Hampshire................ 125
Chesters (G. & J.), Staffordshire 220
David Warnes Books, Herefordshire 129
Delectus Books, London WC...................... 174
Fireside Bookshop, Cumbria 80

Game Advice, Oxfordshire 205
Kenny's Bookshops and Art Galleries Ltd,
  Co. Galway 260
Kingswood Books, Dorset 93
Maghreb Bookshop (The), London WC 175
Mandalay Bookshop, London SW 166
Michael Graves-Johnston, London SW.......... 166
Polczynski (Udo K.H.), Powys..................... 284
Portobello Books, London W 172
R. & A. Books, East Sussex 100
Reading Lasses, Dumfries & Galloway 265
Rhodes, Bookseller (Peter), Hampshire 126
Shapero Rare Books (Bernard J.), London W . 172
Skoob Russell Square, Suffolk..................... 225
Stern Antiquarian Bookseller (Jeffrey), North
  Yorkshire 195
Whitchurch Books Ltd., Cardiff 276
Woburn Books, London N 157
Yesterday's Books, Dorset 91

ANTHROPOSOPHY

Anthroposophical Books, Gloucestershire....... 116
Bridge of Allan Books, Central 263
Greensleeves, Oxfordshire 202
Inner Bookshop (The), Oxfordshire 205
Reads, Dorset.. 94

ANTI-SEMITISM

Dworski Books, Travel & Language Bookshop
  (Marijana), Herefordshire 283

ANTIQUARIAN

Addyman Books, Powys............................ 282
Al Saqi Books, London W 169
Allsop (Duncan M.), Warwickshire 233
Any Amount of Books, London WC............. 174
Apocalypse, Surrey 228
Arden, Bookseller (C.), Powys..................... 282
Ardis Books, Hampshire........................... 126
Arnold (Roy), Suffolk 223
Art Reference Books, Hampshire 125
Austwick Hall Books, Lancaster 190
Autolycus, Shropshire 209
Axe Rare & Out of Print Books (Richard),
  North Yorkshire................................... 190
Baldwin (Jack), Strathclyde 273
Baldwin's Scientific Books, Essex 112
Bardsley's Books, Suffolk.......................... 221
Barmby (C. & A.J.), Kent 140
Bates & Hindmarch, West Yorkshire 243
Bath Old Books, Somerset 212
Baxter (Steve), Surrey 228
Beardsell Books, West Yorkshire 242
Bell (Peter), Strathclyde 270
Bernstein (Nicholas), London W................... 169
Bertram Rota Ltd., London WC 174
Biblion, London W 169
Bookcase, Cumbria 76
Booklore, Leicestershire............................ 146
Books on Spain, London Outer 181

SPECIALITY INDEX

BOOKS4U, Flintshire 279
Bookshop (The), Co. Donegal 258
Bookshop, Kirkstall (The), West Yorkshire 243
Bow Windows Book Shop, East Sussex 102
Bowie Books & Collectables, East Yorkshire ... 106
Bridge of Allan Books, Central 263
Brinded (Scott), Kent 139
Brockwells Booksellers, Lincolnshire 148
Burak (Steve), London WC 174
Byblos Antiquarian & Rare Book, Hampshire . 122
Capes (Books, Maps & Prints) (John L.),
   North Yorkshire 193
Capital Bookshop, Cardiff 276
Castle Hill Books, Herefordshire 128
Celtic Bookshop (The), Co. Limerick 261
Chandos Books, Devon 84
Channel Islands Galleries Limited,
   Channel Islands 253
Chelifer Books, Cumbria 80
Cheshire Book Centre, Cheshire 69
Chris Phillips, Wiltshire 246
Clent Books, Worcestershire 250
Clifford Elmer Books Ltd., Cheshire 68
Cobnar Books, Kent 139
Cobweb Books, North Yorkshire 192
Colin Hancock, Ceredigion 277
Collectable Books, London SE 162
Courtney & Hoff, North Yorkshire 194
Cox Old & Rare Books (Claude), Suffolk 223
Cox Rare Books (Charles), Cornwall 73
Cox, Andrew, Shropshire 211
Craobh Rua Books, Co. Armagh 255
Crouch Rare Books, Surrey 227
Daly (Peter M.), Hampshire 127
Dartmoor Bookshop (The), Devon 83
David (G.), Cambridgeshire 63
Davies Fine Books, Worcestershire 252
Dead Mens Minds.co.uk, Powys 285
Dean Byass, Bristol 60
Demetzy Books, Oxfordshire 203
Derek Stirling Bookseller, Kent 141
Drury Rare Books (John), Essex 111
Duncan & Reid, Lothian 271
Dusty Old Books Ltd., Oxfordshire 204
Dworski Books, Travel & Language Bookshop
   (Marijana), Herefordshire 283
Dylans Bookstore, Glamorgan 286
Eagle Bookshop (The), Bedfordshire 53
Eastleach Books, Berkshire 55
Eastwood Books (David), Cornwall 72
Eggle (Mavis), Hertfordshire 131
Ely Books, Cambridgeshire 65
Eton Antique Bookshop, Berkshire 57
Europa Books, London SW 165
Farahar & Dupre (Clive & Sophie), Wiltshire .. 246
Farquharson, (Hilary), Tayside 275
Farringdon (J.M.), Swansea 287
Fenning (James), Co. Dublin 259
Fine Art, London SE 165
Fine Books at Ilkley, West Yorkshire 243
Fireside Bookshop, Cumbria 80
Fletcher (H.M.), Hertfordshire 131

Fossgate Books, North Yorkshire 194
Foster (Stephen), London NW 158
Foster Bookshop (Paul), London SW 165
Fotheringham (Alex), Northumberland 198
Fox Books (J. & J.), Kent 140
Frew Limited (Robert), London W 170
G. C. Books Ltd., Dumfries & Galloway 264
Gardener & Cook, London SW 165
Gibbs (Jonathan), Worcestershire 251
Gilbert and Son (H.M.), Hampshire 127
Gillmark Gallery, Hertfordshire 131
Glenbower Books, Co. Dublin 259
Golden Books Group, Devon 84
Good for Books, Lincolnshire 149
Goodyer, Natural History Books (Eric),
   Leicestershire 146
Grahame Thornton, Bookseller, Dorset 92
Grampian Books, Grampian 268
Grant & Shaw Ltd., Lothian 271
Grant Books, Worcestershire 250
Green Man Books, East Sussex 100
Gresham Books, Somerset 214
Guildmaster Books, Cheshire 70
Hamish Riley-Smith, Norfolk 188
Hanborough Books, Oxfordshire 205
Hancock (Peter), West Sussex 237
Hanshan Tang Books, London SW 166
Harrington (Adrian), London W 171
Harrington Antiquarian Bookseller (Peter),
   London SW 166
Hava Books, London SE 161
Hawkes (James), Bristol 60
Helston Bookworm (The), Cornwall 73
Hennessey Bookseller (Ray), East Sussex 99
Heritage, West Midlands 234
Hodgson (Judith), London W 171
Hollett and Son (R.F.G.), Cumbria 79
Holtom (Christopher), Cornwall 75
Hornsby, Antiquarian and Secondhand Books
   (Malcolm), Leicestershire 146
Horsham Rare Books, West Sussex 238
Howes Bookshop, East Sussex 101
Humber Books, Lincolnshire 148
Hutchison (Books) (Larry), Fife 265
Ian Briddon, Derbyshire 81
Island Books, Kent 136
Jackdaw Books, Norfolk 185
Jackson (M.W.), Wiltshire 249
Jane Jones Books, Grampian 267
Jarndyce Antiquarian Booksellers, London WC 175
Jiri Books, Co. Antrim 255
John Underwood Antiquarian Books, Norfolk 186
Joppa Books Ltd., Surrey 226
Junk & Spread Eagle, London SE 162
Kerr (Norman), Cumbria 77
Kilgarriff (Raymond), East Sussex 104
Kim's Bookshop, West Sussex 237, 240
Kingswood Books, Dorset 93
Kirkman Ltd., (Robert), Bedfordshire 53
Korn (M. Eric), London N 156
Lake (David), Norfolk 187
Lawson & Company (E.M.), Oxfordshire 203

Laywood (Anthony W.), Nottinghamshire...... 200
Lymelight Books & Prints, Dorset................ 92
Marble Hill Books, Middlesex..................... 181
Marine & Cannon Books, Cheshire 71
Marine and Cannon Books, Cheshire............ 69
Marrin's Bookshop, Kent 138
McConnell Fine Books, Kent 137
McCrone (Audrey), Isle of Arran................ 269
McNaughtan's Bookshop, Lothian............... 271
Mead (P.J.), Shropshire............................ 210
Meads Book Service (The), East Sussex 103
Miller (Stephen), London Outer................... 181
Moore (C.R.), Shropshire 210
Moreton Books, Devon.............................. 86
Murphy (C.J.), Norfolk............................ 187
Muttonchop Manuscripts........................... 239
N V Books, Warwickshire......................... 232
N1 Books, East Sussex............................ 103
Naughton Booksellers, Co. Dublin 259
Neil Summersgill, Lancashire 142
Norton Books, North Yorkshire................... 194
O'Kill (John), Kent................................. 138
Offa's Dyke Books, Shropshire.................... 209
Park Gallery & Bookshop (The),
    Northamptonshire.............................. 197
Pemberley Books, Buckinghamshire............... 62
Period Fine Bindings, Warwickshire.............. 233
Phillips (Nigel), London SW 167
Poetry Bookshop (The), Powys.................... 284
Potterton Books, North Yorkshire 194
Price (John), London N 157
Pringle Booksellers (Andrew), Lothian........... 271
Quaritch Ltd., (Bernard), London W 172
R. & A. Books, East Sussex 100
RGS Books, Surrey................................. 229
Rhos Point Books, Conwy 278
Robertshaw (John), Cambridgeshire............... 66
Robin Doughty - Fine Books, West Midlands. 234
Rochdale Book Company, Greater Manchester 120
Roger Collicott Books, Cornwall 74
Rothwell & Dunworth, Somerset 214
Rowan (H. & S.J.), Dorset......................... 90
Roz Hulse, Conwy.................................. 278
Rye Old Books, East Sussex 103
Saint Philip's Books, Oxfordshire................. 205
Scarthin Books, Derbyshire 81
Schulz–Falster Rare Books (Susanne),
    London N 157
Scrivener's Books & Bookbinding, Derbyshire . 81
Seabreeze Books, Lancashire...................... 144
Shapero Rare Books (Bernard J.), London W . 172
Simpson (Dave), Central........................... 263
Sims Reed Limited, London SW.................. 167
Smith (Clive), Essex 109
Sokol Books Ltd., London W 172
South Downs Book Service, West Sussex 238
Spelman (Ken), North Yorkshire 195
Spooner & Co, Somerset 215
Sterling Books, Somerset 216
Stern Antiquarian Bookseller (Jeffrey), North
    Yorkshire 195
Stone, (G.& R.), Borders 262

Stothert Old Books, Cheshire...................... 68
Taney Books, Co. Dublin 259
Taylor & Son (Peter), Hertfordshire............. 132
Temple (Robert), London N...................... 157
Thomas Rare Books, Suffolk 222
Thomson (Karen), Strathclyde 273
Thornber (Peter M.), North Yorkshire 193
Tiger Books, Kent 137
Tobo Books, Hampshire........................... 124
Tooley, Adams & Co, Oxfordshire 206
Treglown (Roger J.), Cheshire..................... 70
Trinity Rare Books, Co. Leitrim 260
Turton (John), Durham............................. 97
Unsworths Booksellers, London NW 160
Vandeleur Antiquarian Books, Surrey 227
Venables (Morris & Juliet), Bristol 59
Ventnor Rare Books, Isle of Wight 135
Vinovium Books, Durham 96
Wadard Books, Kent............................... 137
Water Lane Bookshop, Wiltshire 248
Waterfield's, Oxfordshire 206
Wembdon Books, Somerset....................... 213
Westcountry Old Books, Cornwall 75
Westcountry Oldbooks, Devon.................... 84
Westfield Books, North Yorkshire 195
Westwood Books Ltd, Cumbria 79
Wilbraham (J. & S.), London NW 160
Woburn Books, London N 157
Worcester Rare Books, Worcestershire 252
Words Etcetera Bookshop, Dorset 92
Worlds End Bookshop, London SW............. 168
Ximenes Rare Books Inc., Gloucestershire...... 115
Yates Antiquarian Books (Tony), Leicestershire 146
York (Graham), Devon............................. 85

ANTIQUES
Abrahams (Mike), Staffordshire................... 219
Ancient Art Books, London SW.................. 164
Antiques on High, Oxfordshire................... 204
Apocalypse, Surrey 228
Arden Books & Cosmographia, Warwickshire. 232
Arnold (Roy), Suffolk............................. 223
Art Reference Books, Hampshire 125
Autumn Leaves, Lincolnshire..................... 150
Aviabooks, Gloucestershire 114
Axe Rare & Out of Print Books (Richard),
    North Yorkshire................................ 190
Barmby (C. & A.J.), Kent......................... 140
Bookcase, Cumbria 76
Books, Kent.. 137
Books & Collectables Ltd., Cambridgeshire 63
Bookworld, Shropshire............................ 210
Browse Books, Lancashire......................... 143
Browzers, Greater Manchester 119
Carningli Centre, Pembrokeshire.................. 281
Carta Regis, Powys................................ 286
Chaucer Bookshop, Kent.......................... 136
Cheshire Book Centre, Cheshire 69
Clark (Nigel A.), London SE..................... 162
Cobbles Books, Somerset......................... 214
Corfe Books, Surrey............................... 227

SPECIALITY INDEX

Cornucopia Books, Lincolnshire 151
Don Kelly Books, London W 170
Duncan & Reid, Lothian 271
Eastcote Bookshop (The), London Outer 178
Eton Antique Bookshop, Berkshire............... 57
Foster (Stephen), London NW 158
Glenwood Books, Surrey 230
Gloucester Road Bookshop, London SW....... 165
Golden Goose Books, Lincolnshire............... 150
Gresham Books, Somerset 214
Hadfield (G.K.), Cumbria 78
Hanshan Tang Books, London SW 166
Heneage Art Books (Thomas), London SW.... 166
Hennessey Bookseller (Ray), East Sussex 99
Hollett and Son (R.F.G.), Cumbria 79
Ives Bookseller (John), London Outer 181
Jackson (M.W.), Wiltshire......................... 249
John R. Hoggarth, North Yorkshire............. 194
Katharine House Gallery, Wiltshire 247
Keeble Antiques, Somerset 215
Keswick Bookshop, Cumbria..................... 78
Leabeck Books, Oxfordshire...................... 205
Malvern Bookshop (The), Worcestershire....... 250
Moss End Bookshop, Berkshire................... 57
Mundy (David), Buckinghamshire................ 61
Nelson (Elizabeth), Suffolk 222
Offa's Dyke Books, Shropshire.................... 209
Park Gallery & Bookshop (The), Northamptonshire................................ 197
Petworth Antique Market (Bookroom), West Sussex 239
Phillips of Hitchin (Antiques) Ltd., Hertfordshire..................................... 131
Pordes Books Ltd., (Henry), London WC 176
Potterton Books, North Yorkshire 194
Prescott - The Bookseller (John), London Outer 181
R. & A. Books, East Sussex 100
Rees & O'Neill Rare Books, London WC 176
Reference Works Ltd., Dorset..................... 94
RGS Books, Surrey................................. 229
Roland Books, Kent................................ 139
Rowan (H. & S.J.), Dorset........................ 90
Smith Books, (Sally), Suffolk 222
Stothert Old Books, Cheshire..................... 68
Studio Bookshop, East Sussex.................... 99
The Glass Key, West Yorkshire................... 242
Thin Read Line, Merseyside 182
Trinders' Fine Tools, Suffolk 222
Water Lane Bookshop, Wiltshire 248
Worlds End Bookshop, London SW............. 168
www.AntiqueWatchStore.com, Hertfordshire... 130
Wychwood Books, Gloucestershire 116

ANTIQUITIES

Apocalypse, Surrey 228
Don Kelly Books, London W 170
Hanshan Tang Books, London SW 166
N1 Books, East Sussex............................. 103
Period Fine Bindings, Warwickshire............. 233

APICULTURE

B. and K. Books, Powys........................... 282
Edmund Pollinger Rare Books, London SW ... 165
Mayhew (Veronica), Berkshire 56

APPLIED ART

Amwell Book Company, London SE............ 154
Ancient Art Books, London SW.................. 164
Anthony Whittaker, Kent 136
Arnold (Roy), Suffolk............................. 223
Ars Artis, Oxfordshire............................. 205
Art Reference Books, Hampshire 125
Artco, Nottinghamshire........................... 201
Aviabooks, Gloucestershire 114
Barmby (C. & A.J.), Kent........................ 140
Batterham (David), London W 169
Biblion, London W 169
Books & Things, London W....................... 169
Butts Books (Mary), Berkshire 56
Cheshire Book Centre, Cheshire 69
Cornucopia Books, Lincolnshire 151
Cover to Cover, Merseyside....................... 183
Dew (Roderick), East Sussex 100
Eastleach Books, Berkshire....................... 55
Fosters Bookshop, London W 170
Handsworth Books, Essex......................... 112
Hay Cinema Bookshop Ltd., Herefordshire 283
Heneage Art Books (Thomas), London SW.... 166
Hennessey Bookseller (Ray), East Sussex 99
High Street Books, Devon 85
Hodgkins and Company Limited (Ian), Gloucestershire 116
Inprint, Gloucestershire 116
Island Books, Kent 136
Keswick Bookshop, Cumbria..................... 78
Mannwaring (M.G.), Bristol 59
Martin - Bookseller (Colin), East Yorkshire.... 106
N1 Books, East Sussex............................. 103
Oopalba Books, Cheshire.......................... 71
Phillips of Hitchin (Antiques) Ltd., Hertfordshire..................................... 131
Potterton Books, North Yorkshire 194
Ray Rare and Out of Print Books (Janette), North Yorkshire.................................. 195
Reads, Dorset...................................... 94
Rees & O'Neill Rare Books, London WC 176
Scrivener's Books & Bookbinding, Derbyshire . 81
Staniland (Booksellers), Lincolnshire............ 152
Trinders' Fine Tools, Suffolk 222
Walden Books, London NW 160
Wyseby House Books, Berkshire................. 55

ARABICA

Apocalypse, Surrey 228
Dworski Books, Travel & Language Bookshop (Marijana), Herefordshire 283
Hamish Riley-Smith, Norfolk 188
Marcet Books, London SE 161

ARCHAEOLOGY

Addyman Books, Powys............................ 282
Alauda Books, Cumbria............................ 76
Ancient Art Books, London SW.................. 164
Atlantis Bookshop, London WC................... 174
Baker Limited (A.P. & R.), Dumfries &
  Galloway... 264
Baldwin's Scientific Books, Essex 112
Barmby (C. & A.J.), Kent........................... 140
Barn Books, Buckinghamshire..................... 61
Berry (L.J.), Kent 138
Bonython Bookshop, Cornwall.................... 75
Books B.C., London Outer 178
Booth Books, Powys 282
Bosco Books, Cornwall 72
Bracton Books, Cambridgeshire................... 63
Burebank Books, Norfolk 184
Castle Bookshop, Powys............................ 285
Castle Bookshop, Essex............................. 109
Castle Hill Books, Herefordshire.................. 128
Cheshire Book Centre, Cheshire 69
Classics Bookshop (The), Oxfordshire 202
Clements (R.W.), London Outer 179
Colin Hancock, Ceredigion 277
Corfe Books, Surrey................................. 227
Crouch Rare Books, Surrey........................ 227
D'Arcy Books, Wiltshire............................ 246
Eastgate Bookshop, East Yorkshire 105
G. C. Books Ltd., Dumfries & Galloway 264
Garfi Books, Ceredigion 282
GfB: the Colchester Bookshop, Essex............ 109
Hanshan Tang Books, London SW 166
Helion & Company, West Midlands 235
Idle Genius Books, London N 156
Island Books, Kent 136
J & J Burgess Booksellers, Cambridgeshire 64
Jackdaw Books, Norfolk 185
John Barton, Hampshire............................ 127
Joppa Books Ltd., Surrey 226
Kalligraphia (formerly Charmouth
  Bounty Books), Isle of Wight..................... 134
Kenny's Bookshops and Art Galleries Ltd,
  Co. Galway 260
Kingswood Books, Dorset 93
Larkham Books (Patricia), Gloucestershire 117
Lowe (John), Norfolk 186
Maghreb Bookshop (The), London WC 175
Malvern Bookshop (The), Worcestershire....... 250
McCrone (Audrey), Isle of Arran.................. 269
medievalbookshop, London Outer................ 179
Michael Graves-Johnston, London SW.......... 166
Miller (Karen), Nottinghamshire................... 200
Moss Books, London NW......................... 159
N1 Books, East Sussex.............................. 103
Nevis Railway Bookshops (The Antique &
  Book Collector), Wiltshire........................ 247
Nonsuch Books, Surrey............................. 229
P. and P. Books, Worcestershire 251
Parrott Books, Oxfordshire 207
Polczynski (Udo K.H.), Powys..................... 284
Pordes Books Ltd., (Henry), London WC 176
Prescott - The Bookseller (John),
  London Outer 181
Prospect House Books, Co. Down 256
Quest Books, East Yorkshire 106
R. & A. Books, East Sussex 100
Reads, Dorset... 94
Saint Mary's Books & Prints, Lincolnshire 152
Samovar Books, Co. Dublin........................ 258
Scrivener's Books & Bookbinding, Derbyshire . 81
Spooner & Co, Somerset 215
Stalagluft Books, Tyne and Wear.................. 231
Staniland (Booksellers), Lincolnshire 152
Taylor & Son (Peter), Hertfordshire............... 132
Tombland Bookshop, Norfolk 188
Unsworths Booksellers, London NW 160
Vickers (Anthony), North Yorkshire.............. 193
Westwood Books Ltd, Cumbria 79
Whitchurch Books Ltd., Cardiff 276

ARCHITECTURE

Addyman Books, Powys............................ 282
Al Saqi Books, London W......................... 169
Amwell Book Company, London SE............ 154
Anne Harris Books & Bags Booksearch, Devon 86
Antiques on High, Oxfordshire.................... 204
Apocalypse, Surrey 228
Ars Artis, Oxfordshire.............................. 205
Art Book Company, (The), Suffolk 223
Art Reference Books, Hampshire.................. 125
Aviabooks, Gloucestershire 114
Barmby (C. & A.J.), Kent........................... 140
Batterham (David), London W 169
Berry (L.J.), Kent 138
Bianco Library, West Sussex....................... 237
Biblion, London W.................................. 169
Bookroom (The), Surrey............................ 229
Books, Kent 137
Bosco Books, Cornwall 72
Bowden Books, Leicestershire 147
Brazenhead Ltd., Norfolk 186
Brighton Books, East Sussex....................... 98
Broadhurst of Southport Ltd., Merseyside...... 182
Broadway Books, Cambridgeshire................ 66
Butts Books (Mary), Berkshire 56
Camden Books, Somerset.......................... 212
Castle Bookshop, Powys............................ 285
Chandos Books, Devon............................. 84
Chevin Books, West Yorkshire.................... 245
Classic Bindings Ltd, London SW................ 164
Clevedon Books, Somerset......................... 214
Coach House Books, Worcestershire............. 251
Collectable Books, London SE.................... 162
Coombes (A.J.), Surrey 226
Corfe Books, Surrey................................. 227
Cornucopia Books, Lincolnshire................... 151
Cottage Books, Leicestershire...................... 145
Country Books, Derbyshire 81
Courtney & Hoff, North Yorkshire 194
Cover to Cover, Merseyside........................ 183
D'Arcy Books, Wiltshire............................ 246
Darkwood Books, Co. Cork....................... 258

SPECIALITY INDEX

Dartmoor Bookshop (The), Devon 83
Dew (Roderick), East Sussex 100
Duck (William), Hampshire 124
Edwards (London) Limited (Francis),
  London WC 175
Edwards in Hay–on–Wye (Francis),
  Herefordshire 283
Elton Engineering Books, London W 170
English (Toby), Oxfordshire 206
Europa Books, London SW 165
Forest Books of Manchester, Cheshire 70
Foster (Stephen), London NW 158
Fosters Bookshop, London W 170
Fotheringham (Alex), Northumberland 198
G. C. Books Ltd., Dumfries & Galloway 264
George St. Books, Derbyshire 82
GfB: the Colchester Bookshop, Essex 109
Gloucester Road Bookshop, London SW 165
Good for Books, Lincolnshire 149
Goodyer (Nicholas), London N 156
Grampian Books, Grampian 268
Gresham Books, Somerset 214
Hadley Bookseller (Peter J.), Essex 110
Hanshan Tang Books, London SW 166
Harrington Antiquarian Bookseller (Peter),
  London SW 166
Hay Castle, Powys 283
Helmsley Antiquarian & Secondhand Books,
  North Yorkshire 191
Heywood Hill Limited (G.), London W 171
Hicks (Ronald C.), Cornwall 73
Hornsey's, North Yorkshire 192
Hu + aunersdorff Rare Books, London SW 166
Inch's Books, North Yorkshire 192
Island Books, Kent 136
Ives Bookseller (John), London Outer 181
Judd Books, London WC 175
Katnap Arts, Norfolk 187
Kelsall (George), Greater Manchester 119
Kenny's Bookshops and Art Galleries Ltd,
  Co. Galway 260
Keswick Bookshop, Cumbria 78
Lighthouse Books (The), Dorset 91
Maghreb Bookshop (The), London WC 175
Malvern Bookshop (The), Worcestershire 250
Mannwaring (M.G.), Bristol 59
Marble Hill Books, Middlesex 181
Marlborough Rare Books Ltd., London W 171
Martin - Bookseller (Colin), East Yorkshire 106
McNaughtan's Bookshop, Lothian 271
Missing Books, Essex 109
Monmouth House Books, Monmouthshire 280
Moss Books, London NW 159
My Back Pages, London SW 167
Nonsuch Books, Surrey 229
Old Town Bookshop (The), Lothian 271
Oopalba Books, Cheshire 71
Pagan Limited (Hugh), London SW 167
Parrott Books, Oxfordshire 207
Patterson (J.D.), Bristol 60
Phillips of Hitchin (Antiques) Ltd.,
  Hertfordshire 131
Pordes Books Ltd., (Henry), London WC 176
Portobello Books, London W 172
Potterton Books, North Yorkshire 194
Prescott - The Bookseller (John),
  London Outer 181
Prospect House Books, Co. Down 256
Quaritch Ltd., (Bernard), London W 172
Quest Books, East Yorkshire 106
Ray Rare and Out of Print Books (Janette),
  North Yorkshire 195
Reads, Dorset 94
Rees & O'Neill Rare Books, London WC 176
Reeves Technical Books, North Yorkshire 193
RGS Books, Surrey 229
Rochdale Book Company, Greater Manchester 120
Roland Books, Kent 139
Rothwell & Dunworth, Somerset 214
Ryeland Books, Northamptonshire 196
Saint Mary's Books & Prints, Lincolnshire 152
Samovar Books, Co. Dublin 258
Scarthin Books, Derbyshire 81
Scrivener's Books & Bookbinding, Derbyshire . 81
Second Edition, Lothian 272
Seydi Rare Books (Sevin), London NW 159
Shapero Rare Books (Bernard J.), London W . 172
Skoob Russell Square, Suffolk 225
Sotheran Limited (Henry), London W 172
Sparrow Books, West Yorkshire 241
Spooner & Co, Somerset 215
Staniland (Booksellers), Lincolnshire 152
Stern Antiquarian Bookseller (Jeffrey), North
  Yorkshire 195
Sturford Books, Wiltshire 248
Sun House Books, Kent 139
Theatreshire Books, North Yorkshire 190
Tilston (Stephen E.), London SE 161
Tobo Books, Hampshire 124
Tombland Bookshop, Norfolk 188
Trinders' Fine Tools, Suffolk 222
Vickers (Anthony), North Yorkshire 193
Walden Books, London W 160
Westwood Books Ltd, Cumbria 79
Wiend Books, Lancashire 143
Woburn Books, London N 157
Worcester Rare Books, Worcestershire 252
Worlds End Bookshop, London SW 168
Wychwood Books, Gloucestershire 116
Wyseby House Books, Berkshire 55

ARMS & ARMOUR

Bookworm, Lothian 270
Cader Idris Books, Gwynedd 280
Caliver Books, Essex 110
Chelifer Books, Cumbria 80
Duck (William), Hampshire 124
Harris (George J.), Co. Derry 255
Helion & Company, West Midlands 235
Heneage Art Books (Thomas), London SW 166
Lost Books, Northamptonshire 197
Meekins Books (Paul), Warwickshire 233
MilitaryHistoryBooks.com, Kent 138

SPECIALITY INDEX

N1 Books, East Sussex............................. 103
Prospect Books, Conwy........................... 278
R. & A. Books, East Sussex 100
Shapero Rare Books (Bernard J.), London W . 172
Spenceley Books (David), West Yorkshire 244
Thin Read Line, Merseyside 182
Wayside Books and Cards, Oxfordshire 203
Wizard Books, Cambridgeshire.................... 67

ARMY, THE
Apocalypse, Surrey 228
Cornucopia Books, Lincolnshire 151
Gaullifmaufry Books, Hertfordshire.............. 131
N1 Books, East Sussex............................. 103
Rothwell & Dunworth, Somerset 214
Thin Read Line, Merseyside 182

ART
- GENERAL
Abacus Books, Greater Manchester 118
Abacus Gallery, Staffordshire...................... 220
Addyman Books, Powys........................... 282
Al Saqi Books, London W 169
Alba Books, Grampian 267
Americanabooksuk, Cumbria....................... 76
Amwell Book Company, London SE 154
Andrew Morton (Books), Powys.................. 281
Andromeda Books, Buckinghamshire............ 62
Anne Harris Books & Bags Booksearch, Devon. 86
Anthony Neville, Kent 138
Antiquary Ltd., (Bar Bookstore), North
  Yorkshire 192
Antiques on High, Oxfordshire.................... 204
Anwoth Books, Dumfries & Galloway 264
Apocalypse, Surrey 228
Arden Books & Cosmographia, Warwickshire . 232
Armchair Books, Lothian 270
Art Reference Books, Hampshire.................. 125
Artco, Nottinghamshire............................. 201
Aurora Books Ltd, Lothian........................ 270
Autumn Leaves, Lincolnshire...................... 150
Aviabooks, Gloucestershire 114
Avonworld Books, Somerset....................... 213
Bardsley's Books, Suffolk.......................... 221
Barmby (C. & A.J.), Kent.......................... 140
Barn Books, Buckinghamshire..................... 61
Bath Old Books, Somerset......................... 212
Berry (L.J.), Kent 138
Bianco Library, West Sussex....................... 237
Biblion, London W 169
Blaenavon Books, Torfaen 287
Book Annex (The), Essex 110
Book Gallery (The), Cornwall..................... 75
Book Palace (The), London SE 161
Bookcase, Cumbria 76
Bookroom (The), Surrey........................... 229
Books, Denbighshire................................ 278
Books, Kent 137
Books & Collectables Ltd., Cambridgeshire 63
Books Antiques & Collectables, Devon.......... 88
Bookworms of Evesham, Worcestershire........ 252

Bosco Books, Cornwall 72
Bowden Books, Leicestershire 147
Brazenhead Ltd., Norfolk 186
Brighton Books, East Sussex....................... 98
Bristol Books, Bristol............................... 60
Broadhurst of Southport Ltd., Merseyside...... 182
Broadway Books, Cambridgeshire................ 66
Brock Books, North Yorkshire.................... 190
Butcher (Pablo), Oxfordshire 203
Butts Books (Mary), Berkshire 56
Caledonia Books, Strathclyde...................... 273
Campbell Art Books (Marcus), London SE 161
Carnforth Bookshop (The), Lancashire........... 142
Carningli Centre, Pembrokeshire.................. 281
Cavern Books, Cheshire 70
Central Bookshop, Warwickshire 232
Chalk (Old & Out of Print Books)
  (Christine M.), W Midlands 234
Chandos Books, Devon............................. 84
Chaucer Bookshop, Kent........................... 136
Cheshire Book Centre, Cheshire 69
Chris Phillips, Wiltshire 246
Classic Bindings Ltd, London SW................ 164
Classics Bookshop (The), Oxfordshire 202
Clements (R.W.), London Outer.................. 179
Clifford Milne Books, Grampian 266
Cobbles Books, Somerset........................... 214
Cofion Books, Pembrokeshire 281
Cooper Hay Rare Books, Strathclyde............. 273
Cover to Cover, Merseyside........................ 183
Cross (Ian), Berkshire 55
Cumming Limited (A. & Y.), East Sussex 102
Dandy Lion Editions, Surrey 228
Darkwood Books, Co. Cork 258
Dartmoor Bookshop (The), Devon............... 83
de Beaumont (Robin), London SW 164
Decorum Books, London N 155
Doorbar (P. & D.), Gwynned 279
Duncan & Reid, Lothian........................... 271
Eastcote Bookshop (The), London Outer 178
Eastleach Books, Berkshire......................... 55
Edwards (London) Limited (Francis),
  London WC..................................... 175
Edwards in Hay-on-Wye (Francis),
  Herefordshire................................... 283
Ellis, Bookseller (Peter), London SE 162
English (Toby), Oxfordshire 206
Europa Books, London SW 165
Evans Books (Paul), West Sussex................. 238
Farnborough Gallery, Hampshire 123
Finch Rare Books Ltd. (Simon), London W ... 170
Fiona Edwards, Nottinghamshire.................. 200
Fireside Bookshop, Cumbria 80
Fisher & Sperr, London N......................... 155
Fortune Green Books, London NW 158
Foster Bookshop (Paul), London SW 165
Fosters Bookshop, London W 170
Fotheringham (Alex), Northumberland.......... 198
Furneaux Books (Lee), Devon..................... 88
Garfi Books, Ceredigion 282
George St. Books, Derbyshire 82
GfB: the Colchester Bookshop, Essex............ 109

SPECIALITY INDEX

Gloucester Road Bookshop, London SW....... 165
Golden Goose Books, Lincolnshire............... 150
Goldman (Paul), Dorset 94
Good for Books, Lincolnshire..................... 149
Goodyer (Nicholas), London N.................... 156
Hall's Bookshop, Kent............................... 141
Hanshan Tang Books, London SW.............. 166
Harrington (Adrian), London W 171
Hatchard & Daughters, West Yorkshire 242
Hay Castle, Powys................................... 283
Hay Cinema Bookshop Ltd., Herefordshire 283
Helmsley Antiquarian & Secondhand Books,
  North Yorkshire..................................... 191
Heneage Art Books (Thomas), London SW.... 166
Hennessey Bookseller (Ray), East Sussex 99
Hicks (Ronald C.), Cornwall 73
Hill House Books, Devon 87
Hodgkins and Company Limited (Ian),
  Gloucestershire 116
Holdsworth Books (Bruce), East Sussex......... 103
Hornsby, Antiquarian and Secondhand Books
  (Malcolm), Leicestershire 146
Horsham Rare Books, West Sussex 238
Idler (The), Suffolk 223
Internet Bookshop UK Ltd., Gloucestershire .. 113
Judd Books, London WC 175
Just Books, Cornwall................................ 75
Katharine House Gallery, Wiltshire 247
Katnap Arts, Norfolk 187
Keeble Antiques, Somerset 215
Keel Row Books, Tyne and Wear................ 231
Keogh's Books, Gloucestershire................... 115
Keswick Bookshop, Cumbria...................... 78
Leabeck Books, Oxfordshire...................... 205
Leigh Gallery Books, Essex 110
Lenton (Alfred), Leicestershire..................... 145
Lymelight Books & Prints, Dorset................ 92
Malvern Bookshop (The), Worcestershire....... 250
Martin - Bookseller (Colin), East Yorkshire.... 106
Mason (Mary), Oxfordshire....................... 202
McNaughtan's Bookshop, Lothian 271
Moorhead Books, West Yorkshire 241
Morley Case, Hampshire 126
Much Ado Books, East Sussex.................... 98
Mundy (David), Buckinghamshire................ 61
Mundy (David), Hertfordshire 130
My Back Pages, London SW 167
N1 Books, East Sussex.............................. 103
Nelson (Elizabeth), Suffolk 222
Newcastle Bookshop, Northumberland.......... 198
Newlyn & New Street Books, Cornwall 74
Niner (Marcus), Gloucestershire 116
Nonsuch Books, Surrey............................. 229
O'Brien Books & Photo Gallery, Co. Limerick 261
Offa's Dyke Books, Shropshire.................... 209
Old Bookshop (The), West Midlands 236
Old Town Bookshop (The), Lothian 271
Oopalba Books, Cheshire........................... 71
Oxfam Books and Music, Hampshire............ 127
Paper Pleasures, Somerset 215
Paton Books, Hertfordshire 132
Peter Lyons Books, Gloucestershire 114

Petworth Antique Market (Bookroom), West
  Sussex 239
Pordes Books Ltd., (Henry), London WC 176
Prescott - The Bookseller (John), London
  Outer 181
Pringle Booksellers (Andrew), Lothian........... 271
Prospect House Books, Co. Down 256
Quaritch Ltd., (Bernard), London W 172
Quinto of Charing Cross Road, London WC.. 176
Quinto of Great Russell Street, London WC... 176
R. & A. Books, East Sussex 100
Reading Lasses, Dumfries & Galloway.......... 265
Reads, Dorset 94
Rees & O'Neill Rare Books, London WC 176
RGS Books, Surrey.................................. 229
Richmond Books, North Yorkshire 192
River Reads Bookshop, Devon.................... 89
Robin Doughty - Fine Books, West Midlands . 234
Roe and Moore, London WC 176
Roger Lucas Booksellers, Lincolnshire........... 150
Roland Books, Kent................................. 139
Rowan (H. & S.J.), Dorset......................... 90
Saint Ann's Books, Worcestershire 251
Sclanders (Beatbooks), (Andrew), London EC. 154
Scott (Peter), East Sussex 103
Scrivener's Books & Bookbinding, Derbyshire . 81
Seabreeze Books, Lancashire...................... 144
Second Edition, Lothian 272
Shapero Rare Books (Bernard J.), London W . 172
Silverman (Michael), London SE 163
Simon Finch Nofolk, Norfolk 186
Sims Reed Limited, London SW.................. 167
Skoob Russell Square, Suffolk 225
Sotheran Limited (Henry), London W........... 172
Staniland (Booksellers), Lincolnshire 152
Sterling Books, Somerset 216
Stern Antiquarian Bookseller (Jeffrey),
  North Yorkshire..................................... 195
Stone Trough Books, North Yorkshire.......... 195
Stothert Old Books, Cheshire..................... 68
Stroma Books, Borders 262
Studio Bookshop, East Sussex..................... 99
Sturford Books, Wiltshire 248
Tilston (Stephen E.), London SE 161
Tombland Bookshop, Norfolk 188
Treasure Chest Books, Suffolk 222
Treasure Island (The), Greater Manchester 120
Trinders' Fine Tools, Suffolk 222
Trinity Rare Books, Co. Leitrim 260
Upper–Room Books, Somerset.................... 214
Venables (Morris & Juliet), Bristol 59
Village Books, Norfolk.............................. 184
Wadard Books, Kent................................ 137
Walden Books, London NW 160
Water Lane Bookshop, Wiltshire 248
Waxfactor, East Sussex 99
Westwood Books Ltd, Cumbria 79
Wetherell (Frances), Cambridgeshire............. 65
Whig Books Ltd., Leicestershire 147
Whitehall Books, East Sussex...................... 102
Wiend Books, Lancashire 143
Woburn Books, London N 157

SPECIALITY INDEX

Wood (Peter), Cambridgeshire 65
Words Etcetera Bookshop, Dorset 92
Worlds End Bookshop, London SW............. 168
Wychwood Books, Gloucestershire............... 116
Wyseby House Books, Berkshire.................. 55

- AFRO-AMERICAN
Apocalypse, Surrey 228

- TECHNIQUE
Apocalypse, Surrey 228
Aviabooks, Gloucestershire 114
Book Annex (The), Essex 110
Cheshire Book Centre, Cheshire 69
Cornucopia Books, Lincolnshire 151
DPE Books, Devon.................................... 86
Europa Books, London SW 165
Farnborough Gallery, Hampshire 123
N1 Books, East Sussex............................... 103
Oopalba Books, Cheshire............................ 71
Peter Lyons Books, Gloucestershire 114
Portobello Books, London W 172
Scrivener's Books & Bookbinding, Derbyshire . 81
Water Lane Bookshop, Wiltshire 248

- THEORY
Amwell Book Company, London SE............. 154
Apocalypse, Surrey 228
Book Annex (The), Essex 110
Book Palace (The), London SE 161
Cheshire Book Centre, Cheshire 69
Europa Books, London SW 165
Orchid Book Distributors, Co. Clare............. 257
Peter Lyons Books, Gloucestershire 114
Scrivener's Books & Bookbinding, Derbyshire . 81
Water Lane Bookshop, Wiltshire 248

ART DECO
Bookshop on the Heath, The, London SE...... 161
Cheshire Book Centre, Cheshire 69
Cornucopia Books, Lincolnshire 151
Don Kelly Books, London W 170
N1 Books, East Sussex............................... 103
Scrivener's Books & Bookbinding, Derbyshire . 81

ART HISTORY
Amwell Book Company, London SE............. 154
Antiques on High, Oxfordshire.................... 204
Apocalypse, Surrey 228
Ars Artis, Oxfordshire................................ 205
Art Book Company, (The), Suffolk 223
Art Reference Books, Hampshire 125
Aviabooks, Gloucestershire 114
Axe Rare & Out of Print Books (Richard),
   North Yorkshire.................................... 190
Bennett & Kerr Books, Oxfordshire.............. 202
Berry (L.J.), Kent 138
Book Annex (The), Essex 110
Book Gallery (The), Cornwall...................... 75
Book Palace (The), London SE 161

Bookroom (The), Surrey............................. 229
Books (For All), North Yorkshire................. 190
Bookworm, Lothian 270
Bosco Books, Cornwall............................... 72
Butts Books (Mary), Berkshire 56
Caledonia Books, Strathclyde...................... 273
Camden Books, Somerset 212
Carnforth Bookshop (The), Lancashire.......... 142
Chaucer Bookshop, Kent............................ 136
Cheshire Book Centre, Cheshire 69
Chevin Books, West Yorkshire..................... 245
Clark (Nigel A.), London SE...................... 162
Clevedon Books, Somerset 214
Cornucopia Books, Lincolnshire 151
Darkwood Books, Co. Cork........................ 258
Dartmoor Bookshop (The), Devon............... 83
Don Kelly Books, London W 170
DPE Books, Devon.................................... 86
Esoteric Dreams Bookshop, Cumbria............ 77
Europa Books, London SW 165
Fisher & Sperr, London N.......................... 155
Ford Books (David), Hertfordshire............... 132
Forest Books of Manchester, Cheshire 70
Foster (Stephen), London NW 158
Goldman (Paul), Dorset 94
Hanshan Tang Books, London SW 166
Heneage Art Books (Thomas), London SW.... 166
Hill House Books, Devon 87
Holdsworth Books (Bruce), East Sussex......... 103
Katnap Arts, Norfolk 187
Kelsall (George), Greater Manchester............ 119
Keogh's Books, Gloucestershire 115
Kingsgate Books & Prints, Hampshire........... 127
Kingswood Books, Dorset 93
Kunkler Books (Paul), Cambridgeshire.......... 64
Marcet Books, London SE......................... 161
Martin - Bookseller (Colin), East Yorkshire.... 106
McCrone (Audrey), Isle of Arran................. 269
Moreton Books, Devon.............................. 86
Naughton Booksellers, Co. Dublin 259
Newcastle Bookshop, Northumberland.......... 198
Nonsuch Books, Surrey.............................. 229
O'Brien Books & Photo Gallery, Co. Limerick 261
Peter Lyons Books, Gloucestershire 114
Pordes Books Ltd., (Henry), London WC 176
Portobello Books, London W 172
Prescott - The Bookseller (John), London
   Outer 181
R. & A. Books, East Sussex 100
Rothwell & Dunworth, Somerset 214
Ryeland Books, Northamptonshire................ 196
Saint Philip's Books, Oxfordshire 205
Savery Books, East Sussex 99
Scrivener's Books & Bookbinding, Derbyshire . 81
Seydi Rare Books (Sevin), London NW......... 159
Shapero Rare Books (Bernard J.), London W . 172
Staniland (Booksellers), Lincolnshire............. 152
Taylor & Son (Peter), Hertfordshire.............. 132
The Sanctuary Bookshop, Dorset 93
Unsworths Booksellers, London NW 160
Walden Books, London NW 160
Water Lane Bookshop, Wiltshire 248

SPECIALITY INDEX

Westwood Books Ltd, Cumbria 79
Whitchurch Books Ltd., Cardiff 276
Words Etcetera Bookshop, Dorset 92
Wyseby House Books, Berkshire................. 55

ART NOUVEAU
Apocalypse, Surrey 228
Don Kelly Books, London W 170
N1 Books, East Sussex 103
Saint Philip's Books, Oxfordshire................ 205

ART REFERENCE
Abbey Books, Cornwall 73
Amwell Book Company, London SE 154
Any Amount of Books, London WC 174
Ars Artis, Oxfordshire........................... 205
Art Reference Books, Hampshire................ 125
Artco, Nottinghamshire......................... 201
Assinder Books, Essex 110
Atlas, London N 155
Aviabooks, Gloucestershire 114
Barlow (Vincent G.), Hampshire................. 126
Barmby (C. & A.J.), Kent....................... 140
Berry (L.J.), Kent 138
Beware of the Leopard, Bristol................... 58
Book Gallery (The), Cornwall 75
Book Palace (The), London SE 161
Bookroom (The), Surrey......................... 229
Books & Things, London W..................... 169
Books on the Bank, Durham 96
Bookworm (The), Lothian 271
Bosco Books, Cornwall 72
Boxwood Books & Prints, Somerset 216
Butts Books (Mary), Berkshire 56
Campbell Art Books (Marcus), London SE 161
Castleton (Pat), Kent............................ 137
Cheshire Book Centre, Cheshire 69
Clark (Nigel A.), London SE 162
Coach House Books, Worcestershire............ 251
Cofion Books, Pembrokeshire 281
Cox Old & Rare Books (Claude), Suffolk....... 223
Darkwood Books, Co. Cork..................... 258
Dartmoor Bookshop (The), Devon............... 83
Decorum Books, London N 155
Don Kelly Books, London W 170
Europa Books, London SW 165
Firth (Bijou Books & Photography)
  (Maureen), South Yorkshire 218
Foster (Stephen), London NW 158
GfB: the Colchester Bookshop, Essex........... 109
Goldman (Paul), Dorset 94
Grosvenor Prints, London WC................... 175
Hanshan Tang Books, London SW 166
Hodgkins and Company Limited (Ian),
  Gloucestershire 116
Holdsworth Books (Bruce), East Sussex......... 103
Ives Bookseller (John), London Outer 181
Jackson (M.W.), Wiltshire....................... 249
John Gorton Booksearch, East Sussex........... 103
Katnap Arts, Norfolk 187
Kelsall (George), Greater Manchester............ 119

Kenny's Bookshops and Art Galleries Ltd,
  Co. Galway 260
Keogh's Books, Gloucestershire.................. 115
Kingsgate Books & Prints, Hampshire........... 127
Martin - Bookseller (Colin), East Yorkshire.... 106
Moreton Books, Devon 86
Murphy (C.J.), Norfolk.......................... 187
N1 Books, East Sussex.......................... 103
Newcastle Bookshop, Northumberland.......... 198
Nonsuch Books, Surrey......................... 229
Old Town Bookshop (The), Lothian............. 271
Parrott Books, Oxfordshire...................... 207
Peter Lyons Books, Gloucestershire.............. 114
Potterton Books, North Yorkshire 194
Priestpopple Books, Northumberland............ 198
R. & A. Books, East Sussex 100
Roe and Moore, London WC.................... 176
Scrivener's Books & Bookbinding, Derbyshire . 81
Skoob Russell Square, Suffolk................... 225
Smith Books, (Sally), Suffolk 222
Staniland (Booksellers), Lincolnshire............ 152
Stevens (Joan), Cambridgeshire 65
Studio Bookshop, East Sussex.................... 99
Sue Lowell Natural History Books, London W 173
The Sanctuary Bookshop, Dorset................. 93
Trinders' Fine Tools, Suffolk 222
Ventnor Rare Books, Isle of Wight 135
Waddington Books & Prints (Geraldine),
  Northamptonshire............................. 196
Water Lane Bookshop, Wiltshire 248
Westwood Books Ltd, Cumbria 79
Wyseby House Books, Berkshire................ 55
York (Graham), Devon.......................... 85

ARTHURIAN
Addyman Books, Powys......................... 282
Apocalypse, Surrey 228
Boer (Louise), Arthurian Books, Powys......... 282
Byre Books, Dumfries & Galloway.............. 264
Cheshire Book Centre, Cheshire 69
Cofion Books, Pembrokeshire 281
Dylans Bookstore, Glamorgan 286
Gildas Books, Cheshire 68
Greer (Robin), London SW...................... 166
Inner Bookshop (The), Oxfordshire 205
Minster Gate Bookshop, North Yorkshire...... 195
R. & A. Books, East Sussex 100
Whitchurch Books Ltd., Cardiff 276
Wizard Books, Cambridgeshire................... 67

ARTISTS
Amwell Book Company, London SE 154
Apocalypse, Surrey 228
Ars Artis, Oxfordshire........................... 205
Art Book Company, (The), Suffolk 223
Art Reference Books, Hampshire................ 125
Artco, Nottinghamshire......................... 201
Aurora Books Ltd, Lothian...................... 270
Aviabooks, Gloucestershire 114
Book Palace (The), London SE 161
Bookroom (The), Surrey......................... 229

Bow Windows Book Shop, East Sussex 102
Brown-Studies, Strathclyde 273
Butts Books (Mary), Berkshire 56
Campbell Art Books (Marcus), London SE 161
Chalk (Old & Out of Print Books)
  (Christine M.), West Midlands 234
Cheshire Book Centre, Cheshire 69
Clark (Nigel A.), London SE 162
Darkwood Books, Co. Cork 258
Dartmoor Bookshop (The), Devon 83
Ellis, Bookseller (Peter), London SE 162
Foster (Stephen), London NW 158
Hodgkins and Company Limited (Ian),
  Gloucestershire 116
Jean Hedger, Berkshire 55
Keogh's Books, Gloucestershire 115
Martin - Bookseller (Colin), East Yorkshire 106
Peter Lyons Books, Gloucestershire 114
R. & A. Books, East Sussex 100
RGS Books, Surrey 229
Rittner Booksearch (Hilary), London SE 162
Roe and Moore, London WC 176
Saint Swithin's Illustrated & Children's Books,
  London W 172
Sephton (A.F.), London W 172
Sims Reed Limited, London SW 167
Studio Bookshop, East Sussex 99
Trinders' Fine Tools, Suffolk 222
Upper–Room Books, Somerset 214
Water Lane Bookshop, Wiltshire 248
Westwood Books Ltd, Cumbria 79
Woodbine Books, West Yorkshire 241
Wyseby House Books, Berkshire 55

ARTS, THE
Addyman Books, Powys 282
All Books, Essex 110
Amwell Book Company, London SE 154
Apocalypse, Surrey 228
Artco, Nottinghamshire 201
Aurora Books Ltd, Lothian 270
Beware of the Leopard, Bristol 58
Book Annex (The), Essex 110
Book Palace (The), London SE 161
Bookbox, Gloucestershire 116
Camilla's Bookshop, East Sussex 100
Carta Regis, Powys 286
Chaucer Bookshop, Kent 136
Collectable Books, London SE 162
Cornucopia Books, Lincolnshire 151
D'Arcy Books, Wiltshire 246
Dolphin Books, Suffolk 221
Don Kelly Books, London W 170
Elephant Books, West Yorkshire 244
Ellis, Bookseller (Peter), London SE 162
Fine Art, London SE 165
Firth (Bijou Books & Photography)
  (Maureen), South Yorkshire 218
Foster (Stephen), London NW 158
Hawley (C.L.), North Yorkshire 193
Holdsworth Books (Bruce), East Sussex 103

Ice House Books, Wiltshire 248
Junk & Spread Eagle, London SE 162
Kim's Bookshop, West Sussex 237, 240
Lenton (Alfred), Leicestershire 145
Little Bookshop (The), Greater Manchester 119
Martin - Bookseller (Colin), East Yorkshire 106
Murch Booksend, (Herbert), London SE 162
N1 Books, East Sussex 103
Naughton Booksellers, Co. Dublin 259
Ouse Valley Books, Bedfordshire 54
Peter Lyons Books, Gloucestershire 114
Pordes Books Ltd., (Henry), London WC 176
R. & A. Books, East Sussex 100
RGS Books, Surrey 229
Richard Thornton Books, London N 157
Segal Books (Joel), Devon 84
Trinders' Fine Tools, Suffolk 222
Trinity Rare Books, Co. Leitrim 260
Tucker (Alan & Joan), Gloucestershire 116
Waterfield's, Oxfordshire 206
Watkins (R.G.), Somerset 213
Williams (Christopher), Dorset 93
Woburn Books, London N 157
Wyseby House Books, Berkshire 55

ASIAN STUDIES
Hanshan Tang Books, London SW 166
Prospect House Books, Co. Down 256
Reading Lasses, Dumfries & Galloway 265

ASSASSINATIONS
Bolland Books (Leslie H.), Bedfordshire 53
Clifford Elmer Books Ltd., Cheshire 68
Crimes Ink, London E 153

ASTROLOGY
Alpha Books, London N 155
Books, Denbighshire 278
Caduceus Books, Leicestershire 145
Cheshire Book Centre, Cheshire 69
Cofion Books, Pembrokeshire 281
Delectus Books, London WC 174
Glyn's Books, Shropshire 209
Greensleeves, Oxfordshire 202
Inner Bookshop (The), Oxfordshire 205
Occultique, Northamptonshire 196
Shapero Rare Books (Bernard J.), London W . 172
Star Lord Books, Greater Manchester 120
Starlord Books, Greater Manchester 118
Waxfactor, East Sussex 99

ASTRONAUTICS
Duck (William), Hampshire 124
K Books, Cheshire 69
Westwood Books Ltd, Cumbria 79

ASTRONOMY
Addyman Books, Powys 282
Altea Antique Maps & Books, London W 169
Andromeda Books, Buckinghamshire 62

SPECIALITY INDEX

Apocalypse, Surrey 228
Aviabooks, Gloucestershire 114
Baldwin's Scientific Books, Essex 112
Cheshire Book Centre, Cheshire 69
Hadfield (G.K.), Cumbria 78
Kalligraphia (formerly Charmouth Bounty
 Books), Isle of Wight............................... 134
Macfarlane (Mr. H.), Essex 112
McCrone (Audrey), Isle of Arran................. 269
Moorside Books, Lancashire....................... 143
N1 Books, East Sussex............................. 103
Phelps (Michael), West Sussex..................... 237
Portobello Books, London W 172
R. & A. Books, East Sussex 100
Turret House, Norfolk 189
Wayside Books and Cards, Oxfordshire......... 203
Westwood Books Ltd, Cumbria 79
Wiend Books, Lancashire 143

ATLASES

Altea Antique Maps & Books, London W 169
Apocalypse, Surrey 228
Bannister (David), Gloucestershire................ 113
Barron (Robert M.), Kent........................... 140
Baynton–Williams Gallery, West Sussex......... 237
Booth Books, Powys 282
Burden Ltd., (Clive A.), Hertfordshire............ 132
Channel Islands Galleries Limited,
 Channel Islands 253
Cheshire Book Centre, Cheshire 69
Corvus Books, Buckinghamshire................... 61
Dworski Books, Travel & Language Bookshop
 (Marijana), Herefordshire 283
Frew Limited (Robert), London W 170
G. C. Books Ltd., Dumfries & Galloway 264
Garwood & Voigt, Kent............................. 140
Gillmark Gallery, Hertfordshire.................... 131
Green (Mrs. D.M.), Surrey......................... 229
Harrington Antiquarian Bookseller (Peter),
 London SW.. 166
Heritage, West Midlands 234
Hogan (F. & J.), London N 156
Hook (Arthur), Bristol 59
Kennedy (Peter), Surrey 230
Kentish (B. & N.), Oxfordshire.................... 202
Lee Jackson, London NW 159
Lymelight Books & Prints, Dorset................. 92
Marshall Rare Books (Bruce), Gloucestershire . 113
Murphy (C.J.), Norfolk 187
Neil Summersgill, Lancashire 142
Nicholson of Chester (Richard), Cheshire....... 68
Paralos Ltd., London WC 175
Potter Limited (Jonathan), London W 172
Preston Book Company, Lancashire 144
R. & A. Books, East Sussex 100
Roz Hulse, Conwy.................................... 278
Russell (Charles), London SW 167
Shapero Rare Books (Bernard J.), London W . 172
Temperley (David), West Midlands 234

AUTHOR

- GENERAL

Aurora Books Ltd, Lothian......................... 270
Cornucopia Books, Lincolnshire 151
Ely Books, Cambridgeshire 65
Harrington (Adrian), London W 171
Hylton Booksearch, Merseyside................... 182
J & J Burgess Booksellers, Cambridgeshire 64
Murphy (C.J.), Norfolk 187
Naughton Booksellers, Co. Dublin 259
Priestpopple Books, Northumberland............ 198
Reading Lasses, Dumfries & Galloway 265

- 20TH CENTURY

Apocalypse, Surrey 228
Aurora Books Ltd, Lothian......................... 270
Barmby (C. & A.J.), Kent.......................... 140
books2books, Devon 87
Cornucopia Books, Lincolnshire 151
Foster Bookshop (Paul), London SW 165
Good for Books, Lincolnshire..................... 149
Island Books, Kent 136
Kenny's Bookshops and Art Galleries Ltd,
 Co. Galway 260
Marble Hill Books, Middlesex..................... 181
Mellon's Books, East Sussex 100
Rhodes, Bookseller (Peter), Hampshire.......... 126
Shapero Rare Books (Bernard J.), London W . 172
The Glass Key, West Yorkshire................... 242

- AHLBERG, JANET & ALLAN

Jean Hedger, Berkshire.............................. 55

- ALCOTTS, THE

Elaine Lonsdale Books, West Yorkshire......... 242

- ALDIN, CECIL

Bookmark (Children's Books), Wiltshire 248
Countryman Books, East Yorkshire 105
Jean Hedger, Berkshire.............................. 55
Lucius Books, North Yorkshire.................... 195
Rothwell & Dunworth, Somerset 214
Saint Mary's Books & Prints, Lincolnshire 152

- ARDIZZONE, EDWARD

Bookmark (Children's Books), Wiltshire 248
Jean Hedger, Berkshire.............................. 55
Key Books (Sarah), Cambridgeshire 64
Mason (Mary), Oxfordshire........................ 202
Periwinkle Press, Kent 139
Rittner Booksearch (Hilary), London SE 162

- ARMOUR, G. D.

Garfi Books, Ceredigion 282

- ASIMOV, ISAAC

Apocalypse, Surrey 228
Esoteric Dreams Bookshop, Cumbria............ 77

SPECIALITY INDEX

- AUSTEN, JANE
Apocalypse, Surrey 228
Cox, Andrew, Shropshire........................... 211
Hodgkins and Company Limited (Ian),
 Gloucestershire 116
Island Books, Kent 136
Jarndyce Antiquarian Booksellers, London WC 175
Sharpe (Mary), Somerset 216
Valentine Rare Books, London W 173
Webb Books (John), South Yorkshire 217

- BADEN-POWELL, LORD ROBERT
John R. Hoggarth, North Yorkshire............. 194

- BAINBRIDGE, BERYL
Apocalypse, Surrey 228
Surprise Books, Gloucestershire.................. 113

- BAKER, DENYS V.
Portus Books, Hampshire 123

- BALLANTYNE, ROBERT M.
Oasis Booksearch, Cambridgeshire 67

- BARING-GOULD, S.
Chapter Two, London SE........................... 161
Island Books, Kent 136
Shacklock Books (David), Suffolk 222

- BARKER, CECILY M.
Fifteenth Century Bookshop (The), East Sussex 102
Jean Hedger, Berkshire............................... 55
Key Books (Sarah), Cambridgeshire 64
Lucius Books, North Yorkshire.................... 195

- BARKER, CLIVE
Apocalypse, Surrey 228
Gildas Books, Cheshire 68

- BARNES, WILLIAM
Antique Map and Bookshop (The), Dorset..... 93

- BARRIE, J.M.
Jean Hedger, Berkshire............................... 55
Orb's Bookshop, Grampian........................ 268

- BATES, H.E.
Emjay Books, Surrey................................. 226
Heppa (Christopher), Essex 108
Park Gallery & Bookshop (The),
 Northamptonshire................................... 197
Webb Books (John), South Yorkshire 217

- BEARDSLEY, AUBREY
Apocalypse, Surrey 228

- BEATON, CECIL
Apocalypse, Surrey 228

- BECKETT, S.
Apocalypse, Surrey 228
Budd (Richard), Somerset 215
Courtwood Books, Co. Laois...................... 260
Norton Books, North Yorkshire.................. 194
Parrott (Jeremy), London E........................ 153
Read Ireland, Co. Dublin 258

- BELL, ADRIAN
Aucott & Thomas, Leicestershire 145

- BELLAIRES, GEORGE
Chapman (Neville), Cornwall...................... 74
Treasure Trove Books, Leicestershire 146

- BELLOC, HILAIRE
Armchair Books, Lothian 270
Island Books, Kent 136

- BENNETT, J.G.
Needham Books, (Russell), Somerset 216

- BENSON, A.C.
Meads Book Service (The), East Sussex 103

- BENSON, E.F.
Meads Book Service (The), East Sussex 103
Parrott (Jeremy), London E........................ 153

- BENSON, R.H.
Meads Book Service (The), East Sussex 103

- BETJEMAN, SIR JOHN
Baker - Books for the Collector (Colin), Devon 88
Island Books, Kent 136
McGee (Terence J.), London Outer 178

- BLACKWOOD, A.
Delectus Books, London WC...................... 174
Fantastic Literature, Essex 111

- BLAKE, N.
Maggs Brothers Limited, London W 171
Sutcliffe (Mark), West Yorkshire.................. 243

- BLOOMSBURY GROUP, THE
Bow Windows Book Shop, East Sussex 102
Evans Books (Paul), West Sussex................. 238
Fifteenth Century Bookshop (The), East Sussex 102
McKelvie (Ian), London N 156
Much Ado Books, East Sussex.................... 98

SPECIALITY INDEX

- BLYTON, ENID
Annie's Books, South Yorkshire 217
Apocalypse, Surrey 228
Badger Books, Somerset 216
Beck (John), East Sussex 102
Chapter Two, London SE 161
Dormouse Bookshop (The), Norfolk 188
Fifteenth Century Bookshop (The), East Sussex 102
Green Meadow Books, Cornwall 74
K Books, Cheshire 69
Key Books (Sarah), Cambridgeshire 64
Little Stour Books, Kent 136
Lucius Books, North Yorkshire 195
Schutte (David), Hampshire 125
Sesemann (Julia), Kent 136
Stella Books, Monmouthshire 281
Surprise Books, Gloucestershire 113
Talisman Books, Cheshire 70
Treasure Trove Books, Leicestershire 146

- BORROW, GEORGE
Orb's Bookshop, Grampian 268
York (Graham), Devon 85

- BOSWELL, JAMES
Island Books, Kent 136

- BRAMAH, ERNEST
Lucius Books, North Yorkshire 195
Webb Books (John), South Yorkshire 217

- BRENT-DYER, ELINOR M.
Badger Books, Somerset 216
Bilski (Gill), Buckinghamshire 61
Bookmark (Children's Books), Wiltshire 248
Fifteenth Century Bookshop (The), East Sussex 102
J & D Jones, Cheshire 70
Key Books (Sarah), Cambridgeshire 64
Lucius Books, North Yorkshire 195
Sims (Sue), Dorset 90
TP Children's Bookshop, West Yorkshire 241
Treasure Trove Books, Leicestershire 146

- BRONTES, THE
Hatchard & Daughters, West Yorkshire 242
Hodgkins and Company Limited (Ian),
  Gloucestershire 116
Idle Booksellers (The), West Yorkshire 241
Sharpe (Mary), Somerset 216

- BROOKE, RUPERT
Apocalypse, Surrey 228

- BROWNING, ROBERT
Cox Rare Books (Charles), Cornwall 73

- BRUCE, MARY GRANT
Fifteenth Century Bookshop (The), East Sussex 102

- BUCHAN, JOHN
Armchair Books, Lothian 270
Avonworld Books, Somerset 213
Bannatyne Books, London N 155
Heppa (Christopher), Essex 108
Orb's Bookshop, Grampian 268

- BUCKERIDGE, A.
Bolland Books (Leslie H.), Bedfordshire 53
Fifteenth Century Bookshop (The), East Sussex 102
Key Books (Sarah), Cambridgeshire 64
Little Stour Books, Kent 136
Schutte (David), Hampshire 125
Treasure Trove Books, Leicestershire 146

- BUKOWSKI, CHARLES
Apocalypse, Surrey 228

- BUNYAN, JOHN
Chapter Two, London SE 161
Kirkman Ltd., (Robert), Bedfordshire 53

- BURNEY, FANNY
Sharpe (Mary), Somerset 216

- BURNS, ROBERT
Orb's Bookshop, Grampian 268

- BURROUGHS, EDGAR R.
Book Palace (The), London SE 161

- BURROUGHS, WILLIAM
Apocalypse, Surrey 228
Lucius Books, North Yorkshire 195
Sclanders (Beatbooks), (Andrew), London EC . 154

- BURTON, R.F.
Campbell Hewson Books (R.), Fife 265
Chas J. Sawyer, Kent 140

- BYRON, LORD
Alec–Smith Books (Alex), East Yorkshire 107
Cox Rare Books (Charles), Cornwall 73
Emjay Books, Surrey 226
Jarndyce Antiquarian Booksellers, London WC 175
Tobo Books, Hampshire 124
Wise (Derek), East Sussex 102

- CALDICOTT, R.
Jean Hedger, Berkshire 55

- CAMERON, JULIA MARGARET
Cameron House Books, Isle of Wight 134

- CARLYLE, THOMAS
Priestpopple Books, Northumberland 198

SPECIALITY INDEX

- CARR, JOHN DICKSON
Lucius Books, North Yorkshire 195

- CARROLL, LEWIS
Apocalypse, Surrey 228
Chas J. Sawyer, Kent 140
Clarke–Hall (J.) Limited, Kent 137
Fifteenth Century Bookshop (The), East Sussex 102
Key Books (Sarah), Cambridgeshire 64
Lucius Books, North Yorkshire 195
Marchpane, London WC 175

- CARTER, FREDERICK
Apocalypse, Surrey 228

- CERVANTES SAAVEDRA, MIGUEL DE
Apocalypse, Surrey 228
Orssich (Paul), London SW 167

- CHANDLER, RAYMOND
Lucius Books, North Yorkshire 195
Sutcliffe (Mark), West Yorkshire 243

- CHAPMAN, ABEL
Chas J. Sawyer, Kent 140

- CHARTERIS, LESLIE
K Books, Cheshire 69
Lucius Books, North Yorkshire 195
Surprise Books, Gloucestershire 113

- CHESTERTON, G.K.
Armchair Books, Lothian 270

- CHRISTIE, AGATHA
Apocalypse, Surrey 228
Classic Crime Collections, Greater Manchester 119
Emjay Books, Surrey 226
Idle Genius Books, London N 156
Lucius Books, North Yorkshire 195
Treasure Trove Books, Leicestershire 146
Williams Rare Books (Nigel), London WC 177

- CHURCHILL, SIR WINSTON
Apocalypse, Surrey 228
Chas J. Sawyer, Kent 140
Churchill Book Specialist (The), London Outer 179
Foster Bookshop (Paul), London SW 165
Frew Limited (Robert), London W 170
Harrington (Adrian), London W 171
Island Books, Kent 136
Junk & Spread Eagle, London SE 162
Kirkman Ltd., (Robert), Bedfordshire 53
Prior (Michael), Lincolnshire 151

- CLARE, JOHN
Peakirk Books, Cambridgeshire 67

- CLARKE, ARTHUR C.
Apocalypse, Surrey 228

- COBBETT, WILLIAM
Island Books, Kent 136

- CONAN DOYLE, SIR ARTHUR
Antique Map and Bookshop (The), Dorset..... 93
Apocalypse, Surrey 228
Armchair Books, Lothian 270
Black Cat Bookshop, Leicestershire 145
Harrington (Adrian), London W 171
Island Books, Kent 136
Lucius Books, North Yorkshire 195
Preston Book Company, Lancashire 144
Rupert Books, Cambridgeshire 64

- COOK, BERYL
Apocalypse, Surrey 228
Jean Hedger, Berkshire............................. 55
Surprise Books, Gloucestershire 113

- CORNWELL, BERNARD
Apocalypse, Surrey 228
Gildas Books, Cheshire 68
Harrington (Adrian), London W 171
Surprise Books, Gloucestershire 113

- COWARD, NOEL
Avonworld Books, Somerset 213

- CRANE, HALL
Norton Books, North Yorkshire 194

- CRANE, WALTER
Bookmark (Children's Books), Wiltshire 248
Hodgkins and Company Limited (Ian),
  Gloucestershire 116
Jean Hedger, Berkshire............................. 55

- CREASEY, JOHN
Classic Crime Collections, Greater Manchester 119

- CROFTS, FREEMAN WILLS
Lucius Books, North Yorkshire 195
Sutcliffe (Mark), West Yorkshire 243

- CROMPTON, RICHMAL
Fifteenth Century Bookshop (The), East Sussex 102
Key Books (Sarah), Cambridgeshire 64
Little Stour Books, Kent 136
Lucius Books, North Yorkshire 195
Schutte (David), Hampshire 125
Silver Trees Books, West Midlands 234
Surprise Books, Gloucestershire 113

SPECIALITY INDEX

- **CROSBY, HARRY & CARESSE**
Norton Books, North Yorkshire 194

- **CROWLEY, ALEISTER**
Atlantis Bookshop, London WC 174
Gildas Books, Cheshire 68
Lucius Books, North Yorkshire 195
Occultique, Northamptonshire 196

- **CRUICKSHANK, G.**
Tobo Books, Hampshire 124

- **CUNARD, NANCY**
Norton Books, North Yorkshire 194

- **DAHL, ROALD**
Bookmark (Children's Books), Wiltshire 248
Fifteenth Century Bookshop (The), East Sussex 102
Jean Hedger, Berkshire 55
Key Books (Sarah), Cambridgeshire 64
Lucius Books, North Yorkshire 195
Surprise Books, Gloucestershire 113

- **DARWIN, CHARLES**
Island Books, Kent 136
Korn (M. Eric), London N 156
Lymelight Books & Prints, Dorset 92

- **DAVID, ELIZABETH**
Talisman Books, Cheshire 70

- **DICK, PHILIP K**
Gildas Books, Cheshire 68
Surprise Books, Gloucestershire 113

- **DICKENS, CHARLES**
Apocalypse, Surrey 228
Boz Books, Powys 282
Childrens Bookshop, West Yorkshire 242
Derek Stirling Bookseller, Kent 141
Golden Books Group, Devon 84
Harrington (Adrian), London W 171
Jarndyce Antiquarian Booksellers, London WC 175
Mr. Pickwick of Towcester, Northamptonshire . 196
Tiger Books, Kent 137
Tobo Books, Hampshire 124
Valentine Rare Books, London W 173

- **DINESEN, ISAK**
Esoteric Dreams Bookshop, Cumbria 77

- **DU MAURIER, DAPHNE**
Apocalypse, Surrey 228
Bonython Bookshop, Cornwall 75
Bookends of Fowey, Cornwall 73

- **DULAC, EDMUND**
Fifteenth Century Bookshop (The), East Sussex 102
Jean Hedger, Berkshire 55
Lucius Books, North Yorkshire 195

- **DURRELL, GERALD**
Apocalypse, Surrey 228

- **DURRELL, LAWRENCE**
Apocalypse, Surrey 228
Barmby (C. & A.J.), Kent 140
Criterion Books, London Outer 180
Island Books, Kent 136
Norton Books, North Yorkshire 194

- **DYMOCK POETS, THE**
Smith Books (Keith), Herefordshire 128

- **EDWARDS, LIONEL**
Rare Books & Berry, Somerset 215
Surprise Books, Gloucestershire 113

- **ELIOT, G.**
Sharpe (Mary), Somerset 216

- **ELIOT, T.S.**
Anglo-American Rare Books, Surrey 228
Apocalypse, Surrey 228
Lucius Books, North Yorkshire 195
Norton Books, North Yorkshire 194

- **FAIRLIE–BRUCE, D.**
Bilski (Gill), Buckinghamshire 61
Fifteenth Century Bookshop (The), East Sussex 102
Key Books (Sarah), Cambridgeshire 64
Sims (Sue), Dorset 90
TP Children's Bookshop, West Yorkshire 241

- **FARNOL, JEFFERY**
Dusty Books, Powys 285

- **FLEMING, IAN**
Apocalypse, Surrey 228
Birmingham Books, West Midlands 234
Black Cat Bookshop, Leicestershire 145
Books, Oxfordshire 202
Bookshop on the Heath, The, London SE 161
Classic Crime Collections, Greater Manchester 119
Harrington (Adrian), London W 171
Lucius Books, North Yorkshire 195
Saint Mary's Books & Prints, Lincolnshire 152
Tobo Books, Hampshire 124
Warrender (Andrew), West Yorkshire 245
Williams Rare Books (Nigel), London WC 177

- **FLINT, WILLIAM RUSSELL**
Webb Books (John), South Yorkshire 217

- FOREST, A.
Badger Books, Somerset 216
Key Books (Sarah), Cambridgeshire 64
Sims (Sue), Dorset 90

- FORESTER, C.S.
Dusty Books, Powys................................. 285
Prior (Michael), Lincolnshire 151
Surprise Books, Gloucestershire 113

- FOWLES, JOHN
Apocalypse, Surrey 228
Barmby (C. & A.J.), Kent.......................... 140
Lymelight Books & Prints, Dorset............... 92
The Sanctuary Bookshop, Dorset................. 93

- FRANCIS, DICK
Apocalypse, Surrey 228
Emjay Books, Surrey................................ 226
firstpagebooks, Norfolk............................ 187
Lucius Books, North Yorkshire................... 195
Orb's Bookshop, Grampian........................ 268

- FREEMAN, R. AUSTIN
Lucius Books, North Yorkshire................... 195

- FREUD, SIGMUND
Apocalypse, Surrey 228

- FROST, ROBERT
Karen Millward, Co. Cork 257

- GASKELL, E.
Hodgkins and Company Limited (Ian),
 Gloucestershire 116
Sharpe (Mary), Somerset 216

- GISSING, GEORGE
Idle Booksellers (The), West Yorkshire 241

- GOREY, EDWARD
Jean Hedger, Berkshire.............................. 55

- GOSS, W.H.
Milestone Publications Goss & Crested China,
 Hampshire.. 124

- GOUDGE, ELIZABETH
Fifteenth Century Bookshop (The), East Sussex 102

- GRAVES, ROBERT
Apocalypse, Surrey 228
Avonworld Books, Somerset....................... 213
Barmby (C. & A.J.), Kent.......................... 140
Island Books, Kent 136

- GREENE, GRAHAM
Anglo-American Rare Books, Surrey 228
Apocalypse, Surrey 228
Birmingham Books, West Midlands.............. 234
firstpagebooks, Norfolk............................ 187
Gloucester Road Bookshop, London SW....... 165
Harrington (Adrian), London W 171
Lucius Books, North Yorkshire................... 195
Tobo Books, Hampshire........................... 124
Williams Rare Books (Nigel), London WC..... 177

- GURDJIEFF, W.I.
Yarwood Rare Books (Edward), Greater
 Manchester 118

- HAGGARD, SIR HENRY RIDER
Lucius Books, North Yorkshire................... 195
Rider Haggard Society (The), Tyne and Wear . 231

- HALL S.C.
Milestone Publications Goss & Crested China,
 Hampshire.. 124

- HAMMETT, DASHIELL
Lucius Books, North Yorkshire................... 195
Sutcliffe (Mark), West Yorkshire.................. 243

- HARDY, THOMAS
Antique Map and Bookshop (The), Dorset..... 93
Apocalypse, Surrey 228
Books Afloat, Dorset............................... 94
Cox Rare Books (Charles), Cornwall 73
Derek Stirling Bookseller, Kent 141
Ferdinando (Steven), Somerset 215
Island Books, Kent 136
Lymelight Books & Prints, Dorset............... 92
Sharpe (Mary), Somerset 216
Valentine Rare Books, London W 173
Walker Fine Books (Steve), Dorset............... 91
Words Etcetera Bookshop, Dorset 92

- HEANEY, SEAMUS
Apocalypse, Surrey 228
Read Ireland, Co. Dublin 258
Words Etcetera Bookshop, Dorset 92

- HEINE, HEINRICH
Apocalypse, Surrey 228

- HEMINGWAY, ERNEST
Anglo-American Rare Books, Surrey 228
Apocalypse, Surrey 228
Norton Books, North Yorkshire.................. 194

- HENTY, G.A.
Antique Map and Bookshop (The), Dorset..... 93
Bookmark (Children's Books), Wiltshire 248

SPECIALITY INDEX

Little Stour Books, Kent 136
Shacklock Books (David), Suffolk 222

- HERBERT, JAMES
Surprise Books, Gloucestershire 113

- HEYER, GEORGETTE
Apocalypse, Surrey 228
Book For All Reasons (A.), Suffolk.............. 224
Boris Books, Hampshire 127
Dusty Books, Powys................................. 285
Fifteenth Century Bookshop (The), East Sussex 102
Orb's Bookshop, Grampian........................ 268
Rider Haggard Society (The), Tyne and Wear . 231

- HILL, LORNA
Fifteenth Century Bookshop (The), East Sussex 102
TP Children's Bookshop, West Yorkshire 241

- HOUSMAN, A.E.
Antiquary Ltd., (Bar Bookstore), North
 Yorkshire 192
Cox Rare Books (Charles), Cornwall 73
Island Books, Kent 136

- HUYSMANS, J.K.
Delectus Books, London WC..................... 174

- INKLINGS, THE
English (Toby), Oxfordshire 206
Saint Philip's Books, Oxfordshire 205

- JAMES, HENRY
Anglo-American Rare Books, Surrey 228
Anthony Neville, Kent 138
Valentine Rare Books, London W 173

- JAMES, M.R.
Island Books, Kent 136

- JEFFERIES, R.
Island Books, Kent 136

- JEWETT, S.O.
Milestone Publications Goss & Crested China,
 Hampshire... 124

- JOHNS, W.E.
Ardis Books, Hampshire........................... 126
Brock Books, North Yorkshire.................... 190
Chapter Two, London SE.......................... 161
Dormouse Bookshop (The), Norfolk............. 188
Fifteenth Century Bookshop (The), East Sussex 102
Harrington (Adrian), London W 171
Key Books (Sarah), Cambridgeshire 64
Little Stour Books, Kent 136
Lucius Books, North Yorkshire................... 195

Schutte (David), Hampshire 125
Stella Books, Monmouthshire 281
TP Children's Bookshop, West Yorkshire 241
Treasure Trove Books, Leicestershire 146

- JOHNSON, SAMUEL
Apocalypse, Surrey 228
Clarke–Hall (J.) Limited, Kent 137
Staffs Bookshop (The), Staffordshire............. 219
Walker Fine Books (Steve), Dorset............... 91

- JOYCE, JAMES
Apocalypse, Surrey 228
Courtwood Books, Co. Laois...................... 260
Karen Millward, Co. Cork......................... 257
Norton Books, North Yorkshire................... 194
Williams Rare Books (Nigel), London WC..... 177

- KEEPING, CHARLES
Bookmark (Children's Books), Wiltshire 248
Cameron House Books, Isle of Wight 134
Jean Hedger, Berkshire............................. 55
Key Books (Sarah), Cambridgeshire 64

- KEROUAC, JACK
Norton Books, North Yorkshire................... 194
Sclanders (Beatbooks), (Andrew), London EC . 154

- KING, STEPHEN
Apocalypse, Surrey 228
Fantastic Literature, Essex 111
Gildas Books, Cheshire 68
Talisman Books, Cheshire......................... 70

- KIPLING, RUDYARD
Apocalypse, Surrey 228
Armchair Books, Lothian 270
Avonworld Books, Somerset...................... 213
Brock Books, North Yorkshire.................... 190
Faversham Books, Kent 138
Fifteenth Century Bookshop (The), East Sussex 102
Harrington (Adrian), London W 171
Macbuiks, North Yorkshire....................... 190
Orb's Bookshop, Grampian........................ 268
Verandah Books, Dorset 94
Wykeham Books, London SW 168

- KOONTZ, DEAN
Gildas Books, Cheshire 68

- LAITHWAITE, ERIC
K.S.C. Books, Cheshire 68

- LANG, ANDREW
Fifteenth Century Bookshop (The), East Sussex 102
Greer (Robin), London SW........................ 166
Hodgkins and Company Limited (Ian),
 Gloucestershire 116

Jean Hedger, Berkshire............................. 55

- LAWRENCE, D.H.
Apocalypse, Surrey 228
Armchair Books, Lothian 270
Norton Books, North Yorkshire................. 194

- LAWRENCE, T.E.
Antique Map and Bookshop (The), Dorset..... 93
Apocalypse, Surrey 228
Avedikian Rare Books, Somerset 213
Branksome Books, Dorset.......................... 93
Coach House Books, Worcestershire............ 251
Lymelight Books & Prints, Dorset................ 92
Moorside Books, Lancashire...................... 143
Watkins (R.G.), Somerset 213
Words Etcetera Bookshop, Dorset 92

- LE CARRE, JOHN
Apocalypse, Surrey 228
Surprise Books, Gloucestershire................... 113

- LEWIS, C.S.
Apocalypse, Surrey 228
Armchair Books, Lothian 270
Key Books (Sarah), Cambridgeshire 64
Lewis First Editions, Kent 137
Lucius Books, North Yorkshire................... 195
Oasis Booksearch, Cambridgeshire 67
Saint Philip's Books, Oxfordshire................. 205

- LEWIS, WYNDHAM
Norton Books, North Yorkshire................. 194

- LOVECRAFT, H.P.
Gildas Books, Cheshire 68

- LOWRY, MALCOLM
Apocalypse, Surrey 228

- MACDONALD, GEORGE
Orb's Bookshop, Grampian....................... 268

- MACHEN, ARTHUR
Apocalypse, Surrey 228
Bass (Ben), Wiltshire 246
Delectus Books, London WC..................... 174

- MACLEAN, ALISTAIR
Little Stour Books, Kent 136

- MADOX FORD, FORD
Meads Book Service (The), East Sussex 103

- MAILER, NORMAN
Anglo-American Rare Books, Surrey 228

Apocalypse, Surrey 228

- MASEFIELD, JOHN
Apocalypse, Surrey 228
Farringdon (J.M.), Swansea....................... 287
Prior (Michael), Lincolnshire 151
Smith Books (Keith), Herefordshire.............. 128

- MASTERS, JOHN
Orb's Bookshop, Grampian....................... 268

- MAUGHAM, SOMERSET
Orb's Bookshop, Grampian....................... 268

- MILLER, HENRY
Apocalypse, Surrey 228
Norton Books, North Yorkshire.................. 194

- MILLIGAN, SPIKE
John R. Hoggarth, North Yorkshire............. 194
Kineton Nooks, Warwickshire 232

- MILNE, A.A.
Fifteenth Century Bookshop (The), East Sussex 102
Harrington (Adrian), London W 171
Surprise Books, Gloucestershire................... 113
Tobo Books, Hampshire........................... 124

- MOORE, JOHN
Aucott & Thomas, Leicestershire 145
Cornell Books, Gloucestershire................... 117
Engaging Gear Ltd., Essex........................ 108
Island Books, Kent 136
Sedgeberrow Books & Framing, Worcestershire 251
Surprise Books, Gloucestershire................... 113

- MORRIS, WILLIAM
Brock Books, North Yorkshire................... 190
Hodgkins and Company Limited (Ian),
    Gloucestershire 116
Upper–Room Books, Somerset................... 214

- MORTON, H.V.
Apocalypse, Surrey 228
Brock Books, North Yorkshire................... 190
Fifteenth Century Bookshop (The), East Sussex 102
Fireside Books, Buckinghamshire................. 62
Island Books, Kent 136
Oasis Booksearch, Cambridgeshire 67
Orb's Bookshop, Grampian....................... 268

- MURDOCH, I.
Apocalypse, Surrey 228
Reaveley Books, Devon............................. 85

- NEEDHAM, V.
Fifteenth Century Bookshop (The), East Sussex 102

Key Books (Sarah), Cambridgeshire 64

- NEWMAN, CARDINAL
Cox Rare Books (Charles), Cornwall 73
Saint Philip's Books, Oxfordshire 205

- NIALL, IAN
Island Books, Kent 136

- NIN, ANAIS
Apocalypse, Surrey 228
Lucius Books, North Yorkshire 195
Norton Books, North Yorkshire 194

- NORTON, MARY
John Underwood Antiquarian Books, Norfolk 186

- O'BRIAN, PATRICK
Harrington (Adrian), London W 171
Lucius Books, North Yorkshire 195
Orb's Bookshop, Grampian 268
Surprise Books, Gloucestershire 113

- ORCZY, BARONESS
Lucius Books, North Yorkshire 195

- ORWELL, GEORGE
Apocalypse, Surrey 228
Lucius Books, North Yorkshire 195

- OSBORNE, JOHN
Apocalypse, Surrey 228

- OXENHAM, ELSIE
Bilski (Gill), Buckinghamshire 61
Fifteenth Century Bookshop (The), East Sussex 102
Key Books (Sarah), Cambridgeshire 64
Little Stour Books, Kent 136
Lucius Books, North Yorkshire 195
Sims (Sue), Dorset 90
TP Children's Bookshop, West Yorkshire 241

- PALIN, MICHAEL
Apocalypse, Surrey 228

- PAUL BOWLES
Riderless Horse Books, Norfolk 184

- PEAKE, MERVYN
Cameron House Books, Isle of Wight 134
Kemp Booksellers, East Yorkshire 106
Lucius Books, North Yorkshire 195

- PEPYS, SAMUEL
Island Books, Kent 136

- PETERS, ELLIS
Surprise Books, Gloucestershire 113

- PICASSO, PABLO
Apocalypse, Surrey 228

- POTTER, BEATRIX
Bookmark (Children's Books), Wiltshire 248
Fifteenth Century Bookshop (The), East Sussex 102
Hodgkins and Company Limited (Ian),
  Gloucestershire 116
Key Books (Sarah), Cambridgeshire 64
Treasure Trove Books, Leicestershire 146

- POWELL, ANTHONY
Apocalypse, Surrey 228

- POWYS FAMILY, THE
Books Afloat, Dorset 94
Ferdinando (Steven), Somerset 215
Green Man Books, East Sussex 100
Words Etcetera Bookshop, Dorset 92

- PRATCHETT, TERRY
Fantastic Literature, Essex 111
Gildas Books, Cheshire 68
Surprise Books, Gloucestershire 113
Talisman Books, Cheshire 70

- PRIESTLEY, J.B.
Greta Books, Durham 96
Orb's Bookshop, Grampian 268

- QUILLER-COUCH, SIR A.T.
Bookends of Fowey, Cornwall 73
Island Books, Kent 136
R & B Graham Trading, Cornwall 73

- RACKHAM, ARTHUR
Apocalypse, Surrey 228
Bow Windows Book Shop, East Sussex 102
Fifteenth Century Bookshop (The), East Sussex 102
Harrington (Adrian), London W 171
Jean Hedger, Berkshire 55
Key Books (Sarah), Cambridgeshire 64
Little Stour Books, Kent 136
Lucius Books, North Yorkshire 195
Saint Mary's Books & Prints, Lincolnshire 152
Stella Books, Monmouthshire 281

- RAND, AYN
Webb Books (John), South Yorkshire 217

- RANKIN, IAN
Apocalypse, Surrey 228
Surprise Books, Gloucestershire 113

SPECIALITY INDEX

- RANSOME, ARTHUR
Farringdon (J.M.), Swansea 287
Fifteenth Century Bookshop (The), East Sussex 102
Key Books (Sarah), Cambridgeshire 64
Kirkland Books, Cumbria 78
Schutte (David), Hampshire 125

- RATCLIFFE, DOROTHY UNA
Brock Books, North Yorkshire 190

- READ, MISS
Baker - Books for the Collector (Colin), Devon 88
Brown-Studies, Strathclyde 273
Fifteenth Century Bookshop (The), East Sussex 102

- RICE, ANNE
Surprise Books, Gloucestershire 113

- RICHARDS, FRANK
Fifteenth Century Bookshop (The), East Sussex 102
Schutte (David), Hampshire 125

- ROBINSON, HEATH W.
Fifteenth Century Bookshop (The), East Sussex 102
Jean Hedger, Berkshire 55

- ROLT, L.T.C.
Baldwin (M. & M.), Shropshire 250
Bird Books (Nigel), Ceredigion 277
Crosby Nethercott Books, London Outer 178
Dales and Lakes Book Centre, Cumbria 79

- ROSSETTI, C.
Cox Rare Books (Charles), Cornwall 73
Hodgkins and Company Limited (Ian),
    Gloucestershire 116

- ROWLING, J.K.
Apocalypse, Surrey 228
Harrington (Adrian), London W 171
Saint Mary's Books & Prints, Lincolnshire 152

- RUSHDIE, SALMAN
Norton Books, North Yorkshire 194

- RUSKIN, JOHN
Apocalypse, Surrey 228
Brock Books, North Yorkshire 190
Cox Rare Books (Charles), Cornwall 73
Hodgkins and Company Limited (Ian),
    Gloucestershire 116

- RUSSELL, W
Karen Millward, Co. Cork 257

- SABATINI, R.
Dusty Books, Powys 285
Lucius Books, North Yorkshire 195

- SACKVILLE-WEST, VITA
Apocalypse, Surrey 228
Bow Windows Book Shop, East Sussex 102
Evans Books (Paul), West Sussex 238
Fifteenth Century Bookshop (The), East Sussex 102
Island Books, Kent 136

- SASSOON, SIEGFRIED
Anglo-American Rare Books, Surrey 228
Island Books, Kent 136

- SAVILLE, M.
Ardis Books, Hampshire 126
Fifteenth Century Bookshop (The), East Sussex 102
Green Meadow Books, Cornwall 74
Key Books (Sarah), Cambridgeshire 64
Lewis First Editions, Kent 137
Schutte (David), Hampshire 125
TP Children's Bookshop, West Yorkshire 241

- SAYERS, DOROTHY
Avonworld Books, Somerset 213
Lucius Books, North Yorkshire 195

- SEARLE, RONALD
Fifteenth Century Bookshop (The), East Sussex 102

- SELOUS, FREDERICK
Edmund Pollinger Rare Books, London SW ... 165

- SENDAK, MAURICE
Jean Hedger, Berkshire 55

- SEYMOUR, JOHN
Mount's Bay Books, Cornwall 74

- SHAKESPEARE, WILLIAM
Apocalypse, Surrey 228
Byre Books, Dumfries & Galloway 264
Chaucer Head Bookshop, Warwickshire 233

- SHAW, GEORGE BERNARD
Apocalypse, Surrey 228
Brock Books, North Yorkshire 190

- SHEPARD, E.H.
Fifteenth Century Bookshop (The), East Sussex 102
Key Books (Sarah), Cambridgeshire 64

- SHUTE, NEVILLE
Dusty Books, Powys 285
Fifteenth Century Bookshop (The), East Sussex 102

Lewis First Editions, Kent 137
Lucius Books, North Yorkshire 195
Orb's Bookshop, Grampian 268
The Sanctuary Bookshop, Dorset 93
Webb Books (John), South Yorkshire 217

- SIMENON, GEORGES
Lucius Books, North Yorkshire 195
Treasure Trove Books, Leicestershire 146

- SIMON, ANDRE L.
Roberts Wine Books (John), Bristol 60

- SITWELL FAMILY
Apocalypse, Surrey 228

- SMITH, WILBUR
Surprise Books, Gloucestershire 113

- SOLZHENITSYN, ALEXANDER
Apocalypse, Surrey 228

- SPARE, AUSTIN OSMAN
Apocalypse, Surrey 228
Atlantis Bookshop, London WC 174
Occultique, Northamptonshire 196

- STEADMAN, RALPH
Barmby (C. & A.J.), Kent 140
Dylans Bookstore, Glamorgan 286
Lucius Books, North Yorkshire 195

- STEIN, GERTRUDE
Norton Books, North Yorkshire 194

- STEINER, RUDOLF
Anthroposophical Books, Gloucestershire 116

- STENDHAL
Apocalypse, Surrey 228

- STEVENSON, ROBERT LOUIS
Apocalypse, Surrey 228
Brock Books, North Yorkshire 190
Parrott (Jeremy), London E 153

- STOKER, B.
Rider Haggard Society (The), Tyne and Wear . 231

- STRATTON PORTER, GENE
Fifteenth Century Bookshop (The), East Sussex 102

- STREET, A.G.
Books for Content, Herefordshire 128

- SWINBURNE, A.C.
Cox Rare Books (Charles), Cornwall 73
Hodgkins and Company Limited (Ian),
  Gloucestershire 116

- TANGYE, D.
Baker - Books for the Collector (Colin), Devon 88
Bonython Bookshop, Cornwall 75
Emjay Books, Surrey 226
Fifteenth Century Bookshop (The), East Sussex 102
Island Books, Kent 136
Mount's Bay Books, Cornwall 74

- TENNYSON, LORD ALFRED
Apocalypse, Surrey 228
Cameron House Books, Isle of Wight 134
Cox Rare Books (Charles), Cornwall 73

- THACKERY, WILLIAM M.
Apocalypse, Surrey 228

- THELWELL, N
Bookstand, Dorset 93

- THIRKELL, ANGELA
Fifteenth Century Bookshop (The), East Sussex 102

- THOMAS, DYLAN
Dylans Bookstore, Glamorgan 286

- THOMAS, EDWARD
Dylans Bookstore, Glamorgan 286
Karen Millward, Co. Cork 257

- THORNDIKE, RUSSELL
Meads Book Service (The), East Sussex 103

- TOLKIEN, J.R.R.
Harrington (Adrian), London W 171
Key Books (Sarah), Cambridgeshire 64
Lucius Books, North Yorkshire 195
Tobo Books, Hampshire 124

- TOURTEL, M
Fifteenth Century Bookshop (The), East Sussex 102
Jean Hedger, Berkshire 55

- TROLLOPE, ANTHONY
Sen Books, Hampshire 127
Tobo Books, Hampshire 124

- TUDOR, TASHA
Fifteenth Century Bookshop (The), East Sussex 102

- TULLY, JIM
Loretta Lay Books, London NW 159

SPECIALITY INDEX

- TWAIN, MARK
Harrington (Adrian), London W 171
Parrott (Jeremy), London E......................... 153

- UPFIELD, ARTHUR
Loretta Lay Books, London NW................. 159

- UTTLEY, ALISON
Bookmark (Children's Books), Wiltshire 248
Fifteenth Century Bookshop (The), East Sussex 102
Jean Hedger, Berkshire............................. 55
Scarthin Books, Derbyshire 81

- VAN VOGT, A. E.
Orb's Bookshop, Grampian........................ 268

- VERNE, JULES
Cox, Andrew, Shropshire........................... 211
Parrott (Jeremy), London E......................... 153

- WAINWRIGHT, ARTHUR
Kirkland Books, Cumbria.......................... 78

- WALLACE, EDGAR
Williams (Bookdealer), (Richard), Lincolnshire 152

- WALSH, M.
Greta Books, Durham 96

- WATKINS, VERNON
Dylans Bookstore, Glamorgan 286

- WATKINS-PITCHFORD, DENYS ('B.B.')
Chalmers Hallam (E.), Hampshire................ 125
Fifteenth Century Bookshop (The), East Sussex 102
Island Books, Kent 136
Key Books (Sarah), Cambridgeshire 64
Lucius Books, North Yorkshire.................... 195
Saint Mary's Books & Prints, Lincolnshire 152
Shakeshaft (Dr. B.), Cheshire..................... 71
Yesterday Tackle & Books, Dorset............... 90

- WEBB, MARY
Woodbine Books, West Yorkshire................. 241

- WELCH, R.
Fifteenth Century Bookshop (The), East Sussex 102
Key Books (Sarah), Cambridgeshire 64

- WELLS, H.G.
Antique Map and Bookshop (The), Dorset..... 93
Brock Books, North Yorkshire.................... 190
Cox, Andrew, Shropshire........................... 211
Fantastic Literature, Essex 111
Harrington (Adrian), London W 171
RGS Books, Surrey................................. 229

- WHARTON, EDITH
Apocalypse, Surrey 228
Meads Book Service (The), East Sussex 103

- WHEATLEY, DENNIS
Apocalypse, Surrey 228
Bookstand, Dorset 93
Heckmondwike Book Shop, West Yorkshire... 244
Lucius Books, North Yorkshire.................... 195
Orb's Bookshop, Grampian........................ 268
Surprise Books, Gloucestershire.................. 113

- WHITE, GILBERT
Sen Books, Hampshire............................. 127

- WHITE, T.H.
Gildas Books, Cheshire 68
John Underwood Antiquarian Books, Norfolk 186

- WILDE, OSCAR
Apocalypse, Surrey 228
Courtwood Books, Co. Laois...................... 260
Cox Rare Books (Charles), Cornwall 73
Harrington (Adrian), London W 171
Karen Millward, Co. Cork......................... 257

- WILLIAMSON, HENRY
Island Books, Kent 136
Tarka Books, Devon 83

- WILSON, COLIN
Apocalypse, Surrey 228
Fifth Element, West Midlands..................... 235
Gildas Books, Cheshire 68
Loretta Lay Books, London NW................. 159
Yarwood Rare Books (Edward), Greater
   Manchester 118

- WODEHOUSE, P.G.
Harrington (Adrian), London W 171
Heppa (Christopher), Essex 108
Little Stour Books, Kent 136
Lucius Books, North Yorkshire.................... 195
Olynthiacs, Shropshire 210
Orb's Bookshop, Grampian........................ 268
Schutte (David), Hampshire 125
Williams Rare Books (Nigel), London WC..... 177

- WOLFE, THOMAS
Idle Genius Books, London N 156

- WOOLF, VIRGINIA
Bookbox, Gloucestershire 116
Bow Windows Book Shop, East Sussex 102
Evans Books (Paul), West Sussex................ 238
Fifteenth Century Bookshop (The), East Sussex 102
Lucius Books, North Yorkshire.................... 195

Orb's Bookshop, Grampian 268
Words Etcetera Bookshop, Dorset 92

- WORDSWORTH, WILLIAM
Apocalypse, Surrey 228
Island Books, Kent 136

- YATES, DORNFORD
Book For All Reasons (A.), Suffolk 224
Fifteenth Century Bookshop (The), East Sussex 102

- YEATS, W.B.
Apocalypse, Surrey 228
Read Ireland, Co. Dublin 258

- YOUNG, FRANCIS BRETT
Orb's Bookshop, Grampian 268
Sedgeberrow Books & Framing, Worcestershire 251

- ZOLA, EMILE
Apocalypse, Surrey 228

AUTHORS
- BRITISH
Shakeshaft (Dr. B.), Cheshire 71
Valentine Rare Books, London W 173

AUTHORS
- LOCAL
Esoteric Dreams Bookshop, Cumbria 77
MK Book Services, Cambridgeshire 66
The Sanctuary Bookshop, Dorset 93

AUTHORS
- NATIONAL
Jane Jones Books, Grampian 267

AUTHORS
- WOMEN
Al Saqi Books, London W 169
Books & Bygones (Pam Taylor),
  West Midlands 236
Crawford (Elizabeth), London EC 154
dgbbooks, West Sussex 239
Dolphin Books, Suffolk 221
Dylans Bookstore, Glamorgan 286
Elaine Lonsdale Books, West Yorkshire 242
Esoteric Dreams Bookshop, Cumbria 77
Hobgoblin Books, Hampshire 125
Johnson Rare Book Collections (C.R.),
  London NW 159
Kenny's Bookshops and Art Galleries Ltd,
  Co. Galway 260
Lane Books (Shirley), Isle of Wight 135
Maghreb Bookshop (The), London WC 175
Reading Lasses, Dumfries & Galloway 265
Scrivener's Books & Bookbinding, Derbyshire . 81

Symes Books (Naomi), Cheshire 71
Treasure Trove Books, Leicestershire 146
Tucker (Alan & Joan), Gloucestershire 116
Willmott Bookseller (Nicholas), Cardiff 276

AUTOBIOGRAPHY
Abacus Gallery, Staffordshire 220
Anthony Spranger, Wiltshire 247
Antiques on High, Oxfordshire 204
Archer (Steve), London Outer 178
Beware of the Leopard, Bristol 58
Bob Mallory (Books), Derbyshire 82
Book Shelf (The), Devon 86
Bookroom (The), Surrey 229
Books, Oxfordshire 202
books2books, Devon 87
Bookworld, Shropshire 210
Booth (Booksearch Service), (Geoff), Cheshire . 68
Castleton (Pat), Kent 137
Chaucer Bookshop, Kent 136
Cheshire Book Centre, Cheshire 69
Church Street Books, Norfolk 184
Clements (R.W.), London Outer 179
Cofion Books, Pembrokeshire 281
Cornucopia Books, Lincolnshire 151
Dolphin Books, Suffolk 221
Family Favourites, East Yorkshire 105
firstpagebooks, Norfolk 187
G. C. Books Ltd., Dumfries & Galloway 264
Grahame Thornton, Bookseller, Dorset 92
Great Oak Bookshop (The), Powys 285
Harris (Books), (Malcolm), West Midlands..... 234
Hurst (Jenny), Kent 138
Kyrios Books, Nottinghamshire 200
Little Bookshop (The), Greater Manchester 119
Lyngheath Books, Norfolk 186
Moreton Books, Devon 86
Murphy (C.J.), Norfolk 187
Oopalba Books, Cheshire 71
Orb's Bookshop, Grampian 268
Poetry Bookshop (The), Powys 284
Politico's.co.uk, Kent 141
Price (R.D.M. & I.M.) (Books), Greater
  Manchester 120
Reading Lasses, Dumfries & Galloway 265
Reads, Dorset 94
Richard Thornton Books, London N 157
Roland Books, Kent 139
Rothwell & Dunworth, Somerset 214
Samovar Books, Co. Dublin 258
Scrivener's Books & Bookbinding,
  Derbyshire 81
Stalagluft Books, Tyne and Wear 231
Tiffin (Tony and Gill), Durham 96
Trinity Rare Books, Co. Leitrim 260
Wiend Books, Lancashire 143
Willmott Bookseller (Nicholas), Cardiff 276

AUTOGRAPHS
Baron (H.), London NW 158
Bertram Rota Ltd., London WC 174

SPECIALITY INDEX

Books & Bygones (Pam Taylor), West
  Midlands.. 236
Bookstand, Dorset 93
Bristow & Garland, Hampshire 123
Chas J. Sawyer, Kent 140
Cox Music (Lisa), Devon........................... 84
Cox Rare Books (Charles), Cornwall 73
Farahar & Dupre (Clive & Sophie), Wiltshire.. 246
Finch Rare Books Ltd. (Simon), London W ... 170
firstpagebooks, Norfolk............................. 187
Ford (Richard), London W 170
Franks Booksellers, Greater Manchester 119
Harrington Antiquarian Bookseller (Peter),
  London SW 166
Ken's Paper Collectables, Buckinghamshire 62
Kirkman Ltd., (Robert), Bedfordshire 53
Maggs Brothers Limited, London W 171
Modern Firsts Etc, Lancashire 142
Neil Summersgill, Lancashire...................... 142
Politico's.co.uk, Kent................................. 141
Rassam (Paul), London NW 159
Silverman (Michael), London SE 163
Wilson (Manuscripts) Ltd., (John),
  Gloucestershire 114

AUTOLITHOGRAPHY
Temperley (David), West Midlands 234

AUTOMOBILIA/AUTOMOTIVE
Bob Mallory (Books), Derbyshire 82
Cornucopia Books, Lincolnshire 151
J & J Burgess Booksellers, Cambridgeshire 64
Wiend Books, Lancashire 143

AVANT-GARDE
Norton Books, North Yorkshire.................. 194
Sclanders (Beatbooks), (Andrew), London EC. 154
Trinity Rare Books, Co. Leitrim.................. 260
Woburn Books, London N 157
Worlds End Bookshop, London SW............. 168

AVIATION
All Books, Essex 110
Anchor Books, Lincolnshire 149
Andron (G.W.), London N 155
Armchair Auctions, Hampshire 122
Askew Books (Vernon), Wiltshire 246
Avedikian Rare Books, Somerset 213
Aviabooks, Gloucestershire 114
Aviation Book Supply, Hertfordshire 130
Baldwin (M. & M.), Shropshire 250
Bancroft (David G.), Isle of Wight 134
Barbican Bookshop, North Yorkshire 194
Barnes (Peter), Wiltshire 248
Beware of the Leopard, Bristol.................... 58
Black Five Books, Shropshire 211
Bonner (John), West Yorkshire 243
Books Afloat, Dorset................................. 94
Books Bought & Sold, Surrey 226
Bookshelf – Aviation Books, Norfolk 187

Bott, (Bookdealers) Ltd., (Martin), Greater
  Manchester 118
Brewin Books Ltd., Warwickshire 233
Camilla's Bookshop, East Sussex 100
Castle Bookshop, Essex............................. 109
Castleton (Pat), Kent................................. 137
Chelifer Books, Cumbria 80
Cheshire Book Centre, Cheshire 69
Chevin Books, West Yorkshire..................... 245
Church Street Books, Norfolk..................... 184
Cobbles Books, Somerset........................... 214
Cobweb Books, North Yorkshire 192
Cocks Books (Brian), Cambridgeshire 66
Coles (T.V.), Cambridgeshire 66
Cotswold Internet Books, Gloucestershire 113
Coulthurst (Richard), Greater Manchester...... 120
Cox (Geoff), Devon 89
D'Arcy Books, Wiltshire............................. 246
Duck (William), Hampshire........................ 124
Edwards (London) Limited (Francis),
  London WC... 175
Ewell Bookshop, Surrey 227
Falconwood Transport & Military Bookshop,
  London Outer 181
Fine Books Oriental Ltd., London WC 175
Gaullifmaufry Books, Hertfordshire.............. 131
Good for Books, Lincolnshire..................... 149
Harris (George J.), Co. Derry 255
Helion & Company, West Midlands 235
Hornsby, Antiquarian and Secondhand Books
  (Malcolm), Leicestershire 146
Hornsey's, North Yorkshire........................ 192
Horsham Rare Books, West Sussex 238
Humm & Co. (Robert), Lincolnshire 151
Internet Bookshop UK Ltd., Gloucestershire .. 113
Invicta Bookshop, Berkshire 56
J & J Burgess Booksellers, Cambridgeshire 64
J.B. Books, Berkshire................................. 56
Keegan's Bookshop, Berkshire 56
Kerr (Norman), Cumbria........................... 77
Lawrence Books, Nottinghamshire 200
Libris (Weston) Books, Somerset 213
Malvern Bookshop (The), Worcestershire....... 250
Marine & Cannon Books, Cheshire 71
Marine and Cannon Books, Cheshire............ 69
Milestone Books, Devon............................ 88
Military Parade Bookshop, Wiltshire 247
MilitaryHistoryBooks.com, Kent 138
Morley Case, Hampshire 126
N1 Books, East Sussex............................... 103
Nelson (Elizabeth), Suffolk......................... 222
Patterson (J.D.), Bristol 60
Phelps (Michael), West Sussex..................... 237
Postings, Surrey 228
Prior (Michael), Lincolnshire 151
Richmond Books, North Yorkshire 192
Rowan (H. & S.J.), Dorset..........................90
Salway Books, Essex 112
Scrivener's Books & Bookbinding, Derbyshire .. 81
Sedgeberrow Books & Framing, Worcestershire 251
Smith Maritime Aviation Books (Frank),
  Tyne and Wear 231

SPECIALITY INDEX

Soldridge Books Ltd, Hampshire 122
Spooner (John E.), Dorset 90
Stour Bookshop, Dorset 92
Suffolk Rare Books, Suffolk 225
Thin Read Line, Merseyside 182
Treasure Chest Books, Suffolk 222
Treasure Island (The), Greater Manchester 120
Vanstone - Aviation Books, (Derek), Suffolk... 225
Wadard Books, Kent 137
War & Peace Books, Hampshire 123
Westwood Books Ltd, Cumbria 79
Wiend Books, Lancashire 143
World War Books, Kent 141
Yeoman Books, Lothian 272

BANKING & INSURANCE
Abrahams (Mike), Staffordshire 219
Collectables (W.H.), Suffolk 225
Old Cathay Fine Books, West Yorkshire 244
Prospect House Books, Co. Down 256
Rainford (Sheila), Hertfordshire 130

BEAT WRITERS
Addyman Books, Powys 282
Elephant Books, West Yorkshire 244
Ellis, Bookseller (Peter), London SE 162
Fifth Element, West Midlands 235
Poetry Bookshop (The), Powys 284
Price (R.W.), Nottinghamshire 200
Sclanders (Beatbooks), (Andrew), London EC. 154
Trinity Rare Books, Co. Leitrim 260
Woburn Books, London N 157
Words Etcetera Bookshop, Dorset 92
Worlds End Bookshop, London SW 168

BELL-RINGING (CAMPANOLOGY)
Church Green Books, Oxfordshire 207
Farringdon (J.M.), Swansea 287
Hadfield (G.K.), Cumbria 78
R. & A. Books, East Sussex 100
Saint Mary's Books & Prints, Lincolnshire 152
Travis & Emery Music Bookshop,
    London WC 177

BELLE-LETTRES
Apocalypse, Surrey 228
Grahame Thornton, Bookseller, Dorset 92

BIBLES
Addyman Books, Powys 282
Ardis Books, Hampshire 126
Barbican Bookshop, North Yorkshire 194
Bardsley's Books, Suffolk 221
Bernstein (Nicholas), London W 169
Biblion, London W 169
Chandos Books, Devon 84
Chapter Two, London SE 161
Copnal Books, Cheshire 68
Derek Stirling Bookseller, Kent 141
G. C. Books Ltd., Dumfries & Galloway 264

Golden Age Books, Worcestershire 251
Harrington Antiquarian Bookseller
    (Peter), London SW 166
Hennessey Bookseller (Ray), East Sussex 99
Humber Books, Lincolnshire 148
Kirkman Ltd., (Robert), Bedfordshire 53
Oasis Booksearch, Cambridgeshire 67
Paper Moon Books, Warwickshire 233
Pendleburys Bookshop, London N 156
Prospect House Books, Co. Down 256
R. & A. Books, East Sussex 100
Roscrea Bookshop, Co. Tipperary 261
Rosemary Pugh Books, Wiltshire 248
Saint Philip's Books, Oxfordshire 205
Scrivener's Books & Bookbinding, Derbyshire . 81
Tuft (Patrick), London W 173

BIBLICAL STUDIES
G. C. Books Ltd., Dumfries & Galloway 264
PsychoBabel Books & Journals, Oxfordshire ... 202
Samovar Books, Co. Dublin 258

BIBLIOGRAPHY
Alec–Smith Books (Alex), East Yorkshire 107
Andron (G.W.), London N 155
Ash Rare Books, London SW 164
Askew Books (Vernon), Wiltshire 246
Barry McKay Rare Books, Cumbria 76
Bettridge (Gordon), Fife 265
Bianco Library, West Sussex 237
Biblion, London W 169
Bookcase, Cumbria 76
Brinded (Scott), Kent 139
Broadhurst of Southport Ltd., Merseyside 182
Caledonia Books, Strathclyde 273
Chandos Books, London Outer 180
Chas J. Sawyer, Kent 140
Cobnar Books, Kent 139
Cox Old & Rare Books (Claude), Suffolk 223
Dew (Roderick), East Sussex 100
Ford (Richard), London W 170
Forest Books, Nottinghamshire 201
Fotheringham (Alex), Northumberland 198
Grampian Books, Grampian 268
Howes Bookshop, East Sussex 101
Island Books, Kent 136
Maggs Brothers Limited, London W 171
Marlborough Rare Books Ltd., London W 171
Mead (P.J.), Shropshire 210
Mills Rare Books (Adam), Cambridgeshire..... 64
Moorhead Books, West Yorkshire 241
Muttonchop Manuscripts 239
O'Connor Fine Books, Lancashire 144
Parrott (Jeremy), London E 153
Quaritch Ltd., (Bernard), London W 172
Quentin Books Ltd, Essex 109
RGS Books, Surrey 229
Rivendale Press, Buckinghamshire 61
Shapero Rare Books (Bernard J.), London W . 172
Smith Books, (Sally), Suffolk 222
Spooner & Co, Somerset 215

SPECIALITY INDEX

Taylor & Son (Peter), Hertfordshire 132
Taylor Rare Books (Michael), Norfolk 184
The Sanctuary Bookshop, Dorset 93
Travis & Emery Music Bookshop,
  London WC 177
Tuft (Patrick), London W 173
Unsworths Booksellers, London NW 160
Ventnor Rare Books, Isle of Wight 135
Wakeman Books (Frances), Nottinghamshire ... 201
Williams (Bookdealer), (Richard), Lincolnshire . 152
Williams (Christopher), Dorset 93
Wykeham Books, London SW 168

BINDINGS

Abacus Gallery, Staffordshire 220
Addyman Annexe (The), Powys 282
Addyman Books, Powys 282
Allsop (Duncan M.), Warwickshire 233
Atholl Fine Books, Tayside 275
Barry McKay Rare Books, Cumbria 76
Bates & Hindmarch, West Yorkshire 243
Baxter (Steve), Surrey 228
Bayntun (George), Somerset 212
Bernstein (Nicholas), London W 169
Biblion, London W 169
Booklore, Leicestershire 146
Camilla's Bookshop, East Sussex 100
Chandos Books, Devon 84
Chas J. Sawyer, Kent 140
Classic Bindings Ltd, London SW 164
Cooper Hay Rare Books, Strathclyde 273
Courtney & Hoff, North Yorkshire 194
Cox Old & Rare Books (Claude), Suffolk 223
Cumming Limited (A. & Y.), East Sussex 102
David (G.), Cambridgeshire 63
Davis, Antiquarian Books (Guy),
  Nottinghamshire 201
de Beaumont (Robin), London SW 164
De Burca Rare Books, Co. Dublin 259
Design Gallery 1850-1950 (The), Kent 141
Edwards (London) Limited (Francis),
  London WC 175
Elgar (Raymond), East Sussex 98
Ely Books, Cambridgeshire 65
Eton Antique Bookshop, Berkshire 57
Finch Rare Books Ltd. (Simon), London W ... 170
Fine Art, London SE 165
Fine Books at Ilkley, West Yorkshire 243
Fletcher (H.M.), Hertfordshire 131
Forest Books, Nottinghamshire 201
Foster Bookshop (Paul), London SW 165
Fosters Bookshop, London W 170
Frew Limited (Robert), London W 170
Garbett Antiquarian Books (Michael),
  Gloucestershire 113
Golden Books Group, Devon 84
Grove Bookshop (The), North Yorkshire 193
Hall's Bookshop, Kent 141
Harrington Antiquarian Bookseller (Peter),
  London SW 166
Hereward Books, Cambridgeshire 65

Heritage, West Midlands 234
Hodgkins and Company Limited (Ian),
  Gloucestershire 116
Horsham Rare Books, West Sussex 238
Howes Bookshop, East Sussex 101
Island Books, Kent 136
Junk & Spread Eagle, London SE 162
Kay Books, London W 171
Kenny's Bookshops and Art Galleries Ltd,
  Co. Galway 260
Kings Bookshop Callander, Central 263
Kirkman Ltd., (Robert), Bedfordshire 53
Maggs Brothers Limited, London W 171
Mair Wilkes Books, Fife 265
Malvern Bookshop (The), Worcestershire 250
Marlborough Rare Books Ltd., London W 171
Maynard & Bradley, Leicestershire 146
McConnell Fine Books, Kent 137
Mead (P.J.), Shropshire 210
Moore (C.R.), Shropshire 210
Moorhead Books, West Yorkshire 241
Moorside Books, Lancashire 143
Muttonchop Manuscripts 239
N1 Books, East Sussex 103
Neil Summersgill, Lancashire 142
Offa's Dyke Books, Shropshire 209
Old Town Bookshop (The), Lothian 271
Paper Moon Books, Warwickshire 233
Petworth Antique Market (Bookroom), West
  Sussex 239
Poetry Bookshop (The), Powys 284
Pordes Books Ltd., (Henry), London WC 176
Quentin Books Ltd, Essex 109
Richard Thornton Books, London N 157
Roger Collicott Books, Cornwall 74
Russell (Charles), London SW 167
Saint Mary's Books & Prints, Lincolnshire 152
Scrivener's Books & Bookbinding, Derbyshire . 81
Seydi Rare Books (Sevin), London NW 159
Sotheran Limited (Henry), London W 172
Staniland (Booksellers), Lincolnshire 152
Sterling Books, Somerset 216
Studio (The), Strathclyde 274
Temperley (David), West Midlands 234
Tobo Books, Hampshire 124
Trinity Rare Books, Co. Leitrim 260
Turton (John), Durham 97
Unsworths Booksellers, London NW 160
Vandeleur Antiquarian Books, Surrey 227
Ventnor Rare Books, Isle of Wight 135
Woodbine Books, West Yorkshire 241

BIOGRAPHY

Abacus Gallery, Staffordshire 220
Alexander's Books, Warwickshire 232
Anthony Spranger, Wiltshire 247
Antiques on High, Oxfordshire 204
Applin (Malcolm), Berkshire 55
Archer (Steve), London Outer 178
Arden Books & Cosmographia, Warwickshire . 232
Askew Books (Vernon), Wiltshire 246

SPECIALITY INDEX

Aurora Books Ltd, Lothian 270
Baldwin's Scientific Books, Essex 112
Bass (Ben), Wiltshire 246
Bell (Peter), Strathclyde 270
Bianco Library, West Sussex 237
Black Five Books, Shropshire 211
Blythswood Bookshop, Highland 269
Bob Mallory (Books), Derbyshire 82
Bonner (John), West Yorkshire 243
Book Shelf (The), Devon 86
Bookroom (The), Surrey 229
Books (For All), North Yorkshire 190
Books Antiques & Collectables, Devon 88
Books for Writers, Monmouthshire 280
books2books, Devon 87
Booth (Booksearch Service), (Geoff), Cheshire . 68
Bosco Books, Cornwall 72
Brighton Books, East Sussex 98
Brimstones, East Sussex 102
Broadhurst of Southport Ltd., Merseyside 182
Brock Books, North Yorkshire 190
Caledonia Books, Strathclyde 273
Camden Books, Somerset 212
Carnforth Bookshop (The), Lancashire 142
Castleton (Pat), Kent 137
Catalyst Booksearch Services, Devon 85
Chaucer Bookshop, Kent 136
Classic Bindings Ltd, London SW 164
Clements (R.W.), London Outer 179
Clifford Elmer Books Ltd., Cheshire 68
Cobbles Books, Somerset 214
Cofion Books, Pembrokeshire 281
Cornucopia Books, Lincolnshire 151
Criterion Books, London Outer 180
Dandy Lion Editions, Surrey 228
Darkwood Books, Co. Cork 258
dgbbooks, West Sussex 239
Dolphin Books, Suffolk 221
Dworski Books, Travel & Language
  Bookshop (Marijana), Herefordshire 283
Eastleach Books, Berkshire 55
Ellis, Bookseller (Peter), London SE 162
Ely Books, Cambridgeshire 65
Esoteric Dreams Bookshop, Cumbria 77
Family Favourites, East Yorkshire 105
Firth (Bijou Books & Photography)
  (Maureen), South Yorkshire 218
Frost (Richard), Hertfordshire 130
Garfi Books, Ceredigion 282
Good for Books, Lincolnshire 149
Graham (John), Dorset 95
Grahame Thornton, Bookseller, Dorset 92
Great Oak Bookshop (The), Powys 285
Hab Books, London W 171
Hall's Bookshop, Kent 141
Hawley (C.L.), North Yorkshire 193
Heraldry Today, Wiltshire 247
Hollett and Son (R.F.G.), Cumbria 79
Holmes (A.), Nottinghamshire 201
Holmes (Harry), East Yorkshire 106
Horsham Rare Books, West Sussex 238
Hurst (Jenny), Kent 138

Kalligraphia (formerly Charmouth
  Bounty Books), Isle of Wight 134
Karen Millward, Co. Cork 257
Kingsmere Books, Bedfordshire 53
Libra Books, Lincolnshire 148
Little Bookshop (The), Cumbria 80
Little Bookshop (The), Greater Manchester 119
Lyngheath Books, Norfolk 186
Malvern Bookshop (The), Worcestershire 250
Martin's Books, Powys 285
McCaughtrie (K.A.), North Yorkshire 190
McCrone (Audrey), Isle of Arran 269
Meads Book Service (The), East Sussex 103
Missing Books, Essex 109
Modlock (Lilian), Dorset 92
Mogul Diamonds, West Midlands 236
Mr. Pickwick of Towcester, Northamptonshire 196
Murch Booksend, (Herbert), London SE 162
Nineteenth Century Books, Oxfordshire 207
Not JUST Books, Lincolnshire 148
O'Brien Books & Photo Gallery, Co. Limerick 261
O'Donoghue Books, Powys 284
Olynthiacs, Shropshire 210
Oopalba Books, Cheshire 71
Orb's Bookshop, Grampian 268
Paperbacks Plus, Bristol 59
Park Gallery & Bookshop (The),
  Northamptonshire 197
Parrott Books, Oxfordshire 207
Poetry Bookshop (The), Powys.................... 284
Politico's.co.uk, Kent 141
Pooks Motor Books, Leicestershire 146
Portobello Books, London W 172
Price (R.D.M. & I.M.) (Books), Greater
  Manchester 120
Primrose Hill Books, London NW 159
Pringle Booksellers (Andrew), Lothian 271
Quentin Books Ltd, Essex 109
R. & A. Books, East Sussex 100
Reading Lasses, Dumfries & Galloway 265
Reads, Dorset 94
Richmond Books, North Yorkshire 192
Rivendale Press, Buckinghamshire 61
Roland Books, Kent 139
Roundstone Books, Lancashire 143
Samovar Books, Co. Dublin 258
Saunders (Tom), Caerphilly 276
Shacklock Books (David), Suffolk 222
Shakeshaft (Dr. B.), Cheshire 71
Skoob Russell Square, Suffolk 225
Smith Books, (Sally), Suffolk 222
Starlord Books, Greater Manchester 118
Stern Antiquarian Bookseller (Jeffrey), North
  Yorkshire 195
Stroma Books, Borders 262
Taylor & Son (Peter), Hertfordshire 132
The Sanctuary Bookshop, Dorset 93
Tiffin (Tony and Gill), Durham 96
Tilston (Stephen E.), London SE 161
Tombland Bookshop, Norfolk 188
Trevorrow (Edwin), Hertfordshire 130
Trinity Rare Books, Co. Leitrim 260

War & Peace Books, Hampshire................... 123
Wayside Books and Cards, Oxfordshire.......... 203
Willmott Bookseller (Nicholas), Cardiff.......... 276
Words Etcetera Bookshop, Dorset............... 92
Worlds End Bookshop, London SW.............. 168
Yarwood Rare Books (Edward), Greater
  Manchester.. 118

BIOLOGY
Alba Books, Grampian............................ 267
Arden, Bookseller (C.), Powys.................... 282
Austwick Hall Books, Lancaster.................. 190
Baron - Scientific Book Sales (P.J.), Somerset.. 213
Bracton Books, Cambridgeshire................... 63
Mogul Diamonds, West Midlands................ 236
Orb's Bookshop, Grampian....................... 268
Parkinsons Books, Merseyside.................... 183
Prospect House Books, Co. Down 256
R. & A. Books, East Sussex 100
Smith (David & Lynn), London Outer 179
Wyseby House Books, Berkshire.................. 55

BLACK STUDIES
Afar Books International, West Midlands 234
Black Voices, Merseyside.......................... 182
Bookshop (The), Greater Manchester............ 119
Oriental and African Books, Shropshire......... 210
R. & A. Books, East Sussex 100
Reading Lasses, Dumfries & Galloway.......... 265
Spurrier (Nick), Kent.............................. 138
Stevens (Joan), Cambridgeshire 65
Woburn Books, London N 157

BOOK ARTS
Alauda Books, Cumbria........................... 76
Barry McKay Rare Books, Cumbria............. 76
Collinge & Clark, London WC 174
Cornucopia Books, Lincolnshire.................. 151
Naughton Booksellers, Co. Dublin 259

BOOK OF HOURS
Addyman Books, Powys.......................... 282
Du Ry Medieval Manuscripts (Marc–Antoine),
  London W... 170
John Underwood Antiquarian Books, Norfolk 186

BOOKBINDING (SEE ALSO HAND BOOK-BINDING)
Alauda Books, Cumbria........................... 76
Andron (G.W.), London N 155
Barry McKay Rare Books, Cumbria............. 76
Beverley Old Bookshop, East Yorkshire 105
Chandos Books, Devon............................ 84
Chas J. Sawyer, Kent.............................. 140
Cheshire Book Centre, Cheshire 69
Coupland (Terry W.), Staffordshire 219
Elgar (Raymond), East Sussex 98
Forest Books, Nottinghamshire 201
Island Books, Kent................................ 136

Scrivener's Books & Bookbinding, Derbyshire. 81
Walker Fine Books (Steve), Dorset............... 91

BOOKS ABOUT BOOKS
Addyman Books, Powys.......................... 282
Alec–Smith Books (Alex), East Yorkshire 107
Andron (G.W.), London N 155
Bardsley's Books, Suffolk......................... 221
Bettridge (Gordon), Fife 265
Biblion, London W 169
Book Palace (The), London SE 161
Bracton Books, Cambridgeshire................... 63
Brian Troath Books, London E.................. 153
Brinded (Scott), Kent.............................. 139
Brock Books, North Yorkshire.................... 190
Chandos Books, Devon............................ 84
Collinge & Clark, London WC 174
Cooper Hay Rare Books, Strathclyde............ 273
Cowley, Bookdealer (K.W.), Somerset........... 214
Cox Old & Rare Books (Claude), Suffolk....... 223
Deverell Books, Bristol............................ 58
Forest Books, Nottinghamshire 201
Island Books, Kent................................ 136
Jean Hedger, Berkshire............................ 55
Malvern Bookshop (The), Worcestershire....... 250
Mead (P.J.), Shropshire 210
Mills Rare Books (Adam), Cambridgeshire..... 64
Mr. Pickwick of Towcester, Northamptonshire 196
Muttonchop Manuscripts.......................... 239
Naughton Booksellers, Co. Dublin 259
Nineteenth Century Books, Oxfordshire......... 207
Parrott (Jeremy), London E....................... 153
Prospect House Books, Co. Down 256
Quentin Books Ltd, Essex......................... 109
R. & A. Books, East Sussex 100
RGS Books, Surrey................................ 229
Rivendale Press, Buckinghamshire................ 61
Rosemary Books, Merseyside..................... 183
Seabreeze Books, Lancashire...................... 144
Solitaire Books, Somerset......................... 212
Trinity Rare Books, Co. Leitrim.................. 260
Unsworths Booksellers, London NW 160
Updike Rare Books (John), Lothian 272
Wakeman Books (Frances), Nottinghamshire .. 201
Walker Fine Books (Steve), Dorset............... 91
Wykeham Books, London SW 168
Zardoz Books, Wiltshire 249

BOOKS IN GREEK
Hellenic Bookservices, London NW.............. 158

BOTANY
Acer Books, Herefordshire 128
Alauda Books, Cumbria........................... 76
Arden, Bookseller (C.), Powys.................... 282
Austwick Hall Books, Lancaster.................. 190
Aviabooks, Gloucestershire 114
Baldwin's Scientific Books, Essex 112
Baron - Scientific Book Sales (P.J.), Somerset.. 213
Bianco Library, West Sussex..................... 237

SPECIALITY INDEX

Blest (Peter), Kent 139
Brown (Books) (P.R.), Durham 97
Burden Ltd., (Clive A.), Hertfordshire 132
Calluna Books, Dorset 94
Camilla's Bookshop, East Sussex 100
Castleton (Pat), Kent 137
Chantrey Books, South Yorkshire 217
Cornucopia Books, Lincolnshire 151
Dales & Lakes Book Centre, Cumbria 79
Dene Barn Books & Prints, Somerset............ 216
Goodyer (Nicholas), London N 156
Harrington Antiquarian Bookseller
 (Peter), London SW 166
Hollingshead (Chris), London Outer 181
Jay Books, Lothian 271
Kennedy (Peter), Surrey 230
Mandalay Bookshop, London SW 166
Mannwaring (M.G.), Bristol 59
Martin's Books, Powys 285
Old Town Bookshop (The), Lothian 271
Park (Mike), London Outer 180
Parkinsons Books, Merseyside..................... 183
Pemberley Books, Buckinghamshire.............. 62
Phelps (Michael), West Sussex..................... 237
Pholiota Books, London WC....................... 176
R. & A. Books, East Sussex 100
Reeves Technical Books, North Yorkshire...... 193
Saint Ann's Books, Worcestershire 251
Steven Simpson Books, Norfolk 188
Sue Lowell Natural History Books, London W 173
Summerfield Books Ltd, Cumbria 76
Tant Yn Ellen Books, Powys 286
Thin Read Line, Merseyside 182
Treasure Trove Books, Leicestershire 146
Woodside Books, Kent 136
Wyseby House Books, Berkshire.................. 55

BREWING

Lucas (Richard), London NW 159
Past & Present Books, Gloucestershire........... 114
Phelps (Michael), West Sussex..................... 237
R. & A. Books, East Sussex 100
Thorne (John), Essex 109

BRIDGE

Beaver Booksearch, Suffolk 221
Bradley–Cox (Mary), Dorset....................... 90
R. & A. Books, East Sussex 100
R. S. & P. A. Scowen, Middlesex 179
Reeves Technical Books, North Yorkshire...... 193

BRITISH BOOKS

Apocalypse, Surrey 228
Cornucopia Books, Lincolnshire 151
Gildas Books, Cheshire 68
Samovar Books, Co. Dublin 258

BROADCASTING

Apocalypse, Surrey 228
Kelly Books, Devon 88

R. & A. Books, East Sussex 100
Wood (Peter), Cambridgeshire 65
Yesterday's News, Conwy 278

BUILDING & CONSTRUCTION

Amwell Book Company, London SE 154
Brown-Studies, Strathclyde........................ 273
Elton Engineering Books, London W............ 170
Greta Books, Durham 96
Inch's Books, North Yorkshire.................... 192
N1 Books, East Sussex.............................. 103
Reeves Technical Books, North Yorkshire...... 193
Scrivener's Books & Bookbinding, Derbyshire. 81
Staniland (Booksellers), Lincolnshire 152
Stobart Davies Limited, Carmarthwnshire 276
Trinders' Fine Tools, Suffolk 222
Whistler's Books, London SW 167

BULL FIGHTING

Askew Books (Vernon), Wiltshire 246
Books on Spain, London Outer................... 181
Orssich (Paul), London SW........................ 167

BUSES/TRAMS

Barbican Bookshop, North Yorkshire 194
Bott, (Bookdealers) Ltd., (Martin), Greater
 Manchester 118
Browse Books, Lancashire 143
Cavern Books, Cheshire 70
Classic Crime Collections, Greater Manchester 119
Dales & Lakes Book Centre, Cumbria 79
Dinnages Transport Publishing, East Sussex.... 98
Milestone Books, Devon........................... 88
R. & A. Books, East Sussex 100
Roland Books, Kent................................. 139
Rolling Stock Books, Greater Manchester 121
Simon Lewis Transport Books, Gloucestershire 115
Tony Pollastrone Railway Books, Wiltshire 246

BUSINESS STUDIES

Ardis Books, Hampshire........................... 126
Boer (Louise), Arthurian Books, Powys 282
Brockwells Booksellers, Lincolnshire 148
Cornucopia Books, Lincolnshire 151
Esoteric Dreams Bookshop, Cumbria............ 77
Reading Lasses, Dumfries & Galloway.......... 265
Roland Books, Kent................................. 139
Stern Antiquarian Bookseller (Jeffrey), North
 Yorkshire 195

BYZANTIUM

Askew Books (Vernon), Wiltshire 246
Caliver Books, Essex 110
Dworski Books, Travel & Language Bookshop
 (Marijana), Herefordshire 283
Hellenic Bookservices, London NW............. 158
Michael Graves-Johnston, London SW.......... 166
Samovar Books, Co. Dublin 258
Unsworths Booksellers, London NW 160
Whitchurch Books Ltd., Cardiff 276

SPECIALITY INDEX

CALLIGRAPHY
Apocalypse, Surrey 228
Barry McKay Rare Books, Cumbria............. 76
Bettridge (Gordon), Fife 265
Cheshire Book Centre, Cheshire 69
Dworski Books, Travel & Language Bookshop
 (Marijana), Herefordshire 283
Eggeling Books (John), West Yorkshire 245
Glacier Books, Tayside............................ 275
Hay Cinema Bookshop Ltd., Herefordshire 283
John Underwood Antiquarian Books, Norfolk 186
Larkham Books (Patricia), Gloucestershire 117
Scrivener's Books & Bookbinding, Derbyshire. 81
Taylor Rare Books (Michael), Norfolk 184
Young (D. & J.), Powys 286

CANADIANA
Yesterday's News, Conwy 278

CANALS/INLAND WATERWAYS
Abrahams (Mike), Staffordshire................... 219
Al Saqi Books, London W 169
Anchor Books, Lincolnshire 149
Anvil Books, West Midlands 235
Archer (Steve), London Outer 178
Arden Books & Cosmographia, Warwickshire. 232
Baldwin (M. & M.), Shropshire 250
Barbican Bookshop, North Yorkshire 194
Bianco Library, West Sussex...................... 237
Bird Books (Nigel), Ceredigion................... 277
Books Afloat, Dorset 94
Bott, (Bookdealers) Ltd., (Martin), Greater
 Manchester 118
Cartographics, Staffordshire....................... 220
Cavern Books, Cheshire 70
Cheshire Book Centre, Cheshire 69
Classic Crime Collections, Greater Manchester 119
Cornucopia Books, Lincolnshire 151
Cottage Books, Leicestershire..................... 145
Coulthurst (Richard), Greater Manchester...... 120
Cox (Geoff), Devon 89
Crosby Nethercott Books, London Outer....... 178
Dales and Lakes Book Centre, Cumbria 79
Duck (William), Hampshire....................... 124
Eastcote Bookshop (The), London Outer 178
Fine Books Oriental Ltd., London WC 175
Gildas Books, Cheshire 68
Hennessey Bookseller (Ray), East Sussex 99
Humm & Co. (Robert), Lincolnshire 151
Island Books, Kent 136
Joppa Books Ltd., Surrey 226
K.S.C. Books, Cheshire 68
Kerr (Norman), Cumbria.......................... 77
Marcet Books, London SE........................ 161
Nevis Railway Bookshops (The Antique &
 Book Collector), Wiltshire....................... 247
Nicolas - Antiquarian Booksellers &
 Art Dealers, London N 156
R. & A. Books, East Sussex 100
Roadmaster Books, Kent.......................... 137
Rochdale Book Company, Greater Manchester 120
Rolling Stock Books, Greater Manchester 121
Salway Books, Essex 112
Scrivener's Books & Bookbinding, Derbyshire. 81
Skyrack Books, West Yorkshire 243
Tony Pollastrone Railway Books, Wiltshire 246
Trinity Rare Books, Co. Leitrim.................. 260

CARICATURE
Apocalypse, Surrey 228
Batterham (David), London W 169
Hogan (F. & J.), London N 156
N1 Books, East Sussex............................. 103
Tooley, Adams & Co, Oxfordshire 206
Trinity Rare Books, Co. Leitrim.................. 260

CARPETS
Abington Bookshop, Suffolk...................... 222
Apocalypse, Surrey 228
Barmby (C. & A.J.), Kent.......................... 140
Byrom Textile Bookroom (Richard), Lancs 142
Don Kelly Books, London W 170
Heneage Art Books (Thomas), London SW.... 166
Potterton Books, North Yorkshire 194
Trinders' Fine Tools, Suffolk 222

CARRIAGES & DRIVING
Joppa Books Ltd., Surrey 226
Keeble Antiques, Somerset 215
Pennymead Books, North Yorkshire............. 191
Phenotype Books, Cumbria 78
R. & A. Books, East Sussex 100

CARTOGRAPHY
Alauda Books, Cumbria 76
Archer (David), Powys............................. 285
Bannister (David), Gloucestershire................ 113
Burden Ltd., (Clive A.), Hertfordshire........... 132
Cartographics, Staffordshire....................... 220
Chas J. Sawyer, Kent 140
Frew Limited (Robert), London W 170
Heritage, West Midlands 234
Hogan (F. & J.), London N 156
InterCol London, London N 156
Kalligraphia (formerly Charmouth
 Bounty Books), Isle of Wight.................... 134
Marcet Books, London SE........................ 161
Paralos Ltd., London WC 175
Potter Limited (Jonathan), London W 172
Taney Books, Co. Dublin 259
Tooley, Adams & Co, Oxfordshire 206

CARTOONS
Apocalypse, Surrey 228
Bates & Hindmarch, West Yorkshire 243
Book Palace (The), London SE 161
Cheshire Book Centre, Cheshire 69
D. & M. Books, West Yorkshire 244
Facet Books, Dorset................................ 90
Fine Books Oriental Ltd., London WC 175
Goldman (Paul), Dorset 94

SPECIALITY INDEX

Longden (George), Cheshire 69
N1 Books, East Sussex............................ 103

CATALOGUES RAISONNES
Apocalypse, Surrey 228
Ars Artis, Oxfordshire............................. 205
Art Book Company, (The), Suffolk 223
Barlow (Vincent G.), Hampshire................. 126
Book Palace (The), London SE 161
Facet Books, Dorset................................ 90
Heneage Art Books (Thomas), London SW.... 166
Old Town Bookshop (The), Lothian............. 271
Reeves Technical Books, North Yorkshire...... 193

CATS
Annie's Books, South Yorkshire 217
Archivist (The), Devon............................. 88
Bookline, Co. Down................................ 256
Castleton (Pat), Kent............................... 137
Cat Lit, Somerset 215
Cheshire Book Centre, Cheshire 69
Cornucopia Books, Lincolnshire 151
Mayhew (Veronica), Berkshire 56
R. & A. Books, East Sussex 100
Roland Books, Kent................................ 139
Saint Swithin's Illustrated & Children's Books,
  London W....................................... 172
Stella Books, Monmouthshire 281

CATTLEMEN
Americanabooksuk, Cumbria...................... 76

CELTICA
Byre Books, Dumfries & Galloway............... 264
Gildas Books, Cheshire 68
Michael J Carroll, Co. Cork 257
Orb's Bookshop, Grampian........................ 268
PsychoBabel Books & Journals, Oxfordshire ... 202

CEMETERIES
Orb's Bookshop, Grampian........................ 268

CERAMICS
Abacus Gallery, Staffordshire..................... 220
Art Reference Books, Hampshire................. 125
Aviabooks, Gloucestershire 114
Axe Rare & Out of Print Books (Richard),
  North Yorkshire................................. 190
Barmby (C. & A.J.), Kent.......................... 140
Bookroom (The), Surrey........................... 229
Clark (Nigel A.), London SE...................... 162
Cornucopia Books, Lincolnshire 151
Cover to Cover, Merseyside....................... 183
Firth (Bijou Books & Photography) (Maureen),
  South Yorkshire................................. 218
Heneage Art Books (Thomas), London SW.... 166
Ives Bookseller (John), London Outer 181
Milestone Publications Goss & Crested China,
  Hampshire....................................... 124

Moss Books, London NW 159
Potterton Books, North Yorkshire 194
R. & A. Books, East Sussex 100
Reference Works Ltd., Dorset..................... 94
Silver Trees Books, West Midlands............... 234

CHARITY
Reading Lasses, Dumfries & Galloway.......... 265

CHEMISTRY
Baron - Scientific Book Sales (P.J.), Somerset.. 213
Parkinsons Books, Merseyside.................... 183
Phelps (Michael), West Sussex.................... 237
Pickering & Chatto, London W................... 172
R. & A. Books, East Sussex 100
Weiner (Graham), London N 157
Westwood Books Ltd, Cumbria 79

CHESS
Bowers Chess Suppliers (Francis),
  Cambridgeshire................................. 66
Caissa Books, Surrey............................... 229
Cheshire Book Centre, Cheshire 69
Peterson (Tony), Essex............................. 111
R. & A. Books, East Sussex 100
R. S. & P. A. Scowen, Middlesex................. 179
Saunders (Tom), Caerphilly....................... 276
Scrivener's Books & Bookbinding, Derbyshire . 81
Treglown (Roger J.), Cheshire.................... 70
Westwood Books Ltd, Cumbria 79
Whistler's Books, London SW 167

CHILDREN'S
- GENERAL
AA1 Books, Dumfries & Galloway 264
Abrahams (Mike), Staffordshire................... 219
Alexander's Books, Warwickshire................. 232
Altshuler (Jean), Cumbria 78
Ampersand Books, Shropshire 209
Andrew Morton (Books), Powys.................. 281
Annie's Books, South Yorkshire 217
Anthony Whittaker, Kent.......................... 136
Antiques on High, Oxfordshire................... 204
Anwoth Books, Dumfries & Galloway 264
Apocalypse, Surrey 228
Arden Books & Cosmographia, Warwickshire . 232
Armitage (Booksearch), (Kate), Devon.......... 83
Assinder Books, Essex 110
Aucott & Thomas, Leicestershire 145
Aurora Books Ltd, Lothian........................ 270
Autolycus, Shropshire 209
Badger Books, Somerset........................... 216
Baker - Books for the Collector (Colin),
  Devon 88
Barlow (Vincent G.), Hampshire................. 126
Bates Books, London Outer 179
Bayntun (George), Somerset...................... 212
Beck (John), East Sussex.......................... 102
Beverley Old Bookshop, East Yorkshire 105
Biblion, London W 169

SPECIALITY INDEX

Bilski (Gill), Buckinghamshire 61
Black Cat Bookshop, Leicestershire 145
Black Five Books, Shropshire 211
Blacket Books, Lothian 270
Book Business (The), London W 169
Book House (The), Cumbria 78
Book Palace (The), London SE 161
Bookline, Co. Down 256
Bookmark (Children's Books), Wiltshire 248
Bookroom (The), Surrey 229
Books & Collectables Ltd., Cambridgeshire 63
Books (For All), North Yorkshire 190
Books Antiques & Collectables, Devon 88
Books Bought & Sold, Surrey 226
books2books, Devon 87
Bookseller (The), Cumbria 79
Bookshop (The), Dorset 92
Bookshop on the Heath, The, London SE 161
Bookworld, Shropshire 210
Bookworm, Essex 110
Booth Books, Powys 282
Border Bookshop, West Yorkshire 245
Boris Books, Hampshire 127
Brazenhead Ltd., Norfolk 186
Bridport Old Books, Dorset 91
Bright (P.G.), Cambridgeshire 65
Brighton Books, East Sussex 98
Broadhurst of Southport Ltd., Merseyside 182
Broadleaf Books, Torfaen 287
Browning Books, Torfaen 287
Bryony Books, West Yorkshire 244
Bufo Books, Hampshire 125
Butts Books (Mary), Berkshire 56
Byre Books, Dumfries & Galloway 264
Camilla's Bookshop, East Sussex 100
Canterbury Bookshop (The), Kent 136
Castleton (Pat), Kent 137
Catalyst Booksearch Services, Devon 85
Chandos Books, Devon 84
Chapter Two, London SE 161
Children's Bookshop (The), Herefordshire 282
Childrens Bookshop, West Yorkshire 242
Clear (Mrs. Patricia), Surrey 226
Clements (R.W.), London Outer 179
Collectables (W.H.), Suffolk 225
Copnal Books, Cheshire 68
Cornell Books, Gloucestershire 117
Cotswold Internet Books, Gloucestershire 113
Countrymans Gallery (The), Leicestershire 145
Coupland (Terry W.), Staffordshire 219
Cranhurst Books, London NW 158
Cygnet Books, East Yorkshire 107
D'Arcy Books, Wiltshire 246
D. & M. Books, West Yorkshire 244
Dandy Lion Editions, Surrey 228
David (G.), Cambridgeshire 63
Dean Illustrated Books (Myra), Powys 281
Deverell Books, Bristol 58
Doorbar (P. & D.), Gwynned 279
Dormouse Bookshop (The), Norfolk 188
Drummond Pleasures of Past Times
 (David), London WC 174

Eastcote Bookshop (The), London Outer 178
Ellis, Bookseller (Peter), London SE 162
Everett (Richard), Norfolk 184
Everett (Richard, at the Southwold
 Antiques Centre, Suffolk 225
Facet Books, Dorset 90
Fifteenth Century Bookshop (The), East Sussex 102
First State Books, London W 170
firstpagebooks, Norfolk 187
Firsts in Print, Isle of Wight 134
Flint (David), Hampshire 122
Foster Bookshop (Paul), London SW 165
Fosters Bookshop, London W 170
Franks Booksellers, Greater Manchester 119
Furneaux Books (Lee), Devon 88
Game Advice, Oxfordshire 205
Gander, (Jacques), Gloucestershire 115
Garfi Books, Ceredigion 282
Gemini–Books, Shropshire 210
Gildas Books, Cheshire 68
Gloucester Road Bookshop, London SW 165
Good Books, Shropshire 210
Good for Books, Lincolnshire 149
Grahame Thornton, Bookseller, Dorset 92
Green Meadow Books, Cornwall 74
Greer (Robin), London SW 166
Harrington (Adrian), London W 171
Harrington Antiquarian Bookseller (Peter),
 London SW 166
Hawley (C.L.), North Yorkshire 193
Heppa (Christopher), Essex 108
Heywood Hill Limited (G.), London W 171
Hodgkins and Company Limited (Ian),
 Gloucestershire 116
Hollett and Son (R.F.G.), Cumbria 79
Holtom (Christopher), Cornwall 75
Hornsey's, North Yorkshire 192
Hurly Burly Books, Wiltshire 249
Hurst (Jenny), Kent 138
Innes Books, Shropshire 209
Intech Books, Northumberland 198
Internet Bookshop UK Ltd., Gloucestershire .. 113
J & D Jones, Cheshire 70
Jane Badger Books, Northamptonshire 196
Jane Jones Books, Grampian 267
JB Books & Collectables, West Sussex 238
Jean Hedger, Berkshire 55
John Underwood Antiquarian Books, Norfolk 186
Jolly Good Read (A.), Tayside 275
Jonkers Rare Books, Oxfordshire 204
Junk & Spread Eagle, London SE 162
K Books, Cheshire 69
Kalligraphia (formerly Charmouth Bounty Books),
 Isle of Wight 134
Katnap Arts, Norfolk 187
Keel Row Books, Tyne and Wear 231
Kellow Books, Oxfordshire 203
Keswick Bookshop, Cumbria 78
Kevin S. Ogilvie Modern First Editions,
 Grampian 266
Key Books (Sarah), Cambridgeshire 64
Kineton Nooks, Warwickshire 232

SPECIALITY INDEX

Leabeck Books, Oxfordshire 205
Leaf Ends, Northumberland 199
Little Stour Books, Kent 136
Lloyd-Davies (Sue), Carmarthenshire 277
Lucius Books, North Yorkshire 195
Macbuiks, North Yorkshire 190
Mainly Fiction, Greater Manchester 118
Malvern Bookshop (The), Worcestershire 250
March House Books, Dorset 94
Marchpane, London WC 175
Mason (Mary), Oxfordshire 202
McCrone (Audrey), Isle of Arran 269
McNaughtan's Bookshop, Lothian 271
Meads Book Service (The), East Sussex 103
Mellon's Books, East Sussex 100
Minster Gate Bookshop, North Yorkshire 195
Modlock (Lilian), Dorset 92
Moorhead Books, West Yorkshire 241
Much Ado Books, East Sussex 98
Murphy (C.J.), Norfolk 187
New Strand Bookshop (The), Herefordshire 128
Old Celtic Bookshop (The), Devon 86
Old Hall Bookshop (The), Northamptonshire .. 196
Old Station Pottery & Bookshop (The),
  Norfolk 189
Old Town Bookshop (The), Lothian 271
Oopalba Books, Cheshire 71
Oxfam Books and Music, Hampshire 127
Paperbacks Plus, Bristol 59
Park Gallery & Bookshop (The),
  Northamptonshire 197
Parrott Books, Oxfordshire 207
Peakirk Books, Cambridgeshire 67
Peter Lyons Books, Gloucestershire 114
Peter's Bookshop, Norfolk 188
Pomes Penyeach, Staffordshire 219
Price (R.W.), Nottinghamshire 200
Priestpopple Books, Northumberland 198
Pyecroft (Ruth), Gloucestershire 116
R. & A. Books, East Sussex 100
RGS Books, Surrey 229
Richard Thornton Books, London N 157
Ripping Yarns, London N 157
River Reads Bookshop, Devon 89
Robertson Books, Lothian 271
Rochdale Book Company,
  Greater Manchester 120
Roe and Moore, London WC 176
Roland Books, Kent 139
Roscrea Bookshop, Co. Tipperary 261
Rose's Books, Herefordshire 284
Rosemary Books, Merseyside 183
Ross & Company Ltd., (Louise),
  Worcestershire 250
Roundstone Books, Lancashire 143
Rowan House Books, Surrey 226
Rye Old Books, East Sussex 103
Ryeland Books, Northamptonshire 196
Saint Mary's Books & Prints, Lincolnshire 152
Saint Swithin's Illustrated & Children's
  Books, London W 172
Saunders (Tom), Caerphilly 276

Savage (Keith A.), Suffolk 224
Schutte (David), Hampshire 125
Scrivener's Books & Bookbinding, Derbyshire . 81
Seabreeze Books, Lancashire 144
Second Edition, Lothian 272
Sesemann (Julia), Kent 136
Shakeshaft (Dr. B.), Cheshire 71
Sharpe (Mary), Somerset 216
Shelley (E. & J.), Buckinghamshire 61
Signature Books, Hampshire 126
Simpson (Dave), Central 263
Sims (Sue), Dorset 90
Siri Ellis Books, Greater Manchester 118
Smith Books, (Sally), Suffolk 222
Sotheran Limited (Henry), London W 172
Staffs Bookshop (The), Staffordshire 219
Stansbury (Rosemary), Devon 87
Stella Books, Monmouthshire 281
Stepping Stones Bookshop, North Yorkshire .. 191
Stinton (Judith), Dorset 91
Stothert Old Books, Cheshire 68
Stroma Books, Borders 262
Surprise Books, Gloucestershire 113
Tant Yn Ellen Books, Powys 286
The Old Children's Bookshelf, Lothian 272
Tiffin (Tony and Gill), Durham 96
TP Children's Bookshop, West Yorkshire 241
Trafalgar Bookshop, East Sussex 99
Transformer, Dumfries & Galloway 265
Treasure Trove Books, Leicestershire 146
Trinity Rare Books, Co. Leitrim 260
Tucker (Alan & Joan), Gloucestershire 116
Updike Rare Books (John), Lothian 272
Wadard Books, Kent 137
Westwood Books Ltd, Cumbria 79
Wilbraham (J. & S.), London NW 160
Words Etcetera Bookshop, Dorset 92
Wright (Norman), Hertfordshire 133
Wychwood Books, Gloucestershire 116
Xanadubooks, Cleveland 96
Yorkshire Relics, West Yorkshire 242

- **EARLY TITLES**

Autolycus, Shropshire 209
Castleton (Pat), Kent 137
Cygnet Books, East Yorkshire 107
Embleton (Paul), Essex 111
Jean Hedger, Berkshire 55
Old Celtic Bookshop (The), Devon 86
Oopalba Books, Cheshire 71
Scrivener's Books & Bookbinding, Derbyshire . 81
Talisman Books, Cheshire 70
Tiffin (Tony and Gill), Durham 96
Wadard Books, Kent 137
Yates Antiquarian Books (Tony), Leicestershire 146

- **ILLUSTRATED**

Allinson (Frank & Stella), Warwickshire 232
Ampersand Books, Shropshire 209
Amwell Book Company, London SE 154
Apocalypse, Surrey 228

SPECIALITY INDEX

Art Reference Books, Hampshire 125
Autolycus, Shropshire 209
Baker - Books for the Collector (Colin), Devon 88
Bath Old Books, Somerset 212
Bayntun (George), Somerset 212
Birmingham Books, West Midlands 234
Book Palace (The), London SE 161
Books & Things, London W 169
books2books, Devon 87
BOOKS4U, Flintshire 279
Bookseller (The), Cumbria 79
Bow Windows Book Shop, East Sussex 102
Browning Books, Torfaen 287
Camilla's Bookshop, East Sussex 100
Castleton (Pat), Kent 137
Chalk (Old & Out of Print Books)
  (Christine M.), West Midlands 234
Chris Phillips, Wiltshire 246
Cooper Hay Rare Books, Strathclyde 273
Cox, Andrew, Shropshire 211
Cygnet Books, East Yorkshire 107
Dandy Lion Editions, Surrey 228
Doorbar (P. & D.), Gwynned 279
Eastwood Books (David), Cornwall 72
Embleton (Paul), Essex 111
Fifteenth Century Bookshop (The), East Sussex 102
Fine Books at Ilkley, West Yorkshire 243
Flint (David), Hampshire 122
Foster Bookshop (Paul), London SW 165
Green Meadow Books, Cornwall 74
Greer (Robin), London W 166
Hennessey Bookseller (Ray), East Sussex 99
Hurly Burly Books, Wiltshire 249
Ian Briddon, Derbyshire 81
J & D Jones, Cheshire 70
Jane Jones Books, Grampian 267
Jean Hedger, Berkshire 55
John Underwood Antiquarian Books, Norfolk 186
Jonkers Rare Books, Oxfordshire 204
Junk & Spread Eagle, London SE 162
Lake (David), Norfolk 187
Lloyd-Davies (Sue), Carmarthenshire 277
Lucius Books, North Yorkshire 195
Lymelight Books & Prints, Dorset 92
Macbuiks, North Yorkshire 190
Mannwaring (M.G.), Bristol 59
N1 Books, East Sussex 103
Old Cathay Fine Books, West Yorkshire 244
Old Celtic Bookshop (The), Devon 86
Oopalba Books, Cheshire 71
Portobello Books, London W 172
R. & A. Books, East Sussex 100
Rhodes, Bookseller (Peter), Hampshire 126
Roscrea Bookshop, Co. Tipperary 261
Rose's Books, Herefordshire 284
Saint Swithin's Illustrated & Children's Books,
  London W 172
Scrivener's Books & Bookbinding, Derbyshire . 81
Shakeshaft (Dr. B.), Cheshire 71
Shapero Rare Books (Bernard J.), London W. 172
Siri Ellis Books, Greater Manchester 118
Stella Books, Monmouthshire 281
Stepping Stones Bookshop, North Yorkshire .. 191
Stroma Books, Borders 262
Studio (The), Strathclyde 274
Tant Yn Ellen Books, Powys 286
The Old Children's Bookshelf, Lothian 272
Tiffin (Tony and Gill), Durham 96
TP Children's Bookshop, West Yorkshire 241
Trafalgar Bookshop, East Sussex 99
Treasure Trove Books, Leicestershire 146
Wadard Books, Kent 137
Worlds End Bookshop, London SW 168

CHRISTMAS

Castleton (Pat), Kent 137
Cygnet Books, East Yorkshire 107
Nostalgia Unlimited, Merseyside 182
R. & A. Books, East Sussex 100
Roscrea Bookshop, Co. Tipperary 261
Saint Swithin's Illustrated & Children's Books,
  London W 172
Samovar Books, Co. Dublin 258

CHURCHILLIANA

Askew Books (Vernon), Wiltshire 246
Baxter (Steve), Surrey 228
Cheshire Book Centre, Cheshire 69
Grahame Thornton, Bookseller, Dorset 92
Guildmaster Books, Cheshire 70
Harrington (Adrian), London W 171
Harrington Antiquarian Bookseller
  (Peter), London SW 166
Island Books, Kent 136
Mellon's Books, East Sussex 100
R. & A. Books, East Sussex 100
RGS Books, Surrey 229
Seabreeze Books, Lancashire 144
Sotheran Limited (Henry), London W 172
Updike Rare Books (John), Lothian 272
Wadard Books, Kent 137
Yesterday's News, Conwy 278

CINEMA/FILM

Abbey Books, Cornwall 73
Apocalypse, Surrey 228
Bardsley's Books, Suffolk 221
Barn Books, Buckinghamshire 61
Beware of the Leopard, Bristol 58
Bob Mallory (Books), Derbyshire 82
Book Palace (The), London SE 161
Bookroom (The), Surrey 229
Books, Denbighshire 278
Books & Collectables Ltd., Cambridgeshire 63
books2books, Devon 87
Brian Troath Books, London E 153
Brighton Books, East Sussex 98
Byre Books, Dumfries & Galloway 264
Caledonia Books, Strathclyde 273
Camilla's Bookshop, East Sussex 100
Capel Mawr Collectors Centre, Gwynedd 280
Cheshire Book Centre, Cheshire 69

SPECIALITY INDEX

Cover to Cover, Merseyside......................... 183
Cowley, Bookdealer (K.W.), Somerset 214
Decorum Books, London N 155
Eastcote Bookshop (The), London Outer 178
Evans (Mark), Lincolnshire 151
firstpagebooks, Norfolk 187
Fitzsimons (Anne), Cumbria 77
Ford Books (David), Hertfordshire 132
Franks Booksellers, Greater Manchester 119
Greenroom Books, West Yorkshire 243
Hay Castle, Powys 283
Hay Cinema Bookshop Ltd., Herefordshire 283
Inprint, Gloucestershire 116
Jade Mountain, Hampshire 125
Judd Books, London WC 175
Junk & Spread Eagle, London SE 162
Kaye - Bookseller (Terence), London NW 159
Keel Row Books, Tyne and Wear 231
Kelly Books, Devon 88
Kenny's Bookshops and Art Galleries
  Ltd, Co. Galway 260
McGee (Terence J.), London Outer 178
Mellon's Books, East Sussex 100
Modlock (Lilian), Dorset 92
Moon's Bookshop (Michael), Cumbria 80
Morris Secondhand & Antiquarian
  Books (Chris), Oxfordshire 205
My Back Pages, London SW 167
Nevitsky (Philip), Greater Manchester 119
O'Brien Books & Photo Gallery, Co. Limerick 261
Paramor (C.D.), Suffolk 224
Pordes Books Ltd., (Henry), London WC 176
Portobello Books, London W 172
Prescott - The Bookseller (John),
  London Outer 181
Priestpopple Books, Northumberland 198
R. & A. Books, East Sussex 100
Reads, Dorset 94
Roland Books, Kent 139
Scrivener's Books & Bookbinding, Derbyshire . 81
Skoob Russell Square, Suffolk 225
Stroma Books, Borders 262
Theatreshire Books, North Yorkshire 190
Till's Bookshop, Lothian 272
Trafalgar Bookshop, East Sussex 99
Treasure Chest Books, Suffolk 222
Waxfactor, East Sussex 99
Williams (Bookdealer), (Richard), Lincolnshire 152
Wood (Peter), Cambridgeshire 65
Worlds End Bookshop, London SW 168
Yesterday's News, Conwy 278
Zardoz Books, Wiltshire 249

CIRCUS

Apocalypse, Surrey 228
Cover to Cover, Merseyside 183
Drummond Pleasures of Past Times (David),
  London WC 174
Fitzsimons (Anne), Cumbria 77
Kaye - Bookseller (Terence), London NW 159
R. & A. Books, East Sussex 100

Saint Swithin's Illustrated & Children's Books,
  London W 172
Webster (D.), Strathclyde 274

CITIES

Amwell Book Company, London SE 154
Duck (William), Hampshire 124
Inch's Books, North Yorkshire 192
R. & A. Books, East Sussex 100

CITY OF LONDON

Apocalypse, Surrey 228
Ash Rare Books, London SW 164
Bookroom (The), Surrey 229
Camilla's Bookshop, East Sussex 100
Chas J. Sawyer, Kent 140
Hook (Arthur), Bristol 59
Junk & Spread Eagle, London SE 162
Marcet Books, London SE 161
Missing Books, Essex 109
Oopalba Books, Cheshire 71
Portobello Books, London W 172
Prospect House Books, Co. Down 256
R. & A. Books, East Sussex 100

CIVIL ENGINEERING

Camden Books, Somerset 212
Duck (William), Hampshire 124
Reeves Technical Books, North Yorkshire 193
Sun House Books, Kent 139

CLASSICAL STUDIES

Andrew Stewart, Cornwall 74
Apocalypse, Surrey 228
Blackwell's Rare Books, Oxfordshire 205
Brian Troath Books, London E 153
Camden Books, Somerset 212
Carnforth Bookshop (The), Lancashire 142
Chthonios Books, East Sussex 101
Classics Bookshop (The), Oxfordshire 202
Crouch Rare Books, Surrey 227
Grahame Thornton, Bookseller, Dorset 92
Hellenic Bookservices, London NW 158
Hill (Peter), Hampshire 123
Howes Bookshop, East Sussex 101
Kings Bookshop Callander, Central 263
Lamb (R.W.), Suffolk 224
Moseley Books, West Midlands 234
Olynthiacs, Shropshire 210
Paralos Ltd., London WC 175
Poole (William), London W 172
Quest Books, East Yorkshire 106
R. & A. Books, East Sussex 100
Sandpiper Books Ltd., London SW 167
Scrivener's Books & Bookbinding, Derbyshire . 81
Seydi Rare Books (Sevin), London NW 159
Skoob Russell Square, Suffolk 225
Sokol Books Ltd., London W 172
Thorntons of Oxford Ltd., Oxfordshire 203
Unsworths Booksellers, London NW 160

Winghale Books, Lincolnshire 151

CLASSICS, THE
Beware of the Leopard, Bristol 58
N1 Books, East Sussex 103

COCKFIGHTING
Blest (Peter), Kent 139
Chalmers Hallam (E.), Hampshire 125
Kilgour (Sporting Books) (Ian), Leicestershire . 147
R. & A. Books, East Sussex 100
Thomas (Barry), Ceredigion 277

COLLECTABLES
Apocalypse, Surrey 228
Book Palace (The), London SE 161
books2books, Devon 87
Cornucopia Books, Lincolnshire 151
Don Kelly Books, London W 170

COLLECTING
Abrahams (Mike), Staffordshire 219
Antiques on High, Oxfordshire 204
Apocalypse, Surrey 228
Art Reference Books, Hampshire 125
Barmby (C. & A.J.), Kent 140
Barn Books, Buckinghamshire 61
Bianco Library, West Sussex 237
Books, Kent 137
Clark (Nigel A.), London SE 162
Collectors Corner, Wiltshire 248
Cornucopia Books, Lincolnshire 151
Don Kelly Books, London W 170
Embleton (Paul), Essex 111
Forest Books of Manchester, Cheshire 70
Hanshan Tang Books, London SW 166
Heneage Art Books (Thomas), London SW 166
Hollett and Son (R.F.G.), Cumbria 79
Ives Bookseller (John), London Outer 181
John R. Hoggarth, North Yorkshire 194
Junk & Spread Eagle, London SE 162
King Street Bookshop (The), Norfolk 185
Nostalgia Unlimited, Merseyside 182
R. & A. Books, East Sussex 100
Restormel Books, Worcestershire 252
Thin Read Line, Merseyside 182
Trinders' Fine Tools, Suffolk 222
Watkins (R.G.), Somerset 213
Westwood Books Ltd, Cumbria 79

COLONIAL
Afar Books International, West Midlands 234
Caliver Books, Essex 110
Collectables (W.H.), Suffolk 225
Eggeling Books (John), West Yorkshire 245
G. Bickford-Smith (formerly Snowden Smith Books), Surrey 228
G. C. Books Ltd., Dumfries & Galloway 264
Kenny's Bookshops and Art Galleries Ltd, Co. Galway 260

Maghreb Bookshop (The), London WC 175
Mandalay Bookshop, London SW 166
Pennymead Books, North Yorkshire 191
Price (R.D.M. & I.M.) (Books), Greater Manchester 120
Winghale Books, Lincolnshire 151
Woolcott Books, Dorset 91

COLOUR-PLATE
Artco, Nottinghamshire 201
Aurelian Books, London NW 158
Bianco Library, West Sussex 237
Biblion, London W 169
Black Cat Books, Norfolk 185
Bolton Books, Hampshire 122
Bowden Books, Leicestershire 147
Chas J. Sawyer, Kent 140
Corvus Books, Buckinghamshire 61
Eastcote Bookshop (The), London Outer 178
Fine Art, London SE 165
Goodyer (Nicholas), London N 156
Grayling (David A.H.), Cumbria 78
Halson Books, Cheshire 71
Harrington (Adrian), London W 171
Harrington Antiquarian Bookseller (Peter), London SW 166
Hodgkins and Company Limited (Ian), Gloucestershire 116
Hodgson (Books) (Richard J.), North Yorkshire 194
Hollett and Son (R.F.G.), Cumbria 79
Lake (David), Norfolk 187
Lymelight Books & Prints, Dorset 92
Marlborough Rare Books Ltd., London W 171
Marshall Rare Books (Bruce), Gloucestershire . 113
Maynard & Bradley, Leicestershire 146
Moorhead Books, West Yorkshire 241
Old Cathay Fine Books, West Yorkshire 244
Preston Book Company, Lancashire 144
R. & A. Books, East Sussex 100
Remington (Reg & Philip), Hertfordshire 132
Roz Hulse, Conwy 278
Sephton (A.F.), London W 172
Shapero Rare Books (Bernard J.), London W . 172
Temperley (David), West Midlands 234

COMEDY
Books Only, Suffolk 222
Facet Books, Dorset 90
firstpagebooks, Norfolk 187
Goldman (Paul), Dorset 94
Greenroom Books, West Yorkshire 243
Price (R.W.), Nottinghamshire 200
R. & A. Books, East Sussex 100
Sarawak Books, East Yorkshire 105

COMIC BOOKS & ANNUALS
Abrahams (Mike), Staffordshire 219
Beck (John), East Sussex 102
Black Cat Bookshop, Leicestershire 145

SPECIALITY INDEX

Bookmark (Children's Books), Wiltshire 248
Books & Collectables Ltd., Cambridgeshire 63
Border Bookshop, West Yorkshire 245
Camilla's Bookshop, East Sussex 100
Cheshire Book Centre, Cheshire 69
Cranhurst Books, London NW 158
Cygnet Books, East Yorkshire 107
D. & M. Books, West Yorkshire 244
Dawlish Books, Devon.............................. 84
Facet Books, Dorset................................ 90
Fifteenth Century Bookshop (The), East Sussex 102
firstpagebooks, Norfolk............................ 187
Franks Booksellers, Greater Manchester 119
Intech Books, Northumberland 198
K Books, Cheshire.................................. 69
Keel Row Books, Tyne and Wear 231
Key Books (Sarah), Cambridgeshire 64
Longden (George), Cheshire 69
Murphy (C.J.), Norfolk 187
Nostalgia Unlimited, Merseyside.................. 182
Old Celtic Bookshop (The), Devon............... 86
Pyecroft (Ruth), Gloucestershire 116
R. & A. Books, East Sussex 100
Savage (Keith A.), Suffolk 224
Scrivener's Books & Bookbinding, Derbyshire . 81
Sesemann (Julia), Kent............................. 136
Till's Bookshop, Lothian 272
Tilleys Vintage Magazine Shop, Derbyshire 81
Tilleys Vintage Magazine Shop, South
    Yorkshire 218
Towers (Mark), Lancashire 143
Wright (Norman), Hertfordshire.................. 133
Yesterday's News, Conwy 278
Yorkshire Relics, West Yorkshire................. 242

COMICS
Ardis Books, Hampshire........................... 126
Beck (John), East Sussex 102
Black Cat Bookshop, Leicestershire 145
Book Palace (The), London SE 161
Books & Collectables Ltd., Cambridgeshire 63
Bookshop (The), Norfolk.......................... 189
Border Bookshop, West Yorkshire 245
Capel Mawr Collectors Centre, Gwynedd....... 280
Collectables (W.H.), Suffolk 225
D. & M. Books, West Yorkshire 244
Facet Books, Dorset................................ 90
Janian Comics / Computer Manuals,
    Buckinghamshire 62
Ken's Paper Collectables, Buckinghamshire 62
Longden (George), Cheshire 69
McGee (Terence J.), London Outer 178
Nostalgia Unlimited, Merseyside.................. 182
Pyecroft (Ruth), Gloucestershire 116
Savage (Keith A.), Suffolk 224
The Old Children's Bookshelf, Lothian.......... 272
Tilleys Vintage Magazine Shop, South
    Yorkshire 218
Towers (Mark), Lancashire 143
Wright (Norman), Hertfordshire.................. 133
Yesterday's News, Conwy 278

Yorkshire Relics, West Yorkshire................. 242

COMMERCE
- GENERAL
Ardis Books, Hampshire........................... 126
Cornucopia Books, Lincolnshire 151

COMMUNICATION
Apocalypse, Surrey 228
Cornucopia Books, Lincolnshire 151

COMMUNISM
G. C. Books Ltd., Dumfries & Galloway 264
PsychoBabel Books & Journals, Oxfordshire ... 202
Reading Lasses, Dumfries & Galloway 265
Samovar Books, Co. Dublin 258

COMPANY HISTORY
Bott, (Bookdealers) Ltd., (Martin), Greater
    Manchester 118
Byrom Textile Bookroom (Richard),
    Lancashire 142
Camden Books, Somerset 212
Cheshire Book Centre, Cheshire 69
Crosby Nethercott Books, London Outer....... 178
Delph Books, Greater Manchester................ 120
Handsworth Books, Essex......................... 112
Kellow Books, Oxfordshire 203
R. & A. Books, East Sussex 100
Roadmaster Books, Kent.......................... 137
Rochdale Book Company, Greater Manchester 120
Roland Books, Kent............................... 139
Salway Books, Essex 112
Spurrier (Nick), Kent.............................. 138
Whistler's Books, London SW 167

COMPUTING
Apocalypse, Surrey 228
Ardis Books, Hampshire........................... 126
Beware of the Leopard, Bristol.................... 58
Cornucopia Books, Lincolnshire 151
Downie Fine Books Ltd., (Robert), Shropshire 211
Game Advice, Oxfordshire 205
Janian Comics / Computer Manuals,
    Buckinghamshire 62
Old Celtic Bookshop (The), Devon............... 86
Plurabelle Books, Cambridgeshire 64
R. & A. Books, East Sussex 100
Roland Books, Kent............................... 139
Roscrea Bookshop, Co. Tipperary................ 261
Skoob Russell Square, Suffolk.................... 225
Stern Antiquarian Bookseller (Jeffrey), North
    Yorkshire 195

CONSERVATION
Acer Books, Herefordshire 128
Arden, Bookseller (C.), Powys 282
Aurelian Books, London NW 158
Coch-y-Bonddu Books, Powys 285

SPECIALITY INDEX

Demar Books (Grant), Kent 140
Heneage Art Books (Thomas), London SW.... 166
Newgate Books and Translations,
  Northumberland 198
Roadmaster Books, Kent 137
Trinders' Fine Tools, Suffolk 222

CONSPIRACY
Apocalypse, Surrey 228
Gildas Books, Cheshire 68

COOKERY - PROFESSIONAL
Bookroom (The), Surrey 229
Books & Bygones, Berkshire 57
Castleton (Pat), Kent 137
Marcet Books, London SE 161
Oopalba Books, Cheshire 71
R & B Graham Trading, Cornwall 73

COOKERY/GASTRONOMY
Abacus Gallery, Staffordshire 220
Abrahams (Mike), Staffordshire 219
Al Saqi Books, London W 169
Apocalypse, Surrey 228
Autumn Leaves, Lincolnshire 150
Axe Rare & Out of Print Books (Richard),
  North Yorkshire 190
Bacon (Josephine), London WC 174
Black Cat Books, Norfolk 185
Books, Oxfordshire 202
Books & Bygones, Berkshire 57
Books & Collectables Ltd., Cambridgeshire 63
Books (For All), North Yorkshire 190
Books for Content, Herefordshire 128
Books Only, Suffolk 222
Books Plus, Devon 83
Bookworld, Shropshire 210
Booth Books, Powys 282
Brown-Studies, Strathclyde 273
Capel Mawr Collectors Centre, Gwynedd 280
Chandos Books, Devon 84
Chantrey Books, South Yorkshire 217
Clarke (Janet), Somerset 212
Cooks Books, East Sussex 98
D'Arcy Books, Wiltshire 246
Dales & Lakes Book Centre, Cumbria 79
Dusty Books, Powys 285
Elmfield Books, West Midlands 234
Esoteric Dreams Bookshop, Cumbria 77
Fiona Edwards, Nottinghamshire 200
Firth (Bijou Books & Photography) (Maureen),
  South Yorkshire 218
Fox Books (J. & J.), Kent 140
Garwood & Voigt, Kent 140
Glenwood Books, Surrey 230
Good for Books, Lincolnshire 149
Grahame Thornton, Bookseller, Dorset 92
Gresham Books, Somerset 214
Harrington (Adrian), London W 171
Harvest Books, Lancashire 144

Hay Cinema Bookshop Ltd., Herefordshire 283
Internet Bookshop UK Ltd., Gloucestershire .. 113
Invicta Bookshop, Berkshire 56
Island Books, Kent 136
Lamb's Tales Books, Devon 85
Lucas (Richard), London NW 159
Maynard & Bradley, Leicestershire 146
Mellon's Books, East Sussex 100
Modlock (Lilian), Dorset 92
Moorhead Books, West Yorkshire 241
Much Ado Books, East Sussex 98
Oopalba Books, Cheshire 71
Parrott Books, Oxfordshire 207
Pholiota Books, London WC 176
Price (John), London N 157
Quaritch Ltd., (Bernard), London W 172
Queen Victoria PH, Torfaen 287
R & B Graham Trading, Cornwall 73
R. & A. Books, East Sussex 100
Rainford (Sheila), Hertfordshire 130
River Reads Bookshop, Devon 89
Scrivener's Books & Bookbinding, Derbyshire. 81
Seeber (Liz), East Sussex 99
Sleepy Elephant Books & Artefacts, Cumbria.. 79
Smith (Clive), Essex 109
Talisman Books, Cheshire 70
Tant Yn Ellen Books, Powys 286
Tilston (Stephen E.), London SE 161
Trinity Rare Books, Co. Leitrim 260
Wadard Books, Kent 137
Whitchurch Books Ltd., Cardiff 276
Williams (Christopher), Dorset 93
Wychwood Books, Gloucestershire 116

COSMOLOGY
Apocalypse, Surrey 228

COUNSELLING
Oast Books, Kent 137
Reading Lasses, Dumfries & Galloway 265
Savery Books, East Sussex 99

COUNTERCULTURE
Atlas, London N 155
Black Cat Bookshop, Leicestershire 145
Capel Mawr Collectors Centre, Gwynedd 280
Church Street Books, Norfolk 184
Fifth Element, West Midlands 235
Gildas Books, Cheshire 68
Invisible Books, East Sussex 98
McGee (Terence J.), London Outer 178
Poetry Bookshop (The), Powys 284
Sclanders (Beatbooks), (Andrew), London EC. 154

COUNTRIES & REGIONS
   - GENERAL
Aurora Books Ltd, Lothian 270
Good for Books, Lincolnshire 149
Naughton Booksellers, Co. Dublin 259

SPECIALITY INDEX

- AFGANISTAN
Bates & Hindmarch, West Yorkshire 243
Daly (Peter M.), Hampshire 127
David Warnes Books, Herefordshire 129
Traveller's Bookshelf (The), Somerset............ 212
Verandah Books, Dorset 94

- AFRICA
Afar Books International, West Midlands 234
Apocalypse, Surrey 228
Ayre (Peter J.), Somerset 216
Bonham (J. & S.L.), London W 169
Bracton Books, Cambridgeshire................... 63
Chalmers Hallam (E.), Hampshire................ 125
Chapter Two, London SE.......................... 161
Chas J. Sawyer, Kent 140
Daly (Peter M.), Hampshire 127
Folios Limited, London SW 165
G. C. Books Ltd., Dumfries & Galloway 264
Halewood & Sons, Lancashire..................... 144
Hall, (Anthony C.) Antiquarian Bookseller,
   London Outer 181
Heritage Books, Isle of Wight 134
Kenny's Bookshops and Art Galleries Ltd,
   Co. Galway 260
Kenya Books, East Sussex 99
Lawson & Company (E.M.), Oxfordshire....... 203
Marble Hill Books, Middlesex..................... 181
Michael Graves-Johnston, London SW.......... 166
Oopalba Books, Cheshire........................... 71
Oriental and African Books, Shropshire......... 210
Popeley (Frank T.), Cambridgeshire............... 67
Probsthain (Arthur), London WC 176
Roland Books, Kent................................. 139
Woolcott Books, Dorset 91
Yesterday's Books, Dorset 91

- ALASKA
David Warnes Books, Herefordshire 129

- ALBANIA
de Visser Books, Cambridgeshire 63
Dworski Books, Travel & Language Bookshop
   (Marijana), Herefordshire 283
Traveller's Bookshelf (The), Somerset............ 212

- ALGERIA
Apocalypse, Surrey 228

- AMERICAS, THE
Americanabooksuk, Cumbria...................... 76
Bracton Books, Cambridgeshire................... 63
Halewood & Sons, Lancashire..................... 144
Lawson & Company (E.M.), Oxfordshire....... 203

- ANDORRA
Books on Spain, London Outer 181
Orssich (Paul), London SW 167

- ANTARCTIC, THE
Bluntisham Books, Cambridgeshire 63
Explorer Books, West Sussex 239
Glacier Books, Tayside............................. 275
Libris (Weston) Books, Somerset 213
Marble Hill Books, Middlesex..................... 181
McEwan Fine Books, Grampian................... 266
Prospect House Books, Co. Down 256

- ARABIA
Apocalypse, Surrey 228
Daly (Peter M.), Hampshire 127
David Warnes Books, Herefordshire 129
Folios Limited, London SW 165
Kenny's Bookshops and Art Galleries Ltd,
   Co. Galway 260
Quest Books, East Yorkshire 106
Traveller's Bookshelf (The), Somerset............ 212

- ARCTIC, THE
Bluntisham Books, Cambridgeshire 63
Explorer Books, West Sussex 239
Prospect House Books, Co. Down 256

- ARMENIA
David Warnes Books, Herefordshire 129
Traveller's Bookshelf (The), Somerset............ 212

- ASIA
Bates & Hindmarch, West Yorkshire 243
Bracton Books, Cambridgeshire................... 63
Chapter Two, London SE.......................... 161
David Warnes Books, Herefordshire 129
Fine Books Oriental Ltd., London WC 175
Hall, (Anthony C.) Antiquarian Bookseller,
   London Outer 181
Kenny's Bookshops and Art Galleries Ltd,
   Co. Galway 260
Rayner (Hugh Ashley), Somerset 212

- ASIA MINOR
Quest Books, East Yorkshire 106
Traveller's Bookshelf (The), Somerset............ 212

- AUSTRALASIA
Eggeling Books (John), West Yorkshire.......... 245
Lawson & Company (E.M.), Oxfordshire....... 203

- AUSTRALIA
Bonham (J. & S.L.), London W 169
Halewood & Sons, Lancashire..................... 144
Moore (Peter), Cambridgeshire.................... 64

- AUSTRIA
de Visser Books, Cambridgeshire 63
Dworski Books, Travel & Language Bookshop
   (Marijana), Herefordshire 283

SPECIALITY INDEX

- BALKANS, THE
David Warnes Books, Herefordshire 129
de Visser Books, Cambridgeshire 63
Dworski Books, Travel & Language Bookshop
  (Marijana), Herefordshire 283
Kenny's Bookshops and Art Galleries Ltd, Co.
  Galway 260
Quest Books, East Yorkshire 106
Traveller's Bookshelf (The), Somerset............ 212

- BALTIC STATES
Baldwin (Jack), Strathclyde 273
de Visser Books, Cambridgeshire 63
Dworski Books, Travel & Language Bookshop
  (Marijana), Herefordshire 283
MK Book Services, Cambridgeshire.............. 66

- BERMUDA
Pennymead Books, North Yorkshire............. 191

- BRITISH NORTH BORNEO
Sarawak Books, East Yorkshire................... 105

- BURMA
Mandalay Bookshop, London SW 166
Rayner (Hugh Ashley), Somerset 212
Verandah Books, Dorset 94

- CANADA
Glacier Books, Tayside............................. 275

- CARIBBEAN, THE
Afar Books International, West Midlands 234
Burton–Garbett (A.), London Outer 180
Leapman Ltd. (G. & R.), Hertfordshire 132
Naughton Booksellers, Co. Dublin 259
Norton Books, North Yorkshire................... 194
Pennymead Books, North Yorkshire............. 191

- CENTRAL AMERICA
Books on Spain, London Outer................... 181
Burton–Garbett (A.), London Outer 180
Orssich (Paul), London SW 167

- CENTRAL ASIA
Al Saqi Books, London W......................... 169
Bates & Hindmarch, West Yorkshire 243
Daly (Peter M.), Hampshire 127
David Warnes Books, Herefordshire............. 129
Hanshan Tang Books, London SW 166
Rayner (Hugh Ashley), Somerset 212
Riddell (Peter), East Yorkshire 105
Traveller's Bookshelf (The), Somerset............ 212

- CHANNEL ISLANDS, THE
Cornucopia Books, Lincolnshire 151

- CHINA
Bow Windows Book Shop, East Sussex 102
Hanshan Tang Books, London SW 166
Hobgoblin Books, Hampshire..................... 125
Kenny's Bookshops and Art Galleries Ltd,
  Co. Galway 260
Mandalay Bookshop, London SW 166
Skoob Russell Square, Suffolk.................... 225
Traveller's Bookshelf (The), Somerset............ 212

- CUBA
Books on Spain, London Outer................... 181
Naughton Booksellers, Co. Dublin 259
Pennymead Books, North Yorkshire............. 191

- CYPRUS
Antique Prints of the World, London N 155
Askew Books (Vernon), Wiltshire 246
Crouch Rare Books, Surrey....................... 227
Hellenic Bookservices, London NW.............. 158
Nicolas - Antiquarian Booksellers & Art
  Dealers, London N 156
Quest Books, East Yorkshire 106

- DOMINICAN REPUBLIC
Pennymead Books, North Yorkshire............. 191

- EAST AFRICA
Samovar Books, Co. Dublin....................... 258

- EAST EUROPE
Apocalypse, Surrey 228
de Visser Books, Cambridgeshire 63
Dworski Books, Travel & Language Bookshop
  (Marijana), Herefordshire 283
Hab Books, London W............................ 171
Hall, (Anthony C.) Antiquarian Bookseller,
  London Outer 181
Orbis Books (London) Ltd., London W 171

- EGYPT
Afar Books International, West Midlands 234
Atlantis Bookshop, London WC.................. 174
Quest Books, East Yorkshire 106
Samovar Books, Co. Dublin....................... 258

- ENGLAND
Broadwater Books, Hampshire 126
Cornell Books, Gloucestershire 117
Cornucopia Books, Lincolnshire 151
Gildas Books, Cheshire 68
Island Books, Kent 136
Missing Books, Essex 109
Naughton Booksellers, Co. Dublin 259
Samovar Books, Co. Dublin....................... 258

- ETHIOPIA
Traveller's Bookshelf (The), Somerset............ 212

SPECIALITY INDEX

- EUROPE
Dworski Books, Travel & Language Bookshop
  (Marijana), Herefordshire 283
Kenny's Bookshops and Art Galleries Ltd, Co.
  Galway 260
Naughton Booksellers, Co. Dublin 259
owenbooks65, Conwy 278
Prospect House Books, Co. Down 256
Shapero Rare Books (Bernard J.), London W . 172

- FALKLANDS, THE
Miles Apart, Suffolk 224

- FAR EAST, THE
Daly (Peter M.), Hampshire 127
Marble Hill Books, Middlesex 181
Oxley (Laurence), Hampshire 122
Robert G Sawers Ltd, London NW 159
Traveller's Bookshelf (The), Somerset 212

- FRANCE
Colwyn Books, Conwy 277
Glacier Books, Tayside 275
Kenya Books, East Sussex 99
owenbooks65, Conwy 278
Roscrea Bookshop, Co. Tipperary 261

- GERMANY
de Visser Books, Cambridgeshire 63
Helion & Company, West Midlands 235
Lee Jackson, London NW 159

- GIBRALTAR
Books on Spain, London Outer 181
Orssich (Paul), London SW 167

- GREAT BRITAIN
G. C. Books Ltd., Dumfries & Galloway 264
Orb's Bookshop, Grampian 268
Oopalba Books, Cheshire 71
Samovar Books, Co. Dublin 258
Shakeshaft (Dr. B.), Cheshire 71

- GREECE
Antique Prints of the World, London N 155
Crouch Rare Books, Surrey 227
Hellenic Bookservices, London NW 158
Kalligraphia (formerly Charmouth Bounty
  Books), Isle of Wight 134
Nicolas - Antiquarian Booksellers &
  Art Dealers, London N 156
Quest Books, East Yorkshire 106
Seydi Rare Books (Sevin), London NW 159
Traveller's Bookshelf (The), Somerset 212

- GREENLAND
Bluntisham Books, Cambridgeshire 63
Explorer Books, West Sussex 239

Glacier Books, Tayside 275

- HIMALAYAS, THE
David Warnes Books, Herefordshire 129
Glacier Books, Tayside 275
Hanshan Tang Books, London SW 166
Rayner (Hugh Ashley), Somerset 212
Traveller's Bookshelf (The), Somerset 212
Verandah Books, Dorset 94

- HUNGARY
de Visser Books, Cambridgeshire 63
Dworski Books, Travel & Language Bookshop
  (Marijana), Herefordshire 283
Parrott (Jeremy), London E 153
Traveller's Bookshelf (The), Somerset 212

- ICELAND
Glacier Books, Tayside 275

- INDIA
Bates & Hindmarch, West Yorkshire 243
Chalmers Hallam (E.), Hampshire 125
Daly (Peter M.), Hampshire 127
David Warnes Books, Herefordshire 129
Donovan Military Books (Tom),
  East Sussex 98
Fine Books Oriental Ltd., London WC 175
G. C. Books Ltd., Dumfries & Galloway 264
Kabristan Archives, Shropshire 211
Mandalay Bookshop, London SW 166
My Back Pages, London SW 167
Oxley (Laurence), Hampshire 122
Rayner (Hugh Ashley), Somerset 212
Rhodes, Bookseller (Peter), Hampshire 126
Roland Books, Kent 139
Traveller's Bookshelf (The), Somerset 212
Verandah Books, Dorset 94
Woolcott Books, Dorset 91

- INDIAN OCEAN, THE
Kenya Books, East Sussex 99

- IRAN
David Warnes Books, Herefordshire 129
Quest Books, East Yorkshire 106
Traveller's Bookshelf (The), Somerset 212

- IRELAND
Abbey Books, Cornwall 73
Apocalypse, Surrey 228
Armchair Books, Lothian 270
Bell Gallery (The), Co. Antrim 255
Celtic Bookshop (The), Co. Limerick 261
Darkwood Books, Co. Cork 258
De Burca Rare Books, Co. Dublin 259
Delectus Books, London WC 174
Foyle Books, Co. Derry 255
Greene's Bookshop Ltd, Co. Dublin 259

Hyland (C.P.), Co. Cork............................ 258
Kabristan Archives, Shropshire 211
Karen Millward, Co. Cork......................... 257
Kenny's Bookshops and Art Galleries Ltd,
   Co. Galway 260
Kenya Books, East Sussex 99
Kernaghans, Merseyside 183
Michael J Carroll, Co. Cork 257
Naughton Booksellers, Co. Dublin 259
Prospect House Books, Co. Down 256
Read Ireland, Co. Dublin 258
Roscrea Bookshop, Co. Tipperary................ 261
Samovar Books, Co. Dublin 258
Skelton (Tony), Kent............................... 141
Taney Books, Co. Dublin 259
Whelan (P. & F.), Kent............................ 141

- ISLE OF MAN
Garretts Antiquarian Books, Isle of Man 254
Mulyan (Don), Merseyside 183

- ISLE OF WIGHT
Apocalypse, Surrey 228
Heritage Books, Isle of Wight 134

- ISRAEL
Samovar Books, Co. Dublin 258

- ITALY
Apocalypse, Surrey 228
Campbell (Fiona), London SE 161
Glacier Books, Tayside............................. 275
McGee (Terence J.), London Outer 178
Seydi Rare Books (Sevin), London NW......... 159

- JAPAN
Bow Windows Book Shop, East Sussex 102
Burebank Books, Norfolk 184
Fine Books Oriental Ltd., London WC 175
Hanshan Tang Books, London SW 166
Hobgoblin Books, Hampshire 125
Orb's Bookshop, Grampian....................... 268
Robert G Sawers Ltd, London NW 159
Traveller's Bookshelf (The), Somerset............ 212

- KENYA
Ayre (Peter J.), Somerset 216
Daly (Peter M.), Hampshire 127
Kenya Books, East Sussex 99
Popeley (Frank T.), Cambridgeshire.............. 67

- KOREA
Hanshan Tang Books, London SW 166
Traveller's Bookshelf (The), Somerset............ 212

- LATIN AMERICA
Books on Spain, London Outer................... 181
Delectus Books, London WC...................... 174

Hodgson (Judith), London W 171
Marble Hill Books, Middlesex.................... 181

- MADEIRA
Chas J. Sawyer, Kent 140

- MALAYSIA
Beardsley (A.E.), Nottinghamshire................ 201
Traveller's Bookshelf (The), Somerset............ 212

- MALTA
Nicolas - Antiquarian Booksellers & Art
   Dealers, London N 156

- MAURITIUS
Chas J. Sawyer, Kent 140

- MELANESIA
Black Cat Bookshop, Leicestershire 145
Books, Denbighshire................................ 278
Bracton Books, Cambridgeshire................... 63
Broadwater Books, Hampshire.................... 126
Modern First Editions, London Outer........... 180
Wayside Books and Cards, Oxfordshire 203

- MEXICO
Baldwin (Jack), Strathclyde 273
Bardsley's Books, Suffolk 221
Black Cat Bookshop, Leicestershire 145
Books on Spain, London Outer................... 181
Booth Books, Powys 282
Burton–Garbett (A.), London Outer 180
Delectus Books, London WC...................... 174
Modern First Editions, London Outer........... 180
Orssich (Paul), London SW....................... 167

- MIDDLE EAST, THE
David Warnes Books, Herefordshire 129
Delectus Books, London WC...................... 174
Fishburn Books, London NW..................... 158
Hall, (Anthony C.) Antiquarian Bookseller,
   London Outer 181
Joppa Books Ltd., Surrey 226
Maghreb Bookshop (The), London WC 175
Oriental and African Books, Shropshire......... 210
Traveller's Bookshelf (The), Somerset............ 212
Trotter Books (John), London N 157

- MONGOLIA
Traveller's Bookshelf (The), Somerset............ 212

- MOROCCO
Books on Spain, London Outer................... 181
Orssich (Paul), London SW....................... 167
Traveller's Bookshelf (The), Somerset............ 212

SPECIALITY INDEX

- NEAR EAST, THE
Marble Hill Books, Middlesex 181
Traveller's Bookshelf (The), Somerset 212

- NEPAL
David Warnes Books, Herefordshire 129
Glacier Books, Tayside 275
Little Bookshop (The), Cumbria 80
Traveller's Bookshelf (The), Somerset 212
Verandah Books, Dorset 94

- NORTH AFRICA
Maghreb Bookshop (The), London WC 175

- NORTH WEST FRONTIER PROVINCE
David Warnes Books, Herefordshire 129

- NORWAY
Apocalypse, Surrey 228
Glacier Books, Tayside 275
Mulyan (Don), Merseyside 183

- PACIFIC, THE
Moore (Peter), Cambridgeshire 64

- PAKISTAN
Glacier Books, Tayside 275
Traveller's Bookshelf (The), Somerset 212
Verandah Books, Dorset 94

- PALESTINE
Samovar Books, Co. Dublin 258
Traveller's Bookshelf (The), Somerset 212

- PAPUA NEW GUINEA
Moore (Peter), Cambridgeshire 64
Traveller's Bookshelf (The), Somerset 212

- PHILIPPINES, THE
Traveller's Bookshelf (The), Somerset 212

- POLAND
Bardsley's Books, Suffolk 221
Caledonia Books, Strathclyde 273
de Visser Books, Cambridgeshire 63
Orbis Books (London) Ltd., London W 171

- POLAR
Bluntisham Books, Cambridgeshire 63
Bonham (J. & S.L.), London W 169
Explorer Books, West Sussex 239
Glacier Books, Tayside 275
McEwan Fine Books, Grampian 266
Riddell (Peter), East Yorkshire 105
Signature Books, Hampshire 126

- POLYNESIA
Bracton Books, Cambridgeshire 63

- PORTUGAL
Baldwin (Jack), Strathclyde 273
Books on Spain, London Outer 181
Hodgson (Judith), London W 171
Orssich (Paul), London SW 167

- PUERTO RICO
Orssich (Paul), London SW 167
Pennymead Books, North
   Yorkshire 191

- PYRENEES, THE
Glacier Books, Tayside 275

- ROMANIA
de Visser Books, Cambridgeshire 63
Dworski Books, Travel & Language
   Bookshop (Marijana), Herefordshire 283
Traveller's Bookshelf (The), Somerset 212

- RUSSIA
Baldwin (Jack), Strathclyde 273
de Visser Books, Cambridgeshire 63
Dworski Books, Travel & Language Bookshop
   (Marijana), Herefordshire 283
Hab Books, London W 171
Hall, (Anthony C.) Antiquarian Bookseller,
   London Outer 181
Kenny's Bookshops and Art Galleries Ltd, Co.
   Galway 260
Orb's Bookshop, Grampian 268
Orbis Books (London) Ltd., London W 171
Traveller's Bookshelf (The), Somerset 212

- SAHARA, THE
Apocalypse, Surrey 228

- SARAWAK
Sarawak Books, East Yorkshire 105
Traveller's Bookshelf (The), Somerset 212

- SCOTLAND
Alba Books, Grampian 267
Armchair Books, Lothian 270
Benny Gillies Books Ltd, Dumfries
   & Galloway 263
Border Books, Borders 262
Bridge of Allan Books, Central 263
Broadwater Books, Hampshire 126
Byre Books, Dumfries & Galloway 264
Clifford Milne Books, Grampian 266
Colonsay Bookshop, Isle of Colonsay 269
Cooper Hay Rare Books, Strathclyde 273
Cornell Books, Gloucestershire 117
Cornucopia Books, Lincolnshire 151

SPECIALITY INDEX

Creaking Shelves, Highland 268
David Houston - Bookseller, London E 153
Farquharson, (Hilary), Tayside 275
G. C. Books Ltd., Dumfries & Galloway 264
Glacier Books, Tayside 275
Grampian Books, Grampian 268
Greta Books, Durham 96
Holmes Books (Harry), East Yorkshire 106
Hughes Rare Books (Spike), Borders 262
Hutchison (Books) (Larry), Fife 265
Iona Bookshop (The), Isle of Iona 269
Leakey's Bookshop, Highland 268
Loch Croispol Bookshop & Restaurant,
  Highland 268
Oopalba Books, Cheshire 71
Orb's Bookshop, Grampian 268
Prospect House Books, Co. Down 256
Quarto Bookshop (The), Fife 266
Samovar Books, Co. Dublin 258
Stroma Books, Borders 262
Wilson (David), Buckinghamshire 61

- SEYCHELLES, THE
Chas J. Sawyer, Kent 140

- SIAM
Pennymead Books, North Yorkshire 191
Traveller's Bookshelf (The), Somerset 212

- SIBERIA
Orb's Bookshop, Grampian 268

- SOUTH AFRICA
Boer War Books, North Yorkshire 194
Chas J. Sawyer, Kent 140
Kenya Books, East Sussex 99
Samovar Books, Co. Dublin 258
Smith (Ray), Hertfordshire 130

- SOUTH AMERICA
Baldwin (Jack), Strathclyde 273
Books on Spain, London Outer 181
Burton–Garbett (A.), London Outer 180
Hünersdorff Rare Books, London SW 166
Orssich (Paul), London SW 167
Prescott - The Bookseller (John),
  London Outer 181

- SOUTH ATLANTIC ISLANDS
Miles Apart, Suffolk 224
MK Book Services, Cambridgeshire 66

- SOUTH EAST ASIA
David Warnes Books, Herefordshire 129
Hanshan Tang Books, London SW 166
Mandalay Bookshop, London SW 166
Traveller's Bookshelf (The), Somerset 212
Verandah Books, Dorset 94

- SPAIN
Baldwin (Jack), Strathclyde 273
Bass (Ben), Wiltshire 246
Books on Spain, London Outer 181
Hodgson (Judith), London W 171
Orssich (Paul), London SW 167
York (Graham), Devon 85

- SRI LANKA
Rayner (Hugh Ashley), Somerset 212
Verandah Books, Dorset 94

- STRAITS SETTLEMENTS, THE
Traveller's Bookshelf (The), Somerset 212

- SUDAN, THE
Michael Graves-Johnston, London SW 166
Traveller's Bookshelf (The), Somerset 212

- SWITZERLAND
Glacier Books, Tayside 275

- TANZANIA
Ayre (Peter J.), Somerset 216
Kenya Books, East Sussex 99
Popeley (Frank T.), Cambridgeshire 67

- TIBET
Bates & Hindmarch, West Yorkshire 243
Daly (Peter M.), Hampshire 127
David Warnes Books, Herefordshire 129
Glacier Books, Tayside 275
Hanshan Tang Books, London SW 166
Traveller's Bookshelf (The), Somerset 212

- TURKEY
Dworski Books, Travel & Language Bookshop
  (Marijana), Herefordshire 283
Nicolas - Antiquarian Booksellers &
  Art Dealers, London N 156
Quest Books, East Yorkshire 106
Seydi Rare Books (Sevin), London NW 159
Traveller's Bookshelf (The), Somerset 212

- U.S.A.
Americanabooksuk, Cumbria 76
Glacier Books, Tayside 275
Marble Hill Books, Middlesex 181
Roland Books, Kent 139
Shakeshaft (Dr. B.), Cheshire 71

- UGANDA
Kenya Books, East Sussex 99
Popeley (Frank T.), Cambridgeshire 67

- VIETNAM
Traveller's Bookshelf (The), Somerset 212

SPECIALITY INDEX

- WALES
Capital Bookshop, Cardiff 276
Carningli Centre, Pembrokeshire 281
Castle Bookshop, Powys............................ 285
Colin Hancock, Ceredigion 277
Cornell Books, Gloucestershire.................... 117
Dworski Books, Travel & Language
  Bookshop (Marijana), Herefordshire 283
Dylans Bookstore, Glamorgan 286
Gildas Books, Cheshire 68
Glacier Books, Tayside.............................. 275
Great Oak Bookshop (The), Powys 285
Island Books, Kent 136
Modern Welsh Publications Ltd.,
  Merseyside... 182
Siop Lyfrau'r Hen Bost, Gwynedd 280
Stella Books, Monmouthshire 281
Thomas (E. Wyn), Conwy 278
Whitchurch Books Ltd., Cardiff 276
Ystwyth Books, Ceredigion 277

- WEST AFRICA
Oopalba Books, Cheshire........................... 71

- WEST INDIES, THE
Pennymead Books, North Yorkshire............. 191

COUNTRY HOUSES
Apocalypse, Surrey 228
Art Reference Books, Hampshire 125
Cornucopia Books, Lincolnshire 151
Dales & Lakes Book Centre, Cumbria 79
Hadley Bookseller (Peter J.), Essex 110
Lighthouse Books (The), Dorset 91
Marlborough Rare Books Ltd., London W 171
Old Town Bookshop (The), Lothian.............. 271
Spenceley Books (David), West Yorkshire 244
Staniland (Booksellers), Lincolnshire............. 152
Trinity Rare Books, Co. Leitrim.................. 260

COUNTY - LOCAL
Benny Gillies Books Ltd, Dumfries
  & Galloway 263
Bury Bookshop, Suffolk 221
Delph Books, Greater Manchester................ 120
Roger Collicott Books, Cornwall 74
Roundstone Books, Lancashire 143

COURTESY
Black Cat Books, Norfolk.......................... 185
Weininger Antiquarian Books (Eva M.),
  London NW 160

COWBOYS
Americanabooksuk, Cumbria....................... 76

CRAFTS
Abacus Books, Greater Manchester............... 118

Andrew Morton (Books), Powys.................. 281
Apocalypse, Surrey 228
Arden Books & Cosmographia, Warwickshire . 232
Baldwin (M. & M.), Shropshire................... 250
Barn Books, Buckinghamshire..................... 61
Books for Content, Herefordshire 128
Bookworld, Shropshire............................. 210
Bosco Books, Cornwall 72
Browse Books, Lancashire 143
Cavern Books, Cheshire 70
Cheshire Book Centre, Cheshire 69
Cornucopia Books, Lincolnshire 151
Cottage Books, Leicestershire..................... 145
Cover to Cover, Merseyside....................... 183
Crouch Rare Books, Surrey........................ 227
Dales & Lakes Book Centre, Cumbria 79
Design Gallery 1850-1950 (The), Kent........... 141
DPE Books, Devon................................. 86
Dusty Books, Powys................................ 285
Footrope Knots, Suffolk........................... 223
Four Shire Bookshops, Oxfordshire.............. 202
Furneaux Books (Lee), Devon 88
Grahame Thornton, Bookseller, Dorset 92
Hay Castle, Powys.................................. 283
Holdsworth Books (Bruce), East Sussex......... 103
Macbuiks, North Yorkshire........................ 190
McCrone (Audrey), Isle of Arran................. 269
N1 Books, East Sussex 103
Priestpopple Books, Northumberland............ 198
R. & A. Books, East Sussex 100
Reeves Technical Books, North Yorkshire...... 193
Roger Lucas Booksellers, Lincolnshire........... 150
Scrivener's Books & Bookbinding, Derbyshire . 81
Smith Books, (Sally), Suffolk 222
Sterling Books, Somerset 216
Stobart Davies Limited, Carmarthwnshire 276
Trinders' Fine Tools, Suffolk 222
Upper–Room Books, Somerset.................... 214
Whittle, Bookseller (Avril), Cumbria 79
Williams (Christopher), Dorset 93

CRIME (TRUE)
Abrahams (Mike), Staffordshire................... 219
Bolland Books (Leslie H.), Bedfordshire 53
Booth (Booksearch Service), (Geoff), Cheshire . 68
Bradley–Cox (Mary), Dorset...................... 90
Cavern Books, Cheshire 70
Cheshire Book Centre, Cheshire 69
Classic Crime Collections, Greater Manchester 119
Clifford Elmer Books Ltd., Cheshire 68
Crimes Ink, London E 153
Eastcote Bookshop (The), London Outer 178
Eastgate Bookshop, East Yorkshire 105
ForensicSearch, Hertfordshire 132
Garfi Books, Ceredigion 282
Hunt (Robin S.), Greater Manchester 120
John Underwood Antiquarian Books, Norfolk 186
Keel Row Books, Tyne and Wear 231
Lawful Occasions, Essex 108
Loretta Lay Books, London NW................. 159
McCaughtrie (K.A.), North Yorkshire 190

Ming Books, Dumfries & Galloway 265
Murder & Mayhem, Powys 284
Not JUST Books, Lincolnshire 148
Porter Bookshop (The), South Yorkshire 217
R. & A. Books, East Sussex 100
Roland Books, Kent 139
Roscrea Bookshop, Co. Tipperary 261
Ruebotham (Kirk), Cheshire 70
Rupert Books, Cambridgeshire 64
Simply Read Books, East Sussex 99
Starlord Books, Greater Manchester 118
Treasure Trove Books, Leicestershire 146
Undercover Books, Lincolnshire 152
Whitehall Books, East Sussex 102
Williams (Bookdealer), (Richard), Lincolnshire 152
Yesterday's News, Conwy 278
Zardoz Books, Wiltshire 249

CRIMINOLOGY
Bolland Books (Leslie H.), Bedfordshire 53
Chesters (G. & J.), Staffordshire 220
Clifford Elmer Books Ltd., Cheshire 68
Crimes Ink, London E 153
Delectus Books, London WC 174
Garfi Books, Ceredigion 282
Lawful Occasions, Essex 108
Loretta Lay Books, London NW 159
Murder & Mayhem, Powys 284
R. & A. Books, East Sussex 100
Reading Lasses, Dumfries & Galloway 265
Roscrea Bookshop, Co. Tipperary 261
Undercover Books, Lincolnshire 152
Whitehall Books, East Sussex 102

CRITICAL THEORY
Reading Lasses, Dumfries & Galloway 265

CROCHET
Byrom Textile Bookroom (Richard),
  Lancashire 142
Cover to Cover, Merseyside 183
Mansfield (Judith), West Yorkshire 245
Whittle, Bookseller (Avril), Cumbria 79

CRYPTOGRAPHY
Baldwin (M. & M.), Shropshire 250

CRYPTOZOOLOGY
Gildas Books, Cheshire 68
Inner Bookshop (The), Oxfordshire 205
SETI Books, Staffordshire 220
Wizard Books, Cambridgeshire 67

CULTS
Samovar Books, Co. Dublin 258

CULTURE
- FOREIGN
Books on Spain, London Outer 181
Dworski Books, Travel & Language Bookshop
  (Marijana), Herefordshire 283
Orssich (Paul), London SW 167
Transformer, Dumfries & Galloway 265
Wadard Books, Kent 137
Weininger Antiquarian Books (Eva M.),
  London NW 160

- NATIONAL
Colin Hancock, Ceredigion 277
De Burca Rare Books, Co. Dublin 259
Guildmaster Books, Cheshire 70
Kenny's Bookshops and Art Galleries Ltd,
  Co. Galway 260
Leakey's Bookshop, Highland 268
Orb's Bookshop, Grampian 268
Samovar Books, Co. Dublin 258
Stokes Books, Co. Dublin 259
Weininger Antiquarian Books (Eva M.),
  London NW 160

- POPULAR
Apocalypse, Surrey 228
Book Palace (The), London SE 161
Bookshop (The), Greater Manchester 119
Pyecroft (Ruth), Gloucestershire 116
R. & A. Books, East Sussex 100
Reid of Liverpool, Merseyside 182

CURIOSA
Edmund Pollinger Rare Books, London SW ... 165
Gildas Books, Cheshire 68

CURIOSITIES
Bernstein (Nicholas), London W 169
Don Kelly Books, London W 170
Dylans Bookstore, Glamorgan 286
Gildas Books, Cheshire 68
N1 Books, East Sussex 103
Philip Hopper, Essex 110
R. & A. Books, East Sussex 100

CYBERNETICS
Dylans Bookstore, Glamorgan 286

D.I.Y. (DO IT YOURSELF)
Brown-Studies, Strathclyde 273
Carningli Centre, Pembrokeshire 281
Junk & Spread Eagle, London SE 162
Larkham Books (Patricia), Gloucestershire 117
R. & A. Books, East Sussex 100
Reeves Technical Books, North Yorkshire 193
Roscrea Bookshop, Co. Tipperary 261
Stobart Davies Limited, Carmarthwnshire 276
Trinity Rare Books, Co. Leitrim 260

SPECIALITY INDEX

DANCE
Baxter - Books (Eddie), Somerset 216
Byre Books, Dumfries & Galloway 264
Dance Books Ltd, Hampshire 122
Fitzsimons (Anne), Cumbria 77
Greenroom Books, West Yorkshire 243
Paramor (C.D.), Suffolk 224
R. & A. Books, East Sussex 100

DECORATIVE ART
Amwell Book Company, London SE 154
Andromeda Books, Buckinghamshire 62
Antiques on High, Oxfordshire 204
Apocalypse, Surrey 228
Art Reference Books, Hampshire 125
Barlow (Vincent G.), Hampshire 126
Barmby (C. & A.J.), Kent 140
Books & Things, London W 169
Butts Books (Mary), Berkshire 56
Cornucopia Books, Lincolnshire 151
Cover to Cover, Merseyside 183
Don Kelly Books, London W 170
Duck (William), Hampshire 124
Foster (Stephen), London NW 158
Goodyer (Nicholas), London N 156
Hadley Bookseller (Peter J.), Essex 110
Heneage Art Books (Thomas), London SW 166
Hodgkins and Company Limited (Ian),
 Gloucestershire 116
Holdsworth Books (Bruce), East Sussex 103
Junk & Spread Eagle, London SE 162
Keswick Bookshop, Cumbria 78
N1 Books, East Sussex 103
Old Town Bookshop (The), Lothian 271
Portobello Books, London W 172
Potterton Books, North Yorkshire 194
R. & A. Books, East Sussex 100
Reference Works Ltd., Dorset 94
Saint Swithin's Illustrated & Children's Books,
 London W 172
Studio (The), Strathclyde 274
Temperley (David), West Midlands 234
Trinders' Fine Tools, Suffolk 222
Whittle, Bookseller (Avril), Cumbria 79
Worlds End Bookshop, London SW 168
Wyseby House Books, Berkshire 55

DEEP SEA DIVING
Green Ltd. (G.L.), Hertfordshire 132
Larkham Books (Patricia), Gloucestershire 117
Lewcock (John), Cambridgeshire 66
R. & A. Books, East Sussex 100
Rods Books, Devon 87
Sub Aqua Prints and Books, Hampshire 124

DESIGN
Amwell Book Company, London SE 154
Apocalypse, Surrey 228
Art Reference Books, Hampshire 125
Berry (L.J.), Kent 138

Bianco Library, West Sussex 237
Blaenavon Books, Torfaen 287
Broadleaf Books, Torfaen 287
Brock Books, North Yorkshire 190
Cover to Cover, Merseyside 183
Decorum Books, London N 155
Don Kelly Books, London W 170
Duck (William), Hampshire 124
Finch Rare Books Ltd. (Simon), London W ... 170
Inch's Books, North Yorkshire 192
Malvern Bookshop (The), Worcestershire 250
Martin - Bookseller (Colin), East Yorkshire 106
Ray Rare and Out of Print Books (Janette),
 North Yorkshire 195
Roe and Moore, London WC 176
Trinders' Fine Tools, Suffolk 222

DIARIES
Camden Books, Somerset 212
Handley (Christopher), Newcastle Upon Tyne . 183
Lawrence Books, Nottinghamshire 200
Piccadilly Rare Books, East Sussex 104
Wembdon Books, Somerset 213

DICTIONARIES
Alec–Smith Books (Alex), East Yorkshire 107
Apocalypse, Surrey 228
Askew Books (Vernon), Wiltshire 246
Bernstein (Nicholas), London W 169
Books & Bygones (Pam Taylor), West
 Midlands 236
Bookworld, Shropshire 210
Chandos Books, Devon 84
Church Street Books, Norfolk 184
Cornucopia Books, Lincolnshire 151
Delectus Books, London WC 174
Dworski Books, Travel & Language
 Bookshop (Marijana), Herefordshire 283
Hava Books, London SE 161
Jade Mountain, Hampshire 125
Murphy (C.J.), Norfolk 187
Portobello Books, London W 172
Scrivener's Books & Bookbinding, Derbyshire . 81
Thomson (Karen), Strathclyde 273
Unsworths Booksellers, London NW 160
Yates Antiquarian Books (Tony), Leicestershire 146

DINOSAURS
Baldwin's Scientific Books, Essex 112
Kalligraphia (formerly Charmouth Bounty
 Books), Isle of Wight 134

DIRECTORIES
- GENERAL
Heritage, West Midlands 234
Roger Collicott Books, Cornwall 74
Sparkes (Books) (Ray), Staffordshire 220

SPECIALITY INDEX

- BRITISH
Sparkes (Books) (Ray), Staffordshire............. 220

DISNEYANA
Book Palace (The), London SE 161
Cygnet Books, East Yorkshire 107
Fifteenth Century Bookshop (The),
  East Sussex 102
Roscrea Bookshop, Co. Tipperary................ 261

DIVINING
Magis Books, Leicestershire........................ 147
McCrone (Audrey), Isle of Arran................. 269
Wizard Books, Cambridgeshire.................... 67

DOCUMENTS - GENERAL
Collectables (W.H.), Suffolk 225
Farahar & Dupre (Clive & Sophie), Wiltshire.. 246
Ford (Richard), London W 170
Junk & Spread Eagle, London SE................. 162
Kenny's Bookshops and Art Galleries Ltd, Co.
  Galway 260
Silverman (Michael), London SE 163
Wilson (Manuscripts) Ltd., (John),
  Gloucestershire 114

DOGS
Apocalypse, Surrey 228
Bookline, Co. Down................................. 256
Castleton (Pat), Kent 137
Cat Lit, Somerset 215
Chalmers Hallam (E.), Hampshire................ 125
Coch-y-Bonddu Books, Powys 285
Countryman Books, East Yorkshire 105
Countrymans Gallery (The), Leicestershire...... 145
Doorbar (P. & D.), Gwynned 279
Evergreen Livres, Gloucestershire................ 115
Halson Books, Cheshire 71
Jane Jones Books, Grampian..................... 267
Kilgour (Sporting Books) (Ian), Leicestershire . 147
London & Sussex Antiquarian Book & Print
  Services, East Sussex.............................. 100
McInnes (P.F. & J.R.), Dorset 90
Oopalba Books, Cheshire.......................... 71
Peel (Valerie), Berkshire........................... 55
Priestpopple Books, Northumberland............ 198
Roger Collicott Books, Cornwall 74
Roland Books, Kent................................. 139
Rolfe (John), London SE........................... 162
Stella Books, Monmouthshire 281
Treasure Trove Books, Leicestershire 146
Wright Trace Books, West Midlands 235

DOLLS & DOLLS' HOUSES
Apocalypse, Surrey 228
Art Reference Books, Hampshire................. 125
Cover to Cover, Merseyside....................... 183
Oopalba Books, Cheshire.......................... 71
Roadmaster Books, Kent........................... 137

Saint Swithin's Illustrated & Children's Books,
  London W.. 172
Staffs Bookshop (The), Staffordshire............. 219
Twigg (Keith), Staffordshire....................... 219

DOMESTICITY
Reading Lasses, Dumfries & Galloway.......... 265
Susan Taylor Books, West Yorkshire............ 243

DRAMA
Apocalypse, Surrey 228
Autumn Leaves, Lincolnshire..................... 150
Bookbox, Gloucestershire 116
Brian Troath Books, London E................... 153
Brighton Books, East Sussex....................... 98
Byre Books, Dumfries & Galloway............... 264
Caledonia Books, Strathclyde..................... 273
Chaucer Head Bookshop, Warwickshire 233
Clements (R.W.), London Outer 179
Cox Rare Books (Charles), Cornwall 73
Dales & Lakes Book Centre, Cumbria 79
Forest Books of Manchester, Cheshire 70
Greenroom Books, West Yorkshire 243
Judd Books, London WC........................... 175
Junk & Spread Eagle, London SE................ 162
Kaye - Bookseller (Terence), London NW...... 159
Kenny's Bookshops and Art Galleries Ltd,
  Co. Galway 260
Mellon's Books, East Sussex...................... 100
Pordes Books Ltd., (Henry), London WC 176
RGS Books, Surrey.................................. 229
Roundstone Books, Lancashire 143
Skoob Russell Square, Suffolk.................... 225
Till's Bookshop, Lothian 272
Trinity Rare Books, Co. Leitrim.................. 260
Updike Rare Books (John), Lothian 272
Willmott Bookseller (Nicholas), Cardiff 276

DRAWING
Apocalypse, Surrey 228
Book Palace (The), London SE 161

DRUGS
Delectus Books, London WC...................... 174

DYES
N1 Books, East Sussex............................. 103

EARLY IMPRINTS
Barry McKay Rare Books, Cumbria............. 76
Dandy Lion Editions, Surrey 228
David (G.), Cambridgeshire....................... 63
Dworski Books, Travel & Language Bookshop
  (Marijana), Herefordshire 283
Edwards (Christopher), Berkshire 55
Finch Rare Books Ltd. (Simon), London W ... 170
Fine Art, London SE................................ 165
House of Figgis Ltd (The), Co. Galway......... 260
Junk & Spread Eagle, London SE................ 162

SPECIALITY INDEX

Maggs Brothers Limited, London W 171
Paralos Ltd., London WC 175
Pickering & Chatto, London W................... 172
Quaritch Ltd., (Bernard), London W 172
Schulz–Falster Rare Books (Susanne),
  London N 157
Seydi Rare Books (Sevin), London NW......... 159
Sokol Books Ltd., London W..................... 172
Treglown (Roger J.), Cheshire.................... 70
Unsworths Booksellers, London NW 160
Zardoz Books, Wiltshire............................ 249

EARTH MYSTERIES
Abrahams (Mike), Staffordshire................... 219
Chthonios Books, East Sussex..................... 101
Gildas Books, Cheshire 68
Inner Bookshop (The), Oxfordshire 205
McCrone (Audrey), Isle of Arran................. 269
Occultique, Northamptonshire..................... 196
Philip Hopper, Essex 110
Pyecroft (Ruth), Gloucestershire 116
SETI Books, Staffordshire.......................... 220
Starlord Books, Greater Manchester 118

EARTH SCIENCES
Baldwin's Scientific Books, Essex 112
Kalligraphia (formerly Charmouth Bounty
  Books), Isle of Wight.............................. 134
Roger Collicott Books, Cornwall 74

EASTER
Saint Swithin's Illustrated & Children's Books,
  London W... 172
Samovar Books, Co. Dublin....................... 258

EASTERN PHILOSOPHY
Orchid Book Distributors, Co. Clare............. 257
Portobello Books, London W 172
PsychoBabel Books & Journals, Oxfordshire ... 202

ECCLESIASTICAL HISTORY & ARCHITECTURE
Apocalypse, Surrey 228
Barbican Bookshop, North Yorkshire 194
Bardsley's Books, Suffolk........................... 221
Bell (Peter), Strathclyde 270
Bennett & Kerr Books, Oxfordshire.............. 202
Birchden Books, London E 153
Carter, (Brian), Oxfordshire....................... 203
Cheshire Book Centre, Cheshire 69
Courtney & Hoff, North Yorkshire 194
Crouch Rare Books, Surrey........................ 227
Edwards (Alan & Margaret), Kent 141
Gage Postal Books, Essex 111
Grampian Books, Grampian....................... 268
Hadley Bookseller (Peter J.), Essex 110
Hedgerow Books, South Yorkshire 217
Island Books, Kent 136
Kyrios Books, Nottinghamshire................... 200

Michael J Carroll, Co. Cork........................ 257
Moss Books, London NW 159
Olynthiacs, Shropshire 210
Pendleburys Bookshop, London N............... 156
PsychoBabel Books & Journals, Oxfordshire ... 202
Rosemary Pugh Books, Wiltshire................. 248
Saint Philip's Books, Oxfordshire................. 205
Salsus Books, Worcestershire 250
Samovar Books, Co. Dublin....................... 258
Scrivener's Books & Bookbinding, Derbyshire . 81
South Downs Book Service, West Sussex 238
Spenceley Books (David), West Yorkshire 244
Spooner & Co, Somerset 215
Staniland (Booksellers), Lincolnshire 152
Sun House Books, Kent 139
Taylor & Son (Peter), Hertfordshire.............. 132
Thornber (Peter M.), North Yorkshire 193
Turton (John), Durham............................ 97
Unsworths Booksellers, London NW 160
Whitchurch Books Ltd., Cardiff 276
Winghale Books, Lincolnshire 151

ECOLOGY
Arden, Bookseller (C.), Powys..................... 282
Baron - Scientific Book Sales (P.J.), Somerset.. 213
Brown-Studies, Strathclyde........................ 273
Cornucopia Books, Lincolnshire 151
Orb's Bookshop, Grampian........................ 268
Rosemary Pugh Books, Wiltshire................. 248
Wildside Books, Worcestershire 250
Wyseby House Books, Berkshire................. 55

ECONOMICS
Bernstein (Nicholas), London W.................. 169
Billing (Brian), Berkshire 57
Booth Books, Powys 282
Camden Books, Somerset 212
Chesters (G. & J.), Staffordshire 220
Clifton Books, Essex 111
Cornucopia Books, Lincolnshire 151
Delectus Books, London WC..................... 174
Drury Rare Books (John), Essex.................. 111
Edwards (London) Limited (Francis),
  London WC.. 175
Edwards in Hay–on–Wye (Francis),
  Herefordshire 283
Hamish Riley-Smith, Norfolk 188
Harrington Antiquarian Bookseller (Peter),
  London SW... 166
Hay Cinema Bookshop Ltd., Herefordshire 283
Herb Tandree Philosophy Books,
  Gloucestershire 116
Jarndyce Antiquarian Booksellers, London WC 175
Kenny's Bookshops and Art Galleries Ltd, Co.
  Galway.. 260
Lawson & Company (E.M.), Oxfordshire....... 203
Lee Rare Books (Rachel), Bristol 59
Maghreb Bookshop (The), London WC 175
Northern Herald Books, West Yorkshire 241
Old Cathay Fine Books, West Yorkshire 244
Pickering & Chatto, London W................... 172

Pollak (P.M.), Devon.................................. 87
PsychoBabel Books & Journals, Oxfordshire ... 202
Quaritch Ltd., (Bernard), London W 172
Rainford (Sheila), Hertfordshire................... 130
Reading Lasses, Dumfries & Galloway 265
Rowan (P. & B.), Co. Antrim 255
Schulz–Falster Rare Books (Susanne),
  London N 157
Skoob Russell Square, Suffolk...................... 225
Spurrier (Nick), Kent.................................. 138
Stern Antiquarian Bookseller (Jeffrey),
  North Yorkshire...................................... 195
Webb Books (John), South Yorkshire 217
Wetherell (Frances), Cambridgeshire 65
Woburn Books, London N 157

EDUCATION & SCHOOL
Alba Books, Grampian 267
Apocalypse, Surrey 228
Barcombe Services, Essex........................... 108
Black Five Books, Shropshire 211
Drury Rare Books (John), Essex................... 111
Game Advice, Oxfordshire 205
Holtom (Christopher), Cornwall 75
Jarndyce Antiquarian Booksellers, London WC 175
Kenny's Bookshops and Art Galleries Ltd, Co.
  Galway.. 260
McGee (Terence J.), London Outer 178
Oopalba Books, Cheshire............................ 71
Pickering & Chatto, London W.................... 172
Priestpopple Books, Northumberland 198
Reading Lasses, Dumfries & Galloway 265
Roland Books, Kent................................... 139
Rutland Bookshop (The), Rutland 208
Saunders (Tom), Caerphilly......................... 276
The Old Children's Bookshelf, Lothian.......... 272
Tiffin (Tony and Gill), Durham.................... 96
Transformer, Dumfries & Galloway............... 265
Wise (Derek), East Sussex.......................... 102
Yates Antiquarian Books (Tony),
  Leicestershire... 146

EGYPTOLOGY
Afar Books International, West Midlands 234
Alpha Books, London N 155
Apocalypse, Surrey 228
Books B.C., London Outer 178
Bookworm, Lothian 270
Byre Books, Dumfries & Galloway............... 264
Cavern Books, Cheshire 70
Chthonios Books, East Sussex...................... 101
Crouch Rare Books, Surrey......................... 227
Dworski Books, Travel & Language Bookshop
  (Marijana), Herefordshire 283
Ford Books (David), Hertfordshire................ 132
Joppa Books Ltd., Surrey 226
Kenny's Bookshops and Art Galleries Ltd, Co.
  Galway.. 260
Kingswood Books, Dorset 93
Michael Graves-Johnston, London SW........... 166
My Back Pages, London SW 167

Occultique, Northamptonshire...................... 196
P. and P. Books, Worcestershire................... 251
Prospect House Books, Co. Down 256
Scrivener's Books & Bookbinding, Derbyshire . 81
Treasure Trove Books, Leicestershire 146
Unsworths Booksellers, London NW 160
Whitchurch Books Ltd., Cardiff 276
Wiend Books, Lancashire 143
Yesterday's Books, Dorset 91

ELECTRONICS
Skoob Russell Square, Suffolk...................... 225
Whistler's Books, London SW 167

EMBLEMATA
John Underwood Antiquarian Books,
  Norfolk... 186
Parikian, Rare Books (Diana), London W...... 171
Seydi Rare Books (Sevin), London NW......... 159

EMBROIDERY
Apocalypse, Surrey 228
Black Cat Books, Norfolk........................... 185
Browse Books, Lancashire 143
Byrom Textile Bookroom (Richard),
  Lancashire 142
Camilla's Bookshop, East Sussex 100
Cover to Cover, Merseyside........................ 183
Crouch Rare Books, Surrey......................... 227
Don Kelly Books, London W 170
DPE Books, Devon................................... 86
Four Shire Bookshops, Oxfordshire 202
Mansfield (Judith), West Yorkshire 245
Old Bookshop (The), West Midlands 236
Oopalba Books, Cheshire............................ 71
Reading Lasses, Dumfries & Galloway 265
Scrivener's Books & Bookbinding, Derbyshire . 81
Sleepy Elephant Books & Artefacts, Cumbria.. 79
Smith Books (Keith), Herefordshire 128
Traveller's Bookshelf (The), Somerset............ 212
Trinders' Fine Tools, Suffolk 222
Warnes (Felicity J.), London Outer 178
Whittle, Bookseller (Avril), Cumbria 79
Young (D. & J.), Powys............................. 286

ENCYCLOPAEDIAS
Apocalypse, Surrey 228
Cornucopia Books, Lincolnshire 151
Frew Limited (Robert), London W 170
PsychoBabel Books & Journals, Oxfordshire ... 202

ENGINEERING
Baron - Scientific Book Sales (P.J.), Somerset.. 213
Bianco Library, West Sussex....................... 237
Book House (The), Cumbria 78
Bott, (Bookdealers) Ltd., (Martin), Greater
  Manchester 118
Brockwells Booksellers, Lincolnshire 148
Courtwood Books, Co. Laois....................... 260
Elton Engineering Books, London W............ 170

Falconwood Transport & Military Bookshop,
London Outer 181
Gaskell Rare Books (Roger), Cambridgeshire.. 66
K.S.C. Books, Cheshire............................. 68
Kerr (Norman), Cumbria............................ 77
Phelps (Michael), West Sussex...................... 237
Skoob Russell Square, Suffolk...................... 225
Sun House Books, Kent............................. 139
Theatreshire Books, North Yorkshire............ 190
Trinders' Fine Tools, Suffolk 222
Westons, Hertfordshire............................. 133
Whistler's Books, London SW 167

ENGLISH
Apocalypse, Surrey 228
Classics Bookshop (The), Oxfordshire 202
Cornucopia Books, Lincolnshire 151
Naughton Booksellers, Co. Dublin 259

ENGRAVING
Apocalypse, Surrey 228
Collinge & Clark, London WC 174
Heritage, West Midlands 234
Waddington Books & Prints (Geraldine),
Northamptonshire................................. 196
Webb Books (John), South Yorkshire 217
Woodbine Books, West Yorkshire................ 241

ENTERTAINMENT
Apocalypse, Surrey 228
Aurora Books Ltd, Lothian......................... 270
Autumn Leaves, Lincolnshire...................... 150
Bookshop (The), Norfolk............................ 189
Cavern Books, Cheshire 70
Dandy Lion Editions, Surrey 228
DaSilva Puppet Books, Dorset 92
Greenroom Books, West Yorkshire 243
Junk & Spread Eagle, London SE................ 162
Katnap Arts, Norfolk................................. 187
Kaye - Bookseller (Terence), London NW...... 159
Nevitsky (Philip), Greater Manchester........... 119
Paramor (C.D.), Suffolk 224
Pyecroft (Ruth), Gloucestershire 116
Roland Books, Kent.................................. 139
Stroma Books, Borders 262
Till's Bookshop, Lothian............................ 272
Wood (Peter), Cambridgeshire 65
Yesterday's News, Conwy.......................... 278

ENTOMOLOGY
Arden, Bookseller (C.), Powys.................... 282
Aurelian Books, London NW 158
Aviabooks, Gloucestershire 114
Blest (Peter), Kent 139
Calluna Books, Dorset 94
Classey Limited (E.W.), Oxfordshire 203
Demar Books (Grant), Kent........................ 140
Edmund Pollinger Rare Books, London SW... 165
Mobbs (A.J.), West Midlands 235
Orb's Bookshop, Grampian........................ 268

Pemberley Books, Buckinghamshire.............. 62
Pendleside Books, Lancashire...................... 143
Tant Yn Ellen Books, Powys 286
Thin Read Line, Merseyside 182
Woodside Books, Kent 136

ENVIRONMENT, THE
Kenny's Bookshops and Art Galleries Ltd, Co.
Galway... 260
Newgate Books and Translations,
Northumberland.................................. 198
Reading Lasses, Dumfries & Galloway.......... 265

EROTICA
Apocalypse, Surrey 228
Delectus Books, London WC...................... 174
Edmund Pollinger Rare Books, London SW... 165
High Street Books, Devon 85
InterCol London, London N 156
N1 Books, East Sussex.............................. 103
Occultique, Northamptonshire..................... 196
Muttonchop Manuscripts............................ 239
Paper Pleasures, Somerset 215
Price (R.W.), Nottinghamshire 200

ESOTERIC
Alpha Books, London N 155
Armchair Books, Lothian 270
Beware of the Leopard, Bristol.................... 58
Book Barrow, Cambridgeshire 63
Books (For All), North Yorkshire 190
Caduceus Books, Leicestershire 145
Central Bookshop, Warwickshire 232
Cofion Books, Pembrokeshire 281
Dawlish Books, Devon.............................. 84
Eastcote Bookshop (The), London Outer 178
Graduate Books, Worcestershire 252
Green Man Books, East Sussex 100
Greensleeves, Oxfordshire 202
IKON, Devon 88
Inner Bookshop (The), Oxfordshire 205
Magis Books, Leicestershire........................ 147
Main Point Books, Lothian........................ 271
Occultique, Northamptonshire..................... 196
Old Aberdeen Bookshop, Grampian 266
Orchid Book Distributors, Co. Clare............. 257
Pyecroft (Ruth), Gloucestershire 116
Reid of Liverpool, Merseyside..................... 182
SETI Books, Staffordshire.......................... 220
Skoob Russell Square, Suffolk..................... 225
Star Lord Books, Greater Manchester 120
Starlord Books, Greater Manchester 118
Treglown (Roger J.), Cheshire..................... 70
Watkins Books Ltd., London WC................. 177
Waxfactor, East Sussex 99
Worlds End Bookshop, London SW............. 168

ESPIONAGE
AA1 Books, Dumfries & Galloway 264
Baldwin (M. & M.), Shropshire................... 250

Corfe Books, Surrey 227
Crimes Ink, London E 153
Grahame Thornton, Bookseller, Dorset 92
Island Books, Kent 136
Loretta Lay Books, London NW 159
MilitaryHistoryBooks.com, Kent 138
Ming Books, Dumfries & Galloway 265
Murphy (C.J.), Norfolk 187
Price (R.W.), Nottinghamshire 200
Transformer, Dumfries & Galloway 265
Trinity Rare Books, Co. Leitrim 260
Undercover Books, Lincolnshire 152

ETHICS
Apocalypse, Surrey 228
Reading Lasses, Dumfries & Galloway 265
Samovar Books, Co. Dublin 258
Skoob Russell Square, Suffolk 225

ETHNOGRAPHY
Bracton Books, Cambridgeshire 63
Butcher (Pablo), Oxfordshire 203
Campbell Hewson Books (R.), Fife 265
Delectus Books, London WC 174
G. Bickford-Smith (formerly Snowden Smith
   Books), Surrey 228
Maghreb Bookshop (The), London WC 175
Michael Graves-Johnston, London SW 166
Reading Lasses, Dumfries & Galloway 265
Traveller's Bookshelf (The), Somerset 212
Yesterday's Books, Dorset 91

ETHNOLOGY
Delectus Books, London WC 174
Deyong Books (J.C.), London SW 164
Maghreb Bookshop (The), London WC 175
Michael Graves-Johnston, London SW 166
Randall (Tom), Somerset 215

ETIQUETTE
Apocalypse, Surrey 228
Black Cat Books, Norfolk 185
Lucas (Richard), London NW 159
Weininger Antiquarian Books (Eva M.),
   London NW 160

EUROPEAN BOOKS
PsychoBabel Books & Journals, Oxfordshire ... 202
Skoob Russell Square, Suffolk 225

EUROPEAN STUDIES
PsychoBabel Books & Journals, Oxfordshire ... 202
Studio Bookshop, East Sussex 99

EVOLUTION
Arden, Bookseller (C.), Powys 282
Austwick Hall Books, Lancaster 190
Baldwin's Scientific Books, Essex 112
Bracton Books, Cambridgeshire 63

Humanist Book Services, Cornwall 72
Ice House Books, Wiltshire 248
Kalligraphia (formerly Charmouth Bounty
   Books), Isle of Wight 134

EX-LIBRIS
Baldwin's Scientific Books, Essex 112
Cox Old & Rare Books (Claude), Suffolk 223
Derek Stirling Bookseller, Kent 141
Heraldry Today, Wiltshire 247
Heritage, West Midlands 234
Hodgson (Books) (Richard J.),
   North Yorkshire 194
Libra Books, Lincolnshire 148
Murphy (C.J.), Norfolk 187
Paper Pleasures, Somerset 215
Reeves Technical Books, North Yorkshire 193
RGS Books, Surrey 229
Stalagluft Books, Tyne and Wear 231
Waddington Books & Prints (Geraldine),
   Northamptonshire 196

EXAMINATION PAPERS
Apocalypse, Surrey 228

EXHIBITIONS
Studio Bookshop, East Sussex 99

EXPEDITIONS
Gildas Books, Cheshire 68
Samovar Books, Co. Dublin 258

EXPLORATION
- GENERAL
Americanabooksuk, Cumbria 76
Austwick Hall Books, Lancaster 190
Byre Books, Dumfries & Galloway 264
Garfi Books, Ceredigion 282
Kirkland Books, Cumbria 78
Marble Hill Books, Middlesex 181
Pinnacle Books, Lothian 271
Samovar Books, Co. Dublin 258

- POLAR REGIONS
Cavendish Rare Books Ltd, London N 155

FABLES
Biblion, London W 169
Byre Books, Dumfries & Galloway 264
Derek Stirling Bookseller, Kent 141
Eggeling Books (John), West Yorkshire 245
Gildas Books, Cheshire 68
Holtom (Christopher), Cornwall 75
Jean Hedger, Berkshire 55
Junk & Spread Eagle, London SE 162
Muttonchop Manuscripts 239
Prescott - The Bookseller (John), London
   Outer 181

Williams Rare Books (Nigel), London WC..... 177

FAIRGROUNDS
Cottage Books, Leicestershire...................... 145
Cover to Cover, Merseyside........................ 183
Kaye - Bookseller (Terence), London NW...... 159

FAIRY/FOLK TALES
Apocalypse, Surrey 228
Byre Books, Dumfries & Galloway............... 264
Castleton (Pat), Kent................................ 137
Fifteenth Century Bookshop (The), East Sussex 102
Gildas Books, Cheshire 68
Jean Hedger, Berkshire.............................. 55
Orb's Bookshop, Grampian........................ 268

FAMILY
Gildas Books, Cheshire 68
Reading Lasses, Dumfries & Galloway.......... 265

FAMOUS PEOPLE
  - BADEN POWELL, LORD & LADY R.S.S.
John R. Hoggarth, North Yorkshire............. 194

  - BEATLES, THE
firstpagebooks, Norfolk............................ 187

  - CHURCHILL, SIR WINSTON
Apocalypse, Surrey 228
Mellon's Books, East Sussex....................... 100

  - KENNEDY, JOHN F
Clifford Elmer Books Ltd., Cheshire 68

FARMING & LIVESTOCK
Barn Books, Shropshire............................. 211
Books for Content, Herefordshire 128
Carningli Centre, Pembrokeshire.................. 281
Cheshire Book Centre, Cheshire 69
Clarke Books (David), Somerset 214
Country Books, Derbyshire 81
Evergreen Livres, Gloucestershire................. 115
Greta Books, Durham 96
Hodgson (Books) (Richard J.),
  North Yorkshire................................... 194
Jane Jones Books, Grampian...................... 267
Kilgour (Sporting Books) (Ian), Leicestershire . 147
Mayhew (Veronica), Berkshire 56
Muttonchop Manuscripts........................... 239
Phenotype Books, Cumbria 78
Rutland Bookshop (The), Rutland 208
Samovar Books, Co. Dublin........................ 258
Scrivener's Books & Bookbinding, Derbyshire . 81
Thornber (Peter M.), North Yorkshire 193

FARRIERS
Austwick Hall Books, Lancaster 190
Jane Jones Books, Grampian...................... 267

Phenotype Books, Cumbria 78
Rutland Bookshop (The), Rutland 208

FASHION & COSTUME
Abrahams (Mike), Staffordshire................... 219
Art Reference Books, Hampshire 125
Batterham (David), London W 169
Black Cat Books, Norfolk........................... 185
Bookroom (The), Surrey............................ 229
Byrom Textile Bookroom (Richard),
  Lancashire 142
Caliver Books, Essex 110
Cheshire Book Centre, Cheshire 69
Duncan & Reid, Lothian............................ 271
Dyson (Anthony), West Midlands................ 235
Forest Books of Manchester, Cheshire 70
Garfi Books, Ceredigion 282
Goodyer (Nicholas), London N................... 156
Greenroom Books, West Yorkshire 243
Gresham Books, Somerset 214
Hornsey's, North Yorkshire........................ 192
Ives Bookseller (John), London Outer 181
King Street Bookshop (The), Norfolk 185
Lighthouse Books (The), Dorset 91
Mansfield (Judith), West Yorkshire 245
Meekins Books (Paul), Warwickshire 233
My Back Pages, London SW...................... 167
N1 Books, East Sussex............................. 103
Pordes Books Ltd., (Henry), London WC 176
Portobello Books, London W 172
Reading Lasses, Dumfries & Galloway.......... 265
Shapero Rare Books (Bernard J.), London W . 172
Trinders' Fine Tools, Suffolk 222
Warnes (Felicity J.), London Outer 178
Whittle, Bookseller (Avril), Cumbria............. 79
Worlds End Bookshop, London SW............. 168
Young (D. & J.), Powys............................ 286

FEMINISM
Delectus Books, London WC...................... 174
Dylans Bookstore, Glamorgan 286
Fortune Green Books, London NW 158
Judd Books, London WC.......................... 175
Kenny's Bookshops and Art Galleries Ltd,
  Co. Galway 260
Lane Books (Shirley), Isle of Wight 135
Reading Lasses, Dumfries & Galloway.......... 265
Rosemary Pugh Books, Wiltshire 248
Spurrier (Nick), Kent............................... 138
Stevens (Joan), Cambridgeshire 65
Susan Taylor Books, West Yorkshire 243
Symes Books (Naomi), Cheshire 71
Till's Bookshop, Lothian........................... 272
Treasure Trove Books, Leicestershire 146
Willmott Bookseller (Nicholas), Cardiff 276
Yesterday's News, Conwy......................... 278

FICTION
  - GENERAL
Abacus Gallery, Staffordshire...................... 220

SPECIALITY INDEX

Abbey Books, Cornwall 73
ahbooks, Merseyside............................... 182
Anglo-American Rare Books, Surrey 228
Antiques on High, Oxfordshire................... 204
Apocalypse, Surrey 228
Applin (Malcolm), Berkshire...................... 55
Aurora Books Ltd, Lothian....................... 270
Autumn Leaves, Lincolnshire..................... 150
Bass (Ben), Wiltshire 246
Beaton (Richard), East Sussex.................... 102
Bernstein (Nicholas), London W 169
Beware of the Leopard, Bristol................... 58
Black Cat Bookshop, Leicestershire 145
Black Five Books, Shropshire 211
Book For All Reasons (A.), Suffolk.............. 224
Book House (The), Cumbria 78
Bookcase, Cumbria 76
Books & Collectables Ltd., Cambridgeshire 63
Books Afloat, Dorset............................... 94
Books Antiques & Collectables, Devon.......... 88
Books for Writers, Monmouthshire 280
books2books, Devon 87
BOOKS4U, Flintshire.............................. 279
Bookshop (The), Dorset 92
Bookworm, Lothian 270
Bookworm (The), Lothian 271
Boris Books, Hampshire 127
Bosco Books, Cornwall 72
Bowie Books & Collectables, East Yorkshire... 106
Boz Books, Powys 282
Brighton Books, East Sussex...................... 98
Broadhurst of Southport Ltd., Merseyside...... 182
Caledonia Books, Strathclyde..................... 273
Capel Mawr Collectors Centre, Gwynedd....... 280
Carnforth Bookshop (The), Lancashire.......... 142
Carningli Centre, Pembrokeshire.................. 281
Celtic Bookshop (The), Co. Limerick 261
Chalk (Old & Out of Print Books)
  (Christine M.), West Midlands 234
Chaucer Bookshop, Kent.......................... 136
Cheshire Book Centre, Cheshire 69
Church Street Books, Norfolk.................... 184
Clarke Books (David), Somerset 214
Clements (R.W.), London Outer 179
Cobbles Books, Somerset......................... 214
Cofion Books, Pembrokeshire 281
Corfe Books, Surrey............................... 227
Cox Rare Books (Charles), Cornwall 73
Crimes Ink, London E............................. 153
D'Arcy Books, Wiltshire........................... 246
Dales & Lakes Book Centre, Cumbria 79
Dartmoor Bookshop (The), Devon............... 83
Dormouse Bookshop (The), Norfolk............. 188
dgbbooks, West Sussex 239
Eastcote Bookshop (The), London Outer 178
Eggeling Books (John), West Yorkshire 245
Ellis, Bookseller (Peter), London SE 162
Ellwood Editions, Wiltshire 247
Fiction First, Cheshire 69
Fireside Bookshop, Cumbria 80
First State Books, London W 170
Ford Books (David), Hertfordshire............... 132

Fortune Green Books, London NW 158
Freya Books & Antiques, Norfolk................ 187
Gemini–Books, Shropshire 210
Gloucester Road Bookshop, London SW....... 165
Greta Books, Durham 96
Grove Bookshop (The), North Yorkshire....... 193
Hardback Hotel, Lancashire 143
Harrington (Adrian), London W 171
Hay Cinema Bookshop Ltd., Herefordshire 283
Heckmondwike Book Shop, West Yorkshire... 244
Hurst (Jenny), Kent 138
Innes Books, Shropshire 209
Intech Books, Northumberland 198
Jade Mountain, Hampshire 125
Jane Jones Books, Grampian 267
Johnson Rare Book Collections (C.R.),
  London NW 159
K Books, Cheshire................................. 69
Kellow Books, Oxfordshire 203
Kim's Bookshop, West Sussex............... 237, 240
Kingfisher Book Service, Nottinghamshire...... 201
Lewis (J.T. & P.), Cornwall 73
Libra Books, Lincolnshire......................... 148
Little Bookshop (The), Greater Manchester 119
Little Stour Books, Kent 136
Main Point Books, Lothian 271
Marble Hill Books, Middlesex.................... 181
Marine Workshop Bookshop, Dorset............ 92
Martin's Books, Powys 285
McKelvie (Ian), London N 156
Meads Book Service (The), East Sussex 103
Modern First Editions, London Outer 180
Moffat Book Exchange, Dumfries & Galloway 264
Mr. Pickwick of Towcester, Northamptonshire 196
Much Ado Books, East Sussex................... 98
Mundy (David), Hertfordshire 130
Murphy (C.J.), Norfolk............................ 187
Naughton Booksellers, Co. Dublin 259
Neil's Books, London NW........................ 159
New Strand Bookshop (The), Herefordshire.... 128
Not JUST Books, Lincolnshire.................... 148
O'Brien Books & Photo Gallery, Co. Limerick 261
Olynthiacs, Shropshire 210
Oxfam Books and Music, Hampshire............ 127
Pamona Books, Lancashire 144
Paperbacks Plus, Bristol 59
Park Gallery & Bookshop (The),
  Northamptonshire................................ 197
Paton Books, Hertfordshire 132
Peter's Bookshop, Norfolk 188
Poor Richard's Books, Suffolk 222
Portobello Books, London W 172
Prescott - The Bookseller (John),
  London Outer 181
Price (R.D.M. & I.M.) (Books),
  Greater Manchester.............................. 120
Price (R.W.), Nottinghamshire 200
Pyecroft (Ruth), Gloucestershire 116
Quinto of Charing Cross Road, London WC.. 176
Quinto of Great Russell Street, London WC... 176
Reading Lasses, Dumfries & Galloway 265
Reid of Liverpool, Merseyside.................... 182

SPECIALITY INDEX

RGS Books, Surrey 229
Richmond Books, North Yorkshire 192
Roger Lucas Booksellers, Lincolnshire 150
Roland Books, Kent 139
Rosemary Books, Merseyside 183
Rutland Bookshop (The), Rutland 208
Rye Old Books, East Sussex 103
Seabreeze Books, Lancashire 144
Shacklock Books (David), Suffolk 222
Shakeshaft (Dr. B.), Cheshire 71
Signature Books, Hampshire 126
Sleepy Elephant Books & Artefacts, Cumbria.. 79
Smith Books, (Sally), Suffolk 222
Sturford Books, Wiltshire 248
Surprise Books, Gloucestershire 113
Temple (Robert), London N 157
Thistle Books, Strathclyde 274
Thomas (E. Wyn), Conwy 278
Till's Bookshop, Lothian 272
Tilston (Stephen E.), London SE 161
Tindley & Chapman, London WC 176
Trevorrow (Edwin), Hertfordshire 130
Trinity Rare Books, Co. Leitrim 260
Valentine Rare Books, Surrey 227
Ventnor Rare Books, Isle of Wight 135
Vokes Books Ltd., North Yorkshire 192
VOL:II, Essex 108
Wadard Books, Kent 137
Ward (R.F. & C.), Norfolk 185
Warrington Book Loft (The), Cheshire 71
Wealden Books, Kent 139
Williams (Bookdealer), (Richard), Lincolnshire 152
Williams Rare Books (Nigel), London WC..... 177
Willmott Bookseller (Nicholas), Cardiff 276
Worlds End Bookshop, London SW 168
Yarborough House Bookshop, Shropshire 209
Zardoz Books, Wiltshire 249

- 18TH CENTURY
Valentine Rare Books, London W 173

- ADVENTURE
Apocalypse, Surrey 228
Onepoundpaperbacks, Cleveland 96
Surprise Books, Gloucestershire 113

- CRIME, DETECTIVE, SPY, THRILLERS
AA1 Books, Dumfries & Galloway 264
Abbey Books, Cornwall 73
Apocalypse, Surrey 228
Aucott & Thomas, Leicestershire 145
Bell (Books) (Mrs. V.S.), Suffolk 223
Beware of the Leopard, Bristol 58
Biblion, London W 169
Birmingham Books, West Midlands 234
Bookshop on the Heath, The, London SE...... 161
Bradley–Cox (Mary), Dorset 90
Cecilia Marsden, London Outer 180
Classic Crime Collections, Greater Manchester 119
Cotswold Internet Books, Gloucestershire 113

Cowley, Bookdealer (K.W.), Somerset 214
Crimes Ink, London E 153
Dyson (Anthony), West Midlands 235
Eggeling Books (John), West Yorkshire 245
Fantastic Literature, Essex 111
Farringdon Books, Essex 109
Fiction First, Cheshire 69
firstpagebooks, Norfolk 187
Firsts in Print, Isle of Wight 134
Garfi Books, Ceredigion 282
Hardback Hotel, Lancashire 143
Harris (Books), (Malcolm), West Midlands..... 234
Heckmondwike Book Shop, West Yorkshire... 244
Heppa (Christopher), Essex 108
Hight (Norman F.), Glamorgan 279
Hill (John S.), Devon 84
J. & J. Books, Lincolnshire 149
John Gorton Booksearch, East Sussex........... 103
Junk & Spread Eagle, London SE 162
Kent (Books) (Mrs. A.), Suffolk 223
Kevin S. Ogilvie Modern First Editions,
  Grampian 266
Libra Books, Lincolnshire 148
Loretta Lay Books, London NW 159
Lucius Books, North Yorkshire 195
Mainly Fiction, Greater Manchester 118
McCaughtrie (K.A.), North Yorkshire 190
McKelvie (Ian), London N 156
Ming Books, Dumfries & Galloway 265
Murder & Mayhem, Powys 284
New Strand Bookshop (The),
  Herefordshire 128
Newgate Books and Translations,
  Northumberland 198
Onepoundpaperbacks, Cleveland 96
Orb's Bookshop, Grampian 268
Paperbacks Plus, Bristol 59
Porcupine Books, London Outer 179
Post Mortem Books, West Sussex 238
Price (R.W.), Nottinghamshire 200
Pyecroft (Ruth), Gloucestershire 116
Reading Lasses, Dumfries & Galloway 265
Richmond Books, North Yorkshire 192
Roland Books, Kent 139
Roscrea Bookshop, Co. Tipperary 261
Ruebotham (Kirk), Cheshire 70
Surprise Books, Gloucestershire 113
Sutcliffe (Mark), West Yorkshire 243
Temple (Robert), London N 157
The Glass Key, West Yorkshire 242
The Sanctuary Bookshop, Dorset 93
Till's Bookshop, Lothian 272
Tindley & Chapman, London WC 176
TP Children's Bookshop, West Yorkshire 241
Transformer, Dumfries & Galloway 265
Treasure Trove Books, Leicestershire 146
Vokes (Jeremiah), Durham 96
Ward (R.F. & C.), Norfolk 185
Wiend Books, Lancashire 143
Williams (Bookdealer), (Richard), Lincolnshire 152

SPECIALITY INDEX

- FANTASY, HORROR

AA1 Books, Dumfries & Galloway 264
Apocalypse, Surrey 228
Beware of the Leopard, Bristol.................... 58
Birmingham Books, West Midlands.............. 234
Books B.C., London Outer 178
Cowley, Bookdealer (K.W.), Somerset........... 214
Dalby (Richard), North Yorkshire 192
Eggeling Books (John), West Yorkshire......... 245
Fantastic Literature, Essex 111
Fantasy Centre, London N 155
Farringdon Books, Essex 109
Fiction First, Cheshire 69
Firsts in Print, Isle of Wight 134
Gildas Books, Cheshire 68
Hight (Norman F.), Glamorgan 279
Interstellar Master Traders, Lancashire.......... 143
Lucius Books, North Yorkshire................... 195
Murder & Mayhem, Powys 284
Occultique, Northamptonshire.................... 196
Onepoundpaperbacks, Cleveland.................. 96
Orb's Bookshop, Grampian........................ 268
Paperbacks Plus, Bristol 59
Porcupine Books, London Outer 179
Price (R.W.), Nottinghamshire 200
Pyecroft (Ruth), Gloucestershire 116
Roland Books, Kent................................. 139
Ruebotham (Kirk), Cheshire 70
Sensawunda Books, Cheshire 68
Solaris Books, East Yorkshire 105
Surprise Books, Gloucestershire.................. 113
Temple (Robert), London N....................... 157
The Glass Key, West Yorkshire................... 242
Till's Bookshop, Lothian 272
Transformer, Dumfries & Galloway.............. 265
Williams (Bookdealer), (Richard), Lincolnshire 152
Zardoz Books, Wiltshire........................... 249

- HISTORICAL

Americanabooksuk, Cumbria...................... 76
Apocalypse, Surrey 228
Black Cat Bookshop, Leicestershire 145
Black Five Books, Shropshire 211
Book For All Reasons (A.), Suffolk.............. 224
Boris Books, Hampshire........................... 127
Cox, Andrew, Shropshire.......................... 211
Eggeling Books (John), West Yorkshire......... 245
Enscot Books, London SE 162
Fantastic Literature, Essex 111
Gildas Books, Cheshire 68
Heppa (Christopher), Essex 108
Libra Books, Lincolnshire......................... 148
Miller (Karen), Nottinghamshire.................. 200
Naughton Booksellers, Co. Dublin 259
Onepoundpaperbacks, Cleveland.................. 96
Orb's Bookshop, Grampian........................ 268
Surprise Books, Gloucestershire.................. 113
Temple (Robert), London N....................... 157
Trevorrow (Edwin), Hertfordshire 130
Valentine Rare Books, Surrey 227
Williams Rare Books (Nigel), London WC..... 177

- ROMANTIC

Book For All Reasons (A.), Suffolk.............. 224
Eggeling Books (John), West Yorkshire......... 245
Onepoundpaperbacks, Cleveland.................. 96
Orb's Bookshop, Grampian........................ 268
Price (R.W.), Nottinghamshire 200
Valentine Rare Books, Surrey 227
Williams (Bookdealer), (Richard), Lincolnshire 152

- SCIENCE FICTION

AA1 Books, Dumfries & Galloway 264
Abbey Books, Cornwall 73
Altshuler (Jean), Cumbria 78
Apocalypse, Surrey 228
Armchair Books, Lothian 270
Beware of the Leopard, Bristol.................... 58
Birmingham Books, West Midlands.............. 234
Black Cat Bookshop, Leicestershire 145
Books & Bygones (Pam Taylor),
    West Midlands................................. 236
Books (For All), North Yorkshire 190
Books B.C., London Outer 178
Booth Books, Powys 282
Carningli Centre, Pembrokeshire 281
Cold Tonnage Books, Surrey 229
Cowley, Bookdealer (K.W.), Somerset........... 214
Cox, Andrew, Shropshire.......................... 211
Crimes Ink, London E............................. 153
Driffield Bookshop (The), West Yorkshire....... 105
Eggeling Books (John), West Yorkshire......... 245
Fantastic Literature, Essex 111
Fantasy Centre, London N 155
Farringdon Books, Essex 109
Fiction First, Cheshire 69
firstpagebooks, Norfolk 187
Gildas Books, Cheshire 68
Hardback Hotel, Lancashire 143
Heckmondwike Book Shop, West Yorkshire... 244
Hight (Norman F.), Glamorgan 279
Hill (John S.), Devon.............................. 84
Idle Genius Books, London N 156
Interstellar Master Traders, Lancashire.......... 143
K Books, Cheshire 69
Libra Books, Lincolnshire......................... 148
Lucius Books, North Yorkshire................... 195
Ming Books, Dumfries & Galloway.............. 265
Modern First Editions, London Outer........... 180
New Strand Bookshop (The), Herefordshire.... 128
Onepoundpaperbacks, Cleveland.................. 96
Orb's Bookshop, Grampian........................ 268
Paperbacks Plus, Bristol 59
Porcupine Books, London Outer 179
Price (R.W.), Nottinghamshire 200
Pyecroft (Ruth), Gloucestershire 116
Rods Books, Devon 87
Roland Books, Kent................................. 139
Ruebotham (Kirk), Cheshire 70
Sensawunda Books, Cheshire 68
Solaris Books, East Yorkshire 105
Surprise Books, Gloucestershire.................. 113
Temple (Robert), London N....................... 157

The Glass Key, West Yorkshire 242
The Sanctuary Bookshop, Dorset 93
Till's Bookshop, Lothian 272
Transformer, Dumfries & Galloway 265
Treasure Trove Books, Leicestershire 146
Trevorrow (Edwin), Hertfordshire 130
Ward (R.F. & C.), Norfolk 185
Waxfactor, East Sussex 99
Wayside Books and Cards, Oxfordshire 203
Wiend Books, Lancashire 143
Williams (Bookdealer), (Richard), Lincolnshire 152
Zardoz Books, Wiltshire 249

- SUPERNATURAL

Dalby (Richard), North Yorkshire 192
Gildas Books, Cheshire 68
Skirrid Books, Monmouthshire 280
Surprise Books, Gloucestershire 113
The Glass Key, West Yorkshire 242

- WESTERNS

AA1 Books, Dumfries & Galloway 264
Adrem Books, Hertfordshire 131
Americanabooksuk, Cumbria 76
Esoteric Dreams Bookshop, Cumbria 77
firstpagebooks, Norfolk 187
Onepoundpaperbacks, Cleveland 96
Price (R.W.), Nottinghamshire 200
Rods Books, Devon 87
Roscrea Bookshop, Co. Tipperary 261
Surprise Books, Gloucestershire 113
Ward (R.F. & C.), Norfolk 185
Zardoz Books, Wiltshire 249

- WOMEN

Apocalypse, Surrey 228
Applin (Malcolm), Berkshire 55
Cheshire Book Centre, Cheshire 69
Eggeling Books (John), West Yorkshire 245
Fortune Green Books, London NW 158
Libra Books, Lincolnshire 148
Paperbacks Plus, Bristol 59
Poor Richard's Books, Suffolk 222
Reading Lasses, Dumfries & Galloway 265
Stevens (Joan), Cambridgeshire 65
Susan Taylor Books, West Yorkshire 243
Symes Books (Naomi), Cheshire 71
Temple (Robert), London N 157
Tiger Books, Kent 137
Tindley & Chapman, London WC 176
Treasure Trove Books, Leicestershire 146
Valentine Rare Books, Surrey 227
Williams (Bookdealer), (Richard), Lincolnshire 152
Yesterday's News, Conwy 278

- YOUNG ADULT MYSTERY & ADVENTURE SERIES

Apocalypse, Surrey 228
Bookroom (The), Surrey 229
Gildas Books, Cheshire 68

FICTIONAL CHARACTERS
Apocalypse, Surrey 228

FINANCE
Aurora Books Ltd, Lothian 270
Beware of the Leopard, Bristol 58

FINE & RARE
Allsop (Duncan M.), Warwickshire 233
Amwell Book Company, London SE 154
Antique Map and Bookshop (The), Dorset 93
Arden, Bookseller (C.), Powys 282
Ardis Books, Hampshire 126
Baldwin's Scientific Books, Essex 112
Barry McKay Rare Books, Cumbria 76
Baxter (Steve), Surrey 228
Bayntun (George), Somerset 212
Biblion, London W 169
Books on Spain, London Outer 181
Brian Troath Books, London E 153
Bristow & Garland, Hampshire 123
Broadhurst of Southport Ltd., Merseyside 182
Byblos Antiquarian & Rare Book, Hampshire . 122
Cameron House Books, Isle of Wight 134
Carnforth Bookshop (The), Lancashire 142
Clent Books, Worcestershire 250
Cooper Hay Rare Books, Strathclyde 273
Cox Rare Books (Charles), Cornwall 73
Dartmoor Bookshop (The), Devon 83
David (G.), Cambridgeshire 63
Dean Byass, Bristol 60
Drury Rare Books (John), Essex 111
Eastwood Books (David), Cornwall 72
Ellwood Editions, Wiltshire 247
Elstree Books, Hertfordshire 131
Fletcher (H.M.), Hertfordshire 131
Grayling (David A.H.), Cumbria 78
Green Man Books, East Sussex 100
Harrington (Adrian), London W 171
Harrington Antiquarian Bookseller (Peter), London SW 166
Heath (A.R.), Bristol 59
Heritage, West Midlands 234
Hughes Rare Books (Spike), Borders 262
Hutchison (Books) (Larry), Fife 265
Ian Briddon, Derbyshire 81
Island Books, Kent 136
Jones (Andrew), Suffolk 223
Kenny's Bookshops and Art Galleries Ltd, Co. Galway 260
Kernaghans, Merseyside 183
Kerr (Norman), Cumbria 77
Kilgarriff (Raymond), East Sussex 104
Lucius Books, North Yorkshire 195
Mair Wilkes Books, Fife 265
Marble Hill Books, Middlesex 181
Marks Limited (Barrie), London N 156
Offa's Dyke Books, Shropshire 209
Orssich (Paul), London SW 167
Paralos Ltd., London WC 175
Parikian, Rare Books (Diana), London W 171

Poetry Bookshop (The), Powys.................... 284
Poole (William), London W 172
Reeves Technical Books, North Yorkshire...... 193
Rochdale Book Company, Greater Manchester 120
Rowan (P. & B.), Co. Antrim 255
Rye Old Books, East Sussex 103
Saint Mary's Books & Prints, Lincolnshire 152
Saintfield Antiques & Fine Books, Co. Down.. 255
Shapero Rare Books (Bernard J.), London W . 172
Sokol Books Ltd., London W 172
Stalagluft Books, Tyne and Wear................. 231
Stern Antiquarian Bookseller (Jeffrey),
    North Yorkshire................................... 195
Taylor & Son (Peter), Hertfordshire.............. 132
Temperley (David), West Midlands 234
Thorntons of Oxford Ltd., Oxfordshire 203
Tobo Books, Hampshire............................ 124
Trinity Rare Books, Co. Leitrim.................. 260
Unsworths Booksellers, London NW 160
Updike Rare Books (John), Lothian 272
Valentine Rare Books, London W 173
Venables (Morris & Juliet), Bristol 59
Wildside Books, Worcestershire................... 250
Woodbine Books, West Yorkshire................ 241
Words Etcetera Bookshop, Dorset 92

FINE ART

Amwell Book Company, London SE 154
Apocalypse, Surrey 228
Ars Artis, Oxfordshire.............................. 205
Art Book Company, (The), Suffolk 223
Art Reference Books, Hampshire................. 125
Berry (L.J.), Kent 138
Book Palace (The), London SE 161
Bookroom (The), Surrey........................... 229
Capes (Books, Maps & Prints) (John L.),
    North Yorkshire................................... 193
Central Bookshop, Warwickshire 232
Cooper Hay Rare Books, Strathclyde............ 273
Cornucopia Books, Lincolnshire 151
Dew (Roderick), East Sussex 100
Don Kelly Books, London W 170
Grosvenor Prints, London WC.................... 175
Handsworth Books, Essex.......................... 112
Heneage Art Books (Thomas), London SW.... 166
Holdsworth Books (Bruce), East Sussex 103
Hollett and Son (R.F.G.), Cumbria 79
Inprint, Gloucestershire 116
Kenny's Bookshops and Art Galleries Ltd,
    Co. Galway 260
Mannwaring (M.G.), Bristol....................... 59
Marlborough Rare Books Ltd., London W 171
Pagan Limited (Hugh), London SW 167
Pordes Books Ltd., (Henry), London WC 176
Potterton Books, North Yorkshire 194
Pugh Books (Ian K.), Worcestershire 251
Ray Rare and Out of Print Books (Janette),
    North Yorkshire................................... 195
Roe and Moore, London WC...................... 176
Second Edition, Lothian............................ 272
Spelman (Ken), North Yorkshire 195

Sykes (Graham), West Yorkshire 244
Trinders' Fine Tools, Suffolk 222
Webb Books (John), South Yorkshire 217
Wyseby House Books, Berkshire.................. 55

FINE PRINTING

Apocalypse, Surrey 228
Bardsley's Books, Suffolk.......................... 221
Barlow (Vincent G.), Hampshire.................. 126
Barnitt (Peter), Wiltshire........................... 248
Barry McKay Rare Books, Cumbria............. 76
Biblion, London W 169
Collinge & Clark, London WC 174
Cox Old & Rare Books (Claude), Suffolk...... 223
Dales & Lakes Book Centre, Cumbria 79
Maggs Brothers Limited, London W 171
Mills Rare Books (Adam), Cambridgeshire..... 64
Pordes Books Ltd., (Henry), London WC 176
Tucker (Alan & Joan), Gloucestershire 116
Updike Rare Books (John), Lothian 272

FIRE & FIRE FIGHTERS

Not JUST Books, Lincolnshire.................... 148
Saint Swithin's Illustrated & Children's Books,
    London W.. 172
Theatreshire Books, North Yorkshire............ 190

FIREARMS/GUNS

Americanabooksuk, Cumbria...................... 76
Bookworm, Lothian 270
Bookworm (The), Lothian 271
Cader Idris Books, Gwynedd...................... 280
Caliver Books, Essex 110
Camilla's Bookshop, East Sussex 100
Chalmers Hallam (E.), Hampshire................ 125
Cornucopia Books, Lincolnshire 151
Duck (William), Hampshire........................ 124
Guildmaster Books, Cheshire 70
Helion & Company, West Midlands 235
Heneage Art Books (Thomas), London SW.... 166
Kilgour (Sporting Books) (Ian), Leicestershire . 147
Meekins Books (Paul), Warwickshire 233
MilitaryHistoryBooks.com, Kent 138
Muttonchop Manuscripts........................... 239
N1 Books, East Sussex.............................. 103
Prospect Books, Conwy............................. 278
Trinders' Fine Tools, Suffolk 222

FIRST EDITIONS

Amwell Book Company, London SE 154
Antiques on High, Oxfordshire.................... 204
Apocalypse, Surrey 228
Armchair Books, Lothian 270
Ash Rare Books, London SW..................... 164
Aurora Books Ltd, Lothian........................ 270
Autolycus, Shropshire............................... 209
Bass (Ben), Wiltshire 246
Bates Books, London Outer 179
Baxter (Steve), Surrey 228
Bayntun (George), Somerset 212

SPECIALITY INDEX

BC Books, Cheshire 69
Bertram Rota Ltd., London WC 174
Bibliophile Books, London E 153
Blythswood Bookshop, Highland 269
Book Barrow, Cambridgeshire 63
Book Gallery (The), Cornwall 75
Books & Collectables Ltd., Cambridgeshire 63
books2books, Devon 87
Bookshop (The), Co. Donegal..................... 258
Boris Books, Hampshire 127
Bowie Books & Collectables, East Yorkshire... 106
Brian Troath Books, London E 153
Brighton Books, East Sussex 98
Budd (Richard), Somerset 215
Cameron House Books, Isle of Wight 134
Carta Regis, Powys 286
Castle Bookshop, Essex 109
Cheshire Book Centre, Cheshire 69
Cobweb Books, North Yorkshire 192
Craobh Rua Books, Co. Armagh 255
Eastcote Bookshop (The), London Outer 178
Ellis, Bookseller (Peter), London SE 162
Elstree Books, Hertfordshire 131
English (Toby), Oxfordshire 206
Enigma Books, Norfolk 186
Farnborough Gallery, Hampshire 123
Fiction First, Cheshire 69
Fifteenth Century Bookshop (The), East Sussex 102
Fine Art, London SE................................ 165
First State Books, London W 170
firstpagebooks, Norfolk 187
Ford Books (David), Hertfordshire 132
Foster Bookshop (Paul), London SW 165
Fosters Bookshop, London W 170
Frost (Richard), Hertfordshire 130
Gekoski (R.A.), London WC 175
Gildas Books, Cheshire 68
Glyn's Books, Shropshire 209
Greta Books, Durham 96
Hadley Bookseller (Peter J.), Essex 110
Hardback Hotel, Lancashire 143
Harrington (Adrian), London W 171
Harrington Antiquarian Bookseller (Peter),
  London SW 166
Heppa (Christopher), Essex 108
Hill (John S.), Devon 84
Ian Briddon, Derbyshire 81
Intech Books, Northumberland 198
Island Books, Kent 136
Jarndyce Antiquarian Booksellers, London WC 175
John Underwood Antiquarian Books, Norfolk 186
Junk & Spread Eagle, London SE 162
K Books, Cheshire 69
Katnap Arts, Norfolk 187
Kendall–Carpenter (Tim), Greater Manchester 119
Kenny's Bookshops and Art Galleries Ltd, Co.
  Galway.. 260
Keswick Bookshop, Cumbria 78
Kevin S. Ogilvie Modern First Editions,
  Grampian... 266
Kirkman Ltd., (Robert), Bedfordshire 53
Leabeck Books, Oxfordshire 205
Little Stour Books, Kent 136
Lloyd-Davies (Sue), Carmarthenshire 277
Lucius Books, North Yorkshire................... 195
Mainly Fiction, Greater Manchester 118
Marcet Books, London SE......................... 161
Martin's Books, Powys 285
McKelvie (Ian), London N 156
Mellon's Books, East Sussex...................... 100
Ming Books, Dumfries & Galloway.............. 265
Modern First Editions, London Outer........... 180
Modern Firsts Etc, Lancashire 142
Murphy (C.J.), Norfolk 187
N V Books, Warwickshire......................... 232
Palladour Books, Hampshire 126
Paton Books, Hertfordshire 132
Poetry Bookshop (The), Powys................... 284
Pomes Penyeach, Staffordshire 219
Prescott - The Bookseller (John),
  London Outer 181
Price (R.W.), Nottinghamshire 200
Primrose Hill Books, London NW 159
Rassam (Paul), London NW 159
Reading Lasses, Dumfries & Galloway 265
Riderless Horse Books, Norfolk 184
Robert (Leslie), London N 172
Rosemary Books, Merseyside..................... 183
Rowan House Books, Surrey 226
Ruebotham (Kirk), Cheshire 70
Sansovino Books, West Sussex 239
Scrivener's Books & Bookbinding, Derbyshire . 81
Sensawunda Books, Cheshire 68
Shakeshaft (Dr. B.), Cheshire 71
Shapero Rare Books (Bernard J.), London W . 172
Shelley (E. & J.), Buckinghamshire 61
Sillem (Anthony), East Sussex 101
Skelton (Tony), Kent............................... 141
Stevens (Joan), Cambridgeshire 65
Surprise Books, Gloucestershire.................. 113
Sutcliffe (Mark), West Yorkshire 243
Sykes (Graham), West Yorkshire................. 244
Temple (Robert), London N...................... 157
The Glass Key, West Yorkshire................... 242
Tiffin (Tony and Gill), Durham................... 96
Till's Bookshop, Lothian 272
Tindley & Chapman, London WC 176
Trevorrow (Edwin), Hertfordshire 130
Trinity Rare Books, Co. Leitrim 260
Updike Rare Books (John), Lothian 272
Ward (R.F. & C.), Norfolk 185
Waterfield's, Oxfordshire 206
Webb Books (John), South Yorkshire 217
Williams (Bookdealer), (Richard), Lincolnshire 152
Williams Rare Books (Nigel), London WC..... 177
Woodbine Books, West Yorkshire................ 241

FISHERIES
Garfi Books, Ceredigion 282

FISHES
Alauda Books, Cumbria 76
Chalmers Hallam (E.), Hampshire................ 125

SPECIALITY INDEX

Coch-y-Bonddu Books, Powys 285
Cornucopia Books, Lincolnshire 151
Edmund Pollinger Rare Books, London SW ... 165
River Reads Bookshop, Devon..................... 89
Steven Simpson Books, Norfolk 188

FLORA & FAUNA

Alauda Books, Cumbria 76
Baldwin's Scientific Books, Essex 112
Carningli Centre, Pembrokeshire.................. 281
Castleton (Pat), Kent............................... 137
Edmund Pollinger Rare Books, London SW ... 165
Garfi Books, Ceredigion 282
Grahame Thornton, Bookseller, Dorset 92
J & J Burgess Booksellers, Cambridgeshire 64
Orb's Bookshop, Grampian........................ 268
Prospect House Books, Co. Down 256
Roger Collicott Books, Cornwall 74
Shakeshaft (Dr. B.), Cheshire...................... 71
Summerfield Books Ltd, Cumbria 76

FLOWER ARRANGING

Blest (Peter), Kent 139
Calendula Horticultural Books, East Sussex.... 101
Court Hay Books, Bristol 58
Park (Mike), London Outer 180
Reading Lasses, Dumfries & Galloway 265
Roadmaster Books, Kent........................... 137

FOLIO SOCIETY, THE

Ardis Books, Hampshire........................... 126
Avery (Alan), North Yorkshire 191
Barbican Bookshop, North Yorkshire 194
Birmingham Books, West Midlands.............. 234
BOOKS4U, Flintshire............................... 279
Camilla's Bookshop, East Sussex 100
Central Bookshop, Warwickshire 232
Cheshire Book Centre, Cheshire 69
Chevin Books, West Yorkshire.................... 245
Coach House Books, Worcestershire............. 251
Cobbles Books, Somerset.......................... 214
Dales & Lakes Book Centre, Cumbria 79
Dandy Lion Editions, Surrey 228
Fifteenth Century Bookshop (The), East Sussex 102
Finn (V. & C.), Merseyside 183
Fisher & Sperr, London N 155
Fossgate Books, North Yorkshire 194
G. C. Books Ltd., Dumfries & Galloway 264
Gildas Books, Cheshire 68
Good for Books, Lincolnshire 149
Junk & Spread Eagle, London SE................ 162
Lighthouse Books (The), Dorset 91
My Back Pages, London SW...................... 167
O'Brien Books & Photo Gallery, Co. Limerick 261
O'Connor Fine Books, Lancashire 144
Parrott Books, Oxfordshire 207
Poetry Bookshop (The), Powys................... 284
Portobello Books, London W 172
Prescott - The Bookseller (John),
   London Outer 181

Ross Old Books & Prints, Herefordshire........ 128
Scrivener's Books & Bookbinding, Derbyshire. 81
Tiffin (Tony and Gill), Durham................... 96
Treasure Trove Books, Leicestershire 146
Trinity Rare Books, Co. Leitrim 260
Waddington Books & Prints (Geraldine),
   Northamptonshire................................ 196
Westwood Books (Mark), Powys 284
Westwood Books Ltd, Cumbria 79

FOLKLORE

Alpha Books, London N 155
Apocalypse, Surrey 228
Books, Denbighshire................................ 278
Books on Spain, London Outer................... 181
Bracton Books, Cambridgeshire.................. 63
Byre Books, Dumfries & Galloway.............. 264
Cottage Books, Leicestershire..................... 145
Country Books, Derbyshire 81
Dancing Goat Bookshop (The), Norfolk........ 184
Delectus Books, London WC..................... 174
DPE Books, Devon 86
Dworski Books, Travel & Language Bookshop
   (Marijana), Herefordshire 283
Edwards (London) Limited (Francis),
   London WC....................................... 175
Edwards in Hay-on-Wye (Francis),
   Herefordshire 283
Fifteenth Century Bookshop (The), East Sussex 102
Gilbert (R.A.), Bristol.............................. 59
Gildas Books, Cheshire 68
Grampian Books, Grampian....................... 268
Green Man Books, East Sussex 100
Hobgoblin Books, Hampshire 125
Holtom (Christopher), Cornwall 75
Hutchison (Books) (Larry), Fife................... 265
Inner Bookshop (The), Oxfordshire 205
Lowe (John), Norfolk 186
Magis Books, Leicestershire....................... 147
Michael J Carroll, Co. Cork 257
Minster Gate Bookshop, North Yorkshire...... 195
Occultique, Northamptonshire.................... 196
Orb's Bookshop, Grampian........................ 268
Orssich (Paul), London SW 167
Philip Hopper, Essex 110
Randall (Tom), Somerset 215
Royal Carbery Books Ltd., Co. Cork 257

FOOD & DRINK

Apocalypse, Surrey 228
Arden Books & Cosmographia, Warwickshire. 232
Aurora Books Ltd, Lothian........................ 270
Black Cat Books, Norfolk......................... 185
Books & Bygones, Berkshire...................... 57
Capel Mawr Collectors Centre, Gwynedd...... 280
Castleton (Pat), Kent............................... 137
Chantrey Books, South Yorkshire 217
Clarke (Janet), Somerset 212
Collectable Books, London SE 162
Cooking = The Books, Gloucestershire......... 115
Cooks Books, East Sussex......................... 98

SPECIALITY INDEX

Dusty Books, Powys... 285
Edmund Pollinger Rare Books, London SW... 165
Elmfield Books, West Midlands..................... 234
Gardener & Cook, London SW..................... 165
Garfi Books, Ceredigion 282
Grahame Thornton, Bookseller, Dorset 92
Gresham Books, Somerset 214
Harvest Books, Lancashire......................... 144
Hurst (Jenny), Kent 138
Ian Briddon, Derbyshire............................ 81
Jade Mountain, Hampshire 125
Junk & Spread Eagle, London SE................ 162
Lucas (Richard), London NW 159
Marcet Books, London SE......................... 161
Much Ado Books, East Sussex.................... 98
N1 Books, East Sussex............................. 103
The Glass Key, West Yorkshire................... 242
The Sanctuary Bookshop, Dorset................. 93

FORE-EDGE PAINTINGS
Carta Regis, Powys................................. 286
Chas J. Sawyer, Kent 140
Cox Old & Rare Books (Claude), Suffolk....... 223
Davis, Antiquarian Books (Guy),
   Nottinghamshire................................. 201
Fine Art, London SE................................ 165
Game Advice, Oxfordshire 205
Harrington (Adrian), London W 171
Harrington Antiquarian Bookseller (Peter),
   London SW 166
Inner Bookshop (The), Oxfordshire 205
Kirkman Ltd., (Robert), Bedfordshire 53
Poetry Bookshop (The), Powys.................... 284

FOREIGN TEXTS
Anthony Neville, Kent 138
Apocalypse, Surrey 228
Artco, Nottinghamshire............................ 201
Atlas, London N 155
Baldwin (Jack), Strathclyde 273
Books on Spain, London Outer.................... 181
Classic Bindings Ltd, London SW................ 164
Colwyn Books, Conwy............................. 277
Crouch Rare Books, Surrey........................ 227
Foyle Books, Co. Derry 255
Hab Books, London W............................. 171
Hellenic Bookservices, London NW.............. 158
Hesketh & Ward Ltd., London SW............... 166
Needham Books, (Russell), Somerset 216
Orbis Books (London) Ltd., London W 171
Orssich (Paul), London SW........................ 167
Owen (J.V.), Conwy 278
Parikian, Rare Books (Diana), London W...... 171
Poetry Bookshop (The), Powys.................... 284
Poole (William), London W 172
Robertshaw (John), Cambridgeshire.............. 66
Sturford Books, Wiltshire 248

FORESTRY
Acer Books, Herefordshire 128

Coch-y-Bonddu Books, Powys 285
Daly (Peter M.), Hampshire 127
Mandalay Bookshop, London SW 166
Park (Mike), London Outer 180
Stobart Davies Limited, Carmarthwnshire...... 276
Summerfield Books Ltd, Cumbria................ 76

FOSSILS
Baldwin's Scientific Books, Essex 112
J & J Burgess Booksellers, Cambridgeshire..... 64
Kalligraphia (formerly Charmouth Bounty Books),
   Isle of Wight 134
Roger Collicott Books, Cornwall 74
The Sanctuary Bookshop, Dorset................. 93

FOURTH WAY
Needham Books, (Russell), Somerset 216

FREE THOUGHT
Church Street Books, Norfolk..................... 184
Forder (R.W.), Hampshire 122
Humanist Book Services, Cornwall............... 72
Kenny's Bookshops and Art Galleries Ltd,
   Co. Galway 260
Northern Herald Books, West Yorkshire 241
Stevens (Joan), Cambridgeshire 65
Turton (John), Durham............................. 97
Turton (John), Durham............................. 97
Webb Books (John), South Yorkshire 217

FREEMASONRY & ANTI-MASONRY
Alpha Books, London N........................... 155
Bibliophile (The), South Yorkshire 217
Bookworm, Lothian................................. 270
Chas J. Sawyer, Kent 140
Fun in Books, Surrey 229
Gilbert (R.A.), Bristol.............................. 59
Gildas Books, Cheshire 68
Holdenhurst Books, Dorset........................ 90
Inner Bookshop (The), Oxfordshire 205
InterCol London, London N 156
Occultique, Northamptonshire..................... 196
Samovar Books, Co. Dublin....................... 258
Yesterday's News, Conwy 278

FRENCH FOREIGN LEGION, THE
Wiend Books, Lancashire 143

FREUDIANA
Apocalypse, Surrey 228

FUNGI
Edmund Pollinger Rare Books, London SW... 165

FUR TRADE
Americanabooksuk, Cumbria...................... 76

FURNITURE
Art Reference Books, Hampshire 125
Cornucopia Books, Lincolnshire 151
Don Kelly Books, London W 170
Hadfield (G.K.), Cumbria 78
Heneage Art Books (Thomas), London SW.... 166
Holdenhurst Books, Dorset 90
N1 Books, East Sussex 103
Reeves Technical Books, North Yorkshire...... 193
Scrivener's Books & Bookbinding, Derbyshire . 81
Sleepy Elephant Books & Artefacts, Cumbria.. 79
Trinders' Fine Tools, Suffolk 222
Upper–Room Books, Somerset 214

GAMBLING
Amos (Denis W.), Hertfordshire 130
Delectus Books, London WC 174
InterCol London, London N 156
Junk & Spread Eagle, London SE 162
Yesterday's News, Conwy 278

GAMES
Baron (Christopher), Greater Manchester 118
Bookmark (Children's Books), Wiltshire 248
Cheshire Book Centre, Cheshire 69
Game Advice, Oxfordshire 205
InterCol London, London N 156
R. S. & P. A. Scowen, Middlesex 179
Saint Swithin's Illustrated & Children's Books, London W 172

GARDENING - GENERAL
Abacus Books, Greater Manchester 118
Abacus Gallery, Staffordshire 220
Apocalypse, Surrey 228
Arden Books & Cosmographia, Warwickshire . 232
Arden, Bookseller (C.), Powys 282
Barn Books, Shropshire 211
Barnhill Books, Isle of Arran 269
Besleys Books, Suffolk 221
Bianco Library, West Sussex 237
Blest (Peter), Kent 139
Book House (The), Cumbria 78
Bookroom (The), Surrey 229
Books, Denbighshire 278
Books & Collectables Ltd., Cambridgeshire 63
Books for Content, Herefordshire 128
Bookworld, Shropshire 210
Bosco Books, Cornwall 72
Brighton Books, East Sussex 98
Brown-Studies, Strathclyde 273
Browse Books, Lancashire 143
Calendula Horticultural Books, East Sussex 101
Camilla's Bookshop, East Sussex 100
Castleton (Pat), Kent 137
Chantrey Books, South Yorkshire 217
Chaucer Bookshop, Kent 136
Cheshire Book Centre, Cheshire 69
Clark (M.R.), West Yorkshire 241
Clarke Books (David), Somerset 214

Court Hay Books, Bristol 58
Cousens (W.C.), Devon 83
D'Arcy Books, Wiltshire 246
Dales & Lakes Book Centre, Cumbria 79
Daly (Peter M.), Hampshire 127
Dartmoor Bookshop (The), Devon 83
Davies Fine Books, Worcestershire 252
Duck (William), Hampshire 124
Dusty Books, Powys 285
Ellis, Bookseller (Peter), London SE 162
Esoteric Dreams Bookshop, Cumbria 77
Evergreen Livres, Gloucestershire 115
Ford Books (David), Hertfordshire 132
Furneaux Books (Lee), Devon 88
Gardener & Cook, London SW 165
Garfi Books, Ceredigion 282
GfB: the Colchester Bookshop, Essex 109
Goodyer (Nicholas), London N 156
Hennessey Bookseller (Ray), East Sussex 99
Hollett and Son (R.F.G.), Cumbria 79
Hollingshead (Chris), London Outer 181
Hünersdorff Rare Books, London SW 166
Inprint, Gloucestershire 116
Internet Bookshop UK Ltd., Gloucestershire .. 113
Jade Mountain, Hampshire 125
Jay Books, Lothian 271
Junk & Spread Eagle, London SE 162
Libra Books, Lincolnshire 148
Macbuiks, North Yorkshire 190
Marble Hill Books, Middlesex 181
My Back Pages, London SW 167
Optimus Books Ltd, West Sussex 240
Park (Mike), London Outer 180
Parrott Books, Oxfordshire 207
Portobello Books, London W 172
Potterton Books, North Yorkshire 194
Queen Victoria PH, Torfaen 287
Rare & Racy, South Yorkshire 217
River Reads Bookshop, Devon 89
Rutland Bookshop (The), Rutland 208
Saint Ann's Books, Worcestershire 251
Savery Books, East Sussex 99
Seeber (Liz), East Sussex 99
Silver Trees Books, West Midlands 234
Staniland (Booksellers), Lincolnshire 152
Sue Lowell Natural History Books, London W 173
Summerfield Books Ltd, Cumbria 76
Tant Yn Ellen Books, Powys 286
Thin Read Line, Merseyside 182
Trinders' Fine Tools, Suffolk 222
Vokes Books Ltd., North Yorkshire 192
Wadard Books, Kent 137
Westwood Books Ltd, Cumbria 79
Wyseby House Books, Berkshire 55

GEMMOLOGY
Baldwin's Scientific Books, Essex 112
Barmby (C. & A.J.), Kent 140
Don Kelly Books, London W 170
Hadfield (G.K.), Cumbria 78
J.G. Natural History Books, Surrey 228

SPECIALITY INDEX 397

Mandalay Bookshop, London SW 166
Nibris Books, London SW 167
Trinders' Fine Tools, Suffolk 222

GENDER STUDIES
PsychoBabel Books & Journals, Oxfordshire ... 202
Reading Lasses, Dumfries & Galloway 265

GENEALOGY
Ambra Books, Bristol 58
Booth Books, Powys 282
Brewin Books Ltd., Warwickshire 233
Cofion Books, Pembrokeshire 281
De Burca Rare Books, Co. Dublin 259
Delph Books, Greater Manchester 120
Farquharson, (Hilary), Tayside 275
Grampian Books, Grampian 268
Hawes Books, Norfolk 187
Hay Cinema Bookshop Ltd., Herefordshire 283
Heraldry Today, Wiltshire 247
Heritage, West Midlands 234
Hill Books (Alan), South Yorkshire 217
Hutchison (Books) (Larry), Fife 265
Idle Booksellers (The), West Yorkshire 241
Island Books, Kent 136
Kingswood Books, Dorset 93
Moore (C.R.), Shropshire 210
Spooner & Co, Somerset 215
Titford (John), Derbyshire 81
Townsend (John), Berkshire 57
Turton (John), Durham 97
Turton (John), Durham 97
Tyger Press, London N 157

GENETICS
Baldwin's Scientific Books, Essex 112

GEOGRAPHY
Acer Books, Herefordshire 128
Altea Antique Maps & Books, London W 169
Archer (David), Powys 285
Chesters (G. & J.), Staffordshire 220
Cornucopia Books, Lincolnshire 151
Harrington Antiquarian Bookseller (Peter),
  London SW 166
Kabristan Archives, Shropshire 211
Kalligraphia (formerly Charmouth Bounty
  Books), Isle of Wight 134
Maghreb Bookshop (The), London WC 175
Roadmaster Books, Kent 137
Sparrow Books, West Yorkshire 241
Tooley, Adams & Co, Oxfordshire 206

GEOLOGY
Archer (David), Powys 285
Austwick Hall Books, Lancaster 190
Baldwin's Scientific Books, Essex 112
Bott, (Bookdealers) Ltd., (Martin), Greater
  Manchester 118
Bow Windows Book Shop, East Sussex 102

Cheshire Book Centre, Cheshire 69
Chesters (G. & J.), Staffordshire 220
Clevedon Books, Somerset 214
Cornucopia Books, Lincolnshire 151
Duck (William), Hampshire 124
Earth Science Books, Wiltshire 247
Esoteric Dreams Bookshop, Cumbria 77
Geophysical Books, Kent 140
Henly (John), West Sussex 239
Holdenhurst Books, Dorset 90
Hollett and Son (R.F.G.), Cumbria 79
K.S.C. Books, Cheshire 68
Kalligraphia (formerly Charmouth Bounty
  Books), Isle of Wight 134
Little Bookshop (The), Cumbria 80
Lymelight Books & Prints, Dorset 92
Maggs Brothers Limited, London W 171
Periplus Books, Buckinghamshire 62
Phelps (Michael), West Sussex 237
Reads, Dorset 94
Roadmaster Books, Kent 137
Roger Collicott Books, Cornwall 74
Sparrow Books, West Yorkshire 241
Stalagluft Books, Tyne and Wear 231
Weiner (Graham), London N 157
Westwood Books Ltd, Cumbria 79
Whitchurch Books Ltd., Cardiff 276
Wiend Books, Lancashire 143

GEOPHYSICS
Geophysical Books, Kent 140

GHOSTS
AA1 Books, Dumfries & Galloway 264
Apocalypse, Surrey 228
Cornucopia Books, Lincolnshire 151
Cowley, Bookdealer (K.W.), Somerset 214
Dalby (Richard), North Yorkshire 192
Enigma Books, Norfolk 186
Esoteric Dreams Bookshop, Cumbria 77
Gildas Books, Cheshire 68
Holdenhurst Books, Dorset 90
Inner Bookshop (The), Oxfordshire 205
Loretta Lay Books, London NW 159
Magis Books, Leicestershire 147
Meads Book Service (The), East Sussex 103
Occultique, Northamptonshire 196
Roger Collicott Books, Cornwall 74
SETI Books, Staffordshire 220
Wizard Books, Cambridgeshire 67

GLAMOUR
Book Palace (The), London SE 161
Fun in Books, Surrey 229
Muttonchop Manuscripts 239
N1 Books, East Sussex 103
Paper Pleasures, Somerset 215
Tilleys Vintage Magazine Shop, Derbyshire 81
Yesterday's News, Conwy 278
Zardoz Books, Wiltshire 249

GLASS
Ancient Art Books, London SW.................. 164
Art Reference Books, Hampshire................. 125
Barmby (C. & A.J.), Kent......................... 140
Heneage Art Books (Thomas), London SW.... 166
Stained Glass Books, Kent........................ 139
Trinders' Fine Tools, Suffolk 222

GNOSTICS
Gilbert (R.A.), Bristol.............................. 59
Rosemary Pugh Books, Wiltshire 248

GOLD RUSH
Americanabooksuk, Cumbria..................... 76
Apocalypse, Surrey 228

GOLDSMITHS
Don Kelly Books, London W 170

GOTHIC REVIVAL
Don Kelly Books, London W 170

GRAND CANYON & COLORADO RIVER, THE
Americanabooksuk, Cumbria..................... 76

GRAPHIC NOVELS
Book Palace (The), London SE 161

GRAPHICS
Amwell Book Company, London SE............ 154
Book Palace (The), London SE 161
Cornucopia Books, Lincolnshire 151
Lawton (J.), Surrey 227

GRAPHOLOGY
Magis Books, Leicestershire...................... 147

GUIDE BOOKS
Abrahams (Mike), Staffordshire.................. 219
Apocalypse, Surrey 228
Arden Books & Cosmographia,
  Warwickshire.................................... 232
Baedekers & Murray Guides, South Yorkshire 217
Bookworld, Shropshire............................ 210
Cavern Books, Cheshire 70
Church Street Books, Norfolk.................... 184
Collectables (W.H.), Suffolk 225
Cornucopia Books, Lincolnshire 151
Hellenic Bookservices, London NW............. 158
Hodgson (Books) (Richard J.),
  North Yorkshire................................. 194
Island Books, Kent................................. 136
Prospect House Books, Co. Down 256
Roger Collicott Books, Cornwall 74
Royal Carbery Books Ltd., Co. Cork 257
Shacklock Books (David), Suffolk............... 222

Shapero Rare Books (Bernard J.), London W . 172
Trinders' Fine Tools, Suffolk 222
Trinity Rare Books, Co. Leitrim 260

GYNAECOLOGY
Alba Books, Grampian 267
Reading Lasses, Dumfries & Galloway 265

GYPSIES
Abrahams (Mike), Staffordshire.................. 219
Cottage Books, Leicestershire.................... 145
Cover to Cover, Merseyside...................... 183
Delectus Books, London WC..................... 174
Doorbar (P. & D.), Gwynned 279
Dworski Books, Travel & Language Bookshop
  (Marijana), Herefordshire 283
Holmes (A.), Nottinghamshire.................... 201
John Underwood Antiquarian Books, Norfolk 186
Philip Hopper, Essex 110
York (Graham), Devon............................ 85

HAIRDRESSING
Black Cat Books, Norfolk......................... 185

HAND BOOKBINDING (SEE ALSO BOOKBINDING)
Barry McKay Rare Books, Cumbria............. 76
John Underwood Antiquarian Books, Norfolk 186

HANDWRITING
Barry McKay Rare Books, Cumbria............. 76

HANDWRITTEN BOOKS
Apocalypse, Surrey 228
John Underwood Antiquarian Books, Norfolk 186

HEALTH
Autumn Leaves, Lincolnshire..................... 150
Cheshire Book Centre, Cheshire 69
Collectable Books, London SE 162
Dworski Books, Travel & Language Bookshop
  (Marijana), Herefordshire 283
Greensleeves, Oxfordshire 202
Hurst (Jenny), Kent 138
Inner Bookshop (The), Oxfordshire 205
Orchid Book Distributors, Co. Clare............ 257
Oxfam Books and Music, Hampshire............ 127
Pickering & Chatto, London W................... 172
Prescott - The Bookseller (John),
  London Outer 181
Reading Lasses, Dumfries & Galloway 265
River Reads Bookshop, Devon.................... 89
Roland Books, Kent................................ 139
Shapero Rare Books (Bernard J.), London W . 172
Till's Bookshop, Lothian 272
Woburn Books, London N 157

SPECIALITY INDEX

HERALDRY
Heraldry Today, Wiltshire.......................... 247
Heritage, West Midlands 234
Marcet Books, London SE......................... 161
McEwan Fine Books, Grampian.................. 266
Moore (C.R.), Shropshire 210
N1 Books, East Sussex.............................. 103
RGS Books, Surrey................................... 229
Scrivener's Books & Bookbinding, Derbyshire. 81
Spooner & Co, Somerset 215
Taylor & Son (Peter), Hertfordshire.............. 132
Townsend (John), Berkshire 57
Turton (John), Durham............................... 97
Turton (John), Durham............................... 97

HERBALISM
Blest (Peter), Kent 139
Brown-Studies, Strathclyde......................... 273
Calendula Horticultural Books, East Sussex.... 101
Chantrey Books, South Yorkshire................. 217
Edmund Pollinger Rare Books, London SW... 165
Greensleeves, Oxfordshire 202
Guildmaster Books, Cheshire 70
Hollingshead (Chris), London Outer 181
IKON, Devon 88
Inner Bookshop (The), Oxfordshire 205
Lucas (Richard), London NW 159
Occultique, Northamptonshire...................... 196
Orchid Book Distributors, Co. Clare............. 257
Park (Mike), London Outer 180
Phelps (Michael), West Sussex.................... 237
Wadard Books, Kent................................. 137

HERITAGE
Cornucopia Books, Lincolnshire 151
G. C. Books Ltd., Dumfries & Galloway 264

HERMETICISM
Alpha Books, London N 155
Chthonios Books, East Sussex..................... 101
Inner Bookshop (The), Oxfordshire 205
Magis Books, Leicestershire........................ 147
Occultique, Northamptonshire...................... 196

HERPETOLOGY
Blest (Peter), Kent 139
J.G. Natural History Books, Surrey.............. 228
Mobbs (A.J.), West Midlands 235
Pemberley Books, Buckinghamshire............... 62
Steven Simpson Books, Norfolk 188

HIMALAYAN KINGDOMS
David Warnes Books, Herefordshire.............. 129

HISTORY
  - GENERAL
AA1 Books, Dumfries & Galloway 264
Abacus Gallery, Staffordshire....................... 220
Abbey Books, Cornwall 73

Addyman Books, Powys............................. 282
Alexander's Books, Warwickshire................. 232
All Books, Essex 110
Anchor Books, Lincolnshire 149
Andrew Morton (Books), Powys.................. 281
Antiquary Ltd., (Bar Bookstore),
  North Yorkshire.................................... 192
Antiques on High, Oxfordshire.................... 204
Apocalypse, Surrey 228
Arden Books & Cosmographia, Warwickshire . 232
Askew Books (Vernon), Wiltshire 246
Aurora Books Ltd, Lothian......................... 270
Autumn Leaves, Lincolnshire...................... 150
Axe Rare & Out of Print Books (Richard),
  North Yorkshire.................................... 190
Baker Limited (A.P. & R.), Dumfries
  & Galloway 264
Barbican Bookshop, North Yorkshire 194
Barcombe Services, Essex.......................... 108
Bardsley's Books, Suffolk........................... 221
Barn Books, Buckinghamshire..................... 61
Barnes (Peter), Wiltshire 248
Baxter (Steve), Surrey 228
Beardsell Books, West Yorkshire 242
Bell (Peter), Strathclyde 270
Bennett & Kerr Books, Oxfordshire.............. 202
Berry (L.J.), Kent 138
Beware of the Leopard, Bristol.................... 58
Black Five Books, Shropshire 211
Bookroom (The), Surrey............................ 229
Books, Denbighshire.................................. 278
Books & Bygones (Pam Taylor),
  West Midlands..................................... 236
Books & Collectables Ltd., Cambridgeshire 63
Books (For All), North Yorkshire................ 190
Books Antiques & Collectables, Devon.......... 88
Books Bought & Sold, Surrey 226
Books on the Bank, Durham...................... 96
books2books, Devon................................. 87
Bookshop (The), Dorset 92
Bookshop (The), Greater Manchester............ 119
Bookshop (The), West Sussex 238
Bookshop at the Plain, Lincolnshire.............. 151
Bookworm, Lothian 270
Bookworm (The), Lothian 271
Bookworms of Evesham, Worcestershire........ 252
Booth Books, Powys 282
Bracton Books, Cambridgeshire................... 63
Brian Troath Books, London E.................... 153
Brimstones, East Sussex............................. 102
Broadhurst of Southport Ltd., Merseyside...... 182
Broadwater Books, Hampshire 126
Broadway Books, Cambridgeshire................. 66
Brockwells Booksellers, Lincolnshire 148
Broughton Books, Lothian.......................... 271
Caledonia Books, Strathclyde...................... 273
Caliver Books, Essex 110
Carnforth Bookshop (The), Lancashire.......... 142
Carningli Centre, Pembrokeshire.................. 281
Castle Hill Books, Herefordshire 128
Castleton (Pat), Kent 137
Catalyst Booksearch Services, Devon 85

SPECIALITY INDEX

Celtic Bookshop (The), Co. Limerick 261
Central Bookshop, Warwickshire 232
Channel Islands Galleries Limited,
　Channel Islands.................................... 253
Chaucer Bookshop, Kent.......................... 136
Cheshire Book Centre, Cheshire 69
Chesters (G. & J.), Staffordshire 220
Clarendon Books, Leicestershire 145
Classic Bindings Ltd, London SW............... 164
Clements (R.W.), London Outer................. 179
Cobbles Books, Somerset.......................... 214
Coombes (A.J.), Surrey 226
Corfe Books, Surrey 227
Cox Old & Rare Books (Claude), Suffolk....... 223
Crouch Rare Books, Surrey....................... 227
D'Arcy Books, Wiltshire........................... 246
Dales & Lakes Book Centre, Cumbria 79
Dandy Lion Editions, Surrey 228
Darkwood Books, Co. Cork 258
Derek Stirling Bookseller, Kent 141
Dolphin Books, Suffolk............................ 221
Driffield Bookshop (The), East Yorkshire....... 105
Dusty Old Books Ltd., Oxfordshire 204
Dworski Books, Travel & Language Bookshop
　(Marijana), Herefordshire 283
Eagle Bookshop (The), Bedfordshire............. 53
Eastern Traveller (The), Somerset................ 216
Eastleach Books, Berkshire........................ 55
Edwards (Christopher), Berkshire................. 55
Edwards (London) Limited (Francis),
　London WC.. 175
Edwards in Hay–on–Wye (Francis),
　Herefordshire 283
Esoteric Dreams Bookshop, Cumbria............ 77
Eton Antique Bookshop, Berkshire............... 57
Farnborough Gallery, Hampshire 123
Fireside Books, Buckinghamshire................. 62
Fireside Bookshop, Cumbria 80
Ford Books (David), Hertfordshire............... 132
Fossgate Books, North Yorkshire 194
Foster (Stephen), London NW 158
Frew Limited (Robert), London W 170
Frost (Richard), Hertfordshire..................... 130
Furneaux Books (Lee), Devon 88
G. C. Books Ltd., Dumfries & Galloway 264
Gildas Books, Cheshire............................ 68
Gloucester Road Bookshop, London SW....... 165
Glyn's Books, Shropshire.......................... 209
Good for Books, Lincolnshire 149
Graham (John), Dorset 95
Grahame Thornton, Bookseller, Dorset 92
Greta Books, Durham 96
Hall's Bookshop, Kent............................. 141
Handsworth Books, Essex......................... 112
Hawley (C.L.), North Yorkshire.................. 193
Hay Cinema Bookshop Ltd., Herefordshire 283
Helion & Company, West Midlands 235
Heraldry Today, Wiltshire......................... 247
Heywood Hill Limited (G.), London W 171
Holmes (A.), Nottinghamshire.................... 201
Hornsby, Antiquarian and Secondhand Books
　(Malcolm), Leicestershire 146

Hornsey's, North Yorkshire....................... 192
Horsham Rare Books, West Sussex 238
Howes Bookshop, East Sussex 101
Hughes Rare Books (Spike), Borders 262
Hunt (Robin S.), Greater Manchester 120
Hurst (Jenny), Kent 138
Hutchison (Books) (Larry), Fife.................. 265
Ice House Books, Wiltshire 248
J & J Burgess Booksellers, Cambridgeshire 64
Jade Mountain, Hampshire 125
Jones (Andrew), Suffolk 223
Judd Books, London WC 175
Junk & Spread Eagle, London SE................ 162
Kalligraphia (formerly Charmouth Bounty
　Books), Isle of Wight............................ 134
Katnap Arts, Norfolk 187
Kelsall (George), Greater Manchester........... 119
Kemp Booksellers, East Yorkshire 106
Kilgarriff (Raymond), East Sussex............... 104
Kim's Bookshop, West Sussex............. 237, 240
King Street Bookshop (The), Norfolk 185
Lawrence Books, Nottinghamshire 200
Leabeck Books, Oxfordshire...................... 205
Lewis (J.T. & P.), Cornwall 73
Libra Books, Lincolnshire......................... 148
Libris (Weston) Books, Somerset................. 213
Little Bookshop (The), Greater Manchester 119
Lost Books, Northamptonshire 197
Marble Hill Books, Middlesex.................... 181
Marcet Books, London SE........................ 161
Marine and Cannon Books, Cheshire............ 69
McCrone (Audrey), Isle of Arran................ 269
Meekins Books (Paul), Warwickshire 233
Mellon's Books, East Sussex...................... 100
Ming Books, Dumfries & Galloway.............. 265
Modern Welsh Publications Ltd., Merseyside .. 182
Morgan (H.J.), Bedfordshire...................... 54
Mundy (David), Buckinghamshire................ 61
Mundy (David), Hertfordshire 130
Murphy (C.J.), Norfolk............................ 187
My Back Pages, London SW...................... 167
N1 Books, East Sussex............................ 103
Naughton Booksellers, Co. Dublin 259
Nicolas - Antiquarian Booksellers & Art
　Dealers, London N 156
Nineteenth Century Books, Oxfordshire......... 207
Nonsuch Books, Surrey........................... 229
Not JUST Books, Lincolnshire................... 148
O'Brien Books & Photo Gallery, Co. Limerick 261
Old Bookshop (The), West Midlands 236
Old Town Bookshop (The), Lothian 271
Olynthiacs, Shropshire 210
Oxfam Books and Music, Hampshire 127
Parkinsons Books, Merseyside.................... 183
Parrott Books, Oxfordshire 207
Paton Books, Hertfordshire 132
Period Fine Bindings, Warwickshire.............. 233
Polmorla Books, Cornwall 75
Pomes Penyeach, Staffordshire.................... 219
Pordes Books Ltd., (Henry), London WC 176
Portobello Books, London W 172
Quentin Books Ltd., Essex........................ 109

SPECIALITY INDEX

Quinto of Charing Cross Road, London WC.. 176
Quinto of Great Russell Street, London WC... 176
Reading Lasses, Dumfries & Galloway 265
RGS Books, Surrey 229
Richard Thornton Books, London N 157
Richmond Books, North Yorkshire 192
Rods Books, Devon 87
Roland Books, Kent 139
Rothwell & Dunworth, Somerset 214
Roundstone Books, Lancashire 143
Rowan (P. & B.), Co. Antrim 255
Royal Carbery Books Ltd., Co. Cork 257
Ryeland Books, Northamptonshire 196
Saint Philip's Books, Oxfordshire 205
Scott (Peter), East Sussex 103
Scrivener's Books & Bookbinding, Derbyshire . 81
Shacklock Books (David), Suffolk 222
Shapero Rare Books (Bernard J.), London W . 172
Silverman (Michael), London SE 163
Singleton (Anthony), South Yorkshire 217
Skoob Russell Square, Suffolk 225
Spelman (Ken), North Yorkshire 195
Spurrier (Nick), Kent 138
Staffs Bookshop (The), Staffordshire 219
Staniland (Booksellers), Lincolnshire 152
Sterling Books, Somerset 216
Stern Antiquarian Bookseller (Jeffrey), North
  Yorkshire 195
Stothert Old Books, Cheshire 68
Sykes (Graham), West Yorkshire 244
Symes Books (Naomi), Cheshire 71
The Dormouse Bookshop, Norfolk 188
The Glass Key, West Yorkshire 242
Thistle Books, Strathclyde 274
Thomas (E. Wyn), Conwy 278
Thorntons of Oxford Ltd., Oxfordshire 203
Till's Bookshop, Lothian 272
Tilston (Stephen E.), London SE 161
Titford (John), Derbyshire 81
Townsend (John), Berkshire 57
Treasure Trove Books, Leicestershire 146
Tuft (Patrick), London W 173
Tyger Press, London N 157
Unsworths Booksellers, London NW 160
Village Books, Norfolk 184
Water Lane Bookshop, Wiltshire 248
Waterfield's, Oxfordshire 206
Watkins (R.G.), Somerset 213
Waxfactor, East Sussex 99
Weiner (Graham), London N 157
Westcountry Old Books, Cornwall 75
Westwood Books (Mark), Powys 284
Westwood Books Ltd, Cumbria 79
Whig Books Ltd., Leicestershire 147
Whitchurch Books Ltd., Cardiff 276
Willmott Bookseller (Nicholas), Cardiff 276
Words Etcetera Bookshop, Dorset 92
Worlds End Bookshop, London SW 168
Yesterday's Books, Dorset 91
Yewtree Books, Cumbria 77

- 19TH CENTURY
Americanabooksuk, Cumbria 76
Apocalypse, Surrey 228
Castleton (Pat), Kent 137
Cox Rare Books (Charles), Cornwall 73
Derek Stirling Bookseller, Kent 141
Helion & Company, West Midlands 235
J & J Burgess Booksellers, Cambridgeshire 64
Junk & Spread Eagle, London SE 162
Kenny's Bookshops and Art Galleries Ltd,
  Co. Galway 260
N1 Books, East Sussex 103
Symes Books (Naomi), Cheshire 71
Whitchurch Books Ltd., Cardiff 276

- AMERICAN
Americanabooksuk, Cumbria 76
Helion & Company, West Midlands 235
Kenny's Bookshops and Art Galleries Ltd, Co.
  Galway 260
Quentin Books Ltd, Essex 109

- AMERICAN REVOLUTION
Americanabooksuk, Cumbria 76

- ANARCHISM
Delectus Books, London WC 174
Helion & Company, West Midlands 235
Red Star Books, Hertfordshire 130

- ANCIENT
Aviabooks, Gloucestershire 114
BC Books, Cheshire 69
Berry (L.J.), Kent 138
Black Five Books, Shropshire 211
Books B.C., London Outer 178
Byre Books, Dumfries & Galloway 264
Classics Bookshop (The), Oxfordshire 202
Crouch Rare Books, Surrey 227
Ford Books (David), Hertfordshire 132
GfB: the Colchester Bookshop, Essex 109
Gildas Books, Cheshire 68
Helion & Company, West Midlands 235
Junk & Spread Eagle, London SE 162
Kingswood Books, Dorset 93
Meekins Books (Paul), Warwickshire 233
Michael Graves-Johnston, London SW 166
Miller (Karen), Nottinghamshire 200
N1 Books, East Sussex 103
Rods Books, Devon 87
Rosanda Books, Leicestershire 146
Thorntons of Oxford Ltd., Oxfordshire 203
Trotter Books (John), London N 157
Unsworths Booksellers, London NW 160
Whitchurch Books Ltd., Cardiff 276

- BRITISH
Apocalypse, Surrey 228
Ardis Books, Hampshire 126

SPECIALITY INDEX

Aviabooks, Gloucestershire 114
Barbican Bookshop, North Yorkshire 194
BC Books, Cheshire 69
Bell (Peter), Strathclyde 270
Black Five Books, Shropshire 211
Clarke Books (David), Somerset 214
Clifton Books, Essex 111
Cobbles Books, Somerset 214
Coombes (A.J.), Surrey 226
Corder (Mark W.), Kent 140
Garfi Books, Ceredigion 282
GfB: the Colchester Bookshop, Essex............ 109
Gildas Books, Cheshire 68
Guildmaster Books, Cheshire...................... 70
Helion & Company, West Midlands 235
Island Books, Kent 136
Jackdaw Books, Norfolk 185
Junk & Spread Eagle, London SE................. 162
K.S.C. Books, Cheshire 68
Lowe (John), Norfolk 186
Meekins Books (Paul), Warwickshire 233
Miller (Karen), Nottinghamshire................... 200
N1 Books, East Sussex.............................. 103
Naughton Booksellers, Co. Dublin 259
Orb's Bookshop, Grampian........................ 268
Ouse Valley Books, Bedfordshire 54
Rods Books, Devon 87
Rosanda Books, Leicestershire 146
Saint Philip's Books, Oxfordshire 205
Samovar Books, Co. Dublin....................... 258
Shakeshaft (Dr. B.), Cheshire...................... 71
Skoob Russell Square, Suffolk..................... 225
Spenceley Books (David), West Yorkshire 244
Stalagluft Books, Tyne and Wear................. 231
Studio Bookshop, East Sussex..................... 99
Symes Books (Naomi), Cheshire 71
Taylor & Son (Peter), Hertfordshire............... 132
Unsworths Booksellers, London NW 160
Whitchurch Books Ltd., Cardiff 276
Wiend Books, Lancashire 143

- BRITISH EMPIRE, THE

Apocalypse, Surrey 228
G. C. Books Ltd., Dumfries & Galloway 264
N1 Books, East Sussex.............................. 103

- BYZANTINE

Camden Books, Somerset 212
Dworski Books, Travel & Language Bookshop
  (Marijana), Herefordshire 283
Helion & Company, West Midlands 235
Kingswood Books, Dorset 93
Unsworths Booksellers, London NW 160

- COLONIAL

N1 Books, East Sussex.............................. 103

- DESIGN

Art Reference Books, Hampshire 125
Black Cat Books, Norfolk.......................... 185

Don Kelly Books, London W 170
Inch's Books, North Yorkshire.................... 192
Sun House Books, Kent 139

- ECONOMIC THOUGHT

Hamish Riley-Smith, Norfolk 188

- EUROPEAN

Apocalypse, Surrey 228
Bell (Peter), Strathclyde 270
Books on Spain, London Outer................... 181
de Visser Books, Cambridgeshire 63
Dworski Books, Travel & Language Bookshop
  (Marijana), Herefordshire 283
Helion & Company, West Midlands 235
IKON, Devon 88
Miller (Karen), Nottinghamshire................... 200
Naughton Booksellers, Co. Dublin 259
Roland Books, Kent.................................. 139
Rosanda Books, Leicestershire 146
Saint Philip's Books, Oxfordshire 205
Symes Books (Naomi), Cheshire 71
Unsworths Booksellers, London NW 160

- FAMILY

Atholl Fine Books, Tayside 275
Delph Books, Greater Manchester................ 120
McEwan Fine Books, Grampian................... 266

- GUILDS & LIVERY COMPANIES

Chas J. Sawyer, Kent 140

- INDUSTRIAL

Anvil Books, West Midlands 235
Barbican Bookshop, North Yorkshire 194
Blanchfield (John), West Yorkshire............... 243
Book House (The), Cumbria 78
Books & Bygones (Pam Taylor),
  West Midlands.................................... 236
Clevedon Books, Somerset 214
Coulthurst (Richard), Greater Manchester...... 120
Cox (Geoff), Devon 89
Crosby Nethercott Books, London Outer....... 178
Dales and Lakes Book Centre, Cumbria 79
Garfi Books, Ceredigion 282
Graham (John), Dorset 95
Hall, (Anthony C.) Antiquarian Bookseller,
  London Outer 181
Hedgerow Books, South Yorkshire................ 217
Helion & Company, West Midlands 235
Humm & Co. (Robert), Lincolnshire 151
Kelsall (George), Greater Manchester............ 119
Kenny's Bookshops and Art Galleries Ltd,
  Co. Galway 260
N1 Books, East Sussex.............................. 103
Rainford (Sheila), Hertfordshire................... 130
Rochdale Book Company, Greater Manchester 120
Scarthin Books, Derbyshire 81
Skyrack Books, West Yorkshire................... 243
Symes Books (Naomi), Cheshire 71

SPECIALITY INDEX

Tony Pollastrone Railway Books, Wiltshire 246
Trinders' Fine Tools, Suffolk 222
Vickers (Anthony), North Yorkshire 193
Whitchurch Books Ltd., Cardiff 276
Ystwyth Books, Ceredigion 277

- IRISH

Abbey Books, Cornwall 73
Apocalypse, Surrey 228
Armchair Books, Lothian 270
Bookline, Co. Down............................... 256
Darkwood Books, Co. Cork....................... 258
Gildas Books, Cheshire 68
Helion & Company, West Midlands 235
Karen Millward, Co. Cork........................ 257
Kenny's Bookshops and Art Galleries Ltd,
  Co. Galway 260
Naughton Booksellers, Co. Dublin 259
Prospect House Books, Co. Down 256
Read Ireland, Co. Dublin 258
Roscrea Bookshop, Co. Tipperary................ 261
Taylor & Son (Peter), Hertfordshire.............. 132

- LABOUR/ RADICAL MOVEMENTS

Cox Rare Books (Charles), Cornwall 73
Delectus Books, London WC..................... 174
Helion & Company, West Midlands 235
Left on The Shelf, Cumbria....................... 78
Reading Lasses, Dumfries & Galloway 265
Red Star Books, Hertfordshire 130
Symes Books (Naomi), Cheshire 71
Woburn Books, London N 157

- LOCAL

Abrahams (Mike), Staffordshire................... 219
Ambra Books, Bristol 58
Arden Books & Cosmographia, Warwickshire . 232
Atholl Fine Books, Tayside 275
Barbican Bookshop, North Yorkshire 194
Barn Books, Shropshire........................... 211
Bear Island Books, Cardiff 276
Beardsell Books, West Yorkshire 242
Beverley Old Bookshop, East Yorkshire 105
Black Five Books, Shropshire 211
Bonython Bookshop, Cornwall................... 75
Book For All Reasons (A.), Suffolk.............. 224
Bookshop (The), Co. Donegal.................... 258
Border Books, Borders............................ 262
Brazenhead Ltd., Norfolk 186
Bridge of Allan Books, Central 263
Brown (Books) (P.R.), Durham 97
Burebank Books, Norfolk 184
Bury Bookshop, Suffolk 221
Carlton Books, Norfolk 187
Carnforth Bookshop (The), Lancashire.......... 142
Castle Bookshop, Essex........................... 109
Castle Hill Books, Herefordshire................. 128
Castleton (Pat), Kent.............................. 137
Chaucer Bookshop, Kent......................... 136
Clarendon Books, Leicestershire 145

Clent Books, Worcestershire 250
Colin Hancock, Ceredigion 277
Compass Books, Devon 84
Coombes (A.J.), Surrey 226
Cornucopia Books, Lincolnshire 151
Cottage Books, Leicestershire.................... 145
Country Books, Derbyshire 81
Courtwood Books, Co. Laois..................... 260
Daly (Peter M.), Hampshire 127
Dinnages Transport Publishing, East Sussex.... 98
Dobson (Bob), Lancashire 142
Dormouse Bookshop (The), Norfolk............ 188
Eastgate Bookshop, East Yorkshire 105
Forest Books of Manchester, Cheshire 70
G. C. Books Ltd., Dumfries & Galloway 264
Garretts Antiquarian Books, Isle of Man 254
Gildas Books, Cheshire 68
Godmanchester Books, Cambridgeshire 65
Graham (John), Dorset 95
Hawes Books, Norfolk............................ 187
Hawley (C.L.), North Yorkshire 193
Helion & Company, West Midlands 235
Hicks (Ronald C.), Cornwall 73
Horsham Rare Books, West Sussex 238
Hughes Rare Books (Spike), Borders 262
hullbooks.com, East Yorkshire 106
Iona Bookshop (The), Isle of Iona 269
J C Books, Devon 86
Jackdaw Books, Norfolk 185
John Barton, Hampshire.......................... 127
Just Books, Cornwall..............................75
Karen Millward, Co. Cork........................ 257
Kingsgate Books & Prints, Hampshire........... 127
Letterbox Books, Nottinghamshire 200
Michael J Carroll, Co. Cork 257
Missing Books, Essex............................. 109
Mogul Diamonds, West Midlands 236
Moon's Bookshop (Michael), Cumbria 80
Orb's Bookshop, Grampian....................... 268
Peter White, Hampshire 122
Polmorla Books, Cornwall 75
Priory Books, Worcestershire 252
Quarto Bookshop (The), Fife 266
Rare & Racy, South Yorkshire................... 217
Rhoda (June), Essex 110
Richard Thornton Books, London N 157
Rods Books, Devon 87
Rose Books, Greater Manchester 120
Ross Old Books & Prints, Herefordshire 128
Royal Carbery Books Ltd., Co. Cork 257
Samovar Books, Co. Dublin 258
Savery Books, East Sussex 99
Scarthin Books, Derbyshire 81
Sedgeberrow Books & Framing, Worcestershire 251
Siop Lyfrau'r Hen Bost, Gwynedd 280
Skyrack Books, West Yorkshire 243
Smith Books (Keith), Herefordshire.............. 128
Spooner & Co, Somerset 215
Stacpoole (George), Co. Limerick 260
Studio (The), Strathclyde......................... 274
Suffolk Rare Books, Suffolk 225
Symes Books (Naomi), Cheshire 71

Taylor & Son (Peter), Hertfordshire 132
Tyger Press, London N 157
Vinovium Books, Durham 96
Wealden Books, Kent 139
Yates Antiquarian Books (Tony), Leicestershire 146

- MIDDLE AGES
Camden Books, Somerset 212
Helion & Company, West Midlands 235
Kingswood Books, Dorset 93
medievalbookshop, London Outer 179
Meekins Books (Paul), Warwickshire 233
Miller (Karen), Nottinghamshire 200
N1 Books, East Sussex 103
Rosanda Books, Leicestershire 146
Spenceley Books (David), West Yorkshire 244
Unsworths Booksellers, London NW 160

- MILITARY (SEE UNDER MILITARY HISTORY)

- MODERN
Naughton Booksellers, Co. Dublin 259
Symes Books (Naomi), Cheshire 71

- NAPOLEONIC
Apocalypse, Surrey 228
N1 Books, East Sussex 103

- NATIONAL
Apocalypse, Surrey 228
Carnforth Bookshop (The), Lancashire 142
Craobh Rua Books, Co. Armagh 255
Davidson Books, Co. Down 256
De Burca Rare Books, Co. Dublin 259
Foyle Books, Co. Derry 255
Fuchsia Books, Co. Wexford 261
Graham (John), Dorset 95
Hawes Books, Norfolk 187
Helion & Company, West Midlands 235
Hughes Rare Books (Spike), Borders 262
Joppa Books Ltd., Surrey 226
Kingswood Books, Dorset 93
Politico's.co.uk, Kent 141
Pringle Booksellers (Andrew), Lothian 271
Siop y Morfa, Denbighshire 279
Thistle Books, Strathclyde 274
Whelan (P. & F.), Kent 141
Winghale Books, Lincolnshire 151
Woolcott Books, Dorset 91

- POSTAL
Apocalypse, Surrey 228
Postings, Surrey 228

- REFORMATION
Apocalypse, Surrey 228

- RENAISSANCE, THE
All Books, Essex 110
Apocalypse, Surrey 228
Art Reference Books, Hampshire 125
Helion & Company, West Midlands 235
medievalbookshop, London Outer 179
Spenceley Books (David), West Yorkshire 244
Unsworths Booksellers, London NW 160

- ROMAN
Apocalypse, Surrey 228
Aviabooks, Gloucestershire 114
Helion & Company, West Midlands 235
N1 Books, East Sussex 103
Unsworths Booksellers, London NW 160

- SCIENCE
Orb's Bookshop, Grampian 268
Polczynski (Udo K.H.), Powys 284

- SCOTTISH
Bell (Peter), Strathclyde 270
Byre Books, Dumfries & Galloway 264
Cooper Hay Rare Books, Strathclyde 273
Grampian Books, Grampian 268
Jane Jones Books, Grampian 267
Loch Croispol Bookshop & Restaurant,
   Highland 268
Orb's Bookshop, Grampian 268
Thistle Books, Strathclyde 274
Till's Bookshop, Lothian 272

- WOMEN
Dolphin Books, Suffolk 221
Reading Lasses, Dumfries & Galloway 265
Scorpio Books, Suffolk 221
Spenceley Books (David), West Yorkshire 244
Symes Books (Naomi), Cheshire 71

HISTORY OF CIVILISATION
Apocalypse, Surrey 228
Camden Books, Somerset 212
Crouch Rare Books, Surrey 227
Helion & Company, West Midlands 235
Michael Graves-Johnston, London SW 166
N1 Books, East Sussex 103
Taylor & Son (Peter), Hertfordshire 132

HISTORY OF IDEAS
Apocalypse, Surrey 228
Bernstein (Nicholas), London W 169
Butler Books, Dorset 90
Clevedon Books, Somerset 214
Dean Byass, Bristol 60
Drury Rare Books (John), Essex 111
Eagle Bookshop (The), Bedfordshire 53
Game Advice, Oxfordshire 205
Gildas Books, Cheshire 68
Helion & Company, West Midlands 235

SPECIALITY INDEX

Herb Tandree Philosophy Books,
  Gloucestershire 116
Kenny's Bookshops and Art Galleries Ltd, Co.
  Galway 260
Lee Rare Books (Rachel), Bristol 59
Mair Wilkes Books, Fife........................... 265
Parkinsons Books, Merseyside.................... 183
Pendleburys Bookshop, London N 156
Phillips (Nigel), London SW 167
Price (John), London N 157
Savery Books, East Sussex 99
Schulz–Falster Rare Books (Susanne),
  London N 157
Seydi Rare Books (Sevin), London NW 159
Sokol Books Ltd., London W 172
Taylor & Son (Peter), Hertfordshire.............. 132
Unsworths Booksellers, London NW 160
Weininger Antiquarian Books (Eva M.),
  London NW 160
Westwood Books Ltd, Cumbria 79

HOBBIES
Cheshire Book Centre, Cheshire 69
Cornucopia Books, Lincolnshire 151
DPE Books, Devon................................... 86
Esoteric Dreams Bookshop, Cumbria............ 77
Reeves Technical Books, North Yorkshire...... 193
River Reads Bookshop, Devon.................... 89

HOLOCAUST
Bookshop (The), Greater Manchester............ 119
Dworski Books, Travel & Language Bookshop
  (Marijana), Herefordshire 283
Fishburn Books, London NW..................... 158
Helion & Company, West Midlands 235
Island Books, Kent 136
Rosemary Pugh Books, Wiltshire 248
Samovar Books, Co. Dublin....................... 258
World War Books, Kent 141

HOMEOPATHY
Edmund Pollinger Rare Books, London SW ... 165
Esoteric Dreams Bookshop, Cumbria............ 77
Greensleeves, Oxfordshire 202
Hinchliffe Books, Bristol............................ 59
Magis Books, Leicestershire....................... 147
Occultique, Northamptonshire 196
Orchid Book Distributors, Co. Clare............. 257
Phelps (Michael), West Sussex................... 237
Scrivener's Books & Bookbinding, Derbyshire ... 81
Till's Bookshop, Lothian 272

HOMOSEXUALITY & LESBIANISM
Bookshop (The), Greater Manchester............ 119
Delectus Books, London WC..................... 174
Esoteric Dreams Bookshop, Cumbria............ 77
Gay's The Word, London WC.................... 175
Ian Briddon, Derbyshire............................ 81
Judd Books, London WC.......................... 175
Paper Pleasures, Somerset 215

Reading Lasses, Dumfries & Galloway.......... 265
Till's Bookshop, Lothian 272
Tsbbooks, London SW 167

HORIZON WRITERS
Criterion Books, London Outer................... 180

HOROLOGY
Barmby (C. & A.J.), Kent.......................... 140
Baron (Christopher), Greater Manchester....... 118
Cheshire Book Centre, Cheshire 69
Clark (Nigel A.), London SE...................... 162
Delph Books, Greater Manchester................ 120
Engaging Gear Ltd., Essex 108
Formby Antiques (Jeffrey), Gloucestershire..... 115
Hadfield (G.K.), Cumbria 78
Nibris Books, London SW......................... 167
Rogers Turner Books, London SE 162
Scrivener's Books & Bookbinding, Derbyshire . 81
Trinders' Fine Tools, Suffolk 222

HORSES
Bob Mallory (Books), Derbyshire 82
Castleton (Pat), Kent............................... 137
Cornucopia Books, Lincolnshire 151
Garfi Books, Ceredigion 282
Jane Badger Books, Northamptonshire.......... 196
Jane Jones Books, Grampian...................... 267

HORTICULTURE
Barn Books, Shropshire............................ 211
Black Five Books, Shropshire 211
Blest (Peter), Kent 139
Books (For All), North Yorkshire................ 190
Books for Content, Herefordshire 128
Calendula Horticultural Books, East Sussex.... 101
Clarke Books (David), Somerset 214
Coach House Books, Worcestershire............. 251
Court Hay Books, Bristol 58
Dales & Lakes Book Centre, Cumbria 79
Daly (Peter M.), Hampshire 127
Eastcote Bookshop (The), London Outer 178
Evergreen Livres, Gloucestershire 115
Garfi Books, Ceredigion 282
Hollingshead (Chris), London Outer 181
Orb's Bookshop, Grampian........................ 268
Park (Mike), London Outer 180
Pugh Books (Ian K.), Worcestershire............ 251
Spelman (Ken), North Yorkshire 195
Summerfield Books Ltd, Cumbria 76
Thin Read Line, Merseyside 182
Vokes Books Ltd., North Yorkshire 192

HOUSEKEEPING
Black Cat Books, Norfolk......................... 185
DPE Books, Devon................................... 86
Susan Taylor Books, West Yorkshire............ 243

HUMANISM

Chthonios Books, East Sussex..................... 101
Forder (R.W.), Hampshire......................... 122
Humanist Book Services, Cornwall............... 72
Poole (William), London W 172
Shapero Rare Books (Bernard J.), London W . 172
Unsworths Booksellers, London NW 160

HUMANITIES

Aurora Books Ltd, Lothian........................ 270
Bristol Books, Bristol.............................. 60
Broughton Books, Lothian........................ 271
Chandos Books, London Outer 180
Crouch Rare Books, Surrey....................... 227
Drury Rare Books (John), Essex.................. 111
Fireside Bookshop, Cumbria 80
Forest Books of Manchester, Cheshire 70
Hadley Bookseller (Peter J.), Essex 110
Hawley (C.L.), North Yorkshire 193
hullbooks.com, East Yorkshire.................... 106
Lee Rare Books (Rachel), Bristol 59
Maghreb Bookshop (The), London WC 175
Moseley Books, West Midlands................... 234
Naughton Booksellers, Co. Dublin 259
Phenotype Books, Cumbria 78
Pickering & Chatto, London W................... 172
Plurabelle Books, Cambridgeshire 64
Porter Bookshop (The), South Yorkshire 217
Reading Lasses, Dumfries & Galloway 265
Till's Bookshop, Lothian 272
Unsworths Booksellers, London NW 160
Waterfield's, Oxfordshire 206

HUMOUR

Apocalypse, Surrey 228
Autumn Leaves, Lincolnshire..................... 150
BC Books, Cheshire 69
Black Five Books, Shropshire 211
Bob Mallory (Books), Derbyshire 82
Book Palace (The), London SE 161
Bookstand, Dorset 93
Bookworld, Shropshire............................ 210
Browse Books, Lancashire 143
Carningli Centre, Pembrokeshire................. 281
Cheshire Book Centre, Cheshire 69
Eastcote Bookshop (The), London Outer 178
Fun in Books, Surrey 229
Goldman (Paul), Dorset 94
Grahame Thornton, Bookseller, Dorset 92
Hay Castle, Powys.................................. 283
Ian Briddon, Derbyshire........................... 81
Poetry Bookshop (The), Powys................... 284
Scrivener's Books & Bookbinding, Derbyshire . 81
Willmott Bookseller (Nicholas), Cardiff 276
Yesterday's News, Conwy 278

HYDROGRAPHY

Earth Science Books, Wiltshire................... 247
Phelps (Michael), West Sussex.................... 237

HYMNOLOGY

Humber Books, Lincolnshire 148
Rosemary Pugh Books, Wiltshire................. 248
Samovar Books, Co. Dublin....................... 258
Stalagluft Books, Tyne and Wear................. 231

HYPNOTISM

Magis Books, Leicestershire....................... 147

ICONOGRAPHY

Bardsley's Books, Suffolk.......................... 221
Baron (H.), London NW........................... 158
Bennett & Kerr Books, Oxfordshire.............. 202
Dworski Books, Travel & Language Bookshop
 (Marijana), Herefordshire 283
Foster (Stephen), London NW 158
Parikian, Rare Books (Diana), London W...... 171
Rosemary Pugh Books, Wiltshire................. 248

ILLUMINATED MANUSCRIPTS

Bardsley's Books, Suffolk.......................... 221
Birchden Books, London E 153
Collectables (W.H.), Suffolk 225
Cox Old & Rare Books (Claude), Suffolk....... 223
Du Ry Medieval Manuscripts (Marc–Antoine),
 London W.. 170
Fine Art, London SE............................... 165
John Underwood Antiquarian Books, Norfolk 186
Maggs Brothers Limited, London W 171
Period Fine Bindings, Warwickshire.............. 233
Taylor & Son (Peter), Hertfordshire.............. 132

ILLUSTRATED

Alexander's Books, Warwickshire................. 232
Anthony Neville, Kent 138
Anthony Whittaker, Kent 136
Antique Map and Bookshop (The), Dorset..... 93
Antiques on High, Oxfordshire................... 204
Art Reference Books, Hampshire................. 125
Artco, Nottinghamshire............................ 201
Assinder Books, Essex 110
Autolycus, Shropshire.............................. 209
Baker - Books for the Collector (Colin), Devon 88
Barlow (Vincent G.), Hampshire.................. 126
Barry McKay Rare Books, Cumbria.............. 76
Bates Books, London Outer 179
Batterham (David), London W 169
Bayntun (George), Somerset 212
Besleys Books, Suffolk............................. 221
Bettridge (Gordon), Fife........................... 265
Beverley Old Bookshop, East Yorkshire 105
Biblion, London W................................. 169
Bolton Books, Hampshire......................... 122
Book Palace (The), London SE 161
Book Shelf (The), Devon 86
Bookline, Co. Down................................ 256
Bookmark (Children's Books), Wiltshire 248
Books & Things, London W....................... 169
Books Bought & Sold, Surrey 226
Bookstand, Dorset 93

SPECIALITY INDEX

Boris Books, Hampshire 127
Boxwood Books & Prints, Somerset 216
Bright (P.G.), Cambridgeshire 65
Brighton Books, East Sussex 98
Burden Ltd., (Clive A.), Hertfordshire 132
Butts Books (Mary), Berkshire 56
Bygone Books, Strathclyde 274
Cameron House Books, Isle of Wight 134
Camilla's Bookshop, East Sussex 100
Canterbury Bookshop (The), Kent 136
Castleton (Pat), Kent 137
Chalk (Old & Out of Print Books)
  (Christine M.), West Midlands 234
Chantrey Books, South Yorkshire 217
Cobweb Books, North Yorkshire 192
Coupland (Terry W.), Staffordshire 219
Cox Old & Rare Books (Claude), Suffolk 223
Criterion Books, London Outer 180
Cumming Limited (A. & Y.), East Sussex 102
D'Arcy Books, Wiltshire 246
David (G.), Cambridgeshire 63
Davies Fine Books, Worcestershire 252
de Beaumont (Robin), London SW 164
Dean Illustrated Books (Myra), Powys 281
Derek Stirling Bookseller, Kent 141
Deverell Books, Bristol 58
Doorbar (P. & D.), Gwynned 279
DPE Books, Devon 86
Drummond Pleasures of Past Times (David),
  London WC 174
Eastcote Bookshop (The), London Outer 178
Eastwood Books (David), Cornwall 72
Elmfield Books, West Midlands 234
Elstree Books, Hertfordshire 131
Ely Books, Cambridgeshire 65
Embleton (Paul), Essex 111
Everett (Richard), Norfolk 184
Ferdinando (Steven), Somerset 215
Fifteenth Century Bookshop (The),
  East Sussex 102
Fine Art, London SE 165
Firth (Bijou Books & Photography) (Maureen),
  South Yorkshire 218
Fletcher (H.M.), Hertfordshire 131
Flint (David), Hampshire 122
Fosters Bookshop, London W 170
Frew Limited (Robert), London W 170
Golden Goose Books, Lincolnshire 150
Goldman (Paul), Dorset 94
Goodyer (Nicholas), London N 156
Green Meadow Books, Cornwall 74
Greer (Robin), London SW 166
Grove Bookshop (The), North Yorkshire 193
Hanborough Books, Oxfordshire 205
Harrington (Adrian), London W 171
Harrington Antiquarian Bookseller (Peter),
  London SW 166
Hava Books, London SE 161
Hennessey Bookseller (Ray), East Sussex 99
Heppa (Christopher), Essex 108
Hereward Books, Cambridgeshire 65
Heywood Hill Limited (G.), London W 171
Hodgkins and Company Limited (Ian),
  Gloucestershire 116
Hodgson (Books) (Richard J.),
  North Yorkshire 194
Hummingbird Books, Herefordshire 128
Hurly Burly Books, Wiltshire 249
Innes Books, Shropshire 209
Island Books, Kent 136
J & D Jones, Cheshire 70
Jane Jones Books, Grampian 267
JB Books & Collectables, West Sussex 238
Jean Hedger, Berkshire 55
Jermy & Westerman, Nottinghamshire 201
Junk & Spread Eagle, London SE 162
Katharine House Gallery, Wiltshire 247
Kennedy (Peter), Surrey 230
Kerr (Norman), Cumbria 77
Keswick Bookshop, Cumbria 78
Key Books (Sarah), Cambridgeshire 64
Kineton Nooks, Warwickshire 232
Lawton (J.), Surrey 227
Leabeck Books, Oxfordshire 205
Leigh Gallery Books, Essex 110
Lenton (Alfred), Leicestershire 145
Little Stour Books, Kent 136
Lloyd-Davies (Sue), Carmarthenshire 277
Lucius Books, North Yorkshire 195
Lymelight Books & Prints, Dorset 92
March House Books, Dorset 94
Marchpane, London WC 175
Marks Limited (Barrie), London N 156
Marlborough Rare Books Ltd., London W 171
Martin Bookshop & Gallery (Richard),
  Hampshire 123
Mason (Mary), Oxfordshire 202
Maynard & Bradley, Leicestershire 146
McCrone (Audrey), Isle of Arran 269
Mereside Books, Cheshire 70
Mills Rare Books (Adam), Cambridgeshire 64
Minster Gate Bookshop, North Yorkshire 195
Modlock (Lilian), Dorset 92
Newcastle Bookshop, Northumberland 198
Nonsuch Books, Surrey 229
O'Kill (John), Kent 138
Old Town Bookshop (The), Lothian 271
Poetry Bookshop (The), Powys 284
Pugh Books (Ian K.), Worcestershire 251
Rees & O'Neill Rare Books, London WC 176
Ripping Yarns, London N 157
Rising Tide Books, Fife 265
Rittner Booksearch (Hilary), London SE 162
Robin Doughty - Fine Books, West Midlands . 234
Rochdale Book Company, Greater Manchester 120
Roe and Moore, London WC 176
Rose's Books, Herefordshire 284
Ross & Company Ltd., (Louise),
  Worcestershire 250
Rowan House Books, Surrey 226
Roz Hulse, Conwy 278
Rye Old Books, East Sussex 103
Sabin (Printed Works) (P.R. & V.), Kent 136
Saint Mary's Books & Prints, Lincolnshire 152

Scrivener's Books & Bookbinding, Derbyshire. 81
Second Edition, Lothian............................ 272
Sephton (A.F.), London W 172
Sesemann (Julia), Kent................................ 136
Seydi Rare Books (Sevin), London NW......... 159
Shakeshaft (Dr. B.), Cheshire....................... 71
Sharpe (Mary), Somerset 216
Shelley (E. & J.), Buckinghamshire................ 61
Sillem (Anthony), East Sussex..................... 101
Simon Finch Nofolk, Norfolk..................... 186
Sims Reed Limited, London SW.................. 167
Siri Ellis Books, Greater Manchester............. 118
Sotheran Limited (Henry), London W............ 172
Stella Books, Monmouthshire 281
Stevens (Joan), Cambridgeshire 65
Stothert Old Books, Cheshire....................... 68
Taylor Rare Books (Michael), Norfolk 184
Temperley (David), West Midlands 234
Ulysses, London WC................................. 177
Updike Rare Books (John), Lothian.............. 272
Waddington Books & Prints (Geraldine),
  Northamptonshire.................................. 196
Whitehall Books, East Sussex...................... 102
Whittle, Bookseller (Avril), Cumbria............. 79
Woodbine Books, West Yorkshire................ 241
Words Etcetera Bookshop, Dorset 92
Xanadubooks, Cleveland 96
Yates Antiquarian Books (Tony), Leicestershire 146

INCUNABULA

De Burca Rare Books, Co. Dublin................ 259
Fine Art, London SE................................. 165
Fletcher (H.M.), Hertfordshire 131
Pickering & Chatto, London W.................... 172
Quaritch Ltd., (Bernard), London W 172
Seydi Rare Books (Sevin), London NW......... 159
Sokol Books Ltd., London W...................... 172
Unsworths Booksellers, London NW 160

INDUSTRIAL DESIGN

Cornucopia Books, Lincolnshire 151
N1 Books, East Sussex............................. 103

INDUSTRY

Anvil Books, West Midlands 235
Blanchfield (John), West Yorkshire............... 243
Book House (The), Cumbria 78
Bott, (Bookdealers) Ltd., (Martin), Greater
  Manchester 118
Byrom Textile Bookroom (Richard),
  Lancashire 142
Cheshire Book Centre, Cheshire 69
Duck (William), Hampshire........................ 124
Hinchliffe Books, Bristol............................ 59
Past & Present Books, Gloucestershire........... 114
PsychoBabel Books & Journals, Oxfordshire ... 202
Rainford (Sheila), Hertfordshire................... 130
Rochdale Book Company, Greater Manchester 120
Salway Books, Essex 112
Whistler's Books, London SW 167

Wiend Books, Lancashire 143

INSTITUTIONS

G. C. Books Ltd., Dumfries & Galloway 264

INTERIOR DESIGN

Barlow (Vincent G.), Hampshire.................. 126
Black Cat Books, Norfolk.......................... 185
Cornucopia Books, Lincolnshire 151
Don Kelly Books, London W 170
Foster (Stephen), London NW..................... 158
Heneage Art Books (Thomas), London SW.... 166
Judd Books, London WC 175
Keswick Bookshop, Cumbria...................... 78
Martin - Bookseller (Colin), East Yorkshire.... 106
N1 Books, East Sussex............................. 103
Phillips of Hitchin (Antiques) Ltd.,
  Hertfordshire.. 131
Portobello Books, London W 172
Potterton Books, North Yorkshire 194
Ray Rare and Out of Print Books (Janette),
  North Yorkshire.................................... 195
Staniland (Booksellers), Lincolnshire 152
Sun House Books, Kent 139
Trinders' Fine Tools, Suffolk 222
Whittle, Bookseller (Avril), Cumbria............. 79

INTERNATIONAL AFFAIRS

Al Saqi Books, London W......................... 169
Brimstones, East Sussex............................ 102
G. Bickford-Smith (formerly Snowden Smith
  Books), Surrey...................................... 228
Melvin Tenner, London W......................... 171

INVENTORS & INVENTIONS

Gildas Books, Cheshire 68
N1 Books, East Sussex............................. 103

IRISH INTEREST

Anglo-American Rare Books, Surrey 228
Ann & Mike Conry, Worcestershire.............. 251
Bell Gallery (The), Co. Antrim.................... 255
Books Ulster, Co. Down 256
Bookshop (The), Co. Donegal..................... 258
Bookshop (The), Greater Manchester............ 119
Byre Books, Dumfries & Galloway............... 264
Caledonia Books, Strathclyde...................... 273
Camilla's Bookshop, East Sussex 100
Carraig Books Ltd., Co. Dublin 258
Chapter Two, London SE........................... 161
Clements (R.W.), London Outer.................. 179
Courtwood Books, Co. Laois...................... 260
Craobh Rua Books, Co. Armagh.................. 255
Darkwood Books, Co. Cork........................ 258
Davidson Books, Co. Down........................ 256
De Burca Rare Books, Co. Dublin................ 259
Drury Rare Books (John), Essex.................. 111
Dublin Bookbrowsers, Co. Dublin................ 259
Ferdinando (Steven), Somerset 215
Foyle Books, Co. Derry 255

SPECIALITY INDEX

Fuchsia Books, Co. Wexford 261
G. C. Books Ltd., Dumfries & Galloway 264
Greene's Bookshop Ltd, Co. Dublin 259
Harris (George J.), Co. Derry 255
House of Figgis Ltd (The), Co. Galway 260
Hyland (C.P.), Co. Cork 258
Jackson (M.W.), Wiltshire 249
Jiri Books, Co. Antrim 255
Karen Millward, Co. Cork 257
Kenny's Bookshops and Art Galleries Ltd, Co. Galway 260
Kenya Books, East Sussex 99
Kernaghans, Merseyside 183
Lighthouse Books (The), Dorset 91
My Back Pages, London SW 167
Naughton Booksellers, Co. Dublin 259
O'Brien Books & Photo Gallery, Co. Limerick 261
Poetry Bookshop (The), Powys 284
Read Ireland, Co. Dublin 258
Roscrea Bookshop, Co. Tipperary 261
Rowan (P. & B.), Co. Antrim 255
Royal Carbery Books Ltd., Co. Cork 257
Rye Old Books, East Sussex 103
Saintfield Antiques & Fine Books, Co. Down.. 255
Samovar Books, Co. Dublin 258
Schull Books, Co. Cork 257
Stokes Books, Co. Dublin 259
Trinity Rare Books, Co. Leitrim 260
Updike Rare Books (John), Lothian 272
Whelan (P. & F.), Kent 141

JEWELLERY

Art Reference Books, Hampshire 125
Barmby (C. & A.J.), Kent 140
Don Kelly Books, London W 170
Edmund Pollinger Rare Books, London SW.... 165
Heneage Art Books (Thomas), London SW 166
Ives Bookseller (John), London Outer 181
Nibris Books, London SW 167
Orchid Book Distributors, Co. Clare 257
Potterton Books, North Yorkshire 194
Trinders' Fine Tools, Suffolk 222
Warnes (Felicity J.), London Outer 178

JOURNALISM

Archivist (The), Devon 88
Bob Mallory (Books), Derbyshire 82
Cornucopia Books, Lincolnshire 151
Kelly Books, Devon 88
Pastmasters, Derbyshire 82

JOURNALS

Autobooks Ltd., East Sussex 100
Baldwin's Scientific Books, Essex 112
Batterham (David), London W 169
Bettridge (Gordon), Fife 265
Border Books, Borders 262
Derek Stirling Bookseller, Kent 141
PsychoBabel Books & Journals, Oxfordshire ... 202
Siop Lyfrau'r Hen Bost, Gwynedd 280

Temple (Robert), London N 157
Turton (John), Durham 97
Wayside Books and Cards, Oxfordshire 203

JUDAICA

Bacon (Josephine), London WC 174
Biblion, London W 169
de Visser Books, Cambridgeshire 63
Delectus Books, London WC 174
Dworski Books, Travel & Language Bookshop (Marijana), Herefordshire 283
Fishburn Books, London NW 158
Inner Bookshop (The), Oxfordshire 205
Kenny's Bookshops and Art Galleries Ltd, Co. Galway 260
Nautical Antique Centre (The), Dorset 94
Occultique, Northamptonshire 196
Pordes Books Ltd., (Henry), London WC 176
Rosemary Pugh Books, Wiltshire 248
Saint Swithin's Illustrated & Children's Books, London W 172
Samovar Books, Co. Dublin 258
Skoob Russell Square, Suffolk 225
Yesterday's News, Conwy 278

JUNGIANA

Apocalypse, Surrey 228

JUVENILE

Barry McKay Rare Books, Cumbria 76
Beck (John), East Sussex 102
Blackwell's Rare Books, Oxfordshire 205
Bookmark (Children's Books), Wiltshire 248
Canterbury Bookshop (The), Kent 136
Cooper Hay Rare Books, Strathclyde 273
Coupland (Terry W.), Staffordshire 219
Demetzy Books, Oxfordshire 203
Fifteenth Century Bookshop (The), East Sussex 102
Freya Books & Antiques, Norfolk 187
Game Advice, Oxfordshire 205
Gildas Books, Cheshire 68
Holtom (Christopher), Cornwall 75
Jean Hedger, Berkshire 55
John R. Hoggarth, North Yorkshire 194
K Books, Cheshire 69
Kirkpatrick (Robert J.), London W 171
Korn (M. Eric), London N 156
Libra Books, Lincolnshire 148
Mason (Mary), Oxfordshire 202
Mead (P.J.), Shropshire 210
Peakirk Books, Cambridgeshire 67
Roe and Moore, London WC 176
Roscrea Bookshop, Co. Tipperary 261
Rosemary Books, Merseyside 183
Saint Swithin's Illustrated & Children's Books, London W 172
Sesemann (Julia), Kent 136
Shacklock Books (David), Suffolk 222
Stour Bookshop, Dorset 92
Temple (Robert), London N 157

The Old Children's Bookshelf, Lothian.......... 272

KABBALA/CABBALA/CABALA
Gildas Books, Cheshire 68
Magis Books, Leicestershire....................... 147

KNITTING
Apocalypse, Surrey 228
Autumn Leaves, Lincolnshire..................... 150
Black Cat Books, Norfolk......................... 185
Brown-Studies, Strathclyde....................... 273
Byrom Textile Bookroom (Richard),
  Lancashire....................................... 142
Cover to Cover, Merseyside....................... 183
DPE Books, Devon................................. 86
Mansfield (Judith), West Yorkshire 245
Reading Lasses, Dumfries & Galloway.......... 265
Sleepy Elephant Books & Artefacts,
  Cumbria.. 79
Warnes (Felicity J.), London Outer 178
Young (D. & J.), Powys 286

KU KLUX KLAN
Loretta Lay Books, London NW.................. 159

LACE
Black Cat Books, Norfolk......................... 185
Byrom Textile Bookroom (Richard),
  Lancashire....................................... 142
Cover to Cover, Merseyside....................... 183
Crouch Rare Books, Surrey....................... 227
Dandy Lion Editions, Surrey 228
Dworski Books, Travel & Language Bookshop
  (Marijana), Herefordshire 283
Ely Books, Cambridgeshire 65
Heneage Art Books (Thomas), London SW.... 166
Hennessey Bookseller (Ray), East Sussex 99
Mansfield (Judith), West Yorkshire 245
Reading Lasses, Dumfries & Galloway.......... 265
Warnes (Felicity J.), London Outer 178
Williams (Christopher), Dorset 93
York (Graham), Devon............................. 85
Young (D. & J.), Powys 286

LANDSCAPE
Acer Books, Herefordshire 128
Apocalypse, Surrey 228
Arden, Bookseller (C.), Powys.................... 282
Burebank Books, Norfolk......................... 184
Calendula Horticultural Books,
  East Sussex 101
Castleton (Pat), Kent.............................. 137
Cottage Books, Leicestershire.................... 145
Duck (William), Hampshire....................... 124
Hollingshead (Chris), London Outer 181
Hünersdorff Rare Books, London SW........... 166
Inch's Books, North Yorkshire................... 192
Marlborough Rare Books Ltd., London W 171
Modlock (Lilian), Dorset 92
Park (Mike), London Outer 180

Ray Rare and Out of Print Books (Janette),
  North Yorkshire.................................. 195

LANGUAGES
- AFRICAN
Dworski Books, Travel & Language Bookshop
  (Marijana), Herefordshire 283
Kenya Books, East Sussex 99
owenbooks65, Conwy 278

- FOREIGN
Al Saqi Books, London W......................... 169
Autumn Leaves, Lincolnshire..................... 150
Bacon (Josephine), London WC 174
Book House (The), Cumbria 78
Bookcase, Cumbria 76
Books on Spain, London Outer................... 181
Booth Books, Powys 282
Carnforth Bookshop (The), Lancashire.......... 142
Crouch Rare Books, Surrey....................... 227
Dworski Books, Travel & Language Bookshop
  (Marijana), Herefordshire 283
Hava Books, London SE........................... 161
Hünersdorff Rare Books, London SW........... 166
Jade Mountain, Hampshire 125
Korn (M. Eric), London N 156
Oopalba Books, Cheshire......................... 71
Orssich (Paul), London SW....................... 167
owenbooks65, Conwy 278
Parkinsons Books, Merseyside.................... 183
Pholiota Books, London WC 176
Priestpopple Books, Northumberland 198
Robertshaw (John), Cambridgeshire.............. 66
Roundstone Books, Lancashire 143
Scrivener's Books & Bookbinding,
  Derbyshire....................................... 81
Stokes Books, Co. Dublin......................... 259
Thorntons of Oxford Ltd., Oxfordshire 203
Transformer, Dumfries & Galloway............. 265

- NATIONAL
Book House (The), Cumbria 78
Browning Books, Torfaen 287
Colin Hancock, Ceredigion 277
Derek Stirling Bookseller, Kent 141
Dworski Books, Travel & Language Bookshop
  (Marijana), Herefordshire 283
Hyland (C.P.), Co. Cork........................... 258
owenbooks65, Conwy 278
Spenceley Books (David), West Yorkshire 244
Treasure Island (The), Greater Manchester 120
Walker Fine Books (Steve), Dorset............... 91

LAW
- GENERAL
Aurora Books Ltd, Lothian....................... 270
Booth Books, Powys 282
Crimes Ink, London E............................. 153
Dean Byass, Bristol 60
Drury Rare Books (John), Essex................. 111

SPECIALITY INDEX

Edwards (London) Limited (Francis), London WC 175
Edwards in Hay–on–Wye (Francis), Herefordshire 283
PsychoBabel Books & Journals, Oxfordshire ... 202
Roscrea Bookshop, Co. Tipperary 261
Rowan (P. & B.), Co. Antrim 255
Skoob Russell Square, Suffolk 225
Undercover Books, Lincolnshire 152
Unsworths Booksellers, London NW 160
Wayside Books and Cards, Oxfordshire 203
Webb Books (John), South Yorkshire 217
Westfield Books, North Yorkshire 195
Wildy & Sons Ltd, London WC 177

- CONSTITUTIONAL
Wildy & Sons Ltd, London WC 177

LEGAL PAPERWORK
John Underwood Antiquarian Books, Norfolk 186

LENINISM
Reading Lasses, Dumfries & Galloway 265

LEPIDOPTEROLOGY
Aurelian Books, London NW 158
Aviabooks, Gloucestershire 114
Edmund Pollinger Rare Books, London SW ... 165
Moss Books, London NW 159
Pemberley Books, Buckinghamshire 62

LETTERING
N1 Books, East Sussex 103

LETTERS
Baron (H.), London NW 158
Camden Books, Somerset 212
Farahar & Dupre (Clive & Sophie), Wiltshire .. 246
Gekoski (R.A.), London WC 175
Hodgkins and Company Limited (Ian), Gloucestershire 116
James Fergusson Books & Manuscripts, London W 170
Lawrence Books, Nottinghamshire 200
Maggs Brothers Limited, London W 171
Neil Summersgill, Lancashire 142
Poetry Bookshop (The), Powys 284
Reading Lasses, Dumfries & Galloway 265
Scrivener's Books & Bookbinding, Derbyshire . 81
Silverman (Michael), London SE 163
Temple (Robert), London N 157

LIBRARY SCIENCE
Skoob Russell Square, Suffolk 225

LIMITED EDITIONS
Apocalypse, Surrey 228
Artco, Nottinghamshire 201

Barlow (Vincent G.), Hampshire 126
Biblion, London W 169
BOOKS4U, Flintshire 279
Brian Troath Books, London E 153
Budd (Richard), Somerset 215
Cameron House Books, Isle of Wight 134
Coach House Books, Worcestershire 251
Collinge & Clark, London WC 174
Cox Old & Rare Books (Claude), Suffolk 223
Eastwood Books (David), Cornwall 72
Ellis, Bookseller (Peter), London SE 162
Elstree Books, Hertfordshire 131
Fine Art, London SE 165
Firth (Bijou Books & Photography) (Maureen), South Yorkshire 218
Hanborough Books, Oxfordshire 205
Hollett and Son (R.F.G.), Cumbria 79
Kirkman Ltd., (Robert), Bedfordshire 53
Lucius Books, North Yorkshire 195
Marks Limited (Barrie), London N 156
McKelvie (Ian), London N 156
Mills Rare Books (Adam), Cambridgeshire 64
Modern First Editions, London Outer 180
N V Books, Warwickshire 232
Rye Old Books, East Sussex 103
Sabin (Printed Works) (P.R. & V.), Kent 136
Scrivener's Books & Bookbinding, Derbyshire . 81
Seabreeze Books, Lancashire 144
Stevens (Joan), Cambridgeshire 65
Temple (Robert), London N 157
Tucker (Alan & Joan), Gloucestershire 116
Updike Rare Books (John), Lothian 272
Words Etcetera Bookshop, Dorset 92

LINGUISTICS
Chesters (G. & J.), Staffordshire 220
Derek Stirling Bookseller, Kent 141
Dworski Books, Travel & Language Bookshop (Marijana), Herefordshire 283
Game Advice, Oxfordshire 205
Judd Books, London WC 175
Kenya Books, East Sussex 99
Olynthiacs, Shropshire 210
Oopalba Books, Cheshire 71
Parkinsons Books, Merseyside 183
Plurabelle Books, Cambridgeshire 64
Reading Lasses, Dumfries & Galloway 265
Schulz–Falster Rare Books (Susanne), London N 157
Skoob Russell Square, Suffolk 225
Unsworths Booksellers, London NW 160

LITERACY
Oopalba Books, Cheshire 71

LITERARY CRITICISM
Alec–Smith Books (Alex), East Yorkshire 107
Apocalypse, Surrey 228
Applin (Malcolm), Berkshire 55
Autumn Leaves, Lincolnshire 150

Axe Rare & Out of Print Books (Richard),
  North Yorkshire.................................... 190
Bennett & Kerr Books, Oxfordshire.............. 202
Berry (L.J.), Kent 138
Boer (Louise), Arthurian Books, Powys 282
Bookcase, Cumbria 76
Books, Denbighshire................................ 278
Bracton Books, Cambridgeshire................... 63
Brian Troath Books, London E.................... 153
Broadhurst of Southport Ltd., Merseyside...... 182
Budd (Richard), Somerset 215
Caledonia Books, Strathclyde...................... 273
Carta Regis, Powys 286
Chaucer Bookshop, Kent........................... 136
Chesters (G. & J.), Staffordshire 220
Clarendon Books, Leicestershire 145
Delectus Books, London WC...................... 174
Dyson (Anthony), West Midlands................. 235
Elaine Lonsdale Books, West Yorkshire......... 242
Ellis, Bookseller (Peter), London SE 162
Ellwood Editions, Wiltshire 247
Fisher & Sperr, London N 155
Fortune Green Books, London NW 158
Frost (Richard), Hertfordshire..................... 130
GfB: the Colchester Bookshop, Essex............ 109
Hadley Bookseller (Peter J.), Essex 110
Handsworth Books, Essex 112
Hawkes (James), Bristol 60
Hawley (C.L.), North Yorkshire 193
Hellenic Bookservices, London NW.............. 158
Island Books, Kent 136
Kingsgate Books & Prints, Hampshire........... 127
Marcet Books, London SE 161
Naughton Booksellers, Co. Dublin 259
Old Aberdeen Bookshop, Grampian 266
Oopalba Books, Cheshire........................... 71
Parkinsons Books, Merseyside..................... 183
Parrott (Jeremy), London E....................... 153
Parrott Books, Oxfordshire 207
Poetry Bookshop (The), Powys................... 284
Polmorla Books, Cornwall 75
Pomes Penyeach, Staffordshire 219
Pordes Books Ltd., (Henry), London WC 176
PsychoBabel Books & Journals, Oxfordshire... 202
Reading Lasses, Dumfries & Galloway 265
Riderless Horse Books, Norfolk 184
Roger Lucas Booksellers, Lincolnshire............ 150
Roundstone Books, Lancashire 143
Rutland Bookshop (The), Rutland 208
Rye Old Books, East Sussex 103
Ryeland Books, Northamptonshire................ 196
Scrivener's Books & Bookbinding, Derbyshire . 81
Skoob Russell Square, Suffolk..................... 225
Staniland (Booksellers), Lincolnshire.............. 152
Stevens (Joan), Cambridgeshire 65
Symes Books (Naomi), Cheshire 71
Temple (Robert), London N....................... 157
The Glass Key, West Yorkshire................... 242
Tombland Bookshop, Norfolk 188
Tucker (Alan & Joan), Gloucestershire 116
Unsworths Booksellers, London NW 160
Venables (Morris & Juliet), Bristol 59

Waterfield's, Oxfordshire 206
Whitehall Books, East Sussex..................... 102
Yesterday's News, Conwy 278

LITERARY TRAVEL

Al Saqi Books, London W........................ 169
Amwell Book Company, London SE 154
Archer (Steve), London Outer 178
Askew Books (Vernon), Wiltshire 246
Books on Spain, London Outer................... 181
Cobbles Books, Somerset........................... 214
Collectables (W.H.), Suffolk 225
Criterion Books, London Outer 180
Hodgkins and Company Limited (Ian),
  Gloucestershire 116
Orb's Bookshop, Grampian........................ 268
Orssich (Paul), London SW 167
Royal Carbery Books Ltd., Co. Cork 257
Shapero Rare Books (Bernard J.), London W . 172
Temple (Robert), London N....................... 157
The Glass Key, West Yorkshire................... 242
Tiger Books, Kent 137
Trinity Rare Books, Co. Leitrim.................. 260
Tucker (Alan & Joan), Gloucestershire 116
War & Peace Books, Hampshire.................. 123
Yesterday's Books, Dorset 91

LITERATURE

Addyman Annexe (The), Powys 282
Addyman Books, Powys............................ 282
Alba Books, Grampian 267
Alec–Smith Books (Alex), East Yorkshire 107
Alexander's Books, Warwickshire................. 232
Andrew Morton (Books), Powys.................. 281
Anglo-American Rare Books, Surrey 228
Antiquary Ltd., (Bar Bookstore),
  North Yorkshire................................... 192
Antique Map and Bookshop (The), Dorset..... 93
Apocalypse, Surrey 228
Archer (Steve), London Outer 178
Archivist (The), Devon............................. 88
Armchair Books, Lothian 270
Artco, Nottinghamshire............................. 201
Aurora Books Ltd, Lothian........................ 270
Autolycus, Shropshire 209
Autumn Leaves, Lincolnshire...................... 150
Avonworld Books, Somerset....................... 213
Axe Rare & Out of Print Books (Richard),
  North Yorkshire.................................... 190
Barbican Bookshop, North Yorkshire 194
Bass (Ben), Wiltshire 246
Bath Old Books, Somerset 212
Baxter (Steve), Surrey 228
Bayntun (George), Somerset....................... 212
BC Books, Cheshire 69
Bernstein (Nicholas), London W 169
Bertram Rota Ltd., London WC 174
Beware of the Leopard, Bristol 58
Black Five Books, Shropshire 211
Blackwell's Rare Books, Oxfordshire............. 205
Book Business (The), London W 169

SPECIALITY INDEX

Books & Collectables Ltd., Cambridgeshire 63
Books (For All), North Yorkshire 190
Books on Spain, London Outer 181
Bookshop at the Plain, Lincolnshire 151
Bookworm, Lothian 270
Bookworms of Evesham, Worcestershire 252
Booth Books, Powys 282
Boris Books, Hampshire 127
Bow Windows Book Shop, East Sussex 102
Bowie Books & Collectables, East Yorkshire ... 106
Boz Books, Powys 282
Bracton Books, Cambridgeshire 63
Brian Troath Books, London E 153
Bridge of Allan Books, Central 263
Bright (P.G.), Cambridgeshire 65
Brinded (Scott), Kent 139
Bristol Books, Bristol 60
Broadhurst of Southport Ltd., Merseyside 182
Broadway Books, Cambridgeshire 66
Brock Books, North Yorkshire 190
Broughton Books, Lothian 271
Budd (Richard), Somerset 215
Butts Books (Mary), Berkshire 56
Caledonia Books, Strathclyde 273
Camden Books, Somerset 212
Cameron House Books, Isle of Wight 134
Carnforth Bookshop (The), Lancashire 142
Carta Regis, Powys 286
Chaucer Bookshop, Kent 136
Cheshire Book Centre, Cheshire 69
Chevin Books, West Yorkshire 245
Chris Phillips, Wiltshire 246
Church Street Books, Norfolk 184
Clarendon Books, Leicestershire 145
Clements (R.W.), London Outer 179
Cobbles Books, Somerset 214
Cofion Books, Pembrokeshire 281
Cox Old & Rare Books (Claude), Suffolk 223
Cox Rare Books (Charles), Cornwall 73
Craobh Rua Books, Co. Armagh 255
Criterion Books, London Outer 180
Crouch Rare Books, Surrey 227
Cumming Limited (A. & Y.), East Sussex 102
D'Arcy Books, Wiltshire 246
Dalby (Richard), North Yorkshire 192
Dales & Lakes Book Centre, Cumbria 79
David (G.), Cambridgeshire 63
Davidson Books, Co. Down 256
De Burca Rare Books, Co. Dublin 259
Dean Byass, Bristol 60
Derek Stirling Bookseller, Kent 141
Dolphin Books, Suffolk 221
Driffield Bookshop (The), East Yorkshire 105
Duncan & Reid, Lothian 271
Dyson (Anthony), West Midlands 235
Eastwood Books (David), Cornwall 72
Edwards (Christopher), Berkshire 55
Edwards (London) Limited (Francis),
  London WC 175
Edwards in Hay–on–Wye (Francis),
  Herefordshire 283
Elaine Lonsdale Books, West Yorkshire 242

Elephant Books, West Yorkshire 244
Ellis, Bookseller (Peter), London SE 162
Esoteric Dreams Bookshop, Cumbria 77
Eton Antique Bookshop, Berkshire 57
Farahar & Dupre (Clive & Sophie), Wiltshire .. 246
Ferdinando (Steven), Somerset 215
Finch Rare Books Ltd. (Simon), London W ... 170
Firsts in Print, Isle of Wight 134
Firth (Bijou Books & Photography)
  (Maureen), South Yorkshire 218
Fortune Green Books, London NW 158
Foster (Stephen), London NW 158
Foster Bookshop (Paul), London SW 165
Fotheringham (Alex), Northumberland 198
Frew Limited (Robert), London W 170
Furneaux Books (Lee), Devon 88
G. C. Books Ltd., Dumfries & Galloway 264
GfB: the Colchester Bookshop, Essex 109
Gibbs Books, (Jonathan), Worcestershire 251
Gilbert and Son (H.M.), Hampshire 127
Gloucester Road Bookshop, London SW 165
Glyn's Books, Shropshire 209
Goldman (Paul), Dorset 94
Good for Books, Lincolnshire 149
Grahame Thornton, Bookseller, Dorset 92
Gregory (George), Somerset 212
Grove Bookshop (The), North Yorkshire 193
Hadley Bookseller (Peter J.), Essex 110
Hall's Bookshop, Kent 141
Harrington (Adrian), London W 171
Harrington Antiquarian Bookseller (Peter),
  London SW 166
Hart (John), Norfolk 188
Hawkes (James), Bristol 60
Hennessey Bookseller (Ray), East Sussex 99
Heppa (Christopher), Essex 108
Heywood Hill Limited (G.), London W 171
Hollett and Son (R.F.G.), Cumbria 79
Holmes Books (Harry), East Yorkshire 106
House of Figgis Ltd (The), Co. Galway 260
Howes Bookshop, East Sussex 101
Hünersdorff Rare Books, London SW 166
Hughes Rare Books (Spike), Borders 262
Hunter–Rare Books (Andrew), London SW 166
Hurst (Jenny), Kent 138
Hutchison (Books) (Larry), Fife 265
Idle Genius Books, London N 156
Innes Books, Shropshire 209
Jade Mountain, Hampshire 125
Jane Jones Books, Grampian 267
Jarndyce Antiquarian Booksellers, London WC 175
JB Books & Collectables, West Sussex 238
Jermy & Westerman, Nottinghamshire 201
Jiri Books, Co. Antrim 255
Johnson Rare Book Collections (C.R.),
  London NW 159
Jonkers Rare Books, Oxfordshire 204
Judd Books, London WC 175
Kalligraphia (formerly Charmouth Bounty
  Books), Isle of Wight 134
Katnap Arts, Norfolk 187
Kilgarriff (Raymond), East Sussex 104

SPECIALITY INDEX

Killeen (John), North Yorkshire 191
Kingsgate Books & Prints, Hampshire 127
Kirkman Ltd., (Robert), Bedfordshire 53
Lawson & Company (E.M.), Oxfordshire 203
Leabeck Books, Oxfordshire 205
Leigh Gallery Books, Essex 110
Lenton (Alfred), Leicestershire 145
Lloyd-Davies (Sue), Carmarthenshire 277
Lymelight Books & Prints, Dorset 92
Maggs Brothers Limited, London W 171
Maghreb Bookshop (The), London WC 175
Main Point Books, Lothian 271
Malvern Bookshop (The), Worcestershire 250
Mannwaring (M.G.), Bristol 59
Marks Limited (Barrie), London N 156
Marlborough Rare Books Ltd., London W 171
McCarty, Bookseller (M.E.), Western Isles 269
McCarty, Bookseller (M.E.), Dumfries &
   Galloway 264
McCrone (Audrey), Isle of Arran 269
McKelvie (Ian), London N 156
McNaughtan's Bookshop, Lothian 271
Mills Rare Books (Adam), Cambridgeshire 64
Minster Gate Bookshop, North Yorkshire 195
Moreton Books, Devon 86
Morgan (H.J.), Bedfordshire 54
Mr. Pickwick of Towcester, Northamptonshire 196
Murch Booksend, (Herbert), London SE 162
Murphy (C.J.), Norfolk 187
Naughton Booksellers, Co. Dublin 259
Needham Books, (Russell), Somerset 216
Niner (Marcus), Gloucestershire 116
Nineteenth Century Books, Oxfordshire 207
Nonsuch Books, Surrey 229
Norton Books, North Yorkshire 194
O'Brien Books & Photo Gallery, Co. Limerick 261
Offa's Dyke Books, Shropshire 209
Old Aberdeen Bookshop, Grampian 266
Old Bookshop (The), West Midlands 236
Old Town Bookshop (The), Lothian 271
Oopalba Books, Cheshire 71
Orangeberry Books, Oxfordshire 204
Orssich (Paul), London SW 167
Over-Sands Books, Cumbria 77
Palladour Books, Hampshire 126
Paper Moon Books, Warwickshire 233
Paper Pleasures, Somerset 215
Parrott (Jeremy), London E 153
Peter's Bookshop, Norfolk 188
Pickering & Chatto, London W 172
Plurabelle Books, Cambridgeshire 64
Polmorla Books, Cornwall 75
Pomes Penyeach, Staffordshire 219
Poor Richard's Books, Suffolk 222
Porter Bookshop (The), South Yorkshire 217
Price (John), London N 157
Pringle Booksellers (Andrew), Lothian 271
PsychoBabel Books & Journals, Oxfordshire ... 202
Quaritch Ltd., (Bernard), London W 172
Quest Booksearch, Cambridgeshire 64
Quinto of Charing Cross Road, London WC .. 176
Quinto of Great Russell Street, London WC ... 176

R. & A. Books, East Sussex 100
Rainford (Sheila), Hertfordshire 130
Rassam (Paul), London NW 159
Rees & O'Neill Rare Books, London WC 176
Richard Thornton Books, London N 157
Richmond Books, North Yorkshire 192
Riderless Horse Books, Norfolk 184
Ripping Yarns, London N 157
Robin Doughty - Fine Books, West Midlands . 234
Ross & Company Ltd., (Louise),
   Worcestershire 250
Roundstone Books, Lancashire 143
Rowan (P. & B.), Co. Antrim 255
Rye Old Books, East Sussex 103
Ryeland Books, Northamptonshire 196
Saint Philip's Books, Oxfordshire 205
Saintfield Antiques & Fine Books, Co. Down .. 255
Sansovino Books, West Sussex 239
Scott (Peter), East Sussex 103
Scrivener's Books & Bookbinding, Derbyshire . 81
Second Edition, Lothian 272
Segal Books (Joel), Devon 84
Shakespeare Books (Colin), Staffordshire 219
Shapero Rare Books (Bernard J.), London W . 172
Sharpe (Mary), Somerset 216
Shelley (E. & J.), Buckinghamshire 61
Sillem (Anthony), East Sussex 101
Silverman (Michael), London SE 163
Simon Finch Nofolk, Norfolk 186
Simpson (Dave), Central 263
Siop Lyfrau'r Hen Bost, Gwynedd 280
Siop y Morfa, Denbighshire 279
Skelton (Tony), Kent 141
Skoob Russell Square, Suffolk 225
Sokol Books Ltd., London W 172
Sotheran Limited (Henry), London W 172
Spelman (Ken), North Yorkshire 195
Staffs Bookshop (The), Staffordshire 219
Staniland (Booksellers), Lincolnshire 152
Stern Antiquarian Bookseller (Jeffrey),
   North Yorkshire 195
Stevens (Joan), Cambridgeshire 65
Stinton (Judith), Dorset 91
Stokes Books, Co. Dublin 259
Stone Trough Books, North Yorkshire 195
Sturford Books, Wiltshire 248
Surprise Books, Gloucestershire 113
Symes Books (Naomi), Cheshire 71
Talisman Books, Cheshire 70
Temple (Robert), London N 157
Tiffin (Tony and Gill), Durham 96
Tiger Books, Kent 137
Till's Bookshop, Lothian 272
Tindley & Chapman, London WC 176
Trafalgar Bookshop, East Sussex 99
Treasure Trove Books, Leicestershire 146
Trevorrow (Edwin), Hertfordshire 130
Trinity Rare Books, Co. Leitrim 260
Tucker (Alan & Joan), Gloucestershire 116
Updike Rare Books (John), Lothian 272
Valentine Rare Books, Surrey 227
Valentine Rare Books, London W 173

SPECIALITY INDEX

Venables (Morris & Juliet), Bristol 59
Ventnor Rare Books, Isle of Wight 135
Walden Books, London NW 160
Walker Fine Books (Steve), Dorset............... 91
War & Peace Books, Hampshire.................. 123
Waterfield's, Oxfordshire 206
Waxfactor, East Sussex 99
Westcountry Old Books, Cornwall 75
Westcountry Oldbooks, Devon.................... 84
Wetherell (Frances), Cambridgeshire............. 65
Whig Books Ltd., Leicestershire 147
Whitehall Books, East Sussex..................... 102
Wilbraham (J. & S.), London NW 160
Williams Rare Books (Nigel), London WC..... 177
Willmott Bookseller (Nicholas), Cardiff 276
Wise (Derek), East Sussex......................... 102
Worlds End Bookshop, London SW.............. 168
Wychwood Books, Gloucestershire............... 116
Yates Antiquarian Books (Tony), Leicestershire 146
Yesterday's Books, Dorset 91
Yesterday's News, Conwy.......................... 278

LITERATURE
- 19TH C
Boz Books, Powys 282
Marble Hill Books, Middlesex..................... 181
The Glass Key, West Yorkshire................... 242
Valentine Rare Books, London W 173

- FRENCH
Baldwin (Jack), Strathclyde 273

- SCOTTISH
Armchair Books, Lothian 270
Atholl Fine Books, Tayside 275
Byre Books, Dumfries & Galloway............... 264
Cheshire Book Centre, Cheshire 69
Cox Rare Books (Charles), Cornwall 73
David Houston - Bookseller, London E......... 153
Greta Books, Durham 96
Jane Jones Books, Grampian...................... 267
Loch Croispol Bookshop & Restaurant,
  Highland... 268
Orb's Bookshop, Grampian........................ 268
Stroma Books, Borders 262
Thistle Books, Strathclyde......................... 274
Till's Bookshop, Lothian 272

- VICTORIAN
Antique Map and Bookshop (The), Dorset..... 93
Apocalypse, Surrey 228
Beaton (Richard), East Sussex.................... 102
Bell (Peter), Strathclyde 270
Brock Books, North Yorkshire.................... 190
Cox Rare Books (Charles), Cornwall 73
Derek Stirling Bookseller, Kent 141
Ely Books, Cambridgeshire........................ 65
Glenwood Books, Surrey 230
Jarndyce Antiquarian Booksellers, London WC 175
Parrott (Jeremy), London E....................... 153

Seabreeze Books, Lancashire...................... 144
Smith Books, (Sally), Suffolk 222
South Downs Book Service, West Sussex 238
Symes Books (Naomi), Cheshire 71
Temple (Robert), London N...................... 157
Tobo Books, Hampshire........................... 124
Valentine Rare Books, London W 173

- WESTERN AMERICAN
Americanabooksuk, Cumbria..................... 76

LITERATURE IN TRANSLATION
AA1 Books, Dumfries & Galloway 264
Atlas, London N 155
Books on Spain, London Outer................... 181
Chthonios Books, East Sussex.................... 101
IKON, Devon 88
Modern Welsh Publications Ltd., Merseyside .. 182
Naughton Booksellers, Co. Dublin 259
Parrott (Jeremy), London E....................... 153
Pholiota Books, London WC..................... 176
Riderless Horse Books, Norfolk 184
Sillem (Anthony), East Sussex.................... 101
Stevens (Joan), Cambridgeshire 65
Temple (Robert), London N...................... 157
Tiger Books, Kent 137
Tucker (Alan & Joan), Gloucestershire 116
Updike Rare Books (John), Lothian............. 272
Valentine Rare Books, Surrey 227

LOCAL STUDIES - SUSSEX
Fifteenth Century Bookshop (The), East Sussex 102
Mellon's Books, East Sussex...................... 100

LOCKS & LOCKSMITHS
Baron (Christopher), Greater Manchester....... 118

LOGGING/LUMBERING
Reeves Technical Books, North Yorkshire...... 193

LOST CIVILISATIONS
Apocalypse, Surrey 228
Byre Books, Dumfries & Galloway............... 264

MAFIA
Clifford Elmer Books Ltd., Cheshire 68
Loretta Lay Books, London NW................. 159

MAGAZINES & PERIODICALS
- GENERAL
Anglo-American Rare Books, Surrey 228
Apocalypse, Surrey 228
Art Reference Books, Hampshire 125
Barnes (Peter), Wiltshire.......................... 248
Bianco Library, West Sussex...................... 237
Black Cat Bookshop, Leicestershire 145
Book Palace (The), London SE 161
Books & Collectables Ltd., Cambridgeshire 63

SPECIALITY INDEX

Books & Things, London W 169
Border Bookshop, West Yorkshire 245
Bracton Books, Cambridgeshire 63
Brian Troath Books, London E 153
Derek Stirling Bookseller, Kent 141
Downie Fine Books Ltd., (Robert), Shropshire 211
Eggeling Books (John), West Yorkshire 245
Franks Booksellers, Greater Manchester 119
Ken's Paper Collectables, Buckinghamshire 62
Lake (Fred), Surrey 229
Mr. Pickwick of Towcester, Northamptonshire 196
Naughton Booksellers, Co. Dublin 259
Norton Books, North Yorkshire 194
Nostalgia Unlimited, Merseyside 182
Palladour Books, Hampshire 126
Paper Pleasures, Somerset 215
Phenotype Books, Cumbria 78
Poetry Bookshop (The), Powys 284
Reading Lasses, Dumfries & Galloway 265
Riderless Horse Books, Norfolk 184
Temple (Robert), London N 157
Tennis Collectables, Cheshire 68
Tiger Books, Kent 137
Tilleys Vintage Magazine Shop, Derbyshire 81
Tilleys Vintage Magazine Shop,
  South Yorkshire 218
Updike Rare Books (John), Lothian 272
Williams (Bookdealer), (Richard), Lincolnshire 152
Williams Rare Books (Nigel), London WC 177
Words Etcetera Bookshop, Dorset 92
Yesterday's News, Conwy 278
Yorkshire Relics, West Yorkshire 242

- WOMEN'S
Black Cat Books, Norfolk 185

MAGIC & CONJURING
Abrahams (Mike), Staffordshire 219
Books & Bygones (Pam Taylor),
  West Midlands 236
Booth (Booksearch Service), (Geoff), Cheshire . 68
Cheshire Book Centre, Cheshire 69
Drummond Pleasures of Past Times (David),
  London WC 174
Edmund Pollinger Rare Books, London SW ... 165
Elgar (Raymond), East Sussex 98
Fitzsimons (Anne), Cumbria 77
Franks Booksellers, Greater Manchester 119
Game Advice, Oxfordshire 205
Harrington (Adrian), London W 171
Harrington (Adrian), London W 171
Hodgson (Books) (Richard J.),
  North Yorkshire 194
N1 Books, East Sussex 103
Saint Swithin's Illustrated & Children's Books,
  London W 172
Scrivener's Books & Bookbinding, Derbyshire . 81
Wiend Books, Lancashire 143
Wizard Books, Cambridgeshire 67

MAGNETICISM
Magis Books, Leicestershire 147

MAMMALS
Austwick Hall Books, Lancaster 190

MANAGEMENT
Bob Mallory (Books), Derbyshire 82
Cornucopia Books, Lincolnshire 151
Reading Lasses, Dumfries & Galloway 265

MANUALS
- GENERAL
Cornucopia Books, Lincolnshire 151

- SEAMANSHIP (SEE ALSO UNDER SEAMANSHIP)
Cheshire Book Centre, Cheshire 69
Lewcock (John), Cambridgeshire 66
McLaren Books, Strathclyde 274
Nautical Antique Centre (The), Dorset 94

MANUSCRIPTS
Aitchison (Lesley), Bristol 58
Apocalypse, Surrey 228
Biblion, London W 169
Bookstand, Dorset 93
Bristow & Garland, Hampshire 123
Cox Music (Lisa), Devon 84
Cox Rare Books (Charles), Cornwall 73
De Burca Rare Books, Co. Dublin 259
Drury Rare Books (John), Essex 111
Du Ry Medieval Manuscripts (Marc–Antoine),
  London W 170
Farahar & Dupre (Clive & Sophie), Wiltshire .. 246
Finch Rare Books Ltd. (Simon), London W ... 170
Fogg Rare Books & Manuscripts (Sam),
  London W 170
Ford (Richard), London W 170
Gekoski (R.A.), London WC 175
Heath (A.R.), Bristol 59
Humber Books, Lincolnshire 148
James Fergusson Books & Manuscripts,
  London W 170
Jarndyce Antiquarian Booksellers, London WC 175
John Underwood Antiquarian Books, Norfolk . 186
Ken's Paper Collectables, Buckinghamshire 62
Kenny's Bookshops and Art Galleries Ltd,
  Co. Galway 260
Kunkler Books (Paul), Cambridgeshire 64
Lucius Books, North Yorkshire 195
Maggs Brothers Limited, London W 171
Marine and Cannon Books, Cheshire 69
Muttonchop Manuscripts 239
Neil Summersgill, Lancashire 142
Pickering & Chatto, London W 172
Quaritch Ltd., (Bernard), London W 172
Rassam (Paul), London NW 159
Rowan (P. & B.), Co. Antrim 255

SPECIALITY INDEX

Seydi Rare Books (Sevin), London NW 159
Silverman (Michael), London SE 163
Taylor & Son (Peter), Hertfordshire.............. 132
Townsend (John), Berkshire 57
Tyger Press, London N 157
Williams Rare Books (Nigel), London WC..... 177
Wilson (Manuscripts) Ltd., (John),
   Gloucestershire 114

MAPS & MAPMAKING
Chas J. Sawyer, Kent 140
Grahame Thornton, Bookseller, Dorset 92

MARINE SCIENCES
Arden, Bookseller (C.), Powys..................... 282
Baldwin's Scientific Books, Essex 112
Cheshire Book Centre, Cheshire 69
Periplus Books, Buckinghamshire................. 62
Sub Aqua Prints and Books, Hampshire........ 124

MARITIME/NAUTICAL - GENERAL
Alba Books, Grampian 267
All Books, Essex 110
Altea Antique Maps & Books, London W 169
Anchor Books, Lincolnshire 149
Andron (G.W.), London N 155
Anvil Books, West Midlands 235
Arden Books & Cosmographia, Warwickshire. 232
Argent (Alan), Isle of Wight 135
Armitage (Booksearch), (Kate), Devon 83
Aviabooks, Gloucestershire 114
Axe Rare & Out of Print Books (Richard),
   North Yorkshire 190
Baldwin (M. & M.), Shropshire 250
Barbican Bookshop, North Yorkshire 194
Barmby (C. & A.J.), Kent........................... 140
Books Afloat, Dorset................................. 94
Bookshop (The), Dorset 92
Bookworld, Shropshire............................. 210
Bookworm, Lothian 270
Bott, (Bookdealers) Ltd., (Martin), Greater
   Manchester 118
Broadhurst of Southport Ltd., Merseyside...... 182
Burebank Books, Norfolk 184
Burroughs (Andrew), Lincolnshire 151
Butterworth (Robert F.), Lancashire 144
Cheshire Book Centre, Cheshire 69
Cofion Books, Pembrokeshire 281
Collectables (W.H.), Suffolk 225
Compass Books, Devon 84
Cornucopia Books, Lincolnshire 151
Cox (Geoff), Devon 89
Crouch Rare Books, Surrey........................ 227
Curtle Mead Books, Isle of Wight................ 134
D'Arcy Books, Wiltshire............................ 246
Dartmoor Bookshop (The), Devon............... 83
Duck (William), Hampshire....................... 124
Falconwood Transport & Military Bookshop,
   London Outer 181

Fireside Bookshop, Cumbria 80
Fisher Nautical, East Sussex 98
Footrope Knots, Suffolk............................ 223
Fox Books (J. & J.), Kent........................... 140
G. C. Books Ltd., Dumfries & Galloway 264
George St. Books, Derbyshire 82
Green Ltd. (G.L.), Hertfordshire.................. 132
Greta Books, Durham 96
Guildmaster Books, Cheshire 70
Hadley Bookseller (Peter J.), Essex 110
Harrington Antiquarian Bookseller (Peter),
   London SW.. 166
Hay Cinema Bookshop Ltd., Herefordshire 283
Helion & Company, West Midlands 235
High Street Books, Devon 85
Humm & Co. (Robert), Lincolnshire 151
Island Books, Kent 136
J & J Burgess Booksellers, Cambridgeshire..... 64
Kalligraphia (formerly Charmouth Bounty
   Books), Isle of Wight............................ 134
Keegan's Bookshop, Berkshire 56
Kellow Books, Oxfordshire 203
Kerr (Norman), Cumbria........................... 77
King Street Bookshop (The), Norfolk 185
Lamb's Tales Books, Devon 85
Larkham Books (Patricia), Gloucestershire 117
Lawrence Books, Nottinghamshire 200
Lee, Maritime Books (Gerald), East Sussex 104
Lewcock (John), Cambridgeshire 66
Marcet Books, London SE......................... 161
Marine and Cannon Books, Cheshire............ 69
Marine Workshop Bookshop, Dorset............ 92
Martin Bookshop & Gallery (Richard),
   Hampshire... 123
McCarty, Bookseller (M.E.), Western Isles 269
McCarty, Bookseller (M.E.), Dumfries &
   Galloway... 264
McConnell Fine Books, Kent 137
McLaren Books, Strathclyde....................... 274
Michael J Carroll, Co. Cork 257
Milestone Books, Devon........................... 88
Military Parade Bookshop, Wiltshire 247
Mothergoose Bookshop, Isle of Wight........... 134
My Back Pages, London SW...................... 167
Nautical Antique Centre (The), Dorset 94
Nelson (Elizabeth), Suffolk 222
Parrott Books, Oxfordshire 207
Portus Books, Hampshire 123
Prior (Michael), Lincolnshire 151
Quentin Books Ltd, Essex.......................... 109
Richmond Books, North Yorkshire 192
Rods Books, Devon 87
Sansovino Books, West Sussex 239
Sea Chest Nautical Bookshop (The), Devon ... 87
Signature Books, Hampshire....................... 126
Simmonds (Anthony J.), London SE 163
Smith Maritime Aviation Books (Frank),
   Tyne and Wear 231
Stroma Books, Borders 262
Sub Aqua Prints and Books, Hampshire........ 124
Suffolk Rare Books, Suffolk 225
Taylor & Son (Peter), Hertfordshire.............. 132

SPECIALITY INDEX

Tilston (Stephen E.), London SE 161
Treasure Island (The), Greater Manchester 120
Trinders' Fine Tools, Suffolk 222
Vanstone - Aviation Books, (Derek), Suffolk... 225
War & Peace Books, Hampshire 123
Warsash Nautical Bookshop, Hampshire 126
Wiend Books, Lancashire 143
Wise (Derek), East Sussex 102
World War Books, Kent 141

- HISTORY
Cavendish Rare Books Ltd, London N 155
Hadley Bookseller (Peter J.), Essex 110

- LOG BOOKS
Hicks (Ronald C.), Cornwall 73
McLaren Books, Strathclyde 274
Nautical Antique Centre (The), Dorset 94
Warsash Nautical Bookshop, Hampshire 126

MARQUE HISTORIES (SEE ALSO MOTORING)
Autobooks Ltd., East Sussex 100
Collectors Carbooks, Northamptonshire 196
Knowles (John), Norfolk 185
Pooks Motor Books, Leicestershire 146

MARXISM
Delectus Books, London WC 174
Killeen (John), North Yorkshire 191
Left on The Shelf, Cumbria 78
Reading Lasses, Dumfries & Galloway 265
Red Star Books, Hertfordshire 130
Spurrier (Nick), Kent 138
Treasure Trove Books, Leicestershire 146
Woburn Books, London N 157

MATHEMATICS
Ænigma Designs (Books), Devon 85
Baron - Scientific Book Sales (P.J.), Somerset.. 213
Camden Books, Somerset 212
Chesters (G. & J.), Staffordshire 220
Eagle Bookshop (The), Bedfordshire 53
Ely Books, Cambridgeshire 65
GfB: the Colchester Bookshop, Essex 109
Hadfield (G.K.), Cumbria 78
Hinchliffe Books, Bristol 59
Holtom (Christopher), Cornwall 75
Hurst (Jenny), Kent 138
John Gorton Booksearch, East Sussex 103
Phelps (Michael), West Sussex 237
Pickering & Chatto, London W 172
Roberts Books, Strathclyde 274
Skoob Russell Square, Suffolk 225
Stroh (M.A.), London E 153
Taylor & Son (Peter), Hertfordshire 132
Transformer, Dumfries & Galloway 265
Treasure Trove Books, Leicestershire 146
Turret House, Norfolk 189

Westwood Books (Mark), Powys 284
Westwood Books Ltd, Cumbria 79
Whistler's Books, London SW 167

MECHANICAL ENGINEERING
N1 Books, East Sussex 103

MEDIA
Aurora Books Ltd, Lothian 270
Cornucopia Books, Lincolnshire 151
Judd Books, London WC 175
Kelly Books, Devon 88
Murch Booksend, (Herbert), London SE 162
Reading Lasses, Dumfries & Galloway 265

MEDICINE
Alba Books, Grampian 267
Axe Rare & Out of Print Books (Richard),
    North Yorkshire 190
Baron - Scientific Book Sales (P.J.), Somerset.. 213
Beware of the Leopard, Bristol 58
Bibliophile (The), South Yorkshire 217
Bookshop (The), Co. Donegal 258
Bracton Books, Cambridgeshire 63
Bradley–Cox (Mary), Dorset 90
Carta Regis, Powys 286
Cheshire Book Centre, Cheshire 69
Childrens Bookshop, West Yorkshire 242
Collectable Books, London SE 162
Dean Byass, Bristol 60
Dusty Old Books Ltd., Oxfordshire 204
Edwards (London) Limited (Francis),
    London WC 175
Edwards in Hay–on–Wye (Francis),
    Herefordshire 283
Erian Books, London N 155
Finch Rare Books Ltd. (Simon), London W ... 170
Game Advice, Oxfordshire 205
Gaskell Rare Books (Roger), Cambridgeshire.. 66
Grahame Thornton, Bookseller, Dorset 92
Hay Cinema Bookshop Ltd., Herefordshire 283
Hünersdorff Rare Books, London SW 166
Hunter–Rare Books (Andrew), London SW 166
Kalligraphia (formerly Charmouth Bounty
    Books), Isle of Wight 134
Lawson & Company (E.M.), Oxfordshire 203
Macfarlane (Mr. H.), Essex 112
Orchid Book Distributors, Co. Clare 257
Outcast Books, Herefordshire 284
Phelps (Michael), West Sussex 237
Phillips (Nigel), London SW 167
Pickering & Chatto, London W 172
Pollak (P.M.), Devon 87
Portobello Books, London W 172
Pratt (B.A. & C.W.M.), Herefordshire 128
Prospect House Books, Co. Down 256
PsychoBabel Books & Journals, Oxfordshire ... 202
Quaritch Ltd., (Bernard), London W 172
Quinto of Charing Cross Road, London WC .. 176
Quinto of Great Russell Street, London WC ... 176

R M Books, Hertfordshire 132
Scrivener's Books & Bookbinding, Derbyshire . 81
Second Edition, Lothian 272
Smith (Clive), Essex 109
Smith (David & Lynn), London Outer 179
Stern Antiquarian Bookseller (Jeffrey), North
  Yorkshire 195
Stroh (M.A.), London E............................ 153
Treasure Island (The), Greater Manchester 120
Turret House, Norfolk 189
Village Books, Norfolk 184
Weiner (Graham), London N 157
Westons, Hertfordshire............................. 133
Westwood Books (Mark), Powys 284
Westwood Books Ltd, Cumbria 79
White (David), Cambridgeshire 65
Worcester Rare Books, Worcestershire 252

MEDICINE - HISTORY OF

Alba Books, Grampian 267
Baldwin's Scientific Books, Essex 112
Biblion, London W 169
Cheshire Book Centre, Cheshire 69
Chesters (G. & J.), Staffordshire 220
Childrens Bookshop, West Yorkshire 242
Erian Books, London N 155
Esplin (David), Hampshire 124
Fireside Bookshop, Cumbria 80
Game Advice, Oxfordshire 205
Kingswood Books, Dorset 93
London & Sussex Antiquarian Book & Print
  Services, East Sussex............................. 100
Maggs Brothers Limited, London W 171
Mair Wilkes Books, Fife 265
Meekins Books (Paul), Warwickshire 233
Phelps (Michael), West Sussex.................... 237
Pordes Books Ltd., (Henry), London WC 176
PsychoBabel Books & Journals, Oxfordshire ... 202
R M Books, Hertfordshire 132
Rowan (P. & B.), Co. Antrim 255
Smith (David & Lynn), London Outer 179
Sue Lowell Natural History Books, London W 173
Taylor & Son (Peter), Hertfordshire.............. 132
Westwood Books (Mark), Powys 284
White (David), Cambridgeshire 65

MEDIEVAL

Alexander's Books, Warwickshire................. 232
Andrew Stewart, Cornwall 74
Bennett & Kerr Books, Oxfordshire.............. 202
Byre Books, Dumfries & Galloway............... 264
Crouch Rare Books, Surrey........................ 227
Du Ry Medieval Manuscripts (Marc–Antoine),
  London W.. 170
Gildas Books, Cheshire 68
Grampian Books, Grampian....................... 268
Hobgoblin Books, Hampshire 125
John Underwood Antiquarian Books, Norfolk 186
medievalbookshop, London Outer................ 179
Meekins Books (Paul), Warwickshire 233
Michael J Carroll, Co. Cork 257

N1 Books, East Sussex.............................. 103
Priestpopple Books, Northumberland............ 198
Sandpiper Books Ltd., London SW.............. 167
Spenceley Books (David), West Yorkshire 244
Taylor & Son (Peter), Hertfordshire.............. 132
Thomson (Karen), Strathclyde 273
Unsworths Booksellers, London NW 160

MEMOIRS

Brimstones, East Sussex............................ 102
Cornucopia Books, Lincolnshire 151
Dolphin Books, Suffolk 221
Firth (Bijou Books & Photography) (Maureen),
  South Yorkshire................................... 218
Kirkpatrick (Robert J.), London W.............. 171
Libra Books, Lincolnshire 148
Mr. Pickwick of Towcester, Northamptonshire 196
Politico's.co.uk, Kent............................... 141
Samovar Books, Co. Dublin 258
Sillem (Anthony), East Sussex 101

MEMORABILIA

Art Reference Books, Hampshire................. 125
Dally Books & Collectables, Powys 285
firstpagebooks, Norfolk............................. 187

METAPHYSICS

Alpha Books, London N 155
Greensleeves, Oxfordshire 202
Inner Bookshop (The), Oxfordshire 205
Old Celtic Bookshop (The), Devon............... 86
SETI Books, Staffordshire......................... 220
Starlord Books, Greater Manchester 118
Trinity Rare Books, Co. Leitrim.................. 260

METEOROLOGY

Periplus Books, Buckinghamshire................ 62

MICROSCOPY

Baron (Christopher), Greater Manchester....... 118
Hadfield (G.K.), Cumbria 78
Phelps (Michael), West Sussex.................... 237
Turret House, Norfolk 189

MILITARY

Abacus Gallery, Staffordshire...................... 220
Addyman Annexe (The), Powys 282
Addyman Books, Powys............................ 282
Albion Books, West Midlands..................... 234
Allinson (Frank & Stella), Warwickshire 232
Anchor Books, Lincolnshire 149
Andrew Morton (Books), Powys.................. 281
Andron (G.W.), London N 155
Anglo-American Rare Books, Surrey 228
Antique Map and Bookshop (The), Dorset..... 93
Apocalypse, Surrey 228
Ardis Books, Hampshire............................ 126
Armchair Auctions, Hampshire 122
Austen (Phillip), Lincolnshire 151

SPECIALITY INDEX

Aviabooks, Gloucestershire 114
Axe Rare & Out of Print Books (Richard), North Yorkshire...................................... 190
B D McManmon, Lancashire 144
Baldwin (M. & M.), Shropshire 250
Barbican Bookshop, North Yorkshire 194
Barn Books, Buckinghamshire..................... 61
Barnes (Peter), Wiltshire 248
Blacket Books, Lothian............................... 270
Boer War Books, North Yorkshire............... 194
Bonner (John), West Yorkshire 243
Books, Denbighshire................................... 278
Books & Collectables Ltd., Cambridgeshire 63
Books Bought & Sold, Surrey 226
Books Plus, Devon 83
Bookworm, Essex....................................... 110
Bookworm (The), Lothian 271
Bookworms of Evesham, Worcestershire........ 252
Booth Books, Powys 282
Border Books, Borders............................... 262
Bosco Books, Cornwall 72
Brazenhead Ltd., Norfolk 186
Bufo Books, Hampshire 125
Burroughs (Andrew), Lincolnshire................ 151
Cader Idris Books, Gwynedd 280
Caliver Books, Essex 110
Camilla's Bookshop, East Sussex 100
Cavern Books, Cheshire 70
Central Bookshop, Warwickshire 232
Chaucer Bookshop, Kent............................. 136
Chelifer Books, Cumbria 80
Cheshire Book Centre, Cheshire 69
Chevin Books, West Yorkshire.................... 245
Churchill Book Specialist (The), London Outer 179
Clent Books, Worcestershire 250
Coach House Books, Worcestershire............. 251
Cobweb Books, North Yorkshire................. 192
Cofion Books, Pembrokeshire 281
Coles (T.V.), Cambridgeshire 66
Collectors Corner, Wiltshire........................ 248
Cornucopia Books, Lincolnshire 151
Cox Old & Rare Books (Claude), Suffolk....... 223
D'Arcy Books, Wiltshire............................. 246
Dally Books & Collectables, Powys 285
Dartmoor Bookshop (The), Devon............... 83
Devanha Military Books, Tayside 275
Donovan Military Books (Tom), East Sussex .. 98
Eastern Traveller (The), Somerset................. 216
Eastgate Bookshop, East Yorkshire 105
Edwards (London) Limited (Francis), London WC... 175
Edwards in Hay–on–Wye (Francis), Herefordshire...................................... 283
Embleton (Paul), Essex 111
Eton Antique Bookshop, Berkshire............... 57
Falconwood Transport & Military Bookshop, London Outer 181
Farnborough Gallery, Hampshire 123
Fireside Bookshop, Cumbria 80
Ford Books (David), Hertfordshire................ 132
Fox Books (J. & J.), Kent............................ 140
G. C. Books Ltd., Dumfries & Galloway 264

Gaullifmaufry Books, Hertfordshire.............. 131
Grahame Thornton, Bookseller, Dorset 92
Hancock (Peter), West Sussex 237
Harlequin Books, Bristol 59
Harris (George J.), Co. Derry 255
Heartland Old Books, Devon....................... 88
Helion & Company, West Midlands 235
High Street Books, Devon 85
Hill (John S.), Devon.................................. 84
Holmes (A.), Nottinghamshire..................... 201
hullbooks.com, East Yorkshire..................... 106
Hurst (Jenny), Kent 138
Hutchison (Books) (Larry), Fife................... 265
Internet Bookshop UK Ltd., Gloucestershire .. 113
Invicta Bookshop, Berkshire........................ 56
Island Books, Kent 136
Joppa Books Ltd., Surrey 226
Keegan's Bookshop, Berkshire 56
Keel Row Books, Tyne and Wear 231
King Street Bookshop (The), Norfolk 185
Kingfisher Book Service, Nottinghamshire...... 201
Lamb's Tales Books, Devon 85
Lawrence Books, Nottinghamshire 200
Lost Books, Northamptonshire 197
Malvern Bookshop (The), Worcestershire........ 250
Mandalay Bookshop, London SW 166
Marcet Books, London SE.......................... 161
Marine & Cannon Books, Cheshire 71
Marine and Cannon Books, Cheshire............ 69
McCrone (Audrey), Isle of Arran................. 269
Meads Book Service (The), East Sussex 103
Meekins Books (Paul), Warwickshire 233
MilitaryHistoryBooks.com, Kent 138
Morley Case, Hampshire 126
Mothergoose Bookshop, Isle of Wight........... 134
Mundy (David), Hertfordshire 130
N1 Books, East Sussex................................ 103
Nelson (Elizabeth), Suffolk 222
Old Aberdeen Bookshop, Grampian 266
Palladour Books, Hampshire 126
Park Gallery & Bookshop (The), Northamptonshire................................ 197
Parlour Bookshop (The), Oxfordshire............ 203
Pedlar's Pack Books, Devon 89
Prior (Michael), Lincolnshire 151
Queen Victoria PH, Torfaen......................... 287
Quinto of Great Russell Street, London WC... 176
Richard Thornton Books, London N............. 157
Rods Books, Devon 87
Royal Carbery Books Ltd., Co. Cork 257
Saint Swithin's Illustrated & Children's Books, London W.. 172
Samovar Books, Co. Dublin........................ 258
Sansovino Books, West Sussex 239
Scrivener's Books & Bookbinding, Derbyshire . 81
Seabreeze Books, Lancashire....................... 144
Sedgeberrow Books & Framing, Worcestershire 251
Shacklock Books (David), Suffolk 222
Shakeshaft (Dr. B.), Cheshire 71
Shapero Rare Books (Bernard J.), London W . 172
Sidey, Bookdealer (Philip), Kent 140
Signature Books, Hampshire....................... 126

SPECIALITY INDEX

Silver Trees Books, West Midlands 234
Skoob Russell Square, Suffolk 225
Smith (Clive), Essex 109
Spink & Son Limited, London WC 176
Spooner (John E.), Dorset 90
Stroma Books, Borders 262
Suffolk Rare Books, Suffolk 225
The Sanctuary Bookshop, Dorset 93
Tiffin (Tony and Gill), Durham 96
Tilston (Stephen E.), London SE 161
Tombland Bookshop, Norfolk 188
Trotman (Ken), Cambridgeshire 66
Vanstone - Aviation Books, (Derek), Suffolk ... 225
Wadard Books, Kent 137
War & Peace Books, Hampshire 123
Warnes (Felicity J.), London Outer 178
Wembdon Books, Somerset 213
Westwood Books Ltd, Cumbria 79
Wiend Books, Lancashire 143
Wise (Derek), East Sussex 102
Wizard Books, Cambridgeshire 67
Woolcott Books, Dorset 91
World War Books, Kent 141
Yeoman Books, Lothian 272
Yesterday's News, Conwy 278

MILITARY HISTORY

Aardvark Books, Wiltshire 249
Albion Books, West Midlands 234
Americanabooksuk, Cumbria 76
Andron (G.W.), London N 155
Antiques on High, Oxfordshire 204
Apocalypse, Surrey 228
Armchair Books, Lothian 270
Armitage (Booksearch), (Kate), Devon 83
Askew Books (Vernon), Wiltshire 246
Avedikian Rare Books, Somerset 213
Baldwin (M. & M.), Shropshire 250
Barbican Bookshop, North Yorkshire 194
Barnes (Peter), Wiltshire 248
Berry (L.J.), Kent 138
Biblion, London W 169
Black Five Books, Shropshire 211
Boer War Books, North Yorkshire 194
Books Afloat, Dorset 94
Books on Spain, London Outer 181
Bookworm, Lothian 270
Bookworm (The), Lothian 271
Brockwells Booksellers, Lincolnshire 148
Burroughs (Andrew), Lincolnshire 151
Caliver Books, Essex 110
Carnforth Bookshop (The), Lancashire 142
Castle Bookshop, Essex 109
Cavern Books, Cheshire 70
Central Bookshop, Warwickshire 232
Chaucer Bookshop, Kent 136
Chelifer Books, Cumbria 80
Cheshire Book Centre, Cheshire 69
Cobbles Books, Somerset 214
Coles (T.V.), Cambridgeshire 66
Corfe Books, Surrey 227

Cornucopia Books, Lincolnshire 151
Dally Books & Collectables, Powys 285
Dandy Lion Editions, Surrey 228
Dartmoor Bookshop (The), Devon 83
David Warnes Books, Herefordshire 129
Delph Books, Greater Manchester 120
Devanha Military Books, Tayside 275
Donovan Military Books (Tom), East Sussex .. 98
Dormouse Bookshop (The), Norfolk 188
Driffield Bookshop (The), East Yorkshire 105
Eastern Traveller (The), Somerset 216
Ewell Bookshop, Surrey 227
Farnborough Gallery, Hampshire 123
firstpagebooks, Norfolk 187
G. C. Books Ltd., Dumfries & Galloway 264
Garfi Books, Ceredigion 282
Gaullifmaufry Books, Hertfordshire 131
Guildmaster Books, Cheshire 70
Handsworth Books, Essex 112
Harlequin Books, Bristol 59
Harris (George J.), Co. Derry 255
Hay Cinema Bookshop Ltd., Herefordshire 283
Helion & Company, West Midlands 235
Heppa (Christopher), Essex 108
Hornsey's, North Yorkshire 192
Hummingbird Books, Herefordshire 128
Island Books, Kent 136
Jackson (M.W.), Wiltshire 249
Keegan's Bookshop, Berkshire 56
Keel Row Books, Tyne and Wear 231
Kellow Books, Oxfordshire 203
Kenny's Bookshops and Art Galleries Ltd,
    Co. Galway 260
Lost Books, Northamptonshire 197
Maggs Brothers Limited, London W 171
Mandalay Bookshop, London SW 166
Marble Hill Books, Middlesex 181
Marcet Books, London SE 161
Marine & Cannon Books, Cheshire 71
Marine and Cannon Books, Cheshire 69
McCrone (Audrey), Isle of Arran 269
Meads Book Service (The), East Sussex 103
Meekins Books (Paul), Warwickshire 233
Military Parade Bookshop, Wiltshire 247
MilitaryHistoryBooks.com, Kent 138
Morten (Booksellers) (E.J.),
    Greater Manchester 119
My Back Pages, London SW 167
N1 Books, East Sussex 103
O'Brien Books & Photo Gallery, Co. Limerick 261
Orssich (Paul), London SW 167
Paperbacks Plus, Bristol 59
Parrott Books, Oxfordshire 207
Pordes Books Ltd., (Henry), London WC 176
Prescott - The Bookseller (John),
    London Outer 181
Priestpopple Books, Northumberland 198
Prior (Michael), Lincolnshire 151
Queen Victoria PH, Torfaen 287
Quinto of Charing Cross Road, London WC .. 176
Richard Thornton Books, London N 157
Richmond Books, North Yorkshire 192

Rochdale Book Company,
  Greater Manchester 120
Rods Books, Devon 87
Roland Books, Kent 139
Savery Books, East Sussex 99
Schull Books, Co. Cork 257
Scorpio Books, Suffolk 221
Second Edition, Lothian 272
Solaris Books, East Yorkshire 105
Sutcliffe (Victor), Norfolk 184
Taylor & Son (Peter), Hertfordshire 132
The Dormouse Bookshop, Norfolk 188
Thin Read Line, Merseyside 182
Tiffin (Tony and Gill), Durham 96
Tilston (Stephen E.), London SE 161
Tombland Bookshop, Norfolk 188
Turton (John), Durham 97
Ventnor Rare Books, Isle of Wight 135
Village Books, Norfolk 184
Vinovium Books, Durham 96
Vokes Books Ltd., North Yorkshire 192
War & Peace Books, Hampshire 123
Water Lane Bookshop, Wiltshire 248
Wise (Derek), East Sussex 102
Wizard Books, Cambridgeshire 67
Words Etcetera Bookshop, Dorset 92
World's End Bookshop, London SW 168
Yeoman Books, Lothian 272
Yesterday's News, Conwy 278

MILITARY UNIFORMS
Chelifer Books, Cumbria 80
N1 Books, East Sussex 103
Thin Read Line, Merseyside 182

MIND, BODY & SPIRIT
Abbey Books, Cornwall 73
Bookshop (The), Dorset 92
Cornucopia Books, Lincolnshire 151
Dales & Lakes Book Centre, Cumbria 79
DPE Books, Devon 86
Esoteric Dreams Bookshop, Cumbria 77
Furneaux Books (Lee), Devon 88
Gildas Books, Cheshire 68
Graduate Books, Worcestershire 252
J & J Burgess Booksellers,
  Cambridgeshire 64
Oasis Booksearch, Cambridgeshire 67
Occultique, Northamptonshire 196
Orchid Book Distributors, Co. Clare 257
Philip Hopper, Essex 110
Reading Lasses, Dumfries & Galloway 265
Reid of Liverpool, Merseyside 182
Savery Books, East Sussex 99
Sedgeberrow Books & Framing,
  Worcestershire 251
SETI Books, Staffordshire 220
Starlord Books, Greater Manchester 118
Till's Bookshop, Lothian 272
Trafalgar Bookshop, East Sussex 99
Treasure Trove Books, Leicestershire 146

Trinity Rare Books, Co. Leitrim 260
Watkins Books Ltd., London WC 177

MINERALOGY
Baldwin's Scientific Books, Essex 112
Henly (John), West Sussex 239
Nibris Books, London SW 167
Phelps (Michael), West Sussex 237

MINIATURE BOOKS
Apocalypse, Surrey 228
Bernstein (Nicholas), London W 169
Demetzy Books, Oxfordshire 203
G. C. Books Ltd., Dumfries & Galloway 264
Garbett Antiquarian Books (Michael),
  Gloucestershire 113
Hennessey Bookseller (Ray), East Sussex 99
Mead (P.J.), Shropshire 210
Moorhead Books, West Yorkshire 241
RGS Books, Surrey 229
Roscrea Bookshop, Co. Tipperary 261
Scrivener's Books & Bookbinding,
  Derbyshire 81
Temperley (David), West Midlands 234

MINING
Book House (The), Cumbria 78
Bott, (Bookdealers) Ltd., (Martin), Greater
  Manchester 118
Browning Books, Torfaen 287
Collectables (W.H.), Suffolk 225
Cox (Geoff), Devon 89
Duck (William), Hampshire 124
G. C. Books Ltd., Dumfries & Galloway 264
Past & Present Books, Gloucestershire 114
Phelps (Michael), West Sussex 237
Salway Books, Essex 112
Turton (John), Durham 97
Vickers (Anthony), North Yorkshire 193
Whitchurch Books Ltd., Cardiff 276

MINORITY STUDIES
Reading Lasses, Dumfries & Galloway 265

MISSIONARIES & MISSIONS
G. C. Books Ltd., Dumfries & Galloway 264
Samovar Books, Co. Dublin 258

MODEL RAILWAYS
Bianco Library, West Sussex 237
Cornucopia Books, Lincolnshire 151
Milestone Books, Devon 88

MODERN ART
Cornucopia Books, Lincolnshire 151
Lucius Books, North Yorkshire 195
Worlds End Bookshop, London SW 168

MODERN FIRST EDITIONS

Addyman Annexe (The), Powys	282
Addyman Books, Powys	282
ahbooks, Merseyside	182
Allinson (Frank & Stella), Warwickshire	232
Amwell Book Company, London SE	154
Anglo-American Rare Books, Surrey	228
Ann & Mike Conry, Worcestershire	251
Annie's Books, South Yorkshire	217
Apocalypse, Surrey	228
Archer (Steve), London Outer	178
Armitage (Booksearch), (Kate), Devon	83
Askew Books (Vernon), Wiltshire	246
Autolycus, Shropshire	209
Avonworld Books, Somerset	213
Bertram Rota Ltd., London WC	174
Biblion, London W	169
Blackwell's Rare Books, Oxfordshire	205
Book Barrow, Cambridgeshire	63
Book Business (The), London W	169
Book Shelf (The), Devon	86
Bookcase, Cumbria	76
Books, Oxfordshire	202
Books & Things, London W	169
BOOKS4U, Flintshire	279
Bookshop on the Heath, The, London SE	161
Bookstand, Dorset	93
Booth (Booksearch Service), (Geoff), Cheshire	68
Bow Windows Book Shop, East Sussex	102
Bowie Books & Collectables, East Yorkshire	106
Broadhurst of Southport Ltd., Merseyside	182
Caledonia Books, Strathclyde	273
Cameron House Books, Isle of Wight	134
Camilla's Bookshop, East Sussex	100
Carta Regis, Powys	286
Castle Bookshop, Essex	109
Central Bookshop, Warwickshire	232
Chris Adam Smith Modern First Editions, West Sussex	238
Church Street Books, Norfolk	184
Clifford Milne Books, Grampian	266
Corfe Books, Surrey	227
Cornucopia Books, Lincolnshire	151
Cranhurst Books, London NW	158
Criterion Books, London Outer	180
Dormouse Bookshop (The), Norfolk	188
Driffield Bookshop (The), East Yorkshire	105
Ellis, Bookseller (Peter), London SE	162
Ellwood Editions, Wiltshire	247
Enscot Books, London SE	162
Fifteenth Century Bookshop (The), East Sussex	102
Finch Rare Books Ltd. (Simon), London W	170
First State Books, London W	170
firstpagebooks, Norfolk	187
Firsts in Print, Isle of Wight	134
Gander, (Jacques), Gloucestershire	115
Gildas Books, Cheshire	68
Hadley Bookseller (Peter J.), Essex	110
Harris (Books), (Malcolm), West Midlands	234
Heppa (Christopher), Essex	108
Hight (Norman F.), Glamorgan	279
Hollett and Son (R.F.G.), Cumbria	79
House of Figgis Ltd (The), Co. Galway	260
Hylton Booksearch, Merseyside	182
Idle Genius Books, London N	156
Innes Books, Shropshire	209
Island Books, Kent	136
Jackson (M.W.), Wiltshire	249
Jonkers Rare Books, Oxfordshire	204
Katharine House Gallery, Wiltshire	247
Kendall–Carpenter (Tim), Greater Manchester	119
Kennedy & Farley, East Sussex	103
Kestrel Books, Powys	283
Kevin S. Ogilvie Modern First Editions, Grampian	266
Lewis (J.T. & P.), Cornwall	73
Lewis First Editions, Kent	137
Libra Books, Lincolnshire	148
Little Stour Books, Kent	136
Lucius Books, North Yorkshire	195
Mainly Fiction, Greater Manchester	118
Mair Wilkes Books, Fife	265
McCrone (Audrey), Isle of Arran	269
McKelvie (Ian), London N	156
Ming Books, Dumfries & Galloway	265
Modern First Editions, London Outer	180
Moore (Sue), Cornwall	73
Moreton Books, Devon	86
Murphy (C.J.), Norfolk	187
N V Books, Warwickshire	232
Needham Books, (Russell), Somerset	216
Neil's Books, London NW	159
Norton Books, North Yorkshire	194
Parker Books (Mike), Cambridgeshire	64
Parrott (Jeremy), London E	153
Peter White, Hampshire	122
Poetry Bookshop (The), Powys	284
Pomes Penyeach, Staffordshire	219
Pordes Books Ltd., (Henry), London WC	176
Portus Books, Hampshire	123
Price (R.W.), Nottinghamshire	200
Pringle Booksellers (Andrew), Lothian	271
R. & A. Books, East Sussex	100
Reading Lasses, Dumfries & Galloway	265
Reaveley Books, Devon	85
Rees & O'Neill Rare Books, London WC	176
Richard Thornton Books, London N	157
Rising Tide Books, Fife	265
Robert (Leslie), London W	172
Rye Old Books, East Sussex	103
Seabreeze Books, Lancashire	144
Second Edition, Lothian	272
Shakeshaft (Dr. B.), Cheshire	71
Sillem (Anthony), East Sussex	101
Silver Trees Books, West Midlands	234
Simply Read Books, East Sussex	99
Simpson (Dave), Central	263
Skelton (Tony), Kent	141
Solaris Books, East Yorkshire	105
Stroma Books, Borders	262
Surprise Books, Gloucestershire	113
Talisman Books, Cheshire	70
Temple (Robert), London N	157

SPECIALITY INDEX

Thistle Books, Strathclyde 274
Thornber (Peter M.), North Yorkshire 193
Till's Bookshop, Lothian 272
Trevorrow (Edwin), Hertfordshire 130
Trinity Rare Books, Co. Leitrim 260
Ulysses, London WC 177
Warrender (Andrew), West Yorkshire 245
Webb Books (John), South Yorkshire 217
Wiend Books, Lancashire 143
Willmott Bookseller (Nicholas), Cardiff 276
Words Etcetera Bookshop, Dorset 92
Wright Trace Books, West Midlands 235
Wychwood Books, Gloucestershire 116

MONOGRAPHS
Barlow (Vincent G.), Hampshire 126
Campbell Art Books (Marcus), London SE 161
Heneage Art Books (Thomas), London SW.... 166
Taylor & Son (Peter), Hertfordshire 132
Trinders' Fine Tools, Suffolk 222

MOTORBIKES / MOTORCYCLES
Autobooks Ltd., East Sussex 100
Chaters Motoring Booksellers, London Outer . 179
Cheshire Book Centre, Cheshire 69
Collectors Carbooks, Northamptonshire 196
Falconwood Transport & Military Bookshop,
  London Outer 181
Holdenhurst Books, Dorset 90
Knowles (John), Norfolk 185
Main–Smith & Co. Ltd. (Bruce), Leicestershire 146
Merlin Books, West Sussex 238
Peake (Robin), Lincolnshire 151
Pooks Motor Books, Leicestershire 146
Simon Lewis Transport Books, Gloucestershire 115
Vintage Motorshop, West Yorkshire 241
Yeoman Books, Lothian 272

MOTORING
Abrahams (Mike), Staffordshire 219
Autobooks Ltd., East Sussex 100
Baldwin (M. & M.), Shropshire 250
Books & Collectables Ltd., Cambridgeshire 63
Books Bought & Sold, Surrey 226
books2books, Devon 87
Brewin Books Ltd., Warwickshire 233
Browse Books, Lancashire 143
Chandos Books, Devon 84
Chaters Motoring Booksellers,
  London Outer 179
Cheshire Book Centre, Cheshire 69
Chevin Books, West Yorkshire 245
Cobweb Books, North Yorkshire 192
Collectors Carbooks, Northamptonshire 196
Corfe Books, Surrey 227
Cornucopia Books, Lincolnshire 151
Cowley, Auto–in–Print (John), Essex 108
Cox (Geoff), Devon 89
Eastcote Bookshop (The), London Outer 178
Emjay Books, Surrey 226

Falconwood Transport & Military Bookshop,
  London Outer 181
Farquharson, (Hilary), Tayside 275
Hames (Peter), Devon 83
Holdenhurst Books, Dorset 90
Hornsey's, North Yorkshire 192
Horsham Rare Books, West Sussex 238
Janus Books, West Midlands 235
Kerr (Norman), Cumbria 77
Knowles (John), Norfolk 185
McGlynn (John), Lancashire 142
Morris Secondhand & Antiquarian Books
  (Chris), Oxfordshire 205
Peake (Robin), Lincolnshire 151
Pooks Motor Books, Leicestershire 146
Roadmaster Books, Kent 137
Roberts (Booksellers), (Ray), Staffordshire...... 219
Rochdale Book Company, Greater Manchester 120
Roland Books, Kent 139
Saint Mary's Books & Prints, Lincolnshire 152
Saint Paul's Street Bookshop, Lincolnshire 152
Scrivener's Books & Bookbinding, Derbyshire . 81
Simon Lewis Transport Books, Gloucestershire 115
Smith Maritime Aviation Books (Frank),
  Tyne and Wear 231
Stour Bookshop, Dorset 92
Thompson (Eric), Surrey 229
Tony Pollastrone Railway Books, Wiltshire 246
Vintage Motorshop, West Yorkshire 241
Volumes of Motoring, Gloucestershire 113
Yeoman Books, Lothian 272

MOUNTAIN MEN
Americanabooksuk, Cumbria 76
Gildas Books, Cheshire 68
Pinnacle Books, Lothian 271

MOUNTAINS
David Warnes Books, Herefordshire 129
Gildas Books, Cheshire 68
Marcet Books, London SE 161
Pinnacle Books, Lothian 271

MOVIE & TELEVISION SCRIPTS
Apocalypse, Surrey 228
Byre Books, Dumfries & Galloway 264

MUSIC - GENERAL
AA1 Books, Dumfries & Galloway 264
Abacus Gallery, Staffordshire 220
Antiques on High, Oxfordshire 204
Apocalypse, Surrey 228
Aurora Books Ltd, Lothian 270
Autumn Leaves, Lincolnshire 150
Axe Rare & Out of Print Books (Richard),
  North Yorkshire 190
Bardsley's Books, Suffolk 221
Baron (H.), London NW 158
Baxter - Books (Eddie), Somerset 216
Beware of the Leopard, Bristol 58

SPECIALITY INDEX

Blackwell's Music Shop, Oxfordshire 205
Bookcase, Cumbria 76
Books, Denbighshire................................ 278
Books & Collectables Ltd., Cambridgeshire 63
Books (For All), North Yorkshire................ 190
Books Plus, Devon 83
books2books, Devon 87
Bookshop (The), Norfolk.......................... 189
Boris Books, Hampshire........................... 127
Byre Books, Dumfries & Galloway............... 264
Carnforth Bookshop (The), Lancashire.......... 142
Carningli Centre, Pembrokeshire................. 281
Carta Regis, Powys................................. 286
Chaucer Bookshop, Kent........................... 136
Cheshire Book Centre, Cheshire 69
Clapham (M. & B.), Hampshire 124
Clements (R.W.), London Outer.................. 179
Colin Hancock, Ceredigion 277
Dales & Lakes Book Centre, Cumbria 79
Decorum Books, London N 155
Dooley (Rosemary), Cumbria 80
East Riding Books, East Yorkshire 106
Elgar (Raymond), East Sussex 98
Esoteric Dreams Bookshop, Cumbria............ 77
Evans (Mark), Lincolnshire 151
Fiona Edwards, Nottinghamshire................. 200
Fitzsimons (Anne), Cumbria...................... 77
Forest Books of Manchester, Cheshire 70
Gibbs Books, (Jonathan), Worcestershire 251
Gloucester Road Bookshop, London SW....... 165
Good for Books, Lincolnshire..................... 149
Goodden (Peter), Somerset........................ 212
Hancock & Monks, Powys........................ 283
Handsworth Books, Essex........................ 112
Hay Cinema Bookshop Ltd., Herefordshire 283
Hurst (Jenny), Kent 138
Internet Bookshop UK Ltd., Gloucestershire .. 113
Jade Mountain, Hampshire 125
Judd Books, London WC 175
Kalligraphia (formerly Charmouth Bounty
 Books), Isle of Wight............................ 134
Kenny's Bookshops and Art Galleries Ltd, Co.
 Galway... 260
Kim's Bookshop, West Sussex............ 237, 240
Libra Books, Lincolnshire......................... 148
Malvern Bookshop (The), Worcestershire....... 250
Marcet Books, London SE........................ 161
Martin Music Books (Philip), North Yorkshire 195
McGee (Terence J.), London Outer 178
Mogul Diamonds, West Midlands................ 236
Morris Secondhand & Antiquarian Books
 (Chris), Oxfordshire.............................. 205
Music By The Score, Cornwall 72
Musicalania, Norfolk.............................. 186
Paramor (C.D.), Suffolk 224
Parrott Books, Oxfordshire 207
Pastmasters, Derbyshire........................... 82
Portobello Books, London W 172
Price (R.W.), Nottinghamshire 200
Priestpopple Books, Northumberland 198
Quinto of Charing Cross Road, London WC.. 176
Quinto of Great Russell Street, London WC... 176
Roland Books, Kent................................ 139
Saint Mary's Books & Prints, Lincolnshire 152
Scarthin Books, Derbyshire 81
Sheet Music Warehouse (The), Devon........... 86
Sherlaw-Johnson (Austin), Oxfordshire.......... 206
Skoob Russell Square, Suffolk.................... 225
Staniland (Booksellers), Lincolnshire............. 152
Stern Antiquarian Bookseller (Jeffrey),
 North Yorkshire................................... 195
Stevens (Joan), Cambridgeshire 65
The Sanctuary Bookshop, Dorset................. 93
Till's Bookshop, Lothian 272
Travis & Emery Music Bookshop,
 London WC....................................... 177
Venables (Morris & Juliet), Bristol 59
Wiend Books, Lancashire 143
Willmott Bookseller (Nicholas), Cardiff 276
Wood (Peter), Cambridgeshire 65
Woodlands Books, West Yorkshire 244
Worlds End Bookshop, London SW............. 168

- CHART HISTORIES & RESEARCH
Sheet Music Warehouse (The), Devon........... 86

- CLASSICAL
Alba Secondhand Music, Strathclyde 273
Barnes - Books (Lyndon), Shropshire............ 209
Biblion, London W 169
Blackwell's Music Shop, Oxfordshire 205
Browne (Christopher I.), West Yorkshire 242
Chesters (G. & J.), Staffordshire 220
East Riding Books, East Yorkshire 106
Ely Books, Cambridgeshire 65
Gibbs Books, (Jonathan), Worcestershire 251
Grahame Thornton, Bookseller, Dorset 92
Hancock & Monks, Powys........................ 283
John R. Hoggarth, North Yorkshire............. 194
Marcan, Bookseller (Peter), London SE......... 162
Newgate Books and Translations,
 Northumberland 198
Pordes Books Ltd., (Henry), London WC 176
Prescott - The Bookseller (John),
 London Outer 181
Reads, Dorset....................................... 94
Scrivener's Books & Bookbinding,
 Derbyshire... 81
Sheet Music Warehouse (The), Devon........... 86
Travis & Emery Music Bookshop,
 London WC....................................... 177
Venables (Morris & Juliet), Bristol 59
Willmott Bookseller (Nicholas), Cardiff 276

- COMPOSERS
Blackwell's Music Shop, Oxfordshire 205
Boris Books, Hampshire........................... 127
East Riding Books, East Yorkshire 106
Hancock & Monks, Powys........................ 283
Marcet Books, London SE........................ 161
Martin Music Books (Philip), North Yorkshire 195

SPECIALITY INDEX

Music By The Score, Cornwall 72
Musicalania, Norfolk 186
Sheet Music Warehouse (The), Devon 86
Sherlaw-Johnson (Austin), Oxfordshire 206
Travis & Emery Music Bookshop,
 London WC... 177
Venables (Morris & Juliet), Bristol 59
Whistler's Books, London SW 167
Willmott Bookseller (Nicholas), Cardiff 276

- COUNTRY & WESTERN
A. & R. Booksearch, Cornwall.................... 73
Barnes - Books (Lyndon), Shropshire............ 209
Sheet Music Warehouse (The), Devon 86

- FOLK & IRISH FOLK
Aucott & Thomas, Leicestershire 145
Church Green Books, Oxfordshire 207
Dancing Goat Bookshop (The), Norfolk........ 184
Green Man Books, East Sussex 100
K.S.C. Books, Cheshire............................. 68
Naughton Booksellers, Co. Dublin 259
Royal Carbery Books Ltd., Co. Cork 257
Sheet Music Warehouse (The), Devon 86
Travis & Emery Music Bookshop,
 London WC... 177

- GREGORIAN CHANTS
Sheet Music Warehouse (The), Devon 86

- ILLUSTRATED SHEET MUSIC
Sheet Music Warehouse (The), Devon 86
The Old Music Master, Bristol 60

- JAZZ & BLUES
A. & R. Booksearch, Cornwall.................... 73
Barnes - Books (Lyndon), Shropshire............ 209
Baxter - Books (Eddie), Somerset................. 216
Bookroom (The), Surrey 229
Courtyard Books, Gloucestershire 113
East Riding Books, East Yorkshire 106
Hames (Peter), Devon............................... 83
Hancock & Monks, Powys......................... 283
My Back Pages, London SW 167
Scorpio Books, Suffolk............................. 221
Sheet Music Warehouse (The), Devon 86
Travis & Emery Music Bookshop,
 London WC... 177

- MUSIC HALL
Browne (Christopher I.), West Yorkshire 242
Fitzsimons (Anne), Cumbria....................... 77
Hancock & Monks, Powys......................... 283
Kaye - Bookseller (Terence), London NW...... 159
McGee (Terence J.), London Outer 178
Music By The Score, Cornwall.................... 72
Sheet Music Warehouse (The), Devon 86
Travis & Emery Music Bookshop,
 London WC... 177

- MUSICIANS
Blackwell's Music Shop, Oxfordshire 205
East Riding Books, East Yorkshire 106
Hancock & Monks, Powys......................... 283
Music By The Score, Cornwall.................... 72
Price (John), London N 157
Sheet Music Warehouse (The), Devon 86
Travis & Emery Music Bookshop,
 London WC... 177
Willmott Bookseller (Nicholas), Cardiff 276
Woodlands Books, West Yorkshire 244

- OPERA
Blackwell's Music Shop, Oxfordshire 205
Browne (Christopher I.), West Yorkshire 242
East Riding Books, East Yorkshire 106
Fitzsimons (Anne), Cumbria....................... 77
Hancock & Monks, Powys......................... 283
Hodgkins and Company Limited (Ian),
 Gloucestershire 116
Marcet Books, London SE......................... 161
Martin Music Books (Philip), North Yorkshire 195
Music By The Score, Cornwall.................... 72
Sheet Music Warehouse (The), Devon 86
Sherlaw-Johnson (Austin), Oxfordshire 206
Travis & Emery Music Bookshop,
 London WC... 177
Whistler's Books, London SW 167
Willmott Bookseller (Nicholas), Cardiff 276

- ORCHESTRAL
Sheet Music Warehouse (The), Devon 86

- POLITICAL SONGS & BALLADS
Barry McKay Rare Books, Cumbria............. 76
Music By The Score, Cornwall.................... 72
Sheet Music Warehouse (The), Devon 86
Travis & Emery Music Bookshop,
 London WC... 177

- POPULAR
A. & R. Booksearch, Cornwall.................... 73
Apocalypse, Surrey 228
Barnes - Books (Lyndon), Shropshire............ 209
Black Cat Bookshop, Leicestershire 145
Dancing Goat Bookshop (The), Norfolk........ 184
firstpagebooks, Norfolk 187
Furneaux Books (Lee), Devon 88
Graduate Books, Worcestershire 252
John R. Hoggarth, North Yorkshire 194
Music By The Score, Cornwall.................... 72
Musicalania, Norfolk 186
Nevitsky (Philip), Greater Manchester 119
Pordes Books Ltd., (Henry), London WC 176
Sheet Music Warehouse (The), Devon 86
Travis & Emery Music Bookshop,
 London WC... 177
Whistler's Books, London SW 167
Willmott Bookseller (Nicholas), Cardiff 276
Yorkshire Relics, West Yorkshire................. 242

SPECIALITY INDEX

- PRINTED, SHEET MUSIC & SCORES
Apocalypse, Surrey 228
Browne (Christopher I.), West Yorkshire 242
Carningli Centre, Pembrokeshire 281
Cox Music (Lisa), Devon 84
Decorum Books, London N 155
Esoteric Dreams Bookshop, Cumbria 77
Gibbs Books, (Jonathan), Worcestershire 251
Hancock & Monks, Powys 283
Martin Music Books (Philip),
 North Yorkshire 195
Music By The Score, Cornwall 72
Sheet Music Warehouse (The), Devon 86
The Old Music Master, Bristol 60
The Sanctuary Bookshop, Dorset 93
Travis & Emery Music Bookshop,
 London WC 177

- ROCK & ROLL
A. & R. Booksearch, Cornwall 73
Barnes - Books (Lyndon), Shropshire 209
Dancing Goat Bookshop (The), Norfolk 184
firstpagebooks, Norfolk 187
Furneaux Books (Lee), Devon 88
Pyecroft (Ruth), Gloucestershire 116
Roland Books, Kent 139
Savery Books, East Sussex 99
Sclanders (Beatbooks), (Andrew), London EC . 154
Sheet Music Warehouse (The), Devon 86
Till's Bookshop, Lothian 272
Travis & Emery Music Bookshop,
 London WC 177
Yorkshire Relics, West Yorkshire 242

- SONGS & BALLADS
Sheet Music Warehouse (The), Devon 86

- THEORY
Sheet Music Warehouse (The), Devon 86

- WESTERNS
Sheet Music Warehouse (The), Devon 86

MUSICAL INSTRUMENTS
Barmby (C. & A.J.), Kent 140
East Riding Books, East Yorkshire 106
Elgar (Raymond), East Sussex 98
Goodden (Peter), Somerset 212
Hancock & Monks, Powys 283
K.S.C. Books, Cheshire 68
Kitley (A.J.), Bristol 59
Martin Music Books (Philip),
 North Yorkshire 195
Orchid Book Distributors, Co. Clare 257
Sherlaw-Johnson (Austin), Oxfordshire 206
Travis & Emery Music Bookshop,
 London WC 177
Trinders' Fine Tools, Suffolk 222

MUSICAL INSTRUMENTS - GUITARS
K.S.C. Books, Cheshire 68

MUSICIANS
Sheet Music Warehouse (The), Devon 86

MYCOLOGY
Hollingshead (Chris), London Outer 181
Pendleside Books, Lancashire 143

MYSTERIES
Apocalypse, Surrey 228
Furneaux Books (Lee), Devon 88
Gildas Books, Cheshire 68
Inner Bookshop (The), Oxfordshire 205
Mostly Mysteries Bookstore, Lincolnshire 150
Occultique, Northamptonshire 196
Philip Hopper, Essex 110
Seabreeze Books, Lancashire 144
Starlord Books, Greater Manchester 118
Temple (Robert), London N 157
Wizard Books, Cambridgeshire 67

MYSTICISM
Bardsley's Books, Suffolk 221
Bygone Books, Strathclyde 274
Cavern Books, Cheshire 70
Esoteric Dreams Bookshop, Cumbria 77
Facet Books, Dorset 90
Gildas Books, Cheshire 68
Greensleeves, Oxfordshire 202
Inner Bookshop (The), Oxfordshire 205
Magis Books, Leicestershire 147
Needham Books, (Russell), Somerset 216
Occultique, Northamptonshire 196
Philip Hopper, Essex 110
Reid of Liverpool, Merseyside 182
Samovar Books, Co. Dublin 258
Starlord Books, Greater Manchester 118
Wizard Books, Cambridgeshire 67

MYTHOLOGY
Alpha Books, London N 155
Apocalypse, Surrey 228
Atlantis Bookshop, London WC 174
Brighton Books, East Sussex 98
Byre Books, Dumfries & Galloway 264
Cheshire Book Centre, Cheshire 69
Esoteric Dreams Bookshop, Cumbria 77
Galloway & Porter Limited, Cambridgeshire ... 63
Gildas Books, Cheshire 68
Green Man Books, East Sussex 100
Greensleeves, Oxfordshire 202
Inner Bookshop (The), Oxfordshire 205
Magis Books, Leicestershire 147
Randall (Tom), Somerset 215
Starlord Books, Greater Manchester 118
Watkins Books Ltd., London WC 177
Wizard Books, Cambridgeshire 67

NATIONAL GEOGRAPHIC

G. C. Books Ltd., Dumfries & Galloway 264
Naughton Booksellers, Co. Dublin 259
Orb's Bookshop, Grampian 268
The Sanctuary Bookshop, Dorset 93

NATIVE AMERICAN

Americanabooksuk, Cumbria 76
Byre Books, Dumfries & Galloway 264
Magis Books, Leicestershire 147
Optimus Books Ltd, West Sussex 240
Orchid Book Distributors, Co. Clare 257

NATURAL HEALTH

Cheshire Book Centre, Cheshire 69
Dandy Lion Editions, Surrey 228
Dworski Books, Travel & Language Bookshop
  (Marijana), Herefordshire 283
Greensleeves, Oxfordshire 202
Hay Cinema Bookshop Ltd., Herefordshire 283
IKON, Devon 88
Mobbs (A.J.), West Midlands 235
Occultique, Northamptonshire 196

NATURAL HISTORY

Abacus Gallery, Staffordshire 220
Acer Books, Herefordshire 128
Alauda Books, Cumbria 76
Allhalland Books, Devon 83
Allinson (Frank & Stella), Warwickshire 232
Andron (G.W.), London N 155
Anthony Whittaker, Kent 136
Antique Map and Bookshop (The), Dorset 93
Antiques on High, Oxfordshire 204
Arden Books & Cosmographia,
  Warwickshire 232
Arden, Bookseller (C.), Powys 282
Aurelian Books, London NW 158
Austwick Hall Books, Lancaster 190
Autumn Leaves, Lincolnshire 150
Aviabooks, Gloucestershire 114
Axe Rare & Out of Print Books (Richard),
  North Yorkshire 190
Ayre (Peter J.), Somerset 216
Baldwin's Scientific Books, Essex 112
Barn Books, Buckinghamshire 61
Barnhill Books, Isle of Arran 269
Baron (Christopher), Greater Manchester 118
Baron - Scientific Book Sales (P.J.), Somerset .. 213
Besleys Books, Suffolk 221
Biblion, London W 169
Billing (Brian), Berkshire 57
Birdnet Optics Ltd., Derbyshire 81
Blest (Peter), Kent 139
Bookcase, Cumbria 76
Books & Collectables Ltd., Cambridgeshire ... 63
Books (For All), North Yorkshire 190
Booth Books, Powys 282
Bow Windows Book Shop, East Sussex 102
Broadhurst of Southport Ltd., Merseyside 182

Broadleaf Books, Torfaen 287
Brock Books, North Yorkshire 190
Brookes (Gerard), Devon 86
Burden Ltd., (Clive A.), Hertfordshire 132
Calluna Books, Dorset 94
Carlton Books, Norfolk 187
Carnforth Bookshop (The), Lancashire 142
Carningli Centre, Pembrokeshire 281
Castle Hill Books, Herefordshire 128
Castleton (Pat), Kent 137
Chandos Books, Devon 84
Channel Islands Galleries Limited,
  Channel Islands 253
Cheshire Book Centre, Cheshire 69
Chevin Books, West Yorkshire 245
Clark (M.R.), West Yorkshire 241
Clarke Books (David), Somerset 214
Classey Limited (E.W.), Oxfordshire 203
Cobbles Books, Somerset 214
Coch-y-Bonddu Books, Powys 285
Collectable Books, London SE 162
Corvus Books, Buckinghamshire 61
Cox Old & Rare Books (Claude), Suffolk 223
Creaking Shelves, Highland 268
Cumming Limited (A. & Y.), East Sussex 102
Curtle Mead Books, Isle of Wight 134
D'Arcy Books, Wiltshire 246
Dales & Lakes Book Centre, Cumbria 79
Daly (Peter M.), Hampshire 127
Dandy Lion Editions, Surrey 228
Dartmoor Bookshop (The), Devon 83
David (G.), Cambridgeshire 63
Davies Fine Books, Worcestershire 252
Demar Books (Grant), Kent 140
Dene Barn Books & Prints, Somerset 216
Earth Science Books, Wiltshire 247
Eastcote Bookshop (The), London Outer 178
Edmund Pollinger Rare Books, London SW ... 165
Edwards (London) Limited (Francis),
  London WC 175
Edwards in Hay–on–Wye (Francis),
  Herefordshire 283
Elmfield Books, West Midlands 234
Evergreen Livres, Gloucestershire 115
Fine Art, London SE 165
Fireside Bookshop, Cumbria 80
firstpagebooks, Norfolk 187
Freader's Books, Tayside 275
Garfi Books, Ceredigion 282
Gaullifmaufry Books, Hertfordshire 131
GfB: the Colchester Bookshop, Essex 109
Gibbard (A. & T.), East Sussex 100
Gildas Books, Cheshire 68
Gillmark Gallery, Hertfordshire 131
Gloucester Road Bookshop, London SW 165
Goodyer (Nicholas), London N 156
Goodyer, Natural History Books (Eric),
  Leicestershire 146
Grayling (David A.H.), Cumbria 78
Hall's Bookshop, Kent 141
Halson Books, Cheshire 71
Harrington (Adrian), London W 171

SPECIALITY INDEX

Hatchard & Daughters, West Yorkshire 242
Hawkridge Books, Derbyshire 81
Hay Cinema Bookshop Ltd., Herefordshire 283
Henly (John), West Sussex 239
Hereward Books, Cambridgeshire 65
Heywood Hill Limited (G.), London W 171
Hodgson (Books) (Richard J.),
    North Yorkshire 194
Hollett and Son (R.F.G.), Cumbria 79
Hollingshead (Chris), London Outer 181
Ice House Books, Wiltshire 248
Island Books, Kent 136
J. & J. Books, Lincolnshire 149
Jackson (M.W.), Wiltshire 249
Jade Mountain, Hampshire 125
Jane Jones Books, Grampian 267
Jay Books, Lothian 271
Just Books, Cornwall 75
Kalligraphia (formerly Charmouth Bounty
    Books), Isle of Wight 134
Katnap Arts, Norfolk 187
Keeble Antiques, Somerset 215
Kellow Books, Oxfordshire 203
Kennedy (Peter), Surrey 230
Kernaghans, Merseyside 183
Kim's Bookshop, West Sussex 237, 240
King Street Bookshop (The), Norfolk 185
Kingsgate Books & Prints, Hampshire 127
Kingshead Books, Wales 286
Kingsmere Books, Bedfordshire 53
Knapton Bookbarn, North Yorkshire 194
Korn (M. Eric), London N 156
Larkham Books (Patricia), Gloucestershire 117
Lenton (Alfred), Leicestershire 145
Libra Books, Lincolnshire 148
Lymelight Books & Prints, Dorset 92
Maggs Brothers Limited, London W 171
Malvern Bookshop (The), Worcestershire 250
Marshall Rare Books (Bruce), Gloucestershire . 113
Martin's Books, Powys 285
McCrone (Audrey), Isle of Arran 269
McEwan Fine Books, Grampian 266
Meads Book Service (The), East Sussex 103
Mobbs (A.J.), West Midlands 235
Moorhead Books, West Yorkshire 241
Moreton Books, Devon 86
Mount's Bay Books, Cornwall 74
Muse Bookshop (The), Gwynedd 279
Neil Summersgill, Lancashire 142
New Strand Bookshop (The), Herefordshire 128
Nineteenth Century Books, Oxfordshire 207
Old Town Bookshop (The), Lothian 271
Orb's Bookshop, Grampian 268
Oxfam Books and Music, Hampshire 127
Page (David), Lothian 271
Pandion Books, North Yorkshire 192
Paralos Ltd., London WC 175
Park (Mike), London Outer 180
Parrott Books, Oxfordshire 207
Pemberley Books, Buckinghamshire 62
Peregrine Books (Leeds), West Yorkshire 244
Phelps (Michael), West Sussex 237

Pordes Books Ltd., (Henry), London WC 176
Priestpopple Books, Northumberland 198
Quentin Books Ltd, Essex 109
Quinto of Great Russell Street, London WC ... 176
R.E. & G.B. Way, Suffolk 224
Richard Thornton Books, London N 157
River Reads Bookshop, Devon 89
Roland Books, Kent 139
Roz Hulse, Conwy 278
Russell (Charles), London SW 167
Rutland Bookshop (The), Rutland 208
Rye Old Books, East Sussex 103
Ryeland Books, Northamptonshire 196
Saint Ann's Books, Worcestershire 251
Second Edition, Lothian 272
Segal Books (Joel), Devon 84
Shakeshaft (Dr. B.), Cheshire 71
Shearwater Bed & Books (formerly John
    Lumby Nat. History Bks), Northumberland.. 198
Signature Books, Hampshire 126
Simon Finch Nofolk, Norfolk 186
Smith (Clive), Essex 109
Smith Books, (Sally), Suffolk 222
Sotheran Limited (Henry), London W 172
Stella Books, Monmouthshire 281
Stone, (G.& R.), Borders 262
Sue Lowell Natural History Books, London W 173
Sykes (Graham), West Yorkshire 244
Tant Yn Ellen Books, Powys 286
Temperley (David), West Midlands 234
Thomas (E. Wyn), Conwy 278
Trinity Rare Books, Co. Leitrim 260
Vokes Books Ltd., North Yorkshire 192
Wadard Books, Kent 137
Westwood Books Ltd, Cumbria 79
Wildside Books, Worcestershire 250
Wilson (David), Buckinghamshire 61
Wise (Derek), East Sussex 102
Woodbine Books, West Yorkshire 241
Woodside Books, Kent 136
Words Etcetera Bookshop, Dorset 92
Wychwood Books, Gloucestershire 116
Wyseby House Books, Berkshire 55

NATURAL SCIENCES

Alauda Books, Cumbria 76
Austwick Hall Books, Lancaster 190
Cheshire Book Centre, Cheshire 69
Cornucopia Books, Lincolnshire 151
Demetzy Books, Oxfordshire 203
Earth Science Books, Wiltshire 247
J & J Burgess Booksellers, Cambridgeshire 64
Lymelight Books & Prints, Dorset 92
Mannwaring (M.G.), Bristol 59
Phelps (Michael), West Sussex 237
Pollak (P.M.), Devon 87
Summerfield Books Ltd, Cumbria 76
Turret House, Norfolk 189
Wildside Books, Worcestershire 250
Wyseby House Books, Berkshire 55

NATURE
Alauda Books, Cumbria 76
Castleton (Pat), Kent 137
Cornucopia Books, Lincolnshire 151
Summerfield Books Ltd, Cumbria 76

NATURISM
Green (Paul), Cambridgeshire 66

NAVAL
AA1 Books, Dumfries & Galloway 264
Alauda Books, Cumbria 76
Anchor Books, Lincolnshire 149
Andron (G.W.), London N 155
Armchair Auctions, Hampshire 122
Aviabooks, Gloucestershire 114
Barnes (Peter), Wiltshire 248
Book For All Reasons (A.), Suffolk 224
Bookends of Fowey, Cornwall 73
books2books, Devon 87
Bookworm, Lothian 270
Bookworm (The), Lothian 271
Bott, (Bookdealers) Ltd., (Martin), Greater
    Manchester 118
Burroughs (Andrew), Lincolnshire 151
Camilla's Bookshop, East Sussex 100
Cavern Books, Cheshire 70
Cheshire Book Centre, Cheshire 69
Cofion Books, Pembrokeshire 281
Coles (T.V.), Cambridgeshire 66
Corfe Books, Surrey 227
Curtle Mead Books, Isle of Wight 134
Edwards (London) Limited (Francis),
    London WC 175
Edwards in Hay-on-Wye (Francis),
    Herefordshire 283
Elton Engineering Books, London W 170
Ewell Bookshop, Surrey 227
Dormouse Bookshop (The), Norfolk 188
Gaullifmaufry Books, Hertfordshire 131
Good for Books, Lincolnshire 149
Green Ltd. (G.L.), Hertfordshire 132
Harris (George J.), Co. Derry 255
Helion & Company, West Midlands 235
Hook (Arthur), Bristol 59
Internet Bookshop UK Ltd., Gloucestershire .. 113
J & J Burgess Booksellers, Cambridgeshire 64
Keegan's Bookshop, Berkshire 56
Lee, Maritime Books (Gerald), East Sussex 104
Lewcock (John), Cambridgeshire 66
Lost Books, Northamptonshire 197
Marcet Books, London SE 161
Marine and Cannon Books, Cheshire 69
McCrone (Audrey), Isle of Arran 269
McLaren Books, Strathclyde 274
Milestone Books, Devon 88
N1 Books, East Sussex 103
Nautical Antique Centre (The), Dorset 94
Prior (Michael), Lincolnshire 151
Rods Books, Devon 87
Savery Books, East Sussex 99
Second Edition, Lothian 272
Simmonds (Anthony J.), London SE 163
Spooner (John E.), Dorset 90
Sub Aqua Prints and Books, Hampshire 124
Surprise Books, Gloucestershire 113
Thin Read Line, Merseyside 182
Tilston (Stephen E.), London SE 161
Wadard Books, Kent 137
War & Peace Books, Hampshire 123
Warwick Leadley Gallery, London SE 163
Webb Books (John), South Yorkshire 217
Wise (Derek), East Sussex 102
Yesterday's News, Conwy 278

NAVIGATION
Anvil Books, West Midlands 235
Books Afloat, Dorset 94
Curtle Mead Books, Isle of Wight 134
Lee, Maritime Books (Gerald), East Sussex 104
Lewcock (John), Cambridgeshire 66
Marcet Books, London SE 161
McLaren Books, Strathclyde 274
Milestone Books, Devon 88
Nautical Antique Centre (The), Dorset 94
Rods Books, Devon 87
Sea Chest Nautical Bookshop (The), Devon ... 87
Warsash Nautical Bookshop, Hampshire 126

NAVY, THE
Marcet Books, London SE 161
Milestone Books, Devon 88
N1 Books, East Sussex 103

NEEDLEWORK
Apocalypse, Surrey 228
Arden Books & Cosmographia, Warwickshire . 232
Axe Rare & Out of Print Books (Richard),
    North Yorkshire 190
Black Cat Books, Norfolk 185
Brown-Studies, Strathclyde 273
Byrom Textile Bookroom (Richard),
    Lancashire 142
Chevin Books, West Yorkshire 245
Cover to Cover, Merseyside 183
Don Kelly Books, London W 170
DPE Books, Devon 86
Four Shire Bookshops, Oxfordshire 202
Good for Books, Lincolnshire 149
Gresham Books, Somerset 214
Heneage Art Books (Thomas), London SW 166
Hennessey Bookseller (Ray), East Sussex 99
Ives Bookseller (John), London Outer 181
Mansfield (Judith), West Yorkshire 245
Old Bookshop (The), West Midlands 236
Reading Lasses, Dumfries & Galloway 265
Scrivener's Books & Bookbinding, Derbyshire . 81
Smith Books (Keith), Herefordshire 128
Trinders' Fine Tools, Suffolk 222
Whittle, Bookseller (Avril), Cumbria 79

SPECIALITY INDEX

NEUROLOGY
Alba Books, Grampian 267
Erian Books, London N 155
Game Advice, Oxfordshire 205
Mair Wilkes Books, Fife 265

NEW AGE
2 Ravens, Cumbria 78
Abacus Gallery, Staffordshire 220
Dandy Lion Editions, Surrey 228
Dawlish Books, Devon 84
DPE Books, Devon 86
Esoteric Dreams Bookshop, Cumbria 77
Gildas Books, Cheshire 68
Greensleeves, Oxfordshire 202
IKON, Devon 88
Inner Bookshop (The), Oxfordshire 205
Invisible Books, East Sussex 98
Magis Books, Leicestershire 147
Occultique, Northamptonshire 196
Orchid Book Distributors, Co. Clare 257
Roger Lucas Booksellers, Lincolnshire 150
SETI Books, Staffordshire 220
Till's Bookshop, Lothian 272
Trinity Rare Books, Co. Leitrim 260
Words Etcetera Bookshop, Dorset 92
Worlds End Bookshop, London SW 168

NEW NATURALIST
Acer Books, Herefordshire 128
Alauda Books, Cumbria 76
Birdnet Optics Ltd., Derbyshire 81
Blest (Peter), Kent 139
Books and Things, Channel Islands 253
BOOKS4U, Flintshire 279
Calluna Books, Dorset 94
Cheshire Book Centre, Cheshire 69
Creaking Shelves, Highland 268
Dales & Lakes Book Centre, Cumbria 79
Hollett and Son (R.F.G.), Cumbria 79
J & J Burgess Booksellers, Cambridgeshire 64
Muse Bookshop (The), Gwynedd 279
Pemberley Books, Buckinghamshire 62
Polmorla Books, Cornwall 75
Poor Richard's Books, Suffolk 222
Roger Collicott Books, Cornwall 74
Scrivener's Books & Bookbinding, Derbyshire . 81
Shakeshaft (Dr. B.), Cheshire 71
Shearwater Bed & Books (formerly John
  Lumby Nat. History Bks), Northumberland.. 198
Sue Lowell Natural History Books, London W 173
Summerfield Books Ltd, Cumbria 76
Westwood Books (Mark), Powys 284
Westwood Books Ltd, Cumbria 79
Wildside Books, Worcestershire 250

NEWSPAPERS
Derek Stirling Bookseller, Kent 141
John Underwood Antiquarian Books, Norfolk 186
Ken's Paper Collectables, Buckinghamshire 62

Mr. Pickwick of Towcester, Northamptonshire 196
Nostalgia Unlimited, Merseyside 182
Tilleys Vintage Magazine Shop, Derbyshire 81
Yesterday's News, Conwy 278

NON-FICTION
Abbey Books, Cornwall 73
Apocalypse, Surrey 228
books2books, Devon 87
Carningli Centre, Pembrokeshire 281
Castleton (Pat), Kent 137
Loretta Lay Books, London NW 159
Marble Hill Books, Middlesex 181
Naughton Booksellers, Co. Dublin 259
Orb's Bookshop, Grampian 268
Reading Lasses, Dumfries & Galloway 265
Savery Books, East Sussex 99
Shakeshaft (Dr. B.), Cheshire 71
Skoob Russell Square, Suffolk 225

NOSTALGIA
Border Bookshop, West Yorkshire 245
Fifteenth Century Bookshop (The), East Sussex 102
Hunt (Robin S.), Greater Manchester 120
McGee (Terence J.), London Outer 178
Nostalgia Unlimited, Merseyside 182
Prior (Michael), Lincolnshire 151
Till's Bookshop, Lothian 272
Yesterday's News, Conwy 278

NUMEROLOGY
Magis Books, Leicestershire 147

NUMISMATICS
Clark (Nigel A.), London SE 162
Heneage Art Books (Thomas), London SW 166
InterCol London, London N 156
Spink & Son Limited, London WC 176
Taylor & Son (Peter), Hertfordshire 132

NURSERY RHYMES
Fifteenth Century Bookshop (The), East Sussex 102
Jean Hedger, Berkshire 55

NURSES/DOCTORS
Reading Lasses, Dumfries & Galloway 265

OCCULT
Alpha Books, London N 155
Anthroposophical Books, Gloucestershire 116
Apocalypse, Surrey 228
Atlantis Bookshop, London WC 174
Books, Denbighshire 278
Bygone Books, Strathclyde 274
Caduceus Books, Leicestershire 145
Cavern Books, Cheshire 70
Central Bookshop, Warwickshire 232
Cheshire Book Centre, Cheshire 69
Chthonios Books, East Sussex 101

SPECIALITY INDEX

Clegg (David), Staffordshire........................ 219
Dandy Lion Editions, Surrey 228
Dartmoor Bookshop (The), Devon............... 83
Dawlish Books, Devon............................... 84
Delectus Books, London WC...................... 174
Dworski Books, Travel & Language Bookshop
  (Marijana), Herefordshire 283
Enigma Books, Norfolk 186
Esoteric Dreams Bookshop, Cumbria............ 77
Gilbert (R.A.), Bristol 59
Gildas Books, Cheshire 68
Green Man Books, East Sussex 100
Greensleeves, Oxfordshire 202
Hay Cinema Bookshop Ltd., Herefordshire 283
Inner Bookshop (The), Oxfordshire 205
J & J Burgess Booksellers, Cambridgeshire..... 64
Loretta Lay Books, London NW.................. 159
Lucius Books, North Yorkshire 195
Magis Books, Leicestershire........................ 147
Needham Books, (Russell), Somerset 216
Occultique, Northamptonshire..................... 196
Philip Hopper, Essex 110
Savery Books, East Sussex 99
SETI Books, Staffordshire.......................... 220
Starlord Books, Greater Manchester 118
Till's Bookshop, Lothian 272
Treasure Chest Books, Suffolk 222
Victoria Bookshop (The), Devon 83
Walker Fine Books (Steve), Dorset................ 91
Watkins Books Ltd., London WC.................. 177
Waxfactor, East Sussex............................... 99
Wizard Books, Cambridgeshire..................... 67
Worlds End Bookshop, London SW.............. 168

OCEAN LINERS
Chas J. Sawyer, Kent 140
Milestone Books, Devon............................ 88

OCEANOGRAPHY
Baldwin's Scientific Books, Essex 112

ODD & UNUSUAL
Book Business (The), London W 169
Delectus Books, London WC...................... 174
Esoteric Dreams Bookshop, Cumbria............ 77
Facet Books, Dorset................................. 90
Gildas Books, Cheshire 68
Good for Books, Lincolnshire 149
Hurst (Jenny), Kent 138
Lewis (J.T. & P.), Cornwall 73
Lighthouse Books (The), Dorset 91
Moss Books, London NW 159
Muttonchop Manuscripts............................ 239
Occultique, Northamptonshire..................... 196
Reid of Liverpool, Merseyside..................... 182
Rutland Bookshop (The), Rutland 208
Treglown (Roger J.), Cheshire..................... 70

OIL LAMPS
Don Kelly Books, London W 170

ORIENTAL
Art Reference Books, Hampshire 125
Books, Denbighshire................................. 278
Butler Books, Dorset 90
Canon Gate Books, West Sussex 239
Hosains Books, London NW...................... 159
Joppa Books Ltd., Surrey 226
Mandalay Bookshop, London SW 166
Probsthain (Arthur), London WC................ 176
RGS Books, Surrey.................................. 229

ORNITHOLOGY
Acer Books, Herefordshire 128
Alauda Books, Cumbria............................ 76
Anwoth Books, Dumfries & Galloway 264
Arden, Bookseller (C.), Powys..................... 282
Aviabooks, Gloucestershire 114
Barnhill Books, Isle of Arran...................... 269
Birdnet Optics Ltd., Derbyshire 81
Blest (Peter), Kent 139
Bosco Books, Cornwall 72
Brown (Books) (P.R.), Durham................... 97
Calendula Horticultural Books, East Sussex.... 101
Calluna Books, Dorset.............................. 94
Carlton Books, Norfolk 187
Coach House Books, Worcestershire............. 251
Coch-y-Bonddu Books, Powys 285
Cornucopia Books, Lincolnshire 151
Countrymans Gallery (The), Leicestershire...... 145
Curtle Mead Books, Isle of Wight................ 134
Daly (Peter M.), Hampshire 127
Dancing Goat Bookshop (The), Norfolk........ 184
Demar Books (Grant), Kent....................... 140
Edmund Pollinger Rare Books, London SW... 165
Goodyer (Nicholas), London N................... 156
Hawkridge Books, Derbyshire..................... 81
Internet Bookshop UK Ltd., Gloucestershire .. 113
Isabelline Books, Cornwall 72
Kellow Books, Oxfordshire 203
Martin's Books, Powys 285
Mayhew (Veronica), Berkshire 56
McEwan Fine Books, Grampian.................. 266
Mobbs (A.J.), West Midlands 235
Moss Books, London NW 159
Pandion Books, North Yorkshire................. 192
Pemberley Books, Buckinghamshire.............. 62
Poor Richard's Books, Suffolk 222
Prospect House Books, Co. Down 256
Rutland Bookshop (The), Rutland 208
Saint Ann's Books, Worcestershire 251
Shearwater Bed & Books (formerly John
  Lumby Nat. History Bks), Northumberland... 198
Sue Lowell Natural History Books, London W 173
Wensum Books, Norfolk 188
Wildside Books, Worcestershire 250
Wilson (David), Buckinghamshire 61
Woodside Books, Kent 136
Wyseby House Books, Berkshire.................. 55

OSTEOPATHY
Phelps (Michael), West Sussex..................... 237

SPECIALITY INDEX

Sue Lowell Natural History Books, London W 173

OTTOMAN EMPIRE
Collectables (W.H.), Suffolk 225
Dworski Books, Travel & Language Bookshop
 (Marijana), Herefordshire 283
Hosains Books, London NW 159

OUT-OF-PRINT
Apocalypse, Surrey 228
Aurora Books Ltd, Lothian........................ 270
Black Cat Books, Norfolk.......................... 185
Book Mad, Lancashire............................... 142
Book Palace (The), London SE 161
Central Bookshop, Warwickshire 232
Clifford Elmer Books Ltd., Cheshire 68
Cornucopia Books, Lincolnshire 151
Fifteenth Century Bookshop (The), East Sussex 102
Good for Books, Lincolnshire..................... 149
J & J Burgess Booksellers, Cambridgeshire 64
Orb's Bookshop, Grampian........................ 268
Reading Lasses, Dumfries & Galloway 265
Samovar Books, Co. Dublin....................... 258
Shakeshaft (Dr. B.), Cheshire....................... 71
Skoob Russell Square, Suffolk..................... 225

OUTDOORS
John R. Hoggarth, North Yorkshire............. 194

OUTLAWS
Americanabooksuk, Cumbria....................... 76
Loretta Lay Books, London NW................. 159

OXFORD MOVEMENT
Carter, (Brian), Oxfordshire....................... 203
Rosemary Pugh Books, Wiltshire................ 248
Samovar Books, Co. Dublin....................... 258

PACIFISM
Dandy Lion Editions, Surrey 228
Larkham Books (Patricia), Gloucestershire 117
Left on The Shelf, Cumbria........................ 78
Moss Books, London NW 159
Spurrier (Nick), Kent................................. 138
Woburn Books, London N 157
Yesterday's Books, Dorset 91
Yesterday's News, Conwy 278

PADDLE BOATS
Milestone Books, Devon............................. 88

PAGANISM
Atlantis Bookshop, London WC.................. 174
Bygone Books, Strathclyde......................... 274
Chthonios Books, East Sussex..................... 101
Inner Bookshop (The), Oxfordshire 205
Occultique, Northamptonshire..................... 196
Starlord Books, Greater Manchester 118

Treasure Trove Books, Leicestershire 146

PAINTING
Apocalypse, Surrey 228
Art Reference Books, Hampshire................. 125
Butts Books (Mary), Berkshire 56
Cheshire Book Centre, Cheshire 69
Don Kelly Books, London W 170
Grosvenor Prints, London WC.................... 175
Heneage Art Books (Thomas), London SW.... 166
Modern Firsts Etc, Lancashire 142
Polmorla Books, Cornwall 75
RGS Books, Surrey.................................... 229
Trinity Rare Books, Co. Leitrim.................. 260

PALAEOGRAPHY
Bennett & Kerr Books, Oxfordshire.............. 202
Brinded (Scott), Kent................................. 139
Earth Science Books, Wiltshire.................... 247
Gildas Books, Cheshire 68
Island Books, Kent 136
Leeds Bookseller, West Yorkshire 244
Taylor & Son (Peter), Hertfordshire.............. 132

PALAEONTOLOGY
Baldwin's Scientific Books, Essex 112
Earth Science Books, Wiltshire.................... 247
Esoteric Dreams Bookshop, Cumbria............ 77
Henly (John), West Sussex 239
Kalligraphia (formerly Charmouth Bounty
 Books), Isle of Wight.............................. 134
Kingswood Books, Dorset 93
Little Bookshop (The), Cumbria 80
Lymelight Books & Prints, Dorset................ 92
Pemberley Books, Buckinghamshire.............. 62
Sykes (Graham), West Yorkshire 244
The Sanctuary Bookshop, Dorset................. 93
Webb Books (John), South Yorkshire 217

PALMISTRY & FORTUNE-TELLING
Alpha Books, London N 155
Cavern Books, Cheshire 70
Inner Bookshop (The), Oxfordshire 205
Magis Books, Leicestershire........................ 147
Occultique, Northamptonshire..................... 196

PAPER COLLECTABLES
Book Palace (The), London SE 161
Embleton (Paul), Essex 111
John Underwood Antiquarian Books, Norfolk 186
Ken's Paper Collectables, Buckinghamshire 62
Murphy (C.J.), Norfolk 187
Wiend Books, Lancashire 143

PAPERMAKING
Barry McKay Rare Books, Cumbria............. 76
Bettridge (Gordon), Fife 265
Brinded (Scott), Kent................................. 139
Coupland (Terry W.), Staffordshire 219

SPECIALITY INDEX

Cox Old & Rare Books (Claude), Suffolk....... 223
Forest Books, Nottinghamshire 201
Wakeman Books (Frances), Nottinghamshire .. 201

PARAPSYCHOLOGY
Atlantis Bookshop, London WC................... 174
Cavern Books, Cheshire 70
Esoteric Dreams Bookshop, Cumbria............ 77
Greensleeves, Oxfordshire 202
Inner Bookshop (The), Oxfordshire 205
Occultique, Northamptonshire..................... 196
Starlord Books, Greater Manchester 118

PARISH REGISTERS
Grampian Books, Grampian....................... 268
Island Books, Kent 136
Taylor & Son (Peter), Hertfordshire.............. 132
Townsend (John), Berkshire 57
Turton (John), Durham............................. 97

PERFORMING ARTS
Anthony Spranger, Wiltshire....................... 247
Book Palace (The), London SE 161
Books & Bygones (Pam Taylor), West
  Midlands... 236
Booth Books, Powys 282
Brian Troath Books, London E.................... 153
Browne (Christopher I.), West Yorkshire 242
Catalyst Booksearch Services, Devon 85
Chaucer Bookshop, Kent........................... 136
Cornucopia Books, Lincolnshire 151
Cover to Cover, Merseyside........................ 183
Cox Rare Books (Charles), Cornwall 73
D'Arcy Books, Wiltshire............................ 246
DaSilva Puppet Books, Dorset 92
Dolphin Books, Suffolk............................. 221
Drummond Pleasures of Past Times (David),
  London WC... 174
Fitzsimons (Anne), Cumbria....................... 77
Franks Booksellers, Greater Manchester 119
Gibbs Books, (Jonathan), Worcestershire 251
Gloucester Road Bookshop, London SW........ 165
Greenroom Books, West Yorkshire 243
Inprint, Gloucestershire 116
Jarndyce Antiquarian Booksellers, London WC 175
Kaye - Bookseller (Terence), London NW...... 159
Libris (Weston) Books, Somerset 213
Malvern Bookshop (The), Worcestershire....... 250
McGee (Terence J.), London Outer 178
N1 Books, East Sussex............................. 103
Paramor (C.D.), Suffolk............................ 224
Poor Richard's Books, Suffolk 222
Price (John), London N 157
Reads, Dorset.. 94
Scorpio Books, Suffolk............................. 221
Scrivener's Books & Bookbinding, Derbyshire . 81
Signature Books, Hampshire....................... 126
Skoob Russell Square, Suffolk.................... 225
Theatreshire Books, North Yorkshire 190
Till's Bookshop, Lothian 272

Treasure Trove Books, Leicestershire 146
Willmott Bookseller (Nicholas), Cardiff 276
Wood (Peter), Cambridgeshire 65

PETROLEUM GEOLOGY
Geophysical Books, Kent........................... 140

PETROLEUM TECHNOLOGY
Geophysical Books, Kent........................... 140

PHARMACY/PHARMACOLOGY
Alba Books, Grampian 267
Baldwin's Scientific Books, Essex 112
Empire Books, North Yorkshire 194
Orchid Book Distributors, Co. Clare............. 257
Phelps (Michael), West Sussex..................... 237
Pickering & Chatto, London W................... 172
Smith (David & Lynn), London Outer 179
White (David), Cambridgeshire 65

PHILATELY
32 Seconds, East Sussex 102
Clark (Nigel A.), London SE...................... 162
Frost (Richard), Hertfordshire..................... 130
Hodgson (Books) (Richard J.), North
  Yorkshire 194
Pennymead Books, North Yorkshire............. 191
Postings, Surrey 228
Spink & Son Limited, London WC 176
Treasure Island (The), Greater Manchester 120

PHILOLOGY
Baldwin (Jack), Strathclyde 273
Bennett & Kerr Books, Oxfordshire.............. 202
Dworski Books, Travel & Language Bookshop
  (Marijana), Herefordshire 283
Ice House Books, Wiltshire........................ 248
Nineteenth Century Books, Oxfordshire......... 207
Olynthiacs, Shropshire 210
Polczynski (Udo K.H.), Powys 284
Seydi Rare Books (Sevin), London NW......... 159
Thomson (Karen), Strathclyde 273
Unsworths Booksellers, London NW 160

PHILOSOPHY
Apocalypse, Surrey 228
Armchair Books, Lothian 270
Bell (Peter), Strathclyde 270
Books, Denbighshire................................ 278
Books Antiques & Collectables, Devon.......... 88
Bookshop (The), Dorset 92
Bookshop (The), Co. Donegal..................... 258
Bookshop (The), Greater Manchester............ 119
Booth Books, Powys 282
Brimstones, East Sussex............................ 102
Caledonia Books, Strathclyde...................... 273
Camden Books, Somerset 212
Carter, (Brian), Oxfordshire........................ 203
Cheshire Book Centre, Cheshire 69

SPECIALITY INDEX

Chesters (G. & J.), Staffordshire 220
Chthonios Books, East Sussex 101
Dean Byass, Bristol 60
Drury Rare Books (John), Essex 111
Edwards (London) Limited (Francis),
    London WC 175
Edwards in Hay–on–Wye (Francis),
    Herefordshire 283
Elephant Books, West Yorkshire 244
Firth (Bijou Books & Photography) (Maureen),
    South Yorkshire 218
Fisher & Sperr, London N 155
Game Advice, Oxfordshire 205
GfB: the Colchester Bookshop, Essex 109
Gloucester Road Bookshop, London SW 165
Graduate Books, Worcestershire 252
Hamish Riley-Smith, Norfolk 188
Handsworth Books, Essex 112
Herb Tandree Philosophy Books,
    Gloucestershire 116
Hughes Rare Books (Spike), Borders 262
Humanist Book Services, Cornwall 72
John Gorton Booksearch, East Sussex 103
Judd Books, London WC 175
Kenny's Bookshops and Art Galleries Ltd,
    Co. Galway 260
Killeen (John), North Yorkshire 191
Kyrios Books, Nottinghamshire 200
Lee Rare Books (Rachel), Bristol 59
Moseley Books, West Midlands 234
My Back Pages, London SW 167
O'Donoghue Books, Powys 284
Occultique, Northamptonshire 196
Orb's Bookshop, Grampian 268
Parkinsons Books, Merseyside 183
Pendleburys Bookshop, London N 156
Pickering & Chatto, London W 172
Plurabelle Books, Cambridgeshire 64
Polczynski (Udo K.H.), Powys 284
Pomes Penyeach, Staffordshire 219
Pordes Books Ltd., (Henry), London WC 176
Portobello Books, London W 172
Price (John), London N 157
Quaritch Ltd., (Bernard), London W 172
Quinto of Charing Cross Road, London WC .. 176
Quinto of Great Russell Street, London WC .. 176
Reading Lasses, Dumfries & Galloway 265
Reads, Dorset 94
Roland Books, Kent 139
Rosemary Pugh Books, Wiltshire 248
Rowan (P. & B.), Co. Antrim 255
Savery Books, East Sussex 99
Schulz–Falster Rare Books (Susanne),
    London N 157
Scrivener's Books & Bookbinding, Derbyshire . 81
Second Edition, Lothian 272
Skoob Russell Square, Suffolk 225
Spurrier (Nick), Kent 138
Staniland (Booksellers), Lincolnshire 152
Stokes Books, Co. Dublin 259
Thorntons of Oxford Ltd., Oxfordshire 203
Till's Bookshop, Lothian 272

Trafalgar Bookshop, East Sussex 99
Unsworths Booksellers, London NW 160
Walden Books, London NW 160
Waterfield's, Oxfordshire 206
Webb Books (John), South Yorkshire 217
Westwood Books (Mark), Powys 284
Wiend Books, Lancashire 143
Winghale Books, Lincolnshire 151
Woburn Books, London N 157
Worcester Rare Books, Worcestershire 252
Worlds End Bookshop, London SW 168
Yarwood Rare Books (Edward), Greater
    Manchester 118

PHOTOGRAPHY

Abacus Gallery, Staffordshire 220
Allsworth Rare Books Ltd., London 164
Amwell Book Company, London SE 154
Apocalypse, Surrey 228
Ars Artis, Oxfordshire 205
Aviabooks, Gloucestershire 114
Berry (L.J.), Kent 138
Biblion, London W 169
Blaenavon Books, Torfaen 287
Books, Denbighshire 278
Books & Collectables Ltd., Cambridgeshire 63
Books & Things, London W 169
Books Only, Suffolk 222
Brighton Books, East Sussex 98
Broadleaf Books, Torfaen 287
Butcher (Pablo), Oxfordshire 203
Cameron House Books, Isle of Wight 134
Cavern Books, Cheshire 70
Cofion Books, Pembrokeshire 281
Collectables (W.H.), Suffolk 225
Derek Stirling Bookseller, Kent 141
Farahar & Dupre (Clive & Sophie), Wiltshire .. 246
Finch Rare Books Ltd. (Simon), London W ... 170
Firth (Bijou Books & Photography) (Maureen),
    South Yorkshire 218
Grays of Westminster, London SW 165
Hay Castle, Powys 283
Hill House Books, Devon 87
Holleyman (J.F.), East Sussex 101
Jill Howell, Kent 138
Judd Books, London WC 175
Keswick Bookshop, Cumbria 78
N1 Books, East Sussex 103
Newcastle Bookshop, Northumberland 198
O'Brien Books & Photo Gallery, Co. Limerick 261
Paper Pleasures, Somerset 215
Photo Books International, London WC 176
Phototitles.com, Essex 109
Pollak (P.M.), Devon 87
Prescott - The Bookseller (John),
    London Outer 181
Quaritch Ltd., (Bernard), London W 172
Ray Rare and Out of Print Books (Janette),
    North Yorkshire 195
Rayner (Hugh Ashley), Somerset 212
Rhodes, Bookseller (Peter), Hampshire 126

Solaris Books, East Yorkshire 105
Soldridge Books Ltd, Hampshire 122
Sykes (Graham), West Yorkshire 244
Treasure Island (The), Greater Manchester 120
Wiend Books, Lancashire 143
Woburn Books, London N 157

PHRENOLOGY
Phelps (Michael), West Sussex 237

PHYSICAL CULTURE
Combat Arts Archive, Durham 96
Webster (D.), Strathclyde 274

PHYSICS
Camden Books, Somerset 212
Eagle Bookshop (The), Bedfordshire 53
Ely Books, Cambridgeshire 65
Freader's Books, Tayside 275
Hinchliffe Books, Bristol 59
Moorside Books, Lancashire 143
Parkinsons Books, Merseyside 183
Phelps (Michael), West Sussex 237
The Sanctuary Bookshop, Dorset 93
Wayside Books and Cards, Oxfordshire 203
Weiner (Graham), London N 157
Whistler's Books, London SW 167

PIRATES
Book Palace (The), London SE 161
Loretta Lay Books, London NW 159

PLANT HUNTING
Alauda Books, Cumbria 76
Anne Harris Books & Bags Booksearch, Devon 86
Arden, Bookseller (C.), Powys 282
Barnhill Books, Isle of Arran 269
Blest (Peter), Kent 139
Calendula Horticultural Books, East Sussex 101
Chantrey Books, South Yorkshire 217
Dales & Lakes Book Centre, Cumbria 79
Daly (Peter M.), Hampshire 127
Edmund Pollinger Rare Books, London SW ... 165
Hollett and Son (R.F.G.), Cumbria 79
Hollingshead (Chris), London Outer 181
Hunter and Krageloh, Derbyshire 82
Mandalay Bookshop, London SW 166
McEwan Fine Books, Grampian 266
Page (David), Lothian 271
Park (Mike), London Outer 180
Summerfield Books Ltd, Cumbria 76
Traveller's Bookshelf (The), Somerset 212

PLAYS
Abbey Books, Cornwall 73
Amwell Book Company, London SE 154
Apocalypse, Surrey 228
Books Antiques & Collectables, Devon 88
Bookshop (The), Dorset 92

Byre Books, Dumfries & Galloway 264
Cheshire Book Centre, Cheshire 69
Derek Stirling Bookseller, Kent 141
G. C. Books Ltd., Dumfries & Galloway 264
Jade Mountain, Hampshire 125
Jarndyce Antiquarian Booksellers, London WC 175
Libra Books, Lincolnshire 148
McKelvie (Ian), London N 156
Pastmasters, Derbyshire 82
Reading Lasses, Dumfries & Galloway 265
Savery Books, East Sussex 99
Scrivener's Books & Bookbinding, Derbyshire . 81
Stalagluft Books, Tyne and Wear 231
Surprise Books, Gloucestershire 113
The Sanctuary Bookshop, Dorset 93
Till's Bookshop, Lothian 272
Willmott Bookseller (Nicholas), Cardiff 276

POETRY
Abacus Gallery, Staffordshire 220
Addyman Books, Powys 282
Amwell Book Company, London SE 154
Anglo-American Rare Books, Surrey 228
Antiques on High, Oxfordshire 204
Anwoth Books, Dumfries & Galloway 264
Apocalypse, Surrey 228
Applin (Malcolm), Berkshire 55
Arden Books & Cosmographia, Warwickshire . 232
Armchair Books, Lothian 270
Ash Rare Books, London SW 164
Barmby (C. & A.J.), Kent 140
Bayntun (George), Somerset 212
Book Shelf (The), Devon 86
Bookroom (The), Surrey 229
Books, Oxfordshire 202
Books, Denbighshire 278
Books & Bygones (Pam Taylor),
  West Midlands 236
Books Antiques & Collectables, Devon 88
Bookshop (The), Dorset 92
Bookstand, Dorset 93
Bracton Books, Cambridgeshire 63
Brian Troath Books, London E 153
Bridge Books, Cumbria 80
Brighton Books, East Sussex 98
Browse Books, Lancashire 143
Budd (Richard), Somerset 215
Byre Books, Dumfries & Galloway 264
Cameron House Books, Isle of Wight 134
Carningli Centre, Pembrokeshire 281
Cheshire Book Centre, Cheshire 69
Classic Bindings Ltd, London SW 164
Clements (R.W.), London Outer 179
Cofion Books, Pembrokeshire 281
Cox Rare Books (Charles), Cornwall 73
Criterion Books, London Outer 180
D'Arcy Books, Wiltshire 246
Dancing Goat Bookshop (The), Norfolk 184
Dandy Lion Editions, Surrey 228
Derek Stirling Bookseller, Kent 141
Eastcote Bookshop (The), London Outer 178

SPECIALITY INDEX

Elaine Lonsdale Books, West Yorkshire 242
Ellwood Editions, Wiltshire 247
Erian Books, London N 155
Eton Antique Bookshop, Berkshire 57
GfB: the Colchester Bookshop, Essex 109
Gloucester Road Bookshop, London SW 165
Good for Books, Lincolnshire 149
Green (Paul), Cambridgeshire 66
Hellenic Bookservices, London NW 158
Hennessey Bookseller (Ray), East Sussex 99
Hurst (Jenny), Kent 138
Jade Mountain, Hampshire 125
Jane Jones Books, Grampian 267
Jiri Books, Co. Antrim 255
Kendall–Carpenter (Tim), Greater Manchester 119
Kingsgate Books & Prints, Hampshire 127
Kingsmere Books, Bedfordshire 53
Lawrence Books, Nottinghamshire 200
Libris (Weston) Books, Somerset 213
Little Bookshop (The), Greater Manchester 119
Loch Croispol Bookshop & Restaurant,
  Highland 268
Lymelight Books & Prints, Dorset 92
Main Point Books, Lothian 271
Malvern Bookshop (The), Worcestershire 250
Marine Workshop Bookshop, Dorset 92
Martin's Books, Powys 285
McCrone (Audrey), Isle of Arran 269
McKelvie (Ian), London N 156
Modlock (Lilian), Dorset 92
Moreton Books, Devon 86
Nineteenth Century Books, Oxfordshire 207
Orangeberry Books, Oxfordshire 204
Palladour Books, Hampshire 126
Paper Moon Books, Warwickshire 233
Poetry Bookshop (The), Powys 284
Polmorla Books, Cornwall 75
Pomes Penyeach, Staffordshire 219
Poor Richard's Books, Suffolk 222
Prescott - The Bookseller (John),
  London Outer 181
Primrose Hill Books, London NW 159
Priory Books, Worcestershire 252
Quest Booksearch, Cambridgeshire 64
Reading Lasses, Dumfries & Galloway 265
Richmond Books, North Yorkshire 192
Riderless Horse Books, Norfolk 184
Rivendale Press, Buckinghamshire 61
Rosemary Books, Merseyside 183
Roundstone Books, Lancashire 143
Rutland Bookshop (The), Rutland 208
Samovar Books, Co. Dublin 258
Savery Books, East Sussex 99
Scrivener's Books & Bookbinding, Derbyshire . 81
Seabreeze Books, Lancashire 144
Shelley (E. & J.), Buckinghamshire 61
Signature Books, Hampshire 126
Skoob Russell Square, Suffolk 225
Smith Books (Keith), Herefordshire 128
Soldridge Books Ltd, Hampshire 122
Staniland (Booksellers), Lincolnshire 152
Stevens (Joan), Cambridgeshire 65
Stone, (G.& R.), Borders 262
Stroma Books, Borders 262
Sturford Books, Wiltshire 248
Tant Yn Ellen Books, Powys 286
Temple (Robert), London N 157
Tiffin (Tony and Gill), Durham 96
Till's Bookshop, Lothian 272
Tilston (Stephen E.), London SE 161
Tindley & Chapman, London WC 176
Tucker (Alan & Joan), Gloucestershire 116
Updike Rare Books (John), Lothian 272
Venables (Morris & Juliet), Bristol 59
War & Peace Books, Hampshire 123
Willmott Bookseller (Nicholas), Cardiff 276
Woburn Books, London N 157
Woodbine Books, West Yorkshire 241
Words Etcetera Bookshop, Dorset 92
Yesterday's News, Conwy 278

POLICE FORCE HISTORIES

Bolland Books (Leslie H.), Bedfordshire 53
Clifford Elmer Books Ltd., Cheshire 68
Crimes Ink, London E 153
Delph Books, Greater Manchester 120
Kenya Books, East Sussex 99
Lawful Occasions, Essex 108
Not JUST Books, Lincolnshire 148
Roscrea Bookshop, Co. Tipperary 261
Undercover Books, Lincolnshire 152

POLITICAL HISTORY

Apocalypse, Surrey 228
Cornucopia Books, Lincolnshire 151
G. C. Books Ltd., Dumfries & Galloway 264
Reading Lasses, Dumfries & Galloway 265
Savery Books, East Sussex 99

POLITICS

Apocalypse, Surrey 228
Barn Books, Buckinghamshire 61
Books, Denbighshire 278
Books Only, Suffolk 222
Bookshop (The), Greater Manchester 119
Booth Books, Powys 282
Bradley–Cox (Mary), Dorset 90
Brimstones, East Sussex 102
Brockwells Booksellers, Lincolnshire 148
Catalyst Booksearch Services, Devon 85
Chas J. Sawyer, Kent 140
Chesters (G. & J.), Staffordshire 220
Chichester Bookshop (The), West Sussex 237
Church Street Books, Norfolk 184
Cornucopia Books, Lincolnshire 151
Dolphin Books, Suffolk 221
Drury Rare Books (John), Essex 111
firstpagebooks, Norfolk 187
G. C. Books Ltd., Dumfries & Galloway 264
Garfi Books, Ceredigion 282
Hab Books, London W 171
Hurst (Jenny), Kent 138

Ice House Books, Wiltshire 248
Internet Bookshop UK Ltd., Gloucestershire.... 113
Jarndyce Antiquarian Booksellers, London WC 175
Joppa Books Ltd., Surrey 226
Judd Books, London WC 175
Keel Row Books, Tyne and Wear 231
Kelsall (George), Greater Manchester............ 119
Libra Books, Lincolnshire 148
Modern Welsh Publications Ltd., Merseyside .. 182
Moseley Books, West Midlands.................... 234
My Back Pages, London SW 167
Northern Herald Books, West Yorkshire 241
Not JUST Books, Lincolnshire...................... 148
O'Donoghue Books, Powys 284
Old Cathay Fine Books, West Yorkshire 244
Politico's.co.uk, Kent 141
Reading Lasses, Dumfries & Galloway 265
Reads, Dorset... 94
Red Star Books, Hertfordshire 130
Roland Books, Kent...................................... 139
Rosemary Pugh Books, Wiltshire 248
Samovar Books, Co. Dublin 258
Saunders (Tom), Caerphilly 276
Signature Books, Hampshire 126
Skoob Russell Square, Suffolk...................... 225
Sparrow Books, West Yorkshire 241
Spurrier (Nick), Kent.................................... 138
Till's Bookshop, Lothian 272
Tilston (Stephen E.), London SE 161
War & Peace Books, Hampshire 123
Webb Books (John), South Yorkshire 217
Winghale Books, Lincolnshire 151
Woburn Books, London N 157

POMOLOGY
Edmund Pollinger Rare Books, London SW ... 165

POP-UP, MOVABLE & CUT OUT
Ampersand Books, Shropshire 209
Bookmark (Children's Books), Wiltshire 248
Castleton (Pat), Kent..................................... 137
Cheshire Book Centre, Cheshire 69
Fifteenth Century Bookshop (The), East Sussex 102
Jean Hedger, Berkshire 55
Kernaghans, Merseyside 183
Roe and Moore, London WC....................... 176
Saint Swithin's Illustrated & Children's Books,
  London W... 172
Scrivener's Books & Bookbinding, Derbyshire . 81
Seabreeze Books, Lancashire 144
Temperley (David), West Midlands 234
The Old Children's Bookshelf, Lothian.......... 272

PORNOGRAPHY
Apocalypse, Surrey 228

POTTERY & GLASS
Apocalypse, Surrey 228
Cornucopia Books, Lincolnshire 151
Don Kelly Books, London W 170

Orchid Book Distributors, Co. Clare............. 257

POULTRY
Blest (Peter), Kent 139
Cheshire Book Centre, Cheshire 69
Countrymans Gallery (The), Leicestershire...... 145
Edmund Pollinger Rare Books, London SW ... 165
Hodgson (Books) (Richard J.),
  North Yorkshire.. 194
Thomas (Barry), Ceredigion 277

PRAYER BOOKS
Barbican Bookshop, North Yorkshire 194
Kyrios Books, Nottinghamshire.................... 200
Oasis Booksearch, Cambridgeshire 67
Paper Moon Books, Warwickshire 233
Pendleburys Bookshop, London N 156
Roscrea Bookshop, Co. Tipperary................. 261
Rosemary Pugh Books, Wiltshire 248
S.P.C.K., Bristol... 59

PRE-RAPHAELITES
Bookstack & D.J. Creece (Bookbinder),
  Shropshire 209

PRECIOUS METALS - SILVER
Art Reference Books, Hampshire 125
Don Kelly Books, London W 170
Trinders' Fine Tools, Suffolk 222

PRINTED TEXTILES
Don Kelly Books, London W 170
N1 Books, East Sussex................................. 103

PRINTING
- GENERAL
Andrew Stewart, Cornwall 74
Andron (G.W.), London N 155
Bettridge (Gordon), Fife 265
Bibliophile (The), South Yorkshire 217
Boxwood Books & Prints, Somerset 216
Brinded (Scott), Kent.................................... 139
Cobnar Books, Kent 139
Collinge & Clark, London WC 174
Coupland (Terry W.), Staffordshire 219
Cox Old & Rare Books (Claude), Suffolk....... 223
Finch Rare Books Ltd. (Simon), London W ... 170
Forest Books, Nottinghamshire 201
Goldman (Paul), Dorset 94
Grosvenor Prints, London WC..................... 175
Judd Books, London WC 175
Macfarlane (Mr. H.), Essex 112
Moore (C.R.), Shropshire 210
O'Connor Fine Books, Lancashire 144
Schulz–Falster Rare Books (Susanne),
  London N 157
Solitaire Books, Somerset............................. 212
Wakeman Books (Frances), Nottinghamshire .. 201

SPECIALITY INDEX

- NORTH OF ENGLAND PROVINCIAL
Barry McKay Rare Books, Cumbria............. 76

PRINTING AND MIND OF MAN
Hamish Riley-Smith, Norfolk 188

PRIVATE PRESS
Anthony Neville, Kent............................. 138
Artco, Nottinghamshire........................... 201
Askew Books (Vernon), Wiltshire 246
Barlow (Vincent G.), Hampshire.................. 126
Barnitt (Peter), Wiltshire........................... 248
Barry McKay Rare Books, Cumbria............. 76
Bertram Rota Ltd., London WC 174
Bettridge (Gordon), Fife........................... 265
Biblion, London W 169
Blackwell's Rare Books, Oxfordshire............ 205
Bookline, Co. Down................................ 256
Books & Things, London W...................... 169
Bookstand, Dorset................................. 93
Bow Windows Book Shop, East Sussex 102
Boxwood Books & Prints, Somerset 216
Brian Troath Books, London E................... 153
Broadhurst of Southport Ltd., Merseyside...... 182
Cameron House Books, Isle of Wight 134
Collinge & Clark, London WC 174
Coupland (Terry W.), Staffordshire 219
Cox Old & Rare Books (Claude), Suffolk....... 223
Dales & Lakes Book Centre, Cumbria 79
Dean Illustrated Books (Myra), Powys 281
Dylans Bookstore, Glamorgan 286
Eastcote Bookshop (The), London Outer 178
Ellis, Bookseller (Peter), London SE 162
Elstree Books, Hertfordshire 131
Emjay Books, Surrey.............................. 226
English (Toby), Oxfordshire 206
Firth (Bijou Books & Photography) (Maureen), South Yorkshire.............................. 218
Franks Booksellers, Greater Manchester 119
Good Books, Shropshire........................... 210
Hadley Bookseller (Peter J.), Essex 110
Hanborough Books, Oxfordshire 205
Heritage, West Midlands 234
Hodgkins and Company Limited (Ian), Gloucestershire 116
Hollett and Son (R.F.G.), Cumbria 79
Keeble Antiques, Somerset 215
Macfarlane (Mr. H.), Essex 112
Marks Limited (Barrie), London N 156
Martin's Books, Powys 285
Maynard & Bradley, Leicestershire............... 146
Mills Rare Books (Adam), Cambridgeshire..... 64
Poetry Bookshop (The), Powys................... 284
R.E. & G.B. Way, Suffolk 224
Rivendale Press, Buckinghamshire............... 61
Robin Doughty - Fine Books, West Midlands. 234
Roz Hulse, Conwy................................. 278
Sabin (Printed Works) (P.R. & V.), Kent 136
Sansovino Books, West Sussex 239
Solitaire Books, Somerset......................... 212
Sotheran Limited (Henry), London W........... 172

Taylor Rare Books (Michael), Norfolk 184
Temple (Robert), London N...................... 157
Updike Rare Books (John), Lothian 272
Waddington Books & Prints (Geraldine), Northamptonshire................................ 196
Wakeman Books (Frances), Nottinghamshire .. 201
Williams Rare Books (Nigel), London WC..... 177
Woodbine Books, West Yorkshire................ 241
Words Etcetera Bookshop, Dorset 92

PROOF COPIES
Firsts in Print, Isle of Wight 134
G. C. Books Ltd., Dumfries & Galloway 264
Kendall–Carpenter (Tim), Greater Manchester 119
Marble Hill Books, Middlesex.................... 181
McKelvie (Ian), London N 156
Scrivener's Books & Bookbinding, Derbyshire . 81
Temple (Robert), London N...................... 157
Williams Rare Books (Nigel), London WC..... 177

PSYCHIC
Alpha Books, London N 155
Cavern Books, Cheshire 70
Dawlish Books, Devon............................ 84
Facet Books, Dorset............................... 90
Fine Books Oriental Ltd., London WC 175
Gilbert (R.A.), Bristol............................. 59
Greensleeves, Oxfordshire 202
Hurst (Jenny), Kent 138
Inner Bookshop (The), Oxfordshire 205
Magis Books, Leicestershire...................... 147
Occultique, Northamptonshire.................... 196
SETI Books, Staffordshire........................ 220
Trafalgar Bookshop, East Sussex 99
Wizard Books, Cambridgeshire................... 67

PSYCHOANALYSIS
Alba Books, Grampian 267
Delectus Books, London WC..................... 174
Game Advice, Oxfordshire 205
Inner Bookshop (The), Oxfordshire 205
Magis Books, Leicestershire...................... 147
Oast Books, Kent.................................. 137
Outcast Books, Herefordshire 284
PsychoBabel Books & Journals, Oxfordshire... 202
Quentin Books Ltd, Essex......................... 109
Reading Lasses, Dumfries & Galloway 265
Rosemary Pugh Books, Wiltshire................. 248
Savery Books, East Sussex 99
Treasure Trove Books, Leicestershire 146

PSYCHOLOGY/PSYCHIATRY
Abbey Books, Cornwall 73
Alba Books, Grampian 267
Barcombe Services, Essex......................... 108
Bookshop (The), Dorset 92
Bracton Books, Cambridgeshire.................. 63
Brimstones, East Sussex 102
Cheshire Book Centre, Cheshire 69
Chesters (G. & J.), Staffordshire 220

SPECIALITY INDEX

Delectus Books, London WC 174
Elephant Books, West Yorkshire 244
Erian Books, London N 155
Fireside Bookshop, Cumbria 80
Game Advice, Oxfordshire 205
GfB: the Colchester Bookshop, Essex 109
Graduate Books, Worcestershire 252
Greensleeves, Oxfordshire 202
Hurst (Jenny), Kent 138
Jade Mountain, Hampshire 125
Judd Books, London WC 175
Mair Wilkes Books, Fife 265
Marathon Books, Greater Manchester 118
O'Donoghue Books, Powys 284
Oast Books, Kent 137
Occultique, Northamptonshire 196
Orchid Book Distributors, Co. Clare 257
Outcast Books, Herefordshire 284
Phelps (Michael), West Sussex 237
Pomes Penyeach, Staffordshire 219
PsychoBabel Books & Journals, Oxfordshire ... 202
Quentin Books Ltd, Essex 109
Reading Lasses, Dumfries & Galloway 265
Reid of Liverpool, Merseyside 182
Rosemary Pugh Books, Wiltshire 248
Savery Books, East Sussex 99
Scrivener's Books & Bookbinding, Derbyshire . 81
Skoob Russell Square, Suffolk 225
Spurrier (Nick), Kent 138
Transformer, Dumfries & Galloway 265
Treasure Trove Books, Leicestershire 146
Victoria Bookshop (The), Devon 83
Waxfactor, East Sussex 99
Westwood Books (Mark), Powys 284
Westwood Books Ltd, Cumbria 79
Wizard Books, Cambridgeshire 67
Worlds End Bookshop, London SW 168

PSYCHOTHERAPY

Alba Books, Grampian 267
Bradley–Cox (Mary), Dorset 90
Greensleeves, Oxfordshire 202
Inner Bookshop (The), Oxfordshire 205
Oast Books, Kent 137
Orchid Book Distributors, Co. Clare 257
Outcast Books, Herefordshire 284
PsychoBabel Books & Journals, Oxfordshire ... 202
Quentin Books Ltd, Essex 109
Reading Lasses, Dumfries & Galloway 265
Rosemary Pugh Books, Wiltshire 248
Savery Books, East Sussex 99
Treasure Trove Books, Leicestershire 146

PUBLIC ADMINISTRATION

Reading Lasses, Dumfries & Galloway 265

PUBLIC HEALTH

Reading Lasses, Dumfries & Galloway 265

PUBLIC HOUSES

Lucas (Richard), London NW 159
Thorne (John), Essex 109

PUBLIC SCHOOLS

Kirkpatrick (Robert J.), London W 171
Oopalba Books, Cheshire 71
Reading Lasses, Dumfries & Galloway 265
Rutland Bookshop (The), Rutland 208
Tiffin (Tony and Gill), Durham 96
Westwood Books Ltd, Cumbria 79
Wise (Derek), East Sussex 102

PUBLISHERS
- GENERAL

Adrem Books, Hertfordshire 131
Apocalypse, Surrey 228
Art Book Company, (The), Suffolk 223
Aurora Books Ltd, Lothian 270
Dinnages Transport Publishing, East Sussex.... 98
G. C. Books Ltd., Dumfries & Galloway 264
Libra Books, Lincolnshire 148
Poole (William), London W 172
Temple (Robert), London N 157
Zardoz Books, Wiltshire 249

- ARABIS BOOKS
Art Book Company, (The), Suffolk 223

- BATSFORD
Hennessey Bookseller (Ray), East Sussex 99
Island Books, Kent 136

- BLACK, A. & C.
Bolton Books, Hampshire 122
Bowden Books, Leicestershire 147
Chapter Two, London SE 161
Missing Books, Essex 109
Paul Hoare, Cornwall 74

- BLACKIE
Bookmark (Children's Books), Wiltshire 248
Jean Hedger, Berkshire 55
Studio (The), Strathclyde 274

- CHAMBERS
Not JUST Books, Lincolnshire 148

PUBLISHERS - COLLINS (CRIME CLUB, THE)
Lucius Books, North Yorkshire 195
Sutcliffe (Mark), West Yorkshire 243

- CUNDALL, JOSEPH
Jean Hedger, Berkshire 55

SPECIALITY INDEX

- DAVID & CHARLES
Ardis Books, Hampshire 126
Roadmaster Books, Kent 137

- FOULIS, T.N.
Bolton Books, Hampshire 122

- GHOST STORY PRESS
Fantastic Literature, Essex 111

- GUINNESS
Not JUST Books, Lincolnshire 148

- HACKER ART BOOKS
Art Book Company, (The), Suffolk 223

- HAYNES PUBLISHING
Colwyn Books, Conwy 277

- HOGARTH PRESS
Evans Books (Paul), West Sussex 238
Fifteenth Century Bookshop (The), East Sussex 102

- JOSEPH LTD., MICHAEL
Archivist (The), Devon 88

- LADYBIRD BOOKS
Armchair Books, Lothian 270
Chapter Two, London SE 161
Dormouse Bookshop (The), Norfolk 188
Fifteenth Century Bookshop (The), East Sussex 102
Kineton Nooks, Warwickshire 232
Rose's Books, Herefordshire 284
Shakeshaft (Dr. B.), Cheshire 71
Treasure Trove Books, Leicestershire 146

- OAKWOOD PRESS
Coulthurst (Richard), Greater Manchester 120

- OBSERVERS BOOKS
Stella Books, Monmouthshire 281

- OXFORD UNIVERSITY PRESS
BOOKS4U, Flintshire 279

- PAN
Castleton (Pat), Kent 137
Heckmondwike Book Shop, West Yorkshire ... 244

- PELICAN
Jade Mountain, Hampshire 125
Orb's Bookshop, Grampian 268
Willmott Bookseller (Nicholas), Cardiff 276

- PENGUIN
Arcadia, Oxfordshire 205
Bettridge (Gordon), Fife 265
Black Cat Bookshop, Leicestershire 145
Books at the Warehouse, North Yorkshire 191
Carningli Centre, Pembrokeshire 281
Grahame Thornton, Bookseller, Dorset 92
Heckmondwike Book Shop, West Yorkshire ... 244
J. & J. Books, Lincolnshire 149
Orb's Bookshop, Grampian 268
Price (R.W.), Nottinghamshire 200
Richmond Books, North Yorkshire 192
Skelton (Tony), Kent 141
The Sanctuary Bookshop, Dorset 93
Willmott Bookseller (Nicholas), Cardiff 276

- POYSERS
Birdnet Optics Ltd., Derbyshire 81

- PUFFIN
Castleton (Pat), Kent 137
Heckmondwike Book Shop,
   West Yorkshire 244
Jean Hedger, Berkshire 55
Treasure Trove Books, Leicestershire 146
Willmott Bookseller (Nicholas), Cardiff 276

- ROUNDWOOD PRESS
Meekins Books (Paul), Warwickshire 233

- STUDIO, THE
Books & Things, London W 169

- THAMES & HUDSON
Ardis Books, Hampshire 126

- WARNES
Everett (Richard), Norfolk 184
Everett (Richard, at the Southwold Antiques
   Centre, Suffolk 225
Hine (Anne), Somerset 214

- WISDENS
Saint Mary's Books & Prints, Lincolnshire 152

PUBLISHING
Bettridge (Gordon), Fife 265
Coupland (Terry W.), Staffordshire 219
Ford (Richard), London W 170
Kabristan Archives, Shropshire 211
Roadmaster Books, Kent 137
Smith Books, (Sally), Suffolk 222
Wakeman Books (Frances), Nottinghamshire .. 201

PULPS
Askew Books (Vernon), Wiltshire 246
Book Palace (The), London SE 161

SPECIALITY INDEX

Bristol Books, Bristol.................................. 60
Cowley, Bookdealer (K.W.), Somerset........... 214
Delectus Books, London WC...................... 174

PUNK FANZINES

Marchpane, London WC........................... 175

PUPPETS & MARIONETTES

DaSilva Puppet Books, Dorset..................... 92
Fitzsimons (Anne), Cumbria....................... 77
Saint Swithin's Illustrated & Children's Books,
  London W.. 172
Westwood Books Ltd, Cumbria 79

PUZZLES

Ænigma Designs (Books), Devon................. 85
Adrem Books, Hertfordshire...................... 131
Saint Swithin's Illustrated & Children's Books,
  London W.. 172

QUAKERS, THE

Hollett and Son (R.F.G.), Cumbria 79
Rosemary Pugh Books, Wiltshire................ 248

RADICAL ISSUES

Forder (R.W.), Hampshire 122
G. C. Books Ltd., Dumfries & Galloway 264
Kenny's Bookshops and Art Galleries Ltd,
  Co. Galway 260
Left on The Shelf, Cumbria........................ 78
Reading Lasses, Dumfries & Galloway.......... 265
Red Star Books, Hertfordshire 130
Spurrier (Nick), Kent............................... 138
Tobo Books, Hampshire........................... 124

RADIO/WIRELESS

Cover to Cover, Merseyside........................ 183
Dormouse Bookshop (The), Norfolk............. 188
Greenroom Books, West Yorkshire 243
Kelly Books, Devon 88
Not JUST Books, Lincolnshire.................... 148
Orb's Bookshop, Grampian........................ 268
Roland Books, Kent................................ 139
Transformer, Dumfries & Galloway............. 265
Whistler's Books, London SW 167

RAILWAYS

Abacus Gallery, Staffordshire..................... 220
Adrem Books, Hertfordshire...................... 131
Anvil Books, West Midlands 235
Apocalypse, Surrey 228
Arden Books & Cosmographia,
  Warwickshire................................... 232
Axe Rare & Out of Print Books (Richard),
  North Yorkshire................................ 190
Baker (Gerald), Bristol............................. 59
Baldwin (M. & M.), Shropshire................... 250
Barbican Bookshop, North Yorkshire 194

Bird Books (Nigel), Ceredigion.................... 277
Black Five Books, Shropshire 211
Book House (The), Cumbria 78
Books & Collectables Ltd.,
  Cambridgeshire................................. 63
Books Afloat, Dorset................................ 94
Books Bought & Sold, Surrey 226
Books Plus, Devon 83
Bott, (Bookdealers) Ltd., (Martin),
  Greater Manchester............................ 118
Brewin Books Ltd., Warwickshire 233
Browning Books, Torfaen 287
Carngili Centre, Pembrokeshire................... 281
Cavern Books, Cheshire 70
Cheshire Book Centre, Cheshire 69
Chevin Books, West Yorkshire.................... 245
Clarke Books (David), Somerset 214
Classic Crime Collections,
  Greater Manchester............................ 119
Cobbles Books, Somerset.......................... 214
Cobweb Books, North Yorkshire................. 192
Cofion Books, Pembrokeshire 281
Collectables (W.H.), Suffolk 225
Collectors Corner, Wiltshire....................... 248
Corfe Books, Surrey 227
Coulthurst (Richard),
  Greater Manchester............................ 120
Cox (Geoff), Devon 89
Crosby Nethercott Books,
  London Outer 178
Dales and Lakes Book Centre, Cumbria 79
Dinnages Transport Publishing,
  East Sussex..................................... 98
Duck (William), Hampshire....................... 124
Eastcote Bookshop (The), London Outer 178
Elton Engineering Books, London W........... 170
Esoteric Dreams Bookshop, Cumbria........... 77
Ewell Bookshop, Surrey 227
Falconwood Transport & Military
  Bookshop, London Outer 181
Garfi Books, Ceredigion 282
Good Books, Shropshire.......................... 210
Harlequin Books, Bristol........................... 59
Hay Castle, Powys 283
Hook (Arthur), Bristol............................. 59
Humm & Co. (Robert), Lincolnshire 151
Internet Bookshop UK Ltd.,
  Gloucestershire 113
Island Books, Kent................................. 136
J C Books, Devon.................................. 86
Jade Mountain, Hampshire....................... 125
Jones (Barry), West Sussex....................... 238
Junk & Spread Eagle, London SE................ 162
Keegan's Bookshop, Berkshire 56
Keel Row Books, Tyne and Wear................ 231
Kerr (Norman), Cumbria.......................... 77
Kirkland Books, Cumbria......................... 78
Milestone Books, Devon.......................... 8
Moreton Books, Devon........................... 86
My Back Pages, London SW..................... 167
Nevis Railway Books, Oxfordshire 204

SPECIALITY INDEX

Nevis Railway Bookshops (The Antique &
   Book Collector), Wiltshire 247
Newband (D.M.), Powys 286
Old Celtic Bookshop (The), Devon 86
Over-Sands Books, Cumbria 77
Park Gallery & Bookshop (The),
   Northamptonshire 197
Parlour Bookshop (The), Oxfordshire 203
Patterson (J.D.), Bristol 60
Peter White, Hampshire 122
Postings, Surrey 228
Priory Books, Worcestershire 252
Railway Book and Magazine Search, Berkshire . 56
Railway Shop (The), Torfaen 287
recollectionsbookshop.co.uk, Cornwall 74
Roadmaster Books, Kent 137
Rochdale Book Company, Greater Manchester 120
Roland Books, Kent 139
Rolling Stock Books, Greater Manchester 121
Saint Swithin's Illustrated & Children's
   Books, London W 172
Salway Books, Essex 112
Scrivener's Books & Bookbinding, Derbyshire .. 81
Sedgeberrow Books & Framing, Worcestershire 251
Simon Lewis Transport Books, Gloucestershire . 115
Skyrack Books, West Yorkshire 243
Soccor Books Limited, Lincolnshire 149
Stella Books, Monmouthshire 281
Suffolk Rare Books, Suffolk 225
Tony Pollastrone Railway Books, Wiltshire 246
Tozer Railway Books (Nick), West Yorkshire . 243
Treasure Island (The), Greater Manchester 120
Trinders' Fine Tools, Suffolk 222
Vailima Books, Dumfries & Galloway 264
Yesteryear Railwayana, Kent 139
Yewtree Books, Cumbria 77

REFERENCE

Adrem Books, Hertfordshire 131
Art Reference Books, Hampshire 125
Axe Rare & Out of Print Books (Richard),
   North Yorkshire 190
Bannister (David), Gloucestershire 113
Books, Denbighshire 278
Books for Writers, Monmouthshire 280
Corder (Mark W.), Kent 140
Downie Fine Books Ltd., (Robert),
   Shropshire 211
Emjay Books, Surrey 226
G. C. Books Ltd., Dumfries & Galloway 264
Hurst (Jenny), Kent 138
Naughton Booksellers, Co. Dublin 259
Potter Limited (Jonathan), London W 172
R. & A. Books, East Sussex 100
Shacklock Books (David), Suffolk 222
Worlds End Bookshop, London SW 168

REGISTERS

Delph Books, Greater Manchester 120

RELIGION
- GENERAL

Adrem Books, Hertfordshire 131
Armchair Books, Lothian 270
Aurora Books Ltd, Lothian 270
Axe Rare & Out of Print Books (Richard),
   North Yorkshire 190
Bardsley's Books, Suffolk 221
Beware of the Leopard, Bristol 58
Blythswood Bookshop, Highland 269
Books, Denbighshire 278
Books (For All), North Yorkshire 190
Bookshop at the Plain, Lincolnshire 151
Bowie Books & Collectables, East Yorkshire ... 106
Brimstones, East Sussex 102
Broadwater Books, Hampshire 126
Butler Books, Dorset 90
Camilla's Bookshop, East Sussex 100
Canon Gate Books, West Sussex 239
Carngili Centre, Pembrokeshire 281
Carta Regis, Powys 286
Cheshire Book Centre, Cheshire 69
Clegg (David), Staffordshire 219
Cofion Books, Pembrokeshire 281
Collectable Books, London SE 162
D'Arcy Books, Wiltshire 246
Ely Books, Cambridgeshire 65
G. C. Books Ltd., Dumfries & Galloway 264
Gage Postal Books, Essex 111
Garfi Books, Ceredigion 282
Geneva Books, London SW 165
Gilbert (R.A.), Bristol 59
Golden Age Books, Worcestershire 251
Good for Books, Lincolnshire 149
Handsworth Books, Essex 112
Hay Cinema Bookshop Ltd., Herefordshire 283
Herb Tandree Philosophy Books,
   Gloucestershire 116
Jade Mountain, Hampshire 125
Kenny's Bookshops and Art Galleries Ltd,
   Co. Galway 260
Kyrios Books, Nottinghamshire 200
Lewis (J.T. & P.), Cornwall 73
Little Bookshop (The), Greater Manchester 119
medievalbookshop, London Outer 179
Moss Books, London NW 159
Murphy (C.J.), Norfolk 187
Naughton Booksellers, Co. Dublin 259
Needham Books, (Russell), Somerset 216
Not JUST Books, Lincolnshire 148
Oxfam Books and Music, Hampshire 127
Parkinsons Books, Merseyside 183
Parrott Books, Oxfordshire 207
Paton Books, Hertfordshire 132
Pendleburys Bookshop, London N 156
Portobello Books, London W 172
Priestpopple Books, Northumberland 198
Prospect House Books, Co. Down 256
PsychoBabel Books & Journals, Oxfordshire ... 202
Quinto of Great Russell Street, London WC ... 176
Reading Lasses, Dumfries & Galloway 265

Reid of Liverpool, Merseyside 182
Robin Doughty - Fine Books, West Midlands . 234
Roland Books, Kent 139
Roscrea Bookshop, Co. Tipperary 261
Rosemary Pugh Books, Wiltshire 248
Rye Old Books, East Sussex 103
Saint Philip's Books, Oxfordshire 205
Salsus Books, Worcestershire 250
Saunders (Tom), Caerphilly 276
Scott (Peter), East Sussex 103
Scrivener's Books & Bookbinding, Derbyshire . 81
Signature Books, Hampshire 126
Skoob Russell Square, Suffolk 225
Starlord Books, Greater Manchester 118
Stroma Books, Borders 262
The Sanctuary Bookshop, Dorset 93
Tobo Books, Hampshire 124
Treasure Trove Books, Leicestershire 146
Trinity Rare Books, Co. Leitrim 260
Walker Fine Books (Steve), Dorset 91
Wayside Books and Cards, Oxfordshire 203
Westwood Books Ltd, Cumbria 79
Wiend Books, Lancashire 143
Wizard Books, Cambridgeshire 67

- BUDDHISM

Inner Bookshop (The), Oxfordshire 205
Occultique, Northamptonshire 196
Parrott (Jeremy), London E 153
Waxfactor, East Sussex 99

- CATHOLIC

Bell (Peter), Strathclyde 270
Britons Catholic Library, Co. Wexford 261
Carraig Books Ltd., Co. Dublin 258
Killeen (John), North Yorkshire 191
Naughton Booksellers, Co. Dublin 259
Oasis Booksearch, Cambridgeshire 67
Prospect House Books, Co. Down 256
Roscrea Bookshop, Co. Tipperary 261
Saint Philip's Books, Oxfordshire 205
Samovar Books, Co. Dublin 258
Sims (Sue), Dorset 90

- CHRISTIAN

Barbican Bookshop, North Yorkshire 194
Bell (Peter), Strathclyde 270
Bevan (John), Wiltshire 247
Blythswood Bookshop, Highland 269
Bookshop (The), Co. Donegal 258
Bookworm Alley, Devon 87
Butler Books, Dorset 90
Canon Gate Books, West Sussex 239
Carnforth Bookshop (The), Lancashire 142
Chapter Two, London SE 161
Chthonios Books, East Sussex 101
Classic Bindings Ltd, London SW 164
Crouch Rare Books, Surrey 227
Facet Books, Dorset 90
Golden Age Books, Worcestershire 251

Greensleeves, Oxfordshire 202
Holmes Books (Harry), East Yorkshire 106
Humber Books, Lincolnshire 148
Inner Bookshop (The), Oxfordshire 205
Kernaghans, Merseyside 183
Kyrios Books, Nottinghamshire 200
Libra Books, Lincolnshire 148
Naughton Booksellers, Co. Dublin 259
Oasis Booksearch, Cambridgeshire 67
Orb's Bookshop, Grampian 268
Parkinsons Books, Merseyside 183
Pendleburys Bookshop, London N 156
Roscrea Bookshop, Co. Tipperary 261
Rose Books, Greater Manchester 120
Rosemary Books, Merseyside 183
S.P.C.K., Hampshire 127
S.P.C.K., Bristol 59
Saint Philip's Books, Oxfordshire 205
Salsus Books, Worcestershire 250
Samovar Books, Co. Dublin 258
Stalagluft Books, Tyne and Wear 231
Thornber (Peter M.), North Yorkshire 193
Tuft (Patrick), London W 173

- HEBRAICA

Fishburn Books, London NW 158
Samovar Books, Co. Dublin 258

- ISLAM

Al Saqi Books, London W 169
Books on Spain, London Outer 181
Delectus Books, London WC 174
Folios Limited, London SW 165
Inner Bookshop (The), Oxfordshire 205
Joppa Books Ltd., Surrey 226
Occultique, Northamptonshire 196
Pendleburys Bookshop, London N 156
Quaritch Ltd., (Bernard), London W 172

- JEWISH

Books on Spain, London Outer 181
Butler Books, Dorset 90
Crouch Rare Books, Surrey 227
Delectus Books, London WC 174
Fishburn Books, London NW 158
Golden Age Books, Worcestershire 251
Inner Bookshop (The), Oxfordshire 205
Occultique, Northamptonshire 196
Pendleburys Bookshop, London N 156
Samovar Books, Co. Dublin 258
Trotter Books (John), London N 157

- METHODISM

Barbican Bookshop, North Yorkshire 194
Humber Books, Lincolnshire 148
MK Book Services, Cambridgeshire 66
Oasis Booksearch, Cambridgeshire 67
Samovar Books, Co. Dublin 258

SPECIALITY INDEX

- MUSLIM
Salsus Books, Worcestershire 250

- NON CONFORMITY
Humber Books, Lincolnshire 148
Samovar Books, Co. Dublin....................... 258

- ORIENTAL
Fine Books Oriental Ltd., London WC 175
Greensleeves, Oxfordshire 202
Inner Bookshop (The), Oxfordshire 205
Occultique, Northamptonshire..................... 196

- PRE-VATICAN II CATHOLICISM
Samovar Books, Co. Dublin....................... 258

- PRESBYTERIAN
Bell (Peter), Strathclyde 270
Prospect House Books, Co. Down 256
Samovar Books, Co. Dublin....................... 258

- PROTESTANTISM
Humber Books, Lincolnshire 148
Prospect House Books, Co. Down 256
Samovar Books, Co. Dublin....................... 258

- PURITANISM
Humber Books, Lincolnshire 148
Samovar Books, Co. Dublin....................... 258

- QUAKERS
Barbican Bookshop, North Yorkshire 194
Prospect House Books, Co. Down 256
Robin Doughty - Fine Books,
   West Midlands..................................... 234
Samovar Books, Co. Dublin....................... 258

- SALVATION ARMY
Bookworm Alley, Devon 87
Prospect House Books, Co. Down 256
Samovar Books, Co. Dublin....................... 258

- TAOISM
Occultique, Northamptonshire..................... 196

RELIGIOUS TEXTS
Apocalypse, Surrey 228
Brimstones, East Sussex............................ 102
Magis Books, Leicestershire........................ 147
Rosemary Pugh Books, Wiltshire................. 248
Samovar Books, Co. Dublin....................... 258

RIVER THAMES
Apocalypse, Surrey 228
Tooley, Adams & Co, Oxfordshire 206
Way Booksellers (Richard), Oxfordshire 204

ROCK ART
Book Palace (The), London SE 161

ROMANCE
Apocalypse, Surrey 228

ROSICRUCIANISM
Gildas Books, Cheshire 68
Magis Books, Leicestershire........................ 147

ROYALTY
- GENERAL
Barn Books, Buckinghamshire..................... 61
Books & Collectables Ltd.,
   Cambridgeshire 63
Dworski Books, Travel & Language Bookshop
   (Marijana), Herefordshire 283
Farahar & Dupre (Clive & Sophie),
   Wiltshire 246
Hay Cinema Bookshop Ltd.,
   Herefordshire 283
Heraldry Today, Wiltshire.......................... 247
Heritage, West Midlands 234
Hunt (Robin S.), Greater Manchester 120
Libra Books, Lincolnshire.......................... 148
Piccadilly Rare Books, East Sussex............... 104
Saint Swithin's Illustrated & Children's Books,
   London W... 172
Ventnor Rare Books, Isle of Wight 135
Yesterday's News, Conwy.......................... 278

- EUROPEAN
Dworski Books, Travel & Language Bookshop
   (Marijana), Herefordshire 283
Orb's Bookshop, Grampian........................ 268
Piccadilly Rare Books, East Sussex............... 104

RUBAIYAT OF OMAR KHAYYAM
N1 Books, East Sussex.............................. 103

RUGS
Apocalypse, Surrey 228
Byrom Textile Bookroom (Richard),
   Lancashire... 142
Cover to Cover, Merseyside....................... 183
Don Kelly Books, London W 170
Reading Lasses, Dumfries & Galloway 265
Sleepy Elephant Books & Artefacts,
   Cumbria.. 79
Smith Books (Keith), Herefordshire.............. 128
Trinders' Fine Tools, Suffolk 222
Whittle, Bookseller (Avril), Cumbria 79

RURAL LIFE
2 Ravens, Cumbria 78
Acer Books, Herefordshire......................... 128
Arden Books & Cosmographia,
   Warwickshire....................................... 232

SPECIALITY INDEX

Arnold (Roy), Suffolk 223
Barn Books, Shropshire 211
Blest (Peter), Kent 139
Books for Content, Herefordshire 128
Books on the Bank, Durham 96
Campbell Hewson Books (R.), Fife 265
Carningli Centre, Pembrokeshire 281
Chantrey Books, South Yorkshire 217
Church Green Books, Oxfordshire 207
Clarke Books (David), Somerset 214
Cobbles Books, Somerset 214
Coch-y-Bonddu Books, Powys 285
Cottage Books, Leicestershire 145
Country Books, Derbyshire 81
Cover to Cover, Merseyside 183
Dolphin Books, Suffolk 221
Doorbar (P. & D.), Gwynned 279
Dusty Books, Powys 285
Fireside Books, Buckinghamshire 62
Fireside Bookshop, Cumbria 80
Furneaux Books (Lee), Devon 88
Grove Bookshop (The), North Yorkshire .. 193
Harvest Books, Lancashire 144
J & J Burgess Booksellers, Cambridgeshire .. 64
Keeble Antiques, Somerset 215
Kilgour (Sporting Books) (Ian), Leicestershire . 147
King Street Bookshop (The), Norfolk 185
Libra Books, Lincolnshire 148
Meekins Books (Paul), Warwickshire 233
Missing Books, Essex 109
Moss End Bookshop, Berkshire 57
Mount's Bay Books, Cornwall 74
Murphy (C.J.), Norfolk 187
Orb's Bookshop, Grampian 268
Park (Mike), London Outer 180
Periwinkle Press, Kent 139
Petworth Antique Market (Bookroom),
 West Sussex 239
Roadmaster Books, Kent 137
Rods Books, Devon 87
Rutland Bookshop (The), Rutland 208
Singleton (Anthony), South Yorkshire 217
Wildside Books, Worcestershire 250
Woodbine Books, West Yorkshire 241

SALVATION ARMY

Earth Science Books, Wiltshire 247
Hollett and Son (R.F.G.), Cumbria 79
Lawful Occasions, Essex 108
Roscrea Bookshop, Co. Tipperary 261

SATIRE

Adrem Books, Hertfordshire 131
Yesterday's News, Conwy 278

SCHOOL REGISTERS/
ROLLS OF HONOUR

Camilla's Bookshop, East Sussex 100
Coach House Books, Worcestershire 251
Delph Books, Greater Manchester 120

Heraldry Today, Wiltshire 247
Palladour Books, Hampshire 126
Tiffin (Tony and Gill), Durham 96
Townsend (John), Berkshire 57
Turton (John), Durham 97
Wise (Derek), East Sussex 102
World War Books, Kent 141

SCIENCE
- GENERAL

Ænigma Designs (Books), Devon 85
Alba Books, Grampian 267
Aurora Books Ltd, Lothian 270
Baldwin's Scientific Books, Essex 112
Barcombe Services, Essex 108
Baron (Christopher), Greater Manchester 118
Baron - Scientific Book Sales (P.J.), Somerset .. 213
Beware of the Leopard, Bristol 58
Book Annex (The), Essex 110
Bookcase, Cumbria 76
Books & Collectables Ltd., Cambridgeshire 63
Bookshop (The), Co. Donegal 258
Booth Books, Powys 282
Camden Books, Somerset 212
Carningli Centre, Pembrokeshire 281
Carta Regis, Powys 286
Cheshire Book Centre, Cheshire 69
Eagle Bookshop (The), Bedfordshire 53
Finch Rare Books Ltd. (Simon), London W ... 170
Gaskell Rare Books (Roger), Cambridgeshire .. 66
GfB: the Colchester Bookshop, Essex 109
Hay Cinema Bookshop Ltd., Herefordshire 283
Hinchliffe Books, Bristol 59
Hollett and Son (R.F.G.), Cumbria 79
Hünersdorff Rare Books, London SW 166
Hunter–Rare Books (Andrew), London SW.... 166
Hurst (Jenny), Kent 138
Ice House Books, Wiltshire 248
J C Books, Devon 86
Jay Books, Lothian 271
Lawson & Company (E.M.), Oxfordshire 203
Lenton (Alfred), Leicestershire 145
Lewis (J.T. & P.), Cornwall 73
Libra Books, Lincolnshire 148
Little Stour Books, Kent 136
Lymelight Books & Prints, Dorset 92
Macfarlane (Mr. H.), Essex 112
McGee (Terence J.), London Outer 178
Mollie's Loft, Swansea 287
Moorside Books, Lancashire 143
Orangeberry Books, Oxfordshire 204
Parkinsons Books, Merseyside 183
Phillips (Nigel), London SW 167
Pickering & Chatto, London W 172
Plurabelle Books, Cambridgeshire 64
Pollak (P.M.), Devon 87
Pomes Penyeach, Staffordshire 219
Prospect House Books, Co. Down 256
PsychoBabel Books & Journals, Oxfordshire ... 202
Quaritch Ltd., (Bernard), London W 172
Quinto of Charing Cross Road, London WC.. 176

SPECIALITY INDEX

Quinto of Great Russell Street, London WC... 176
R M Books, Hertfordshire 132
Roberts Books, Strathclyde 274
Rogers Turner Books, London SE 162
Scrivener's Books & Bookbinding, Derbyshire . 81
Signature Books, Hampshire....................... 126
Skoob Russell Square, Suffolk.................... 225
Smith (David & Lynn), London Outer 179
Stern Antiquarian Bookseller (Jeffrey),
  North Yorkshire.................................... 195
Stroh (M.A.), London E............................. 153
The Sanctuary Bookshop, Dorset................. 93
Transformer, Dumfries & Galloway.............. 265
Turret House, Norfolk 189
Wayside Books and Cards, Oxfordshire 203
Weiner (Graham), London N 157
Westons, Hertfordshire.............................. 133
Westwood Books Ltd, Cumbria 79
Whistler's Books, London SW 167
Worcester Rare Books, Worcestershire 252

- FORENSIC
Cheshire Book Centre, Cheshire 69
ForensicSearch, Hertfordshire 132
Lawful Occasions, Essex 108

- HISTORY OF
Axe Rare & Out of Print Books (Richard),
  North Yorkshire.................................... 190
Baldwin's Scientific Books, Essex 112
Baron (Christopher), Greater Manchester....... 118
Camden Books, Somerset 212
Cheshire Book Centre, Cheshire 69
Chesters (G. & J.), Staffordshire 220
Clevedon Books, Somerset 214
Dean Byass, Bristol 60
Earth Science Books, Wiltshire.................... 247
Erian Books, London N............................ 155
Esplin (David), Hampshire 124
Fireside Bookshop, Cumbria 80
Hamish Riley-Smith, Norfolk 188
Jay Books, Lothian.................................. 271
Judd Books, London WC 175
Kingswood Books, Dorset 93
Mair Wilkes Books, Fife........................... 265
McGee (Terence J.), London Outer 178
Moorside Books, Lancashire....................... 143
N1 Books, East Sussex.............................. 103
Orb's Bookshop, Grampian........................ 268
Phelps (Michael), West Sussex 237
Phillips (Nigel), London SW 167
Plurabelle Books, Cambridgeshire 64
Pollak (P.M.), Devon................................ 87
Pordes Books Ltd., (Henry), London WC 176
R M Books, Hertfordshire 132
Roberts Books, Strathclyde 274
Roger Collicott Books, Cornwall 74
Rogers Turner Books, London SE 162
Rowan (P. & B.), Co. Antrim 255
Skoob Russell Square, Suffolk.................... 225
Smith (David & Lynn), London Outer 179

Sokol Books Ltd., London W..................... 172
Sue Lowell Natural History Books, London W 173
Turret House, Norfolk 189
Wayside Books and Cards, Oxfordshire 203
Weiner (Graham), London N 157
Westwood Books (Mark), Powys 284
Westwood Books Ltd, Cumbria 79
Worcester Rare Books, Worcestershire 252
Wyseby House Books, Berkshire................. 55

- PURE & APPLIED
Baldwin's Scientific Books, Essex 112
Book Annex (The), Essex 110
Parkinsons Books, Merseyside.................... 183
The Sanctuary Bookshop, Dorset................. 93

SCIENTIFIC INSTRUMENTS
Arnold (Roy), Suffolk............................... 223
Baron (Christopher), Greater Manchester....... 118
Formby Antiques (Jeffrey), Gloucestershire..... 115
Hadfield (G.K.), Cumbria 78
Phelps (Michael), West Sussex 237
Pollak (P.M.), Devon................................ 87
Rogers Turner Books, London SE 162
Smith (David & Lynn), London Outer 179
Trinders' Fine Tools, Suffolk 222
Turret House, Norfolk 189

SCIENTISTS
Baldwin's Scientific Books, Essex 112
K.S.C. Books, Cheshire............................ 68

SCOTTISH ENLIGHTENMENT
Grampian Books, Grampian....................... 268
Hamish Riley-Smith, Norfolk 188
Leakey's Bookshop, Highland..................... 268
Loch Croispol Bookshop & Restaurant,
  Highland... 268
Orb's Bookshop, Grampian........................ 268

SCOTTISH INTEREST
Adrem Books, Hertfordshire....................... 131
Alba Books, Grampian 267
Anwoth Books, Dumfries & Galloway 264
Armchair Books, Lothian 270
Atholl Browse, Tayside 275
Atholl Fine Books, Tayside 275
Aurora Books Ltd, Lothian........................ 270
Axe Rare & Out of Print Books (Richard),
  North Yorkshire.................................... 190
Bell (Peter), Strathclyde 270
Benny Gillies Books Ltd, Dumfries &
  Galloway.. 263
Blacket Books, Lothian............................. 270
Bookworm, Lothian................................. 270
Bookworm (The), Lothian......................... 271
Byre Books, Dumfries & Galloway.............. 264
Caledonia Books, Strathclyde..................... 273
Cheshire Book Centre, Cheshire 69
Chesters (G. & J.), Staffordshire 220

Coleman (Tom), Highland 268
Colonsay Bookshop, Isle of Colonsay 269
Cooper Hay Rare Books, Strathclyde............ 273
Cornucopia Books, Lincolnshire 151
Cottage Books, Leicestershire..................... 145
Craobh Rua Books, Co. Armagh................. 255
Duncan & Reid, Lothian........................... 271
Farquharson, (Hilary), Tayside.................... 275
Freader's Books, Tayside 275
G. C. Books Ltd., Dumfries & Galloway 264
Grampian Books, Grampian 268
Grayling (David A.H.), Cumbria 78
Greta Books, Durham 96
Hunter–Rare Books (Andrew), London SW.... 166
Jane Jones Books, Grampian 267
Kings Bookshop Callander, Central.............. 263
Leakey's Bookshop, Highland 268
Loch Croispol Bookshop & Restaurant,
  Highland... 268
Mactaggart (Caroline), Dorset..................... 91
Main Point Books, Lothian........................ 271
Mair Wilkes Books, Fife............................ 265
McCrone (Audrey), Isle of Arran................. 269
McNaughtan's Bookshop, Lothian 271
Ming Books, Dumfries & Galloway.............. 265
Old Bookshelf (The), Strathclyde 273
Old Town Bookshop (The), Lothian 271
Oopalba Books, Cheshire........................... 71
Orb's Bookshop, Grampian........................ 268
Pinnacle Books, Lothian............................ 271
Poetry Bookshop (The), Powys.................... 284
Price (John), London N 157
Pringle Booksellers (Andrew), Lothian........... 271
Reading Lasses, Dumfries & Galloway 265
RGS Books, Surrey.................................. 229
Rising Tide Books, Fife............................. 265
Roberts Books, Strathclyde 274
Second Edition, Lothian............................ 272
Stroma Books, Borders 262
Temple (Robert), London N....................... 157
Thistle Books, Strathclyde.......................... 274
Updike Rare Books (John), Lothian 272
Winram's Bookshop, Grampian 266

SCOUTS & GUIDES
Adrem Books, Hertfordshire....................... 131
Askew Books (Vernon), Wiltshire 246
Books & Bygones (Pam Taylor),
  West Midlands...................................... 236
Collectables (W.H.), Suffolk 225
Fifteenth Century Bookshop (The), East Sussex 102
John R. Hoggarth, North Yorkshire.............. 194
The Old Children's Bookshelf, Lothian.......... 272
Yesterday's News, Conwy 278

SCRIMSHAW
Don Kelly Books, London W 170

SCULPTURE
Birchden Books, London E 153

Don Kelly Books, London W 170
Heneage Art Books (Thomas), London SW.... 166
Holdsworth Books (Bruce), East Sussex......... 103
Jones (Madalyn S.), West Yorkshire 242
Lighthouse Books (The), Dorset 91
Martin - Bookseller (Colin), East Yorkshire.... 106
Trinders' Fine Tools, Suffolk 222

SEAFARING & SHIPPING
Carningli Centre, Pembrokeshire.................. 281
Loch Croispol Bookshop & Restaurant,
  Highland... 268
Milestone Books, Devon............................ 88

SEAMANSHIP
Argent (Alan), Isle of Wight 135
Cornucopia Books, Lincolnshire 151

SECRET SOCIETIES
Apocalypse, Surrey 228
Gildas Books, Cheshire 68

SELF-HELP
Reading Lasses, Dumfries & Galloway 265

SELF-IMPROVEMENT
Esoteric Dreams Bookshop, Cumbria............ 77
Reading Lasses, Dumfries & Galloway 265

SELF-SUFFICIENCY
Coch-y-Bonddu Books, Powys 285
Cornucopia Books, Lincolnshire 151
Greta Books, Durham 96
Mount's Bay Books, Cornwall 74
Reading Lasses, Dumfries & Galloway 265
Savery Books, East Sussex 99

SETS OF BOOKS
Apocalypse, Surrey 228
Baxter (Steve), Surrey 228
Bernstein (Nicholas), London W.................. 169
Browse Books, Lancashire 143
Cheshire Book Centre, Cheshire 69
Crouch Rare Books, Surrey........................ 227
Ely Books, Cambridgeshire 65
Eton Antique Bookshop, Berkshire............... 57
Fisher & Sperr, London N 155
Fosters Bookshop, London W 170
Frew Limited (Robert), London W 170
Grove Bookshop (The), North Yorkshire....... 193
Harrington (Adrian), London W 171
Harrington Antiquarian Bookseller (Peter),
  London SW 166
Hava Books, London SE........................... 161
Kirkman Ltd., (Robert), Bedfordshire 53
Old Town Bookshop (The), Lothian 271
Poetry Bookshop (The), Powys.................... 284
Sotheran Limited (Henry), London W........... 172

SPECIALITY INDEX

Treasure Trove Books, Leicestershire 146

SETTE OF ODD VOLUMES
N1 Books, East Sussex............................. 103

SEXOLOGY
Apocalypse, Surrey 228
Delectus Books, London WC...................... 174
Paper Pleasures, Somerset 215
Reading Lasses, Dumfries & Galloway.......... 265

SHEEP/SHEPHERDING
Byrom Textile Bookroom (Richard),
   Lancashire 142
Greta Books, Durham 96
Hodgson (Books) (Richard J.),
   North Yorkshire................................... 194

SHERLOCKIANA
Askew Books (Vernon), Wiltshire 246
Black Cat Bookshop, Leicestershire 145
Ming Books, Dumfries & Galloway.............. 265
Murder & Mayhem, Powys 284
Preston Book Company, Lancashire 144
Rupert Books, Cambridgeshire.................... 64
Scrivener's Books & Bookbinding, Derbyshire . 81
Vokes (Jeremiah), Durham......................... 96
Williams Rare Books (Nigel),
   London WC.. 177
Yesterday's News, Conwy.......................... 278

SHIP MODELLING
Aviabooks, Gloucestershire 114
Curtle Mead Books, Isle of Wight................ 134
Lee, Maritime Books (Gerald), East Sussex 104
McLaren Books, Strathclyde....................... 274
Milestone Books, Devon........................... 88
Prior (Michael), Lincolnshire 151
Trinders' Fine Tools, Suffolk 222

SHIPBUILDING AND SHIPPING
Anvil Books, West Midlands 235
Cheshire Book Centre, Cheshire 69
Curtle Mead Books, Isle of Wight................ 134
G. C. Books Ltd., Dumfries & Galloway 264
Green Ltd. (G.L.), Hertfordshire................... 132
Kerr (Norman), Cumbria........................... 77
Lee, Maritime Books (Gerald), East Sussex 104
Lewcock (John), Cambridgeshire 66
Marine and Cannon Books, Cheshire............ 69
McLaren Books, Strathclyde....................... 274
Milestone Books, Devon........................... 88
N1 Books, East Sussex............................. 103
Nautical Antique Centre (The), Dorset 94
Phelps (Michael), West Sussex..................... 237
Prior (Michael), Lincolnshire 151
Railway Shop (The), Torfaen...................... 287
Roadmaster Books, Kent........................... 137
Rods Books, Devon 87

Smith Maritime Aviation Books (Frank),
   Tyne and Wear.................................... 231
Stalagluft Books, Tyne and Wear................. 231
Trinders' Fine Tools, Suffolk 222

SHIPWRECKS
Cornucopia Books, Lincolnshire 151
Milestone Books, Devon........................... 88

SHORTHAND
Ainslie Books, Strathclyde......................... 273
Naughton Booksellers, Co. Dublin 259

SIGILLOGRAPHY
Taylor & Son (Peter), Hertfordshire.............. 132

SIGNED EDITIONS
Acer Books, Herefordshire 128
Adrem Books, Hertfordshire...................... 131
Apocalypse, Surrey 228
Bibliophile Books, London E...................... 153
Black Cat Bookshop, Leicestershire 145
Book Barrow, Cambridgeshire 63
BOOKS4U, Flintshire............................... 279
Bookstand, Dorset.................................. 93
Cameron House Books, Isle of Wight 134
Corfe Books, Surrey................................ 227
Eastwood Books (David), Cornwall.............. 72
Ellis, Bookseller (Peter), London SE 162
Ellwood Editions, Wiltshire 247
Elstree Books, Hertfordshire...................... 131
Ely Books, Cambridgeshire 65
Farahar & Dupre (Clive & Sophie),
   Wiltshire 246
firstpagebooks, Norfolk............................ 187
Firsts in Print, Isle of Wight 134
Fosters Bookshop, London W 170
Greta Books, Durham 96
Harrington Antiquarian Bookseller (Peter),
   London SW.. 166
Harris (Books), (Malcolm), West Midlands..... 234
Heppa (Christopher), Essex 108
Ian Briddon, Derbyshire........................... 81
Jean Hedger, Berkshire............................. 55
Kevin S. Ogilvie Modern First Editions,
   Grampian.. 266
Kirkman Ltd., (Robert), Bedfordshire 53
Little Stour Books, Kent........................... 136
McKelvie (Ian), London N 156
N V Books, Warwickshire......................... 232
Poetry Bookshop (The), Powys.................... 284
Portobello Books, London W 172
Richard Thornton Books, London N............ 157
Scrivener's Books & Bookbinding, Derbyshire . 81
Sensawunda Books, Cheshire 68
Shakeshaft (Dr. B.), Cheshire...................... 71
Signature Books, Hampshire 126
Simpson (Dave), Central........................... 263
Temple (Robert), London N...................... 157
Till's Bookshop, Lothian 272

Updike Rare Books (John), Lothian 272
Williams Rare Books (Nigel), London WC..... 177
Woodbine Books, West Yorkshire................ 241
Words Etcetera Bookshop, Dorset 92

SILVERSMITHS
Don Kelly Books, London W 170

SIXTIES, THE
Cornucopia Books, Lincolnshire 151

SLAVERY
Kenny's Bookshops and Art Galleries Ltd,
 Co. Galway 260
N1 Books, East Sussex............................. 103
Reading Lasses, Dumfries & Galloway.......... 265

SMALL PRESS PUBLISHED BOOKS
Samovar Books, Co. Dublin....................... 258

SOCIAL ECONOMICS
Adrem Books, Hertfordshire...................... 131
Hamish Riley-Smith, Norfolk 188
PsychoBabel Books & Journals, Oxfordshire ... 202
Reading Lasses, Dumfries & Galloway.......... 265

SOCIAL HISTORY
Adrem Books, Hertfordshire...................... 131
Apocalypse, Surrey 228
Bell (Peter), Strathclyde 270
Bibliophile Books, London E..................... 153
Black Cat Books, Norfolk.......................... 185
Brimstones, East Sussex............................ 102
Byrom Textile Bookroom (Richard),
 Lancashire 142
Castleton (Pat), Kent................................ 137
Chesters (G. & J.), Staffordshire 220
Clifton Books, Essex 111
Cottage Books, Leicestershire..................... 145
Cox (Geoff), Devon 89
Delectus Books, London WC...................... 174
Drury Rare Books (John), Essex.................. 111
Duck (William), Hampshire 124
Eggeling Books (John), West Yorkshire 245
Eggle (Mavis), Hertfordshire...................... 131
Elaine Lonsdale Books, West Yorkshire........ 242
Fireside Bookshop, Cumbria 80
Forest Books of Manchester, Cheshire 70
Graham (John), Dorset 95
Harvest Books, Lancashire........................ 144
Helion & Company, West Midlands 235
Hughes Rare Books (Spike), Borders 262
Hunt (Robin S.), Greater Manchester 120
Jarndyce Antiquarian Booksellers, London WC 175
Judd Books, London WC........................... 175
Kelsall (George), Greater Manchester........... 119
Maghreb Bookshop (The), London WC 175
Marcan, Bookseller (Peter), London SE......... 162
Murphy (C.J.), Norfolk............................. 187

N1 Books, East Sussex............................. 103
Naughton Booksellers, Co. Dublin 259
Northern Herald Books, West Yorkshire 241
Not JUST Books, Lincolnshire.................... 148
Pollak (P.M.), Devon............................... 87
Reading Lasses, Dumfries & Galloway.......... 265
Red Star Books, Hertfordshire 130
Roadmaster Books, Kent........................... 137
Russell (Charles), London SW 167
Scrivener's Books & Bookbinding, Derbyshire. 81
Segal Books (Joel), Devon 84
Sephton (A.F.), London W 172
South Downs Book Service, West Sussex 238
Stern Antiquarian Bookseller (Jeffrey), North
 Yorkshire 195
Stevens (Joan), Cambridgeshire 65
Symes Books (Naomi), Cheshire 71
Unsworths Booksellers, London NW 160
Warnes (Felicity J.), London Outer 178
Weininger Antiquarian Books (Eva M.),
 London NW 160
Westwood Books Ltd, Cumbria 79
Wetherell (Frances), Cambridgeshire 65
Whitchurch Books Ltd., Cardiff 276
Whittle, Bookseller (Avril), Cumbria 79
Woburn Books, London N 157

SOCIAL SCIENCES
Adrem Books, Hertfordshire...................... 131
Brimstones, East Sussex............................ 102
Cheshire Book Centre, Cheshire 69
Chesters (G. & J.), Staffordshire 220
Delectus Books, London WC...................... 174
Hamish Riley-Smith, Norfolk 188
hullbooks.com, East Yorkshire 106
Ice House Books, Wiltshire 248
Judd Books, London WC........................... 175
Northern Herald Books, West Yorkshire 241
O'Donoghue Books, Powys....................... 284
Old Cathay Fine Books, West Yorkshire 244
Orb's Bookshop, Grampian....................... 268
Outcast Books, Herefordshire 284
PsychoBabel Books & Journals, Oxfordshire ... 202
Reading Lasses, Dumfries & Galloway.......... 265
Reid of Liverpool, Merseyside.................... 182
Westwood Books Ltd, Cumbria 79
Woburn Books, London N 157

SOCIALISM
Adrem Books, Hertfordshire...................... 131
Left on The Shelf, Cumbria....................... 78
Naughton Booksellers, Co. Dublin 259
Northern Herald Books, West Yorkshire 241
Old Cathay Fine Books, West Yorkshire 244
Reading Lasses, Dumfries & Galloway.......... 265
Red Star Books, Hertfordshire 130
Spurrier (Nick), Kent............................... 138
Symes Books (Naomi), Cheshire 71
Woburn Books, London N 157

SPECIALITY INDEX

SOCIOLOGY
Apocalypse, Surrey 228
Brimstones, East Sussex............................ 102
Chesters (G. & J.), Staffordshire 220
PsychoBabel Books & Journals, Oxfordshire ... 202
Reading Lasses, Dumfries & Galloway 265

SOUTH SEAS
Adrem Books, Hertfordshire....................... 131

SPACE
Adrem Books, Hertfordshire....................... 131

SPECIAL COLLECTIONS
Downie Fine Books Ltd., (Robert), Shropshire 211
Kohler (C.C.), Surrey 226
Murphy (C.J.), Norfolk............................. 187
Temple (Robert), London N....................... 157

SPIRITUAL
Susan Taylor Books, West Yorkshire 243

SPIRITUALISM
Cavern Books, Cheshire 70
Chthonios Books, East Sussex..................... 101
Dawlish Books, Devon 84
Esoteric Dreams Bookshop, Cumbria............ 77
Facet Books, Dorset.................................. 0
Fine Books Oriental Ltd., London WC 175
Forest Books of Manchester, Cheshire 70
Greensleeves, Oxfordshire 202
Holmes Books (Harry), East Yorkshire 106
Hurst (Jenny), Kent 138
Jade Mountain, Hampshire 125
Loretta Lay Books, London NW.................. 159
Magis Books, Leicestershire........................ 147
Needham Books, (Russell), Somerset 216
Occultique, Northamptonshire.................... 196
Orchid Book Distributors, Co. Clare............. 257
PsychoBabel Books & Journals,
  Oxfordshire.. 202
Reading Lasses, Dumfries & Galloway 265
Saint Swithin's Illustrated & Children's Books,
  London W.. 172
Tilleys Vintage Magazine Shop,
  South Yorkshire................................... 218
Waxfactor, East Sussex 99
Wizard Books, Cambridgeshire.................... 67

SPORT
- GENERAL
Abacus Gallery, Staffordshire...................... 220
Adrem Books, Hertfordshire....................... 131
Allinson (Frank & Stella), Warwickshire 232
Amos (Denis W.), Hertfordshire 130
Ann & Mike Conry, Worcestershire.............. 251
Antique Map and Bookshop (The), Dorset..... 93
Archways Sports Books, Lothian 269
Aurora Books Ltd, Lothian........................ 270
Autumn Leaves, Lincolnshire...................... 150
Axe Rare & Out of Print Books (Richard),
  North Yorkshire................................... 190
Bob Mallory (Books), Derbyshire 82
Bodyline Books, Surrey............................. 227
Bookcase, Cumbria 76
Books Plus, Devon 83
books2books, Devon 87
Capel Mawr Collectors Centre, Gwynedd....... 280
Carningli Centre, Pembrokeshire................. 281
Carta Regis, Powys.................................. 286
Chandos Books, Devon 84
Chaucer Bookshop, Kent........................... 136
Clements (R.W.), London Outer.................. 179
Cofion Books, Pembrokeshire 281
Eastcote Bookshop (The), London Outer 178
Elmo Books, East Sussex........................... 98
Esoteric Dreams Bookshop, Cumbria............ 77
Eton Antique Bookshop, Berkshire............... 57
Evans (Mark), Lincolnshire 151
Fiona Edwards, Nottinghamshire................. 200
Garfi Books, Ceredigion 282
Gathern (D.), Conwy............................... 278
Good for Books, Lincolnshire 149
Hay Cinema Bookshop Ltd., Herefordshire 283
Hollett and Son (R.F.G.), Cumbria 79
Hornsey's, North Yorkshire........................ 192
Hummingbird Books, Herefordshire 128
Hurst (Jenny), Kent 138
Jackson (M.W.), Wiltshire......................... 249
Libra Books, Lincolnshire.......................... 148
Lyngheath Books, Norfolk......................... 186
Marble Hill Books, Middlesex..................... 181
McCrone (Audrey), Isle of Arran................. 269
Mead (P.J.), Shropshire 210
Mellon's Books, East Sussex....................... 100
Moore (C.R.), Shropshire 210
Morten (Booksellers) (E.J.),
  Greater Manchester................................ 119
Mr. Pickwick of Towcester, Northamptonshire 196
Mundy (David), Hertfordshire 130
Murphy (C.J.), Norfolk............................. 187
Oopalba Books, Cheshire.......................... 71
Portobello Books, London W 172
Price (R.W.), Nottinghamshire 200
Priestpopple Books, Northumberland............ 198
Quinto of Charing Cross Road, London WC .. 176
Quinto of Great Russell Street, London WC... 176
Richard Thornton Books, London N............. 157
Roland Books, Kent................................. 139
Rutland Bookshop (The), Rutland 208
Scrivener's Books & Bookbinding, Derbyshire . 81
Signature Books, Hampshire...................... 126
Stothert Old Books, Cheshire..................... 68
Stroma Books, Borders............................. 262
Tiffin (Tony and Gill), Durham................... 96
Trafalgar Bookshop, East Sussex 99
Treasure Trove Books, Leicestershire 146
Wadard Books, Kent................................ 137
Wiend Books, Lancashire 143
Yewtree Books, Cumbria........................... 77

SPECIALITY INDEX

- **AMERICAN FOOTBALL**
Archways Sports Books, Lothian 269
Saunders (Tom), Caerphilly 276

- **ANGLING/FISHING**
Aucott & Thomas, Leicestershire 145
Baron (Christopher), Greater Manchester 118
Biblion, London W 169
Blest (Peter), Kent 139
Bodyline Books, Surrey 227
Bolland Books (Leslie H.), Bedfordshire 53
Branksome Books, Dorset 93
Chalmers Hallam (E.), Hampshire 125
Chevin Books, West Yorkshire 245
Classics Bookshop (The), Oxfordshire 202
Coch-y-Bonddu Books, Powys 285
Cornucopia Books, Lincolnshire 151
Countryman Books, East Yorkshire 105
Countrymans Gallery (The), Leicestershire 145
Darkwood Books, Co. Cork 258
David Way Angling Books, Devon 86
Dusty Books, Powys 285
Edmund Pollinger Rare Books, London SW ... 165
Eggle (Mavis), Hertfordshire 131
Garfi Books, Ceredigion 282
Good Books, Shropshire 210
Grayling (David A.H.), Cumbria 78
Grove Bookshop (The), North Yorkshire 193
Head (John & Judith), Wiltshire 247
Hereward Books, Cambridgeshire 65
Internet Bookshop UK Ltd., Gloucestershire .. 113
Jane Jones Books, Grampian 267
Kilgour (Sporting Books) (Ian), Leicestershire . 147
Lion Books, Worcestershire 250
McEwan Fine Books, Grampian 266
Murphy (C.J.), Norfolk 187
Petersfield Bookshop (The), Hampshire 125
Petworth Antique Market (Bookroom),
  West Sussex 239
Rare Books & Berry, Somerset 215
Richard Thornton Books, London N 157
River Reads Bookshop, Devon 89
Rothwell & Dunworth, Somerset 214
Saint Mary's Books & Prints, Lincolnshire 152
Treasure Island (The), Greater Manchester 120
Vinovium Books, Durham 96
Worlds End Bookshop, London SW 168
Yesterday Tackle & Books, Dorset 90

- **ARCHERY**
Bodyline Books, Surrey 227
Cader Idris Books, Gwynedd 280
Chalmers Hallam (E.), Hampshire 125
Lake (Fred), Surrey 229

- **ATHLETICS**
Archways Sports Books, Lothian 269
Bob Mallory (Books), Derbyshire 82
Bodyline Books, Surrey 227
Bookzone, Berkshire 55

Marathon Books, Greater Manchester 118

- **BADMINTON**
Bodyline Books, Surrey 227
Pennymead Books, North Yorkshire 191

- **BALLOONING**
J.B. Books, Berkshire 56
Postings, Surrey 228

- **BASEBALL**
Gathern (D.), Conwy 278

- **BASKETBALL**
Adrem Books, Hertfordshire 131
Archways Sports Books, Lothian 269
Bodyline Books, Surrey 227

- **BIG GAME HUNTING**
Allsworth Rare Books Ltd., London 164
Ayre (Peter J.), Somerset 216
Barnhill Books, Isle of Arran 269
Bates & Hindmarch, West Yorkshire 243
Campbell Hewson Books (R.), Fife 265
Chalmers Hallam (E.), Hampshire 125
Countryman Books, East Yorkshire 105
Edmund Pollinger Rare Books, London SW ... 165
Farahar & Dupre (Clive & Sophie), Wiltshire .. 246
Grayling (David A.H.), Cumbria 78
McEwan Fine Books, Grampian 266
Popeley (Frank T.), Cambridgeshire 67
R.E. & G.B. Way, Suffolk 224
Vandeleur Antiquarian Books, Surrey 227

- **BILLIARDS/SNOOKER/POOL**
Ben–Nathan (Jack), London Outer 178
Bodyline Books, Surrey 227
R. S. & P. A. Scowen, Middlesex 179
Richard Thornton Books, London N 157

- **BOWLS**
Bodyline Books, Surrey 227
Cornucopia Books, Lincolnshire 151

- **BOXING**
Archways Sports Books, Lothian 269
Askew Books (Vernon), Wiltshire 246
Bodyline Books, Surrey 227
Bookzone, Berkshire 55
Combat Arts Archive, Durham 96
Derek Stirling Bookseller, Kent 141
Franks Booksellers, Greater Manchester 119
Hedgerow Books, South Yorkshire 217
McInnes (P.F. & J.R.), Dorset 90
Roland Books, Kent 139
Rugby Relics, West Glamorgan 281

SPECIALITY INDEX

- CANOEING/KAYAKS
Baldwin (M. & M.), Shropshire 250
McLaren Books, Strathclyde 274

- CAVING (SPELAEOLOGY)
Letterbox Books, Nottinghamshire 200

- CLIMBING & TREKKING
George St. Books, Derbyshire 82
Gildas Books, Cheshire 68
Glacier Books, Tayside 275
Hunter and Krageloh, Derbyshire 82
Little Bookshop (The), Cumbria 80
Main Point Books, Lothian 271
O'Reilly - Mountain Books (John), Derbyshire 82

- COURSING
Chalmers Hallam (E.), Hampshire 125
Wychwood Books, Gloucestershire 116

- CRICKET
Aardvark Books, Lincolnshire 150
Acumen Books, Staffordshire 220
Archways Sports Books, Lothian 269
Barbican Bookshop, North Yorkshire 194
Bardsley's Books, Suffolk 221
Barmby (C. & A.J.), Kent 140
Black Five Books, Shropshire 211
Bob Mallory (Books), Derbyshire 82
Bodyline Books, Surrey 227
Bookzone, Berkshire 55
Border Bookshop, West Yorkshire 245
Bright (P.G.), Cambridgeshire 65
Chas J. Sawyer, Kent 140
Chevin Books, West Yorkshire 245
Christopher Saunders (Orchard Books),
   Gloucestershire 115
Classic Crime Collections, Greater Manchester 119
Coach House Books, Worcestershire 251
Cobbles Books, Somerset 214
David Summerfield Books, East Sussex 98
Derek Stirling Bookseller, Kent 141
Esoteric Dreams Bookshop, Cumbria 77
firstpagebooks, Norfolk 187
GS Cricket Books / The Old Book Shop, West
   Midlands 236
Internet Bookshop UK Ltd., Gloucestershire .. 113
Invicta Bookshop, Berkshire 56
Lion Books, Worcestershire 250
Maynard & Bradley, Leicestershire 146
McEwan Fine Books, Grampian 266
McKenzie (J.W.), Surrey 227
Mellon's Books, East Sussex 100
My Back Pages, London SW 167
Poor Richard's Books, Suffolk 222
Prescott - The Bookseller (John),
   London Outer 181
Roberts (William H.), West Yorkshire 243
Roland Books, Kent 139
Rugby Relics, West Glamorgan 281

Saint Mary's Books & Prints, Lincolnshire 152
Tiffin (Tony and Gill), Durham 96
Treasure Island (The), Greater Manchester 120
Treasure Trove Books, Leicestershire 146
Wood Cricket Books (Martin), Kent 140
Yesterday's News, Conwy 278

- CROQUET
Bodyline Books, Surrey 227
Edmund Pollinger Rare Books, London SW ... 165

- CYCLING
Archways Sports Books, Lothian 269
Bodyline Books, Surrey 227
Engaging Gear Ltd., Essex 108
Larkham Books (Patricia), Gloucestershire 117
Ouse Valley Books, Bedfordshire 54

- DIVING/SUB-AQUA
Internet Bookshop UK Ltd., Gloucestershire .. 113
Sidey, Bookdealer (Philip), Kent 140
Underwater Books, East Sussex 101

- DUELLING
Combat Arts Archive, Durham 96

- FALCONRY
Barnhill Books, Isle of Arran 269
Blest (Peter), Kent 139
Chalmers Hallam (E.), Hampshire 125
Coch-y-Bonddu Books, Powys 285
Countryman Books, East Yorkshire 105
Hereward Books, Cambridgeshire 65
Walker (Adrian), Bedfordshire 53
Wildside Books, Worcestershire 250

- FENCING
Bodyline Books, Surrey 227
Chalmers Hallam (E.), Hampshire 125
Combat Arts Archive, Durham 96

- FIELD SPORTS
Barnhill Books, Isle of Arran 269
Blest (Peter), Kent 139
Bookline, Co. Down 256
Border Books, Borders 262
Branksome Books, Dorset 93
Cat Lit, Somerset 215
Chalmers Hallam (E.), Hampshire 125
Cornucopia Books, Lincolnshire 151
Countrymans Gallery (The), Leicestershire 145
Daly (Peter M.), Hampshire 127
Edmund Pollinger Rare Books, London SW ... 165
Garfi Books, Ceredigion 282
Good Books, Shropshire 210
Grayling (David A.H.), Cumbria 78
Grove Bookshop (The), North Yorkshire 193
Head (John & Judith), Wiltshire 247
Heartland Old Books, Devon 88

Hereward Books, Cambridgeshire 65
Hollett and Son (R.F.G.), Cumbria 79
Jane Jones Books, Grampian 267
Kilgour (Sporting Books) (Ian), Leicestershire . 147
Lake (Fred), Surrey 229
Maynard & Bradley, Leicestershire 146
McEwan Fine Books, Grampian 266
Moss End Bookshop, Berkshire 57
Neil Summersgill, Lancashire 142
Petworth Antique Market (Bookroom), West
  Sussex 239
R.E. & G.B. Way, Suffolk 224
Simon Finch Nofolk, Norfolk 186
Stacpoole (George), Co. Limerick 260
Vinovium Books, Durham 96
Wychwood Books, Gloucestershire 116

- FOOTBALL (SOCCER)
Amos (Denis W.), Hertfordshire 130
Ann & Mike Conry, Worcestershire.............. 251
Archways Sports Books, Lothian 269
Bob Mallory (Books), Derbyshire 82
Bodyline Books, Surrey 227
BOOKS4U, Flintshire 279
Bookzone, Berkshire 55
Border Bookshop, West Yorkshire 245
Chevin Books, West Yorkshire 245
Eden Books, Lincolnshire 150
Elmo Books, East Sussex 98
Esoteric Dreams Bookshop, Cumbria............ 77
firstpagebooks, Norfolk 187
Footballana, Berkshire 56
Franks Booksellers, Greater Manchester 119
Gathern (D.), Conwy 278
Hedgerow Books, South Yorkshire............... 217
Lion Books, Worcestershire 250
Moore (C.R.), Shropshire 210
Peter White, Hampshire 122
Richard Thornton Books, London N 157
Roland Books, Kent 139
Rugby Relics, West Glamorgan 281
Soccer Books Limited, Lincolnshire.............. 149
Treasure Trove Books, Leicestershire 146
Yesterday's News, Conwy 278

- GOLF
Abrahams (Mike), Staffordshire................... 219
Archways Sports Books, Lothian 269
Bob Mallory (Books), Derbyshire 82
Bodyline Books, Surrey 227
Bookzone, Berkshire 55
Bradley–Cox (Mary), Dorset....................... 90
Classic Crime Collections, Greater Manchester 119
Clifford Milne Books, Grampian 266
Coupland (Terry W.), Staffordshire 219
Esoteric Dreams Bookshop, Cumbria............ 77
Garfi Books, Ceredigion 282
Grant Books, Worcestershire 250
Gresham Books, Somerset 214
Hennessey Bookseller (Ray), East Sussex 99
McEwan Golf Books (Rhod), Grampian 266

Morley Case, Hampshire 126
Murphy (C.J.), Norfolk 187
Poor Richard's Books, Suffolk 222
Quarto Bookshop (The), Fife 266
Roland Books, Kent 139
Rugby Relics, West Glamorgan 281
Schofield Golf Books (Steve), West Yorkshire . 245
Seabreeze Books, Lancashire 144

- GYMNASTICS
Archways Sports Books, Lothian 269
Bodyline Books, Surrey 227

- HIGHLAND GAMES
Archways Sports Books, Lothian 269
Webster (D.), Strathclyde 274

- HOCKEY
Archways Sports Books, Lothian 269
Bodyline Books, Surrey 227
Bookworld, Shropshire 210
Pennymead Books, North Yorkshire............. 191
Yesterday's Books, Dorset 91

- HORSE RACING (INC. RIDING/ BREEDING/EQUESTRIAN)
Amos (Denis W.), Hertfordshire 130
Archways Sports Books, Lothian 269
Askew Books (Vernon), Wiltshire 246
Aucott & Thomas, Leicestershire 145
Bob Mallory (Books), Derbyshire 82
Bodyline Books, Surrey 227
Bookzone, Berkshire 55
Brown (Books) (Steve), Staffordshire............. 219
Browzers, Greater Manchester 119
Carters (Janet), Suffolk 222
Castleton (Pat), Kent 137
Cobbles Books, Somerset 214
Cornucopia Books, Lincolnshire 151
Day (J.H.), Hampshire 124
Garfi Books, Ceredigion 282
Gibbs Books, (Jonathan), Worcestershire 251
Jane Badger Books, Northamptonshire.......... 196
Jane Jones Books, Grampian 267
Karen Millward, Co. Cork 257
Kennedy & Farley, East Sussex 103
Leeper (Romilly), London SW 166
MK Book Services, Cambridgeshire.............. 66
Roland Books, Kent 139
Treasure Island (The), Greater Manchester 120
Wychwood Books, Gloucestershire 116

- HUNTING
Cobbles Books, Somerset 214
Coch-y-Bonddu Books, Powys 285
Cornucopia Books, Lincolnshire 151
Countryman Books, East Yorkshire 105
Countrymans Gallery (The), Leicestershire...... 145
Darkwood Books, Co. Cork 258

SPECIALITY INDEX

Edmund Pollinger Rare Books, London SW ... 165
Garfi Books, Ceredigion 282
Grove Bookshop (The), North Yorkshire 193
Jane Badger Books, Northamptonshire 196
Jane Jones Books, Grampian 267
Kennedy & Farley, East Sussex 103
Kilgour (Sporting Books) (Ian), Leicestershire . 147
Rare Books & Berry, Somerset 215
Saint Mary's Books & Prints, Lincolnshire 152
Wychwood Books, Gloucestershire 116

- ICE HOCKEY
Archways Sports Books, Lothian 269
Bodyline Books, Surrey 227

- ICE-SKATING
Archways Sports Books, Lothian 269
Bodyline Books, Surrey 227

- MARTIAL ARTS
Archways Sports Books, Lothian 269
Combat Arts Archive, Durham 96

- MOTOR RACING
Archways Sports Books, Lothian 269
Bob Mallory (Books), Derbyshire 82
Bodyline Books, Surrey 227
books2books, Devon 87
Collectors Carbooks, Northamptonshire 196
Elmo Books, East Sussex 98
Heritage, West Midlands 234
Knowles (John), Norfolk 185
Lion Books, Worcestershire 250
Morris Secondhand & Antiquarian Books
  (Chris), Oxfordshire 205
Richard Thornton Books, London N 157
Saint Paul's Street Bookshop, Lincolnshire 152
Simon Lewis Transport Books, Gloucestershire 115
Volumes of Motoring, Gloucestershire 113

- OLYMPIC GAMES, THE
Amos (Denis W.), Hertfordshire 130
Archways Sports Books, Lothian 269
Bob Mallory (Books), Derbyshire 82
Bodyline Books, Surrey 227

- PIG-STICKING
Chalmers Hallam (E.), Hampshire 125
Edmund Pollinger Rare Books, London SW ... 165

- POLO
Askew Books (Vernon), Wiltshire 246
Blacklock's, Surrey 227
Bodyline Books, Surrey 227
Countryman Books, East Yorkshire 105

- POTHOLING
Glacier Books, Tayside 275

Letterbox Books, Nottinghamshire 200

- RACING
Bob Mallory (Books), Derbyshire 82

- RACKET SPORTS
Bodyline Books, Surrey 227

- REAL TENNIS
Bodyline Books, Surrey 227
Edmund Pollinger Rare Books, London SW ... 165

- ROWING
Archways Sports Books, Lothian 269
Bodyline Books, Surrey 227
McLaren Books, Strathclyde 274
Vandeleur Antiquarian Books, Surrey 227
Way Booksellers (Richard), Oxfordshire 204

- RUGBY
Archways Sports Books, Lothian 269
Bodyline Books, Surrey 227
Bookzone, Berkshire 55
Chas J. Sawyer, Kent 140
Dylans Bookstore, Glamorgan 286
Eden Books, Lincolnshire 150
Franks Booksellers, Greater Manchester 119
Lion Books, Worcestershire 250
Poor Richard's Books, Suffolk 222
Roland Books, Kent 139
Rugby Relics, West Glamorgan 281
Saunders (Tom), Caerphilly 276
Treasure Island (The), Greater Manchester 120

- RUNNING
Archways Sports Books, Lothian 269

- SAILING
Argent (Alan), Isle of Wight 135
Portus Books, Hampshire 123

- SHOOTING
Blest (Peter), Kent 139
Chalmers Hallam (E.), Hampshire 125
Countryman Books, East Yorkshire 105
Countrymans Gallery (The), Leicestershire 145
Daly (Peter M.), Hampshire 127
Darkwood Books, Co. Cork 258
Edmund Pollinger Rare Books, London SW ... 165
Garfi Books, Ceredigion 282
Grayling (David A.H.), Cumbria 78
Kilgour (Sporting Books) (Ian), Leicestershire . 147
Roland Books, Kent 139
Wychwood Books, Gloucestershire 116

- SKIING
Archways Sports Books, Lothian 269
Frew Limited (Robert), London W 170

Pinnacle Books, Lothian............................ 271

- SQUASH
Bodyline Books, Surrey 227

- SWIMMING
Bodyline Books, Surrey 227

- TENNIS
Amos (Denis W.), Hertfordshire 130
Archways Sports Books, Lothian 269
Bodyline Books, Surrey 227
Bookzone, Berkshire................................. 55
Tennis Collectables, Cheshire 68

- WATERSPORTS
Archways Sports Books, Lothian 269

- WEIGHTLIFTING/BODYBUILDING
Archways Sports Books, Lothian 269
Bodyline Books, Surrey............................. 227
Combat Arts Archive, Durham 96
Webster (D.), Strathclyde.......................... 274

- WRESTLING
Bodyline Books, Surrey 227
Combat Arts Archive, Durham 96
Webster (D.), Strathclyde.......................... 274

- YACHTING
Baldwin (M. & M.), Shropshire 250
Bookends of Fowey, Cornwall 73
Books Afloat, Dorset................................. 94
Clapham (M. & B.), Hampshire 124
Cornucopia Books, Lincolnshire 151
Crouch Rare Books, Surrey........................ 227
Curtle Mead Books, Isle of Wight................ 134
Footrope Knots, Suffolk............................ 223
G Collins Bookdealers, Hertfordshire............ 131
Internet Bookshop UK Ltd., Gloucestershire .. 113
Lewcock (John), Cambridgeshire 66
McLaren Books, Strathclyde...................... 274
Milestone Books, Devon............................ 88
Prior (Michael), Lincolnshire 151
Roland Books, Kent................................ 139
Sea Chest Nautical Bookshop (The), Devon ... 87
Smith Maritime Aviation Books (Frank),
    Tyne and Wear 231

STAINED GLASS
Barmby (C. & A.J.), Kent.......................... 140
Birchden Books, London E 153
Don Kelly Books, London W 170
Heneage Art Books (Thomas), London SW.... 166
Stained Glass Books, Kent........................ 139
Staniland (Booksellers), Lincolnshire............ 152
Taylor & Son (Peter), Hertfordshire.............. 132
Trinders' Fine Tools, Suffolk 222

Venables (Morris & Juliet), Bristol 59

STATES OF AMERICA - LOUISIANA
Apocalypse, Surrey 228

STATISTICS
Adrem Books, Hertfordshire....................... 131

STEAM ENGINES
Abrahams (Mike), Staffordshire................... 219
All Books, Essex 110
Autobooks Ltd., East Sussex 100
Biblion, London W 169
Bott, (Bookdealers) Ltd., (Martin), Greater
    Manchester 118
Brewin Books Ltd., Warwickshire 233
Browning Books, Torfaen 287
Cornucopia Books, Lincolnshire 151
Coulthurst (Richard), Greater Manchester...... 120
Cox (Geoff), Devon 89
Dales and Lakes Book Centre, Cumbria 79
Duck (William), Hampshire........................ 124
Kerr (Norman), Cumbria........................... 77
N1 Books, East Sussex............................. 103
Nautical Antique Centre (The), Dorset 94
Newband (D.M.), Powys 286
Roadmaster Books, Kent........................... 137
Roland Books, Kent................................. 139

STONE MASONRY
Courtney & Hoff, North Yorkshire 194

SUFFRAGETTES
Reading Lasses, Dumfries & Galloway 265

SUFISM
Portobello Books, London W 172
The Sanctuary Bookshop, Dorset................. 93

SUPERNATURAL
Adrem Books, Hertfordshire....................... 131
Caduceus Books, Leicestershire 145
Cowley, Bookdealer (K.W.), Somerset........... 214
Eggeling Books (John), West Yorkshire 245
Enigma Books, Norfolk 186
Facet Books, Dorset................................. 90
Gildas Books, Cheshire 68
Loretta Lay Books, London NW................... 159
Occultique, Northamptonshire..................... 196
Temple (Robert), London N....................... 157

SURGERY
Demetzy Books, Oxfordshire 203
G. C. Books Ltd., Dumfries & Galloway 264

SURREALISM
Atlas, London N 155

SPECIALITY INDEX

Delectus Books, London WC 174
Ellis, Bookseller (Peter), London SE 162

SYMBOLISM
Apocalypse, Surrey 228

TAPESTRY
Abington Bookshop, Suffolk 222
Art Reference Books, Hampshire 125
Books, Oxfordshire 202
Byrom Textile Bookroom (Richard),
    Lancashire 142
Dandy Lion Editions, Surrey 228
Don Kelly Books, London W 170
Glacier Books, Tayside 275
Heneage Art Books (Thomas), London SW 166
Hennessey Bookseller (Ray), East Sussex 99
Trinders' Fine Tools, Suffolk 222
Whittle, Bookseller (Avril), Cumbria 79

TAXIDERMY
Blest (Peter), Kent 139
Chalmers Hallam (E.), Hampshire 125

TEACHING
Ice House Books, Wiltshire 248
Reading Lasses, Dumfries & Galloway 265
Sun House Books, Kent 139

TECHNICAL
Adrem Books, Hertfordshire 131
Brimstones, East Sussex 102
Duck (William), Hampshire 124
Fine Books at Ilkley, West Yorkshire 243
Moorhead Books, West Yorkshire 241
Parkinsons Books, Merseyside 183
Roberts Books, Strathclyde 274
Savery Books, East Sussex 99

TECHNOLOGY
Baron (Christopher), Greater Manchester 118
Batterham (David), London W 169
Book House (The), Cumbria 78
Booth Books, Powys 282
Bott, (Bookdealers) Ltd., (Martin),
    Greater Manchester 118
Camden Books, Somerset 212
Chris Phillips, Wiltshire 246
Eagle Bookshop (The), Bedfordshire 53
Eggle (Mavis), Hertfordshire 131
Esplin (David), Hampshire 124
Gaskell Rare Books (Roger),
    Cambridgeshire 66
Hinchliffe Books, Bristol 59
Jay Books, Lothian 271
K.S.C. Books, Cheshire 68
Mollie's Loft, Swansea 287
Orangeberry Books, Oxfordshire 204
Parkinsons Books, Merseyside 183

Phelps (Michael), West Sussex 237
Phillips (Nigel), London SW 167
Pollak (P.M.), Devon 87
Roberts Books, Strathclyde 274
Rogers Turner Books, London SE 162
Skoob Russell Square, Suffolk 225
Stroh (M.A.), London E 153
Trinders' Fine Tools, Suffolk 222
Weiner (Graham), London N 157
Westons, Hertfordshire 133
Westwood Books (Mark), Powys 284
Whistler's Books, London SW 167
Ystwyth Books, Ceredigion 277

TEDDY BEARS
Bookmark (Children's Books), Wiltshire 248
DPE Books, Devon 86
Saint Swithin's Illustrated & Children's Books,
    London W 172

TELEVISION
Byre Books, Dumfries & Galloway 264
Cover to Cover, Merseyside 183
Evans (Mark), Lincolnshire 151
firstpagebooks, Norfolk 187
Fitzsimons (Anne), Cumbria 77
Greenroom Books, West Yorkshire 243
Kaye - Bookseller (Terence), London NW 159
Kelly Books, Devon 88
McGee (Terence J.), London Outer 178
Morris Secondhand & Antiquarian Books
    (Chris), Oxfordshire 205
Mr. Pickwick of Towcester, Northamptonshire 196
Not JUST Books, Lincolnshire 148
Paramor (C.D.), Suffolk 224
Pyecroft (Ruth), Gloucestershire 116
Williams (Bookdealer), (Richard), Lincolnshire 152
Yesterday's News, Conwy 278
Zardoz Books, Wiltshire 249

TEXANA
Americanabooksuk, Cumbria 76

TEXTBOOKS
Cornucopia Books, Lincolnshire 151
Oopalba Books, Cheshire 71
Stalagluft Books, Tyne and Wear 231
The Sanctuary Bookshop, Dorset 93

TEXTILES
Abington Bookshop, Suffolk 222
Art Reference Books, Hampshire 125
Black Cat Books, Norfolk 185
Brock Books, North Yorkshire 190
Byrom Textile Bookroom (Richard),
    Lancashire 142
Cover to Cover, Merseyside 183
Crouch Rare Books, Surrey 227
Delph Books, Greater Manchester 120
Don Kelly Books, London W 170

Forest Books of Manchester, Cheshire 70
Heneage Art Books (Thomas), London SW.... 166
Hennessey Bookseller (Ray), East Sussex 99
Ives Bookseller (John), London Outer 181
Mansfield (Judith), West Yorkshire 245
Potterton Books, North Yorkshire 194
Reading Lasses, Dumfries & Galloway 265
Sleepy Elephant Books & Artefacts, Cumbria.. 79
Susan Taylor Books, West Yorkshire 243
Trinders' Fine Tools, Suffolk 222
Warnes (Felicity J.), London Outer 178
Whittle, Bookseller (Avril), Cumbria 79
Young (D. & J.), Powys 286

THEATRE
Addyman Books, Powys 282
Brock Books, North Yorkshire 190
Byre Books, Dumfries & Galloway 264
Carta Regis, Powys 286
Clark (Nigel A.), London SE 162
Cobbles Books, Somerset 214
Cover to Cover, Merseyside 183
Cox Rare Books (Charles), Cornwall 73
DaSilva Puppet Books, Dorset 92
Decorum Books, London N 155
Ely Books, Cambridgeshire 65
Evans (Mark), Lincolnshire 151
Fitzsimons (Anne), Cumbria 77
Forest Books of Manchester, Cheshire 70
Greenroom Books, West Yorkshire 243
Harris (Books), (Malcolm), West Midlands..... 234
J.C. Books, Norfolk 188
Jarndyce Antiquarian Booksellers, London WC 175
Junk & Spread Eagle, London SE 162
Kaye - Bookseller (Terence), London NW...... 159
Keel Row Books, Tyne and Wear 231
McGee (Terence J.), London Outer 178
My Back Pages, London SW 167
Oopalba Books, Cheshire 71
Paramor (C.D.), Suffolk 224
Pastmasters, Derbyshire 82
Pordes Books Ltd., (Henry), London WC 176
Portobello Books, London W 172
Prescott - The Bookseller (John),
    London Outer 181
Primrose Hill Books, London NW 159
Reading Lasses, Dumfries & Galloway 265
Reads, Dorset 94
RGS Books, Surrey 229
Rhodes, Bookseller (Peter), Hampshire 126
Richard Thornton Books, London N 157
Saint Swithin's Illustrated & Children's Books,
    London W 172
Scrivener's Books & Bookbinding, Derbyshire . 81
Sleepy Elephant Books & Artefacts, Cumbria.. 79
Temple (Robert), London N 157
Theatreshire Books, North Yorkshire 190
Whittle, Bookseller (Avril), Cumbria 79
Willmott Bookseller (Nicholas), Cardiff 276
Wood (Peter), Cambridgeshire 65
Yesterday's News, Conwy 278

THEOLOGY
Addyman Books, Powys 282
Andrew Stewart, Cornwall 74
Andrews Books & Collectables, Derbyshire 82
Apocalypse, Surrey 228
Axe Rare & Out of Print Books (Richard),
    North Yorkshire 190
Barbican Bookshop, North Yorkshire 194
Bardsley's Books, Suffolk 221
Beckham Books Ltd., Suffolk 225
Bell (Peter), Strathclyde 270
Beware of the Leopard, Bristol 58
Blythswood Bookshop, Highland 269
Book Aid, Durham 96
Bookcase, Cumbria 76
Bookshop (The), Co. Donegal 258
Booth Books, Powys 282
Brimstones, East Sussex 102
Broadwater Books, Hampshire 126
Butler Books, Dorset 90
Capel Mawr Collectors Centre, Gwynedd 280
Carta Regis, Powys 286
Carter, (Brian), Oxfordshire 203
Chesters (G. & J.), Staffordshire 220
Colwyn Books, Conwy 277
Copnal Books, Cheshire 68
Corder (Mark W.), Kent 140
Crouch Rare Books, Surrey 227
Edwards (Alan & Margaret), Kent 141
Edwards (London) Limited (Francis),
    London WC 175
Edwards in Hay–on–Wye (Francis),
    Herefordshire 283
Fotheringham (Alex), Northumberland 198
Foyle Books, Co. Derry 255
G. C. Books Ltd., Dumfries & Galloway 264
Gage Postal Books, Essex 111
Gilbert (R.A.), Bristol 59
Golden Age Books, Worcestershire 251
Hab Books, London W 171
Hellenic Bookservices, London NW 158
Heritage Books, Isle of Wight 134
Howes Bookshop, East Sussex 101
Humber Books, Lincolnshire 148
Jade Mountain, Hampshire 125
Kernaghans, Merseyside 183
Kyrios Books, Nottinghamshire 200
Lewis (J.T. & P.), Cornwall 73
Magis Books, Leicestershire 147
Main Point Books, Lothian 271
Martin's Books, Powys 285
Modern Welsh Publications Ltd., Merseyside .. 182
Moss Books, London NW 159
Oasis Booksearch, Cambridgeshire 67
Old Bookshop (The), West Midlands 236
Olynthiacs, Shropshire 210
Parkinsons Books, Merseyside 183
Quinto of Charing Cross Road, London WC.. 176
Rose Books, Greater Manchester 120
Rosemary Pugh Books, Wiltshire 248
S.P.C.K., Hampshire 127

SPECIALITY INDEX

S.P.C.K., Bristol 59
Saint Philip's Books, Oxfordshire 205
Salsus Books, Worcestershire 250
Samovar Books, Co. Dublin 258
Shacklock Books (David), Suffolk 222
Singleton (Anthony), South Yorkshire 217
Spooner & Co, Somerset 215
Staffs Bookshop (The), Staffordshire 219
Stalagluft Books, Tyne and Wear 231
Sterling Books, Somerset 216
Stokes Books, Co. Dublin 259
Thornber (Peter M.), North Yorkshire 193
Thorntons of Oxford Ltd., Oxfordshire 203
Westcountry Oldbooks, Devon 84
Westwood Books (Mark), Powys 284

THEOSOPHY

Alpha Books, London N 155
Bookcase, Cumbria 76
Gildas Books, Cheshire 68
Inner Bookshop (The), Oxfordshire 205
Occultique, Northamptonshire 196
Rosemary Pugh Books, Wiltshire 248
Starlord Books, Greater Manchester 118
The Sanctuary Bookshop, Dorset 93

THERAPY - MARITAL & FAMILY

Reading Lasses, Dumfries & Galloway 265
Savery Books, East Sussex 99

TIMBER TECHNOLOGY

Reeves Technical Books, North Yorkshire 193

TOPOGRAPHY
- GENERAL

Abacus Gallery, Staffordshire 220
Acer Books, Herefordshire 128
Addyman Books, Powys 282
Adrem Books, Hertfordshire 131
Alexander's Books, Warwickshire 232
Allhalland Books, Devon 83
Altea Antique Maps & Books, London W 169
Andrews Books & Collectables, Derbyshire 82
Andron (G.W.), London N 155
Antiquary Ltd., (Bar Bookstore),
    North Yorkshire 192
Antiques on High, Oxfordshire 204
Anvil Books, West Midlands 235
Arden Books & Cosmographia, Warwickshire . 232
Arts & Antiques Centre (The), Cheshire 69
Atholl Fine Books, Tayside 275
Autolycus, Shropshire 209
Baker - Books for the Collector (Colin), Devon 88
Bardsley's Books, Suffolk 221
Barnes (Peter), Wiltshire 248
Beardsley (A.E.), Nottinghamshire 201
Bolton Books, Hampshire 122
Bonham (J. & S.L.), London W 169
Bookbox, Gloucestershire 116
Books, Denbighshire 278

Books & Collectables Ltd., Cambridgeshire 63
Books (For All), North Yorkshire 190
Books Afloat, Dorset 94
books2books, Devon 87
BOOKS4U, Flintshire 279
Bookshop (The), Norfolk 189
Booth Books, Powys 282
Bowden Books, Leicestershire 147
Brinded (Scott), Kent 139
Broadhurst of Southport Ltd., Merseyside 182
Broadway Books, Cambridgeshire 66
Brock Books, North Yorkshire 190
Burden Ltd., (Clive A.), Hertfordshire 132
Carnforth Bookshop (The), Lancashire 142
Carta Regis, Powys 286
Castle Bookshop, Essex 109
Castle Hill Books, Herefordshire 128
Castleton (Pat), Kent 137
Cavern Books, Cheshire 70
Channel Islands Galleries Limited,
    Channel Islands 253
Chaucer Bookshop, Kent 136
Cheshire Book Centre, Cheshire 69
Chevin Books, West Yorkshire 245
Clarke (J.&D), Norfolk 187
Clarke Books (David), Somerset 214
Classic Bindings Ltd, London SW 164
Coach House Books, Worcestershire 251
Cobweb Books, North Yorkshire 192
Cofion Books, Pembrokeshire 281
Coles (T.V.), Cambridgeshire 66
Coombes (A.J.), Surrey 226
Cornucopia Books, Lincolnshire 151
Craobh Rua Books, Co. Armagh 255
Cumming Limited (A. & Y.), East Sussex 102
D'Arcy Books, Wiltshire 246
Dales & Lakes Book Centre, Cumbria 79
Dandy Lion Editions, Surrey 228
Dartmoor Bookshop (The), Devon 83
De Burca Rare Books, Co. Dublin 259
Edwards (Alan & Margaret), Kent 141
Elaine Lonsdale Books, West Yorkshire 242
Ellwood Editions, Wiltshire 247
Elmfield Books, West Midlands 234
Elstree Books, Hertfordshire 131
Eton Antique Bookshop, Berkshire 57
Ewell Bookshop, Surrey 227
Farquharson, (Hilary), Tayside 275
Fine Art, London SE 165
Fireside Books, Buckinghamshire 62
Fisher & Sperr, London N 155
Ford Books (David), Hertfordshire 132
Freader's Books, Tayside 275
Frost (Richard), Hertfordshire 130
G. C. Books Ltd., Dumfries & Galloway 264
Garfi Books, Ceredigion 282
Gilbert and Son (H.M.), Hampshire 127
Gillmark Gallery, Hertfordshire 131
Good for Books, Lincolnshire 149
Goodyer (Nicholas), London N 156
Green (Mrs. D.M.), Surrey 229
Grove Bookshop (The), North Yorkshire 193

Guildmaster Books, Cheshire 70
Hall's Bookshop, Kent 141
Handsworth Books, Essex 112
Harrington Antiquarian Bookseller (Peter),
   London SW 166
Hawes Books, Norfolk 187
Hay Cinema Bookshop Ltd., Herefordshire 283
High Street Books, Devon 85
Hinchliffe Books, Bristol 59
Hollett and Son (R.F.G.), Cumbria 79
Hornsey's, North Yorkshire 192
Hummingbird Books, Herefordshire 128
InterCol London, London N 156
Jackson (M.W.), Wiltshire 249
Jade Mountain, Hampshire 125
Janus Books, West Midlands 235
Junk & Spread Eagle, London SE 162
Kalligraphia (formerly Charmouth Bounty
   Books), Isle of Wight 134
Kay Books, London W 171
Keegan's Bookshop, Berkshire 56
Kellow Books, Oxfordshire 203
Kemp Booksellers, East Yorkshire 106
Kim's Bookshop, West Sussex 237, 240
King Street Bookshop (The), Norfolk 185
Kingsmere Books, Bedfordshire 53
Kingswood Books, Dorset 93
Knapton Bookbarn, North Yorkshire 194
Letterbox Books, Nottinghamshire 200
Lewis (J.T. & P.), Cornwall 73
Libra Books, Lincolnshire 148
Libris (Weston) Books, Somerset 213
Lowe (John), Norfolk 186
Malvern Bookshop (The), Worcestershire 250
Marcan, Bookseller (Peter), London SE 162
Marlborough Rare Books Ltd., London W 171
Martin Bookshop & Gallery (Richard),
   Hampshire 123
Maynard & Bradley, Leicestershire 146
Missing Books, Essex 109
Modlock (Lilian), Dorset 92
Mundy (David), Buckinghamshire 61
Mundy (David), Hertfordshire 130
Murphy (C.J.), Norfolk 187
Newlyn & New Street Books, Cornwall 74
Nicolas - Antiquarian Booksellers & Art
   Dealers, London N 156
Nineteenth Century Books, Oxfordshire 207
Old Cathay Fine Books, West Yorkshire 244
Old Station Pottery & Bookshop (The),
   Norfolk 189
Oopalba Books, Cheshire 71
Ouse Valley Books, Bedfordshire 54
Over-Sands Books, Cumbria 77
Oxfam Books and Music, Hampshire 127
Oxley (Laurence), Hampshire 122
Paralos Ltd., London WC 175
Park Gallery & Bookshop (The),
   Northamptonshire 197
Parlour Bookshop (The), Oxfordshire 203
Parrott Books, Oxfordshire 207
Past & Present Books, Gloucestershire 114
Peter White, Hampshire 122
Poor Richard's Books, Suffolk 222
Pordes Books Ltd., (Henry), London WC 176
Prescott - The Bookseller (John),
   London Outer 181
Priory Books, Worcestershire 252
Quentin Books Ltd, Essex 109
Quinto of Charing Cross Road, London WC .. 176
Quinto of Great Russell Street, London WC ... 176
R. & A. Books, East Sussex 100
Reads, Dorset 94
Richard Thornton Books, London N 157
Robin Doughty - Fine Books, West Midlands . 234
Roger Collicott Books, Cornwall 74
Roland Books, Kent 139
Ross Old Books & Prints, Herefordshire 128
Royal Carbery Books Ltd., Co. Cork 257
Saint Mary's Books & Prints, Lincolnshire 152
Samovar Books, Co. Dublin 258
Saunders (Tom), Caerphilly 276
Sedgeberrow Books & Framing, Worcestershire 251
Segal Books (Joel), Devon 84
Shacklock Books (David), Suffolk 222
Shakeshaft (Dr. B.), Cheshire 71
Shakespeare Books (Colin), Staffordshire 219
Sharpe (Mary), Somerset 216
Signature Books, Hampshire 126
Singleton (Anthony), South Yorkshire 217
Smith (Clive), Essex 109
Sparrow Books, West Yorkshire 241
Stalagluft Books, Tyne and Wear 231
Stella Books, Monmouthshire 281
Sterling Books, Somerset 216
Stothert Old Books, Cheshire 68
Suffolk Rare Books, Suffolk 225
Sykes (Graham), West Yorkshire 244
Temperley (David), West Midlands 234
Thorntons of Oxford Ltd., Oxfordshire 203
Tilston (Stephen E.), London SE 161
Titford (John), Derbyshire 81
Townsend (John), Berkshire 57
Treasure Trove Books, Leicestershire 146
Trinders' Fine Tools, Suffolk 222
Turton (John), Durham 97
Tyger Press, London N 157
Unsworths Booksellers, London NW 160
Ventnor Rare Books, Isle of Wight 135
Vokes Books Ltd., North Yorkshire 192
Wadard Books, Kent 137
Water Lane Bookshop, Wiltshire 248
Wealden Books, Kent 139
Westcountry Oldbooks, Devon 84
Yewtree Books, Cumbria 77

TOPOGRAPHY - LOCAL

2 Ravens, Cumbria 78
Abacus Books, Greater Manchester 118
Abacus Gallery, Staffordshire 220
Abrahams (Mike), Staffordshire 219
Aitchison (Lesley), Bristol 58

SPECIALITY INDEX

Alec–Smith Books (Alex), East Yorkshire 107
Altea Antique Maps & Books, London W 169
Ambra Books, Bristol 58
Andrews Books & Collectables, Derbyshire 82
Andron (G.W.), London N 155
Anthony Whittaker, Kent 136
Antiquary Ltd., (Bar Bookstore),
  North Yorkshire................................... 192
Antique & Book Shop, Powys.................... 286
Arden Books & Cosmographia, Warwickshire . 232
Atholl Fine Books, Tayside 275
Axe Rare & Out of Print Books (Richard),
  North Yorkshire................................... 190
Baker - Books for the Collector (Colin), Devon 88
Barbican Bookshop, North Yorkshire 194
Barmby (C. & A.J.), Kent.......................... 140
Barn Books, Shropshire............................ 211
Barnes (Peter), Wiltshire 248
Bath Old Books, Somerset 212
Bear Island Books, Cardiff........................ 276
Benny Gillies Books Ltd, Dumfries &
  Galloway.. 263
Beware of the Leopard, Bristol................... 58
Birchden Books, London E 153
Bird (Tony), Powys 286
Black Cat Bookshop, Leicestershire 145
Bonython Bookshop, Cornwall.................... 75
Book For All Reasons (A.), Suffolk.............. 224
Book Gallery (The), Cornwall 75
Bookbox, Gloucestershire 116
Bookcase, Cumbria 76
Bookends of Fowey, Cornwall 73
Books & Collectables Ltd., Cambridgeshire 63
Books Afloat, Dorset............................... 94
Books Bought & Sold, Surrey 226
Books on the Bank, Durham 96
Books Only, Suffolk 222
BOOKS4U, Flintshire 279
Bookshop (The), Co. Donegal..................... 258
Bookshop on the Heath, The, London SE...... 161
Bookworms of Evesham, Worcestershire........ 252
Border Books, Borders............................. 262
Bowdon Books, Lancashire 143
Brewin Books Ltd., Warwickshire 233
Bridge Books, Cumbria 80
Bridge of Allan Books, Central 263
Burden Ltd., (Clive A.), Hertfordshire 132
Bury Bookshop, Suffolk 221
Capes (Books, Maps & Prints) (John L.),
  North Yorkshire................................... 193
Carlton Books, Norfolk 187
Carnforth Bookshop (The), Lancashire.......... 142
Cassidy (Bookseller) (P.), Lincolnshire 149
Castle Bookshop, Essex............................ 109
Castle Hill Books, Herefordshire 128
Castleton (Pat), Kent 137
Cavern Books, Cheshire 70
Chandos Books, Devon............................ 84
Channel Islands Galleries Limited,
  Channel Islands................................... 253
Chapman (Neville), Cornwall..................... 74
Chapter & Verse, Lincolnshire 150

Chaucer Bookshop, Kent.......................... 136
Chaucer Head Bookshop, Warwickshire 233
Cheshire Book Centre, Cheshire 69
Chevin Books, West Yorkshire.................... 245
Chichester Bookshop (The), West Sussex 237
Church Green Books, Oxfordshire 207
Clarke (J.&D), Norfolk 187
Clarke Books (David), Somerset 214
Classic Bindings Ltd, London SW................ 164
Classic Crime Collections, Greater Manchester 119
Clent Books, Worcestershire 250
Coach House Books, Worcestershire............. 251
Cobbles Books, Somerset.......................... 214
Cobnar Books, Kent 139
Cofion Books, Pembrokeshire 281
Collectors Corner, Wiltshire....................... 248
Compass Books, Devon 84
Coombes (A.J.), Surrey 226
Copnal Books, Cheshire 68
Corder (Mark W.), Kent 140
Cornucopia Books, Lincolnshire 151
Courtwood Books, Co. Laois...................... 260
Cousens (W.C.), Devon............................ 83
Cox Old & Rare Books (Claude), Suffolk....... 223
Curtle Mead Books, Isle of Wight 134
D'Arcy Books, Wiltshire........................... 246
Dales & Lakes Book Centre, Cumbria 79
Dandy Lion Editions, Surrey 228
Dartmoor Bookshop (The), Devon 83
Davidson Books, Co. Down....................... 256
Debbage (John), Norfolk 187
Delph Books, Greater Manchester................ 120
Dene Barn Books & Prints, Somerset............ 216
Dobson (Bob), Lancashire 142
Eastgate Bookshop, East Yorkshire 105
Ellwood Editions, Wiltshire 247
Elmfield Books, West Midlands 234
English (Toby), Oxfordshire 206
Everett (Richard), Norfolk 184
Everett (Richard, at the Southwold Antiques
  Centre, Suffolk.................................... 225
Ewell Bookshop, Surrey 227
Exeter Rare Books, Devon........................ 84
Farquharson, (Hilary), Tayside.................... 275
Ferdinando (Steven), Somerset 215
Fine Art, London SE............................... 165
Fireside Books, Buckinghamshire 62
Ford Books (David), Hertfordshire............... 132
Freader's Books, Tayside 275
Furneaux Books (Lee), Devon 88
G Collins Bookdealers, Hertfordshire 131
G. C. Books Ltd., Dumfries & Galloway 264
Garretts Antiquarian Books, Isle of Man 254
GfB: the Colchester Bookshop, Essex............ 109
Gibbard (A. & T.), East Sussex 100
Gilbert and Son (H.M.), Hampshire 127
Gildas Books, Cheshire 68
Gillmark Gallery, Hertfordshire................... 131
Glenwood Books, Surrey 230
Godmanchester Books, Cambridgeshire 65
Good for Books, Lincolnshire 149
Greta Books, Durham 96

SPECIALITY INDEX

Grove Bookshop (The), North Yorkshire....... 193
Hames (Peter), Devon............................. 83
Harlequin Books, Bristol 59
Helmsley Antiquarian & Secondhand Books,
  North Yorkshire.................................. 191
Helston Bookworm (The), Cornwall 73
Hennessey Bookseller (Ray), East Sussex 99
Heritage, West Midlands 234
High Street Books, Devon 85
Hill Books (Alan), South Yorkshire.............. 217
Hollett and Son (R.F.G.), Cumbria 79
Holmes Books (Harry), East Yorkshire 106
Hornsey's, North Yorkshire....................... 192
Horsham Rare Books, West Sussex 238
Howes Bookshop, East Sussex 101
Hutchison (Books) (Larry), Fife.................. 265
Idle Booksellers (The), West Yorkshire 241
Idle Genius Books, London N 156
Intech Books, Northumberland 198
Invicta Bookshop, Berkshire...................... 56
Iona Bookshop (The), Isle of Iona 269
J C Books, Devon 86
J. & J. Books, Lincolnshire 149
Jackdaw Books, Norfolk 185
Jane Jones Books, Grampian..................... 267
Janus Books, West Midlands 235
Jermy & Westerman, Nottinghamshire 201
John Barton, Hampshire.......................... 127
Junk & Spread Eagle, London SE................ 162
Just Books, Cornwall.............................. 75
Keeble Antiques, Somerset 215
Keegan's Bookshop, Berkshire 56
Kellow Books, Oxfordshire 203
Kelsall (George), Greater Manchester............ 119
Kemp Booksellers, East Yorkshire 106
Kernaghans, Merseyside 183
Kerr (Norman), Cumbria.......................... 77
Key Books (Sarah), Cambridgeshire 64
Killeen (John), North Yorkshire 191
Kim's Bookshop, West Sussex............... 237, 240
Kirkland Books, Cumbria......................... 78
Lake (David), Norfolk 187
Lawrence Books, Nottinghamshire 200
Leakey's Bookshop, Highland 268
Leigh Gallery Books, Essex 110
Letterbox Books, Nottinghamshire 200
Little Bookshop (The), Cumbria 80
Lymelight Books & Prints, Dorset................ 92
M. & D. Books, Worcestershire................... 250
Mair Wilkes Books, Fife.......................... 265
Malvern Bookshop (The), Worcestershire....... 250
Marcan, Bookseller (Peter), London SE......... 162
Marrin's Bookshop, Kent 138
McCrone (Audrey), Isle of Arran................. 269
Meads Book Service (The), East Sussex 103
Missing Books, Essex.............................. 109
Modlock (Lilian), Dorset 92
Mogul Diamonds, West Midlands................ 236
Moon's Bookshop (Michael), Cumbria 80
Moore (C.R.), Shropshire 210
Moorhead Books, West Yorkshire 241
Moreton Books, Devon............................ 86

Mount's Bay Books, Cornwall 74
Mulyan (Don), Merseyside........................ 183
Mundy (David), Hertfordshire 130
Naughton Booksellers, Co. Dublin 259
Newlyn & New Street Books, Cornwall 74
Niner (Marcus), Gloucestershire 116
Oakwood Books, Gloucestershire................. 115
Old Bookshop (The), West Midlands 236
Old Hall Bookshop (The), Northamptonshire.. 196
Old Town Bookshop (The), Lothian 271
Orb's Bookshop, Grampian....................... 268
Ouse Valley Books, Bedfordshire 54
Over-Sands Books, Cumbria...................... 77
Oxley (Laurence), Hampshire..................... 122
Park Gallery & Bookshop (The),
  Northamptonshire................................ 197
Past & Present Books, Gloucestershire........... 114
Peakirk Books, Cambridgeshire 67
Pendleside Books, Lancashire 143
Periwinkle Press, Kent 139
Poor Richard's Books, Suffolk 222
Postings, Surrey 228
Quarto Bookshop (The), Fife..................... 266
Randall (Tom), Somerset 215
Rare & Racy, South Yorkshire.................... 217
Rare Books & Berry, Somerset 215
Reads, Dorset...................................... 94
recollectionsbookshop.co.uk, Cornwall 74
Restormel Books, Worcestershire 252
Richard Thornton Books, London N............ 157
Richmond Books, North Yorkshire............... 192
Roadmaster Books, Kent.......................... 137
Robin Doughty - Fine Books, West Midlands . 234
Rochdale Book Company, Greater Manchester 120
Roger Collicott Books, Cornwall 74
Rowan (H. & S.J.), Dorset....................... 90
Rutland Bookshop (The), Rutland 208
Saint Paul's Street Bookshop, Lincolnshire 152
Salway Books, Essex 112
Scarthin Books, Derbyshire 81
Second Edition, Lothian 272
Sedgeberrow Books & Framing, Worcestershire 251
Segal Books (Joel), Devon 84
Skyrack Books, West Yorkshire 243
Sleepy Elephant Books & Artefacts, Cumbria.. 79
Smith (Clive), Essex............................... 109
Smith Books (Keith), Herefordshire.............. 128
Sparrow Books, West Yorkshire 241
Spooner & Co, Somerset 215
Staffs Bookshop (The), Staffordshire 219
Staniland (Booksellers), Lincolnshire 152
Stella Books, Monmouthshire 281
Stinton (Judith), Dorset 91
Stothert Old Books, Cheshire 68
Suffolk Rare Books, Suffolk 225
Summerfield Books Ltd, Cumbria 76
Taylor & Son (Peter), Hertfordshire.............. 132
Temperley (David), West Midlands 234
Thomas (E. Wyn), Conwy 278
Tiffin (Tony and Gill), Durham.................. 96
Tombland Bookshop, Norfolk 188
Townsend (John), Berkshire 57

SPECIALITY INDEX

Trafalgar Bookshop, East Sussex 99
Treasure Chest Books, Suffolk 222
Treasure Trove Books, Leicestershire 146
Tucker (Alan & Joan), Gloucestershire 116
Turton (John), Durham............................ 97
Unsworths Booksellers, London NW 160
Ventnor Rare Books, Isle of Wight 135
Vickers (Anthony), North Yorkshire............. 193
Vinovium Books, Durham 96
Wadard Books, Kent.............................. 137
Wealden Books, Kent 139
Wembdon Books, Somerset...................... 213
Whitchurch Books Ltd., Cardiff 276
Williams (Christopher), Dorset................... 93
Wilson (David), Buckinghamshire 61
Words Etcetera Bookshop, Dorset 92
Wychwood Books, Gloucestershire 116
Yates Antiquarian Books (Tony), Leicestershire 146
Yewtree Books, Cumbria......................... 77
Ystwyth Books, Ceredigion 277

TOPOLOGY

Trinity Rare Books, Co. Leitrim.................. 260
Vickers (Anthony), North Yorkshire............. 193

TOWN PLANNING

Bookroom (The), Surrey.......................... 229
Duck (William), Hampshire...................... 124
Inch's Books, North Yorkshire................... 192
Reads, Dorset..................................... 94
Sun House Books, Kent 139
Vickers (Anthony), North Yorkshire............. 193

TOWN PLANS

Burden Ltd., (Clive A.), Hertfordshire........... 132

TOYS

Addyman Books, Powys.......................... 282
Adrem Books, Hertfordshire..................... 131
Barmby (C. & A.J.), Kent........................ 140
Bianco Library, West Sussex..................... 237
Bookmark (Children's Books), Wiltshire 248
Saint Swithin's Illustrated & Children's Books, London W..................................... 172
Twigg (Keith), Staffordshire...................... 219
Whittle, Bookseller (Avril), Cumbria 79

TRACTION ENGINES

Autobooks Ltd., East Sussex 100
Bott, (Bookdealers) Ltd., (Martin), Greater Manchester 118
Cottage Books, Leicestershire.................... 145
Cox (Geoff), Devon 89
Dales and Lakes Book Centre, Cumbria 79
Falconwood Transport & Military Bookshop, London Outer 181
Jones (Barry), West Sussex 238
Kerr (Norman), Cumbria......................... 77
Muttonchop Manuscripts......................... 239
N1 Books, East Sussex............................ 103

Randall (Tom), Somerset......................... 215
Roadmaster Books, Kent......................... 137
Roberts (Booksellers), (Ray), Staffordshire...... 219
Salway Books, Essex 112
Simon Lewis Transport Books, Gloucestershire 115
Vintage Motorshop, West Yorkshire............. 241

TRADE CATALOGUES

Black Cat Books, Norfolk........................ 185
Don Kelly Books, London W 170
G. C. Books Ltd., Dumfries & Galloway 264
Reeves Technical Books, North Yorkshire...... 193

TRADE UNIONS

Adrem Books, Hertfordshire..................... 131
Byrom Textile Bookroom (Richard), Lancashire 142
Clifton Books, Essex 111
Delectus Books, London WC.................... 174
Left on The Shelf, Cumbria...................... 78
Northern Herald Books, West Yorkshire 241
Reading Lasses, Dumfries & Galloway 265
Red Star Books, Hertfordshire 130
Spurrier (Nick), Kent............................. 138
Symes Books (Naomi), Cheshire 71
Woburn Books, London N 157

TRADES & PROFESSIONS

Adrem Books, Hertfordshire..................... 131
N1 Books, East Sussex............................ 103

TRADITIONAL CHINESE MEDICINE

Orchid Book Distributors, Co. Clare............ 257

TRADITIONS

Gildas Books, Cheshire 68
Philip Hopper, Essex 110

TRANSPORT

Addyman Books, Powys.......................... 282
Adrem Books, Hertfordshire..................... 131
Allinson (Frank & Stella), Warwickshire 232
Anvil Books, West Midlands 235
Archer (David), Powys........................... 285
Arden Books & Cosmographia, Warwickshire . 232
Aurora Books Ltd, Lothian....................... 270
Autobooks Ltd., East Sussex 100
Autumn Leaves, Lincolnshire.................... 150
Baldwin (M. & M.), Shropshire 250
Barbican Bookshop, North Yorkshire 194
Bianco Library, West Sussex..................... 237
Bird Books (Nigel), Ceredigion................... 277
Black Five Books, Shropshire 211
Book House (The), Cumbria 78
Bookcase, Cumbria 76
Books, Denbighshire.............................. 278
Books & Bygones (Pam Taylor), West Midlands.................................. 236
Books Afloat, Dorset.............................. 94

SPECIALITY INDEX

Bookworms of Evesham, Worcestershire 252
Border Books, Borders 262
Bosco Books, Cornwall 72
Bott, (Bookdealers) Ltd., (Martin), Greater Manchester 118
Brewin Books Ltd., Warwickshire 233
Browning Books, Torfaen 287
Browse Books, Lancashire 143
Castle Bookshop, Essex 109
Cavern Books, Cheshire 70
Chaucer Bookshop, Kent 136
Cheshire Book Centre, Cheshire 69
Chevin Books, West Yorkshire 245
Classic Crime Collections, Greater Manchester 119
Clements (R.W.), London Outer 179
Clevedon Books, Somerset 214
Clifton Books, Essex 111
Cobweb Books, North Yorkshire 192
Collectables (W.H.), Suffolk 225
Collectors Carbooks, Northamptonshire 196
Collectors Corner, Wiltshire 248
Cornucopia Books, Lincolnshire 151
Coulthurst (Richard), Greater Manchester 120
Dales & Lakes Book Centre, Cumbria 79
Dandy Lion Editions, Surrey 228
Dinnages Transport Publishing, East Sussex.... 98
Duck (William), Hampshire 124
Elton Engineering Books, London W 170
Ewell Bookshop, Surrey 227
Falconwood Transport & Military Bookshop, London Outer 181
Fireside Bookshop, Cumbria 80
Hay Castle, Powys 283
Humm & Co. (Robert), Lincolnshire 151
J C Books, Devon 86
Jade Mountain, Hampshire 125
Jones (Barry), West Sussex 238
Kelsall (George), Greater Manchester 119
Kerr (Norman), Cumbria 77
Kim's Bookshop, West Sussex 237, 240
Kirkland Books, Cumbria 78
Knowles (John), Norfolk 185
Malvern Bookshop (The), Worcestershire 250
Marine & Cannon Books, Cheshire 71
Marine and Cannon Books, Cheshire 69
McGlynn (John), Lancashire 142
Milestone Books, Devon 88
My Back Pages, London SW 167
Muttonchop Manuscripts 239
Newband (D.M.), Powys 286
Paton Books, Hertfordshire 132
Periwinkle Press, Kent 139
Peter White, Hampshire 122
Pooks Motor Books, Leicestershire 146
Postings, Surrey 228
Prior (Michael), Lincolnshire 151
Railway Shop (The), Torfaen 287
Randall (Tom), Somerset 215
Richard Thornton Books, London N 157
Roadmaster Books, Kent 137
Rochdale Book Company, Greater Manchester 120
Rods Books, Devon 87

Roland Books, Kent 139
Rolling Stock Books, Greater Manchester 121
Segal Books (Joel), Devon 84
Signature Books, Hampshire 126
Simon Lewis Transport Books, Gloucestershire 115
Stothert Old Books, Cheshire 68
Suffolk Rare Books, Suffolk 225
The Glass Key, West Yorkshire 242
Tony Pollastrone Railway Books, Wiltshire 246
Treasure Chest Books, Suffolk 222
Vailima Books, Dumfries & Galloway 264
Ventnor Rare Books, Isle of Wight 135
Vintage Motorshop, West Yorkshire 241
Weiner (Graham), London N 157
Westwood Books Ltd, Cumbria 79

TRAVEL
- GENERAL

Abacus Gallery, Staffordshire 220
Addyman Books, Powys 282
Adrem Books, Hertfordshire 131
Allsworth Rare Books Ltd., London 164
Altea Antique Maps & Books, London W 169
Andron (G.W.), London N 155
Ann & Mike Conry, Worcestershire 251
Anne Harris Books & Bags Booksearch, Devon.. 86
Antique Map and Bookshop (The), Dorset 93
Antiques on High, Oxfordshire 204
Arden Books & Cosmographia, Warwickshire . 232
Askew Books (Vernon), Wiltshire 246
Aurora Books Ltd, Lothian 270
Autolycus, Shropshire 209
Autumn Leaves, Lincolnshire 150
Aviabooks, Gloucestershire 114
B D McManmon, Lancashire 144
Baedekers & Murray Guides, South Yorkshire 217
Barnhill Books, Isle of Arran 269
Baynton–Williams Gallery, West Sussex 237
Beardsley (A.E.), Nottinghamshire 201
Bianco Library, West Sussex 237
Biblion, London W 169
Billing (Brian), Berkshire 57
Black Five Books, Shropshire 211
Blackwell's Rare Books, Oxfordshire 205
Bonham (J. & S.L.), London W 169
Book Business (The), London W 169
Book Shelf (The), Devon 86
Bookcase, Cumbria 76
Books & Collectables Ltd., Cambridgeshire 63
Books Afloat, Dorset 94
books2books, Devon 87
Bookshop (The), Dorset 92
Bookshop (The), Co. Donegal 258
Bookshop at the Plain, Lincolnshire 151
Bookworld, Shropshire 210
Bookworms of Evesham, Worcestershire 252
Booth Books, Powys 282
Border Books, Borders 262
Bowden Books, Leicestershire 147
Bracton Books, Cambridgeshire 63
Broadhurst of Southport Ltd., Merseyside 182

SPECIALITY INDEX

Broadwater Books, Hampshire 126
Broadway Books, Cambridgeshire 66
Brockwells Booksellers, Lincolnshire 148
Burden Ltd., (Clive A.), Hertfordshire 132
Byre Books, Dumfries & Galloway 264
Campbell (Fiona), London SE 161
Carnforth Bookshop (The), Lancashire 142
Carningli Centre, Pembrokeshire 281
Castleton (Pat), Kent 137
Chalmers Hallam (E.), Hampshire 125
Chandos Books, Devon 84
Chaucer Bookshop, Kent 136
Cheshire Book Centre, Cheshire 69
Church Street Books, Norfolk 184
Clegg (David), Staffordshire 219
Clements (R.W.), London Outer 179
Clevedon Books, Somerset 214
Collectable Books, London SE 162
Collectables (W.H.), Suffolk 225
Corvus Books, Buckinghamshire 61
Cox Old & Rare Books (Claude), Suffolk 223
Craobh Rua Books, Co. Armagh 255
Cumming Limited (A. & Y.), East Sussex 102
D'Arcy Books, Wiltshire 246
D.C. Books, Lincolnshire 150
Dartmoor Bookshop (The), Devon 83
David (G.), Cambridgeshire 63
David Warnes Books, Herefordshire 129
Davies Fine Books, Worcestershire 252
Demetzy Books, Oxfordshire 203
Driffield Bookshop (The), East Yorkshire 105
Dusty Old Books Ltd., Oxfordshire 204
Dworski Books, Travel & Language Bookshop
 (Marijana), Herefordshire 283
Eastern Traveller (The), Somerset 216
Edwards in Hay–on–Wye (Francis),
 Herefordshire 283
Elstree Books, Hertfordshire 131
Ely Books, Cambridgeshire 65
Empire Books, North Yorkshire 194
Esoteric Dreams Bookshop, Cumbria 77
Farahar & Dupre (Clive & Sophie), Wiltshire .. 246
Ferdinando (Steven), Somerset 215
Fireside Books, Buckinghamshire 62
Firth (Bijou Books & Photography) (Maureen),
 South Yorkshire 218
Ford Books (David), Hertfordshire 132
Fosters Bookshop, London W 170
Frew Limited (Robert), London W 170
Frost (Richard), Hertfordshire 130
Furneaux Books (Lee), Devon 88
Garfi Books, Ceredigion 282
Gibbard (A. & T.), East Sussex 100
Glacier Books, Tayside 275
Gloucester Road Bookshop, London SW 165
Goodyer (Nicholas), London N 156
Grahame Thornton, Bookseller, Dorset 92
Hall's Bookshop, Kent 141
Harrington (Adrian), London W 171
Harrington Antiquarian Bookseller (Peter),
 London SW 166
Hay Cinema Bookshop Ltd., Herefordshire 283

Heartland Old Books, Devon 88
Hereward Books, Cambridgeshire 65
High Street Books, Devon 85
Hill (Peter), Hampshire 123
Hodgson (Books) (Richard J.),
 North Yorkshire 194
Hollett and Son (R.F.G.), Cumbria 79
Holmes (A.), Nottinghamshire 201
Howes Bookshop, East Sussex 101
Hurst (Jenny), Kent 138
Internet Bookshop UK Ltd., Gloucestershire .. 113
Jackson (M.W.), Wiltshire 249
Jade Mountain, Hampshire 125
Jiri Books, Co. Antrim 255
Junk & Spread Eagle, London SE 162
Kalligraphia (formerly Charmouth Bounty
 Books), Isle of Wight 134
Kay Books, London W 171
Keeble Antiques, Somerset 215
Kenny's Bookshops and Art Galleries Ltd, Co.
 Galway 260
Kernaghans, Merseyside 183
Killeen (John), North Yorkshire 191
Kingswood Books, Dorset 93
Knapton Bookbarn, North Yorkshire 194
Larkham Books (Patricia), Gloucestershire 117
Leabeck Books, Oxfordshire 205
Lewis (J.T. & P.), Cornwall 73
Libra Books, Lincolnshire 148
Lighthouse Books (The), Dorset 91
Little Bookshop (The), Greater Manchester 119
Lloyd-Davies (Sue), Carmarthenshire 277
Lucas (Richard), London NW 159
Lymelight Books & Prints, Dorset 92
Maggs Brothers Limited, London W 171
Malvern Bookshop (The), Worcestershire 250
Marble Hill Books, Middlesex 181
Marcet Books, London SE 161
Marco Polo Travel & Adventure Books, Dorset 91
Marshall Rare Books (Bruce), Gloucestershire .. 113
Martin Bookshop & Gallery (Richard),
 Hampshire 123
McCarty, Bookseller (M.E.), Western Isles 269
McCarty, Bookseller (M.E.), Dumfries &
 Galloway 264
Miles Apart, Suffolk 224
Modlock (Lilian), Dorset 92
Moreton Books, Devon 86
Morgan (H.J.), Bedfordshire 54
Morten (Booksellers) (E.J.),
 Greater Manchester 119
Mundy (David), Buckinghamshire 61
Murphy (C.J.), Norfolk 187
Muse Bookshop (The), Gwynedd 279
My Back Pages, London SW 167
Naughton Booksellers, Co. Dublin 259
Neil Summersgill, Lancashire 142
Nicolas - Antiquarian Booksellers & Art
 Dealers, London N 156
Niner (Marcus), Gloucestershire 116
Old Hall Bookshop (The), Northamptonshire .. 196
Oopalba Books, Cheshire 71

Orangeberry Books, Oxfordshire 204
Oxfam Books and Music, Hampshire 127
Page (David), Lothian 271
Parrott Books, Oxfordshire 207
Paton Books, Hertfordshire 132
Peregrine Books (Leeds), West Yorkshire 244
Petersfield Bookshop (The), Hampshire 125
Pordes Books Ltd., (Henry), London WC 176
Portobello Books, London W 172
Portus Books, Hampshire 123
Prescott - The Bookseller (John),
  London Outer 181
Preston Book Company, Lancashire 144
Price (R.W.), Nottinghamshire 200
Prospect House Books, Co. Down 256
Quaritch Ltd., (Bernard), London W 172
Quest Books, East Yorkshire 106
Quinto of Charing Cross Road, London WC.. 176
Reading Lasses, Dumfries & Galloway 265
Richard Thornton Books, London N 157
Richmond Books, North Yorkshire 192
Roberts (Booksellers), (Ray), Staffordshire...... 219
Rochdale Book Company, Greater Manchester 120
Roland Books, Kent 139
Roundstone Books, Lancashire 143
Rowan (P. & B.), Co. Antrim 255
Roz Hulse, Conwy 278
Russell (Charles), London SW 167
Saintfield Antiques & Fine Books, Co. Down.. 255
Samovar Books, Co. Dublin 258
Second Edition, Lothian 272
Shapero Rare Books (Bernard J.), London W . 172
Signature Books, Hampshire 126
Simply Read Books, East Sussex 99
Singleton (Anthony), South Yorkshire 217
Smith (Clive), Essex 109
Smith Books, (Sally), Suffolk 222
Sokol Books Ltd., London W 172
Sotheran Limited (Henry), London W 172
Spearman Books, East Sussex 103
Sterling Books, Somerset 216
Stothert Old Books, Cheshire 68
Stroma Books, Borders 262
Sturford Books, Wiltshire 248
Sue Lowell Natural History Books, London W 173
Sykes (Graham), West Yorkshire 244
Temperley (David), West Midlands 234
Temple (Robert), London N 157
The Glass Key, West Yorkshire 242
Thorntons of Oxford Ltd., Oxfordshire 203
Till's Bookshop, Lothian 272
Tilston (Stephen E.), London SE 161
Travel Bookshop (The), London W 173
Treasure Island (The), Greater Manchester 120
Treasure Trove Books, Leicestershire 146
Valentine Rare Books, Surrey 227
Vokes Books Ltd., North Yorkshire 192
Wembdon Books, Somerset 213
Westwood Books Ltd, Cumbria 79
Words Etcetera Bookshop, Dorset 92
Worlds End Bookshop, London SW 168
Yesterday's Books, Dorset 91

Yesterday's News, Conwy 278
Yewtree Books, Cumbria 77

- AFRICA

Ayre (Peter J.), Somerset 216
Bonham (J. & S.L.), London W 169
Bow Windows Book Shop, East Sussex 102
Butcher (Pablo), Oxfordshire 203
Campbell Hewson Books (R.), Fife 265
Chalmers Hallam (E.), Hampshire 125
Chandos Books, Devon 84
Daly (Peter M.), Hampshire 127
Dartmoor Bookshop (The), Devon 83
Deyong Books (J.C.), London SW 164
Eastern Traveller (The), Somerset 216
Edmund Pollinger Rare Books, London SW... 165
Empire Books, North Yorkshire 194
Farahar & Dupre (Clive & Sophie), Wiltshire.. 246
Fine Books at Ilkley, West Yorkshire 243
G. Bickford-Smith (formerly Snowden Smith
  Books), Surrey 228
Glacier Books, Tayside 275
Grayling (David A.H.), Cumbria 78
Hall, (Anthony C.) Antiquarian Bookseller,
  London Outer 181
Hosains Books, London NW 159
Joppa Books Ltd., Surrey 226
Kenya Books, East Sussex 99
Maghreb Bookshop (The), London WC 175
Michael Graves-Johnston, London SW 166
Oriental and African Books, Shropshire 210
Page (David), Lothian 271
Remington (Reg & Philip), Hertfordshire 132
Samovar Books, Co. Dublin 258
Shapero Rare Books (Bernard J.), London W . 172
Smith (Ray), Hertfordshire 130
Vandeleur Antiquarian Books, Surrey 227
Woolcott Books, Dorset 91
Yesterday's Books, Dorset 91

- AMERICAS

Americanabooksuk, Cumbria 76
Bonham (J. & S.L.), London W 169
Books on Spain, London Outer 181
Burden Ltd., (Clive A.), Hertfordshire 132
Butcher (Pablo), Oxfordshire 203
Chalmers Hallam (E.), Hampshire 125
Dartmoor Bookshop (The), Devon 83
Empire Books, North Yorkshire 194
Farahar & Dupre (Clive & Sophie), Wiltshire.. 246
Fine Books at Ilkley, West Yorkshire 243
Glacier Books, Tayside 275
Grayling (David A.H.), Cumbria 78
Leapman Ltd. (G. & R.), Hertfordshire 132
Orssich (Paul), London SW 167
Pinnacle Books, Lothian 271
Remington (Reg & Philip), Hertfordshire 132
Shapero Rare Books (Bernard J.), London W . 172
Vandeleur Antiquarian Books, Surrey 227

SPECIALITY INDEXE

- ASIA

Abington Bookshop, Suffolk....................... 222
Allsworth Rare Books Ltd., London.............. 164
Alpha Books, London N 155
Bates & Hindmarch, West Yorkshire 243
Bonham (J. & S.L.), London W 169
Bow Windows Book Shop, East Sussex 102
Chalmers Hallam (E.), Hampshire................. 125
Daly (Peter M.), Hampshire 127
Dartmoor Bookshop (The), Devon................ 83
David Warnes Books, Herefordshire 129
Deyong Books (J.C.), London SW 164
Dworski Books, Travel & Language Bookshop
  (Marijana), Herefordshire 283
Eastern Traveller (The), Somerset................. 216
Eastgate Bookshop, East Yorkshire 105
Empire Books, North Yorkshire 194
Farahar & Dupre (Clive & Sophie), Wiltshire.. 246
Fine Books Oriental Ltd., London WC 175
G. Bickford-Smith (formerly Snowden Smith
  Books), Surrey..................................... 228
Glacier Books, Tayside............................. 275
Grayling (David A.H.), Cumbria 78
Hall, (Anthony C.) Antiquarian Bookseller,
  London Outer 181
Hunter and Krageloh, Derbyshire 82
Joppa Books Ltd., Surrey 226
Moorside Books, Lancashire....................... 143
O'Reilly - Mountain Books (John), Derbyshire 82
Page (David), Lothian.............................. 271
Parrott (Jeremy), London E........................ 153
Pinnacle Books, Lothian........................... 271
Rayner (Hugh Ashley), Somerset 212
Remington (Reg & Philip), Hertfordshire 132
Shapero Rare Books (Bernard J.), London W . 172
Smith (Clive), Essex 109
Traveller's Bookshelf (The), Somerset............ 212
Vandeleur Antiquarian Books, Surrey 227
Woolcott Books, Dorset 91

- ASIA, SOUTH EAST

Butcher (Pablo), Oxfordshire 203
David Warnes Books, Herefordshire 129
Deyong Books (J.C.), London SW 164
Dworski Books, Travel & Language Bookshop
  (Marijana), Herefordshire 283
Fine Books at Ilkley, West Yorkshire............ 243
Leeper (Romilly), London SW 166
Mandalay Bookshop, London SW 166
Michael Graves-Johnston, London SW.......... 166

- AUSTRALASIA/AUSTRALIA

Bonham (J. & S.L.), London W 169
Burden Ltd., (Clive A.), Hertfordshire........... 132
Chalmers Hallam (E.), Hampshire................. 125
Dartmoor Bookshop (The), Devon................ 83
Deyong Books (J.C.), London SW 164
Empire Books, North Yorkshire 194
Farahar & Dupre (Clive & Sophie), Wiltshire.. 246
Michael Graves-Johnston, London SW.......... 166
Moore (Peter), Cambridgeshire.................... 64

Pinnacle Books, Lothian........................... 271
Remington (Reg & Philip), Hertfordshire 132
Shapero Rare Books (Bernard J.), London W . 172

- BALKANS

G. Bickford-Smith (formerly Snowden Smith
  Books), Surrey..................................... 228

- BURMA

Mandalay Bookshop, London SW 166
Pinnacle Books, Lothian........................... 271

- CHINA

Fine Books at Ilkley, West Yorkshire............ 243
Mandalay Bookshop, London SW 166

- EUROPE

Bonham (J. & S.L.), London W 169
Books on Spain, London Outer.................... 181
Campbell (Fiona), London SE 161
Daly (Peter M.), Hampshire 127
Dartmoor Bookshop (The), Devon................ 83
de Visser Books, Cambridgeshire 63
Dworski Books, Travel & Language Bookshop
  (Marijana), Herefordshire 283
Empire Books, North Yorkshire 194
Fine Books at Ilkley, West Yorkshire............ 243
Glacier Books, Tayside............................. 275
Hall, (Anthony C.) Antiquarian Bookseller,
  London Outer 181
Naughton Booksellers, Co. Dublin 259
Orssich (Paul), London SW....................... 167
Samovar Books, Co. Dublin....................... 258
Shapero Rare Books (Bernard J.), London W . 172
Undercover Books, Lincolnshire 152
Vandeleur Antiquarian Books, Surrey 227
York (Graham), Devon............................. 85

- FAR EAST

Fine Books at Ilkley, West Yorkshire............ 243

- GREECE

Hellenic Bookservices, London NW.............. 158

- INDIA

Butcher (Pablo), Oxfordshire 203
Fine Books at Ilkley, West Yorkshire............ 243
Glacier Books, Tayside............................. 275
Mandalay Bookshop, London SW 166
N1 Books, East Sussex............................. 103

- ISLAMIC WORLD

Butcher (Pablo), Oxfordshire 203
Clarke Books (David), Somerset 214
David Warnes Books, Herefordshire 129
Deyong Books (J.C.), London SW 164
Dworski Books, Travel & Language Bookshop
  (Marijana), Herefordshire 283

G. Bickford-Smith (formerly Snowden Smith
  Books), Surrey 228
Kingswood Books, Dorset 93

- JAPAN
Fine Books at Ilkley, West Yorkshire 243
Murphy (C.J.), Norfolk 187

- MEXICO
Fine Books at Ilkley, West Yorkshire 243

- MIDDLE EAST
Al Saqi Books, London W 169
Allsworth Rare Books Ltd., London 164
Bonham (J. & S.L.), London W 169
Chalmers Hallam (E.), Hampshire 125
Clarke Books (David), Somerset 214
Daly (Peter M.), Hampshire 127
Dartmoor Bookshop (The), Devon 83
David Warnes Books, Herefordshire 129
Deyong Books (J.C.), London SW 164
Eastern Traveller (The), Somerset 216
Empire Books, North Yorkshire 194
Farahar & Dupre (Clive & Sophie), Wiltshire .. 246
Fine Books at Ilkley, West Yorkshire 243
Fine Books Oriental Ltd., London WC 175
G. Bickford-Smith (formerly Snowden Smith
  Books), Surrey 228
Hall, (Anthony C.) Antiquarian Bookseller,
  London Outer 181
Joppa Books Ltd., Surrey 226
Maghreb Bookshop (The), London WC 175
Michael Graves-Johnston, London SW 166
Moorside Books, Lancashire 143
Oriental and African Books, Shropshire 210
P. and P. Books, Worcestershire 251
Page (David), Lothian 271
Pholiota Books, London WC 176
Quest Books, East Yorkshire 106
Remington (Reg & Philip), Hertfordshire 132
Shapero Rare Books (Bernard J.), London W . 172
Traveller's Bookshelf (The), Somerset 212
Trotter Books (John), London N 157
Valentine Rare Books, Surrey 227
Woolcott Books, Dorset 91
Worlds End Bookshop, London SW 168

- POLAR
Bluntisham Books, Cambridgeshire 63
Bonham (J. & S.L.), London W 169
Chalmers Hallam (E.), Hampshire 125
Daly (Peter M.), Hampshire 127
Dartmoor Bookshop (The), Devon 83
David Warnes Books, Herefordshire 129
Empire Books, North Yorkshire 194
Explorer Books, West Sussex 239
Farahar & Dupre (Clive & Sophie), Wiltshire .. 246
Fine Books at Ilkley, West Yorkshire 243
Glacier Books, Tayside 275
Holmes Books (Harry), East Yorkshire 106

Hunter and Krageloh, Derbyshire 82
Internet Bookshop UK Ltd., Gloucestershire .. 113
Miles Apart, Suffolk 224
O'Reilly - Mountain Books (John), Derbyshire 82
Page (David), Lothian 271
Pinnacle Books, Lothian 271
Remington (Reg & Philip), Hertfordshire 132
Shapero Rare Books (Bernard J.), London W . 172
Vandeleur Antiquarian Books, Surrey 227
Walcot (Patrick), West Midlands 235

- REGIONAL
Samovar Books, Co. Dublin 258

- THAILAND
Apocalypse, Surrey 228
Mandalay Bookshop, London SW 166

TRIALS
Clifford Elmer Books Ltd., Cheshire 68
Loretta Lay Books, London NW 159

TRIBAL
Bracton Books, Cambridgeshire 63
David Warnes Books, Herefordshire 129
Deyong Books (J.C.), London SW 164
G. Bickford-Smith (formerly Snowden Smith
  Books), Surrey 228
Michael Graves-Johnston, London SW 166
Popeley (Frank T.), Cambridgeshire 67
Traveller's Bookshelf (The), Somerset 212
Yesterday's Books, Dorset 91

TROTSKYISM
Reading Lasses, Dumfries & Galloway 265

TYPOGRAPHY
Andron (G.W.), London N 155
Batterham (David), London W 169
Bettridge (Gordon), Fife 265
BOOKS4U, Flintshire 279
Brinded (Scott), Kent 139
Canterbury Bookshop (The), Kent 136
Collinge & Clark, London WC 174
English (Toby), Oxfordshire 206
Forest Books, Nottinghamshire 201
Fox Books (J. & J.), Kent 140
Hanborough Books, Oxfordshire 205
Katnap Arts, Norfolk 187
Mills Rare Books (Adam), Cambridgeshire 64
Oopalba Books, Cheshire 71
Solitaire Books, Somerset 212
Taylor Rare Books (Michael), Norfolk 184
Wakeman Books (Frances), Nottinghamshire .. 201

U.F.O.S
Alpha Books, London N 155
Cavern Books, Cheshire 70
Dawlish Books, Devon 84

Dworski Books, Travel & Language Bookshop
(Marijana), Herefordshire 283
Facet Books, Dorset 90
Gildas Books, Cheshire 68
Greensleeves, Oxfordshire 202
Inner Bookshop (The), Oxfordshire 205
Occultique, Northamptonshire..................... 196
SETI Books, Staffordshire 220
Starlord Books, Greater Manchester 118
Wizard Books, Cambridgeshire.................... 67

U.S. PRESIDENTS
Shakeshaft (Dr. B.), Cheshire..................... 71

UMBRELLAS/PARASOLS
Adrem Books, Hertfordshire...................... 131

UNEXPLAINED, THE
Dawlish Books, Devon............................. 84
Esoteric Dreams Bookshop, Cumbria............ 77
Fantastic Literature, Essex 111
Gildas Books, Cheshire 68
Inner Bookshop (The), Oxfordshire 205
Occultique, Northamptonshire..................... 196
Old Celtic Bookshop (The), Devon............... 86
SETI Books, Staffordshire 220
Till's Bookshop, Lothian 272

UNIVERSITY HISTORIES
G. C. Books Ltd., Dumfries & Galloway 264

UNIVERSITY PRESS
Adrem Books, Hertfordshire...................... 131
Book Annex (The), Essex 110
G. C. Books Ltd., Dumfries & Galloway 264
Stalagluft Books, Tyne and Wear................. 231

UNIVERSITY TEXTS
Book Annex (The), Essex 110
Downie Fine Books Ltd., (Robert), Shropshire 211
G. C. Books Ltd., Dumfries & Galloway 264
Hurst (Jenny), Kent 138
Murphy (C.J.), Norfolk 187
Pomes Penyeach, Staffordshire 219
Scrivener's Books & Bookbinding, Derbyshire . 81
Stalagluft Books, Tyne and Wear................. 231
Warrington Book Loft (The), Cheshire 71

URBAN HISTORY
Inch's Books, North Yorkshire.................... 192
Reading Lasses, Dumfries & Galloway 265
Stern Antiquarian Bookseller (Jeffrey), North
Yorkshire 195
Sun House Books, Kent 139
Symes Books (Naomi), Cheshire 71

VATICAN AND PAPAL HISTORY, THE
Adrem Books, Hertfordshire...................... 131

Samovar Books, Co. Dublin....................... 258
Scrivener's Books & Bookbinding, Derbyshire . 81
Shapero Rare Books (Bernard J.), London W . 172
Taylor & Son (Peter), Hertfordshire.............. 132
Tuft (Patrick), London W 173

VETERINARY
Alba Books, Grampian 267
Dusty Old Books Ltd., Oxfordshire 204
Grahame Thornton, Bookseller, Dorset 92
Jane Jones Books, Grampian 267
Phenotype Books, Cumbria 78

VICTORIAN MULTI-DECKERS
Valentine Rare Books, London W 173

VICTORIANA
Art Reference Books, Hampshire 125
Bell (Peter), Strathclyde 270
Book Shelf (The), Devon 86
Bosco Books, Cornwall 72
Castleton (Pat), Kent 137
Cornucopia Books, Lincolnshire 151
de Beaumont (Robin), London SW 164
Don Kelly Books, London W 170
Goldman (Paul), Dorset 94
Kenny's Bookshops and Art Galleries Ltd,
Co. Galway 260
N1 Books, East Sussex............................. 103
Saint Swithin's Illustrated & Children's Books,
London W 172
Shacklock Books (David), Suffolk 222
Symes Books (Naomi), Cheshire 71
Yesterday's News, Conwy 278

VINTAGE CARS
Autobooks Ltd., East Sussex 100
Baldwin (M. & M.), Shropshire 250
Brewin Books Ltd., Warwickshire 233
Camilla's Bookshop, East Sussex 100
Collectors Carbooks, Northamptonshire 196
Cornucopia Books, Lincolnshire 151
Cox (Geoff), Devon 89
Falconwood Transport & Military Bookshop,
London Outer 181
Peake (Robin), Lincolnshire....................... 151
Pooks Motor Books, Leicestershire 146
Roadmaster Books, Kent........................... 137
Roberts (Booksellers), (Ray), Staffordshire...... 219
Simon Lewis Transport Books, Gloucestershire 115
Stour Bookshop, Dorset 92
Vintage Motorshop, West Yorkshire............. 241

VINTAGE PAPERBACKS
Black Cat Bookshop, Leicestershire 145
Castleton (Pat), Kent 137
Cowley, Bookdealer (K.W.), Somerset........... 214
Dancing Goat Bookshop (The), Norfolk........ 184
Eggeling Books (John), West Yorkshire 245
Esoteric Dreams Bookshop, Cumbria............ 77

Gildas Books, Cheshire 68
Heckmondwike Book Shop, West Yorkshire... 244
J. & J. Books, Lincolnshire 149
Katnap Arts, Norfolk 187
Murphy (C.J.), Norfolk 187
Onepoundpaperbacks, Cleveland.................. 96
Roscrea Bookshop, Co. Tipperary................ 261
Ruebotham (Kirk), Cheshire....................... 70
Scrivener's Books & Bookbinding, Derbyshire. 81
Trevorrow (Edwin), Hertfordshire 130
Yorkshire Relics, West Yorkshire................. 242

VITICULTURE
Lucas (Richard), London NW 159
Roberts Wine Books (John), Bristol.............. 60
Thorne (John), Essex 109

VOYAGES & DISCOVERY
Adrem Books, Hertfordshire....................... 131
Afar Books International, West Midlands 234
Allsworth Rare Books Ltd., London............. 164
Altea Antique Maps & Books, London W 169
Americanabooksuk, Cumbria...................... 76
Avedikian Rare Books, Somerset 213
Barn Books, Buckinghamshire..................... 61
Books on Spain, London Outer.................... 181
Brockwells Booksellers, Lincolnshire 148
Campbell Hewson Books (R.), Fife 265
Castleton (Pat), Kent............................... 137
Cavendish Rare Books Ltd, London N 155
Dartmoor Bookshop (The), Devon............... 83
Eastern Traveller (The), Somerset................. 216
Edwards (London) Limited (Francis),
  London WC.. 175
Edwards in Hay–on–Wye (Francis),
  Herefordshire 283
Explorer Books, West Sussex 239
Farahar & Dupre (Clive & Sophie), Wiltshire.. 246
Glacier Books, Tayside.............................. 275
Harrington (Adrian), London W 171
Harrington Antiquarian Bookseller (Peter),
  London SW 166
Holmes Books (Harry), East Yorkshire 106
Hosains Books, London NW...................... 159
Keel Row Books, Tyne and Wear 231
Lawson & Company (E.M.), Oxfordshire....... 203
Lee, Maritime Books (Gerald), East Sussex 104
Lewcock (John), Cambridgeshire 66
Marine and Cannon Books, Cheshire............ 69
N1 Books, East Sussex.............................. 103
O'Reilly - Mountain Books (John), Derbyshire 82
Orssich (Paul), London SW....................... 167
Prior (Michael), Lincolnshire 151
Quinto of Charing Cross Road, London WC.. 176
Quinto of Great Russell Street, London WC... 176
Remington (Reg & Philip), Hertfordshire 132
Rowan (P. & B.), Co. Antrim 255
Roz Hulse, Conwy 278
Saint Mary's Books & Prints, Lincolnshire 152
Saint Swithin's Illustrated & Children's Books,
  London W... 172

Shapero Rare Books (Bernard J.), London W . 172
Smith (Clive), Essex 109
Vandeleur Antiquarian Books, Surrey 227

WAR
- GENERAL
Adrem Books, Hertfordshire....................... 131
Albion Books, West Midlands..................... 234
Andron (G.W.), London N 155
Aurora Books Ltd, Lothian........................ 270
Barbican Bookshop, North Yorkshire 194
Barnes (Peter), Wiltshire 248
Beware of the Leopard, Bristol.................... 58
Bookcase, Cumbria 76
books2books, Devon 87
Bookworm, Lothian 270
Bookworm (The), Lothian 271
Bowland Bookfinders, Lancashire 142
Broadhurst of Southport Ltd., Merseyside...... 182
Bufo Books, Hampshire 125
Caliver Books, Essex 110
Cavern Books, Cheshire 70
Chelifer Books, Cumbria 80
Cofion Books, Pembrokeshire 281
Criterion Books, London Outer................... 180
Dally Books & Collectables, Powys 285
Daly (Peter M.), Hampshire 127
Dartmoor Bookshop (The), Devon.............. 83
Eastcote Bookshop (The), London Outer 178
Esoteric Dreams Bookshop, Cumbria............ 77
G. C. Books Ltd., Dumfries & Galloway 264
Good for Books, Lincolnshire..................... 149
Grahame Thornton, Bookseller, Dorset 92
Handsworth Books, Essex......................... 112
Harrington Antiquarian Bookseller (Peter),
  London SW 166
Harris (George J.), Co. Derry 255
Hay Cinema Bookshop Ltd., Herefordshire 283
Hurst (Jenny), Kent 138
Janus Books, West Midlands 235
Keel Row Books, Tyne and Wear 231
Kingfisher Book Service, Nottinghamshire...... 201
Lewis (J.T. & P.), Cornwall 73
Libra Books, Lincolnshire 148
Lost Books, Northamptonshire 197
Marine & Cannon Books, Cheshire 71
Marine and Cannon Books, Cheshire............ 69
McCrone (Audrey), Isle of Arran................. 269
Meekins Books (Paul), Warwickshire 233
MilitaryHistoryBooks.com, Kent 138
Murphy (C.J.), Norfolk............................. 187
N1 Books, East Sussex.............................. 103
Palladour Books, Hampshire 126
Poetry Bookshop (The), Powys................... 284
Priestpopple Books, Northumberland............ 198
Prior (Michael), Lincolnshire 151
Quinto of Charing Cross Road, London WC.. 176
Quinto of Great Russell Street, London WC... 176
Richard Thornton Books, London N............ 157
Rods Books, Devon 87
Roland Books, Kent................................ 139

SPECIALITY INDEX

Scrivener's Books & Bookbinding, Derbyshire ... 81
Shapero Rare Books (Bernard J.), London W . 172
Smith Books, (Sally), Suffolk 222
Spurrier (Nick), Kent................................. 138
Stevens (Joan), Cambridgeshire 65
Stothert Old Books, Cheshire....................... 68
Thin Read Line, Merseyside 182
Tiffin (Tony and Gill), Durham.................... 96
Treasure Trove Books, Leicestershire 146
Ward (R.F. & C.), Norfolk 185
Wiend Books, Lancashire 143
World War Books, Kent 141
Yeoman Books, Lothian............................. 272
Yesterday's News, Conwy 278
Zardoz Books, Wiltshire............................ 249

- AMERICAN CIVIL

Adrem Books, Hertfordshire....................... 131
Americanabooksuk, Cumbria....................... 76
Broadhurst of Southport Ltd., Merseyside...... 182
Helion & Company, West Midlands 235
Marble Hill Books, Middlesex..................... 181
Meekins Books (Paul), Warwickshire 233
Rods Books, Devon 87
Savery Books, East Sussex 99
Shakeshaft (Dr. B.), Cheshire...................... 71

- BOER, THE

Helion & Company, West Midlands 235
Kenya Books, East Sussex 99
Meekins Books (Paul), Warwickshire 233
N1 Books, East Sussex.............................. 103
Thin Read Line, Merseyside 182

- CIVIL

Clifford Elmer Books Ltd., Cheshire 68

- ENGLISH CIVIL WARS

Caliver Books, Essex 110
Helion & Company, West Midlands 235
John Underwood Antiquarian Books, Norfolk 186
Meekins Books (Paul), Warwickshire 233
N1 Books, East Sussex.............................. 103
Roger Collicott Books, Cornwall 74
Shakeshaft (Dr. B.), Cheshire...................... 71
Spenceley Books (David), West Yorkshire 244
Taylor & Son (Peter), Hertfordshire.............. 132

- NAPOLEONIC

Adrem Books, Hertfordshire....................... 131
Armchair Books, Lothian........................... 270
Books on Spain, London Outer.................... 181
Donovan Military Books (Tom), East Sussex .. 98
Dworski Books, Travel & Language Bookshop
  (Marijana), Herefordshire 283
Helion & Company, West Midlands 235
Lost Books, Northamptonshire 197
Meekins Books (Paul), Warwickshire 233
Miles Apart, Suffolk 224
N1 Books, East Sussex.............................. 103

Orssich (Paul), London SW 167
Prior (Michael), Lincolnshire 151
Thin Read Line, Merseyside 182

- SPANISH CIVIL WAR

Books on Spain, London Outer.................... 181
Helion & Company, West Midlands 235
Left on The Shelf, Cumbria......................... 78
Meekins Books (Paul), Warwickshire 233
Orssich (Paul), London SW 167
Red Star Books, Hertfordshire 130
York (Graham), Devon.............................. 85

- VIETNAM

Anglo-American Rare Books, Surrey 228
Helion & Company, West Midlands 235
Meekins Books (Paul), Warwickshire 233

- WORLD WAR I

Aardvark Books, Wiltshire......................... 249
Albion Books, West Midlands..................... 234
Anglo-American Rare Books, Surrey 228
Armchair Auctions, Hampshire 122
Avedikian Rare Books, Somerset 213
Aviabooks, Gloucestershire 114
Barbican Bookshop, North Yorkshire 194
Berry (L.J.), Kent 138
Burroughs (Andrew), Lincolnshire................ 151
Caliver Books, Essex 110
Churchill Book Specialist (The), London Outer 179
Dally Books & Collectables, Powys 285
Dormouse Bookshop (The), Norfolk............. 188
Garfi Books, Ceredigion 282
Gaullifmaufry Books, Hertfordshire.............. 131
Green Ltd. (G.L.), Hertfordshire.................. 132
Helion & Company, West Midlands 235
Heppa (Christopher), Essex 108
Joppa Books Ltd., Surrey 226
Lost Books, Northamptonshire 197
Meekins Books (Paul), Warwickshire 233
My Back Pages, London SW....................... 167
N1 Books, East Sussex.............................. 103
Palladour Books, Hampshire 126
Prior (Michael), Lincolnshire 151
Rods Books, Devon 87
Smith Books (Keith), Herefordshire.............. 128
Symes Books (Naomi), Cheshire 71
Thin Read Line, Merseyside 182
Tiffin (Tony and Gill), Durham.................... 96
Tilston (Stephen E.), London SE 161
Updike Rare Books (John), Lothian 272

- WORLD WAR II

Aardvark Books, Wiltshire......................... 249
Aviabooks, Gloucestershire 114
Baldwin (M. & M.), Shropshire................... 250
Barbican Bookshop, North Yorkshire 194
Berry (L.J.), Kent 138
Book For All Reasons (A.), Suffolk.............. 224
Burroughs (Andrew), Lincolnshire................ 151

Caliver Books, Essex 110
Chaucer Bookshop, Kent 136
Churchill Book Specialist (The), London Outer 179
Dally Books & Collectables, Powys 285
Donovan Military Books (Tom), East Sussex .. 98
Dormouse Bookshop (The), Norfolk 188
Garfi Books, Ceredigion 282
Gaullifmaufry Books, Hertfordshire 131
Green Ltd. (G.L.), Hertfordshire 132
Helion & Company, West Midlands 235
Lost Books, Northamptonshire 197
Mandalay Bookshop, London SW 166
Meekins Books (Paul), Warwickshire 233
My Back Pages, London SW 167
Palladour Books, Hampshire 126
Prior (Michael), Lincolnshire 151
Rods Books, Devon 87
Roland Books, Kent 139
Symes Books (Naomi), Cheshire 71
Thin Read Line, Merseyside 182
Tilston (Stephen E.), London SE 161
Updike Rare Books (John), Lothian 272
Wembdon Books, Somerset 213
World War II Books, Surrey 230

- WWII HOME FRONT UK (1939-45)
Marchpane, London WC 175

- ZULU
Thin Read Line, Merseyside 182

WARGAMES
Bardsley's Books, Suffolk 221
Barnes (Peter), Wiltshire 248
Bookworm (The), Lothian 271
Caliver Books, Essex 110
Chelifer Books, Cumbria 80
Helion & Company, West Midlands 235
Meekins Books (Paul), Warwickshire 233
MilitaryHistoryBooks.com, Kent 138

WATERCOLOURS
Don Kelly Books, London W 170

WEIRD & WONDERFUL
Adrem Books, Hertfordshire 131
Delectus Books, London WC 174
Gildas Books, Cheshire 68
Inner Bookshop (The), Oxfordshire 205
N1 Books, East Sussex 103
Starlord Books, Greater Manchester 118

WELSH INTEREST
Adrem Books, Hertfordshire 131
Bear Island Books, Cardiff 276
BOOKS4U, Flintshire 279
Browning Books, Torfaen 287
Cader Idris Books, Gwynedd 280
Carta Regis, Powys 286

Castle Bookshop, Powys 285
Chapter Two, London SE 161
Cheshire Book Centre, Cheshire 69
Coch-y-Bonddu Books, Powys 285
Cofion Books, Pembrokeshire 281
Colin Hancock, Ceredigion 277
Dally Books & Collectables, Powys 285
Dusty Books, Powys 285
Dworski Books, Travel & Language Bookshop
  (Marijana), Herefordshire 283
Gildas Books, Cheshire 68
Great Oak Bookshop (The), Powys 285
Kingshead Books, Wales 286
Libra Books, Lincolnshire 148
Lighthouse Books (The), Dorset 91
Lloyd-Davies (Sue), Carmarthenshire 277
Mollie's Loft, Swansea 287
Naughton Booksellers, Co. Dublin 259
Oopalba Books, Cheshire 71
Poetry Bookshop (The), Powys 284
PsychoBabel Books & Journals, Oxfordshire ... 202
Rhos Point Books, Conwy 278
Siop Lyfrau'r Hen Bost, Gwynedd 280
Siop y Morfa, Denbighshire 279
Stothert Old Books, Cheshire 68
Willmott Bookseller (Nicholas), Cardiff 276

WESTERN AMERICANA
Adrem Books, Hertfordshire 131
Americanabooksuk, Cumbria 76
Clifford Elmer Books Ltd., Cheshire 68

WHALING
Bluntisham Books, Cambridgeshire 63
Glacier Books, Tayside 275
Marine and Cannon Books, Cheshire 69
McLaren Books, Strathclyde 274
Prior (Michael), Lincolnshire 151

WHISKY
Edmund Pollinger Rare Books, London SW ... 165
Lucas (Richard), London NW 159
McEwan Fine Books, Grampian 266
Roberts Wine Books (John), Bristol 60
Thorne (John), Essex 109

WINDMILLS & WATERMILLS
Arnold (Roy), Suffolk 223
Cottage Books, Leicestershire 145
Island Books, Kent 136
Paramor (C.D.), Suffolk 224
Reads, Dorset 94
Vickers (Anthony), North Yorkshire 193

WINE
Apocalypse, Surrey 228
Clarke (Janet), Somerset 212
Collectable Books, London SE 162
Dusty Books, Powys 285
Gresham Books, Somerset 214

SPECIALITY INDEX

Lucas (Richard), London NW 159
Macbuiks, North Yorkshire........................ 190
Moorhead Books, West Yorkshire 241
Pholiota Books, London WC...................... 176
Roberts Wine Books (John), Bristol.............. 60
Thorne (John), Essex 109

WITCHCRAFT
Adrem Books, Hertfordshire...................... 131
Alpha Books, London N 155
Caduceus Books, Leicestershire 145
Chthonios Books, East Sussex.................... 101
Daly (Peter M.), Hampshire 127
Edmund Pollinger Rare Books, London SW... 165
Esoteric Dreams Bookshop, Cumbria............ 77
Gilbert (R.A.), Bristol............................. 59
Gildas Books, Cheshire 68
Inner Bookshop (The), Oxfordshire 205
Occultique, Northamptonshire..................... 196
Philip Hopper, Essex 110
SETI Books, Staffordshire......................... 220
Shapero Rare Books (Bernard J.), London W . 172
Starlord Books, Greater Manchester 118
Walker Fine Books (Steve), Dorset............... 91
Waxfactor, East Sussex 99
Wizard Books, Cambridgeshire.................... 67

WOMEN
Adrem Books, Hertfordshire...................... 131
Black Cat Books, Norfolk......................... 185
Book Annex (The), Essex 110
Books & Bygones (Pam Taylor),
 West Midlands..................................... 236
Chesters (G. & J.), Staffordshire 220
Crawford (Elizabeth), London EC................ 154
Drury Rare Books (John), Essex.................. 111
Dylans Bookstore, Glamorgan 286
Elaine Lonsdale Books, West Yorkshire......... 242
Fortune Green Books, London NW 158
Hobgoblin Books, Hampshire 125
Jarndyce Antiquarian Booksellers, London WC 175
Lane Books (Shirley), Isle of Wight 135
Northern Herald Books, West Yorkshire 241
Orssich (Paul), London SW 167
Pickering & Chatto, London W................... 172
Polmorla Books, Cornwall 75
Reading Lasses, Dumfries & Galloway........... 265
Schulz–Falster Rare Books (Susanne),
 London N 157
Scorpio Books, Suffolk............................. 221
Shapero Rare Books (Bernard J.), London W . 172
Spurrier (Nick), Kent.............................. 138
Stevens (Joan), Cambridgeshire 65
Stone, (G.& R.), Borders 262
Susan Taylor Books, West Yorkshire 243
Symes Books (Naomi), Cheshire 71
Willmott Bookseller (Nicholas), Cardiff 276
Woburn Books, London N 157

WOODLAND CRAFTS
Adrem Books, Hertfordshire...................... 131

WOODWORK
Adrem Books, Hertfordshire...................... 131
Arnold (Roy), Suffolk.............................. 223
Bookends of Fowey, Cornwall 73
Brown-Studies, Strathclyde........................ 273
Camilla's Bookshop, East Sussex 100
Cavern Books, Cheshire 70
Cheshire Book Centre, Cheshire 69
N1 Books, East Sussex............................. 103
Phillips of Hitchin (Antiques) Ltd.,
 Hertfordshire...................................... 131
Stobart Davies Limited, Carmarthwnshire 276
Trinders' Fine Tools, Suffolk 222
Upper–Room Books, Somerset.................... 214
Whittle, Bookseller (Avril), Cumbria............. 79

WORLD FAIRS & EXHIBITIONS
Don Kelly Books, London W 170

WRITING
Adrem Books, Hertfordshire...................... 131
Apocalypse, Surrey 228
Byre Books, Dumfries & Galloway............... 264
Cornucopia Books, Lincolnshire 151

YEARBOOKS
Adrem Books, Hertfordshire...................... 131

YOGA
Greensleeves, Oxfordshire 202
Inner Bookshop (The), Oxfordshire 205
Magis Books, Leicestershire....................... 147
Occultique, Northamptonshire..................... 196
Orchid Book Distributors, Co. Clare............. 257
Portobello Books, London W 172
Till's Bookshop, Lothian 272

YOUTH MOVEMENTS
Reading Lasses, Dumfries & Galloway 265

ZOOLOGY
Adrem Books, Hertfordshire...................... 131
Alba Books, Grampian 267
Arden, Bookseller (C.), Powys.................... 282
Baldwin's Scientific Books, Essex 112
Baron - Scientific Book Sales (P.J.), Somerset.. 213
Blest (Peter), Kent 139
Bracton Books, Cambridgeshire................... 63
Daly (Peter M.), Hampshire 127
Demar Books (Grant), Kent....................... 140
Grayling (David A.H.), Cumbria 78
Harrington Antiquarian Bookseller (Peter),
 London SW 166
Orb's Bookshop, Grampian........................ 268
Parkinsons Books, Merseyside.................... 183

Pemberley Books, Buckinghamshire 62
Phelps (Michael), West Sussex 237
Saint Ann's Books, Worcestershire 251
Steven Simpson Books, Norfolk 188
Sue Lowell Natural History Books, London W 173
Wildside Books, Worcestershire 250
Wyseby House Books, Berkshire 55

ZOOS
Adrem Books, Hertfordshire 131

BOOKSEARCH
Index of dealers who offer a booksearch service

Acer Books, Herefordshire	128
Adrem Books, Hertfordshire	131
Afar Books International, West Midlands	234
Ainslie Books, Strathclyde	273
Albion Books, West Midlands	234
Alexander's Books, Warwickshire	232
Alton Secondhand Books, Hampshire	122
Americanabooksuk, Cumbria	76
Annie's Books, South Yorkshire	217
Antiquary Ltd., (Bar Bookstore), North Yorkshire	192
Anvil Books, West Midlands	235
Archer (Steve), London Outer	178
Armchair Auctions, Hampshire	122
Arnold (Roy), Suffolk	223
Askew Books (Vernon), Wiltshire	246
Autolycus, Shropshire	209
Ayre (Peter J.), Somerset	216
Baggins Book Bazaar Ltd., Kent	139
Bardsley's Books, Suffolk	221
Barn Books, Buckinghamshire	61
Bass (Ben), Wiltshire	246
Bath Book Exchange, Somerset	212
Baxter (Steve), Surrey	228
Baxter - Books (Eddie), Somerset	216
Beardsley (A.E.), Nottinghamshire	201
Beaver Booksearch, Suffolk	221
Bell (Books) (Mrs. V.S.), Suffolk	223
Ben–Nathan (Jack), London Outer	178
Bertram Rota Ltd., London WC	174
Bilski (Gill), Buckinghamshire	61
Birmingham Books, West Midlands	234
Black Cat Bookshop, Leicestershire	145
Black Voices, Merseyside	182
Blue Penguin (The), Gloucestershire	116
Blythswood Bookshop, Highland	269
Bolland Books (Leslie H.), Bedfordshire	53
Bonython Bookshop, Cornwall	75
Book Depot (The), London NW	158
Book House (The), Cumbria	78
Bookcase, Cumbria	76
Bookends, Hampshire	123
Bookline, Co. Down	256
BookLovers.co.uk, Somerset	215
Bookmark (Children's Books), Wiltshire	248
Bookquest, Devon	83
Books Bought & Sold, Surrey	226
Books for Writers, Monmouthshire	280
books2books, Devon	87
Bookseeker, Tayside	275
Bookshelf – Aviation Books, Norfolk	187

BOOKSEARCH need not be frustrating

A new method is now available

Bookdealers who have their stock shown on the Internet seldom have the time and financial resources to upload all their titles in specialist subjects. So buyers have to write or telephone.

Sheppard's World offers an alternative method of searching. By selecting the subject of the book, users can send copies of a prepared e-mail with the search details to dealers specialising in that subject. Using our e-mail editor this is a very quick method - and enquiries can be sent to as many, or as few, as the user needs.

Visit www.sheppardsworld.co.uk today to find out more

Bookshop (The), Co. Donegal 258	Eton Antique Bookshop, Berkshire 57
Bookshop (The), Greater Manchester 119	Evans (Mark), Lincolnshire 151
Bookshop (The), West Sussex 238	Ewell Bookshop, Surrey 227
Booktrace International, Devon 85	Exedra Booksearch Ltd., London SW 165
Bookworld, Shropshire 210	
Booth (Booksearch Service), (Geoff), Cheshire . 68	Facet Books, Dorset 90
Border Books, Borders 262	Fantastic Literature, Essex 111
Bott, (Bookdealers) Ltd., (Martin), Greater Manchester 118	Farquharson, (Hilary), Tayside 275
	Farringdon (J.M.), Swansea 287
Bowland Bookfinders, Lancashire 142	Ferguson (Elizabeth), Grampian 266
Bridge of Allan Books, Central 263	Find That Book, West Yorkshire 244
Broadhurst of Southport Ltd., Merseyside 182	Fiona Edwards, Nottinghamshire 200
Butts Books (Mary), Berkshire 56	Fireside Books, Buckinghamshire 62
Byblos Antiquarian & Rare Book, Hampshire . 122	Firth (Bijou Books & Photography) (Maureen), South Yorkshire 218
Caliver Books, Essex 110	
Cameron House Books, Isle of Wight 134	Fisher Nautical, East Sussex 98
Candle Lane Books, Shropshire 210	ForensicSearch, Hertfordshire 132
Canon Gate Books, West Sussex 239	Forest Books, Rutland 208
Capital Bookshop, Cardiff 276	Four Shire Bookshops, Oxfordshire 202
Carta Regis, Powys 286	Foyle Books, Co. Derry 255
Chandos Books, Devon 84	Freya Books & Antiques, Norfolk 187
Chapter House Books, Dorset 94	Fuchsia Books, Co. Wexford 261
Chapter Two, London SE 161	Fullerton's Booksearch, Norfolk 185
Chaters Motoring Booksellers, London Outer . 179	
Cheshire Book Centre, Cheshire 69	G. C. Books Ltd., Dumfries & Galloway 264
Children's Bookshop (The), Herefordshire 282	Game Advice, Oxfordshire 205
Christine's Book Cabin, Leicestershire 147	Gaullifmaufry Books, Hertfordshire 131
Chthonios Books, East Sussex 101	Gillmark Gallery, Hertfordshire 131
Church Green Books, Oxfordshire 207	Glenwood Books, Surrey 230
Church Street Books, Norfolk 184	Gloucester Road Bookshop, London SW 165
Clark (M.R.), West Yorkshire 241	Glyn's Books, Shropshire 209
Clark (Nigel A.), London SE 162	Godmanchester Books, Cambridgeshire 65
Clarke Books (David), Somerset 214	Goldsworth Books, Surrey 230
Classey Limited (E.W.), Oxfordshire 203	Graham (John), Dorset 95
Classic Crime Collections, Greater Manchester 119	Great Oak Bookshop (The), Powys 285
Coach House Books, Worcestershire 251	Greensleeves, Oxfordshire 202
Coch-y-Bonddu Books, Powys 285	
Cocks Books (Brian), Cambridgeshire 66	Hadfield (G.K.), Cumbria 78
Collectors Carbooks, Northamptonshire 196	Halewood & Sons, Lancashire 144
Colwyn Books, Conwy 277	Hall's Bookshop, Kent 141
Corfe Books, Surrey 227	Harlequin Books, Bristol 59
Coulthurst (Richard), Greater Manchester 120	Harries (Pauline), Hampshire 124
Cousens (W.C.), Devon 83	Harris (Books), (Malcolm), West Midlands..... 234
Cowley, Auto–in–Print (John), Essex 108	Harvest Books, Lancashire 144
Craobh Rua Books, Co. Armagh 255	Hawley (C.L.), North Yorkshire 193
Curtle Mead Books, Isle of Wight 134	Helion & Company, West Midlands 235
	Hencotes Books & Prints, Northumberland 198
D'Arcy Books, Wiltshire 246	Heneage Art Books (Thomas), London SW.... 166
D. & M. Books, West Yorkshire 244	Heppa (Christopher), Essex 108
D.C. Books, Lincolnshire 150	Heraldry Today, Wiltshire 247
Dales and Lakes Book Centre, Cumbria 79	Heywood Hill Limited (G.), London W 171
Dolphin Books, Suffolk 221	Hicks (Ronald C.), Cornwall 73
Dusty Books, Powys 285	Hill (John S.), Devon 84
	Holdsworth Books (Bruce), East Sussex 103
Eastern Books of London, London SW 165	Hollingshead (Chris), London Outer 181
Eastgate Bookshop, East Yorkshire 105	Holmes Books (Harry), East Yorkshire 106
Elstree Books, Hertfordshire 131	Hoovey's Books, East Sussex 101
Embleton (Paul), Essex 111	HP Bookfinders, Central 263
Emjay Books, Surrey 226	Hutchison (Books) (Larry), Fife 265
English (Toby), Oxfordshire 206	Hylton Booksearch, Merseyside 182
Erian Books, London N 155	
	Idler (The), Suffolk 223

Intech Books, Northumberland	198
J. & J. Books, Lincolnshire	149
Jackson (M.W.), Wiltshire	249
Jean Hedger, Berkshire	55
Jobson (N.W.), Oxfordshire	204
Jones (Madalyn S.), West Yorkshire	242
Kalligraphia (formerly Charmouth Bounty Books), Isle of Wight	134
Katnap Arts, Norfolk	187
Kaye - Bookseller (Terence), London NW	159
Keeble Antiques, Somerset	215
Kenny's Bookshops and Art Galleries Ltd, Co. Galway	260
Kent (Books) (Mrs. A.), Suffolk	223
Kerr (Norman), Cumbria	77
Kingfisher Book Service, Nottinghamshire	201
Lawful Occasions, Essex	108
Leapman Ltd. (G. & R.), Hertfordshire	132
Lee Rare Books (Rachel), Bristol	59
Left on The Shelf, Cumbria	78
Letterbox Books, Nottinghamshire	200
Little Bookshop (The), Greater Manchester	119
Lloyd-Davies (Sue), Carmarthenshire	277
Lymelight Books & Prints, Dorset	92
Maghreb Bookshop (The), London WC	175
Malvern Bookshop (The), Worcestershire	250
Marine & Cannon Books, Cheshire	71
Marine and Cannon Books, Cheshire	69
Mayhew Books, Norfolk	184
Maynard & Bradley, Leicestershire	146
Meads Book Service (The), East Sussex	103
Meekins Books (Paul), Warwickshire	233
Mellon's Books, East Sussex	100
Melvin Tenner, London W	171
Merlin Books, West Sussex	238
MilitaryHistoryBooks.com, Kent	138
Minster Gate Bookshop, North Yorkshire	195
MK Book Services, Cambridgeshire	66
Modlock (Lilian), Dorset	92
Monmouth House Books, Monmouthshire	280
Moon's Bookshop (Michael), Cumbria	80
Moore (Sue), Cornwall	73
Moorland Books, Greater Manchester	120
Morris Secondhand & Antiquarian Books (Chris), Oxfordshire	205
Mr. Pickwick of Towcester, Northamptonshire	196
Murphy (C.J.), Norfolk	187
Newband (D.M.), Powys	286
Nineteenth Century Books, Oxfordshire	207
Not JUST Books, Lincolnshire	148
Occultique, Northamptonshire	196
Old Hall Bookshop (The), Northamptonshire	196
Orbis Books (London) Ltd., London W	171
Over-Sands Books, Cumbria	77
Oxfam Books and Music, Hampshire	127
Palladour Books, Hampshire	126
Paramor (C.D.), Suffolk	224
Park (Mike), London Outer	180
Park Gallery & Bookshop (The), Northamptonshire	197
Pedlar's Pack Books, Devon	89
Peel (Valerie), Berkshire	55
Petersfield Bookshop (The), Hampshire	125
Phillips of Hitchin (Antiques) Ltd., Hertfordshire	131
Poetry Bookshop (The), Powys	284
Pomes Penyeach, Staffordshire	219
Potterton Books, North Yorkshire	194
Price (R.D.M. & I.M.) (Books), Greater Manchester	120
Professional Book Services, North Yorkshire	190
Quarto Bookshop (The), Fife	266
Quest Books, East Yorkshire	106
Quest Booksearch, Cambridgeshire	64
Raftery Books (Michael D.), Leicestershire	145
Randall (Tom), Somerset	215
Rider Haggard Society (The), Tyne and Wear	231
Rittner Booksearch (Hilary), London SE	162
Roadmaster Books, Kent	137
Rods Books, Devon	87
Rolling Stock Books, Greater Manchester	121
Rosemary Pugh Books, Wiltshire	248
Roundstone Books, Lancashire	143
Rowan (H. & S.J.), Dorset	90
Ruskin Books, Kent	136
S.P.C.K., Hampshire	127
Saint Mary's Books & Prints, Lincolnshire	152
Saltburn Bookshop, North Yorkshire	192
Sansovino Books, West Sussex	239
Scarthin Books, Derbyshire	81
Schull Books, Co. Cork	257
Scrivener's Books & Bookbinding, Derbyshire	81
Sea Chest Nautical Bookshop (The), Devon	87
Seeber (Liz), East Sussex	99
Sen Books, Hampshire	127
Shacklock Books (David), Suffolk	222
Shapero Rare Books (Bernard J.), London W	172
Simmonds (Anthony J.), London SE	163
Simply Read Books, East Sussex	99
Sims (Sue), Dorset	90
Skelton (Tony), Kent	141
Skyrack Books, West Yorkshire	243
Solaris Books, East Yorkshire	105
Sparrow Books, West Yorkshire	241
Spelman (Ken), North Yorkshire	195
Spenceley Books (David), West Yorkshire	244
Spooner & Co, Somerset	215
Spurrier (Nick), Kent	138
Stacpoole (George), Co. Limerick	260
Sterling Books, Somerset	216
Sturford Books, Wiltshire	248
Symes Books (Naomi), Cheshire	71
Tarka Books, Devon	83
Temperley (David), West Midlands	234

Tennis Collectables, Cheshire 68
The Sanctuary Bookshop, Dorset 93
Thompson (Eric), Surrey 229
Thorntons of Oxford Ltd., Oxfordshire 203
Tiger Books, Kent 137
Titford (John), Derbyshire 81
Tozer Railway Books (Nick), West Yorkshire . 243
TP Children's Bookshop, West Yorkshire 241
Trevorrow (Edwin), Hertfordshire 130
Trinity Rare Books, Co. Leitrim 260
Trotter Books (John), London N 157
Tsbbooks, London SW 167
Twiggers Booksearch, Kent 141

Undercover Books, Lincolnshire 152

Vokes (Jeremiah), Durham 96
Vokes Books Ltd., North Yorkshire 192

Walden Books, London NW 160
Warsash Nautical Bookshop, Hampshire 126
Watkins (R.G.), Somerset 213
Webster (D.), Strathclyde 274
Wells (Mary), London SW 167
Wembdon Books, Somerset 213
Wetherell (Frances), Cambridgeshire 65
Whistler's Books, London SW 167
Whitchurch Books Ltd., Cardiff 276
Woolcott Books, Dorset 91
Worrallo (J. & M.A.), West Midlands 235
Wright Trace Books, West Midlands 235

LARGE PRINT
Dealers who stock books in large print

Yesterday's News, Conwy 278
Apocalypse, Surrey 228
Arden Books & Cosmographia, Warwickshire . 232
Family Favourites, East Yorkshire 105
Jade Mountain, Hampshire 125
Oxfam Books and Music, Hampshire............ 127
Peter's Bookshop, Norfolk 188
Shapero Rare Books (Bernard J.), London W . 172

INDEX OF ADVERTISERS

Abrams – Books, Harvey	52
Adrian Harrington	Bookmark
atlanticweb.co.uk	50
Book Collector	27
Bookdealer	31
Game Advice	206
Gazelle Book Services	43
Humber Books	148
P.B.F.A	21, 38
Project Portmanteaux	204
The Old Town Bookshop	270
Rare Book Review	44
Ripping Yarns	156
Stella Books	280
Temple Bookbinders	Bookmark
Textualties	41
Thurbans Publishing Services	30
TL Dallas (City) Ltd	35